WESTERN
CIVILIZATIONS

W · W · NORTON & COMPANY · NEW YORK · LONDON

EDWARD MCNALL BURNS
ROBERT E. LERNER
STANDISH MEACHAM

WESTERN CIVILIZATIONS

Their History and Their Culture

TENTH EDITION

Tenth Edition 1984

First Edition, Copyright 1941
Second Edition, Copyright 1947
Third Edition, Copyright 1949
Fourth Edition, Copyright 1954
Fifth Edition, Copyright © 1958
Sixth Edition, Copyright © 1963
Seventh Edition, Copyright © 1968
Eighth Edition, Copyright © 1973
Ninth Edition, Copyright © 1980

BY W. W. NORTON & COMPANY, INC.

Book Design by Antonina Krass
Layout by Ben Gamit

Cartography by Harold K. Faye

W. W. Norton & Company, Inc.,
500 Fifth Avenue, New York, N.Y. 10110
W. W. Norton & Company Ltd.,
37 Great Russell Street, London WC1B 3NU

3 4 5 6 7 8 9 0

ISBN 0-393-95315-7

For Joseph R. Strayer;
Edith, Louisa, and Samuel Meacham

CONTENTS

Chapter 16   A Century of Crisis for Early–Modern Europe (c. 1560–c. 1660)   501

Chapter 17   The Economy and Society of Early–Modern Europe   543

Chapter 18   The Age of Absolutism (1660–1789)   587

Chapter 19   The Scientific Revolution and Enlightenment   629

Part Six   THE WEST AT THE WORLD'S CENTER

MAPS

Maps in Color

(Maps appear facing or following the pages indicated)

Maps in Black and White

XVI

Maps

ILLUSTRATIONS IN COLOR

ILLUSTRATIONS IN THE TEXT

PREFACE

The first eight enormously successful editions of *Western Civilizations,* appearing between 1941 and 1973, were brought out single-handedly by Edward McNall Burns. Professor Burns not only had the courage, vision, and fortitude to write a coherent survey of Western history from primeval times to his own day without collaborators, but he was a pioneer in conceiving of his textbook as a history of *civilizations* rather than as a chronicle of events. Thus although he penned a colorful and vigorous narrative, he laid as much stress on the evolution of ideas and institutions as on political developments. Not surprisingly, then, his *Western Civilizations* withstood passing historiographical fads. With periodic revisions it outlasted all its original competitors to become the preeminent and longest lived introductory survey in the field.

In accepting the assignment to revise *Western Civilizations* for the ninth edition in 1977 we accordingly had no doubts that we wished to retain the work's basic physiognomy. Yet the expansion of historical research over previously neglected subject matters as well as the progress of research in more traditional areas made it necessary to revise substantial portions. Realizing that we could not do everything at once, we brought Professor Burns's account up to the most recent state of knowledge wherever we perceived inadequacies, but concentrated our attentions especially on the Middle Ages and the nineteenth and twentieth centuries.

For this tenth edition we have followed the same strategy, concentrating our attentions now on Europe's early-modern era. More specifically, the chapter on the Renaissance (14) has been thoroughly overhauled and the five following chapters completing the early-modern unit have been almost entirely rewritten. The most important changes in Chapter 14 are the introduction of a new section on "The Italian Background," which examines the social and economic contexts of Italian Renaissance developments; the introduction of coverage of Lorenzo Valla and the place of women in the writings of Alberti and Castiglione; revised discussions of Michelangelo and Vesalius; and a fully rewritten treatment of the northern Renaissance which proceeds topically rather than geographically and emphasizes the centrality of Erasmus and Christian humanism. In Chapter 15 overseas discoveries and the Protestant and Catholic Reformations are brought together in one unit: whereas treatment of the Portuguese and Spanish voyages and colonizing activities was slighted in earlier editions of *Western Civilizations,* this material is now fully covered in what we hope is an engaging narrative. Thereafter the Lutheran upheaval is analyzed from the points of view of theology and politics, and the succeeding sections on other major developments in sixteenth-century religious history are fully reconceived with the aims of pursuing new organizational strategies, distilling the results of the best recent research, and paying special attention to the effects of the Protestant and Catholic Reformations on the history of women.

Chapter 16 on "the iron century" falling between about 1560 and 1660 is an addition to our table of contents. This chapter attempts to respond to the challenge of how to treat the period between Luther and Louis XIV by adopting the prevalent recent scholarly view that Early-Modern Europe experiences a thoroughgoing "general crisis." Pursuit of this interpretation has enabled us to unite otherwise refractory material in an integrated manner. Thus Chapter 16 not only presents a narrative of religious wars and constitutional struggles against the backdrop of economic pressures and regionalist resentments of nationalizing tendencies but interrelates treatment of thought, literature, and art in ways which hitherto had been impossible.

While Chapters 17 through 19 correspond ostensibly to Chapters 16 through 18 of the Ninth Edition, they too have been substantially rewritten. Chapter 17 contrasts the dynamic world of the Commercial Revolution with the traditional institutions and assumptions of an ordered, hierarchical society, and suggests the dimensions and tensions of the social, economic, and demographic changes that occurred during the seventeenth and eighteenth centuries. Material on capitalism and mercantilism has been sharpened and expanded, and now includes a full treatment of the slave trade. The section on agriculture and industry has been rewritten to emphasize the fact that the Industrial Revolution did not emerge *de novo* at the end of the eighteenth century, but was a logical conclusion to the economic expansionism experienced in the Early-Modern period. Recent scholarly research on demographic trends has been added to the chapter, as have materials concerning the patterns of daily life within all ranks of society. Poverty, education, and literacy, subjects dealt with heretofore in only the broadest terms, now receive their due. Chapter 18 contains an extended and comparative discussion of absolutism. We have expanded our coverage of the history of eastern Europe and of the important subjects of warfare, diplomacy, and the development of the state system. We have also attempted to treat the political developments of the eighteenth century in a way that we hope will assist students to master the historical intricacies of the French Revolution by avoiding a sharp and potentially confusing break with pre-revolutionary Europe.

Chapter 19 represents another major change in the treatment of Early-Modern Europe. It covers seventeenth- and eighteenth-century intellectual achievements but focuses far more sharply than before on the Scientific Revolution and Enlightenment. In this chapter new emphasis is placed on the achievements of Bacon, Descartes, and Newton; treatment of the ways in which the scientific revolution laid the groundwork for eighteenth-century thought is expanded; the coverage of all the foremost Enlightenment thinkers is reconceived (note too that Montesquieu and Adam Smith are now treated here rather than in the French Revolution chapter); and the coverage of art, literature, and music is reconceived (e.g., a new section on the rise of the novel, culminating in Jane Austen) and rewritten in order to convey the fullest possible measure of aesthetic appreciation integrated with historical analysis.

Of course, in concentrating on Early-Modern Europe we have not neglected to review all the rest of *Western Civilizations'* coverage, and where necessary have made some fundamental changes. In the chapter on Ancient Egypt the narrative of political history has been expanded to include treatment of the archaic period, and greater attention has been paid to the role of women. Occasional streamlining and revision of chronology have been introduced in several other chapters of Parts One and Two, and the title of Chapter 6 has been changed from "Hellenic Civilization" to "Greek Civilization" in order to avoid terminological confusion with the Hellenistic Civilization that followed. In view of the prior slighting of early Russian and eastern European history, an entirely new section on "The Formation of the Empire of Russia" has been added to Chapter 13 on the Later Middle Ages.

In the chapters on the nineteenth and twentieth centuries, additions and innovations begin with an expanded treatment of the causes of the French Revolution and the inclusion of a discussion of the Vienna Settlement in Chapter 20. We have also increased our coverage of the social history of women, the spread of literacy, and the demographic shifts of the nineteenth century. The section on imperialism in Chapter 25 has been greatly expanded, as have those on the coming of the First World War in Chapter 27. In both cases we have introduced the historiographical controversies that have arisen over the interpretation of those events. As in earlier chapters we have added to our accounts of the history of eastern Europe, the expanded sections on Russia in the late-nineteenth and twentieth centuries being the most notable examples. Chapter 29 now contains a fuller—and, we hope, clearer—discussion of the varieties of totalitarianism that emerged in Europe during the interwar years. Finally, the treatment of the post–Second

World War world has been systematically revised and updated to accommodate new interpretations and recent developments.

In conjunction with the textual revisions the map and illustration programs have received serious attention. Five new maps have been added and the remaining maps have been amended as necessary. Nearly 40 percent of the over 800 illustrations are new to this edition, having been culled from a wide range of European and American archives. The text was the first to include color illustrations and continues to include far more color plates than any other book in the field. The new edition, like its predecessors, is available in a one-volume and a two-volume edition. Both the Instructor's Manual and the Study Guide, which includes numerous extracts from original and secondary sources, have undergone thorough revision as well.

Robert Lerner has had primary responsibility for Chapters 1 through 16 as well as Chapter 19, while Standish Meacham's province has lain with Chapters 17 and 18, and Chapters 20 through 32. The revision of Parts One and Two was facilitated greatly by criticisms offered by Edward W. Kase (Loyola University of Chicago) and Patrick F. O'Mara (Los Angeles City College). Firm bibliographical aid for Chapter 1 was provided by Loretta F. Smith, for Chapter 4 by Robert L. Cohn (Northwestern University), and for Chapters 6 and 7 by Brook Manville. Extraordinarily helpful suggestions for improving the early-modern coverage were provided by Carolyn C. Lougee (Stanford University; who no doubt would still prefer a very different Renaissance chapter than the one here presented), Paul J. Hauben (University of the Pacific), and David Longfellow (Rice University). Expert bibliographical guidance for early-modern art and music history came respectively from Richard Wendorf and William V. Porter (both of Northwestern University), helpful tips for illustrations came from Theresa Gross-Diaz and Klaus Arnold (University of Hamburg), and Vita Maniscalco and Tiina Ruus were argus-eyed readers. The later chapters have benefited from the careful and perceptive criticisms of Lamar Cecil (Washington and Lee University), Maarten Ultee (University of Alabama in Tuscaloosa), Margaret George (Northern Illinois University), John W. Carson (University of Wisconsin–Oshkosh), and John C. Olin (Fordham University). Valuable bibliographical assistance for modern art and music history was supplied by Charlotte Gomolak. At W. W. Norton, Ruth Mandel, as always, has been a resourceful picture-gatherer, and Ben Gamit an imaginative makeup artist. Without question, however, our greatest debt on this round is to Robert E. Kehoe, by title an editor but really Castiglione's ideal diplomat, man of letters, art connoisseur, impresario, and stage manager, all rolled into one.

Robert E. Lerner
Standish Meacham

WESTERN CIVILIZATIONS

Part One

THE DAWN OF HISTORY

No one knows the place of origin of the human species. There is evidence, however, that it may have been south-central Africa or possibly central or south-central Asia. Here climatic conditions were such as to favor the evolution of a variety of human types from primate ancestors. From their place or places of origin members of the human species wandered to southeastern and eastern Asia, northern Africa, Europe, and eventually, to America. For hundreds of centuries they remained primitive, leading a life which was at first barely more advanced than that of the higher animals. About 3500 B.C., a few of them, enjoying special advantages of location and climate, slowly developed superior civilizations. These civilizations, which attained knowledge of writing and considerable advancement in the arts and sciences and in social organization, began in that part of the world known as the Near East. This region extends from modern-day Iran to the Mediterranean Sea and to the farther bank of the Nile. Here flourished, at different periods between 3000 and 300 B.C., the mighty empires of the Egyptians, the Babylonians, the Assyrians, the Chaldeans, and the Persians, together with the smaller states of such peoples as the Hittites, the Phoenicians, and the Hebrews. The only other very early civilization existed in India in the area of the Indus valley from about 2500 to 1500 B.C. The earliest signs of civilization in China date from about 1800 B.C., and the earliest civilizations in Europe—on the island of Crete and mainland Greece—similarly date from around that time.

The Earliest Development of Humanity

	CULTURE PERIOD	TYPE OF HUMAN	CHARACTERISTIC ACHIEVEMENTS
2 million years ago	Earlier Paleolithic (Early Old Stone Age)	*Homo habilis*	Walking erect; use of objects taken from nature as tools; hunting
500,000 years ago		Java Man; Peking Man	Larger brains: greater intelligence
50,000 years ago		Neanderthal Man: first *Homo sapiens*	Speech; ability to think in the abstract; earliest tool-making
20,000 years ago	Later Paleolithic (Late Old Stone Age)	Cro-Magnon Man	Variety of tools and weapons made from stone and bone; cooked food; cave-painting
12,000 years ago	Mezolithic (Middle Stone Age)	Modern physical types	More settled living conditions; earliest transition from food-gathering to food-raising
7,000 years ago	Neolithic (New Stone Age)		Agriculture; domestication of animals; pottery; earliest village life; origin of states
5,500 years ago	Bronze Age		Earliest civilizations in Egypt and Mesopotamia; writing; bronze metallurgy; developed political, social, and economic institutions

Chapter 1

THE EARLIEST BEGINNINGS

As we turn to the past itself . . . we might well begin with a pious tribute to our nameless [preliterate] ancestors, who by inconceivably arduous and ingenious effort succeeded in establishing a human race. They made the crucial discoveries and inventions, such as the tool, the seed, and the domesticated animal; their development of agriculture, the "neolithic revolution" that introduced a settled economy, was perhaps the greatest stride forward that man has ever taken. They created the marvelous instrument of language, which enabled man to discover his humanity, and eventually to disguise it. They laid the foundations of civilization: its economic, political, and social life, and its artistic, ethical, and religious traditions. Indeed, our "savage" ancestors are still very near to us, and not merely in our capacity for savagery.

—Herbert J. Muller, *The Uses of the Past*

1. THE NATURE OF HISTORY

Catherine Morland, the heroine of Jane Austen's novel *Northanger Abbey,* complained that history "tells me nothing that does not either vex or weary me. The quarrels of popes and kings, with wars or pestilences in every page; the men all so good for nothing, and hardly any women at all, it is very tiresome." Although Jane Austen's heroine said this around 1800, she might have lodged the same complaint until quite recently, for until deep into the twentieth century most historians considered history to be little more than "past politics"—and a dry chronicle of past politics at that. The content of history was restricted primarily to battles and treaties, the personalities and politics of statesmen, the laws and decrees of rulers. But important as such data are, they by no means constitute the whole substance of history. Especially within the last few decades historians have come to recognize that history comprises a record of past human activities in every sphere—not just political developments, but also social, economic, and intellectual ones. Women as well as men, the ruled as well as the rulers, the poor as well as the rich, are part of his-

History more than battles and treaties

tory. So too are the social and economic institutions that men and women have created and that in turn have shaped their lives: family and social class; manorialism and city life; capitalism and industrialism. Ideas and attitudes too, not just of intellectuals but also of people whose lives may have been virtually untouched by "great books," are all part of the historian's concern. And, most important, history includes an inquiry into the causes of events and patterns of human organization and ideas—a search for the forces that impelled humanity toward its great undertakings, and the reasons for its successes and failures.

New historical methods

As historians have extended the compass of their work, they have also equipped themselves with new methods and tools, the better to practice their craft. No longer do historians merely pore over the same old chronicles and documents to ask whether Charles the Fat was at Ingelheim or Lustnau on July 1, 887. To introduce the evidence of statistics they learn the methods of the computer scientist. To interpret the effect of a rise in the cost of living, they study economics. To deduce marriage patterns or evaluate the effect upon an entire population of wars and plagues, they master the skills of the demographer. To explore the phenomena of cave-dwelling or modern urbanization, they become archeologists, studying fossil remains, fragments of pots, or modern city landscapes. To understand the motives of the men and women who have made history, they draw on the insights of social psychologists and cultural anthropologists. To illuminate the lives of the poor and of those who have left few written records, they look for other cultural remains—folk songs, for example, and the traditions embodied in oral history.

Necessity for studying past on its own terms

Perhaps the most important lesson historians have learned is that they must no longer condescend to the past, no longer assume that their civilization is worthier than those that have come before. History is primarily the study of change over time, but that does not mean that it is a tale of uninterrupted progress from past to present or that all change was ordained to produce our own modern world. Those who write history and those who study it must look to see how one event led to another and how the entire past is prologue to the present, but they must also appreciate the past on its own terms, examining it, so far as possible, through the eyes and with the minds of those who lived it.

2. HISTORY AND PREHISTORY

The so-called prehistoric era

It is the custom among many historians to distinguish between historic and prehistoric periods in the evolution of human society. By the former they mean history based upon written records. By the latter they mean the record of human achievement before the invention of writing. But this distinction is not altogether satisfactory because it implies that human accomplishments before they were recorded in characters representing words or concepts were not important. On the contrary, however, many of the greatest accomplishments of human technology, and even of social and political systems, were laid before people could write a word. It is preferable, therefore, that the whole period of human life on earth be regarded as historic, and that the era before the invention of writing be designated by a term such as "pre-literate." The records of preliterate societies are, of course, not books and documents, but tools, weapons, fossils, utensils, paintings, and fragments of jewelry and ornamentation. These, commonly known as "artifacts," are often almost as valuable as the written word in providing knowledge of a people's deeds and modes of living.

The entire span of human history can be divided roughly into two periods, the Age of Stone and the Age of Metals. The former is roughly coterminous with the Preliterate Age, or the period before the invention of writing. The latter coincides roughly with the period of history based upon written records. The Preliterate Age covered all but the smallest fraction of humanity's existence and did not come to an end until about 3500 B.C., although some Stone Age cultures persisted after that time and a few tribes still exist in remote areas. The Age of Metals practically coincides with the history of civilized nations. The Age of Stone is subdivided into the Paleolithic, or Old Stone Age, and the Neolithic, or New Stone Age. Each takes its name from the type of stone tools and weapons manufactured during the period. Thus during the greater part of the Paleolithic Age implements were commonly made by chipping pieces off a large stone or flint and using the core that remained as a hand ax or "fist hatchet." Toward the end of the period the chips themselves were used as knives or spearheads, and the core thrown away. The Neolithic Age witnessed the supplanting of chipped stone tools by implements made by grinding and polishing stone.

Fist Hatchet

3. THE CULTURE OF THE EARLIER PALEOLITHIC PEOPLES

The Paleolithic period can be dated from roughly 2,000,000 B.C. to 10,000 B.C. It is commonly divided into two stages, an earlier and a later one. The earlier Paleolithic period was vastly the longer of the two, covering about 99 percent of the entire Old Stone Age. During this time at least four species of humanlike creatures inhabited the earth. Momentous discoveries pertaining to the earliest of these have been made very recently by scientific teams working in East Africa. In 1961, the anthropologist Jonathan Leakey uncovered in Tanzania parts

Homo habilis

The Skull (left) *of a Young Woman of the Species Homo habilis,* believed to have lived in Tanzania, East Africa, about 1,750,000 years ago. On the right is the skull of a present-day African. Though *Homo habilis* was smaller than a pygmy, the brain casing was shaped like that of modern humans.

Java Man

of a skull that was about 1.8 million years old, far older than any humanlike skull previously known. (Chemical tests such as the carbon-14 method or the potassium-argon method are used in determining the age of the geological strata in which bones are found and sometimes the age of the bones themselves.) Then, in 1972, a team led by Jonathan's brother Richard discovered in Kenya a similar and nearly complete skull that was more than 2 million years old. The species which left behind these remains has been named *Homo habilis,* or "man having ability." *Homo habilis* may be counted as a true ancestor of modern man because he walked erect, possessed a brain that was larger than that of any apes, and was intelligent enough to use tools. Of course, his tools were extremely primitive. For the most part they consisted of objects taken from nature: bones of animals, limbs from trees, and chunks of stone, perhaps broken or crudely chipped. But they allowed *Homo habilis* to survive in times of food shortage as a hunter rather than as a food gatherer or forager. It must not be thought that reliance on hunting led these earliest ancestors to kill each other. Quite to the contrary, their survival depended upon cooperation. Most likely only after the development of agriculture and herding—more than a million years later—did humans start warring with each other for the possession of territory. The cooperation necessary in hunting made *Homo habilis* the first truly social creature and led toward the use of language. *Homo habilis* was, therefore, clearly in the vanguard of the human race.

Two subsequent inhabitants of the earlier Paleolithic period were Java man and Peking man. Java man was long thought to be the oldest of humanlike creatures, but it is now generally agreed that the date of his origin was about 500,000 B.C. His skeletal remains were found on the island of Java in 1891. The remains of Peking man were found in China between 1926 and 1930. Since the latter date, fragments of no fewer than thirty-two skeletons of the Peking type have been located, making possible a complete reconstruction of at least the head of this ancient species. Anthropologists generally agree that Peking man and Java man are of approximately the same antiquity, and that both probably descended from the same ancestral type.

Peking Man

During the last 25,000 years of the earlier Paleolithic period a fourth species of ancient man made an appearance. He was Neanderthal man, famous as an early caveman. Although first discovered a few years earlier at Gibraltar, Neanderthal man is named after a find of skeletal fragments in 1856 in the valley of the Neander, near Düsseldorf, in Germany. Since then numerous other discoveries have been made, in some cases complete skeletons, in such widely separated regions as Spain, Italy, Yugoslavia, Russia, and Israel. So closely did Neanderthal man resemble modern man that he is classified as a member of the same species, *Homo sapiens.* The resemblance, however, was by no means perfect. Neanderthalers, on the average, were only about five feet, four inches in height. They had receding chins and heavy eyebrow ridges. Although their foreheads sloped back and their brain cases were low-vaulted, their average cranial capacity was slightly greater than that of modern Caucasians. What this may have signified with respect to their intelligence cannot be determined.

Neanderthal Man

Although we know little about Neanderthal culture, it is certain that Neanderthalers progressed far beyond the apes, above all because they had the capacity for speech which enabled them to communicate with their fellows and to pass on what they had learned to succeeding generations. In addition they had some ability to think in the abstract, as evidenced by their burial of their dead with objects intended for use in an afterlife. The Neanderthalers also progressed beyond *Homo habilis* by fashioning their own tools instead of just using the ones they found. They discovered that stones could be chipped in such a way as to give them cutting edges. Thus were developed spearheads, borers, and much superior knives and scrapers. Indications have been found also of a degree of advancement in nonmaterial culture. In the entrances to caves where Neanderthalers lived, or at least took refuge, evidence has been discovered of flint-working floors and stone hearths where huge fires appear to have been made. These would suggest the origins of cooperative group life and possibly the crude beginnings of social institutions.

Accomplishments of earlier Paleolithic peoples

Cro-Magnon Man

Later Paleolithic Fishhook

4.. LATER PALEOLITHIC CULTURE

About 30,000 B.C. the culture of the Old Stone Age passed to the later Paleolithic stage. This period lasted for only about two hundred centuries, or from 30,000 to 10,000 B.C. A new and superior type of human being dominated the earth in this time. Biologically these peoples were closely related to modern humans. Their foremost predecessors, Neanderthal men, had ceased to exist as a distinct variety. What became of the Neanderthalers is not known.

The name used to designate the prevailing breed of later Paleolithic humans is Cro-Magnon, from the Cro-Magnon cave in southern France where some of the most typical remains were discovered. These people lived by hunting reindeer, bison, and mammoths, which freely roamed through southern Europe and Asia because the climate, dominated by glaciers, was very cold. The Cro-Magnon people were tall, broad-shouldered, and walked erect, the males averaging over six feet. They had high foreheads, well-developed chins, and a cranial capacity about equal to the modern average. The heavy eyebrows so typical of earlier species were absent. Whether Cro-Magnon men left any survivors is a debatable question. They do not seem to have been exterminated but appear to have been driven into mountainous regions and to have been ultimately absorbed into other breeds.

Later Paleolithic culture was markedly more advanced than that which had gone before. Not only were tools and implements better made, they existed in greater variety. They were not fashioned merely from flakes of stone and an occasional shaft of bone; other materials were used in abundance, particularly reindeer horn and ivory. Examples of the more complicated tools included the fishhook, the harpoon, and, at the very end of the period, the bow and arrow. That later Paleolithic people wore clothing is indicated by the fact that they invented the needle (made out of bone). They did not know how to weave cloth, but animal skins sewn together proved a satisfactory substitute. It is certain that they cooked their food, for enormous hearths, evidently used for roasting meat, have been discovered. In the vicinity of one at Solutré, in southern France, was a mass of charred bones, estimated to contain the remains of a hundred thousand large animals. Although Cro-Magnon people built no houses, except a few simple huts in regions where natural shelters did not abound, their life was not wholly nomadic. Evidence found in caves that served as homes indicate that they must have been used, seasonally at least, for years at a time.

With respect to nonmaterial elements there are also indications that later Paleolithic culture represented a marked advancement. Group life became more highly organized than ever before. The profusion of charred bones at Solutré and elsewhere probably indicates cooperative enterprise in the hunt and sharing of the results in community feasts.

The amazing workmanship displayed in tools and weapons and highly developed techniques in the arts scarcely could have been achieved without some division of labor. It appears certain, therefore, that later Paleolithic communities included professional artists and skilled craftsmen. In order to acquire such talents, certain members of the communities must have gone through long periods of training and given all their time to the practice of their specialties.

Substantial proof exists that the Cro-Magnons had highly developed notions of a world with supernatural aspects. They bestowed more care upon the bodies of the dead than did the Neanderthalers, painting the corpses, folding the arms over the heart, and depositing pendants, necklaces, and richly carved weapons in the graves. The Cro-Magnons also formulated an elaborate system of sympathetic magic designed to increase their food supply. Sympathetic magic is based upon the principle that imitating a desired result will bring about that result. Applying this principle, Cro-Magnon people

Sympathetic magic

Later Paleolithic Engraving and Sculpture. The two objects at the top and upper right are dart-throwers. At the lower right is the famous Venus of Willendorf.

The Venus of Laussel

Significance of later Paleolithic art

painted murals on the walls of their caves depicting, for example, the capture of reindeer in the hunt. At other times they fashioned clay models of the bison or mammoth and mutilated them with dart thrusts. The purpose of such representation was probably to facilitate the results portrayed and thereby to increase the hunter's success and make easier the struggle for existence. Possibly incantations or ceremonies accompanied the making of these pictures or images, and it is likely that the work of producing them was carried on while the actual hunt was in progress.

In fact, the supreme achievement of the Cro-Magnon people was their art—an achievement so original and resplendent that it ought to be counted among the Seven Wonders of the World. Nothing else illustrates so well the great gulf between their culture and that of their predecessors. Later Paleolithic art included nearly every branch that the material culture of the time made possible. Sculpture, painting, and carving were all represented. The ceramic arts and architecture were lacking; pottery had not yet been invented; and the only buildings erected were of simple design. The Cro-Magnon art par excellence was cave painting. On cave walls were exhibited the greatest number and variety of their talents—their discrimination in the use of color, their meticulous attention to detail, their capacity for the employment of scale in depicting a group, and above all, their genius for imitating natural detail. Especially noteworthy was their skill in representing movement. Almost all of the murals depict animals running, leaping, chewing their cud, or facing the hunter at bay. Ingenious devices were often employed to give the impression of motion. Chief among them was the drawing of additional outlines to indicate the areas in which the legs or the head of the animal had moved. The scheme was so shrewdly executed that no appearance whatever of artificiality resulted.

Cave painting throws a flood of light on many problems relating to primitive mentalities. To a certain extent Cro-Magnon art was undoubtedly an expression of a true aesthetic sense. Cro-Magnon people did obviously delight in a graceful line or symmetrical pattern or brilliant color. The fact that they painted and tattooed their bodies and wore ornaments gives evidence of this. But their chief works of art can scarcely have been produced primarily for the sake of creating beautiful objects. Such an interpretation must be excluded for several reasons. To begin with, the best of the paintings and drawings are usually to be found on the walls and ceilings of the darkest and most inaccessible parts of the caves. The gallery of paintings at Niaux, for instance, is more than half a mile from the entrance of the cave. No one could see the artists' creations except in the imperfect light of torches or primitive lamps, which must have smoked and sputtered badly, for the only illuminating fluid available was animal fat. Furthermore, there is evidence that Cro-Magnon people were largely indifferent to their murals after they were finished. Numerous exam-

Cave Drawings at Lascaux, France. On the left are characteristic examples of the realism of Cro-Magnon art. On the right, a view of the entrance to the caves.

ples have been found of paintings or drawings superimposed upon earlier ones of the same or of different types. Evidently the important thing was not the finished work itself, but the act of making it.

The real purpose of nearly all Cro-Magnon art was apparently not to delight the senses but to increase the supply of animals useful for food. The artist was not an aesthete but a magician, and art was a form of magic designed to promote the hunter's success. In this purpose lay its chief significance and the foundation of most of its special qualities. It suggests, for example, the real reason why game animals were almost the exclusive subjects of the great murals and why plant life and inanimate objects were seldom represented. It aids us in understanding the Cro-Magnons' neglect of finished paintings and the predominant interest in the process of making them. The placing of the art in the most inaccessible part of the cave is further proof of a religious motivation on the part of the artist—the art then becomes secreted in a sacred place.

Art an aid in the struggle for existence

Later Paleolithic culture ended around 10,000 B.C. because of a disappearance of the food supply. As the last glacier retreated north, the climate of southern Europe became too warm for the reindeer, and they gradually migrated to the shores of the Baltic. The mammoth, whether for the same or for different reasons, became extinct. Cro-Magnon people probably followed the reindeer northward, but any later cultural achievements remain unknown to us.

The end of later Paleolithic culture

5. NEOLITHIC CULTURE

From roughly 10,000 B.C. to roughly 5000 B.C., varying very much according to location, ensued the Mesolithic, or Middle Stone Age. This was a transitional period in which peoples became more sedentary and found new sources of food, such as shellfish and edible grasses, now that most of the world was freed from ice. The Mesolithic stage was succeeded by the Neolithic, or New Stone Age. This name is applied because stone weapons and tools were now generally made by grinding and polishing instead of by chipping or fracturing as in the preceding periods. The bearers of Neolithic culture were new varieties of modern peoples who poured into Africa and southern Europe from Asia. Since no evidence exists of their later extermination or wholesale migration, they must be regarded as the immediate ancestors of most of the peoples now living in Europe.

It is impossible to fix exact dates for the Neolithic period because different peoples passed through the Neolithic stage of development at different rates in different areas. Exciting recent archeological discoveries on the west bank of the Jordan River give evidence of Neolithic settlements in their earliest forms around 7500 B.C. Fully developed Neolithic culture existed in Mesopotamia and Egypt by 5000 B.C., but the culture was not well established in Europe until about 3000 B.C. There is also variation in the dates of its ending. It was superseded in Mesopotamia and Egypt by the first literate civilizations around 3500 B.C., but except on the island of Crete it did not come to an end anywhere in Europe before 2000, and in northern Europe much later still. In a few regions of the world it has not ended yet. The peoples of some islands of the Pacific, the Arctic regions of North America, and the jungles of Brazil are still in the Neolithic culture stage except for a few customs acquired from explorers and missionaries.

In many respects the New Stone Age was the most significant in the history of the world thus far. The level of material progress rose to new heights. Neolithic peoples had a better mastery of their environment than any of their predecessors. They were less likely to perish from a shift in climatic conditions or from the failure of some part of their food supply. This decided advantage was the result primarily of the development of agriculture and the domestication of animals. Whereas all of the peoples who had lived heretofore were mere food-gatherers, Neolithic peoples were *food-producers*. Tilling the soil and keeping flocks and herds provided them with much more dependable food resources and at times even yielded them a surplus. The development of agriculture, one of the most important of all transitions in human history, promoted a settled existence and made possible an increase in population. Such were the elements of a great social and economic revolution whose importance it would be difficult to exaggerate.

The new culture also derives significance from the fact that it was the first to be distributed over the *entire* world. Although some earlier cultures, especially those of the Neanderthalers and Cro-Magnons, were widely dispersed, they were confined chiefly to the accessible mainland areas of the Old World. Neolithic culture penetrated into every habitable area of the earth's surface—from Arctic wastes to the jungles of the tropics. Neolithic peoples apparently made their way from a number of centers of origin to every region of both hemispheres. They traveled enormous distances by water as well as by land, and eventually occupied every major island of the oceans, no matter how remote.

Migration over long distances was not the only example of Neolithic achievements. Neolithic peoples developed the arts of knitting and weaving. They made the first pottery and knew how to produce fire by friction. They built houses of wood and sun-dried mud. Toward the end of the period they discovered the possibilities of metals, and a few implements of copper and gold were added to their stock. Since nothing was yet known of the arts of smelting and refining, the use of metals was limited to the more malleable ones occasionally found in the pure state in the form of nuggets.

But the real foundations of Neolithic culture were the domestication of animals and the development of agriculture, for these advances above all made possible a settled mode of existence and the growth of villages and social institutions. The first animal to be domesticated is generally thought to have been the dog, on the assumption that he

Activities Around a Neolithic Dwelling. This model represents part of a Neolithic village that was located at Troldebjerg, Denmark, about 2700 B.C. Note the hunters, the wood-gatherer, the potter, the weaver, the grain-grinder, and the carver.

Neolithic Flint Sickles

The beginning of agriculture

The nature of institutions

The family

would be continually hanging around the hunter's camp to pick up bones and scraps of meat. Eventually it would be discovered that he could be put to use in hunting, or possibly in guarding the camp. After achieving success in domesticating the dog, Neolithic peoples would logically turn their attention to other animals, especially those used for food. Before the period ended, at least five species—the cow, the dog, the goat, the sheep, and the pig—had been made to serve their needs.

The exact spot where agriculture originated has never been determined. All we know is that wild grasses resembling modern cereal grains have been found in a number of places. Types of wheat grow wild in the Near East and southern Russia. Wild ancestors of barley have been reported in North Africa, the Near East, and central Asia. Though it is probable that these were the first crops of Neolithic agriculture, they were by no means the only ones. Millet, vegetables, and numerous fruits were also grown. Flax was cultivated in the Eastern Hemisphere for its textile fiber, and in some localities the growing of the poppy for opium had already begun. In the Western Hemisphere maize (Indian corn) was the only cereal, but the American Indians cultivated numerous other crops, including tobacco, beans, squashes, tomatoes, and potatoes.

The most important consequence of Neolithic settled life was the development of lasting institutions. An institution may be defined as a combination of group beliefs and activities organized in a relatively permanent fashion for the purpose of fulfilling some group need. It ordinarily includes a body of customs and traditions, a code of rules and standards, and physical extensions such as buildings, punitive devices, and facilities for communication and indoctrination. Since humans are social beings, some of these elements probably existed from earliest times, but institutions in their fully developed form seem to have been an achievement of the Neolithic Age.

One of the most ancient of human institutions is the family. Sociologists do not agree upon how it should be defined. Historically, however, the family has always meant a more or less permanent unit composed of parents and their offspring, which serves the purposes of care of the young, division of labor, acquisition and transmission of property, and preservation and transmission of beliefs and customs. The family is not now, and never has been, exclusively biological in character. Like most institutions, it has evolved through a long period of changing conventions which have given it a variety of functions and forms. No doubt there were primitive families in Paleolithic times, but we know practically nothing about them and they probably were not very stable. In Neolithic times the family clearly emerges and appears to have been dominated by the male patriarch who had one or more wives depending upon region.

A second institution known earlier but developed in more complex form by Neolithic peoples was religion. On account of its infinite variations, it is hard to define, but perhaps the following would be accepted as an accurate definition of the institution in at least its basic character: "Religion is everywhere an expression in one form or another of a sense of dependence on a power outside ourselves, a power which we may speak of as a spiritual or moral power."[1] Modern anthropologists emphasize the fact that early religion was not so much a matter of belief as a matter of rites. For the most part, the rites came first; the myths, dogmas, and theologies were later rationalizations. Primitive people were universally dependent upon nature—on the regular succession of the seasons, on the rain falling when it should, on the growth of plants and the reproduction of animals. Unless they performed sacrifices and rites these natural phenomena, according to this notion, would not occur. For this reason they developed rainmaking ceremonies in which water was sprinkled on ears of corn to imitate the falling of the rain. The members of a whole village or even a whole tribe would attire themselves in animal skins and mimic the habits and activities of some species they depended upon for food. They apparently had an idea that by imitating the life pattern of the species they were helping to guarantee its continuance.

Primitive religion; rites and ceremonies

Still another of the great institutions to be developed by Neolithic peoples was the state. This may be defined as an organized society occupying a specific territory and possessing an authoritative government independent of external control. The essence of the state is the power to make and administer laws and to preserve social order by punishing people for infractions of those laws. Except in time of crisis the state does not exist in a very large proportion of preliterate societies—a fact which probably indicates that it originated rather late in the Neolithic culture stage.

The state: definition

The major explanation for the development of states in the Neolithic period lies in the development of agriculture. In areas such as the Nile valley, where a large population lived by cultivating intensively a limited area of fertile soil, a high degree of social organization was absolutely essential. Ancient customs would not suffice for the definition of rights and duties in such a society, with its high standard of living, its unequal distribution of wealth, and its wide scope for the clash of personal interests. New measures of social control would become necessary, which could scarcely be achieved in any other way than by setting up a government of sovereign authority and submitting to it; in other words, by establishing a state.

Role of agriculture in the origin of states

6. FACTORS RESPONSIBLE FOR THE ORIGIN AND GROWTH OF CIVILIZATIONS

Sometime around 3500 B.C. the earliest *civilizations* emerged out of Neolithic culture. We may say that civilization is a stage in human his-

---

[1] A. R. Radcliffe-Brown, *Structure and Function in Primitive Society*, p. 157.

torical development when writing is used to a considerable extent; some progress has been made in the arts and sciences; and political, social, and economic institutions have developed sufficiently to conquer at least some of the problems of order, security, and efficiency in a complex society. What causes contributed to the rise of civilizations? What factors account for their growth? Why do some civilizations reach much higher levels of development than others? Inquiry into these questions is one of the chief pursuits of historians and social scientists. Some decide that factors of geography are most important. Others stress economic resources, food supply, contact with older civilizations, and so on. Usually a variety of causes is acknowledged, but one is commonly singled out by historians as deserving special emphasis.

The meaning of civilization

Probably the most popular of the theories accounting for the rise of advanced cultures are those which come under the heading of geography. Prominent among them is the hypothesis of climate. The climatic theory, advocated by such philosophers as Aristotle and Montesquieu, received its most developed exposition in the writings of an American geographer, Ellsworth Huntington. Huntington acknowledged the importance of other factors, but he insisted that no nation, ancient or modern, rose to the highest cultural status except under the influence of a climatic stimulus. He described the ideal climate as one in which the mean temperature seldom falls below 38 degrees or rises above 64 degrees Fahrenheit. But temperature is not alone important. Moisture is also essential, and the humidity should average about 75 percent. Finally, the weather must not be uniform: cyclonic storms, or ordinary storms resulting in weather changes from day to day, must have sufficient frequency and intensity to clear the atmosphere every once in a while and produce those sudden variations in temperature which seem to be necessary to exhilarate and revitalize human beings.[2]

Geographic theories: the climatic hypothesis

Much can be said in favor of the climatic hypothesis. Certainly some parts of the earth's surface, under existing atmospheric conditions, could never give rise to a superior culture. They are either too hot, too humid, too cold, or too dry. Such is the case in regions beyond the Arctic Circle, the larger desert areas, and the rain forests of India, Central America, and Brazil. Evidence is available, moreover, to show that some of these places have not always existed under climate so adverse as that now prevalent. Desolate sections of Asia, Africa, and America contain unmistakable traces of better days in the past. Here and there are the ruins of towns and cities where now the supply of water is totally inadequate, or which are entrapped by growths of dense foliage. Roads traverse deserts which at present are impassable, or come to an end at the mouth of a jungle.

Evidence in favor of the climatic hypothesis

The best-known evidences of the cultural importance of climatic change are those pertaining to the civilization of the Mayas. Mayan

[2] Ellsworth Huntington, *Civilization and Climate*, 3d ed., pp. 220–23.

civilization flourished in Guatemala, Honduras, and on the peninsula of Yucatan in Mexico from about 400 to 1500 A.D. Numbered among its achievements were the making of paper, the perfection of a solar calendar, and the development of a system of writing partly phonetic. Great cities were built; marked progress was made in astronomy; and sculpture and architecture reached advanced levels. At present most of the civilization is in ruins. No doubt many factors conspired to produce its end, including deadly wars between tribes, but climatic change was also probably involved. The remains of most of the great Mayan cities are now surrounded by jungles, where malaria is prevalent and agriculture difficult. That the Mayan civilization or any other could have grown to maturity under present-day conditions is hard to believe.

The Mayan civilization

Related to the climatic hypothesis is the soil-exhaustion theory. A group of modern conservationists has advanced this theory as the primary explanation of the decay and collapse of the great empires of the past and as a universal threat to the nations of the present. At best it is only a partial hypothesis, since it offers no theory of the birth or growth of civilizations. But its proponents seem to think that almost any environment not ruined by humans is capable of nourishing a superior culture. The great deserts and barren areas of the earth, they maintain, are not natural but artificial, created by improper grazing and farming practices. Ecologists discover innumerable evidences of waste and neglect that have wrought havoc in such areas as Mesopotamia, Palestine, Greece, Italy, China, and Mexico. The mighty civilizations that once flourished in these countries were ultimately doomed by the fact that their soil would no longer provide sufficient food for the population. As a consequence, the more intelligent and enterprising citizens migrated elsewhere and left others to sink into stagnation and apathy. But the fate that overtook the latter was not of their making alone. The whole nation had been guilty of plundering the forests, mining the soil, and pasturing flocks on the land until the grass was eaten down to the very roots. Among the tragic results were floods alternating with droughts, since there were no longer any forests to regulate the run-off of rain or snow. At the same time, much of the top soil on the close-cropped or excessively cultivated hillsides was blown away or washed into the rivers to be carried eventually down to the sea. The damage done was irreparable, since about three hundred years are required to produce a single inch of topsoil.

The soil-exhaustion theory

A recent hypothesis of the origin of civilizations is the British historian Arnold J. Toynbee's adversity theory. According to this, conditions of hardship or adversity are the real causes which have brought superior cultures into existence. Such conditions constitute a *challenge* which not only stimulates humans to try to overcome it but generates additional energy for new achievements. The challenge may take the form of a desert, a jungle area, rugged topography, or a grudging soil. The Hebrews and Arabs were challenged by the first, the Indians of the Andes by the last. The challenge may also take the

The adversity theory of Arnold J. Toynbee

form of defeat in war or even enslavement. Thus the Carthaginians, as a result of defeat in the First Punic War, were stimulated to conquer a new empire in Spain. In general it is true that the greater the challenge, the greater the achievement. Nevertheless, there are limits: if the challenge is too severe it will deal a crushing blow to all who attempt to meet it.

7. WHY THE EARLIEST CIVILIZATIONS BEGAN WHERE THEY DID

Egypt and Mesopotamia

Which of the great civilizations of antiquity was the oldest is still a sharply debated question. The judgment of some scholars inclines toward the Egyptian, though a larger body of authority supports the claims of Mesopotamia. These two areas were geographically the most favored sections in the Near East. In both, larger numbers of artifacts of undoubted antiquity have been found than in any other regions. Furthermore, progress in the arts and sciences had reached unparalleled heights in both of these areas as early as 3000 B.C., when most of the rest of the world was backward in the extreme. If the foundations of this progress were really laid elsewhere, it seems strange that they should have disappeared, although of course there is no telling what archeologists may uncover in the future.

A limited area of fertile soil in the Nile valley

Of the several causes responsible for the earliest rise of civilizations in Egypt and Mesopotamia, the existence of fertile river valleys was certainly the most important. Both regions were endowed with a limited area of exceedingly fertile soil. Although the Egyptian valley of the Nile extended for a distance of 750 miles, the valley was only 10 miles wide in some places, and its maximum width was 31 miles. The total area was less than 10,000 square miles, or roughly the equivalent of Maryland. Through countless centuries the Nile had carved a vast canyon, bounded on either side by towering cliffs. Between the river itself and the cliffs lay narrow shores covered with a rich alluvial deposit, which in places reached a depth of more than thirty feet. The soil here was so productive that as many as three crops could be raised each year. This river valley constituted virtually all the arable land of ancient Egypt, for beyond the cliffs lay nothing but desert.

A similar condition in Mesopotamia

In Mesopotamia similar conditions prevailed, although here two rivers—the Tigris and the Euphrates—played the role that the Nile alone played in Egypt. Indeed, Mesopotamia is simply an ancient Greek word for "between the rivers," alluding to the fact that the territory was defined by its position between the roughly parallel flow of the Tigris and Euphrates. Not only was the soil of the region fertile, but the distance between the two rivers at one point was less than twenty miles and elsewhere was not much greater. Since the surrounding country was desert, the Mesopotamian people were kept from scattering over too great an expanse of territory. The result, as in Egypt, was the welding of the inhabitants into a compact society, under conditions that facilitated the interchange of ideas. As the population increased, the need for agencies of social control became ever more urgent. Numbered among these were government, schools, legal and moral codes, and institutions for the production and distribution of wealth. At the same time conditions of living became more complex and artificial and necessitated the keeping of records of things accomplished and the perfection of new techniques. Among the consequences were the invention of writing, the practice of smelting metals, the performance of mathematical operations, and the development of astronomy and the rudiments of physics. With these achievements the first great milestone of civilization was passed.

Climatic influences also played their part in both regions. The atmosphere of Egypt is dry and invigorating. Even the hottest days produce none of the oppressive discomfort which is often experienced during the summer seasons in more northern countries. The mean temperature in winter varies from 56 degrees Fahrenheit in the Nile Delta to 66 degrees in the valley above. The summer mean is 83 degrees and an occasional maximum of 122 is reached, but the nights are always cool and the humidity is extremely low. Except in the Delta, rainfall occurs in negligible quantities, but the deficiency of moisture is counteracted by the annual floods of the Nile from July to October. Also very significant from the historical standpoint is the total absence of malaria in Upper Egypt, while even in the coastal region it is practically unknown. The direction of the prevailing winds is likewise a favorable factor. For more than three-quarters of the year the wind comes from the north, blowing against the force of the Nile current. The effect of this is to simplify immensely the problem of transportation. Upstream traffic, with the propulsion of the wind to counteract the force of the river, presents no greater difficulty than downstream traffic. In ancient times this circumstance must have been of enormous advantage in promoting communication among the Egyptian peoples stretched out along the length of the Nile.

Climatic advantages in
Egypt

Climatic conditions in Mesopotamia do not seem to have been quite so favorable as in Egypt. The summer heat is more relentless; the humidity is somewhat higher; and tropical diseases take their toll. Nevertheless, the torrid winds from the Indian Ocean, while enervating to human beings, blow over the valley at just the right season to ripen the fruit of the date palm. More than anything else the excellent yield of dates, the dietary staple of the Near East, encouraged the settlement of large numbers of people in the valley of the two rivers. Furthermore, the melting of the snows in the mountains of the north produced an annual flooding of the Babylonian plain similar to that in Egypt. The effect was to provide the soil with moisture and to cover it over with a layer of mud of unusual fertility. At the same time, it should be noted that water conditions in Mesopotamia were less dependable than in Egypt. Floods were sometimes catastrophic, a factor which left its mark on the development of culture.

Climatic influences in
Mesopotamia

Most significant of all of the geographic influences, however, was the fact that the scanty rainfall in both regions provided a spur to initiative and inventive skill. In spite of the yearly floods of the rivers there was insufficient moisture left in the soil to produce abundant harvests. A few weeks after the waters had receded, the earth was baked to a stony hardness. Irrigation was accordingly necessary if full advantage was to be taken of the richness of the soil. As a result, in both Egypt and Mesopotamia elaborate systems of dams and irrigation canals were constructed as long as five thousand years ago. The mathematical skill, engineering ability, and social cooperation necessary for the development of these projects were available for other uses and so fostered the achievement of civilization.

Uncertainty as to which civilization was older

Which of the two civilizations, the Egyptian or the Mesopotamian, was the older? Until recently most historians assumed that the Egyptian one took precedence. Between the two world wars of the twentieth century, however, facts were unearthed which seemed to prove a substantial Mesopotamian influence in the Nile valley as early as 3500 B.C. This influence was exemplified by the use of cylinder seals, methods of building construction, art motifs, and elements of a system of writing of undoubted Mesopotamian origin. That such achievements could have radiated into Egypt from the Tigris-Euphrates valley at so early a date indicated beyond doubt that the Mesopotamian civilization was one of vast antiquity. It did not necessarily prove, though, that it was older than the Egyptian because the achievements mentioned were not taken over and copied slavishly. Instead, the Egyptians modified them radically to suit their own culture pattern. On the basis of this evidence, it would seem that the only conclusion which can be safely drawn is that both civilizations were very old, and that to a large extent they developed concurrently. With them both we begin the story of the history of Western civilizations.

SELECTED READINGS

• *Items so designated are available in paperback editions.*

• Childe, V. Gordon, *What Happened in History?* New York, 1943. Emphasizes materialistic explanations for the emergence of the earliest civilizations. A modern classic.
• Fagan, Brian, *Archaeology: A Brief Introduction,* 2nd ed., Boston, 1983. Defines the terminology and describes some of the basic methods of archeology. Clear and concise.
• ———, *People of the Earth,* 4th ed., Boston, 1982. The most accessible survey of all cultures without written records, ranging from the earliest humans to the Incas.
• Harris, Marvin, *Cannibals and Kings: The Origins of Cultures,* New York, 1977. A materialistic interpretation of the emergence of primitive societies as a process of interaction with environmental and economic determinants.

- Lamberg-Karlovsky, C. C., and J. Sabloff, *Ancient Civilizations: The Near East and Mesoamerica*, Menlo Park, Calif., 1979. A lucid discussion of how the earliest states were formed and of how the earliest civilizations became increasingly complex over time.

  Leakey, Richard E., *The Making of Mankind*, New York, 1981. Describes the most recent discoveries (including Leakey's own) concerning the ancestors of man and posits environmental explanations of the human species. An extremely valuable account.

- Malinowski, B., *Magic, Science and Religion*, New York, 1954. Essays by one of the founders of modern anthropology.

  Marshack, A., *Roots of Civilization: The Cognitive Beginnings of Man's First Art, Symbol, and Notation*, New York, 1972. A basic interpretation of the origins of art and writing as a product of the human capacity for making symbols.

- Mauss, Marcel, *The Gift: Forms and Functions of Exchange in Archaic Societies*, New York, 1967. Originally written in 1927, this book offers enduring insights into the nature of social interaction between individuals and among groups.

  Norbeck, Edward, *Religion in Primitive Society*, New York, 1961. A clear introductory analysis of primitive religious rituals, beliefs, and symbols.

- Pfeiffer, John, *The Emergence of Man*, 3rd ed., New York, 1978. The fullest review of various theories offered by anthropologists to explain human beginnings.

- Sandars, N. K., *Prehistoric Art in Europe*, Baltimore, 1968.

- Turner, Victor, *The Ritual Process*, Chicago, 1969. A concise and fascinating exploration of how rituals can be "read" like a book.

Ancient Civilizations of the Near East and the Aegean World

	POLITICAL	ECONOMIC
3000 B.C.	Archaic period in Egypt, c. 3100–c. 2770 Old Kingdom in Egypt, c. 2770–c. 2200 Supremacy of Sumerian cities in Mesopotamia, c. 2800–c. 2340 Dominance of Akkadian Empire in Mesopotamia, 2334–c. 2200 First intermediate period in Egypt, c. 2200–c. 2050 Sumerian revival, c. 2200–c. 2000 Middle Kingdom in Egypt, c. 2050–1786	Development of irrigation and large-scale farming in Egypt and Mesopotamia, c. 3500–c. 2500
2000 B.C.	Old Babylonian Empire in Mesopotamia, c. 2000–c. 1550 Height of Minoan civilization under leadership of Knossos and Phaistos, c. 2000–c. 1500 Second intermediate period in Egypt, 1786–c. 1560 Mycenaean civilization on mainland Greece, c. 1600–c. 1200 Hittite Empire in Asia Minor, c. 1600–c. 1200 The New Kingdom in Egypt, c. 1560–1087 Kassites overthrow Babylonians, c. 1550	Extended commerce in Egypt and Crete, c. 2000 Slavery in Egypt, c. 1575
1500 B.C.	Mycenaean dominance on Crete, c. 1500–c. 1400 Destruction of Knossos and end of Minoan civilization, c. 1400 Hebrew occupation of Canaan, c. 1300–c. 1025	Use of iron by Hittites, c. 1500
1000 B.C.	Trojan War, c. 1250 Collapse of Mycenaean civilization in Greece, c. 1200–c. 1100 Unified Hebrew monarchy under Saul, David, and Solomon, c. 1025–922 Height of Phoenician civilization, c. 1000–c. 700 Kingdom of Israel, 922–722 Kingdom of Judah, 922–586 Height of Assyrian Empire, c. 750–612 Chaldean Empire, 612–539 Nebuchadnezzar conquers Jerusalem, 586 Persian Empire, 559–330 Height of Lydia under Croesus, c. 550 Persian conquest of Egypt, 525	Mediterranean trade of Phoenicians, c. 1000–c. 700 Invention of coinage by Lydians, c. 625
500 B.C.	Darius the Great, height of Persia, 522–486	Royal Road of Persians, c. 500

CULTURAL	RELIGIOUS	
Egyptian hieroglyphic writing, c. 3100	Egyptian sun worship, c. 3000	**3000** **B.C.**
Sumerian cuneiform writing, c. 3000		
Construction of first pyramid in Egypt, c. 2770		
Development of Indus Valley writing, c. 2500	Egyptian belief in personal immortality, c. 2500	
Sumerian legal codes, c. 2100		
Gilgamesh epic, c. 2000		**2000** **B.C.**
Code of Hammurabi, c. 1790	Ethical religion in Egypt, c. 1800	
Egyptian diagnostic medicine, c. 1700		
Egyptian temple architecture, c. 1580–c. 1090		
Development of alphabet by Phoenicians, c. 1500		**1500** **B.C.**
Naturalistic art in Egypt under Akhenaton, c. 1375	Religious revolution of Akhenaton, c. 1375	
	Hebrew worship of Yahweh, c. 1000	**1000** **B.C.**
Realistic sculpture of Assyrians, c. 750	Hebrew prophetic revolution, c. 750–c. 600	
	Astral religion of Chaldeans, c. 600–c. 500	
Deuteronomic code, c. 600	Zoroaster, c. 600	
		500 **B.C.**
Book of Job, c. 400		

Chapter 2

THE EGYPTIAN CIVILIZATION

Thou makest the Nile in the Nether World,
Thou bringest it as thou desirest,
To preserve alive the people of Egypt.
For thou hast made them for thyself,
Thou lord of them all, who weariest thyself for them;
Thou sun of day, great in glory. . . .

 —Hymn to Aton, from reign of the Pharaoh Akhenaton

Modern crowds that flood museums to view fabled treasures of Egyptian art are still caught by the spell of one of the oldest and most fascinating civilizations in history. Although the Egyptian civilization was not necessarily the oldest in the ancient world, it was certainly of great antiquity; its origins date from about 3500 B.C. We may consider it here first because somewhat more is known about its accomplishments than about those of most other early peoples. It should be borne in mind while reading this chapter, however, that Mesopotamian and, later, other civilizations were developing simultaneously and sometimes influenced Egyptian developments.

Chronological primacy of Egypt and Mesopotamia

The hallmark of Egyptian civilization was the sense of stability offered by the Nile valley. The fact that the Nile flooded regularly year after year gave Egyptians a feeling that nature was predictable and benign. Moreover, the fertility of the soil in the valley provided for great agricultural wealth, and the fact that the valley was surrounded by deserts and the sea meant that Egypt was comparatively free from threats of foreign invasion. For all these reasons Egyptian civilization was both very advanced and remarkably peaceful. The Greek historian Herodotus was undoubtedly correct when he referred to Egypt as "the gift of the Nile."

Favorable conditions for the development of Egyptian civilization

1. POLITICAL HISTORY UNDER THE PHARAOHS

The ancient history of Egypt is usually divided into six eras: the archaic (or "early dynastic") period, the Old Kingdom, the first intermediate period, the Middle Kingdom, the second intermediate period, and the New Kingdom. Even before the beginning of the archaic period the Egyptians had taken some extremely important steps in the direction of creating an advanced civilization. Above all, they had begun their earliest attempts at irrigation and drainage, and they had learned to use copper tools in place of stone ones, thereby benefiting from the advantages that copper was more durable than stone and could easily be sharpened or recast when blunted.

About 3100 B.C. two of the greatest achievements in all Egyptian history occurred: the unification of the country and the invention of writing. Until then separate powers had ruled in Upper (or southern) Egypt, and Lower (or northern) Egypt, but unity was essential for Egypt's future because a single government was necessary in order to ensure centralized direction of irrigation projects along the entire length of the Nile. Tradition attributes the unification of Egypt to one individual, called Menes by the Greeks and Narmer by the Egyptians, but modern experts lean toward the view that the work of unification was accomplished over several generations. Whatever the case, just around the time when one or more rulers of the "First Dynasty" were forging Egyptian unity, the earliest form of Egyptian writing was invented. Probably this was not coincidental, for the use of writing must have been inspired by the record-keeping needs of the new state.

The first two dynasties of united Egypt were succeeded around 2770 by the rule of the mighty Zoser, the first king of the Third Dynasty and therewith the founder of the Old Kingdom. While it is difficult to be certain how the governmental system of the Old Kingdom differed in details from that of the archaic period, there is no doubt whatsoever that Zoser's reign initiated a period of much greater royal absolutism, best symbolized by the fact that Zoser commissioned the first pyramid. Under Zoser and his leading successors of the Old Kingdom the power of the pharaoh, or king, was virtually unlimited. (Egyptian rulers are called "pharaohs" as the result of biblical usage, even though the ancient Egyptians themselves did not use this term.) The pharaoh was considered to be the son of the sun god, and by custom married one of his sisters to keep the divine blood from becoming contaminated. No separation of religious and political life existed. The pharaoh's chief subordinates were priests, and he himself was the chief priest.

The government of the Old Kingdom was founded upon a policy of peace and nonaggression. In this respect it was virtually unique among ancient states. The pharaoh had no standing army, nor was there anything that could be called a national militia. Each local area had its own militia, but militias were commanded by civil officials, and when

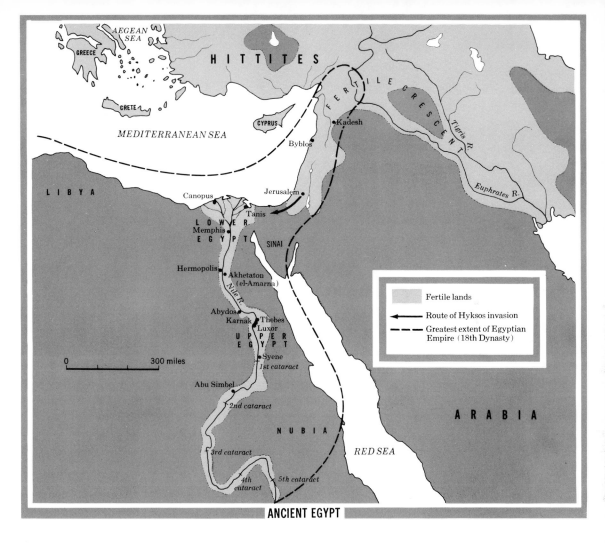

ANCIENT EGYPT

called into active service generally devoted their energies to labor on the public works. In case of a threat of invasion the various local units were assembled at the call of the pharaoh and placed under the command of one of his civil subordinates. At no other time did the head of the government have a military force at his disposal. The Egyptians of the Old Kingdom were content for the most part to work out their own destinies and to let other nations alone. The reasons for this attitude lie in the protected position of their country, in their possession of land of inexhaustible fertility, and in the fact that their state was a product of cooperative need instead of being grounded in exploitation.

The nonmilitaristic character of the Old Kingdom

After centuries of peace and relative prosperity the Old Kingdom came to an end with the downfall of the Sixth Dynasty about 2200 B.C. Several causes were responsible. Governmental revenues became exhausted because the pharaohs invested heavily in such grandiose projects as pyramid-building. To make matters worse, overall Egyp-

End of the Old Kingdom

tian prosperity was adversely affected by climatic disasters which created crop failures. In the meantime provincial nobles usurped more and more power until central authority virtually disappeared. The era which followed is called the first intermediate period. Anarchy now prevailed. The nobles created their own rival principalities, and political chaos was aggravated by internal brigandage and invasion by desert tribes. The first intermediate period did not end until the rise of the Eleventh Dynasty, which restored centralized rule around 2050 B.C. The next great stage of Egyptian history, known as the Middle Kingdom, ensued.

The Middle Kingdom

Throughout most of its life the government of the Middle Kingdom was more socially responsible than that of the Old Kingdom. The Eleventh Dynasty could not withstand the power of the nobles, but the Twelfth, which followed around 1990 and lasted until 1786 B.C., ruled strongly by means of an alliance with a middle class composed of officials, merchants, artisans, and farmers. This alliance kept the nobility in check and laid the foundations for unprecedented prosperity. During the rule of the Twelfth Dynasty there were advances in social justice and much intellectual achievement. Public works that benefited the whole population, such as extensive drainage and irrigation projects, replaced the building of pyramids, which had no practical use. There was also a democratization of religion which extended to common people a hope for salvation that they had not been granted before. Religion now emphasized proper moral conduct instead of ritual dependent on wealth. For all these reasons the reign of the Twelfth Dynasty is commonly considered to be Egypt's classical or golden age.

The invasion of the Hyksos

Immediately afterward, however, Egypt entered its second intermediate period. This was another era of internal chaos and foreign invasion which lasted for more than two centuries, or from 1786 to about 1560 B.C. The contemporary records are scanty, but they seem to show that the internal disorder was the result of a counterrevolt of the nobles. The pharaohs were again reduced to impotence, and much of the social progress of the Twelfth Dynasty was destroyed. About 1750 the land was invaded by the Hyksos, or "Rulers of Foreign Lands," a mixed horde originating in western Asia. Their military prowess is commonly ascribed to the fact that they possessed horses and war chariots, but their victory was certainly made easier by the dissension among the Egyptians themselves. Their rule had profound effects upon Egyptian history. Not only did they introduce the Egyptians to new methods of warfare, but by providing them with a common grievance in the face of foreign tyranny they also enabled them to forget their differences and unite in a common cause.

Near the end of the seventeenth century B.C. the rulers of southern (Upper) Egypt launched a revolt against the Hyksos, a movement which was eventually joined by all of Egypt. By about 1560 the last conquerors who had not been killed or enslaved had been driven from the country. The hero of this victory, Ahmose, founder of the Eighteenth Dynasty, thereafter established a regime which was much more highly consolidated than any that had hitherto existed. In the great outpouring of patriotism which had accompanied the struggle against the Hyksos, local loyalties were reduced, and with them the power of the nobles.

The period which followed the accession of Ahmose is called the New Kingdom, and by some, the period of the Empire. It lasted from about 1560 to 1087 B.C., during which time Egypt was ruled by three dynasties of pharaohs in succession: the Eighteenth, Nineteenth, and Twentieth. No longer was the prevailing state policy pacific and isolationist; a spirit of aggressive imperialism rapidly pervaded the nation, for the military ardor generated by the successful war against the Hyksos whetted an appetite for further victories. Moreover, a vast military machine had been created to expel the invader, which proved to be too valuable an adjunct to the pharaoh's power to be discarded immediately.

Ramses II (XIXth Dynasty)

The first steps in the direction of the new policy were taken by the immediate successors of Ahmose in making extensive raids into Palestine and claiming sovereignty over Syria. With one of the most formidable armies of ancient times, the new pharaohs speedily annihilated all opposition in Syria and eventually made themselves masters of a vast domain extending from the Euphrates to the farther cataracts of the Nile. But they never succeeded in welding the conquered peoples into loyal subjects, and weakness was the signal for widespread revolt in Syria. Their successors suppressed the uprising and managed to hold the Empire together for some time, but ultimate disaster could not be averted. More territory had been annexed than could be managed successfully. The influx of wealth into Egypt weakened the national fiber by fostering corruption and luxury, and the constant revolts of the vanquished eventually sapped the strength of the state beyond all hope of recovery. By the twelfth century most of the conquered provinces had been permanently lost.

Failures of the Empire

The government of the New Kingdom or Empire resembled that of the Old Kingdom, except for the fact that it was even more absolute. Military power now provided the basis of the pharaoh's rule. A professional army was always available with which to overawe his subjects. Most of the former nobles now became courtiers or members of the royal bureaucracy under the complete domination of the king.

The government of the Empire

The last of the great pharaohs was Ramses III, who ruled from 1182 to 1151 B.C. He was succeeded by a long line of nonentities who inherited his name but not his ability. By the middle of the twelfth century Egypt had fallen prey to renewed barbarian invasions and social decadence. About the same time the Egyptians appear to have lost most of their creative talents. To win immortality by magic devices was now the commanding interest of people of every class. The process of

The last of the pharaohs

decline was hastened also by the growing power of the priests, who finally usurped the royal prerogatives and dictated the pharaoh's decrees.

From the middle of the tenth century to nearly the end of the eighth a dynasty of Libyan barbarians occupied the throne of the pharaohs. The Libyans were followed by a line of Ethiopians or Nubians, who came in from the desert regions west of the Upper Nile. In 670 Egypt was conquered by the Assyrians, who succeeded in maintaining their supremacy for only eight years. After the collapse of Assyrian rule the Egyptians regained their independence, and a brilliant renaissance of culture ensued. It was doomed to an untimely end, however, for in 525 B.C. the country was conquered by the Persians. The ancient civilization was never again revived.

2. EGYPTIAN RELIGION

Religion played a dominant role in the life of the ancient Egyptians, leaving its impress upon almost everything. The art was an expression of religious symbolism. The literature and philosophy were suffused with religious teachings. The government of the Old Kingdom was a theocracy, and even the military pharaohs of the Empire professed to rule in the name of the gods. Material resources in considerable amounts were expended in providing elaborate tombs and in supporting priests.

The religion of the ancient Egyptians went through various stages: from simple polytheism to the earliest known expression of monotheism, and then back to polytheism. In the beginning each city or district appears to have had its local deities, who were guardian gods of the locality or personifications of nature powers. The unification of the country resulted not only in a consolidation of territory but in a fusion of divinities as well. All of the guardian deities were merged into the great sun god Re. Under the Middle Kingdom, with the establishment of Theban dynasties in control of the government, this deity was commonly called Amon or Amon-Re from the name of the chief god of Thebes. The gods who personified the vegetative powers of nature were fused into a deity called Osiris, who was also the god of the Nile. Thereafter these two great powers who ruled the universe, Amon and Osiris, vied with each other for supremacy. Other deities, as we shall see, were recognized also, but they occupied a distinctly subordinate place.

During the period of the Old Kingdom the solar faith, embodied in the worship of Re, was the dominant system of belief. It served as an official religion whose chief function was to give immortality to the state and to the people collectively. The pharaoh was the living representative of this faith on earth; through his rule the rule of the god was maintained. But Re was not only a guardian deity. He was in addition

Funerary Papyrus. The scene shows the heart of a princess of the XXIst Dynasty being weighed in a balance before the god Osiris. On the other side of the balance are the symbols for life and truth.

the god of righteousness, justice, and truth, and the upholder of the moral order of the universe. He offered no spiritual blessings or even material rewards to people as individuals. The solar faith was not a religion for the masses as such, except insofar as their welfare coincided with that of the state.

The cult of Osiris, as already observed, began its existence as a nature religion. The god personified the growth of vegetation and the life-giving powers of the Nile. The career of Osiris was wrapped about with an elaborate legend. In the remote past, according to belief, he had been a benevolent ruler, who taught his people agriculture and other practical arts and gave them laws. After a time he was treacherously slain by his wicked brother Set, and his body cut into pieces. His wife Isis, who was also his sister, went in search of the pieces, put them together, and miraculously restored his body to life. The risen god regained his kingdom and continued his beneficent rule for a time, but eventually descended to the nether world to serve as judge of the dead. Horus, his posthumous son, finally grew to manhood and avenged his father's death by killing Set.

Originally this legend seems to have been little more than a nature myth. The death and resurrection of Osiris symbolized the recession of the Nile in the autumn and the coming of the flood in the spring. But in time the Osiris legend began to take on a deeper significance. The human qualities of the deities concerned—the paternal solicitude

The Osiris cult

Significance of the Osiris legend

Akhenaton. Above is a profile sketch, surviving from a sculptor's workshop; below, a full-sized weathered bust.

of Osiris for his subjects, the faithful devotion of his wife and son—appealed to the emotions of average Egyptians, who were now able to see their own tribulations and triumphs mirrored in the lives of the gods. More important still, the death and resurrection of Osiris came to be regarded as conveying a promise of personal immortality. As the god had triumphed over death and the grave, so might also the individual who followed him faithfully inherit everlasting life. Finally, the victory of Horus over Set appeared to foreshadow the ultimate ascendancy of good over evil.

Egyptian ideas of the hereafter attained their full development in the later history of the Middle Kingdom. For this reason elaborate preparations had to be made to prevent the extinction of one's earthly remains. Not only were bodies mummified but wealthy men left munificent endowments to provide their mummies with food and other essentials. As the religion advanced toward maturity, however, a less naive conception of the afterlife was adopted. The dead were now believed to appear before Osiris to be judged according to their deeds on earth.

All of the departed who met the tests included in this system of judgment entered a celestial realm of physical delights and simple pleasures. Here in marshes of lilies and lotus-flowers they would hunt wild geese and quail with never-ending success. Or they might build houses in the midst of orchards with luscious fruits of unfailing yield. They would find lily-lakes on which to sail, pools of sparkling water in which to bathe, and shady groves inhabited by singing birds and every manner of gentle creature. The unfortunate victims whose hearts revealed their vicious lives were utterly destroyed.

The Egyptian religion attained its fullest development about the end of the Middle Kingdom. By this time the solar faith and the cult of Osiris had been merged in such a way as to preserve the best features of both. The province of Amon as the god of the living, as the champion of good in this world, was accorded almost equal importance with the functions of Osiris as the giver of personal immortality and the judge of the dead. The religion was now quite clearly an ethical one. People repeatedly avowed their desire to do justice because such conduct was pleasing to the great sun god.

Soon after the establishment of the Empire the religion which has just been described underwent a serious debasement. Its ethical significance was largely destroyed, and superstition and magic gained the ascendancy. The chief cause seems to have been that the long and bitter war for the expulsion of the Hyksos fostered the growth of irrational attitudes and correspondingly depreciated the intellect. The result was a marked increase in the power of the priests, who preyed upon the fears of the masses to promote their own advantage. They inaugurated the practice of selling magical charms, which were supposed to have the effect of preventing the heart of the deceased from betraying his or her real character. They also sold formulas which, inscribed on rolls of

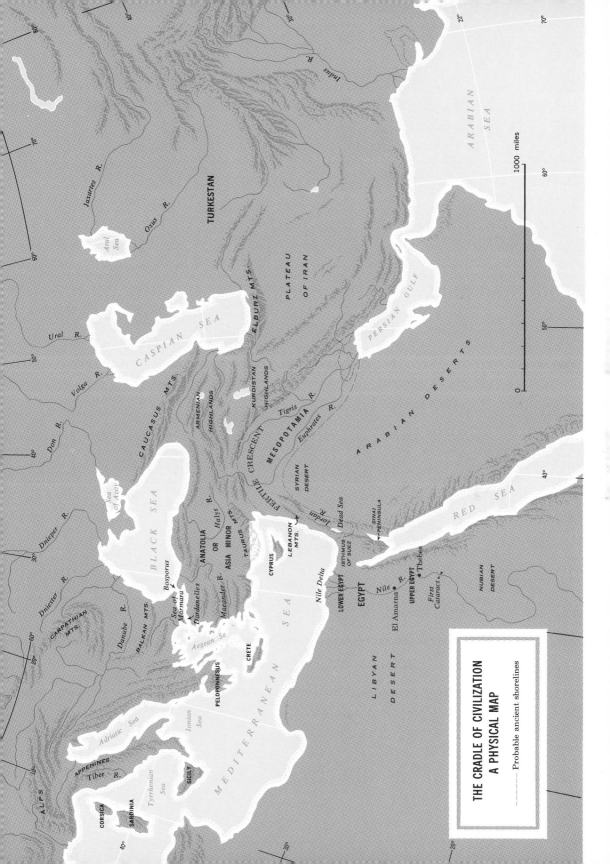

THE CRADLE OF CIVILIZATION
A PHYSICAL MAP

——— Probable ancient shorelines

1000 miles

ARABIAN SEA

TURKESTAN

Jaxartes R.

Oxus R.

Aral Sea

Ural R.

CASPIAN SEA

Volga R.

Don R.

CAUCASUS MTS.

ELBURZ MTS.

PLATEAU OF IRAN

ARMENIAN HIGHLANDS

KURDISTAN HIGHLANDS

Tigris R.

MESOPOTAMIA

Euphrates R.

PERSIAN GULF

ARABIAN DESERTS

FERTILE CRESCENT

SYRIAN DESERT

Sea of Azov

BLACK SEA

Dnieper R.

Dniester R.

CARPATHIAN MTS.

Danube R.

BALKAN MTS.

Bosporus

Sea of Marmara

Dardanelles

Meander R.

Halys R.

ANATOLIA OR ASIA MINOR

TAURUS MTS.

CYPRUS

LEBANON MTS.

Jordan R.

Dead Sea

SINAI PENINSULA

ISTHMUS OF SUEZ

RED SEA

Aegean Sea

CRETE

PELOPONNESUS

MEDITERRANEAN SEA

Nile Delta

LOWER EGYPT

EGYPT

Nile R.

El Amarna

UPPER EGYPT

Thebes

First Cataract

NUBIAN DESERT

LIBYAN DESERT

Ionian Sea

Adriatic Sea

APPENINES

Tiber R.

SICILY

Tyrrhenian Sea

CORSICA

SARDINIA

ALPS

Egyptian Pottery Jar, c. 3600 B.C. It was filled with food or water and placed in the tomb to provide for the afterlife. (MMA)

An Egyptian Official and His Son. Painted limestone, c. 2500 B.C.

Gold and Inlay Pendant of Princess Sit Hat Hor Yunet. Egyptian, Twelfth Dynasty.

Farmhand Plowing. Egyptian tomb figures, c. 1900 B.C.

Thutmose III as Amon, 1450 B.C. The Pharaoh wears the crown and the beard of the god, and carries a scimitar and the symbol of "life."

Jeweled Headdress of Gold, Carnelian and Glass. Egyptian, 1475 B.C.

Part of the Egyptian "Book of the Dead." A collection of magic formulas to enable the deceased to gain admission to the realm of Osiris and to enjoy its eternal benefits.

Silversmiths Working on a Stand and a Jar. Egyptian, c. 1450 B.C.

A scribe writing on a papyrus roll. Egyptian, c. 1415 B.C.

awabty ("to answer") Figures, c. ?00 B.C. These were put in the ?mb to do any degrading work ?e rich man might be called ?on to do in the next world.

Stele or Grave Marker. It shows the deceased being presented to the Sun god on his throne. She is holding her heart in her hand.

Scarab or Beetle-Shaped Charm of a Pharaoh, c. 1395 B.C. The beetle was sacred in ancient Egypt.

Wall painting of an Egyptian house, c. 1400 B.C.

Painted limestone figures, c. 1300 B.C.

Head of Ramses II, 1324–1258 B.C.

ainted Wood Shrine Box for ?hawabty Figures, c. 1200 ?.C.

A hieroglyphic character for the idea "Millions of Years," 500–330 B.C.

A carved sandstone capital, c. 370 B.C., representing a bundle of papyrus reeds.

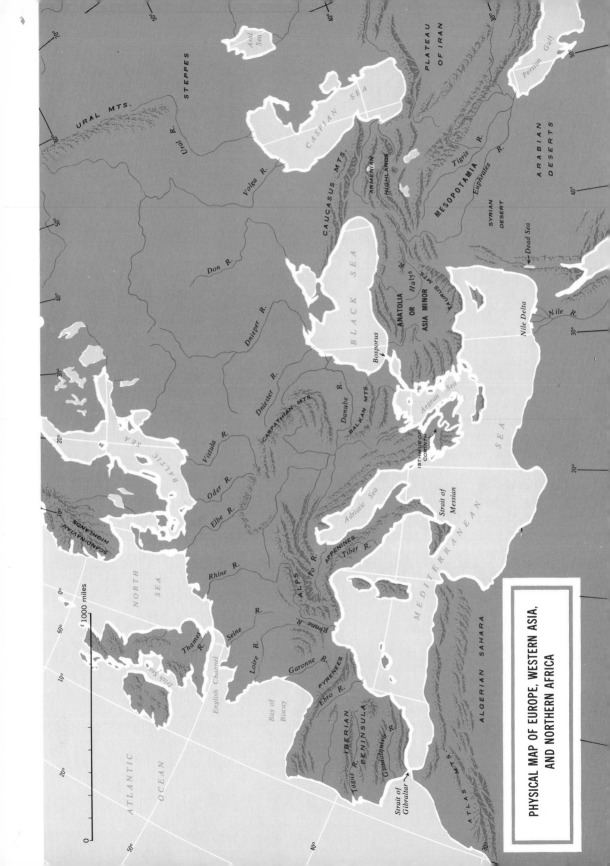

PHYSICAL MAP OF EUROPE, WESTERN ASIA, AND NORTHERN AFRICA

papyrus and placed in the tomb, were alleged to be effective in facilitating the passage of the dead to the celestial realm. The aggregate of these formulas constituted what is referred to as the Book of the Dead. Contrary to the general impression, it was not an Egyptian Bible, but merely a collection of mortuary inscriptions.

This degradation of the religion at the hands of the priests into a system of magical practices finally resulted in a great religious upheaval. The leader of this movement was the Pharaoh Amenhotep IV, who began his reign about 1375 B.C. and died or was murdered about fifteen years later. After some fruitless attempts to correct the most flagrant abuses, he resolved to crush the system entirely. He drove the priests from the temples, hacked the names of the traditional deities from the public monuments, and initiated the worship of a new god whom he called "Aton," an ancient designation for the physical sun. He changed his own name from Amenhotep ("Amon rests") to Akhenaton, which meant "Aton is satisfied." His wife Nefertiti became Nefer-nefru-aton: "Beautiful is the beauty of Aton." In keeping with his desire to begin entirely anew, Akhenaton built a new capital, El-Amarna, which he dedicated to the worship of the new deity.

Akhenaton, His Wife Nefertiti, and Their Children. The god Aton is depicted here as a sun-disk, raining down his power on the royal family.

More important than these physical changes was the new set of doctrines enunciated by the reforming pharaoh. He taught first of all a religion of qualified monotheism. Aton and Akhenaton himself were the only gods in existence. Like none of the gods before him, Aton had no human or animal shape but was to be conceived in terms of the lifegiving, warming rays of the sun. He was the creator of all, and thus god not merely of Egypt but of the whole universe. Akhenaton deemed himself to be Aton's heir and co-regent; while the pharaoh and his wife worshiped Aton, others were to worship Akhenaton as a living deity. Aside from this important qualification Akhenaton restored the ethical quality of Egyptian religion at its best by insisting that Aton was the author of the moral order of the world and the rewarder of mankind for integrity and purity of heart. He envisaged the new god as the sustainer of all that is of benefit to humanity, and as a heavenly father who watches with benevolent care over all his creatures. Conceptions like these of the unity, righteousness, and benevolence of God were not attained again until the time of the Hebrew prophets some 600 years later.

Despite the energy with which Akhenaton pursued his religious revolution it was still a failure. The religion of Aton gained little popular following because the masses remained devoted to their old gods. The new religion was too strange for them and lacked the greatest attraction of the older faith: the promise of an afterlife. Moreover, the pharaohs who followed Akhenaton were allied with the priests of Amon and accordingly restored the older modes of worship. Akhenaton's successor, the pharaoh whom we refer to as "King Tut," changed his name from Tutankhaton to Tutankhamen, abandoned El-Amarna for the old capital of Thebes, and presided over a return to all

Tutankhamen or "King Tut." This solid-gold coffin weighs 2,500 pounds.

the old ways. His own burial was a lavish demonstration of commitment to the old rituals and belief in life after death. Thereafter Egyptian religion was characterized by growing faith in ritualism and magic. Priests sold formulas and charms which were supposed to trick the gods into granting salvation: thus even the cult of Osiris lost most of its elevated moral quality.

3. EGYPTIAN INTELLECTUAL ACHIEVEMENTS

The general character of Egyptian philosophy

The philosophy of ancient Egypt was chiefly ethical and political, although traces of broader philosophic conceptions are occasionally to be found. The idea that the universe is controlled by mind or intelligence, for example, is a notion that appeared from time to time in the writings of priests. Other philosophic ideas of the ancient Egyptians included the conception of an eternal universe, the notion of constantly recurring cycles of events, and the doctrine of natural cause and effect. No Egyptian writers could be classified as "pure" philosophers. They were concerned primarily with religion and with questions of individual conduct and social justice.

The earliest ethical philosophy

The earliest examples of Egyptian ethical philosophy were maxims similar to those of the Book of Proverbs in the Old Testament. They went little beyond practical wisdom, but occasionally they enjoined tolerance, moderation, and justice.

The Plea of the Eloquent Peasant

As political philosophers the Egyptians developed a concept of the state as a welfare institution presided over by a benevolent ruler. This concept was embodied especially in the *Plea of the Eloquent Peasant,* written about 2050 B.C. It sets forth the idea of a ruler committed to benevolence and justice for the good of his subjects. He is urged to act as the father of the orphan, the husband of the widow, and the brother of the forsaken. He is supposed to judge impartially and to execute punishment upon whom it is due; and to promote such an order of harmony and prosperity that no one will be deprived of basic human necessities.

Nature of Egyptian science

The branches of science which most absorbed the attention of the Egyptians were astronomy, mathematics, and medicine. All were developed for practical ends—astronomy primarily to compute the time of the Nile floods, mathematics for building purposes, and medicine for healing. By no means pure scientists, the Egyptians had little interest in the nature of the universe as such, a fact which probably accounts for their failure to advance very far in the science of astronomy. Nonetheless they did perfect a calendar based on the annual appearance of Sirius, the brightest star in the sky, whose yearly rising usually preceded the overflowing of the Nile. In addition they worked out a lunar calendar to mark the succession of religious rites.

Mathematics was more highly developed. The Egyptians laid the foundations for arithmetic and geometry. They devised the arithmetical operations of addition, subtraction, and division, but never discovered how to multiply except through a series of additions. They invented the decimal system, but had no symbol for zero. Fractions caused them some difficulty: all those with a numerator greater than one had to be broken down into a series, each with *one* as the numerator, before they could be used in mathematical calculations. The only exception was the fraction two-thirds, which the scribes had learned to use as it stood. The Egyptians also achieved a surprising degree of skill in the mathematics of measurement, computing with accuracy the areas of triangles, rectangles, and hexagons. The ratio of the circumference of a circle to its diameter they calculated to be 3.16, thereby coming very close to the modern calculation of 3.14. They learned how to compute the volume of the pyramid, the cylinder, and the hemisphere.

The Egyptians also did some remarkable work in medicine. Early medical practice was conservative and profusely corrupted by superstition, but a document dating from about 1700 B.C. reveals a fairly adequate conception of scientific diagnosis and treatment. Egyptian physicians were frequently specialists: some were oculists; others were dentists, surgeons, specialists in diseases of the stomach, and so on. In the course of their work they made many discoveries of lasting value. They recognized the importance of the heart and had some appreciation of the significance of the pulse. They acquired a degree of skill in the treatment of fractures and performed simple operations. Unlike some peoples of later date they ascribed disease to natural causes. They discovered the value of cathartics, noted the curative properties of numerous drugs, and compiled the first *materia medica,* or catalogue of medicines. Many of their remedies were later carried into Europe by the Greeks and are still employed by the peasantry of isolated regions.

In other scientific fields the Egyptians contributed less. Although they achieved great building feats, they possessed but the scantiest knowledge of physics. They knew the principle of the inclined plane, which they applied to the building of pyramids, but they were ignorant of the pulley. To their credit, on the other hand, must be assigned considerable progress in metallurgy, the invention of the sundial, and the making of papyrus and glass. With all their deficiencies as pure scientists, they equaled or surpassed in actual accomplishment most of the other peoples of the ancient Near East.

The Egyptians developed their first form of writing concurrently with the foundation of their first unified state around 3100 B.C. This system, known as the *hieroglyphic,* from the Greek words meaning sacred carving, was originally composed of pictographic signs denoting concrete objects. Gradually, certain of these signs were conventionalized and used to represent abstract concepts. Other characters were introduced to designate separate syllables which could be combined to form words. Finally, twenty-four symbols, each representing a single consonant sound of the human voice, were added early in the

Old Kingdom. Thus the hieroglyphic system of writing had come to include at an early date three separate types of characters, the pictographic, syllabic, and alphabetic.

The ultimate step in this evolution of writing would have been the complete separation of the alphabetic from the nonalphabetic characters and the exclusive use of the former in written communication. But the Egyptians, although they made frequent use of the consonant signs, did not commonly employ them as an independent system of writing. It was left for the Phoenicians to do this some 1,500 years later. Nevertheless, the Egyptians must be credited with the invention of the principle of the alphabet. It was they who first perceived the value of single symbols for the individual sounds of the human voice. The Phoenicians merely copied this principle, based their own system of writing on it, and diffused the idea among neighboring nations. In the final analysis it is therefore true that the Egyptian alphabet was the parent of every other that has ever been used in the Western world.

4. THE MEANING OF EGYPTIAN ART

No single interpretation will suffice to explain the meaning of Egyptian art. In general, it expressed the aspirations of a collectivized national life. It was not art for art's sake, nor did it serve to convey the individual's reactions to the problems of his or her personal world. Yet there were times when the conventions of a communal society broke down, and the supremacy was accorded to a spontaneous individual art that expressed the beauty of a flower or caught the radiant idealism of a youthful face. Seldom was the Egyptian genius for faithful reproduction of nature entirely suppressed. Even the rigid formalism of official architecture was commonly relieved by touches of naturalism—columns in imitation of palm trunks, lotus-blossom capitals, and occasional statues of pharaohs that were not stylized types but true individual portraits.

In most civilizations where the interests of society are exalted above those of individuals, architecture tends to be the most typical and the most highly developed of the arts. Egypt was no exception. Whether in the Old, Middle, or New Kingdom, it was the problems of building construction that most absorbed the talent of the artist. Although sculpture and painting were by no means primitive, they nevertheless had as their primary function the embellishment of temples. Only at times did they rise to the status of independent arts.

The characteristic examples of Old Kingdom architecture were the pyramids, the first of which was built as early as 2770 B.C. An amazing amount of labor and skill were expended in their construction. The Greek historian Herodotus estimated that 100,000 workers were employed for twenty years to complete the single pyramid of Khufu

The Pyramids of Gizeh with the Sphinx in the Foreground

(or Cheops) at Gizeh. Its height was 481 feet, and the more than 2 million limestone blocks it contains are fitted together with a precision which few modern masons could duplicate. Each of the blocks weighs between 2.5 and 15 tons. They were evidently hewn out of rock cliffs with drills and wedges and then dragged by gangs of workers without the aid of wheeled vehicles (as yet unknown) up earthen ramps and fitted into place.

Several theories have been advanced to explain the building of the pyramids. They may have been intended for the economic purpose of providing employment opportunities. This explanation would assume that the population had increased to overcrowding, and that the resources of agriculture, mining, industry, and commerce were no longer adequate to provide a livelihood for all the people. There may be some validity to this theory, but it is certain that the pyramids had primarily religious and political significance for those who ordered them built. The pyramids were unquestionably meant to be the tombs of the divine pharaohs: the mightier the pharaoh, the larger his resting place was supposed to be. And since the pharaoh stood for the state the pyramids certainly were also political statements. Not only did they glorify the rulers but they probably helped enhance the idea that the might of the Egyptian state was indestructible.

Later, when concern for personal salvation became predominant, the temple displaced the pyramid as the leading architectural form. The most noted examples were the great temples at Karnak and Luxor,

Significance of the pyramids

built during the period of the New Kingdom. Many of their gigantic, richly carved columns still stand as silent witness to a splendid architectural talent. Egyptian temples were characterized by massive size. The temple at Karnak, with a length of about 1,300 feet, covered the largest area of any religious edifice ever built. Its central hall alone could contain almost any of the Gothic cathedrals of Europe. The columns used in the temples had stupendous proportions. The largest of them were seventy feet high, with diameters in excess of twenty feet. It has been estimated that the capitals which surmounted them could furnish standing room for a hundred men.

The temples

As already mentioned, Egyptian sculpture and painting served primarily as adjuncts to architecture. The former was heavily laden with conventions that governed its style and meaning. Statues of pharaohs were commonly of colossal size. Those produced during the New Kingdom ranged in height from seventy-five to ninety feet. Some of them were colored to enhance the portrait, and the eyes were frequently inlaid with rock crystal. The figures were nearly always rigid, with the arms folded across the chest or fixed to the sides of the body and with the eyes staring straight ahead. Countenances were generally represented as impassive, utterly devoid of emotional expression. Anatomical distortion was frequently practiced: the natural length of the thighs might be increased, the squareness of the shoulders accentuated, or all of the fingers of the hand made equal in length. A familiar example of nonnaturalistic sculpture was the Sphinx, of which there were thousands in Egypt; the best-known example was the Great Sphinx at Gizeh. This represented the head of a pharaoh on the

Egyptian sculpture

The Temple at Karnak. Most of this building has collapsed or been carried away, but the huge pylons give an idea of the massiveness of Egyptian temples.

body of a lion. The purpose was probably to symbolize the notion that the pharaoh possessed the lion's qualities of strength and courage. The figures of sculpture in relief were even less in conformity with nature. The head was presented in profile, with the eye full-face; the torso was shown in the frontal position, while the legs were rendered in profile.

The meaning of Egyptian sculpture is not hard to perceive. The colossal size of the statues of pharaohs was doubtless intended to symbolize their power and the power of the state they represented. It is significant that the size of these statues increased as the empire expanded and the government became more absolute. The conventions of rigidity and impassiveness were meant to express the timelessness and stability of the national life. Here was a nation which, according to the ideal, was not to be torn loose from its moorings by the uncertain mutations of fortune but was to remain fixed and imperturbable. The portraits of its chief men consequently must betray no anxiety, fear, or triumph, but an unvarying calmness throughout the ages. In similar fashion, the anatomical distortion can probably be interpreted as a deliberate attempt to express some national ideal.

An intriguing exception to the mainstream of Egyptian artistic development is the art produced during the reign of Akhenaton. Because the pharaoh wished to break with all manifestations of the ancient Egyptian religion, including its artistic conventions, he presided over an artistic revolution. The new style he patronized was naturalistic because his new religion reverenced nature as the handiwork of Aton. Accordingly portrait busts of the pharaoh himself and his queen Nefertiti abandoned the earlier grandiloquent impassivity and distortion in favor of more realistic detail. A surviving bust of Nefertiti which reveals her slightly quizzical and haunting femininity is one of the greatest monuments in the history of art. For the same reasons painting under the patronage of Akhenaton also emerged as a highly expressive art form. Murals of this period display the world of experience above all in terms of movement. They catch the instant action of the wild bull leaping in the swamp, the headlong flight of the frightened stag, and the effortless swimming of ducks in a pond. But just as Akhenaton's religious reform was not lasting, neither was the more naturalistic art of his reign.

5. SOCIAL AND ECONOMIC LIFE

During the greater part of the history of Egypt the population was divided into five classes: the royal family; the priests; the nobles; the middle class of scribes, merchants, artisans, and wealthy farmers; and the peasants, who comprised by far the bulk of the population. During the New Kingdom a sixth class, the professional soldiers, was added, ranking immediately below the nobles. Thousands of slaves

Pharaoh Mycerinus and His Queen. Sculpture from the IVth Dynasty, c. 2590 B.C.—an example of the impassive, grandiloquent style.

Nefertiti. The famous portrait bust executed in Akhenaton's studios at El-Amarna.

Fishing and Fowling: Wall Painting, Thebes, XVIIIth Dynasty. Most of the women appear to belong to the prosperous classes, while the simple garb and insignificant size of the men indicates that they are probably slaves.

The principal classes of Egyptian society

were also captured in this period, and for a time these formed a seventh class. Despised by all, they were forced to labor in the government quarries and on the temple estates. Gradually, however, they were allowed to enlist in the army and even in the personal service of the pharaoh. With these developments they ceased to constitute a separate class. The position of the various ranks of society shifted from time to time. In the Old Kingdom the nobles and priests among all of the pharaoh's subjects held the supremacy. During the Middle Kingdom the classes of commoners came into their own. Merchants, artisans, and farmers gained concessions from the government. Particularly impressive is the dominant role played by the merchants and artisans in this period. The establishment of the Empire, accompanied as it was by the extension of government functions, resulted in the ascendancy of a new nobility, made up primarily of officials. The priests also gained more power with the growth of magic and ritualism.

The gulf between rich and poor

The gulf that separated the standards of living of the upper and lower classes of Egypt was perhaps even wider than it is today in Europe and America. The wealthy nobles lived in splendid villas that opened onto fragrant gardens and shady groves. Their food had all the richness and variety of sundry kinds of meat, poultry, cakes, fruit, wine, and sweets. They ate from vessels of alabaster, gold, and silver, and adorned themselves with expensive fabrics and costly jewels. By contrast, the life of the poor was wretched. The laborers in the towns inhabited congested quarters composed of mud-brick hovels whose only furnishings were stools, boxes, and a few crude pottery jars. The peasants on the great estates enjoyed a less crowded but no more abundant life.

Gold Shrine Depicting Akhenaton's Son, "King Tut," and His Queen. Note the more naturalistic style held over from Akhenaton's reign. As opposed to the rigid formality otherwise characteristic of Egyptian art, curved lines predominate and both figures seem completely at ease. The young king is pouring water for his bride, who cups it with her hand.

Although polygamy was permitted, normally the basic social unit was the monogamous family. Even the pharaoh, who could keep a harem of secondary wives and concubines, had a chief wife. Concubinage, however, was a socially reputable institution. Yet compared to women in most other ancient societies, Egyptian women were not entirely subordinated to men. Wives were not secluded; women could own and inherit property and engage in business. Almost alone among ancient peoples the Egyptians permitted women to succeed to the throne: Queen Sobeknofru reigned during the Twelfth Dynasty and Queen Hatshepsut during the Eighteenth.

Egyptian women

The Egyptian economic system rested primarily upon an agrarian basis. Agriculture was diversified and highly developed, and the soil yielded excellent crops of wheat, barley, millet, vegetables, fruits, flax, and cotton. Theoretically the land was the property of the pharaoh, but in the earlier periods he granted most of it to his subjects, so that in actual practice it was largely in the possession of individuals. Com-

Agriculture, trade, and industry

Sowing Seed and Working It into the Soil. From a bag which he wears over his left shoulder, the sower casts seed under the feet of cattle yoked to a plow. The plow is here used to harrow the soil. While one laborer guides the cows with a stick, another guides the plow straight and keeps the plowshare in the ground by bearing down on the handles. Sheep are then driven across the field to trample in the seed. From wall paintings at Sheikh Saîd, about 2700 B.C.

merce grew steadily after about 2000 B.C. to a position of first-rate importance. A flourishing trade was carried on with the island of Crete, with Phoenicia, Palestine, and Syria. Gold mines in Libya controlled by Egypt were an important source of wealth. The chief articles of export consisted of gold, wheat, and linen fabrics, with imports being confined primarily to silver, ivory, and lumber. Of no less significance than commerce was manufacturing. As early as 3000 B.C. large numbers of people were already engaged in artisanal crafts. In later times factories were established, employing twenty or more persons under one roof, and with some degree of division of labor. The leading industries were quarrying, shipbuilding, and the manufacture of pottery, glass, and textiles.

*The development of
instruments of business*

From an early date the Egyptians made progress in the development of instruments of business. They knew the elements of accounting and bookkeeping. Their merchants issued orders and receipts for goods. They invented deeds for property, written contracts, and wills. While they had no system of coinage, they had nevertheless attained a money economy. Rings of copper or gold of definite weight circulated as media of exchange. This Egyptian ring-money is apparently the oldest currency in the history of civilizations. Probably it was not used except for larger transactions. The simple dealings of the peasants and poorer townsfolk doubtless continued on a basis of barter.

Economic collectivism

The Egyptian economic system was always collective. From the very beginning the energies of the people had been drawn into socialized channels. The interests of the individual and the interests of society were conceived as identical. The productive activities of the entire nation revolved around huge state enterprises, and the government remained by far the largest employer of labor. But this collectivism was not all-inclusive; a considerable sphere was left for private initia-

Sculptors at Work. From a tomb of the VIth Dynasty, c. 2300 B.C.

tive. Merchants conducted their own businesses; many of the craftsmen had their own shops; and as time went on, larger and larger numbers of peasants gained the status of independent farmers. The government continued to operate the quarries and mines, to build pyramids and temples, and to farm the royal estates.

The extreme development of state control came with the founding of the New Kingdom. The growth of a military absolutism and the increasing frequency of wars of conquest augmented the need for revenue and for unlimited production of goods. To fulfill this need the government extended its control over economic life. The services of craftsmen were conscripted for the erection of magnificent temples and for the manufacture of implements of war, while foreign trade became a state monopoly. As the New Kingdom staggered toward its downfall, the government absorbed more and more of the economic activities of the people.

The extreme development of state control under the New Kingdom

6. THE EGYPTIAN ACHIEVEMENT

Few civilizations of ancient times surpassed the Egyptian in impressive accomplishments. Important elements of mathematics and science had their beginnings in the Nile valley. The Egyptians also perfected techniques of irrigation, engineering, and the making of pottery and glass. They were one of the first peoples to have any clear conception of art for other than utilitarian purposes, and they originated architectural principles that were destined for extensive use in subsequent ages.

Egyptian contributions: (1) intellectual and artistic

Equally noteworthy were Egyptian religious and ethical ideas. Aside from the Persians, the dwellers on the banks of the Nile were the only peoples of the ancient world to build a national religion around the doctrine of personal immortality and the idea of rewards and punishments after death. Beyond that, Akhenaton's experiment in the cult of Aton was the first example in history of a religion of universal monotheism. Egyptian ethical prescriptions, moreover, were remarkably advanced in embracing not only the ordinary prohibitions of lying, theft, and murder, but in including exalted ideals of justice, benevolence, and equal rights. Egyptian thought had little direct influence on subsequent formulations because the Egyptian language and writing were hardly understood by others, but all told the Egyptian civilization stands as a remarkable and ever-fascinating monument of human accomplishments at the dawn of recorded time.

(2) religious and ethical

SELECTED READINGS

• *Items so designated are available in paperback editions.*
  Aldred, Cyril, *The Egyptians,* New York, 1963. A short but reliable account covering culture as well as political history.

Bibby, Geoffrey, *Four Thousand Years Ago*, Baltimore, 1961. Egyptian developments from 2000 to 1000 B.C. seen from the perspective of contemporary events elsewhere.

• Breasted, James H., *The Development of Religion and Thought in Ancient Egypt*, New York, 1912. Stimulating, but exaggerated in its claims for the work of Akhenaton; should be read in conjunction with Wilson.

———, *History of Egypt*, New York, 1912. The standard older work by America's first great Egyptologist. Full of valuable information but now regarded as being out of date in its extreme claims for Egyptian originality and influence.

• Childe, V. Gordon, *New Light on the Most Ancient East*, 4th ed., New York, 1957. Covers origins of civilization not just in Egypt but also in Mesopotamia and India.

Cottrell, Leonard, *Life under the Pharaohs*, New York, 1960. Fascinating account of life during the period of the Empire.

Desroches-Noblecourt, C., *Egyptian Wall Paintings*, New York, 1962.

• Edwards, I. E. S., *The Pyramids of Egypt*, Baltimore, 1961. Traces evolution of the form and speculates on the meaning of the pyramids.

Emery, Walter, *Archaic Egypt*, Baltimore, 1961. Controversial account of the earliest period.

• Frankfort, Henri, *Ancient Egyptian Religion: An Interpretation*, New York, 1948. A penetrating, profound study.

Hayes, William C., *The Sceptre of Egypt*, 2 vols., New York, 1953–1959. Written with special reference to the Egyptian holdings of the Metropolitan Museum of Art in New York.

• Mertz, B., *Temples, Tombs and Hieroglyphs*, New York, 1965. Intriguing approach by means of archeological discoveries.

• Smith, W. S., *Art and Architecture of Ancient Egypt*, Baltimore, 1958.

• Steindorff, G., and K. C. Seele, *When Egypt Ruled the East*, Chicago, 1963. Best account of political history of the Empire.

• Wilson, John H., *The Burden of Egypt*, Chicago, 1951. (Paperback edition under the title, *The Culture of Ancient Egypt*.) In a class by itself as the one book to read on Egypt if the student only wishes to read one book. Scintillating and masterful.

SOURCE MATERIALS

Grayson, A. Kirk, and D. B. Redford, eds., *Papyrus and Tablet*, Englewood Cliffs, N.J., 1973. Sources from both ancient Egypt and Mesopotamia. The best short collection for the beginner.

• Pritchard, James B., *The Ancient Near East: An Anthology of Texts and Pictures*, Princeton, N.J., 1965. Also covers both Egypt and Mesopotamia. An excellent selection.

Chapter 3

THE MESOPOTAMIAN AND PERSIAN CIVILIZATIONS

If a son strike his father, they shall cut off his hand.
If a man destroy the eye of an aristocrat, they shall destroy his eye.
If one break an aristocrat's bone, they shall break his bone.
If one destroy the eye of a commoner, or break the bone of a commoner,
   he shall pay one mina of silver.
If one destroy the eye of a slave, or break a bone of a slave, he shall pay
   one-half his price.

            —The Code of Hammurabi, lines 195–199

The other of the most ancient civilizations was that which began in the Tigris-Euphrates valley at least as early as 3500 B.C. This civilization was formerly called the Babylonian or Babylonian-Assyrian civilization. It is now known, however, that the civilization was not founded by either the Babylonians or the Assyrians but by an earlier people called the Sumerians. It seems better, therefore, to use the geographical term "Mesopotamian" to cover the whole civilization.

Origin of the Mesopotamian civilization

The Mesopotamian civilization differed from the Egyptian in many fundamental respects. Because the Tigris and Euphrates rivers—unlike the Nile—flooded irregularly, and sometimes disastrously, the Mesopotamians, unlike the Egyptians, could not take nature for granted. Furthermore, the Mesopotamians were not naturally protected, as the Egyptians were, from foreign incursions. In general, therefore, life in the Tigris-Euphrates regions was far more of a struggle. The results of this can be seen in both political and cultural history. The political history of the Mesopotamian area was marked by much sharper interruptions than transpired in Egypt, as the dominance of one people succeeded that of another. Mesopotamian culture too was more warlike and far more gloomy and pessimistic than the Egyptian.

Comparisons with Egypt

Moreover, whereas the native of Egypt believed in immortality and dedicated a large part of his energy to preparing for the life to come, his Mesopotamian counterpart lived in the present and cherished few hopes regarding human fate beyond the grave. Further religious differences were that the Mesopotamians never advanced as far as the Egyptians did toward monotheism and conceived of their divinities more in terms of fear than of love. Finally, Mesopotamian art was fiercer and less personal than the Egyptian.

Similarities

But there were also important similarities between the two. Both civilizations made progress in ethical theory and in concepts of social justice. Both had their evils of slavery and imperialism, of oppressive kings and priests. Both had common problems of irrigation and land boundaries; and, as a result, both made notable progress in the sciences, especially in mathematics. Finally, rivalry among small states led eventually to consolidation and to the growth of mighty empires, especially in the case of Mesopotamia.

*See color map facing
page 65*

1. FROM THE SUMERIAN TO THE PERSIAN CONQUEST

The Sumerians

The pioneers in the development of the Mesopotamian civilization were the people known as Sumerians, who settled in the lower Tigris-Euphrates valley around 3500 B.C. Their exact place of origin is obscure, but it seems likely that they came from the plateau of central Asia. They spoke a language unrelated to any now known, although their culture bore a certain resemblance to the earliest civilization of India. By a process of peaceful interaction they gradually began to guide the natives hitherto living in the lower valley, a mysterious people who were already advancing well beyond the Neolithic cultural stage. From around 2800 to 2340 B.C. a number of independent Sumerian city-states, the most important of which were Ur and Lagash, flourished in Lower Mesopotamia. Then, however, the period of Sumerian predominance was interrupted by a successful invasion from the north led by the mighty Sargon of Akkad (c. 2334–2279).[1] The Akkadians were Semites, a large grouping of peoples of the Near East who spoke related languages (the leading Semitic peoples today are Arabs and Jews). Under Sargon's leadership the Akkadians established the first extensive military empire in Mesopotamia, but this declined around 2200 B.C. and was supplanted by a Sumerian revival led by the city of Ur.

The period of Sumerian revival did not last long. Around 2000 B.C. the Amorites, another tribe of Semites, advanced from the west, conquered the Sumerian cities, and established a new empire in the Meso-

*Hammurabi: King of Babylon and
Law-Giver*

[1]Here, and throughout, dates following a ruler's name refer to dates of reign.

potamian region. Since the Amorites made the village of Babylon the capital of their empire they are commonly called the Babylonians, or the Old Babylonians, to distinguish them from the Neo-Babylonians or Chaldeans, who occupied the Tigris-Euphrates valley much later. The rise of the Old Babylonians inaugurated the second important stage of Mesopotamian civilization after the Sumerian stage. Although most of the Sumerian culture survived, Sumerian dominance was now at an end. The Babylonians established an autocratic state and during the reign of their most famous king, Hammurabi (c. 1792–1750 B.C.), extended their dominion north to Assyria. But after his time their empire gradually declined until it was finally overthrown by the Kassites about 1550 B.C.

With the downfall of Old Babylonia a period of retrogression set in which lasted for 600 years, for the Kassites were barbarians with no interest in the cultural achievements of their predecessors. Indeed, the old culture probably would have died out entirely had it not been for its partial adoption by another Semitic people who, as early as 3000 B.C., had founded a tiny kingdom on the plateau of Assur some 500 miles up the Tigris River. These people came to be called the Assyrians, and their rise to power marked the beginning of the third stage in the development of the Mesopotamian civilization. They began to expand about 1300 B.C. and soon afterward made themselves masters of the whole northern valley. In the tenth century they overturned what was left of Kassite power in Babylonia. Their empire reached its height in the eighth and seventh centuries under Sargon II (722–705 B.C.) and Sennacherib (705–681), who built Nineveh, a magnificent new capital on the Tigris. The Assyrian Empire had now come to include nearly all of the Near East, since the Assyrians had conquered, one after another, Syria, Phoenicia, the Kingdom of Israel, and Egypt.

Brilliant though the successes of the Assyrians were, they did not endure. So rapidly were new territories annexed that the empire soon reached an unmanageable size. The Assyrians' ability at government was far inferior to their appetite for conquest. Subjugated nations chafed under the despotism that had been forced upon them and, as the empire gave signs of cracking from within, determined to regain their freedom. The death blow was delivered by the Chaldeans (pronounced Kaldeans), a nation of Semites who had settled southeast of the valley of the two rivers. Under the leadership of Nabopolassar, who had served the Assyrian emperors in the capacity of a provincial governor, they organized a revolt and finally captured Nineveh in 612 B.C. The most famous of the Chaldeans was Nebuchadnezzar (605–562 B.C.), who conquered Jerusalem and made his capital of Babylon the leading city of the Near East.

In 539 B.C. the empire of the Chaldeans fell, after an existence of less than a century. It was overthrown by Cyrus the Persian, as he himself declared, "without a battle and without fighting." The easy victory appears to have been made possible by assistance from the Jews, who

The rise and fall of the Old Babylonians

The Kassites and the Assyrians

Assyrians Storming an Enemy City

The downfall of the Chaldeans

were being held captive in Babylon, and by a conspiracy of the priests of Babylon to deliver the city to Cyrus as an act of vengeance against the Chaldean king, whose policies they did not like. Members of other influential classes appear also to have looked upon the Persians as deliverers.

The Persians

Although the Persian state incorporated all of the territories that had once been embraced by the Mesopotamian empires, it included many other provinces besides. It was the vehicle, moreover, of a new and different culture. The downfall of Chaldea must therefore be taken as marking the end of Mesopotamian political history.

2. SUMERIAN ORIGINS OF MESOPOTAMIAN CIVILIZATION

Formative influence of the Sumerians

More than to any other people, the Mesopotamian civilization owed its character to the Sumerians. Much of what used to be ascribed to the Babylonians and Assyrians is now known to have been developed by the nation that preceded them. The system of writing was of Sumerian origin; likewise the religion, the laws, and a great deal of the science and commercial practice. Only in the evolution of government and military tactics and in the development of the arts was the originating talent of the later conquerors particularly manifest.

The Sumerian political system

Through the greater part of their history the Sumerians lived in a loose confederation of city-states, united only for military purposes. At the head of each was a *patesi,* who combined the functions of chief priest, commander of the army, and superintendent of the irrigation system. Occasionally one of the more ambitious of these rulers would extend his power over a number of cities and assume the title of king,

Diorama of a Part of Ur about 2000 B.C. A modern archeologist's conception. Walls are omitted to show interiors at left.

but no true empire was ever created like those of the Akkadians, or subsequent Babylonians, Assyrians, or Chaldeans.

The Sumerian economic pattern was relatively simple and permitted a wider scope for individual enterprise than was generally allowed in Egypt. The land was never the exclusive property of the ruler either in theory or in practice. Neither was trade or industry a monopoly of the government. The temples, however, seem to have fulfilled many of the functions of a collectivist state. They owned a large portion of the land and operated business enterprises. Because the priests alone had the technical knowledge to calculate the coming of the seasons and lay out canals, they controlled the irrigation system. The masses of the people had little they could call their own. Many of them were serfs, but even those who were technically free were little better off, forced as they were to pay high rents and to labor on public works. Slavery in the strict sense of the word was not an important institution.

The Sumerian economic pattern

Agriculture was the chief economic pursuit of most of the citizens, and the Sumerians were excellent farmers. By virtue of their knowledge of irrigation they produced large crops of cereal grains and subtropical fruits. Since most of the land was divided into large estates held by the rulers, the priests, and the army officers, the average rural citizen was either a tenant farmer or a serf. Commerce was the second most important source of Sumerian wealth. A flourishing trade was established with all of the surrounding areas, revolving around the exchange of metals and timber from the north and west for agricultural products and handicrafted goods from the lower valley. Nearly all of the familiar adjuncts of business were highly developed; bills, receipts, notes, and letters of credit were regularly used.

Agriculture

The most distinctive achievement of the Sumerians was their system of law. It was the product of a gradual evolution of local usage merging together with ideas absorbed from neighboring Semitic peoples. Only a few fragments of this law have survived in their original form, but the famous Code of Hammurabi, the Babylonian king, is now recognized to have been a variant of the code of the Sumerians. Ultimately this code became the basis of the laws of nearly all of the Semites—Babylonians, Assyrians, Chaldeans, and Hebrews.

Mesopotamian law

The following may be regarded as the essential features of the Mesopotamian law:

(1) The *lex talionis,* or law of retaliation in kind—"an eye for an eye, a tooth for a tooth, a limb for a limb." This fundamental concept was one that the Sumerians learned from the Semites.

Essential features of Mesopotamian law

(2) Semiprivate administration of justice. It was incumbent upon the victim or his family to bring the offender to justice. The court served principally as an umpire in the dispute between the plaintiff and defendant, not as an agency of the state to maintain public security, although constables attached to the court might assist in the execution of the sentence.

(3) Inequality before the law. Mesopotamian law divided the population into three classes: patricians or aristocrats; burghers or commoners; serfs and slaves. Penalties were graded according to the rank of the victim, but also in some cases according to the rank of the offender. The killing or maiming of a patrician was a much more serious offense than a similar crime committed against a burgher or a slave. On the other hand, when a patrician was the offender he was punished *more severely* than a person of inferior status would be for the same crime. The origin of this curious rule was probably to be found in considerations of military discipline. Since the patricians were army officers and therefore the chief defenders of the state, they could not be permitted to give vent to their passions or to indulge in riotous conduct.

(4) Inadequate distinction between accidental and intentional homicide. A person responsible for killing another accidentally did not escape penalty, as under modern law, but had to pay a fine to the family of the victim, apparently on the theory that children were the property of their fathers and wives the property of their husbands.

Quite as much as their law, the religion of the Sumerians illuminates their social attitudes and the character of their culture. They did not succeed in developing a very exalted religion; yet it occupied an important place in their lives. To begin with, it was polytheistic and anthropomorphic. They believed in a number of gods and goddesses, each a distinct personality with human attributes. The sun god, the lord of the rain and wind, the goddess of the generative powers of nature were only a few of them. All of these numerous deities were thought to be capable of performing both good and evil.

Sumerian religion

The Sumerian religion was a religion for this world exclusively; it offered no hope for a blissful, eternal afterlife. The afterlife was a mere temporary existence in a dreary, shadowy place which later came to be called Sheol. Here the ghosts of the dead lingered for a time, perhaps a generation or so, and then disappeared. No one could look forward to resurrection in another world and a joyous eternal existence as a recompense for the evils of this life; the victory of the grave was complete. In accordance with these beliefs the Sumerians bestowed only limited care upon the bodies of their dead. They practiced no mummification and built no elaborate tombs. Corpses were commonly interred beneath the floor of the house without a coffin and with comparatively few articles for the use of the ghost.

*A religion neither ethical
nor spiritual*

There was little spiritual content in Sumerian religion. As we have seen, the gods were not spiritual beings but creatures cast in the human mold, with most of the weaknesses and passions of mortals. Nor were the purposes of the religion any more spiritual. It provided no blessings in the form of solace, uplift of the soul, or oneness with God. If it benefited humanity at all, it did so chiefly in the form of material gain—abundant harvests and prosperity in business. The re-

Sumerian Praying Figures. These statues dating from about 2700 B.C. show the immobile bodies and huge staring eyes characteristic of much of Mesopotamian art.

ligion did have some ethical content. All the major deities in the Sumerian pantheon were extolled in hymns as lovers of truth, goodness, and justice. The goddess Nanshe, for example, was said "to comfort the orphan, to make disappear the widow, to set up a place of destruction for the mighty." Yet the same deities who personified these noble ideals created such evils as falsehood and strife, and endowed every human being with a sinful nature. "Never," it was said, "has a sinless child been born to its mother."

In the field of intellectual endeavor the Sumerians achieved no small distinction. They produced a system of writing which was destined to be used for two thousand years after the downfall of their nation. This was the celebrated *cuneiform* writing, consisting of wedge-shaped characters (*cuneus* is Latin for wedge) imprinted on clay tablets with a square-tipped reed. At first a pictographic system, it was gradually transformed into an aggregate of syllabic and phonetic signs, some 350 in number. No alphabet was ever developed out of it, but cuneiform nonetheless became the standard medium for commercial transactions throughout most of the Near East (often including Egypt) from about 3000 to about 500 B.C. The Sumerians wrote nothing that could be called philosophy, but they did make some notable beginnings in science. In mathematics, for example, they surpassed the Egyptians in every field except geometry. They discovered the processes of multiplication and division and even the extraction of square and cube root. Their systems of numeration and of weights and measures were duodecimal, with the number sixty as the most common unit. They invented the water clock and the lunar calendar, the latter an inaccurate division of the year into months based upon cycles of the

The intellectual level of Sumerian culture

See color plates
following page 64

moon. In order to bring it into harmony with the solar year, an extra month had to be added from time to time. The Sumerians were the first known peoples to believe in astrology—the belief that that human fates are determined by the courses of the stars—and this interest led them to pioneer in astronomical observations and predictions of planetary movements. Their medicine was a curious compound of herbalism and magic. The repertory of the physician consisted primarily of charms to exorcise the evil spirits which were believed to be the cause of the disease.

As artists, the Sumerians excelled in metalwork, gem carving, and sculpture. They produced some remarkable specimens of naturalistic art in their weapons, vessels, jewelry, and animal representations, which revealed alike a technical skill and a gift of imagination. Evidently religious conventions had not yet imposed any paralyzing influence, and consequently the artist was still free to follow his own impulses. Architecture, on the other hand, was distinctly inferior, probably because of the limitations enforced by the scarcity of good building materials. Since there was no stone in the valley, the architect had to depend upon sun-dried brick. The characteristic Sumerian edifice, extensively copied by their Semitic successors, was the *ziggurat,* a terraced tower set on a platform and surmounted by a shrine. Its construction was massive, its lines were monotonous, and little architectural ingenuity was exhibited in it. The royal tombs and private houses showed more originality. It was in them that the Sumerian inventions of the arch, the vault, and the dome were regularly employed, and the column was used occasionally.

3. OLD BABYLONIAN DEVELOPMENTS

Although the Old Babylonians were an alien nation, they had lived long enough in close contact with the Sumerians to be influenced profoundly by them. They had little culture of their own when they came into the valley, and in general they only appropriated and modified what the Sumerians had already developed. Thus the changes in Mesopotamian culture during the Old Babylonian period were essentially variations on Sumerian themes.

First among the alterations which the Old Babylonians made in their inheritance may be mentioned the political and legal. As military conquerors holding in subjection numerous vanquished nations, they found it necessary to establish a consolidated state. Vestiges of the old system of local autonomy were swept away, and the power of the king of Babylon was made supreme. Kings became gods, or at least claimed divine origin. A system of royal taxation was adopted as well as compulsory military service. The system of law was also changed to conform to the new condition of centralized despotism. The list of crimes against the state was enlarged, and the king's officers assumed a

Two Portraits from Lagash. Although these Sumerian votive statues are separated by some seven centuries, dating from about 2700 B.C. and 2000 B.C. respectively, they show the barest minimum of artistic evolution.

The Great Ziggurat at Ur

Gold Jewelry from Ur, c. 3500–2800 B.C.

more active role in apprehending and punishing offenders, although it was still impossible for any criminal to be pardoned without the consent of the victim or the victim's family. The severity of penalties was decidedly increased, particularly for crimes involving any suggestion of treason or sedition. Such apparently trivial offenses as "vagabondage" and "disorderly conduct at a tavern" were made punishable by death, probably on the assumption that they would be likely to foster disloyal activities. Whereas under the Sumerian law the harboring of fugitive slaves was punishable merely by a fine, the Babylonian law made it a capital crime. According to the Sumerian code, the slave who disputed his master's rights over him was to be sold; the Code of Hammurabi prescribed that he should have his ear cut off. Adultery was also made a capital offense, whereas under the Sumerian law it did not even necessarily result in divorce. In a few particulars the new system of law revealed some improvement. Wives and children sold for debt could not be held in bondage for longer than four years, and a female slave who had borne her master a child could not be sold at all.

The Old Babylonian laws also reflect a more extensive development of business than that which existed in the preceding culture. That an influential merchant class traded for profit and enjoyed a privileged position in society is evidenced by the fact that the commercial provisions of Hammurabi's code were based upon the principle of "Let the buyer beware." The Babylonian rulers did not believe in a regime of free competition, however. Trade and industry were subject to elaborate regulation by the state. There were laws regarding partnership, storage, and agency; laws respecting deeds, wills, and the taking of in-

Scenes from the Epic of Gilgamash. A Sumerian inlaid shell panel.

terest on money; and a host of others. For a deal to be negotiated without a written contract or without witnesses was punishable by death. Agriculture, which was still the occupation of a majority of the citizens, did not escape regulation. The code provided penalties for failure to cultivate a field and for neglect of dikes and canals. Both government ownership and private tenure of land were permitted; but, regardless of the status of the owner, the tenant farmer was required to pay two-thirds of all he produced as rent.

Religion under the Old Babylonians underwent only superficial changes. Deities that had been venerated by the Sumerians were now neglected and new ones exalted in their stead. Above all, a new god, Marduk, was imported to head the Mesopotamian pantheon. He and the other new deities carried no spiritual significance, however, conveying no promise of resurrection from the dead or of personal immortality. The Old Babylonians were no more otherworldly in their outlook than the Sumerians. The religions of both peoples were fundamentally materialistic.

Although there was some decline in artistic accomplishments during the period of Babylonian rule, this was by no means true of developments in literature. Building upon legends and myths already evolving under the Sumerians, the Babylonians contributed to world literature one of the greatest epics of all time, the epic of *Gilgamesh*. This long poem, comparable in sweep and power to the Greek *Iliad* and *Odyssey,* is a compilation of stories that were told and re-told over many generations. Its hero, Gilgamesh, is a Mesopotamian king who experiences many adventures. In one he seeks the secret of immortality from an old man and his wife who had been saved when the gods had decided to destroy the world by a flood. Many of the elements of this story are strikingly similar to the Old Testament story of Noah,

Panel of Glazed Brick, Babylon, Sixth Century B.C. An ornamental relief on a background of earth brown. The lion is in blue, white, and yellow glazes.

including the details that the couple had survived the flood by floating in an ark. But the message is rather different, for the Babylonian hero learns only resignation from the old couple: the gods will preserve those whom they please and there is nothing mankind can do to understand divine decisions. Gilgamesh does learn from the old pair of a plant that will at least bring back his youth, but after gaining it with great effort from the floor of the sea he leaves it unguarded while asleep, and a snake eats it instead. According to the epic, this is why snakes gain new life every year when they shed their skins. But the human hero is finally forced to recognize that he himself can never transcend old age and death. As the epic states in resigned summary: "When the gods created man, they let death be his share, and life they kept in their own hands."

4. THE METAMORPHOSIS UNDER ASSYRIA

Of all the peoples of the Mesopotamian area after the time of the Sumerians, the Assyrians went through the most completely independent evolution. For several centuries they had lived a comparatively isolated existence on top of their small plateau in the upper valley of the Tigris. Eventually they came under the influence of the Babylonians, but not until after the course of their own history had been partially fixed. As a consequence, the period of Assyrian supremacy (from about 1300 B.C. to 612 B.C.) had a more peculiar character than any other era of Mesopotamian history.

The evolution of Assyrian supremacy

The Assyrians were preeminently a nation of warriors because of the special conditions of their own environment. The limited resources of their original home and the constant danger of attack from hostile nations around them forced the development of warlike habits and imperial ambitions. It is therefore not strange that their hunger for territory should have known no limits. The more they conquered, the more they felt they had to conquer, in order to protect what they had already gained. Every success excited ambition and riveted the chains of militarism more firmly than ever. Disaster was inevitable.

A nation of warriors

The exigencies of war determined the whole character of the Assyrian system. The state was a great military machine. The army commanders were at once the richest and the most powerful class in the country. Not only did they share in the plunder of war, but they were frequently granted huge estates as rewards for victory. At least one of them, Sargon II, dared to usurp the throne. The military establishment itself represented the last word in preparedness. The standing army greatly exceeded in size that of any other nation of the Near East. New and improved armaments and techniques of fighting gave to the Assyrian soldiers unparalleled advantages. Iron swords, heavy bows, long lances, battering rams, fortresses on wheels, and metal breastplates, shields, and helmets were only a few examples of their superior equipment.

Features of Assyrian militarism

Assyrian Winged Human-Headed Bull.
This relief was found in the palace of
King Sargon II (722–705 B.C.). It measures 16 feet wide by 16 feet high and
weighs approximately 40 tons.

Frightfulness

But swords and spears and engines of war were not their only instruments of combat. As much as anything else the Assyrians depended upon frightfulness as a means of overcoming their enemies.
Upon soldiers captured in battle, and sometimes upon noncombatants
as well, they inflicted unspeakable cruelties—skinning them alive, im-
paling them on stakes, cutting off ears, noses, and sex organs, and
then exhibiting the mutilated victims in cages for the benefit of cities
that had not yet surrendered. Accounts of these cruelties are not taken
from atrocity stories circulated by their enemies; they come from the
records of the Assyrians themselves. Their chroniclers boasted of
them as evidences of valor, and the people believed in them as guaranties of security and power. It is clear why the Assyrians were the most
hated of all the nations of antiquity.

The tragedy of Assyrian militarism

Seldom has the decline of an empire been so complete as was that of
Assyria. In spite of its magnificent armaments and its wholesale destruction of its foes, Assyria's period of imperial splendor lasted little
more than a century. Nation after nation conspired against the Assyrians and finally accomplished their downfall. Their enemies took
frightful vengeance. The whole land was so thoroughly sacked and
the people so completely enslaved or exterminated that it has been difficult to trace any subsequent Assyrian influence upon history. The
power and security which military strength was supposed to provide
proved a mockery in the end. If Assyria had been utterly defenseless,
its fate could hardly have been worse.

With so complete an absorption in military pursuits, it was inevitable that the Assyrians should have neglected in some measure the arts of peace. Industry and commerce appear to have declined under the regime of the Assyrians, for such pursuits were generally scorned as beneath the dignity of a soldierly people. The minimum of manufacturing and trade which had to be carried on was left quite largely to the Arameans, a people closely related to the Phoenicians and the Hebrews. The Assyrians themselves preferred to derive their living from agriculture. The land system included both public and private holdings. The temples held the largest share of the landed wealth. Although the estates of the crown were likewise extensive, they were constantly being diminished by grants to army officers.

Neither the economic nor the social order was sound. The frequent military campaigns depleted the energies and resources of the nation. In the course of time the army officers became a pampered aristocracy, delegating their duties to their subordinates and devoting themselves to luxurious pleasures. The stabilizing influence of a prosperous and intelligent merchant class was precluded by the rule that only foreigners and slaves could engage in commercial activities. Yet more serious was the treatment accorded to the lower classes, the serfs and the slaves. The former comprised the bulk of the rural population. Some of them cultivated definite portions of their master's estates and retained a part of what they produced for themselves. Others were "empty" men, without even a plot to cultivate and dependent on the need for seasonal labor to provide for their means of subsistence. All were extremely poor and were subject to the additional hardships of labor on public works and compulsory military service. The slaves, who were chiefly an urban working class, were of two different types: the domestic slaves, who performed household duties and sometimes engaged in business for their masters; and the war captives. The former were not numerous and were allowed a great deal of freedom, even to the extent of owning property. The latter suffered much greater miseries. Bound by heavy shackles, they were compelled to labor to the point of exhaustion in building roads, canals, and palaces.

An Assyrian King of the Ninth Century B.C.

Defects in the economic system

Whether the Assyrians adopted the law of the Old Babylonians has never been settled. Undoubtedly they were influenced by it, but several of the features of Hammurabi's code are entirely absent. Notable among these are the *lex talionis* and the system of gradation of penalties according to the rank of the victim and the offender. Whereas the Babylonians prescribed the most drastic punishments for crimes suggestive of treason or sedition, the Assyrians reserved theirs for such offenses as abortion and homosexuality, probably for the military reason of preventing a decline in the birth rate. Another contrast is the more complete subjection of Assyrian women. Wives were treated as chattels of their husbands, polygamy was permitted, and the right of divorce was placed entirely in the hands of the male.

Assyrian law

That a military nation like the Assyrians should not have taken first rank in intellectual achievement is easily understandable. The atmosphere of a military campaign is not favorable to reflection or disinterested research. Yet the demands of successful campaigning may lead to a certain accumulation of knowledge, for practical problems have to be solved. Under such circumstances the Assyrians accomplished some measure of scientific progress. They appear to have divided the circle into 360 degrees and to have estimated locations on the surface of the earth in something resembling latitude and longitude. They recognized and named five planets and achieved some success in predicting eclipses. Since the health of armies is important, medicine received considerable attention. More than five hundred drugs, both vegetable and mineral, were catalogued and their uses indicated. Symptoms of various diseases were described and were generally interpreted as due to natural causes, although incantations and the prescription of disgusting compounds to drive out demons were still commonly employed as methods of treatment.

In the domain of art the Assyrians surpassed the Old Babylonians and at least equaled the work of the Sumerians, although in different form. Sculpture was the art most highly developed, particularly in the low reliefs. These portrayed dramatic incidents of war and the hunt with the utmost fidelity to nature and a vivid description of movement. The Assyrians delighted in depicting the cool bravery of the hunter in the face of terrific danger, the ferocity of lions at bay, and the death agonies of wounded beasts. Unfortunately this art was limited almost entirely to the two themes of war and sport. Its purpose was to glorify the exploits of the ruling class. Architecture ranked second to sculpture from the standpoint of artistic excellence. Assyrian palaces and temples were built of stone, obtained from the mountainous areas of the north, instead of the mud brick of former times. Their principal features were the arch and the dome. The column was also used but never very successfully. The chief demerit of this architecture was its hugeness, which the Assyrians appeared to regard as synonymous with beauty.

Assyrian Relief Sculpture. This panel depicts the Emperor Assurbanipal (668–626 B.C.) hunting lions.

5. THE CHALDEAN RENASCENCE

The Mesopotamian civilization entered its final stage with the over-throw of Assyria and the establishment of Chaldean supremacy. This stage is often called the Neo-Babylonian, because Nebuchadnezzar and his followers restored the capital at Babylon and attempted to revive the culture of Hammurabi's time. As might have been ex-pected, their attempt was not wholly successful. The Assyrian meta-morphosis had altered that culture in various profound and ineffaceable ways. Besides, the Chaldeans themselves had a history of their own which they could not entirely escape. Nevertheless, they did manage to revive certain of the old institutions and ideals. They re-stored the ancient law and literature, the essentials of the Old Baby-lonian form of government, and the economic system of earlier times with its dominance of industry and trade. Farther than this they were unable to go.

It was in religion that the failure of the Chaldean renascence was most conspicuous. Although Marduk was restored to his traditional place at the head of the pantheon, the system of belief was little more than superficially Babylonian. What the Chaldeans really did was to develop an astral religion. The gods were divested of their human qualities and exalted into transcendent, omnipotent beings. They were actually identified with the planets themselves. Though still not en-tirely aloof from humans, they certainly lost their character as beings who could be cajoled and threatened and coerced by magic. They ruled the universe almost mechanically. While their immediate inten-tions were sometimes discernible, their ultimate purposes were in-scrutable.

Two significant results flowed from these conceptions. The first was an even greater attitude of fatalism than before. Since the ways of the gods were past comprehension, all that humans could do was to resign themselves to their fate. It behooved them therefore to submit abso-lutely to the gods, to trust in them implicitly, in the vague hope that the results in the end would be good. Thus arose for the first time in history the concept of piety as submission—a concept which was adopted in several other religions, as we shall see in succeeding chap-ters. For the Chaldeans it implied no otherwordly significance; one did not resign oneself to calamities in this life in order to be justified in the next. The Chaldeans had no interest in a life to come. Submission might bring certain earthly rewards, but in the main, as they con-ceived it, it was not a means to an end at all. It was rather the expres-sion of an attitude of despair, of humility in the face of mysteries that could not be fathomed.

The second great result which came from the growth of an astral religion was the development of a stronger spiritual consciousness.

This is revealed in the penitential hymns of unknown authors and in the prayers which were ascribed to Nebuchadnezzar and other kings as the spokesmen for the nation. In most of them the gods are addressed as exalted beings who are concerned with justice and righteous conduct on the part of humanity, although the distinction between ceremonial and genuine morality is not always sharply drawn. It has been asserted by one scholar that these hymns could have been used by the Hebrews with little modification except for the substitution of the name of Yahweh for that of the Chaldean god.

With the gods promoted to so lofty a plane, it was perhaps inevitable that human beings should have been abased. Mortal creatures could not be compared with the timeless beings who dwelt in the heavens and guided the destinies of the earth. Humans were lowly creatures, sunk in iniquity and vileness, and hardly worthy of approaching the gods. The consciousness of sin already present in the Babylonian and Assyrian religions now reached a stage of almost pathological intensity. Chaldean hymns compare people to prisoners, bound hand and foot, languishing in darkness, whose transgressions are "seven times seven." Their misery is increased by the fact that their evil nature has prompted them to sin unwittingly. Never before had humans been regarded as so hopelessly depraved.

Curiously enough, the pessimism of the Chaldeans does not appear to have affected their morality very much. So far as the evidence reveals, they indulged in no rigors of asceticism. Apparently they took it for granted that humans could not avoid sinning, no matter how hard they tried. They seem to have been just as deeply committed to enjoying creature comforts as any of the earlier nations. Occasional references were made in their hymns to reverence, kindness, and purity of heart as virtues, and to oppression, slander, and anger as vices, but these were intermingled with ritualistic conceptions of cleanness and uncleanness and with expressions of desire for physical satisfactions. When the Chaldeans prayed, it was not always that their gods would make them good, but more often that they would grant long life, abundant offspring, and material well-being.

Aside from religion, the Chaldean culture differed from that of the Sumerians, Babylonians, and Assyrians chiefly in regard to astronomical achievements. Without doubt the Chaldeans were the most capable astronomers in all of Mesopotamian history. They worked out the most elaborate system for recording the passage of time that had yet been devised, with their invention of the seven-day week and their division of the day into twelve double-hours of 120 minutes each. They kept accurate records of eclipses and other celestial occurrences for more than 350 years—until long after the downfall of their empire. The motivating force behind Chaldean astronomy was religion. The chief purpose of mapping the heavens and collecting celestial data was to discover the future the gods had prepared for mankind. Since the planets were gods themselves, that future could best be divined in the movements of the heavenly bodies. Astronomy was therefore primarily astrology.

Aside from astronomy, Chaldean culture showed little advance beyond the stage it had reached under the Assyrians. Art differed only in its greater magnificence. Literature, dominated by the antiquarian spirit, revealed a lack of originality. The writings of the Old Babylonians were extensively copied and reedited, but they were supplemented by little that was new.

6. THE PERSIAN EMPIRE AND ITS HISTORY

Comparatively little is known of the Persians before the sixth century B.C. Up to that time they appear to have led an obscure and peaceful existence on the eastern shore of the Persian Gulf. They were not Semites but spoke an Indo-European language, that is, one of a group that includes Sanskrit (the language of ancient India), Greek, Latin, and most of the modern European tongues. Their homeland afforded only modest advantages. On the east it was hemmed in by mountains, and its coastline lacked harbors. The fertile valleys of the interior, however, were capable of providing adequate subsistence for a limited population. Save for the development of an elaborate religion, the people had made little progress. At the dawn of their history they were not independent but were vassals of the Medes, a kindred people who ruled over a territory north and east of the Tigris.

The Persian background

In 559 B.C. a prince by the name of Cyrus became king of a southern Persian tribe. About five years later he made himself ruler of all the Persians, overthrew the domination of the Medes, and then began to conquer neighboring areas. As Cyrus the Great he has gone down in history as one of the most sensational conquerors of all time. Within the short space of twenty years he founded a vast empire, larger than any that had previously existed.

The rise of Cyrus

The first of the conquests of Cyrus was the kingdom of Lydia, which occupied the western half of Asia Minor and was separated from the lands of the Medes by the River Halys, in what is now northern Turkey. Perceiving the ambitions of the Persians, Croesus, the fabulously rich Lydian king, decided to wage a preventive war to preserve his own nation from conquest. According to the Greek historian Herodotus, Croesus consulted the oracle at Delphi as to the advisability of an immediate attack and gained the reply that if he would cross the Halys and assume the offensive he would destroy a great nation. He did, but that nation was his own. His forces were completely overwhelmed, and his prosperous realm was annexed as a province of the Persian state. Seven years later, in 539 B.C., Cyrus took advantage of discontent and conspiracies in the Chaldean Empire to capture the city of Babylon. His victory was easy, for he had the assistance of the Jews within the city and of the Chaldean priests, who were dissatisfied

The conquests of Cyrus

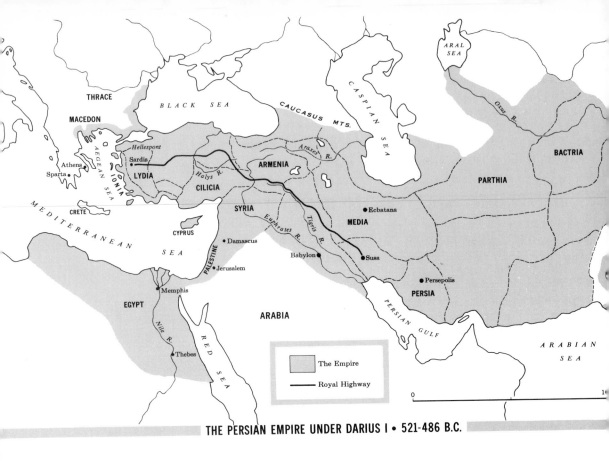

THE PERSIAN EMPIRE UNDER DARIUS I • 521-486 B.C.

with the policies of their king. The conquest of Babylon thereupon enabled Cyrus to gain control over the whole Chaldean Empire.

The successors of Cyrus

Cyrus the Great died in 529 B.C., as the result of wounds received in a war with barbarian tribes. Soon afterward a succession of troubles overtook the state he had founded. Like so many other empire-builders both before and since, he had devoted too much energy to conquest and not enough to internal development. He was succeeded by his son Cambyses, who conquered Egypt in 525 B.C. During the new king's absence revolt spread throughout his Asiatic possessions. Chaldeans and Medes strove to regain their independence. The chief minister of the realm, abetted by the priests, organized a movement to gain the throne for a pretender who was one of their puppets. Upon learning of conditions at home, Cambyses set out from Egypt with his most dependable troops, but he was murdered on the way. The most serious of the revolts was finally crushed by Darius, a powerful noble, who killed the pretender and seized the throne for himself.

Darius the Great

Darius I, or the Great, as he is often called, ruled the empire from 522 to 486 B.C. The early years of his reign were occupied in suppressing the revolts of subject peoples and in improving the administrative organization of the state. He completed the division of the empire into satrapies, or provinces, and fixed the annual tribute due from each province. He standardized the currency and weights and measures. He repaired and completed a primitive canal from the Nile to the Red Sea. He followed the example of Cyrus in tolerating and protecting the institutions of subject peoples. Not only did he restore ancient temples and foster local cults, but he ordered his satrap of Egypt to codify the Egyptian laws in consultation with the native priests. But in some of his military exploits Darius overreached himself. In order to check the incursions of the Scythians, who lived on the European shore of the Black Sea, he crossed the Hellespont and conquered a large part of the Thracian coast. In addition, he increased the oppression of the Greeks on the shore of Asia Minor, who had fallen under Persian domination with the conquest of Lydia. He collected heavier tribute from them, and forced them to serve in his armies. The immediate result was a revolt of the Greek cities with the assistance of Athens. And when Darius attempted to punish the Athenians for their part in the rebellion, he found that they offered stiff resistance.

Darius the Great died before the war with Athens and allied Greek cities had come to an end. The struggle was prosecuted vigorously but unsuccessfully by his successor, Xerxes I. By 479 B.C. the Persians had been driven from all of Greece. Though they continued to hold sway as a major power in Asia, their attempt to extend their dominion into Europe was thwarted. The last century and a half of the empire's existence was marked by frequent assassinations, revolts of provincial governors, and barbarian invasions, until finally, in 330 B.C., its independence was terminated by the armies of Alexander the Great.

The end of the Persian Empire

Although the Persian government had its defects, it was certainly superior to most of the others that had existed in the Near East. The Persian rulers did not imitate the terrorism of the Assyrians. They levied tribute upon conquered peoples, but they generally allowed them to keep their own customs, religions, and laws. Indeed, the chief accomplishment of the Persian Empire lay in the fact that it achieved a synthesis of Near Eastern cultures, including those of Persia itself, Mesopotamia, Asia Minor, the Syria-Palestine coast, and Egypt.

Persian government

The Persian rulers built excellent roads to help hold their empire together. Most famous was the Royal Road, some 1,600 miles in length. It extended from Susa near the Persian Gulf to Sardis near the western coast of Asia Minor. So well kept was this highway that royal messengers, traveling day and night, could cover all its length in less than a week. Other roads linked the various provinces with one or another of the four leading Persian cities: Susa, Persepolis, Babylon, and Ecbatana. Although they naturally contributed to ease of trade, the highways were built primarily to facilitate governmental control over the outlying sections of the empire.

Persian roadways

7. PERSIAN CULTURE

The culture of the Persians, in the narrower sense of intellectual and artistic achievements, was largely derived from that of previous civilizations. Much of it came from Mesopotamia, but a great deal of it from Egypt, and some from Lydia and northern Palestine. Their system of writing was originally the cuneiform, but in time they devised an alphabet of thirty-nine letters, based upon the alphabet of the Arameans who traded within their borders. In science they accomplished nothing, except to adopt with some slight modifications the solar calendar of the Egyptians and to encourage exploration as an aid to commerce. They deserve credit also for diffusing a knowledge of the Lydian coinage throughout many parts of western Asia.

It was the architecture of the Persians which gave the most positive expression of the eclectic character of their culture. They copied the raised platform and the terraced building style that had been standard in Babylonia and Assyria. They imitated also the winged bulls, the brilliantly colored glazed bricks, and other decorative motifs of Mesopotamian architecture. But at least two of the leading features of Mesopotamian construction were not used by the Persians—the arch and the vault. In place of them they adopted the column and the colonnade from Egypt. In addition, interior arrangement and the use of palm and lotus designs at the base of columns also came from Egyptian influence. On the other hand, the fluting of the columns and the volutes or scrolls beneath the capitals were not Egyptian but Greek, adopted not from the mainland of Greece itself but from the Ionian cities of Asia Minor. If there was anything unique about Persian architecture, it was the fact that it was purely secular. The great Persian structures were not temples but palaces. They served to glorify not gods, but the "King of Kings." The most famous were the magnificent residences of Darius and Xerxes at Persepolis. The latter, built in imitation of the temple at Karnak, had an enormous central audience-hall containing a hundred columns and surrounded by innumerable

The Great Palace of Darius and Xerxes at Persepolis. Persian architecture made use of fluted columns, copied from the Greeks, and reliefs resembling those of the Assyrians,

Silver Figurine of a Kneeling Bull Holding a Vessel. Elamite, c. 3000 B.C.

Gold, Silver, Shell, and Lapis Lazuli Statuette of a Ram in a Thicket. Sumerian, 2500 B.C.

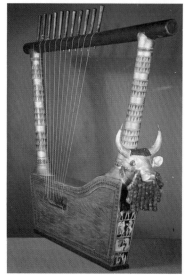

Gold and Lapis Lazuli Lyre with Bull's Head. Sumerian, c. 2500 B.C.

Stone Head of Ur-Ningirsu, Son of Gudea of Lagash. Sumerian, c. 2100 B.C.

Gold Plaque with Animals and Stylized Trees in Relief. Persian, VII cent. B.C.

Bronze Bull, Symbol of Strength. Arabian, VI cent. B.C.

Ivory Screen of Four Winged Figures. Assyrian, VIII cent. B.C.

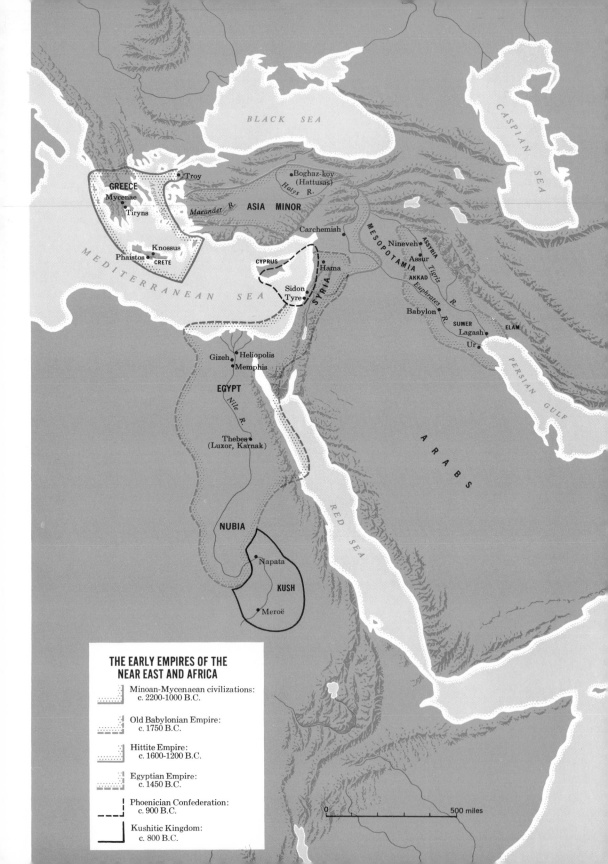

BLACK SEA

CASPIAN SEA

GREECE
Troy
Mycenae
Tiryns
Maeander R.
ASIA MINOR
Boghaz-koy
(Hattusas)
Halys R.

Carchemish

MESOPOTAMIA
Nineveh
ASSYRIA
Assur
Tigris R.
AKKAD

Phaistos
Knossus
CRETE
CYPRUS
Hama
SYRIA
Sidon
Tyre

MEDITERRANEAN SEA

Euphrates R.
Babylon
SUMER
Lagash
Ur
ELAM

PERSIAN GULF

Gizeh
Heliopolis
Memphis

EGYPT

Nile R.

Thebes
(Luxor, Karnak)

A R A B S

RED SEA

NUBIA

Napata

KUSH

Meroë

THE EARLY EMPIRES OF THE NEAR EAST AND AFRICA

Minoan-Mycenaean civilizations:
c. 2200-1000 B.C.

Old Babylonian Empire:
c. 1750 B.C.

Hittite Empire:
c. 1600-1200 B.C.

Egyptian Empire:
c. 1450 B.C.

Phoenician Confederation:
c. 900 B.C.

Kushitic Kingdom:
c. 800 B.C.

0   500 miles

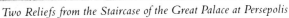
Two Reliefs from the Staircase of the Great Palace at Persepolis

rooms which served as offices and as quarters for the eunuchs and
members of the royal harem.

8. THE ZOROASTRIAN RELIGION

By far the most enduring influence left by the ancient Persians was
that of their religion. Their system of faith was of ancient origin. It
was already highly developed when they began their conquests. So
strong was its appeal, and so ripe were the conditions for its acceptance, that it spread through most of western Asia. Its doctrines
turned other religions inside out, displacing beliefs which had been
held for ages.

*The religion of the
Persians*

Although the roots of this religion can be traced as far back as the
fifteenth century B.C., its real founder was Zoroaster (the Greek form
of the Persian name Zarathustra), who appears to have lived shortly
before 600 B.C. From him the religion derives its name of Zoroastrianism. Zoroaster was probably the first real theologian in history,
the first known person to devise a completely developed system of
religious belief. He seems to have conceived it as his mission to purify
the traditional customs of his people—to eradicate polytheism, animal
sacrifice, and magic—and to establish their worship on a more spiritual and ethical plane. But in spite of his reforming efforts many of the
old superstitions survived and were gradually fused with the new
ideals.

*The founding of
Zoroastrianism*

Zoroastrianism had a character unique among the religions of the
world up to that time. It was dualistic—not monistic like the Sumerian and Babylonian religions, in which the same gods were capa-

*Characteristics of
Zoroastrianism: (1)
dualism*

ble of both good and evil; but it did not go as far in the direction of
monotheism as did the religion of the Hebrews. According to Zoroaster, two spiritual principles ruled the universe: one, Ahura-Mazda,
supremely good, embodied the principles of light, truth, and righteousness; the other, Ahriman, treacherous and malignant, presided
over the forces of darkness and evil. The two were engaged in a desperate struggle for supremacy. Although they were about evenly
matched in strength, the god of light would eventually triumph. On
the last great day Ahura-Mazda would overpower Ahriman and cast
him down into the abyss. The dead would then be raised from their
graves to be judged according to their deserts. The righteous would
enter into immediate bliss, while the wicked would be sentenced to
the flames of hell. Ultimately, though, all would be saved; for the
Persian hell, unlike the Christian, did not last forever.

(2) an ethical religion

The Zoroastrian religion was definitely an ethical one. Although it
contained suggestions of predestination, of the election of some from
all eternity to be saved, in the main it rested upon the assumption that
humans possessed free will, that they were free to sin or not to sin, and
that they would be rewarded or punished in the afterlife in accordance
with their conduct on earth. Ahura-Mazda commanded that people
should be truthful, that they should love and help one another to the
best of their power, that they should befriend the poor and practice
hospitality. The essence of these broader virtues was perhaps expressed
in another of the god's decrees: "Whosoever shall give meat to one of
the faithful . . . he shall go to Paradise." The forms of conduct forbidden were sufficiently numerous and varied to cover the whole list
of sins of medieval Christianity and a great many more. Pride, gluttony, sloth, covetousness, wrathfulness, lust, adultery, abortion, slander, and waste were among the more typical. The taking of interest on
loans to others of the same faith was described as the "worst of sins,"
and the accumulation of riches was condemned. The restraints which
believers were to practice included also a kind of negative Golden Rule:
"That nature alone is good which shall not do unto another whatever
is not good for its own self."

9. THE MYSTICAL AND OTHERWORLDLY HERITAGE FROM PERSIA

The religion of the Persians as taught by Zoroaster did not long continue in its original state. It was corrupted, first of all, by the persistence of primitive superstitions, of magic and priestcraft. The farther
the religion spread, the more of these relics of barbarism were engrafted upon it. As the years passed, additional modification resulted
from the influence of alien faiths, particularly that of the Chaldeans.
The outcome was the growth of a powerful synthesis in which the
dualism of the Persians was combined with the pessimism and fatalism of the Chaldeans.

Out of this debased Zoroastrianism gradually emerged a profusion of cults, alike in their basic dogmas but according them different emphases. The oldest was Mithraism, deriving its name from Mithras, a lieutenant of Ahura-Mazda in the struggle against the powers of evil. At first only a minor deity in the religion of Zoroastrianism, Mithras finally won recognition by many of the Persians as the god most deserving of worship. The reason for this change was probably the emotional appeal made by the incidents of his career. He was believed to have lived an earthly existence involving great suffering and sacrifice. He performed miracles giving bread and wine to man and ending a drought and also a disastrous flood. Finally, he created much of the ritual of Zoroastrianism, proclaiming Sunday as the most sacred day of the week and the twenty-fifth of December as the most sacred day of the year. Since the sun was the giver of light and the faithful ally of Mithras, his day was naturally the most sacred. The twenty-fifth of December also possessed its solar significance: as the approximate date of the winter solstice it marked the return of the sun from its long journey south of the Equator. It was in a sense the "birthday" of the sun, since it connoted the revival of its life-giving powers for the benefit of humanity.

Exactly when Mithraism became an independent cult is unknown, but it was certainly not later than the fourth century B.C. Its spread thereafter was rapid. In the last century B.C. it was introduced into Rome, although it was of little importance in Italy itself until after 100 A.D. It drew its converts especially from the lower classes, from the ranks of soldiers, foreigners, and slaves. Ultimately it rose to the status of one of the most popular religions of the empire, the chief competitor of Christianity and of old Roman paganism. After 275, however, its strength rapidly waned. How much influence Mithraism exerted is impossible to say. Its superficial resemblance to Christianity is obvious, but this does not mean, of course, that the two were identical, or that one was an offshoot of the other. Nevertheless, it is probably true that Christianity as the younger of the two rivals borrowed some of its externals from Mithraism, at the same time preserving its own philosophy essentially untouched.

One of the principal successors of Mithraism in transmitting the legacy from Persia was Manicheism, founded around 250 A.D. by Mani, a high-born priest of Ecbatana. Like Zoroaster he became dedicated to reforming the prevailing religion, but he received scant sympathy in his own country and had to be content with missionary ventures in India and western China. About 276 A.D. he was condemned and executed by his Persian opponents. Following his death his teachings were carried by his disciples into practically every country of western Asia and finally into Italy about 330 A.D.

Of all the Zoroastrian teachings, the one that made the deepest impression upon the mind of Mani was dualism. But Mani gave to this doctrine a broader interpretation than it had ever received in the earlier religion. He conceived not merely of two deities engaged in a relentless struggle for supremacy, but of a whole universe divided into two kingdoms, each the antithesis of the other. The first was the kingdom of spirit ruled over by a God eternally good. The second was the kingdom of matter under the dominion of Satan. Only "spiritual" substances such as fire, light, and the souls of human beings were created by God. Darkness, sin, desire, and all things bodily and material owed their origin to Satan.

The moral implications of this rigorous dualism were profound. Since everything connected with sensation or desire was the work of Satan, humanity should strive to free itself as completely as possible from enslavement to physical needs. Humans should refrain from all forms of sensual enjoyment, the eating of meat, the drinking of wine, the gratification of sexual desire. Even marriage was prohibited, for this would result in the begetting of more physical bodies to people the kingdom of Satan. In addition, humans should subdue the flesh by prolonged fasting and infliction of pain. Recognizing that this program of austerities would be too difficult for ordinary mortals, Mani divided the human race into the "perfect" and the "hearers." Only the former would be obliged to adhere to the full program as the ideal of what all should hope to attain. To aid humanity in its struggle against the powers of darkness, God had sent prophets and redeemers from time to time to give comfort and inspiration. Noah, Abraham, Zoroaster, Jesus, and Paul were among these divine emissaries; but the last and greatest of them was Mani. Since Mani called himself "the apostle of Jesus Christ," many Manicheans in the West, including the great St. Augustine during his early career, considered themselves to be radical Christians. The faith had many followers in the Roman Empire around 400, but it died out thereafter as a result of persecution.

The third most important cult which developed as an element in the Persian heritage was Gnosticism (from the Greek *gnosis,* meaning knowledge). It had no single founder but evolved out of Persian and Greek religious ideas and came to full fruition around the first century A.D., reaching the height of its popularity in the latter half of the second century. Although it gained some followers in Italy, it flourished primarily in the Near East. The feature which most sharply distinguished Gnosticism from the other cults was mysticism. The Gnostics denied that religious truths could be discovered by reason or could even be made intelligible. They regarded themselves as the exclusive possessors of a secret spiritual knowledge revealed to them directly by God. This knowledge was alone important as a guide to faith and conduct.

The combined influence of these several Persian-derived religions was enormous. Most of them were launched at a time when political and social conditions were particularly conducive to their spread. The breakup of Alexander the Great's empire about 300 B.C. inaugurated a peculiar period in the history of the ancient world. International barriers were broken down; there was an extensive migration and intermingling of peoples; and the collapse of the old social order gave rise to disillusionment with life on earth and a yearning for individual salvation. People's attentions were centered as never before upon compensations in a life to come. Under such circumstances religions of the kind described were bound to thrive. Otherworldly and mystical, they offered the very escape that people were seeking from a world of anxiety and confusion.

The combined influence of the several offshoots of Zoroastrianism

Although not exclusively religious, the heritage left by the Persians contained few elements of a secular nature. Their form of government was adopted by the later Roman monarchs, not in its purely political aspect, but in its character of a divine-right despotism. When such emperors as Diocletian and Constantine I invoked divine authority as a basis for their absolutism and required their subjects to prostrate themselves in their presence, they were really following patterns laid down by the Persians. At the same time the Romans were impressed by the Persian idea of a world empire. Darius and his successors conceived of themselves as the rulers of the whole civilized world, with a mission to reduce it to unity and, under Ahura-Mazda, to govern it justly. For this reason they generally conducted their wars with a minimum of savagery and treated conquered peoples humanely. Their ideal was a kind of prototype of the Roman peace. Traces of Persian influence upon certain Hellenistic philosophies are also discernible; but here again it was essentially religious, for it was confined almost entirely to spiritual and mystical theories.

Persian legacy

SELECTED READINGS

- Items so designated are available in paperback editions.
- Chiera, Edward, *They Wrote on Clay*, Chicago, 1956. An engrossing account of the discovery and decipherment of cuneiform tablets.
- Contenau, G., *Everyday Life in Babylonia and Assyria*, New York, 1954. Based on archeological evidence and well illustrated.
- Frankfort, H., *The Art and Architecture of the Ancient Orient*, rev. ed., Baltimore, 1971.
    ———, *The Birth of Civilization in the Near East*, Bloomington, Ind., 1951. Brief but useful.
    ———, et al., *The Intellectual Adventure of Ancient Man*, Chicago, 1946. Essays by leading experts on ancient myths; see that by T. Jakobsen on Mesopotamia.
  Frye, R. N., *The Heritage of Persia*, New York, 1963. A fascinating history of Persia from earliest times to the triumph of Islam in the seventh century A.D.
- Ghirshman, R., *Iran*, Baltimore, 1954.
- Hallo, W. W., and W. K. Simpson, *The Ancient Near East: A History*, New York, 1971. An authoritative survey.
  Kramer, S. N., *History Begins at Sumer*, New York, 1959.

• ———, *Sumerian Mythology,* New York, 1961. Develops different point of view about early myth than that found in Frankfort et al., *Intellectual Adventure.*

• ———, *The Sumerians: Their History, Culture, and Character,* Chicago, 1963. Best general treatment of Sumerian civilization.

Lloyd, Seton, *Foundations in the Dust,* Baltimore, 1955. Describes the development and accomplishments of Mesopotamian archeology.

Moscati, S., *The Face of the Ancient Orient,* New York, 1962. Deals with Assyrians and Chaldeans.

Neugebauer, Otto, *The Exact Sciences in Antiquity,* Princeton, N.J., 1952. Excellent on Mesopotamian mathematical accomplishments.

• Olmstead, A. T., *History of the Persian Empire,* Chicago, 1948. Detailed but somewhat uncritical.

• Oppenheim, A. Leo, *Ancient Mesopotamia,* Chicago, 1964. Concentrates on Babylonian and Assyrian culture.

• Roux, G., *Ancient Iraq,* London, 1964.

Russell, Jeffrey B., *The Devil: Perceptions of Evil from Antiquity to Primitive Christianity,* Ithaca, N.Y., 1977. Particularly strong on the religious revolution accomplished by Zoroaster.

• Saggs, H. W. F., *The Greatness That Was Babylon,* London, 1962.

Widengren, G., *Mani and Manicheism,* London, 1965.

• Woolley, C. L., *The Sumerians,* New York, 1928. A pioneer work, brief and interestingly written.

Zaehner, R. C., *The Dawn and Twilight of Zoroastrianism,* New York, 1961. The standard treatment.

SOURCE MATERIALS

• *Epic of Gilgamesh,* tr. N. Sandars, Baltimore, 1960.

Grayson, A. K., and D. B. Redford, *Papyrus and Tablet,* Englewood Cliffs, N.J., 1973.

Herodotus, *The Persian Wars,* tr. A. de Sélincourt, Baltimore, 1954.

Luckenbill, D. D., *Ancient Records of Assyria and Babylonia,* Chicago, 1926, 2 vols.

Pritchard, James B., *Ancient Near Eastern Texts Relating to the Old Testament,* rev. ed., Princeton, N.J., 1969.

Chapter 4

THE HEBREW CIVILIZATION

I am the Lord thy God, which brought thee out of the land of Egypt from
the house of bondage.
Thou shalt have none other gods before me.
Thou shalt not make thee any graven image, or any likeness of any thing
that is in heaven above, or that is in the earth beneath, or that is in the
waters beneath the earth . . .
Thou shalt not take the name of the Lord thy God in vain.

—Deuteronomy 5:6–11

Of all the peoples of the ancient Near East, none has been of
greater importance to the modern world than the Hebrews.
It was the Hebrews, of course, who provided much of the
background of the Christian religion—its view of the Creation, its
Commandments, its concept of a single, transcendent God as law-
giver and judge, and more than two-thirds of its Bible. Hebrew conceptions of morality and political theory have also profoundly influenced modern nations. For these reasons we tend today to think of the
Hebrew accomplishment as unique, and there is much truth in that
assumption. But although Hebrew culture gradually came to differ
greatly from that of neighboring Egypt and Mesopotamia it is necessary to remember that the Hebrews did not develop their culture in a
vacuum. No more than any other people were they able to escape the
influence of nations around them.

*Importance of the Hebrew
civilization*

1. HEBREW ORIGINS AND RELATIONS WITH OTHER PEOPLES

The origin of the Hebrews is still a puzzling problem. Certainly they
did not have any physical characteristics sufficient to distinguish them
clearly from their neighbors, and their language belonged to the Near

Eastern Semitic family. Most scholars agree that the original home of the Hebrews was the Arabian Desert. The first definite appearance of the founders of the nation of Israel, however, was in northwestern Mesopotamia. Apparently as early as 1900 B.C. a group of Hebrews under the leadership of Abraham had settled there. Later Abraham's grandson Jacob led a migration westward and began the occupation of Palestine. It was from Jacob, subsequently called Israel, that the Israelites derived their name. Sometime before 1600 B.C. certain tribes of Israelites, together with other Hebrews, moved into Egypt to escape the consequences of famine. According to the biblical account they were gradually enslaved by the Egyptian government, although there is no record of this in the Egyptian evidence. At any rate, around 1300–1250 B.C. their descendants found a leader in the indomitable Moses, who led them to the Sinai peninsula and persuaded them to become worshipers of Yahweh, a god whose name was much later written erroneously as Jehovah. Hitherto Yahweh had been the deity of Hebrew shepherd folk in the Sinai area. Making use of a Yahwist cult as a nucleus, Moses welded the various tribes of his followers into a confederation, which thereupon occupied Palestine, or the land of Canaan.

With its scanty rainfall and rugged terrain, Palestine was a barren and inhospitable place. But compared with the arid wastes of Arabia it seemed a veritable paradise, and it is not surprising that the leaders should have pictured it as a "land flowing with milk and honey." Most of it was already occupied by the Canaanites, another Semitic people who had lived there for centuries. Through contact with the Babylonians, Hittites, and Egyptians they had built up a culture which was no longer primitive. They practiced agriculture and carried on trade. They knew the art of writing, and they had adapted the laws of Hammurabi's code to the needs of their simpler existence. Their religion, which was also derived in large part from Babylonia, was cruel and sensual, including human sacrifice and temple prostitution.

The Hebrew occupation of the land of Canaan was a slow and difficult process. Seldom did the tribes unite in a combined attack, and even when they did, the enemy cities were well enough fortified to resist capture. After several generations of sporadic fighting the Hebrews had succeeded in taking only the limestone hills and a few of the less fertile valleys. In the intervals between wars they mingled freely with the Canaanites and adopted no small amount of their culture. Before they had a chance to complete the conquest they found themselves confronted by a new and more formidable enemy, the Philistines, who appear to have entered Palestine from Asia Minor. Stronger than either the Hebrews or Canaanites, especially because they used iron weapons while the others used bronze, these invaders rapidly overran the country and forced the Hebrews to surrender much of the territory they had already gained. It is from the Philistines that Palestine derives its name.

2. THE RECORD OF POLITICAL HOPES AND FRUSTRATIONS

The crisis produced by the Philistine conquests served not to discourage the Hebrews but to unite them and to intensify their ardor for battle. Moreover, it led directly to the founding of the Hebrew monarchy about 1025 B.C. Up to this time the nation had been ruled by "judges," who possessed little more than the authority of religious leaders over twelve independent Hebrew tribes. But now with a greater need for organization and discipline, the people demanded a king to rule them and lead them in war. The man selected as the first incumbent of the office was Saul, a member of the tribe of Benjamin, who at first gained considerable success.

The founding of the Hebrew monarchy

But the reign of King Saul ultimately was not a happy one, either for the nation or for the ruler himself. Only a few suggestions of the reasons are given in the Old Testament account. Evidently Saul incurred the displeasure of Samuel, the last of the great judges, who had expected to remain the power behind the throne. Before long there appeared on the scene the ambitious David, who, with the encouragement of Samuel, carried on skillful maneuvers to draw popular support from the king. Waging his own military campaigns, he achieved one bloody triumph after another. By contrast, the armies of Saul met disastrous reverses. Finally the king, being critically wounded, requested his armor-bearer to kill him. When the latter would not, Saul drew his own sword, fell upon it, and died.

The reign of King Saul

David now became king and ruled for forty years. His reign was one of the most glorious periods in Hebrew history. He smote the Philistines hip and thigh and reduced their territory to a narrow strip of coast in the south. He united the twelve tribes into a consolidated state under an absolute monarch, and he began the construction of a magnificent capital at Jerusalem. But strong government, military glory, and material splendor were not unmixed blessings for the people. Their inevitable accompaniments were high taxation and conscription. As a consequence, before David died, rumblings of discontent were plainly to be heard in certain parts of his kingdom.

The mighty David

David was succeeded by his son Solomon, the last of the kings of the united monarchy. As a result of the nationalist aspirations of later times, Solomon has been pictured in Hebrew lore as one of the wisest and most enlightened rulers in all history. The facts of his career furnish little support for such a belief. About all that can be said in his favor is that he was a shrewd diplomat and an active patron of trade. Most of his policies were oppressive, although of course not deliberately so. Ambitious to copy the luxury and magnificence of other Oriental despots, he established a harem of 700 wives and 300 concubines and completed the construction of sumptuous palaces, stables for 4,000 horses, and a costly temple in Jerusalem. Since Palestine was

Solomon aspires to Oriental magnificence

Model of King Solomon's Temple. Significant details are: A, royal gates; B, treasury; C, royal palace; D, people's gate; E, western (wailing) wall; F, priests' quarters; G, courthouse; H, Solomon's porch.

poor in resources, most of the materials for the building projects had to be imported. Gold, silver, bronze, and cedar were brought in in such quantities that the revenues from taxation and from the tolls levied upon trade were insufficient to pay for them. To make up the deficit Solomon ceded twenty towns and resorted to a system of conscripting labor. Every three months 30,000 Hebrews were drafted and sent into Phoenicia to work in the forests and mines of King Hiram of Tyre, from whom the most expensive materials had been purchased.

The secession of the Ten Tribes

Solomon's extravagance and oppression produced acute discontent among his subjects. His death in 922 B.C. was the signal for open revolt. The ten northern tribes, refusing to submit to his son Rehoboam, seceded and set up their own kingdom. Sectional differences played their part also in the disruption of the nation. The northern Hebrews were sophisticated and accustomed to urban living. They benefited from their location at the crossroads of Near Eastern trade. While this factor increased their prosperity, it also caused them to be steeped in foreign influences. By contrast, the two southern tribes were composed very largely of pastoral and agricultural folk, loyal to the religion of their fathers, and hating the ways of the foreigner. Perhaps these differences alone would have been sufficient in time to have destroyed the Hebrews' national unity.

Roman Coin Celebrating the Destruction of Jerusalem. This coin, struck about 70 A.D., bears the inscription "IVDAEA CAPTA" (Captive Judea), and shows a female personification of the Jews propping her head in an attitude of dejection.

The northern kingdom came to be known as the Kingdom of Israel, having its capital in Samaria, while the two southern tribes comprised the Kingdom of Judah, which continued to have its capital in Jerusalem. For more than two centuries the two little states maintained their separate existences. But in 722 B.C. the Kingdom of Israel was conquered by the Assyrians. Its inhabitants were scattered throughout the vast empire of their conquerors and were eventually absorbed by the more numerous population around them. Ever since they have been referred to as the Ten Lost Tribes of Israel. The Kingdom of Judah managed to survive for more than a hundred years longer, successfully outlasting the Assyrian menace. But in 586 B.C. it was

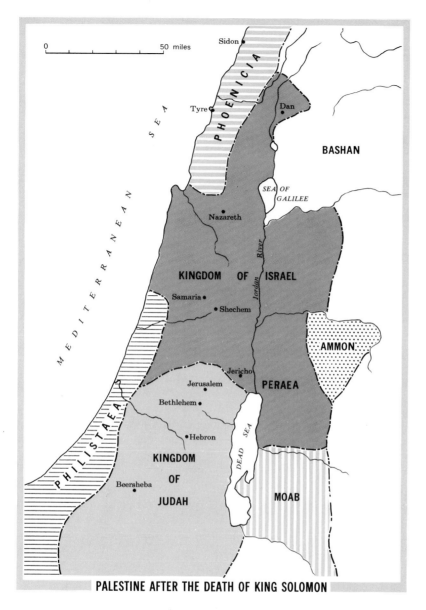

PALESTINE AFTER THE DEATH OF KING SOLOMON

overthrown by the Chaldeans under Nebuchadnezzar. Jerusalem was plundered and burned, and its leading citizens were carried off into captivity in Babylon. When Cyrus the Persian conquered the Chaldeans, he freed the Jews and permitted them to return to their native land. Few were willing to go, and considerable time elapsed before it was possible to rebuild the temple. From 539 to 332 B.C. Palestine was a vassal state of Persia. In 332 B.C. it was conquered by Alexander the Great and after his death was placed under the rule of Egypt. In 63 B.C. it became a Roman protectorate. Its political history as a Jewish commonwealth was ended in 70 A.D. after a desperate revolt which the

Masada. This ancient mountaintop fortress, which towers above the western shore of the Dead Sea in Israel, was the final outpost of the Jews in their war against Roman domination. The fortress, occupied by 1,000 men, women, and children, was besieged by the Roman army for two years before it fell in 73 A.D. Defiant to the end, almost all of the Jewish defenders killed themselves rather than be captured and enslaved by the Romans.

Romans punished by destroying Jerusalem and annexing the country as a province. The inhabitants were gradually diffused through other parts of the Roman Empire.

The Diaspora

The destruction of Jerusalem and annexation of the country by the Romans were the principal factors in the so-called Diaspora, or dispersion of the Jews from Palestine. Even earlier large numbers of them had fled into various parts of the Greco-Roman world on account of difficulties in their homeland. In their new environment they rapidly accepted foreign influences, a fact which was of tremendous importance in promoting a fusion of Greek and Oriental ideas. It was a Hellenized Jew, St. Paul, who was mainly responsible for remolding Christianity in accordance with Greek philosophical doctrines.

3. THE HEBREW RELIGIOUS EVOLUTION

Reasons for the varied evolution of Hebrew religion

Few peoples in history have gone through a religious evolution comparable to that of the Hebrews. Its cycle of development ranged all the way from the crudest superstitions to the loftiest spiritual and ethical conceptions. Part of the explanation lies in the peculiar geographic position occupied by the Hebrew people. Located as they were after their conquest of Canaan on the highroad between Egypt and the major civilizations of Asia, they were bound to be affected by an extraordinary variety of influences.

At least four different stages can be distinguished in the growth of the Hebrew religion. The first we can call the pre-Mosaic stage, from the earliest beginnings of the people to approximately 1250 B.C. This stage was characterized at first by animism, the worship of spirits that dwelt in trees, mountains, sacred wells and springs, and even in stones of peculiar shape. Diverse forms of magic were practiced also at this time—necromancy, imitative magic, and scapegoat sacrifices. Many traces of these early beliefs and rites are preserved in the Old Testament.

The pre-Mosaic stage

Gradually animism gave way to belief in anthropomorphic gods. How this transition occurred cannot be determined. Perhaps it was related to the fact that Hebrew society had become patriarchal, that is, the father exercised absolute authority over the family and descent was traced through the male line. The gods may have been thought to occupy a similar position in the clan or tribe. Apparently few of the new deities were as yet given names; each was usually referred to merely by the generic name of "El," that is, "god." They were guardians of particular places and probably of separate tribes. No *national* worship of Yahweh was known at this time.

Anthropomorphic gods

The second stage, which lasted from the thirteenth century B.C. to the ninth, is frequently called the stage of national monolatry. The term may be defined as the exclusive worship of one god but without denial that other gods exist. Due chiefly to the influence of Moses, the Hebrews gradually adopted as their national deity during this period a god whose name appears to have been written "Yhwh." How it was pronounced no one knows, but scholars generally agree that it was probably uttered as if spelled "Yahweh." The meaning is also a mystery. When Moses inquired of Yahweh what he should tell the people when they demanded to know what god had sent him, Yahweh replied: "I AM THAT I AM: and he said, Thus shalt thou say unto the children of Israel, I AM hath sent me unto you" (Exodus 3:13–14).

The stage of national monolatry

During the time of Moses and for two or three centuries thereafter Yahweh was a somewhat peculiar deity. He was conceived almost exclusively in anthropomorphic terms. He possessed a physical body and the emotional qualities of men. He was capricious on occasions, and somewhat irascible—as capable of evil and wrathful judgments as he was of good. His decrees were often quite arbitrary, and he would punish someone who sinned unwittingly just about as readily as one whose guilt was real. By way of illustration, Yahweh reportedly struck Uzza dead merely because that unfortunate individual placed his hand upon the Ark of the Covenant to steady it while it was being transported to Jerusalem (I Chronicles 13:9–10). Yahweh was hardly omnipotent, for his power was limited to the territory occupied by the Hebrews. Nonetheless, some of the most important Hebrew contributions to subsequent Western thought were first formulated during this time. It was during this period that the Hebrews came to believe that God was not part of nature but entirely outside of it, and that humans, while part of nature, became the rulers of nature by divine dispensation. This "transcendent" theology meant that God

Characteristics of Yahweh

could gradually be understood in purely intellectual or abstract terms, and that humanity could be regarded as having the potential for altering nature as it pleased.

The supremacy of law and ritual

The religion of this stage was neither primarily ethical nor profoundly spiritual. Yahweh was revered as a supreme law-giver and as the stern upholder of the moral order of the universe. According to the biblical account, he issued the Ten Commandments to Moses on top of Mount Sinai. Old Testament scholars, however, do not generally accept this tradition. They admit that a primitive set of commandments may have existed in Mosaic times, but they doubt that the Ten Commandments in the form in which they are preserved in the Book of Exodus go back any farther than the seventh century. In any event, it is clear that Moses's God was interested just about as much in sacrifice and in ritualistic observances as he was in good conduct or in purity of heart. Moreover, the religion was not vitally concerned with spiritual matters. It offered nothing but material rewards in this life and none at all in a life to come. Finally, the belief in monolatry was corrupted by certain elements of fetishism, magic, and even grosser superstitions that lingered from more primitive times or that were gradually acquired from neighboring peoples. These varied all the way from serpent worship to bloody sacrifices and fertility orgies.

The stage of the prophetic revolution

The really important work of religious reform was accomplished by the great prophets—Amos, Hosea, Isaiah,[1] and Micah. And their achievements represented the third stage in the development of the Hebrew religion, the stage of the prophetic revolution, which occupied the eighth and seventh centuries B.C. The great prophets were men of broader vision than any of their forerunners. Three basic doctrines made up the substance of their teachings: (1) rudimentary monotheism—Yahweh is the ruler of the universe; He even makes use of nations other than the Hebrews to accomplish His purposes; the gods of other peoples are false gods and should not be worshiped for any reason; (2) Yahweh is a god of righteousness exclusively; He is not really omnipotent, but His power is limited by justice and goodness; the evil in the world comes from humanity not from God; (3) the purposes of religion are chiefly ethical; Yahweh cares nothing for ritual and sacrifice, but that His followers should "seek justice, relieve the oppressed, judge the fatherless, plead for the widow." Or as Micah expressed it: "What doth the Lord require of thee, but to do justly, and to love mercy, and to walk humbly with thy God?" (Micah 6:8).

Although these doctrines contradicted nearly everything the older religion had stood for, the prophets genuinely thought that they were

---

[1] Most Old Testament authorities consider the Book of Isaiah the work of three authors. They ascribe the first part to Isaiah, the second part from Chapters 40 to 55 to Deutero-Isaiah, or the second Isaiah, and the end to someone who wrote after the return to Jerusalem. The second Isaiah was more emphatic than the first in denying the existence of the gods of other peoples.

Remains of an Ancient Synagogue at Capernaum. Capernaum was supposed to have been the scene of many of the miracles attributed to Jesus. Here also he called out Peter, Andrew, and Matthew to be his disciples.

restoring Hebrew beliefs to their ancient purity, for they assumed that the crudities they opposed were foreign corruptions. Thus their actual accomplishments went so far beyond their conscious objectives that they amounted to a religious revolution. To a considerable extent this revolution also had its social and political aspects. Wealth had become concentrated in the hands of a few. Thousands of small farmers had lost their freedom to rich proprietors. If we can believe the testimony of Amos, bribery was so rife in the law courts that the plaintiff in a suit for debt had merely to give the judge a pair of shoes and the defendant would be handed over as a slave (Amos 2:6). Overshadowing all was the threat of Assyrian domination. To enable the Hebrews to cope with that threat, the prophets believed that social abuses should be stamped out and the people united under a religion purged of its alien corruptions.

Contrasts with the older religion; political and social aspects

The results of this revolution must not be misinterpreted. It did eradicate some of the most flagrant forms of oppression, and it rooted out permanently most of the barbarities that had crept into the religion from foreign sources. But the Hebrew faith did not yet bear much resemblance to modern Judaism. Instead of being otherworldly, it was oriented toward this life. Its purposes were social and ethical—to promote a just and harmonious society and to abate man's inhumanity to man—not to confer individual salvation in an afterlife. As yet there was no belief in heaven and hell or in Satan as a powerful opponent of God. The shades of the dead went down into Sheol to linger there for a time in the dust and gloom and then disappear.

The religion not yet otherworldly or mystical

The final significant stage in Hebrew religious evolution was the post-Exilic stage or the period of Persian influence. This may be considered to have covered the years from 539 to about 300 B.C. Perhaps enough has been said already to indicate the character of the influence from Persia. It will be recalled from the preceding chapter that

The post-Exilic stage

Zoroastrianism was a dualistic, messianic, and otherworldly religion. In the period following the exile in Babylon these influences gained wide acceptance among the Jews. They adopted a belief in Satan as the Great Adversary and the author of evil. They developed an eschatology (a set of doctrines concerning the end of the world) which included such notions as the coming of a spiritual savior, the resurrection of the dead, and a last judgment. They turned their attention to salvation in an afterworld as more important than enjoyment of this life. Last, they embraced the conception of a revealed religion, that is, they regarded the books of their Bible as having been directly inspired by God Himself.

4. HEBREW CULTURE

The limitations of the Hebrew accomplishment

In some respects Hebrew culture was inferior to that of other great nations of antiquity. In the first place, the Hebrews revealed no talent for science. Nor were they adept at appropriating the technological knowledge of others. They could not build a bridge or a tunnel except of the crudest sort. In the second place, they seem to have been almost entirely devoid of artistic skill. In part because of religious prohibitions concerning "graven images" they had no sculpture, but they also had no architecture or painting worthy of mention. The famous temple at Jerusalem was not a Hebrew building at all but a product of Phoenician skill, for Solomon imported artisans from Tyre to finish the more complicated tasks.

Hebrew law

It was rather in law, literature, and philosophy that the Hebrew genius was most perfectly expressed. Although all of these subjects were closely allied with religion, they did have their secular aspects. The foremost example of Jewish law was the Deuteronomic Code, which forms the core of the Book of Deuteronomy. Despite claims of its great antiquity, it was probably an outgrowth of the prophetic revolution. It was based in part upon an older Code of the Covenant, which was derived in considerable measure from the laws of the Canaanites and the Old Babylonians. In general, its provisions were more enlightened than those of Hammurabi's code. One of them enjoined liberality to the poor and to the stranger. Another commanded that the Hebrew slave who had served six years should be freed, and insisted that he must not be sent away empty. A third provided that judges and other officers should be chosen by the people and forbade them to accept gifts or to show partiality in any form. A fourth condemned witchcraft and divination. A fifth denounced the punishment of children for the guilt of their fathers and affirmed the principle of individual responsibility for sin. A sixth prohibited the taking of interest on any kind of loan made by one Jew to another. A seventh required that at the end of every seven years there should be a "release" of debts. "Every creditor that lendeth aught unto his neighbour shall release it; he shall not exact it of his neighbour, or of his brother . . . save when there shall be no poor among you" (Deuteronomy 15:1–4).

The literature of the Hebrews was the finest that the ancient Near East produced. Nearly all of it now extant is preserved in the Old Testament and in the books of the Apocrypha (ancient Hebrew works not recognized as scriptural because of doubtful religious authority). Except for a few fragments like the Song of Deborah in Judges 5, it is not really so old as is commonly supposed. Scholars now recognize that the Old Testament was built up through a series of collections and revisions in which old and new parts were merged and generally assigned to an ancient author—Moses, for example. But the oldest of these revisions was not prepared any earlier than 850 B.C. The majority of the books of the Old Testament were of still later origin, excepting some of the chronicles. Although the bulk of the Psalms were ascribed to King David, a good many of them refer to events of the Babylonian Captivity and it is certain that the collection of Psalms as a whole was the work of several centuries. Most recent of all were the books of Ecclesiastes, Esther, and Daniel, composed no earlier than the third century B.C. Likewise, the Apocryphal books did not see the light of day until Hebrew civilization was almost extinct. Some, like Maccabees I and II, relate events of the second century B.C. Others, including the Wisdom of Solomon and the Book of Enoch, were written under the influence of Greco-Oriental philosophy.

Hebrew literature

Granted that many parts of the Old Testament consist of dull, repetitious chronicles, many others, whether taking the form of battle song, prophecy, love lyric, or drama, are rich in rhythm, concrete images, and emotional vigor. Few passages in any language can surpass the scornful indictment of social abuses voiced by the prophet Amos:

Amos's indictment of social abuses

> Hear this, O ye that swallow up the needy, even to make the
>   poor of the land to fail,
> Saying, when will the new moon be gone, that we may sell
>   corn?
> And the sabbath that we may set forth wheat,
> Making the ephah small, and the shekel great,
> And falsifying the balances by deceit?
> That we may buy the poor for silver, and the need for a pair
>   of shoes;
> Yea, and sell the refuse of the wheat?

The most beautiful of Hebrew love lyrics is the Song of Songs, or Song of Solomon. Its theme was probably derived from an old Canaanite hymn of spring, celebrating the passionate affection of the Shulamith or fertility goddess for her lover, but it had long since lost its original meaning. The following verses are typical of its sensuous beauty:

The Song of Songs

King David as a Musician. A much later conception of David from the eighth century A.D. shows the Hebrew king playing his lyre and charming animals. According to tradition, David was the author of the Psalms, which he sung to his lyre (also known as a *psaltery*).

I am the rose of Sharon
and the lily of the valleys.
As the lily among thorns,
so is my love among the daughters.

.   .   .   .

My beloved is white and ruddy,
the chiefest among ten thousand.
His head is as the most fine gold;
his locks are bushy and black as a raven:
His eyes are as the eyes of doves by the rivers of waters,
washed with milk and fitly set.
His cheeks are as a bed of spices, as sweet flowers;
his lips like lilies, dropping sweet smelling myrrh.

.   .   .   .

How beautiful are thy feet with shoes, O prince's daughter!
The joints of thy thighs are like jewels,
the work of the hands of a cunning workman.

The Book of Job

One other of the supreme Hebrew literary achievements is the Book of Job, written sometime between 500 and 300 B.C. In form the work is a drama of the tragic struggle between man and fate. Its central theme is the problem of evil: how it can be that the righteous suffer while the wicked prosper. The story was an old one, adapted very probably from an Old Babylonian writing of similar content. But the Hebrews introduced into it a much deeper realization of philosophical possibilities. The main character, Job, a man of unimpeachable virtue, is suddenly overtaken by a series of disasters: he is despoiled of his property, his children are killed, and his body is afflicted with a painful disease. His attitude at first is one of stoic resignation; the evil must be accepted along with the good. But as his sufferings increase he is plunged into despair. He curses the day of his birth and praises death, where "the wicked cease from troubling and the weary be at rest."

Then follows a lengthy debate between Job and his friends over the meaning of evil. The latter take the traditional Hebraic view that all suffering is a punishment for sin, and that those who repent are forgiven and strengthened in character. But Job is not satisfied with any of their arguments. Torn between hope and despair, he strives to review the problem from every angle. He even considers the possibility that death may not be the end, that there may be some adjustment of the balance hereafter. But the mood of despair returns, and he decides that God is an omnipotent demon, destroying without mercy wherever His caprice or anger directs. Finally, in his anguish he appeals to the Almighty to reveal Himself and make known His ways to him. God answers him out of the whirlwind with a magnificent exposition of the tremendous works of nature. Convinced of his own insignificance and of the unutterable majesty of God, Job despises himself and repents in dust and ashes. In the end no solution is given of the problem of individual suffering. No promise is made of recompense in a life hereafter, nor does God make any effort to refute the hopeless pessimism of Job. Humans must take comfort in the philosophic reflection that the universe is greater than themselves, and that God in the pursuit of His sublime purposes cannot really be limited by human standards of equity and goodness.

The problem of evil

As philosophers the Hebrews surpassed all other peoples before the Greeks. Although they were not brilliant metaphysicians and constructed no great theories of the universe, they did concern themselves with most of the problems relating to human life and destiny. Their thought was essentially personal rather than abstract. Probably the earliest of their writings of a distinctly philosophical character were the Book of Proverbs and the Book of Ecclesiasticus. In their final form both were of late composition, but much of the material they contain was doubtless quite ancient. These have as their basic teaching: be temperate, diligent, wise, and honest, and you will surely be rewarded with prosperity, long life, and a good reputation. Only in such isolated passages as the following is any recognition given to higher motives of sympathy or respect for the rights of others: "Whoso mocketh the poor reproacheth his Maker; and he that is glad at calamities shall not be unpunished" (Proverbs 17:5).

Hebrew philosophy: early examples

A much more profound and critical philosophy is contained in Ecclesiastes, an Old Testament book, not to be confused with the Ecclesiasticus mentioned above. The author of Ecclesiastes is unknown. In some way it came to be attributed to Solomon, but he certainly did not write it, for it includes doctrines and forms of expression unknown to the Hebrews for hundreds of years after his death. Scholars now date it no earlier than the third century B.C. The basic ideas of its philosophy may be summarized as follows:

(1) Mechanism. The universe is a machine that rolls on forever without evidence of any purpose or goal. Sunrise and sunset, birth and death are but phases of constantly recurring cycles and "there is nothing new under the sun."

(2) Fatalism. Humans are victims of the whims of fate. There is no necessary relation between effort and success. "The race is not to the swift, nor the battle to the strong, neither yet bread to the wise . . . but time and chance happeneth to them all."

(3) Pessimism. "All is vanity and vexation of spirit." Fame, riches, extravagant pleasure are snares and delusions in the end. Although wisdom is better than folly, even it is not a sure key to happiness, for an increase in knowledge brings a keener awareness of suffering.

(4) Moderation. Extremes of asceticism and extremes of indulgence are both to be avoided. "Be not righteous over much . . . be not over much wicked: why shouldest thou die before thy time?"

5. THE MAGNITUDE OF THE HEBREW INFLUENCE

The influence of the Hebrews has been chiefly religious and ethical. While it is true that the Old Testament has served as a source of inspiration for some of the literature and art of medieval and early modern civilizations, this has resulted largely because the Bible was familiar material as a part of the religious heritage. The same explanation can be applied to the use of the Old Testament as a source of law and political theory by Protestants in the sixteenth century, and by many other Christians both before and since.

But these facts do not mean that the Hebrew influence has been slight. On the contrary, the history of nearly every Western civilization during the past two thousand years would have been radically different without the heritage from Israel. For it must be remembered that the Hebrews developed the first sustained monotheism known to mankind and that Hebrew beliefs were among the principal foundations of Christianity. The relationship between the two religions is frequently misunderstood. The movement inaugurated by Jesus of Nazareth is commonly represented as a revolt against Judaism; but such was only partly the case. On the eve of the Christian era the Jewish nation had come to be divided into several different religious parties, including a majority group of Pharisees, and minority groups of Sadducees and Essenes. The Pharisees represented the middle classes and some of the better educated common folk. They believed in the resurrection, in rewards and punishments after death, and in the coming of a political messiah. Intensely nationalistic, they advocated participation in government and faithful observance of the ancient ritual. They regarded all parts of the law as of virtually equal importance, whether they applied to matters of ceremony or to obligations of social ethics. Their concern for the law was so great that they debated such questions as whether one could eat an egg laid on the Sabbath.

Representing altogether different strata of society, the minority parties disagreed with the Pharisees on both religious and political issues. The Sadducees, including the priests and the wealthier classes, were most famous for their denial of the resurrection and of rewards and punishments in an afterlife. Although they favored the temporary acceptance of Roman rule, their attitude toward the ancient law was even more inflexible than that of the Pharisees. The Essenes, who were not even a unified party but consisted of various similar but separate communities, drew their members from the lower classes, practiced asceticism, and preached otherworldliness as means of protest against the wealth and power of priests and rulers. They ate and drank only enough to keep themselves alive, held all their goods in common, and looked upon marriage as a necessary evil. Far from being fanatical patriots, they regarded government with indifference and refused to take oaths under any conditions. They emphasized the spiritual aspects of religion rather than the ceremonial, and stressed particularly the immortality of the soul, the coming of a religious messiah, and the early destruction of the world.

Until recently scholars were dependent for their knowledge of the Essenes almost entirely upon secondary sources. But in 1947 an Arab shepherd unwittingly opened the way to a spectacular documentary discovery. Searching for a lost sheep on the shore of the Dead Sea, he threw a stone that entered a hole in the rocks and made such a strange noise that he ran away in fright. He returned, however, with a friend to investigate and discovered a cave in which were stored about fifty cylindrical earthen jars stuffed with writings on papyrus scrolls. Studied by scholars, the scrolls revealed the existence of a monastic community which flourished from about 130 B.C. to 67 A.D. Its members lived a life of self-denial, holding their goods in common, and devoting their time to prayer and sacraments and to studying and copying biblical texts. They looked forward confidently to the coming of a messiah, the overthrow of evil, and the establishment of God's kingdom on earth. That they belonged to the same general movement that fostered the growth of the Essenes seems beyond question.

All branches of Judaism except the Sadducees strongly influenced the development of Christianity. From Jewish sources Christianity obtained its cosmogony, or theory of the origin of the universe; the Ten Commandments; and a large portion of its theology, including the "transcendent" view of God as outside of nature and humanity as master of nature. Jesus himself, although he condemned the Pharisees for their legalism and hypocrisy, did not repudiate all of their tenets.

The Sa..ees ..d the Essenes

The Dead Sea scr..

Hebrew influence up.. Christianity

The Dead Sea Scrolls. Now on display in an underground vault at the Hebrew University in Jerusalem. The oldest extant examples of Hebrew religious literature, they furnish us with evidence of the activities of the Essenes and mystical and otherworldly sects about the beginning of the Christian era.

Instead of abolishing the ancient law, as he is popularly supposed to have done, he demanded its fulfillment, insisting, however, that it should not be made the essential part of religion. In the first flush of enthusiasm at the discovery of the Dead Sea Scrolls it seemed as if Christianity might have been most directly influenced by the Essenes. Scholars now, however, speak less of direct influences than of similarities, for early Christians, like the Essenes, practiced asceticism, regarded government with indifference and the Roman Empire with hostility, held their goods in common, and believed in the imminent end of the world. These parallels do not mean, of course, that Christianity was a mere adaptation of beliefs and practices emanating from Judaism. There was much in it that was unique; but that is a subject which will be discussed later on.[2]

The ethical and political influence of the Hebrews has also been substantial. Their moral conceptions have been a leading factor in the development of the negative approach toward ethics which has prevailed for so long in Western countries. For the early Hebrews, "righteousness" consisted primarily in the observance of taboos or prohibitions. "Thou shalt not . . ." is a major theme of many parts of the Old Testament. But a positive morality of charity and social justice made rapid headway during the time of the prophets and has had its great influence as well. With respect to political thought, Hebrew ideals of the

tical

Hebrews

on

[2] See Chapter 9.

sovereignty of law, and regard for the dignity and worth of the individual have been among the major formative influences which have shaped the growth of modern democracy. It is now almost universally recognized that the traditions of Judaism contributed equally with the influence of Christianity and Stoic philosophy in fostering recognition of human rights and in promoting the development of free society.

SELECTED READINGS

• *Items so designated are available in paperback editions.*

• Albright, W. F., *From the Stone Age to Christianity,* New York, 1957. Emphasizes the development of Hebrew monotheism.

Anderson, Bernard, *Understanding the Old Testament,* 3rd ed., Englewood Cliffs, N.J., 1975.

Baron, Salo W., *A Social and Religious History of the Jews,* rev. ed., 17 vols, New York, 1952–1980. A modern classic: almost all work on Jewish history takes Baron as a point of departure.

• Bickermann, E., *From Ezra to the Last of the Maccabees: Foundations of Post-Biblical Judaism,* New York, 1962.

Bright, John, *A History of Israel,* 3rd ed., Philadelphia, 1981. A standard account.

Harrison, R. K., *The Dead Sea Scrolls: An Introduction,* New York, 1961. A valuable guide for the beginner.

Hermann, Siegfried, *A History of Israel in Old Testament Times,* London, 1975. Iconoclastic and challenging.

• Kaufmann, Yehezkel, *The Religion of Israel,* New York, 1972. Stresses the uniqueness of the Hebrew religious accomplishment.

• McCullough, W. S., *The History of the Palestinian Jews from Cyrus to Herod, 550B.C. to 4 B.C.,* Toronto, 1976.

Noth, Martin, *The History of Israel,* 2nd ed., New York, 1960. A provocative reappraisal.

• Orlinsky, H. M., *Ancient Israel,* 2nd ed., Ithaca, N.Y., 1960. A good brief overview of ancient Hebrew history.

Rowley, H. H., *Growth of the Old Testament,* New York, 1963. A helpful survey of scholarly opinion concerning the circumstances of origin of the various Old Testament books.

• Schürer, E., *The History of the Jewish People in the Age of Jesus Christ (175 B.C.–A.D. 135),* rev. ed., 3 vols., Edinburgh, 1973–1983. A new edition of an irreplaceable nineteenth-century narrative.

• Vaux, Roland de, *Ancient Israel: Its Life and Institutions,* New York, 1962. Especially valuable for archeological data.

SOURCE MATERIALS

Baron, Salo W., and J. L. Blau, eds., *Judaism: Post-Biblical and Talmudic Periods,* New York, 1954.

Gaster, T. H., tr., *The Dead Sea Scriptures in English Translation,* New York, 1964.

The *Old Testament* and the *Apocrypha,* many editions.

Pritchard, J. B., ed., *Ancient Near Eastern Texts Relating to the Old Testament,* rev. ed., Princeton, N.J., 1969.

Chapter 5

THE HITTITE, MINOAN, MYCENAEAN, AND LESSER CIVILIZATIONS

But for them among these gods will be bled for annual food:
to the god Karnua one steer and one sheep;
to the goddess Kupapa one steer and one sheep;
to the divinity Sarku one sheep;
and a Kutupalis sheep to the male divinities.

> —Hittite sacrifice formula, translated
> from a hieroglyph by
> H. T. Bossert

A few other ancient civilizations require more than passing attention. Chief among them are the Hittite, the Minoan, the Mycenaean, the Lydian, and the Phoenician. The Hittites served primarily as intermediaries between East and West, linking the civilizations of Egypt and Mesopotamia with the region of the Aegean Sea. The Minoan and the Mycenaean civilizations were the oldest ones of Europe, significant above all for their remarkable achievements in the arts and as the starting points of Greek history. As for the Lydians, no one could overlook their importance as the originators of the first system of coinage. Finally, the Phoenicians were impressive traders who also invented an alphabet which lies behind all those used in the modern Western world.

Importance of these civilizations

1. THE HITTITES

Until about a century ago little was known of the Hittites except their name. They were commonly assumed to have played no role of any significance in the drama of history. The slighting references to them in the Bible give the impression that they were little more than a half-barbarian tribe. But in 1870 the discovery of some curiously inscribed

The discovery of remains of the Hittite civilization

stones found at Hama in Syria began an extensive inquiry which has continued with few interruptions to the present day. It was not long until scores of other monuments and clay tablets were discovered over most of Asia Minor and through the Near East as far as the Tigris-Euphrates valley. In 1907 some evidences of an ancient city were unearthed near the village of Boghaz-Koy in Turkey. Further excavation eventually revealed the ruins of a great fortified capital known as Hattusas or Hittite City, within whose walls were discovered more than 20,000 clay tablets.

The Hittite Empire

On the basis of these finds it has become clear that the Hittites were once the rulers of a mighty empire covering most of Asia Minor, extending to the upper reaches of the Euphrates, and, at its height, even including Syria and portions of Palestine. The Hittites reached the zenith of their power during the years from 1600 to 1200 B.C. In the last century of this period they waged a long war with Egypt, which probably contributed to the downfall of both empires. Neither was able to regain its strength. After 1200 B.C. Carchemish on the Euphrates for a time became the leading Hittite city, but as a commercial center rather than as the capital of a great unified state. Finally, after 717 B.C., all the remaining Hittite territories were conquered and absorbed by the Assyrians, Lydians, and Phrygians.

See color map facing
page 65

*The mystery of the race
and language of the
Hittites*

Where the Hittites came from and what their relationships were to other peoples are problems which still defy solution. Most modern scholars trace their place of origin to Turkestan and consider them related to the Greeks. Their language was Indo-European. Its secret was unlocked during World War I by the Czech scholar Bedrich Hrozny. Since then thousands of clay tablets making up the laws and official records of the emperors have been deciphered. They reveal a civilization resembling more closely the Old Babylonian than any other.

*The economic life of the
Hittites*

Insufficient evidence has yet been collected to make possible an accurate appraisal of Hittite civilization. Certainly, however, the Hittites had an extensive knowledge of agriculture and a highly developed economic life in general. They mined great quantities of silver, copper, and lead, which they sold to surrounding nations. They discovered the mining and use of iron and made that material available for the rest of the civilized world. Trade was also one of their principal pursuits. In fact, they seem to have depended almost as much upon commercial penetration as upon war for the expansion of their empire.

*The intellectual level of
Hittite culture*

The literature of the Hittites consisted chiefly of mythology, including adaptations of creation and flood legends from the Old Babylonians. They had nothing that could be described as philosophy, nor is there any evidence of scientific originality outside of the metallurgical arts. They evidently possessed some talent for the perfection of writing, for in addition to a modified cuneiform adapted from Mesopotamia they also developed a hieroglyphic system which was partly phonetic in character.

One of the most significant achievements of the Hittites was their system of law. Approximately two hundred separate paragraphs or decrees, covering a great variety of subjects, have been translated. They reflect a society comparatively urbane and sophisticated but subject to rigorous governmental control. The title to all land was vested in the king or in the governments of the cities. Grants were made to individuals only in return for military service and under the strict requirement that the land be cultivated. Prices were fixed in the laws themselves for an enormous number of commodities—not only for articles of luxury and the products of industry, but even for food and clothing. All wages and fees for services were likewise prescribed, with the pay of women fixed at less than half the rate for men.

Hittite law

On the whole, the Hittite law was more humane than that of the Old Babylonians. Death was the punishment for only eight offenses—such as witchcraft, and theft of property from the palace. Even premeditated murder was punishable only by a fine. Mutilation was not specified as a penalty at all except for arson or theft when committed by a slave. The contrast with the cruelties of Assyrian law was more striking. Not a single example is to be found in the Hittite decrees of such sadistic punishments as flaying, castration, and impalement, which the rulers at Nineveh seemed to think necessary for maintaining their authority.

Humane character of Hittite law

The art of the Hittites was not of outstanding excellence. So far as we know, it included only sculpture and architecture. The former was generally crude but not entirely lacking in freshness and vigor. Most of it was in the form of reliefs depicting scenes of war and mythology. Architecture was ponderous and huge. Temples and palaces were squat, unadorned structures with small, two-columned porches and great stone lions guarding the entrance.

The art of the Hittites

Not a great deal is known about the Hittite religion except that it had an elaborate mythology, innumerable deities, and forms of wor-

Hittite Sculpture. Perhaps the most highly conventionalized sculpture of the ancient world is found in Hittite reliefs.

Hittite religion

The importance of the Hittites

ship of Mesopotamian origin. A sun god was worshiped, along with a host of other deities, some of whom appear to have had no particular function at all. The Hittites seem to have welcomed into the divine company practically all of the gods of the peoples they conquered and even of the nations that bought their wares. The practices of the religion included divination, sacrifice, and purification ceremonies. Nothing can be found in the records to indicate that the religion was in any sense ethical.

The chief historical importance of the Hittites lies in the role which they played as intermediaries between the Tigris-Euphrates valley and the westernmost portions of the Near East. Doubtless in this way certain culture elements from Mesopotamia were transmitted to the Canaanites and to the peoples of the Aegean islands.

2. THE MINOAN AND MYCENAEAN CIVILIZATIONS

Long-forgotten civilizations

By a strange coincidence the discovery of the existence of the Hittite, Minoan, and Mycenaean civilizations was made at just about the same time. Before 1870 scarcely anyone dreamed that great civilizations had flourished on the Aegean islands and on the shores of Asia Minor for hundreds of years prior to the rise of classical Greek civilization. Students of the *Iliad* knew, of course, of the references to a strange people who were supposed to have dwelt in Troy, to have kidnaped the fair Helen, and to have been punished by the Greeks for this act by the siege and destruction of their city. But it was commonly supposed that these accounts were mere figments of a poetical imagination. Today we are certain that Greek history, and thus European history, began over one thousand years before the Golden Age of Athens.

The discoveries by Schliemann and others

The first discovery of a highly developed Aegean culture center was made not by a professional archeologist but by a retired German businessman, Heinrich Schliemann. Fascinated from early youth by the stories of the Homeric epics, he determined to dedicate his life to archeological research as soon as he had sufficient income to enable him to do so. Luckily for him and for the world he accumulated a fortune in Russian business ventures and then retired to spend both time and money in the pursuit of his boyhood dreams. In 1870 he began excavating at Troy. Within a few years he had uncovered portions of nine different cities, each built upon the ruins of its predecessor. The second of these cities he identified as the Troy of the *Iliad,* although it has been proved since then that Troy was the seventh city. After fulfilling his first great ambition, he started excavations on the mainland of Greece and eventually uncovered two other Aegean cities, Mycenae (pronounced My-sée-nee) and Tiryns. The work of Schliemann was soon followed by that of other investigators, notably the Englishman Sir Arthur Evans, who discovered Knossos, the resplendent capital of

See color map facing page 65

the Minoan kings of Crete. Up to the present time more than half of the ancient Aegean sites have been carefully searched, and a wealth of knowledge has been accumulated about various aspects of the culture.

The Minoan and Mycenaean civilizations originated on the island of Crete. (See the map on p. 122, below.) In few other cases in history does the geographic interpretation of culture origins fit so neatly. Crete has a benign and equable climate. While the soil is fertile, it is not of unlimited area; consequently, as the population increased, people were impelled to sharpen their wits and to contrive new means of earning a living. Some emigrated; others took to the sea; but a larger number remained at home and developed articles for export. The latter included wine and olive oil, pottery, gems and seals, knives and daggers, and objects of skilled craftsmanship. The chief imports were foodstuffs and metals. As a result of such trade, prosperity increased and extensive contacts were made with the surrounding civilized world. Added to these factors of a favorable environment were the beauties of nature which abounded almost everywhere, stimulating the development of a marvelous art.

The favorable natural environment of Crete

The Minoan civilization, named after the legendary Cretan ruler Minos, was founded by peoples who emigrated from Asia Minor to Crete around 3000 B.C. In the millennium thereafter they made the transition from the Neolithic stage to the age of metals; by 2000 B.C. they had developed cities and an early form of writing. From then until about 1500 B.C. their civilization developed under the leadership of the cities of Knossos and Phaistos. Recently, evidence has been found of the existence of another great city, Kato Zakros, on the east coast of Crete. Here was a huge palace of 250 rooms, with a swimming pool, parquet floors, and thousands of decorated vases. Only severe earthquakes, which periodically shook the island, interrupted the serene existence of the sophisticated Cretans. These quakes caused much devastation, but after each one the inhabitants of the Cretan cit-

Origins and flowering of Minoan civilization

Central Staircase of the Palace at Knossos

A Linear B Tablet from Knossos

ies set about the work of rebuilding and usually managed to construct even more splendid palaces than the ones which had been destroyed. So confident were the inhabitants of Knossos that they faced no threat of foreign invasion that they left their magnificent city without any protective walls.

Ultimately such confidence proved to be mistaken. While Cretan civilization was flourishing, a related one was emerging on the mainland of Greece. Around 1900 B.C. Indo-European peoples who spoke the earliest form of Greek invaded the Greek peninsula, and by 1600 B.C. they were beginning to form settled communities. After around 1600 they became greatly influenced in their cultural development by the neighboring civilization of Minoan Crete, with which they had been developing trading relations. The civilization that resulted from the fusion of Greek and Minoan elements is usually called *Mycenaean,* after Mycenae, the leading city of Greece from about 1600 to 1200 B.C. It was this civilization that became dominant in the Aegean world after about 1500 and even gained predominance on the island of Crete itself.

One of the greatest scholarly accomplishments of recent times has radically altered our understanding of Cretan and Greek history in the century between 1500 and 1400. It used to be thought that Greece throughout that time was still a semibarbarous economic colony of splendid Crete and that internal changes on Crete between 1500 and 1400 could be attributed to the rise of a "new dynasty." It was known that numerous specimens of the same linear script (called "Linear B") could be found on both Crete and the Greek mainland, but it was simply assumed that the script was Cretan in origin and spread from Crete to Greece. But in 1952 a brilliant young Englishman, Michael Ventris, who was then only thirty years old (and tragically died in an automobile accident four years later), succeeded in deciphering Linear B and demonstrating that it expressed an early form of Greek. Ventris's discovery revolutionized preclassical Greek studies by showing that the mainlanders dominated Crete in the late Minoan period and not vice versa.

The new scholarly consensus is that the Mycenaeans supplanted the Minoans as rulers of the Aegean world sometime shortly after 1500

Origin of the Mycenaean civilization

Linear B

B.C. Around 1500 a great earthquake on Crete probably brought about sufficient weakness to allow the mainlanders to take control of the island. These Mycenaean Greeks helped to rebuild Knossos and presided over roughly a century of continued prosperity and artistic accomplishment on Crete. Around 1400, however, another wave of Greek invaders crossed over to the island, destroyed Knossos entirely, and put a cataclysmic end to the Minoan civilization. Why this invasion was so destructive cannot be known, but it left mainland Greece unrivaled as the center of civilization in the Aegean world for about another 200 years. Around 1250 B.C. the Mycenaeans waged their successful war with the Trojans of western Asia Minor, but their own demise was now in the offing. In the course of the century between 1200 B.C. and 1100 B.C., the Mycenaeans, whose civilization seems to have been decaying from within, succumbed to the Dorians—barbaric northern Greeks who had iron weapons. (Iron weapons may not at first have been much superior to the bronze ones used by the Mycenaeans, but they were far cheaper, thereby allowing many more fighters to wield them.) Because the Dorians were primitive in all but their weaponry their ascendancy initiated a dark age in Greek history which lasted until about 800 B.C.

As can be seen from the foregoing account, the Minoan and Mycenaean civilizations were closely interrelated; even the greatest experts have difficulty in determining exactly where one left off and the other began. The problem is complicated by the fact that two forms of writing which predate Linear B and have been found on Crete alone have not yet been deciphered. (Anyone who wishes to become as famous as Schliemann, Evans, or Ventris may take the decipherment of Cretan writing as his or her goal.) Accordingly, discussions of Minoan civilization before about 1500 B.C. rely exclusively on visual and archeological evidence, leaving much to the realm of speculation. Such evidence, however, does suggest that Cretan civilization was one of the most progressive in all of early history.

The Minoan ruler was no bristling warlord like the Assyrian and Persian kings. He does seem to have commanded a large navy, but this was not for war but for the maintenance of trade. In fact, the king was the chief entrepreneur in the country. The workshops located near his palace turned out great quantities of fine pottery, textiles, and metal goods. Although private enterprise apparently was not prohibited it seems to have been heavily taxed. Nevertheless there were some privately owned workshops, especially in smaller towns, and much agriculture was also in private hands.

The Cretan state is probably best described as a bureaucratic monarchy. The ruler of each leading city and its surrounding territory appears to have been absolute, and toward the end of Minoan history (exactly when is hard to say) the ruler of Knossos appears to have taken over the entire island. The absolute Cretan ruler governed by means of a large administrative class. Scribes, who seem to have had a

Mycenaean Warrior Vase, c. 1250 B.C. Found in the ruins of Mycenae, this vase displays the warlike aspects of Mycenaean culture: the men might be marching off to the Trojan War.

Difficulty of distinguishing between early Minoan and Mycenaean characteristics

A Minoan Vase, c. 1400 B.C. The potter's wheel, probably invented by the Minoans, allowed a greater variety of shapes for vessels and encouraged Minoan artists to employ new styles and methods of decoration.

Scenes from the Bull Ring: Minoan Mural, c. 1500 B.C. Evident are the youth, skill, and agility of the Cretan athletes, the center one a male, the other two female. The body and horns of the bull are exaggerated, as are the slenderness of the athletes and their full-face eyes in profile heads. There is probably also some exaggeration in content: modern experts in bullfighting insist that it is impossible to somersault over the back of a charging bull.

monopoly of learning, kept close accounts of all aspects of economic life. All agricultural production and manufacturing was closely supervised for purposes of gathering or taxing whatever was owed to the king. Foreign trade too seems to have been closely supervised by the state; most likely the large Cretan ships that put into ports as far away as Syria and Egypt were owned or at least heavily taxed by the ruler and carefully watched over by the bureaucratic administration.

Despite such close supervision, the Cretan people of nearly all classes appear to have led fairly prosperous lives. Although there were great social and economic distinctions between the rulers and the ruled, there were apparently few gradations of wealth or status among the common people. If slavery existed at all, it certainly occupied an unimportant place. The dwellings in the poorest quarters of smaller towns such as Gournia were well built and commodious, often with as many as six or eight rooms, but we do not know how many families resided in them. Women seem to have enjoyed equality with men. Regardless of class there was no public activity from which they were debarred, and no occupation which they could not enter. In this the Minoans were the exception in the ancient world. Crete had female bullfighters and even female pugilists. Women of the upper strata devoted much time to fashion and other leisure activities.

The natives of Crete delighted in games and sports of every description. Dancing, running matches, and boxing rivaled each other in their attraction for the people. The Cretans were the first to build stone theaters where processions and music entertained large audiences.

A bureaucratic monarchy

Evidences of social equality

The love of sports and games

So far as we know, Minoan religion was a medley of strange characteristics. First of all it was apparently matriarchal. The chief deity was not a god but a goddess, who was the ruler of the entire universe—the sea and the sky as well as the earth. Originally no male deity appears to have been worshiped, but later a god was associated with the goddess as her son and consort. Although, like the divine sons in several other religions, he apparently died and rose from the dead, he was never regarded by the Cretans as of particular importance. In the second place, the Minoan religion was thoroughly monistic. The mother goddess was the source of evil as well as of good, but not in any morbid or terrifying sense. Though she brought the storm and spread destruction in her path, these served for the replenishment of nature. Death itself was interpreted as the prerequisite for life. Whether the religion had any body of ethical precepts is unknown.

Other features of the religion of the Minoans included the worship of animals and birds (the bull, the snake, and the dove); the worship of sacred trees; the veneration of sacred objects which were probably reproductive symbols (the double-axe, the pillar, and the cross); and, in accordance with the matriarchal nature of the belief system, the employment of priestesses instead of priests to administer sacred rites.

Since we cannot yet decipher the early Cretan scripts it is impossible to tell whether the Minoans had any literature or philosophy, although the existence of either seems extremely unlikely because there is none written in Linear B. The problem of scientific achievements is easier to solve, since we have material remains for our guidance. Archeological discoveries on the island of Crete indicate that the ancient inhabitants were gifted inventors and engineers. They built excellent stone roads about eleven feet wide. Nearly all the basic principles of modern sanitary engineering were known to the designers of the palace of Knossos, with the result that the royal family of Crete in the seventeenth century B.C. enjoyed comforts and conveniences, such as indoor running water, that were not available to the wealthiest rulers of Western countries in the seventeenth century A.D.

Minoan Snake Goddess, Sixteenth Century B.C. A statuette made of ivory and gold.

If any single achievement of the Minoans appears most to emphasize the vitality and freedom of their culture, it was their art. With the exception of the classical Greek, no other art of the ancient world was its equal. Its distinguishing features were delicacy, spontaneity, and naturalism. It served not to glorify the ambitions of an arrogant ruling class or to inculcate the doctrines of a religion, but to express the delight of the individual in the beauty and splendor of the Minoan world. As a result, it was remarkably free from the retarding influence of ancient tradition. It was unique, moreover, in the universality of its application, for it extended not merely to paintings and statues but even to the humblest objects of ordinary use.

Of the major arts, architecture was the least developed. The great palaces were not remarkably beautiful buildings but rambling struc-

Architecture

"La Parisienne"

Similarities between the Minoan and Mycenaean civilizations

tures designed primarily for capaciousness and comfort. As more and more functions were absorbed by the state, the palaces were enlarged to accommodate them. New quarters were annexed to those already built or piled on top of them without regard for order or symmetry. The interiors, however, were decorated with beautiful paintings and furnishings. The architecture of Crete may be said to have resembled the modern international style in its subordination of form to utility and in its emphasis upon a pleasing and livable interior as more important than external beauty.

Painting was the supreme Cretan art. Nearly all of it consisted of murals done in fresco, although painted reliefs were occasionally to be found. The murals in the palaces of Crete were by all odds the best that have survived from ancient times. They revealed almost perfectly the remarkable gifts of the Minoan artist—an instinct for the dramatic, a sense of rhythm, a feeling for nature in its most characteristic moods. So sophisticated and elegant was Cretan art that a Frenchman who was unearthing the remains of a fresco at Knossos could not help exclaiming when he saw a painting of a striking woman portrayed with curls, vivid eyes, and sensuous lips: "Mais, c'est la Parisienne!" ("Why, she's just like a woman from Paris!").

Sculpture and the ceramic and gem-carving arts were also developed to a high stage of perfection. The sculpture of the Cretans differed from that of any other people in the ancient Near East. It never relied upon size as a device to convey the idea of power. The Cretans produced no colossi like those of Egypt or reliefs like those of Babylonia depicting a king of gigantic proportions smiting his puny enemies. Instead, they preferred sculpture in miniature. Nearly all of the statues of human beings or of deities that the archeologists have found are smaller than life-size.

Mycenaean civilization appears to have been more warlike and less refined than the Minoan, but the most recent scholarship warns us to beware of exaggerating these differences. As on Crete, so on mainland Greece, the city was the center of civilization—the leading Mycenaean cities being Mycenae itself (according to Homer the home of the leading Greek king Agamemnon), Pylos (according to Homer the home of the wise Nestor), and Tiryns. Each city and its surrounding area was ruled over by a king called a *wanax,* who in many respects ruled like an Oriental despot. As on Crete, the Mycenaean state was a bureaucratic monarchy. We know for certain about some of the workings of this monarchy because of the decipherment of numerous Linear B tablets, all of which are records of a highly regulatory bureaucratic apparatus. Linear B tablets from Pylos report the minutest details of the economic lives of the king's subjects: the exact acreage of a given estate; the number of cooking utensils owned by so-and-so; the personal names given to somebody else's two oxen ("Glossy" and "Blackie"). Such detailed inventories show us that the state was highly centralized and that it was as supreme in its control over the economic activities of its citizens as any other in the Near East.

Although the bureaucratic monarchies of Crete and Mycenaean Greece were probably similar, there were still at least a few notable differences between the two related civilizations. One was that the Mycenaeans definitely had a slave system. Mycenaean society too was geared much more toward warfare. Because Mycenaean cities frequently fought with one another they were built on hilltops and were heavily fortified. In keeping with a somewhat more rugged and barbaric style of life than that of Crete, Mycenaean kings built themselves ostentatious graves in which they buried their best inlaid bronze daggers and other signs of their power and wealth.

It is also true that Mycenaean art is less elegant than Minoan. Without question the Mycenaeans never equaled the artistic delicacy and grace of their Minoan predecessors. Nevertheless, Mycenaean artwork done in Knossos between 1500 and 1400 B.C., while stiffer and more symmetrical in composition than earlier Minoan work, is by no means wholly different in kind. Moreover, the "Parisian woman" of Minoan Knossos has some very close stylistic relatives in a female procession fresco from about 1300 B.C. found in Mycenaean Tiryns. Nor should it be thought that all the best traits of Mycenaean art can merely be seen as debased borrowings from the Minoans: the superbly executed and exquisite Mycenaean inlaid daggers have no antecedents anywhere on Crete.

Detail from a Procession Fresco at Tiryns, c. 1300 B.C. Note the similarity of this Mycenaean female profile to the Minoan "La Parisienne" shown on p. 98.

The significance of the Minoan and the Mycenaean civilizations should not be estimated primarily in terms of subsequent influences. Minoan culture hardly influenced any peoples other than the Mycenaeans and it was then destroyed more or less without a trace after about 1400 B.C. The Mycenaeans left behind a few more traces, but still not very many. Later Greeks retained some Mycenaean gods and goddesses like Zeus, Hera, Hermes, and Poseidon, but they completely altered their role in the religious pantheon. It may also be that the later Greeks gained from the Mycenaeans their devotion to athletics and their system of weights and measures, but these connections remain uncertain. Homer definitely remembered the successful Mycenaean siege of Troy, but it is just as important to realize how much Homer forgot: writing in the eighth century B.C. Homer (actually several different writers who have come down to us under that name) entirely forgot the whole pattern of Mycenaean bureaucratic monarchy which we know from the Linear B tablets. It may well be that the break between the Mycenaeans and Homer was all for the good. Some historians maintain that the destruction of despotic Mycenae by the Dorians was a necessary prelude to the emergence of the freer and more enlightened later Greek outlook.

Influence of the Minoan and Mycenaean civilizations

Although the Minoan and Mycenaean civilizations had little subsequent influence, they are still noteworthy for at least four reasons. First of all, they were the earliest civilizations of Europe. Before the

Importance of the Minoan and Mycenaean civilizations

Cretan accomplishments all civilizations had existed farther east, but afterward Europe was to witness the development of one highly impressive civilization after another. Second, in some respects the Minoans and the Mycenaeans seem to have looked forward to certain later European values and accomplishments even if they did not directly influence them. Minoan and Mycenaean political organization was similar to that of many Asian states but Minoan art in particular seems very different and more characteristic of later European patterns. Unlike most ancient Near Eastern artists, the Minoan gloried not in portraying the slaughter of armies or the sacking of cities but in picturing flowery landscapes, joyous festivals, thrilling exhibitions of athletic prowess, and similar scenes of a free and peaceful existence. Third, the Minoan civilization, and to a lesser degree also the Mycenaean one, is significant for its worldly and progressive outlook. This is exemplified in the devotion of the Aegean peoples to comfort and opulence, in their love of amusement, zest for life, and courage for experimentation. And finally, the Minoan civilization is particularly remarkable for having flourished for so long in peace. If there has never again been as peaceful a civilization as the Minoan then that is a fact we should not celebrate but deplore.

3. THE LYDIANS AND THE PHOENICIANS

The Kingdom of Lydia

After the last remnants of the Hittite Empire fell in the eighth century B.C., one of the successor states in Asia Minor was the Kingdom of Lydia. The Lydians established their rule in what is now the western part of Turkey. They quickly secured control of the Greek cities on the coast of Asia Minor and of the entire plateau west of the Halys River. But their power was short-lived. In 547 B.C. their king, Croesus, fancied he saw a good opportunity to add to his domain the territory of the Medes east of the Halys. The Median king had just been deposed by Cyrus the Great of Persia. Thinking this meant an easy triumph for his own armies, Croesus set out to capture the territory beyond the river. After an indecisive battle with Cyrus, he returned to his own capital (Sardis) for reinforcements. Here Cyrus caught him unprepared in a surprise attack and captured and burned the city. The Lydians never recovered from the blow, and soon afterward all of their territory, including the Greek cities on the coast, passed under the dominion of Cyrus.

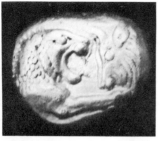

An Early Lydian Coin, Probably Struck during the Reign of Croesus

The Lydians, a people of Indo-European speech, were probably a mixture of native peoples of Asia Minor with migrant stocks from eastern Europe. Benefiting from the advantages of favorable location and abundance of resources, they enjoyed one of the highest standards of living of ancient times. They were famous for the splendor of their armored chariots and the quantities of gold and articles of luxury possessed by the citizens. The wealth of their kings was legendary, as shown by the simile "rich as Croesus." The chief sources of this prosperity were gold from the streams, wool from the thousands of sheep on the hills, and the profits of the extensive commerce which passed overland from the Tigris-Euphrates valley to the Aegean Sea. But with all their wealth and opportunities for leisure, they succeeded in making only one original contribution to civilization. This was the coinage of money from electrum or "white gold," a natural mixture of gold and silver found in the sands of one of their rivers. Hitherto all systems of money had consisted of weighed rings or bars of metal. The new coins, of varying sizes, were stamped with a definite value more or less arbitrarily given by the ruler who issued them.

The Lydian people and their culture

In contrast with the Lydians, who gained their ascendancy as a result of the downfall of the Hittites, were the Phoenicians, who benefited from the break-up of Aegean supremacy. But the Phoenicians were neither conquerors nor the builders of an empire. They exerted their influence through the arts of peace, especially through commerce. During most of their history their political system was a loose confederation of city-states, which frequently bought their security by paying tribute to foreign powers. The territory they occupied was the narrow strip north of Palestine between the Lebanon Mountains and the Mediterranean Sea and the islands off the coast. With good harbors and a central location, it was admirably situated for trade. The great centers of commerce included Tyre and Sidon. Under the leadership of Tyre, Phoenicia reached the zenith of its accomplishments from the tenth to the eighth century B.C. During the sixth century it passed under the domination of the Chaldeans and then of the Persians. In 332 B.C. Tyre was destroyed by Alexander the Great after a siege of seven months.

The Phoenician cities and confederation

See color map facing page 65

The Phoenicians were a Semitic people, closely related to the Canaanites. They displayed little creative genius, but were remarkable adapters of the achievements of others. They produced no original art worthy of the name, and they made but slight contributions to literature. Their religion, like that of the Canaanites, was characterized by human sacrifice to the god Moloch and by licentious fertility rites. They excelled, however, in specialized manufactures, in geography and navigation. They founded colonies at Carthage in North Africa, near modern-day Palermo on the island of Sicily, on the Balearic Islands, and at Cadiz and Malaga in Spain. They were renowned throughout the ancient world for their glass and metal industries and for their purple dye obtained from a mollusk in the adjacent seas. They developed the art of navigation to such a stage that they could sail by the stars at night. To less venturesome peoples, the North Star was known for some time as the Phoenicians' star. Phoenician ships and sailors were recruited by all the great powers. The most lasting achievement of the Phoenicians, however, was the invention and diffusion of an alphabet based upon principles set forth by the Egyptians.

Achievements of the Phoenicians

The Phoenician contribution was the adoption of a system of signs representing the sounds of the human voice, and the elimination of all pictographic and syllabic characters. This alphabet was taken up by the Greeks, who adapted it for their own language, and from the Greek alphabet was derived the modern Latin one, used throughout the West today.

4. LESSONS FROM THE HISTORY OF THE NEAR EASTERN STATES

Defects of the Near Eastern empires

Like most other periods in world history, the period of the states we have studied thus far was an era of contention and strife. Nearly all of the great empires, and the majority of the smaller states as well, devoted most of their energies to expansion and aggression. The only notable exceptions were the Minoan and Egyptian, but even the Egyptians in the later period of their history were imperialistic. The causes were largely geographic. Each nation grew accustomed to the pursuit of its own interests in some fertile river valley or on some easily defended plateau. Isolation bred fear of foreigners and an incapacity to think of one's own people as members of a common humanity. The feelings of insecurity that resulted seemed to justify aggressive foreign policies and the annexation of neighboring states to serve as buffers against a hostile world.

Results of Near Eastern imperialism

It seems possible to trace nearly all of the woes of the Near Eastern nations to wars of aggression. Arnold J. Toynbee has shown this in devastating fashion in the case of the Assyrians. He contends that it was no less true of such later peoples as the Spartans, the Carthaginians, the Macedonians, and the Ottoman Turks. Each made militarism and conquest its gods and wrought such destruction upon itself that when it made its last heroic stand against its enemies, it was a mere "corpse in armor." Not death by foreign conquest but national suicide was the fate which befell it.[1] The way of the warrior brought racism, a love of ease and luxury, crime, and crushing burdens of taxation. Expansion of empire promoted a fictitious prosperity, at least for the upper classes, and aroused enough envy among poorer nations to make them willing conspirators against a rich neighbor who could easily be portrayed as an oppressor. The use of hungry and discontented allies against powerful rivals is not new in history.

SELECTED READINGS

• *Items so designated are available in paperback editions.*
 Alsop, Joseph, *From the Silent Earth: A Report on the Greek Bronze Age,* New York, 1964. An enthusiastic account by a modern political reporter of

[1] D. C. Somervell (ed.), A. J. Toynbee's *A Study of History,* I, 338–43.

some of the most exciting recent discoveries and hypotheses. Favors the Mycenaeans in discussions of their relationships to the Minoans.

Blegen, C. W., *Troy and the Trojans,* New York, 1963. The most reliable archeological appraisal.

• Ceram, C. W., *The Secret of the Hittites,* New York, 1956. The best popular account.

• Chadwick, John, *The Decipherment of Linear B,* 2nd ed., New York, 1968. Chadwick was a research colleague of Michael Ventris and here gives the most accessible account of Ventris's brilliant work.

———, *The Mycenaean World,* New York, 1976. A lively account of the society based on the evidence of the Linear B tablets.

Finley, M. I., *Early Greece: The Bronze and Archaic Ages,* New York, 1970. An excellent survey that spans two different eras.

• Gordon, Cyrus H., *The Ancient Near East,* New York, 1965.

•———, *The Common Background of Greek and Hebrew Civilizations,* New York, 1965. Very controversial. Gordon believes that Greek culture was in its origins Semitic.

Gurney, O. R., *The Hittites,* Baltimore, 1961. More scholarly than Ceram.

Harden, Donald, *The Phoenicians,* New York, 1962. Best account of the Phoenicians at home and abroad.

• Higgins, Reynold, *Minoan and Mycenaean Art,* New York, 1967.

History of the Hellenic World, Vol. I, *Prehistory and Protohistory,* University Park, Pa., 1974.

Hutchinson, R. W., *Prehistoric Crete,* Baltimore, 1962.

Lloyd, Seton, *Early Anatolia,* Baltimore, 1956.

• MacDonald, William A., *Progress into the Past: The Rediscovery of Mycenaean Civilization,* New York, 1967.

Palmer, L. R., *Mycenaeans and Minoans,* New York, 1962. Includes bold statements on many debatable problems of interpretation.

Starr, C. G., *The Origins of Greek Civilization,* New York, 1961.

Trump, David, *The Prehistory of the Mediterranean,* New Haven, Conn., 1980. Treats the earliest European cultures from 5000 B.C. to 1000 B.C.

• Vermeule, Emily, *Greece in the Bronze Age,* Chicago, 1964. The best book on the subject.

Part Two

THE CLASSICAL CIVILIZATIONS OF GREECE AND ROME

After 600 B.C. the centers of civilization in the Western world were no longer mainly located in the Near East. By that time new cultures were already growing to maturity in Greece and in Italy. Both had started their evolution considerably earlier, but the civilization of Greece did not begin to ripen until about 600 B.C., while the Romans showed little promise of original achievement before 500. About 300 B.C. Greek civilization, properly speaking, came to an end and was superseded by a new culture representing a fusion of elements derived from Greece and the Near East. This was the Hellenistic civilization, which lasted until about the beginning of the Christian era and included not only the Greek peninsula but Egypt and most of Asia west of the Indus River. The outstanding characteristic which serves to distinguish these three civilizations from the ones that had gone before is secularism. No longer does religion absorb the interests of humans to the extent that it did in ancient Egypt or in the nations of Mesopotamia. The state is now above the church, and the power of the priests to determine the direction of cultural evolution has been greatly reduced. Furthermore, ideals of human freedom and an emphasis on the welfare of the individual have largely superseded the despotism and collectivism of the ancient Near East. Only late in Roman history, around the third century A.D., did Near Eastern despotism begin to reassert itself within the confines of imperial Rome. Around that time too, a new religion, Christianity, began to reshape the life of the West.

The Classical Civilizations of Greece and Rome

	POLITICS	PHILOSOPHY AND SCIENCE
800 **B.C.**	Dark Ages of Greek history, 1100–800	
	Beginning of city-states in Greece, c. 800 Rome founded, c. 750	Thales of Miletus, c. 640–546 Pythagoras, c. 582–c. 507
	Age of the tyrants in Greece, c. 650–c. 500 Reforms of Solon in Athens, 594 Tyranny of Peisistratus, 560 Reforms of Cleisthenes, 508	
500 **B.C.**	Establishment of Roman Republic, c. 500 Greco-Persian War, 490–479	Protagoras, c. 490–c. 420 Socrates, 469–399
	Delian League, 479–404 Perfection of Athenian democracy, 461–429 Law of the Twelve Tables, Rome, c. 450 Peloponnesian War, 431–404	Hippocrates, 460–c. 377 Democritus, c. 460–c. 362 The Sophists, c. 450–c. 400
400 **B.C.**		Plato, 427–347 Aristotle, 384–322
	Theban supremacy in Greece, 371–362 Macedonian conquest of Greece, 338–337 Conquests of Alexander the Great, 336–323 Division of Alexander's empire, 323	Epicurus, 342–270 Zeno the Stoic, c. 320–c. 250 Euclid, c. 323–285 Aristarchus, 310–230
300 **B.C.**		Archimedes, c. 287–212 Eratosthenes, c. 276–c. 195
		Herophilus, c. 220–c. 150 Polybius, c. 205–118
200 **B.C.**		The Skeptics, c. 200–c. 100
	Punic Wars between Rome and Carthage, 264–146 Reforms of the Gracchi, 133–121 Dictatorship of Julius Caesar, 46–44 Principate of Augustus Caesar, 27 B.C.–14 A.D.	Introduction of Stoicism into Rome, c. 140 Cicero, 106–43
100 **B.C.**	Dictatorship of Julius Caesar, 46–44 Principate of Augustus Caesar, 27 B.C.–14 A.D.	
		Lucretius, 98–55
100 **A.D.**	"Five Good Emperors," 96–180	Seneca, 34 B.C.–65 A.D. Marcus Aurelius, 121–180
200 **A.D.**	Completion of Roman jurisprudence by great jurists, c. 200 Civil war in Roman Empire, 235–284	Galen, 130–c. 200 Plotinus, c. 204–270
	Diocletian, 284–305	
300 **A.D.**	Constantine I, 306–337	
400 **A.D.**	Theodosius I, 379–395 Visigoths sack Rome, 410	
500 **A.D.**	Deposition of last of Western Roman emperors, 476 Theodoric the Ostrogoth king of Italy, 493–526 Justinian, 527–565 *Corpus* of Roman law, c. 550	Boethius, c. 480–524

ECONOMICS	RELIGION	ARTS AND LETTERS	
			800 **B.C.**
Economic revolution and colonization in Greece, c. 750–c. 600			
Rise of middle class in Greece, c. 750–c. 600		*Iliad* and *Odyssey*, c. 750	
		Doric architectural style, c. 650–c. 500	
	Orphic and Eleusinian mystery cults, c. 500–c. 100	Aeschylus, 525–456	**500** **B.C.**
		Phidias, c. 500–c. 432	
		Ionic architectural style, c. 500–c. 400	
		Sophocles, 496–406	
		Herodotus, c. 484–c. 420	
		Euripides, 480–406	
		Thucydides, c. 471–c. 400	
		The Parthenon, c. 460	**400** **B.C.**
		Aristophanes, c. 448–c. 380	
		Corinthian architectural style, c. 400–c. 300	
Hellenistic international trade and growth of large cities, c. 300 B.C.–c. 100 A.D.		Praxiteles, c. 370–c. 310	
			300 **B.C.**
Growth of slavery, rise of middle class, decline of small farmer in Rome, c. 250–100	Oriental mystery cults in Rome, c. 250–50		
			200 **B.C.**
	Spread of Mithraism in Rome, 27 B.C.–270 A.D.	Virgil, 70–19	**100** **B.C.**
	The Crucifixion, c. 30 A.D.	Horace, 65–8	
Decline of slavery in Rome, c. 120–c. 476	St. Paul's missionary work, c. 35–c. 67	Livy, 59 B.C.–17 A.D.	
Growth of serfdom in Rome, c. 200–500		Ovid, c. 43 B.C.–17 A.D.	
		Tacitus, c. 55 A.D.–c. 117 A.D.	**100** **A.D.**
Sharp economic contraction in Rome, c. 200–c. 300		The Colosseum, c. 80 A.D.	**200** **A.D.**
		The Pantheon, c. 120	
	Beginning of toleration of Christians in the Roman Empire, 311	Height of Roman portrait statuary, c. 120–c. 250	
			300 **A.D.**
	St. Augustine, 354–430		**400** **A.D.**
	Christianity made official Roman religion, 380		
			500 **A.D.**
	Benedictine monastic rule, c. 520		

GREEK CIVILIZATION

We love beauty without extravagance, and wisdom without weakness of will. Wealth we regard not as a means for private display but rather for public service; and poverty we consider no disgrace, although we think it is a disgrace not to try to overcome it. We believe a man should be concerned about public as well as private affairs, for we regard the person who takes no part in politics not as merely uninterested but as useless.

—Pericles, *Funeral Oration,* on the ideals of Athens

Now, what is characteristic of any nature is that which is best for it and gives most joy. Such to man is the life according to reason, since it is this that makes him man.

—Aristotle, *Nicomachean Ethics*

Among all the peoples of the ancient world, the one whose culture most clearly exemplified the spirit of Western society was the Greek or Hellenic. No one of these nations had so strong a devotion to liberty or so firm a belief in the nobility of human achievement. The Greeks glorified humanity as the most important creation in the universe and refused to submit to the dictation of priests or despots or even to humble themselves before their gods. Their attitude was essentially secular and rationalistic; they exalted the spirit of free inquiry and made knowledge supreme over faith. Largely for these reasons their culture advanced to the highest stage which the ancient world was destined to reach.

The character of Greek civilization

1. THE GREEK DARK AGES

The fall of the Mycenaean civilization was a major catastrophe for the Greek world. It ushered in a period usually called by historians the Dark Ages, which lasted from about 1100 to 800 B.C. Written records disappeared, except where accidentally preserved, and culture reverted to simpler forms than had been known for centuries. Toward

The Dark Ages

Bronze Centaur and Man. These figures date from about 750 B.C. They are no more than about five inches high.

Bronze Statuette. Perhaps representing Apollo, this work dates from about 750 B.C.

the end of the period some decorated pottery and skillfully designed metal objects began to appear on the islands of the Aegean Sea, but essentially the period was a long night. Aside from the development of writing at the very end, intellectual accomplishment was limited to ballads, and short epics sung and embellished by bards as they wandered from one village to another. A large part of this material was finally woven into a great epic cycle by one or more poets in the eighth century B.C. Though not all the poems of this cycle have come down to us, the two most important, the *Iliad* and the *Odyssey*, the so-called Homeric epics, provide us with a rich store of information about many of the customs and institutions of the Dark Ages.

The political institutions of the Dark Ages were exceedingly primitive. Each little community of villages was independent of external control, but political authority was so tenuous that it would not be too much to say that the state scarcely existed at all. The *basileus* or ruler was not much more than a tribal leader. He could not make or enforce laws or administer justice. He received no remuneration of any kind, and had to cultivate his farm for a living the same as any other citizen. Practically his only functions were military and priestly. He commanded the army in time of war and offered sacrifices to keep the gods on the good side of the community. Although each little community had its council of nobles and assembly of warriors, neither of these bodies had any definite membership or status as an organ of government. Almost without exception custom took the place of law, and the administration of justice was private. Even willful murder was punishable only by the family of the victim. While it is true that disputes were sometimes submitted to the ruler for settlement, he acted in such cases merely as an arbitrator, not as a judge. As a matter of fact, the political consciousness of the Greeks of this time was so poorly developed that they had no conception of government as an indispensable agency for the preservation of social order. When Odysseus, ruler of Ithaca, was absent for twenty years, no regent governed in his place and no session of the council or assembly was held. No one seemed to think that the complete suspension of government, even for so long a time, was a matter of critical importance.

The pattern of social and economic life was remarkably simple. Though the general tone of the society portrayed in the epics is aristocratic, no rigid stratification of classes existed. Manual labor was not looked upon as degrading, and there were apparently no idle rich. That there were dependent laborers who worked on the lands of the nobles and served them as faithful warriors seems clear from the Homeric epics, but they appear to have been serfs rather than slaves. The slaves were chiefly women, employed as servants, wool-processors, or concubines. Many were war captives, but they do not appear to have been badly treated. Agriculture and herding were the basic occupations of free men. Except for a few skilled crafts like those of wagonmaker, swordsmith, goldsmith, and potter, there was no specialization of labor. For the most part every household made its own tools, wove its own clothing, and raised its own food. So far were the Greeks of this time from being a trading people that they had no word in their language for "merchant," for barter was the only method of exchange.

To the Greeks of the Dark Ages religion meant chiefly a system for: (1) explaining the physical world in such a way as to remove its awesome mysteries and give people a feeling of intimate relationship with it; (2) accounting for the tempestuous passions that seized human nature; and (3) obtaining such tangible benefits as good fortune, long life, skill in craftsmanship, and abundant harvests. The Greeks did not expect that their religion would save them from sin or endow them with spiritual blessings. As they conceived it, piety was neither a matter of conduct nor of faith. Their religion, accordingly, had no commandments, dogmas, or sacraments. All were at liberty to believe what they pleased and to conduct their own lives as they chose without fear of divine wrath.

Religious conceptions in the Dark Ages

As is commonly known, the deities of the early Greek religion were merely human beings writ large. It was really necessary that this should be so if the Greeks were to feel at home in the world over which they ruled. Remote, omnipotent beings like the gods of most oriental religions would have inspired fear rather than a sense of security. What the Greeks wanted was not necessarily gods of great power, but deities who could be bargained with on equal terms. Consequently gods were endowed with attributes similar to human ones—with human bodies and human weaknesses and wants. The early Greeks imagined the great company of divinities as frequently quarreling with one another, mingling freely with mortals, and even occasionally procreating children by mortal women. They differed from humans only in the fact that they subsisted on ambrosia and nectar, which made them immortal. They dwelt not in the sky or in the stars but on the summit of Mount Olympus, a peak in northern Greece with an altitude of about 10,000 feet.

Human qualities of the deities

The religion was thoroughly polytheistic, with no one deity elevated very high above any of the others. Zeus, the sky god and wielder of the thunderbolt, who was sometimes referred to as the father of the gods and of men, frequently received less attention than did Poseidon, the sea god, Aphrodite, goddess of love, or Athena, variously considered goddess of wisdom and war and patroness of handicrafts. Since the Greeks had no Satan, their religion cannot be described as dualistic. All of the deities were deemed capable of malevolence as well as good.

The Greeks of the Dark Ages were almost completely indifferent to what happened to them after death. They did assume, however, that shades or ghosts survived for a time after the death of their bodies. All, with a few exceptions, went to the same abode—to the murky realm of Hades situated beneath the earth. This was neither a paradise

Poseidon or Zeus. Detail from an Athenian statue of about 470 B.C., larger than life size.

nor a hell: no one was rewarded for good deeds, and no one was punished for sins. Each of the shades appeared to continue the same kind of life its human embodiment had lived on earth. The Homeric poems make casual mention of two other realms, the Elysian Plain and the realm of Tartarus, which seem at first glance to contradict the idea of no rewards and punishments in the hereafter. But the few individuals who enjoyed the ease and comfort of the Elysian Plain had done nothing to deserve such blessings: they were simply persons whom the gods had chosen to favor. The realm of Tartarus was not really an abode of the dead but a place of imprisonment for rebellious deities.

Worship in early Greek religion consisted primarily of sacrifice. The offerings were made, however, not as an atonement for sin, but chiefly in order to please the gods and induce them to grant favors. In other words, religious practice was external and mechanical and not far removed from magic. Reverence, humility, and purity of heart were not essentials in it. The worshiper just made the proper sacrifice and then hoped for the best. For a religion such as this no elaborate institutions were required. Even a professional priesthood was unnecessary. Since there were no mysteries and no sacraments, one man could perform the simple rites about as well as another. The Greek temple was not a church or place of religious assemblage, and no ceremonies were performed within it. Instead it was a shrine which the god might visit occasionally and use as a temporary house.

As intimated already, the morality of the Greeks in the Dark Ages had only the vaguest connection with their religion. While it is true that the gods were generally disposed to support the right, they did not consider it their duty to combat evil and make righteousness prevail. In meting out rewards to humans, they appear to have been influenced more by their own whims and by gratitude for sacrifices offered than by any consideration for moral character. The only crime they punished was perjury, and that none too consistently. Nearly all the virtues extolled in the epics were those which would make the individual a better soldier—bravery, self-control, patriotism, wisdom (in the sense of cunning), love of one's friends, and hatred of one's enemies. There was no conception of sin in the Christian sense of wrongful acts to be repented of or atoned for.

At the end of the Dark Ages the Greeks already had started along the road of social ideals that they would follow in later centuries. They were optimists, convinced that life was worth living for its own sake, and could see no reason for looking forward to death as a glad release. They were egotists striving for the fulfillment of self. As a consequence, they rejected mortification of the flesh and all forms of denial which implied the frustration of life. They could see no merit in humility or in turning the other cheek. Finally, they were humanists, who worshiped the finite and the natural rather than the otherworldly or sublime. For this reason they refused to invest their gods with awe-

Man Carrying a Calf for Sacrifice. A life-size Athenian sculpture from about 570 B.C.

Battle between the Gods and the Giants. This frieze dates from before 525 B.C. and is from the sanctuary of Apollo at Delphi.

inspiring qualities, or to invent any conception of humans as depraved and sinful creatures.

2. THE EVOLUTION OF THE CITY-STATES

About 800 B.C. the village communities which had been founded mainly upon tribal or clan organization, began to give way to larger political units. As trade and the need for defense increased, cities grew up around marketplaces and defensive fortifications as seats of government for whole communities. Thus emerged the city-state, the most famous unit of political society developed by the Greeks. Examples could be found in almost every section of the Hellenic world: Athens, Thebes, and Megara on the mainland; Sparta and Corinth on the Peloponnesus; Miletus on the shore of Asia Minor; and Mitylene and Samos on the islands of the Aegean Sea. They varied enormously in both area and population. Sparta with more than 3,000 square miles and Athens with 1,060 had by far the greatest extent; the others averaged less than 100. At the peak of their power Athens and Sparta, each with a population of about 400,000, had approximately three times the numerical strength of most of their neighboring states.

The origin and nature of the city-states

More important is the fact that the Greek city-states varied widely in cultural evolution. From 800 to 500 B.C., commonly called the Archaic period, the Peloponnesian cities of Corinth and Argos were leaders in the development of literature and the arts. In the seventh century Sparta outshone many of its rivals. Preeminent above all were the Greek-speaking cities on the coast of Asia Minor and the islands of the Aegean Sea. Foremost among them was Miletus, where a brilliant

Variations among the city-states

flowering of philosophy and science occurred as early as the sixth century. Athens lagged behind until at least one hundred years later.

With a few exceptions the Greek city-states went through a similar political evolution. They began their histories as monarchies. During the eighth century they were changed into oligarchies. About a hundred years later, on the average, most of the oligarchies were overthrown by dictators, or "tyrants," as the Greeks called them, meaning usurpers who ruled without legal right whether oppressively or not. Finally, in the sixth and fifth centuries, democracies were set up, or in some cases "timocracies," that is, governments based upon a property qualification for the exercise of political rights.

On the whole, it is not difficult to determine the causes of this political evolution. The first change came about as a result of the concentration of landed wealth. As the owners of great estates gained ever-greater economic power, they determined to wrest political authority from the ruler, now commonly called king, and vest it in the council, which they generally controlled. In the end they abolished the kingship entirely. Then followed a period of sweeping economic changes and political turmoil.

One of the Earliest Minted Greek Coins. Struck around 700 B.C. on the island of Aegina, near Athens, this coin shows a sea turtle, a symbol of the Greeks' ability to flourish by sea.

These developments affected not only Greece itself but many other parts of the Mediterranean world. For they were accompanied and followed by a vast overseas expansion. The chief causes were an increasing scarcity of land, internal strife, and a general temper of restlessness and discontent. The Greeks rapidly learned of numerous areas, thinly populated, with climate and soil similar to those of the homelands. The parent states most active in the expansive movement were Corinth, Chalcis, and Miletus. Their citizens founded colonies along the Aegean shores and even in Italy and Sicily. Of the latter the best known were Taras (modern Taranto) and Syracuse. They also established trading centers on the coast of Egypt and as far east as Babylon. The results of this expansionist movement were momentous. Commerce and industry became leading pursuits and the urban population increased. Merchants and artisans now joined with dispossessed farmers in an attack upon the landholding oligarchy. The natural fruit of the bitter class conflicts that ensued was dictatorship. By encouraging extravagant hopes and promising relief from chaos, ambitious demagogues attracted enough popular support to ride into power in defiance of constitutions and laws. Ultimately, however, dissatisfaction with tyrannical rule and the increasing economic might and political consciousness of the common citizens led to the establishment of democracies or timocracies.

A Coin from Selinus, a Greek City in Sicily. Depicted is a sacrifice to Asclepius, god of healing, who is represented in the form of a cock.

See color map facing page 160

Internal development widely similar

Unfortunately space does not permit an analysis of the political history of each of the Greek city-states. Except in the more backward sections of Thessaly and the Peloponnesus, it is safe to conclude that the internal development of all of them paralleled the account given above, although minor variations due to local conditions doubtless occurred. The two most important of the Hellenic states, Sparta and Athens, deserve more detailed study.

3. THE ARMED CAMP OF SPARTA

The history of Sparta[1] was the great exception to the political evolution of the city-states. Despite the fact that its citizens sprang from the same origins as most of the other Greeks, Sparta failed to make any progress in the direction of democratic rule. Instead, its government gradually evolved into a form more closely resembling a modern elite dictatorship. Culturally, also, the nation stagnated after the sixth century. The causes were due partly to isolation. Hemmed in by mountains on the northeast and west and lacking good harbors, the Spartan people had little opportunity to profit from the advances made in the outside world. Besides, no middle class arose to aid the masses in the struggle for freedom.

The peculiar development of Sparta

The major explanation is to be found, however, in militarism. The Spartans were originally Dorians who had come into the eastern Peloponnesus as an invading army. Though by the end of the ninth century they had gained dominion over all of Laconia, they were not satisfied. West of the Taygetus Mountains lay the fertile plain of Messenia. The Spartans determined to conquer it. The venture was successful, and the Messenian territory was annexed to Laconia. About 640 B.C. the Messenians enlisted the aid of Argos and launched a revolt. The war that followed was desperately fought, Laconia itself was invaded, and only the death of the Argive commander and the patriotic pleas of the fire-eating poet Tyrtaeus saved the day for the Spartans. This time the victors took no chances. They confiscated the lands of the Messenians, murdered or expelled their leaders, and turned the masses into serfs called *helots*. Thereafter Spartan foreign policy was defensive. Following the Messenian wars the Spartans feared that further foreign warfare would provide the opportunities for a helot uprising; consequently Sparta devoted itself to keeping what it had already gained.

The Spartan desire for conquest

Almost all the major features of Spartan life resulted from their wars with the Messenians. In subduing and despoiling their enemies they unwittingly enslaved themselves, for they lived through the remaining centuries of their history in deadly fear of insurrections. This fear explains their conservatism, their stubborn resistance to change, lest any innovation result in a fatal weakening of the system. Their pro-

The results of Spartan militarism

---

[1] Sparta was the leading city of a district called Laconia or Lacedaemonia; sometimes the *state* was referred to by one or the other of these names. The people, also, were frequently called Laconians or Lacedaemonians. (The modern adjective "laconic" comes from the reputation of the ancient Spartans for being sparing with words.)

vincialism can also be attributed to the same cause. Frightened by the prospect that dangerous ideas might be brought into the country, they discouraged travel and prohibited trade with the outside world. The necessity of maintaining the absolute supremacy of the citizen class over an enormous population of serfs required an iron discipline and a strict subordination of the individual; hence the Spartan collectivism, which extended into every branch of the social and economic life. Finally, much of the cultural backwardness of Sparta grew out of the atmosphere of restraint which inevitably resulted from the bitter struggle to conquer the Messenians and hold them under stern repression.

The Spartan government

The Spartan constitution provided for a government preserving the forms of the old system of the Dark Ages. Instead of one king, however, there were two, representing separate families of exalted rank. The Spartan kings enjoyed but few powers and those were chiefly of a military and priestly character. A second branch of the government was the council, composed of the two kings and twenty-eight nobles sixty years of age and over. This body supervised the work of administration, prepared measures for submission to the assembly, and served as the highest court for criminal trials. The third organ of government, the assembly, composed of all adult male citizens, approved or rejected the proposals of the council and elected all public officials except the kings. But the highest authority under the Spartan constitution was vested in a board of five men known as the *ephorate.* The ephors virtually were the government. They presided over the council and the assembly, controlled the educational system and the distribution of property, censored the lives of the citizens, and exercised a veto power over all legislation. They had power also to determine the fate of newborn infants, to conduct prosecutions before the council, and even to depose the kings if the religious omens appeared unfavorable. The Spartan government dominated by the ephors was thus in effect an oligarchy.

The class system in Sparta

The population of Sparta was divided into three main classes. The ruling element was made up of the Spartiates, or descendants of the original conquerors. Though never exceeding one-twentieth of the total population, the Spartiates alone had political privileges. Next in order of rank were the *perioeci,* or "dwellers around." The origin of this class is uncertain, but it was probably composed of peoples that had at one time been allies of the Spartans or had submitted voluntarily to Spartan domination. In return for service as a buffer population between the ruling class and the helots, the perioeci were allowed to carry on trade and to engage in manufacturing. At the bottom of the scale were the helots, or serfs, bound to the soil.

Perioeci and helots

Among these classes only the perioeci enjoyed any appreciable measure of comfort and freedom. While it is true that the economic condition of the helots cannot be described in terms of absolute misery, since they were permitted to keep for themselves a good share of what they produced on the estates of their masters, they were personally subjected to such degrading treatment that they were constantly wretched and rebellious. To guard against rebellion young Spartiates were sometimes sent to live among the helots in disguise and act like a secret police with the power to murder whom they pleased. The brutalizing effects on both sides can be easily imagined.

Discipline for the benefit of the state

Those who were born into the Spartiate class were doomed to a respectable slavery for the major part of their lives. Forced to submit to the severest discipline and to sacrifice individual interests, they were little more than cogs in a vast machine. Spartan babies were examined for hardiness at birth and those who were thought to be potential weaklings were carried off to the hills to die of neglect. The education of Spartan males was limited almost entirely to military training, which began at the age of seven, supplemented by merciless floggings to harden the boys for the duties of war. Between the ages of twenty and sixty the men gave almost all their time to state service. Although marriage was practically compulsory there was little family life: young men had to live in barracks, and after the age of thirty they still had to eat in military messes. The husbands carried off their wives on their wedding nights by a show of force. Because they saw so little of them afterwards it sometimes happened that men "had children before they ever saw their wives' faces in daylight."[2] The production of vigorous offspring was the wives' main duty, but mothers had to accept the fact that children were virtually the property of the state. It may be doubted that the Spartiates resented these hardships and deprivations. Pride in their status as the ruling class probably compensated in their minds for harsh discipline and denial of privileges.

Economic regulations

The economic organization of Sparta was designed almost solely for the ends of military efficiency and the supremacy of the citizen class. The best land was owned by the state and was originally divided into equal plots which were assigned to the Spartiate class as inalienable estates. Later these holdings as well as the inferior lands were permitted to be sold and exchanged, with the result that some of the citizens became richer than others. The helots, who did all the work of cultivating the soil, also belonged to the state and were assigned to their masters along with the land. Their masters were forbidden to emancipate them or to sell them outside of the country. The labor of the helots provided for the support of the whole citizen class, whose members were not allowed to be associated with any economic enterprise other than agriculture. The minimal trade and industry of the Spartan state were reserved exclusively for the perioeci. Thus the Spartan economy was as static as Sparta's government was repressive.

[2] Plutarch, "Lycurgus," *Lives of Illustrious Men,* I, 81.

4. THE ATHENIAN TRIUMPH AND TRAGEDY

Athens began its history under conditions quite different from those which prevailed in Sparta. The district of Attica in which Athens is situated had not been the scene of an armed invasion or of bitter conflict between opposing peoples. As a result, no military caste imposed its rule upon a vanquished nation. Furthermore, the wealth of Attica consisted of mineral deposits and splendid harbors in addition to agricultural resources. Athens, consequently, never remained a predominantly agrarian state but rapidly developed a prosperous trade and an essentially urban culture.

Until the middle of the eighth century B.C. Athens, like the other Greek states, had a monarchical form of government. During the century that followed, the council of nobles, or Council of the Areopagus, as it came to be called, gradually divested the king of his powers. The transition to rule by the few was both the cause and the result of an increasing concentration of wealth. The introduction of vine and olive culture about this time led to the growth of agriculture as a large-scale enterprise. Since vineyards and olive orchards require considerable time to become profitable, only those farmers with abundant resources were able to survive in the business. Their poorer and less thrifty neighbors sank rapidly into debt, especially since grain was now coming to be imported at ruinous prices. The small farmer had no alternative but to mortgage his land, and then his family and himself, in the vain hope that some day a way of escape would be found. Ultimately many of this class became serfs when the mortgages could not be paid; those without land to mortgage were sold into slavery.

Bitter cries of distress now arose. The urban middle classes espoused the cause of the peasants in demanding liberalization of the government. Finally, in 594 B.C., all parties agreed upon the appointment of the aristocrat Solon as chief magistrate with absolute power to carry out reforms. The measures Solon enacted provided for both political and economic adjustments. The former included: (1) the establishment of a new council, the Council of Four Hundred, and the admission of the middle classes to membership in it; (2) the enfranchisement of the lower classes by making them eligible for service in the assembly; and (3) the organization of a final court of appeals in criminal cases, open to all citizens and elected by universal manhood suffrage. The economic reforms benefited the poor farmers by canceling existing mortgages, prohibiting enslavement for debt in the future, and limiting the amount of land any one individual could own. Nor did Solon neglect the middle classes. He introduced a new system of coinage designed to give Athens an advantage in foreign trade, imposed heavy penalties for idleness, ordered every man to teach his son a trade, and offered full privileges of citizenship to alien craftsmen who would become permanent residents of the country.

Significant though these reforms were, they did not allay the discontent. The nobles were disgruntled because some of their privileges had been taken away. The middle and lower classes were dissatisfied because they were still excluded from the offices of magistracy, and because the Council of the Areopagus was left with its powers intact. The chaos and disillusionment that followed paved the way in 560 B.C. for the triumph of Peisistratus, the first of the Athenian tyrants. Although he proved to be a benevolent despot who patronized culture, reduced the power of the aristocracy, and raised the standard of living of the average Athenian, his son Hippias, who succeeded him, was a ruthless and spiteful oppressor.

The rise of tyranny

In 510 B.C. Hippias's tyranny was overthrown by a group of nobles with aid from Sparta. Factional conflict raged for another two years until Cleisthenes, an intelligent aristocrat, enlisted the support of the masses to eliminate his rivals from the scene. Having promised concessions to the people as a reward for their help, he proceeded to reform the government in so sweeping a fashion that he has since been known as the father of Athenian democracy. Cleisthenes, who dominated Athenian politics from 508 to 502, enlarged the citizen population by granting full rights to all free men who resided in the country at that time. He established a new council and made it the chief organ of government with power to prepare measures for submission to the assembly and with supreme control over executive and administrative functions. Members of this body were to be chosen by lot. Any male citizen over thirty years of age was eligible. Cleisthenes also expanded the authority of the assembly, giving it power to debate and pass or reject the measures submitted by the Council, to declare war, to appropriate money, and to audit the accounts of retiring magistrates.

The reforms of Cleisthenes

Greeks at War. A battle scene from the interior of a drinking cup, done in Athens between about 530 and 500 B.C.

The Owl of Athens. An Athenian silver coin of around 470 B.C., showing the owl, thought to be sacred to Athens's protectress, the goddess Athena. The name Athens appears in the Greek letters AΘE.

The perfection of Athenian democracy

Athenian democracy compared with modern democracy

Lastly, not long after the time of Cleisthenes, in 487, the Athenians instituted the device of ostracism, whereby any citizen considered dangerous to the state could be sent into honorable exile for a ten-year period. The device was meant to eliminate men suspected of cherishing dictatorial ambitions, but too often its effect was to eliminate exceptional personalities and to allow mediocrity to flourish.

The Athenian democracy attained its full perfection in the Age of Pericles (461–429 B.C.). It was during this period that the assembly acquired the authority to initiate legislation in addition to its power to ratify or reject proposals of the council. During this time also the Board of Ten Generals rose to a position roughly comparable to that of the British cabinet. The generals were chosen by the assembly for one-year terms and were eligible for reelection indefinitely. Pericles held the position of chief strategus or president of the Board of Generals for more than thirty years. The generals were not simply commanders of the army but the chief legislative and executive officials in the state. Though wielding enormous power, they could not become tyrants, for their policies were subject to review by the assembly, and they could easily be recalled at the end of their one-year terms or indicted for malfeasance at any time. Finally, in the Age of Pericles the Athenian system of courts reached its completion. No longer was there merely a supreme court to hear appeals from the decisions of magistrates, but an array of popular courts were formed to try all kinds of cases. At the beginning of each year a list of 6,000 citizens was chosen by lot from the various sections of the country. From this list separate juries, varying in size from 201 to 1,001, were made up for particular trials. Each of these juries constituted a court with power to decide by majority vote every question involved in the case. Although one of the magistrates presided, he had none of the prerogatives of a judge; the jury itself was the judge, and from its decision there was no appeal.

The Athenian democracy differed from the modern form in various ways. First of all, it entirely excluded women. Even taking that into account, it did not extend to the whole population, but only to the citizen class. While it is true that in the time of Cleisthenes the citizens probably included a majority of the inhabitants because of his enfranchisement of resident aliens, in the Age of Pericles the citizens were distinctly a minority. It may be well to observe, however, that within its limits Athenian democracy was more thoroughly applied than is the modern form. The choice by lot of nearly all magistrates except the Ten Generals, the restriction of all terms of public officials to one year, and the uncompromising adherence to the principle of majority rule even in judicial trials were examples of a confidence in the political capacity of the citizen which few modern nations would be willing to accept. The democracy of Athens differed from the contemporary ideal also in the fact that it was direct, not representative. The Athenians were not interested in being governed by a few men of reputation and ability; what vitally concerned them was the assurance to every citizen of an actual voice in the control of all public affairs.

In the century of its greatest expansion and creativity, Athens fought two major wars. The first, the war with Persia, was an outgrowth of the expansion of that empire into the eastern Mediterranean area. The Athenians resented the oppression of the Greek-speaking cities in Asia Minor and aided them in their struggle for freedom. (These cities shared with Athens a common Greek dialect—Ionian—a fact which made the Athenians feel a particularly close kinship with them.) The Persians retaliated by sending a powerful army and fleet to attack the Greeks. Although all Greece was in danger of conquest, Athens bore the chief burden of repelling the invader. The war, which began in 490 B.C. and lasted with interludes of peace until 479, is commonly regarded as one of the most significant in the history of the world. The heroic victories of the Greeks in such battles as Marathon (490) and Salamis (480) put an end to the menace of Persian conquest and forestalled the submergence of Hellenic ideals of freedom in Near Eastern despotism. The war also strengthened democracy in Athens and made that state the leading power in Greece.

The other of the great struggles, the Peloponnesian War with Sparta, had results of a quite different character. Instead of being another milestone in the Athenian march to power, it ended in tragedy. The causes of this war are of particular interest to the student of the downfall of civilizations. First and most important was the growth of Athenian imperialism. In the last year of the war with Persia, Athens had joined with a number of other Greek states in the formation of an offensive and defensive alliance known as the Delian League. When peace was concluded the league was not dissolved, for many of the Greeks feared that the Persians might come back. As time went on, Athens gradually transformed the league into a naval empire for the advancement of its own interests. It used some of the funds in the common treasury for its own purposes. It tried to reduce all the other members to a condition of vassalage, and when one of them rebelled, Athens overwhelmed it by force, seized its navy, and imposed tribute upon it as if it were a conquered state. Such high-handed methods aroused the suspicions of the Spartans, who feared that an Athenian hegemony would soon be extended over all of Greece.

A second major cause was to be found in the social and cultural differences between Athens and Sparta. Athens was democratic, progressive, urban, imperialist, and intellectually and artistically advanced. Sparta was aristocratic, conservative, agrarian, provincial, and culturally backward. Where such sharply contrasting systems exist side by side, conflicts are almost bound to occur. The attitude of the Athenians and Spartans had been hostile for some time. The former looked upon the latter as uncouth barbarians. The Spartans accused the Athenians of attempting to gain control over the northern Peloponnesian states and of encouraging the helots to rebel. Economic fac-

The Persian War and its results

Athenian imperialism and the Peloponnesian War

Other causes of the Peloponnesian War

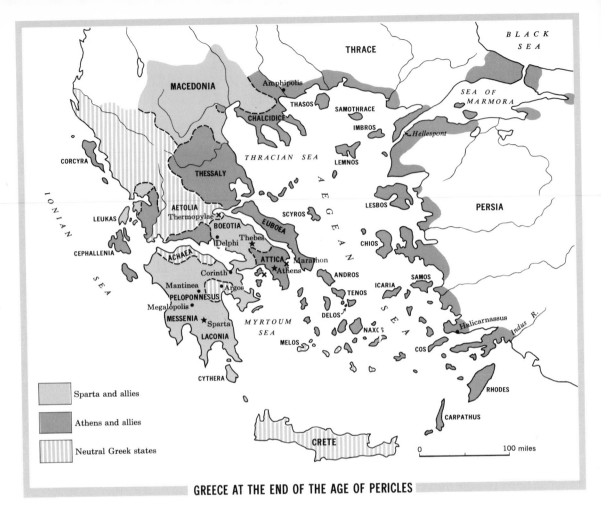

GREECE AT THE END OF THE AGE OF PERICLES

The defeat of Athens

tors also played a large part in bringing the conflict to a head. Athens sought to dominate the Corinthian Gulf, the principal avenue of trade with Sicily and southern Italy. This made Athens the deadly enemy of Corinth, the chief ally of Sparta.

The war, which broke out in 431 B.C. and lasted until 404, was a record of frightful calamities for Athens. Athenian trade was destroyed, its democracy overthrown, and the population decimated by a terrible pestilence. Quite as bad was the moral degradation which followed in the wake of the military reverses. Treason, corruption, and brutality were among the hastening ills of the last few years of the conflict. On one occasion the Athenians even slaughtered the whole male population of the island of Melos, and enslaved the women and children, for no other crime than refusing to abandon neutrality. Ultimately, deserted by all its allies except Samos and with its food supply cut off, Athens was left with no alternative but to surrender or starve. The terms imposed upon the Athenians were drastic enough: destruction of their fortifications, surrender of all foreign possessions and practically their entire navy, and submission to Sparta as a subject state. Though Athens recovered its leadership for a time in the fourth century, its period of glory was approaching its end.

5. POLITICAL DEBACLE—THE LAST DAYS

Not only did the Peloponnesian War put an end to the political supremacy of Athens, it annihilated freedom throughout the Greek world and sealed the doom of the Hellenic political genius. Following the war, Sparta asserted its power over all of Greece. Oligarchies supported by Spartan troops replaced democracies wherever they existed. Confiscation of property and assassination were the methods regularly employed to combat opposition. Although in Athens the tyrants were overthrown after a time and free government restored, Sparta was able to dominate the remainder of Greece for more than thirty years. In 371 B.C., however, Epaminondas of Thebes defeated the Spartan army at Leuctra and thereby inaugurated a period of Theban supremacy. Unfortunately Thebes showed little more wisdom and tolerance in governing than Sparta, and nine years later a combination was formed to free the Greek cities from their new oppressor. Failing to break up the alliance, the Thebans gave battle on the field of Mantinea. Both sides claimed the victory, but Epaminondas was slain, and his empire soon afterward collapsed.

The long succession of wars had now brought the Greek states to the point of exhaustion. Though the glory of their culture was yet undimmed, politically they were prostrate and helpless. Their fate was soon decided for them by the rise of Philip of Macedon. Except for a thin veneer of Hellenic culture, the Macedonians were barbarians; but Philip, before becoming their king, had learned how to lead an army while a hostage at Thebes. Perceiving the weakness of the states to the south, he determined to conquer them. A series of early successes led to a decisive victory in 338 B.C. and soon afterward to dominion over all of Greece except Sparta. Two years later Philip was murdered as the sequel to a family brawl.

Rule over Greece now passed into the hands of his son Alexander, a youth of twenty years. After putting to death all possible aspirants to the throne and quelling some feeble revolts of the Greeks, Alexander, subsequently known as "the Great," conceived the grandiose scheme of conquering Persia. One victory followed another until, in the short space of twelve years, all the eastern territory from the Indus River to the Nile had been annexed to Greece as the personal domain of one man. Alexander did not live to enjoy it long. In 323 B.C. he fell ill of Babylonian swamp fever and died at the age of thirty-two.

It is difficult to gauge the significance of Alexander's career. Historians have differed widely in their interpretations. Some have seen him as one of the supreme galvanizing forces in history. Others would limit his genius to military strategy and organization and deny that he made a single major contribution of benefit to humanity. There can be no doubt that he was a master of the art of war (he never lost a battle), and that he was intelligent and endowed with charm and physical courage. Unquestionably, also, he was a man of vibrant energy and overpowering ambitions. Just what these ambitions were is not certain. Evidence eludes us that he aspired to conquer the world or to advance the Hellenic ideals of freedom and justice. It seems doubtful that he had much interest in lofty ideals or in using military force to extend them. His main goal was to enhance his own power and glory. The primary significance of his military accomplishment lay in the fact that he carried the Hellenic drive into Asia farther and faster than would otherwise have occurred. At the same time he appears to have placed too great a strain upon Hellenism with the result of encouraging a sweeping tide of Eastern influences into the West. Within a short period Hellenic and Eastern cultures interpenetrated to such an extent as to produce a new civilization. This was the Hellenistic civilization, to be discussed in the chapter that follows.

6. GREEK THOUGHT AND CULTURE

From what has been said in preceding chapters it should be clear that the popular notion that all philosophy originated with the Greeks is fallacious. Centuries earlier the Egyptians had given much thought to the nature of the universe and to the social and ethical problems of humanity. The achievement of the Greeks was rather the development of philosophy in a more inclusive manner than it had ever possessed before. They attempted to find answers to every conceivable question about the nature of the universe, the problem of truth, and the meaning and purpose of life. The magnitude of their accomplishment is attested by the fact that philosophy ever since has been largely a debate over the validity of their conclusions.

Greek philosophy had its origins in the sixth century B.C. in the work of the so-called Milesian school, whose members were natives of the commercial city of Miletus. Their philosophy was fundamentally scientific and materialistic. The problem which chiefly engaged them was to discover the nature of the physical world. They believed that all things could be reduced to some primary substance which was the source of worlds, stars, animals, plants, and humans, and to which all would ultimately return. Thales, the founder of the school, perceiving that all things contained moisture, taught that the primary substance is water. Anaximander insisted that it could not be any particular thing such as water or fire but something "uncreated and imperishable." He called this substance the Indefinite or the Boundless. A third Milesian, Anaximenes, declared that the original material of the universe is air. Air when rarefied becomes fire; when condensed it turns successively to wind, vapor, water, earth, and stone.

Although seemingly naive in its conclusions, the philosophy of the Milesian school was of real significance. It broke through the mythological beliefs of the Greeks about the origin of the world and substituted purely rational explanations. It expanded the Egyptian ideas of the eternity of the universe and the indestructibility of matter. It suggested very clearly, especially in the teachings of Anaximander, the concept of evolution in the sense of rhythmic change, of continuing creation and decay.

Significance of the teachings of the Milesian school

Before the end of the sixth century Greek philosophy developed a metaphysical turn; it ceased to be occupied solely with problems of the physical world and shifted its attention to abstruse questions about the nature of being, the meaning of truth, and the position of the divine in the scheme of things. First to exemplify the new tendency were the Pythagoreans, who interpreted philosophy largely in terms of religion. Little is known about them except that their leader, Pythagoras, migrated from Greece to southern Italy, where he founded a religious community at Croton in 530 B.C. He and his followers taught that the speculative life is the highest good, but that in order to pursue it, the individual must be purified of the evil desires of the flesh. They held that the essence of things is not a material substance but an abstract principle, number. Their chief significance lies in the sharp distinctions they drew between spirit and matter, harmony and discord, good and evil, which made them the founders of dualism in Greek thought.

The Pythagoreans

A consequence of the work of the Pythagoreans was to intensify the debate over the nature of the universe. One of their contemporaries, Parmenides, argued that stability or permanence is the real nature of things; change and diversity are simply illusions of the senses. Directly opposed to this was the position taken by Heraclitus, who argued that permanence is an illusion, that change alone is real. The universe, he maintained, is in a condition of constant flux; therefore "it is impossible to step twice into the same stream." Creation and destruction, life and death, are but the obverse and reverse sides of the same picture. In other words, Heraclitus believed that the things we see, hear, and feel are all there is to reality. Evolution or constant change is the law of the universe. The tree or the stone that is here today is gone tomorrow; no underlying substance exists immutable through all eternity.

Renewal of the debate over the nature of the universe

A final alternative to the question of the underlying character of the universe was provided by the atomists. The philosopher chiefly responsible for the development of the atomic theory was Democritus, who lived in Abdera on the Thracian coast in the second half of the fifth century. As their name implies, the atomists held that the ultimate constituents of the universe are atoms, infinite in number, indestructible, and indivisible. Although these differ in size and shape, they are exactly alike in composition. Because of the motion inherent in them, they are eternally uniting, separating, and reuniting in different arrangements. Every individual object or organism in the universe is thus the product of a fortuitous concourse of atoms. The only dif-

The atomists

ference between a human and a tree is the difference in the number and arrangement of their atoms. This philosophy represented the final fruition of the materialistic tendencies of early Greek thought. Democritus denied the immortality of the soul and the existence of any spiritual world. Strange as it may appear to some people, he was a moral idealist, affirming that "good means not merely not to do wrong, but rather not to desire to do wrong."

The intellectual revolution begun by the Sophists

About the middle of the fifth century B.C. an intellectual revolution began in Greece. It accompanied the high point of democracy in Athens. The rise in the power of the citizen, the growth of individualism, and the demand for the solution of practical problems produced a reaction against the old ways of thinking. As a result philosophers abandoned the study of the physical universe and turned to consideration of subjects more intimately related to the individual. The first exponents of the new intellectual trend were the Sophists. Originally the term meant "those who are wise," but later it came to be used in the derogatory sense of men who employ specious reasoning. Since most of our knowledge of the Sophists comes from Plato, one of their severest critics, they were commonly viewed as the enemies of all that was best in Hellenic culture. Modern research has rejected so extreme a conclusion, while conceding that some members of the group did lack a sense of social responsibility and were quite unscrupulous in "making the worse appear the better case."

The doctrines of Protagoras

One of the leading Sophists was Protagoras, a native of Abdera who did most of his teaching in Athens. His famous dictum, "Man is the measure of all things," contains the essence of the Sophist philosophy. By this he meant that goodness, truth, justice, and beauty are relative to the needs and interests of man. There are no absolute truths or eternal standards of right and justice. Since sense perception is the exclusive source of knowledge, there can be only particular truths valid for a given time and place. Morality likewise varies from one people to another, for there are no absolute canons of right and wrong eternally decreed in the heavens to fit all cases.

The extremist doctrines of the later Sophists

Some of the later Sophists went far beyond the teachings of Protagoras. The individualism implicit in the teachings of Protagoras was twisted by Thrasymachus into the doctrine that all laws and customs are merely expressions of the will of the strongest and shrewdest for their own advantage, and that therefore the wise man is the "perfectly unjust man" who is above the law and concerned with the gratification of his own desires. (It should also be mentioned that man, in the sense of the male, was the primary focus of this and all other Greek philosophy dealing with the individual.)

The valuable contributions of the Sophists

Yet there was much that was admirable in the teachings of the Sophists, even of those who were the most extreme. All of them condemned slavery and the racial exclusiveness of the Greeks. They were champions of liberty, the rights of the common man, and the practical and progressive point of view. They perceived the folly of war and ridiculed the chauvinism of many Athenian citizens. Perhaps most important, they broadened philosophy to include not only physics and metaphysics, but ethics and politics. As the Roman Cicero expressed it, they "brought philosophy down from heaven to the dwellings of men."

Inevitably the relativism, skepticism, and individualism of the Sophists aroused strenuous opposition. In the judgment of the more conservative Greeks these doctrines appeared to lead straight to atheism and anarchy. If there is no final truth, and if goodness and justice are merely relative to the whims of the individual, then neither religion, morality, the state, nor society itself can long be maintained. The result of this conviction was the growth of a new philosophic movement grounded upon the theory that truth is real and that absolute standards do exist. The leaders of this movement were perhaps the three most famous individuals in the history of thought—Socrates, Plato, and Aristotle.

Socrates was born in Athens in 469 B.C. of humble parentage; his father was a sculptor, his mother a midwife. How he obtained an education no one knows, but he was certainly familiar with the teachings of earlier Greek thinkers. The impression that he was a mere gabbler in the marketplace is quite unfounded. He became a philosopher on his own account chiefly to combat the doctrines of the Sophists. In 399 B.C. he was condemned to death on a charge of "corrupting the youth and introducing new gods." The real reason for the unjust sentence was the tragic outcome for Athens of the Peloponnesian War. Overwhelmed by resentment, the Athenian citizens turned against Socrates because of his associations with aristocrats, including the traitor Alcibiades, and because of his criticism of popular belief. There is also evidence that he disparaged democracy and contended that no government was worthy of the name except intellectual aristocracy.

Socrates. According to Plato, Socrates looked like a goatman but spoke like a god.

Because Socrates wrote nothing himself, historians find it difficult to determine the exact scope of his teachings. He is generally regarded as primarily a teacher of ethics with no interest in abstract philosophy. Certain passages in Plato, however, raise the possibility that Plato's abstract doctrine of Ideas was ultimately of Socratic origin. At any rate we can be reasonably sure that Socrates believed in a stable and universally valid knowledge, which humans could possess if they pursued the right method. This would consist in the exchange and analysis of opinions, in the setting up and testing of provisional definitions, until finally an essence of truth recognizable by all could be distilled from them. Socrates argued that in similar fashion man could discover enduring principles of right and justice independent of the selfish desires of human beings. He believed, moreover, that the discovery of such rational principles of conduct would prove an infallible guide to virtuous living, for he denied that anyone who knows the good can choose the evil.

The philosophy of Socrates

By far the most distinguished of Socrates's pupils was Plato, who

Plato's philosophy of Ideas

Plato

Plato's ethical and religious philosophy

Plato as a political philosopher

was born in Athens around 429 B.C., the son of noble parents. At the age of twenty Plato joined the Socratic circle, remaining a member until the tragic death of his teacher. Unlike his great mentor, he was a prolific writer. The most noted of his works are such dialogues as the *Apology*, the *Phaedo*, the *Phaedrus*, the *Symposium*, and the *Republic*. He was engaged in the completion of the *Laws* when death overtook him in his eighty-first year.

Plato's objectives were similar to those of Socrates although somewhat broader: (1) to combat the theory of reality as a disordered flux and to substitute an interpretation of the universe as essentially spiritual and purposeful; (2) to refute the Sophist doctrines of relativism and skepticism; and (3) to provide a secure foundation for ethics. In order to realize these aims he developed his doctrine of Ideas. He admitted that relativity and change are characteristics of the world of physical things, of the world we perceive with our senses. But he denied that this world is the complete universe. A higher, spiritual realm exists, composed of eternal forms or Ideas which only the mind can conceive. These are not, however, mere abstractions invented by the mind, but spiritual things. Each is the pattern of some particular class of objects or relation between objects on earth. Thus there are Ideas of man, tree, shape, color, proportion, beauty, and justice. Highest of them all is the Idea of the Good, the active cause and guiding purpose of the universe. The things we perceive through our senses are merely imperfect copies of the supreme realities, Ideas.

Plato's ethical and religious philosophy was closely related to his doctrine of Ideas. Like Socrates he believed that true virtue has its basis in knowledge. But the knowledge derived from the senses is limited and variable; hence true virtue must consist in rational apprehension of the eternal Ideas of goodness and justice. By relegating the physical to an inferior place, he gave to his ethics an ascetic tinge. He regarded the body as a hindrance to the mind and taught that only the rational part of man's nature is noble and good. Yet in contrast with some of his later followers, he did not demand that appetites and emotions should be denied altogether, but urged that they should be strictly subordinated to reason. Plato never made his conception of God entirely clear, but it is certain that he conceived of the universe as spiritual in nature and governed by intelligent purpose. He rejected both materialism and mechanism. As for the soul, he regarded it not only as immortal but as preexisting through all eternity.

As a political philosopher Plato was motivated by the ideal of constructing a state which would be free from turbulence and self-seeking on the part of individuals and classes. Neither democracy nor liberty but harmony and efficiency were the ends he desired to achieve. Accordingly, he proposed in his *Republic* a famous plan for society which would have divided the population into three principal classes corresponding to the functions of the soul. The lowest class, representing the appetitive function, would include the farmers, artisans, and merchants. The second class, representing the spirited element or will, would consist of the soldiers. The highest class, representing the function of reason, would be composed of the intellectual aristocracy. Each of these classes would perform those tasks for which it was best fitted. The function of the lowest class would be the production and distribution of goods for the benefit of the whole community; that of the soldiers, defense; the aristocracy, by reason of special aptitude for philosophy, would enjoy a monopoly of political power. The division of the people into these several ranks would not be made on the basis of birth or wealth, but through a sifting process that would take into account the ability of each individual to profit from education. Thus the farmers, artisans, and merchants would be those who had shown the least intellectual capacity, whereas the philosopher-kings would be those who had shown the greatest.

The last of the great champions of the Socratic tradition was Aristotle, a native of Stagira, born in 384 B.C. At the age of seventeen he entered Plato's Academy,[3] continuing as student and teacher there for twenty years. In 343 he was invited by Philip of Macedon to serve as tutor to the young Alexander. History affords few more conspicuous examples of wasted effort, except for the fact that the young prince acquired an enthusiasm for science and for some other elements of Hellenic culture. Seven years later Aristotle returned to Athens, where he conducted a school of his own, known as the Lyceum, until his death in 322 B.C. Aristotle wrote even more voluminously than Plato and on a greater variety of subjects. His principal works include treatises on logic, metaphysics, rhetoric, ethics, natural sciences, and politics.

Aristotle

Though Aristotle was as much interested as Plato and Socrates in absolute knowledge and eternal standards, his philosophy differed from theirs in several outstanding respects. To begin with, he had a higher regard for the concrete and the practical. In contrast with Plato, the aesthete, and Socrates, who declared he could learn nothing from trees and stones, Aristotle was an empirical scientist with a compelling interest in biology, physics, and astronomy. Moreover, he was less inclined than his predecessors to a spiritual outlook. And last, he did not share their strong aristocratic sympathies.

Aristotle compared with Plato and Socrates

Aristotle agreed with Plato that universals, Ideas (or forms as he called them), are real, and that knowledge derived from the senses is limited and inaccurate. But he refused to go along with his teacher in ascribing an independent existence to universals and in reducing material things to pale reflections of their spiritual patterns. On the contrary, he asserted that form and matter are of equal importance; both are eternal, and neither can exist without the other. The union of these two gives the universe its character. Forms are the causes of all things;

Aristotle's conception of the universe

[3] So called from the grove of Academus, where Plato and his disciples met to discuss philosophic problems.

they are the purposive forces that shape the world of matter into the infinitely varied objects and organisms around us. All evolution, both cosmic and organic, results from the interaction of form and matter. Thus the presence of the form *man* in the human embryo molds and directs the development of the latter until it ultimately evolves as a human being. Aristotle's philosophy may be regarded as halfway between the spiritualism and transcendentalism of Plato on the one hand, and the mechanistic materialism of the atomists on the other. His conception of the universe was *teleological*—that is, governed by purpose; but he refused to regard the spiritual as overshadowing its material embodiment.

Aristotle's religious doctrines

Aristotle's scientific attitude led him to conceive of God primarily as a First Cause. Aristotle's God was simply the Prime Mover, the original source of the purposive motion contained in the forms. In no sense was he a personal God, for his nature was pure intelligence, devoid of all feelings, will, or desire. Aristotle seems to have left no place for individual immortality: all the functions of the soul, except the creative reason which is not individual at all, depend upon the body and perish with it.

Aristotle's ethical philosophy of the golden mean

Aristotle's ethical philosophy was less ascetic than Plato's. He did not regard the body as the prison of the soul, nor did he believe that physical appetites are necessarily evil in themselves. He taught that the highest good consists in self-realization, that is, in the exercise of that part of man's nature which most truly distinguishes him as a human being. Self-realization would therefore be identical with the life of reason. But the life of reason is dependent upon the proper combination of physical and mental conditions. The body must be kept in good health and the emotions under adequate control. The solution is to be found in the *golden mean,* in preserving a balance between excessive indulgence on the one hand and ascetic denial on the other. This was simply a reaffirmation of the characteristic Greek ideal of *sophrosyne,* "nothing too much."

The golden mean applied to politics

Although Aristotle included in his *Politics* much descriptive and analytical material on the structure and functions of government, he dealt primarily with the broader aspects of political theory. He considered the state as the supreme institution for the promotion of the good life, and he was therefore vitally interested in its origin and development and in the best forms it could be made to assume. Declaring that man is by nature a political animal, he denied that the state is an artificial product of the ambitions of the few or of the desires of the many. On the contrary, he asserted that it is rooted in the instincts of man himself, and that civilized life outside of its limits is impossible. He considered the best state to be neither a monarchy, an aristocracy, nor a democracy, but a *polity*—which he defined as a commonwealth intermediate between oligarchy and democracy. Essentially it would be a state under the control of the middle class, but Aristotle intended to make sure that the members of that class would be fairly numerous, for he advocated measures to prevent the concentration of wealth. He defended the institution of private property, but he opposed the heaping up of riches beyond what is necessary for intelligent living. He recommended that the government provide the poor with money to buy small farms or to "make a beginning in trade and husbandry" and thus promote their prosperity and self-respect.

Contrary to popular belief, the period of Greek civilization before the time of Alexander the Great was not a great age of science. The vast majority of the scientific achievements commonly thought of as Greek were made during the Hellenistic period, when the culture was no longer predominantly Greek but a mixture of Greek and Near Eastern. The interests of the Greeks in the Periclean Age and in the century that followed were chiefly speculative and artistic; they were not deeply concerned with material comforts or with mastery of the physical universe. Consequently, with the exception of some important developments in mathematics, biology, and medicine, scientific progress was relatively slight.

Greek thought not primarily scientific

The most significant Greek mathematical work was accomplished by the Pythagoreans. These followers of Pythagoras developed an elaborate theory of numbers, classifying them into various categories, such as odd, even, prime, composite, and perfect. They are also supposed to have discovered the theory of proportion and to have proved for the first time that the sum of the three angles of any triangle is equal to two right angles. But the most famous of their achievements was the discovery of the theorem attributed to Pythagoras himself: the square of the hypotenuse of any right-angled triangle is equal to the sum of the squares of the other two sides.

Pythagorean mathematics

The first of the Greeks to manifest an interest in biology was the philosopher Anaximander, who developed a crude theory of organic evolution based upon the principle of survival through progressive adaptations to the environment. The earliest ancestral animals, he asserted, lived in the sea, which originally covered the whole face of the earth. As the waters receded, some organisms were able to adjust themselves to their new environment and became land animals. The final product of this evolutionary process was man himself. The real founder of the science of biology, however, was Aristotle. Devoting many years of his life to painstaking study of the structure, habits, and growth of animals, he made many remarkable observations. The metamorphoses of various insects, the reproductive habits of the eel, the embryological development of the dog-fish—these are only samples of the wide extent of his knowledge. Unfortunately, however, Aristotle's biology was also heavily laden with misconceptions: he denied the sexuality of plants, for example, and he believed in the spontaneous generation of certain species of worms and insects.

Biology

Greek medicine also had its origin with the philosophers. A pioneer was Empedocles, exponent of the theory of the four elements (earth, air, fire, and water). He discovered that blood flows to and from the heart, and that the pores of the skin supplement the work of the respiratory passages in breathing. More important was the work of Hippocrates of Cos in the fifth and fourth centuries. By general consensus he is regarded as the father of medicine. He dinned into the ears of his pupils the doctrine that "Every disease has a natural cause, and without natural causes, nothing ever happens." In addition, by his methods of careful study and comparison of symptoms he laid the foundations for clinical medicine. He discovered the phenomenon of crisis in disease and improved the practice of surgery. Though he had a wide knowledge of drugs, his chief reliances in treatment were diet and rest. The main fact to his discredit was his development of the theory of the four humors—the notion that illness is due to excessive amounts of yellow bile, black bile, blood, and phlegm in the system. The practice of bleeding the patient was the regrettable outgrowth of this theory.

Medicine

Generally the most common medium of literary expression in the formative age of a people is the epic of heroic deeds. The most famous of the Greek epics, the *Iliad* and the *Odyssey,* were put into written form at the end of the Dark Ages and commonly attributed to Homer. The first, which deals with the Trojan War, has its theme in the wrath of Achilles; the second describes the wanderings and return of Odysseus. Both have supreme literary merit in their carefully woven plots, in the realism of their character portrayals, and in their mastery of the full range of emotional intensity. They exerted an almost incalculable influence upon later writers. Their style and language inspired the fervid emotional poetry of the sixth century, and they were an unfailing source of plots and themes for the great tragedians of the Golden Age of the fifth century.

The Homeric epics

The three centuries which followed the Dark Ages were distinguished, as we have already seen, by tremendous social changes. The

Interior of a Greek Cup. Depicted is the friendship of leading characters from the *Iliad:* Patroklus and Achilles. Here Achilles is bandaging Patroklus's wounds.

rural pattern of life gave way to an urban society of steadily increasing complexity. The founding of colonies and the growth of commerce provided new interests and habits of living. Inevitably these changes were reflected in new forms of literature, especially of a more personal type. The first to be developed was the elegy, which was probably intended to be declaimed rather than sung to the accompaniment of music. Elegies varied in theme from individual reactions toward love to the idealism of patriots and reformers. Generally, however, they were devoted to melancholy reflection on the disillusionments of life or to bitter lament over the loss of prestige. Outstanding among the authors of elegiac verse was Solon the legislator.

Development of the elegy

In the sixth century and the early part of the fifth, the elegy was gradually displaced by the lyric, which derives its name from the fact that it was sung to the music of the lyre. The new type of poetry was particularly well adapted to the expression of passionate feelings, the violent loves and hates engendered by the strife of classes. It was employed for other purposes also. Both Alcaeus and Sappho, the latter a woman poet from the island of Lesbos, used it to describe the poignant beauty of love, the delicate grace of spring, and the starlit splendor of a summer night. Meanwhile other poets developed the choral lyric, intended to express the feelings of the community rather than the sentiments of any one individual. Greatest of all the writers of this group was Pindar of Thebes, who wrote during the first half of the fifth century. The lyrics of Pindar took the form of odes celebrating the victories of athletes and the glories of Greek civilization.

Lyric poetry

The supreme literary achievement of the Greeks was the tragic drama. Like so many of their other great works, it had its roots in religion. At the festivals dedicated to the worship of Dionysus, the god of spring and of wine, a chorus of men dressed as satyrs, or goat-men, sang and danced around an altar, enacting the various parts of a dithyramb or choral lyric that related the story of the god's career. In time a leader came to be separated from the chorus to recite the main parts of the story. The true drama was born about the beginning of the fifth century when Aeschylus introduced a second "actor" and relegated the chorus to the background. The name "tragedy," which came to be applied to this drama, was probably derived from the Greek word *tragos* meaning "goat."

The origins of tragic drama

Greek tragedy stands out in marked contrast to the tragedies of Shakespeare or modern playwrights. There was, first of all, little action presented on the stage; the main business of the actors was to recite the incidents of a plot which was already familiar to the audience, for the story was drawn from popular legends. Second, Greek tragedy devoted little attention to the study of complicated individual personality. There was no development of character as shaped by the vicissitudes of a long career. Those involved in the plot were scarcely individuals at all, but types. On the stage they wore masks to disguise any characteristics which might serve to distinguish them too sharply

Greek tragedy compared with modern tragedy

Greek Theater in Epidauros. The construction, to take advantage of the slope of the hill, and the arrangement of the stage are of particular interest. Greek dramas were invariably presented in the open air.

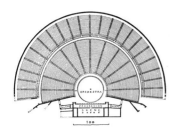

Epidauros Plan

Aeschylus and Sophocles

Euripides

from the rest of humanity. In addition, Greek tragedies differed from the modern variety in having as their theme the conflict between the individual and the universe, not the clash between personalities, or the internal conflicts of one person. The tragic fate that befell the main characters in these plays was external to individuals. It was brought on by the fact that someone had committed a crime against society, or against the gods, thereby violating the scheme of the universe. Punishment must follow in order to balance the scale of justice. Finally, the purpose of Greek tragedies was not merely to depict suffering and to interpret human actions, but to purify the emotions of the audience by representing the triumph of justice.

As already indicated, the first of the tragic dramatists was Aeschylus (525–456 B.C.). Though he is known to have written about eighty plays, only seven have survived in complete form, among them *Prometheus Bound* and a trilogy known as *The Oresteia*. Guilt and punishment is the recurrent theme of nearly all of them. The second of the leading tragedians, Sophocles (496–406), is often considered the greatest. His style was more polished and his philosophy more profound than that of his predecessor. He was the author of over a hundred plays. More than any other Greek writer he expressed the ideal of "nothing too much." His attitude was distinguished by love of harmony and peace, intelligent respect for democracy, and profound sympathy for human weakness. The most famous of his plays are *Oedipus Rex* and *Antigone*.

The work of the last of the great tragedians, Euripides (480–406), reflects a different spirit. He was a skeptic and individualist who took delight in ridiculing the ancient myths and the "sacred cows" of his time. An embittered pessimist who suffered from the barbs of his conservative critics, he loved to humble the proud in his plays and exalt the lowly. He was the first to give the ordinary man, even the beggar and the peasant, a place in the drama. Euripides is also noted for his sympathy for the slave, for his condemnation of war, and for his protests against the exclusion of women from social and intellectual life. Because of his humanism, his tendency to portray men as they actually were (or even a little worse), and his introduction of the love motif into drama, he is often considered a modernist. It must be remembered, however, that in other respects his plays were perfectly consistent with the Greek model. They did not exhibit the evolution of individual character or the conflict of egos to any greater extent than did the works of Sophocles or Aeschylus. Nevertheless, he has been called the most tragic of the Greek dramatists because he dealt with situations having analogues in real life. Among the best-known tragedies of Euripides are *Alcestis, Medea,* and *The Trojan Women.*

Greek comedy, in common with tragedy, appears to have grown out of the Dionysiac festivals, but it did not attain full development until late in the fifth century B.C. Its outstanding representative was Aristophanes (448?–380?), a somewhat coarse and belligerent aristocrat who lived in Athens. Most of his plays satirized the political and intellectual ideals of the radical democracy of his time. In *The Knights* he pilloried the incompetent and greedy politicians for their reckless adventures in imperialism. In *The Frogs* he lampooned Euripides's innovations in the drama. *The Clouds* he reserved for ridicule of the Sophists, ignorantly or maliciously classifying Socrates as one of them. While he was undoubtedly an imaginative and humorous writer, his ideas were founded largely upon prejudice. He deserves much credit, however, for his sharp criticisms of the policies of the warhawks of Athens during the struggle with Sparta. Though written as a farce, his *Lysistrata* cleverly pointed a way—however infeasible—to the termination of any war: in this play wives refuse to have sexual relations with their husbands until the latter agree to make peace with their foreign enemies.

No account of Greek literature would be complete without some mention of the two great historians of the Golden Age. Herodotus, the "father of history" (c. 484–c. 420), was a native of Halicarnassus in Asia Minor. He traveled extensively through the Persian empire, Egypt, Greece, and Italy, collecting a multitude of interesting data about various peoples. His famous account of the great war between the Greeks and the Persians included so much background that the work seems almost a history of the world. He regarded that war as an epic struggle between East and West, with Zeus giving victory to the Greeks against a mighty host of barbarians.

If Herodotus deserves to be called the father of history, much more does his younger contemporary, Thucydides (c. 460–c. 400), deserve to be considered the founder of scientific history. Influenced by the skepticism and practicality of the Sophists, Thucydides chose to work

Greek comedy

The Greek historians: Herodotus

Thucydides

on the basis of carefully sifted evidence, rejecting legends and hearsay. The subject of his *History* was the war between Sparta and Athens, which he described scientifically and dispassionately, emphasizing the complexity of causes which led to the clash. His aim was to present an accurate record which could be studied with profit by statesmen and generals of all time, and it must be said that he was extremely successful. If there were any defects in his historical method, they consisted in overemphasizing political factors to the neglect of the social and economic and in failing to consider the importance of emotions in history.

7. THE MEANING OF GREEK ART

Greek art as an expression of the Greek spirit

Art as well as literature reflected the basic character of Hellenic civilization. The Greeks were essentially materialists who conceived of the world in physical terms. Plato and the followers of the mystic religions were exceptions, but few other Greeks believed in a universe of spiritual realities. It would be natural therefore to find that the material emblems of architecture and sculpture exemplified best the ideals the Greeks maintained.

The ideals embodied in Greek art

What did Greek art express? Above all, it symbolized humanism—the glorification of man as the most important creature in the universe. Though much of the sculpture depicted gods, and also goddesses, this did not detract in the slightest from its humanistic quality. The Greek deities existed for the benefit of man; in glorifying them he thus glorified himself. Both architecture and sculpture embodied the ideals of balance, harmony, order, and moderation. Anarchy and excess were abhorrent to the mind of the Greek, but so was absolute repression. Consequently, Greek art exhibited qualities of simplicity and dignified restraint—free from decorative extravagance on the one hand, and from restrictive conventions on the other. Moreover, Greek art was an expression of the national life. Its purpose was not merely aesthetic but political: to symbolize the pride of the people in their city and to enhance their consciousness of unity. The Parthenon at Athens, for example, was the temple of Athena, the protecting goddess who presided over the corporate life of the state. In providing her with a beautiful shrine which she might frequently visit, the Athenians were giving evidence of their love for their city and their hope for its continuing welfare.

See color plates following page 160

Greek art compared with that of later peoples

The art of the Greeks differed from that of nearly every people since their time in a variety of ways. Like the tragedies of Aeschylus and Sophocles, it was universal. It included few portraits either in sculpture or in painting. (Most of the portrait busts commonly considered Greek really belong to the Hellenistic Age.) The human beings depicted were generally types, not individuals. Again, Greek art differed from

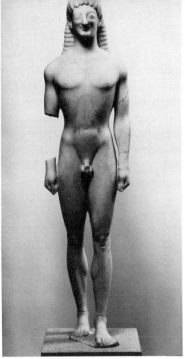  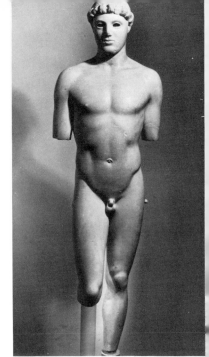

Apollo of Tenea; Apollo of Piombino; "The Critian Boy." These three statues, dating from about 560, 500, and 480 B.C. respectively, display the progressive "unfreezing" of Greek statuary art. The first stiff and symmetrical statue is imitative of Egyptian sculpture (see statue of the Pharoah Mycerinus, p. 39 above). Roughly half a century later it is succeeded by a figure which begins to display motion, as if awakening from a sleep of centuries in a fairy tale. The last figure introduces genuine naturalism in its delicate twists and depiction of the subject's weight resting on one leg.

that of most later peoples in its ethical purpose. It was not art for the sake of mere decoration or for the expression of the artist's own ideas, but a medium for the ennoblement of humanity. This does not mean that its merit depended upon the moral lesson it taught, but rather that it was supposed to exemplify qualities of living essentially artistic in themselves. The Athenian, at least, drew no sharp distinction between the ethical and aesthetic spheres; the beautiful and the good were really identical. True morality, therefore, consisted in rational living, in the avoidance of grossness, sensual excesses, and other forms of conduct aesthetically offensive. Finally, although the utmost attention was given to the depiction of beautiful bodies, this had little to do with fidelity to nature. The Greek was not interested in interpreting nature for its own sake, but in expressing *human* ideals.

The history of Greek art can be divided into three periods. The first covered the seventh and sixth centuries. During the greater part of this so-called archaic period sculpture was dominated by Egyptian influence, as can be seen in the frontality and rigidity of the statues, with their square shoulders and one foot slightly advanced. Toward

The three periods of Greek art

the end, however, these conventions were thrown aside. The chief architectural styles also had their origin in this period, and several crude temples were built. The second period, which occupied the fifth century, witnessed the full perfection of both architecture and sculpture. The art of this time was completely idealistic. During the fourth century, the last period of Greek art, architecture lost some of its balance and simplicity and sculpture assumed new characteristics. It came to reflect more clearly the reactions of the individual artist, to incorporate more realism, and to lose some of its quality as an expression of civic pride.

Greek architecture

For all its artistic excellence, Greek temple architecture was extremely simple. Greek temples consisted of only five elements: (1) the cella or nucleus of the building, which was a rectangular chamber to house the statue of the god; (2) the columns, which formed the porch and surrounded the cella; (3) the entablature, which rested upon the columns and supported the roof; (4) the gabled roof itself; and (5) the pediment or triangular section under the gable of the roof. Two different architectural styles were developed, representing modifications of certain of these elements. The more common was the Doric, which made use of a rather heavy, sharply fluted column surmounted by a plain capital. The other, the Ionic, had more slender and more graceful columns with flat flutings, a triple base, and a scroll or volute capital. The so-called Corinthian style, which was chiefly Hellenistic, differed from the Ionic primarily in being more ornate. The three styles differed also in their treatment of the entablature. In the Ionic style it was left almost plain. In the Doric and Corinthian styles it bore sculptured reliefs. The Parthenon, the best example of Greek architecture, was essentially a Doric building, but it reflected some of the grace and subtlety of Ionic influence.

Greek sculpture

According to the prevailing opinion among his contemporaries, Greek sculpture attained its height in the work of Phidias (c. 500–c. 432). His masterpieces were the statue of Athena in the Parthenon and the statue of Zeus in the Temple of Olympian Zeus. In addition, he

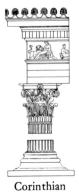

Corinthian

Ionic

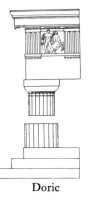

Doric

Details of the Three Orders of Greek Architecture

The Parthenon. The largest and most famous of Athenian temples, the Parthenon is considered the classic example of Doric architecture. Its columns were made more graceful by tapering them in a slight curve toward the top. Its friezes and pediments were decorated with lifelike sculptures of prancing horses (see above), fighting giants, and benign and confident deities.

designed the Parthenon reliefs. The main qualities of his work are grandeur of conception, patriotism, proportion, dignity, and restraint. Nearly all of his figures are idealized representations of deities and mythological creatures in human form. The second most renowned fifth-century sculptor was Myron, noted for his statue of the discus thrower and for his glorification of other athletic types. The names of three great sculptors in the fourth century have come down to us. The most gifted was Praxiteles, renowned for his portrayal of humanized deities with slender, graceful bodies and countenances of philosophic repose. His older contemporary, Scopas, gained distinction as an emotional sculptor. One of his most successful creations was the statue of a religious ecstatic, a worshiper of Dionysus, in a condition of mystic frenzy. At the end of the century Lysippus pioneered in sculptural realism and individualism. He was the first great master of the realistic portrait as a study of personal character.

Parthenon Frieze

8. ATHENIAN LIFE IN THE GOLDEN AGE

The population of Athens in the fifth and fourth centuries comprised three groups: the citizens, the metics, and the slaves. The citizens, who numbered at the most about 160,000, included only those males born of citizen parents, except for the few who were oc-

Athenian classes

Left: *The Discobolus or Discus Thrower of Myron.* The statue reflects the glorification of the human body characteristic of Athens in the Golden Age. Now in the Vatican Museum. Right: *Hermes with the Infant Dionysus, by Praxiteles, Fourth Century B.C.* Original in the Olympia Museum, Greece.

casionally enfranchised by special law. The metics, who probably did not exceed a total of 35,000, were resident aliens, chiefly non-Athenian Greeks. Save for the fact that they had no political privileges and generally were not permitted to own land, male metics had equal opportunities with citizens. They could engage in any occupation they desired and participate in any social or intellectual activities. Contrary to a popular tradition, the slaves in Athens were never a majority of the population. Their maximum number did not exceed 110,000. Urban slaves, at least, were very well treated and were sometimes rewarded for faithful service by being set free. The males could work for wages and own property, and some of them held responsible positions as minor public officials. The treatment of slaves who worked in the mines, however, was often cruel.

Life in Athens stands out in sharp contrast to that in most other civilizations. One of its leading features was the great amount of social and economic equality that prevailed among all the inhabitants. Although there were many who were poor, there were few who were very rich. Nearly everyone, whether citizen, metic, or slave, ate the same kind of food, wore the same kind of clothing, and participated in the same kind of amusement. This substantial equality was enforced

The amazing degree of social and economic equality.

in part by the system of *liturgies,* which were services to the state rendered by wealthy men, chiefly in the form of contributions to support the drama, equip the navy, or provide for the poor.

A second outstanding characteristic of Athenian life was its lack of comforts and luxuries. Part of this was a result of the low income of the mass of the people. Teachers, sculptors, masons, carpenters, and common laborers all received the same low standard wage. Part of it may have been a consequence also of the mild climate, which allowed for a life of simplicity. But whatever the cause, the fact remains that, in comparison with modern standards, the Athenians made do with the barest essentials. They knew nothing of such commodities as clocks, soap, newspapers, cotton cloth, sugar, tea, or coffee. Their beds had no springs, their houses had no drains, and their food consisted chiefly of barley cakes, onions, and fish, washed down with diluted wine. From the standpoint of clothing they were no better off. A rectangular piece of cloth wrapped around the body and fastened with pins at the shoulders and with a rope around the waist served as the main garment. A larger piece was draped around the body as an extra garment for outdoor wear. No one wore either stockings or socks, and few had any footgear except sandals.

The poverty of Athenian life

But lack of luxury was a matter of little consequence to the Athenian citizen. Instead his aim was to live as interestingly and contentedly as possible without spending all his days working for the sake of a little more comfort for his family or of piling up riches as a source of power or prestige. What each citizen really wanted was a small farm or business that would provide him with a reasonable income and at the same time allow him an abundance of leisure for politics, for gossip in the marketplace, and for intellectual or artistic activities if he had the talent to enjoy them.

Indifference toward material comforts and wealth

In spite of the expansion of trade, Athenian economic organization never became very complex. Agriculture and commerce were by far

Young Men Baiting a Dog and Cat. This Athenian relief from about 510 B.C. depicts an odd form of leisure-time amusement.

the most important enterprises. Even in Pericles's day the majority of the citizens still lived in the country. Industry was not highly developed. Few examples of large-scale production are on record, and those chiefly in the manufacture of pottery and implements of war. The largest establishment that ever existed was apparently a shield factory owned by a metic and employing 120 slaves. No other was more than half as large. The enterprises which absorbed the most labor were the mines, but they were owned by the state and leased in sections to small contractors to be worked by slaves. The bulk of industry was carried on in shops owned by individual craftsmen who produced their wares directly to the order of the consumer.

Religion underwent some notable changes in the Golden Age of the fifth and fourth centuries. The polytheism and anthropomorphism of the Homeric myths were largely supplanted by a belief in one God as the creator and sustainer of the moral law. Other significant consequences flowed from the mystery cults. These new forms of religion first became popular in the sixth century because of the craving for an emotional faith to make up for the disappointments of life. One was the Orphic cult, which revolved around the myth of the death and resurrection of Dionysus. Another, the Eleusinian cult, had as its central theme the abduction of Persephone by Hades, god of the nether world, and her ultimate redemption by Demeter, the great Earth Mother. Both of these cults had as their original purpose worship of the life-giving powers of nature, but in time they came to express a much deeper significance. They communicated to their followers the ideas of vicarious atonement, salvation in an afterlife, and ecstatic union with the divine. Although entirely inconsistent with the spirit of the ancient religion, they made a powerful appeal to certain classes and were largely responsible for the spread of the belief in personal immortality. The more thoughtful Greeks, however, seem to have persisted in their adherence to the worldly, optimistic, and mechanical faith of their ancestors and to have shown little concern about sin or a desire for salvation in a life to come.

Head of Persephone. Obverse of a coin struck by the Greek city of Syracuse on the island of Sicily around 310 B.C.

It remains to consider briefly the position of the family in Athens in the fifth and fourth centuries. Though marriage was still an important institution for the procreation of children who would become citizens of the state, there is reason to believe that family life had declined. Men of the more prosperous classes, at least, now spent the greater part of their time away from their families. Wives were relegated to an inferior position and required to remain secluded in their homes. Their place as social and intellectual companions for their husbands was taken by alien women, the *hetaerae,* many of whom were highly cultured natives of the Ionian cities of Asia Minor. Marriage itself assumed the character of a political and economic arrangement devoid of romantic elements. Men married wives so as to ensure that at least some of their children would be legitimate and in order to obtain property in the form of a dowry. It was important also, of course, to have someone to care for the household. But husbands did not consider their wives as their equals and did not appear in public with them or encourage their participation in any form of social or intellectual activity.

9. THE GREEK ACHIEVEMENT AND ITS SIGNIFICANCE FOR US

No historian would deny that the achievement of the Greeks was one of the most remarkable in the history of the world. With no great expanse of fertile soil or abundance of mineral resources, they succeeded in developing a higher and more varied civilization than any of the most richly favored nations of the Near East. With only a limited cultural inheritance from the past to build upon, they produced intellectual and artistic achievements which have served ever since as models of perfection for the culture of the West. It may be argued as well that the Greeks achieved a more leisured and rational mode of living than most other peoples who strutted and fretted their hour upon this planet. The infrequency of brutal crimes and the contentment with simple amusements and modest wealth all point to a comparatively happy and satisfied existence.

The magnitude of the Greek achievement

It is necessary to be on guard, however, against uncritical adulation of the ancient Greeks. We must not assume that all of the natives of Hellas were as cultured, wise, and free as the citizens of Athens and of the Ionian states across the Aegean. The Spartans, the Arcadians, the Thessalians, and the majority of the Boeotians remained much less culturally advanced. Further, Athenian civilization itself was not without its defects. It permitted some exploitation of the weak, especially of the slaves who toiled in the mines. It was based upon a principle of racial exclusiveness which reckoned every man a foreigner whose parents were not both Athenians, and consequently denied political rights to the majority of the inhabitants. It was also characterized by the overt repression of the female members of the society. Its statecraft was not sufficiently enlightened to avoid the pitfalls of imperialism and aggressive war. Finally, the attitude of its citizens was not always tolerant and just. Socrates was put to death for his opinions, and two other philosophers, Anaxagoras and Protagoras, were forced to leave the city. It must be conceded, however, that the record of the Athenians for tolerance was better than that of most other nations, both ancient and modern. There was probably more freedom of expression in Athens during the war with Sparta than there was in the United States during World War I.

Undesirable features of Greek life

Nor is it true that the Greek influence has been as great as is often supposed. No well-informed student could accept the sentimental verdict of Shelley: "We are all Greeks; our laws, our literature, our religion, our arts have their roots in Greece." Our laws do not really

*Greek influence
sometimes exaggerated*

have their roots in Greece but chiefly in Hellenistic and Roman sources. Much of our poetry is undoubtedly Greek in inspiration, but such is not the case with most of our prose literature. Our religion is no more than partly Greek; except as it was influenced by Plato and the Romans, it reflects primarily the spirit of the Near East. Even our arts derive from other sources almost as much as from Greece. Actually, modern civilization has been the result of the convergence of numerous influences coming from many different periods and places.

*The influence of the
Greeks on the West*

In spite of all this, the Hellenic adventure was of profound significance for the history of the world. For the Greeks were the founders of nearly all those ideals commonly thought of as peculiar to the West. The civilizations of the ancient Near East, with the exception, to a certain extent, of the Hebrew and Egyptian, were dominated by absolutism, supernaturalism, ecclesiasticism, the denial of both body and mind, and the subjection of the individual to the group. It is noteworthy that the Greek word for freedom—*eleutheria*—cannot be translated into any ancient Near Eastern language, not even Hebrew. The typical political regime of the Near East was that of an absolute monarch supported by a powerful priesthood. Culture in the Near Eastern empires served mainly as an instrument to magnify the power of the state and to enhance the prestige of rulers and priests.

*Contrast of Greek and
Near Eastern ideals*

In contrast, the civilization of Greece, notably in its Athenian form, was founded upon ideals of freedom, optimism, secularism, rationalism, the glorification of both body and mind, and a high regard for the dignity and worth of the individual. Insofar as anyone other than a slave was repressed, his subjection was to the rule of the majority. This, of course, was not always good, especially in times of crisis, when the majority might be swayed by prejudice. Religion was worldly and practical, serving the interests of human beings. Worship of the gods was a means for the ennoblement of man. As opposed to the ecclesiasticism of the Near East, the Greeks had no organized priesthood at all. They kept their priests in the background and refused to allow them to define dogma or to govern the realm of intellect. In addition, they excluded them from control over the sphere of moral-

The Acropolis Today. Occupying the commanding position is the Parthenon. To the left is the Erechtheum with its Porch of the Maidens facing the Parthenon.

ity. The culture of the Greeks was the first to be based upon the primacy of intellect—upon the supremacy of the spirit of free inquiry. There was no subject they feared to investigate, or any question they regarded as beyond the province of reason. To an extent never before realized, mind was supreme over faith, logic and science over superstition.

The supreme tragedy of the Greeks was, of course, their failure to solve the problem of political conflict. To a large degree, this conflict was the product of social and cultural dissimilarities. Because of different geographic and economic conditions the Greek city-states developed at an uneven pace. Some went forward rapidly to high levels of cultural superiority, while others lagged behind and made little or no intellectual progress. The consequences were discord and suspicion, which gave rise eventually to hatred and fear. Though some of the more advanced thinkers attempted to propagate the notion that the Hellenes were one people who should reserve their contempt for non-Hellenes, or "barbarians," the conception never became part of a national ethos. Athenians hated Spartans, and vice versa, almost as vehemently as they hated Persians. Not even the danger of Asian conquest sufficed to dispel the distrust and antagonism of Greeks for one another. Thus the war that finally broke out between Athens and Sparta sealed the doom of Hellenic civilization even though Greece remained undefeated by foreigners.

The tragedy of Hellenic history

SELECTED READINGS

• *Items so designated are available in paperback editions.*

• Andrewes, A., *The Greeks,* New York, 1967. An excellent, up-to-date account of archaic and classical Greek history from about 750 to 350 B.C.

  Austin, M., and P. Vidal-Naquet, *The Economic and Social History of Ancient Greece,* Berkeley, Calif., 1977.

• Boardman, J., *Greek Art,* New York, 1964.

• ———, *The Greeks Overseas,* rev. ed., London, 1982. The standard treatment of Greek colonization.

  Burn, A. R., *The Lyric Age of Greece,* New York, 1961. A lively introduction to the seventh and sixth centuries.

  Davies, J. K., *Democracy and Classical Greece,* Glasgow, 1978.

• Dodds, E. R., *The Greeks and the Irrational,* Berkeley, Calif., 1963. A novel approach to classical Greek culture.

• Dover, K. J., *Greek Homosexuality,* Cambridge, Mass., 1978. A serious analysis of a basic aspect of classical Greek life.

• ———, et al., *Ancient Greek Literature,* Oxford, 1980.

• Ehrenberg, V., *From Solon to Socrates,* New York, 1967. An excellent treatment of early Athenian history by one of the twentieth century's leading authorities.

• Finley, M. I., *The Ancient Greeks: An Introduction to Their Life and Thought,* New York, 1963. An expert brief introduction to the Greeks.

• ———, *The World of Odysseus,* rev. ed., New York, 1978. Attempts to use the Homeric poems as a guide to Dark Ages Greece.

Forrest, W. G., *The Emergence of Greek Democracy,* London, 1966. An engaging account of the origins of democratic ideas and practices.

• ———, *A History of Sparta, 950–152 B.C.,* London, 1968.

• Guthrie, W. K. C., *The Greeks and Their Gods,* Boston, 1965.

Jones, A. H. M., *Athenian Democracy,* New York, 1957. Concentrates on actual political practice.

• Kitto, H. D. F., *The Greeks,* Baltimore, 1957. A delightfully written, highly personal interpretation.

• Lloyd, G. E. R., *Early Greek Science: Thales to Aristotle,* London, 1970.

• Marrou, H. I., *A History of Education in Antiquity,* New York, 1964. A modern classic that covers the entire ancient world.

• Meiggs, R., *The Athenian Empire,* Oxford, 1972. The major study of fifth-century Athenian imperialism; a monumental work.

Michell, H., *The Economics of Ancient Greece,* rev. ed., Cambridge, 1956.

Murray, D., *Early Greece,* Glasgow, 1980. An excellent analytical narrative of early Greek history before the fifth century.

Nilsson, M. P., *A History of Greek Religion,* New York, 1964.

• Pollitt, J. J., *Art and Experience in Classical Greece,* Cambridge, 1972. The best introduction to the social and intellectual forces behind Greek art.

• Pomeroy, Sarah B., *Goddesses, Whores, Wives, and Slaves: Women in Classical Antiquity,* New York, 1975. The best treatment of the role of women in Greece and Rome. Relies on a variety of source material and covers women of all classes.

Rose, H. J., *A Handbook of Greek Literature,* New York, 1960.

• ———, *A Handbook of Greek Mythology,* 6th ed., New York, 1960.

• Sealey, R., *A History of the Greek City States, ca. 700–338 B.C.,* Berkeley, Calif., 1977. A provocative account that reconsiders older assumptions about Greek political life.

Sinclair, T. A., *A History of Greek Political Thought,* London, 1951.

Snell, Bruno, *The Discovery of the Mind: The Greek Origins of European Thought,* Cambridge, Mass., 1953. Stimulating essays.

• Snodgrass, A. M., *Archaic Greece,* London, 1980.

• Starr, C. G., *The Economic and Social Growth of Early Greece: 800–500 B.C.,* New York, 1978. An excellent study of this difficult but important topic.

——— , *The Origins of Greek Civilization, 1100–650 B.C.,* New York, 1961. The best detailed treatment of the early periods.

Zimmern, A. E., *The Greek Commonwealth,* 5th ed., New York, 1931. A classic study, perhaps too uncritical of the Athenians.

SOURCE MATERIALS

Most Greek authors have been translated in the appropriate volumes of the Loeb Classical Library, Harvard University Press.

In addition the following may be helpful:

Barnstone, Willis, tr., *Greek Lyric Poetry,* New York, 1962.

Kagan, Donald, *Sources in Greek Political Thought,* Glencoe, Ill., 1965.

Kirk, G. S., and J. E. Raven, *The Presocratic Philosophers,* Cambridge, 1957.

Lattimore, R., tr., *Greek Lyrics,* Chicago, 1960.

——— , tr., *The Iliad,* Chicago, 1961.

——— , tr., *The Odyssey,* New York, 1968.

Chapter 7

THE HELLENISTIC CIVILIZATION

Beauty and virtue and the like are to be honored, if they give pleasure, but
if they do not give pleasure, we must bid them farewell.

—Epicurus, "On the End of Life"

I agree that Alexander was carried away so far as to copy oriental luxury. I
hold that no mighty deeds, not even conquering the whole world, is of
any good unless the man has learned mastery of himself.

—Arrian, *Anabasis of Alexander*

The death of Alexander the Great in 323 B.C. constituted a wa-
tershed in the development of world history. Greek civilization
as it had existed in its prime now came to an end. Of course, the
old institutions and ways of life did not suddenly disappear, but Alexander's career had cut so deeply into the old order that it could not be
restored intact. The fusion of cultures and intermingling of peoples
resulting from Alexander's conquests accomplished the overthrow of
many of the ideals developed in the Golden Age of the fifth and fourth
centuries. Gradually a new pattern of civilization emerged, based upon
a mixture of Greek and Eastern elements. To this new civilization,
which lasted until about the beginning of the Christian era, the name
Hellenistic is most commonly applied.

*A new stage in world
history*

Although the break between the Hellenic and Hellenistic eras was
sharp, it would be a mistake to deny all continuity. The language of
the new cultured classes was predominantly Greek, and even the peoples whose heritage was non-Greek considered it desirable to have
some Hellenic culture. Hellenic achievements in science provided a
foundation for the great scientific advances of the Hellenistic Age.
Greek emphasis upon logic was likewise carried over into Hellenistic

*Comparison of the
Hellenistic Age with the
Golden Age of Greece*

philosophy, though the objectives of the latter were in many cases quite different. In the spheres of the political, social, and economic the resemblances were few indeed. The classical ideal of democracy was now superseded by despotism perhaps as rigorous as any that Egypt or Persia had ever produced. The Greek city-state survived in some parts of Greece itself, but elsewhere it was replaced by large-scale monarchy, and in the minds of some leaders by notions of a world state. The Hellenic devotion to simplicity and the golden mean gave way to extravagance in the arts and to a love of luxury. In the economic realm there was a growing stress on big business and vigorous competition for profits. In view of these changes it seems valid to conclude that the Hellenistic Age was sufficiently distinct from the Golden Age of Greece to justify its being considered the era of a new civilization.

1. POLITICAL HISTORY AND INSTITUTIONS

The Hellenistic states

When Alexander died in 323 B.C., he left no legitimate heir to succeed him save a feeble-minded half-brother. Tradition relates that when his friends requested him on his deathbed to designate a successor, he replied "To the strongest." After his death his highest-ranking generals proceeded to divide the empire among them. Some of the younger commanders contested this arrangement, and a series of wars followed which culminated in the decisive battle of Ipsus in 301 B.C. The

Alexander in Battle. A scene from a sarcophagus of about 300 B.C. Alexander is shown on horseback at the left.

result of this battle was a new division among the victors. Seleucus took possession of Persia, Mesopotamia, and Syria; Lysimachus assumed control over Asia Minor and Thrace; Cassander established himself in Macedonia; and Ptolemy added Phoenicia and Palestine to his original domain of Egypt. Twenty years later these four states were reduced to three when Seleucus defeated and killed Lysimachus in battle and appropriated his territory in Asia Minor. In the meantime most of the Greek states had revolted against the attempts of Macedon to extend its power over them. By banding together in defensive leagues several of them succeeded in maintaining their independence for nearly a century. Finally, between 146 and 30 B.C. nearly all of the Hellenistic territory passed under Roman rule.

The dominant form of government in the Hellenistic Age was the despotism of rulers who represented themselves as at least semi-divine. Alexander himself was recognized as a son of God in Egypt and was worshiped as a god in Greece. His most powerful successors, the Seleucid kings in western Asia and the Ptolemies in Egypt, made systematic attempts to deify themselves. A Seleucid monarch, Antiochus IV, adopted the title "Epiphanes" or "God Manifest." The later members of the dynasty of the Ptolemies signed their decrees "Theos" (God) and revived the practice of sister marriage which had been followed by the pharaohs as a means of preserving the divine blood of the royal family from contamination. Only in the kingdom of Macedonia was despotism tempered by a modicum of respect for the liberties of the citizens.

Two other political institutions developed as by-products of Hellenistic civilization: the Achaean and Aetolian Leagues. We have already seen that most of the Greek states rebelled against Macedonian rule following the division of Alexander's empire. The better to preserve their independence, several of these states formed alliances among themselves, which were gradually expanded to become confederate leagues. The organization of these leagues was essentially the same in all cases. Each had a federal council composed of representatives of the member cities with power to enact laws on subjects of general concern. An assembly which all of the citizens in the federated states could attend decided questions of war and peace and elected officials. Executive and military authority was vested in the hands of a general, elected for one year and eligible for reelection only in alternate years. Although these leagues are frequently described as federal states, they were scarcely more than confederacies, for the central authority depended upon the local governments for contributions of revenue and troops. Furthermore, the powers delegated to the central government were limited primarily to matters of war and peace, coinage, and weights and measures. The chief significance of these leagues lies in the fact that they constituted the nearest approach ever made in Greece to voluntary national union before modern times.

Alexander the Great. Shown here is a silver coin struck in Thrace by King Lysimachus about 300 B.C.

The Achaean and Aetolian Leagues

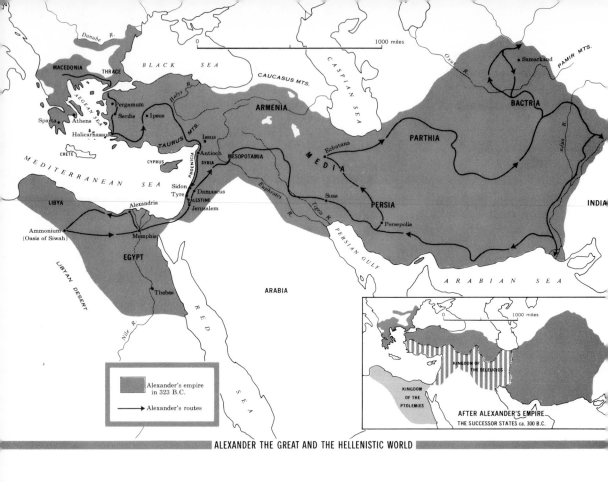

Map labels: Danube R., MACEDONIA, THRACE, BLACK SEA, CAUCASUS MTS., CASPIAN SEA, Samarkand, PAMIR MTS., Pergamum, Sardis, Ipsus, Halys R., ARMENIA, BACTRIA, Sparta, Athens, AEGEAN SEA, Oxus R., Halicarnassus, TAURUS MTS., Issus, Antioch, MESOPOTAMIA, MEDIA, Ecbatana, PARTHIA, Indus R., CRETE, CYPRUS, PHOENICIA, SYRIA, Euphrates R., Tigris R., Susa, PERSIA, INDIA, MEDITERRANEAN SEA, Sidon, Tyre, Damascus, PALESTINE, Jerusalem, LIBYA, Alexandria, PERSIAN GULF, Persepolis, Ammonium (Oasis of Siwah), Memphis, ARABIAN SEA, EGYPT, LIBYAN DESERT, Thebes, ARABIA, Nile R., RED SEA

0 — 1000 miles

Alexander's empire in 323 B.C.
→ Alexander's routes

Inset map: KINGDOM OF THE SELEUCIDS, KINGDOM OF THE PTOLEMIES, 0 — 1000 miles, AFTER ALEXANDER'S EMPIRE. THE SUCCESSOR STATES ca. 300 B.C.

2. SIGNIFICANT ECONOMIC AND SOCIAL DEVELOPMENTS

The economic revolution and its causes

Hellenistic civilization witnessed economic transformations second only in magnitude to the Industrial Revolution of the modern era. Several important causes can be distinguished: (1) the opening up of a vast area of trade from the Indus River to the Nile as a result of the Alexandrian conquests; (2) the rise in prices as a consequence of the release of an enormous Persian hoard of gold and silver into the channels of circulation, resulting in the growth of investment and speculation; and (3) the promotion of trade and industry by governments as a means of augmenting their revenues. The result was the growth of a system of large-scale production, trade, and finance, with the state as the principal entrepreneur.

The concentration of land ownership

Agriculture was as profoundly affected by the new developments as any other branch of economic life. The most dramatic changes were the concentration of landholdings and the degradation of the agricultural laborers. The successors of Alexander immediately confiscated the estates of the chief landowners and added them to their own domains. The lands thus acquired were then either granted to royal favorites or leased to tenants under an arrangement calculated to ensure an abundant income for the crown. The tenants were generally forbidden to leave the lands they cultivated until after the harvest and were not allowed to dispose of their grain until after the ruler had had a chance to sell the share he received as rent at the highest price the market would bring. When some of the tenants went on strike or attempted to run away, they were all bound to the soil as hereditary serfs. Many of the small independent farmers also became serfs when they got into debt as a result of inability to compete with large-scale production.

In an effort to make all of the resources of the state contribute to the profit of the government, the rulers of Egypt and the Seleucid Empire promoted and regulated industry and trade. The Ptolemies established factories and shops in nearly every village and town to be owned and operated by the government for its own financial benefit. In addition, they assumed control over all privately owned enterprises, fixing the prices the owners could charge and manipulating markets to the advantage of the crown. A similar plan of regimentation for industry, although not on quite so ambitious a scale, was enforced by the Seleucid rulers of western Asia. Trade was left by both of these governments very largely in private hands, but it was heavily taxed and regulated in such a way as to make sure that an ample share of the profits went to the ruler. Every facility was provided by the government for the encouragement of new trading ventures. Harbors were improved, warships were sent out to police the seas, and roads and canals were built. Moreover, the Ptolemies employed famous geographers to discover new routes to distant lands and thereby open up valuable markets. As a result of such methods Egypt developed a flourishing commerce in the widest variety of products. Into the port of Alexandria came spices from Arabia, copper from Cyprus, gold from Ethiopia and India, tin from Britain, elephants and ivory from Nubia, silver from the northern Aegean and Spain, fine carpets from Asia Minor, and even silk from China. Profits for the government and for some of the merchants were often as high as 20 or 30 percent.

State regimentation of industry and trade

Further evidence of the significant economic development of the Hellenistic Age is to be found in the growth of finance. An international money economy, based upon gold and silver coins, now became general throughout the Near East. Banks, usually owned by the government, developed as the chief institutions of credit for business ventures of every description. Speculation, cornering of markets, intense competition, the growth of large business houses, and the development of insurance and advertising were other significant phenomena of this remarkable age.

The growth of finance

According to the available evidence, the Hellenistic Age was a period of prosperity. Although serious crises frequently followed the collapse of speculative booms, they appear to have been of short duration. But

Hellenistic Coins. Obverse and reverse sides of the silver tetradrachma of Macedon, 336–323 B.C. Objects of common use from this period often show as much beauty of design as formal works of art.

The disparity between rich and poor

the prosperity that existed seems to have been limited chiefly to the rulers, the upper classes, and the merchants. It certainly did not extend to the peasants or even to the workers in the towns. The daily wages of both skilled and unskilled workers in Athens in the third century had dropped to less than half of what they had been in the Age of Pericles. The cost of living, on the other hand, had risen considerably. To make matters worse, unemployment in the large cities posed so serious a problem that the government had to provide free grain for many of the poor. Slavery declined in the Hellenistic world, partly because of the influence of the Stoic philosophy, but mainly for the reason that wages had fallen so low that it was cheaper to hire a free laborer than to purchase and maintain a slave.

The growth of large cities

A primary result of social and economic conditions in the Hellenistic Age was the growth of large cities. Despite the fact that most people still lived in the country, urbanization increased because of the expansion of industry and commerce, the enlargement of governmental functions, and the desire of former independent farmers to escape the hardships of serfdom. Cities multiplied and grew in the Hellenistic empires almost as rapidly as in nineteenth- and twentieth-century America. The population of Antioch in Syria quadrupled during a single century. Seleucia on the Tigris grew from nothing to a metropolis of several hundred thousand in less than two centuries. The largest and most famous of all the Hellenistic cities was Alexandria in Egypt, with over 500,000 inhabitants and possibly as many as 1,000,000. No other city in ancient times before imperial Rome surpassed it in size or in magnificence. Its streets were well paved and laid out in regular order. It had splendid public buildings and parks, a museum, and a library of 700,000 scrolls. It was the most brilliant center of Hellenistic cultural achievement, especially in the field of scientific research. The masses of its people, however, had no share in the brilliant and luxurious life around them, although it was paid for in part out of the fruits of their labor.

3. HELLENISTIC CULTURE: PHILOSOPHY, LITERATURE, AND ART

Hellenistic philosophy exhibited two trends that ran almost parallel throughout the civilization. The major trend, exemplified by Stoicism and Epicureanism, showed a fundamental regard for reason as the key to the solution of human problems. This trend was a manifestation of Greek influence, though philosophy and science, as combined in Aristotle, had now come to a parting of the ways. The minor trend, exemplified by the Cynics, Skeptics, and various Asian cults, tended to reject reason, to deny the possibility of attaining truth, and in some cases to turn toward mysticism and a reliance upon faith. Despite the differences in their teachings, the philosophers of the Hellenistic Age generally agreed upon one thing: the necessity of finding some release from the hardships and evils of human existence.

Trends in philosophy

The first of the Hellenistic philosophers were the Cynics, who arose about 350 B.C. Their foremost leader, Diogenes, won fame by his ceaseless quest for an "honest" man. The Cynics argued for the adoption of the "natural" life and the repudiation of everything conventional and artificial. Their principal goal was the cultivation of "self-sufficiency": everyone should cultivate within himself the ability to satisfy his own needs. Obviously the Cynics bore some resemblance to other movements that have cropped up through the ages—the hippie movement of the 1960s, for example. There were notable differences, however. The Cynics spurned music and art as manifestations of artificiality, and they were not representative of a youth generation. But all such movements seem to reflect a sense of frustration and hopeless conflict in society. According to one story, Alexander the Great once asked Diogenes's disciple Crates whether the city of Thebes, recently destroyed in war, should be rebuilt: "Why?" replied the Cynic, "Another Alexander will surely tear it down again."

The Cynics

Epicureanism and Stoicism both originated about 300 B.C. The founders were, respectively, Epicurus (c. 342–270) and Zeno (fl. after 300), who were residents of Athens. Epicureanism and Stoicism had several features in common. Both were individualistic, concerned not with the welfare of society but with the good of the individual. Both were materialistic, denying categorically the existence of any spiritual substances; even divine beings and the soul were declared to be formed of matter. Moreover, Stoicism and Epicureanism alike contained elements of universalism, since both taught that people are the same the world over and recognized no distinctions between Greeks and "barbarians."

Epicureanism and Stoicism

But in many ways the two systems were quite different. Zeno and his disciples taught that the cosmos is an ordered whole in which all contradictions are resolved for ultimate good. Evil is, therefore, relative; the particular misfortunes which befall human beings are but necessary incidents to the final perfection of the universe. Everything that happens is rigidly determined in accordance with rational purpose. No individual is master of his fate; human destiny is a link in an unbroken chain. People are free only in the sense that they can accept their fate or rebel against it. But whether they accept or rebel, they cannot overcome it. Their supreme duty is to submit to the order of the universe in the knowledge that that order is good; in other words, to resign themselves as graciously as possible to their fate. Through such an act of resignation the highest happiness will be attained, which consists in tranquility of mind. The individual who is most truly happy is therefore the one who by the assertion of his rational nature has accomplished a perfect adjustment of his life to the cosmic purpose and has purged his soul of all bitterness and whining protest against evil turns of fortune.

The Stoics developed an ethical and social theory that accorded well with their general philosophy. Believing that the highest good consists in serenity of mind, they naturally emphasized duty and self-discipline as cardinal virtues. Recognizing the prevalence of particular evil, they taught tolerance for and forgiveness of one another. Unlike the Cynics, they did not recommend withdrawal from society but urged participation in public affairs as a duty for the citizen of rational mind. They condemned slavery and war, but it was far from their purpose to preach any crusade against these evils. They believed that the results that might arise from violent measures of social change would be worse than the diseases they were meant to cure. Besides, what difference did it make if the body were in bondage so long as the mind was free? Despite its negative character, the Stoic philosophy was the noblest product of the Hellenistic Age. Its equalitarianism, pacifism, and humanitarianism were important factors in mitigating the harshness not only of that time but of later centuries as well.

The Epicureans derived their metaphysics chiefly from Democritus. Epicurus taught that the basic ingredients of all things are minute, indivisible atoms, and that change and growth are the results of the combination and separation of these particles. Nevertheless, while accepting the materialism of the atomists, Epicurus rejected their absolute mechanism. He denied that an automatic, mechanical motion of the atoms can be the cause of all things in the universe. Though he taught that the atoms move downward in perpendicular lines because of their weight, he insisted upon endowing them with a spontaneous ability to swerve from the perpendicular and thereby to combine with one another. This modification of the atomic theory made possible a belief in human freedom. If the atoms were capable only of mechanical motion, then a human being, also made up of atoms, would be reduced to the status of an automaton, and fatalism would be the law of the universe. In this repudiation of the mechanistic interpretation of life, Epicurus was probably closer to the Hellenic spirit than either Democritus or the Stoics.

The ethical philosophy of the Epicureans was based upon the doctrine that the highest good is pleasure. But they did not include all forms of indulgence in the category of genuine pleasure. The so-called pleasures of the flesh should be avoided, since every excess of carnality must be balanced by its portion of pain. On the other hand, a moderate satisfaction of bodily appetites is permissible and may be regarded as a good in itself. Better than this is mental pleasure, sober contemplation of the reasons for the choice of some things and the avoidance of others, and mature reflection upon satisfactions previously enjoyed. The highest of all pleasures, however, consists in serenity of soul, in the complete absence of both mental and physical pain. This end can be best achieved through the elimination of fear, especially fear of the supernatural, since that is the sovereign source of mental pain. The individual must recognize from the study of philosophy that the soul is material and therefore cannot survive the body, that the universe operates of itself, and that the gods do not intervene in human affairs. The gods live remote from the world and are too intent upon their own happiness to bother about what takes place on earth. Since they do not reward or punish mortals either in this life or in a life to come there is no reason why they should be feared. The Epicureans thus came by a different route to the same general conclusion as the Stoics—the supreme good is tranquillity of mind.

The Epicurean pursuit of tranquility of mind through overcoming fear of the supernatural

The ethics of the Epicureans as well as their political theory rested squarely upon a utilitarian basis. In contrast with the Stoics, they did not insist upon virtue as an end in itself but taught that the only reason why one should be good is to increase his own happiness. In like manner, they denied that there is any such thing as absolute justice: laws and institutions are just only insofar as they contribute to the welfare of the individual. Certain rules have been found necessary in every complex society for the maintenance of security and order. These rules are obeyed solely because it is to each individual's advantage to do so. Epicurus held no high regard for either political or social life. He considered the state as a mere convenience and taught that the wise man should take no active part in politics. Unlike the Cynics, he did not propose that civilization should be abandoned; yet his conception of the happiest life was essentially passive and defeatist. Epicurus taught that the thinking person will recognize that evils in the world cannot be eradicated by human effort; the individual will therefore withdraw to study philosophy and enjoy the fellowship of a few congenial friends.

The ethical and political theories of the Epicureans

A more radically defeatist philosophy was that propounded by the Skeptics. Skepticism reached the zenith of its popularity about 200 B.C. under the influence of Carneades. The chief source of its inspiration was the Sophist teaching that all knowledge is derived from sense perception and therefore must be limited and relative. From this was deduced the conclusion that we cannot prove anything. Since the im-

The defeatist philosophy of the Skeptics

pressions of our senses deceive us, no truth can be certain. All we can say is that things *appear* to be such and such; we do not know what they really *are*. We have no definite knowledge of the supernatural, of the meaning of life, or even of right and wrong. It follows that the sensible course to pursue is suspension of judgment: this alone can lead to happiness. If we will abandon the fruitless quest for absolute truth and cease worrying about good and evil, we will attain that equanimity of mind which is the highest satisfaction that life affords. The Skeptics were even less concerned than the Epicureans with political and social problems. Their ideal was the typically Hellenistic one of escape for the individual from a world neither understandable nor capable of reform.

The new religious philosophies

The nonrational trend in Hellenistic thought reached its farthest extreme in the philosophies of Philo Judaeus and the Neo-Pythagoreans in the last century B.C. and the first century A.D. The proponents of the two systems generally agreed in their basic teachings. They believed in a transcendent God so far removed from the world as to be utterly unknowable to mortal minds. They conceived of the universe as being sharply divided between spirit and matter. They considered everything physical and material as evil; the soul is imprisoned in the body, from which an escape can be effected only through rigorous denial and mortification of the flesh. Their attitude was mystical and nonintellectual: truth comes neither from science nor from reason but from revelation. Philo, a Jew who lived in Alexandria, maintained that the books of the Old Testament were of absolute divine authority and contained all truth; the ultimate aim in life is to accomplish a mystic union with God, to lose one's self in the divine. Both Philo and the Neo-Pythagoreans influenced the development of Christian theology—Philo, in particular, with his dualism of matter and spirit and his doctrine of the Logos, the word, or highest intermediary between God and the universe.

The profusion of ephemeral literature

Hellenistic literature is significant mainly for the light it throws upon the character of the civilization. Most of the writings showed little originality or depth of thought. But they poured forth from the hands of the copyists in a profusion that is almost incredible when we consider that the art of printing by movable type was unknown. We know the names of at least 1,100 authors. Much of what they wrote was trash, comparable to some of the cheap novels of our own day. Nevertheless, there were several works of more than mediocre quality and a few which met the highest standards ever set by the Greeks.

Hellenistic poetry

Among the leading types of Hellenistic literature were the drama and the pastoral. Drama was almost exclusively comedy, represented mainly by the plays of Menander. His plays were very different from the comedy of Aristophanes. They were distinguished by naturalism rather than by satire, by preoccupation with the seamy side of life rather than with political or intellectual issues. Their dominant theme was romantic love, with its pains and pleasures, its intrigues and seductions, and its culmination in happy marriage. The greatest author of pastorals was Theocritus of Syracuse, who wrote in the first half of the third century B.C. His pastorals, as the name implies, celebrate the charm of life in the country and idealize the simple pleasures of rustic folk. Theocritus later found greater imitators in the Roman poet Virgil and the Elizabethan poet Edmund Spenser.

The field of prose literature was dominated by the historians, the biographers, and the authors of utopias. By far the ablest of the writers of history was Polybius of Megalopolis, who lived during the second century B.C. From the standpoint of his scientific approach and his zeal for truth, he probably deserves to be ranked second only to Thucydides among all the historians in ancient times; but he excelled Thucydides in his grasp of the importance of social and economic forces. Although most of the biographies were of a light and gossipy character, their tremendous popularity bears eloquent testimony to the literary tastes of the time. Even more significant was the popularity of the utopias, or descriptive accounts of ideal states. Virtually all of them depicted a life of social and economic equality, free from greed, oppression, and strife, on an imaginary island or in some distant, unfamiliar region. Generally in these paradises money was considered to be unknown, trade was prohibited, all property was held in common, and all were required to work with their hands in producing the necessities of life. We are probably justified in assuming that the profusion of this utopian literature was a direct result of the evils and injustices of Hellenistic society and a consciousness of the need for reform.

Historians, biographers, and authors of utopias

Hellenistic art did not preserve all of the characteristic qualities of

The Dying Gaul. A good example of Hellenistic realism in sculpture, which often reflected a preoccupation with the morbid and sensational. Every detail of the warrior's agony is dramatically portrayed. Now in the Capitoline Museum, Rome.

Left: *The Winged Victory of Samothrace*. In this figure, done around 200 B.C., a Hellenistic sculptor preserved some of the calmness and devotion to grace and proportion characteristic of Hellenic art in the Golden Age. Right: *Laocoön*. In sharp contrast to the serenity of the Winged Victory is this famous sculpture group from the late second century B.C., depicting the death of Laocoön. According to legend, Laocoön warned the Trojans not to touch the wooden horse sent by the Greeks and was punished by Poseidon, who sent two serpents to kill him and his sons. The intense emotionalism of this work later had a great influence on western European art from Michelangelo onward. See, for example, the painting by El Greco on page 535.

Hellenistic art

the art of the Greeks. In place of the humanism, balance, and restraint which had distinguished the architecture and sculpture of the Golden Age, qualities of exaggerated realism, sensationalism, and voluptuousness now became dominant. The simple and dignified Doric and Ionic temples gave way to luxurious palaces, costly mansions, and elaborate public buildings and monuments symbolic of power and wealth. A typical example was the great lighthouse of Alexandria, which rose to a height of nearly four hundred feet, with three diminishing stories and eight columns to support the light at the top. Sculpture likewise exhibited extravagant and sentimental tendencies. Many of the statues and figures in relief were huge and some of them almost grotesque. Violent emotionalism and exaggerated realism were features common to the majority. But by no means all of Hellenistic sculpture was overwrought. Some of it was distinguished by a calmness and compassion for human suffering reminiscent of the best work of the great fourth-century artists. Statues which exemplify these superior qualities include the *Aphrodite of Melos* (*Venus de Milo*) and the *Winged Victory of Samothrace*.

4. THE FIRST GREAT AGE OF SCIENCE

The most brilliant age in the history of science prior to the seventeenth century A.D. was the period of the Hellenistic civilization. Indeed, many modern scientific achievements would scarcely have been possible without the discoveries of the scientists of Alexandria, Syracuse, Pergamum, and other great Hellenistic cities. The reasons for the impressive development of science in the centuries after the downfall of Alexander's empire are manifold. Alexander himself had given some financial encouragement to scientific research. More important was the stimulus provided for intellectual inquiry by the fusion of Chaldean and Egyptian science with the learning of the Greeks. Possibly a third factor was the new interest in material comfort and a fourth the demand for practical knowledge that would enable the scientific thinker to solve the problems of a disordered and unsatisfying existence.

Factors responsible for the remarkable progress of science

The major Hellenistic sciences were astronomy, mathematics, geography, medicine, and physics. Chemistry, aside from metallurgy, was practically unknown. Except for the work of Theophrastus, who was the first to recognize the sexuality of plants, biology was also largely neglected. Neither chemistry nor biology bore any definite relationship to trade or to the forms of industry then in existence and hence were not regarded as having much practical value.

The most popular sciences

The most renowned of the earlier Hellenistic astronomers was Aristarchus of Samos (310–230 B.C.), sometimes called the "Hellenistic Copernicus." His chief accomplishment was his deduction that the earth and the other planets revolve around the sun. Unfortunately this view was not accepted by his successors because it conflicted with the teachings of Aristotle and with the conviction of the Greeks that man, and therefore the earth, must be at the center of the universe. Another important Hellenistic astronomer was Hipparchus, who flourished in Alexandria in the latter half of the second century B.C. His chief contributions were the invention of the astrolabe and the approximately correct calculation of the diameter of the moon and its distance from the earth. His fame was eventually overshadowed, however, by the reputation of Ptolemy of Alexandria (second century A.D.). Although Ptolemy made few original discoveries, he systematized the work of others. His principal writing, the *Almagest,* based upon the geocentric theory (the view that all heavenly bodies revolve around the earth), was handed down to medieval Europe as the classic summary of ancient astronomy. Ptolemy's geography too had a considerable influence on medieval and Renaissance thought.

Astronomy

Closely allied with astronomy were two other sciences, mathemat-

*Mathematics and
geography*

ics and geography. The Hellenistic mathematician of greatest renown was Euclid (c. 323–c. 285 B.C.), the master of geometry. Until the middle of the nineteenth century his *Elements of Geometry* remained the accepted basis for the study of that branch of mathematics. Much of the material in this work was not original but was a synthesis of the discoveries of others. The most original of the Hellenistic mathematicians was probably Hipparchus, who laid the foundations of both plane and spherical trigonometry. Hellenistic geography owed most of its development to Eratosthenes (c. 276–c. 196 B.C.), astronomer, poet, and librarian of Alexandria. By means of sundials placed some hundreds of miles apart, he calculated the circumference of the earth with an error of less than 200 miles. He produced the most accurate map that had yet been devised, with the surface of the earth divided into degrees of latitude and longitude. He propounded the theory that all of the oceans are really one, and he was the first to suggest the possibility of reaching India by sailing west. One of his successors divided the earth into the five climatic zones which are still recognized, and explained the ebb and flow of the tides as due to the influence of the moon.

*Medicine: the
development of anatomy*

Perhaps none of the Hellenistic advances in science surpassed in importance the progress in medicine. Especially significant was the work of Herophilus of Chalcedon, who conducted his researches in Alexandria about the beginning of the second century. Without question he was the greatest anatomist of antiquity and probably the first to practice human dissection. Among his most important achievements were a detailed description of the brain, with an attempt to distinguish between the functions of its various parts; the discovery of the significance of the pulse and its use in diagnosing illness; and the discovery that the arteries contain blood alone, not a mixture of blood and air as Aristotle had taught, and that their function is to carry blood from the heart to all parts of the body.

Physiology

The ablest of the colleagues of Herophilus was Erasistratus, who flourished in Alexandria about the middle of the third century. He is considered the founder of physiology as a separate science. Not only did he practice dissection, but he is believed to have gained a great deal of his knowledge of bodily functions from vivisection. He discovered the valves of the heart, distinguished between motor and sensory nerves, and taught that the ultimate branches of the arteries and veins are connected. He was the first to reject absolutely the humoral theory of disease and to condemn excessive blood-letting as a method of cure. Unfortunately this theory was revived by Galen, the great encyclopedist of medicine who lived in the Roman Empire in the second century A.D.

Physics

Prior to the third century B.C. physics had been a branch of philosophy. It was made a separate experimental science by Archimedes of Syracuse (c. 287–212 B.C.). Archimedes discovered the law of floating bodies, or specific gravity, and formulated with scientific exactness

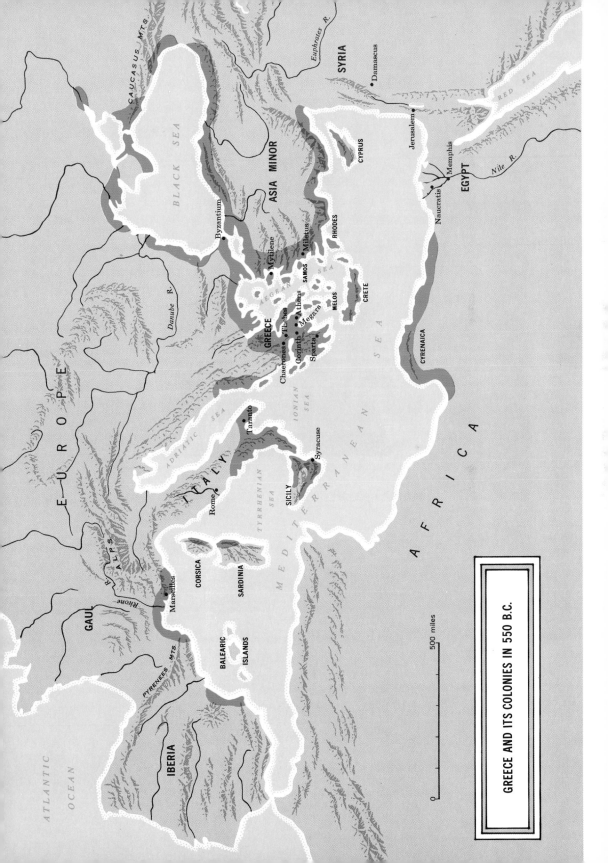

ATLANTIC OCEAN

EUROPE

GAUL

Marseilles

PYRENEES MTS.

IBERIA

BALEARIC ISLANDS

CORSICA

SARDINIA

ALPS

Rhone R.

Rome

ITALY

Taranto

SICILY

Syracuse

TYRRHENIAN SEA

MEDITERRANEAN SEA

ADRIATIC SEA

IONIAN SEA

CAUCASUS MTS.

BLACK SEA

Danube R.

Byzantium

ASIA MINOR

Mytilene

SAMOS

Miletus

RHODES

AEGEAN SEA

GREECE

Thebes

Chaeronea

Corinth

Megara

Athens

Sparta

MELOS

CRETE

Euphrates R.

SYRIA

Damascus

CYPRUS

Jerusalem

Memphis

Naucratis

EGYPT

Nile R.

RED SEA

CYRENAICA

AFRICA

AEGEAN SEA

500 miles

0

GREECE AND ITS COLONIES IN 550 B.C.

Geometric Horse, VIII cent. B.C. Greek art of this early period was angular, formal, and conventionalized.

Geometric Jar, VIII cent. B.C. Another example of the stylized decorative patterns of early Greek art.

Sphinx, c. 540–530 B.[.] Though doubtless of Orie[n]tal derivation, Greek sphi[n]es had a softer and m[ore] human aspect than the O[ri]ental.

Statue of an Amazon, one of the fabled tribe of women warriors, V cent. B.C. (Roman copy)

Departure of a Warrior. Gravestone, c. 530 B.C., a period when naturalism was the dominant note of Greek art.

Athena, c. 460 B.C. T[he] young, graceful patro[n] goddess of Athens is ab[out] to send forth an owl a[s a] sign of victory.

Jar, 500–490 B.C. The figures depicted in a fine black glaze on the natural red clay show athletes in the Panathenaic games.

Chorus of Satyrs, c. 420 B.C. The background is black with the figures in red clay. The satyrs, dressed in fleecy white, with flowing tails, are the chorus of a play.

Toilet Box, 465–460 B.C. T[he] scene shows the judgment [of] Paris, an event which touched [off] the Trojan War.

Bronze Mirror Case, V cent. B.C. Greek articles of everyday use were commonly finished with the same delicacy and precision as major works of art.

Diadoumenos, after Polykleitos, V cent. B.C. An idealized statue of a Greek athlete tying the "diadem," or band of victory, around his head.

Bracelet Pendant, IV–III cent. B.C. This tiny figure of the god Pan is a masterpiece of detail and expression.

Woman Arranging Her Hair, 400–300 B.C. Sculptors of antiquity took pride in these statuettes of ordinary people in ordinary activities, which were usually made of terracotta painted soft blue, pink, or yellow.

Head of an Athlete, c. 440–420 B.C. The sculptor aimed to express manly beauty in perfect harmony with physical and intellectual excellence.

Statuette of Hermarchos, III cent. B.C. An example of the realism of Hellenistic sculpture.

Sleeping Eros, 250–150 B.C. Along with a penchant for realism, Hellenistic sculptors were fond of portraying serenity or repose.

Comic Actor, 200–100 B.C. Hellenistic realism often included portrayal of ugly and even deformed individuals.

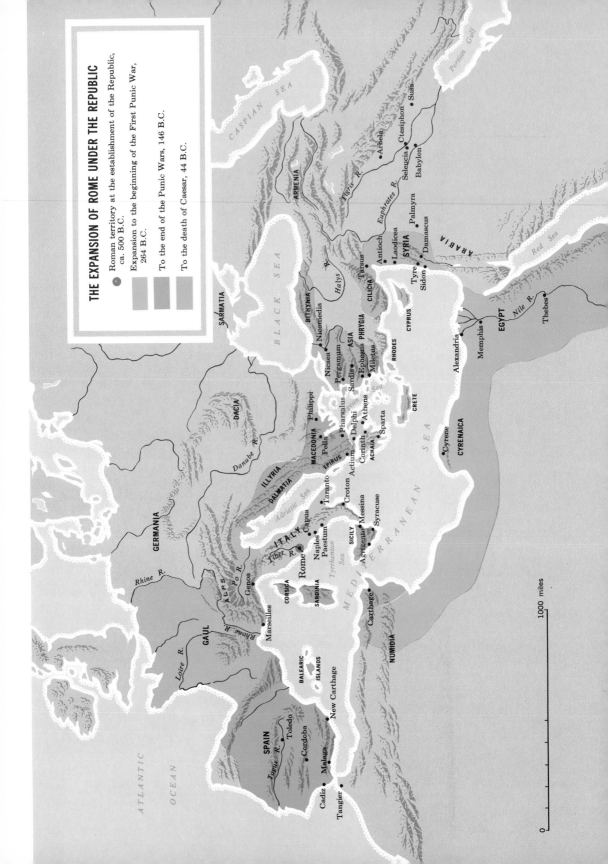

THE EXPANSION OF ROME UNDER THE REPUBLIC

- Roman territory at the establishment of the Republic, ca. 500 B.C.

  Expansion to the beginning of the First Punic War, 264 B.C.

  To the end of the Punic Wars, 146 B.C.

  To the death of Caesar, 44 B.C.

ATLANTIC OCEAN

CASPIAN SEA

SARMATIA

BLACK SEA

ARMENIA

GERMANIA

DACIA

Danube R.

Rhine R.

Loire R.

Rhône R.

ALPS

GAUL

Tagus R.

SPAIN

Toledo

Cordoba

Malaga

Cadiz

Tangier

New Carthage

BALEARIC ISLANDS

Marseilles

Genoa

CORSICA

SARDINIA

Tiber R.

Rome

ITALY

Naples

Paestum

Capua

Taranto

Croton

Tyrrhenian Sea

Adriatic Sea

ILLYRIA

DALMATIA

EPIRUS

MACEDONIA

Pella

Philippi

Pharsalus

Delphi

Actium

Athens

Corinth

Sparta

ACHAIA

Carthage

NUMIDIA

SICILY

Messina

Syracuse

Agrigentum

MEDITERRANEAN SEA

Aegean Sea

BITHYNIA

Nicomedia

Nicaea

Pergamum

Sardis

ASIA

Ephesus

Miletus

PHRYGIA

RHODES

CRETE

CYRENAICA

Cyrene

Halys R.

Tarsus

CILICIA

Antioch

Laodicea

SYRIA

Damascus

Tyre

Sidon

CYPRUS

Euphrates R.

Tigris R.

Palmyra

Seleucia

Ctesiphon

Babylon

Susa

Arbela

ARABIA

Red Sea

Persian Gulf

EGYPT

Alexandria

Memphis

Nile R.

Thebes

0   1000 miles

the principles of the lever, the pulley, and the screw. Among his memorable inventions were the compound pulley, the tubular screw for pumping water, the screw propeller for ships, and the burning lens. Although he has been called the "technical Yankee of antiquity," there is evidence that he set no high value upon his ingenious mechanical contraptions and preferred to devote his time to pure scientific research.

Certain other individuals in the Hellenistic Age also devoted themselves to applied science. Preeminent among them was Hero of Alexandria, who lived in the last century B.C. The record of inventions credited to him almost passes belief. The list includes a fire engine, a siphon, a jet engine, a hydraulic organ, a slot machine, and a catapult operated by compressed air. How many of these inventions were really his own is impossible to say, but there appears to be no question that such contrivances were actually in existence in his time or soon thereafter. Nevertheless, the total progress in applied science was comparatively slight, probably for the reason that human labor continued to be so abundant and cheap that it was not worthwhile to substitute the work of machines.

Applied science

5. RELIGION IN THE HELLENISTIC AGE

If there was one aspect of the Hellenistic civilization which served more than others to accent the contrast with Hellenic culture, it was the new trend in religion. The civic religion of the Greeks as it was in the age of the city-states had now almost entirely disappeared. For the majority of the intellectuals its place was taken by the philosophies of Stoicism, Epicureanism, and Skepticism. Some who were less philosophically inclined turned to the worship of Fortune.

The new trend in religion

Among the common people a tendency to embrace emotional religions was even more dominant. The Orphic and Eleusinian mystery cults attracted more votaries than ever before. The worship of the Egyptian mother-goddess, Isis, threatened for a time to predominate throughout the Near East. The astral religion of the Chaldeans likewise spread rapidly, with the result that its chief product, astrology, was received with intense enthusiasm throughout the Hellenistic world. But the most powerful influence of all came from the offshoots of Zoroastrianism, especially from Mithraism and Gnosticism. While all of the cults of Oriental origin resembled each other in their promises of salvation in a life to come, Mithraism and Gnosticism had a more ethically exalted mythology, a deeper contempt for this world, and a more clearly defined doctrine of redemption through a personal savior. These were the ideas which satisfied the emotional cravings of the common people, convinced as they were of the worthlessness of this life and ready to be lured by extravagant promises of better things in a world to come.

The popularity of mystical religions

A factor by no means unimportant in the religious developments of the Hellenistic Age was the dispersion of the Jews. As a result of Alexander's conquest of Palestine in 332 B.C. and the Roman conquest about three centuries later, thousands of Jews migrated to various sections of the Mediterranean world. It has been estimated that 1,000,000 of them lived in Egypt in the first century A.D. and 200,000 in Asia Minor. They mingled freely with other peoples, adopting the Greek language and no small amount of the Hellenic culture which still survived from earlier days. At the same time they played a major part in the diffusion of Eastern beliefs. Some of the Hellenistic Jews eventually became converts to Christianity and were instrumental in the spread of that religion outside of Palestine. A notable example was Saul of Tarsus, known in Christian history as St. Paul.

6. A FORETASTE OF MODERNITY?

With the possible exception of the Roman, no great culture of ancient times resembles the modern age quite so much as does the Hellenistic civilization. Here, as in the twentieth century, were to be found a considerable variety of forms of government, the growth of militarism, and a trend in the direction of authoritarian rule. Many of the characteristic economic and social developments of the Hellenistic Age are equally suggestive of contemporary experience: the growth of big business, the expansion of trade, the zeal for exploration and discovery, the interest in technology, the devotion to material prosperity, the growth of cities with congested slums, and the widening gulf between rich and poor. In the realms of intellect and art the Hellenistic civilization also had a distinctly modern flavor. This was exemplified by the emphasis upon science, the narrow specialization of learning, the penchant for realism and naturalism, the vast production of mediocre literature, and the popularity of mysticism side by side with extreme skepticism and dogmatic unbelief.

Because of these resemblances there has been a tendency among certain writers to regard our own civilization as decadent. But this is based partly upon a false conception of Hellenistic culture as merely a degenerate phase of Greek civilization. Instead, it was a new social and cultural organism born of a fusion of Greek and Near Eastern elements. Moreover, the differences between the Hellenistic civilization and that of the contemporary world ultimately outweigh the resemblances. The Hellenistic political outlook was essentially cosmopolitan; nothing comparable to the national patriotism of modern times really prevailed. Despite the remarkable expansion of trade in the Hellenistic Age, no industrial revolution ever took place. Finally, Hellenistic science was more limited than that of the present day. Modern pure science is to a very large extent a species of philosophy—

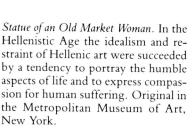

Statue of an Old Market Woman. In the Hellenistic Age the idealism and restraint of Hellenic art were succeeded by a tendency to portray the humble aspects of life and to express compassion for human suffering. Original in the Metropolitan Museum of Art, New York.

an adventure of the mind in the realm of the unknown. Notwithstanding frequent assertions to the contrary, much of it is gloriously impractical and will probably remain so.

SELECTED READINGS

• *Items so designated are available in paperback editions.*

Cary, Max, *The Legacy of Alexander: A History of the Greek World from 323 to 146 B.C.*, New York, 1932. A firm guide to the complicated political history of the period.

Clagett, M., *Greek Science in Antiquity*, New York, 1963. A solid and dependable introduction.

Festugière, A. J., *Epicurus and His Gods*, Cambridge, Mass., 1956.

• Finley, M. I., *The Ancient Economy*, Berkeley, Calif., 1973. A fundamental topical treatment by a brilliant scholar.

Grant, F. C., *Hellenistic Religions*, New York, 1963. A standard work.

Hamilton, J. R., *Alexander the Great*, London, 1973. The best concise scholarly biography currently available.

Lane Fox, R., *Alexander the Great,* London, 1973. Longer and more interpretative than Hamilton but highly recommended.

Larsen, J. A. O., *Greek Federal States,* Oxford, 1968.

Rostovtzeff, M., *The Social and Economic History of the Hellenistic World,* 3 vols., Oxford, 1941. An authoritative mine of information.

• Tarn, W. W., *Alexander the Great,* Cambridge, 1948. Tarn was the leading English expert on Hellenistic history of the earlier part of this century.

———, and G. T. Griffith, *Hellenistic Civilization,* 3rd ed., London, 1952. Still indispensible.

Walbank, F. W., *The Hellenistic World,* Cambridge, Mass., 1982. An excellent college-level survey by one of the world's most prominent experts.

• Wilcken, U., *Alexander the Great,* New York, 1932. A fundamental older interpretation, translated from the German.

SOURCE MATERIALS

Greek source materials for the Hellenistic period are available in the appropriate volumes of the Loeb Classical Library, Harvard University Press.

Chapter 8

ROMAN CIVILIZATION

My city and country, so far as I am Antoninus, is Rome, but so far as I am
a man, it is the world.

— Marcus Aurelius Antoninus, *Meditations*

For the categories into which you divide the world are not Hellenes and
Barbarians. . . . The division which you substituted is one into Romans
and non-Romans. To such a degree have you expanded the name of your
city.

— Aelius Aristides, *Oration to Rome*

W ell before the glory that was Greece had begun to fade,
another civilization, ultimately much influenced by Greek
culture, had started its growth in the West on the banks of
the Tiber. Around the time of Alexander's conquests the new civilization of Rome was already a dominant force on the Italian peninsula.
For five centuries thereafter Rome's power increased. By the end of
the first century B.C. it had imposed its rule over the entire Hellenistic
world as well as over most of western Europe. By conquering the old
Hellenistic states and destroying the North African civilization of Carthage, Rome was able to make the Mediterranean a "Roman lake." In
so doing it brought Greek institutions and ideas to the western half of
the Mediterranean world. And by pushing northward to the Rhine
and Danube rivers it brought Mediterranean urban culture to lands
still sunk in the Iron Age. Rome, then, was the builder of a great
historical bridge between East and West.

The rise of Rome

Of course Rome would not have been able to play this role had it
not followed its own peculiar course of development. This was
marked by the tension between two different cultural outlooks. On
the one hand Romans throughout most of their history tended to be
conservative: they revered their old agricultural traditions, household
gods, and ruggedly warlike ways. But they also strove to be builders
and could not resist the attractions of Greek culture. For a few centu-

The Roman synthesis

ries their greatness was based on a synthesis of these different traits: respect for tradition, order, and military prowess, together with Greek urbanization and cultivation of the mind. The synthesis could not last forever, but as long as it did the glory that was Greece was replaced by the grandeur that was Rome.

1. EARLY ITALY AND THE ROMAN MONARCHY

The impact of geography on Roman history

The geographical character of the Italian peninsula contributed significantly to the course of Roman history. Except for some excellent marble and small quantities of tin, copper, iron, and gold, Italy has no mineral resources. The extensive coastline is broken by few good harbors. On the other hand, the amount of fertile land is greater than that of Greece. As a result, the Romans remained a predominantly agrarian people through the greater part of their history. They seldom enjoyed the intellectual stimulus which comes from extensive trading with other areas. In addition, the Italian peninsula was more open to invasion than was Greece. The Alps posed no effective barrier to the influx of peoples from central Europe, and the low-lying coast in many places invited conquest by sea. Domination of the territory by force was therefore more common than peaceful intermingling of immigrants with original settlers. The Romans became absorbed in military pursuits almost from the moment of their settlement on Italian soil, for they were forced to defend their own conquests against other invaders.

An Etruscan Musician. This well-coordinated flutist appears in an Etruscan wall painting dating from about 480 B.C.

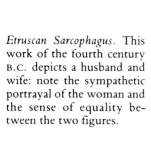

Etruscan Sarcophagus. This work of the fourth century B.C. depicts a husband and wife: note the sympathetic portrayal of the woman and the sense of equality between the two figures.

Archeological evidence indicates that Italy was inhabited at least as far back as the later Paleolithic Age. At this time the territory was occupied by a people closely related to the Cro-Magnons of southern France. In the Neolithic period people of Mediterranean stock entered the land, some coming in from northern Africa and others from Spain and Gaul. The beginning of the Bronze Age witnessed several new incursions. From north of the Alps came the first of the immigrants of the Indo-European language group. They were herdsmen and farmers, who brought the horse and the wheeled cart into Italy. Their culture was based upon the use of bronze, although after about 900 B.C. they appear to have acquired a knowledge of iron. These Indo-Europeans seem to have been the ancestors of most of the so-called Italic peoples, including the Romans, and they were probably related to the Hellenic invaders of Greece.

The earliest inhabitants of Italy

Probably during the eighth century B.C. two other nations of immigrants occupied different portions of the Italian peninsula: the Etruscans and the Greeks. Where the Etruscans came from is a question which has never been satisfactorily answered, although it is certain that they were not Indo-Europeans. Most authorities believe that they were natives of Asia Minor. Whatever their origins, by the sixth century B.C. they had established a great federation of cities that stretched over most of northern and central Italy. Although their writing has never been completely deciphered, enough materials survive to indicate the nature of their culture. They had an alphabet based upon the Greek, a high degree of skill in metalwork, great artistic talents, a flourishing trade with the East, and a religion based upon the worship of gods in human form. They bequeathed to the Romans a knowledge of the arch and the vault, the cruel amusement of gladiatorial combats, and the practice of foretelling the future by supernatural means such as studying the entrails of animals or the flight of

The Etruscans and the Greeks

birds. One of their most distinctive traits was the comparatively great respect they showed for women. Etruscan wives, unlike those in other contemporary societies, ate with their husbands, and some Etruscan families listed descent through the maternal line.

The Greeks settled mainly along the southern and southwestern shores of Italy and the island of Sicily, as well as along the southern coast of Gaul. Their most important settlements were Taranto, Naples, and Syracuse, each of which was an independent city-state. Greek civilization in Italy and Sicily was as advanced as in Greece itself. Such famous Greeks as Pythagoras, Archimedes, and even Plato for a time, lived in the Italian West. From the Greeks the Romans derived their alphabet, a number of their religious concepts, and much of their art and mythology.

The founders of Rome itself were Italic peoples who lived in the area south of the Tiber River. Though the exact year of the founding of the city is unknown, recent archeological research places the event quite near the traditional date of 753 B.C. By reason of its strategic location, Rome came to exercise an effective suzerainty over several of the most important neighboring cities. One conquest followed another until, by the sixth century B.C., Rome came to dominate most of the surrounding area. But just then Etruscans took over power in Rome.

At first Roman government aimed far more at establishing stability than at creating liberty. The original Roman state was essentially an application of the idea of the patriarchal family to the whole community, with the king exercising a jurisdiction over his subjects comparable to that of the head of the family over the members of his household. But just as the authority of the father was limited by custom and by the requirement that he respect the wishes of his adult sons, the authority of the king was limited by the ancient constitution, which he was powerless to change without the consent of the chief men of the realm. His prerogatives were not primarily legislative but executive, priestly, military, and judicial. He judged all civil and criminal cases, but he had no authority to pardon without the consent of the assembly. Although his accession to office had to be confirmed by the people, he could not be deposed, and there was no one who could really challenge the exercise of his powers.

In addition to the kingship, the Roman government of this time included an assembly and a Senate. The former was composed of all the male citizens of military age. As one of the chief sources of sovereign power, according to the theory, this body could veto any proposal for a change in the law which the king might make. Moreover, it determined whether pardons should be granted and whether aggressive war should be declared. But it was essentially a ratifying body with no right to initiate legislation or recommend changes of policy. The Senate, or council of elders, comprised in its membership the heads of the various clans which formed the community. Even more than the common citizens, the rulers of the clans embodied the sovereign power of the state. The king was only one of their number to whom they had delegated the active exercise of their authority. When the royal office became vacant, the powers of the king immediately reverted to the Senate until the succession of a new monarch had been confirmed by the people. In ordinary times the chief function of the Senate was to examine proposals of the king which had been ratified by the assembly and to veto them if they violated rights established by ancient custom. It was thus almost impossible for fundamental changes to be made in the law even when the majority of the citizens were ready to sanction them. This extremely conservative attitude of the ruling classes persisted until the end of Roman history.

Toward the end of the sixth century (the date traditionally given is 509 B.C.) the monarchy was overthrown and replaced by a republic. Legend has it that this revolution was provoked by the crimes of the Tarquins, an Etruscan family that had taken over the kingship in Rome around the middle of the century. After suffering numerous indignities, the last and worst of which was the rape and subsequent suicide of a virtuous Roman matron, Lucretia, by a lustful Tarquin prince, the native Romans could stand no more and rose up to expel their alien oppressors. In fact the story of the rape of Lucretia is fictional but the change in government was probably in part a native uprising against foreigners, as well as a successful movement of the Roman senatorial aristocracy to gain full power for itself. The result was the beginning of Etruscan decline in Italy, as well as a lasting conviction among Romans that kingship was evil.

End of the monarchy

2. THE EARLY REPUBLIC

The history of the Roman Republic for more than two centuries after its establishment was one of almost constant warfare. Many of the most familiar Roman legends, such as that of the brave Horatio, who with only two friends held off an entire army in front of a bridge, date from this period. At first the Romans were on the defensive. The overthrow of the Tarquins resulted in acts of reprisal by their allies in neighboring regions, and other peoples on the borders took advantage of the confusion accompanying the change of regime to slice off portions of Roman territory. After Rome managed to ward off these attacks it began to expand in order to gain more land and satisfy a rapidly growing population. As time went on Rome steadily conquered all the Etruscan territories and then took over all the Greek cities in the southernmost portion of the Italian mainland. Not only did the latter add to the Roman domain, they also brought the Romans into fruitful contact with Greek culture. The Romans were then frequently confronted with revolts of peoples previously conquered. The suppression of these revolts awakened the suspicions of surrounding states

Early Roman expansion

See color map facing page 161

Roman Battle Sarcophagus. This relief displays the glories of war and expresses the Roman military ideal.

and sharpened the appetite of the victors for further triumphs. New wars followed each other in what seemed an unending succession, until by 265 B.C. Rome had conquered the entire Italian peninsula.

Effects of the early military conflicts

This long series of military conflicts had profound social, economic, and cultural effects upon the subsequent history of Rome. It affected adversely the interests of the poorer citizens and furthered the concentration of land in the possession of wealthy proprietors. Long service in the army forced the ordinary farmers to neglect the cultivation of the soil, with the result that they fell into debt and frequently lost their farms. Many took refuge in the city, until they were settled later as tenants on great estates in the conquered territories. The wars had the effect also of confirming the agrarian character of the Roman nation. The repeated acquisition of new lands made it possible to absorb the entire population into agricultural pursuits. As a consequence Romans saw no need for the development of industry and commerce. Last, the continual warfare of this formative period served to develop among the Romans a strong military ideal: along with Horatio, another of Rome's great early legendary heroes was Cincinnatus, who supposedly left his farm at a moment's notice for the battlefield.

Political changes following the overthrow of the monarchy

During this same period of the early Republic, Rome underwent some significant political changes. These were not products so much of the revolution of the sixth century as of the developments of later years. The revolution which overthrew the monarchy was about as conservative as it is possible for a revolution to be. Its chief effect was to substitute two elected officials called consuls for the king and to exalt the position of the Senate by granting it control over the public funds and a veto on all actions of the assembly. The consuls themselves were usually senators and acted as the agents of their class. They did not rule jointly, but each was supposed to possess the full executive and judicial authority which had previously been wielded by the king. If a conflict arose between them, the Senate might be called upon to decide; or, in time of grave emergency, a dictator might be appointed for a term not greater than six months. In other respects the government remained the same as in the days of the monarchy.

Not long after the establishment of the Republic a struggle for power began among factions of the common citizens. Before the end of the monarchy the Roman population had come to be divided into two great classes—the patricians and the plebeians. The former were the aristocracy, wealthy landowners who monopolized the seats in the Senate and the offices of magistracy. Among the plebeians were some wealthy families who were barred from the patriciate because they were of recent foreign origin, but most plebeians were common people—small farmers, craftsmen, and tradesmen. Many were clients or dependents of the patricians, obliged to fight for them, to render them political support, and to cultivate their estates in return for protection. The grievances of the plebeians were numerous. Compelled to pay heavy taxes and forced to serve in the army in time of war, they were nevertheless excluded from all part in the government except membership in the assembly. Moreover, they felt themselves the victims of discriminatory decisions in judicial trials. They did not even know what legal rights they were supposed to enjoy, for the laws were unwritten, and no one but the consuls had the power to interpret them. In suits for debt the creditor was frequently allowed to sell the debtor into slavery.

In order to obtain a redress of these grievances the plebeians rebelled soon after the beginning of the fifth century B.C. They gained their first victory about 494 B.C., when they forced the patricians to agree to the election of a number of officers known as tribunes with power to protect the citizens by means of a veto over unlawful acts of the magistrates. This victory was followed by a successful demand for codification of the laws about 450 B.C. The result was the publication of the famous Law of the Twelve Tables, so called because it was written on tablets of wood. Although the Twelve Tables came to be revered by the Romans of later times as a kind of charter of the people's liberties, they were really nothing of the sort. For the most part they merely perpetuated ancient custom without even abolishing enslavement for debt. They did, however, enable the people to know where they stood in relation to the law, and they permitted an appeal to the assembly against a magistrate's sentence of capital punishment. About a generation later the plebeians won eligibility to positions as lesser magistrates, and about 367 B.C. the first plebeian consul was elected. Since ancient custom provided that, upon completing their term of office, consuls should automatically enter the Senate, the patrician monopoly of seats in that body was broken. The final plebeian victory came in 287 B.C. with the passage of a law which provided that measures enacted by the assembly should become binding upon the state whether the Senate approved them or not.

The significance of these changes must not be misinterpreted. They did not constitute a revolution to gain more liberty for the individual but merely to curb the power of the magistrates and to win for the plebeians a larger share in government. The state as a whole remained as despotic as ever, for its authority over the citizens was not even challenged. Indeed, the Romans of the early Republic "never really abandoned the principle that the people were not to govern but to be governed."[1] Because of this attitude the grant of full legislative powers to the assembly seems to have meant little more than a formality; the Senate continued to rule as before. Nor did the admission of plebeians to membership in the Senate have any effect in liberalizing that body. So high was its prestige and so deep was the veneration of the Roman for authority, that the new members were soon swallowed up in the conservatism of the old. Moreover, the fact that the magistrates received no salaries prevented most of the poorer citizens from seeking public office.

Intellectually and culturally the Romans developed very slowly. Life in Rome was still harsh and crude. Though writing had been adopted as early as the sixth century, little use was made of it except for the copying of laws, treaties, and funerary inscriptions. Inasmuch as education was limited to instruction imparted by the father in manly sports, practical arts, and soldierly virtues, the great majority of the people were still illiterate. War and agriculture continued as the chief occupations for the bulk of the citizens. A few craftsmen were to be found in the cities, and a minor development of trade had occurred. But the fact that the country had no standard system of coinage until 269 B.C. clearly demonstrates the comparative insignificance of Roman commerce at this time.

During the period of the early Republic Roman religion assumed the character it retained through the greater part of Roman history. In several ways this religion resembled that of the Greeks, partly for the reason that the Etruscan religion was deeply indebted to the Greek, and the Romans, in turn, were influenced by the Etruscans. Both the Greek and Roman religions emphasized the performances of rites in order to gain benefits from the gods or keep them from anger. The deities in both religions performed similar functions: Jupiter corresponded to Zeus as god of the sky, Minerva to Athena as goddess of wisdom and patroness of crafts, Venus to Aphrodite as goddess of love, Neptune to Poseidon as god of the sea, and so on. The Roman religion, like the Greek, had no dogmas or sacraments or belief in rewards and punishments in an afterlife.

But there were significant differences also. The Roman religion was distinctly more political and less humanist in purpose. It served not to glorify humanity or establish a comfortable relationship between human beings and their world but to protect the state from its enemies

---

[1] Theodor Mommsen, *The History of Rome,* I, 313.

Intervention of Jupiter. This scene from the first century A.D. depicts Jupiter, god of the sky, supporting the Romans in a battle against Germanic barbarians.

and to augment its power and prosperity. The gods were less human; indeed, it was only as a result of Greek and Etruscan influences that they were made personal deities at all, having previously been worshiped as animistic spirits. The Romans never conceived of their deities as quarreling among themselves or mingling with human beings after the fashion of the Homeric divinities. Finally, the Roman religion contained a much stronger element of priestliness than the Greek. The priests, or pontiffs as they were called, formed an organized class, a branch of the government itself. They not only supervised the offering of sacrifices, they were also guardians of an elaborate body of sacred traditions and laws which they alone could interpret. It must be understood, however, that these pontiffs were not priests in the sense of intermediaries between the individual Roman and the gods; they heard no confessions, forgave no sins, and administered no sacraments.

The morality of the Romans in this as in later periods had almost no connection with religion. The Romans did not ask their gods to make them good, but to bestow upon the community and upon their families material blessings. Morality was a matter of patriotism and of respect for authority and tradition. The chief virtues were bravery, honor, self-discipline, reverence for the gods and for one's ancestors, and duty to country and family. Loyalty to Rome took precedence over everything else. For the good of the state the citizen had to be ready to sacrifice not only his own life but, if necessary, the lives of his family and friends. The courage of certain consuls who dutifully put their sons to death for breaches of military discipline was a subject of

Morality in the Early Republic

profound admiration. Few peoples in European history with the exception of the Spartans and modern totalitarians have ever taken the problems of national interest so seriously or subordinated the individual so completely to the welfare of the state.

3. THE FATEFUL WARS WITH CARTHAGE

The beginning of imperialism on a major scale

By 265 B.C. Rome had conquered and annexed almost the entire Italian mainland. Proud and confident of its strength, it was almost certain to strike out into new fields of empire. The prosperous island of Sicily was not yet within its grasp, nor could it regard with indifference the situation in other parts of the Mediterranean world. Rome was now prone to interpret almost any change in the status quo as a threat to its own power and security. It was for such reasons that Rome soon became involved in a series of wars with other great nations which decidedly altered the course of its history.

Carthage

The first and most important of these wars was the struggle with Carthage, a great maritime empire that stretched along the northern coast of Africa from modern-day Tunisia to the Strait of Gibraltar. Carthage had originally been founded about 800 B.C. as a Phoenician colony. In the sixth century it severed its ties with the homeland and gradually developed into a rich and powerful state. The prosperity of its upper classes was founded upon commerce and upon exploitation of the silver and tin resources of Spain and the tropical products of north central Africa. Carthaginian government was oligarchic. The real rulers were thirty merchant princes who constituted an inner council of the Senate. These men controlled elections and dominated every other branch of the government. The remaining 270 members of the Senate appear to have been summoned to meet only on special occasions. In spite of these political deficiencies and a cruel religion that demanded blood sacrifices, Carthage had a civilization superior in luxury and scientific attainment to that of Rome when the struggle between the two states began.

Causes of the First Punic War

The initial clash with Carthage started in 264 B.C.[2] The primary cause was Roman jealousy over Carthaginian expansion in Sicily. Carthage already controlled the western portion of the island and was threatening the Greek cities of Syracuse and Messina on the eastern coast. If these cities were captured, all chances of Roman occupation of Sicily would be lost. Faced with this danger, Rome declared war upon Carthage with the hope of forcing it back into its African domain. Twenty-three years of fighting finally brought victory to the Roman generals. Carthage was compelled to surrender its possessions in Sicily and to pay a very large indemnity.

[2] The wars with Carthage are known as the Punic Wars. The Romans called the Carthaginians *Poeni,* i.e., Phoenicians, whence is derived the adjective "Punic."

But the Romans had exerted such heroic efforts to defeat Carthage that when victory was finally secured it made them more arrogant and acquisitive than ever. As a result, the struggle with Carthage was renewed on two subsequent occasions. In 218 B.C., the Romans interpreted the Carthaginian attempt to rebuild an empire in Spain as a threat to their interests and responded with a declaration of war. This struggle raged through a period of sixteen years. Italy was ravaged by the armies of Hannibal, the famous Carthaginian commander, who crossed the Alps with sixty elephants, and whose tactics have been copied by military experts to the present day. Rome escaped defeat by the narrowest of margins. Only the durability of its system of alliances in Italy saved the day. As long as these alliances held, Hannibal dared not besiege the city of Rome itself for fear of being attacked from the rear. In the end Carthage was more completely humbled than before, being compelled to abandon all its possessions except the capital city and its surrounding territory in Africa, and to pay an indemnity three times greater than that paid at the end of the First Punic War.

Roman vindictiveness reached its peak about the middle of the second century B.C. By this time Carthage had recovered a modicum of its former prosperity—enough to excite the displeasure of its conquerors. Nothing would now satisfy the senatorial magnates but the complete destruction of Carthage and the expropriation of its land. In 149 B.C. the Senate dispatched an ultimatum demanding that the Carthaginians abandon their city and settle at least ten miles from the coast. Since this demand was tantamount to a death sentence for a nation dependent upon commerce, it was refused—as the Romans probably hoped it would be. The result was the Third Punic War, a brutal conflict which was fought between 149 and 146 B.C. The final Roman assault upon the city was carried into the houses of the inhabitants and a frightful butchery took place. When the victorious Roman general saw Carthage going up in flames he said: "It is a glorious moment, but I have a strange feeling that some day the same fate will befall my own homeland." With the resistance of the Carthaginians finally broken, the few citizens left to surrender were sold into slavery, their once magnificent city was razed, and the ground was plowed over with salt. Carthaginian territory was then organized into a Roman province, with the best areas parceled out as senatorial estates.

The wars with Carthage had momentous effects on Rome. First, victory in the Second Punic War led to Roman occupation of Spain. This not only brought great new wealth—above all from Spanish silver—but was the beginning of a policy of westward expansion that proved to be one of the great formative influences on the history of Europe. Then too the wars brought Rome into conflict with eastern Mediterranean powers and thereby paved the way for still greater dominion. During the Second Punic War, Philip V of Macedon had entered into an alliance with Carthage and had plotted with the king of Syria to divide Egypt between them. In order to forestall the execu-

The Second Punic War

Hannibal. A coin from Carthage representing Hannibal as a victorious general, with an elephant on the reverse.

The Third Punic War and the destruction of Carthage

See color map facing page 161

Results of the wars with Carthage: (1) conquest of Spain and the Hellenistic East

tion of Philip's plans, Rome sent an army into the East. The result was
the conquest of Greece and Asia Minor and the establishment of a protectorate over Egypt. Thus before the end of the second century B.C.
virtually the entire Mediterranean area had been brought under
Roman control. The conquest of the Hellenistic East led to the introduction of Greek ideas and customs into Rome. Despite formidable
resistance, these novelties exerted considerable influence in changing
some aspects of social and cultural life.

Still another effect of the Punic Wars was a great social and economic revolution that swept over Rome in the third and second centuries B.C. The changes wrought by this revolution may be enumerated as follows: (1) a marked increase in slavery due to the capture
and sale of prisoners of war; (2) the decline of the small farmer as a
result of the establishment of the plantation system in conquered areas
and the influx of cheap grain from the provinces; (3) the growth of a
disgruntled urban element composed of impoverished farmers and
workers displaced by slave labor; (4) the appearance of a middle class
comprising merchants, moneylenders, and men who held government contracts to operate mines, build roads, or collect taxes; and (5)
an increase in luxury and vulgar display, particularly among the newly
rich who fattened themselves on the profits of war.

*Cato's attempt to prevent
the transformation of
Roman society*

As a consequence of this social and economic revolution, Rome was
changed from a republic of yeoman farmers into a complex society
with new habits of luxury and indulgence. Though property had
never been evenly distributed, the gulf which separated rich and poor
now yawned more widely than before. The old-fashioned ideals of
discipline and devotion to the service of the state were weakened, and
people began to live more for pleasure. A few members of the senatorial aristocracy exerted efforts to check these tendencies and to restore
the simple virtues of the past. The leader of this movement was the
dour Cato the Elder, who inveighed against the new rich for their soft
living and strove to set an example to his countrymen by performing
hard labor on his farm and dwelling in a house with a dirt floor and no
plaster on the walls. In addition he was a prude who showed contempt
for women and boasted that his wife never came into his arms except
during great thunder. Cato also strove, often cantankerously, to prevent the influx of Greek intellectual influences. But his efforts on all
fronts had no lasting effect because the clock could not be turned back.

4. THE SOCIAL STRUGGLES OF THE LATE REPUBLIC

The period from the end of the Punic Wars in 146 B.C. to about 30 B.C.
was one of the most turbulent in the history of Rome. It was between
these years that the nation reaped the full harvest of the seeds of violence sown during the wars of conquest. Bitter class conflicts, assassinations, desperate struggles between rival dictators, wars, and insur-

rections were the all too common occurrences of this time. Even the slaves contributed to the general disorder: first, in 104 B.C. when they ravaged Sicily; and again in 73 B.C. when 70,000 of them under the leadership of a slave named Spartacus held the consuls at bay for more than a year. Spartacus was finally slain in battle and 6,000 of his followers were captured and left crucified along the length of a long road to provide a warning for others.

The first stage in the conflict between classes of citizens began with the revolt of the Gracchi brothers. The Gracchi were leaders of the liberal, pro-Greek elements in Rome and had the support of the middle classes and a number of influential senators as well. Though of aristocratic lineage themselves, they strove for a program of reforms to alleviate the country's ills. They considered these to be a result of the decline of the free peasantry, and proposed the simple remedy of dividing state lands among the landless. The first of the brothers to take up the cause of reform was Tiberius. Elected tribune in 133 B.C., he proposed a law that restricted the current renters or holders of state lands to a maximum of 640 acres. The excess was to be confiscated by the government and given to the poor in small plots. Conservative aristocrats bitterly opposed this proposal and brought about its veto by Tiberius's colleague in the tribunate, Octavius. Tiberius removed Octavius from office, and when his own term expired attempted to stand for reelection. Both of these moves were unconstitutional and gave the conservative senators an excuse for violence. Armed with clubs, they went on a rampage during the elections and murdered Tiberius and 300 of his followers.

*The revolt of the Gracchi:
the land program of
Tiberius*

Nine years later Gaius Gracchus, the younger brother of Tiberius, renewed the struggle for reform. Though Tiberius's land law had finally been enacted by the Senate, Gaius believed that the campaign had to go further. Elected tribune in 123 B.C., and reelected in 122, he procured the enactment of various laws for the benefit of the less privileged. The first provided for stabilizing the price of grain in Rome. For this purpose great public granaries were built along the Tiber. A second law proposed to extend the franchise to Roman allies, giving them the rights of Latin citizens. Still a third gave the middle class the right to make up the juries that tried governors accused of exploiting the provinces. These and similar measures provoked so much anger and contention among the classes that civil war broke out. Gaius was proclaimed an enemy of the state, and the Senate authorized the consuls to take all necessary steps for the defense of the Republic. In the ensuing conflict Gaius committed suicide and about 3,000 of his followers were killed.

*Gaius Gracchus and the
renewed fight for reform*

The Gracchan revolt had a broad significance. It demonstrated, first of all, that the Roman Republic had outgrown its constitution. Over the years the assembly had gained powers almost equal to those of the Senate. Instead of working out a peaceful accommodation to these changes, both sides resorted to violence. By so doing they set a prece-

*Significance of the
Gracchan revolt*

Pompey

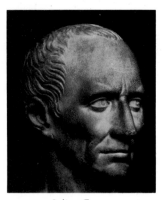

Julius Caesar

Pompey and Julius Caesar

See color map facing page 161

dent for the unbridled use of force by any politician ambitious for supreme power and thereby paved the way for the destruction of the Republic. The Romans had shown a remarkable capacity for organizing an empire and for adapting the Greek idea of a city-state to a large territory, but the narrow conservatism of their upper classes was a fatal hindrance to the health of the state. Regarding all reform as evil, they failed to understand the reasons for internal discord and seemed to think that repression was its only remedy.

After the downfall of the Gracchi, two military leaders who had won fame in foreign wars successively made themselves rulers of the state. The first was Marius, who was elevated to the consulship by the masses in 107 B.C. and reelected six times thereafter. Unfortunately, Marius was no statesman and accomplished nothing for his followers beyond demonstrating the ease with which a general with an army at his back could override opposition. Following his death in 86 B.C. the aristocrats took a turn at government by force. Their champion was Sulla, another victorious commander. Appointed dictator in 82 B.C. for an unlimited term, Sulla ruthlessly proceeded to exterminate his opponents and to restore to the Senate its original powers. Even the senatorial veto over acts of the assembly was revived, and the authority of the tribunes was sharply curtailed. After three years of rule Sulla decided to exchange the pomp of power for the pleasures of the senses and retired to a life of luxury and ease on his country estate.

It was not to be expected that the "reforms" of Sulla would stand unchallenged after he had relinquished his office, for the effect of his decrees was to give control to a selfish aristocracy. Several new leaders now emerged to espouse the cause of the people. The most famous of them were Pompey (106–48 B.C.) and Julius Caesar (100–44 B.C.). For a time they pooled their energies and resources in a plot to gain control of the government, but later they became rivals and sought to outdo each other in bids for popular support. Pompey won fame as the conqueror of Syria and Palestine, while Caesar devoted his talents to a series of brilliant forays against the Gauls, adding to the Roman state the territory of modern Belgium, Germany west of the Rhine, and France. In 52 B.C., after a series of mob disorders in Rome, the Senate turned to Pompey and caused his election as sole consul. Caesar, stationed in Gaul, was eventually branded an enemy of the state, and Pompey conspired with the senatorial faction to deprive him of political power. The result was a deadly war between the two men. In 49 B.C. Caesar crossed the Rubicon River into Italy (ever since then an image for a fateful decision) and marched on Rome. Pompey fled to the East in the hope of gathering an army large enough to regain control of Italy. In 48 B.C. the forces of the two rivals met at Pharsalus in Greece. Pompey was defeated and soon afterward was murdered by agents of the ruler of Egypt.

Caesar then intervened in Egyptian politics at the court of Cleopatra (whom he left pregnant). Then he conducted another military campaign in Asia Minor in which victory was so swift that he could report "I came, I saw, I conquered" (*veni, vidi, vici*). After that Caesar returned to Rome. There was now no one who dared to challenge his power. With the aid of his veterans he cowed the Senate into granting his every desire. In 46 B.C. he became dictator for ten years, and two years later for life. In addition, he assumed nearly every other title that could augment his power. He obtained from the Senate full authority to make war and peace and to control the revenues of the state. For all practical purposes he was above the law, and the other agents of the government were merely his servants. Unquestionably he had little respect for the constitution, and rumors spread that he intended to make himself king. At any rate, it was on such a charge that he was assassinated on the Ides of March in 44 B.C. by a group of conspirators, under the leadership of Brutus and Cassius, who hoped to rid Rome of the dictatorship.

Although Caesar used to be revered by historians as a superhuman hero, it is now customary to dismiss him as insignificant. But both extremes of interpretation should be avoided. Certainly he did not "save Rome" and was not the greatest statesman of all time, for he treated the Republic with contempt and made the problem of governing more difficult for those who came after him. Yet some of the measures he took as dictator did have lasting effects. With the aid of a Greek astronomer he revised the calendar so as to make a year last for 365 days (with an extra day added every fourth year). This "Julian" calendar—subject to adjustments made by Pope Gregory XIII in 1582—is still with us. It is thus only proper that the seventh month is named after Julius as "July." By conferring citizenship upon thousands of Spaniards and Gauls, Caesar took an important step toward eliminating the distinction between Italians and provincials. He also helped relieve economic inequities by settling many of his veterans and some of the urban poor on unused lands. Vastly more important than these reforms, however, was Caesar's far-sighted resolve, made before he seized power, to invest his efforts in the West. While Pompey, and before him Alexander, went to the East to gain fame and fortune, Caesar was the first great leader to recognize the potential significance of northwestern Europe. By incorporating Gaul into the Roman world he brought Rome great agricultural wealth and helped bring urban life and culture to what was then the wild West. Western European civilization, later to be anchored in just those regions that Caesar conquered, might not have been the same without him.

Caesar's achievements

Ides of March Coin. This coin was struck by Brutus to commemorate the assassination of Julius Caesar. Brutus is depicted on the obverse; on the reverse is a liberty cap between two daggers and the Latin abbreviation for the Ides of March.

5. ROME BECOMES SOPHISTICATED

The culture that Rome brought to Gaul was itself taken from the Greek East. During the last two centuries of republican history Rome came under the influence of Hellenistic civilization. The result was a flowering of intellectual activity and a further impetus to social change beyond what the Punic Wars had produced. The fact must be noted, however, that several of the components of the Hellenistic pattern of culture were never adopted by the Romans. The science of the Hellenistic Age, for example, was largely ignored, and the same was true of some of its art.

One of the most notable effects of Hellenistic influence was the adoption of Epicureanism and, above all, Stoicism by numerous Romans of the upper classes. The most renowned of the Roman exponents of Epicureanism was Lucretius (98–55 B.C.), author of a book-length philosophical poem entitled *On the Nature of Things*. In writing this work Lucretius was moved to explain the universe in such a way as to remove all fear of the supernatural, which he regarded as the chief obstacle to peace of mind. Worlds and all things in them, he taught, are the results of fortuitous combinations of atoms. Though he admitted the existence of the gods, he conceived of them as living in eternal peace, neither creating nor governing the universe. Everything is a product of mechanical evolution, including human beings, and their habits, institutions, and beliefs. Since mind is indissolubly linked with matter, death means utter extinction; consequently, no part of the human personality can survive to be rewarded or punished in an afterlife. Lucretius's conception of the good life was simple: what one needs, he asserted, is not enjoyment but "peace and a pure heart." Whether one agrees with Lucretius's philosophy or not, there is no doubt that he was an extraordinarily fine poet. In fact his musical cadences, sustained majesty of expression, and infectious enthusiasm earn him a rank among the greatest poets who ever lived.

Stoicism was introduced into Rome about 140 B.C. and soon came to include among its converts numerous influential leaders of public life. The greatest of these was Cicero (106–43 B.C.), the "father of Roman eloquence." Although Cicero adopted doctrines from a number of philosophers, including both Plato and Aristotle, he derived more of his ideas from the Stoics than from any other source. Cicero's ethical philosophy was based on the Stoic premises that virtue is sufficient for happiness and that tranquility of mind is the highest good. He conceived of the ideal human being as one who has been guided by reason to an indifference toward sorrow and pain. Where Cicero diverged from the Greek Stoics was in his greater approval of the active, political life. To this degree he still spoke for the older Roman tradition of service to the state. Cicero never claimed to be an original philosopher but rather conceived his goal to be that of bringing the best of Greek philosophy to the West. In this he was remarkably successful, for he wrote in a rich and elegant Latin prose style that has never been surpassed. Cicero's prose immediately became a standard for composition and has remained so until the present century. Thus even though not a truly great thinker Cicero was the most influential Latin transmitter of ancient thought to the medieval and modern western European worlds.

Lucretius and Cicero were the two leading exponents of Greek thought but not the only two fine writers of the later Roman Republic. It now became the fashion among the upper classes to learn Greek and to strive to reproduce in Latin some of the more popular forms of Greek literature. Some results of enduring literary merit were the ribald comedies of Plautus (257?–184 B.C.), the passionate love poems of Catullus (84?–54? B.C.), and the crisp military memoirs of Julius Caesar, the opening of which all beginning students of Latin used to know as well as the pledge of allegiance.

Roman literary achievements

The conquest of the Hellenistic world accelerated the process of social change which the Punic Wars had begun. The effects were most clearly evident in the growth of luxury, in a widened cleavage between classes, and in a further increase in slavery. The Italian people, numbering about eight million at the end of the Republic, had come to be divided into four main castes: the aristocracy, the equestrians, the common citizens, and the slaves. The aristocracy included the senatorial class with a total membership of 300 citizens and their families. The majority of them inherited their status, although occasionally a plebeian would gain admission to the Senate through serving a term as consul. Most of the aristocrats gained their living as office-holders and as owners of great landed estates. The equestrian order was made up of government contractors, bankers, and the wealthier merchants. Originally this class had been composed of those citizens with incomes sufficient to enable them to serve in the cavalry at their own ex-

Social conditions in the late Republic

Left: *Atrium of an Upper-class House in Pompeii, Seen from the Interior.* Around the atrium or central court were grouped suites of living rooms. The marble columns and decorated walls still give an idea of the luxury and refinement enjoyed by the privileged minority. Right: *Orpheus Floor Mosaic.* This luxurious adornment to an upper-class Roman dwelling, in what is today Arles in southern France, represents the inspired musician soothing lions and tigers as well as numerous other representatives of the animal kingdom.

pense, but the term equestrian had now come to be applied to all outside of the senatorial class who possessed property in substantial amount. The equestrians were the chief offenders in the indulgence of vulgar tastes and in the exploitation of the poor and the provincials. As bankers they regularly charged exorbitant interest rates whenever they could get them. By far the largest number of the citizens were mere commoners or plebeians. Some of these were independent farmers, a few were industrial workers, but the majority were members of the city mob. When Julius Caesar became dictator, 320,000 citizens were receiving free grain from the state.

The status of the slaves

The Roman slaves were scarcely considered people at all but instruments of production like cattle or horses to be worked for the profit of their masters. Notwithstanding the fact that some of them were cultivated foreigners taken as prisoners of war, they had none of the privileges granted to slaves in Athens. The policy of many of their owners was to get as much work out of them as possible during their prime and then to turn them loose to be fed by the state when they became old and useless. Of course, there were exceptions, especially as a result of the civilizing effects of Stoicism. Cicero, for example, reported himself very fond of his slaves. It is, nevertheless, a sad commentary on Roman civilization that nearly all of the productive labor in the country was done by slaves. They produced practically all of the nation's food supply, for the amount contributed by the few surviving independent farmers was quite insignificant. At least 80 percent of the workers employed in shops were slaves or former slaves. But many of the members of the servile population were engaged in nonproductive activities. A lucrative form of investment for the business classes was ownership of slaves trained as gladiators, who could be rented to the government or to aspiring politicians for the amusement of the people. The growth of luxury also required the employment of thousands of slaves in domestic service. The man of great wealth must have his doorkeepers, his litter-bearers, his couriers (for the government of the Republic had no postal service), his valets, and his tutors for his children. In some great households there were special servants with no other duties than to rub the master down after his bath or to care for his sandals.

Changes in religion

The religious beliefs of the Romans were altered in various ways in the last two centuries of the Republic—again mainly because of the extension of Roman power over most of the Hellenistic states. First of all, the upper classes tended to abandon the traditional religion for the philosophies of Stoicism and, to a lesser degree, Epicureanism. But many of the common people also found worship of the ancient gods no longer satisfying because it was too formal and mechanical and demanded too much in the way of duty and self-sacrifice to meet their needs. Furthermore, Italy had attracted a stream of immigrants from the East, most of whom had a religious background totally different from that of the Romans. The result was the spread of Eastern mystery cults, which satisfied the craving for a more emotional religion and offered the reward of immortality to the wretched and downtrodden of the earth. From Egypt came the cult of Osiris (or Serapis, as the god was now more commonly called), while from Phrygia in Asia Minor was introduced the worship of the Great Mother, with her eunuch priests and wild, symbolic orgies. So strong was the appeal of these cults that the decrees of the Senate against them proved almost impossible to enforce. In the last century B.C. the Persian cult of Mithraism, which came to surpass all the others in popularity, gained a foothold in Italy.

6. THE PRINCIPATE OR EARLY EMPIRE (27 B.C.–180 A.D.)

Shortly before his death in 44 B.C., Julius Caesar had adopted as his sole heir his grandnephew Octavian (63 B.C.–14 A.D.), then a young man of eighteen quietly pursuing his studies in Illyria across the Adriatic Sea. Upon learning of his uncle's death, Octavian hastened to Rome to take control of the government. He soon found that he had to share his ambition with two of Caesar's powerful friends, Mark Antony and Lepidus. The following year the three men formed an alliance for the purpose of crushing the power of the aristocratic group responsible for Caesar's murder. The methods employed were not to the new leaders' credit. Prominent members of the aristocracy were hunted down and slain and their property confiscated. The most noted of the victims was Cicero, brutally slain by Mark Antony's thugs though he had taken no part in the conspiracy against Caesar's life. The real murderers, Brutus and Cassius, escaped and organized an army, but were finally defeated by Octavian and his colleagues near Philippi in 42 B.C.

An alliance to avenge Caesar's death

Thereafter a quarrel developed between the members of the alliance, inspired primarily by Antony's jealousy of Octavian. The subsequent struggle became a contest between East and West. Antony went to the East and made an alliance with Cleopatra that was dedicated to introducing principles of Oriental despotism into Roman rule. Octavian consolidated the forces of the West and came forward as the champion of Greek cultural traditions. As in the earlier contest between Caesar and Pompey the victory again went to the West. In the naval battle of Actium (31 B.C.) Octavian's forces defeated those of Antony and Cleopatra, both of whom soon afterward committed suicide. It was now clear that Rome would not be swallowed up by the East. Actium guaranteed that there would be several more centuries for the consolidation of Greek ideals and urban life, a development important above all for the future of western Europe.

The victory of Octavian ushered in a new period in Roman history, the most glorious and the most prosperous that the nation experienced. Although problems of peace and order were still far from being

Enchained Crocodile. This bizarre coin from the Roman city of Nîmes in southern France symbolizes Augustus's victory at Actium. The crocodile stands for Egyptian prisoners whom Augustus sent as colonists to Nîmes.

completely solved, the deadly civil strife was over, and the people now had their first opportunity to show what their talents could achieve. Octavian was determined to preserve the forms if not the substance of constitutional government. He accepted the titles of Augustus and emperor (which then only meant "victorious general") conferred upon him by the Senate and the army. He held the authority of proconsul and tribune permanently; but he refused to make himself dictator or even consul for life, despite the pleas of the populace that he do so. In his view the Senate and the people were the supreme sovereigns, as they had been under the early Republic. The title by which he preferred to have his authority designated was princeps, or first citizen of the state. For this reason the period of his rule and that of his successors is properly called the Principate, or early Empire, to distinguish it from the periods of the Republic (sixth century B.C. to 27 B.C.), the time of upheavals (180 A.D. to 284 A.D.), and the period of the late Empire (284 A.D. to 610 A.D.).

Octavian, or Augustus as he was now more commonly called, ruled over Italy and the provinces for forty-four years (31 B.C.–14 A.D.). At the beginning of the period he governed by military power and by common consent, but in 27 B.C. the Senate bestowed upon him the series of offices and titles described above. His work as a statesman at least equaled in importance that of Julius Caesar. Among the reforms of Augustus were the establishment of a new coinage system, the creation of a centralized system of courts under his own supervision, and the bestowal of a large measure of local self-government upon cities and provinces. He insisted upon experience and intelligence as qualifi-

The Emperor Augustus Receiving the Submission of German Barbarians. A drinking cup of the first century A.D.

cations for appointment to administrative office. By virtue of his pro-consular authority he assumed direct control over the provincial governors and punished them severely for graft and extortion. He abolished the old system of farming out the collection of taxes in the provinces, which had led to great abuses, and appointed his own personal representatives as collectors at regular salaries. But he did not stop with political reforms. He enacted laws designed to check the more glaring social and moral evils of the time. By his own example of temperate living he sought to discourage luxurious habits and to set the precedent for a return to the ancient virtues.

After the death of Augustus in 14 A.D. until almost the end of the century Rome had no really capable rulers, with the single exception of Claudius (41–54). Several of Augustus's successors, most infamously Caligula (37–41) and Nero (54–68), were brutal tyrants who squandered the resources of the state and kept the city of Rome in an uproar by their deeds of bloody violence. But starting in 96 A.D., a period of strong and stable government returned with the advent of "five good emperors": Nerva (96–98), Trajan (98–117), Hadrian (117–138), Antoninus Pius (138–161), and Marcus Aurelius (161–180). These five ruled in harmony with the Senate, displayed great gifts as administrators, and, each in their turn, were able to bequeath a well-ordered and united realm to their designated successors.

Augustus

From the time of Augustus until that of Trajan, the Roman Empire continued to expand. Augustus gained more land for Rome than did any other Roman ruler. His generals advanced into central Europe, conquering the territories known today as Switzerland, Austria, and Bulgaria. Only in modern-day central Germany did Roman troops meet defeat, a setback which convinced Augustus to hold the Roman borders at the Rhine and Danube. Subsequently, in 43 A.D., the Emperor Claudius began the conquest of Britain, and at the beginning of the next century Trajan pushed beyond the Danube to add Dacia (now Rumania) to the Roman realms. Trajan also conquered territories in Mesopotamia but thereby incurred the enmity of the Persians, causing his successor Hadrian to embark on a defensive policy. The Roman Empire had now reached its ultimate territorial limits; in the third century these limits would begin to recede.

Trajan

Rome's peaceful sway over a vast empire for about two centuries from the time of Augustus to that of Marcus Aurelius was certainly one of its most impressive accomplishments. As the historian Gibbon said, "the Empire of Rome comprehended the fairest part of the earth and the most civilized portion of mankind." The celebrated *Pax Romana,* or Roman peace, was unprecedented. The Mediterranean was now under the control of one power (as it has never been before or since) and experienced the passage of centuries without a single naval battle. On land one rule held without contention from the borders of Scotland to those of Persia. A contemporary orator justly boasted that "the whole civilized world lays down the arms which were its ancient

The Pax Romana

load, as if on holiday . . . all places are full of gymnasia, fountains, monumental approaches, temples, workshops, schools; one can say that the civilized world, which had been sick from the beginning . . . , has been brought by the right knowledge to a state of health." But much of this health, as we will see, proved illusory.

7. CULTURE AND LIFE IN THE PERIOD OF THE PRINCIPATE

Cultural progress under the Principate

From the standpoint of variety of intellectual and artistic interests the period of the Principate outshone all other ages in the history of Rome. From 27 B.C. to about 200 A.D. Roman philosophy attained its most characteristic form. The same period also witnessed the production of outstanding literary works, the growth of a distinctive architecture and art, and the greatest triumphs of Roman engineering.

Roman Stoicism

The form of philosophy that appealed most strongly to the Romans was Stoicism. The reasons for Stoicism's popularity are easy to discover. With its emphasis upon duty, self-discipline, and subjection to the natural order of things, it accorded well with the ancient virtues of the Romans and with their habits of conservatism. Moreover, its insistence upon civic obligations and its doctrine of cosmopolitanism appealed to the Roman political-mindedness and pride in world empire. It is necessary to observe, however, that the Stoicism developed in the days of the Principate was somewhat different from that of Zeno and his school. The old physical theories borrowed from Heraclitus were now discarded and replaced by a broader interest in politics and ethics. Roman Stoicism also tended to assume a more distinctly religious tone than that which had characterized the original philosophy.

See color map facing page 193

Three eminent apostles of Stoicism lived and taught in Rome in the

Marcus Aurelius. The mounted figure of the emperor-philosopher, now standing on the Piazza del Campidoglio in Rome, is the only full-sized equestrian statue surviving from the ancient world. The Christians destroyed other such statues because they seemed to stand for ruler worship, but they saved this one on the mistaken assumption that it represented Constantine, the first Christian Roman emperor.

two centuries that followed the rule of Augustus: Seneca (4 B.C.–65 A.D.), millionaire adviser for a time to Nero; Epictetus, the slave (60?–120 A.D.); and the Emperor Marcus Aurelius (121–180 A.D.). All of them agreed that inner serenity is the ultimate goal to be sought, that true happiness can be found only in surrender to the benevolent order of the universe. They preached the ideal of virtue for virtue's sake, deplored the sinfulness of human nature, and urged obedience to conscience as the voice of duty. Seneca and Epictetus adulterated their philosophy with such deep mystical yearnings as to make it almost a religion. They worshiped the cosmos as divine, governed by an all-powerful Providence who ordains all that happens for ultimate good. The last of the Roman Stoics, Marcus Aurelius, was more fatalistic and less hopeful. Although he did not reject the conception of an or-dered and rational universe, he shared neither the faith nor the dogma-tism of the earlier Stoics. He was confident of no blessed immortality to balance the sufferings of one's earthly career and was inclined to think of humans as creatures buffeted by evil fortune for which no dis-tant perfection of the whole could fully atone. He urged, nevertheless, that people should continue to live nobly, that they should neither abandon themselves to gross indulgence nor break down in angry protest, but that they should derive what contentment they could from dignified resignation to suffering and tranquil submission to death.

The literary achievements of the Romans bore a definite relation to their philosophy. This was especially true of the works of the most distinguished writers of the Augustan Age. Horace (65–8 B.C.), for ex-ample, in his famous *Odes* drew copiously from the teachings of both Epicureans and Stoics. He confined his attention, however, to their doctrines of a way of life, for like most of the Romans he had little cu-riosity about the workings of the universe. He developed a philosophy which combined the Epicurean justification of pleasure with the Stoic bravery in the face of trouble. While he never reduced pleasure to the mere absence of pain, he was sophisticated enough to know that the highest enjoyment is possible only through the exercise of rational control.

Virgil (70–19 B.C.) likewise reflects a measure of the philosophical temper of his age. Though his *Eclogues* convey something of the Epi-curean ideal of quiet pleasure, Virgil was much more of a Stoic. His utopian vision of an age of peace and abundance, his brooding sense of the tragedy of human fate, and his idealization of a life in harmony with nature indicate an intellectual heritage similar to that of Seneca and Epictetus. Virgil's most noted work, the *Aeneid,* like several of the *Odes* of Horace glorified Roman imperialism. The *Aeneid* in fact was an epic of empire recounting the toils and triumphs of the found-ing of the state, its glorious traditions, and its magnificent destiny. Other major writers of the Augustan Age were Ovid (43 B.C.?–17 A.D.) and Livy (59 B.C.–17 A.D.). The former was the chief representative of the cynical and individualist tendencies of his day. His brilliant and witty writings often reflected the dissolute tastes of the time. The chief claim of Livy to fame rests upon his skill as a prose stylist. As a historian he was woefully deficient. His main work, a history of Rome, is replete with dramatic and picturesque narrative, designed to appeal to the patriotic emotions rather than to present an accurate record of events.

Petronius, Apuleius, Martial, Juvenal, and Tacitus

The literature of the period which followed the death of Augustus also exemplified conflicting social and intellectual tendencies. The tales of Petronius and Apuleius and the epigrams of Martial describe the more exotic and sometimes sordid aspects of Roman life. The aim of the authors is not to instruct or uplift but chiefly to tell an entertaining story or turn a witty phrase. An entirely different viewpoint is presented in the works of the other most important writers of this age: Juvenal, the satirist (60?–140 A.D.), and Tacitus, the historian (55?–117? A.D.). Juvenal wrote under the influence of the Stoics but with narrow vision. Convinced that the troubles of the nation were due to moral degeneracy, he censured the vices of his countrymen with the fury of an evangelist. A somewhat similar attitude characterized the writing of his younger contemporary, Tacitus. The best-known of Roman historians, Tacitus described the events of his age not with a view to dispassionate analysis but largely for the purpose of moral indictment. His description of the customs of the ancient Germans in his *Germania* served to heighten the contrast between the manly virtues of an unspoiled race and the effeminate vices of the decadent Romans. Whatever his failings as a historian, he was a master of ironic wit and brilliant aphorism. Referring to the boasted *Pax Romana,* he makes a barbarian chieftain say: "They create a wilderness and call it peace."

Achievements in art

Roman art first assumed its distinctive character during the period of the Principate. Before this time what passed for an art of Rome was really an importation from the Hellenistic East. Conquering armies brought back to Italy wagonloads of statues, reliefs, and marble columns as part of the plunder from Greece and Asia Minor. These became the property of wealthy businessmen and were used to embellish their sumptuous mansions. As the demand increased, hundreds of copies were made, with the result that Rome came to have by the end of the Republic a profusion of objects of art which had no more cultural significance than the Picassos in the home of some modern stockbroker. The aura of national glory which surrounded the early Principate stimulated the growth of an art that was more indigenous. Augustus himself boasted that he found Rome a city of brick and left it a city of marble. Nevertheless, much of the old Hellenistic influence remained until the talent of the Romans themselves was exhausted.

See color plates following page 192

The arts most truly expressive of the Roman character were architecture and sculpture. Architecture was monumental, designed to symbolize power and grandeur. It contained as its leading elements

The Pantheon in Rome. Built by the Emperor Hadrian it boasted the largest dome without interior supports of the ancient world. The dome forms a perfect sphere, exactly as high as it is wide.

the round arch, the vault, and the dome, although at times the Corinthian column was employed, especially in the construction of temples. The materials most commonly used were brick, squared stone blocks, and concrete, the last a Roman invention. As a further adornment of public buildings, sculptured entablatures and facades, built up of tiers of colonnades or arcades, were frequently added. Roman architecture was devoted primarily to utilitarian purposes. The foremost examples were government buildings, amphitheaters, baths, race courses, and private houses. Nearly all were of massive proportions and solid construction. Among the largest and most noted were the Pantheon, with its dome having a diameter of 142 feet, and the Colosseum, which could accommodate 65,000 spectators at the gladiatorial combats. Roman sculpture included as its main forms triumphal arches and columns, narrative reliefs, altars, and portrait busts and statues. Its distinguishing characteristics were individuality and naturalism. Sometimes Roman statues and busts served only to express the vanity of the aris-

The Baths of Caracalla, Rome. The gigantic scale is typical of late empire buildings. Elaborate and luxurious public baths like these were often presented to the public by the emperor or rich citizens. The floor plan above indicates the separate chambers for hot tub baths.

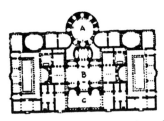

Floor Plan of the Baths of Caracalla

Pliny

tocracy, but the best Roman sculptured portraiture succeeded in conveying qualities of simple human dignity similar to those espoused in the philosophy of the Stoics.

Closely related to their achievements in architecture were Roman triumphs in engineering and public services. The imperial Romans built marvelous roads and bridges, many of which still survive. In the time of Trajan eleven aqueducts brought water into Rome from the nearby hills and provided the city with 300 million gallons daily for drinking and bathing as well as for flushing a well-designed sewage system. Water was cleverly funneled into the homes of the rich for their private gardens, fountains, and pools. Romans also established the first hospitals in the Western world and the first system of state medicine for the benefit of the poor.

For all their achievements in engineering, the Romans accomplished little in science. They excelled, as has been jokingly but not inaccurately said, in drains, not brains. Scarcely an original discovery of fundamental importance was made by anyone of Latin nationality. This fact seems strange when we consider that the Romans had the advantage of Hellenistic science as a foundation upon which to build. But they neglected their opportunity almost completely because they had no vigorous curiosity about the natural world in which they lived. Roman writers on scientific subjects were hopelessly devoid of critical intelligence. The most renowned and typical of them was Pliny the Elder (23–79 A.D.), who completed about 77 A.D. a voluminous encyclopedia of "science" which he called *Natural History*. The subjects discussed varied from cosmology to economics. Despite the wealth of material it contains, Pliny's work is of limited value, for he was totally unable to distinguish between fact and fable.

The only real scientific advance made during the period of the Principate was the work of Hellenistic scientists who lived in Italy or in the provinces. One of these was the astronomer Ptolemy, who flourished in Alexandria around the middle of the second century (see above, p. 159). Another was the physician Galen, active in Rome at various times during the latter half of the second century. While Galen's fame rests primarily on his medical encyclopedia, systematizing the learning of others, he deserves more credit for his own experiments which brought him close to a discovery of the circulation of the blood. He not only taught but proved that the arteries carry blood, and that severance of even a small one is sufficient to drain away all of the blood of the body in little more than half an hour.

Roman society exhibited the same general tendencies under the Principate as in the last days of the Republic. One of the least attractive of its traits was the low status it accorded to women. The historian M. I. Finley has remarked that the two most famous women in Roman history were Cleopatra, who was not even a Roman, and the fictional Lucretia, who earned her fame by being raped and killing herself. Seldom have women been so confined to domesticity and obscurity. Roman women did not even really have their own names but were given family names with feminine endings—for example, Julia from Julius, Claudia from Claudius, and Livia from Livius. When there were two daughters in a family they would be distinguished only as "Julia the elder" and "Julia the younger," and when several as "Julia the first," "second," and "third." Women were expected to be subservient to their fathers and husbands, were valued to the degree they produced progeny, and were expected to stay at home. A typical tomb epitaph might say: "She loved her husband . . . she bore two sons . . . she was pleasant to talk with . . . she kept the house and

Galen

Roman women

Roman Aqueduct at Segovia, Spain. Aqueducts conveyed water from mountains to the larger cities.

Gladiatorial combat

worked in wool. That is all." During the Principate Roman women from imperial families not surprisingly tried to escape these limitations by taking a backstage and often literally murderous role in politics. Less highly placed women sought outlets in the excitement of gladiatorial shows—making gladiators the equivalent of modern rock-and-roll stars—or in the ceremonies of religious cults.

Along with the confinement of women, the most serious indictment which can be brought against the age was the further growth of the passion for cruelty. Whereas the Greeks entertained themselves with theater, the Romans more and more preferred "circuses," which were really exhibitions of human slaughter. In the period of the Principate the great games and spectacles became bloodier than ever. The Romans could no longer obtain a sufficient thrill from mere exhibitions of athletic prowess: pugilists were now required to have their hands wrapped with thongs of leather loaded with iron or lead. The most popular amusement of all was watching the gladiatorial combats in the Colosseum or in other amphitheaters capable of accommodating thousands of spectators. Fights between gladiators were nothing new, but they were now presented on a much more elaborate scale. Not only the common people attended them, but wealthy aristocrats also, and frequently the head of the government himself. The

The Colosseum. Built by the Roman emperors between 75 and 80 A.D. as a place of entertainment, it was the scene of gladiatorial combats. The most common form of Greek secular architecture was the theater (see p. 134), but the most common Roman form was the amphitheater.

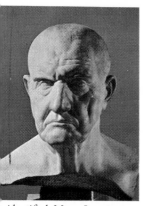

nidentified Man, I cent. B.C. *he* Romans excelled in por*aits* of sharp individuality.

Augustus, Reigned 31 B.C.–A.D. *14.* This portrait suggests the contradictory nature of the genius who gave Rome peace after years of strife.

Constantine, Reigned A.D. *306–337.* The head is from a statue sixteen feet in height.

Mummy Portrait, II cent. A.D. A Roman woman buried in Egypt.

Mosaic, I cent. A.D. A floor design composed of small pieces of colored marble fitted together to form a picture.

Wall Painting of a Satyr Mask, I cent. B.C. The belief in satyrs, thought to inhabit forests and pastures, was taken over from the Greeks.

Architectural Wall Painting from a Pompeiian Villa, I cent. B.C. Such paintings suggest the Greek origin of Roman forms of architecture.

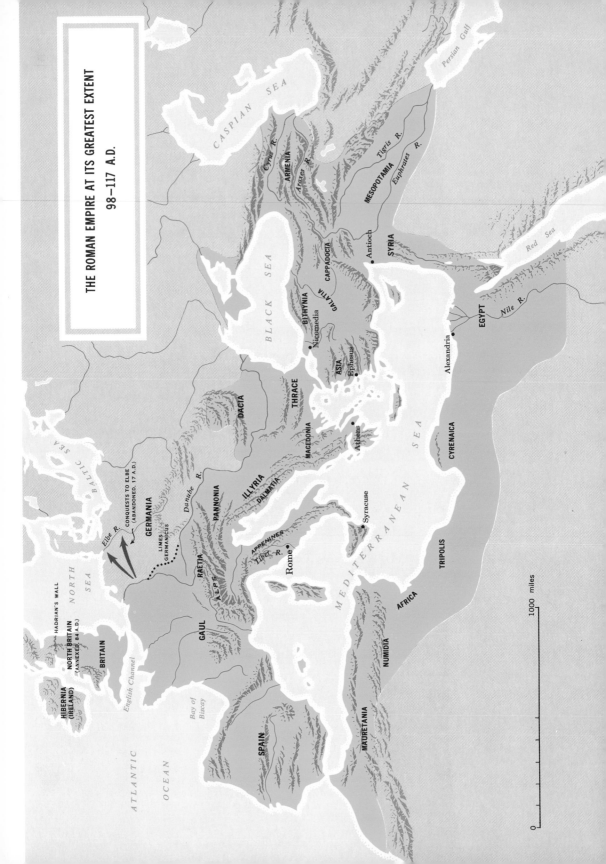

THE ROMAN EMPIRE AT ITS GREATEST EXTENT
98–117 A.D.

CASPIAN SEA

Cyrus R.

ARMENIA

Araxes R.

Tigris R.

Euphrates R.

MESOPOTAMIA

CAPPADOCIA

SYRIA

Antioch

BITHYNIA

GALATIA

Nicomedia

Persian Gulf

Red Sea

BLACK SEA

ASIA

Ephesus

EGYPT

Nile R.

Alexandria

THRACE

MACEDONIA

Athens

CYRENAICA

DACIA

ILLYRIA

DALMATIA

PANNONIA

Danube R.

Syracuse

MEDITERRANEAN SEA

GERMANIA

CONQUESTS TO ELBE
(ABANDONED, 17 A.D.)

Elbe R.

LIMES
GERMANICUS

RAETIA

APPENNINES

Tiber R.

Rome

TRIPOLIS

AFRICA

ALPS

GAUL

NUMIDIA

BALTIC SEA

NORTH SEA

HADRIAN'S WALL

NORTH BRITAIN
(ANNEXED, 84 A.D.)

BRITAIN

English Channel

Bay of Biscay

MAURETANIA

SPAIN

HIBERNIA (IRELAND)

ATLANTIC OCEAN

1000 miles

0

The Maison Carrée at Nîmes, France. The most perfect example of a Roman temple extant. Reflecting possible Etruscan influence, it was built on a high base or podium with great steps leading to the entrance. It dates from the beginning of the Christian era.

gladiators fought to the accompaniment of savage cries and curses from the audience. When one went down with a disabling wound, the crowd was asked to decide whether his life should be spared or whether the weapon of his opponent should be plunged into his heart. One contest after another, often featuring the sacrifice of men to wild animals, was staged in the course of a single exhibition. Should the arena become too sodden with blood, it was covered over with a fresh layer of sand, and the revolting performance went on. Most of the gladiators were condemned criminals or slaves, but some were volunteers even from the respectable classes. Commodus, the worthless son of Marcus Aurelius, entered the arena several times for the sake of the plaudits of the mob: this was his idea of a Roman holiday.

Notwithstanding its low moral tone, the age of the Principate was characterized by an even deeper interest in salvationist religions than that which had prevailed under the Republic. Mithraism now gained adherents by the thousands, absorbing many of the followers of the cults of the Great Mother and of Serapis. About 40 A.D. the first Christians appeared in Rome. The new sect grew steadily and eventually succeeded in displacing Mithraism as the most popular of the salvationist faiths. More will be said about its nature and success in the next chapter.

The spread of Mithraism and Christianity

The establishment of stable government by Augustus ushered in a

*Economic prosperity
during the first two
centuries*

Portrait Bust of a Roman Lady.
The ostentatiousness of upper-
class culture during the period
of the Principate is well displayed by this sculpture, done
around 90 A.D.

*The early development of
Roman law*

*Roman law under the
Principate; the great
jurists*

period of prosperity for Italy which lasted for more than two centuries. Trade was now extended to all parts of the known world, even
to Arabia, India, and China. Manufacturing increased somewhat, especially in the production of pottery, textiles, and articles of metal and
glass. In spite of all this, the economic order was far from healthy.
Prosperity was not evenly distributed but was confined primarily to
the upper classes. Since the stigma attached to manual labor persisted
as strongly as ever, production was bound to decline as the supply of
slaves diminished. Perhaps worse was the fact that Italy had a decidedly unfavorable balance of trade. The meager industrial development was by no means sufficient to provide enough articles of export
to meet the demand for luxuries imported from the provinces and
from the outside world. As a consequence, Italy was gradually drained
of its supply of precious metals. By the third century the Western
Roman economy began to collapse.

8. ROMAN LAW

There is general agreement that one of the most important legacies
which the Romans left to succeeding cultures was their system of law.
This resulted from a gradual evolution which began roughly with the
publication of the Twelve Tables about 450 B.C. In the later centuries
of the Republic the law of the Twelve Tables was modified and practically superseded by the growth of new precedents and principles.
These emanated from different sources: from changes in custom, from
the teachings of the Stoics, from the decisions of judges, but especially
from the edicts of the *praetors*. The Roman praetors were magistrates
who had authority to define and interpret the law in a particular suit
and issue instructions to the jury for the decision of the case. The jury
merely decided questions of fact; all issues of law were settled by the
praetor, and generally his interpretations became precedents for the
decision of similar cases in the future.

It was under the Principate, however, that the Roman law attained
its highest stage of development. This later progress was the result in
part of the extension of the law over a wider field of jurisdiction, over
the lives and properties of aliens in strange environments as well as
over the citizens of Italy. But the major reason was the fact that
Augustus and his successors gave to certain eminent jurists the right to
deliver opinions on the legal issues of cases under trial in the courts.
The most prominent of the men thus designated from time to time
were Gaius, Ulpian, Papinian, and Paulus. Although most of them
held high judicial office, they had gained their reputations primarily as
lawyers and writers on legal subjects. The responses of these jurists
came to embody a science and philosophy of law and were accepted as
the basis of Roman jurisprudence.

The Roman law as it was developed under the influence of the jurists comprised three great branches or divisions: the civil law, the law of peoples, and the natural law. The civil law was the law of Rome and its citizens. As such it existed in both written and unwritten forms. It included the statutes of the Senate, the decrees of the princeps, the edicts of the praetors, and also certain ancient customs operating with the force of law. The law of peoples was the law held to be common to all people regardless of nationality. This law authorized the institutions of slavery and private ownership of property and defined the principles of purchase and sale, partnership, and contract. It was not superior to the civil law but supplemented it as especially applicable to the alien inhabitants of the empire.

The most interesting and in many ways the most important branch of the Roman law was the natural law, a product not of judicial practice, but of philosophy. The Stoics had developed the idea of a rational order of nature which is the embodiment of justice and right. They had affirmed that all men are by nature equal, and that they are entitled to certain basic rights which governments have no authority to transgress. The father of the law of nature as a legal principle, however, was not one of the Hellenistic Stoics, but Cicero. "True law," he declared, "is right reason consonant with nature, diffused among all men, constant, eternal. To make enactments infringing this law, religion forbids, neither may it be repealed even in part, nor have we power through Senate or people to free ourselves from it." This law is prior to the state itself, and any ruler who defies it automatically becomes a tyrant. Most of the great jurists subscribed to conceptions of the law of nature very similar to those of the philosophers. Although the jurists did not regard this law as an automatic limitation upon the civil law, they thought of it nevertheless as a great ideal to which the statutes and decrees of men ought to conform. This development of the concept of abstract justice as a legal principle was one of the noblest achievements of the Roman civilization.

9. THE CRISIS OF THE THIRD CENTURY (180–284 A.D.)

With the death of Marcus Aurelius in 180 A.D. the period of beneficent imperial rule came to an end. One reason for the success of the "five good emperors" was that the first four designated particularly promising young men, rather than sons or close relatives, for the succession. But Marcus Aurelius broke this pattern with results that were to prove fateful. Although he was one of the most philosophic and thoughtful rulers who ever reigned, he was not wise enough to recognize that his son Commodus was a vicious incompetent. Made emperor by his father's wishes, Commodus indulged his taste for perversities, showed

Commodus. The self-deluded ruler encouraged artists to portray him as the equal of the superhuman Hercules.

open contempt for the Senate, and ruled so brutally that a palace clique finally had him murdered by strangling in 192. Matters thereafter became worse. With the lack of an obvious successor to Commodus, the armies of the provinces raised their own candidates and civil war ensued. Although a provincial general, Septimius Severus (193–211), emerged victorious, it now became clear that provincial armies could interfere in imperial politics at will. Severus and some of his successors aggravated the problem by eliminating even the theoretical rights of the Senate and ruling frankly as military dictators. Once the role of brute force was openly revealed any aspiring general could try his luck at seizing power. Hence civil war became endemic. From 235 to 284 there were no less than twenty-six "barracks emperors," of whom only one managed to escape a violent death.

Consequences of civil war

The half-century between 235 and 284 was certainly the worst for Rome since its rise to world power. In addition to political chaos, a number of other factors combined to bring the empire to the brink of ruin. One was that civil war had disastrous economic effects. Not only did constant warfare interfere with agriculture and trade, but the rivalry of aspirants to rule led them to drain the wealth of their territories in order to gain favor with their armies. Following the maxim of "enriching the soldiers and scorning the rest," they could only raise funds by debasing the coinage and by nearly confiscatory taxation of civilians. Landlords, small tenants, and manufacturers thus had little motive to produce at a time when production was most necessary. In human terms the poorest, as is usual in times of economic contraction, suffered the most. Often they were driven to the most abject destitution. In the wake of war and hunger, disease then became rampant.

Arch of Septimius Severus. This monument to the feats of Septimius Severus was constructed about 200 A.D.

Already in the reign of Marcus Aurelius a terrible plague had swept through the empire, decimating the army and the population at large. In the middle of the third century pestilence returned and struck at the population with its fearful scythe for fifteen years.

The resulting strain on human resources came at a time when Rome could least afford it, for still another threat to the empire in the middle of the third century was the advance of Rome's external enemies. With Roman ranks thinned by disease and Roman armies fighting each other, Germans in the West and Persians in the East broke through the old Roman defense lines. In 251 the Goths defeated and slew the Emperor Decius, crossed the Danube, and marauded at will in the Balkans. A more humiliating disaster came in 260 when the Emperor Valerian was captured in battle by the Persians and made to kneel as a footstool for their ruler. When he died his body was stuffed and hung on exhibition. Clearly the days of Caesar and Augustus were very far off.

The Emperor Decius. The extreme naturalism and furrowed brow is typical of the portraits of this period.

Understandably enough the culture of the third century was marked by pervasive anxiety. One can even see expressions of worry in the surviving statuary, as in the bust of the Emperor Philip (244–249) who appears almost to realize that he would soon be killed in battle. Suiting the spirit of the age, the Neoplatonic philosophy of otherworldlyism came to the fore. Neoplatonism (meaning "New Platonism") drew the spiritualist tendency of Plato's thought to extremes. The first of its basic teachings was emanationism: everything that exists proceeds from God in a continuing stream of emanations. The initial stage in the process is the emanation of the world-soul. From this come the divine Ideas or spiritual patterns, and then the souls of particular things. The final emanation is matter. But matter has no form or quality of its own; it is simply the privation of spirit, the residue which is left after the spiritual rays from God have burned themselves out. It follows that matter is to be despised as the symbol of evil and darkness. The second major doctrine was mysticism. The human soul was originally a part of God, but it has become separated from its divine source through its union with matter. The highest goal of life should be mystic reunion with the divine, which can be accomplished through contemplation and through emancipation of the soul from bondage to matter. Human beings should be ashamed of the fact that they possess a physical body and should seek to subjugate it in every way possible. Asceticism was therefore the third main teaching of this philosophy.

The Emperor Philip the Arab. An artistic legacy of the Roman "age of anxiety."

The real founder of Neoplatonism was Plotinus, who was born in Egypt about 204 A.D. In the later years of his life he taught in Rome and won many followers among the upper classes before he died in 270. His principal successors diluted the philosophy with more and more bizarre superstitions. In spite of its antirational viewpoint and its utter indifference to the state, Neoplatonism became so popular in Rome in the third and fourth centuries A.D. that it almost completely

Plotinus

supplanted Stoicism. No fact could have expressed more eloquently the turn of Rome away from the realities of the here and now.

10. CAUSES FOR ROME'S DECLINE

Turning point in 284

As Rome was not built in a day, so it was not lost in one. As we will see in the next chapter, strong rule returned in 284. Thereafter the Roman Empire endured in the West for two hundred years more and in the East for a millennium. But the restored Roman state differed greatly from the old one—so much so that it is proper to end the story of characteristically Roman civilization here and review the reasons for Rome's decline.

Theories of decline

More has been written on the fall of Rome than on the death of any other civilization. The theories offered to account for the decline have been many and varied. A popular recent one is that Rome fell from the effects of lead poisoning, but this cannot be accepted for many reasons, one of which is that most Roman pipes were not made of lead but of terracotta. Moralists have found the explanation for Rome's fall in the descriptions of lechery and gluttony presented in the writings of such authors as Juvenal and Petronius. Such an approach, however, overlooks the facts that much of this evidence is patently overdrawn, and that nearly all of it comes from the period of the early Principate: in the later centuries, when the empire was more obviously collapsing, morality became more austere through the influence of ascetic religions. One of the simplest explanations is that Rome fell only because of the severity of German attacks. But barbarians had always stood ready to attack Rome throughout its long history: German pressures indeed mounted at certain times but German invasions would never have succeeded had they not come at moments when Rome was already weakened internally.

Internal causes of decline

It is best then, to concentrate on Rome's most serious internal problems. Some of these were political. The most obvious political failing of the Roman constitution under the Principate was the lack of a clear law of succession. Especially when a ruler died suddenly there was no certainty about who was to follow him. In modern America the deaths of a Lincoln or Kennedy might shock the nation, but people at least knew what would happen next; in imperial Rome no one knew and civil war was generally the result. From 235 to 284 such warfare fed upon itself. Civil war was also nurtured by the lack of constitutional means for reform. If regimes became unpopular, as most did after 180, the only means to alter them was to overthrow them. But the resort to violence always bred more violence. In addition to those problems, imperial Rome's greatest political weakness may ultimately have been that it did not involve enough people in the work of government. The vast majority of the empire's inhabitants were subjects who did not participate in the government in any way. Hence they

Slaves Towing a Barge. This relief shows very graphically how heavily Roman civilizations relied on slave labor.

looked on the empire at best with indifference and often with hostility, especially when tax-collectors appeared. Loyalty to Rome was needed to keep the empire going, but when the tests came such loyalty was lacking.

Even without political problems the Roman Empire would probably have been fated to extinction for economic reasons. Rome's worst economic problems derived from its slave system and from manpower shortages. Roman civilization was based on cities, and Roman cities existed largely by virtue of an agricultural surplus produced by slaves. Slaves were worked so hard that they did not normally reproduce to fill their own ranks. Until the time of Trajan Roman victories in war and fresh conquests provided fresh supplies of slaves to keep the system going, but thereafter the economy began to run out of human fuel. Landlords could no longer be so profligate of human life, barracks slavery came to an end, and the countryside produced less of a surplus to feed the towns. The fact that no technological advance took up the slack may also be attributed to slavery. Later in Western history agricultural surpluses were produced by technological revolutions, but Roman landlords were indifferent to technology because interest in it was thought to be demeaning. As long as slaves were present to do the work there was no interest in labor-saving devices, and attention to any sort of machinery was deemed a sign of slavishness. Landlords proved their nobility by their interest in "higher things," but while they were contemplating these heights their agricultural surpluses gradually became depleted.

Manpower shortages greatly aggravated Rome's economic problems. With the end of foreign conquests and the decline of slavery there was a pressing need for people to stay on the farm, but because of constant barbarian pressures there was also a steady need for men to serve in the army. The plagues of the second and third centuries

Economic causes

Inadequate manpower

sharply reduced the population just at the worst time. It has been estimated that between the reign of Marcus Aurelius and the restoration of strong rule in 284 the population of the Roman Empire was reduced by one third. (Demoralization seems also to have lowered the birthrate.) The result was that there were neither sufficient forces to work the land nor men to fight Rome's enemies. No wonder Rome began to lose battles as it had seldom lost them before.

Lack of civic ideals

Enormous dedication and exertion on the part of large numbers might just possibly have saved Rome, but few were willing to work hard for the public good. For this cultural explanations may be posited. Most simply stated the Roman Empire of the third century could not draw upon commonly shared civic ideals. By then the old republican and senatorial traditions had been rendered manifestly obsolete. Worse, provincials could hardly be expected to fight or work hard for Roman ideals of any sort, especially when the Roman state no longer stood for beneficent peace but only brought recurrent war and oppressive taxation. Regional differences, the lack of public education, and social stratification were further barriers to the development of any unifying public spirit. As the empire foundered new ideals indeed emerged, but these were religious, otherworldly ones. Ultimately, then, the decline of Rome was accompanied by disinterest, and the Roman world slowly came to an end not so much with a bang as with a whimper.

11. THE ROMAN HERITAGE

Comparison of Rome with the modern world

It is tempting to believe that we today have many similarities to the Romans: first of all, because Rome is nearer to us in time than any of the other civilizations of antiquity; and second, because Rome seems to bear such a close kinship to the modern temper. The resemblances between Roman history and the history of Great Britain or the United States in the nineteenth and twentieth centuries have often been noted. The Roman economic evolution progressed all the way from a simple agrarianism to a complex urban system with problems of unemployment, gross disparities of wealth, and financial crises. The Roman Empire, in common with the British, was founded upon conquest. It must not be forgotten, however, that the heritage of Rome was an ancient heritage and that consequently, the similarities between the Roman and modern civilizations are not so important as they seem. As noted already, the Romans disdained industrial activities, and they were not interested in science. Neither did they have any idea of the modern national state; the provinces were really colonies, not integral parts of a body politic. The Romans also never developed an adequate system of representative government. Finally, the Roman conception of religion was vastly different from our own. Their system of wor-

The Forum, the Civic Center of Ancient Rome. In addition to public squares, the Forum included triumphal arches, magnificent temples, and government buildings. In the foreground is the Temple of Saturn. Behind it is the Temple of Antoninus and Faustina. The three columns at the extreme right are what is left of the Temple of Castor and Pollux, and in the farthest background is the arch of Titus.

ship, like that of the Greeks, was external and mechanical, not inward or spiritual. What Christians consider the highest ideal of piety—an emotional attitude of love for the divine—the Romans regarded as gross superstition.

Nevertheless, the civilization of Rome exerted a great influence upon later cultures. The form, if not the spirit, of Roman architecture was preserved in the ecclesiastical architecture of the Middle Ages and survives to this day in the design of many of our government buildings. The sculpture of the Augustan Age also lives on in the equestrian statues, the memorial arches and columns, and in the portraits in stone of statesmen and generals that adorn our streets and parks. Although subjected to new interpretations, the law of the great jurists became an important part of the Code of Justinian and was thus handed down to the Middle Ages and modern times. American judges frequently cite maxims originally invented by Gaius or Ulpian. Further, the legal systems of nearly all continental European countries today incorporate much of the Roman law. This law was one of the grandest of the Romans' achievements and reflected their genius for governing a vast and diverse empire. It should not be forgotten either that Roman liter-

The influence of Roman civilization

ary achievements furnished much of the inspiration for the revival of learning that spread over Europe in the twelfth century and reached its zenith in the Renaissance. Perhaps not so well known is the fact that the organization of the Catholic Church, to say nothing of part of its ritual, was adapted from the structure of the Roman state and the complex of the Roman religion. For example, the pope still bears the title of supreme pontiff (*pontifex maximus*), which was used to designate the authority of the emperor as head of the civic religion.

Rome's role as conveyor of Greek civilization

Most important of all Rome's contributions to the future was the transmission of Greek civilization to the European West. The development in Italy of a culture that was highly suffused by Greek ideals from the second century B.C. onward was in itself an important counterweight to the earlier predominance of Greek-oriented civilization in the East. Then, following the path of Julius Caesar, this culture advanced still further West. Before the coming of Rome the culture of northwestern Europe (modern France, the Benelux countries, western and southern Germany, and England) was tribal. Rome brought cities and Greek ideas, above all conceptions of human freedom and individual autonomy that went along with the development of highly differentiated urban life. It is true that ideals of freedom were often ignored in practice—they did not temper Roman dependence on slavery and subjugation of women, or prevent Roman rule in conquered territories from being exploitive and sometimes oppressive. Nonetheless, Roman history is the real beginning of Western history as we now know it. Greek civilization brought to the East by Alexander was not enduring, but the same civilization brought West by the work of such men as Caesar, Cicero, and Augustus was the starting point for many of the subsequent accomplishments of western Europe. As we will see, the development was not continuous and there were many other ingredients to later European success, but the influence of Rome was no less profound.

SELECTED READINGS

• *Items so designated are available in paperback editions.*

POLITICAL HISTORY

• Adcock, F. E., *Roman Political Ideas and Practice,* Ann Arbor, Mich., 1964.
  Bloch, Raymond, *The Origins of Rome,* New York, 1960.
  Cary, M., and H. H. Scullard, *A History of Rome,* 3rd ed., New York, 1975.
    A basic college-level textbook.
• Chambers, M., ed., *The Fall of Rome,* New York, 1970. A collection of readings on this perennially fascinating subject.
  Cowell, F. R., *Cicero and the Roman Republic,* New York, 1948.
  Grant, M., *The Etruscans,* New York, 1980.

Gruen, E. S., *The Last Generation of the Roman Republic*, Berkeley, Calif., 1964.

Haywood, R. M., *The Myth of Rome's Fall*, New York, 1962.

Mommsen, Theodor, *The History of Rome*, Chicago, 1957. An abridged reissue of one of the greatest historical works of the nineteenth century. Emphasizes personalities, especially that of Julius Caesar.

Ogilvie, R. M., *Early Rome and the Etruscans*, Atlantic Highlands, N.J., 1976. Now the best specialized review of the earliest period.

• Scullard, H. H., *From the Gracchi to Nero*, New York, 1959. Good survey of events in this central period.

Sinnigen, W., and A. E. R. Boak, *A History of Rome to A.D. 565*, 6th ed., New York, 1977. A good alternative to Cary and Scullard as a basic textbook.

• Starr, C. G., *The Emergence of Rome*, Ithaca, N.Y., 1953. A brief elementary introduction.

• Syme, Ronald, *The Roman Revolution*, New York, 1939. A pathfinding work on the late Republic and early empire that stresses power politics and the role of factions rather than the clash of institutional principles. Also extremely well written.

• Taylor, Lily Ross, *Party Politics in the Age of Caesar*, Berkeley, Calif., 1949. Still the best introduction to society and politics in the late republican period.

Warmington, B. H., *Carthage*, Baltimore, 1965.

CULTURAL AND SOCIAL HISTORY

Africa, T., *Rome of the Caesars*, New York, 1965. An entertaining approach to the history of imperial Rome by means of short biographies.

Arnold, E. V., *Roman Stoicism*, New York, 1911.

• Badian, Ernst, *Roman Imperialism in the Late Republic*, Oxford, 1967. Very sophisticated analysis.

Bailey, Cyril, ed., *The Legacy of Rome*, New York, 1924. An older collection of readings on different aspects of the Roman legacy to later times.

Balston, J. P. V. D., *Life and Leisure in Ancient Rome*, New York, 1969.

• Brunt, P. A., *Social Conflicts in the Roman Republic*, London, 1971.

• Carcopino, Jerome, *Daily Life in Ancient Rome*, New Haven, Conn., 1960.

Dill, Samuel, *Roman Society from Nero to Marcus Aurelius*, New York, 1905.

Duff, J. W., *A Literary History of Rome in the Golden Age*, New York, 1964.

———, *A Literary History of Rome in the Silver Age*, New York, 1960.

Earl, Donald, *The Moral and Political Tradition of Rome*, Ithaca, N.Y., 1967.

Frank, Tenney, *Economic History of Rome*, Baltimore, 1927. Still valuable.

Grant, M., *Roman Literature*, New York, 1954.

Laistner, M. L. W., *The Greater Roman Historians*, Berkeley, Calif., 1947.

McMullen, R., *Enemies of the Roman Order*, Cambridge, Mass., 1966.

• ———, *Roman Social Relations, 50 B.C. to A.D. 284*, New Haven, Conn., 1974.

Rostovtzeff, M. I., *Social and Economic History of the Roman Empire*, 2nd ed., 2 vols., New York, 1957. By one of the greatest historians of the early twentieth century. Important both for its interpretations and the wealth of information it contains.

• Sandbach, F. H., *The Stoics*, London, 1975.

Scullard, H. H., *The Etruscan Cities and Rome,* Ithaca, N.Y., 1967.
- Starr, C. G., *Civilization and the Caesars,* Ithaca, N.Y., 1954. Surveys Roman intellectual developments in the four centuries after Cicero.
Toynbee, A. J., *Hannibal's Legacy,* 2 vols., London, 1965.
Westermann, W. L., *The Slave Systems of Greek and Roman Antiquity,* Philadelphia, 1955. The best overview of this basic subject.
- Wheeler, Mortimer, *The Art of Rome,* New York, 1964.
Yavetz, Z., *Plebs and Princeps,* London, 1969.

SOURCE MATERIALS

Translations of Roman authors are available in the appropriate volumes of the Loeb Classical Library, Harvard University Press.

See also:

- Lewis, Naphtali, and M. Reinhold, *Roman Civilization,* 2 vols., New York, 1955.
MacKendrick, P., *The Roman Mind at Work,* Princeton, N.J., 1958.

Chapter 9

CHRISTIANITY AND THE TRANSFORMATION OF THE ROMAN WORLD

Who will hereafter credit the fact . . . that Rome has to fight within her own borders not for glory but for bare life? . . . The poet Lucan describing the power of the city in a glowing passage says: "If Rome be weak, where shall we look for strength?" We may vary his words and say: "If Rome be lost, where shall we look for help?"

For mortals this life is a race: we run it on earth that we may receive our crown elsewhere. No man can walk secure amid serpents and scorpions.

—St. Jerome, *Letters*

The Roman Empire declined after 180 A.D., but it did not collapse. In 284 the vigorous soldier-emperor Diocletian began a reorganization of the empire which gave it a new lease on life. Thereafter, throughout the fourth century the Roman state continued to surround the Mediterranean. In the fifth century the western half of the empire did fall to invading Germans, but even then Roman institutions were not entirely destroyed, and in the sixth century the eastern half of the empire managed to reconquer a good part of the western Mediterranean shoreline. Only in the seventh century did it become fully evident that the Roman Empire could only hope to survive by turning away from the West and consolidating its strength in the East. When that happened antiquity clearly came to an end.

The protracted decline of the Roman Empire

Historians used to underestimate the longevity of Roman institutions and begin their discussions of medieval history in the third, fourth, or fifth century. Since historical periodization is always approximate and depends largely on which aspects of development a historian wishes to emphasize, this approach cannot be dismissed. Certainly the transition from the ancient to the medieval world was gradual and many "medieval" ways were slowly emerging in the West

The age of late antiquity (284–610)

206

Christianity and the
Transformation of the
Roman World

as early as the third century. But it is now more customary to conceive of ancient history as continuing after 284 and lasting until the Roman Empire lost control over the Mediterranean in the seventh century. The period from 284 to about 610, although transitional (as, of course, all ages are), has certain themes of its own and is perhaps best described as neither Roman nor medieval but as the age of late antiquity.

Rise of Christianity and decline of urban life

The major cultural trend of late-antique history was the spread and triumph of Christianity throughout the Roman world. At first Christianity was just one of several varieties of otherworldlyism which appealed to increasing numbers of persons during the later empire. But in the fourth century it was adopted as the Roman state religion and thereafter became one of the greatest shaping forces in the development of the West. While Christianity was spreading, the Roman Empire was indubitably declining. Central to this decline was a contraction of the urban life on which the empire had been based. As the empire began to experience severe pressures, urban contraction was most pronounced in the European northwest because city civilization there was least deeply rooted and most distant from the empire's major trade and communications lifelines on the Mediterranean. Contraction was also felt in parts of the West that were closer to the Mediterranean because western cities depended far more on declining agricultural production than eastern ones, which relied more on trade in luxury goods and industry. Consequently the entire period saw a steady shift in the weight of civilization and imperial government from West to East. The most visible manifestations of this shift were the German successes of the fifth century. These surely helped open a new chapter in Western political history, but their immediate impact should not be exaggerated. Even with the influx of Germans, Roman institutions continued to decline gradually. Particularly in areas that were on or close to the Mediterranean, Roman city life persisted, albeit with steadily declining vigor, until the Mediterranean was no longer a Roman lake.

1. THE REORGANIZED EMPIRE

The reforms of Diocletian

Before we examine the emergence and triumph of Christianity, it is best to survey the nature of the government and society in which the new religion became a dominant force. The fifty years of chaos that threatened to destroy Rome in the third century were ended by the energetic work of a remarkable soldier named Diocletian, who ruled as emperor from 284 to 305. Conscious of some of the more obvious problems that had undone his predecessors, Diocletian embarked on a number of fundamental political and economic reforms. Recognizing that the dominance of the army in the life of the state had hitherto been too great, he introduced measures to separate military from civilian administrative chains of command. Aware that new pressures, both external and internal, had made it nearly impossible for one man to govern the entire Roman Empire, he divided his realm in half, granting the western part to a trusted colleague, Maximian, who recognized Diocletian as the senior ruler. The two then chose lieutenants, called *caesars,* to govern large subsections of their territories. This system was also meant to provide for an orderly succession, for the caesars were supposed to inherit the major rule of either East or West and then appoint new caesars in their stead. In the economic sphere Diocletian stabilized the badly debased currency, introduced a new system of taxation, and issued legislation designed to keep agricultural workers and town-dwellers at their jobs so that the basic work necessary to support the empire would continue to be done.

Diocletian. His short hair is in the Roman military style.

Although Diocletian's program of reorganization was remarkably successful in restoring an empire that had been on the verge of expiring, it also transformed the empire by "orientalizing" it in three primary and lasting ways. Most literally, Diocletian began a geographical orientalization of the empire by shifting its administrative weight toward the East. Since he was a "Roman" emperor we might assume that he ruled from Rome, but in fact between 284 and 303 he was never there, ruling instead from Nicomedia, a city in modern-day Turkey. This he did in tacit recognition of the fact that the wealthier and more vital part of the empire was clearly in the East. Second, as befitting one who turned his back on Rome, Diocletian adopted the titles and ceremonies of an Oriental potentate. Probably he did this less because he had Eastern tastes than because he wished to avoid the fate of his predecessors who were insufficiently respected. Most likely he thought that if he were feared and worshiped he would stand a greater chance of dying in bed. Accordingly, Diocletian completely abandoned Augustus's policy of appearing to be a constitutional ruler and came forward as an undisguised autocrat. He took the title not of *princeps,* or first citizen, but of *dominus,* or lord, and he introduced Oriental ceremony into his court. He wore a diadem and a purple gown of silk interwoven with gold. Those who gained an audience had to prostrate themselves before him; a privileged few were allowed to kiss his robe.

Diocletian's easternizing policy

The third aspect of orientalization in Diocletian's policy was his growing reliance on an imperial bureaucracy. By separating civilian from military commands and legislating on a wide variety of economic and social matters, Diocletian created the need for many new officials. Not surprisingly, by the end of his reign subjects were complaining that "there were more tax-collectors than taxpayers." The officials did keep the empire going, but the new bureaucracy was prone—as all are—to graft and corruption; worse, the growth of officialdom called for reservoirs of manpower and wealth at a time when the Roman Empire no longer had large supplies of either. Taken together, the various aspects of Diocletian's easternizing made him

The growth of imperial bureaucracy

208

*Christianity and the
Transformation of the
Roman World*

The Emperor Honorius. An example of the impassive portrait sculpture brought in by the age of Diocletian. Compare the lack of individuality of this bust to the portraits of Decius and Philip the Arab, above, p. 197.

The reign of Constantine

seem more like a pharaoh than a Roman ruler: it was almost as if the defeat of Antony and Cleopatra at Actium was now being avenged.

The new coercive regime of Diocletian left no room for the cultivation of individual spontaneity or freedom. The results can be seen most clearly in the architecture and art of the age. Diocletian himself preferred a colossal bombastic style of building that was meant to emphasize his own power. The baths he had constructed in Rome, when he finally arrived there in 303, were the largest yet known, encompassing about thirty acres. When he retired in 305 Diocletian built a palace for himself in what is now Split (Yugoslavia) that was laid out along a rectilinear grid like an army camp. A plan of this palace shows clearly how Diocletian favored regimentation in everything.

Also in the age of Diocletian, Roman portrait statuary, which had hitherto featured striking naturalism and individuality, became impersonal. Human faces became impassive and symmetrical rather than reflecting a free play of emotions. Porphyry, a particularly hard and dark stone that had to be imported from Egypt—itself a sign of easternization—often replaced marble for imperial busts. Porphyry groups of Diocletian, Maximian, and their two caesars show the new hardness and symmetry at their fullest, for the figures were made to look so similar that they are indistinguishable from each other.

In 305 Diocletian decided to abdicate to raise cabbages—an unprecedented achievement for a late-Roman ruler. At the same time he obliged his colleague Maximian to retire as well, and their two caesars moved peacefully up the ladders of succession. Such concord, however, could not last. Soon civil war broke out among Diocletian's successors and continued until Constantine, the son of one of the original caesars, emerged victorious. From 312 until 324 Constantine ruled only in the West, but from the latter year until his death in 337 he did away with the sharing of powers and ruled over a reunited empire. Except for the fact that he favored Christianity, an epoch-making decision to be examined in the next section, Constantine otherwise con-

Diocletian's Palace in Split. An artistic reconstruction.

Left: *Porphyry Sculptures of Diocletian and His Colleagues in Rule.* Every effort is made to make the two senior rulers and their two junior colleagues look identical by means of stylization. Note also the emphasis on military strength. Right: *Colossal Head of Constantine.* In the head of Constantine the eyes are enlarged as if to emphasize the ruler's spiritual vision. The head is approximately ten times larger than life.

tinued to govern along the lines laid down by Diocletian. Bureaucracy proliferated and the state became so vigilant in keeping town-dwellers and agricultural laborers at their posts that society began to harden into a caste system. Although Constantine was a Christian, he never thought for a moment of acting with any Christlike humility: on the contrary, he made court ceremonials more elaborate and generally behaved as if he were a god. In keeping with this he built a new capital in 330 and named it Constantinople, after himself. Although he declared that he moved his government from Rome to Constantinople in order to demonstrate his abandonment of paganism, self-esteem was no doubt a major factor, and the shift was the most visible manifestation of the continued move of Roman civilization to the East. Situated on the border of Europe and Asia, Constantinople had commanding advantages as a center for Eastern-oriented communications, trade, and defense. Surrounded on three sides by water and protected on land by walls, it was to prove nearly impregnable and would remain the center of "Roman" government for as long as the Roman Empire was to endure.

Constantine also made the succession hereditary. By so doing he brought Rome back to the principle of dynastic monarchy that it had thrown off about eight hundred years earlier. But Constantine, who treated the empire as if it were his private property, did not pass on

Two Contemporary Representations of Theodosius. Above is a detail from a silver plate. Theodosius is shown here with an orb in his hand, symbolizing his worldly power, and a halo, symbolizing his supernatural strength. In both the plate and the coin shown below the emperor is depicted in military garb.

united rule to one son. Instead he divided his realm among three of them. Not surprisingly his three sons started fighting each other upon their father's death, a conflict exacerbated by religious differences. The warfare and succeeding dynastic squabbles that continued on and off for most of the fourth century need not detain us here. Suffice it to say that they were not as serious as the civil wars of the third century, and that from time to time one or another contestant was able to reunite the empire for a period of years. The last to do so was Theodosius I (379–395), who butchered thousands of innocent citizens of Thessalonica in retribution for the death of one of his officers, but whose energies in preserving the empire by holding off Germanic barbarians still gave him some claim to his surname "the Great."

The period between Constantine and Theodosius saw the steady development of earlier tendencies. With Constantinople now the leading city of the empire, the center of commerce and administration was located clearly in the East. Regionalism too grew more pronounced: the Latin-speaking West was losing a sense of rapport and contact with the Greek-speaking East, and in both West and East local differences were becoming accentuated. In economic life the hallmark of the age was the growing gap between rich and poor. In the West large landowners were able to consolidate their holdings, and in the East some individuals became prosperous by rising through the bureaucracy and enriching themselves with graft, or by trading in luxury goods. But the taxation system initiated by Diocletian and maintained throughout the fourth century weighed down heavily on the poor, forcing them to carry the burden of supporting the bureaucracy, the army, and the lavish imperial court or courts. The poor, moreover, had no chance to escape their poverty, for legislation demanded that they and their heirs stay at their unrewarding and heavily taxed jobs. Since most people in the fourth century were poor, most people lived in desperate and unrelenting poverty against a backdrop of ostentatious wealth. The Roman Empire may have been restored in the years from 284 to 395, but it was nonetheless a fertile breeding-ground for a new religion of otherworldly salvation.

2. THE EMERGENCE AND TRIUMPH OF CHRISTIANITY

The origins and spread of Christianity

Christian beginnings of course go back several centuries before Constantine to the time of Jesus. Christianity was formed primarily by Jesus and St. Paul and gained converts steadily thereafter. But the new religion only became widespread during the chaos of the third century and only triumphed in the Roman Empire during the demoralization of the fourth. At the time of its humble beginnings nobody could have known that Christianity would be decreed the sole religion of the Roman Empire by the year 380.

Jesus of Nazareth was born in Bethlehem, a small town of Judea, sometime near the beginning of the Christian era (but not exactly in the "year one"—we owe this mistake in our dating system to a sixth-century monk). While Jesus was growing up Judea was under Roman rule. The atmosphere of the country was charged with religious emotionalism and political discontent. Some of the people, notably the Pharisees, concentrated on preserving the Jewish law and looked forward to the coming of a political messiah who would rescue the country from Rome. Most extreme of those who sought hope in politics were the "Zealots," who wished to overthrow the Romans by means of armed force. Some groups, on the other hand, were not interested in politics at all. Typical of these were the Essenes, who hoped for spiritual deliverance through asceticism, repentance, and mystical union with God. The ministry of Jesus was clearly more allied to this pacific orientation.

When Jesus was about thirty years old, he was acclaimed by an ascetic evangelist, John the Baptist, as one "mightier than I, whose shoes I am not worthy to bear." Thenceforth for about three years his career, according to the New Testament accounts, was a continuous course of preaching and teaching and of healing the sick, "casting out devils," restoring sight to the blind, and raising the dead. He not only denounced shame, greed, and licentious living but set the example himself by a life of humility and self-denial. Though the conception he held of himself is somewhat obscure, he apparently believed that he had a mission to save humanity from error and sin. His preaching and other activities eventually aroused the antagonism of some of the chief priests and conservative rabbis. They disliked his caustic references to the legalism of the Pharisees, his contempt for form and ceremony, and his scorn for pomp and luxury. They feared also that his active leadership would cause trouble with the Romans. Accordingly, they brought him into the highest court in Jerusalem, where he was solemnly condemned for blasphemy and for setting himself up as "king of the Jews" and turned over to Pontius Pilate, the Roman governor, for execution of the sentence. After hours of agony he died on the cross between two thieves on the hill of Golgotha outside Jerusalem.

The crucifixion of Jesus marked a great climax in Christian history. At first his death was viewed by his followers as the end of their hopes. Their despair soon vanished, however, for rumors began to spread that the Master was alive and had been seen by some of his faithful disciples. The remainder of his followers were quickly convinced that he had risen from the dead and that he was truly a divine being. With their courage restored, they organized their little band and began preaching and testifying in the name of their martyred leader. Thus one of the world's great religions was launched on a course that would ultimately convert an empire no less mighty than Rome.

Jesus of Nazareth; his milieu

Jesus's career

Jesus Christ. An artist's conception from a sixth-century mosaic in Ravenna.

212

*Christianity and the
Transformation of the
Roman World*

*A Carved Tablet, c. 400 A.D.,
Depicting Christ's Tomb and As-
cension into Heaven*

St. Paul. From a Ravenna
mosaic.

There has never been complete agreement among Christians as to
the precise teachings of Jesus of Nazareth. The only dependable records are the four Gospels, but the earliest of these was not written
until at least a generation after Jesus's death. According to the beliefs
of his orthodox followers, the founder of Christianity revealed himself as the Christ, the divine Son of God, who was sent on this earth
to suffer and die for the sins of humanity. They were convinced that
after three days in the tomb, he had risen from the dead and ascended
into heaven, whence he would come again to judge the world. The
Gospels at least make it clear that he included the following among his
basic teachings: (1) the fatherhood of God and the brotherhood of
humanity; (2) the Golden Rule; (3) forgiveness and love of one's enemies; (4) repayment of evil with good; (5) self-denial; (6) condemnation of hypocrisy and greed; (7) opposition to ceremonialism as the
essence of religion; (8) the imminent approach of the end of the world;
and (9) the resurrection of the dead and the establishment of the kingdom of heaven. Recent research has tended to emphasize the last two
of these points as being at the center of Jesus's mission.

Christianity was broadened and invested with a more elaborate theology by some of the successors of Jesus, above all the Apostle Paul,
originally known as Saul of Tarsus (10?–67?A.D.). Paul was not a native
of Palestine but a Jew born in the city of Tarsus in southeastern Asia
Minor. Originally a persecutor of Christians, he later converted to
Christianity and devoted his limitless energy to propagating that faith
throughout the Near East. It would be almost impossible to overestimate the significance of his work. Denying that Jesus was sent merely
as the redeemer of the Jews, Paul proclaimed Christianity to be a universal religion. Furthermore, he placed major emphasis on the idea of
Jesus as the Christ, as the anointed God-man whose death on the cross
was an atonement for the sins of humanity. Not only did he reject the
works of the Law (i.e., Jewish ritualism) as of primary importance in
religion, but he declared them to be utterly worthless in procuring
salvation. Sinners by nature, human beings can be saved only by faith
and by the grace of God "through the redemption that is in Christ
Jesus." It follows, according to Paul, that human fate in the life to
come is almost entirely dependent upon the will of God; for "Hath
not the potter power over the clay, of the same lump to make one
vessel unto honor, and another unto dishonor?" (Romans 9:21). God
has mercy "on whom He will have mercy, and whom He will He
hardeneth" (Romans 9:18).

Although it may be something of a simplification, it seems basically
true to say that whereas Jesus proclaimed the imminent coming of the
kingdom of God, Paul laid the basis for a religion of personal salvation
through Christ and the ministry of the Church. Therefore, after Paul
Christianity developed both ceremonies, or sacraments, to bring the
believer closer to Christ and an organization of priests to administer
those sacraments. In teaching that priests who administered sacra-

ments were endowed with supernatural powers, Christianity gradually posited a distinction between clergy and laity much sharper than that which had existed in most earlier religions. This would become the basis of subsequent Western controversies and divisions between "Church" and "State." In the meantime, Christianity's emphasis on otherworldly salvation ministered by a worldly priestly organization helped it greatly to grow and ultimately to flourish.

Christianity grew steadily in the first two centuries after Christ but only really began to flourish in the third. To understand this we must recall that the third century in Roman history was an "age of anxiety." At a time of extreme political turbulence and economic hardship people understandably began to treat life on earth as an illusion and place their hopes in the beyond. The human body and the material world were more and more regarded as either evil or basically unreal. As the Neoplatonic philosopher and leading thinker of that age, Plotinus, wrote, "when I come to myself, I wonder how it is that I have a body . . . by what deterioration did this happen?" Plotinus devised a whole philosophical system to answer this question, but this system was far too abstruse to have much meaning for large numbers of people. Instead, several religions that emphasized the dominance in this world of spiritual forces and the absolute preeminence of otherworldly salvation gained hold as never before.

At first Christianity was just another of these religions; Mithraism, Gnosticism, and the cults of Isis and Serapis were others. It is natural to ask, therefore, why Christianity gained converts in the third century at the expense of its rivals. A number of answers may be posited. One of the simplest, but not the least important, is that even though Christianity borrowed elements from older religions—above all Judaism and Gnosticism—it was new and hence possessed a sense of dynamism lacking among the salvationist religions which had existed for centuries. (It is noteworthy in this regard that one of Christianity's most serious rivals in the period from 276 to about 400 was Manicheanism, which was even newer than the Christian faith.) Christianity's dynamism was also enhanced by its rigorous exclusiveness. Hitherto people had adopted religions as people today take on insurance policies, piling one on another in order to feel more secure. The fact that Christianity prohibited this, demanding that the Christian God be worshiped alone, made the new religion most appealing at a time when people were searching desperately for absolutes. Similarly, Christianity alone among its rivals (with the later exception of Manicheanism) had an all-embracing theory to explain evil on earth, namely as the work of demons governed by the devil. When Christian missionaries sought converts they successfully emphasized the new faith's ability to combat these demons by reputed miracles.

An Early-Christian Woman. A wall-painting from the catacomb of Priscilla, Rome, third century A.D.

Although Christianity's novelty, exclusiveness, and theory of evil help greatly to explain its success, probably the greatest attractions of the religion had to do with three other traits: its view of salvation, its

214

*Christianity and the
Transformation of the
Roman World*

social dimensions, and its organizational structure. Exorcism of demons might help to make life more tolerable on earth, but ultimately people in the later Roman Empire were most concerned with other-worldly salvation. Rival religions also promised an afterlife, but Christianity's doctrine on this subject was the most far-reaching. Christian preachers who warned that nonbelievers would "liquefy in fierce fires" for eternity and that believers would enjoy eternal blessedness understandably made many converts in an age of fears. They made converts too among all classes because Christianity had from its origins been a religion of the humble—carpenters, fishermen, and tent-makers—which promised the exaltation of the lowly. As the religion grew it gained a few wealthy patrons, but it continued to find its greatest strength among the lower and middle classes who comprised the greatest numbers in the Roman Empire. Moreover, while Christianity forbade women to become priests or discuss the faith and, as we will see, adopted many attitudes hostile to women, it at least accorded women some rights of participation in worship and equal hope for salvation. This fact gave it an advantage over Mithraism, which excluded women from its cult entirely. In addition to all these considerations, a final reason for Christianity's success lay in its organization. Unlike the rival mystery religions, it had by the third century developed an organized hierarchy of priests to direct the life of the faith. More than that, Christian congregations were tightly knit communities that provided services to their members—such as nursing, support of the unprotected, and burial—that went beyond strictly religious concerns. Those who became Christians found human contacts and a sense of mission while the rest of the world seemed to be collapsing about them.

Jonah under the Gourd. A Christian marble statue done around the time of Constantine's conversion. Jonah resting after leaving the whale's belly was a symbol for the risen Christ.

Christianity was never as brutally persecuted by the Roman state as used to be thought. In fact the attitude of Rome was usually one of indifference: Christians were customarily tolerated unless certain magistrates decided to prosecute them for refusing to worship the official state gods. From time to time there were more concerted persecutions, but these were too intermittent and short-lived to do irreparable damage: on the contrary, they served to give Christianity some helpful publicity. To this degree the blood of martyrs really was the seed of the Church, but only because the blood did not flow too freely. One last great persecution took place toward the end of the reign of Diocletian and was continued by one of his immediate successors, a particularly bitter enemy of Christianity named Galerius. But by then the religion was far too strong to be wiped out by persecution, a fact that Galerius finally recognized by issuing an edict of toleration right before his death in 311. Thereafter Christianity was to be supported by the Roman state rather than persecuted by it.

*Roman persecution of
Christians relatively
moderate*

The adoption of Christianity by the Roman Empire was initiated by Constantine and completed by Theodosius. Constantine did not yet make Christianity the official religion of the empire, but he clearly favored it. Probably he did so both because he associated his own conversion to the faith (around the year 312) with a rise of his political fortunes, and because he hoped that Christianity might bring a spiritual unity to an empire that had been badly demoralized and religiously divided. Some of his successors, who were brought up in the Christian religion, pursued this end by ordering the persecution of pagans even more ruthlessly than some pagan emperors had formerly persecuted Christians. Christianity probably would have triumphed merely with official support because aspiring functionaries were usually quick to accept the religion of their rulers. The masses too were easily converted to the faith once it was supported by the state because, even though the fourth century was politically more stable than the third, the reorganization of the empire weighed most heavily on the lower classes and made them as desperate for otherworldly salvation as they had been in the century before. Substantial numbers, too, simply followed the lead of authority. Christians probably comprised no more than a fifth of the population of the Roman Empire at the time of the conversion of Constantine; with state support they quickly became an overwhelming majority. When Theodosius the Great forbade the worship of all religions other than Christianity by an edict of 380, paganism, already disappearing, was soon wiped out in all but the most rural backlands of the Roman realms.

*The triumph of
Christianity*

3. THE NEW CONTOURS OF CHRISTIANITY

Once the new faith became dominant within the Roman Empire it underwent some major changes in forms of thought, organization, and

216

*Christianity and the
Transformation of the
Roman World*

conduct. These changes all bore relationships to earlier tendencies, but the triumph of the faith greatly accelerated certain trends and altered the course of others. The result was that in many respects the Christianity of the late fourth century was a very different religion from the one persecuted by Diocletian and Galerius.

One consequence of Christianity's triumph was the flaring up of bitter doctrinal disputes. These brought great turmoil to the Church but resulted in the hammering out of dogma and discipline. Before the conversion of Constantine there had of course been disagreements among Christians about doctrinal matters, but as long as Christianity was a minority religion it managed to control its internal divisions in order to present a united front against hostile outsiders. Hardly had the new faith emerged victorious, however, than sharp splits developed within its own ranks. These were due partly to the fact that there had always been a tension between the intellectual and emotional tendencies within the religion which could now come more fully into the open, and partly to the fact that different regions of the empire tried to preserve a sense of their separate identities by preferring different theological formulas.

The first of the bitter disputes was between the Arians and Athanasians over the nature of the Trinity. The Arians—not to be confused with Aryans (a racial term)—were followers of a priest named Arius and were the more intellectual group. Under the influence of Greek philosophy they rejected the idea that Christ could be equal with God. Instead they maintained that the Son was created by the Father and therefore was not co-eternal with Him or formed of the same substance. The followers of St. Athanasius, indifferent to human logic, held that even though Christ was the Son he was fully God: that Father, Son, and Holy Ghost were all absolutely equal and composed of an identical substance. After protracted struggles Athanasius's side won out and the Athanasian doctrine became the Christian dogma of the Trinity, as it remains today.

The struggle between the Arians and Athanasians was followed by numerous other doctrinal quarrels during the next few centuries. The issues at stake were generally too abstruse to warrant explaining here, but the results were momentous. One was that the dogmas of the Catholic faith gradually became fixed. It should be emphasized that this was a slow development and that many basic tenets of Catholicism were only defined much later (for example, the theory of the Mass was not formally promulgated until 1215; the doctrine of the Immaculate Conception of the Virgin Mary until 1854; and that of the Bodily Assumption of the Virgin until 1950). Nonetheless, the faith was beginning to take on a sharply defined form unprecedented in the history of earlier religions. Above all, this meant that any who differed from a certain formulation would be excluded from the community and often persecuted as a heretic. In the subsequent history of Christianity this concern for doctrinal uniformity was to result in both strengths and weaknesses for the Church.

A second result of the doctrinal quarrels was that they aggravated regional hostilities. In the fourth century differences among Christians increased alienation between West and East and also aggravated hostilities among regions within the East. Although the Roman Empire was evolving toward regionalism for many different reasons, including economic and administrative ones, and although regionalism was partly a cause of religious differences, the sharper and more frequent doctrinal quarrels became, the more they served to intensify regional hostilities.

Regionalism

Finally, the doctrinal quarrels provoked the interference of the Roman state in the governance of the Church. The same Constantine who favored Christianity as a unifying force was horrified by the prompt emergence of the Arian conflict and intervened in it by calling the Council of Nicea (325), which condemned Arius. It is noteworthy that this council—the first general council of the Church—was convened by a Roman emperor and that Constantine served during its meetings as a presiding officer. Thereafter secular interference in Church matters continued, above all in the East. There were two major reasons for this. First, religious disputes were more prevalent in the East than the West and quarreling parties often appealed to the emperor for support. Second, the weight of imperial government was generally heavier in the East, and after 476 there were no Roman emperors in the West at all. When Eastern emperors were not appealed to by quarreling parties they interfered in religious disputes themselves, as Constantine had done before them, in order to preserve unity. The result was that in the East the emperor assumed great religious authority and control, while in the West the future of relations between State and Church was more open.

*Imperial involvement in
religious conflicts*

Even while emperors were interfering in religious matters, however, the Church's own internal organization was becoming more complex and articulated. We have seen that a clear distinction between clergy and laity was already a hallmark of the early Christian religion after the time of St. Paul. The next step was the development of a hierarchical organization within the ranks of the clergy. The superiority of bishops over priests was recognized before Christianity's triumph. Christian organization was centered in cities and one bishop in each important city became the authority to which all the clergy in the surrounding vicinity answered. This organization was sufficient for a minority religion, but as the number of congregations multiplied and as the influence of the Church increased due to the adoption of Christianity as the official religion of Rome, distinctions of rank among the bishops themselves began to appear. Those who had their headquarters in the larger cities came to be called metropolitans (today known in the West as archbishops), with authority over the clergy of an entire province. In the fourth century the still higher rank of patriarch was established to designate those bishops who ruled over the oldest and largest of Christian communities—such cities as Rome, Jerusalem, Constantinople, Antioch, and Alexandria, and their sur-

*The organization
of the clergy*

*Christianity and the
Transformation of the
Roman World*

The rise of the papacy

rounding districts. Thus the Christian clergy by 400 A.D. had come to embrace a definite hierarchy of patriarchs, metropolitans, bishops, and priests.

The climax of all this development—still largely in the future—was the growth of the primacy of the bishop of Rome, or in other words the rise of the papacy. For several reasons the bishop of Rome enjoyed a preeminence over the other patriarchs of the Church. The city in which he ruled was venerated by the faithful as a scene of the missionary activities of the Apostles Peter and Paul. The tradition was widely accepted that Peter had founded the bishopric of Rome and that therefore all of his successors were heirs of his authority and prestige. This tradition was supplemented by the theory that Peter had been commissioned by Christ as his vicar on earth and had been given the keys of the kingdom of heaven with power to punish people for their sins and even to absolve them from guilt (Matthew 16:18–19). This theory, known as the doctrine of the Petrine Succession, has been used by popes ever since as a basis for their claims to authority over the Church. The bishops of Rome had an advantage also in the fact that after the transfer of the imperial capital to Constantinople there was seldom any emperor with effective sovereignty in the West. Finally, in 445 the Emperor Valentinian III issued a decree commanding all western bishops to submit to the jurisdiction of the pope. It must not be supposed, however, that the Church was by any means yet under a monarchical form of government. The patriarchs in the East regarded the extreme assertions of papal claims as brazen effrontery, and even many bishops in the West continued to ignore them for some time. The clearest example of the papacy's early weakness is the fact that the popes did not even attend the first eight general councils of the Church (from 325 to 869), although later they were to convene and preside over all the others.

*Effects of the
rationalization of
ecclesiastical
administration*

The growth of ecclesiastical organization helped the Church to conquer the Roman world in the fourth century and to minister to the needs of the faithful thereafter. The existence of an episcopal administrative structure was particularly influential in the West as the Roman Empire decayed and finally collapsed in the fifth century. Since every city had a bishop trained to some degree in the arts of administration, the Church in the West took over many of the functions of government and helped to preserve order amid the deepening chaos. But the new emphasis on administration also had its inevitably deleterious effects: as the Church developed its own rationalized administrative structure it inevitably became more worldly and distant in spirit from the simple faith of Jesus and the Apostles.

The rise of monasticism

The clearest reaction to this trend was expressed in the spread of monasticism. Today we are accustomed to thinking of monks as groups of priests who live communally in order to dedicate themselves primarily to lives of contemplation and prayer. In their origins, however, monks were not priests but laymen who almost always

lived alone and who sought extremes of self-torture rather than ordered lives of spirituality. Monasticism began to emerge in the third
century as a response to the anxieties of that age, but it only became a
dominant movement within Christianity in the fourth century. Two
obvious reasons for this fact stand out. First of all, the choice of extreme hermitlike asceticism was a substitute for martyrdom. With the
conversion of Constantine and the abandonment of persecution, most
chances of winning a crown of glory in heaven by undergoing death
for the faith were eliminated. But the desire to prove one's religious
ardor by self-abasement and suffering was still present. Second, as the
fourth century progressed the priesthood became more and more
immersed in worldly concerns. Those who wished to avoid secular
temptations fled to the deserts and woods to practice an asceticism that
priests and bishops were forgetting. (Monks customarily became priests
only later during the Middle Ages.) In this way even while Christianity
was accommodating itself to practical needs, monasticism satisfied the
inclinations of ascetic extremists who otherwise might have become
Gnostics or Manicheans and who looked forward to lives of torture
and deprivation that far outstripped those of Christ and the Apostles.

Monasticism first emerged in the East, where for about one
hundred years after Constantine's conversion it spread like a mania.
Hermit monks of Egypt and Syria vied with each other in their pursuit
of the most inhuman and humiliating excesses. Some grazed in the
fields after the manner of cows, others penned themselves into small
cages, and others hung heavy weights around their necks. A monk
named Cyriacus stood for hours on one leg like a crane until he could
bear it no more. The most extravagant of these monastic ascetics was
St. Simeon Stylites, who performed self-punishing exercises—such as
touching his feet with his head 1,244 times in succession—on top of a
high pillar for thirty-seven years, while crowds gathered below to
worship "the worms that dropped from his body."

*The extremes of
monastic asceticism*

In time such ascetic hysteria subsided and it became recognized that
monasticism would be more enduring if monks lived in a community
and did not concentrate on self-torture. The most successful architect
of communal monasticism in the East was St. Basil (330?–379), who
started his monastic career as a hermit and ascetic extremist but came
to prefer communal and more moderate forms of life. Basil expressed
this preference in writings for monks that laid down the basic guidelines for eastern monasticism down to the present. Rather than
encouraging extremes of self-torture, Basil encouraged monks to discipline themselves by useful labor. Although his teachings were still
extremely severe by modern standards, he prohibited monks from
engaging in prolonged fasts or lacerating their flesh. Instead he urged
them to submit to obligations of poverty and humility, and to spend
many hours of the day in silent religious meditation. With the triumph
of St. Basil's ideas, eastern monasticism became more organized and
subdued, but even so Basilian monks preferred to live as far away

*The communal
monasticism of St. Basil*

220

*Christianity and the
Transformation of the
Roman World*

The rule of St. Benedict

*The significance of
Benedictine monasticism:
(1) missionary activities;
(2) attitude toward manual
labor*

from the "world" as they could and never had the same civilizing influence on external society as did their brothers in western Europe.

Monasticism did not at first spread so quickly in the West as it did in the East because the appeal of asceticism was much weaker there. This situation changed only in the sixth century when St. Benedict (480?–547?) drafted his famous Latin rule which ultimately became the guide for nearly all the monks in the West. Recent research has shown that Benedict copied much of his rule from an earlier Latin text, but he still produced a document notable for its brevity, flexibility, and moderation. The Benedictine rule imposed obligations similar to those laid down by St. Basil: poverty, obedience, labor, and religious devotion. Yet Benedict prescribed less austerity than Basil did: the monks were granted a sufficiency of simple food, clothing, and enough sleep; they were even allowed to drink a small amount of wine, although meat was only granted to the sick. The abbot's authority was absolute and the abbot was allowed to flog monks for disobedience, yet Benedict urged him to try "to be loved rather than feared," and ordained that the abbot take counsel before making decisions "because the Lord often reveals to a younger member what is best." For such reasons the Benedictine monastery became a center of deep religious enrichment rather than a school for punishment.

We will have occasion for continuing the story of Benedictine monasticism later on, but here we may point in advance to some of its greatest contributions to the development of Western civilization. One was that Benedictine monks were committed from an early date to missionary work: they were primarily responsible for the conversion of England and later most of Germany. Such activities not only helped to spread the faith but also served to create a sense of cultural unity for western Europe. Another positive contribution lay in the at-

A Monastery of the Basilian Order on Mt. Athos. The asceticism of the Basilian monks caused them to build their monasteries in almost inaccessible places on lofty crags or on the steep sides of rugged mountains.

St. Benedict Offering His Rule to Grateful Monks. A late-medieval conception from an Austrian manuscript of about 1355.

titude of the Benedictines toward work. Whereas the highest goal for ancient philosophers and aristocrats was to have enough leisure time for unimpeded contemplation, St. Benedict wanted his monks always to keep busy, for he believed that "idleness is an enemy of the soul." Therefore he prescribed that they should be occupied at certain times in manual labor, a prescription that would have horrified most thinkers of earlier times. Accordingly, early Benedictines worked hard themselves and spread the idea of the dignity of labor to others. With Benedictine support, this idea would become one of the most distinctive traits of Western culture. We read of Benedictines who gladly milked cows, threshed, plowed, and hammered: in so doing they increased the prosperity of their own monasteries and provided good examples for others. Benedictine monasteries became particularly successful in farming and later in estate-managing. Thus they often helped to advance the level of the western European economy and sometimes even to provide wealth that could be drawn upon by emerging western European states.

The fact that Benedictine monasteries were often islands of culture when literacy and learning were all but forgotten in the secular world is better known. St. Benedict himself was no admirer of classical culture. Quite to the contrary, he wanted his monks to serve only Christ—not literature or philosophy. But he did assume that monks would have to read well enough to say their prayers. That meant that some teaching in the monasteries was necessary because it was seldom available outside, and because boys were often given over from birth to the monastic profession. Once there was teaching there would obviously be at least a few writing implements and books. This explains why Benedictines always maintained some literacy but not why some of them became devoted to perpetuating classical culture. The impetus

(3) the preservation of classical culture; Cassiodorus

222

*Christianity and the
Transformation of the
Roman World*

behind the latter development was the work of a monastic thinker named Cassiodorus (477?–570?). Inspired by St. Augustine, whom we will treat in more detail later, Cassiodorus believed that some basic classical learning was necessary for the proper understanding of the Bible; this justified the study of the classics by monks. Furthermore, Cassiodorus recognized that copying manuscripts was in itself "manual labor" (literally work with the hands) and might be even more appropriate for monks than hard work in the fields. As Benedictines began to subscribe to these ideas, Benedictine monasteries became centers for learning and transcribing that were without rival for centuries. No work of classical Latin literature, including such "licentious" writings as the poems of Catullus and Ovid, would survive today had they not been copied and preserved during the early Middle Ages by Benedictine monks.

Love of women was of course, however, not a Benedictine preference. Returning to our original subject—the changes that took place in Christian institutions and attitudes during the fourth century—a final fateful trend was the development of a negative attitude toward the role of women in human life. Compared to most other religions, Christianity was favorable to women. Female souls were regarded as equal to male ones in the eyes of God, and human nature was deemed to be complete only in both sexes. St. Paul even went so far as to say that after baptism "there is neither male nor female" (Galatians 3:28), a spiritual equalitarianism which meant that women could be saved as fully as men. But Christians from earliest times shared the view of their contemporaries that in everyday life and in marriage women were to be strictly subject to men. Not only did early Christians believe, with all male supremacists of the ancient world, that women should be excluded from positions of leadership or decision-making, meaning that they should be "silent in Church" (I Corinthians 14:34–35) and could never be priests, but they added to this the view that women were more "fleshly" than men and therefore should be subjected to men as the flesh is subjected to the spirit (Ephesians 5:21–33).

With the growth of the ascetic movement in the third and fourth centuries, the denigration of women as dangerously "fleshly" creatures became more and more pronounced. Since sexual abstinence lay at the heart of asceticism, the most perfect men were expected to shun women. Monks, of course, shunned women the most. This was a primary reason why they fled to deserts and forests. One eastern ascetic was struck by the need for virginity in the midst of his marriage ceremony, ran off to a hermit's cell, and blocked the entrance; another monk who was forced to carry his aged mother across a stream swaddled her up as thoroughly as he could so that he would not catch any "fire" and no thoughts of other women attack him. With monks taking such an uncompromising attitude, the call for continence was extended to the priesthood. Originally priests could be married; it seems that even some of the Apostles had wives (I Corinthians 9:5). But

Monks Chopping Down Trees (above) *and Harvesting Grain* (below). From a twelfth-century French manuscript.

223

*The Germanic Invasions and the
Fall of the Roman Empire in the
West*

in the course of the fourth century the doctrine spread that priests could not be married after ordination, and that those already married were obliged to live continently with their wives afterward.

Once virginity was accepted as the highest standard, marriage was taken to be only second-best. St. Jerome expressed this view most earthily when he said that virginity was wheat, marriage barley, and fornication cow-dung: since people should not eat cow-dung he would permit them barley. The major purposes of marriage were to keep men from "burning" and to propagate the species. (St. Jerome went so far as to praise marriage above all because it brought more virgins into the world!) Thus Christianity reinforced the ancient view that woman's major earthly purpose was to serve as mother. Men and women were warned not to take pleasure even in marital intercourse but to indulge in it only for the purpose of procreation. Women were to be "saved in childbearing" (I Timothy 2:15). Since they could not become priests and only a very few could become nuns (female monasticism was regarded as a very expensive luxury in the premodern world), almost all women were expected to become submissive wives and mothers. As wives they were not expected to have their own careers and were not meant to be educated or even literate. Hence even though they had full hopes for salvation, they were treated as inferiors in the everyday affairs of the world, a treatment that would endure until modern times.

4. THE GERMANIC INVASIONS AND THE FALL OF THE ROMAN EMPIRE IN THE WEST

While Christianity was conquering the Roman Empire from within, another force, that of the Germanic barbarians, was threatening it from without. The Germans, who had already almost brought Rome to its knees in the third century, were held off from the time of Diocletian until shortly before the reign of Theodosius the Great. But thereafter they demolished Western Roman resistance and, by the end of the fifth century, succeeded in conquering all of the Roman West. Germanic kingdoms then became the new form of government in territories once ruled over by Caesar and Augustus.

It is customary to think, perhaps with the encouragement of grade-B movies, that the Germans who destroyed the Western Roman Empire were fierce and thoroughly uncouth savages. But that is a misunderstanding. The Germans were barbarians in the sense that they did not live in cities and were customarily illiterate, but they were not therefore savages. On the contrary, they often practiced settled agriculture—although they preferred hunting and grazing—and were adept at making iron tools and weapons as well as jewelry and pottery. Physically they looked enough like Romans to intermarry without causing much comment, and their Indo-European language was related to Latin and Greek. Prolonged interaction with the Romans had a decisive civilizing influence on the Germans before they started their final conquests. Germans and Romans who shared common borders along the Rhine and Danube had steady trading relations with each other. Even during times of war Romans were often allied with some German tribes while they fought others. By the fourth century, moreover, German tribes often served as auxiliaries of depleted Roman armies and were sometimes allowed to settle on borderlands of the empire where Roman farmers had given up trying to cultivate the land. Finally, many German tribes had been converted to Christianity in the fourth century, although the Christianity they accepted was of the heretical Arian version. All these interactions made the "barbarians" very familiar with Roman civilization and substantially favorable to it.

The Visigoths and the Vandals

The Germans began their final push not to destroy Rome but to find more and better land. The first breakthrough occurred in 378 when one tribe, the Visigoths, who had recently settled on some Roman lands in the Danube region, revolted against mistreatment by Roman officials and then decisively defeated a punitive Roman army in the Battle of Adrianople. The Visigoths did not immediately follow up this victory because they were cleverly bought off and made allies of the empire by Theodosius the Great. But when Theodosius died in 395 he divided his realm between his two sons, neither of whom was as competent as he, and both halves of the empire were weakened by political intrigues. The Visigoths under their leader Alaric took advantage of this situation to wander through Roman realms almost at will, looking for the best land and provisions. In 410 they sacked Rome itself—a great shock to some contemporaries—and in the following years marched into southern Gaul. Meanwhile, in December of 406, a group of allied Germanic tribes led by the Vandals crossed the frozen Rhine and capitalized on Roman preoccupation with the Visigoths by streaming through Gaul into Spain. Later they were able to cross the straits into northwest Africa, then one of the richest agricultural regions of the empire. From Africa they took control of the central Mediterranean, even sacking Rome from the sea in 455. By 476 the entirely ineffectual Western Roman emperor, a mere boy derisively nicknamed Augustulus ("little Augustus"), was easily deposed by a leader of a mixed band of Germans who then assumed the title of king of Rome. Accordingly, 476 is conventionally given as the date for the end of the Western Roman Empire. But it must be remembered that a Roman emperor, who maintained some claims to authority in the West, continued to rule in Constantinople.

Reasons for the German success

Two questions that historians of the German invasions customarily ask are: How did the Germans manage to triumph so easily? Why was it that they were particularly successful in the West rather than the East? The ease of the German victories appears particularly striking when it is recognized that the German armies were remarkably small:

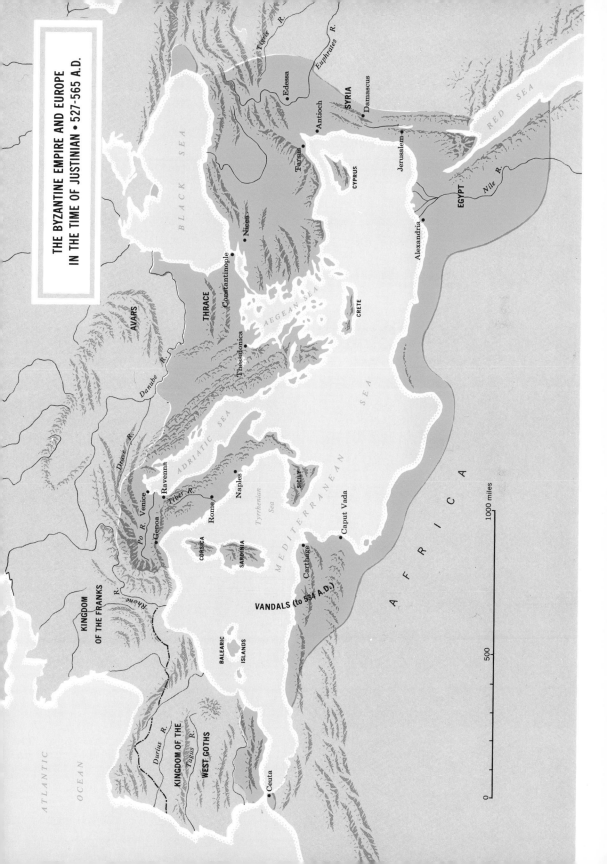

ATLANTIC
OCEAN

KINGDOM
OF THE FRANKS

Rhône R.

Durius R.

Tagus R.

KINGDOM OF THE
WEST GOTHS

Ceuta

BALEARIC
ISLANDS

CORSICA

SARDINIA

Carthage

VANDALS (to 534 A.D.)

A   F   R   I   C   A

Po R.

Venice
Genoa

Ravenna

Tiber R.

Rome

Naples

SICILY

Caput Vada

Tyrrhenian
Sea

MEDITERRANEAN

SEA

Drave R.

Danube R.

AVARS

ADRIATIC SEA

Thessalonica

THRACE

Constantinople

Nicea

AEGEAN SEA

CRETE

BLACK SEA

Tyras R.

Edessa

Euphrates R.

Antioch

SYRIA

Damascus

Tarsus

CYPRUS

Jerusalem

Alexandria

EGYPT

Nile R.

RED SEA

1000 miles

500

0

Byzantine Gold Cup, VI–IX cent.
The relief shows Constantinople
personified as a queen holding the
sceptre of imperial rule. (MMA)

Merovingian Fibula or Brooch, VII cent. A
fabulous gold-plated animal set with
garnets and colored paste. (MMA)

*Sienese Madonna and Child, Byzantine School,
XIII cent.* The painters of Siena in Italy imitated the opulent style of Byzantine art. Their
madonnas were not earthly mothers, but
celestial queens reigning in dignified splendor. (National Gallery)

Saint John Writing His Gospel. From a Carolingian illuminated manuscript, c. 850. The monastic artist was
indifferent to perspective, but excelled in coloring and
conveying a sense of vitality and energy. (Morgan
Library)

225

*The Germanic Invasions and the
Fall of the Roman Empire in the
West*

the Goths who won at Adrianople numbered no more than 10,000 men, and the total number of the Vandal "hordes" (including women and children) was about 80,000—a population about the same as that of an average-sized American suburb. But the Roman armies themselves were depleted because of declining population and the need for manpower in other occupations, above all in the new bureaucracies. More than that, German armies often won by default (Adrianople was one of the few pitched battles in the history of their advance) because the Romans were no longer zealous about defending themselves. Germans were seldom regarded with horror—many German soldiers had even risen to positions of leadership within Roman ranks—and the coercive regime begun by Diocletian was not deemed to be worth fighting for.

The reasons why the Germans fared best in the West are complex—some having to do with personalities and mistakes of the moment, and others with geographical considerations. But the primary explanation why the Eastern Roman Empire survived while the Western did not is that the East was simply richer. By the fifth century most Western Roman cities had shrunk in terms of both population and space to a small fraction of their earlier size and were often little more than empty administrative shells or fortifications. The economy of the West was becoming more and more strictly agricultural, and agricultural produce served only to feed farm laborers and keep rich landlords in luxuries. In the East, on the other hand, cities like Constantinople, Antioch, and Alexandria were still teeming metropolises because of their trade and industry. Because the eastern state had greater reserves of wealth to tax, it was more vigorous. It could also afford to buy off the barbarians with tribute money, which it did with increasing regularity. So Constantinople was able to stay afloat while Rome floundered and then sank.

*Why the Eastern Roman
Empire survived and the
Western collapsed*

The effects of the Germanic conquests in the West were not cataclysmic. The greatest difference between the Germans and the Romans had been that the former did not live in cities, but since the Western Roman cities were already in a state of decline, the invasions only served at most to accelerate the progress of urban decay. On the land Germans replaced Roman landlords without interrupting basic Roman agricultural patterns. Moreover, since the Germans never comprised very large numbers, they usually never took over more than a part of Roman lands. Germans also tried to avail themselves of Roman administrative apparatuses, but these tended to diminish gradually because of the diminishing of wealth and literacy. Thus the only major German innovation was to create separate tribal kingdoms in the West in place of a united empire.

*Consequences of the
Germanic invasions*

The map of western Europe around the year 500 reveals the following major political divisions. Germanic tribes of Anglo-Saxons, who had crossed the English Channel in the middle of the fifth century, were extending their rule on the island of Britain. In the northern part

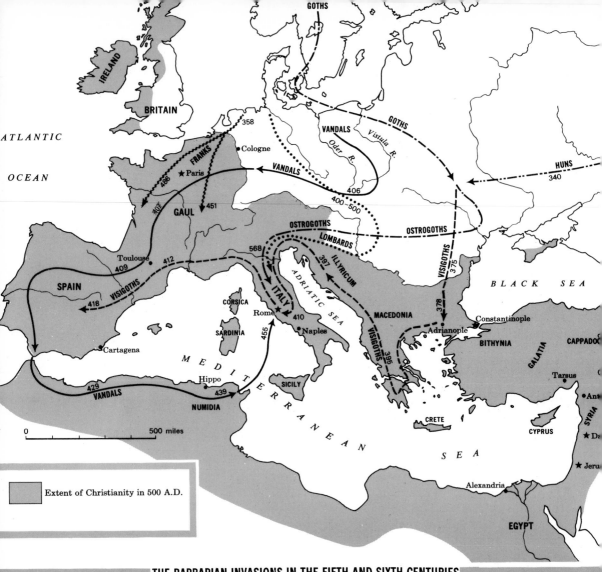

THE BARBARIAN INVASIONS IN THE FIFTH AND SIXTH CENTURIES

Germanic kingdoms in the year 500

of Gaul, around Paris and east to the Rhine, the growing kingdom of the Franks was ruled by a crafty warrior named Clovis. South of the Franks stood the Visigoths, who ruled the southern half of Gaul and most of Spain. South of them were the Vandals, who ruled throughout previously Roman northwest Africa. In all of Italy the Ostrogoths, eastern relatives of the Visigoths, held sway under their impressive King Theodoric. Of these kingdoms the Frankish would be the most promising for the future (for that reason it will be taken up in the next chapter) and the seemingly strongest for the present was that of the Ostrogoths.

Theodoric the Ostrogoth, who ruled in Italy from 493 to 526, was a great admirer of Roman civilization; this he tried to preserve as best he could. He fostered agriculture and commerce, repaired public buildings and roads, patronized learning, and maintained a policy of religious toleration. In short he gave Italy a more enlightened rule than it had known under most of its earlier emperors. But since Theodoric and his sparsely numbered Ostrogoths were Arian Christians while the local bishops and native population were Catholics, his rule, no matter how tolerant and benign, was viewed with some hostility. The "Roman" rulers in Constantinople were also hostile to Theodoric because he was an Arian and because they had not given up hopes of reconquering Italy themselves. All these circumstances led to the demise of Theodoric's Ostrogothic kingdom not long after his death. In fact, none of the continental barbarian kingdoms would last long except for that of the Franks.

5. THE SHAPING OF WESTERN CHRISTIAN THOUGHT

The period of the decline and fall of the Roman Empire in the West was also the time when a few Western Christian thinkers formulated an approach to the world and to God that was to guide the thought of the West for roughly the next 800 years. This concurrence of political decline and theological advance was not coincidental. With the empire falling and being replaced by barbarian kingdoms, it seemed clearer than ever to thinking Christians both that the classical inheritance had to be reexamined and that God had not intended the world to be anything more than a transitory testing place. The consequences of these assumptions accordingly became urgent questions. Between about 380 and 525 answers were worked out by Western Christian thinkers whose accomplishments were intimately interrelated. The towering figure among them was St. Augustine, but some others had great influence as well.

Three contemporaries who knew and influenced each other—St. Jerome (340?–420), St. Ambrose (340?–397), and St. Augustine (354–430)—count as three of the four greatest "fathers" of the Western, Latin Church. (The fourth, St. Gregory the Great, came later and will be discussed in the next chapter.) St. Jerome's greatest single contribution to the future was his translation of the Bible from Hebrew and Greek into Latin. His version, known as the "Vulgate" (or "common" version), became the standard Latin Bible used throughout the Middle Ages; with minor variations it continued to be used long afterward by the Roman Catholic Church. Fortunately Jerome was one of the best writers of his day, and he endowed his translation with vigorous, often colloquial prose and, occasionally, fine poetry. Since the Vulgate was the most widely read work in Latin for centuries, Jerome's writing had as much influence on Latin style and thought as the

Theodoric the Ostrogoth. The barbarian ruler is shown here in Roman dress, with an ornate Roman hairstyle and a Roman symbol of victory in his hand. The inscription reads REX THEODERICVS PIVS PRINCIS, Latin for King Theodoric, pious prince.

St. Jerome

Mosaic of Theodoric's Palace at Ravenna. At the right is a stylized conception of the ruler's palace, with the Latin inscription PALA TIVM; to the left of it is a row of saints, who would be indistinguishable were it not for the initials on their clothing: for early Christian artists, supernatural merits rather than individual personality traits were of the essence.

King James Bible has had on English literature. Jerome, who was the least original thinker of the great Latin fathers, also influenced the Western Christian future by his contentious but eloquent formulations of contemporary views. Among the most important of these were the beliefs that much of the Bible was to be understood allegorically rather than literally, that classical learning could be valid for Christians if it was thoroughly subordinated to Christian aims, and that the most perfect Christians were rigorous ascetics. In keeping with the last position Jerome avidly supported monasticism. He also taught that women should not take baths so that they would not see their own bodies naked.

St. Ambrose

Unlike Jerome, who was primarily a scholar, St. Ambrose was most active in the concerns of the world. As archbishop of Milan, Ambrose was the most influential Church official in the West—more so even than the pope. Guided by practical concerns, he wrote an ethical work, *On the Duties of Ministers,* which followed closely upon Cicero's *On Duties* in title and form, and also drew heavily on Cicero's Stoic ethics. But Ambrose differed from Cicero and most of traditional classical thought on two major points. One was that the beginning and end of human conduct should be the reverence and search for God rather than any self-concern or interest in social adjustment. The other— Ambrose's most original contribution—was that God helps some Christians but not others in this pursuit by the gift of grace, a point that was to be greatly refined and amplified by St. Augustine. Ambrose put his concern for proper conduct into action by his most famous act, his confrontation with the Emperor Theodosius the Great for massacring innocent civilians. Ambrose argued that by violating divine commandments Theodosius had made himself subject to Church discipline. Remarkably the archbishop succeeded in forcing the sovereign emperor to do penance. This was the first time that a churchman had subordinated the Roman secular power in matters of morality. Consequently it symbolized the Church's claim to preeminence in this sphere, and particularly the *Western* Church's developing sense of autonomy and moral superiority that would subsequently make it so much more independent and influential on the secular world than the Eastern Church.

St. Ambrose's disciple, St. Augustine, was the greatest of all the Latin fathers; indeed he was one of the most powerful Christian intellects of all time. Augustine's influence on subsequent medieval thought was incalculable. Even after the Middle Ages his theology had a profound influence on the development of Protestantism; in the twentieth century many leading Christian thinkers have called themselves Neo-Augustinians. It may be that one reason why Augustine's Christianity was so searching was because he began his career by searching for it. Nominally a Christian from birth, he hesitated until the age of thirty-three to be baptized, passing from one system of thought to another without being able to find intellectual or spiritual satisfaction in any. Only increasing doubts about all other alternatives, the appeals of St. Ambrose's teachings, and a mystical experience movingly described in his *Confessions* led Augustine to embrace the faith wholeheartedly in 387. Thereafter he advanced rapidly in ecclesiastical positions, becoming bishop of the North African city of Hippo in 395. Although he led a most active life in this office, he still found time to write a large number of profound, complex, and powerful treatises in which he set forth his convictions concerning the most fundamental problems of Christian thought and action.

St. Augustine

St. Augustine's theology revolved around the principles of divine omnipotence and the profound sinfulness of humanity. Ever since Adam and Eve turned away from God in the Garden of Eden humans have remained basically sinful. One of Augustine's most vivid illustrations of human depravity appears in the *Confessions,* where he tells how he and some other boys once were driven to steal pears from a neighbor's garden, not because they were hungry or because the pears were beautiful, but for the sake of the evil itself. God would be purely just if He condemned all human beings to hell, but since He is also merciful He has elected to save a few. Ultimately human will has nothing to do with this choice: although one has the power to choose between good and evil, one does not have the power to decide whether he will be saved. God alone, from eternity, predestined a portion of the human race to be saved and sentenced the rest to be damned. In other words, God fixed for all time the number of human inhabitants of heaven. If any mere mortals were to respond that this seems unfair, the answer is first that strict "fairness" would confine all to perdition,

Augustine's theology

*Christianity and the
Transformation of the
Roman World*

*The doctrine of
predestination*

and second that the basis for God's choice is a mystery shrouded in His omnipotence—far beyond the realm of human comprehension.

Even though it might seem to us that the practical consequences of this rigorous doctrine of predestination would be lethargy and fatalism, Augustine and subsequent medieval Christians did not see it that way at all. Humans themselves must do good, and if they are "chosen" they usually will do good; since no one knows who is chosen and who is not, all should try to do good in the hope that they are among the chosen. For Augustine the central guide to doing good was the doctrine of "charity," which meant leading a life devoted to loving God and loving one's neighbor for the sake of God. Seen from the opposite, humans should avoid "cupidity," or loving earthly things for their own sake. Put in other terms, Augustine taught that humans should behave on earth as if they were travelers or "pilgrims," keeping their eyes at all times on their heavenly home and avoiding all materialistic concerns.

On the City of God

Augustine built an interpretation of history on this view in one of his major works, *On the City of God*. In this, he argued that the entire human race from the Creation until the Last Judgment was and will be composed of two warring societies, those who "live according to man" and love themselves, and those who "live according to God." The former belong to the "City of Earth" and will be damned, while the blessed few who compose the "City of God" will on Judgment Day put on the garment of immortality. This reading of history subsequently went unquestioned throughout the Middle Ages.

*Augustine's view of
classical learning*

Although Augustine worked out for the first time major new aspects of Christian theology, he believed that he was only putting together truths found in the Bible. Indeed, he was convinced that the Bible alone contained all the wisdom worth knowing. But he also believed that much of the Bible was expressed obscurely, and that it was therefore necessary to have a certain amount of education in order to understand it thoroughly. This conviction led him to a modified acceptance of classical learning. The ancient world had already worked out an educational system based on the "liberal arts," or those subjects necessary for the worldly success and intellectual growth of free men. Augustine argued that privileged Christians could learn the fundamentals of these subjects, but only in a limited way and for a completely different end—study of the Bible. Since nonreligious schools existed in his day which taught these subjects, he permitted a Christian elite to attend them; later, when such schools died out, their place was taken by schools in monasteries and cathedrals. Thus Augustine's teaching laid the groundwork for some continuity of educational practice as well as for the theory behind the preservation of some classical treatises. But we must qualify this by remarking that Augustine intended liberal education only for an elite; all others were simply to be catechized, or drilled, in the faith. He also thought it far worse that anyone should become engaged in classical thought for its own sake than that someone might not know any classical thought at all. The true wisdom of mortals, he insisted, was piety.

Augustine had many followers, of whom the most interesting and influential was Boethius, a Roman aristocrat who lived from about 480 to 524. To say that Boethius was a follower of St. Augustine might until recently have been regarded as controversial because some of his works make no explicit mention of Christianity. Indeed, since Boethius was indisputably interested in ancient philosophy, wrote in a polished, almost Ciceronian style, and came from a noble Roman family, it has been customary to view him as the "last of the Romans." But in fact he intended the classics to serve Christian purposes, just as Augustine had prescribed, and his own teachings were basically Augustinian.

Because Boethius lived a century after Augustine he could see far more clearly that the ancient world was coming to an end. Therefore he made it his first goal to preserve as much of the best ancient learning as possible by a series of handbooks, translations, and commentaries. Accepting a contemporary division of the liberal arts into seven subjects—grammar, rhetoric, logic, arithmetic, geometry, astronomy, and music—he wrote handbooks on two: arithmetic and music. These summaries were meant to convey all the basic aspects of the subject matter that a Christian might need to know. Had Boethius lived longer he probably would have written similar treatments of the other liberal arts, but as it was he concentrated his efforts on his favorite subject: logic. In order to preserve the best of classical logic, he translated from Greek into Latin some of Aristotle's logical treatises as well as an introductory work on logic by Porphyry (another ancient philosopher). He also wrote his own explanatory commentaries on these works in order to help beginners. Since Latin writers had never been interested in logic, even in the most flourishing periods of Roman culture, Boethius's translations and commentaries became a crucial link between the Greeks and the Middle Ages. Boethius helped endow the Latin language with a logical vocabulary, and when interest in logic was revived in the twelfth-century West it rested first on a Boethian basis.

Although Boethius was an exponent of Aristotle's logic, his worldview was not Aristotelian but Augustinian. This can be seen both in his several orthodox treatises on Christian theology and above all in his masterpiece, *The Consolation of Philosophy*. Boethius wrote the *Consolation* at the end of his life, after he had been condemned to death for treason by Theodoric the Ostrogoth, whom he had served as an official. (Historians are unsure about the justice of the charges.) In it Boethius asks the age-old question of what is human happiness and concludes that it is not found in earthly rewards such as riches or fame but only in the "highest good," which is God. Human life, then, should be spent in pursuit of God. Since Boethius speaks in the *Consolation* as a philosopher rather than a theologian, he does not refer to

Boethius

Boethius's intellectual contributions

Boethius. A twelfth-century artist's conception of Boethius as a musician, a reputation he earned because of his treatise on music.

*Christianity and the
Transformation of the
Roman World*

The Consolation of
Philosophy

Christian revelation or to the role of divine grace in salvation. But his basically Augustinian message is unmistakable. *The Consolation of Philosophy* became one of the most popular books of the Middle Ages because it was extremely well written, because it showed how classical expression and some classical ideas could be appropriated and subordinated into a clearly Christian framework, and most of all, because it seemed to offer a real meaning to life. In times when all earthly things really did seem crude or fleeting it was genuinely consoling to be told eloquently and "philosophically" that life has purpose if led for the sake of God.

The myth of Orpheus as a symbol for Christian truths

At a climactic moment in the *Consolation* Boethius retold in verse the myth of Orpheus in a way that might stand for the common position of the four writers just discussed; i.e., how Christian thinkers were willing to accept and maintain some continuity with the classical tradition. But Boethius also made new sense of the story. According to Boethius Orpheus's wife, Eurydice, symbolized hell; since Orpheus could not refrain from looking at her he was forced to die and was condemned to hell himself. In other words, Orpheus was too worldly and material; he should not have loved a woman but should have sought God. True Christians, on the other hand, know that "happy is he who can look into the shining spring of good [i.e., the divine vision]; happy is he who can break the heavy chains of earth."

6. EASTERN ROME AND THE WEST

Boethius's execution a turning point

Boethius's execution by Theodoric the Ostrogoth in 524 was in many ways an important historical turning point. For one, Boethius was both the last noteworthy philosopher and last writer of cultivated Latin prose the West was to have for many hundreds of years. Then too Boethius was a layman, and for hundreds of years afterward almost all western European writers would be priests or monks. In the political sphere Boethius's execution was symptomatic as well because it was the harbinger of the collapse of the Ostrogothic kingdom in Italy. Whether or not he was justly condemned, Boethius's execution showed that the Arian Ostrogoths could not live in perfect harmony with Catholic Christians such as himself. Soon afterward, therefore, the Ostrogoths were overthrown by the Eastern Roman Empire. That event in turn was to be a major factor in the ultimate divorce between East and West and the consequent final disintegration of the old Roman World.

The Emperor Justinian

The conquest of the Ostrogoths was part of a larger plan for Roman revival conceived and directed by the Eastern Roman Emperor Justinian (527–565). Eastern Rome, with its capital at Constantinople, had faced many external pressures from barbarians and internal religious dissensions since the time of Theodosius. But throughout the fifth century it had managed to weather these, and by the time of Justinian's accession had regained much of its strength. Although the Eastern Roman Empire—which then encompassed the modern-day territories of Greece, Turkey, most of the Middle East, and Egypt— was largely Greek- and Syriac-speaking, Justinian himself came from a westernmost province (modern-day Yugoslavia) and spoke Latin. Not surprisingly, therefore, he concentrated his interests on the West. He saw himself as the heir of imperial Rome, whose ancient power and western territory he was resolved to restore. Aided by his astute and determined wife Theodora, who, unlike earlier imperial Roman consorts, played an influential role in his reign, Justinian took great strides toward this goal. But ultimately his policy of recovering the West proved unrealistic.

One of Justinian's most impressive and lasting accomplishments was his codification of Roman law. This project was part of his attempt to emphasize continuities with earlier imperial Rome and was also meant to enhance his own prestige and absolute power. Codification of the law was necessary because between the third and sixth centuries the volume of statutes had continued to grow, with the result that the vast body of enactments contained many contradictory or obsolete elements. Moreover, conditions had changed so radically that many of the old legal principles could no longer be applied, due to the establishment of an Oriental despotism and the adoption of Christianity as the official religion. When Justinian came to the throne in 527, he immediately decided upon a revision and codification of the existing law to bring it into harmony with the new conditions and to establish it as an authoritative basis of his rule. To carry out the actual work he appointed a commission of lawyers under the supervision of his minister, Tribonian. Within two years the commission published the first result of its labors. This was the Code, a systematic revision of all of the statutory laws which had been issued from the reign of Hadrian to the reign of Justinian. The Code was later supplemented by the Novels, which contained the legislation of Justinian and his immediate successors. By 532 the commission had completed the Digest, a summary of all of the writings of the great jurists. The final product of the work of revision was the Institutes, a textbook of the legal principles reflected in both the Digest and the Code. The combination of all four of these results of the program of revision constitutes the *Corpus Juris Civilis,* or the body of the civil law.

Justinian's *Corpus* was a brilliant achievement in its own terms: the Digest alone has been justly called "the most remarkable and important lawbook that the world has ever seen." In addition, the *Corpus* had an extraordinarily great influence on subsequent legal and governmental history. Revived and restudied in western Europe from the eleventh century on, Justinian's *Corpus* became the basis of all the law

Codification and revision of Roman law; the Corpus Juris Civilis

General significance of Justinian's Corpus

Justinian and Theodora. Sixth-century mosaics from the church of San Vitale, Ravenna. The emperor and empress are conceived here to have supernatural, almost priestly powers: they are advancing toward the altar, bringing the communion dish and chalice respectively. Both rulers are set off from their

and jurisprudence of European states, exclusive of England (which followed its own "common law"). The nineteenth-century Napoleonic Code, which provided the basis for the laws of modern European countries and also of Latin America, is fundamentally the Institutes of Justinian in modern dress.

Other influences   Only a few of the more specific influences of Justinian's legal work can be enumerated here. One is that in its basic governmental theory it was a bastion of absolutism. Starting from the maxim that "what pleases the prince has the force of law," it granted untrammeled powers to the imperial sovereign and therefore was adopted with alacrity by later European monarchs and autocrats. But the *Corpus* also provided some theoretical support for constitutionalism because it maintained that the sovereign originally obtained his powers from the people rather than from God. Since government came from the people it could in theory be given back to them. Perhaps most important and influential was the *Corpus*'s view of the state as an abstract public and secular entity. In the Middle Ages rival views of the state as the private property of the ruler or as a supernatural creation meant to control sin often predominated. The modern conception of the state as a public entity concerned not with the future life but with everyday affairs gained strength toward the end of the Middle Ages largely because of the revival of assumptions found in Justinian's legal compilations.

Justinian aimed to be a full Roman emperor in geographical practice as well as in legal theory. To this end he sent out armies to reconquer

retinues by their haloes. The observant viewer is also meant to note the representation of the "three wise kings from the East" at the hem of Theodora's gown: just as the "three magi" once had supernatural knowledge of Christ, so now do their counterparts, Justinian and Theodora.

the West. At first they were quickly successful. In 533 Justinian's brilliant general Belisarius conquered the Vandal kingdom in northwest Africa, and in 536 Belisarius seemed to have won all Italy, where he was welcomed by the Catholic subjects of the Ostrogoths. But the first victories of the Italian campaign were illusory. After their initial defeats the Ostrogoths put up stubborn resistance and the war dragged on for decades until the exhausted Eastern Romans finally reduced the last Gothic outposts in 563. Shortly before he died Justinian became master of all Italy as well as northwest Africa and coastal parts of Spain that his troops had also managed to recapture. The Mediterranean was once more briefly a "Roman" lake. But the cost of the endeavor was soon going to call the very existence of the Eastern Roman Empire into question.

Justinian's policy of reconquest in the West

There were two major reasons why Justinian's Western campaigns were ill-advised. One was that his realm really could not afford them. Belisarius seldom had enough troops to do his job properly: he began his Italian campaign with only 8,000 men. Later, when Justinian did grant his generals enough troops, it was only at the cost of oppressive taxation. But additional troops would probably have been insufficient to hold the new lines in the West because the empire had greater interests, as well as enemies, to the East. While the Eastern Roman Empire was exhausting itself in Italy the Persians were gathering strength. Justinian's successors had to pull away from the West in order to meet the threat of a revived Persia, but even so, by the beginning of the seventh

The Western campaigns unwise

The end of Roman unity

century, it seemed as if the Persians would be able to march all the way to the waters that faced Constantinople. Only a heroic reorganization of the empire after 610 saved the day, but it was one that helped withdraw Eastern Rome from the West and helped the West begin to lead a life of its own.

In the meantime Justinian's wars had left most of Italy in a shambles. In the course of the protracted fighting much devastation had been wrought. Around Rome aqueducts were cut and the countryside returned to marshes that would not be drained until the time of Mussolini. In 568, only three years after Justinian's death, another Germanic tribe, the Lombards, invaded the country and took much of it away from the Eastern Romans. They met little resistance because the latter were now properly paying more attention to the East, but the Lombards were still too weak to conquer the whole Italian peninsula. Instead, Italy became divided between Lombard, Eastern Roman, and papal territories. At the same time Slavs took advantage of Eastern Roman weakness to sweep into the Balkans. Farther west the Franks in Gaul were fighting among themselves, and it would be only a matter of time before northwest Africa and most of Spain would fall to Arabs. So the Roman unity had finally come to an end. The future in this decentralized world may have looked bleak, but new forces in the separate areas would soon be gathering strength.

SELECTED READINGS

• *Items so designated are available in paperback editions.*

Anderson, Hugh, *Jesus*, Englewood Cliffs, N.J., 1967. An excellent collection of readings displaying many different scholarly points of view.

Bonner, Gerald, *St. Augustine of Hippo*, London, 1963. The best biography for beginners.

Brown, Peter, *Augustine of Hippo*, Berkeley, Calif., 1967. An extremely subtle study.

———, *The World of Late Antiquity*, New York, 1971. A survey that approaches the period in its own terms rather than as a prelude to the Middle Ages.

• Bultmann, Rudolf, *Primitive Christianity in Its Contemporary Setting*, New York, 1956. Summarizes the ideas of one of our century's most important biblical scholars.

• Bury, J. B., *The Invasion of Europe by the Barbarians*, London, 1928. A straightforward narrative.

• Chadwick, Henry, *The Early Church*, Baltimore, 1967.

• Cochrane, C. N., *Christianity and Classical Culture*, Oxford, 1940. Difficult but fundamental.

Daniélou, J., and H. I. Marrou, *The Christian Centuries; I: The First Six Hundred Years*, London, 1964. A survey from the Roman Catholic perspective.

Dill, Samuel, *Roman Society in the Last Century of the Western Empire*, London, 1921.

- Dodds, E. R., *Pagan and Christian in an Age of Anxiety,* Cambridge, 1965. A short but brilliant study of what pagans and Christians had in common as well as what made Christianity ultimately successful.
- Enslin, M. S., *The Prophet from Nazareth,* New York, 1961.
- Jones, A. H. M., *The Decline of the Ancient World,* New York, 1966. A survey that emphasizes economic and social factors.
- Katz, Solomon, *The Decline of Rome,* Ithaca, N.Y., 1955. The best brief introduction.
- Knowles, David, *Christian Monasticism,* New York, 1969.
- Latourette, K. S., *A History of Christianity,* New York, 1953.
- L'Orange, H. P., *Art Forms and Civic Life in the Late Roman Empire,* Princeton, N.J., 1965. An imaginative and stimulating essay displaying how developments in art reflected developments in political and social life.
  Lot, Ferdinand, *The End of the Ancient World,* New York, 1931. The best detailed treatment of the political history of the period.
- Lyon, Bryce, *The Origins of the Middle Ages,* New York, 1971.
  MacMullen, Ramsay, *Constantine,* New York, 1969. A good popular biography.
  Markus, R. A., *Christianity in the Roman World,* New York, 1974.
- Mattingly, Harold, *Christianity in the Roman Empire,* New York, 1967.
  Momigliano, A., *The Conflict between Paganism and Christianity,* New York, 1963.
  Pelikan, J., *The Christian Tradition; I: The Emergence of the Catholic Tradition,* Chicago, 1971. An advanced survey of doctrine.
- Rand, E. K., *Founders of the Middle Ages,* Cambridge, Mass., 1928. A thoroughly engaging account of the early Christian reactions to the classics.
- Riché, Pierre, *Education and Culture in the Barbarian West,* Columbia, S.C., 1976. A magisterial survey of learning in the Christian West from the fall of Rome to about 800.
- White, Lynn T., Jr., *The Transformation of the Roman World,* Berkeley, Calif., 1966. Stimulating essays.
  Workman, H. B., *The Evolution of the Monastic Ideal,* London, 1913. Highly interpretative but still one of the best works on the subject.

SOURCE MATERIALS

- St. Augustine, *City of God,* tr. H. Bettenson, Baltimore, 1972.
- ———, *Confessions,* tr. R. S. Pine-Coffin, Baltimore, 1961.
- ———, *The Enchiridion on Faith, Hope and Love,* ed. H. Paolucci, Chicago, 1961.
- ———, *On Christian Doctrine,* tr. D. W. Robertson, Jr., New York, 1958.
- Boethius, *The Consolation of Philosophy,* tr. R. Green, Indianapolis, 1962.
- Cassiodorus, *An Introduction to Divine and Human Readings,* tr. L. W. Jones, New York, 1946.
- *Early Christian Writings: The Apostolic Fathers,* tr. M. Staniforth, Baltimore, 1968.
- Eusebius, *The History of the Church,* tr. G. A. Williamson, Baltimore, 1965.
  Procopius, *The Secret History,* tr. G. A. Williamson, Baltimore, 1966.

Part Three

THE MIDDLE AGES

The term "Middle Ages" was coined by Europeans in the seventeenth century to express their view that a long and dismal period of interruption extended between the glorious accomplishments of classical Greece and Rome and their own "modern age." Because the term became so widespread, it is now an ineradicable part of our historical vocabulary; but no serious scholar uses it with the sense of contempt it once had. Between about 600 and 1500—the rough opening and closing dates of the Middle Ages—too many different things happened to be characterized in any single way. In the eastern parts of the old Roman Empire two new civilizations emerged, the Byzantine and the Islamic, which must rank among the most impressive civilizations of all time. Although the Byzantine civilization came to an end in 1453, the Islamic one has continued to exist without major interruption right up to the present. Seen from an Islamic perspective, therefore, the "Middle Ages" was not a middle period at all but a marvelous time of birth and vigorous early youth. The history of western Europe in the Middle Ages is conventionally divided into three parts: the early Middle Ages; the High Middle Ages; and the later Middle Ages. Throughout the early, High, and later Middle Ages the Christian religion played an extraordinarily important role in human life, but otherwise there are few common denominators. The early Middle Ages, from about 600 to about 1050, came closest to appearing like an interval of darkness, for the level of material and intellectual accomplishment was, in fact, very low. Nonetheless, even during the early Middle Ages important foundations were being laid for the future: above all, western Europe was beginning to develop its own distinct sense of cultural identity. The High Middle Ages, from about 1050 to 1300, was one of the most creative epochs in the history of human endeavor. Europeans greatly improved their standard of living, established enduring national states, developed new institutions of learning and modes of thought, and created magnificent works of literature and art. During the later Middle Ages, from about 1300 to 1500, the survival of many high-medieval accomplishments was threatened by numerous disasters, particularly profound economic depression and lethal plague. But people in the later Middle Ages rose above adversity, tenaciously held on to what was most valuable in their inheritance, and, where necessary, created new institutions and thought-patterns to fit their altered circumstances. The Middle Ages thus were really many hundred years of enormous diversity. They may be studied profitably both for their own intrinsic interest and for the fundamental contributions they made to the development of the modern world.

The Middle Ages

POLITICS	PHILOSOPHY AND SCIENCE	
Byzantine Emperor Heraclius, 610–641		**600**
Muhammad enters Mecca in triumph, 630		
Muslims conquer Syria, Persia, and Egypt, 636–651		
Muslims conquer Spain, 711		
Muslim attack on Constantinople repulsed, 717		**700**
Charles Martel defeats Muslims at Poitiers, 732		
Abbasid dynasty in Islam, 750–1258		
Pepin the Short anointed king of the Franks, 751		
Charlemagne, 768–814		
Charlemagne crowned emperor, 800		**800**
Carolingian Empire disintegrates, c. 850–911		
Alfred the Great of England, 871–899		
High point of Viking raids in Europe, c. 880–911	Al-Farabi, d. 950	
Otto the Great of Germany, 936–973	Avicenna, d. 1037	**900**
Foundation of Kievan state in Russia, c. 950	Peter Abelard, 1079–1142	**1000**
Norman Conquest of England, 1066		
Seljuk Turks defeat Byzantines at Manzikert, 1071		
Penance of Henry IV at Canossa, 1077		
Henry I of England, 1100–1135	Origins of universities in the West, c. 1100–c. 1300	**1100**
Louis VI of France, 1108–1137	Translation of Aristotle's works into Latin, c. 1140–c. 1260	
Frederick I (Barbarossa) of Germany, 1152–1190	Peter Lombard's *Sentences,* c. 1155	
Henry II of England, 1154–1189	Robert Grosseteste, c. 1168–1253	
Philip Augustus of France, 1180–1223	Windmill invented, c. 1180	
	Averroës, d. 1198	
Crusaders take Constantinople (Fourth Crusade), 1204	Maimonides, d. 1204	**1200**
Spanish victory over Muslims at Las Navas de Tolosa, 1212		
Frederick II of Germany and Sicily, 1212–1250	Roger Bacon, c. 1214–1294	
	St. Thomas Aquinas, 1225–1274	
Magna Carta, 1215	Height of Scholasticism, c. 1250–c. 1277	
Louis IX (St. Louis) of France, 1226–1270	William of Ockham, c. 1285–1349	
	Mechanical clock invented, c. 1290	
Edward I of England, 1272–1307		
Philip IV (the Fair) of France, 1285–1314	Master Eckhart, active c. 1300–c. 1327	**1300**
	Height of nominalism, c. 1320–c. 1500	
Hundred Years' War, 1337–1453		
Political chaos in Germany, c. 1350–c. 1450		
		1400
Appearance of Joan of Arc, 1429–1431		
Reassertion of royal power in France, c. 1143–c. 1513	Printing with movable type, c. 1450	
Rise of princes in Germany, c. 1450–c. 1500	Heavy artillery helps Turks capture Constantinople and French end Hundred Years' War, 1453	
Capture of Constantinople by Ottoman Turks, 1453		
Wars of the Roses in England, 1455–1485		
Peace among northern Italian states, 1454–1485		
Marriage of Ferdinand and Isabella, 1469		
Ivan III lays groundwork for Russian Empire, 1462–1505		
Strong Tudor dynasty in England, 1485–1603		

	ECONOMICS	RELIGION	ARTS AND LETTERS
600	Decline of towns and trade in the West, c. 500–c. 700	Muhammad, c. 570–632 Pope Gregory I, 590–604 Muhammad's *Hijrah*, 622	Byzantine church of Santa Sophia, 532–537
700	Height of Islamic commerce and industry, c. 700–c. 1300 Predominantly agrarian economy in the West, c. 700–c. 1050	Split in Islam between Shiites and Sunnites, c. 656 Missionary work of St. Boniface in Germany, c. 715–754 Iconoclasm in Byzantine Empire, 726–843	The Venerable Bede, d. 735 *Beowulf*, c. 750 Irish "Book of Kells," c. 750 Carolingian Renaissance, c. 800–c. 850
800 **900**	Height of Byzantine commerce and industry, c. 800–c. 1000	Foundation of Cluny, 910 Byzantine conversion of Russia, c. 988	
1000	Destruction of Byzantine free peasantry, c. 1025–c. 1100 Agricultural advance, revival of towns and trade in the West, c. 1050– c. 1300	Beginning of Reform Papacy, 1046 Schism between Roman and Eastern Orthodox Churches, 1054 Pope Gregory VII, 1073–1085 St. Bernard of Clairvaux, 1090–1153 First Crusade, 1095–1099	Romanesque style in architecture and art, c. 1000–c. 1200
1100		Height of Cistercian monasticism, c. 1115–c. 1153 Concordat of Worms ends investiture struggle, 1122 Crusaders lose Jerusalem to Saladin, 1187 Pope Innocent III, 1198–1216 Albigensian Crusade, 1208–1213 Founding of Franciscan Order, 1210 Fourth Lateran Council, 1215 Founding of Dominican Order, 1216	*Song of Roland*, c. 1095 Troubadour poetry, c. 1100–c. 1220 *Rubaiyat* of Umar Khayyam, c. 1120 Anna Comnena's biography of Alexius, 1148 Gothic style in architecture and art, c. 1150–c. 1500 Poetry of Chretien de Troyes, c. 1165–c. 1190 Development of polyphony in Paris, c. 1170 Wolfram von Eschenbach, c. 1200 Gottfried von Strassburg, c. 1210
1200			
1300	European economic depression, c. 1300–c. 1450	Fall of last Christian outposts in Holy Land, 1291 Pope Boniface VIII, 1294–1303 Babylonian Captivity of papacy, 1305–1378 John Wyclif, c. 1330–1384	Persian poetry of Sadi, c. 1250 *Romance of the Rose*, c. 1270 Paintings of Giotto, c. 1305–1337
1400	Floods through western Europe, 1315 Black Death, 1347–1350 Height of Hanseatic League, c. 1350–c. 1450 English Peasants' Revolt, 1381 Medici Bank, 1397–1494	Great Schism of papacy, 1378–1417 John Hus preaches in Bohemia, c. 1408–1415 Council of Constance, 1414–1417 Hussite Revolt, 1420–1434 *Imitation of Christ*, c. 1427 Council of Basel, defeat of conciliarism, 1431–1449	Dante's *Divine Comedy*, c. 1310 Boccaccio's *Decameron*, c. 1350 Persian poetry of Hafiz, c. 1370 Chaucer's *Canterbury Tales*, c. 1390 Paintings of Jan van Eyck, c. 1400–c. 1441

Chapter 10

ROME'S THREE HEIRS: THE BY-ZANTINE, ISLAMIC, AND EARLY-MEDIEVAL WESTERN WORLDS

Constantinople is a bustling city, and merchants come to it from all over, by sea or land, and there is none like it in the world except Baghdad, the great city of Islam. In Constantinople is the church of Santa Sophia, and the seat of the Pope of the Greeks, since the Greeks do not obey the Pope of Rome. There are also as many churches as there are days of the year. A quantity of wealth is brought to them from the islands, and the like of this wealth is not to be found in any other church in the world.

—Benjamin of Tudela, *Travels*

You have become the best community ever raised up for mankind, enjoining the right and forbidding the wrong, and having faith in God.

—The Koran, III, 110

He who ordains the fate of kingdoms and the march of events, the almighty Disposer, having destroyed one extraordinary image, that of the Romans, which had feet of iron, or even feet of clay, then raised up among the Franks the golden head of a second image, just as remarkable, in the person of the glorious Charlemagne.

—A monk of St. Gall

A new period in the history of Western civilizations began in the seventh century, when it became clear that there would no longer be a single empire ruling over all the territories bordering on the Mediterranean. By about 700 A.D., in place of a united Rome, there were three successor civilizations that stood as rivals on different Mediterranean shores: the Byzantine, the Islamic, and the Western Christian. Each of these had its own language and distinctive forms of life. The Byzantine civilization, which descended directly from the Eastern Roman Empire, was Greek-speaking and dedicated to combining Roman governmental traditions with intense pursuit of

The successors of Rome

the Christian faith. The Islamic civilization was based on Arabic and inspired in government as well as culture by the idealism of a dynamic new religion. Western Christian civilization in comparison to the others was a laggard. It was the least economically advanced and faced organizational weaknesses in both government and religion. But it did have some base of unity in Christianity and the Latin language, and would soon begin to find greater political and religious cohesiveness.

Because the Western Christian civilization ultimately outstripped its rivals, Western writers until recently have tended to denigrate the Byzantine and Islamic civilizations as backward and even irrational. Of the three, however, the Western Christian was certainly the most backward from about the seventh to the eleventh centuries. For some four or five hundred years the West lived in the shadow of Constantinople and Mecca. Scholars are only now beginning to recognize the full measure of Byzantine and Islamic accomplishments. These greatly merit our attention both for their own sakes and because they influenced western European development in many direct and indirect ways.

I. THE BYZANTINE EMPIRE AND ITS CULTURE

Once dismissed by the historian Gibbon as "a tedious and uniform tale of weakness and misery," the story of Byzantine civilization is today recognized as a most interesting and impressive one. It is true that the Byzantine Empire was in many respects not very innovative; it was also continually beset by grave external threats and internal weaknesses. Nonetheless it managed to survive for a millennium. In fact the empire did not just survive, it frequently prospered and greatly influenced the world around it. Among many other achievements, it helped preserve ancient Greek thought, created magnificent works of art, and brought Christian culture to pagan peoples, above all the Slavs. Simply stated it was one of the most enduring and influential empires the world has ever known.

It is impossible to date the beginning of Byzantine history with any precision because the Byzantine Empire was the uninterrupted successor of the Roman state. For this reason different historians prefer different beginnings. Some argue that "Byzantine" characteristics already emerged in Roman history as a result of the easternizing policy of Diocletian, and others that Byzantine history began when Constantine moved his capital from Rome to Constantinople, the city which subsequently became the center of the Byzantine world. (The old name for the site on which Constantinople was built was Byzantium, from which we get the adjective Byzantine; it would be more accurate but cumbersome to say Constantinopolitine.) Diocletian and Constantine, however, continued to rule a united Roman Empire. As we have seen, as late as the sixth century, after the western part of the empire had fallen to the Germans, the Eastern Roman Emperor Justinian thought of himself as an heir to Augustus and fought hard to win back the West. Justinian's reign was clearly an important turning point in the direction of Byzantine civilization because it saw the crystallization of new forms of thought and art that can be considered more "Byzantine" than "Roman." But this still remains a matter of subjective emphasis: some scholars emphasize these newer forms, while others respond that Justinian continued to speak Latin and dreamed of restoring old Rome. Only after 610 did a new dynasty emerge that came from the East, spoke Greek, and maintained a fully Eastern or properly "Byzantine" policy. Hence although good arguments can be made for beginning Byzantine history with Diocletian, Constantine, or Justinian, we will begin here with the accession in 610 of the Emperor Heraclius.

It is also convenient to begin in 610 because from then until 1071 the main lines of Byzantine military and political history were determined by resistance against successive waves of invasions from the East. When Heraclius came to the throne the very existence of the Byzantine Empire was being challenged by the Persians, who had conquered almost all of the empire's Asian territories. As a symbol of their triumph the Persians in 614 even carried off the relic believed to be part of the original cross from Jerusalem. By enormous effort Heraclius rallied Byzantine strength and turned the tide, routing the Persians and retrieving the cross in 627. Persia was then reduced to subordination and Heraclius reigned in glory until 641. But in his last years new armies began to invade Byzantine territory, swarming out of hitherto placid Arabia. Inspired by the new religion of Islam and profiting from Byzantine exhaustion after the struggle with Persia, the Arabs made astonishingly rapid gains. By 650 they had taken most of the Byzantine territories the Persians had occupied briefly in the early seventh century, had conquered all of Persia itself, and were making their way westward across North Africa. Having become a Mediterranean power, the Arabs also took to the sea. In 677 they tried to conquer Constantinople with a fleet. Failing that, they attempted to take the city again in 717 by means of a concerted land and sea operation.

The Arab threat to Constantinople in 717 was a new low in Byzantine fortunes, but the threat was countered by the Emperor Leo the Isaurian (717–741) with as much resolution as Heraclius had met the Persian threat a century before. With the help of a secret incendiary device known as "Greek fire"[1] and great military ability, Leo was able

The reign of Heraclius; the rise of Islam

The Byzantine Emperor Heraclius, Shown Together with His Son. Comparison to coins of Trajan and Theodosius (above, pp. 185, 210) shows at a glance that a new style of civilization has emerged with much less attachment to naturalistic portraiture.

---

[1] This is believed to have been a mixture of sulfur, naphtha, and quicklime. Bronze tubes placed on the prows of ships, and also on the walls of Constantinople, released this liquid fire at the enemy.

Greek Fire

to defeat the Arab forces on sea and land. Leo's relief of Constantinople in 717 was one of the most significant battles in European history, not just because it allowed the Byzantine Empire to endure for centuries more, but also because it helped to save the West: had the Islamic armies taken Constantinople there would have been little to stop them from sweeping through the rest of Europe. Over the next few decades the Byzantines were able to reconquer most of Asia Minor. This territory, together with Greece, became the heartland of their empire for the next three hundred years. Thereafter the Byzantines achieved a stalemate with Islam until they were able to take the offensive against a decaying Islamic power in the second half of the tenth century. In that period—the greatest in Byzantine history—Byzantine troops reconquered most of Syria. But in the eleventh century a different Islamic people, the Seljuk Turks, cancelled out all the prior Byzantine gains. In 1071 the Seljuks annihilated a Byzantine army at Manzikert in Asia Minor, a stunning victory which allowed them to overrun the remaining Byzantine eastern provinces. Constantinople was now thrown back upon itself more or less as it had been in the days of Heraclius and Leo.

After Manzikert the Byzantine Empire managed to survive, but never regained its earlier vigor. One major reason for this was the fact that, from 1071 until the final destruction of the empire in 1453, Byzantine fortunes were greatly complicated by the rise of western Europe. Hitherto the West had been far too weak to present any major challenge to Byzantium, but that situation changed entirely in the course of the eleventh century. In 1071, the same year that saw the victory of the Seljuks over the Byzantines in Asia Minor, westerners known as Normans expelled the Byzantines from their last holdings in southern Italy. Despite this clear sign of Western enmity, in 1095 a Byzantine emperor named Alexius Comnenus issued a call for Western help against the Turks. He could hardly have made a worse mistake: his call helped inspire the Crusades, and the Crusades became a major cause for the fall of the Byzantine state. Westerners on the First Crusade did help the Byzantines win back Asia Minor but they also carved out territories for themselves in Syria, which the Byzantines considered to be their own. As time went on frictions mounted and the westerners, now militarily superior, looked more and more upon Constantinople as a fruit ripe for the picking. In 1204 they finally picked it: Crusaders who should have been intent on conquering Jerusalem conquered Constantinople instead and sacked the city with ruthless ferocity. A greatly reduced Byzantine government was able to survive nearby and return to Constantinople in 1261, but thereafter the Byzantine state was an "empire" in name and recollection of past glories only. After 1261 it eked out a reduced existence in parts of Greece until 1453, when powerful Turkish successors to the Seljuks, the Ottomans, completed the Crusaders' work of destruction by conquering the last vestiges of the empire and taking Constantinople. Turks rule in Constantinople—now Istanbul—even today.

That Constantinople was finally taken was no surprise. What *is* a cause for wonder is that the Byzantine state survived for so many centuries in the face of so many different hostile forces. This wonder becomes all the greater when it is recognized that the internal political history of the empire was exceedingly tumultuous. Because Byzantine rulers followed their late-Roman predecessors in claiming the powers of divinely appointed absolute monarchs, there was no way of opposing them other than by intrigue and violence. Hence Byzantine history was marked by repeated palace revolts; mutilations, murders, and blindings were almost commonplace. Byzantine politics became so famous for their behind-the-scenes complexity that we still use the word "Byzantine" to refer to highly complex and devious backstage machinations. Fortunately for the empire some very able rulers did emerge from time to time to wield their untrammeled powers with efficiency, and, even more fortunately, a bureaucratic machinery always kept running during times of palace upheaval.

Efficient bureaucratic government indeed was one of the major elements of Byzantine success and longevity. The Byzantines could count on having an adequate supply of manpower for their bureaucracy because Byzantine civilization preserved and encouraged the practice of education for the laity. This was one of the major differences between the Byzantine East and the early Latin West: from about 600 to about 1200 there was practically no literate laity in Western Christendom, while lay literacy in the Byzantine East was the basis of governmental accomplishment. Byzantine officialdom regulated many aspects of life, far more than we would think proper

Factors of the stability of the Byzantine Empire: (1) occasional able rulers

(2) efficient bureaucratic administration

today. Bureaucrats helped supervise education and religion and presided over all forms of economic endeavor. Urban officials in Constantinople, for example, regulated prices and wages, maintained systems of licensing, controlled exports, and enforced the observance of the Sabbath. What is more, they usually did this with comparative efficiency and did not stifle business initiative. Bureaucratic methods too helped regulate the army and navy, the courts, and the diplomatic service, endowing them with organizational strengths incomparable for their age.

(3) firm economic base

Another explanation for Byzantine endurance was the comparatively sound economic base of the state until the eleventh century. As the historian Sir Steven Runciman has said, "if Byzantium owed her strength and security to the efficiency of her Services, it was her trade that enabled her to pay for them." While long-distance trade and urban life all but disappeared in the West for hundreds of years, commerce and cities continued to flourish in the Byzantine East. Above all, in the ninth and tenth centuries Constantinople was a vital trade emporium for Far Eastern luxury goods and Western raw materials. The empire also nurtured and protected its own industries, most notably that of silk-making, and it was renowned until the eleventh century for its stable gold and silver coinage. Among its great urban centers was not only Constantinople, which at times may have had a population of close to a million, but also in certain periods Antioch, and up until the end of Byzantine history the bustling cities of Thessalonica and Trebizond.

The significance of Byzantine agricultural history

Historians emphasize Byzantine trade and industry because these were so advanced for the time and provided most of the surplus wealth which supported the state. But agriculture was really at the heart of the Byzantine economy as it was of all premodern ones. The story of Byzantine agricultural history is mainly one of a struggle of small peasants to stay free of the encroachments of large estates owned by wealthy aristocrats and monasteries. Until the eleventh century the free peasantry just managed to maintain its existence with the help of state legislation, but after 1025 the aristocracy gained power in the government and began to transform the peasants into impoverished tenants. This had many unfortunate results, not the least of which was that the peasants became less interested in resisting the enemy. The defeat at Manzikert was the inevitable result. The destruction of the free peasantry was accompanied and followed in the last centuries of Byzantine history by foreign domination of Byzantine trade. Primarily the Italian cities of Venice and Genoa established trading outposts and privileges within Byzantine realms after 1204, which channeled off much of the wealth on which the state had previously relied. In this way the empire was defeated by the Venetians from within before it was destroyed by the Turks from without.

So far we have spoken about military campaigns, government, and economics as if they were at the center of Byzantine survival. Seen from hindsight they were, but what the Byzantines themselves cared about most was usually religion. Remarkable as it might seem, Byzantines fought over abstruse religious questions as vehemently as we today might argue about politics and sports—indeed more vehemently because the Byzantines were often willing to fight and even die over some words in a religious creed. The intense preoccupation with questions of doctrine is well illustrated by the report of an early Byzantine writer who said that when he asked a baker for the price of bread, the answer came back, "the Father is greater than the Son," and when he asked whether his bath was ready, was told that "the Son proceeds from nothing." Understandably such zealousness could harm the state greatly during times of religious dissension but endow it with a powerful sense of confidence and mission during times of religious concord.

Byzantine religious dissensions were greatly complicated by the fact that the emperors took an active role in them. Because the emperors carried great power in the life of the Church—emperors were sometimes deemed by churchmen to be "similar to God"—they exerted great influence in religious debates. Nonetheless, especially in the face of provincial separatism, rulers could never force all their subjects to believe what they did. Only after the loss of many eastern provinces and the refinement of doctrinal formulae did religious peace seem near in the eighth century. But then it was shattered for still another century by what is known as the Iconoclastic Controversy.

Imperial participation in religious controversies

The Iconoclasts were those who wished to prohibit the worship of icons—that is, images of Christ and the saints. Since the Iconoclastic movement was initiated by the Emperor Leo the Isaurian, and subsequently directed with even greater energy by his son Constantine V (740–775), historians have discerned in it different motives. One was certainly theological. The worship of images seemed to the Iconoclasts to smack of paganism. They believed that nothing made by human beings should be worshiped by them, that Christ was so divine that he could not be conceived of in terms of human art, and that the prohibition of worshiping "graven images" in the Ten Commandments (Exodus 20:4) placed the matter beyond dispute.

Iconoclasts' Cross. The Iconoclasts covered over beautiful apse mosaics with unadorned crosses. This example survives in St. Irene's church, Greece.

In addition to these theological points, there were probably other considerations. Since Leo the Isaurian was the emperor who saved Constantinople from the onslaught of Islam, and since Muslims zealously shunned images on the grounds that they were "the work of Satan" (Koran, V. 92), it has been argued that Leo's Inconoclastic policy was an attempt to answer one of Islam's greatest criticisms of Christianity and thereby deprive Islam of some of its appeal. There may also have been certain internal political and financial motives. By proclaiming a radical new religious movement the emperors may have wished to reassert their control over the Church and combat the

Political and financial motives

Christ as Ruler of the Universe. A twelfth-century Byzantine mosaic from the cathedral of Cefalù in Sicily. Although the Byzantines did not rule in Sicily in the twelfth century, the Norman rulers employed Byzantine workmen. Note the use of Greek—the Byzantine language—on the left-handed Bible page and Latin—the Norman language—on the right.

growing strength of monasteries. In the event, the monasteries did rally behind the cause of images and as a result were bitterly persecuted by Constantine V, who took the opportunity to appropriate much monastic wealth.

Significance of the Iconoclastic Controversy

The Iconoclastic Controversy was resolved in the ninth century by a return to the status quo, namely the worship of images, but the century of turmoil over the issue had some profound results. One was the destruction by imperial order of a large amount of religious art. Pre–eighth-century Byzantine religious art that survives today comes mostly from places like Italy or Palestine, which were beyond the easy reach of the Iconoclastic emperors. When we see how great this art is we can only lament the destruction of the rest. A second consequence of the controversy was the opening of a serious religious breach between East and West. The pope, who until the eighth century had usually been a close ally of the Byzantines, could not accept Iconoclasm for many reasons. The most important of these was that extreme Iconoclasm tended to question the cult of saints, and the claims of papal primacy were based on an assumed descent from St. Peter. Accordingly, the eighth-century popes combated Byzantine Iconoclasm and turned to the Frankish kings for support. This "about-face of the papacy" was both a major step in the worsening of East-West relations and a landmark in the history of western Europe.

Other results: (1) reaffirmation of tradition

Those were some consequences of Iconoclasm's temporary victory; a major consequence of its defeat was the reassertion of some major traits of Byzantine religiosity, which from the ninth century until the end of Byzantine history remained predominant. One of these was the reemphasis of a faith in traditionalism. Even when Byzantines were experimenting in religious matters they consistently stated that they were only restating or developing the implications of tradition. Now, after centuries of turmoil, they abandoned experiment almost entirely and reaffirmed tradition more than ever. As one opponent of Iconoclasm said: "If an angel or an emperor announces to you a gospel other than the one you have received, close your ears." This view gave strength to Byzantine religion internally by ending controversy and heresy, and helped it gain new adherents in the ninth and tenth centuries. But it also inhibited free speculation not just in religion but also in related intellectual matters.

Allied to this development was the triumph of Byzantine contemplative piety. Supporters defended the use of icons not on the grounds that they were meant to be worshiped for themselves but because they helped lead the mind from the material to the immaterial. The emphasis on contemplation as a road to religious enlightenment thereafter became the hallmark of Byzantine spirituality. While westerners did not by any means reject such a path, the typical Western saint was an activist who saw sin as a vice and sought salvation through good works. Byzantine theologians on the other hand saw sin more as ignorance and believed that salvation was to be found in illumination. This led to a certain religious passivity and mysticism in Eastern Christianity which makes it seem different from Western varieties up to the present time.

(2) the triumph of Byzantine contemplative piety

Since religion was so dominant in Byzantine life, certain secular aspects of Byzantine civilization often go unnoticed, but there are good reasons why some of these should not be forgotten. One is Byzantine cultivation of the classics. Commitment to Christianity by no means inhibited the Byzantines from revering their ancient Greek inheritance. Byzantine schools based their instruction on classical Greek literature to the degree that educated people could quote Homer more extensively than we today can quote Shakespeare. Byzantine scholars studied and commented on the philosophy of Plato and Aristotle, and Byzantine writers imitated the prose of Thucydides. Such dedicated classicism both enriched Byzantine intellectual and literary life, which is too often dismissed entirely by moderns because it generally lacked originality, and helped preserve the Greek classics for later ages. The bulk of classical Greek literature that we have today survives only because it was copied by Byzantine scribes.

Byzantine classicism

Byzantine classicism was a product of an educational system for the laity which extended to the education of women as well as men. Given attitudes and practices in the contemporary Christian West and Islam, Byzantine commitment to female education was truly unusual. Girls from aristocratic or prosperous families did not go to schools but were relatively well educated at home by private tutors. We are told, for example, of one Byzantine woman who could discourse like Plato or Pythagoras. The most famous Byzantine female intellectual was the Princess Anna Comnena, who described the deeds of her father Alexius in an urbane biography in which she freely cited Homer and the ancient tragedians. In addition to such literary figures there were

The education of women

Santa Sophia. The greatest monument of Byzantine architecture. The four minarets were added after the fall of the Byzantine Empire, when the Turks turned the church into a mosque. As the diagram shows, the central dome rests on four massive arches.

*Byzantine architecture;
the Church of Santa
Sophia*

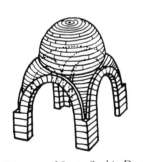

Diagram of Santa Sophia Dome

Novel structural design

women doctors in the Byzantine Empire, a fact which may serve to remind us that there have hardly been any in America almost to the present day.

Byzantine achievements in the realms of architecture and art are more familiar. The finest example of Byzantine architecture was the Church of Santa Sophia (Holy Wisdom), built at enormous cost in the sixth century. Although built before the date taken here as the beginning of Byzantine history, it was typically Byzantine in both its style and subsequent influence. Though designed by architects of Hellenic descent, it was vastly different from any Greek temple. Its purpose was not to express human pride in the power of the individual, but to symbolize the inward and spiritual character of the Christian religion. For this reason the architects gave little attention to the external appearance of the building. Nothing but plain brick covered with plaster was used for the exterior walls; there were no marble facings, graceful columns, or sculptured entablatures. The interior, however, was decorated with richly colored mosaics, gold leaf, colored marble columns, and bits of tinted glass set on edge to refract the rays of sunlight after the fashion of sparkling gems. To emphasize a sense of the miraculous, the building was constructed in such a way that no light appeared to come from the outside at all but to be manufactured within.

The structural design of Santa Sophia was something altogether new in the history of architecture. Its central feature was the application of the principle of the dome to a building of square shape. The church was designed, first of all, in the form of a cross, and then over the central square was to be erected a magnificent dome, which would dominate the entire structure. The main problem was how to fit the round circumference of the dome to the square area it was supposed to cover. The solution consisted in having four great arches spring from pillars at the four corners of the central square. The rim of the dome was then made to rest on the keystones of the arches, with the curved triangular spaces between the arches filled in with masonry. The result was an architectural framework of marvelous strength, which at the same time made possible a style of imposing grandeur and even some delicacy of treatment. The great dome of Santa Sophia has a diameter of 107 feet and rises to a height of nearly 180 feet from the floor. So many windows are placed around its rim that the dome appears to have no support at all but to be suspended in mid-air.

As in architecture, so in art the Byzantines profoundly altered the earlier Greek classical style. Byzantines excelled in ivory-carving, manuscript illumination, jewelry-making, and, above all, the creation of mosaics—that is, designs of pictures produced by fitting together small pieces of colored glass or stone. Human figures in these mosaics were usually distorted and elongated in a very unclassical fashion to create the impression of intense piety or extreme majesty. Most Byzantine art is marked by highly abstract, formal, and jewel-like qualities. For this reason many consider Byzantine artistic culture to be a model of timeless perfection. The modern poet W. B. Yeats expressed this point of view most eloquently when he wrote in his "Sailing to Byzantium" of artificial birds made by Byzantine goldsmiths ". . . to sing / To lords and ladies of Byzantium / Of what is past, or passing, or to come."

See color plates facing page 225

Probably the single greatest testimony to the vitality of Byzantine civilization at its height was the conversion of many Slavic peoples, especially those of Russia. According to the legend, which has a basic kernel of fact, a Russian ruler named Vladimir decided around 988 to abandon the paganism of his ancestors. Accordingly, he sent emissaries to report on the religious practices of Islam, Roman Catholicism, and Byzantine Christianity. When they returned to tell him that only among the Byzantines did God seem to "dwell among men," he promptly agreed to be baptized by a Byzantine missionary. The event was momentous because Russia thereupon became a cultural province of Byzantium. From then until the twentieth century Russia remained a bastion of the Eastern Orthodox religion.

After Constantinople fell in 1453 Russians began to feel that they were chosen to carry on both the faith and the imperial mission of the fallen Byzantine Empire. Thus their ruler took the title of tsar—which simply means caesar—and Russians asserted that Moscow was "the third Rome": "Two Romes have fallen," said a Russian spokesman, "the third is still standing, and a fourth there shall not be." Such ideology helps explain in part the later growth of Russian imperialism. Byzantine traditions also may help explain the dominance of the ruler in the Russian state. Without question Byzantine stylistic principles influenced Russian religious art, and Byzantine ideas influenced the thought of modern Russia's greatest writers, Dostoevsky and Tolstoy.

Byzantine Metalwork. This dish, from about 620, represents literally David and Goliath, and figuratively the New Dispensation (David was the ancestor of Christ) overcoming the Old. The New, Christian, Dispensation is also symbolized by the sun, and the Old by a crescent moon.

Russian Icon. This early–seventeenth-century Russian painting depicts an angel in a distinctly Byzantine style.

Unfortunately, just at the time when relations between Constantinople and Russia were solidifying, relations with the West were deteriorating to a point of no return. After the skirmishes of the Iconoclastic period relations between Eastern and Western Christians remained tense, partly because Constantinople resented Western claims (initiated by Charlemagne in 800) of creating a rival empire, but most of all because cultural and religious differences between the two were growing. From the Byzantine point of view westerners were uncouth and ignorant, while to western European eyes Byzantines were effeminate and prone to heresy. Once the West started to revive, it began to take the offensive against a weakened East in theory and practice. In 1054 extreme papal claims of primacy over the Eastern Church provoked a religious schism which since then has never been healed. Thereafter the Crusades drove home the dividing wedge.

After the sack of Constantinople in 1204 Byzantine hatred of westerners became understandably intense. "Between us and them," one Byzantine wrote, "there is now a deep chasm: we do not have a single thought in common." Westerners called easterners "the dregs of the dregs . . . unworthy of the sun's light," while easterners called westerners the children of darkness, alluding to the fact that the sun sets in the West. The beneficiaries of this hatred were the Turks, who not only conquered Constantinople in 1453, but soon after conquered most of southeastern Europe up to Vienna.

St. Mark's Church, Venice. The most splendid example of Byzantine architecture in Italy.

The Interior of St. Mark's, Venice

In view of this sad history of hostility it is best to end our treatment of Byzantine civilization by recalling how much we owe to it. In simple physical terms the Byzantine Empire acted as a bulwark against Islam from the seventh to the eleventh centuries, thus helping to preserve an independent West. If the Byzantines had not prospered and defended Europe, Western Christian civilization might well have been snuffed out. Then too we owe an enormous amount in cultural terms to Byzantine scholars who helped preserve classical Greek learning. The most famous moment of communication between Byzantine and western European scholars came during the Italian Renaissance, when Byzantines helped introduce Italian humanists to the works of Plato. But westerners were already learning from Byzantines before then, and they continued to gain riches from Byzantine manuscripts until the sixteenth century. Similarly, Byzantine art exerted a great influence on the art of western Europe over a long period of time. To take only some of the most famous examples, St. Mark's basilica in Venice was built in close imitation of the Byzantine style, and the art of such great Western painters as Giotto and El Greco owes much in different ways to Byzantine influences. Nor should we stop at listing influences because the great surviving monuments of Byzantine culture retain their imposing appeal in and of themselves. Travelers who view Byzantine mosaics in such cities as Ravenna and Palermo are continually awe-struck; others who make their way to Istanbul still find Santa Sophia to be a marvel. In such jeweled beauty, then, the light from the Byzantine East, which once glowed so brightly, continues to shimmer.

The Byzantine contribution to Western civilization

2. THE FLOWERING OF ISLAM

In contrast to Byzantine history, which has no clearly datable beginning but a definite end in 1453, the history of Islamic civilization has a clear point of origin, beginning with the career of Muhammad in the seventh century, but no end since Islam, Muhammad's religion, is still a major force in the modern world. Believers in Islam, known as Muslims, currently comprise about one-seventh of the global population: in their greatest concentrations they extend from Africa through the Middle East and the Soviet Union to India, Bangladesh, and Indonesia. All these Muslims subscribe both to a common religion and a common way of life, for Islam has always demanded from its followers not just adherence to certain forms of worship but also adherence to set social and cultural norms. Indeed, more than Judaism or Christianity, Islam has been a great experiment in trying to build a worldwide society based on the fullest harmony between religious requirements and precepts for everyday existence. In practice, of course, that experiment has differed in its success and quality according to time and place, but it is still being tested, and it accounts for the fact that there remains an extraordinary sense of community between all Muslims regardless of race, language, and geographical distribution. In this section we will trace the early history of the Islamic experiment with primary emphasis on its orientation toward the West. But it must always be remembered that Islam expanded in many directions and that it ultimately had as much influence on the history of Africa and India as it did on that of Europe or western Asia.

Although Islam spread to many lands it was born in Arabia, so the story of its history must begin there. Arabia, a peninsula of deserts, had been so backward before the founding of Islam that the two dominant neighboring empires, the Roman and the Persian, had not deemed it worthwhile to extend their rule over Arabian territories. Most Arabs were Bedouins, wandering camel herdsmen who lived off the milk of their animals and the produce, such as dates, that was grown in desert oases. In the second half of the sixth century there was a quickening of economic life owing to a shift in long-distance trade routes. The protracted wars between the Byzantine and Persian Empires made Arabia a safer transit route for caravans going between Africa and Asia than were other areas, and some towns grew to direct and take advantage of this growth of trade. Most prominent of these was Mecca, which not only lay on the junction of major trade routes, but also had long been a local religious center. In Mecca was located the Kabah, a pilgrimage shrine which served as a central place of worship for many different Arabian clans and tribes. (Within the Kabah was the Black Stone, a meteorite worshiped as a miraculous relic by adherents of many different divinities.) The men who controlled this shrine and also directed the economic life of the Meccan area belonged to the tribe of Quraish, an aristocracy of traders and entrepreneurs who provided the area with whatever little government it knew.

Muhammad, the founder of Islam, was born in Mecca to a family of the Quraish about 570. Orphaned early in life, he entered the service of a rich widow whom he later married, thereby attaining financial security. Until middle age he lived as a prosperous trader, behaving little differently from his fellow townsmen, but around 610 he underwent a religious experience which changed the course of his life and ultimately that of a good part of the world. Although most Arabs until then had been polytheists who recognized at most the vague superiority of a more powerful god they called Allah, Muhammad in 610 believed he heard a voice from heaven tell him that there was no god but Allah alone. In other words, as the result of a conversion experience he became an uncompromising monotheist. Thereafter he received further messages which served as the basis for a new religion and which commanded him to accept the calling of "Prophet" to proclaim the monotheistic faith to the Quraish. At first he was not very successful in gaining converts beyond a limited circle, perhaps because the leading Quraish tribesmen believed that establishment of a new religion would deprive the Kabah, and therewith Mecca, of its central place in local worship. The town of Yathrib to the north, however, had no such concerns, and its representatives invited Muhammad to emigrate there so that he could serve as a neutral arbiter of local rivalries. In 622 Muhammad and his followers accepted the invitation. Because their migration—called in Arabic the *Hijrah* (or Hegira)—saw the beginning of an advance in Muhammad's fortunes, it is considered by Muslims to mark the beginning of their era: as Christians begin their era with the birth of Christ so Muslims begin their dating system with the *Hijrah* of 622.

Muhammad changed the name of Yathrib to Medina (the "city of the Prophet") and quickly succeeded in establishing himself as ruler of the town. In the course of doing this he consciously began to organize his converts into a political as well as religious community. But he still needed to find some means of support for his original Meccan fol-

The consolidation of Muhammad's religion

The Kabah. It contains the black stone which was supposed to have been miraculously sent down from heaven, and rests in the courtyard of the great mosque in Mecca.

lowers, and he also desired to wreak vengeance on the Quraish for not heeding his calls for conversion. Accordingly, he started leading his followers in raids on Quraish caravans traveling beyond Mecca. The Quraish endeavored to defend themselves, but after a few years Muhammad's band, fired by religious enthusiasm, succeeded in defeating them. In 630, after several desert battles, Muhammad entered Mecca in triumph. The Quraish thereupon submitted to the new faith and the Kabah was not only preserved but made the main shrine of Islam, as it remains today. With the taking of Mecca other tribes throughout Arabia in turn accepted the new faith. Thus, although Muhammad died in 632, he lived long enough to see the religion he had founded become a success.

The doctrines of Islam

The doctrines of Islam are very simple. The word *islam* itself means submission, and the faith of Islam called for absolute submission to God. Although the Arabic name for the one God is Allah, it is mistaken to believe that Muslims worship a god like Zeus or Jupiter who is merely the first among many: Allah for Muslims means the Creator God Almighty—the same omnipotent deity worshiped by Christians and Jews. Instead of saying, then, that Muslims believe "there is no god but Allah," it is more correct to say they believe that "there is no divinity but God." In keeping with this, Muslims believe that Muhammad himself was God's last and greatest prophet, but not that he was God himself. In addition to strict monotheism Muhammad taught above all that men and women must surrender themselves entirely to God because divine judgment was imminent. Mortals must make a fundamental choice about whether to begin a new life of divine service: if they decide in favor of this, God will guide them to blessedness, but if they do not, God will turn away from them and they will become irredeemably wicked. On judgment day the pious will be granted eternal life in a fleshly paradise of delights, but the damned will be sent to a realm of eternal fire and torture. The practical steps the believer can take are found in the Koran, the compilation of the revelations purportedly sent by God to Muhammad, and hence the definitive Islamic scripture. These steps include thorough dedication to moral rectitude and compassion, and fidelity to set religious observances: i.e., a regimen of prayers and fasts, pilgrimage to Mecca, and frequent recitation of parts of the Koran.

Judeo-Christian influence on Islam

The fact that much in the religion of Islam resembles Judaism and Christianity is not just coincidental; Muhammad was definitely influenced by the two earlier religions. (There were many Jews in Mecca and Medina; Christian thought was also known to Muhammad, although more indirectly.) Islam most resembles the two earlier religions in its strict monotheism, its stress on personal morality and compassion, and its reliance on written, revealed scripture. Muhammad proclaimed the Koran as the ultimate source of religious authority but accepted both the Old and New Testaments as divinely inspired. From Christianity Muhammad seems to have derived his doctrines of

The Archangel Gabriel Brings Revelation to Muhammad. A much later Persian conception.

the last judgment, the resurrection of the body with subsequent rewards and punishments, and his belief in angels (he thought that God's first message to him had been sent by the angel Gabriel). But although Muhammad accepted Jesus Christ as one of the greatest of a long line of prophets, he did not believe in Christ's divinity and himself laid claim to no miracles other than the writing of the Koran. He also ignored the Christian doctrine of sacrificial love, and most important, preached a religion without sacraments or priests. For Muslims every believer has direct responsibility for living the life of the faith without intermediaries; instead of priests there are only religious scholars who may comment on problems of Islamic faith and law. Muslims are expected to pray together in mosques, but there is nothing like a Muslim mass. The absence of clergy makes Islam more like Judaism, a similarity which is enhanced by Islamic stress on the inextricable connection between the religious and sociopolitical life of the divinely inspired community. But, unlike Judaism, Islam laid claim to universalism and a unique role in uniting the world as it started to spread far beyond the confines of Arabia.

This move toward world influence began immediately upon Muhammad's death. Since he had made no provision for the future, and since the Arabs had no clear concept of political succession, it was unclear whether Muhammad's community would survive at all. But his closest followers, led by his father-in-law Abu-Bakr and a zealous early convert named Umar, quickly took the initiative by naming Abu-Bakr *caliph* meaning "deputy of the Prophet." Thereafter, for about three hundred years, the caliph was to serve as the supreme religious and political leader of all Muslims. Immediately after becoming caliph Abu-Bakr began a military campaign to subdue various Arabian tribes which had followed Muhammad but were not willing to accept his

The unification of Arabia after Muhammad: the caliphs

Two Views of the Dome of the Rock, Jerusalem. According to Muslim tradition, Muhammad made a miraculous journey to Jerusalem before his death and left a footprint in a rock. The mosque which was erected over the site in the seventh century is, after the Kabah, Islam's second-holiest shrine.

successor's authority. In the course of this thoroughly successful military action Abu-Bakr's forces began to spill northward over the borders of Arabia. Probably to their surprise they found that they met minimal resistance from Byzantine and Persian forces.

Arab expansion and conquests

Abu-Bakr died two years after his accession but was succeeded as caliph by Umar, who continued to direct the Arabian invasions of the neighboring empires. In the following years triumph was virtually uninterrupted. In 636 the Arabs routed a Byzantine army in Syria and then quickly swept over the entire area, occupying the leading cities of Antioch, Damascus, and Jerusalem; in 637 they destroyed the main army of the Persians and marched into the Persian capital of Ctesiphon. Once the Persian administrative center was taken, the Persian Empire offered scarcely any more resistance: by 651 the Arabian conquest of the entire Persian realm was complete. Since Byzantium was centered around distant Constantinople, the Arabs were not similarly able to stop its imperial heart from beating. But they did quickly manage to deprive the Byzantine Empire of Egypt by 646 and then swept west across North Africa. In 711 they crossed from there into Spain and quickly took almost all of that area too. Thus within less than a century Islam had conquered all of ancient Persia and much of the old Roman world.

How can we explain this prodigious expansion? The best approach is to see first what impelled the conquerors and then to see what circumstances helped to ease their way. Contrary to widespread belief the early spread of Islam was not achieved through a religious crusade. At first the Arabs were not at all interested in converting other peoples: to the contrary, they hoped that conquered populations would not convert so that they could maintain their own identity as a community of rulers and tax-gatherers. But although their motives for expansion were not religious, religious enthusiasm played a crucial role in making the hitherto unruly Arabs take orders from the caliph and in instilling a sense that they were carrying out the will of God. What really moved the Arabs out of the desert was the search for richer territory and booty, and what kept them moving ever farther was the ease of acquiring new wealth as they progressed. Fortunately for the Arabs their inspiration by Islam came just at the right time in terms of the weakness of their enemies. The Byzantines and Persians had become so exhausted by their long wars that they could hardly rally for a new effort. Moreover, Persian and Byzantine local populations were hostile to the financial demands made by their bureaucratic empires; also, in the Byzantine lands of Syria and Egypt "heretical" Christians were at odds with the persecuting orthodoxy of Constantinople. Because the Arabs did not demand conversion and exacted fewer taxes than the Byzantines and Persians, they were often welcomed as preferable to the old rulers. One Christian writer in Syria went so far as to say "the God of vengeance delivered us out of the hands of the Romans [i.e., the Byzantine Empire] by means of the Arabs." For all these reasons Islam quickly spread over the vast extent of territory between Egypt and Iran, and has been rooted there ever since.

While the Arabs were extending their conquests they ran into their first serious political divisions. In 644 the Caliph Umar died; he was replaced by one Uthman, a weak ruler who had the added drawback for many of belonging to the Umayyad family, a wealthy clan from Mecca which had not at first accepted Muhammad's call. Those dissatisfied with Uthman rallied around the Prophet's cousin and son-in-law Ali, whose blood, background, and warrior spirit made him seem a more appropriate leader of the cause. When Uthman was murdered in 656 by mutineers, Ali's partisans raised him up as caliph. But Uthman's powerful family and supporters were unwilling to accept Ali. In subsequent disturbances Ali was murdered and Uthman's party emerged triumphant. In 661 a member of the Umayyad family took over as caliph and that house ruled Islam until 750. Even then, however, Ali's followers did not accept defeat. As time went on they hardened into a minority religious party known as Shiites; this group insisted that only descendants of Ali could be caliphs or have any authority over the Muslim community. Those who stood instead for the actual historical development of the caliphate and became committed to its customs were called Sunnites. The cleft between the two parties has been a lasting one in Islamic history. Often persecuted, Shiites developed great militancy and a deep sense of being the only true

Reasons for the spread of Islam

Division between Shiites and Sunnites

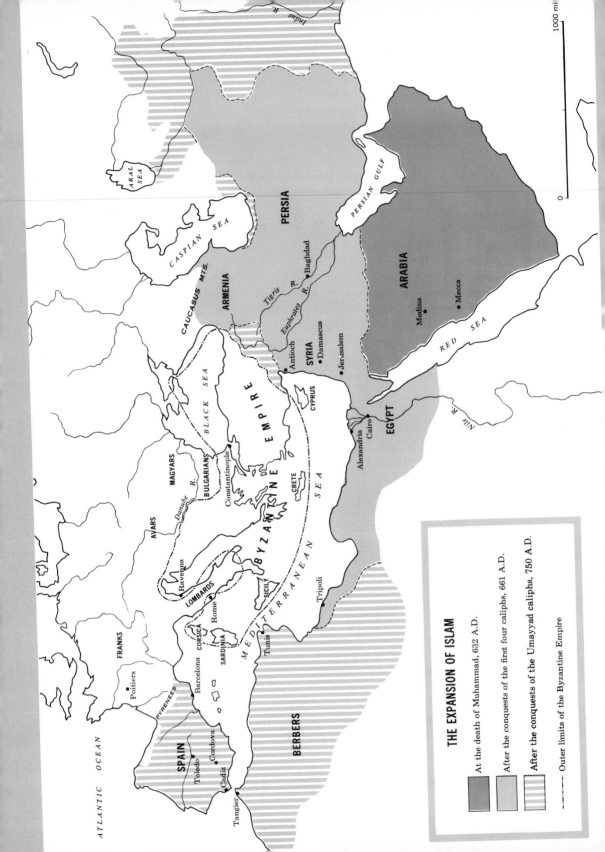

ATLANTIC OCEAN

SPAIN
Toledo
Cordova
Cadiz
Tangier

FRANKS
Poitiers
PYRENEES
Barcelona

BERBERS

MEDITERRANEAN SEA

Tunis
SARDINIA
CORSICA
Rome
LOMBARDS
Ravenna
SICILY
Tripoli

AVARS
MAGYARS
BULGARIANS
Danube R.
Constantinople
BYZANTINE EMPIRE
CRETE
CYPRUS

BLACK SEA

CAUCASUS MTS.
ARMENIA

CASPIAN SEA

ARAL SEA

Indus R.

PERSIA

Tigris R.
Euphrates R.
Baghdad
Antioch
SYRIA
Damascus
Jerusalem

PERSIAN GULF

ARABIA
Medina
Mecca

RED SEA

Alexandria
Cairo
EGYPT
Nile R.

1000 miles
0

THE EXPANSION OF ISLAM

At the death of Muhammad, 632 A.D.

After the conquests of the first four caliphs, 661 A.D.

After the conquests of the Umayyad caliphs, 750 A.D.

Outer limits of the Byzantine Empire

preservers of the faith. From time to time they were able to seize power in one or another area, but they never succeeded in converting the majority of Muslims. Today they rule in Iran and are very numerous in Iraq but comprise only about one-tenth of the worldwide population of Islam.

The triumph of the Umayyads in 661 began a more settled period in the history of the caliphate, lasting until 945. During that time there were two major governing orientations: that represented by the rule of the Umayyads, and that represented by their successors, the Abbasids. The Umayyads centered their strength in the old Byzantine territories in Syria and continued to use local officials who were not Muslims for their administration. For these reasons the Umayyad caliphate appears to some extent like a Byzantine successor state. With their more Western orientation the Umayyads concentrated their energies on dominating the Mediterranean and conquering Constantinople. When their most massive attack on the Byzantine capital failed in 717, Umayyad strength was seriously weakened; it was only a matter of time before a new orientation would develop.

The Umayyads

This was represented by the takeover of a new family, the Abbasids, in 750. Their rule may be said to have stressed Persian more than Byzantine elements. Characteristic of this change was a shift in capitals, for the second Abbasid caliph built his new capital of Baghdad in Iraq near the ruins of the old Persian capital and even appropriated stones from the ruins. The Abbasids developed their own Muslim administration and imitated Persian absolutism. Abbasid caliphs ruthlessly cut down their enemies, surrounded themselves with elaborate court ceremonies, and lavishly patronized sophisticated literature. This is the world described in the *Arabian Nights,* a collection of stories of dazzling Oriental splendor written in Baghdad under the Abbasids. The dominating presence in those stories, Harun al-Rashid, actually reigned as caliph from 786 to 809 and behaved as extravagantly as he was described, tossing coins in the streets, passing out sumptuous gifts to his favorites and severe punishments to his enemies. From a Western point of view the Abbasid caliphate was of significance not just in creating legends and literature but also because its Eastern orientation took much pressure off the Mediterranean. The Byzantine state, accordingly, was able to revive, and the Franks in the far West began to develop some strength of their own. (The greatest Frankish ruler, Charlemagne, maintained diplomatic relations with the caliphate of Harun al-Rashid, who patronizingly sent the much poorer westerner a gift of an elephant.)

The Abbasids

When Abbasid power began to decline in the tenth century there followed an extended period of decentralization. The major cause for growing Abbasid weakness was the gradual impoverishment of their primary economic base, the agricultural wealth of the Tigris-Euphrates basin. Their decline was further accelerated by the later Abbasids' practice of surrounding themselves with Turkish soldiers, who

Islamic political history after the fall of the Abbasid Empire

soon realized that they could take over actual power in the state. In 945 the Abbasid Empire fell apart when a Shiite tribe seized Baghdad. Thereafter the Abbasids became powerless figureheads until their caliphate was completely destroyed with the destruction of Baghdad by the Mongols in 1258. From 945 until the sixteenth century Islamic political life was marked by localism, with different petty rulers, most often Turkish, taking command in different areas. It used to be thought that this decentralization also meant decay, but in fact Islamic civilization greatly prospered in the "middle period," above all from about 900 to about 1250, a time also when Islamic rule expanded into modern-day Turkey and India. Later, new Islamic empires developed, the leading one in the West being that of the Ottoman Turks, who controlled much of eastern Europe and the Near East from the fifteenth century until 1918. It is therefore entirely false to believe that Islamic history descended upon an ever-downward course sometime shortly after the reign of Harun al-Rashid.

The character of Islamic culture and society

For those who approach Islamic civilization with modern preconceptions, the greatest surprise is to realize that from the time of Muhammad until at least about 1500 Islamic culture and society was extraordinarily cosmopolitan and dynamic. Muhammad himself was not a desert Arab but a town-dweller and trader imbued with advanced ideals. Subsequently, Muslim culture became highly cosmopolitan for several reasons: it inherited the sophistication of Byzantium and Persia; it remained centered at the crossroads of long-distance trade between the Far East and West; and the prosperous town life in most Muslim territories counterbalanced agriculture. Because of the importance of trade there was much geographical mobility. Muhammad's teachings furthermore encouraged social mobility because the Koran stressed the equality of all Muslims. The result was that at the court of Baghdad, and later at those of the decentralized Muslim states, careers were open to those with talent. Since literacy was remarkably widespread—a rough estimate for around the year 1000 is 20 percent of all Muslim males—many could rise through education. Offices were seldom regarded as being hereditary and "new men" could arrive at the top by enterprise and skill. Muslims were also remarkably tolerant of other religions. As stated above, they rarely sought forced conversions, and they generally allowed a place within their own states for Jews and Christians, whom they accepted as "people of the book" because the Bible was seen as a precursor of the Koran. In keeping with this attitude of toleration an early caliph employed a Christian as his chief secretary, the Umayyads patronized a Christian who wrote poetry in Arabic, and Muslim Spain saw the greatest flowering of Jewish culture between ancient and modern times. The greatest fruit of this Jewish flowering was the work of Moses Maimonides (1135–1204), a profound religious thinker, sometimes called "the second Moses," who wrote both in Hebrew and Arabic.

There was one major exception to this rule of Muslim equalitarianism and tolerance: the treatment of women. Perhaps because social status was so fluid, successful men were extremely anxious to preserve and enhance their positions and their "honor." They could accomplish this by maintaining and/or expanding their worldly possessions, which category included women. For a man's females to be most "valuable" to his status, their inviolability had to be assured. The Koran allowed a man to marry four wives, so women were at a premium, and married ones were segregated from other males. A prominent man would also have a number of female servants and concubines, and he kept all these women in a part of his residence called the harem, where they were guarded by eunuchs, i.e., castrated men. Within these enclaves women vied with each other for preeminence and engaged in intrigues to advance the fortunes of their children. Although large harems could be kept only by the wealthy, the system was imitated as far as possible by all classes. Based on the principle that women were chattel, these practices did much to debase women and to emphasize attitudes of domination in sexual life. Male homosexual relations were tolerated in upper-class society, yet they too were based on patterns of domination, usually that of a powerful adult over an adolescent.

Women in Islam

There were two major Islamic avenues for devotion to the particularly religious life. One was that of the *ulama,* learned men who came closest to being like priests. Their job was to study and offer advice on all aspects of religion and religious law. Not surprisingly they usually stood for tradition and rigorous maintenance of the faith; most often they exerted great influence on the conduct of public life. But complementary to them were the *sufis,* religious mystics who might be equated with Christian monks were it not for the fact that they were not committed to celibacy and seldom withdrew from the life of the community. Sufis stressed contemplation and ecstasy as the ulama stressed religious law: they had no common program and in practice behaved very differently. Some sufis were "whirling dervishes," so known in the West because of their dances; others were *faqirs,* associated in the West with snake-charming in marketplaces; and others were quiet meditative men who practiced no exotic rites. Sufis were usually organized into "brotherhoods," which did much to convert outlying areas such as Africa and India. Throughout the Islamic world sufism provided a channel for the most intense religious impulses. The ability of the ulama and sufis to coexist is in itself a remarkable index of Islamic cultural pluralism.

Islamic religious life: the ulama *and the* sufis

More remarkable still is the fact that these two groups often coexisted with representatives of yet another worldview, students and practitioners of philosophy and science. Islamic philosophers were actually called *faylasufs* in Arabic because they were dedicated to the cultivation of what the Greeks had called *philosophia.* Islamic philosophy was based on the study of earlier Greek thought, above all the Aris-

Islamic philosophy

totelian and Neoplatonic strains. Around the time when the philosophical schools were closed in Athens by order of the Emperor Justinian, Greek philosophers migrated east, and the works of Aristotle and others were translated into Syriac, a Semitic dialect. From that point of transmission Greek philosophy gradually entered the life of Islam and became cultivated by the class of faylasufs, who believed that the universe is rational and that a philosophical approach to life was the highest god-given calling. The faylasufs' profound knowledge of Aristotle can be seen, for example, in the fact that Avicenna (d. 1037), one of the greatest of them, read practically all of Aristotle's works in the Far Eastern town of Bukhara before he reached the age of eighteen.

The problem of reconciling Greek ideas with Islamic religion

The most serious problem faced by the faylasufs was that of reconciling Greek philosophy with Islamic religion because they followed their Greek sources in believing—in opposition to Islamic doctrine—that the world is eternal and that there is no immortality for the individual soul. Different faylasufs reacted to this problem in different ways. Of the three greatest, Al-Farabi (d. 950), who lived mainly in Baghdad, was least concerned by it; he taught that an enlightened elite could philosophize without being distracted by the binding common beliefs of the masses. Even so, he never attacked these beliefs, considering them necessary to hold society together.

Avicenna and Averroës

Unlike Al-Farabi, Avicenna, who was active farther east, taught a less rationalistic philosophy that came close in many points to sufi mysticism. (A later story held that Avicenna said of a sufi "all I know, he sees," while the sufi replied "all I see, he knows.") Finally, Averroës (1126–98) of Cordova, in Spain, was a thoroughgoing Aristotelian who led two lives, one in private as an extreme rationalist and the other in public as a believer in the official faith, indeed even as an official censor. Averroës was the last really important Islamic philosopher: after him rationalism either blended into sufism, the direction pointed to by Avicenna, or became too constrained by religious orthodoxy to lead an independent existence. But in its heyday between about 850 and 1200 Islamic philosophy was far more advanced and sophisticated than anything found in either the Byzantine or Western Christian realms.

Islamic science; the practice of astrology

Before their decline Islamic faylasufs were as distinguished in studying natural science as they were in philosophical speculation. Usually the same men were both philosophers and scientists because they could not make a living by commenting on Aristotle (there were no universities in which to teach) but could rise to positions of wealth and power by practicing astrology and medicine. Astrology sounds to us today less like science than superstition, but among the Muslims it was an "applied science" intimately related to accurate astronomical observation: after an Islamic astrologer carefully studied and foretold the courses of the heavenly bodies, he would endeavor to apply his knowledge to the course of human events, particularly the fortunes of

The Planetary Constellation of Andromeda as Visualized by the Muslims. This manuscript illumination executed in western Iran in 1009 A.D. shows clearly how Muslim culture reconceived Greek learning.

wealthy patrons. In order to account most simply for heavenly motions, some Muslims considered the possibilities that the earth rotates on its axis and revolves around the sun, but these theories were not accepted because they did not fit in with ancient preconceptions such as the assumption of circular planetary orbits. It was therefore not in these suggestions that Muslim astrologers later influenced the West, but rather in their extremely advanced observations and predictive tables that often went beyond the most careful work of the Greeks.

Islamic accomplishments in medicine were equally remarkable. Faylasufs serving as physicians appropriated the knowledge contained in the medical writings of the Hellenistic Age but were rarely content with that. Avicenna discovered the contagious nature of tuberculosis, described pleurisy and several varieties of nervous ailments, and pointed out that disease can be spread through contamination of water and soil. His chief medical writing, the *Canon,* was accepted in Europe as authoritative until late in the seventeenth century. Avicenna's older contemporary, Rhazes (865–925), was the greatest clinical physician of the medieval world. His major achievement was the discovery of the difference between measles and smallpox. Other Islamic physicians discovered the value of cauterization and of styptic agents, diagnosed cancer of the stomach, prescribed antidotes for cases of poisoning, and made notable progress in treating diseases of the eyes. In addition,

Islamic contributions to medicine

they recognized the infectious character of bubonic plague, pointing out that it could be transmitted by clothes. Finally, the Muslims excelled all other medieval peoples in the organization of hospitals and in the control of medical practice. There were at least thirty-four great hospitals located in the principal cities of Persia, Syria, and Egypt, which appear to have been organized in a strikingly modern fashion. Each had wards for particular cases, a dispensary, and a library. The chief physicians and surgeons lectured to the students and graduates, examined them, and issued licenses to practice. Even the owners of leeches, who in most cases were also barbers, had to submit them for inspection at regular intervals.

Optics, chemistry, and mathematics

Other great Islamic scientific achievements were in optics, chemistry, and mathematics. Islamic physicists founded the science of optics and drew a number of significant conclusions regarding the theory of magnifying lenses and the velocity, transmission, and refraction of light. Islamic chemistry was an outgrowth of alchemy, an invention of the Hellenistic Greeks, the system of belief that was based upon the principle that all metals were the same in essence, and that baser metals could therefore be transmuted into gold if only the right instrument, the philosopher's stone, could be found. But the efforts of scientists in this field were by no means confined to this fruitless quest; some even denied the whole theory of transmutation of metals. As a result of experiments by Muslim scientists, various new substances and compounds were discovered, among them carbonate of soda, alum, borax, nitrate of silver, saltpeter, and nitric and sulphuric acids. In addition, Islamic scientists were the first to describe the chemical processes of distillation, filtration, and sublimation. In mathematics Islam's greatest accomplishment was to unite the geometry of the Greeks with the number science of the Hindus. Borrowing what westerners know as "Arabic numerals," including the zero, from the Hindus, Islamic mathematicians were able to develop an arithmetic based on the decimal system and also make advances in algebra (itself an Arabic word). Building upon Greek geometry with reference to heavenly motions, they made great progress in spherical trigonometry. Thus they brought together and advanced all the areas of mathematical knowledge which would later be further developed in the Christian West.

In addition to its philosophers and scientists Islam had its poets too. The primitive Arabs themselves had excelled in writing poetry, and literary accomplishment became recognized as a way to distinguish oneself at court. Probably the greatest of Islamic poets were the Persians (who wrote in their own language), the best known of whom in the West is Umar Khayyam (d. 1123) because his *Rubaiyat* was turned into a popular English poem by the Victorian Edward Fitzgerald. Although Fitzgerald's translation distorts much, Umar's hedonism ("a jug of wine, a loaf of bread—and thou") shows us that all Muslims were by no means dour puritans. Actually Umar's poetry was excelled by the works of Sadi (1193–1292) and Hafiz (d. 1389). And far

The Great Mosque, Qayrawan, Tunisia. This ninth-century minaret, from which the criers call the faithful to prayer, is a leading monument of the North African Islamic architectural style.

The Court of the Lions in the Alhambra, Granada, Spain. The palace-fortress of the Alhambra is one of the finest monuments of the Islamic architectural style. Notable are the graceful columns, the horseshoe arches, and the delicate tracery in stone that surmounts the arches.

from Persia lush poetry was cultivated as well in the courts of Muslim Spain. This poetry too was by no means inhibited, as can be seen from lines like "such was my kissing, such my sucking of his mouth / that he was almost made toothless."

In their artistic endeavors Muslims were highly eclectic. Their main source of inspiration came from the art of Byzantium and Persia. The former contributed many of the structural features of Islamic architecture, especially the dome, the column, and the arch. Persian influence was probably responsible for the intricate, nonnaturalistic designs which were used as decorative motifs in practically all of the arts. From both Persia and Byzantium came the tendency to subordinate form to rich and sensuous color. Architecture was the most important of the Islamic arts; the development of both painting and sculpture was inhibited by religious prejudice against representation of the human form. By no means all of the examples of this architecture were mosques; many were palaces, schools, libraries, private dwellings, and hospitals. Indeed, Islamic architecture had a much more decidedly secular character than any in medieval Europe. Among its principal elements were bulbous domes, minarets, horseshoe arches, and twisted columns, together with the use of tracery in stone, alternating stripes of black and white, mosaics, and Arabic script as decorative devices. As in the Byzantine style, comparatively little attention was given to exterior ornamentation. The so-called minor arts of the Muslims included the weaving of gorgeous pile carpets and rugs, magnificent leather tooling, and the making of brocaded silks and tapestries, inlaid metalwork, enameled glassware, and painted pottery. Most of the products of these arts were embellished with compli-

The eclectic art of the Muslims

cated patterns of interlacing geometric designs, plants and fruits and flowers, Arabic script, and fantastic animal figures. In general, art laid particular emphasis on pure visual design. Separated from any role in religious teaching, it became highly abstract and nonrepresentational. For these reasons Islamic art often seems more secular and "modern" than any other art of premodern times.

The economic development of the Islamic Empire: (1) commerce

The economic life of the Islamic world varied greatly according to time and place, but underdevelopment was certainly not one of its primary characteristics. On the contrary, in the central areas of Islamic civilization from the first Arab conquests until about the fourteenth century mercantile life was extraordinarily advanced. The principal reason for this was that the Arabs inherited in Syria and Persia an area that was already marked by an enterprising urban culture and that was at the crossroads of the world, lying athwart the major trade routes between Africa, Europe, India, and China. Islamic traders and entrepreneurs built venturesomely on these earlier foundations. Muslim merchants penetrated into southern Russia and even into the equatorial regions of Africa, while caravans of thousands of camels traveled to the gates of India and China. (The Muslims used camels as pack animals instead of building roads and drawing wheeled carts.) Ships from Islam established new routes across the Indian Ocean, the Persian Gulf, and the Caspian Sea. For periods of time Islamic ships also dominated parts of the Mediterranean. Indeed, one reason for subsequent Islamic decline was that the Western Christians took hold of the Mediterranean in the eleventh and twelfth centuries and wrested control of the Indian Ocean in the sixteenth century.

The great Islamic expansion of commerce would scarcely have been possible without a corresponding development of industry. It was the

Interior of the Great Mosque at Cordova, Spain. This splendid specimen of Moorish architecture gives an excellent view of the cusped arches and alternating stripes of black and white so commonly used by Islamic architects.

ability of the people of one region to turn their natural resources into finished products for sale to other regions which provided a basis for a large part of the trade. Nearly every one of the great cities specialized in some particular variety of manufactures. Mosul, in Syria, was a center of the manufacture of cotton cloth; Baghdad specialized in glassware, jewelry, pottery, and silks; Damascus was famous for its fine steel and for its "damask" or woven figured silk; Morocco was noted for the manufacture of leather; and Toledo, in Spain, for its excellent swords. The products of these cities did not exhaust the list of manufactures. Drugs, perfumes, carpets, tapestries, brocades, woolens, satins, metal products, and a host of others were turned out by the craftsmen of many cities. From the Chinese the Muslims learned the art of papermaking, and the products of that industry were in great demand, not only within the empire itself but in Europe as well.

(2) industry

In all the areas we have reviewed Islamic civilization so overshadowed that of the Christian West until about the twelfth century that there can be no comparison. When the West did move forward it was able to do so partly because of what it learned from Islam. In the economic sphere westerners profited from absorbing many accomplishments of Islamic technology, such as irrigation techniques, the raising of new crops, papermaking, and the distillation of alcohol. The extent of our debt to Islamic economic influence is well mirrored in the large number of common English words which were originally of Arabic or Persian origin. Among these are traffic, tariff, magazine, alcohol, muslin, orange, lemon, alfalfa, saffron, sugar, syrup, and musk. (Our word admiral also comes from the Arabic—in this case deriving from the title of emir.)

Islamic economic influence on the West

The West was as much indebted to Islam in intellectual and scientific as in economic life. In those areas, too, borrowed words tell some of the story: algebra, cipher, zero, nadir, amalgam, alembic, alchemy, alkali, soda, almanac, and names of many stars such as Aldebaran and Betelgeuse. Islamic civilization both preserved and expanded Greek philosophical and scientific knowledge when such knowledge was almost entirely forgotten in the West. All the important Greek scientific works surviving from ancient times were translated into Arabic and most of these in turn were translated in the medieval West from Arabic into Latin. Above all, the preservation and interpretation of the works of Aristotle was one of Islam's most enduring accomplishments. Not only was Aristotle first reacquired in the West by means of the Arabic translations, but Aristotle was interpreted with Islamic help, above all that of Averroës, whose prestige was so great that he was simply called "the Commentator" by medieval Western writers. Of course Arabic numerals, too, rank as a tremendously important intellectual legacy, as anyone will discover by trying to balance a checkbook with Roman ones.

Intellectual and scientific contributions

Aside from all these specific contributions, the civilization of Islam probably had its greatest influence on the West merely by standing as a powerful rival and spur to the imagination. Byzantine civilization was at once too closely related to the Christian West and too weak to serve this function. Westerners usually, for right or wrong, looked down on the Byzantine Greeks, but they more often respected and feared the Muslims. And right they were as well, for Islamic civilization at its zenith (to use another Arabic word) was surely one of the world's greatest. Though loosely organized, it united peoples as diverse as Arabs, Persians, Turks, various African tribes, and Hindus by means of a great religion and common institutions. Unity within multiplicity was an Islamic hallmark, which created both a splendid diverse society and a splendid legacy of original discoveries and achievements.

3. WESTERN CHRISTIAN CIVILIZATION IN THE EARLY MIDDLE AGES

Western Europeans in the early Middle Ages (the period between about 600 and 1050) were so backward in comparison to their Byzantine and Islamic neighbors that a tenth-century Arabic geographer could write of them that "they have large bodies, gross natures, harsh manners, and dull intellects . . . those who live farthest north are particularly stupid, gross, and brutish." Material conditions throughout this period were so primitive that one can almost speak of five centuries of camping-out. Yet new and promising patterns were definitely taking shape. Above all, a new center of civilization was emerging in the North Atlantic regions. Around 800 the Frankish monarchy, based in agriculturally rich northwestern Europe, managed to create a western European empire in alliance with the Western Christian Church. Although this empire did not last long, it still managed to hew out a new Western cultural unity that was to be an important building block for the future.

Once the Eastern Romans under Justinian had destroyed the Ostrogothic and Vandal kingdoms in Italy and Africa, and the Arabs had eliminated the Visigothic kingdom in Spain, the Frankish rulers in Gaul remained as the major surviving barbarian power in western Europe. But it took about two centuries before they began to exercise their full hegemony. The founder of the Frankish state was the brutal and wily chieftain Clovis, who conquered most of modern-day France and Belgium around 500 and cleverly converted to western Catholic Christianity, the religion of the local bishops and indigenous population. Clovis founded the Merovingian dynasty (so called from Merovech, the founder of the family to which he belonged). He did not, however, pass on a united realm but followed the typical barbarian custom of dividing up his kingdom among his sons. More or less without interruption for the next two hundred years sons fought sons for a larger share of the Merovingian inheritance. Toward the end of that period the line also began to degenerate, and numerous so-called do-nothing kings left their government and fighting to their chief ministers, known as "mayors of the palace." Throughout this era, one of the darkest in the recorded history of Europe, trade contracted, towns declined, literacy was almost forgotten, and violence was endemic. Minimal agricultural self-sufficiency coexisted with the rule of the battle-axe.

Largely unnoticed, however, some hope for the future was coalescing around the institutions of the Roman papacy and Benedictine monasticism. The architect of a new western European religious policy that was based on an alliance between these two institutions was Pope Gregory I (reigned 590–604), known as St. Gregory the Great. Until his time the Roman popes were generally subordinate to the emperors in Constantinople and to the greater religious prestige of the Christian East, but Gregory sought to counteract this situation by creating a more autonomous western-oriented Latin Church. This he tried to do in many ways. As a theologian—the fourth great "Latin father" of the Church—he built upon the work of his three predecessors, Jerome, Ambrose, and especially Augustine, in articulating a theology that had its own distinct characteristics. Among these were emphasis on the idea of penance and the concept of purgatory as a place for purification before admission into heaven. (Western belief in purgatory was thereafter to become one of the major differences in the dogmas of the Eastern and Western Churches.) In addition to his theological work, Gregory pioneered in the writing of a simplified unadorned Latin prose that corresponded to the actual spoken language of his contemporaries, and presided over the creation of a powerful Latin liturgy. If Gregory did not actually invent the "Gregorian chant," it was under his impetus that this new plainsong—forever after a central part of the Roman Catholic ritual—developed. All of these innovations helped to make the Christian West religiously and culturally more independent of the Greek-speaking East than it had ever been before.

Gregory the Great was as much a statesman as he was a theologian and shaper of Latin. Within Italy he assured the physical survival of the papacy in the face of the barbarian Lombard threat of his day by clever diplomacy and expert management of papal landed estates. He also began to reemphasize earlier claims of papal primacy, especially over Western bishops, that were in danger of being forgotten. Above all, he patronized the order of Benedictine monks and used them to help evangelize new Western territories. Gregory himself had been a Benedictine—perhaps the first Benedictine monk to become pope—and he wrote the standard life of St. Benedict. Because the Benedictine order was still very young and the times were turbulent, Gregory's patronage helped the order to survive and later to become for centuries the only monastic order in the West. In return the pope could profit from using the Benedictines to carry out special projects. The

Pope Gregory the Great. In this tenth-century German ivory panel the pope is receiving inspiration from the Holy Spirit in the form of a dove.

Gregory's religious policies

most significant of these was the conversion of Anglo-Saxon England to Christianity. This was a long-term project which took about a century to complete, but its great result was that it left a Christian outpost to the far northwest that was thoroughly loyal to the papacy and that would soon help to bring together the papacy and the Frankish state. Gregory the Great himself did not live to see that union, but it was his policy of invigorating the Western Church that most helped to bring it about.

Around 700, when the Benedictines were completing their conversion of England, the outlook for Frankish Gaul was becoming somewhat brighter. The most profound reason for this was that the long, troubled period of transition between the ancient and medieval worlds was finally coming to an end. The ancient Roman civilization of cities and Mediterranean trade was in its last gasps in Gaul in the time after Clovis. Then, when the Arabs conquered the southern Mediterranean shore and took to the sea in the seventh century, northwestern Europe was finally thrown back upon itself and forced to look away from the Mediterranean. In fact the lands of the north—modern-day northern France, the Low Countries, Germany, and England—were extremely fertile: with adequate farming implements they could yield great natural wealth. Given the proper circumstances, a new power could emerge in the north to make the most of a new pattern of life based predominantly on agrarianism instead of urban commerce and Mediterranean trade. Around 700 that is exactly what happened in Merovingian Gaul.

The proper circumstances were the triumph of a succession of able rulers and their alliance with the Church. In 687 an energetic Merovingian mayor of the palace, Pepin of Heristal, managed to unite all the Frankish lands under his rule and build a new power base for his own family in the region of Belgium and the Rhine. He was succeeded by his aggressive son, Charles Martel ("the Hammer"), who is sometimes considered a second founder of the Frankish state. Charles's claim to this title is twofold. First, in 732 he turned back a Muslim force from Spain at the Battle of Poitiers, some 150 miles from Paris. Although the Muslim contingent was not a real army but merely a marauding band, the incursion was the high-water mark of their progress toward the northwest and Charles's victory won him great prestige. Equally important, around the end of his reign Charles began to develop an alliance with the Church, particularly with the Benedictines of England. Having finished most of their conversion work on their island, the Benedictines, under their idealistic leader St. Boniface, were moving across the English Channel in an attempt to convert central Germany. Charles Martel realized that he and they had common interests, for after he had guarded his southern flank against the Muslims he was seeking to direct Frankish expansion eastward in the direction of Germany. Missionary work and Frankish expansion

could go hand in hand, so Charles offered St. Boniface and his Benedictines material aid in return for their support of his territorial aims.

Once allied with the Franks, St. Boniface provided further service
in the next reign in helping to contribute to one of the most momentous events in Western history. Charles Martel had never assumed the
royal title, but his son, Pepin the Short, wished to take it. Even
though Pepin and not the reigning "do-nothing king" was the real
power, Pepin needed the prestige of the Church for supporting a
change in dynasties. Fortunately for him the times were highly propitious for obtaining Church support. St. Boniface supported Pepin
because the young ruler continued his father's policy of collaborating
with the Benedictines in Germany. And Boniface had great influence
in Rome because the Anglo-Saxon Benedictines had remained in the
closest touch with the papacy since the time of Gregory the Great.

The papacy was now fully prepared to cast its own lots with a
strong Frankish ruler because it was in the midst of a bitter fight with
the Byzantine emperors over Iconoclasm. The Byzantines until then
had offered papal territories in Italy some protection against the Lombards, but the increasingly powerful Franks were now fully able to
take over that role. The papacy accordingly made an epochal about-
face, turning once and for all to the West. In 750 the pope encouraged
Pepin to depose the Merovingian figurehead, and in 751 St. Boniface,
acting as papal emissary, anointed Pepin as a divinely sanctioned king.
Thus the Frankish monarchy attained a spiritual mandate and was fully
integrated into the papal-Benedictine orbit. Shortly afterward Pepin
paid his debt to the pope by conquering the Lombards in Italy. The
West was now achieving its own unity based on the Frankish state and
the Latin church, not coincidentally just at the time when the Abbasid
caliphate was being founded in the East and the Byzantines were going
their own fully Greek way.

The ultimate consolidation of the new pattern took place in the
reign of Pepin's son, Carolus Magnus or Charlemagne (768–814), from
whom the new dynasty takes its name of "Carolingian." Without
question Charlemagne ranks as one of the most important rulers of the
whole medieval period. Had it been possible to ask him what his
greatest accomplishment was, he almost certainly would have replied
that it lay in greatly increasing the Frankish realm. Except for the English, there was scarcely a people of western Europe against whom he
did not fight. Most of his campaigns were successful; he annexed the
greater part of central Europe and northern and central Italy to the
Frankish domain. To rule this vast area he bestowed all the powers of
local government upon his own appointees, called counts, and tried to
remain in control of them by sending representatives of the court to
observe them. Among the counts' many duties were the administration of justice and the raising of armies. Although Charlemagne's system in practice was far from perfect, it led to the best government that

*Solidification of the
alliance in the time of
Pepin the Short*

*The "about-face" of the
papacy*

Charlemagne. A silver penny
struck between 804 and 814 in
Mainz (as indicated by the letter M at the bottom) showing
Charlemagne in a highly stylized fashion as emperor with
Roman military cloak and lau-
rel. The inscription reads
KAROLVS IMP AVG (Charles,
Emperor, Augustus). See p.
185, above, for the variety of
late-Roman coin portraiture
that must have served as the
Carolingian minter's model.

The Carolingian Renaissance

Europe had seen since the Romans. Because of the military triumphs and internal peace of his reign, Charlemagne was long remembered and revered as a western European folk hero.

Primarily to aid his territorial expansion and help administer his realm Charlemagne presided over a revival of learning known as the "Carolingian Renaissance." Charlemagne extended his rule into Germany in the name of Christianity, but in order to proselytize he needed educated monks and priests. More than that, in order to administer his far-flung territories he needed at least a few people who could read and write. Amazing as it may seem to us, at first hardly any people in his entire realm were literate, so thoroughly had the rudiments of learning been forgotten since the decay of Roman city life. Only in Anglo-Saxon England had literacy been cultivated by the Benedictine monks. The reason for this was that the Anglo-Saxons spoke a form of German but the monks needed to learn Latin in order to say their offices and study the Bible. Since they knew no Latin to begin with they had to go about learning it by a very self-conscious program of studies. The greatest Anglo-Saxon Benedictine scholar before Charlemagne's time was the Venerable Bede (d. 735), whose *History of the English Church and People,* written in Latin, was one of the best historical writings of the early-medieval period and can still be read with pleasure. When Charlemagne came to the throne he invited the Anglo-Saxon Benedictine Alcuin—a student of one of Bede's students—to direct a revival of studies on the continent. With Charlemagne's active support Alcuin helped establish new schools to teach reading, directed the copying and correcting of important Latin works, including many Roman classics, and inspired the formulation of a new clear handwriting that is the ancestor of our modern "Roman" print. These were the greatest achievements of the Carolingian Renaissance, which stressed practicality rather than original literary or intellectual endeavors. Thoroughly unpretentious as they were, they

Carolingian Handwriting. Even the untrained reader has little difficulty in reading this excerpt from a Carolingian manuscript.

established a bridgehead for literacy on the Continent which thereafter would never be completely lost. They also helped to preserve Latin literature, and they made the Latin language the language of state and diplomacy for all of western Europe, as it remained until comparatively recent times.

The climax of Charlemagne's career came in the year 800 when he was crowned emperor on Christmas Day in Rome by the pope. Historians continue to debate whether this was Charlemagne's or the pope's idea, but there is no doubt that the pope did not gain any immediate power from it. Once the Franks ruled Italy they came to dominate the papacy, and indeed the whole Church, to such a degree that by 800 the pope was very close to being Charlemagne's puppet. Charlemagne did not gain any actual new power by taking the imperial title either, but the significance of the event is nonetheless great. Up until 800 the only emperor ruled in Constantinople and could lay claim to being the direct heir of Augustus. Although the Byzantines had lost most of their interest in the West, they still continued to regard it vaguely as an outlying province and were actively opposed to any westerner calling himself emperor. Charlemagne's assumption of the title was virtually a declaration of Western self-confidence and independence. Since Charlemagne's vast realm was fully as large as that of the Byzantines, had great reserves of agricultural wealth, and was defining its own culture based on Western Christianity and the Latin linguistic tradition, the claim to empire was largely justified. More than that, it was never forgotten. Both for its symbolism and for its contribution toward giving westerners a sense of unity and purpose it was a major landmark on the road to the making of a great western Europe.

*Charlemagne's coronation
as emperor*

Although the claim to empire was bold and memorable, Charlemagne's actual empire disintegrated quickly after his death for many reasons. The simplest was that hardly any of his successors were as competent and decisive as he was. In order to rule an empire in those still extremely primitive times, one had to have enormous reserves of strength and energy—one had to travel on horseback over enormous distances, fight and win battles at the head of unruly armies, and know how to delegate power to others yet guard against its abuse. Unfortunately for western Europe few of Charlemagne's heirs had such combinations of energy and talent. To make matters worse, Charlemagne's sole surviving son, Louis the Pious, who inherited the Frankish realm intact, divided his inheritance among his own three sons, thereby bringing civil war back to Frankish Europe. And to make matters worst of all, new waves of invasions began just as Charlemagne's grandsons and great-grandsons started fighting each other: from the north came the Scandinavian Vikings; from the east came the Asiatic Magyars (or Hungarians); and from the south came new attacks by marauding Muslims, attacking now from the sea. Under these pressures the Carolingian Empire completely fell apart and a new political map of Europe was drawn in the tenth century.

Viking Dragon Head. Wooden carvings like these on the stemposts of Viking ships were calculated to inspire terror.

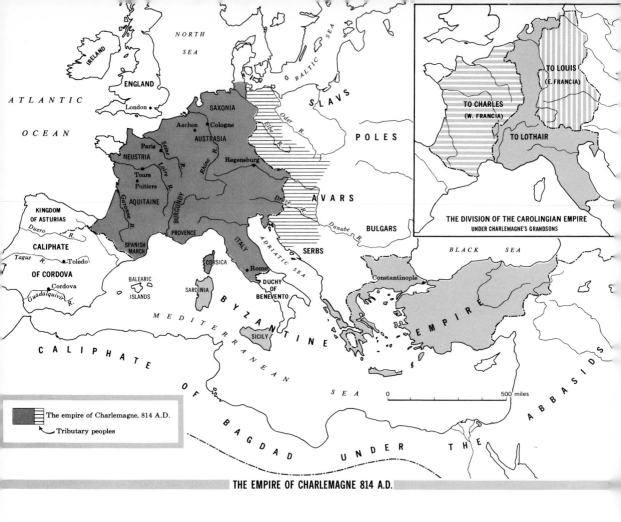

THE EMPIRE OF CHARLEMAGNE 814 A.D.

Map labels: NORTH SEA, BALTIC SEA, ATLANTIC OCEAN, IRELAND, ENGLAND, London, SAXONIA, Aachen, Cologne, AUSTRASIA, Paris, NEUSTRIA, Seine R., Loire R., Tours, Poitiers, AQUITAINE, Garonne R., BURGUNDY, Rhine R., Regensburg, Danube R., Drave R., AVARS, BULGARS, SERBS, ITALY, PROVENCE, SPANISH MARCH, CORSICA, Rome, DUCHY OF BENEVENTO, KINGDOM OF ASTURIAS, Duero R., CALIPHATE OF CORDOVA, Tagus R., Toledo, Cordova, Guadalquivir R., BALEARIC ISLANDS, SARDINIA, SICILY, MEDITERRANEAN SEA, ADRIATIC SEA, BYZANTINE EMPIRE, Constantinople, BLACK SEA, CALIPHATE OF BAGDAD UNDER THE ABBASIDS, SLAVS, POLES, Oder R., Elbe R.

THE DIVISION OF THE CAROLINGIAN EMPIRE
UNDER CHARLEMAGNE'S GRANDSONS
TO LOUIS (E. FRANCIA), TO CHARLES (W. FRANCIA), TO LOTHAIR

■ The empire of Charlemagne, 814 A.D.
⌐ Tributary peoples

England in the time of Alfred the Great

As the Carolingian period was crucial for marking the beginnings of a common North Atlantic western European civilization, so the tenth century was crucial for marking the beginnings of the major modern European political entities. England, which never had been part of Charlemagne's empire, and which hitherto had been divided among smaller warring Anglo-Saxon states, became unified in the late ninth and the tenth century owing to the work of King Alfred the Great (871–899) and his direct successors. Alfred and his heirs reorganized the army, infused new vigor into local government, and codified the English laws. In addition, Alfred founded schools and fostered an interest in Anglo-Saxon writing and other elements of a national culture.

Political conditions in France and Germany

Across the Channel, France (now the name for the main part of Roman Gaul because it was the original seat of the Frankish monarchy) was most devastated by the invasions of Vikings, who had sailed up the French rivers. For that reason France broke up into small principalities rather than developing a strong national monarchy on the pattern of England. Nonetheless there was a king in France, who, however weak, was recognized as the ruler of the western part of Charlemagne's former territories. Directly to the east, the kings of Germany were the strongest continental monarchs of the tenth century, ruling over an essentially united realm. In addition to Germany, their lands encompassed most of the Low Countries and a good part of modern eastern France.

The most important German ruler of the period was Otto the Great. He became king in 936, resoundingly defeated the Hungarians in 955—thereby relieving Germany of its greatest foreign threat—and took the title of emperor in Rome in 962. By this last act Otto strengthened his claim to being the greatest continental monarch since Charlemagne. Otto and his successors, who continued to call themselves emperors, tried to rule over Italy but barely succeeded in doing so. Instead, Italy in the tenth century saw the greatest western European development of urban life, a pattern on which the Italians would subsequently build.

*Otto the Great of
Germany*

Although Italy did develop some city life in the tenth century, this was by no means typical of the early-medieval period in western Europe as a whole. Quite to the contrary, from the eighth to the eleventh century the European economy was based almost entirely on agriculture and very limited local trade. Roads deteriorated and barter widely replaced the use of money. Whatever cities survived from Roman days were usually empty shells that served at most as administrative centers for bishops and fortified places in case of common danger. The main economic unit throughout the period was the self-supporting large landed estate, usually owned by kings, warrior aristocrats, or large-scale monasteries. Although the northern European soil was rich, farming tools in most places were still too primitive to bring in a fully adequate return on the enormous investment of effort expended by the laboring masses. Agricultural yields in all but the most fertile Carolingian heartlands (and often even in them) were pitifully low, and Europeans, except the rulers and the higher clergy, lived on the edge of subsistence. It is true that some increase in agricultural income had underpinned the Carolingian successes and some progress in farming might have continued had the peace of Charlemagne's reign endured. But the subsequent invasions of the ninth and tenth centuries set agricultural life back and new beginnings would have to be made in the years thereafter.

*The economy of western
Europe in the early
Middle Ages*

Given the low level of early-medieval economic life, it is not surprising that the age was not a prosperous time for learning or the arts: with scarcely enough wealth to keep most people alive, there is not going to be much to support schools or major artistic projects. Throughout the period, even in the best of years, learning was a privilege for the few: the masses received no formal education, and even most members of the secular aristocracy were illiterate. Learning also consisted mostly of memorization, without regard for criticism or

*The low level of
intellectual life*

refutation. We have seen that there was some revival of learning under Charlemagne that may be called a "renaissance" but that it did not issue into any real intellectual creativity. Its major accomplishment was the founding of enough schools to educate the clergy in the rudiments of reading and the training of enough monastic scribes to recopy and preserve some major works of Roman literature. Even this accomplishment was jeopardized in the period of invasions that accompanied the fall of the Carolingian Empire. Fortunately just enough schools and manuscripts survived to become the basis for another—far greater—revival of learning that began in the eleventh and twelfth centuries.

Literature

In the realm of literature the early Middle Ages had an extremely meager production. This was because few Christians could write and those who could were usually monks and priests, who were not supposed to engage in purely literary endeavors. There was some impressive writing of history in Latin, most notably that of Bede and Charlemagne's eloquent biographer, Einhard, but otherwise Latin composition was little cultivated. Toward the close of the period, however, the vernacular languages, which were either Germanic or based on different regional dialects of Latin (the "Romance" languages, so-called because they were based on "Roman" speech) began to be employed for crude poetic expression, usually first by oral transmission.

Beowulf

The best-known example of this literature in the vernacular is the Anglo-Saxon epic poem *Beowulf.* First put into written form about the eighth century, this poem incorporates ancient legends of the Germanic peoples of northwestern Europe. It is a story of fighting and seafaring and of heroic adventure against deadly dragons and the forces of nature. The background of the epic is pre-Christian, but the author of the work introduced into it some qualities of Christian idealism. *Beowulf* is important not only as one of the earliest specimens of Anglo-Saxon or Old English poetry, but also for the picture it gives of the society of the English and their ancestors in the early Middle Ages.

The artistic history of the early Middle Ages was a story of isolated and interrupted accomplishments because artistic life relied most of all on brief moments of local peace or royal patronage. The earliest enduring monuments of early-medieval art were those created by monks in Ireland—which had its own unique culture—between the sixth and the eighth centuries. Above all in manuscript illumination (i.e., painted illustrations) the Irish monks developed a thoroughly anticlassical and almost surrealistic style, whose origins are most difficult to account for. The greatest surviving product from this school is the stunning "Book of Kells," an illuminated Gospel book that has been called "the most sophisticated work of decorative art in the history of painting." The Irish school declined without subsequent influence and was followed by artistic products of the Carolingian Renaissance.

The art of Charlemagne's period returned for much of its inspira-

Irish Art. The opening of a gospel page that shows the Irish style at its most surrealistic.

Carolingian Art. The fountain of life: an illuminated manuscript page from Gottschalk's Evangeliary (book with four gospels), dating from 781.

tion to classical models, yet it also retained some of the spontaneous vitality of barbarian decoration. When Charlemagne's empire declined and disintegrated there was a corresponding decline and then interruption in the history of Western art. In the tenth century, however, new regional schools emerged. The greatest of these were the English, which emphasized restless fluency in manuscript illumination; the German, which was more grave but still managed to communicate extreme religious ecstasy; and the northern Spanish, which, though Christian, created a rather strange and independent style mostly influenced by the decorative style of Islamic art.

Regional variations in early-medieval art

See color plates facing page 225

Undoubtedly, there is no single, obvious terminal date for early-medieval history as a whole. The date 1000 is sometimes given because it is a convenient round number, but even as late as 1050 Europe had not changed on the surface very much from the way it had been since the end of the Carolingian period. Indeed, looking at Europe as late as 1050 it would at first seem that not much progress had been made over the entire course of the early-medieval centuries. Except for Germany there was hardly any centralized government because by 1050 the Anglo-Saxon English state created by King Alfred and his successors was falling apart. Throughout Europe, all but the most privileged individuals continued to live on the brink of starvation and cultural attainments were minimal and sparse. But actually much had been accomplished. By shifting its main weight to the Atlantic northwest, European civilization became centered in lands that would soon harvest great agricultural wealth. By preserving some of the traditions developed by Gregory the Great, St. Boniface, Pepin, and Charle-

A distinct western European civilization evident in 1050

Left: *Utrecht Psalter.* This Carolingian manuscript of the Psalms from about 820 later provided the basis for the "nervous expressiveness" of the tenth-century English regional school. Right: *Bamberg Apocalypse.* In this manuscript illumination from about 1000 A.D. the fall of Babylon in the Book of Revelation (18: 1–20) is displayed by depicting the city upside down. An example of the grave regional German style.

magne, European civilization had also developed an enduring sense of cultural unity based on Western Christianity and the Latin inheritance. And in the tenth century the beginnings of the future European kingdoms and city-states started to coalesce. Western European civilization was thus for the first time becoming autonomous and distinctive. From then on it would become a leading force in the history of the world.

SELECTED READINGS

• *Items so designated are available in paperback editions.*

BYZANTINE CIVILIZATION

Beckwith, John, *The Art of Constantinople,* 2nd ed., London, 1968. A standard account.

• Diehl, Charles, *Byzantium: Greatness and Decline,* New Brunswick, N.J., 1957. Evaluates strengths and weaknesses of Byzantine civilization.

Hussey, J. M., *The Byzantine World,* London, 1957. Half-narrative, half-topical; a useful short introduction.

• Krautheimer, R., *Early Christian and Byzantine Architecture,* Baltimore, 1970.

Magoulias, H. J., *Byzantine Christianity: Emperor, Church and the West*, Chicago, 1970. Limited to three themes mentioned in title.

Miller, D. A., *The Byzantine Tradition*, New York, 1966. The briefest introduction.

Ostrogorsky, George, *History of the Byzantine State*, New Brunswick, N.J., 1957. The most authoritative longer account of political developments; very scholarly.

• Pelikan, J., *The Christian Tradition; II: The Spirit of Eastern Christendom*, Chicago, 1974. An advanced treatment of religious doctrines.

Runciman, S., *Byzantine Civilization*, New York, 1933. A topical approach; well written but in parts outdated.

——, *Byzantine Style and Civilization*, Baltimore, 1975. A fine study of Byzantine art.

• Vasiliev, A. A., *History of the Byzantine Empire*, 2 vols., Madison, Wisc., 1928. Supplements Ostrogorsky; valuable for its detail on social and intellectual as well as political history.

Vryonis, S., *Byzantium and Europe*, New York, 1967. Noteworthy for its illustrations.

ISLAMIC CIVILIZATION

Arnold, Thomas, and A. Guillaume, *The Legacy of Islam*, New York, 1931.

Gabrieli, F., *Muhammad and the Conquests of Islam*, New York, 1968.

Gibb, H. A. R., *Arabic Literature: An Introduction*, 2nd ed., Oxford, 1963. An excellent survey.

——, *Mohammedanism: An Historical Survey*, 2nd ed., Oxford, 1953. The best brief interpretation of Islamic religion.

• Goitein, S. D., *Jews and Arabs, Their Contacts through the Ages*, New York, 1955.

Grube, E. J., *The World of Islam*, New York, 1966.

• Hodgson, M., *The Venture of Islam*, 3 vols., Chicago, 1974. A masterwork. One of the greatest works of history written by a modern American. Advanced and sometimes difficult, but always rewarding.

Kennedy, Hugh, *The Early Abbasid Caliphate: A Political History*, Totowa, N.J., 1981.

• Lewis, Bernard, *The Arabs in History*, rev. ed., New York, 1966. The best short survey of the conquests and political fortunes of the Arabs.

Lombard, Maurice, *The Golden Age of Islam*, New York, 1975.

Peters, F. E., *Aristotle and the Arabs*, New York, 1968. A well-written and engaging account.

Watt, W. Montgomery, *Islamic Philosophy and Theology*, Edinburgh, 1962.

• ——, *Muhammad: Prophet and Statesman*, Oxford, 1961. A good short biography.

Watt, W. M., and P. Cachia, *A History of Islamic Spain*, Edinburgh, 1965. Briefly covers an undeservedly neglected subject.

EARLY-MEDIEVAL WESTERN CHRISTIAN CIVILIZATION

• Barraclough, G., *The Crucible of Europe: The Ninth and Tenth Centuries in European History*, Berkeley, Calif., 1976. A controversial and sometimes wrongheaded but clear and stimulating interpretation of political developments.

- Dawson, Christopher, *The Making of Europe,* London, 1932. A brilliant interpretation that emphasizes cultural and religious developments by one of this century's most eminent Catholic historians.
- Duby, G., *The Early Growth of the European Economy,* Ithaca, N.Y., 1974. Emphasizes role of lords and peasants; very sophisticated economic history.

  Fichtenau, H., *The Carolingian Empire,* Oxford, 1957. A highly interpretative account that aims to whittle its subject down to size.
- Ganshof, F. L., *Frankish Institutions under Charlemagne,* Providence, 1958. A straightforward technical exposition.

  Halphen, L., *Charlemagne and the Carolingian Empire,* New York, 1977. An older French survey recently translated into English.
- Kitzinger, Ernst, *Early Medieval Art,* London, 1940. A very short but masterful introduction.
- Laistner, M. L. W., *Thought and Letters in Western Europe, A. D. 500–900,* rev. ed., Ithaca, N.Y., 1957. An old-fashioned but standard account; should be supplemented by Wolff.
- Pirenne, Henri, *Mohammed and Charlemagne,* New York, 1939. A bold interpretation, now no longer widely accepted but still thought-provoking.

  Stenton, Frank, *Anglo-Saxon England,* 3rd ed., Oxford, 1971. A standard work.
- Sullivan, Richard E., *Heirs of the Roman Empire,* Ithaca, N.Y., 1960. An elementary introduction.
- Wallace-Hadrill, J. M., *The Barbarian West, A. D. 400–1000,* 2nd ed., London, 1962. A sophisticated short account that emphasizes analysis of the historical sources and questions earlier scholarly assumptions.

  Wemple, S. F., *Women in Frankish Society: Marriage and the Cloister, 500–900,* Philadelphia, 1981. Describes changing attitudes toward marriage among the early Franks.

  Wolff, Philippe, *The Awakening of Europe,* Baltimore, 1968. The "new intellectual history": emphasizes interrelations between the development of thought and material foundations. Masterfully written and organized.

SOURCE MATERIALS

- Arberry, A. J., *The Koran Interpreted,* 2 vols., London, 1955.
- Bede, *A History of the English Church and People,* tr. L. Sherley-Price, Baltimore, 1955.

  Brand, Charles M., ed., *Icon and Minaret: Sources of Byzantine and Islamic Civilization,* Englewood Cliffs, N.J., 1969.
- Brentano, Robert, ed., *The Early Middle Ages: 500–1000,* New York, 1964. The best shorter anthology of the Western Christian sources, enlivened by the editor's subjective commentary.
- Einhard and Notker the Stammerer, *Two Lives of Charlemagne,* tr. L. Thorpe, Baltimore, 1969.
- Gregory Bishop of Tours, *History of the Franks,* tr. E. Brehaut, New York, 1965.

Chapter 11

THE HIGH MIDDLE AGES (1050–1300): ECONOMIC, SOCIAL, AND POLITICAL INSTITUTIONS

I judge those who write at this time to be in a certain measure happy. For, after the turbulence of the past, an unprecedented brightness of peace has dawned again.

—The historian Otto of
Freising, writing around 1158

The period between about 1050 and 1300, termed by historians the High Middle Ages, was the time when western Europe first clearly emerged from backwardness to become one of the greatest powers on the globe. Around 1050 the West was still less developed in most respects than the Byzantine Empire or the Islamic world, but by 1300 it had forged ahead of these two rivals. From a global perspective, only China was its equal in economic, political, and cultural prosperity. Given the sorry state of western Europe around 1050, this startling leap forward was certainly one of the most impressive achievements of human history. Those who think that the entire Middle Ages were times of stagnation could not be more wrong.

Western Europe emerges from backwardness

The reasons for Europe's enormous progress in the High Middle Ages are predictably complex, yet medieval historians agree upon certain broad lines of interpretation. One is that Europe between 900 and 1050 was already poised for growth and could finally begin to live up to its potential once the devastating invasions of Vikings, Hungarians, and Muslims had ceased. Most of these invasions had tapered off by around 1000, but in the eleventh century England was still troubled by the Danes: the year 1066, more famous as the year of the Norman Conquest, was also the year of the last Viking invasion of England.

Reasons for the "great leap forward"

Once foreign invasions were no longer imminent, western Europeans could concentrate on developing their economic life with much less fear of interruption than before. Because of the relative continuity allowed by this change, extraordinarily important technological breakthroughs were made, above all those that contributed to the first great western European "agricultural revolution." The revolution in agriculture made food more bountiful and provided a solid basis for economic development and diversification in other spheres. Population grew rapidly, and towns and cities grew to such a degree that we can speak also of an "urban revolution," even though western Europe remained predominantly agrarian. At the same time political life in the West became more stable. In the course of the High Middle Ages strong new secular governments began to provide more and more internal peace for their subjects and became the foundations of our modern nation-states. In addition to all these advances, there were also striking new religious and intellectual developments, to be treated in the next chapter, which helped give the West a new sense of mission and self-confidence. Although in this chapter we will treat only the economic, social, and political accomplishments of the High Middle Ages, it is well to bear in mind that religion played a pervasive role in all of medieval life, and that all aspects of the high-medieval "great leap forward" were inextricably interrelated.

1. THE FIRST AGRICULTURAL REVOLUTION

The state of agriculture before 1050

The agricultural worker, the "Man with the Hoe," supported European civilization materially by his labors more than anyone else until the industrialization of modern times. Yet, amazing as it seems, until about 1050 he had hardly so much as a hoe. Inventories of farm implements from the Carolingian period reveal that metal tools on the wealthiest rural estates were extremely rare, and even wooden implements were so few in number that many laborers must have had to grapple with nature quite literally with only their bare hands. Between about 1050 and 1250 all that changed. In roughly those two centuries an agricultural revolution took place which entirely altered the nature and vastly increased the output of western European farming.

Prerequisities for the medieval agricultural revolution: (1) shift in area of cultivation

Many of the prerequisites for the medieval agricultural revolution had been present before the middle of the eleventh century. The most important was the shift in the weight of European civilization from the Mediterranean to the North Atlantic regions. Most of northern Europe from southern England to the Urals is a vast, wet, and highly fertile alluvial plain. The Romans had hardly begun to cultivate this area because they only ruled part of it, because it lay too far away from the center of their civilization, and because they did not have the proper tools and systems to work the soil. Starting around the time of the Carolingians much more attention was paid to colonizing and cultivating the great alluvial plain. The Carolingians opened up all of western and central Germany to agricultural settlement and started experimenting with new tools and methods that would be most appropriate for cultivating the newly settled lands. The results helped support other Carolingian achievements, but the Carolingian peace, as we have seen, was too brief to allow for any cumulative development. After the invasions of the tenth century, it was necessary to start again in a systematic attempt to exploit the potential wealth of the north. As long as Western civilization was centered in England, northern France, the Low Countries, and Germany, however, the rich lands remained available for cultivation.

Another prerequisite for agricultural development was improved climate. We know far less about European climatic patterns in past centuries than we would like to, but historians of climate are reasonably certain that there was an "optimum," or period of improved climate for western Europe, lasting from about 700 to 1200. This meant not only that during those centuries the temperature on the average was somewhat warmer than it had been before (at most only a rise of about 1° Centigrade), but also that the weather was somewhat drier. Dryness was of primary advantage to northern Europe, where lands were, if anything, usually too wet for good farming, whereas it was disadvantageous to the Mediterranean south, which was already dry enough. Among other things, the occurrence of this optimum helps explain why there was more agricultural cultivation in northern climes such as Iceland than there has been since then. (Also, with fewer icebergs in the northern seas, Norsemen were able to reach Greenland and Newfoundland, and Greenland then was probably indeed more green than white.) Although the optimum began around 700 and continued through the ninth and tenth centuries, it could not by itself counteract the deleterious effects of the tenth-century invasions. Fortunately the weather stayed propitious when Europeans again were able to take advantage of it.

Similar remarks apply to the fact that the Carolingians knew about many of the technological devices to be discussed presently that later helped western Europeans accomplish their first agricultural revolution. Although the most basic new devices were known before 1050, all came into widespread use and were brought to greatest perfection between then and about 1200 because only then was there a conjunction of the most favorable circumstances. Not only did the invasions end and good climate continue, but better government gradually provided the more lasting peace necessary for agricultural expansion. Landlords too became more interested in profit-making than mere consumption. Above all, from about 1050 to 1200 there was a greater consolidation of wealth for further investment as one advance helped support another; quite simply, technological devices could now be afforded.

One of the first and most important breakthroughs in agriculture

(2) improved climate

(3) technology in conjunction with favorable circumstances

Light Plow and Heavy Plow. Note that the peasant using the light plow had to press his foot on it to give it added weight. The major innovation of the heavy plow (often wheeled, as shown here) was the long moldboard, which turned

Technological innovations: (1) the heavy plow

was the use of the heavy plow. The plow itself, of course, is an ancient tool, but the Romans knew only a light "scratch plow" that broke up the surface of the ground without fully turning it over. This implement was sufficient for the light soil of the Mediterranean regions but was virtually useless with the much heavier, wetter soil of the European north. During the course of the early Middle Ages a much heavier and more efficient plow was developed that could cultivate the northern lands. Not only could this heavier plow deal with heavier soils, but it was fitted with new parts that enabled it to turn over furrows and fully aerate the ground. The benefits were immeasurable. In addition to the fact that the plow allowed for the cultivation of hitherto unworkable lands, the furrows it made provided excellent drainage systems for water-logged territories. It also saved labor: whereas the Roman scratch plow had to be dragged over the fields twice in two different directions, the heavy plow did more thorough work in one operation. In short, the opening up of northern Europe for intensive agriculture and everything that followed would have been inconceivable without the heavy plow.

(2) the three-field system

Closely allied to the use of the heavy plow was the introduction of the three-field system of crop rotation. Before modern times, farmers always let a large part of their arable land lie fallow for a year to avoid exhaustion of the soil because there was not enough fertilizer to support more intensive agriculture, and nitrogen-fixing crops such as clover and alfalfa were almost unknown. But the Romans represented an unproductive extreme in their inability to cultivate any more than half of their arable land in any year. The medieval innovation was to reduce the fallow to one-third by introducing a three-field system. In a given year one third of the land would lie fallow, one third would be

over the ground after the plowshare cut into it. The picture on the right depicts a second crucial medieval invention as well—the padded horse collar which allowed horses to throw their full weight into pulling.

given to cereal that was sown in the fall and harvested in early summer, and one third to a new crop—oats, barley, or legumes—that would be planted in the late spring and harvested in August or September. The fields were then rotated over a three-year cycle. The major innovation was the planting of the new crop which grew over the summer. The Romans could not have supported this system because their lands were poorer and especially because the Mediterranean area is too dry to support much summer growth at all. In this respect the wetter north obviously had a great advantage. The benefits of the new crop were that it did not deplete the soil as much as cereal like wheat and rye (in fact, it restored nitrogen taken from the soil by these crops); that it provided some insurance against loss from natural disasters by diversifying the growth of the fields; and that it produced new types of food. If the third field was planted with oats, the crop could be consumed by both humans and horses; if planted with legumes, it helped to balance the human diet by providing a source of protein to balance the major intake of cereal carbohydrates. Since the new system also helped to diversify labor over the course of the year and raised production from one-half to two-thirds, it was nothing short of an agricultural miracle.

A third major innovation was the use of mills. The Romans had known about water mills but hardly used them, partly because they had enough slaves to be indifferent to labor-saving devices and partly because most Roman territories were not richly endowed with swiftly flowing streams. Starting around 1050, however, there was a veritable craze in northern Europe for building increasingly efficient water mills. One French area saw a growth from 14 water mills in the eleventh century to 60 in the twelfth; in another part of France about 40

(3) use of mills

mills were built between 850 and 1080, 40 more between 1080 and 1125, and 245 between 1125 and 1175. Once Europeans had mastered the complex technology of building water mills, they turned their attention to harnessing the power of wind: around 1170 they constructed the first European windmills. Thereafter, in flat lands like Holland that had no swiftly flowing streams, windmills proliferated as rapidly as water-powered ones had spread elsewhere. Although the major use of mills was to grind grain, they were soon adapted for a variety of other important functions: for example, they were employed to drive saws, process cloth, press oil, brew beer, provide power for iron forges, and crush pulp for manufacturing paper. Paper had been made in China and the Islamic world before this but never with the aid of paper mills, which is evidence of the technological sophistication the West was achieving in comparison to other advanced civilizations.

(4) other technological developments

Other important technological breakthroughs that gathered force around 1050 should be mentioned. Several related to providing the means for using horses as farm animals. Around 800 a padded collar was first introduced into Europe; this allowed the horse to put his full weight into pulling without choking himself. Roughly a century later iron horseshoes were first used to protect hooves, and perhaps around 1050 tandem harnessing was developed to allow horses to pull behind each other. With these advances and the greater abundance of oats due to the three-field system, horses replaced oxen as farm animals in some parts of Europe and brought with them the advantages of working more quickly and working longer hours. Further inventions were the wheelbarrow and the harrow, a tool drawn over the field after the plow to level the earth and mix in the seed. Important for most of these inventions was the greater use of iron in the High Middle Ages to reinforce all sorts of agricultural implements, most crucially the parts of the heavy plow that came into contact with the soil.

Peasants Bringing Grain to Windmills. Shown here are two different kinds of mills: those set to operate by prevailing winds (at left) and those that are pivoted to face into chance winds (middle and right).

So far we have been speaking of technological developments as if they alone account for the high-medieval agricultural revolution. But that is by no means the case. Along with improved technology came a great extension in the amount of land made arable and more intensive cultivation of the land already cleared. Although the Carolingians had begun to open the rich plain of northwestern Europe to tillage, they had only chosen to clear the most easily workable patches: a map of Carolingian agricultural settlements would show numerous tiny islands of cultivated lands surrounded by vast stretches of forests, swamps, and wastes. Starting around 1050, and greatly accelerating in the twelfth century, movements of land-clearing entirely changed the topography of northern Europe. First, greater peace and stability allowed farm workers in northern France and western Germany to begin pushing beyond the islands of settlement, clearing little bits of land at a time. At first they did this surreptitiously because they were poaching on territories that were actually owned by aristocratic lords. In time the aristocratic landowners gave their support to the clearing activities because they demanded their own profits from them. When that happened the work of clearing forests and draining swamps was carried on more swiftly. Thus, as the twelfth century progressed the isolated arable islands of Carolingian times expanded to meet each other. While this was going on, and continuing somewhat later, entirely new areas were colonized and opened to cultivation, for example, in northern England, Holland, and above all the eastern parts of Germany. Finally, in the twelfth and thirteenth centuries, peasants began working all the lands they had cleared more efficiently and intensively in order to gain more income for themselves. They harrowed after plowing, hoed frequently to keep down weeds, and added extra plowings to their yearly cycle, thereby greatly helping to renew the fertility of the soil.

*Extension and intense
cultivation of arable land*

The result of all these changes was an enormous increase in agricultural production. With more land opened for cultivation obviously more crops were raised, but the increase was magnified by the introduction of more efficient farming methods. Thus, average yields from grains of seed sown increased from at best twofold in Carolingian times to three- or fourfold by around 1300. And all the additional grain could be ground far more rapidly than before because a mill could grind grain in the same time that it would have taken forty men to do the same job. Europeans, therefore, could for the first time begin to rely on a regular and stable food supply.

*Enormous increase in
agricultural productivity*

That fact in turn had the profoundest consequences for the further development of European history. To begin with, it meant that more land could be given over to uses other than raising grain. Accordingly, as the High Middle Ages progressed, there was greater agricultural diversification and specialization. Large areas were turned over to sheep-raising, others to viniculture, and others to raising cotton and dyestuffs. Many of the products of these new enterprises were con-

*Consequences of the
agricultural revolution*

sumed locally, but many were also traded over long distances or used to provide the raw materials for new industries—above all those of cloth-making. The growth of this trade and manufacturing helped initiate and support, as we will see, the growth of towns. The agricultural boom also helped sustain the growth of towns in another way: by supporting a great spurt in population. With more food and a better diet (above all the increase in proteins) life expectancy increased from perhaps as low as an average of thirty years for the poor of Carolingian Europe to between forty and fifty years in the High Middle Ages. Healthier people also increased their birthrate. For these reasons the population of the West grew about threefold between about 1050 and 1300. More people and more labor-saving devices meant that not everybody had to stay on the farm: some could migrate to new towns and cities where they found a new way of life.

Other results   Still other results of the agricultural revolution were that it raised the incomes of lords, thereby underpinning a great increase in the sophistication of aristocratic life, and raised the incomes of monarchs, underpinning the growth of states. European-wide prosperity also helped support the growth of the Church and paid the way for the burgeoning of schools and intellectual enterprises. One final, more intangible, result was that Europeans apparently became more optimistic, more energetic, and more willing to experiment and take risks than any of their rivals on the world scene.

2. LORD AND SERF: SOCIAL CONDITIONS AND QUALITY OF LIFE IN THE MANORIAL REGIME

The meaning of the term *manorialism*   While agriculture was being transformed, social and economic conditions began to change for both landowners and agricultural laborers. Since for much of the High Middle Ages, however, rural life revolved around the institution of the manor owned by lords and worked by serfs, it is best to describe this manorial regime in its most typical form before describing basic changes. In reading the following it should be understood that the term manorialism is not synonymous with feudalism: manorialism was an economic system in which large agricultural estates were worked by serfs, whereas feudalism, in the sense the word is used by most medieval historians, was a political system in which government was greatly decentralized (see the fourth section of this chapter). It should also be borne in mind that when scholars talk about manorialism based on a "typical manor" they are resorting to a historical approximation: no two manors were ever exactly alike; indeed many differed enormously in size and basic characteristics. Moreover, in those parts of Europe farthest away from the original centers of Carolingian settlement between the Seine and the Rhine, there were few, if any, manors at all. In Italy there was still much agriculture based on slavery, and in central and eastern Germany there were many smaller farms worked by free peasants.

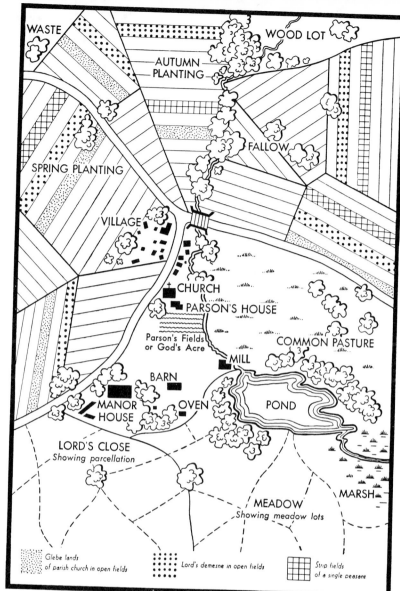

WASTE

WOOD LOT

AUTUMN PLANTING

FALLOW

SPRING PLANTING

VILLAGE

CHURCH

PARSON'S HOUSE

Parson's Fields or God's Acre

COMMON PASTURE

MILL

BARN

OVEN

POND

MANOR HOUSE

LORD'S CLOSE
Showing parcellation

MARSH

MEADOW
Showing meadow lots

Glebe lands of parish church in open fields

Lord's demesne in open fields

Strip fields of a single peasant

Diagram of a Manor

The manor first clearly emerged in Carolingian times and continued to be the dominant form of agrarian social and economic organization in most of northwestern Europe until about the thirteenth century. It descended from the large Roman landed estate, but, unlike the Roman estate, the manor was worked by serfs (sometimes called villeins) and not slaves. Serfs were definitely not free in the modern sense: above all, they could not leave their lands, were forced to work for their lords regularly without pay, and were subject to numerous humiliating dues and to the jurisdiction of the lord's court. But they were much better off than slaves insofar as they were allocated land which they culti-

The manor; serfs

*The manorial system of
agriculture*

vated to support themselves and which normally could not be taken away from them. Thus, when agricultural improvements took place the serfs themselves could hope to profit at least a little from them. More than that, although the lord theoretically had the right to levy dues at will, in practice obligations tended to remain fixed. Although the lot of the serfs was surely terribly hard, they were seldom entirely at their lord's whim.

The lands of the manor, which might run from several hundred to several thousand acres, were divided into those that belonged to the lord and those that were allocated to the serfs. The former, called the lord's *demesne* (pronounced demean), usually comprised between a third and a half of the arable land. It was worked by the serfs on certain days, perhaps three days a week. The demesne did not consist of big parcels but was made up of narrow strips alternating with strips belonging to different peasants (and sometimes also strips set aside for the Church). All these strips were long and narrow because a heavy plow drawn by a yoke of horses or oxen could not be turned around easily. Because all the strips were generally separated only by a narrow band of unplowed turf, the whole regime is sometimes called the *open-field system*. Even when the serfs tilled their own lands they almost always worked together because they usually owned farm animals and implements in common. For the same reason, grazing lands were called "commons" because the commonly owned herds grazed there together. In addition to cultivated fields and pastures, the serfs usually had their own small gardens. Most manors also had forests set aside primarily for the lord's hunting which were also useful for the foraging of pigs and the gathering of firewood. Insofar as serfs were allowed

Sowing Seed. When the peasant sows his seed broadcast, the crows are not far off to help themselves. Here, one is bold enough to peck at the sack while another is momentarily chased off by a dog.

Medieval Peasants Slaughtering a Pig. Deep in winter, probably around Christmas, it is finally time to slaughter the household pig. But nothing can be wasted, so even the blood is caught in a pan to make blood pudding.

to take advantage of such opportunities they did that too in common: indeed, the entire manorial system emphasized communal enterprise and solidarity.

Communalism must have helped make a barely endurable life seem slightly more bearable. Even though the lot of the medieval serf was surely far superior to that of the Roman slave, and even though it improved from around 1050 to 1300, it was still primitive and pitiful beyond modern comprehension. Dwellings were usually miserable hovels constructed of wattle—braided twigs—smeared over with mud. As late as the thirteenth century an English peasant was convicted of destroying his neighbor's house simply by sawing apart one central beam. The floors of most huts were usually no more than the bare earth, often cold or damp. For beds there was seldom more than bracken, and beyond that there was hardly any furniture. Not entirely jokingly it may be said that a good meal often consisted of two courses: one a porridge very much like gruel and the other a gruel very much like porridge. Fruit was almost unheard of, and meager vegetables were limited to such fare as onions, leeks, turnips, and cabbages— all boiled to make a thin soup. Meat came at most a few times a year, either on holidays or deep in winter, when all the fodder for a scrawny ox or pig had run out. Cooking utensils were never cleaned, so as to make sure that there was never any waste. In addition, there was always the possibility of crop failures, which affected the serfs far more than their lords, since the lords demanded the same income as always. At such times the serfs were forced to surrender whatever grain they had and watched their children die slowly of starvation. It is particularly heart-rending to realize that children might be dying

Living conditions of serfs

while there was still a bit of grain in the granaries: but that grain could not be touched because it was set aside as next year's seed, and without that there would be no future at all.

To counterbalance this grim picture we may now turn to patterns of change and improvement. One, as we have already seen, was dietary. In the High Middle Ages famines were actually far rarer than before and people grew stronger because some protein, mostly in the form of legumes, was added to their fare. There was also a widespread enfranchisement (i.e., freeing) of serfs for many reasons. Once landlords started opening up new lands, they could only attract laborers by guaranteeing their freedom. New centers of free labor usually attracted runaway serfs and became models of a new system whereby landlords asked for fixed rents rather than demanding services. Then, even on the old manors, lords began to realize that they might be able to raise profits by demanding rents instead of duties. Alternatively, by selling their excess produce at free markets serfs might become sufficiently rich to buy their freedom.

In these different ways serfdom gradually came to an end throughout most of Europe in the course of the thirteenth century. The process, however, moved more or less swiftly in different areas—it was somewhat delayed in England and was seldom so complete that former serfs did not owe some remnant of labor service and dues to powerful local lords. In France some of these obligations continued to exist as nagging indignities right down to the French Revolution in 1789. Serfs who became enfranchised often continued to work communally, but they were now free peasants who produced more for the open market than for their own subsistence.

The lords profited even more than their serfs from the agricultural revolution for several reasons. One was that whenever lords enfranchised serfs they obtained large sums of cash, usually about all the wealth that the serfs had hitherto amassed. Afterward the lords lived mainly on their rents. Since some of these were levied on lands that the lords had once owned but had never been cultivated, noble income rose greatly. Even more than that, once the lords began to prefer rents to services, they found that rents were easier to increase. In their capacity as rent-collectors the lords did not personally supervise their lands as much as before but traveled more freely, sometimes going off crusading and sometimes living at royal courts. Consequently, added wealth allowed them to live better, and greater mobility gave them new ideas for improving their style of life.

Increased sophistication of the nobility was much enhanced by the fact that in the High Middle Ages there was less tumultuous local warfare than before. Until around 1100 the typical European noble was a crude and brutal warrior who spent most of his time engaging in combat with his neighbors and pillaging the defenseless. Much of this violence slackened off in the twelfth century as a result of ecclesiastical constraints, because emerging states were more effectively enforcing

Jousting in a Tournament

local peace, and because the nobles themselves were beginning to enjoy a more settled existence. Nobles continued to go on crusades and to fight in national wars, but they engaged in petty quarrels with each other less frequently. Apparently as an unconscious surrogate for the old fighting spirit the code of *chivalry* was developed. This channeled martial conduct into relatively benign activities. Chivalry literally means "horsemanship," and the chivalrous noble was expected to be thoroughly adept at the equestrian arts. Chivalry also imposed the obligation of fighting in defense of honorable causes; if none was to be found there were opportunities for combat in tournaments, mock battles that at first were quite savage but later became elaborate ceremonial affairs. Above all, the chivalric lord—typically a "knight" who owned less land than the upper aristocracy—was expected to be not only brave and loyal but generous, truthful, reverent, kind to the poor, and disdainful of unfair advantage or sordid gain.

By-products of the increase in noble wealth and the rise of chivalry were improvements in the quality of living conditions and the treatment of women. Until around 1100 most noble dwellings were made of wood, and burned down frequently because of primitive heating and cooking methods. With increasing wealth and more advanced technology, castles after 1100 were usually built of stone and were thus far less flammable. Moreover, they were now equipped with chimneys and mantled fireplaces, both medieval inventions, which meant that instead of having one large fire in a central great hall, indi-

Improvements in the quality of noble life

Aristocratic Table Manners. There are knives but no forks or napkins on the table. The large stars mark these nobles as members of a chivalric order.

vidual rooms could be heated and individuals gained some privacy. Nobles customarily ate fewer vegetables than peasants, but their diet was laden with meat; increased luxury trade also brought costly exotic spices like pepper and saffron to their tables. Although table manners were still atrocious—all used only knives and spoons but no forks and blew their noses on their sleeves—nobles tried to show their superiority to others by dressing elegantly, indeed ostentatiously. During this period snug-fitting clothing also became available because both knitting and the button and buttonhole had just been invented.

Changes in noble attitudes toward women

The history of noble attitudes toward women in the High Middle Ages is somewhat controversial for two reasons. One is that most of our evidence comes from literature, and historians differ as to what degree literature actually reflects life. The other is that according to some scholars women were at best put on a pedestal, whereas modern women rightly prefer to move "up from the pedestal." Nonetheless, there can be no question that as the material quality of noble life improved it did so for women as well as men. More than that, there definitely was a revolution in some verbalized attitudes toward the female sex. Until the twelfth century, aside from a few female saints, women were virtually ignored in literature: the typical French epic told of bloody warlike deeds that either made no mention of women or portrayed them only in passing as being totally subservient. But within a few decades after 1100 noblewomen were suddenly turned into objects of veneration by lyric poets and writers of romances (see the following chapter). A typical troubadour poet could write of his lady that "all I do that is fitting I infer from her beautiful body," and that "she is the tree and the branch where joy's fruit ripens."

Changes in the status of noblewomen

Although the new "courtly" literature was extremely idealistic and somewhat artificial, it surely expressed the values of a gentler culture wherein upper-class women were in practice more respected than before. Moreover, there is no question that certain royal women in the twelfth and thirteenth centuries actually did rule their states on various occasions when their husbands or sons were dead or unable to do so.

The indomitable Eleanor of Aquitaine, wife of Henry II, for example, helped rule England even though she was over seventy years old when her son Richard I went on a crusade from 1190 to 1194, and the strong-willed Blanche of Castile ruled France extremely well twice in the thirteenth century, once during the minority of her son Louis IX and again when he was off crusading. No doubt from a modern perspective high-medieval women were still very constrained, but from the point of view of the past the High Middle Ages was a time of progress for the women of the upper classes. The most striking symbol comes from the history of the game of chess: before the twelfth century chess was played in Eastern countries, but there the equivalent of the queen was a male figure, the king's chief minister, who could only move diagonally one square at a time; in twelfth-century western Europe, however, this piece was turned into a queen, and sometime before the end of the Middle Ages she began to move all over the board.

3. THE REVIVAL OF TRADE AND THE URBAN REVOLUTION

Inseparable from the agricultural revolution, the enfranchisement of serfs, and the growing sophistication of noble life was the revival of trade and the burgeoning of towns. Reviving trade was of many different sorts. Most fundamental was the mundane trade at local markets, where serfs or free peasants sold their excess grain or perhaps a few dozen eggs. But with growing specialization, produce like wine or cotton might be shipped over longer distances. River and sea routes were used wherever possible, but land transport was also necessary, and this was aided by improvements in road-building, the introduction of packhorses and mules, and the building of bridges. Whereas the Romans were really only interested in land *communications,* medieval people, starting in the eleventh century, concentrated on land *transport* to the degree that they were much better able to maintain a vigorous land-based trade. And that is not to say that they ignored Mediterranean communications either. On the contrary, starting again in the eleventh century they began to make the former Roman "lake" the intermediary for an extensive seaborne trade that stretched over shorter and longer distances. Between 1050 and 1300 the Italian city-states of Genoa, Pisa, and Venice freed much of the Mediterranean from Muslim control, started monopolizing trade on formerly Byzantine waters, and began to establish in eastern Mediterranean outposts a flourishing commerce with the Orient. As a result, luxury goods such as spices, gems, perfumes, and fine cloths began to appear in Western markets and stimulated economic life by inspiring nobles to accelerate the agricultural revolution in order to pay for them.

Patterns of trade

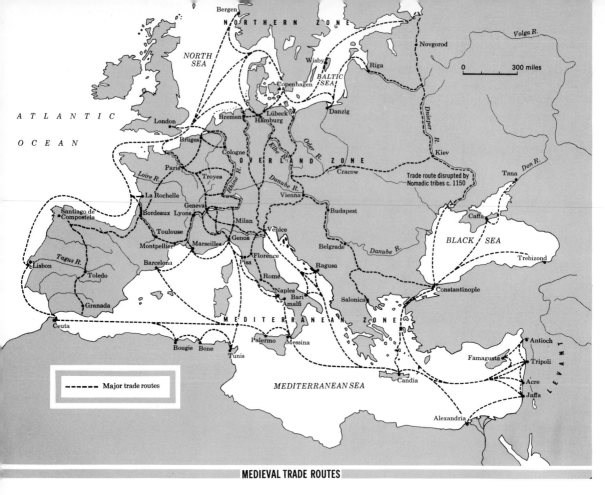

MEDIEVAL TRADE ROUTES

This revival of trade called for new patterns of payment and the development of new commercial techniques. Most significantly, western Europe returned to a money economy after about four centuries when coined money was hardly used as a medium of exchange. The traditional manor had been almost self-sufficient and the few external items needed could be bartered for. But with the growth of markets coins became indispensable. At first these were coins of only the smallest denominations, but as luxury trade grew in the West the denominations increased apace; by the thirteenth century gold coins were minted by Italian states such as Florence and Venice.

The revival of a money economy

In a similar pattern of development, long-distance traders were first itinerant merchants, often not unlike peddlers, but gradually they found it best to exhibit and sell their wares at international trade fairs. The most prosperous of these fairs were held in the French province of Champagne, where, for example, cloths from Flanders and spices brought by Italians from the East were exhibited and sold. Later, by around 1300, trade fairs declined because prosperous merchants were now sending out whole fleets from Italy to the North Atlantic and staying at home themselves. To facilitate this more sedentary pattern

Long-distance trade and new commercial techniques

of business life, merchants perfected modern techniques of business partnerships, letters of credit, and accounting. Because such entrepreneurs invested in trade intentionally for profit and devised and used sophisticated credit mechanisms, most modern historians agree in calling them the first Western commercial capitalists.

In addition to the expansion of money and credit, trade was vastly facilitated by the rapid growth of towns. If we could imagine an aerial view of twelfth-century Europe, the mushrooming of towns would be the most strikingly visible phenomenon after the clearing of forests and wastes. Some historians misleadingly include under the heading of towns the numerous new agricultural village communities of peasants that were established in clearings. These, however, were not really urban in any sense. Putting them aside, many urban agglomerations were built from the ground up in the High Middle Ages, and existing towns that had barely survived from the Roman period grew enormously in size. To take some examples, in central and eastern Germany, which had not been part of the old Roman area of settlement, new towns such as Freiburg, Lübeck, Munich, and Berlin were founded in the twelfth century. Farther west, where old Roman towns had become little more than episcopal residences or stockades, formerly insignificant towns like Paris, London, and Cologne roughly doubled in size between 1100 and 1200 and doubled again in the next century. Urban life was above all concentrated in Italy, which encompassed most of Europe's largest cities: Venice, Genoa, Milan, Bologna, Palermo, Florence, and Naples. In the thirteenth century the population of the largest of these—Venice, Genoa, and Milan—was in the range of 100,000. We lack accurate growth figures for other Italian cities, but it seems likely that many at least trebled in population between about 1150 and 1300 because we do know that the smaller Italian town of Imola, near Bologna, grew from some 4,200 in 1210 to 11,500 in 1312. Considering that town life had come very close to disappearing in most of Europe between 750 and 1050, it is warranted to speak of a high-medieval urban revolution. Moreover, from the High Middle Ages until now a vigorous urban life has been a major characteristic of western European and subsequently modern world civilization.

It used to be thought that the primary cause of the medieval urban revolution was the revival of long-distance trade. Theoretically, itinerant peddlers, who had no secure place in the dominantly agrarian society of Europe, gradually settled together in towns in order to offer each other much-needed protection and establish markets to sell their wares. In fact, the picture is far more complicated than that. While some towns did receive great stimulus from long-distance trade, and the growth of a major city such as Venice would have been unthinkable without it, most towns relied for their origin and early economic vitality far more on the wealth of their surrounding areas. These brought them surplus agricultural goods, raw materials for manufac-

Growth of towns

Venetian Coin. Minted between 1280 and 1289 this obverse depicts the patron saint of Venice, Saint Mark, granting a banner symbolizing worldly rule to the Venetian doge.

Causes of the urban revolution

View of Paris. The city looked this way at the end of the Middle Ages, around 1480. Note the prominence of the cathedral of Notre Dame in the center and the large number of other church spires; note, too, how closely all the buildings are packed behind the walls.

Old Houses in Strassburg. In the Middle Ages food was stored in attics, with special openings for ventilation, as insurance against famine. Of course there was still much spoilage.

ture, and an influx of population. In other words, the quickening of economic life in general was the major cause of urban growth: towns existed in a symbiotic relationship with the countryside by providing markets and also wares made by artisans, while they lived off the rural food surplus and grew with the migration of surplus serfs or peasants who were seeking a better life. (Escaped serfs were guaranteed their freedom if they stayed in a town a year and a day.) Once towns started to flourish, many of them began to specialize in certain enterprises. Paris and Bologna gained considerable wealth by becoming the homes of leading universities; Venice, Genoa, Cologne, and London became centers of long-distance trade; and Milan, Ghent, and Bruges specialized in manufactures. The most important urban industries were those devoted to cloth-making. Cloth manufacturers sometimes developed techniques of large-scale production and investment that are ancestors of the modern factory system and industrial capitalism. But it must be emphasized that large industrial enterprises were atypical of medieval economic life as a whole.

Medieval cities and towns were not smaller scale facsimiles of modern ones; to our own eyes they would still have seemed half-rural and uncivilized. Streets were often unpaved, houses had gardens for raising vegetables, and cows and pigs were kept in stables and pigsties. Passing along the streets of a major metropolis one might be stopped by a flock of bleating sheep or a crowd of honking geese. Sanitary conditions were often very poor and the air must often have reeked of excrement—both animal and human. Town-dwellers were cursed by the frequency of fires that swept quickly through closely settled wooden or straw quarters and went unstopped by the lack of fire stations. People were also highly susceptible to contagious diseases bred by unsanitary conditions and crowding. Still another problem was that economic tensions and family rivalries could lead to bloody riots. Yet for all this, urban folk took great pride in their new cities and ways of life. A famous paean to London, for example, written by a twelfth-century denizen of that city, boasted of its prosperity, piety, and perfect climate (!), and claimed that except for frequent fires, London's only nuisance was "the immoderate drinking of fools."

The most distinctive form of economic and social organization in the medieval towns was the guild. This was, roughly speaking, a professional association organized to protect and promote special interests. The main types were merchant guilds and craft guilds. The primary functions of the merchant guild were to maintain a monopoly of the local market for its members and to preserve a stable economic system. To accomplish these ends the merchant guild severely restricted trading by foreigners in the city, guaranteed to its members the right to participate in sales offered by other members, enforced uniform pricing, and did everything possible to ensure that no individual would corner the market for goods produced by its members.

A Medieval Shoemaker

Craft guilds similarly regulated the affairs of artisans. Usually their only full-fledged voting members were so-called master craftsmen, who were experts at their trades and ran their own shops. Hence if these guilds were anything like modern trade unions, they were unions of bosses. Second-class members of craft guilds were journeymen, who had learned their trades but still worked for the masters (*journeyman* is from the French *journée,* meaning "day," or by extension "day's work"), and apprentices. Terms of apprenticeship were carefully regulated: if an apprentice wished to become a master he often had to produce a "masterpiece" for judging by the masters of the guild. Craft guilds, like merchant guilds, sought to preserve monopo-

The Great Crane at Bruges. A pulley device operated by human energy. Animals wander through the narrow street in the background.

A Medieval Weaver

Medieval attitudes toward
merchants

lies and to limit competition. Thus they established uniformity of prices and wages, prohibited working after hours, and formulated detailed regulations governing methods of production and quality of materials. In addition to all their economic functions, both kinds of guilds served important social ones. Often they acted in the capacity of religious associations, benevolent societies, and social clubs. Wherever possible guilds tried to minister to the human needs of their members. Thus in some cities they came close to becoming miniature governments.

Town merchants and artisans were particularly concerned to protect themselves because they had no accepted role in the older medieval scheme of things. Usually merchants were disdained by the landed aristocracy because they could claim no ancient lineages and were not versed in the ways of chivalry. Worst of all, they were too obviously concerned with pecuniary gain. Although nobles too were gradually becoming interested in making profits, they displayed this less openly: they paid little attention in their daily lives to accounts and made much of their free-spending largesse. Still another reason why medieval merchants were on the defensive was that the Church, opposed to illicit gain, taught a doctrine of the "just price" that was often at variance with what the merchants thought they deserved. Clergymen too condemned usury—i.e., the lending of money for interest—even though it was often essential for doing business. A decree of the Second Lateran Council of 1139, to take one example, excoriated the "detestable, shameful, and insatiable rapacity of moneylenders." As time went on, however, attitudes slowly changed. In Italy it often became hard to tell merchants from aristocrats because the latter customarily lived in towns and often engaged in trade themselves. In the rest of Europe, the most prosperous town-dwellers, called patricians, developed their own sense of pride verging on that of the nobility. The medieval Church never abandoned its prohibition of usury, but it did

Medieval Walled City of
Carcassonne, France.
These walls date from
1240 to 1285.

come to approve making profits on commercial risks, which was often close to the same thing. Moreover, starting around the thirteenth century leading churchmen came to speak more favorably of merchants. St. Bonaventure, a leading thirteenth-century churchman, argued that God showed special favors to shepherds like David in the time of the Old Testament, to fishers like Peter in the time of the New, and to merchants like St. Francis in the thirteenth century.

All in all, the importance of the high-medieval urban revolution can scarcely be overestimated. The fact that the new towns were the vital pumps of the high-medieval economy has already been sufficiently emphasized: in providing markets and producing wares they kept the entire economic system thriving. In addition, cities and towns made important contributions to the development of government because in many areas they gained their own independence and ruled themselves as city-states. Primarily in Italy, where urban life was by far the most advanced, city governments experimented with new systems of tax-collecting, record-keeping, and public participation in decision-making. Italian city-states were particularly advanced in their administrative techniques and thereby helped influence a general European-wide growth in governmental sophistication.

Significance of the urban revolution: (1) development of the economy and government

Finally, the rise of towns contributed greatly to the quickening of intellectual life in the West. New schools were invariably located in towns because towns afforded domiciles and legal protection for scholars. At first, students and teachers were always clerics, but by the thirteenth century the needs of merchants to be trained in reading and accounting led to the foundation of numerous lay primary schools. Equally momentous for the future was the fact that the stimulating urban environment helped make advanced schools more open to intellectual experimentation than any in the West since those of the Greeks. Not coincidentally, Greek intellectual life too was based on thriving cities. Thus it seems that without commerce in goods there can be little exciting commerce in ideas.

(2) towns as a foundation for intellectual life

4. FEUDALISM AND THE RISE OF THE NATIONAL MONARCHIES

If any western European city of around 1200 epitomized Europe's greatest new accomplishments it was Paris: that city was not only a bustling commercial center and an important center of learning, it was also the capital of what was becoming Europe's most powerful government. France, like England and the new Christian kingdoms of the Iberian peninsula, was taking shape in the twelfth and thirteenth centuries as a *national monarchy,* a new form of government which was to dominate Europe's political future. Because the developing national monarchies were the most successful and promising European governments we must concentrate on them. But before we do it is well

A Medieval Tailor

*The political decline of
medieval Germany an
intriguing historical
problem*

*The German monarchy in
the tenth and eleventh
centuries*

to see what was happening from the political point of view in Germany and Italy.

Around 1050 Germany was unquestionably the most centralized and best-ruled territory in Europe, but by 1300 it had fallen into a congeries of warring petty states. Since most other areas of Europe were gaining stronger rule in the very same period, the political decline of Germany becomes an intriguing historical problem. It is also a problem of fundamental importance because from a political point of view Germany only caught up with the rest of Europe in the nineteenth century and its belated efforts to gain its full place in the European political system created difficulties that have just come to be resolved in our own age.

The major sources of Germany's strength from the reign of Otto the Great in the middle of the tenth century until the latter part of the eleventh century were its succession of strong rulers, its resistance to political fragmentation, and the close alliance of its crown with the Church. By resoundingly defeating the Hungarians and taking the title of emperor, Otto kept the country from falling prey to further invasions and won great prestige for the monarchy. For over a century afterward there was a nearly uninterrupted succession of rulers as able and vigorous as Otto. Their nearest political rivals were the dukes, military leaders of five large German territories (Lorraine, Saxony, Franconia, Swabia, and Bavaria), but throughout most of this period the dukes were overawed by the emperors' greater power. The latter, in order to rule their wide territories—which included Switzerland, eastern France, and most of the Low Countries, as well as claims to northern Italy—relied heavily on cooperation with the Church. The leading royal administrators were archbishops and bishops whom the emperors appointed without interference from the pope and who often came from their own families. The German emperors were so strong that, when they chose to do so, they could come down to Italy and name their own popes. The archbishops and bishops ran the German government fairly well for the times without any elaborate administrative machinery, and they counterbalanced the strength of the dukes. In the course of the eleventh century the emperors were starting tentatively to develop their own secular administration. Had they been allowed to continue this policy, it might have provided a really solid governmental foundation for the future. But just then the whole system shaped by Otto the Great and his successors was dramatically challenged by a revolution within the Church.

The challenge to the German government came in the reign of Henry IV (1056–1106) and was directed by Pope Gregory VII (1073–1085). For reasons that will be discussed in the next chapter, Gregory wished to free the Church from secular control and launched a struggle to achieve this aim against Henry IV. Gregory immediately placed Henry on the defensive by forging an alliance with the dukes and other German princes, who only needed a sufficient pretext to rise

*The struggle between
Henry IV and Gregory
VII*

up against their ruler. When the princes threatened to depose Henry because of his disobedience to the pope, the hitherto mighty ruler was forced to seek absolution from Gregory VII in one of the most melodramatic scenes of the Middle Ages. In the depths of winter in 1077 Henry hurried over the Alps to abase himself before the pope in the north Italian castle of Canossa. As Gregory described the scene in a letter to the princes: "There on three successive days, standing before the castle gate, laying aside all royal insignia, barefooted and in coarse attire, Henry ceased not with many tears to beseech the apostolic help and comfort." No German ruler had ever been so humiliated. Although the events at Canossa forestalled Henry's deposition, they robbed him of his great prestige. By the time his struggle with the papacy, continued by his son, was over, the princes had won far more practical independence from the crown than they had ever had. More than that, in 1125 they made good their claims to be able to elect a new ruler regardless of hereditary succession—a principle that would thereafter often lead them to choose the weakest successors or to embroil the country in civil war. Meanwhile, the crown had lost much of its control of the Church and thus in effect had its administrative rug pulled out from under it. While France and England were gradually consolidating their centralized governmental apparatuses, Germany was losing its own.

Frederick Barbarossa. A stylized contemporary representation.

A major attempt to stem the tide running against the German monarchy was made in the twelfth century by Frederick I (1152–1190), who came from the family of Hohenstaufen. Frederick, called "Barbarossa" (meaning "red beard"), tried to reassert his imperial dignity by calling his realm the "Holy Roman Empire," on the theory that it was a universal empire descending from Rome and blessed by God. Laying claim to Roman descent, he promulgated old Roman imperial laws—preserved in the Code of Justinian—that gave him much theoretical power. But he could not hope to enforce such laws unless he had his own material base of support. Therefore the major policy of his reign was to balance the power of the princes by carving out his own geographical domain from which he might draw wealth and strength.

Unfortunately for Frederick, his ancestral lands were located in Swabia, a poorer part of Germany that even today still consists of relatively unproductive hill country and the Black Forest. So Frederick decided to make northern Italy his power base in addition to Swabia. In this he could hardly have made a worse decision. Northern Italy was certainly wealthy, but it was also fiercely independent. Its rich towns and cities, led by Milan, offered stiff resistance. They were further lent helpful moral support by the papacy, which had no wish to see a strong German emperor ruling powerfully in Italy. Frederick came very close to overpowering the urban-papal alliance but ultimately the Alps proved to be too great a barrier to allow him to enforce his will in Italy and hope to rule in Germany as well. Whenever

Frederick's Italian policy

he subdued the towns he would shortly afterward have to leave for home, and the towns, with papal encouragement, would then rise up again. Finally, in 1176, insufficient German imperial forces were resoundingly defeated by the troops of a north Italian urban coalition at Legnano, and Barbarossa was forced to concede the area's de facto independence. In the meantime, the princes in Germany were continuing to gather strength, especially by colonizing the rich agricultural lands east of the Elbe where Frederick really should have busied himself, and the emperor's struggle with the popes further alienated elements within the German church. Because Barbarossa was a dashing figure he was well remembered by Germans, but his reign virtually made it certain that the German empire would not rise again during the medieval period.

The reign of Barbarossa's equally famous grandson, Frederick II (1212–1250), was merely a playing out of Germany's fate. In terms of his personality Frederick was probably the most fascinating of all medieval rulers. Because his father, Henry VI, had inherited through marriage the kingdom of southern Italy and Sicily (later called the Kingdom of the Two Sicilies), Frederick grew up in Palermo, where he absorbed elements of Islamic culture. (Arabs had ruled in Sicily for two and a half centuries, from 831 to 1071.) Frederick II spoke five or six languages, was a patron of learning, and wrote his own book on falconry, which takes an honored place in the early history of Western observational science. He also performed bizarre and brutal "experiments," such as disemboweling men to observe the comparative effects of rest and exercise upon digestion. Such practices corresponded to Frederick's overall policy of trying to rule like an Oriental despot. In his autonomous kingdom of southern Italy he introduced Eastern forms of absolutist and bureaucratic government. He established a professional army, levied direct taxation, and promulgated uniform Roman law. Typically, Frederick tried to create a ruler cult and decreed it an act of sacrilege even to discuss his statutes or judgments. For a while these policies seemed successful in ruling southern Italy, but Frederick's power base in Italy led to renewed conflicts with the papacy and the north Italian cities. These dragged on indecisively until his death, but thereafter the papacy was resolved to see no further Hohenstaufens ruling in Italy and proceeded to eliminate the remaining contenders from the line by calling crusades against them. Overtaxed by Frederick's ruthlessness and subsequent wars, southern Italy gradually sank into the backwardness from which it is only barely emerging today. And Frederick's reign was as damaging to Germany as well. Bent on pursuing his Italian policies without hindrance, Frederick formally wrote Germany off to the princes by granting them large areas of sovereignty. Although titular "emperors" afterward continued to be elected, the princes were the real rulers of the country. Yet they fought with each other so much that peace was rare, and they subdivided their lands among their heirs to such an extent that the

The Emperor Frederick II. He is shown holding a *fleur de lis,* as a symbol of rule, with a falcon, his favorite bird, at his side.

map of Germany began to look like a jig-saw puzzle. As the French philosopher Voltaire later said, the German "Holy Roman Empire" had become neither holy, nor Roman, nor an empire.

The story of high-medieval Italian politics may be told more quickly. Southern Italy and Sicily had been welded together into a strong monarchical state in the twelfth century by Norman-French descendants of the Vikings. But then, as we have seen, the area went to the Hohenstaufens and was subsequently brought to ruin. Central Italy was largely ruled by the papacy in the High Middle Ages, but the popes were seldom strong enough to create a really well-governed state, partly because they were at constant loggerheads with the German emperors. Farthest north were the rich commercial and manufacturing cities which had successfully fought off Barbarossa. These were usually organized politically in the form of republics or "communes." They offered much participation in governmental life to their more prosperous inhabitants. But because of diverse economic interests and family antagonisms, the Italian cities were usually riven with internal strife. Moreover, although they could unite in leagues against foreign threats such as those represented by Barbarossa or Frederick II, the cities often fought each other when foreign threats were absent. The result was that although economic and cultural life was very far advanced in the Italian cities, and although the cities made important experiments in administrative techniques, political stability was widely lacking in northern Italy throughout most of the high-medieval period.

If one looks for the centers of growing political stability in Europe, then one has to seek them in high-medieval France and England. Ironically, some of the most basic foundations for future political achievement in France were established without any planning just when that area was most politically unstable. These foundations were aspects of a level of political decentralization often referred to by historians as the system of "feudalism." The use of this word is controversial because ever since Marx some historians prefer to use it as a term to describe an agrarian economic and social system wherein large estates are worked by a dependent peasantry. The difficulty with this usage is that it is too imprecise, for such large estates existed in many times and places beyond the European Middle Ages and the medieval agrarian system can best be called manorialism. Some historians on the other extreme argue that even if the word feudalism is used to describe a medieval political system, medieval realities were so diverse that no one definition of feudalism can accurately or even usefully be extended to cover more than a single case. Nonetheless, for convenience we can retain the use of the word here and apply it to a specific point in medieval political development so long as we bear in mind that, like manorialism, it is only meant to serve as an approximation and that other historians may use it as a term for economic or sociological analysis.

GERMAN EMPIRE c. 1200 A.D.

Political feudalism

Political feudalism was essentially a system of extreme political decentralization wherein what we today would call public power was widely vested in private hands. From a historical perspective it was most fully experienced in France during the tenth century when the Carolingian empire had disintegrated and the area was being buffeted by devastating Viking invasions. The Carolingians had maintained a modicum of public authority, but they proved to be no help whatsoever in warding off the invasions. So local landlords had to fend for themselves. In the end, the landlords turned out to offer the best defense against the Vikings and accordingly were able to acquire practically all the old governmental powers. They raised their own small armies, dispensed their own crude justice, and occasionally issued their own primitive coins. Despite such decentralization, however, it was never forgotten that there once had been higher and larger units of government. Above all, no matter how weak the king was (and he was indeed usually very weak), there always remained a king in France who descended directly or indirectly from the western branch of the Carolingians. There also were scattered remaining dukes or counts, who in theory were supposed to have more power and authority than petty landlords or knights. So, by a complicated and hard-to-trace process of rationalization, a vague theory was worked out in the course of the tenth and eleventh centuries that tried to establish some order within feudalism. According to this, minor feudal lords did not hold their powers outright but only held them as so-called *fiefs* (rhymes with reefs), which could be revoked upon noncompliance with certain obligations. In theory—and much of this theory was ignored in practice for long periods of time—the king or higher lords granted fiefs, that is, governmental rights over various lands, to lesser lords in return for a stipulated amount of military service. In turn, the lesser lords could grant some of those fiefs to still lesser lords for military services until the chain stopped at the lowest level of knights. The holder of a fief was called a *vassal* of the granter, but this term had none of the demeaning connotations that it has gained today. Vassalage—much unlike serfdom—was a purely honorable status and all fief-holders were "noble."

Since feudalism was originally a form of decentralization, it once was considered by historians to have been a corrosive or divisive historical force; in common speech today many use the word feudal as a synonym for backward. But scholars more recently have come to the conclusion that feudalism was a force for progress and a fundamental point of departure for the growth of the modern state. They note that in areas such as Germany and Italy, where there was hardly any feudalism, political stabilization and unification came only in later times, whereas in the areas of France and England, which saw full feudalization, stabilization and governmental centralization came rapidly afterward. Scholars now posit several reasons for this. Because feudalism was originally spontaneous and makeshift, it was highly flexible. Local lords, instead of being bound by anachronistic, procrustean principles, could rule as seemed best at the moment, or could bend to the dictates of particular local customs. Thus their governments, however crude, worked the best for their times and could be used for building an even stronger government as time went on. A second reason for the effectiveness of feudalism was that it drew more people into direct contact with the actual workings of political life than had the old Roman or Carolingian systems. Government on the most local level could most easily be seen or experienced; as it became

*Feudalism as a cause of
political progress*

tangible people began to appreciate and identify with it far more than they had appreciated empires. The result was that feudalism inculcated growing governmental loyalty, and once that loyalty was developed it could be drawn upon by still larger units. Third, feudalism helped lead to certain more modern institutions by its emphasis on courts. As the feudal system became more regularized, it became customary for vassals to appear at the court of their overlords at least once a year. There they were expected to "pay court," i.e., show certain ceremonial signs of loyalty, and also to serve on "courts" in the sense of participating in trials and offering counsel. Thus they became more and more accustomed to performing governmental business and began to behave more like courtiers or politicians. As the monarchical states of France and England themselves developed, kings saw how useful the feudal court was and made it the administrative kernel of their expanding governmental systems. A final reason why feudalism led to political progress is not really intrinsic to the system itself. Because the theory of larger units was never forgotten, it could be drawn upon by greater lords and kings when the right time came to reacquire their rights.

The Norman Conquest

The greatest possibilities for the use of feudalism were first demonstrated in England after the Norman Conquest of 1066. We have seen that England became unified and enjoyed strong kingship under the Saxon Alfred and his successors in the late ninth and tenth centuries. But then the Saxon kingship began to weaken, primarily as the result of renewed Viking invasions and poor leadership. In 1066 William, the duke of Normandy (in western France), laid claim to the English crown and crossed the Channel to conquer what he had claimed. Fortunately for him the newly installed English king, Harold, had just warded off a Viking attack in the north and thus could not offer resistance at full strength. At the Battle of Hastings Harold and his Saxon troops fought bravely, but ultimately could not withstand the on-

Battle of Hastings. A scene from the Bayeux tapestry, embroidered shortly after William the Conqueror's victory. The inscription reads in translation: "Here the English and French have fallen together in battle."

slaught of the fresher Norman troops. As the day waned Harold fell, mortally wounded by a random arrow, his forces dispersed, and the Normans took the field and with it, England. Duke William now became King William, the Conqueror, and proceeded to rule his new prize as he wished.

With hindsight we can say that the Norman Conquest came at just the right time to preserve and enhance political stability. Before 1066 England was threatened with disintegration under warrior aristocrats called earls, but William destroyed their power entirely. In its place he substituted the feudal system, whereby all the land in England was newly granted in the form of fiefs held directly or indirectly from the king. Fief-holders had most of the governmental rights they had obtained less formally on the Continent, but William retained the prerogatives of coining money, collecting a land tax, and supervising justice in major criminal cases. He also retained the Anglo-Saxon officer of local government, known as the sheriff, to help him administer and enforce these rights. In order to make sure that none of his barons (the English term for major fief-holders) became too powerful, William was careful to scatter the fiefs granted to them throughout various parts of the country. In these ways William used feudal practices to help govern England when there were not yet enough trained administrators to allow any real governmental professionalization. But he also retained much royal power and kept the country thoroughly unified under the crown.

*The feudal system in
Norman England*

The history of English government in the two centuries after William is primarily a story of kings tightening up the feudal system to their advantage until they superseded it and created a strong national monarchy. The first to take steps in this direction was the Conqueror's energetic son Henry I (1100–1135). One of his most important accomplishments was to start a process of specialization at the royal court whereby certain officials began to take full professional responsibility for supervising financial accounts; these officials became known as clerks of the *Exchequer*. Another accomplishment was to institute a system of traveling circuit-judges to administer justice as direct royal representatives in various parts of the realm.

*The growth of national
monarchy in England; the
reign of Henry I*

After an intervening period of civil war Henry I was succeeded by his grandson Henry II (1154–1189), who was very much in his grandfather's activist mold. Henry II's reign was certainly one of the most momentous in all of English history. One reason for this was that it saw a great struggle between the king and the flamboyant archbishop of Canterbury, Thomas Becket, over the status of Church courts and Church law. In Henry's time priests and other clerics were tried for any crimes in Church courts under the rules of canon law. Punishment in these courts was notoriously lax. Even murderers were seldom sentenced to more than penance and loss of their clerical status. Also, decisions handed down in English Church courts could be appealed to the papal *curia* in Rome. Henry, who wished to have royal law prevail

*The struggle between
Henry II and Thomas
Becket*

Martyrdom of Thomas Becket. From a thirteenth-century English Psalter. One of the knights has struck Becket so mightily that he has broken his sword.

as far as possible and maintain judicial standards for all subjects in his realm, tried to limit these practices by the Constitutions of Clarendon of 1164. On the matter of clerics accused of crime he was willing to compromise by allowing them to be judged in Church courts but then have them sentenced in royal ones. Becket, however, resisted all attempts at change with great determination. The quarrel between king and archbishop was made more bitter by the fact that the two had earlier been close friends. It reached a tragic climax when Becket was murdered in Canterbury Cathedral by four of Henry's knights, after the king, in an outburst of anger, had rebuked them for doing nothing to rid him of his antagonist. The crime so shocked the English public that Becket was quickly revered as a martyr and became the most famous English saint. More important for the history of government, Henry had to abandon most of his program of bringing the Church courts under royal control, and his aims were only fulfilled in the sixteenth century with the coming of the English Reformation.

Despite this major setback, Henry II made enormous governmental gains in other areas, so much so that some historians maintain that Henry was the greatest king that England has ever known. His most important contributions were judicial. He greatly expanded the use of the itinerant judges instituted by Henry I and began the practice of commanding sheriffs to bring before these judges groups of men who were familiar with local conditions. These were then required to report under oath every case of murder, arson, robbery, or other major

The judicial reforms of Henry II

crimes known to them to have occurred since the judges' last visit. This was the origin of the grand jury. Henry also for the first time allowed parties in civil disputes to obtain royal justice. In the most prevalent type of case, someone who claimed to have been recently dispossessed of his land could obtain a writ from the crown, which would order the sheriff to bring twelve men who were assumed to know the facts before a judge. The twelve were then asked under oath if the plaintiff's claim was true, and the judge rendered his decision in accordance with their answers. Out of such practices grew the institution of the trial jury, although the trial jury was not used in criminal cases until the thirteenth century.

The benefits of Henry's legal work

Henry II's legal innovations benefited both the crown and the country in several ways. Most obviously, they made justice more uniform and equitable throughout the realm. They also thereby made royal justice sought after and popular. Particularly in disputes over land—the most important and frequent disputes of the day—the weaker party was no longer at the mercy of a strong-arming neighbor. Usually the weaker parties were knights, with whom the crown before then had not been in close touch. In helping defend their rights Henry gained valuable allies in his policy of keeping the stronger barons in tow. Finally, the widespread use of juries in Henry's reign brought more and more people into actual participation in royal government. In so doing it got them more interested in government and more loyal to government. Since these people served without pay, Henry brilliantly managed to expand the competence and popularity of his government at very little cost.

The most concrete proof of Henry II's success is that after his death his government worked so well that it more or less ran on its own. Henry's son, the swashbuckling Richard I, the "Lionhearted," ruled for ten years, from 1189 to 1199, but in that time he only stayed in England for six months because he was otherwise engaged in crusading or defending his possessions on the Continent. Throughout the time of Richard's absence governmental administration actually became more efficient, owing to the work of capable ministers. The country also raised two huge sums for Richard by taxation: one to pay for his crusade to the Holy Land and the other to buy his ransom when he was captured by an enemy on his return. But later when a new king needed still more money, most Englishmen were disinclined to pay it.

King John. An effigy in Worcester cathedral.

The new king was Richard's brother, John (1199–1216), who has the reputation of being a villain but was more a victim of circumstances. Ever since the time of William the Conqueror, English kings had continued to rule in large portions of modern-day France, but by John's reign the kings of France were becoming strong enough to take back much of these territories. John had the great misfortune of facing the able French King Philip Augustus, who won back Normandy and neighboring lands by force of arms in 1204 and reinsured this victory by military successes in 1214. John needed money both to govern Eng-

The reign of John;
Magna Carta

The progress of
centralized government in
the reign of Henry III

Origins of the English
Parliament

land and to fight in France, but his defeats made his subjects disinclined to give it to him. The barons particularly resented John's financial exigencies and in 1215 they made him renounce these in the subsequently famous Magna Carta (Great Charter), a document which was also designed to redress all the other abuses the barons could think of. Most common conceptions of Magna Carta are erroneous. It was not intended to be a bill of rights or a charter of liberties for the common man. On the contrary, it was basically a feudal document in which the king as overlord pledged to respect the traditional rights of his vassals. Nonetheless, it did enunciate in writing the important principles that large sums of money could not be raised by the crown without consent given by the barons in a common council, and that no free man could be punished by the crown without judgment by his equals and by the law of the land. Above all, Magna Carta was important as an expression of the principle of limited government and of the idea that the king is bound by the law.

As the contemporary American medievalist J. R. Strayer has said, "Magna Carta made arbitrary government difficult, but it did not make centralized government impossible." In the century following its issuance, the progress of centralized government continued apace. In the reign of John's son, Henry III (1216–1277), the barons vied with the weak king for control of the government but did so on the assumption that centralized government itself was a good thing. Throughout that period administrators continued to perfect more efficient legal and administrative institutions. Whereas in the reign of Henry I financial administration began to become a specialized bureau of the royal court, in the reign of Henry III this became true of legal administration (the creation of permanent High Courts) and administration of foreign correspondence (the so-called Chancery). English central government was now fully developing a trained officialdom.

The last and most famous branch of the medieval English governmental system was Parliament. This gradually emerged as a separate branch of government in the decades before and after 1300, above all owing to the wishes of Henry III's son, Edward I (1272–1307). Although Parliament later became a check against royal absolutism, nothing could be further from the truth than to think that its first meetings were "demanded by the people." In its origins Parliament actually had little to do with popular representation, but was rather the king's feudal court in its largest gathering. Edward I was a strong king who called Parliaments frequently to raise money as quickly and efficiently as possible in order to help finance his foreign wars. Those present at Parliaments were not only expected to give their consent to taxation—in fact, it was virtually inconceivable for them to refuse—but while they were there they were told why taxes were necessary so that they would pay them less grudgingly. They could also agree upon details of collection and payment. At the same meetings Edward could take advice about pressing concerns, have justice done for exceptional cases, review local administration, and promulgate new laws. Probably the most unusual trait of Edward's Parliaments in comparison to similar assemblies on the Continent was that they began to include representatives from the counties and towns in addition to the higher nobility. These representatives, however, scarcely spoke for "the people" because most of the people of England were unfranchised serfs and peasants—not to mention women, who were never consulted in any way. Most likely, Edward had predominantly financial motives for calling representatives from the "commons." He probably also realized the propaganda value of overawing local representatives with royal grandeur at impressive parliamentary meetings so that they would then spread a favorable impression of the monarchy back home. As time went on, commoners were called to Parliament so often that they became a recognized part of its organization: by the middle of the fourteenth century they sat regularly in their own "house." But they still represented only the prosperous people of countryside and towns and were usually manipulated by the crown or the nobles.

Edward I's reign also saw the culmination of the development of a strong national monarchy in other aspects. By force of arms Edward nearly unified the entire island of Britain, conquering Wales and almost subduing Scotland (which, however, was to rise up again soon after his death). Edward began the practice of regularly issuing statute law, that is, original public legislation designed to apply indefinitely to the entire realm. Because of his role as a law-giver, Edward is sometimes referred to as the "English Justinian." Most important, Edward also curtailed the feudal powers of his barons by limiting their rights to hold private courts and to grant their own lands as fiefs. Thus, by the end of his reign much of the independent power once consciously vested with the barons by William the Conqueror was being taken away from them. The explanation for this is that in the intervening high-medieval centuries the king was developing his own royal institutions of government to the degree that old-fashioned feudalism was now no longer of any real service. Because Edward pressed his strong government and financial demands somewhat excessively for the spirit of the age, there was an antimonarchical reaction after his death. But it is striking that after Edward's time whenever there were baronial rebellions they were always made on the assumption that England would remain a unified country, governed by the basic high-medieval monarchical institutions. England was unified around the crown in the High Middle Ages and would remain a basically well-governed and unified country right up to modern times.

While the process of governmental centralization was making impressive strides in England, it developed more slowly in France. But by around 1300 it had come close to reaching the same point of completion. French governmental unification proceeded more slowly because France in the eleventh century was more decentralized than England

*The English monarchy
under Edward I*

*The process of political
centralization in France*

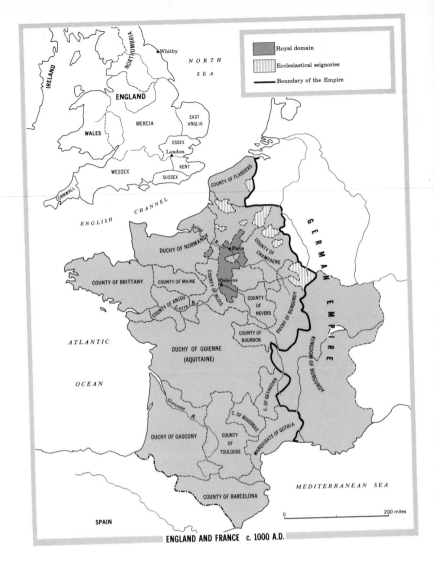

ENGLAND AND FRANCE c. 1000 A.D.

and faced greater problems. The last of the weak Carolingian monarchs was replaced in 987 by Hugh Capet, the count of Paris, but the new Capetian dynasty—which was to rule without interruption until 1328—was at first no stronger than the old Carolingian one. Even through most of the twelfth century the kings of France ruled directly only in a small area around Paris known as the Ile-de-France, roughly the size of Vermont. Beyond that territory the kings had shadowy claims to being the feudal overlords of numerous counts and dukes throughout much of the area of modern France, but for practical purposes those counts and dukes were almost entirely independent. It was said that when the king of France demanded homage from the first duke of Normandy, the duke had one of his warriors pretend to kiss the king's foot but then seize the royal leg and pull the king over backwards, to the mockery of all those present. While the French kingship was so weak, the various parts of France were developing their own distinct local traditions and dialects. Thus, whereas William the Conqueror inherited in England a country that had already been unified and was just on the verge of falling apart, the French kings of the High Middle Ages had to unify their country from scratch, with only a vague reminiscence of Carolingian unity to build upon.

In many respects, however, luck was on their side. First of all, they were fortunate for hundreds of years in having direct male heirs to succeed them. Consequently, there were no deadly quarrels over the right of succession. In the second place, most of the French kings lived to an advanced age, the average period of rule being about thirty years. That meant that sons were already mature men when they came to the throne and there were few regencies to squander the royal power during the minority of a prince. More than that, the kings of France were always highly visible, if sometimes not very imposing, when there were power struggles elsewhere, so people in neighboring areas became accustomed to thinking of the kingship as a force for stability in an unstable world. A third favorable circumstance for the French kings was the growth of agricultural prosperity and trade in their home region; this provided them with important sources of revenue. A fourth fortuitous development was that the kings were able to gain the support of the popes because the latter usually needed allies in their incessant struggles with the German emperors. The popes lent the French kings prestige, as they earlier had done for the Carolingians, and they also allowed them much direct power over the local Church, thereby bringing the kings further income and influence from patronage. A fifth factor in the French king's favor was the growth in the twelfth and thirteenth centuries of the University of Paris as the leading European center of studies. As foreigners came flocking to the university, they learned of the French king's growing authority and spread their impressions when they returned home. Finally, and by no means least of all, great credit must be given to the shrewdness and vigor of several of the French kings themselves.

The first noteworthy Capetian king was Louis VI, "the Fat" (1108–1137). While accomplishing nothing startling, Louis at least managed to pacify his home base, the Ile-de-France, by driving out or subduing its turbulent "robber barons." Once this was accomplished, agriculture and trade could prosper and the intellectual life of Paris could start to flourish. Thereafter, the French kings had a geographical source of power of exactly the kind that the German ruler Barbarossa sought but never found. The really startling additions to the realm were made by Louis's grandson, Philip Augustus (1180–1223). Philip was wily enough to know how to take advantage of certain feudal rights in order to win large amounts of western French territory from the English King John. He was also decisive enough to know how to defend his gains in battle. Most impressive of all, Philip worked out an excellent formula for governing his new acquisitions. Since these in-

*Factors facilitating the
growth of the French
monarchy*

*Foundations of the French
monarchy; Louis VI and
Philip Augustus*

A Seal Depicting Philip Augustus

St. Louis

King Philip the Fair of France

creased his original lands close to fourfold, and since each new area had its own highly distinct local customs, it would have been hopeless to try to enforce strict governmental standardization by means of what was then a very rudimentary administrative system. Instead, Philip allowed his new provinces to maintain most of their indigenous governmental practices but superimposed on them new royal officials known as *baillis*. These officials were entirely loyal to Philip because they never came from the regions in which they served and were paid impressive salaries for the day. They had full judicial, administrative, and military authority in their bailiwicks: on royal orders they tolerated regional diversities but guided them to the king's advantage. Thus there were no revolts in the conquered territories and royal power was enhanced. This pattern of local diversity balanced against bureaucratic centralization was to remain the basic pattern of French government. Thus Philip Augustus can be seen as an important founder of the modern French state.

In the brief reign of Philip's son, Louis VIII (1223–1226), almost all of southern France was added to the crown in the name of intervention against religious heresy. Once incorporated, this territory was governed largely on the same principles laid down by Philip. The next king, Louis IX (1226–1270), was so pious that he was later canonized by the Church and is commonly referred to as St. Louis. He ruled strongly and justly (except for great intolerance of Jews and heretics), decreed a standardized coinage for the country, perfected the judicial system, and brought France a long, golden period of internal peace. Because he was so well-loved, the monarchy lived off his prestige for many years afterward.

That prestige, however, came close to being squandered by St. Louis's more ruthless grandson, Philip IV, "the Fair" (1285–1314). Philip fought many battles at once, seeking to round out French territories in the northeast and southwest and to gain full control over the French Church instead of sharing it with the pope in Rome. All these activities forced him to accelerate the process of governmental centralization, especially with the aim of trying to raise money. Thus his reign saw the quick formulation of many administrative institutions that came close to completing the development of medieval French government, as the contemporary reign of Edward I did in England. Philip's reign also saw the calling of assemblies that were roughly equivalent to the English Parliaments, but these—later called "Estates General"—never played a central role in the French governmental system. Philip the Fair was successful in most of his ventures; above all, as we will later see, in reducing the pope to the level of a virtual French figurehead. After his death there would be an antimonarchical reaction, as there was at the same time in England, but by his reign France was unquestionably the strongest power in Europe. With only a sixteenth-century interruption, it would remain so until the nineteenth century.

While England and France followed certain similar processes of monarchical centralization and nation-building, they were also marked by basic differences that are worth describing because they were to typify differences in development for centuries after. England, a far smaller country than France, was much better unified. Aside from Wales and Scotland, there were no regions in Britain that had such different languages or traditions that they thought of themselves as separate territories. Correspondingly, there were no aristocrats who could move toward separatism by drawing on regional resentments. This meant that England never really had to face the threat of internal division and could develop strong institutions of united national government such as Parliament. It also meant that the English kings, starting primarily with Henry II, could rely on numerous local dignitaries, above all, the knights, to do much work of local government without pay. The obvious advantage was that local government was cheap, but the hidden implication of the system was that government also had to be popular, or else much of the voluntary work would grind to a halt. This doubtless was the main reason why English kings went out of their way to seek formal consent for their actions. When they did not they could barely rule, so wise kings learned the lesson and as time went on England became most clearly a limited monarchy. The French kings, much to the contrary, ruled a richer and larger country, which gave them—at least in times of peace—sufficient wealth to pay for a more bureaucratic, salaried administration at both the central and local levels. French kings therefore could rule more absolutely. But they were continually faced with serious threats of regional separatism. Different regions continued to cherish their own traditions and often supported centrifugalism in league with the upper aristocracy. So French kings often had to struggle with attempts at regional breakaways and take various measures to subdue their aristocrats. Up to around 1700 the monarchy had to fight a steady battle against regionalism, but it had the resources to win consistently and thereby managed to grow from strength to strength.

The only continental state that would rival France until the rise of Germany in the nineteenth century was Spain. The foundations of Spain's greatness were also laid in the High Middle Ages on the principle of national monarchy, but in the Middle Ages there was not yet one monarchy that ruled through most of the Iberian peninsula. After the Christians started pushing back the forces of Islam around 1100 there were four Spanish Christian kingdoms: the tiny northern mountain state of Navarre, which would always remain comparatively insignificant; Portugal in the west; Aragon in the northeast; and Castile in the center. The main Spanish occupation in the High Middle Ages was the *Reconquista*, i.e., the reconquest of the peninsula for Christianity. This reached its culmination in the year 1212 in a major victory of a combined Aragonese-Castilian army over the Muslims at Las Navas de Tolosa. The rest was mostly mopping up. By the end of the thirteenth century all that remained of earlier Muslim domination

*Comparison of England
and France*

Medieval Spain

Bullfighting in a Thirteenth-Century Spanish Arena. Times do not seem to have changed much, although here the spectators are taking a rather unsporting part in the action.

was the small state of Granada in the extreme south, and Granada existed largely because it was willing to pay tribute to the Christians. Because Castile had the largest open frontier, it became by far the largest Spanish kingdom, but it was balanced in wealth by the more urban and trade-oriented Aragon. Both kingdoms developed institutions in the thirteenth century that roughly paralleled those of France. But until the union of Aragon and Castile under King Ferdinand and Queen Isabella in the fifteenth century, the Iberian states individually could not hope to be as strong as the much richer and more populous France.

Historical role of the national monarchies

Before concluding this chapter it is best to assess the general significance of the rise of the national monarchies in high-medieval western Europe. Until their emergence there had been two basic patterns of government in Europe: city-states and empires. City-states had the advantage of drawing heavily upon citizen participation and loyalty and thus were able to make highly efficient use of their human potential. But they were often divided by economic rivalries and they were not sufficiently large or militarily strong to defend themselves against imperial forces. The empires, on the other hand, could win battles and often had the resources to support an efficient bureaucratic administrative apparatus, but they drew on little voluntary participation and were too far-flung or rapacious to inspire any deep loyalties. The new national monarchies were to prove the "golden mean" between these extremes. They were large enough to have adequate military strength and they developed administrative techniques that would rival and eventually surpass those of the Roman or Byzantine Empires. More than that, building at first upon the bases of feudalism, they drew upon sufficient citizen participation and loyalty to help support them in times of stress when empires would have foundered. By about 1300 the monarchies of England, France, and the Iberian peninsula had gained the primary loyalties of their subjects, superseding loyalties to communities, regions, or to the government of the Church. For all these reasons they brought much internal peace and stability to large parts of Europe where there had been little stability before. Thus they contributed greatly to making life fruitful. The medieval national monarchies were also the ancestors of the modern nation-states—the most effective and equitable governments of our day (the current Soviet Union being something more like an empire). In short, they were one of the Middle Ages' most beneficial bequests to modern times.

SELECTED READINGS

• *Items so designated are available in paperback editions.*

GENERAL STUDIES

• Bloch, Marc, *Feudal Society,* Chicago, 1961. A modern classic, first published in France in 1940. Full of valuable insights but outdated in some respects.
• Heer, Friedrich, *The Medieval World,* London, 1961. A controversial interpretation that opposes an "open" twelfth century to a "closed" thirteenth century. Very detailed.
• Southern, R. W., *The Making of the Middle Ages,* New Haven, Conn., 1953. A subtle and brilliant reading of eleventh- and twelfth-century developments. Difficult but most rewarding.
• Strayer, J. R., *Western Europe in the Middle Ages,* 3rd ed., Glenview, Ill., 1982. In a class by itself as the best short introduction to medieval political and cultural history.
 Wood, Charles T., *The Age of Chivalry* (also published as *The Quest for Eternity*), London, 1970. A lively work for the beginner that supplements Strayer in its emphasis on economic and social history.

ECONOMIC AND SOCIAL CONDITIONS

• Barber, Richard, *The Knight and Chivalry,* 2nd ed., London, 1974.
 Bautier, R. H., *The Economic Development of Medieval Europe,* London, 1971.
• Duby, G., *Rural Economy and Country Life in the Medieval West,* London, 1968. The best work on agrarian history. Highly recommended as an example of recent French historiography at its highest level.
 Ennen, E., *The Medieval Town,* New York, 1979. Complements Duby on urban development.
• Gies, J. and F., *Life in a Medieval City,* New York, 1973. An engaging popular account concentrating on life in thirteenth-century Troyes.
 Labarge, M. W., *A Baronial Household of the Thirteenth Century,* New York, 1965. Particularly valuable for its emphasis on the career of a woman.
• Lopez, Robert S., *The Commercial Revolution of the Middle Ages,* Englewood Cliffs, N.J., 1971.

- Pirenne, H., *Economic and Social History of Medieval Europe*, London, 1936. Many of Pirenne's ideas are no longer accepted but this is still an extremely useful brief account.
  Postan, M. M., *The Medieval Economy and Society: An Economic History of Britain, 1100–1500*, Berkeley, Calif., 1972.
- Power, Eileen, *Medieval Women*, Cambridge, 1975. Very brief but informative.
- White, Lynn, Jr., *Medieval Technology and Social Change*, Oxford, 1962. Controversial but excellently written and thought-provoking.

POLITICAL DEVELOPMENTS

- Barraclough, G., *The Origins of Modern Germany*, 2nd ed., Oxford, 1947. Highly interpretative, should be read in conjunction with Hampe.
  Douglas, David, *The Norman Achievement, 1050–1100*, Berkeley, Calif., 1969.
  ————, *The Norman Fate, 1100–1154*, Berkeley, Calif., 1976.
- Fawtier, R., *The Capetian Kings of France*, London, 1962. The best single volume on medieval French politics.
  Hampe, K., *Germany under the Salian and Hohenstaufen Emperors*, Totowa, N.J., 1973. An older, reliable German work recently translated.
  Hyde, J. K., *Society and Politics in Medieval Italy*, New York, 1973. An excellent survey that integrates political and social history.
  Loyn, H. R., *The Norman Conquest*, London, 1965.
  O'Callaghan, Joseph F., *A History of Medieval Spain*, Ithaca, N.Y., 1975.
  Petit-Dutaillis, Charles, *The Feudal Monarchy in France and England*, London, 1936. An excellent essay in comparative history.
  Poole, Austin L., *From Domesday Book to Magna Carta, 1087–1216*, 2nd ed., Oxford, 1955. Very detailed yet clear.
- Sayles, G. O., *The King's Parliament of England*, New York, 1974. Emphasizes the role of the crown and downplays the importance of the commons.
  ————, *The Medieval Foundations of England*, London, 1952. An excellent interpretation of medieval English political developments.
- Stephenson, Carl, *Mediaeval Feudalism*, Ithaca, N.Y., 1942. Very elementary.
- Strayer, J. R., *On the Medieval Origins of the Modern State*, Princeton, N.J., 1970. A distillation of the ideas of one of America's greatest medievalists.

SOURCE MATERIALS

Herlihy, David, ed., *The History of Feudalism*, New York, 1970.
- Lopez, Robert S., and I. W. Raymond, eds., *Medieval Trade in the Mediterranean World*, New York, 1955.
- Lyon, Bryce, ed., *The High Middle Ages*, New York, 1964.
- Otto of Freising, *The Deeds of Frederick Barbarossa*, tr. C. C. Mierow, New York, 1953. A contemporary chronicle that is interesting enough to read from start to finish.
  Strayer, J. R., ed., *Feudalism*, Princeton, N.J., 1965.

Chapter 12

THE HIGH MIDDLE AGES (1050–1300): RELIGIOUS AND INTELLECTUAL DEVELOPMENTS

You would see men and women dragging carts through marshes . . . everywhere miracles daily occurring, jubilant songs rendered to God. . . . You would say that the prophecy was fulfilled, "The Spirit of Life was in the wheels."

—Abbot Robert of Torigni,
on the building of the cathedral
of Chartres, 1145

The religious and intellectual changes that transpired in the West between 1050 and 1300 were as important as the economic, social, and political ones. In the sphere of religion, the most fundamental organizational development was the triumph of the *papal monarchy.* Before the middle of the eleventh century certain popes had laid claim to primacy within the Church, but very few were able to come close to making good on such claims. Indeed, most popes before about 1050 were hardly able to rule effectively as bishops of Rome. But then, most dramatically, the popes emerged as the supreme religious leaders of Western Christendom. They centralized the government of the Church, challenged the sway of emperors and kings, and called forth the crusading movement. By 1300 the temporal success of the papacy had proven to be its own nemesis, but the popes still ruled the Church internally, as they continue to rule the Roman Catholic Church today.

Religious changes

While the papacy was assuming power, a new vitality infused the Christian religion itself, enabling Christianity to capture the human imagination as never before. At the same time too there was a remarkable revival of intellectual and cultural life. In education, thought, and

Intellectual changes

the arts, as in economics and politics, the West before 1050 had been a backwater. Thereafter it emerged swiftly from backwardness to become an intellectual and artistic leader of the globe. Westerners boasted that learning and the arts had moved northwest to them from Egypt, Greece, and Rome—a boast that was largely true. In the High Middle Ages Europeans first started building on ancient intellectual foundations and also contributed major intellectual and artistic innovations of their own.

1. THE CONSOLIDATION OF THE PAPAL MONARCHY

The sorry state of religious life in the tenth and early eleventh centuries

To understand the origins and appreciate the significance of the western European religious revival of the High Middle Ages it is necessary to have some idea of the level to which religion had sunk in the tenth and early eleventh centuries. Around 800 the Emperor Charlemagne had made some valiant attempts to enhance the religious authority of bishops, introduce the parish system into rural regions where there had hardly been any priests before, and provide for the literacy of the clergy. But with the collapse of the Carolingian Empire, religious decentralization and ensuing corruption prevailed throughout most of Europe. Most churches and monasteries became the private property of strong local lords. The latter disposed of Church offices under their control as they wished, often by selling them or by granting them to close relatives. Obviously this was not the best way to find the most worthy candidates, and many priests were quite unqualified for their jobs. They were almost always illiterate, and often they lived openly with concubines. When archbishops or bishops were able to control appointments the results were not much better because such officials were usually close relatives of secular lords who followed their practices of financial or family aggrandizement. As for the popes, they were usually incompetent or corrupt, the sons or tools of powerful families who lived in or around the city of Rome. Some were astonishingly debauched. John XII may have been the worst of them. He was made pope at the age of eighteen in 955 because of the strength of his family. It is certain that he ruled for nine years as a thorough profligate, but there is some uncertainty about the cause of his death: either he was caught *in flagrante delicto* by a jealous husband and murdered on the spot, or else he died in the midst of a carnal act from sheer amorous exertion.

Religious revival: (1) Cluny and monastic reform

Once Europe began to catch its breath from the wave of external invasions that peaked in the tenth century, the wide extent of religious corruption or indifference was bound to call forth some reaction. The first successful measures of reform were taken in the monasteries because the work of a bishop was limited to what he could do in his lifetime, and even more because most archbishops and bishops were unable to disentangle themselves from the political affairs of their day. Monasteries could be somewhat more independent and could count more on the support of their reforms by lay lords, insofar as lords feared for the health of their souls if monks did not serve their proper function in saying offices (i.e., prayers). The movement for monastic reform began with the foundation of the monastery of Cluny in Burgundy in 910 by a pious nobleman. Cluny was a Benedictine house but it introduced two constitutional innovations. One was that, in order to remain free from domination by either local secular or ecclesiastical powers, it was made directly subject to the pope. The other was that it undertook the reform or foundation of numerous "daughter monasteries": whereas formerly all Benedictine houses had been independent and equal, Cluny founded a monastic "family," whose members were subordinate to it. Owing to the succession of a few extremely pious, active, and long-lived abbots, the congregation of Cluniac houses grew so rapidly that there were sixty-seven by 1049. In all of them dedicated priors were chosen who followed the dictates of the abbot of Cluny rather than being responsible to local potentates. Cluniac monks accordingly became famous for their industry in the saying of offices. And Cluny was only the most famous of the new congregations. Other similar ones spread just as rapidly in the years around 1000 and succeeded in making the reformed monasteries vital centers of religious life and prayer.

Around the middle of the eleventh century, after so many monasteries had been taken out of the control of secular authorities, the leaders of the monastic reform movement started to lobby for the reform of the clerical hierarchy as well. They centered their attacks upon *simony*—i.e., the buying and selling of positions in the Church—and they also demanded celibacy for all levels of clergy. Their entire program was directed toward depriving secular powers of their ability to dictate appointments of bishops, abbots, and priests, and toward making the clerical estate as "pure" and as distinct from the secular one as possible. Once this reform program was appropriated by the papacy, it would begin to change the face of the entire Church.

(2) reform of the secular clergy

Considering that the reformers were greatly opposed to lay interference, it is ironic that their party was first installed in the papacy by a German emperor, namely Henry III. In 1046 this ruler came to Italy, deposed three rival Italian claimants to the papal title, and named as pope a German reformer from his own retinue. Henry III's act brought in a series of reforming popes, who started to promulgate decrees against simony, clerical marriage, and immorality of all sorts throughout the Church. These popes also insisted upon their own role as primates and universal spiritual leaders in order to give strength to their actions. One of the most important steps they took was the issuance in 1059 of a decree on papal elections. This vested the right of naming a new pope solely with the cardinals, thereby depriving the

Emperor Henry III and reform of the papacy

Roman aristocracy or the German emperor of the chance to interfere in the matter. The decree preserved the independence of papal elections thereafter. In granting the right of election to cardinals the decree also became a milestone in the evolution of a special body within the Church. Ever since the tenth century a number of bishops and clerics, known as cardinals, from sees in and near Rome had taken on an important role as advisors and administrative assistants of the popes, but the election decree of 1059 first gave them their clearest powers. Thereafter the "college of cardinals" took on more and more administrative duties and helped create continuity in papal policy, especially when there was a quick succession of pontiffs. The cardinals still elect the pope today.

*The ideals of Pope
Gregory VII*

A new and most momentous phase in the history of the reform movement was initiated during the pontificate of Gregory VII (1073–1085). Scholars disagree about how much Gregory was indebted to the ideas and policies of his predecessors in the reform movement and how much he departed from them. The answer seems to be that Gregory supported reform as much as others, indeed he explicitly renewed his predecessors' decrees against simony and clerical marriage. Yet he was not only more zealous in trying to enforce these decrees—a contemporary even called him a "Holy Satan"—but he brought with him a basically new conception of the role of the Church in human life. Whereas the older Christian ideal had been that of withdrawal, and the perfect "athlete of Christ" had been a passive contemplative, or ascetic monk, Gregory VII conceived of Christianity as being much more activist and believed that the Church was responsible for creating "right order in the world." To this end he demanded absolute obedience and strenuous chastity from his clergy: some of his clerical opponents complained that he wanted clerics to live like angels. Equally important, he thought of kings and emperors as his inferiors, who would carry out his commands obediently and help him reform and evangelize the world. Gregory allowed that secular princes would continue to rule directly and make their own decisions in purely secular matters, but he expected them to accept ultimate papal overlordship. Put in other terms, in contrast to his predecessors who had sought merely a duality of ecclesiastical and secular authority, Gregory VII wanted to create a papal monarchy over both. When told that his ideas were novel, he and his immediate followers replied: "The Lord did not say 'I am custom'; the Lord said 'I am truth.' " Since no pope had spoken like this before, it is proper to accept the judgment of a modern historian who called Gregory "the great innovator, who stood quite alone."

The investiture struggle

Gregory's actual conduct as pope was nothing short of revolutionary. From the start he was determined to enforce a decree against "lay investiture," the practice whereby secular rulers ceremonially granted clerics the symbols of their office. The German Emperor

Henry IV was bound to resist this because the ceremony was a manifestation of his long-accepted rights to appoint and control churchmen: without these his own authority would be greatly weakened. The ensuing fight is often called "the investiture struggle" because the problem of investitures was a central one, but the struggle was really about the relative obedience and strength of pope and emperor. The larger issue was immediately joined when Henry IV flouted Gregory's injunctions against appointing prelates. Whereas earlier popes might have tried to deal with such insubordination diplomatically, Gregory rapidly took the entirely unprecedented step of excommunicating the emperor and suspending him from all his powers as an earthly ruler. This bold act amazed all who learned of it. Between 955 and 1057 German emperors had deposed five and named twelve out of twenty-five popes; now a pope dared to dismiss an emperor! We have seen in the previous chapter that in 1077 Henry IV abased himself before the pope in order to forestall a formal deposition: that act amazed contemporaries even more. Thereafter Henry was able to rally some support and sympathy for himself and a terrible war of words ensued, while on the actual battlefield the emperor was able to place troops supporting the pope on the defensive. In 1085 Gregory died, seemingly defeated. But Gregory's successors continued the struggle with Henry IV and later with his son, Henry V.

The long and bitter contest on investiture only came to an end with the Concordat of Worms (a city in Germany) of 1122. Under this compromise the German emperor was forbidden to invest prelates with *Results of the conflict* the religious symbols of their office but was allowed to invest them with the symbols of their rights as temporal rulers because the emperor was recognized as their temporal overlord. That settlement was ultimately less significant than the fact that the struggle had lastingly impaired the prestige of the emperors and raised that of the popes. In addition, the dramatic struggle helped rally the Western clergy behind the pope and galvanized the attentions of all onlookers. As one contemporary reported, nothing else was talked about "even in the women's spinning-rooms and the artisans' workshops." This meant that people who had earlier been largely indifferent to or excluded from religious issues became much more absorbed by them.

Gregory VII's successors and most of the popes of the twelfth century were fully committed to the goal of papal monarchy. But they were far less impetuous than Gregory had been and were more inter- *The growth of papal* ested in the everyday administration of the Church. They apparently *monarchy* recognized that there was no point in claiming to rule as papal monarchs unless they could avail themselves of a governmental apparatus to support their claims. To this end they presided over an impressive growth of law and administration. Under papal guidance the twelfth century saw the basic formulation of the canon law of the Church. Canon law claimed ecclesiastical jurisdiction for all sorts of cases per-

Pope Innocent III. A mosaic dating from the thirteenth century.

taining not only to the clergy but also to problems of marriage, inheritance, and rights of widows and orphans. Most of these cases were supposed to originate in the courts of bishops, but the popes insisted that they alone could issue dispensations from the strict letter of the law and that the papal *consistory*—comprised of the pope and cardinals—should serve as a final court of appeals. As the power of the papacy and the prestige of the Church mounted, cases in canon law courts and appeals to Rome rapidly increased; after the middle of the twelfth century legal expertise became so important for exercising the papal office that most popes were trained canon lawyers, whereas previously they had usually been monks. Concurrent with this growth of legalism was the growth of an administrative apparatus to keep records and collect income. As the century wore on, the papacy developed a bureaucratic government that was far in advance of most of the secular governments of the day. This allowed it to become richer, more efficient, and ever stronger. Finally, the popes asserted their powers within the Church by gaining greater control over the election of bishops and by calling general councils in Rome to promulgate laws and demonstrate their leadership.

By common consent the most capable and successful of all high-medieval popes was Innocent III (1198–1216). Innocent, who was elected at the age of thirty-seven, was one of the youngest and most vigorous individuals ever to be raised to the papacy; more than that, he was expertly trained in theology and had also studied canon law. His major goal was to unify all Christendom under papal hegemony and to bring in the "right order in the world" so fervently desired by Gregory VII. He never questioned the right of kings and princes to rule directly in the secular sphere but believed that he could step in and discipline kings whenever they "sinned," a wide opening for interference. Beyond that, he saw himself as the ultimate overlord of all. In his own words he said that "as every knee is bowed to Jesus . . . so all men should obey His Vicar [i.e., the pope]."

Innocent sought to implement his goals in many different ways. In order to give the papacy a solid territorial base of support, like the one drawn upon by the French kings, he tried to initiate strong rule in the papal territories around Rome by consolidating them where possible and providing for efficient and vigilant administration. For this reason Innocent is often considered to be the real founder of the Papal States. But because some urban communities tenaciously sought to maintain their independence, he never came close to dominating the papal lands in Italy so completely as the French kings controlled the Ile-de-France. In other projects he was more completely successful. He intervened in German politics assertively enough to engineer the triumph of his own candidate for the imperial office, the Hohenstaufen Frederick II. He disciplined the French King Philip Augustus for his marital misconduct and forced John of England to accept an unwanted candidate as archbishop of Canterbury. To demonstrate his superiority and also gain income, Innocent forced John to grant England to the papacy as a fief, and he similarly gained the feudal overlordship of Aragon, Sicily, and Hungary. When southern France was threatened by the spread of the Albigensian heresy (to be discussed later) the pope effectively called a crusade that would extinguish it by force. He also levied the first income tax on the clergy to support a crusade to the Holy Land. The crown of Innocent's religious achievement was the calling of the Fourth Lateran Council in Rome in 1215. This defined central dogmas of the faith and made the leadership of the papacy within Christendom more apparent than ever. The pope was now clearly both disciplining kings and ruling over the Church without hindrance.

Innocent's reign was certainly the zenith of the papal monarchy, but it also sowed some of the seeds of future ruin. Innocent himself could administer the Papal States and seek new sources of income without seeming to compromise the spiritual dignity of his office. But future popes who followed his policies had less of his stature and thus began to appear more like ordinary acquisitive rulers. Moreover, because the Papal States bordered on the Kingdom of Sicily, Innocent's successors quickly came into conflict with the neighboring ruler, who was none other than Innocent's protégé Frederick II. Although Innocent had raised up Frederick, he never dreamed that Frederick would later become an inveterate opponent of papal power in Italy.

Problems for Innocent's successors

At first these and other problems were not fully apparent. The popes of the thirteenth century continued to enhance their powers and centralize the government of the Church. They gradually asserted the right to name candidates for ecclesiastical benefices, both high and low, and they asserted control over the curriculum and doctrine taught at the University of Paris. But they also became involved in a protracted political struggle which led to their own demise as temporal powers. This struggle began with the attempt of the popes to destroy Frederick II. To some degree they were acting in self-defense because Frederick threatened their own rule in central Italy. But in combating him they overemployed their spiritual weapons. Instead of merely excommunicating and deposing Frederick, they also called a crusade against him—the first time a crusade was called on a large scale for blatantly political purposes.

The papacy's struggle with Frederick II and his heirs; political crusades

After Frederick's death in 1250 a succession of popes made a still worse mistake by renewing and maintaining their crusade against all of the emperor's heirs, whom they called the "viper brood." In order to implement this crusade they became preoccupied with raising funds, and they sought and won as their military champion a younger son from the French royal house, Charles of Anjou. But the latter only helped the popes for the purely political motive of winning the Kingdom of Sicily for himself. Charles in fact won Sicily in 1268 by defeating the last of Frederick II's male heirs. But he then taxed the realm so excessively that the Sicilians revolted in the "Sicilian Vespers" of 1282 and offered their crown to the king of Aragon, who had married Fred-

The effects of the political crusades

Pope Boniface VIII. From a portrait by Giotto.

Two crucial disputes: (1) the issue of clerical taxation

(2) quarrel with the king of France

erick II's granddaughter. The king of Aragon accordingly entered the Italian arena and came close to winning Frederick's former kingdom for himself. To prevent this Charles of Anjou and the reigning pope prevailed upon the king of France—then Philip III (1270–1285)—to embark on a crusade against Aragon. This crusade was a terrible failure and Philip III died on it. In the wake of these events Philip's son, Philip IV, resolved to alter the traditional French pro-papal policy. By that time France had become so strong that such a decision was fateful. More than that, by misusing the institution of the crusade and trying to raise increasingly large sums of money to support it, the popes had lost much of their prestige. The denouement would be played out at the very beginning of the next century.

The temporal might of the papacy was toppled almost melodramatically in the reign of Boniface VIII (1294–1303). Many of Boniface's troubles were not of his own making. His greatest obstacle was that the national monarchies had gained more of their subjects' loyalties than the papacy could draw upon because of the steady growth of royal power and erosion of papal prestige. Boniface also had the misfortune to succeed a particularly pious, although inept, pope who resigned his office within a year. Since Boniface was entirely lacking in conventional piety or humility, the contrast turned many Christian observers against him. Some even maintained—incorrectly—that Boniface had convinced his predecessor to resign and had murdered him shortly afterward. Boniface ruled assertively and presided over the first papal "jubilee" in Rome in 1300. This was an apparent, but, as events would show, hollow demonstration of papal might.

Two disputes with the kings of England and France proved to be Boniface's undoing. The first concerned the clerical taxation that had been initiated by Innocent III. Although Innocent had levied this tax to support a crusade and had collected it himself, in the course of the thirteenth century the kings of England and France had begun to levy and collect clerical taxes on the pretext that they would use them to help the popes on future crusades to the Holy Land or aid in papal crusades against the Hohenstaufens. Then, at the end of the century, the kings started to levy their own war taxes on the clergy without any pretexts at all. Boniface understandably tried to prohibit this step, but quickly found that he had lost the support of the English and French clergy. Thus when the kings offered resistance he had to back down.

Boniface's second dispute was with the king of France alone. Specifically it concerned Philip IV's determination to try a French bishop for treason. As in the earlier struggle between Gregory VII and Henry IV of Germany, the real issue was the comparative strength of papal and secular power, but this time the papacy was decisively defeated. As before, there was a bitter propaganda war, but now hardly anyone listened to the pope. The king instead pressed absurd charges of heresy against Boniface and sent his minions to arrest the pope to stand trial. At the papal residence of Anagni in 1303 Boniface, who was in his eighties, was captured and mistreated before he was released by the local citizens. These events exhausted the old man's strength and he died a month later. Immediately thereupon it was said that he had entered the papacy like a fox, reigned like a lion, but died like a dog.

After Boniface VIII's death the papacy became virtually a pawn of French temporal authority for most of the fourteenth century. But the emergence and success of the papal monarchy in the High Middle Ages had several beneficial effects during the course of that period. One was that the international rule of the papacy over the Church enhanced international communications and uniformity of religious practices. Another was that the papal cultivation of canon law aided a growing respect for law of all sorts and often helped protect the causes of otherwise defenseless subjects, like widows and orphans. The popes also managed to advance very far in their campaigns to eliminate the sale of Church offices and to raise the morals of the clergy. By centralizing appointments they made it easier for worthy candidates who had no locally influential relatives to gain advancement. There was of course corruption in the papal government too, but in an age of entrenched localism the triumph of an international force was mainly beneficial. Finally, as we will see later, the growth of the papal monarchy helped bring vitality to popular religion and helped support the revival of learning.

Beneficial effects of the papal monarchy

2. THE CRUSADES

The rise and fall of the crusading movement was closely related to the fortunes of the high-medieval papal monarchy. The First Crusade was initiated by the papacy, and its success a great early victory for the papal monarchy. But the later decline of the crusading movement helped undermine the pope's temporal authority. Thus the Crusades can be seen as part of a chapter in papal and religious history. In addition, the Crusades opened the first chapter in the history of Western colonialism.

Two themes of the crusading movement

The immediate cause of the First Crusade was an appeal for aid in 1095 by the Byzantine Emperor Alexius Comnenus. Alexius hoped to reconquer Byzantine territory in Asia Minor which had recently been lost to the Turks. Since he had already become accustomed to using Western mercenaries as auxiliary troops, he asked the pope to help rally some Western military support. But the emperor soon found, no doubt to his great surprise, that he was receiving not just simple aid but a *crusade*. In other words, instead of a band of mercenaries to fight in Asia Minor, the West sent forth an enormous army of volunteers whose goal was to wrest Jerusalem away from Islam. Since the decision to turn Alexius's call for aid into a crusade was made by the pope, it is well to examine the latter's motives.

The direct cause of the First Crusade

The Roman pope in 1095 was Urban II, an extremely competent

Political boundaries are those sh[own]
at the time of the First Crusade

Population predominantly Christian

Population predominantly Moslem

→——→ First Crusade
·······→ Second Crusade
– – → Third Crusade
–·–·→ Fourth Crusade

THE MAJOR CRUSADES

*The Gregorian theory of
Christian Warfare*

disciple of Gregory VII. Without question, Urban called the First Crusade to help further the policies of the Gregorian papacy. Urban's very patronage of Christian warfare was Gregorian. Early Christianity had been pacifistic: St. Martin, for example, a revered Christian saint of the fourth century, gave up his career as a soldier when he converted with the statement "I am Christ's soldier; I cannot fight." The Latin fathers St. Augustine and St. Gregory worked out theories to justify Christian warfare but only in the eleventh century, with the triumph of the Gregorian movement, were these put into practice. Gregory VII engineered papal support for the Norman Conquest even before he became pope, and he, or popes under his influence, blessed Christian campaigns against Muslims in Spain, Greeks in Italy, and Slavs in the German east. All these campaigns were considered by Gregory VII and his followers to be steps toward gaining "right order in the world."

Following in Gregory VII's footsteps, Urban II probably conceived of a great crusade to the Holy Land as a means for achieving at least four ends. One was to bring the Greek Orthodox Church back into the fold. By sending a mighty volunteer army to the East, Urban might overawe the Byzantines with Western strength and convince them to reaccept Roman primacy. If he was successful in that, he would gain a great victory for the Gregorian program of papal monarchy. A second motive was to embarrass the pope's greatest enemy, the German emperor. In 1095 Henry IV had become so militarily strong that Urban had been forced to flee Italy for France. By calling a mighty crusade of all westerners but Germans, Urban might hope to show up the emperor as a narrow-minded, un-Christian persecutor, and demonstrate his own ability to be the spiritual leader of the West. Third, by sending off a large contingent of fighters Urban might help to achieve peace at home. Earlier, the local French Church had supported a "peace movement" which prohibited attacks on noncombatants (the "Peace of God") and then prohibited fighting on certain holy days (the "Truce of God"). Right before he called the First Crusade Urban promulgated the first full papal approval and extension of this peace movement. Clearly the crusade was linked to the call for peace: in effect, Urban told unruly warriors that if they really wished to fight they could do so justly for a Christian cause overseas. Finally, the goal of Jerusalem itself must have genuinely inspired Urban. Jerusalem was thought to be the center of the earth and was the most sacred shrine of the Christian religion. It must have seemed only proper that pilgrimages to Jerusalem should not be impeded and that Christians should rule the city directly. "Right order in the world" could scarcely mean less.

When Urban called his crusade at a Church council in the French town of Clermont in 1095, the response was more enthusiastic than he could possibly have expected. Many in the crowd interrupted the pope's speech with spontaneous cries of "God wills it," and many impetuously rushed off to the East shortly thereafter. All told, there were probably about a hundred thousand men in the main crusading army, an enormous number for the day. Accordingly, the question arises as to why Urban's appeal was so remarkably successful. Certainly there were economic and political reasons. Many of the poorer people who went crusading came from areas that by 1095 were already becoming overpopulated: these crusaders may have hoped to do better for themselves in the East than they could on their crowded lands. Similarly, some lords were feeling the pressures of growing political stability and a growing acceptance of *primogeniture* (inheritance limited to the eldest male heir). Hitherto younger sons might have hoped to make their own fortune in endemic warfare, or at least inherit a small piece of territory for themselves, but now there were more and longer-lived siblings, warfare was becoming limited, and only the eldest son in-

Urban II's motives

Economic and political causes of the First Crusade

*Religion the dominant
motive: crusades as armed
pilgrimages*

herited his father's lands. Clearly, leaving for the East was an attractive alternative to chafing at home.

But the dominant motive for going on the First Crusade was definitely religious. Nobody could have gone crusading out of purely calculating motives because nobody could have predicted for certain that new lands would be won. Indeed, any rational caculation would have predicted at best an unremunerative return trip, or, more likely, death at the hands of the Muslims. But the journey offered great solace for the Christian soul. For centuries pilgrimages had been the most popular type of Christian penance, and the pilgrimage to Jerusalem was considered to be the most sacred and efficacious one of all. Obviously the greatest of all spiritual rewards would come from going on an armed pilgrimage to Jerusalem in order to win back the holiest of sacred places for Christianity. To make this point explicit, Urban II at Clermont promised that Crusaders would be freed from all other penances imposed by the Church. Immediately afterward some Crusade preachers went even further by promising, without Urban's authorization, what became known as a *plenary indulgence*. This was the promise that all Crusaders would be entirely freed from otherworldly punishments in purgatory and that their souls would go straight to heaven if they died on the Crusade. The plenary indulgence was a truly extraordinary offer and crowds streamed in to take advantage of it. As they flocked together they were further whipped up by preachers into a religious frenzy that approached mass hysteria. They were convinced that they had been chosen to cleanse the world of unbelievers. One terrible consequence was that even before they had fully set out for the East they started slaughtering European Jews in the first really virulent outbreak of Western anti-Semitism.

Burning of Jews. From a late-medieval German manuscript. After the persecutions of the First Crusade, treatment of Jews in western Europe became worse and worse. These Jews were set upon by the populace because they were suspected of poisoning wells.

King Louis VII of France and His Queen, Eleanor of Aquitaine, Embarking for the Second Crusade. This late-medieval conception is idealized inasmuch as Louis did not travel to the Holy Land by sea but took a land route.

Against great odds the First Crusade was a thorough success. In 1098 the Crusaders captured Antioch and with it most of Syria; in 1099 they took Jerusalem. Their success came mainly from the facts that their Muslim opponents just at that time were internally divided and that the appearance of the strange, uncouth, and terribly savage westerners took the Muslims by surprise. From the start the Crusaders in the Holy Land acted like imperialists. As soon as they conquered new territories they claimed them as property for themselves, carving out their acquisitions into four different principalities. They also exulted in their own ferocity. When they captured Antioch, instead of taking prisoners they killed all the Turks they laid their hands on. Similarly, when they conquered Jerusalem they ignored Christ's own pacifistic precepts, mercilessly slaughtering all the Muslim inhabitants of the city. Some Crusaders actually boasted in a joint letter home that "in Solomon's Porch and in his temple our men rode in the blood of the Saracens up to the knees of their horses." Those Crusaders who stayed on in the Holy Land gradually became more civilized and tolerant, but new waves of armed pilgrims from the West continued to act brutally. Moreover, even the settled Crusaders never became fully integrated with the local population but remained a separate, exploiting foreign element in the heart of the Islamic world.

The brutal conduct of the Crusaders

Given the fact that the Christian states comprised only an underpopulated, narrow strip of colonies along the coastline of Syria and Palestine, it was only a matter of time before they would be won back for Islam. By 1144 the northernmost principality fell. When Christian warriors led by the king of France and emperor of Germany came East in the Second Crusade to recoup the losses, they were too internally

Failure of subsequent crusades; the triumph of Frederick II's diplomacy

divided to win any victories. Not long afterward the Islamic lands of the region were united from Egypt by the Sultan Saladin, who recaptured Jerusalem in 1187. Again a force from the West tried to repair the damages: this was the Third Crusade, led by the German Emperor Frederick Barbarossa, the French King Philip Augustus, and the English King Richard the Lionhearted. Even this glorious host, however, could not triumph, above all because rival leaders again quarreled among themselves. When Innocent III became pope his main ambition was to win back Jerusalem. He called the Fourth Crusade to that end, but that Crusade was an unprecedented disaster from the point of view of a united Christendom. The pope could not control its direction and the Crusaders in 1204 wound up seizing Orthodox Christian Constantinople instead of marching on the Holy Land. As we have seen, the ultimate result of this act was to help destroy the Byzantine Empire and open up eastern Europe to the Ottoman Turks. Innocent convened the Fourth Lateran Council in 1215 partially to prepare for yet another crusade that would be more directly under papal guidance. That crusade, the fifth, was launched from the sea against Egypt in order to penetrate Muslim power at its base, but after a promising start it too was a failure. Only the Sixth Crusade, led from 1228 to 1229 by the Emperor Frederick II, was a success; this, however, was not for any military reasons. Frederick, who knew Arabic and could communicate easily with the Egyptian sultan, did not fight but skillfully negotiated a treaty whereby Jerusalem and a narrow access route were restored to the Christians. Thus diplomacy triumphed where warfare had failed. But the Christians could not hold on to their gains and Jerusalem fell again in 1244, never to be recaptured by the West until 1917. The Christian "states" were now only a small enclave around the Palestinian city of Acre.

The papacy's sacrifice of the crusading ideal to political interests

While Frederick II was negotiating for Jerusalem, he was under excommunication by the pope; therefore, when he entered the city, he had to crown himself king of Jerusalem in the Church of the Holy Sepulcher with his own hands. This was indicative of the fact that by then the papacy was becoming more intent on advancing European political aims than on reconquering the Holy Land. The victory of the First Crusade had greatly enhanced the prestige and strength of the papal monarchy, but the subsequent failures were increasingly calling into question the papal ability to unite the West for a great enterprise. The Albigensian Crusade, called by Innocent III in 1208, established the crucial precedent that a believer could receive the same spiritual rewards by crusading within Europe as by going on a much longer and more risky crusade to the East. The Albigensian Crusade did not damage the papacy's religious image, however, because the Albigensian heretics (whose beliefs will be discussed later) were a clear religious threat to the Church. Once the papacy launched its crusade against Frederick II and his heirs, however, it fully sacrificed the crusading ideal to political interests.

It was then that the decline of the crusading movement and the decline of the papacy became most closely interrelated. In the crusades against Frederick and his successors, and later against the king of Aragon, the popes offered the same plenary indulgence that was by then officially offered to all Crusaders against Islam. Worse, they granted the same indulgence to anyone who simply contributed enough money to arm a Crusader for the enterprise. This created a great inflation in indulgences. By 1291 the last Christian outposts in the Holy Land had fallen without any Western help while the papacy was still trying to salvage its losing crusade against Aragon. Boniface VIII's papal jubilee of 1300, which offered a plenary indulgence to all those who made a pilgrimage to Rome, was a tacit recognition that the Eternal City and not the Holy Land would henceforth have to be the central goal of Christian pilgrimage. Boniface fell from power three years later for many reasons, but one was certainly that the prestige of the papacy had become irreparably damaged by the misuses and failures of crusading.

The decline of the crusading movement and the decline of the papacy interrelated

So, while the crusading idea helped build up the papal monarchy, it also helped destroy it. Other than that, what practical significance did the Crusades have? On the credit side, the almost incredible success of the First Crusade greatly helped raise the self-confidence of the medieval West. For centuries western Europe had been on the defensive against Islam; now a Western army could march into a center of Islamic power and take a coveted prize seemingly at will. This dramatic victory contributed to making the twelfth century an age of extraordinary buoyancy and optimism. To Western Christians it must have seemed as if God was on their side and that they could accomplish almost anything they wished. The Crusades also helped broaden Western horizons. Few westerners in the Holy Land ever bothered to learn Arabic or profit from specific Islamic institutions or ideas—the most profitable cultural communications between Christians and Muslims took place in Spain and Sicily—but Crusaders who traveled long dis-

Positive effects of the Crusades

Krak des Chevaliers. This Crusader castle in northern Syria is one of the best preserved fortresses of the Middle Ages. The word *krak* comes from the Arabic *karak,* meaning strong fort.

tances through foreign lands were bound to become somewhat more sophisticated. The Crusades certainly stimulated interest in hitherto unknown luxury goods and presented a wealth of subjects for literature and fable.

Commerce and taxation

From an economic point of view, the success of the First Crusade helped open up the eastern Mediterranean to Western commerce. The Italian cities of Venice and Genoa particularly began to dominate trade in that area, thereby helping to enhance Western prosperity as a whole. The need to transfer money over long distances also stimulated early experiments in banking techniques. Politically, the precedent of taxing the clergy for financing crusades was not only quickly turned to the advantage of the Western monarchies, it also stimulated the development of various forms of national taxation. More than that, the very act of organizing a country to help support a royal crusade by raising funds and provisions was an important stimulus to the development of efficient administrative institutions in the emerging nation-states.

Negative consequences

But there was a debit as well as a credit side to the crusading balance sheet. There is no excusing the Crusaders' savage butchery—of Jews at home and of Muslims abroad. As we have seen too in Chapter 10, the Crusades greatly accelerated the deterioration of Western relations with the Byzantine Empire and contributed fundamentally to the destruction of that realm, with all the disastrous consequences that followed. And Western colonialism in the Holy Land was only the beginning of a long history of colonialism that has continued until modern times.

3. THE OUTBURST OF RELIGIOUS VITALITY

The awakening of religious interest

The First Crusade would never have succeeded if westerners had not become enthusiastic about religion. The growth of that enthusiasm itself was a most remarkable development. Had the First Crusade been called about fifty years earlier it is doubtful that many people would have joined it. But the eleventh-century reform movement and the pontificate of Gregory VII awakened interest in religion in all quarters. Thereafter the entire high-medieval period was to be marked by extraordinary religious vitality.

The impact of the Gregorian reform movement on religious revival

The reformers and Gregory VII stimulated a European religious revival for two reasons. One was that the campaign to cleanse the Church actually achieved a large measure of success: the laity could now respect the clergy more and increasingly large numbers of people were inspired to join the clergy themselves. According to a reliable estimate, the number of people who joined monastic orders in England increased tenfold between 1066 and 1200, a statistic that does not include the increase in priests. The other reason why the work of Gregory VII in particular helped inspire a revival was that Gregory explicitly called upon the laity to help discipline their priests. In letters of great propagandistic power he denounced the sins of "fornicating priests" (by which he really meant just married ones) and urged the laity to drive them from their pulpits or boycott their services. Not surprisingly, this touched off something close to a vigilante movement in many parts of Europe. This excitement, taken together with the fact that the papal struggle with Henry IV was really the first European event of universal interest, increased religious commitment immensely. Until about 1050 most western Europeans were Christians in name, but religiosity seems to have been lukewarm and attendance at church services quite rare; after the Gregorian period Christianity was becoming an ideal and practice which really began to direct human lives.

One of the most visible manifestations of the new religiosity was the spread of the Cistercian movement in the twelfth century. By around 1100 the Cluniac monks had begun to sink into the same morass of worldliness and corruption that had engulfed their older Benedictine brothers whom they had set about to reform. The result was the founding of new orders to provide for the fullest expression of monastic idealism. One was the Carthusian order, whose monks were required to live in separate cells, abstain from meat, and fast three days each week on bread, water, and salt. The Carthusians never sought to attract great numbers and therefore remained a small group. But the same was by no means true of the Cistercians. The latter were monks who were first organized around 1100 and who sought to follow the Benedictine Rule in the purest and most austere way possible. In order

The new religiosity: the Carthusian and Cistercian orders; St. Bernard of Clairvaux

St. Bernard of Clairvaux. Here the saint, in the white habit of the Cistercians, has a miraculous vision of Christ during Mass. From a manuscript of about 1290.

to avoid the worldly temptations to which the Cluniacs had succumbed, they founded new monasteries in forests and wastelands as
far away from civilization as possible. They shunned all unnecessary
church decoration and ostentatious utensils, abandoned the Cluniac
stress on an elaborate liturgy in favor of more contemplation and
private prayer, and seriously committed themselves to hard manual
labor. Under the charismatic leadership of St. Bernard of Clairvaux
(1090–1153), a spellbinding preacher, brilliant writer, and the most influential European religious personality of his age, the Cistercian order
grew exponentially. There were only 5 houses in 1115 but no less than
343 on St. Bernard's death in 1153. This growth not only meant that
many more men were becoming monks—the older houses did not
disappear—but that many pious laymen were donating funds and
lands to support the new monasteries.

*New forms of religious
belief and practice*

As more people were entering or patronizing new monasteries, the
very nature of religious belief and devotion was changing. One of
many examples was a shift away from the cult of saints to emphasis on
the worship of Jesus and veneration of the Virgin Mary. Older Benedictine monasteries encouraged the veneration of the relics of local
saints that they housed in order to attract pilgrims and donations. But
the Cluniac and Cistercian orders were both centralized congregations
that allowed only one saintly patron for all their houses: respectively,
St. Peter (to honor the founder of the papacy) and the Virgin. Since
these monasteries contained few relics (the Virgin was thought to have
been taken bodily into heaven, so there were no corporeal relics for
her at all) they deemphasized their cult. The veneration of relics was
replaced by a concentration on the Eucharist, or the sacrament of the
Lord's Supper. Of course celebration of the Eucharist had always been
an important part of the Christian faith, but only in the twelfth century was it made really central, for only then did theologians fully
work out the doctrine of *transubstantiation*. According to this the priest
during mass cooperates with God in the performance of a miracle
whereby the bread and wine on the altar are changed or "transubstantiated" into the body and blood of Christ. Popular reverence for the
Eucharist became so great in the twelfth century that for the first time
the practice of elevating the consecrated host was initiated so that the
whole congregation could see it. The new theology of the Eucharist
greatly enhanced the dignity of the priest and also encouraged the
faithful to meditate on the Passion of Christ. As a result many developed an intense sense of identification with Christ and tried to imitate his life in different ways.

*The cult of the Virgin
Mary*

Coming a very close second to the renewed worship of Christ in the
twelfth century was veneration of the Virgin Mary. This development
was more unprecedented because until then the Virgin had been only
negligibly honored in the Western Church. Exactly why veneration of
the Virgin became so pronounced in the twelfth century is not fully
clear, but, whatever the explanation, there is no doubt that in the

Christ Blessing the Coronation of His Mother, the Virgin Mary. A relief from the cathedral of Notre Dame, Paris.

twelfth century the cult of Mary blossomed throughout all of western Europe. The Cistercians made her their patron saint, St. Bernard constantly taught about her life and virtues, and practically all the magnificent new cathedrals of the age were dedicated to her: there was Notre Dame ("Our Lady") of Paris, and also a "Notre Dame" of Chartres, Rheims, Amiens, Rouen, Laon, and many other places. Theologically, Mary's role was that of intercessor with her son for the salvation of human souls. It was held that Mary was the mother of all, an infinite repository of mercy who urged the salvation even of sinners so long as they were loving and ultimately contrite. Numerous stories circulated about seeming reprobates who were saved because they venerated Mary and because she then spoke for them at the hour of death.

The significance of the new cult was manifold. For the first time a woman was given a central and honored place in the Christian religion. Theologians still taught that sin had entered the world through the woman, but they now counterbalanced this by explaining how the triumph over sin transpired with the help of Mary. Moreover, this emphasis on Mary gave women a religious figure with whom they could identify, thereby enhancing their own religiosity. A third result was that artists and writers who portrayed Mary were able to concentrate on femininity and scenes of human tenderness and family life. This contributed greatly to a general softening of artistic and literary style. But perhaps most important of all, the rise of the cult of Mary was closely associated with a general rise of hopefulness and optimism in the twelfth-century West.

Significance of the cult

The Virgin in Majesty. A representation from a stained-glass window in the cathedral of Chartres.

Sometimes the great religious enthusiasm of the twelfth century went beyond the bounds approved by the Church. After Gregory VII had called upon the laity to help discipline their clergy it was difficult to control lay enthusiasm. As the twelfth century progressed and the papal monarchy concentrated on strengthening its legal and financial administration, some lay people began to wonder whether the Church, which had once been so inspiring, had not begun to lose sight of its idealistic goals. Another difficulty was that the growing emphasis on the miraculous powers of priests tended to inhibit the religious role of the laity and place it in a distinct position of spiritual inferiority. The result was that in the second half of the twelfth century large-scale movements of popular heresy swept over western Europe for the first time in its history. The two major twelfth-century heresies were Albigensianism and Waldensianism. The former, which had its greatest strength in Italy and southern France, was a recrudescence of Eastern dualism. Like the Zoroastrians, Gnostics, and Manicheans before them, the Albigensians believed that all matter was created by an evil principle and that therefore the flesh should be thoroughly mortified. This teaching was completely at variance with Christianity, but it seems that most Albigensians believed themselves to be Christians and subscribed to the heresy mainly because it challenged the authority of insufficiently zealous Catholic priests and provided an outlet for intense lay spirituality. More typical of twelfth-century mainstream religious protest was Waldensianism, a heresy that originated in southern France and spread throughout most of Europe. Waldensians wished to imitate the life of Christ and the Apostles to the fullest possible extent. Therefore, they translated and studied the Gospels, and dedicated themselves to lives of poverty and preaching. Since the Waldensians did not attack any actual doctrines or practices of the Church, the ecclesiastical hierarchy did not at first interfere with them. But it was soon recognized that they were becoming too independent and that their simple piety could prove an embarrassing contrast to the life of worldly prelates. So the papacy forbade them to preach without authorization; when they refused to accept this they were condemned for heresy. This only made them more radical, and they began to teach that people could be saved by living the simple apostolic life without any need for the sacraments administered by priests.

Innocent III's response to heresy

When Innocent III became pope in 1198 he was faced with a very serious challenge from growing heresies. His response was characteristically decisive and fateful for the future of the Church. Simply stated it was two-pronged. On the one hand, Innocent resolved to crush all disobedience to papal authority, but on the other, he decided to patronize whatever idealistic religious groups he could find that were willing to acknowledge obedience. Papal monarchy could thus be protected without frustrating all dynamic spirituality within the Church. Innocent not only launched a full-scale crusade against the Albigensians, he also encouraged the use against heresy of judicial procedures that included ruthless techniques of religious "inquisi-tion." In 1252 the papacy first approved the use of torture in inquisi-torial trials, and burning at the stake became the prevalent punishment for religious disobedience. Neither the crusade nor the inquisitorial procedures were fully successful in uprooting the Albigensian heresy in Innocent's own lifetime, but the extension of such measures did result in destroying the heresy by fire and sword after about the mid-dle of the thirteenth century. Waldensians, like Albigensians, were hunted down by inquisitors and their numbers reduced, but scattered Waldensian groups did manage to survive until modern times.

Another aspect of Innocent's program was to pronounce formally the new religious doctrines that enhanced the special status of priests and the ecclesiastical hierarchy. Thus at the Fourth Lateran Council of 1215 he reaffirmed the doctrine that the sacraments administered by the Church were the indispensable means of procuring God's grace, and that no one could be saved without them. The decrees of the Lateran Council emphasized two sacraments: the Eucharist and pen-ance. The doctrine of transubstantiation was formally defined and it was made a requirement—as it remains today—that all Catholics con-fess their sins to a priest at least once a year. The council also promul-gated other doctrinal definitions and disciplinary measures which served both to oppose heresy and to assert the unique dignity of the clergy.

*Innocent III's emphasis on
the sacraments*

As stated above, the other side of Innocent's policy was to support obedient idealistic movements within the Church. The most impor-tant of these were the new orders of *friars*—the Dominicans and the Franciscans. Friars resembled monks in vowing to follow a rule, but they differed greatly from monks in their actual conduct. Above all, they did not retreat from society into monasteries. Assuming that the way of life originally followed by Christ and the Apostles was the most holy, they wandered through the countryside and espec-ially the towns ministering to the sick and poor, preaching, and teach-ing. In imitation of Christ they also resolved to wed themselves to poverty. In many respects they resembled the Waldensian heretics, but they professed absolute obedience to the pope and sought to fight heresy themselves.

The new orders of friars

The Dominican order, founded by St. Dominic in 1216 with In-nocent III's approval, was particularly dedicated to the fight against heresy and also to the conversion of Jews and Muslims. At first the Dominicans hoped to achieve these ends by preaching and public debate. Hence they became intellectually oriented. Many members of the order gained teaching positions in the infant European universities and contributed much to the development of philosophy and theol-ogy. The most influential thinker of the thirteenth century, St. Thomas Aquinas, was a Dominican who addressed one of his major theologi-cal works to converting the "gentiles" (i.e., all non-Christians). The Dominicans always retained their reputation for learning, but they

The Dominican order

St. Francis of Assisi. By the great
Italian painter of the late thirteenth century, Cimabue.

*The working relationship
between the papal
monarchy and the friars*

The age of faith

also came to believe that stubborn heretics were best controlled by
legal procedures. Accordingly, they became the leading medieval
administrators of inquisitorial trials.

The Franciscan order was in many respects quite different and more
radical. Its founder, St. Francis of Assisi (1182–1226), behaved at first
remarkably like a social rebel and heretic. The son of a rich Italian
merchant, he became dissatisfied with the values of his father and determined to become a servant of the poor. Giving away all of his property, he threw off all of his clothes in public, donned the simple garb
of a beggar, and began to preach salvation and minister to outcasts in
the darkest corners of Italian cities. He rigorously imitated the life of
Christ and displayed indifference to doctrine, form, and ceremony.
But he did wish to gain the support of the pope. One day in 1210 he
appeared in Rome with a small ragged band to request that Innocent
III approve a primitive "rule" that was little more than a collection of
Gospel precepts. Some other pope might have rejected the layman
Francis as a hopelessly unworldly, perhaps even demented, religious
anarchist. But Francis was thoroughly willing to profess obedience,
and Innocent had the genius to approve Francis's rule and give him
permission to preach. With papal support the Franciscan movement
spread rapidly. Thus Innocent managed to harness a vital new force
that would help maintain a sense of religious enthusiasm within the
Church.

Until the end of the thirteenth century both the Franciscans and
Dominicans worked closely together with the papal monarchy in a
mutually supportive relationship. The popes helped the friars establish
themselves throughout Europe and often allowed them to infringe on
the duties of parish priests. On their side the friars combated heresy,
helped preach papal crusades, were active in missionary work, and
otherwise undertook special missions for the popes. Above all, by the
power of their examples and by their vigorous preaching the friars
helped maintain religious intensity throughout the thirteenth century.

The entire period from 1050 to 1300 was hence unquestionably a
great "age of faith." The products of this faith were both tangible and
intangible. We will examine the tangible products—works of theology, literature, art, and architecture—presently. Great as these were,
the intangible products were equally important. Until the Christian
religion became deeply felt in the High Middle Ages hardly any common ideals inspired average men and women. Life in the Middle Ages
was extraordinarily hard, and until about 1050 there was not much to
give it meaning. Then, when people began to take Christianity more
seriously, an impetus was provided for performing hard work of all
sorts. As we have seen in the last chapter, Europeans after 1050 literally had better food than before, and now we have seen that they were
better fed figuratively as well. With more spiritual as well as material
nourishment they accomplished great feats in all forms of human
endeavor.

The major intellectual accomplishments of the High Middle Ages were of four related but different sorts: the spread of primary education and literacy; the origin and spread of universities; the acquisition of classical and Islamic knowledge; and the actual progress in thought made by westerners. Any one of these accomplishments would have earned the High Middle Ages a signal place in the history of Western learning; taken together they began the era of Western intellectual predominance which became a hallmark of modern times.

*Four major intellectual
accomplishments*

Around 800 Charlemagne ordered that primary schools be established in every bishopic and monastery in his realm. Although it is doubtful that this command was carried out to the letter, many schools were certainly founded during the Carolingian period. But their continued existence was later endangered by the Viking invasions. Primary education in some monasteries and cathedral towns managed to survive, but until around 1050 the extent and quality of basic education in the European West were meager. Thereafter, however, there was a blossoming that paralleled the efflorescence we have seen in other human activities. Even contemporaries were struck by the rapidity with which schools sprang up all over Europe. One French monk writing in 1115 stated that when he was growing up around 1075 there was "such a scarcity of teachers that there were almost none in the villages and hardly any in the cities," but that by his maturity there was "a great number of schools," and the study of grammar was "flourishing far and wide." Similarly, a Flemish chronicle referred to an extraordinary new passion for the study and practice of rhetoric around 1120. Clearly, the economic revival, the growth of towns, and the emergence of strong government allowed Europeans to dedicate themselves to basic education as never before.

*The spread of primary
education*

The high-medieval educational boom was more than merely a growth of schools, for the nature of the schools changed, and as time went on so did the curriculum and the clientele. The first basic mutation was that monasteries in the twelfth century abandoned their practice of educating outsiders. Earlier, monasteries had taught a few privileged nonmonastic students how to read because there were no other schools for such pupils. But by the twelfth century sufficient alternatives existed. The main centers of European education became the cathedral schools located in the growing towns. The papal monarchy energetically supported this development by ordering in 1179 that all cathedrals should set aside income for one schoolteacher, who could then instruct all who wished, rich or poor, without fee. The papacy believed correctly that this measure would enlarge the number of well-trained clerics and potential administrators.

*Changes in medieval
education: (1) the
development of cathedral
schools*

At first the cathedral schools existed almost exclusively for the basic training of priests, with a curriculum designed to teach only such literacy necessary for reading the Church offices. But soon after 1100

Two Medieval Advertisements for Elementary Education. On the left an illumination from a twelfth-century Austrian manuscript depicts a kneeling student saying "I wish to study, dear master," which is perhaps not too surprising given the fact that his teacher seems to be threatening to beat and kick him. Grammar school education is advertised more gently on the right, a late-medieval scene in which a woman personifying the alphabet leads a willing boy into a palace of learning wherein the stories ascend from grammar through logic and rhetoric to the heights of theology.

(2) the broadening of the curriculum

the curriculum was broadened, for the growth of both ecclesiastical and secular governments created a growing demand for trained officials who had to know more than how to read a few prayers. The revived reliance on law especially made it imperative to improve the quality of primary education in order to train future lawyers. Above all, a thorough knowledge of Latin grammar and composition began to be inculcated, often by studying some of the Roman classics such as the works of Cicero and Virgil. The revived interest in these texts, and attempts to imitate them, have led scholars to refer to a "Renaissance of the Twelfth Century."

(3) the growth of lay education

Until about 1200 the students in the urban schools remained predominantly clerical. Even those who hoped to become lawyers or administrators rather than mere priests usually found it advantageous to take Church orders. But afterward more pupils entered schools who were not in the clergy and never intended to be. Some were children of the upper classes who began to regard literacy as a badge of status. Others were future notaries (i.e., men who drew up official documents) or merchants who needed some literacy and/or computational skills to advance their own careers. Customarily, the latter groups would not go to cathedral schools but to alternate ones which were more practically oriented. Such schools grew rapidly in the course of the thirteenth century and became completely independent of ecclesiastical control. Not only were their students recruited from the laity, their teachers were usually laymen as well. As time went on instruction ceased being in Latin, as had hitherto been the case, and was offered in the European vernacular languages instead.

The rise of lay education was an enormously important development in western European history for two related reasons. The first was that the Church lost its monopoly over education for the first time in almost a millennium. Learning and resultant attitudes could now become more secular, and they did just that increasingly over the course of time. Laymen could not only evaluate and criticize the ideas of priests, they could also pursue entirely secular lines of inquiry. Western culture therefore ultimately became more independent of religion, and much of the traditionalism associated with religion, than any other culture in the world. Second, the growth of lay schools, taken together with the growth of church schools which trained the laity, led to an enormous growth of lay literacy: by 1340 roughly 40 percent of the Florentine population could read; by the later fifteenth century about 40 percent of the total population of England was literate as well. (These figures include women, who were usually taught to read by paid tutors or male family members at home rather than in schools.) When one considers that literacy around 1050 was almost entirely limited to the clergy and that the literate comprised less than 1 percent of the population of western Europe, it can be appreciated that an astonishing revolution had taken place. Without it, many of Europe's other accomplishments would have been inconceivable.

*Significance of the rise of
lay education*

The emergence of universities was part of the same high-medieval educational boom. Originally, universities were institutions that gave specialized instruction in advanced studies which could not be pursued in average cathedral schools. In Italy the earliest universities took shape in the eleventh and twelfth centuries: those of Salerno, which specialized in medicine, and Bologna, which specialized in law—both Roman law and the canon law of the Church. North of the Alps the earliest and for a long time the most prominent university was that of Paris. The University of Paris started out as a cathedral school like many others, but in the twelfth century it began to become a recognized center of northern intellectual life. One reason for this was that scholars there found necessary conditions of peace and stability provided by the increasingly strong French kingship; another was that food was plentiful because the area was rich in agricultural produce; and another was that the cathedral school of Paris in the first half of the twelfth century boasted the most charismatic and controversial teacher of the day, Peter Abelard (1079–1142). Abelard, whose intel-

The origins of universities

See color map facing
page 353

lectual accomplishments we will discuss later, attracted students from all over Europe in droves. According to an apocryphal story that was told at the time, he was such an exciting teacher that when he was forbidden to teach in French lands, because of his controversial views, he climbed a tree and students flocked under it to hear him lecture; when he was then forbidden to teach from the air he started lecturing from a boat and students massed to hear him from the banks. As a result of his reputation many other teachers settled in Paris and began to offer much more varied and advanced instruction than anything offered in other French cathedral schools. By 1200 Paris was evolving into a university that specialized in liberal arts and theology. Around then Innocent III, who had studied in Paris himself, called the school "the oven that bakes the bread for the entire world."

Nature of the medieval university

It should be emphasized that the institution of the university was really a medieval invention. Of course advanced schools existed in the ancient world, but they did not have fixed curricula or organized faculties, and they did not award degrees. At first, medieval universities themselves were not so much places as groups of scholars. The term university originally meant a corporation or guild. In fact, all of the medieval universities were corporations, either of teachers or students, organized like other guilds to protect their interests and rights. But gradually the word university came to mean an educational institution with a school of liberal arts and one or more faculties in the professional subjects of law, medicine, and theology. Salerno never became more than a medical school, but Bologna and Paris after about 1200 were regarded as the prototypic universities. During the thirteenth century such famous institutions as Oxford, Cambridge, Montpellier, Salamanca, and Naples were founded or granted formal recognition. In Germany there were no universities until the fourteenth century—a reflection of the disorganized condition of that area—but in 1385 Heidelberg, the first university on German soil, was founded and many others quickly followed.

Organization of universities

Every university in medieval Europe was patterned after one or the other of two different models. Throughout Italy, Spain, and southern France the standard was generally the University of Bologna, in which the students themselves constituted the corporation. They hired the teachers, paid their salaries, and fined or discharged them for neglect of duty or inefficient instruction. The universities of northern Europe were modeled after Paris, which was not a guild of students but of teachers. It included four faculties—arts, theology, law, and medicine—each headed by a dean. In the great majority of the northern universities arts and theology were the leading branches of study. Before the end of the thirteenth century separate colleges came to be established within the University of Paris. The original college was nothing more than an endowed home for poor students, but eventually the colleges become centers of instruction as well as residences. While most of these colleges have disappeared from the Continent, the

A Lecture Class in a Medieval University. Some interesting similarities and contrasts may be observed between this scene and a modern classroom.

universities of Oxford and Cambridge still retain the pattern of federal organization copied from Paris. The colleges of which they are composed are semi-independent educational units.

Most of our modern degrees as well as our modern university organization derive from the medieval system, but actual courses of study have been greatly altered. No curriculum in the Middle Ages included history or anything like the modern social sciences. The medieval student was assumed to know Latin grammar thoroughly before entrance into a university—this he learned in the primary, or "grammar," schools. Upon admission, limited to males, he was required to spend about four years studying the basic liberal arts, which meant doing advanced work in Latin grammar and rhetoric, and mastering the rules of logic. If he passed his examinations he received the preliminary degree of bachelor of arts (the prototype of our B.A.), which conferred no unusual distinction. To assure himself a place in professional life he then usually had to devote additional years to the pursuit of an advanced degree, such as master of arts (M.A.), or doctor of laws, medicine, or theology. For the M.A. degree three or four years had to be given to the study of mathematics, natural science, and philosophy. This was accomplished by reading and commenting on standard ancient works, such as those of Euclid and especially Aristotle. Abstract analysis was emphasized and there was no such thing as laboratory science. The requirements for the doctors' degrees included more specialized training. Those for the doctorate in theology were particularly arduous: by the end of the Middle Ages the course for the doctorate in theology at the University of Paris had been extended to twelve or thirteen years after the roughly eight years taken for the M.A.! Continuous residence was not required and it was accordingly

The courses of study

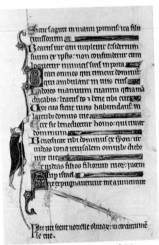

A Scribe with a Sense of Humor.
An English scribe of around
1300, having noticed that he left
out a whole line in a luxurious
prayerbook, devised this ingenious way to rectify the error.

*Acquisition of Greek and
Arabic knowledge*

rare to become a doctor of theology before the age of forty; statutes in
fact forbade awarding the degree to anyone under thirty-five. Strictly
speaking, doctor's degrees, including even the one in medicine, only
conferred the right to teach. But in practice university degrees of all
grades were recognized as standards of attainment and became
pathways to nonacademic careers.

Student life in medieval universities was often very rowdy. Many
students were very immature because it was customary to begin university studies between the ages of twelve and fifteen. Moreover, all
university students believed that they comprised an independent and
privileged community, set aside from that of the local townspeople.
Since the latter tried to reap financial profits from the students and the
students were naturally boisterous, there were frequent riots and
sometimes pitched battles between "town" and "gown." But actual
study was very intense. Because the greatest emphasis was placed on
the value of authority and also because books were prohibitively expensive (they were handwritten and made from rare parchment), there
was an enormous amount of rote memorization. As students advanced in their disciplines they were also expected to develop their
own skills in formal, public disputations. Advanced disputations
could become extremely complex and abstract; sometimes they might
also last for days. The most important fact pertaining to medieval university students was that, after about 1250, there were so many of them.
The University of Paris in the thirteenth century numbered about
seven thousand students and Oxford somewhere around two thousand in any given year. This means that a relatively appreciable proportion of male Europeans who were more than peasants or artisans
were gaining at least some education at the higher levels.

As the numbers of those educated at all levels vastly increased during the High Middle Ages, so did the quality of learning. This was
owing first and foremost to the reacquisition of Greek knowledge and
to the absorption of intellectual advances made by the Muslims. Since
practically no western Europeans knew Greek or Arabic, works in
those languages had to be transmitted by means of Latin translations.
But there were very few of these before about 1140: of all the many
works of Aristotle only a few logical treatises were available in Latin
translations before the middle of the twelfth century. But then, suddenly, an enormous burst of translating activity made almost all of ancient Greek and Arabic scientific knowledge accessible to western Europeans. This activity transpired in Spain and Sicily because Christians
there lived in close proximity with Arabic speakers, or Jews who
knew Latin and Arabic, either of whom could aid them in their tasks.
Greek works were first translated into Latin from earlier Arabic translations; then many were retranslated directly from the Greek by a few
westerners who had managed to learn that language, usually by traveling in Greek-speaking territories. The result was that by about 1260

Ivory Plaque, German, X cent. The plaque shows Otto the Great presenting a church to Christ while St. Peter watches, a reference to Otto's building an empire by cooperating with the Church. (MMA)

Aquamanile, German, XII–XIII cent. Aquamaniles were water jugs used for handwashing during Church ritual, or at mealtimes. (MMA)

Chalice, German, XIII cent. A beautifully embellished cup used to hold the wine in the sacrament of the Eucharist. (MMA)

Kings in Battle, French, c. 1250. A scene depicting Joshua's fight against the five kings of Canaan. In the center Joshua raises his hand, commanding the sun and moon to stand still to enable him to complete his victory. Since the artist was oblivious to the concept of anachronism all these Old Testament figures are shown in contemporary medieval armor. (Morgan Library)

The French King, Louis IX, XIII cent. Although Louis was later recognized as a saint, the artist here depicts him as a young and earthly ruler. (Morgan Library)

0   500 miles

NORWAY

SWEDEN

Upsala

NORTH
SEA

SCOTLAND

△ Aberdeen

△ St. Andrews

△ Glasgow

DENMARK

Copenhagen

BALTIC SEA

ENGLAND

Rostock

Greifswald

Elbe R.

Vistula R.

Frankfurt

POLAND

Cambridge

△ Oxford

Rhine R.

Wittenberg

Leipzig

Oder R.

Louvain

Cologne

Erfurt

Cracow

Trier

HOLY ROMAN

Prague

ATLANTIC

OCEAN

△ Caen

Seine R.

△ Paris

Mainz

Würzburg

Heidelberg

EMPIRE

Danube R.

Pressburg

Orléans

Freiburg

Ingolstadt

Vienna

AUSTRIA

Buda

Angers

Tübingen

Nantes

Bourges

Besançon

Basel

Poitiers

Dôle

SWITZ.

HUNGARY

Fünfkirchen

FRANCE

Lyons

Grenoble

Vercelli

Turin

Pavia

Vicenza

Treviso

Padua

VENETIAN REPUBLIC

Cahors

Valence

Piacenza

Ferrara

Bologna

Bordeaux

Orange

Reggio

ADRIATIC SEA

Avignon

Florence

Arezzo

Montpellier

Aix

Siena

Perugia

Toulouse

PAPAL STATES

Rome

Ebro R.

Palencia

Huesca

CORSICA

Valladolid

Saragossa

Perpignan

Lérida

Salamanca

Siguenza

Barcelona

Coimbra

△ Avila

Naples

PORTUGAL

Tagus R.

SPAIN

Toledo

BALEARIC

SARDINIA

Salerno

Lisbon

Valencia

Palma △ MAJORCA

THE TWO

ISLANDS

Palermo

SICILIES

Seville

MEDITERRANEAN

Catania

SEA

THE RISE OF THE MEDIEVAL UNIVERSITY

△ Founded in the 12th century

■ Founded in the 13th century

● Founded in the 14th century   —··—··— Boundaries ca. 1500 A.D.

△ Founded in the 15th century

almost the entire Aristotelian corpus that is known today was made available in Latin. So also were basic works of such important Greek scientific thinkers as Euclid, Galen, and Ptolemy. Only the milestones of Greek literature and the works of Plato were not yet translated because they had not been made available to the Arabs; they existed only in inaccessible Byzantine manuscripts. But in addition to the thought of the Greeks, Western scholars became familiar with the accomplishments of all the major Islamic philosophers and scientists such as Avicenna and Averroës.

Having acquired the best of Greek and Arabic scientific and speculative thought, the West was able to build on it and make its own advances. This progress transpired in different ways. When it came to natural science, westerners were able to start building on the acquired learning without much difficulty because it seldom conflicted with the principles of Christianity. But when it came to philosophy, the basic question arose as to how thoroughly Greek and Arabic thought was compatible with the Christian faith. The most advanced thirteenth-century scientist was the Englishman Robert Grosseteste (c. 1168–1253), who was not only a great thinker but was also very active in public life as bishop of Lincoln. Grosseteste became so proficient at Greek that he translated all of Aristotle's *Ethics*. More important, he made very significant theoretical advances in mathematics, astronomy, and optics. He formulated a sophisticated scientific explanation of the rainbow, and he posited the use of lenses for magnification. Grosseteste's leading disciple was Roger Bacon (c. 1214–1294), who is today more famous than his teacher because he seems to have predicted automobiles and flying machines. Bacon in fact had no real interest in machinery, but he did follow up on Grosseteste's work in optics, discussing, for example, further properties of lenses, the rapid speed of light, and the nature of human vision. Grosseteste, Bacon, and some of their followers at the University of Oxford argued that natural knowledge was more certain when it was based on sensory evidence than when it rested on abstract reason. To this degree they can be seen as early forerunners of modern science. But the important qualification remains that they did not perform any real laboratory experiments.

The growth of western scientific and speculative thought; Robert Grosseteste and Roger Bacon

The story of the high-medieval encounter between Greek and Arabic philosophy and Christian faith is basically the story of the emergence of Scholasticism. This word can be, and has been, defined in many ways. In its root meaning Scholasticism was simply the method of teaching and learning followed in the medieval schools. That meant that it was highly systematic and also that it was highly respectful of authority. Yet Scholasticism was not only a method of study: it was a worldview. As such, it taught that there was a fundamental compatability between the knowledge humans can obtain naturally, i.e., by experience or reason, and the teachings imparted by

The meaning of Scholasticism

Peter Abelard

Abelard. A late-medieval conception.

Abelard's autobiography

Sic et Non *and the Scholastic method*

Divine Revelation. Since medieval scholars believed that the Greeks were the masters of natural knowledge and that all revelation was in the Bible, Scholasticism consequently was the theory and practice of reconciling classical philosophy with Christian faith.

One of the most important thinkers who paved the way for Scholasticism without yet being fully a Scholastic himself was the stormy petrel Peter Abelard. As a student Abelard was so adept in logic and theology that he publicly humiliated his teachers in and around Paris in debate. Such arrogant conduct made him many enemies. These engineered his first conviction for heresy in 1121. To complicate matters, Abelard entered upon an affair with a young woman, Heloise, herself a scholar, without marrying her. Abelard had been hired to be Heloise's tutor by her uncle, Fulbert, canon of Notre Dame of Paris. A child was the result of the affair, and Heloise's uncle took revenge upon Abelard by having him castrated. Heloise became a nun and Abelard a monk, but Abelard was too restless and cantankerous a personality to find real peace in a monastery. After quarreling and breaking with the monks of two different communities, he set himself up as a teacher in Paris from about 1132 until 1141. This was the peak of his career. In 1141, however, he was again charged with heresy, this time by the highly influential St. Bernard, and condemned by a Church council. Not long afterward the persecuted thinker abjured, and in 1142 he died in retirement.

Abelard recounted many of these trials in a letter called *The Story of My Calamities,* one of the first autobiographical accounts written in the West since St. Augustine's *Confessions.* On first reading, this work appears "modern" because Abelard seems to revel in himself and boast a great deal. But actually he did not write about his calamities in order to boast. Rather, his main intention was to moralize about how he had been appropriately punished for his intellectual pride by his first condemnation and for his "lechery" by the loss of those parts which had "offended." Abelard certainly represents a reawakening interest in personal introspection, but in this he did not differ much from St. Augustine. More important is the fact that he was the first westerner who sought to make a full profession out of the life of the mind.

Abelard's greatest contributions to the subsequent development of Scholasticism were made in his *Sic et Non* (Yes and No) and in a number of original theological works. In the *Sic et Non* Abelard prepared the way for the Scholastic method by gathering a collection of statements from the church fathers that spoke for both sides of 150 theological questions. It used to be thought that the brash Abelard did this in order to embarrass authority, but the contrary is true. What Abelard really hoped to do was begin a process of careful study whereby it could be shown that the highest authority of the Bible was infallible and that the best authorities, despite any appearances to the contrary, really agreed with each other. Later Scholastics would follow his method of studying theology by raising fundamental questions and arraying the answers that had been put forth in authoritative texts. Abelard did not propose any solutions of his own in the *Sic et Non,* but he did start to do this in his original theological writings. In these he proposed to treat theology like a science, by studying it as comprehensively as possible and by applying to it the tools of logic, of which he was a master. He did not even shrink from applying logic to the mystery of the Trinity, one of the excesses for which he was condemned. Thus he was one of the first to try to harmonize religion with rationalism and was in this capacity a herald of the Scholastic outlook.

Immediately after Abelard's death two further steps were taken to prepare for mature Scholasticism. One was the writing of the *Book of Sentences* between 1155 and 1157 by Abelard's student Peter Lombard. This raised all the most fundamental theological questions in rigorously consequential order, adduced answers from the Bible and Christian authorities on both sides of each question, and then proposed a judgment on every case. By the thirteenth century Peter Lombard's work became a standard text. Once formal schools of theology were established in the universities, all aspirants to the doctorate were required to study and comment upon it; not surprisingly, theologians also followed its organizational procedures in their own writings. Thus the full Scholastic method was born.

Peter Lombard's Book of Sentences

Peter Lombard

The other basic step in the development of Scholasticism, as mentioned above, was the reacquisition of classical philosophy that occurred after about 1140. Abelard would probably have been glad to have drawn upon the thought of the Greeks, but he could not because few Greek works were yet available in translation. Later theologians, however, could avail themselves fully of the new knowledge, above all, the works of Aristotle and his Arabic commentators. By around 1250 Aristotle's authority in purely philosophical matters became so great that he was referred to as "the Philosopher" pure and simple. Scholastics of the mid–thirteenth century accordingly adhered to Peter Lombard's organizational method, but added the consideration of Greek and Arabic philosophical authorities to that of purely Christian theological ones. In doing this they tried to construct systems of understanding the entire universe that most fully harmonized the earlier separate realms of faith and natural knowledge.

Influence of Aristotle

By far the greatest accomplishments in this endeavor were made by St. Thomas Aquinas (1225–1274), the leading Scholastic theologian of the University of Paris. As a member of the Dominican order, St. Thomas was committed to the principle that faith could be defended by reason. More important, he believed that natural knowledge and the study of the created universe were legitimate ways of approaching theological wisdom because "nature" complements "grace." By this he meant to say that because God created the natural world He can be

St. Thomas Aquinas

St. Thomas Aquinas. A fifteenth-century painting by Justus of Ghent, after an earlier copy.

The achievements of the thirteenth century

approached through its terms even though ultimate certainty about the highest truths can only be obtained through the supernatural revelation of the Bible. Imbued with a deep confidence in the value of human reason and human experience, as well as in his own ability to harmonize Greek philosophy with Christian theology, Thomas was the most serene of saints. In a long career of teaching at the University of Paris and elsewhere he indulged in few controversies and worked quietly on his two great *Summaries* of theology: the *Summa contra Gentiles* and the much larger *Summa Theologica.* In these he hoped to set down all that could be said about the faith on the firmest of foundations.

Most experts think that St. Thomas came extremely close to fulfilling this extraordinarily ambitious goal. His vast *Summaries* are awesome for their rigorous orderliness and intellectual penetration. He admits in them that there are certain "mysteries of the faith," such as the doctrines of the Trinity and the Incarnation, that cannot be approached by the unaided human intellect; otherwise, he subjects all theological questions to philosophical inquiry. In this, St. Thomas relied heavily on the work of Aristotle, but he is by no means merely "Aristotle baptized." Instead, he fully subordinated Aristotelianism to basic Christian principles and thereby created his own original philosophical and theological system. Scholars disagree about how far this system diverges from the earlier Christian thought of St. Augustine, but there seems little doubt that Aquinas placed a higher value on human reason, on human life in this world, and on the abilities of humans to participate in their own salvation. Not long after his death St. Thomas was canonized, for his intellectual accomplishments seemed like miracles. His influence lives on today insofar as he helped to revive confidence in rationalism and human experience. More directly, philosophy in the modern Roman Catholic Church is supposed to be taught according to the Thomistic method, doctrine, and principles.

With the achievements of St. Thomas Aquinas in the middle of the thirteenth century, Western medieval thought reached its pinnacle. Not coincidentally, other aspects of medieval civilization were reaching their pinnacles at the same time. France was enjoying its ripest period of peace and prosperity under the rule of St. Louis, the University of Paris was defining its basic organizational forms, and the greatest French Gothic cathedrals were being built. Some ardent admirers of medieval culture have fixed on these accomplishments to call the thirteenth the "greatest of centuries." Such a judgment, of course, is a matter of taste, and many might respond that life was still too harsh and requirements for religious orthodoxy too great to justify this extreme celebration of the lost past. Whatever our individual judgments, it seems wise to end this section by correcting some false impressions about medieval intellectual life.

It is often thought that medieval thinkers were excessively conservative, but in fact the greatest thinkers of the High Middle Ages were astonishingly receptive to new ideas. As committed Christians they could not allow doubts to be cast upon the principles of their faith, but otherwise they were glad to accept whatever they could from the Greeks and Arabs. Considering that Aristotelian thought differed radically from anything accepted earlier in its emphasis on rationalism and the fundamental goodness and purposefulness of nature, its rapid acceptance by the Scholastics was a philosophical revolution. Another false impression is that Scholastic thinkers were greatly constrained by authority. Certainly they revered authority more than we do today, but Scholastics like St. Thomas did not regard the mere citation of texts—except biblical revelation concerning the mysteries of the faith—as being sufficient to clinch an argument. Rather, the authorities were brought forth to outline the possibilities, but reason and experience then demonstrated the truth. Finally, it is often believed that Scholastic thinkers were "antihumanistic," but modern scholars are coming to the opposite conclusion. Scholastics unquestionably gave primacy to the soul over the body and to the otherworldly salvation over life in the here and now. But they also exalted the dignity of human nature because they viewed it as a glorious divine creation, and they believed in the possibility of a working alliance between themselves and God. Moreover, they had extraordinary faith in the powers of human reason—probably more than we do today.

False impressions concerning Scholastic thinkers

5. THE BLOSSOMING OF LITERATURE, ART, AND MUSIC

The literature of the High Middle Ages was as varied, lively, and impressive as that produced in any other period in Western history. The revival of grammatical studies in the cathedral schools and universities led to the production of some excellent Latin poetry. The best examples were secular lyrics, especially those written in the twelfth century by a group of poets known as the Goliards. How these poets got their name is uncertain, but it possibly meant followers of the devil. That would have been appropriate because the Goliards were riotous poets who wrote parodies of the liturgy and burlesques of the Gospels. Their lyrics celebrated the beauties of the changing seasons, the carefree life of the open road, the pleasures of drinking and sporting, and especially the joys of love. The authors of these rollicking and satirical songs were mainly wandering students, although some were men in more advanced years. The names of most are unknown. Their poetry is particularly significant both for its robust vitality and for being the first clear counterstatement to the ascetic ideal of Christianity.

Medieval Latin literature; the poetry of the Goliards

Charlemagne Weeping for His Knights. A scene from the *Song of Roland.*

In addition to the use of Latin, the vernacular languages of French, German, Spanish, and Italian became increasingly popular as media of literary expression. At first, most of the literature in the vernacular languages was written in the form of the heroic epic. Among the leading examples were the French *Song of Roland,* the Norse eddas and sagas, the German *Song of the Nibelungs,* and the Spanish *Poem of the Cid.* Practically all of these works were originally composed between 1050 and 1150, although some were first set down in writing afterward. These epics portrayed a virile but unpolished warrior society. Blood flowed freely, skulls were cleaved by battleaxes, and heroic warfare, honor, and loyalty were the major themes. If women were mentioned at all, they were subordinate to men. Brides were expected to die for their betrotheds, but husbands were free to beat their wives. In one French epic a queen who tried to influence her husband met with a blow to the nose; even though blood flowed she replied: "Many thanks, when it pleases you, you may do it again." Despite the repugnance we find in such passages, the best of the vernacular epics have much unpretentious literary power. Above all, the *Song of Roland,* though crude, is like an uncut gem.

In comparison to the epics, an enormous change in both subject matter and style was introduced in twelfth-century France by the troubadour poets and the writers of courtly romances. The dramatic nature of this change represents further proof that high-medieval culture was not at all conservative. The troubadours were courtier poets who came from southern France and wrote in a language related to French known as Provençal. The origin of their inspiration is debated, but there can be no doubt that they initiated a movement of profound importance for all subsequent Western literature. Their style was far more finely wrought and sophisticated than that of the epic poets, and the most eloquent of their lyrics, which were meant to be sung to music, originated the theme of romantic love. The troubadours idealized women as marvelous beings who could grant intense spiritual and sensual gratification. Whatever greatness the poets found in themselves they usually attributed to the inspiration they found in love. But they also assumed that their love would lose its magic if it were too easily or frequently gratified. Therefore, they wrote more often of longing than of romantic fulfillment.

In addition to their love lyrics, the troubadours wrote several other kinds of short poems. Some were simply bawdy. In these, love is not mentioned at all, but the poet revels in thoughts of carnality, comparing, for example, the riding of his horse to the "riding" of his mistress. Other troubadour poems treat of feats of arms, others comment on contemporary political events, and a few even meditate on matters of religion. But whatever the subject matter, the best troubadour poems were always cleverly and innovatively expressed. The literary tradition originated by the southern French troubadours was continued by the *trouvères* in northern France and by the *minnesingers* in Germany. Thereafter many of their innovations were developed by later lyric poets in all Western languages. Some of their poetic devices were consciously revived in the twentieth century by such "modernists" as Ezra Pound.

Other troubadour poems

An equally important twelfth-century French innovation was the composition of longer narrative poems known as romances. These were the first clear ancestors of the modern novel: they told engaging stories, they often excelled in portraying character, and their subject matter was usually love and adventure. Some romances elaborated on classical Greek themes, but the most famous and best were "Arthurian." These took their material from the legendary exploits of the Celtic hero King Arthur and his many chivalrous knights. The first great writer of Arthurian romances was the northern Frenchman Chrétien de Troyes, who was active between about 1165 and 1190. Chrétien did much to help create and shape the new form, and he also introduced innovations in subject matter and attitudes. Whereas the troubadours exalted unrequited, extramarital love, Chrétien was the first to hold forth the ideal of romantic love within marriage. He also described not only the deeds but the thoughts and emotions of his characters.

The Arthurian romances; Chrétien de Troyes

A generation later, Chrétien's work was continued by the great German poets Wolfram von Eschenbach and Gottfried von Strassburg. These are recognized as the greatest writers in the German language before the eighteenth century. Wolfram's *Parzival,* a story of love and the search for the Holy Grail, is more subtle, complex, and greater in scope than any other high-medieval literary work except Dante's *Divine Comedy.* Like Chrétien, Wolfram believed that true love could only be fulfilled in marriage, and in *Parzival,* for the first time in West-

A Thirteenth-Century Miniature. From a manuscript of Wolfram von Eschenbach's *Parzival.*

*Wolfram von Eschenbach
and Gottfried von
Strassburg*

ern literature since the Greeks, one can see a full psychological development of the hero. Gottfried von Strassburg's *Tristan* is a more somber work, which tells of the hopeless adulterous love of Tristan and Isolde. Indeed, it might almost be regarded as the prototype of modern tragic romanticism. Gottfried was one of the first to develop fully the idea of individual suffering as a literary theme and to point out the indistinct line which separates pleasure from pain. For him, to love is to yearn, and suffering and unfulfilled gratification are integral chapters of the book of life. Unlike the troubadours, he could only see complete fulfillment of love in death. *Parzival* and *Tristan* have become most famous today in the form of their operatic reconceptions by the nineteenth-century German composer Richard Wagner.

The fabliaux

Not all high-medieval narratives were so elevated as the romances in either form or substance. A very different new narrative form was the *fabliau,* or verse fable. Although *fabliaux* derived from the moral animal tales of Aesop, they quickly evolved into short stories that were written less to edify or instruct than to amuse. Often they were very coarse, and sometimes they dealt with sexual relations in a broadly humorous and thoroughly unromantic manner. Many were also strongly anticlerical, making monks and priests the butts of their jokes. Because the *fabliaux* are so "uncourtly" it used to be thought that they were written solely for the new urban classes. But there is now little doubt that they were addressed at least equally to the "refined" aristocracy who liked to have their laughs too. They are significant as expressions of growing worldliness and as the first manifestations of the robust realism which was later to be perfected by Boccaccio and Chaucer.

Completely different in form but similar as an illustration of growing worldliness was the sprawling *Romance of the Rose.* As its title indicates, this was begun as a romance, specifically around 1230 by the courtly Frenchman William of Lorris. But William left his rather flowery, romantic work unfinished, and it was completed around 1270 by another Frenchman, John of Meun. The latter changed its nature greatly. He inserted long, biting digressions in which he skewered religious hypocrisy, and made his major theme the need for procreation. Not love, but the service of "Dame Nature" in sexual fecundity is urged in numerous witty but extremely earthy images and metaphors. At the climax the originally dreamy hero seizes his mistress, who is allegorically depicted as a rose, and rapes her. Since the work became enormously popular, it seems fair to conclude that tastes, then as now, were very diverse.

Nature Perpetuates the Species. A miniature from a manuscript of the *Romance of the Rose.*

In a class by itself as the greatest work of medieval literature is Dante's *Divine Comedy.* Not much is known about the life of Dante Alighieri (1265–1321), except that he was active during the early part of his career in the political affairs of his native city of Florence. Despite his engagement in politics and the fact that he was a layman, he managed to acquire an awesome mastery of the religious, philosophic, and literary knowledge of his time. He not only knew the Bible and the church fathers, but—most unusual for a layman—he also absorbed the most recent Scholastic theology. In addition, he was thoroughly familiar with Virgil, Cicero, Boethius, and numerous other classical writers, and was fully conversant with the poems of the troubadours and the Italian poetry of his own day. In 1302 he was expelled from Florence after a political upheaval and was forced to live the rest of his life in exile. The *Divine Comedy,* his major work, was written during this final period.

Dante's *Divine Comedy* is a monumental narrative in powerful rhyming Italian verse, which describes the poet's journey through hell, purgatory, and paradise. At the start Dante tells of how he once found himself in a "dark wood," his metaphor for a deep personal mid-life crisis. He is led out of this forest of despair by the Roman Virgil, who stands for the heights of classical reason and philosophy. Virgil guides Dante on a trip through hell and purgatory, and afterward Dante's deceased beloved, Beatrice, who stands for Christian wisdom and blessedness, takes over and guides him through paradise. In the course of this progress Dante meets both historical beings and the poet's contemporaries, all of whom have already been assigned places in the afterlife, and he is instructed by them and his guides as to why they met their several fates. As the poem progresses the poet himself leaves the condition of despair to grow in wisdom and ultimately to reach assurance of his own salvation.

The Divine Comedy

Every reader finds a different combination of wonder and satisfaction in Dante's magnificent work. Some—especially those who know Italian—marvel at the vigor and inventiveness of Dante's language and images. Others are awed by his subtle complexity and poetic symmetry; others by his array of learning; others by the vitality of his characters and individual stories; and still others by his soaring imagination. The historian finds it particularly remarkable that Dante could sum up the best of medieval learning in such an artistically satisfying manner. Dante stressed the precedence of salvation, but he viewed the earth as existing for human benefit. He allowed humans free will to choose good and avoid evil, and accepted Greek philosophy as authoritative in its own sphere; for example, he called Aristotle "the master of them that know." Above all, his sense of hope and his ultimate faith in humanity—remarkable for a defeated exile—most powerfully expresses the dominant mood of the High Middle Ages and makes Dante one of the two or three most stirringly affirmative writers who ever lived.

Quarter Barrel Vaults, Typical of Romanesque Architecture. St. Etienne, Nevers.

The closest architectural equivalents of the *Divine Comedy* are the great high-medieval Gothic cathedrals, for they too have qualities of vast scope, balance of intricate detail with careful symmetry, soaring height, and affirmative religious grandeur. But before we approach the Gothic style, it is best to introduce it by means of its high-medieval predecessor, the style of architecture and art known as the Roman-

Medieval architecture: (1) *the Romanesque style*

Romanesque Sculpture. Shown here is Jesus with two of his Apostles. The elongation and distortion is typical. From a church in Spain.

esque. This style had its origins in the tenth century, but became fully formed in the eleventh and first half of the twelfth centuries, when the religious reform movement led to the building of many new monasteries and large churches. The Romanesque was primarily a building style: it aimed to manifest the glory of God in ecclesiastical construction by rigorously subordinating all architectural details to a uniform system. In this it was very severe: we may think of it as the architectural analogue of the unadorned hymn. Aside from its primary stress on systematic construction, the essential features of the Romanesque style were the rounded arch, massive stone walls, enormous piers, small windows, and the predominance of horizontal lines. The plainness of interiors was sometimes relieved by mosaics or frescoes in bright colors, and, a very important innovation for Christian art, the introduction of sculptural decoration, both within and without. For the first time, full-length human figures appeared on facades. These are usually grave and elongated far beyond natural dimensions, but they have much evocative power and represent the first manifestations of a revived interest in sculpting the human form.

In the course of the twelfth and thirteenth centuries the Romanesque style was supplanted throughout most of Europe by the Gothic. Although trained art historians can see how certain traits of the one style led to the development of the other, the actual appearance of the two styles is enormously different. In fact, the two seem as different as the epic is different from the romance, an appropriate analogy because the Gothic style emerged in France in the mid–twelfth century exactly when the romance did, and because it was far more sophisticated,

Worms Cathedral, Eleventh-Century Romanesque

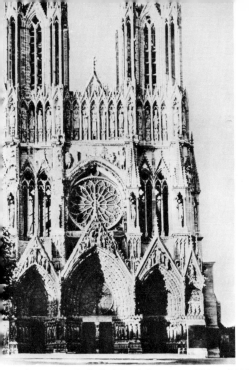

Left: *Rheims Cathedral.* Built between 1220 and 1299, this High Gothic cathedral places great stress on the vertical elements. The gabled portals, the windows above the doorways, the gallery of royal statues, and the multitude of pinnacles all accentuate the height of the structue. Right: *The High Chapel of La Sainte-Chapelle, Paris.* High Gothic is here carried to its logical extreme. Slender columns, tracery, and stained-glass windows take the place of walls.

graceful, and elegant than its predecessor, in the same way that the romance compared with the epic. The rapid development and acceptance of the Gothic shows for a last time—if any more proof be needed—that the twelfth century was experimental and dynamic, arguably at least as much as the twentieth. When the abbey church of St. Denis, venerated as the shrine of the French patron saint and burial place of French kings, was torn down in 1144 in order to make room for a much larger one in the strikingly new Gothic style, it was as if the president of the United States were to tear down the White House and replace it with a Mies van der Rohe or Frank Lloyd Wright edifice. Such an act today would be highly improbable, or at least would create an enormous uproar. But in the twelfth century the equivalent actually happened and was taken in stride.

Gothic architecture was one of the most intricate of building styles. Its basic elements were the pointed arch, groined and ribbed vaulting, and the flying buttress. These devices made possible a much lighter and loftier construction than could ever have been achieved with the round arch and the engaged pier of the Romanesque. In fact, the Gothic cathedral could be described as a skeletal framework of stone enclosed by enormous windows. Other features included lofty spires,

(2) the development of the Gothic style

Elements of the Gothic style

Gothic Sculpture. The three kings bearing gifts, from the thirteenth-century cathedral of Amiens. Note the greater naturalism in comparison to the Romanesque sculpture shown on p. 362.

rose windows, delicate tracery in stone, elaborately sculptured facades, multiple columns, and the use of gargoyles, or representations of mythical monsters, as decorative devices. Ornamentation in the best of the cathedrals was generally concentrated on the exterior. Except for the stained-glass windows and the intricate carving on woodwork and altars, interiors were kept rather simple and occasionally almost severe. But the inside of the Gothic cathedral was never somber or gloomy. The stained-glass windows served not to exclude the light but to glorify it, to catch the rays of sunlight and suffuse them with a richness and warmth of color which nature itself could hardly duplicate even in its happiest moods.

Many people still think of the Gothic cathedral as the expression of purely ascetic otherworldliness, but this estimation is highly inaccurate. Certainly all churches are dedicated to the glory of God and hope for life everlasting, but Gothic ones sometimes included stained-glass scenes of daily life that had no overt religious significance at all. More important, Gothic sculpture of religious figures such as Jesus, the Virgin, and the saints was becoming far more naturalistic than anything hitherto created in the medieval West. So also was the sculptural representation of plant and animal life, for interest in the human person and in the world of natural beauty was no longer considered sinful. Moreover, Gothic architecture was also an expression of the medieval intellectual genius. Each cathedral, with its mass of symbolic figures, was a kind of encyclopedia of medieval knowledge carved in stone for

The significance of Gothic architecture

See color plates facing page 352

those who could not read. Finally, Gothic cathedrals were manifestations of urban pride. Always located in the growing medieval cities, they were meant to be both centers of community life and expressions of a town's greatness. When a new cathedral went up the people of the entire community participated in erecting it, and rightfully regarded it as almost their own property. Many of the Gothic cathedrals were the products of urban rivalries. Each city or town sought to overawe its neighbor with ever bigger or taller buildings, to the degree that ambitions sometimes got out of bounds and many of the cathedrals were left unfinished. But most of the finished ones are still vast enough. Built to last into eternity, they provide the most striking visual manifestation of the soaring exuberance of their age.

Surveys of high-medieval accomplishments often omit drama and music, but such oversights are unfortunate. Our own modern drama descends at least as much from the medieval form as from the classical one. Throughout the medieval period some Latin classical plays were known in manuscript but were never performed. Instead drama was born all over again within the Church. In the early Middle Ages certain passages in the liturgy began to be acted out. Then, in the twelfth century, primarily in Paris, these were superseded by short religious plays in Latin, performed inside the Church. Rapidly thereafter, and still in twelfth-century Paris, the Latin plays were supplemented or supplanted by ones in the vernacular so that the whole congregation could understand them. Then, around 1200, these started to be performed outside, in front of the Church, so that they would not take time away from the services. As soon as that happened, drama entered the everyday world: nonreligious stories were introduced, character portrayal was expanded, and the way was fully prepared for the Elizabethans and Shakespeare.

As the drama grew out of developments within the liturgy and then moved far beyond them, so did characteristically Western music. Until the High Middle Ages Western music was *homophonic,* as is most non-Western music even today. That is, it developed only one melody at a time without any harmonic background. The great high-medieval invention was *polyphony,* or the playing of two or more harmonious melodies together. Some experiments along these lines may have been made in the West as early as the tenth century, but the most fundamental breakthrough was achieved in the cathedral of Paris around 1170, when the Mass was first sung by two voices weaving together two different melodies in "counterpoint." Roughly concurrently, systems of musical notation were invented and perfected so that performance no longer had to rely on memory and could become more complex. All the greatness of Western music followed from these first steps.

It may have been noticed that many of the same people who made such important contributions to learning, thought, literature, architecture, drama, and music, must have intermingled with each other in

The revival of drama

Medieval music: polyphony

the Paris of the High Middle Ages. Some of them no doubt prayed together in the cathedral of Notre Dame. The names of the leading scholars are remembered, but the names of most of the others are forgotten. Yet taken together they did as much for civilization and created as many enduring monuments as their counterparts in ancient Athens. If their names are forgotten, their achievements in many different ways live on still.

SELECTED READINGS

• *Items so designated are available in paperback editions.*

RELIGION AND THE CRUSADES

• Barraclough, G., *The Medieval Papacy,* New York, 1968. A forcefully argued analytical treatment. Noteworthy too for its illustrations.

Daniel-Rops, H., *Cathedral and Crusade,* 2 vols., New York, 1963. The best survey from a Roman Catholic perspective.

Erdmann, Carl, *The Origin of the Idea of Crusade,* Princeton, N.J., 1978. A brilliant advanced work on the background to the First Crusade.

Lambert, Malcolm, *Medieval Heresy,* London, 1977. A masterful synthesis.

Leclercq, Jean, *Bernard of Clairvaux and the Cistercian Spirit,* Kalamazoo, Mich., 1976.

• Mayer, Hans Eberhard, *The Crusades,* New York, 1972. The best one-volume survey.

Moorman, J. R. H., *A History of the Franciscan Order from its Origins to the Year 1517,* Oxford, 1968. Exhaustive.

Runciman, S., *A History of the Crusades,* 3 vols., Cambridge, 1951–54. Colorful and engrossing.

Southern, R. W., *Western Society and the Church in the Middle Ages,* Baltimore, 1970. An extremely insightful and well-written interpretation of the interplay between society and religion.

Tellenbach, G., *Church, State and Christian Society at the Time of the Investiture Contest,* Oxford, 1940. Stresses revolutionary aspects of Gregory VII's thought and career.

Ullmann, Walter, *A Short History of the Papacy in the Middle Ages,* 2nd ed., London, 1974.

THOUGHT, LETTERS, AND THE ARTS

• Baldwin, John W., *The Scholastic Culture of the Middle Ages,* Lexington, Mass., 1971. A fine introduction.

Bergin, T. G., *Dante,* New York, 1965.

Chenu, M. D., *Toward Understanding St. Thomas,* Chicago, 1964. An excellent approach to St. Thomas's work by a contemporary Dominican.

Cobban, Alan B., *The Medieval Universities,* London, 1975. The best shorter treatment in English.

Curtius, E. R., *European Literature and the Latin Middle Ages,* New York, 1953. An exhaustive treatment of medieval Latin literature in terms of its classical background and influence on later times.

Frankl, P., *Gothic Architecture*, Baltimore, 1962.

• Gilson, E., *Reason and Revelation in the Middle Ages*, New York, 1938. A brief but illuminating treatment by the greatest modern student of Scholasticism.

• Haskins, C. H., *The Renaissance of the Twelfth Century*, Cambridge, Mass., 1927. Treats Latin writings in many different genres.

• Henderson, George, *Gothic*, Baltimore, 1967.

Holmes, Urban T., *A History of Old French Literature*, 2nd ed., London, 1948.

Hoppin, Richard H., *Medieval Music*, New York, 1978.

• Knowles, David, *The Evolution of Medieval Thought*, New York, 1962. A very authoritative and well-written but often difficult survey.

Leclercq, Jean, *The Love of Learning and the Desire for God*, New York, 1961. About monastic culture, with special reference to St. Bernard.

Leff, G., *Paris and Oxford Universities in the Thirteenth and Fourteenth Centuries*, New York, 1968. Covers both thought and institutions of learning.

• Lewis, C. S., *The Discarded Image*, Cambridge, 1964.

• Lindberg, David C., ed., *Science in the Middle Ages*, Chicago, 1978. A collection of introductory essays by leading authorities in their respective fields.

• Mâle, E., *The Gothic Image*, New York, 1913.

• Morris, Colin, *The Discovery of the Individual*, London, 1972. A provocative interpretation which sees "individualism" as a twelfth-century discovery.

Southern, R. W., *Medieval Humanism*, New York, 1970. A collection of essays, almost all of which are exciting. Most exciting is the title piece.

Ullmann, W., *Medieval Political Thought*, rev. ed., Baltimore, 1976. The best short survey.

Van Steenberghen, F., *Aristotle in the West*, New York, 1970. A short account of the recovery of Aristotelian thought in the High Middle Ages.

• Von Simson, O., *The Gothic Cathedral*, New York, 1956. A controversial argument that Gothic architecture was meant to be "scientific."

SOURCE MATERIALS

• *An Aquinas Reader*, ed. Mary T. Clark, New York, 1972.

• Chrétien de Troyes, *Arthurian Romances*, tr. W. W. Comfort, New York, 1914.

• Dante, *The Divine Comedy*, tr. J. Ciardi, New York, 1977.

• Goldin, F., ed., *Lyrics of the Troubadours and Trouvères*, New York, 1973.

• Gottfried von Strassburg, *Tristan*, tr. A. T. Hatto, Baltimore, 1960.

• Joinville and Villehardouin, *Chronicles of the Crusades*, tr. M. R. B. Shaw, Baltimore, 1963.

• *The Letters of Abelard and Heloise* (includes Abelard's *Story of My Calamities*), tr. B. Radice, Baltimore, 1974.

• Peters, Edward, ed., *The First Crusade: The Chronicle of Fulcher of Chartres and Other Source Materials*, Philadelphia, 1971.

The Romance of the Rose, tr. Harry W. Robbins, New York, 1962.

- *The Song of Roland,* tr. F. Goldin, New York, 1978.
- Thorndike, Lynn, ed., *University Records and Life in the Middle Ages,* New York, 1944.
- Tierney, Brian, ed., *The Crisis of Church and State, 1050–1300,* Englewood Cliffs, N.J., 1964. An excellent anthology of readings introduced and connected by masterful commentary.
- Wolfram von Eschenbach, *Parzival,* tr. H. M. Mustard and C. E. Passage, New York, 1961.

Chapter 13

THE LATER MIDDLE AGES
(1300–1500)

My lot has been to live amidst a storm
Of varying disturbing circumstances.
For you . . . a better age awaits.
Our descendants—the darkness once dispersed—
Can come again to the old radiance.

> —The poet Petrarch,
> writing in the 1340s

I f the High Middle Ages were "times of feasts," then the late Middle Ages were "times of famine." From about 1300 until the
middle or latter part of the fifteenth century calamities struck
throughout western Europe with appalling severity and dismaying
persistence. Famine first prevailed because agriculture was impeded
by soil exhaustion, colder weather, and torrential rainfalls. Then, on
top of those "acts of God," came the most terrible natural disaster of
all: the dreadful plague known as the "Black Death," which cut broad
swaths of mortality throughout western Europe. As if all that were
not enough, incessant warfare continually brought hardship and desolation. Common people suffered most because they were most exposed to raping, stabbing, looting, and burning by soldiers and organized bands of freebooters. After an army passed through a region one
might see miles of smoldering ruins littered with putrefying corpses;
in many places the desolation was so great that wolves roamed the
countryside and even entered the outskirts of the cities. In short, if the
serene Virgin symbolized the High Middle Ages, the grinning
death's-head symbolized the succeeding period. For these reasons we
should not look to the later Middle Ages for the dramatic progress we
saw transpiring earlier; but this is not to say that there was no progress
at all. In the last two centuries of the Middle Ages Europeans dis-

*The later Middle Ages:
catastrophe and adaptation*

played a tenacious perseverance in the face of adversity. Instead of abandoning themselves to apathy, they resolutely sought to adjust themselves to changed circumstances. Thus there was no collapse of civilization as there was with the fall of the Roman Empire, but rather a period of transition that resulted in preserving and building upon what was most solid in Europe's earlier legacy.

1. ECONOMIC DEPRESSION AND THE EMERGENCE OF A NEW EQUILIBRIUM

Economic crisis

By around 1300 the agricultural expansion of the High Middle Ages had reached its limits. Thereafter yields and areas under cultivation began to decline, causing a decline in the whole European economy that was accelerated by the disruptive effects of war. Accordingly, the first half of the fourteenth century was a time of growing economic depression. The coming of the Black Death in 1347 made this depression particularly acute because it completely disrupted the affairs of daily life. Subsequent recurrences of the plague and protracted warfare continued to depress most of the European economy until deep into the fifteenth century. But between roughly 1350 and 1450 Europeans learned how to adjust to the new economic circumstances and succeeded in placing their economy on a sounder basis. This became most evident after around 1450, when the tapering off of disease and warfare permitted a slow, but steady economic recovery. All told, therefore, despite a prolonged depression of roughly 150 years, Europe emerged in the later fifteenth century with a healthier economy than it had known earlier.

Agricultural adversity

The limits to agricultural expansion reached around 1300 were natural ones. There was a limit to the amount of land that could be cleared and a limit to the amount of crops that could be raised without the introduction of scientific farming. In fact, Europeans had gone further in clearing and cultivating than they should have: in the enthusiasm of the high-medieval colonization movement, marginal lands had been cleared that were not rich enough to sustain intense cultivation. In addition, even the best plots were becoming overworked. To make matters worse, after around 1300 the weather deteriorated. Whereas western Europe had been favored with a drying and warming trend in the eleventh and twelfth centuries, in the fourteenth century the climate became colder and wetter. Although the average decline in temperature over the course of the century was only at most 1° Centigrade, this was sufficient to curtail viticulture in many northern areas such as England. Cereal farming too became increasingly impractical in far northern regions because the growing season became too short: in Greenland and parts of Scandinavia agricultural settlements were abandoned entirely. Increased rainfall also took its toll.

Terrible floods that deluged all of northwestern Europe in 1315 ruined crops and caused a prolonged, deadly famine. For three years peasants were so driven by hunger that they ate their seed grain, ruining their chances for a full recovery in the following season. In desperation they also ate cats, dogs, and rats. Many peasants were so exposed to unsanitary conditions and weakened by malnutrition that they became highly susceptible to disease. Thus there was an appalling death rate. In one Flemish city a tenth of the population was buried within a six-month period of 1316 alone. Relatively settled farming conditions returned after 1318, but in many parts of Europe heavy rains or other climatic disasters came again. In Italy floods swept away Florentine bridges in 1333 and a tidal wave destroyed the port of Amalfi in 1343. With nature so recurrently capricious economic life could only suffer.

Although ruinous wars combined with famine to kill off many, Europe remained overpopulated until the middle of the fourteenth century. The reason for this was that population growth was still outstripping food supply. Since people continued to multiply while cereal production declined, there was just not enough food to go around. Accordingly, grain prices soared and the poor throughout Europe paid the penalty in hunger. And then a disaster struck which was so appalling that it seemed to many to presage the end of the world.

This was the Black Death, a combined onslaught of bubonic and pneumonic plague which first swept through Europe from 1347 to 1350, and returned at periodic intervals for roughly the next hundred years. This calamity was fully comparable—in terms of the death, dislocation, and horror it wrought—to the two world wars of the twentieth century. The clinical effects of the plague were hideous. Once infected with bubonic plague by a flea-bite, the diseased person would develop enormous swellings in the groin or armpits; black spots might appear on the arms and legs, diarrhea would ensue, and the victim would die between the third and fifth day. If the infection came in the pneumonic form, i.e., caused by inhalation, there would be coughing of blood instead of swellings, and death would follow within three days. Some people went to bed healthy and were dead the next morning after a night of agony; ships with dead crews floated aimlessly on the seas. Although the successive epidemics left a few localities unscathed, the overall demographic effects of the plague were devastating. To take just a few examples: the population of Toulouse declined from roughly 30,000 in 1335, to 26,000 in 1385, to 8,000 in 1430; the total population of eastern Normandy fell by 30 percent between 1347 and 1357, and again by 30 percent before 1380; in the rural area around Pistoia a population depletion of about 60 percent occurred between 1340 and 1404. Altogether, the combined effects of famine, war, and, above all, plague reduced the total population of western Europe by at least one half and probably more like two-thirds between 1300 and 1450.

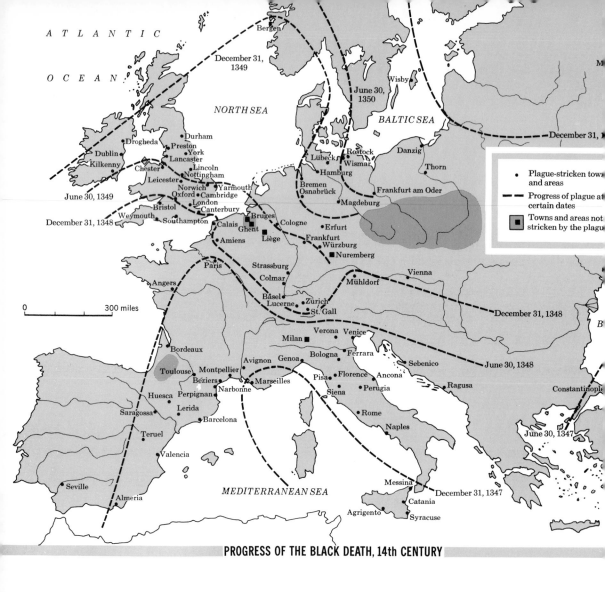

ATLANTIC

OCEAN

NORTH SEA

Bergen

December 31,
1349

June 30,
1350

Wisby

BALTIC SEA

December 31,

Durham
Drogheda
Preston
Dublin
York
Kilkenny
Lancaster
Chester
Lincoln
Leicester
Nottingham
Norwich
Oxford
Yarmouth
Cambridge
London
Bristol
Canterbury
Weymouth
Southampton
Calais
Ghent
Bruges
Cologne
Amiens
Liège

Rostock
Lübeck
Wismar
Danzig
Hamburg
Thorn
Bremen
Osnabrück
Magdeburg
Frankfurt am Oder

June 30, 1349

December 31, 1348

Erfurt
Frankfurt
Würzburg
Nuremberg

Paris
Strassburg
Colmar
Vienna
Angers
Bâsel
Lucerne
Zürich
St. Gall
Mühldorf

0   300 miles

December 31, 1348

B

Bordeaux
Milan
Verona
Venice
Toulouse
Avignon
Genoa
Bologna
Ferrara
Montpellier
Béziers
Pisa
Florence
Ancona
Sebenico
Marseilles
Perpignan
Narbonne
Siena
Perugia
Ragusa
Huesca
Lerida
Rome
Saragossa
Barcelona
Naples
Teruel

June 30, 1348

Constantinople

June 30, 1347

Valencia

Seville

Almeria

MEDITERRANEAN SEA

Messina
Catania
Agrigento
Syracuse

December 31, 1347

Legend:
- Plague-stricken town and areas
- - - Progress of plague at certain dates
▪ Towns and areas not stricken by the plague

PROGRESS OF THE BLACK DEATH, 14th CENTURY

The Black Death disrupts society and economy

At first, the Black Death caused great hardships for most of the survivors. Since panic-stricken people wished to avoid contagion, many fled from their jobs to seek isolation. Town-dwellers fled to the country and country-dwellers fled from each other. Even the pope retreated to the interior of his palace and allowed no one entrance. With large numbers dead and others away from their posts, harvests were left rotting, manufacturing was disrupted, and conveyance systems were abandoned. Hence basic commodities became scarcer and prices rose. For these reasons the onslaught of the plague greatly intensified Europe's economic crisis.

But after around 1400 the new demographic realities began to turn prices around and alter basic economic patterns. Particularly, the prices of staple foodstuffs began to decline because production gradually returned to normal and there were fewer mouths to feed. Recurrent reappearances of the plague or natural disasters sometimes caused prices to fluctuate greatly in certain years, but overall prices of basic commodities throughout most of the fifteenth century went down or remained stable. This trend led to new agricultural specialization. Since cereals were cheaper, people could afford to spend a greater percentage of their income on comparative luxuries such as dairy products, meat, and wine. Hitherto farmers all over Europe had concentrated on cereals because bread was the staff of life, but now it was wisest, particularly in areas of poorer soil or unpropitious climate, to shift to specialized production. Depending upon whatever seemed most feasible, land might be used for the raising of livestock for milk, grapes for wine, or malt for beer. Specialized regional economies resulted: parts of England were given over to sheep-raising or beer production, parts of France concentrated on wine, and Sweden traded butter for cheap German grain. Most areas of Europe turned to what they could do best, and reciprocal trade of basic commodities over long distances created a sound new commercial equilibrium.

Another economic result of the Black Death was an increase in the relative importance of towns and cities. Urban manufacturers usually could respond more flexibly than landlords to drastically changed economic conditions because their production capabilities were more elastic. When markets shrank, manufacturers could cut back supply more easily to match demand; they could also raise production more easily when circumstances warranted. Thus urban entrepreneurs bounced back from disaster more quickly than landowners. Often they took advantage of their greater strength to attract rural labor by

Economic consequences of the Black Death: (1) agricultural specialization

(2) the growth in importance of urban centers

A Late-Medieval Funeral Scene

The towns of northern Germany and northern Italy

means of higher salaries. Thereby the population balance between countryside and town was shifted slightly in favor of the latter.

Certain urban centers, especially those in northern Germany and northern Italy, profited the most from the new circumstances. In Germany a group of cities and towns under the leadership of Lübeck and Bremen allied in the so-called Hanseatic League to control long-distance trade in the Baltic and North Seas. Their fleets transported German grain to Scandinavia and brought back dairy products, fish, and furs. The enhanced European per capita ability to buy luxury goods brought new wealth to the northern Italian trading cities of Genoa and, especially, Venice because these cities controlled the importation of spices from the East. Greater expenditures on luxury also aided the economies of Florence, Venice, Milan, and other neighboring cities because those cities concentrated on the manufacture of silks and linens, light woolens, and other fine cloths. Milan, in addition, prospered from its armaments industry, which kept the warring European states supplied with armor and weapons. Because of varying local conditions, some cities and towns, above all those of Flanders, became economically depressed, but altogether European urban centers profited remarkably well from the new economic circumstances and emphasis on specialization.

The growth of advanced business and financial techniques

The changed circumstances also helped stimulate the development of sophisticated business, accounting, and banking techniques. Because sharp fluctuations in prices made investments precarious, new forms of partnerships were created to minimize risks. Insurance contracts were also invented to take some of the risk out of shipping. Europe's most useful accounting invention, double-entry bookkeeping, was first put into use in Italy in the mid–fourteenth century and spread rapidly thereafter north of the Alps. This allowed for quick discovery of computational errors and easy overview of profits and losses, credits and debits. Large-scale banking had already become common after the middle of the thirteenth century, but the economic crises of the later Middle Ages encouraged banks to alter some of their ways of doing business. Most important was the development of prudent branch-banking techniques, especially by the Florentine house of the Medici. Earlier banks had built branches, but the Medici bank, which flourished from 1397 to 1494, organized theirs along the lines of a modern holding company. The Medici branches, located in London, Bruges, and Avignon, as well as several Italian cities, were dominated by senior partners from the Medici family who followed common policies. Formally, however, each branch was a separate partnership which did not carry any other branch down with it if it collapsed. Other Italian banks experimented with advanced credit techniques. Some even allowed their clients to transfer funds between each other without any real money changing hands. Such "book transfers" were at first executed only by oral command, but around 1400 they started to be carried out by written orders. These were the earliest ancestors of the modern check.

An Artisan Making Chain Mail. One can easily see why late-medieval knightly armor was terribly expensive.

In surveying the two centuries of late-medieval economic history, both the role of nature and that of human beings must be emphasized. The premodern history of all parts of the globe tends to show that whenever population becomes excessive natural controls manage to reduce it. Bad weather and disease may come at any time, but when humans are already suffering from hunger and conditions of over-crowding, the results of natural disasters will be particularly devastating. That certainly is what happened in the fourteenth century. Nature intervened cruelly in human affairs, but no matter how cruel the immediate effects, the results were ultimately beneficial. By 1450 a far smaller population had a higher average standard of living than the population of 1300. In this result humans too played their part. Because people were determined to make the best of the new circumstances and avoid a recurrence of economic depression, they managed to reorganize their economic life and place it on a sounder footing. The gross European product of about 1450 was probably smaller than it was in 1300, but this is not surprising given the much smaller population. In fact, per capita output had risen with per capita income, and the European economy was ready to move on to new conquests.

2. SOCIAL AND EMOTIONAL DISLOCATION

Before the healthy new equilibrium was reached, the economic crises of the later Middle Ages contributed from about 1300 to 1450 to provoking a rash of lower-class rural and urban insurrections more numerous than Europe had ever known before or has ever known since. It used to be thought that these were all caused by extreme deprivation, but as we will see, that was not always the case.

The one large-scale rural uprising that was most clearly caused by extreme poverty was the northern French "Jacquerie" of 1358. This took its name from the prototypical French peasant, "Jacques Bonhomme," who had finally suffered more than he could endure. In 1348 and 1349 the Black Death had brought its terror and wreaked havoc with the economy and with people's lives. Then a flare-up of war between England and France had spread great desolation over the countryside. The peasants, as usual in late-medieval warfare, suffered most from the pillaging and burning carried out by the rapacious soldiers. To make matters even less endurable, after the English decisively defeated the French in 1356 at the Battle of Poitiers the French king, John II, and numerous aristocrats had to be ransomed. As always in such cases, the peasants were asked to bear the heaviest share of the burden, but by 1358 they had had enough and rose up with astounding ferocity. Without any clear program they burned down castles, murdered their lords, and raped their lords' wives. Undoubtedly their intense (and justified) economic resentments were the major cause for the uprising, but it should be said too that 1358 was a year of deep political uncertainty for northern France, thus making an uprising of peasants possible. While the king was in captivity in England, groups of townsmen were trying to reform the governmental system by limiting monarchical powers, and certain aristocrats were plotting to seize power. In the meantime, John II's son, Charles, was trying both to raise a large ransom for his father and subdue the crown's enemies. Although we can never be certain, it seems unlikely that the peasants would have revolted had they not sensed an opportunity to take advantage of France's political confusion. But in fact the opportunity was not as great as they may have thought: within a month the privileged powers closed ranks, massacred the rebels, and quickly restored order.

Background of the English Peasants' Revolt

The English Peasants' Revolt of 1381—the most serious lower-class rebellion in English history—is frequently bracketed with the Jacquerie, but its causes were very different. Instead of being a revolt of abject desperation, it was one of frustrated rising expectations. By 1381 the effects of the Black Death should have been working in favor of the peasants. Above all, a shortage of labor should have placed their services in demand. In fact, the incidence of the plague did help to increase manumissions (i.e., freeings) of serfs and raise salaries or lower rents of free farm laborers. But aristocratic landlords fought back to preserve their own incomes. They succeeded in passing legislation that aimed to keep wages at pre-plague levels and force landless laborers to work at the lower rates. Aristocrats furthermore often tried to exact all their old dues and unpaid services. Because the peasants were unwilling to be pushed down into their previous poverty and subservience, a collision was inevitable.

The course of the revolt

The spark that ignited the great revolt of 1381 was an attempt to collect a national tax levied equally on every head instead of being made proportional to wealth. This was an unprecedented development in English tax-collecting that the peasants understandably found unfair. Two head-taxes were levied without resistance in 1377 and 1379, but when agents tried to collect a third in 1381 the peasantry rose up to resist and seek redress of all their grievances. First they burned local records and sacked the dwellings of those they considered their exploiters; then they marched on London, where they executed the lord chancellor and treasurer of England. Recognizing the gravity of the situation, the fifteen-year-old king, Richard II, went out to meet the peasants and won their confidence by promising to abolish serfdom and keep rents low; meanwhile, during negotiations, the peasant leader, Wat Tyler, was murdered in a squabble with the king's escort. Lacking leadership, the peasants, who mistakenly thought they had achieved their aims, rapidly dispersed. But once the boy-king was no longer in danger of his life he kept none of his promises. Instead, the scattered peasant forces were quickly hunted down and a few alleged trouble-makers were executed without any mass reprisals. The revolt itself therefore accomplished nothing, but within a few decades the natural play of economic forces caused serfdom to disappear and considerably improved the lot of the rural wage laborer.

Other rural revolts took place in other parts of Europe, but we may now look at some urban ones. Conventionally, the urban revolts of the later Middle Ages are viewed as uprisings of exploited proletarians who were more oppressed than ever because of the effects of economic depression. But this is probably too great a simplification because each case differed and complex forces were always at work. For example, an uprising in the north German town of Brunswick in 1374 was much less a movement of the poor against the rich than a political upheaval in which one political alliance replaced another. A different north German uprising, in Lübeck in 1408, has been aptly described as a "taxpayer's" revolt. This again was less a confrontation of the poor versus the rich than an attempt of a faction that was out of power to initiate less costly government.

The nearest thing to a real proletarian revolt was the uprising in 1378 of the Florentine *Ciompi* (pronounced "cheeompi"). The Ciompi were wool-combers who had the misfortune to be engaged in an industry that had become particularly depressed. Some of them had lost their jobs and others were frequently cheated or underpaid by the masters of the woolen industry. The latter wielded great political power in Florence, and thus could pass economic legislation in their own favor. This fact in itself meant that if there were to be economic reforms, they would have to go together with political changes. As events transpired it was a political crisis that called the Ciompi into direct action. In 1378 Florence had become exhausted by three years of war with the papacy. Certain patrician leaders overthrew the old regime to alter the war policy and gain their own political advantage. Circumstances led them to seek the support of the lower classes and, once stirred up, the Ciompi became emboldened after a few months to launch their own far more radical rebellion. This was inspired primarily by economic hardship and grievances, but personal hatreds also played a role. The Ciompi gained power for six weeks, during which they tried to institute tax relief, fuller employment, and representation of themselves and other proletarian groups in the Florentine government. But they could not maintain their hold on power and a new oligarchical government revoked all their reforms.

Tombstone of a Leader of a Fourteenth-Century German Peasant Uprising. In 1336 a petty knight from Franconia (central Germany) marched at the head of impoverished peasants who vented their resentments by robbing and murdering all the Jews they could find in the nearby towns. After several months of leading this rampage the knight was finally apprehended and executed by governing authorities. His tombstone shows him with bound hands at the moment of his beheading, but the inscription calls him "blessed," a sign that some wished to view him as a martyred saint.

If we try to draw any general conclusions about these various uprisings, we can certainly say that few if any of them would have occurred had there not been an economic crisis. But political considerations always had some influence, and the rebels in some uprisings were more prosperous than in others. It is noteworthy that all the genuinely lower-class uprisings of economically desperate groups quickly failed. This was certainly because the upper classes were more accustomed to wielding power and giving orders; even more important, they had access to the money and troops necessary to quell revolts. Sometimes

General observations on the nature of popular uprisings

elements within the lower classes might fight among themselves, whereas the privileged always managed to rally into a united front when faced by a lower-class threat to their domination. In addition, lower-class rebels were usually more intent on redressing immediate grievances than on developing fully coherent long-term governmental programs; inspiring ideals for cohesive action were generally lacking. The case of the Hussite Revolution in Bohemia—to be treated later—shows that religion in the later Middle Ages was a more effective rallying ground for large numbers of people than political, economic, and social demands.

The crisis of the late-medieval aristocracy

Although the upper classes succeeded in overcoming popular uprisings, they perceived the economic and emotional insecurities of the later Middle Ages and the possibility of revolt as a constant threat, and became obsessed with maintaining their privileged social status. Late-medieval aristocrats were in a precarious economic position because they gained most of their income from land. In times when grain prices and rents were falling and wages rising, landowners were obviously in economic trouble. Some aristocrats probably also felt threatened by the rapid rise of merchants and financiers who could make quick killings because of sharp market fluctuations. In practice, really wealthy merchants bought land and were absorbed into the aristocracy. Moreover, most landowning aristocrats were able to stave off economic threats by expert estate management; in fact, many of them actually became richer than ever. But most still felt more exposed to social and economic insecurities than before. The result was that they tried to set up artificial barriers behind which they separated themselves from other classes.

A Party of Late-Medieval Aristocrats. Notice the pointed shoes and the women's pointed hats, twice as high as their heads.

Two of the most striking examples of this separation were the aristocratic emphasis on luxury and the formation of exclusive chivalric orders. The late Middle Ages was the period par excellence of aristocratic ostentation. While famine or disease raged, aristocrats regaled themselves with lavish banquets and magnificent pageants. At one feast in Flanders in 1468 a table decoration was forty-six feet high. Aristocratic clothing too was extremely ostentatious: men wore long, pointed shoes, and women ornately festooned headdresses. Throughout history rich people have always enjoyed dressing up, but the aristocrats of the later Middle Ages seem to have done so obsessively to comfort themselves and convey the message that they were entirely different from others. The insistence on maintaining a sharply defined social hierarchy also accounts for the late-medieval proliferation of chivalric orders, such as those of the Knights of the Garter or the Golden Fleece. By joining together in exclusive orders which prescribed special conduct and boasted special insignia of membership, aristocrats who felt threatened by social pressures again tried to set themselves off from others, in effect, by putting up a sign that read "for members only."

Another explanation for the exorbitant stress on luxury is that it was a form of escapism. Aristocrats who were continually exposed to the sight and smell of death must have found it emotionally comforting to retreat into a dream-world of elegant manners, splendid feasts, and multicolored clothes. In a parallel fashion, nonaristocrats who could not afford such luxuries often sought relief from the vision of death in crude public entertainments: for example, crowds would watch blind beggars try to catch a squealing pig but beat each other with clubs instead, or they would cheer on boys to clamber up greasy poles in order to win prizes of geese.

Duke Philip the Good of Burgundy. The duke proudly wears the emblem of the Order of the Golden Fleece around his neck.

It must not be thought, however, that late-medieval Europeans gave themselves over to riotous living without interruption. In fact, the same people who sought elegant or boisterous diversions just as often went to the other emotional extreme when faced by the psychic stress caused by the troubles of the age, and abandoned themselves to sorrow. Throughout the period grown men and women shed tears in abundance. The queen mother of France wept in public when she first viewed her grandson; the great preacher Vincent Ferrer had to interrupt his sermons on Christ's Passion and the Last Judgment because he and his audience were sobbing too convulsively; and the English king, Edward II, supposedly wept so much when imprisoned that he gushed forth enough hot water for his own shave. The last story taxes the imagination, but it does illustrate well what contemporaries thought was possible. We know for certain that the Church encouraged crying because of the survival of moving statuettes of weeping St. Johns, which were obviously designed to call forth tears from their viewers.

Tears and sorrow

People also were encouraged by preachers to brood on the Passion of Christ and on their own mortality. Fearsome crucifixes abounded,

A Late-Medieval Crucifixion Scene. The Virgin has to be held up to keep from swooning, and the angels are weeping.

and the figure of the Virgin Mary was less a smiling madonna than a sorrowing mother: now she was most frequently depicted slumping with grief at the foot of the cross, or holding the dead Christ in her lap. The late-medieval obsession with mortality can also still be seen in sculptures, frescoes, and book illustrations that reminded viewers of the brevity of life and the torments of hell. The characteristic tombs of the High Middle Ages were mounted with sculptures that either showed the deceased in some action that had been typical of his or her accomplishments in life, or else in a state of repose that showed death to be nothing more than peaceful sleep. But in the late fourteenth century, tombs appeared that displayed the physical ravages of death in the most gruesome ways imaginable: emaciated corpses were displayed with protruding intestines or covered with snakes or toads. Some tombs bore inscriptions stating that the viewer would soon be "a fetid cadaver, food for worms"; some warned chillingly: "What you are, I was; what I am, you will be." Omnipresent illustrations displayed figures of grinning Death, with his scythe, carrying off elegant and healthy men and women, or sadistic devils roasting pain-wracked humans in hell. Because people who painted or brooded on such pictures might the next day indulge in excessive revels, late-medieval culture often

Left: *A Dead Man Before His Judge.* A late-medieval reminder of human mortality. Right: *Tomb of François de la Sarra.* This late–fourteenth-century Swiss nobleman is shown with snakes around his arms and toads littering his face.

seems to border on the manic-depressive. But apparently such extreme reactions were necessary to help people cope with their fears.

3. TRIALS FOR THE CHURCH AND HUNGER FOR THE DIVINE

The intense concentration on the meaning of death was also a manifestation of a very deep and pervasive religiosity. The religious enthusiasm of the High Middle Ages by no means flagged after 1300; if anything, it became more intense. But religious enthusiasm took on new forms of expression because of the institutional difficulties of the Church and the turmoils of the age.

After the humiliation and death of Pope Boniface VIII in 1303, the Church experienced a period of institutional crisis that was as severe and prolonged as the contemporary economic crisis. We may distinguish three phases: the so-called Babylonian Captivity of the papacy, 1305–1378; the Great Schism, 1378–1417; and the period of the Italian territorial papacy, 1417–1517. During the Babylonian Captivity the papacy was located in Avignon instead of Rome and was generally subservient to the interests of the French crown. There were several reasons for this: the most obvious was that since the test of strength between Philip the Fair and Boniface VIII had resulted in a clear victory for the French king, subsequent popes were unwilling to risk French royal ire. In fact, once the popes recognized that they could not give orders to the French kings, they found that they could gain certain advantages from currying their favor. One was a safe home in southern France, away from the tumult of Italy. Central Italy and the city of Rome in the fourteenth century had become so politically turbulent and rebellious that the pope could not even count on finding personal safety there, let alone sufficiently peaceful conditions to maintain orderly ecclesiastical administration. But no such danger existed in Avignon. Even though Avignon was not then part of the French kingdom—it was the major city of a small papal territory—French military might was close enough to guarantee the pope his much-needed security. Another advantage of papal subservience to French power was help from the French in pursuing mutually advantageous policies in Germany and southern Italy. Perhaps most important was a working agreement whereby the French king would propose his own candidates to become bishops and the pope would then name them, thereby gaining sizable monetary payments. After 1305 the pro-French system became so entrenched that a majority of cardinals and all the popes until 1378 were themselves French.

At Avignon the popes were more successful than ever in pursuing their policy of centralizing the government of the Church. For the first time they worked out a really sound system of papal finance, based on the systematization of dues collected from the clergy throughout

The Prince of the World. A stone figure from the church of St. Sebald, Nuremberg, from about 1330. From the front the man is smiling and master of all he surveys; from the rear he is crawling with vermin.

Europe. The papacy also succeeded in appointing more candidates to vacant benefices than before (in practice often naming candidates proposed by the French and English kings), and they proceeded against heresy with great determination, indeed with ruthlessness. But whatever the popes achieved in power they lost in respect and loyalty. The clergy became alienated as a result of being asked to pay so much money, and much of the laity was horrified by the corruption and unbridled luxury displayed at the papal court: there the cardinals lived more splendidly than lords, dining off peacocks, pheasants, grouse, and swans, and drinking from elaborately sculptured fountains that spouted the finest wines. Most of the Avignonese popes themselves were personally upright and abstemious, but one, Clement VI (1342–1352), was worse than his cardinals. Clement was ready to offer any spiritual benefit for money, boasted that he would appoint even a jackass as bishop if political circumstances warranted, and defended his incessant sexual transgressions by insisting that he fornicated on doctors' orders.

As time went on the pressures of informed public opinion forced the popes to promise that they would return to Rome. After one abortive attempt by Urban V in 1367, Pope Gregory XI finally did return to the Holy City in 1377. But he died a year later and then disaster struck. The college of cardinals, surrounded in Rome by clamoring Italians, yielded to local sentiment by naming an Italian as pope, who took the title of Urban VI. But most of the cardinals were Frenchmen and quickly regretted their decision, especially because Urban VI immediately began quarreling with them and revealing what were probably paranoid tendencies. Therefore, after only a few months, the French cardinals met again, declared the previous election void, and replaced Urban with one of their own number, who called himself Clement VII.

Unfortunately, however, Urban VI did not meekly resign. On the contrary, he named an entirely new Italian college of cardinals and remained entrenched in Rome. Clement VII quickly retreated with his own party to Avignon and the so-called Great Schism ensued. France and other countries in the French political orbit—such as Scotland, Castile, and Aragon—recognized Clement, while the rest of Europe recognized Urban as the true pope. For three decades Christians looked on helplessly while the rival pontiffs hurled curses at each other and the international monastic orders became divided into Roman and Avignonese camps. The death of one or the other pope did not end the schism; each camp had its own set of cardinals which promptly named either a French or Italian successor. The desperateness of the situation led a council of prelates from both camps to meet in Pisa in 1409 to depose both popes and name a new one instead. But neither the Italian nor the French pope accepted the council's decision and both had enough political support to retain some obedience. So after 1409 there were three rival claimants hurling curses instead of two.

The Great Schism was finally ended in 1417 by the Council of Constance, the largest ecclesiastical gathering in medieval history. This time the assembled prelates made certain to gain the crucial support of secular powers and also to eliminate the prior claimants before naming a new pope. After the council's election of Martin V in 1417, European ecclesiastical unity was thus fully restored. But a struggle over the nature of Church government followed immediately. The members of the Council of Constance challenged the prevailing medieval theory of papal monarchy by calling for balanced, "conciliar," government. In two momentous decrees they stated that a general council of prelates was superior in authority to the pope, and that such councils should meet regularly to govern the Church. Not surprisingly, subsequent popes—who had now returned to Rome—sought to nullify these decrees. When a new council met in Basel in 1431, in accordance with the principles laid down at Constance, the reigning pope did all he could to sabotage its activities. Ultimately he was successful: after a protracted struggle the Council of Basel dissolved in 1449 in abject failure, and the attempt to institute constitutional government in the Church was completely defeated. But the papacy only won this victory over conciliarism by gaining the support of the rulers of the European states. In separate concordats with kings and princes the popes granted the secular rulers much authority over the various local churches. The popes thus became assured of theoretical supremacy at the cost of surrendering much real power. To compensate for this they concentrated on consolidating their own direct rule in central Italy. Most of the fifteenth-century popes ruled very much like any other princes, leading armies, jockeying for alliances, and building magnificent palaces. Hence, although they did succeed for the first time in creating a viable political state, their reputation for disinterested piety remained low.

*The end of the Schism;
conciliarism*

While the papacy was undergoing these vicissitudes, the local clergy throughout Europe was undergoing a loss of prestige for several reasons. One was that the pope's greater financial demands forced the clergy to demand more from the laity, but such demands were bitterly resented, especially during times of prevailing economic crisis. Then too during outbreaks of plague the clergy sometimes fled their posts just like everyone else, but in so doing they lost whatever claim they had for being morally superior. Probably the single greatest reason for growing dissatisfaction with the clergy was the increase in lay literacy. The continued proliferation of schools and the decline in the cost of books—a subject we will treat later—made it possible for large numbers of lay people to learn how to read. Once that happened, the laity could start reading parts of the Bible, or, more frequently, popular religious primers. These made it clear that their local priests were not living according to the standards set by Jesus and the Apostles. In the meantime, the upheavals and horrors of the age drove people to seek religious solace more than ever. Finding the conventional channels of church attendance, confession, and submission to clerical au-

*The decline of clerical
prestige*

A *German Flagellant Procession.*
These penitents hoped they could
ward off the Black Death by their
mutually inflicted tortures.

The growth of lay piety:
(1) devotional practices

thority insufficient, the laity sought supplementary or alternate routes
to piety. These differed greatly from each other, but they all aimed to
satisfy an immense hunger for the divine.

The most widely-traveled route was that of performing repeated
acts of external devotion in the hope that they would gain the devotee
divine favor on earth and salvation in the hereafter. People flocked to
go on pilgrimages as never before and participated regularly in barefooted religious processions: the latter were often held twice a month
and occasionally as often as once a week. Men and women also eagerly
paid for thousands of masses to be said by full-time "mass priests" for
the souls of their dead relatives and left legacies for the reading of
numerous requiem masses to save their own souls after death. Obsession with repeating prayers reached a peak when some pious individuals tried to compute the number of drops of blood that Christ
shed on the cross so that they could say the same number of Our
Fathers. The most excessive and repugnant form of religious ritual in
the later Middle Ages was flagellation. Some women who lived in
communal houses beat themselves with the roughest animal hides,
chains, and knotted thongs. A young girl who entered such a community in Poland in 1331 suffered extreme internal injuries and became
completely disfigured within eleven months. Flailings were not usually performed in public, but during the first onslaught of the Black
Death in 1348 and 1349, whole bands of lay people marched through
northern Europe chanting and beating each other with metal-tipped
scourges in the hope of appeasing the apparent divine wrath.

Building Operations. From a French picture Bible, c. 1250. Note the treadmill, with wheel, ropes, and pulley, by means of which a basket of stones is brought to the construction level. (Morgan Library)

Siege of a City, c. 1470. The use of cannon would soon put an end to traditional medieval fortifications. (Morgan Library)

Stained Glass, German, c. 1300. One of the kings from the House of David, Christ's royal ancestry. (MMA)

The Virgin and Chancellor Rolin, Jan van Eyck (1390–1444). The early Flemish painters loved to present scenes of piety in the sumptuous surroundings of wealthy burghers. (Louvre)

Vespers of the Holy Ghost, with a View of Paris,
Jean Fouquet. From the *Book of Hours* of
Etienne Chevalier, 1461. Demons in the sky are
sent flying by the divine light from heaven.
The cathedral is Notre Dame. (Robert Lehman)

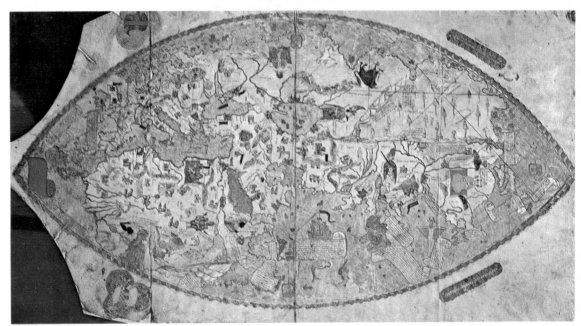

A Fifteenth-Century Map of the World. The European continent is in the upper left, China and Japan are at the far
right, and a western hemisphere is lacking. (Scala)

An opposite route to godliness was the inward path of mysticism. Throughout the European continent, but particularly in Germany and England, male and female mystics, both clerical and lay, sought union with God by means of "detachment," contemplation, or spiritual exercises. The most original and eloquent late-medieval mystical theorist was the German Dominican, Master Eckhart (c. 1260–1327), who taught that there was a power or "spark" deep within every human soul that was really the dwelling-place of God. By renouncing all sense of selfhood one could retreat into one's innermost recesses and there find divinity. Eckhart did not recommend ceasing attendance at church—he hardly could have because he preached in churches—but he made it clear that outward rituals were of comparatively little importance in reaching God. He also gave the impression to his lay audiences that they might attain godliness largely on their own volition. Thus ecclesiastical authorities charged him with inciting "ignorant and undisciplined people to wild and dangerous excesses." Although Eckhart pleaded his own doctrinal orthodoxy, some of his teachings were condemned by the papacy.

(2) mysticism

That Eckhart's critics were not entirely mistaken in their worries is shown by the fact that some lay people in Germany who were influenced by him did fall into the heresy of believing that they could become fully united with God on earth without any priestly intermediaries. But these so-called heretics of the Free Spirit were few in number. Much more numerous were later orthodox mystics, sometimes influenced by Eckhart and sometimes not, who placed greater emphasis on the divine initiative in the meeting of the soul with God and made certain to insist that the ministrations of the Church were a necessary contribution to the mystic way. Even they, however, believed that "churches make no man holy, but men make churches holy." Most of the great teachers and practitioners of mysticism in the fourteenth century were clerics, nuns, or hermits, but in the fifteenth century a modified form of mystical belief spread among lay people. This "practical mysticism" did not aim for full ecstatic union with God, but rather for an ongoing sense of some divine presence during the conduct of daily life. The most popular manual that pointed the way to this goal was the Latin *Imitation of Christ,* written around 1427, probably by the north German canon Thomas à Kempis. Because this was written in a simple but forceful style and taught how to be a pious Christian while still living actively in the world, it was particularly attractive to lay readers. Thus it quickly became translated into the leading European vernaculars. From then until today it has been more widely read by Christians than any other religious work outside of the Bible. The *Imitation* urges its readers to participate in one religious ceremony—the sacrament of the Eucharist—but otherwise it emphasizes inward piety. According to its teachings, the individual Christian is best able to become the "partner" of Jesus Christ both by taking communion and also by engaging in biblical meditation and leading a simple, moral life.

*Heterodox and orthodox
mysticism*

*(3) Heresy: John Wyclif
and the Lollards*

A third distinct form of late-medieval piety was outright religious protest or heresy. In England and Bohemia especially, heretical movements became serious threats to the Church. The founder of heresy in late-medieval England was an Oxford theologian named John Wyclif (c. 1330–1384). Wyclif's rigorous adherence to the theology of St. Augustine led him to believe that a certain number of humans were predestined to be saved while the rest were irrevocably damned. He thought the predestined would naturally live simply, according to the standards of the New Testament, but in fact he found most members of the Church hierarchy indulging in splendid extravagances. Hence he concluded that most Church officials were damned. For him the only solution was to have secular rulers appropriate ecclesiastical wealth and reform the Church by replacing corrupt priests and bishops with men who would live according to apostolic standards. This position was obviously attractive to the aristocracy of England, who may have looked forward to enriching themselves with Church spoils and at least saw nothing wrong with using Wyclif as a bulldog to frighten the pope and the local clergy. Thus Wyclif at first received influential aristocratic support. But toward the end of his life he moved from merely calling for reform to attacking some of the most basic institutions of the Church, above all the sacrament of the Eucharist. This radicalism frightened off his influential protectors, and Wyclif probably would have been formally condemned for heresy had he lived longer. His death brought no respite for the Church, however, because he had attracted numerous lay followers—called Lollards—who zealously continued to propagate some of his most radical ideas. Above all, the Lollards taught that pious Christians should shun the corrupt Church and instead study the Bible and rely as far as possible on their individual consciences. Lollardy gained many adherents in the last two decades of the fourteenth century, but after the introduction in England of the death penalty for heresy in 1399 and the failure of a Lollard uprising in 1414 the heretical wave greatly receded. Nonetheless, a few Lollards did continue to survive underground, and their descendants helped contribute to the Protestant Reformation of the sixteenth century.

John Hus

Much greater was the influence of Wyclifism in Bohemia. Around 1400, Czech students who had studied in Oxford brought back Wyclif's ideas to the Bohemian capital of Prague. There Wyclifism was enthusiastically received by an eloquent preacher named John Hus (c. 1373–1415), who had already been inveighing in well-attended sermons against "the world, the flesh, and the devil." Hus employed Wyclifite theories to back up his own calls for the end of ecclesiastical corruption, and rallied many Bohemians to the cause of reform in the years between 1408 and 1415. Never alienating anyone as Wyclif had done by criticizing the doctrine of the Eucharist, Hus gained support from many different directions. The politics of the Great Schism prompted the king of Bohemia to lend Hus his protection, and influential aristocrats supported Hus for motives similar to those of their English counterparts. Above all, Hus gained a mass following because of his eloquence and concern for social justice. Accordingly, most of Bohemia was behind him when Hus in 1415 agreed to travel to the Council of Constance to defend his views and try to convince the assembled prelates that only thoroughgoing reform could save the Church. But although Hus had been guaranteed his personal safety, this assurance was revoked as soon as he arrived at the Council: rather than being given a fair hearing, the betrayed idealist was tried for heresy and burned.

Hus's supporters in Bohemia were justifiably outraged and quickly raised the banner of open revolt. The aristocracy took advantage of the situation to seize Church lands, and poorer priests, artisans, and peasants rallied together in the hope of achieving Hus's goals of religious reform and social justice. Between 1420 and 1424 armies of lower-class Hussites, led by a brilliant blind general, John Zizka, amazingly defeated several invading forces of well-armed "crusading" knights from Germany. In 1434 more conservative, aristocratically dominated Hussites overcame the radicals, thereby ending attempts to initiate a purified new religious and social dispensation. But even the conservatives refused to return to full orthodoxy. Thus Bohemia never came back to the Catholic fold until after the Catholic Reformation in the seventeenth century. The Hussite declaration of religious independence was both a foretaste of what was to come one hundred years later with Protestantism and the most successful late-medieval expression of dissatisfaction with the government of the Church.

The Hussite revolt

4. POLITICAL CRISIS AND RECOVERY

The story of late-medieval politics at first seems very dreary because throughout most of the period there was incessant strife. Almost everywhere neighbors fought neighbors and states fought states. But on closer inspection it becomes clear that despite the turmoil there was ultimate improvement in almost all the governments of Europe. In the course of the fifteenth century peace returned to most of the continent, the national monarchies in particular became stronger, and the period ended on a new note of strength just as it had from the point of view of economics.

Progress in late-medieval politics despite turmoil

Starting our survey with Italy, it must first be explained that the Kingdom of Naples in the extreme south of the Italian peninsula was sunk in endemic warfare or maladministration more or less without interruption throughout the fourteenth and fifteenth centuries. Otherwise, Italy emerged from the prevailing political turmoil of the late Middle Ages earlier than any other part of Europe. The fourteenth century was a time of troubles for the Papal States, comprising most of central Italy, because forces representing the absent or divided pa-

The political situation in Italy

pacy were seldom able to overcome the resistance of refractory towns and rival leaders of marauding military bands. But after the end of the Great Schism in 1417 the popes concentrated more on consolidating their own Italian territories and gradually became the strong rulers of most of the middle part of the peninsula. Farther north some of the leading city-states—such as Florence, Venice, Siena, and Genoa—had experienced at least occasional and most often prolonged social warfare in the fourteenth century because of the economic pressures of the age. But sooner or later the most powerful families or interest groups overcame internal resistance. By around 1400 the three leading cities of the north—Venice, Milan, Florence—had fixed definitively upon their own different forms of government: Venice was ruled by a merchant oligarchy, Milan by a dynastic despotism, and Florence by a complex, supposedly republican system that was actually controlled by the rich. (After 1434 the Florentine republic was in practice dominated by the banking family of the Medici.)

Peace established in the fifteenth century

Having settled their internal problems, Venice, Milan, and Florence proceeded from about 1400 to 1454 to expand territorially and conquer almost all the other northern Italian cities and towns except Genoa, which remained prosperous and independent but gained no new territory. Thus, by the middle of the fifteenth century Italy was divided into five major parts: the states of Venice, Milan, and Florence in the north; the Papal States in the middle; and the backward Kingdom of Naples in the south. A treaty of 1454 initiated a half-century of peace between these states: whenever one threatened to upset the "balance of power," the others usually allied against it before serious warfare could break out. Accordingly, the last half of the fifteenth century was a fortunate age for Italy. But in 1494 a French invasion initiated a period of renewed warfare in which the French attempt at dominating Italy was successfully countered by Spain.

Germany: the triumph of the princes

North of the Alps political turmoil prevailed throughout the fourteenth century and lasted longer into the fifteenth. Probably the worst instability was experienced in Germany. There the virtually independent princes continually warred with the greatly weakened emperors, or else they warred with each other. Between about 1350 and 1450 near-anarchy prevailed, because while the princes were warring and subdividing their inheritances into smaller states, petty powers such as free cities and knights who owned one or two castles were striving to shake off the rule of the princes. Throughout most of the German west these attempts met with enough success to fragment political authority more than ever, but in the east after about 1450 certain stronger German princes managed to assert their authority over divisive forces. After they did so they started to govern firmly over middle-sized states on the model of the larger national monarchies of England and France. The strongest princes were those who ruled in eastern territories such as Bavaria, Austria, and Brandenburg, because there towns were fewer and smaller and the princes had earlier been able to take advantage of imperial weakness to preside over the colonization of large tracts of land. Especially the Habsburg princes of Austria and the Hohenzollern princes of Brandenburg—a territory joined in the sixteenth century with the easternmost lands of Prussia—would be the most influential powers in Germany's future.

The great nation-states did not escape unscathed from the late-medieval turmoil either. France was strife-ridden for much of the period, primarily in the form of the Hundred Years' War between France and England. The Hundred Years' War was actually a series of conflicts that lasted for even more than one hundred years—from 1337 to 1453. There were several different causes for this prolonged struggle. The major one was the long-standing problem of French territory held by the English kings. At the beginning of the fourteenth century the English kings still ruled much of the rich southern French lands of Gascony and Aquitaine as vassals of the French crown. The French, who since the reign of Philip Augustus had been expanding and consolidating their rule, obviously hoped to expel the English, making war inevitable. Another cause for strife was that the English economic interests in the woolen trade with Flanders led them to support the frequent attempts of Flemish burghers to rebel against French rule. Finally, the fact that the direct Capetian line of succession to the French throne died out in 1328, to be replaced thereafter by the related Valois dynasty, meant that the English kings, who themselves descended from the Capetians as a result of intermarriage, laid claim to the French crown itself.

France: causes of the Hundred Years' War

France should have had no difficulty in defeating England at the start: it was the richest country in Europe and outnumbered England in population by some fifteen million to fewer than four million. Nonetheless, throughout most of the first three-quarters of the Hundred Years' War the English won most of the pitched battles. One reason for this was that the English had learned superior military tactics, using well-disciplined archers to fend off and scatter the heavily armored mounted French knights. In the three greatest battles of the long conflict—Crécy (1346), Poitiers (1356), and Agincourt (1415)—the outnumbered English relied on tight discipline and effective use of the longbow to inflict crushing defeats on the French. Another reason for English success was that the war was always fought on French soil. That being the case, English soldiers were eager to fight because they could look forward to rich plunder, while their own homeland suffered none of the disasters of war. Worst of all for the French was the fact that they often were badly divided. The French crown had always had to fear provincial attempts to assert autonomy: especially during the long period of warfare, when there were several highly inept kings and the English encouraged internal French dissensions, many aristocratic provincial leaders took advantage of the confusion to ally with the enemy and seek their own advantage. The most dramatic and fateful instance was the breaking away of Burgundy,

The course of the war: factors in the initial English success

Joan of Arc

whose dukes from 1419 to 1435 allied with the English, an act which called the very existence of an independent French crown into question.

It was in this dark period that the heroic figure of Joan of Arc came forth to rally the French. In 1429 Joan, an illiterate but extremely devout peasant girl, sought out the uncrowned French ruler, Charles VII, to announce that she had been divinely commissioned to drive the English out of France. Charles was persuaded to let her take command of his troops, and her piety and sincerity made such a favorable impression on the soldiers that their morale was raised immensely. In a few months Joan had liberated much of central France from English domination and had brought Charles to Rheims, where he was crowned king. But in May 1430 she was captured by the Burgundians and handed over to the English, who accused her of being a witch and tried her for heresy. Condemned in 1431 after a predetermined trial, she was publicly burned to death in the market square at Rouen. Nonetheless, the French, fired by their initial victories, continued to move on the offensive. When Burgundy withdrew from the English alliance in 1435, and the English king, Henry VI, proved to be totally incompetent, there followed an uninterrupted series of triumphs for the French side. In 1453 the capture of Bordeaux, the last of the English strongholds in the southwest, finally brought the long war to an end. The English now held no land in France except for the Channel port of Calais, which they ultimately lost in 1558.

More than merely expelling the English from French territory, the Hundred Years' War resulted in greatly strengthening the powers of the French crown. Although many of the French kings during the long war had been ineffective personalities—one, Charles VI, was even insane—the monarchy demonstrated remarkable staying power because it provided France with the strongest institutions it knew and therefore offered the only realistic hope for lasting stability and peace. Moreover, warfare emergencies allowed the kings to gather new powers, above all, the rights to collect national taxes and maintain a standing army. Hence after Charles VII succeeded in defeating the English, the crown was able to renew the high-medieval royal tradition of ruling the country assertively. In the reigns of Charles's successors, Louis XI (1461–1483) and Louis XII (1498–1515), the monarchy became ever stronger. Its greatest single achievement was the destruction of the power of Burgundy in 1477 when the Burgundian duke, Charles the Bold, fell in the battle of Nancy at the hands of the Swiss, whom Charles had been trying to dominate. Since Charles died without a male heir, Louis XI of France was able to march into Burgundy and reabsorb the breakaway duchy. Later, when Louis XII gained Brittany by marriage, the French kings ruled powerfully over almost all of what is today included in the borders of France.

Although the Hundred Years' War was fought on French instead of English soil, England also experienced great turmoil during the later

Louis XI of France. A portrait by Fouquet.

Middle Ages because of internal instability. Indeed, England was a hot-bed of insurrection: of the nine English kings who came to the throne between 1307 and 1485, five died violently because of revolts or conspiracies. Most of these slain kings had proven themselves to be incapable rulers, but there were other reasons for England's political troubles as well. One was that the crown had been too ambitious in trying both to hold on to its territories in France and also to subdue Scotland. This policy often made it necessary to resort to heavy taxation and to grant major political concessions to the aristocracy. When English arms in France were successful, the crown rode the crest of popularity and the aristocracy prospered from military spoils and ransoms; but whenever the tides of battle turned to defeat, the crown became financially embarrassed and thrown on the political defensive. To make matters worse, the English aristocracy was particularly unruly throughout the period, not just because the aristocrats often had reason to distrust the inept kings, but because the economic pressures of the age made them seek to enlarge their agricultural estates at the expense of each other. This led to factionalism, and factionalism often led to civil war.

After the English presence in France was virtually eradicated and the aristocracy could no longer hope to enrich itself on the spoils of foreign warfare, England's political situation became particularly desperate. As bad luck would have it, the reigning king, Henry VI (1422–1461), was one of the most incompetent that England has ever had. According to one recent authority, Henry "paralyzed and confused the whole process of English government with a royal irresponsibility and inanity which had no precedent." Henry's willfulness helped provoke the Wars of the Roses that flared on and off from 1455 to 1485. These wars received their name from the emblems of the two competing factions: the red rose of Henry's family of Lancaster and the white rose of the rival house of York. The Yorkists for a time gained the kingship, under such monarchs as Richard III, but in 1485 they were replaced by a new dynasty, that of the Tudors, who began a new period in English history. The first Tudor king, Henry VII, steadily eliminated rival claimants to the throne, avoided expensive foreign wars, built up a financial surplus, and gradually reasserted royal power over the aristocracy. When he died in 1509 he was therefore able to pass on to his son, Henry VIII (1509–1547), a royal power as great as it had ever been before.

It is tempting to view the entire period of English history between 1307 and the accession of Henry VII in 1485 as one long, dreary interregnum which accomplished nothing positive. But that would not quite be doing justice to the time: in the first place, the fact that England did not entirely fall apart during the recurrent turbulence was an accomplishment in itself. Remarkably, the rebellious aristocrats of the later Middle Ages never tried to proclaim the independence of any of their regions; only once, in 1405, did they seek unsuccessfully to divide the country between them. Discounting that insignificant exception, aristocratic rebels always sought to control the central government rather than destroy or break away from it. Thus when Henry VII came to the throne, he did not have to win back any English territories as Louis XI of France had had to win back Burgundy. More than that, the antagonisms of the Hundred Years' War had the ultimately beneficial effect of enhancing an English sense of national identity. From the Norman Conquest until deep into the fourteenth century, French was the preferred language of the English crown and aristocracy, but mounting anti-French sentiment contributed to the complete triumph of English by around 1400. The loss of lands in France was also ultimately beneficial because thereafter the crown was freed from the inevitability of war with the French. This freedom gave England more diplomatic maneuverability in sixteenth-century continental politics and later helped strengthen England's ability to invest its energies in overseas expansion in America and elsewhere. Yet another positive development was the steady growth of effective governmental institutions; despite the shifting fortunes of kings, the central governmental administration expanded and became more sophisticated. Parliament too became stronger, largely because both the crown and the aristocracy believed that they could use it for their own ends. In 1307 Parliament had not yet become a regular part of the English governmental system, but by 1485 it definitely had. Later kings who tried to govern without it ran into severe difficulties.

Around the time when Louis XI of France and Henry VII of England were reasserting royal power in their respective countries, the Spanish monarchs, Ferdinand and Isabella, were doing the same on the Iberian peninsula. In the latter area there had also been incessant strife in the later Middle Ages; Aragon and Castile had often fought each other, and aristocratic factions within those kingdoms had continually fought the crown. But in 1469 Ferdinand, the heir of Aragon, married Isabella, the heiress of Castile, and thereby created a union which laid the basis for modern Spain.

Although Spain did not become a fully united nation until 1716 because Aragon and Castile retained their separate institutions, at least warfare between the two previously independent kingdoms ended and the new country was able to embark on united policies. Isabella and Ferdinand, ruling respectively until 1504 and 1516, annexed Granada, the last Muslim state in the peninsula, expelled the Jews, whom they regarded as a divisive element in their society, and thoroughly subdued their aristocracies. Having dealt with their major internal obstacles, the Spanish rulers also started to embark on an ambitious foreign policy: not only did they turn to overseas expansion, as most famously in their support of Christopher Columbus, but they also entered decisively into the arena of Italian politics. Enriched by the influx of American gold and silver after the conquest of Mexico and Peru, and nearly invincible on the battlefields, Spain quickly became Europe's most powerful state in the sixteenth century.

Ultimately the clearest result of political developments throughout Europe in the late Middle Ages was the preservation of basic high-medieval patterns. The areas of Italy and Germany which had been politically divided before 1300 remained politically divided thereafter. The emergence of middle-sized states in both of these areas in the fifteenth century brought more stability than had existed before, but events would show that Italy and Germany would still be the prey of the Western powers. The latter were clearly much stronger because they were consolidated around stronger national monarchies. The trials of the later Middle Ages put the existence of these monarchies to the test, but after 1450 they emerged stronger than ever. The clearest illustration of their superiority is shown by the history of Italy in the years immediately following 1494. Until then the Italian states appeared to be relatively well governed and prosperous. They experimented with advanced techniques of administration and diplomacy. But when France and Spain invaded the peninsula the Italian states fell over like houses of cards. The Western monarchies could simply draw on greater resources and thus inherited the future of Europe.

5. THE FORMATION OF THE EMPIRE OF RUSSIA

Just as the half century after 1450 witnessed the definitive consolidation of the power of the western European nation-states, so it saw the rise to prominence of the state that henceforth was to be the dominant power in the european East—Russia. But Russia was not at all like a Western nation-state; rather, by about 1500 Russia had taken the first decisive steps on its way to becoming Europe's leading Eastern-style empire.

Had it not been for a combination of late-medieval circumstances, one or several Russian states might well have developed along typical Western lines. Indeed, the founders of the first political entity located in the territories of modern-day Russia were themselves Westerners— Swedish Vikings who in the tenth century established a principality centered around Kiev for the purposes of protecting their lines of trade between Scandinavia and Constantinople. (The very word *Rus* is Slavic for Swede.) Within two or three generations these Vikings became linguistically assimilated by their Slavic environment, but the Kievan state they founded remained until about 1200 very much part of the greater European community of nations. Since Kiev lay on the westernmost extremity of the Russian plain (properly speaking, Kiev is not in Russia at all but is the center of a territory known as the Ukraine) it was natural for the Kievan state of the High Middle Ages to maintain close and cordial diplomatic and trading relations with western

A Swedish Viking. An elk-horn carving showing the sort of Viking warrior who founded the Kievan state.

Europe. For example, in the eleventh century King Henry I of France was married to a Kievan princess, Anne, and their son was consequently given the Kievan name of Philip, a christening that marked the introduction of this hitherto foreign first name into the West. Aside from such direct links with Western culture, Kievan government bore some similarity to Western limited monarchy inasmuch as the ruling power of the Kievan princes was limited by the institution of the *veche,* or popular assembly.

Reasons for retreat from the West: (1) the Mongol conquests in Russia

But after 1200 four epoch-making developments conspired to drive a wedge between Russia and western European civilization. The first was the conquest of most of Russia by the Mongols, or Tartars, in the thirteenth century. As early as the mid–twelfth century Kiev had been buffeted by the incursions of an Asiatic tribe known as Cumans, but Kiev and other loosely federated Russian principalities ultimately managed to hold the Cumans at bay. The utterly savage Mongols, who crossed the Urals from Asia into Russia in 1237, however, were quite another matter. Commanded by Batu, a grandson of the dreaded Genghis Khan, the Mongols cut such swaths of devastation as they advanced westward that, according to one contemporary, "no eye remained open to weep for the dead." In 1240 the Mongols overran Kiev, and two years later they created their own state on the lower Volga River—the Khanate of the Golden Horde—that exerted suzerainty over almost all of Russia for roughly the following two centuries. Unwilling or unable to institute governmental arrangements that would permit them to rule the vast expanses of Russia directly, the Mongol Khans instead tolerated the existence of several native Russian states, from whom they demanded obeisance and regular monetary tribute. Under this "Tartar yoke," the normal course of Russian political development was inevitably impeded.

The native Russian principality which finally emerged to defeat the Mongols and unify much of Russia in the fifteenth century was the Grand Duchy of Moscow, situated deep in the northeastern Russian

Kievans Chasing Cumans. From a fifteenth–century Russian manuscript.

interior. Inasmuch as Moscow was located very far away from the Mongol power base on the lower Volga, the Muscovite dukes had greater freedom of initiative to consolidate their strength free from Mongol interference than did some of their rivals, and when the Mongol Khans began to realize what was happening, it was too late to stem the Muscovite tide. But Moscow's remote location also placed it extremely far from western Europe: about 600 miles (often snow covered) farther away from France or Italy than the distance separating those countries from Kiev. This added distance alone would have presented an appreciable obstacle to the establishment of close relations between Moscow and the West, but, to make matters far worse, the rise of Poland-Lithuania after 1386 and the fall of Constantinople in 1453 rendered cordial relations all but impossible.

Throughout most of the Middle Ages the Kingdom of Poland had been a second-rate power, usually on the defensive against German encroachments. But in the fourteenth century that situation changed dramatically, partly because German strength had by then become a ghost of its former self, and above all because the marriage in 1386 of Poland's reigning queen, Jadwiga, to Jagiello, grand duke of Lithuania, more than doubled Poland's size and enabled it to become a major expansionist state. Even before 1386 the Grand Duchy of Lithuania had begun to carve out an extensive territory for itself, not just on the shores of the Baltic where the present territory of Lithuania lies, but in the western Russian regions of Byelorussia and the Ukraine. Obviously, Lithuania's expansionist momentum increased after the union with Poland: in 1410 combined Polish-Lithuanian forces inflicted a stunning defeat on the German military order of Teutonic Knights who ruled neighboring Prussia at the battle of Tannenberg, and Poland-Lithuania extended its borders so far east in the early fifteenth century that the new power seemed on the verge of conquering all of Russia. But Poland-Lithuania subscribed to Roman Catholicism in religion, whereas many of the Russian peoples it had conquered were Eastern Orthodox who accordingly resented the sway of their new rulers. Eastern Orthodox Moscow was the obvious beneficiary of such discontent, becoming a center of religious resistance to Poland. Thus when Moscow was able to move on the offensive against Poland-Lithuania in the late fifteenth century, it appealed to religious as well as national sentiments. Prolonged warfare ensued, greatly exacerbating antagonisms, and since Poland-Lithuania stood in the Muscovites' minds for all the West, Moscow's attitude toward all of Western civilization became ever more etched by hostility.

Finally, interrelated with this trend were the incalculable effects wrought by the fall of Constantinople to the Turks in 1453. We have seen in Chapter 10 that missionaries from the Byzantine Empire had been responsible for converting Russia to the Eastern Orthodox faith in the late tenth century. During the Kievan period Russia's commitment to Eastern Orthodoxy posed no barrier to cordial communica-

NORWAY

SWEDEN

WHITE
SEA

•Archangel

FINLAND

BALTIC SEA

LIVONIA

TEUTONIC
ORDERS

REP. OF NOVGOROD
•Novgorod

URAL MOUNTAINS

TEUTONIC
ORDER
PRUSSIA

LITHUANIA

Tannenberg

BYELORUSSIA

KAZAN

Smolensk•

DUCHY OF
MOSCOW

•Moscow

Nizhny
Novgorod

Kazan•

POLAND

KINGDOM OF POLAND
AND LITHUANIA

Cracow•

UKRAINE

Kiev•

Dnieper R.

KHANATE OF
THE GOLDEN HORDE

HUNGARY

MOLDAVIA

Volga R.

VALLACHIA

CRIMEA

ASTRAKHAN

BLACK SEA

OTTOMAN

Constantinople•

EMPIRE

CASPIAN
SEA

	Moscow c. 1300
	Expansion to 1389
	Expansion to 1462
	Expansion to 1505
- - -	Kievan Russia (10-11th centuries)

RUSSIA TO 1505

tions with western Europe because there was as yet no insuperable religious enmity between Orthodox Byzantium and the West. But embittered hatred is the only expression to describe Byzantine attitudes toward Rome after 1204 when the Western Fourth Crusaders sacked Constantinople. Eastern Orthodox Russians came to sympathize with their Byzantine mentors thereafter, and felt all the more that they had extraordinarily good reason to shun the "Roman infection" after the debacle of 1453. This was because in 1438 the Byzantines in Constantinople, sensing correctly that a mighty Turkish onslaught was in the offing, swallowed their pride and agreed to a submissive religious compromise with the papacy in the hope that this might earn them Western military support for their last-ditch stand. But despite this submission, no Western help was forthcoming and Constantinople fell to the Turks in 1453 without any Roman Catholic knight lifting a hand. Meanwhile, however, the Orthodox hierarchy of Moscow had refused to follow Byzantium in its religious submission for the obvious reason that Moscow was in no way threatened by the Turks. Once Constantinople fell, therefore, the Muscovites reached the conclusion that the Turkish victory was a divine chastisement for the Byzantines' religious perfidy and the Muscovite state became the center of a particularly zealous anti-Roman ideology.

It is against this backdrop that we can examine the reign of the man who did the most to turn the Grand Duchy of Moscow into the nascent empire of Russia, Ivan III (1462–1505), customarily known as Ivan the Great. Ivan's immediate predecessor, Vasily II, had already gained the upper hand in Moscow's struggle to overthrow the domination of the Mongols, but Ivan was the one who completed this process by formally renouncing all subservience to the Mongol Khanate in 1480, by which time the Mongols were too awed by Muscovy's strength to offer any resistance. Concurrently, between 1462 and 1485, Ivan annexed one by one all the independent Russian principalities that remained between Moscow and Poland-Lithuania. And finally, as the result of two successive invasions of Lithuania (1492 and 1501), the mighty conqueror wrested away a whole stretch of Byelorussian and Ukranian territory along his western border. Thus when Ivan the Great died in 1505, it had become clear that Muscovy was a power to be reckoned with on the European scene.

Ivan the Great

But it also would have been clear to any observer that Russian culture and government were now almost completely non-Western. Having been divorced from the West for all practical purposes since about 1200, Russia had not kept up with the most basic Western intellectual and cultural developments. For example, there was virtually no secular literature, arithmetic was barely known, Arabic numerals were not used, and merchants made their calculations with the abacus. Nor were manners and customs comparable to those of the West. Women of the upper classes were veiled and secluded, and flowing beards and skirted garments were universal for men.

Russia's isolation from the West

Perhaps most important, during the reign of Ivan III Russia was evolving in the direction of Eastern-style political autocracy and imperialism. This can be seen most clearly in Ivan's assumption of the title "tsar of all the Russias." The word *tsar* (sometimes spelled czar) is Russian for Caesar, and Ivan's appropriation of it meant that he was claiming to be the successor of the defunct Byzantine emperors, who themselves had been heirs of the Roman Caesars. To reinforce this claim, Ivan married the niece of the last Byzantine ruler, adopted as his insignia the Byzantine double-headed eagle, encouraged his churchmen to proclaim Moscow as "the third Rome," and rebuilt Moscow's fortified princely residence, the Kremlin, in magnificent style to manifest his imperial splendor. Ivan's appropriation of the Byzantine model was fateful for Russia's future political development because it enabled him and his successors to imitate the Byzantine emperors in behaving like Oriental despots who assumed without discussion that "what pleases the prince has the force of law." Moreover, as "tsar of all the Russias," Ivan conceived of himself as the autocratic potentate not just of the Russians of Moscow but of all Russians, and even of Byelorussians and Ukrainians. As the subsequent course of events would show, this was the beginning of an expansionist policy by which future Russian tsars would incorporate both Russian and a wide variety of non-Russian peoples into Europe's largest empire.

6. THOUGHT, LITERATURE, AND ART

Although it might be guessed that the extreme hardships of the later Middle Ages in western Europe should have led to the decline or stagnation of intellectual and artistic endeavors, in fact the period was an extremely fruitful one in the realms of thought, literature, and art. In this section we will postpone treatment of certain developments most closely related to the early history of the Italian Renaissance, but will discuss some of western Europe's other important late-medieval intellectual and artistic accomplishments.

Theology and philosophy after about 1300 faced a crisis of doubt. This doubt did not concern the existence of God and His supernatural powers, but was rather doubt about human ability to comprehend the supernatural. Whereas St. Thomas Aquinas and other Scholastics in the High Middle Ages had serenely delimited the number of "mysteries of the faith" and believed that everything else, both in heaven and earth, could be thoroughly understood by humans, the floods, frosts, wars, and plagues of the fourteenth century helped undermine such confidence in the powers of human understanding. Once human beings experienced the universe as arbitrary and unpredictable, fourteenth-century thinkers began to wonder whether there was not far more in heaven and earth than could be understood by their philosophies. The result was a thoroughgoing reevaluation of the prior theological and philosophical outlook.

The leading late-medieval abstract thinker was the English Franciscan William of Ockham, who was born around 1285 and died in 1349, apparently from the Black Death. Traditionally, Franciscans had always had greater doubts than Dominicans like St. Thomas concerning the abilities of human reason to comprehend the supernatural; Ockham, convinced by the events of his age, expressed these most formidably. He denied that the existence of God and numerous other theological matters could be demonstrated apart from scriptural revelation, and he emphasized God's freedom and absolute power to do anything He wished. In the realm of human knowledge per se Ockham's searching intellect drove him to look for absolute certainties instead of mere theories. In investigating earthly matters he developed the position, known as *nominalism,* that only individual things, but not collectivities, are real, and that one thing therefore cannot be understood by means of another: to know a chair one has to see and touch it rather than just know what several other chairs are like. Ockham also formulated a logic which was based upon the assumption that words stood only for themselves rather than for real things. Such logic might not say much about the real world, but at least it could not be refuted, since it was as internally valid in its own terms as Euclidean geometry.

William of Ockham; nominalism

Ockham's outlook, which gained widespread adherence in the late-medieval universities, today often seems overly methodological and verging on the arid, but it had several important effects on the development of Western thought. Ockham's concern about what God *might* do led to the raising by his followers of some of the seemingly absurd questions for which medieval theology has been mocked, for example, asking whether God can undo the past, or whether an infinite number of pure spirits can simultaneously inhabit the same place (the nearest medieval thinkers actually came to asking how many angels can dance on the head of a pin). Nonetheless, Ockham's emphasis on preserving God's autonomy led to a stress on divine omnipotence that became one of the basic presuppositions of sixteenth-century Protestantism. Further, Ockham's determination to find certainties in the realm of human knowledge ultimately helped make it possible to discuss human affairs and natural science without reference to supernatural explanations—one of the most important foundations of the modern scientific method. Finally, Ockham's opposition to studying collectivities and his refusal to apply logic to real things helped encourage *empiricism,* or the belief that knowledge of the world should rest on sense experience rather than abstract reason. This too is a presupposition for scientific progress: thus it is probably not coincidental that some of Ockham's fourteenth-century followers made significant advances in the study of physics.

The significance of Ockham's thought

Ockham's search for reliable truths finds certain parallels in the realm of late-medieval literature, although Ockham surely had no direct influence in that field. The major trait of the best late-medieval literature was *naturalism,* or the attempt to describe things the way they really are. This was more a development from high-medieval precedents—such as the explorations of human conduct pursued by Chrétien de Troyes, Wolfram von Eschenbach, and Dante—than a reaction against them. The steady growth of a lay reading public furthermore encouraged authors to avoid theological and philosophical abstractions and seek more to entertain by portraying people realistically with all their strengths and foibles. Another main characteristic of late-medieval literature, the predominance of composition in the European vernaculars instead of Latin, also developed out of high-medieval precedents but gained great momentum in the later Middle Ages for two different reasons. One was that international tensions and hostilities, including the numerous wars of the age and the trials of the universal papacy, led to need for security and a pride of self-identification reflected by the use of vernacular tongues. Probably more important was the fact that continued spread of education for the laity greatly increased a public that could read in a given vernacular language but not in Latin. Hence although much poetry was written during the High Middle Ages in the vernacular, in the later Middle Ages use of the vernacular was widely extended to prose. Moreover, countries such as Italy and England, which had just begun to cultivate their own vernacular literatures around 1300, subsequently began to employ their native tongues to the most impressive literary effect.

The greatest writer of vernacular prose fiction of the later Middle Ages was the Italian Giovanni Boccaccio (1313–1375). Although Boccaccio would have taken an honored place in literary history for some of his lesser works, which included courtly romances, pastoral poems, and learned treatises, by far the most impressive of his writings is the *Decameron,* written between 1348 and 1351. This is a collection of one hundred stories, mostly about love and sex, adventure, and clever trickery, supposedly told by a sophisticated party of seven young ladies and three men who are sojourning in a country villa outside Florence in order to escape the ravages of the Black Death. Boccaccio by no means invented all one hundred plots, but even when he borrowed the outlines of his tales from earlier sources he retold the stories in his own characteristically exuberant, masterful, and extremely witty fashion. There are many reasons why the *Decameron* must be counted as epoch-making from a historical point of view. The first is that it was the earliest ambitious and successful work of vernacular creative literature ever written in western Europe in narrative prose. Boccaccio's prose is "modern" in the sense that it is brisk, for unlike the medieval authors of flowery romances, Boccaccio purposely wrote in an unaffected, colloquial style. Simply stated, in the *Decameron* he was less interested in being "elevated" or elegant than in being unpretentiously entertaining. From the point of view of content, Boccaccio wished to portray men and women as they really are rather than as they ought to be. Thus when he wrote about the clergy he showed them to be as susceptible to human appetites and failings as other mortals. His women are not pallid playthings, distant goddesses, or steadfast virgins, but flesh-and-blood creatures with intellects, who interact more comfortably and naturally with men and with each other than any women in Western literature had ever done before. Boccaccio's treatment of sexual relations is often graphic, often witty, but never demeaning. In his world the natural desires of both women and men are not meant to be thwarted. For all these reasons the *Decameron* is a robust and delightful appreciation of all that is human.

Similar in many ways to Boccaccio as a creator of robust, naturalistic vernacular literature was the Englishman Geoffrey Chaucer (c. 1340–1400). Chaucer was the first major writer of an English that can still be read today with relatively little effort. Remarkably, he was both a founding father of England's mighty literary tradition and one of the four or five greatest contributors to it: most critics rank him just behind Shakespeare, and in a class with Milton, Wordsworth, and Dickens. Chaucer wrote several highly impressive works, but his masterpiece is unquestionably the unfinished *Canterbury Tales,* dating from the end of his career. Like the *Decameron,* this is a collection of stories held together by a frame, in Chaucer's case the device of having a group of people tell stories while on a pilgrimage from London to Canterbury. But there are also differences between the *Decameron* and the *Canterbury Tales.* Chaucer's stories are told in sparkling verse instead of prose and they are recounted by people of all different classes—from a chivalric knight to a dedicated university student to a thieving miller with a wart on his nose. Lively women are also represented, most memorably the gap-toothed, oft-married "Wife of Bath," who knows all "the remedies of love." Each character tells a story which is particularly illustrative of his or her own occupation and outlook on the world. By this device Chaucer is able to create a highly diverse "human comedy." His range is therefore greater than Boccaccio's and although he is as witty, frank, and lusty as the Italian, he is sometimes more profound.

As naturalism was a dominant trait of late-medieval literature, so it was of late-medieval art. Already by the thirteenth century Gothic sculptors were paying far more attention than their Romanesque predecessors had done to the way plants, animals, and human beings really looked. Whereas medieval art had previously emphasized abstract design, the stress was now increasingly on realism: thirteenth-century carvings of leaves and flowers must have been done from direct observation and are the first to be clearly recognizable as distinct species. Statues of humans also gradually became more naturally proportioned and realistic in their portrayals of facial expressions. By around 1290 the concern for realism had become so great that a sculptor working on a tomb-portrait of the German Emperor Rudolf of Habsburg allegedly made a hurried return trip to view Rudolf in person, because he

Chaucer

Naturalism in late-medieval art

Painting

The naturalistic style of Giotto

See color plates facing page 448 for *The Flight into Egypt* by Giotto

had heard that a new wrinkle had appeared on the emperor's face.

In the next two centuries the trend toward naturalism continued in sculpture and was extended to manuscript illumination and painting. The latter was in certain basic respects a new art. Ever since the caveman, painting had been done on walls, but walls of course were not easily movable. The art of wall-painting continued to be cultivated in the Middle Ages and long afterward, especially in the form of *frescoes,* or paintings done on wet plaster. But in addition to frescoes, Italian artists in the thirteenth century first started painting pictures on pieces of wood or canvas. These were first done in tempera (pigments mixed with water and natural gums or eggwhites), but around 1400 painting in oils was introduced in the European north. These new technical developments created new artistic opportunities. Artists were now able to paint religious scenes on altarpieces for churches and for private devotions practiced by the wealthier laity at home. Artists also painted the first Western portraits, which were meant to gratify the self-esteem of monarchs and aristocrats. The earliest surviving example of a naturalistic painted portrait is one of a French king, John the Good, executed around 1360. Others followed quickly, so that within a short time the art of portraiture done from life was highly developed. Visitors to art museums will notice that some of the most realistic and sensitive portraits of all time date from the fifteenth century.

The most pioneering and important painter of the later Middle Ages was the Florentine Giotto (c. 1267–1337). He did not engage in individual portraiture, but he brought deep humanity to his religious images done on both walls and movable panels. Giotto was preeminently a naturalist, i.e., an imitator of nature. Not only do his human beings and animals look more natural than those of his predecessors, they seem to do more natural things. When Christ enters Jerusalem on Palm Sunday, boys climb trees to get a better view; when St. Francis is laid out in death, one onlooker takes the opportunity to see whether the saint had really received Christ's wounds; and when the Virgin's parents, Joachim and Anna, meet after a long separation, they actually embrace and kiss—perhaps the first deeply tender kiss in Western art. It was certainly not true, as one fanciful storyteller later reported, that an onlooker found a fly Giotto had painted so real that he attempted to brush it away with his hand, but Giotto in fact accomplished something more. Specifically, he was the first to conceive of the painted space in fully three-dimensional terms: as one art historian has put it, Giotto's frescoes were the first to "knock a hole into the wall." After Giotto's death a reaction in Italian painting set in. This was probably caused by a new reverence for the awesomely supernatural brought about by the horrors of the plague. Whatever the explanation, artists of the mid–fourteenth century briefly moved away from naturalism and painted stern, forbidding religious figures who seemed to float in space. But by around 1400 artists came back down to earth and started

The Meeting of Joachim and Anna at the Golden Gate. A fresco by Giotto. Note how the haloes merge: this old and barren couple will soon miraculously have a child, none other than Mary, the mother of Jesus.

to build upon Giotto's influence in ways that led to the great Italian renaissance in painting.

In the north of Europe painting did not advance impressively beyond manuscript illumination until the early fifteenth century, but then it suddenly came very much into its own. The leading northern European painters were Flemish, first and foremost the brothers Hubert and Jan van Eyck (c. 1366–1426; c. 1380–1441), Roger van der Weyden (c. 1400–1464), and Hans Memling (c. 1430–1494). The van Eycks used to be credited with the invention of oil painting; while that is now open to question, they certainly were its greatest early practitioners. The use of oils allowed them and the other fifteenth-century Flemish painters to engage in brilliant coloring and sharp-focused realism. The van Eycks and van der Weyden excelled most at two things: communicating a sense of deep religious piety and portraying minute details of familiar everyday experience. These may at first seem incompatible, but it should be remembered that contemporary manuals of practical mysticism such as *The Imitation of Christ* also sought to link deep piety with everyday existence. Thus it was by no means blasphemous when a Flemish painter would portray behind a tender Madonna and Child a vista of contemporary life with people going about their usual business and a man even urinating against a wall. This union between the sacred and profane tended to fall apart in the work of Memling, who excelled in either straightforward religious pictures or secular portraits, but it would return in the work of the greatest painters of the Low Countries, Brueghel and Rembrandt.

The Flemish painters

See color plates facing page 384 for *The Virgin and Chacellor Rollin* by Jan van Eyck

7. ADVANCES IN TECHNOLOGY

Late-medieval technological achievements: (1) the weapons of war

No account of enduring late-medieval accomplishments would be complete without mention of certain epoch-making technological advances. Sadly, but probably not unexpectedly, treatment of this subject has to begin with reference to the invention of artillery and firearms. The prevalence of warfare stimulated the development of new weaponry. Gunpowder itself was a Chinese invention, but it was first put to particularly devastating uses in the late-medieval West. Heavy cannons, which made terrible noises "as though all the dyvels of hell had been in the way," were first employed around 1330. The earliest cannons were so primitive that it often was more dangerous to stand behind than in front of them, but by the middle of the fifteenth century they were greatly improved and began to revolutionize the nature of warfare. In one year, 1453, heavy artillery played a leading role in determining the outcome of two crucial conflicts: the Ottoman Turks used German and Hungarian cannons to breach the defenses of Constantinople—hitherto the most impregnable in Europe—and the French used heavy artillery to take the city of Bordeaux, thereby ending the Hundred Years' War. Cannons thereafter made it difficult for rebellious aristocrats to hole up in their stone castles, and thus they aided in the consolidation of the national monarchies. Placed aboard ships, cannons enabled European vessels to dominate foreign waters in the subsequent age of overseas expansion. Guns, also invented in the fourteenth century, were gradually perfected afterward. Shortly after 1500 the most effective new variety of gun, the musket, allowed foot-soldiers to end once and for all the earlier military dominance of heavily armored mounted knights. Once lance-bearing cavalries became outmoded and fighting could more easily be carried on by all, the monarchical states that could turn out the largest armies completely subdued internal resistance and dominated the battlefields of Europe.

(2) optical and navigational instruments

Other late-medieval technological developments were more life-enhancing. Eyeglasses, first invented in the 1280s, were perfected in the fourteenth century. These allowed older people to keep on reading when nearsightedness would otherwise have stopped them. For example, the great fourteenth-century scholar Petrarch, who boasted excellent sight in his youth, wore spectacles after his sixtieth year and was thus enabled to complete some of his most important works. Around 1300 the use of the magnetic compass helped ships to sail farther away from land and venture out into the Atlantic. One immediate result was the opening of direct sea commerce between Italy and the North. Subsequently, numerous improvements in shipbuilding, map making, and navigational devices contributed to Europe's ability to start expanding overseas. In the early fourteenth century the Azores and Cape Verde Islands were reached; then, after a long pause caused

Cannons Being Used to Breach the Walls of a Castle. This scene depicts a late engagement of the Hundred Years' War.

by Europe's plagues and wars, the African Cape of Good Hope was rounded in 1487, the West Indies discovered in 1492, India reached by the sea route in 1498, and Brazil discovered in 1500. Partly as a result of technology the world was thus suddenly made much smaller.

Among the most familiar implements of our modern life that were invented by Europeans in the later Middle Ages were clocks and printed books. Mechanical clocks were invented shortly before 1300 and proliferated in the years immediately thereafter. The earliest clocks were too expensive for private purchase, but towns quickly vied with each other to install the most elaborate clocks in their prominent public buildings. These clocks not only told the time but showed the courses of sun, moon, and planets, and performed mechanical tricks on the striking of the hours. The new invention ultimately had two profound effects. One was the further stimulation of European interest in complex machinery of all sorts. This interest had already been awakened by the high-medieval proliferation of mills, but clocks ultimately became even more omnipresent than mills because after about 1650 they became quite cheap and were brought into practically every European home. Household clocks served as models of marvelous machines. Equally if not more significant was the fact that clocks began to rationalize the course of European daily affairs. Until the advent of clocks in the late Middle Ages time was flexible. Men and women had only a rough idea of how late in the day it was and rose and retired more or less with the sun. Especially people who lived in the country performed different jobs at different rates according to the rhythm of the seasons. Even when hours were counted, they were measured at different lengths according to the amount of light in the

(3) mechanical clocks

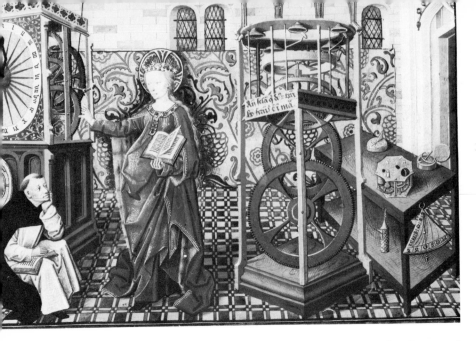

Horloge de Sapience. This miniature, from an early–fifteenth-century French manuscript, reflects the growing fascination with machines of all sorts and clocks in particular.

different seasons of the year. In the fourteenth century, however, clocks first started relentlessly striking equal hours through the day and night. Thus they began to regulate work with new precision. People were expected to start and end work "on time" and many came to believe that "time is money." This emphasis on time-keeping brought new efficiencies but also new tensions: Lewis Carroll's white rabbit, who is always looking at his pocket watch and muttering, "how late it's getting," is a telling caricature of time-obsessed Western man.

(4) the invention of printing

The invention of printing with movable type was equally momentous. The major stimulus for this invention was the replacement of parchment by paper as Europe's primary writing material between 1200 and 1400. Parchment, made from the skins of valuable farm animals, was extremely expensive: since it was possible to get only about four good parchment leaves from one animal, it was necessary to slaughter between two to three hundred sheep or calves to gain enough parchment for a Bible! Paper, made from rags turned into pulp by mills, brought prices down dramatically. Late-medieval records show that paper sold at one-sixth the price of parchment. Accordingly, it became cheaper to learn how to read and write. With literacy becoming ever more widespread, there was a growing market for still cheaper books, and the invention of printing with movable type around 1450 fully met this demand. By greatly saving labor, the invention made printed books about one-fifth as expensive as handwritten ones within about two decades.

The effects of printing

As soon as books became easily accessible, literacy increased even more and book-culture became a basic part of the European way of life. After about 1500 Europeans could afford to read and buy books of all sorts—not just religious tracts, but instructional manuals, light ententertainment, and, by the eighteenth century, newspapers. Printing ensured that ideas would spread quickly and reliably; moreover, revolutionary ideas could no longer be easily extinguished once they were set down in hundreds of copies of books. Thus the greatest religious reformer of the sixteenth century, Martin Luther, gained an immediate following throughout Germany by employing the printing press to run off pamphlets: had printing not been available to him, Luther might have died like Hus. The spread of books also helped stimulate the growth of cultural nationalism. Before printing, regional dialects in most European countries were often so diverse that people who supposedly spoke the same language often could barely understand each other. Such a situation hindered governmental centralization because a royal servant might be entirely unable to communicate with inhabitants of the provinces. Shortly after the invention of printing, however, each European country began to develop its own linguistic standards which were disseminated uniformly by books. The "King's English" was what was printed in London and carried to Yorkshire or Wales. Thus communications were enhanced and governments were able to operate ever more efficiently.

In conclusion it may be said that clocks and books as much as guns and ocean-going ships helped Europe to dominate the globe after 1500. The habits inculcated by clocks encouraged Europeans to work

Left: *Paper-Making at a Paper Mill*. Right: *A Printing Press*. From a title page of a Parisian printer, 1520.

efficiently and to plan precisely; the prevalence of books enhanced communications and the flow of progressive ideas. Once accustomed to reading books, Europeans communicated and experimented intellectually as no other peoples in the world. Thus it was not surprising that after 1500 Europeans could start to make the whole world their own.

SELECTED READINGS

• *Items so designated are available in paperback editions.*

Breisach, E., *Renaissance Europe, 1300–1517*, New York, 1973. The best college-level textbook on the period.

Bridbury, A. R., *Economic Growth: England in the Later Middle Ages*, 2nd ed., New York, 1975. A controversial argument against the dominant theory of economic depression.

• Brucker, G., *Renaissance Florence*, New York, 1969. An excellent introduction by one of America's foremost experts.

• Cipolla, C. M., *Clocks and Culture, 1300–1700*, London, 1967. Treats both technological developments and the importance of clocks as items of trade.

• Cole, Bruce, *Giotto and Florentine Painting, 1280–1375*, New York, 1976. A clear and stimulating introduction.

Dollinger, P., *The German Hansa*, Stanford, Calif., 1970.

Florinsky, M. T., *Russia: A History and Interpretation*, Vol. I, New York, 1961. The best narrative in English of early Russian developments.

Hale, John R., et al., *Europe in the Late Middle Ages*, Evanston, Ill., 1965. Specialized essays on numerous subjects.

Herlihy, David, *Medieval and Renaissance Pistoia: The Social History of an Italian Town*, New Haven, Conn., 1967. Important for its use of statistical evidence.

• Holmes, George, *The Later Middle Ages, 1272–1485*, New York, 1962.

• Huizinga, J., *The Waning of the Middle Ages*, London, 1924. An evocatively written classic on forms of thought and art in the Low Countries.

• Johnson, Jerah, and W. Percy, *The Age of Recovery: The Fifteenth Century*, Ithaca, N.Y., 1970.

Kaminsky, H., *A History of the Hussite Revolution*, Berkeley, Calif., 1967. Detailed and difficult but far and away the best treatment of the subject.

• Lerner, R. E., *The Age of Adversity: The Fourteenth Century*, Ithaca, N.Y., 1968.

Lewis, P. S., *Later Medieval France: The Polity*, London, 1968.

McFarlane, K. B., *The Nobility of Later Medieval England*, Oxford, 1973. An excellent collection of essays by a late master of the field.

• Meiss, M., *Painting in Florence and Siena After the Black Death*, Princeton, N.J., 1951. A stimulating attempt to relate art history to the spirit of an age.

• Miskimin, H. A., *The Economy of Early Renaissance Europe, 1300–1460*, Englewood Cliffs, N.J., 1969. The best short work on the subject.

Mollat, G., *The Popes at Avignon, 1305–1378,* London, 1963.

Mollat, M., and P. Wolff, *The Popular Revolts of the Late Middle Ages,* London, 1973.

Oakley, F., *The Western Church in the Later Middle Ages,* Ithaca, N.Y., 1979.

• Panofsky, E., *Early Netherlandish Painting,* 2 vols., Cambridge, Mass., 1953. A brilliant specialized history by a master art historian.

• Pernoud, R., *Joan of Arc,* New York, 1966. Joan viewed through the eyes of her contemporaries.

Perroy, E., *The Hundred Years War,* Bloomington, Ind., 1959. The standard account.

Scaglione, A., *Nature and Love in the Late Middle Ages,* Berkeley, Calif., 1963.

• Smart, Alastair, *The Dawn of Italian Painting, 1250–1400,* Ithaca, N.Y., 1978. More detailed than Cole.

Trinkaus, C., and H. A. Oberman, eds., *The Pursuit of Holiness in Late Medieval and Renaissance Religion,* Leiden, 1974. Essays that reveal the most recent trends in research.

Vaughan, Richard, *Valois Burgundy,* London, 1975.

SOURCE MATERIALS

Allmand, C. T., ed., *Society at War: The Experience of England and France During the Hundred Years War,* Edinburgh, 1973. An outstanding collection of documents.

• Boccaccio, G., *The Decameron,* tr. M. Musa and P. E. Bondanella, New York, 1977.

• Chaucer, G., *The Canterbury Tales.* (Many editions.)

Colledge, E., ed., *The Mediaeval Mystics of England,* New York, 1961.

• Froissart, J., *Chronicles,* tr. G. Brereton, Baltimore, 1968. A selection from the most famous contemporary account of the Hundred Years' War. Reads more like a novel than like history.

The Imitation of Christ, tr. L. Sherley-Price, Baltimore, 1952.

John Hus at the Council of Constance, tr. M. Spinka, New York, 1965. The translation of a Czech chronicle with an expert introduction and appended collection of documents.

Meister Eckhart, tr. R. B. Blakney, New York, 1941.

Memoirs of a Renaissance Pope: The Commentaries of Pius II (abridged ed.), tr. F. A. Gragg, New York, 1959. A fascinating insight into the Renaissance papacy.

A Parisian Journal, 1405–1449, tr. J. Shirley, Oxford, 1968. A marvelous panorama of Parisian life recorded by an eyewitness.

• Pitti, B., and G. Dati, *Two Memoirs of Renaissance Florence,* tr. J. Martines, New York, 1967.

Part Four

THE EARLY-MODERN WORLD

Historians tend to agree that the Middle Ages ended sometime roughly around 1500 and were followed by an "early-modern" period of European history that lasted until the concurrent outbreaks of the French and Industrial Revolutions at the very end of the eighteenth century. As early as about 1350 in Italy representatives of a new cultural movement, usually called the Renaissance, began to challenge certain basic medieval assumptions and offer alternatives to medieval modes of literary and artistic expression. By around 1500 Renaissance ideals had not only triumphed fully in Italy, but they were also spreading to northern Europe where they were reconceived to produce the highly influential movement of Christian humanism. At the same time, in the early sixteenth century western Europe lost much of its medieval appearance by expanding and dividing. Intrepid mariners and conquista-dores *ended Europe's millennium of geographical self-containment by venturing onto the high seas of the Atlantic and Indian Oceans and by planting Europe's flag throughout the world. Concurrently, however, Europe lost its religious uniformity as a result of the Protestant Reformation, which divided the continent up into hostile religious camps. Thereafter, from about 1560 to about 1660 western Europe experienced a period of grave economic, political, and spiritual crisis but emerged from this century of testing with renewed energy and confidence. A commercial revolution spurred the development of overseas colonies and trade, and encouraged agricultural and industrial expansion. Though monarchs continued to meet with opposition from the various estates within their realms, they asserted their power as absolute rulers, stabilizing domestic unrest by continually expanding state bureaucracies.*

Warfare remained the chief instrument of their foreign policies; yet by the end of the period, the mutually recognized goal of those policies was more often the maintenance of a general balance of power than the pursuit of unrestrained aggrandizement. Finally, in the later seventeenth century the scientific revolution, initiated earlier by Copernicus, was completed by Sir Isaac Newton, and was followed during the eighteenth century by the "Enlightenment," or enthronement of a new secular faith in humanity's ability to master nature and better itself by its own efforts.

The Early Modern World

POLITICS	PHILOSOPHY AND SCIENCE	
	Civic humanism in Italy, c. 1400–c. 1450	*1400*
	Lorenzo Valla, 1407–1457	
Renaissance popes, 1447–1521	Florentine Neoplatonism, c. 1450–c. 1600	
French invade Italy, 1494	Erasmus, c. 1467–1536	
	Machiavelli, 1469–1527	
	Nicholas Copernicus, 1473–1543	*1500*
Henry VIII of England, 1509–1547	Andreas Vesalius, 1514–1564	
Charles V, Holy Roman Emperor, 1519–1546	More's *Utopia,* 1516	
Troops of Charles V sack Rome, 1527		
Spanish gain supremacy in Italy, 1529	Jean Bodin, 1530–1596	
	Michel de Montaigne, 1533–1592	
Philip II of Spain, 1556–1598		
Elizabeth I of England, 1558–1603	Francis Bacon, 1561–1626	
Revolt of the Netherlands, 1566–1609	Galileo, 1564–1642	
Defeat of Spanish Armada, 1588	Johann Kepler, 1571–1630	
Henry IV of France, 1589–1610	William Harvey, 1578–1657	
	Thomas Hobbes, 1588–1679	
Edict of Nantes, 1598	René Descartes, 1596–1650	*1600*
Thirty Years' War, 1618–1648	Bacon's *Novum Organum,* 1620	
Supremacy of Richelieu in France, 1624–1642	Blaise Pascal, 1623–1662	
	John Locke, 1632–1704	
English Civil War, 1642–1649	Descartes' *Discourse on Method,* 1637	
Fronde revolts in France, 1648–1653	Isaac Newton, 1642–1727	
Commonwealth and Protectorate in England, 1649–1660		
Louis XIV of France, 1651–1715		
Frederick William, Elector of Brandenburg, 1640–1688		
Louis XIV of France, 1643–1715		
Leopold I, Habsburg emperor, 1658–1705		
Restoration of Stuart dynasty in England, 1660		
Charles II of England, 1660–1685		
Peter the Great of Russia, 1682–1725		
Revocation of the Edict of Nantes, 1685		
James II of England, 1685–1688	Newton's *Mathematical Principles of Natural Philoso-phy,* 1687	
"Glorious" revolution in England, 1688	Montesquieu, 1689–1755	
War of the League of Augsburg, 1688–1697		
John Locke, *Two Treatises of Government,* 1690		
War of the Spanish Succession, 1702–1714	Voltaire, 1694–1778	*1700*
Jacques Bossuet, *Politics Drawn from the Very Words of Holy Scripture,* 1708		
Treaty of Utrecht, 1713	Linnaeus, 1707–1778	
Frederick William I of Prussia, 1713–1740	David Hume, 1711–1776	
Louis XV of France, 1715–1774	Diderot, 1713–1784	
Ascendency of Robert Walpole as Britain's "first minister," 1720–1743		
Frederick the Great of Prussia, 1740–1786		
Maria Theresa of Austria, 1740–1780		
Seven Years' War, 1756–1763	Condorcet, 1743–1794	
George III of Britain, 1760–1820	Antoine Lavoisier, 1743–1794	
Catherine the Great of Russia, 1762–1796	French *Encyclopedia,* 1751–1772	
Louis XVI of France, 1774–1792	Edward Jenner introduces vaccination, 1796	
War of American Independence, 1776–1783		
Joseph II of Austria, 1780–1790		
Beginning of the French Revolution, 1789		

The Early Modern World (continued)

ECONOMICS	RELIGION	ARTS AND LETTERS
		Francis Petrarch, 1304–1374
1400		Italian Renaissance, c. 1350–c. 1550
Portugal gains control of East Indian spice trade, 1498–1511		Masaccio, 1401–1428
	Martin Luther, 1483–1546	Botticelli, 1444–1510
	Ulrich Zwingli, 1484–1531	Leonardo da Vinci, 1452–151•
	Ignatius Loyola, 1491–1556	Erasmus, c. 1467–1536
		Albrecht Dürer, 1471–1528
		Ariosto, 1474–1533
		Raphael, 1483–1520
1500	John Calvin, 1509–1564	Michelangelo, 1485–1564
	Letters of Obscure Men, 1515	Rabelais, c. 1494–1553
	Erasmus's Greek New Testament, 1516	Michelangelo's main work on Sistine Chapel, 1508–1512
	Luther attacks indulgences, 1517	Peter Brueghel, c. 1525–1569
		Palestrina, c. 1525–1594
Spain gains control of Central and South America, c. 1520–c. 1550	Henry VIII of England breaks with Rome, 1527–1534	El Greco, c. 1541–c. 1614
	Anabaptists seize Münster, 1534	Cervantes, 1547–1616
	Loyola's Society of Jesus approved by Pope Paul III, 1540	Shakespeare, 1564–1616
	Calvin takes over Geneva, 1541	Claudio Monteverdi, 1567–16.
	Council of Trent, 1545–1563	Rubens, 1577–1640
	Peace of Augsburg divides Germany into Lutheran and Catholic areas, 1555	Bernini, 1598–1680
"Price Revolution" in Europe, c. 1560–c. 1600		Velásquez, 1599–1660
Economic decline of Italy, c. 1580–c. 1700	Elizabethan religious compromise in England, c. 1558–c. 1570	
1600 Chartering of English East India Company, 1600		Rembrandt, 1606–1669
English Poor Law, 1601		John Milton, 1608–1674
Chartering of Dutch East India Company, 1602		Molière, 1622–1673
Settlement of Jamestown, 1607		Christopher Wren, 1632–172•
Height of mercantilism in Europe, 1650–1750		
Colbert's economic reforms in France, 1664–1683		Watteau, 1684–1721
Founding of Bank of England, 1694		J. S. Bach, 1685–1750
1700 Introduction of maize and potato crops in Europe, c. 1700		G. F. Handel, 1685–1759
Mississippi Bubble, 1715	John Wesley, 1703–1789	Voltaire, 1694–1778
South Sea Bubble, 1720		The Enlightenment, c. 1700–c. 1790
Last appearance of bubonic plague in western Europe, 1720		Henry Fielding, 1707–1754
Enclosure movement in England, 1730–1810		
General European population increase beginning 1750		Joseph Haydn, 1732–1809
		Edward Gibbon, 1737–1794
Adam Smith, *The Wealth of Nations,* 1776		W. A. Mozart, 1756–1791
		Jane Austen, 1775–1817

Chapter 14

THE CIVILIZATION
OF THE RENAISSANCE
(c. 1350—c. 1550)

Now may every reflecting spirit thank God he has chosen to live in this new age, so full of hope and promise, which already exults in a greater array of nobly-gifted souls than the world has seen in the thousand years before.

—Matteo Palmieri, *On the Civil Life,* c. 1435

Whatever was done by man with genius and with a certain grace he held to be almost divine.

—L. B. Alberti, *Self-Portrait,* c. 1460

The prevalent modern notion that a "Renaissance period" followed western Europe's medieval age was first expressed by numerous Italian writers who lived between 1350 and 1550. According to them, one thousand years of unrelieved darkness had intervened between the Roman era and their own times. During these "dark ages" the Muses of art and literature had fled Europe before the onslaught of barbarism and ignorance. Almost miraculously, however, in the fourteenth century the Muses suddenly returned and Italians happily collaborated with them to bring forth a glorious "renaissance of the arts."

"A renaissance of the arts"

Ever since this periodization was advanced historians have taken for granted the existence of some sort of "Renaissance," intervening between medieval and modern times. Indeed, in the late nineteenth and early twentieth centuries many scholars went so far as to argue that the Renaissance was not just an epoch in the history of learning and culture but that a unique "Renaissance spirit" transformed all aspects of life—political, economic, and religious, as well as intellec-

Limits of the term "Renaissance"

tual and artistic. Today, however, most experts no longer accept this characterization because they find it impossible to locate any truly distinctive "Renaissance" politics, economics, or religion. Instead, scholars tend to agree that the term "Renaissance" should be reserved to describe certain exciting trends in thought, literature, and the arts that emerged in Italy from roughly 1350 to 1550 and then spread to northern Europe during the first half of the sixteenth century. That is the approach that will be followed here: accordingly, when we refer to a "Renaissance period" in this chapter we mean to limit ourselves to an epoch in intellectual and cultural history.

Further qualifications

Granted this restriction, some further qualifications are still necessary. Since the word "renaissance" literally means "rebirth," it is sometimes thought that after about 1350 certain Italians who were newly cognizant of Greek and Roman cultural accomplishments initiated a classical cultural rebirth after a long period of "death." In fact, however, the High Middle Ages witnessed no "death" of classical learning. St. Thomas Aquinas, for example, considered Aristotle to be "the Philosopher" and Dante revered Virgil. Similarly, it would be completely false to oppose an imaginary "Renaissance paganism" to a medieval "age of faith" because however much most Renaissance personalities loved the classics, none went so far as to worship classical gods. And finally, all discussions of the postmedieval Renaissance must be qualified by the fact that there was no single Renaissance position on any given subject.

The continuing rediscovery and spread of classical learning

Nonetheless, in the realms of thought, literature, and the arts important distinguishing traits may certainly be found which make the concept of a "Renaissance" meaningful for intellectual and cultural history. First, regarding knowledge of the classics, there was indubitably a significant quantitative difference between the learning of the Middle Ages and that of the Renaissance. Medieval scholars knew many Roman authors, such as Virgil, Ovid, and Cicero, but in the Renaissance the works of others such as Livy, Tacitus, and Lucretius were rediscovered and made familiar. Equally if not more important was the Renaissance discovery of the literature of classical Greece. In the twelfth and thirteenth centuries Greek scientific and philosophical treatises were made available to Westerners in Latin translations, but none of the great Greek literary masterpieces and practically none of the major works of Plato were yet known. Nor could more than a handful of medieval Westerners read the Greek language. In the Renaissance, on the other hand, large numbers of Western scholars learned Greek and mastered almost the entire Greek literary heritage that is known today.

New uses for classical learning

Second, Renaissance thinkers not only knew many more classical texts than their medieval counterparts, but they used them in new ways. Whereas medieval writers tended to employ their ancient sources for the purposes of complementing and confirming their own preconceived Christian assumptions, Renaissance writers customarily drew on the classics to reconsider their preconceived notions and alter their modes of expression. Firm determination to learn from classical antiquity, moreover, was even more pronounced in the realms of architecture and art, areas in which classical models contributed most strikingly to the creation of fully distinct "Renaissance" artistic styles.

Third, although Renaissance culture was by no means pagan, it certainly was more secular in its orientation than the culture of the Middle Ages. The evolution of the Italian city-states in the fourteenth and fifteenth centuries created a supportive environment for attitudes that stressed the attainment of success in the urban political arena and living well in this world. Inevitably such secular ideals helped create a culture that was increasingly nonecclesiastical. To be sure, the Church retained its wealth and some of its influence, but it adjusted to the spread of secularity by becoming more secular itself.

A secular Renaissance culture

One word above all comes closest to summing up the most common and basic Renaissance intellectual ideals, namely humanism. This word has two different meanings, one technical and one general, but both apply to the cultural goals and ideals of a large number of Renaissance thinkers. In its technical sense humanism was a program of studies which aimed to replace the medieval Scholastic emphasis on logic and metaphysics with the study of language, literature, history, and ethics. Ancient literature was always preferred: the study of the Latin classics was at the core of the curriculum, and, whenever possible, the student was expected to advance to Greek. Humanist teachers argued that Scholastic logic was too arid and irrelevant to the practical concerns of life; instead, they preferred the "humanities," which were meant to make their students virtuous and prepare them for contributing best to the public functions of the state. (Women, as usual, were generally ignored, but sometimes aristocratic women were given humanist training in order to make them appear more polished.) The broader sense of humanism lies in a stress on the "dignity" of man as the most excellent of all God's creatures below the angels. Some Renaissance thinkers argued that man was excellent because he alone of earthly creatures could obtain knowledge of God; others stressed man's ability to master his fate and live happily in the world. Either way, Renaissance humanists had a firm belief in the nobility and possibilities of the human race.

Humanism

1. THE ITALIAN BACKGROUND

The Renaissance originated in Italy for several reasons. The most fundamental was that Italy in the later Middle Ages encompassed the most advanced urban society in all of Europe. Unlike aristocrats north of the Alps, Italian aristocrats customarily lived in urban centers rather than in rural castles and consequently became fully involved in urban public affairs. Moreover, since the Italian aristocracy built its palaces

The erosion of distinctions between the aristocracy and upper bourgeoisie in Italy

in the cities, the aristocratic class was less sharply set off from the class of rich merchants than in the north. Hence whereas in France or Germany there was never any appreciable variation from the rule that aristocrats lived off the income from their landed estates while rich town dwellers (*bourgeois*) gained their living from trade, in Italy so many town-dwelling aristocrats engaged in banking or mercantile enterprises and so many rich mercantile families imitated the manners of the aristocracy that by the fourteenth and fifteenth centuries the aristocracy and upper bourgeoisie were becoming virtually indistinguishable. The noted Florentine family of the Medici, for example, emerged as a family of physicians (as the name suggests), made its fortune in banking, and rose imperceptibly into the aristocracy in the fifteenth century. The results of these developments for the history of education are obvious: not only was there a great demand for education in the skills of reading and counting necessary to become a successful merchant, but the richest and most prominent families sought above all to find teachers who would impart to their offspring the knowledge and skills necessary to argue well in the public arena. Consequently, Italy produced a large number of secular educators, many of whom not only taught students but demonstrated their learned attainments in the production of political and ethical treatises and works of literature. The schools of these educators, moreover, created the best educated upper-class public in all of Europe and inevitably therewith a considerable number of wealthy patrons who were ready to invest in the cultivation of new ideas and new forms of literary and artistic expression.

The special appeal of the classical past

A second reason why late-medieval Italy was the birthplace of an intellectual and artistic Renaissance lay in the fact that it had a far greater sense of rapport with the classical past than any other territory in western Europe. Given the Italian aristocratic commitment to an educational curriculum which stressed success in urban politics, the best teachers understandably sought inspiration from ancient Latin and Greek texts because politics and political rhetoric were classical rather than medieval arts. Elsewhere, resort to classical knowledge and classical literary style might have seemed intolerably antiquarian and artificial, but in Italy the classical past appeared most "relevant" because ancient Roman monuments were omnipresent throughout the peninsula and ancient Latin literature referred to cities and sites that Renaissance Italians recognized as their own. Moreover, Italians became particularly intent on reappropriating their classical heritage in the fourteenth and fifteenth centuries because Italians then were seeking to establish an independent cultural identity in opposition to a Scholasticism most closely associated with France. Not only did the removal of the papacy to Avignon for most of the fourteenth century, and then the prolonged Great Schism from 1378 to 1415, heighten antagonisms between Italy and France, but during the fourteenth century there was an intellectual reaction against Scholasticism on all fronts which made it natural for Italians to prefer the intellectual alternatives offered by classical literary sources. Naturally too, once Roman literature and learning became particularly favored in Italy, so did Roman art and architecture, for Roman models could help Italians create a splendid artistic alternative to French Gothicism just as Roman learning offered an intellectual alternative to French Scholasticism.

Finally, the Italian Renaissance obviously could not have occurred without the underpinning of Italian wealth. Oddly enough, the Italian economy as a whole was probably more prosperous in the thirteenth century than it was in the fourteenth and fifteenth. But late-medieval Italy was wealthier in comparison to the rest of Europe than it had been before, a fact which meant that Italian writers and artists were more likely to stay at home than seek employment abroad. Moreover, in late-medieval Italy unusually intensive investment in culture arose from an intensification of urban pride and the concentration of per capita wealth. Although these two trends overlapped somewhat, most scholars tend to agree that a phase of predominantly public urban support for culture came first in Italy from roughly 1250 to about 1400 or 1450, depending on place, with the private sector taking over thereafter. In the first phase the richest cities vied with each other in building the most splendid public monuments and in supporting writers whose role was to glorify the urban republics in letters and speeches as full of magniloquent Ciceronian prose as possible. But in the course of the fifteenth century, when most Italian city-states succumbed to the hereditary rule of princely families, patronage was monopolized by the princely aristocracy. It was then that the great princes—the Visconti and Sforza in Milan; the Medici in Florence; the Este in Ferrara; and the Gonzaga in Mantua—patronized art and literature in their courts to glorify themselves, while lesser aristocratic families imitated those princes on a smaller scale. Not least of the great princes in Italy from about 1450 to about 1550 were the popes in Rome, who were dedicated to a policy of basing their strength on temporal control of the Papal States. Hence the most worldly of the Renaissance popes— Alexander VI (1492–1503); Julius II (1503–1513); and Leo X (1513– 1521), son of the Florentine ruler Lorenzo de' Medici—obtained the services of the greatest artists of the day and for a few decades made Rome the unrivaled artistic capital of the Western world.

Patronage of the arts rooted in urban pride and private wealth

2. THE RENAISSANCE OF THOUGHT AND LITERATURE IN ITALY

In surveying the greatest accomplishments of Italian Renaissance scholars and writers it is natural to begin with the work of Francis Petrarch (1304–1374), the earliest of the humanists in the technical

Pope Julius II. A portrait by Raphael.

Petrarch, the first humanist

Civic humanism

The civic humanists and classical Greek studies

sense of the term. Petrarch was a deeply committed Christian who believed that Scholasticism was entirely misguided because it concentrated on abstract speculation rather than teaching people how to behave properly and attain salvation. Petrarch thought that the Christian writer must above all cultivate literary eloquence so that he could inspire people to do good. For him the best models of eloquence were to be found in the ancient literary classics, which he thought repaid study doubly inasmuch as they were filled with ethical wisdom. So Petrarch dedicated himself to searching for undiscovered ancient Latin texts and writing his own moral treatises in which he imitated classical style and quoted classical phrases. Thereby he initiated a program of "humanist" studies that was to be influential for centuries. Petrarch also has a place in purely literary history because of his poetry. Although he prized his own Latin poetry over the poems he wrote in the Italian vernacular, only the latter have proved enduring. Above all, the Italian sonnets—later called Petrarchan sonnets—which he wrote for his beloved Laura in the chivalrous style of the troubadours, were widely imitated in form and content throughout the Renaissance period.

Because he was a very traditional Christian, Petrarch's ultimate ideal for human conduct was the solitary life of contemplation and asceticism. But in subsequent generations, from about 1400 to 1450, a number of Italian thinkers and scholars, located mainly in Florence, developed the alternative of what is customarily called "civic humanism." Civic humanists like the Florentines Leonardo Bruni (c. 1370–1444) and Leon Battista Alberti (1404–1472) agreed with Petrarch on the need for eloquence and the study of classical literature, but they also taught that man's nature equipped him for action, for usefulness to his family and society, and for serving the state—ideally a republican city-state after the classical or contemporary Florentine model. In their view ambition and the quest for glory were noble impulses which ought to be encouraged. They refused to condemn the striving for material possessions, for they argued that the history of human progress is inseparable from mankind's success in gaining mastery over the earth and its resources. Perhaps the most vivid of the civic humanists' writings is Alberti's *On the Family* (1443), in which he argued that the nuclear family was instituted by nature for the well-being of humanity. Not surprisingly, however, Alberti consigned women to purely domestic roles within this framework, for he believed that "man [is] by nature more energetic and industrious," and that woman was created "to increase and continue generations, and to nourish and preserve those already born."

In addition to differing with Petrarch in their preference for the active over the solitary or contemplative life, the civic humanists went far beyond him in their study of the ancient literary heritage. Many of them discovered important new Latin texts, but far more important was their success in opening up the field of classical Greek studies. In this they were greatly aided by the cooperation of several Byzantine scholars who had migrated to Italy in the first half of the fifteenth century. These men gave instruction in the Greek language and taught about the achievements of their ancient forebears. In doing so they inspired Italian scholars to make trips to Constantinople and other cities in the Near East in search of Greek manuscripts. In 1423 one Italian humanist, Giovanni Aurispa, alone brought back 238 manuscript books, including works of Sophocles, Euripides, and Thucydides. In this way most of the Greek classics, particularly the writings of Plato, the dramatists, and the historians, were first made available to western Europe.

Related in his textual interests to the civic humanists, but by no means a full adherent of their movement, was the atypical yet highly influential Renaissance thinker, Lorenzo Valla (1407–1457). Born in Rome and active primarily as a secretary in the service of the king of Naples, Valla had no inclination to espouse the ideas of republican political engagement as the Florentine civic humanists did. Instead, he preferred to advertise his skills as an expert in grammar, rhetoric, and the painstaking analysis of Greek and Latin texts by showing how the thorough study of language could discredit old verities. Most decisive in this regard was Valla's brilliant demonstration that the so-called Donation of Constantine was a medieval forgery. Whereas papal propagandists had argued ever since the early thirteenth century that the papacy possessed rights to temporal rule in western Europe on the grounds of a charter purportedly granted by the Emperor Constantine in the fourth century, Valla proved beyond dispute that the document in question was full of nonclassical Latin usages and anachronistic terms. Hence he concluded that the "Donation" was the work of a medieval forger whose "monstrous impudence" was exposed by the "stupidity of his language." This demonstration not only discredited a prize specimen of "medieval ignorance," but, more importantly, introduced the concept of anachronism into all subsequent textual study and historical thought. Valla also employed his skills in linguistic analysis and rhetorical argumentation to challenge a wide variety of philosophical positions, but his ultimate goals were by no means purely destructive, for he revered the literal teachings of the Pauline Epistles. Accordingly, in his *Notes on the New Testament* he applied his expert knowledge of Greek to elucidating the true meaning of St. Paul's words, which he believed had been obscured by the Latin Vulgate translation. This work was to prove an important link between Italian Renaissance scholarship and the subsequent Christian humanism of the north.

*Lorenzo Valla and
linguistic analysis*

From about 1450 until about 1600 dominance in the world of Italian thought was assumed by a school of Neoplatonists, who sought to blend the thought of Plato, Plotinus, and various strands of ancient mysticism with Christianity. Foremost among these were Marsilio Ficino (1433–1499) and Giovanni Pico della Mirandola (1463–1494),

*Renaissance
Neoplatonism: Ficino and
Pico*

both of whom were members of the Platonic Academy founded by Cosimo de' Medici in Florence. The academy was a loosely organized society of scholars who met to hear readings and lectures. Their hero was unquestionably Plato: sometimes they celebrated Plato's birthday by holding a banquet in his honor, after which everybody gave speeches as if they were characters in a Platonic dialogue. Ficino's greatest achievement was the translation of Plato's works into Latin, thereby making them widely available to western Europeans for the first time. It is debatable whether Ficino's own philosophy may be called humanist because he moved away from ethics to metaphysics and taught that the individual should look primarily to the other world. In Ficino's opinion, "the immortal soul is always miserable in its mortal body." The same problem holds for Ficino's disciple Giovanni Pico della Mirandola, whose most famous work is the *Oration on the Dignity of Man.* Pico was certainly not a civic humanist since he saw little worth in mundane public affairs. But he did believe that there is "nothing more wonderful than man" because he believed that man is endowed with the capacity to achieve union with God if he so wills.

Hardly any of the Italian thinkers between Petrarch and Pico were really original: their greatness lay mostly in their manner of expression, their accomplishments in technical scholarship, and their popularization of different themes of ancient thought. The same, however, can by no means be said of Renaissance Italy's greatest political philosopher, Niccolò Machiavelli (1469–1527), who belonged to no school and stood in a class by himself. No man did more than Machiavelli to overturn all earlier views of the ethical basis of politics or to pioneer in the dispassionate direct observation of political life. Machiavelli's writings reflect the unhappy condition of Italy in his time. At the end of the fifteenth century Italy had become the cockpit of international struggles. Both France and Spain had invaded the peninsula and were competing with each other for the allegiance of the Italian states. The latter, in many cases, were torn by internal dissension which made them easy prey for foreign conquerors. In 1498 Machiavelli entered the service of the newly founded republic of Florence as second chancellor and secretary. His duties largely involved diplomatic missions to other states. While in Rome he became fascinated with the achievements of Cesare Borgia, son of Pope Alexander VI, in cementing a solidified state out of scattered elements. He noted with approval Cesare's combination of ruthlessness with shrewdness and his complete subordination of morality to political ends. In 1512 the Medici returned to overthrow the republic of Florence, and Machiavelli was deprived of his position. Disappointed and embittered, he spent the remainder of his life in exile, devoting his time primarily to writing. In his *Discourses on Livy* he praised the ancient Roman republic as a model for all time. He lauded constitutionalism, equality, liberty, in the sense of freedom from outside interference, and subordination of religion to the interests of the state. But Machiavelli also wrote *The Prince* in

Niccolò Machiavelli.

which he described the policies and practices of government, not in accordance with some lofty ideal, but as they actually were. The supreme obligation of the ruler, he avowed, was to maintain the power and safety of the country over which he ruled. No consideration of justice or mercy or the sanctity of treaties should be allowed to stand in his way. Cynical in his views of human nature, Machiavelli maintained that all men are prompted exclusively by motives of self-interest, particularly by desires for personal power and material prosperity. The head of the state should therefore not take for granted the loyalty or affection of his subjects. The one ideal Machiavelli kept before him in his later years was the unification of Italy. But this he believed could only be achieved through ruthlessness.

Far more congenial to contemporary tastes than the shocking political theories of Machiavelli were the guidelines for proper aristocratic conduct offered in *The Book of the Courtier* (1516) by the diplomat and count Baldesar Castiglione. This cleverly written forerunner of modern handbooks of etiquette stands in sharp contrast to the earlier civic humanist treatises of Bruni and Alberti, for whereas they taught the sober "republican" virtues of strenuous service in behalf of the city-state and family, Castiglione, writing in an Italy dominated by magnificent princely courts, taught how to attain the elegant and seemingly effortless qualities necessary for acting like a "true gentleman." More than anyone else, Castiglione popularized the ideal of the "Renaissance man": one who is accomplished in many different pursuits and is also brave, witty, and "courteous," meaning civilized and learned. By no means ignoring the female sex, Castiglione, much unlike Alberti, was silent about woman's role in "hearth and home," but stressed instead the ways in which court ladies could be "gracious entertainers." Thereby he was one of the first European male writers to offer women an independent role outside of the household, a fact which should not be underrated even though he was offering such a role merely to the richest of the rich and even though his stress on "pleasing affability" today seems demeaning. Widely read throughout Europe for over a century after its publication, Castiglione's *Courtier* spread Italian ideals of "civility" to princely courts north of the Alps, resulted in the ever-greater patronage of art and literature by the European aristocracy, and gave currency to the hitherto novel proposition that all women other than nuns were not fated to be passive vessels of reproduction and nutrition.

*Castiglione's ideal courtier
and court lady*

Had Castiglione's ideal courtier wished to show off his knowledge of contemporary Italian literature, he would have had many works from which to choose, for sixteenth-century Italians were highly accomplished in the creation of imaginative prose and verse. Among the many impressive writers who might be mentioned, Machiavelli himself wrote a delightful short story, "Belfagor," and an engaging bawdy play, *Mandragola;* the great artist Michelangelo wrote many moving sonnets; and the most eminent of sixteenth-century Italian

*Other sixteenth-century
Italian literary
achievements*

The Expulsion of Adam and Eve from the Garden of Eden. Masaccio built on the artistic tradition established by Giotto in stressing emotion and psychological study.

Italian painting in the fifteenth century

epic poets was Ludovico Ariosto (1474–1533), author of a lengthy verse narrative called *Orlando Furioso* (*The Madness of Roland*). Although woven substantially from materials taken from the medieval Charlemagne cycle, this work differed radically from any of the medieval epics because it introduced elements of lyrical fantasy and above all because it was totally devoid of heroic idealism. Ariosto wrote to make readers laugh and to charm them with felicitous descriptions of the quiet splendor of nature and the passions of love. His work represents the disillusionment of the late Renaissance, the loss of hope and faith, and the tendency to seek consolation in the pursuit of pleasure and aesthetic delight.

3. THE ARTISTIC RENAISSANCE IN ITALY

Despite numerous intellectual and literary advances, the most long-lived achievements of the Italian Renaissance were made in the realm of art. Of all the arts, painting was undoubtedly supreme. We have already seen that around 1300 very impressive beginnings were made in the history of Italian painting by the artistic genius of Giotto, but it was not until the fifteenth century that Italian painting began to attain its majority. One reason for this was that in the early fifteenth century the laws of linear perspective were discovered and first employed to give the fullest sense of three dimensions. Fifteenth-century artists also experimented with effects of light and shade (*chiaroscuro*) and for the first time carefully studied the anatomy and proportions of the human body. By the fifteenth century, too, increase in private wealth and the partial triumph of the secular spirit had freed the domain of art to a large extent from the service of religion. As we have noted above, the Church was no longer the only patron of artists. While subject matter from biblical history was still commonly employed, it was frequently infused with nonreligious themes. The painting of portraits for the purpose of revealing the hidden mysteries of the soul now became popular. Paintings intended to appeal primarily to the intellect were paralleled by others whose main purpose was to delight the eye with gorgeous color and beauty of form. The fifteenth century was characterized also by the introduction of painting in oil, probably from Flanders. The use of the new technique doubtless had much to do with the artistic advance of this period. Since oil does not dry so quickly as fresco pigment, the painter could now work more leisurely, taking time with the more difficult parts of the picture and making corrections if necessary as he went along.

The majority of the painters of the fifteenth century were Florentines. First among them was the precocious Masaccio (1401–1428). Although he died at the age of twenty-seven, Masaccio inspired the work of Italian painters for a hundred years. Masaccio's greatness as a painter is based on his success in "imitating nature," which became a primary value in Renaissance painting. To achieve this effect he employed perspective, perhaps most dramatically in his fresco of the *Trinity;* he also used *chiaroscuro* with originality, leading to a dramatic and moving outcome. In the *Expulsion of Adam and Eve from the Garden,* he records the shame and guilt felt by the individuals in the biblical story.

The best known of the painters who directly followed the tradition begun by Masaccio was the Florentine Sandro Botticelli (1444–1510), who depicted both religious and classical themes. Botticelli's work excels in beautiful and accurate depiction of natural detail; he is a master, for example, at painting the female nude. But his major contribution to Renaissance painting derives from the philosophical basis of much of his work, for he was closely associated with the Florentine Neoplatonists. Two of his most famous paintings are *The Allegory of Spring* and *The Birth of Venus,* which illustrate Neoplatonic concepts regarding the classical goddess of love, Venus or Aphrodite. Later in his life Botticelli became a follower of the evangelical priest Savonarola, who came to Florence from Ferrara to preach fire-and-brimstone sermons against worldliness. Botticelli's *Mystic Nativity* was probably painted as a result of Savonarola's influence; it is a profoundly moving religious painting, in which he anticipates the end of the world. The last years of Botticelli's life are shadowy; his popularity declined and it is believed he died in poverty.

Botticelli

See color plates facing page 448 for *The Birth of Venus*

Perhaps the greatest of the Florentine artists was Leonardo da Vinci (1452–1519), one of the most versatile geniuses who ever lived. Leonardo was practically the personification of the "Renaissance man": he was a painter, architect, musician, mathematician, engineer, and inventor. The illegitimate son of a lawyer and a peasant woman, Leonardo set up an artist's shop in Florence by the time he reached twenty-five and gained the patronage of the Medici ruler of the city, Lorenzo the Magnificent. But if Leonardo had any weakness, it was his slowness in working and difficulty in finishing anything. This naturally displeased Lorenzo and other Florentine patrons, who thought an artist was little more than an artisan, commissioned to produce a certain piece of work of a certain size for a certain price on a certain date. Leonardo, however, strongly objected to this view because he considered himself to be no menial craftsman but an inspired creator. Therefore in 1482 he left Florence for the Sforza court of Milan where he was given freer rein in structuring his time and work. He remained there until the French invaded Milan in 1499; after that he wandered about Italy, finally accepting the patronage of the French king, Francis I, under whose auspices Leonardo lived and worked in France until his death.

Leonardo da Vinci

Lorenzo de' Medici. The leading patron of Florentine art and literature in the latter part of the fifteenth century.

The paintings of Leonardo da Vinci began what is known as the High Renaissance in Italy. His approach to painting was that it should be the most accurate possible imitation of nature. Leonardo was like a naturalist, basing his work on his own detailed observations of a blade

Studies of the Shoulder by Leonardo da Vinci

See color plates following page 448 for the *Virgin on the Rocks,* the *Last Supper,* and the *Mona Lisa*

The Venetian painters

See color plates following page 448 for *Pope Paul III and His Nephews* and *Charles V* by Titian

of grass, the wing of a bird, a waterfall. He obtained human corpses for dissection—by which he was breaking the law—and reconstructed in drawing the minutest features of anatomy, which knowledge he carried over to his paintings. Leonardo worshiped nature, and was convinced of the essential divinity in all living things. It is not surprising, therefore, that he was a vegetarian, and that he went to the marketplace to buy caged birds which he released to their native habitat.

It is generally agreed that Leonardo's masterpieces are the *Virgin of the Rocks* (which exists in two versions), the *Last Supper,* and the *Mona Lisa.* The first represents not only his marvelous technical skill but also his passion for science and his belief in the universe as a well-ordered place. The figures are arranged in geometric composition with every rock and plant depicted in accurate detail. The *Last Supper,* painted on the walls of the refectory of Santa Maria delle Grazie in Milan, is a study of psychological reactions. A serene Christ, resigned to his terrible fate, has just announced to his disciples that one of them will betray him. The purpose of the artist is to portray the mingled emotions of surprise, horror, and guilt revealed in the faces of the disciples as they gradually perceive the meaning of their master's statement. The third of Leonardo's major triumphs, the *Mona Lisa,* reflects a similar interest in the varied moods of the human soul. Although it is true that the *Mona Lisa* is a portrait of an actual woman, the wife of Francesco del Giocondo, a Neapolitan, it is more than a mere photographic likeness. The distinguished art critic Bernard Berenson has said of it, "Who like Leonardo has depicted . . . the inexhaustible fascination of the woman in her years of mastery? . . . Leonardo is the one artist of whom it may be said with perfect literalness: 'Nothing that he touched but turned into a thing of eternal beauty.' "

The beginning of the High Renaissance around 1490 also witnessed the rise of the so-called Venetian school, the major members of which were Giovanni Bellini (c. 1426–1516), Giorgione (1478–1510), and Titian (c. 1477–1576). The work of all these men reflected the luxurious life and the pleasure-loving interests of the thriving commercial city of Venice. Most Venetian painters had little of the concern with philosophical and psychological themes that characterized the Florentine school. Their aim was to appeal primarily to the senses rather than to the mind. They delighted in painting idyllic landscapes and gorgeous symphonies of color. For their subject matter they chose not merely the natural beauty of Venetian sunsets and the shimmering silver of lagoons in the moonlight but also the artificial splendor of sparkling jewels, richly colored satins and velvets, and gorgeous palaces. Their portraits were invariably likenesses of the rich and the powerful. In the subordination of form and meaning to color and elegance there were mirrored not only the sumptuous tastes of wealthy merchants, but also definite traces of Eastern influence which had filtered through from Byzantium during the Middle Ages.

The remaining great painters of the High Renaissance all accomplished their most important work in the first half of the sixteenth century. It was in this period that Renaissance Italian art reached its peak. Rome was now the major artistic center of the Italian peninsula, although the traditions of the Florentine school still exerted a potent influence. Among the eminent painters of this period at least two must be given more than passing attention. One was Raphael (1483–1520), a native of Urbino, and perhaps the most beloved artist of the entire Renaissance. The lasting appeal of his style is due primarily to his ennobling humanism, for he portrayed the members of the human species as temperate, wise, and dignified beings. Although Raphael was influenced by Leonardo da Vinci and copied many features of his work, he cultivated a much more symbolical or allegorical approach. His *Disputà* symbolized the dialectical relationship between the Church in heaven and the Church on earth. In a wordly setting against a brilliant sky, theologians debate the meaning of the Eucharist, while in the clouds above, saints and the Trinity repose in the possession of a holy mystery. Raphael's *School of Athens* is an allegorical representation of the conflict between the Platonist and Aristotelian philosophies. Plato (painted as a portrait of Leonardo) is shown pointing upward to emphasize the spiritual basis of his world of Ideas, while Aristotle gestures toward the earth to exemplify his belief that concepts or ideas are inseparably linked with their material embodiments. Raphael is noted also for his portraits and Madonnas. To the latter, especially, he gave a softness and warmth that seemed to endow them with a sweetness and piety quite different from the enigmatic and somewhat distant Madonnas of Leonardo da Vinci.

The last towering figure of the High Renaissance was Michelangelo (1475–1564) of Florence. If Leondardo was a naturalist, Michelangelo was an idealist; where the former sought to recapture and interpret

The painters of the late Renaissance: Raphael

See color plates following page 448 for the *Madonna of the Chair* by Raphael

Michelangelo

The School of Athens by Raphael

The Creation of Adam by Michelangelo. One of a series of frescoes on the ceiling of the Sistine Chapel in Rome. Suggesting philosophical inquiries into the meaning of life and the universe, it represents Renaissance realism at its height.

fleeting natural phenomena, Michelangelo, who embraced Neoplatonism as a philosophy, was more concerned with expressing enduring, abstract truths. Michelangelo was a painter, sculptor, architect, and poet—and he expressed himself in all these with a similar power and in a similar manner. At the center of all of his paintings is the human figure, which is always powerful, colossal, magnificent. If man, and the potential of the individual, lay at the center of Italian Renaissance culture, then Michelangelo, who depicted the human, and particularly the male, figure without cease, is the supreme Renaissance artist.

The Sistine Chapel

Michelangelo's greatest achievements in painting appear in a single location—the Sistine Chapel in Rome—yet conveniently enough for the spectator they are products of two different periods in the artist's life and consequently exemplify two different artistic styles and outlooks on the human condition. Most famous are the sublime frescoes Michelangelo painted on the ceiling of the Sistine Chapel from 1508 to 1512, depicting scenes from the book of Genesis. All the panels in this series, including *God Dividing the Light from Darkness, The Creation of Adam,* and *The Flood,* exemplify the younger artist's commitment to classical Greek aesthetic principles of harmony, solidity, and dignified restraint. Correspondingly, all exude as well a sense of sublime affirmation regarding Creation and the heroic qualities of mankind. (When one considers that Michelangelo executed these magnificent scenes while lying on his back on a scaffold, one can begin to imagine the exalted mood of creativity that must have possessed him.) But a quarter of a century later, when Michelangelo returned to work in the Sistine Chapel, both his style and mood had changed dramatically. In the enormous *Last Judgment,* a fresco done for the

See color plates following page 448 for detail from the *Last Judgement*

Sistine Chapel's altar wall in 1536, Michelangelo repudiated classical restraint and substituted a style that emphasized tension and distortion in order to communicate the older man's pessimistic conception of a humanity wracked by fear and bowed by guilt.

In the realm of sculpture the Italian Renaissance took a great step forward by creating statues that were no longer carved as parts of columns or doorways on church buildings or as effigies on tombs. Instead, Italian sculptors for the first time since antiquity carved free-standing statues "in the round." These freed sculpture from its bondage to architecture and established its status as a separate art frequently devoted to secular purposes.

The first great master of Renaissance sculpture was Donatello (c. 1386?–1466). He emancipated his art from Gothic mannerisms and introduced a new vigorous note of individualism. His bronze statue of David triumphant over the body of the slain Goliath, the first free-standing nude since antiquity, established a precedent of glorifying the life-size nude. Donatello's *David,* moreover, represents a first step in the direction of imitating classical sculpture, not just in the depiction of a nude body but also in the subject's posture of resting his weight on one leg. Yet this David is clearly a lithe adolescent rather than a muscular Greek athlete. Later in his career, Donatello more fully imitated ancient statuary in his commanding portrayal of the proud warrior Gattamelata—the first monumental equestrian statue in bronze executed in the West since the time of the Romans. Here, in addition to drawing very heavily on the legacy of antiquity, the sculptor most clearly expressed his dedication to immortalizing the earthly accomplishments of a contemporary secular hero.

Certainly the greatest sculptor of the Italian Renaissance—indeed, probably the greatest sculptor of all time—was Michelangelo. Believ-

David by Donatello. The first free-standing nude statue executed in the West since antiquity.

Gattamelata by Donatello. Note the debt to the Roman equestrian statue of Marcus Aurelius, shown above, p. 186.

David by Michelangelo. Over thirteen feet high, this serenely self-confident affirmation of the beauty of the human form was placed prominently by the Florentine government in front of Florence's city hall to proclaim the city's humanistic values.

ing with Leonardo that the artist was an inspired creator, Michelangelo pursued this conviction to the conclusion that sculpture was the most exalted of the arts because it allowed the artist to imitate God most fully in recreating human forms. Furthermore, in Michelangelo's view the most God-like sculptor disdained slavish naturalism, for anyone could make a plaster cast of a human figure, but only an inspired creative genius could endow his sculpted figures with a sense of life. Accordingly, Michelangelo subordinated naturalism to the force of his imagination and sought restlessly to express his ideals in ever more arresting forms.

As in his painting, Michelangelo's sculpture followed a course from classicism to anticlassicism, that is, from harmonious modeling to dramatic distortion. The sculptor's most noted early work, his *David,* executed in 1501 when he was just twenty-six, is surely his most perfect classical statue in style and inspiration. Choosing, like Donatello, to depict a life-size male nude, Michelangelo nonetheless decided to make his own *David* heroic rather than merely graceful and hence conceived his nude in the purest, well-proportioned Greek terms. The resulting portrait in marble epitomizes for many the Italian Renaissance's facility for employing classical style to express the serenest confidence in human attainments. Deep serenity, however, is no longer

Left: *Moses* by Michelangelo. Far less classical in style than Michelangelo's *David,* this statue stresses a sense of drama. (Moses was depicted with horns in medieval and renaissance art on account of a faulty translation of a passage from the Book of Exodus.) Right: *Descent from the Cross* by Michelangelo. This portrayal of tragedy was made by the sculptor for his own tomb. Note the distortion for effect exemplified by the elongated body and left arm of the figure of Christ. The figure in the rear is Nicodemus, but was probably intended to represent Michelangelo himself. The original is in the cathedral of Florence.

St. Peter's, Rome. Built to a square cross plan originally conceived by Bramante and revised by Michelangelo. Completed in 1626, the church rises to a total height of 450 feet.

prominent in the works of Michelangelo's middle period; rather, in a work such as the *Moses* of about 1515, the sculptor has begun to explore the use of anatomical distortion to create effects of emotional intensity—in this case the biblical prophet's righteous rage. While such statues remain awesomely heroic, as Michelangelo's life drew to a close he experimented ever more with exaggerated stylistic mannerisms for the purpose of communicating moods of brooding pensiveness or outright pathos. The culmination of this trend in Michelangelo's statuary is his moving *Descent from the Cross,* a depiction of the Virgin Mary grieving over the body of the dead Christ, intended for the artist's own tomb.

To a much greater extent than either sculpture or painting, Renaissance architecture had its roots in the past. The new building style was eclectic, a compound of elements derived from the Middle Ages and from antiquity. It was not the Greek or the Gothic, however, but the Roman and the Romanesque which provided the inspiration for the architecture of the Italian Renaissance. Neither the Greek nor the Gothic had ever found a congenial soil in Italy. The Romanesque, by contrast, was able to flourish there, since it was more in keeping with Italian traditions, while the persistence of a strong admiration for Latin culture made possible a revival of the Roman style. Accordingly, the great architects of the Renaissance generally adopted their building plans from the Romanesque churches and monasteries and copied their decorative devices from the ruins of ancient Rome. The result was an architecture based on the cruciform floor plan of transept and nave and embodying the decorative features of the column and arch, or the column and lintel, the colonnade, and frequently the dome. Horizontal lines predominated; and, though many of the buildings were churches, the ideals they expressed were the secular ones of joy in this

The eclecticism of Renaissance architecture

The Villa Rotonda of Palladio. A highly influential Renaissance private dwelling near Vicenza. Note how Palladio drew for inspiration on the Roman Pantheon, pictured above, p. 189.

life and pride in human achievement. Renaissance architecture also emphasized harmony and proportion because Italian builders, under the influence of Neoplatonism, concluded that perfect proportions in man reflect the harmony of the universe, and that, therefore, the parts of a building should be related to each other and to the whole in the same way as the parts of the human body. A fine example of Renaissance architecture is St. Peter's Basilica in Rome, built under the patronage of Popes Julius II and Leo X and designed by some of the most celebrated architects of the time, including Donato Bramante (c. 1444–1514) and Michelangelo. Equally impressive are the artfully proportioned aristocratic country houses of the northern Italian architect Andrea Palladio (1518–1580), who redesigned ancient temples, such as the Roman Pantheon, to create secular miniatures meant to glorify the aristocrats who dwelled within them.

4. THE WANING OF THE ITALIAN RENAISSANCE

Political factors in the decline of the Italian Renaissance: the French invasion of 1494

Around 1550 the Renaissance in Italy began to decline after some two hundred glorious years. The causes of this decline were varied. Perhaps at the head of the list should be placed the French invasion of 1494 and the incessant warfare that ensued. The French king Charles VIII, who ruled the richest and most powerful kingdom in Europe, viewed Italy as an attractive prey for his grandiose ambitions. Accordingly, in 1494 he led an army of 30,000 well-trained troops across the Alps. The Medici of Florence fled before him, abandoning their city to immediate capture. Halting only long enough to establish peace with a subservient new republican government, the French resumed their advance and conquered Naples. By so doing, however, they aroused the suspicions of the rulers of Spain, who feared an attack on their own possession of Sicily. An alliance among Spain, the Papal States, the Holy Roman Empire, Milan, and Venice finally forced Charles to withdraw whence he had come. Yet upon his death his successor, Louis XII, launched a second invasion, and from 1499 until

1529 warfare in Italy was virtually uninterrupted. Alliances and counteralliances followed each other in bewildering succession, but they only managed to prolong the hostilities. The French won a great victory at Marignano in 1515, but they were decisively defeated by the Spanish at Pavia in 1525. The worst disaster came in 1527 when unruly Spanish and German troops, nominally under the command of the Spanish ruler and Holy Roman Emperor Charles V, but in fact entirely out of control, sacked the city of Rome, causing irreparable destruction. Only in 1529 did Charles finally manage to gain control over most of the Italian peninsula, putting the fighting to an end for a time. Once triumphant, Charles retained two of the largest portions of Italy for Spain—the Duchy of Milan and the Kingdom of Naples—and installed favored princes as the rulers of almost all the other Italian political entities exclusive of Venice and the Papal States. These protégés of the Spanish crown continued to preside over their own courts, to patronize the arts, and to adorn their cities with luxurious buildings, but in fact they were puppets of a foreign power and unable to inspire their retinues with a sense of vigorous cultural independence.

To the Italian political disasters was added a waning of Italian prosperity. Whereas Italy's virtual monopoly of trade with Asia in the fifteenth century had been one of the chief economic supports for the cultivation of Italian Renaissance culture, the gradual shifting of trade routes from the Mediterranean to the Atlantic region following the overseas discoveries of around 1500 slowly but surely cost Italy its supremacy as the center of world trade. Since the incessant warfare of the sixteenth century also contributed to Italy's economic hardships, as did Spanish financial exactions in Milan and Naples, there was gradually less and less of a surplus to support artistic endeavors.

The waning of Italian prosperity

The Entrance of Charles VIII into Florence. A painting by Francesco Granacci.

THE STATES OF ITALY DURING THE RENAISSANCE c. 1494

Giordano Bruno

A final cause of the decline of the Italian Renaissance was the Counter-Reformation. During the sixteenth century the Roman Church sought increasingly to exercise firm control over thought and art as part of a campaign to combat worldliness and the spread of Protestantism. In 1542 the Roman Inquisition was established; in 1564 the Council of Trent issued the first Index of Prohibited Books. The extent of ecclesiastical interference in cultural life was enormous. For example, Michelangelo's great *Last Judgment* in the Sistine Chapel was criticized by some straitlaced fanatics for looking like a bordello because it showed too many naked bodies. Therefore, Pope Paul IV ordered a second-rate artist to paint in clothing wherever possible. (The unfortunate artist was afterward known as "the underwear-maker.") While this incident may appear merely grotesquely humorous, the determination of ecclesiastical censors to enforce doctrinal uniformity could lead to death, as in the case of the unfortunate Neoplatonic philosopher Giordano Bruno, whose insistence on maintaining that there may be more than one world in contravention of the book of Genesis resulted in his being burned at the stake by the Roman Inquisition in 1600.

The most notorious example of inquisitorial censorship of free intellectual speculation was the disciplining of the great scientist Galileo, whose achievements we will discuss in more detail later on. In 1616 the Holy Office in Rome condemned the new astronomical theory that the earth moves around the sun as "foolish, absurd, philosophically false, and formally heretical." Accordingly, the Inquisition proceeded immediately against Galileo when he published a brilliant defense of the heliocentric system in 1632. In short order the Inquisition made Galileo recant his "errors" and sentenced him to house arrest for the duration of his life. Galileo was not willing to face death for his beliefs, but after he publicly retracted his view that the earth revolves around the sun he supposedly whispered, "despite everything, it still moves." Not surprisingly, Galileo was the last great Italian contributor to the development of astronomy and physics until modern times.

In conclusion, it should be emphasized that cultural and artistic achievement was by no means extinguished in Italy after the middle of the sixteenth century. On the contrary, an impressive new artistic style known as Mannerism was cultivated between about 1550 and 1600 by painters who drew on traits found in the later work of Michelangelo, and in the seventeenth century Mannerism was supplanted by the dazzling Baroque style, which was born in Rome under ecclesiastical auspices. Similarly, Italian music registered enormous accomplishments virtually without interruption from the sixteenth to the twentieth century. But whatever seemed threatening to the Church could not be tolerated and the free spirit of Renaissance culture was found no more.

5. THE RENAISSANCE IN THE NORTH

It was inevitable that after about 1500 the Renaissance which originated in Italy should have spread to other European countries. Throughout the fifteenth century a continuous procession of northern European students had come down to Italy to study in Italian universities such as Bologna or Padua, and an occasional Italian writer or artist traveled briefly north of the Alps. Such interchanges helped spread ideas, but only after around 1500 did most of northern Europe become sufficiently prosperous and politically stable to provide a truly congenial environment for the widespread cultivation of art and literature. Intellectual interchanges, moreover, became much more extensive after 1494, when France and Spain started fighting on Italian battlefields. The result of this development was that more and more northern Europeans began to learn what the Italians had been accomplishing (Spain's forces came not just from Spain but also from Germany and the Low Countries). Then too leading Italian thinkers and artists, like Leonardo, began to enter the retinues of northern kings or aristocrats. Accordingly, the Renaissance became an international movement and

The religious roots of the northern Renaissance

Northern Christian humanism

Erasmus

continued to be vigorous in the north even as it started to wane on its native ground.

The Renaissance outside Italy, however, was by no means identical to the Renaissance within Italy. Above all, the northern European Renaissance was generally less secular. The main explanation for this difference lies in the different social and cultural traditions Italy and northern Europe had inherited from the Middle Ages. As we have seen, late-medieval Italy's vigorous urban society fostered a secular educational system which led, in union with a revival of classicism, to the evolution of new and more secular forms of expression. The north, on the other hand, had a far less mercantile and urban-oriented economy than did Italy and no northern cities ever attained the political dominance of their surrounding countrysides as did Florence, Venice, and Milan. Instead, political power was coalescing around the nation-states (or in Germany the princedoms), whose rulers were willing until about 1500 to acknowledge the educational and cultural hegemony of the clergy. Consequently, northern European universities tended to specialize in theological studies, and the most prominent buildings in almost all the leading northern towns were cathedrals.

Simply stated, the northern Renaissance was the product of an engrafting of certain Italian Renaissance ideals upon preexisting northern traditions. This can be seen very clearly in the case of the most prominent northern Renaissance intellectual movement, *Christian humanism*. Agreeing with Italian humanists that medieval Scholasticism was too ensnarled in logical hair-splitting to have any value for the practical conduct of life, northern Christian humanists nonetheless looked for practical guidance from purely biblical, religious precepts. Like their Italian counterparts, they sought wisdom from antiquity, but the antiquity they had in mind was Christian rather than in any way pagan—the antiquity, that is, of the New Testament and the early Christian fathers. Similarly, northern Renaissance artists were moved by the accomplishments of Italian Renaissance masters to turn their backs on medieval Gothic artistic styles and became determined instead to learn how to employ classical techniques. Yet these same artists depicted classical subject matter far less frequently than did the Italians, and, inhibited by the greater northern European attachment to Christian asceticism, virtually never dared to portray completely undressed nudes.

Any discussion of northern Renaissance accomplishments in the realm of thought and literary expression must begin with the career of Desiderius Erasmus (c. 1467–1536), "the prince of the Christian humanists." The illegitimate son of a priest, Erasmus was born near Rotterdam in Holland, but later, as a result of his wide travels, became in effect a citizen of all northern Europe. Placed as a teenager against his will into a monastery, the young Erasmus found there little religion or formal instruction of any kind but plenty of freedom to read what he liked. He devoured all the classics he could get his hands on and the writings of many of the church fathers. When he was about thirty years of age, he obtained permission to leave the monastery and enroll in the University of Paris, where he completed the requirements for the degree of bachelor of divinity. But Erasmus subsequently rebelled against what he considered the arid learning of Parisian Scholasticism. In one of his later writings he reported the following exchange: "Q. Where do you come from? A. The College of Montaigu. Q. Ah, then you must be bowed down with learning. A. No, with lice." Erasmus also never entered into the active duties of a priest, choosing rather to make his living by teaching and writing. Ever on the lookout for new patrons, he changed his residence at frequent intervals, traveling often to England, staying once for three years in Italy, and residing in several different cities in the Netherlands before settling finally toward the end of his life in Basel, Switzerland. By means of a voluminous correspondence he kept up with learned friends he made wherever he went, Erasmus became the leader of a northern European humanist coterie. And by means of the popularity of his numerous publications, he became the arbiter of "advanced" northern European cultural tastes during the first quarter of the sixteenth century.

Erasmus's many-sided intellectual activity may best be appraised from two different points of view: the literary and the doctrinal. As a Latin prose stylist, Erasmus was probably without peer since the days of Cicero. Extraordinarily learned and witty, he revelled in tailoring his mode of discourse to fit his subject, creating dazzling verbal effects when appropriate, and coining puns that took on added meaning if one knew Greek as well as Latin. Above all, Erasmus excelled in the deft use of irony, poking fun at all and sundry, including himself. For example, in his *Colloquies* (Latin for *Discussions*) he had a fictional character lament the evil signs of the times thus: "kings make war, priests strive to line their pockets, theologians invent syllogisms, monks roam outside their cloisters, the commons riot, and Erasmus writes colloquies."

Erasmus's literary accomplishments

But although Erasmus's urbane Latin style and wit earned him a wide audience for purely literary reasons, he by no means thought of himself as a mere entertainer. Rather, he intended everything he wrote to propagate in one form or another what he called the "philosophy of Christ." The essence of Erasmus's Christian humanist convictions was his belief that the entire society of his day was caught up in corruption and immorality as a result of having lost sight of the simple teachings of the Gospels. Accordingly, he offered to his contemporaries three different categories of publication: clever satires meant to show people the error of their ways, serious moral treatises meant to offer guidance toward proper Christian behavior, and scholarly editions of basic Christian texts.

His "philosophy of Christ"

In the first category belong the works of Erasmus that are still most widely read today—the *Praise of Folly* (1509), in which he pilloried

Knight, Death, and Devil by Dürer. This engraving of 1513 illustrates the ideal figure of Erasmus's *Handbook of a Christian Knight*. The steadfast knight is able to advance through the world on his charger, his loyal dog at his side, despite intimations of mortality and the snares of the devil.

The satires and moral treatises

Scholastic pedantry and dogmatism as well as the ignorance and superstitious credulity of the masses; and the *Colloquies* (1518), in which he held up contemporary religious practices for examination in a more serious but still pervasively ironic tone. In such works Erasmus let fictional characters do the talking, and hence his own views can only be determined by inference. But in his second mode Erasmus did not hesitate to speak clearly in his own voice. The most prominent treatises in this second genre are the quietly eloquent *Handbook of the Christian Knight* (1501), which urged the laity to pursue lives of serene inward piety, and the *Complaint of Peace* (1517), which pleaded movingly for Christian pacifism.

Erasmus's edition of the New Testament

Despite this highly impressive literary production, however, Erasmus probably considered his textual scholarship his single greatest achievement. Revering the authority of the early Latin Fathers, Augustine, Jerome, and Ambrose, he brought out reliable editions of all their works, and revering the authority of the Bible most of all, he applied his extraordinary skills as a student of Latin and Greek to producing a reliable edition of the New Testament. After reading Lorenzo Valla's *Notes on the New Testament* in 1505, Erasmus became convinced that nothing was more imperative than divesting the text of the entire New Testament of the myriad errors in transcription and translation that had piled up during the Middle Ages, for no one could be a good Christian without being certain of exactly what Christ's message really was. Hence he spent ten years studying and comparing all the best early Greek biblical manuscripts he could find in order to establish an authoritative text. Finally appearing in 1516, Erasmus's Greek New Testament, published together with explanatory notes and his own new Latin translation, was one of the most important landmarks of biblical scholarship of all time.

One of Erasmus's closest friends, and a close second to him in distinction among the ranks of the Christian humanists, was the Englishman Sir Thomas More (1478–1535). Following a successful career as a lawyer and as speaker of the House of Commons, in 1529 More was appointed lord chancellor of England. He was not long in this position, however, before he incurred the wrath of his royal master, King Henry VIII, because More, who was loyal to Catholic universalism, opposed the king's design to establish a national church under subjection to the state. Finally, in 1534, when More refused to take an oath acknowledging Henry as head of the Church of England, he was thrown into the Tower, and a year later met his death on the scaffold as a Catholic martyr. Much earlier, however, in 1516, long before More had any inkling of how his life was to end, he published the one work for which he will ever be best remembered, the *Utopia*. Creating the subsequently popular genre of "utopian fiction," More's *Utopia* expressed an Erasmian critique of contemporary society. Purporting

Sir Thomas More and Utopia

A Map of Thomas More's Imaginary Island of Utopia. "Utopia's" fictional discoverer, Hythlodaeus, whose name means "dispenser of nonsense" in Greek, points to the island of Utopia, which means "no place." From an early edition.

to describe an ideal community on an imaginary island, the book is really an indictment of the glaring abuses of the time—of poverty undeserved and wealth unearned, of drastic punishments, religious persecution, and the senseless slaughter of war. The inhabitants of Utopia hold all their goods in common, work only six hours a day so that all may have leisure for intellectual pursuits, and practice the natural virtues of wisdom, moderation, fortitude, and justice. Iron is the precious metal "because it is useful," war and monasticism are abolished, and toleration is granted to all who recognize the existence of God and the immortality of the soul. Although More advanced no explicit arguments in his *Utopia* in favor of Christianity, he clearly meant to imply that if the "Utopians" could manage their society so well without the benefit of Christian Revelation, Europeans who knew the Gospels ought to be able to do even better.

Whereas Erasmus and More were basically conciliatory in their temperaments and preferred to express themselves by means of wry understatements, a third representative of the Christian humanist movement, Erasmus's German disciple Ulrich von Hutten (1488–1523) was of a much more combative disposition. Dedicated to the cause of German cultural nationalism, von Hutten in translations from the Roman historian Tacitus employed his command of classical scholarship to demonstrate how "proud and free" Germanic tribes had once triumphed heroically over Roman legions. In other writings he spoke up truculently in his own words to defend the German people against foreigners. But von Hutten's chief claim to fame was his collaboration with another German humanist, Crotus Rubianus, in the authorship of the *Letters of Obscure Men* (1515), one of the most stinging satires in the history of literature. This was written as part of a propaganda war in favor of a scholar named Johann Reuchlin who wished to pursue his study of Hebrew writings, above all, the Talmud. When Scholastic theologians from the University of Cologne and the German inquisitor general tried to have all Hebrew books in Germany destroyed, Reuchlin and his party strongly opposed the move. After a while it became apparent that direct argument was accomplishing nothing, so Reuchlin's supporters resorted to ridicule. Von Hutten and Rubianus published a series of letters, written in intentionally bad Latin, purportedly by some of Reuchlin's Scholastic opponents from the University of Cologne. These were given such ridiculous names as Goatmilker, Baldpate, and Dungspreader, and shown to be learned fools who paraded forth examples of absurd religious literalism or grotesque erudition. Heinrich Sheep's-mouth, for example, the supposed writer of one of the letters, professed to be worried that he had sinned grievously by eating on Friday an egg that contained the yolk of a chick. The author of another boasted of his "brilliant discovery" that Julius Caesar could not have written Latin histories because he was too busy with his military exploits ever to have learned Latin. Although immediately banned by the Church, the letters circulated nonetheless and were widely read, giving ever more currency to the Erasmian proposition that Scholastic theology and Catholic religious ritual had to be set aside in favor of the most earnest dedication to the pursuit of apostolic Christianity.

With Erasmus, More, and von Hutten the list of energetic and eloquent Christian humanists is by no means exhausted, for the Englishman John Colet (c. 1467–1519), the Frenchman Jacques Lefèvre d'Étaples (c. 1455–1529), and the Spaniards Cardinal Francisco Ximénez de Cisneros (1436–1517) and Juan Luis Vives (1492–1540), among still many others, all made signal contributions to the collective enterprise of editing biblical and early Christian texts and expounding Gospel morality. But despite a host of achievements, the Christian humanist movement, which possessed such an extraordinary degree of international solidarity and vigor from about 1500 to 1525, was thrown into disarray by the rise of Protestantism and subsequently lost its momentum. The irony here is obvious, for the Christian humanists' emphasis on the literal truth of the Gospels and their devastating criticisms of clerical corruption and excessive religious ceremonialism certainly helped pave the way for the Protestant Reformation initiated by Martin Luther in 1517. But, as will be seen in the following chapter, very few Christian humanists were willing to go the whole route with Luther in rejecting the most fundamental principles on which Catholicism was based, and the few who did became such ardent Protestants that they lost all the sense of quiet irony that earlier had been a hallmark of Christian humanist expression. Most Christian humanists tried to remain within the Catholic fold while still espousing their ideal of nonritualistic inward piety, but as time went on the leaders of Catholicism had less and less tolerance for them because lines were hardening in the war with Protestantism and any suggestion of internal criticism of Catholic religious practices seemed like giving covert aid to "the enemy." Erasmus himself, who remained a Catholic, died early enough to escape opprobrium, but several of his less fortunate followers lived on to suffer as victims of the Spanish Inquisition.

The decline of Christian humanism

Yet if Christian humanism faded rapidly after about 1525, the northern Renaissance continued to flourish throughout the sixteenth century in primarily literary and artistic forms. In France, for example, the highly accomplished poets Pierre de Ronsard (c. 1524–1585) and Joachim du Bellay (c. 1525–1560) wrote elegant sonnets in the style of Petrarch, and in England the poets Sir Philip Sidney (1554–1586) and Edmund Spenser (c. 1552–1599) drew impressively on Italian literary innovations as well. Indeed, Spenser's *The Faerie Queene,* a long chivalric romance written in the manner of Ariosto's *Orlando Furioso,* communicates as well as any Italian work the gorgeous sensuousness typical of Italian Renaissance culture.

Northern Renaissance poetry

More intrinsically original than any of the aforementioned poets was the French prose satirist François Rabelais (c. 1494–1553), probably

François Rabelais

His affirmativeness

the best loved of all the great European creative writers of the sixteenth century. Like Erasmus, whom he greatly admired, Rabelais was educated as a monk, but soon after taking holy orders he left his monastery to study medicine. Becoming thereafter a practicing physician in Lyons, Rabelais from the start interspersed his professional activities with literary endeavors of one sort or another. He wrote almanacs for the common people, satires against quacks and astrologers, and burlesques of popular superstitions. But by far his most enduring literary legacy consists of his five volumes of "chronicles" published under the collective title of *Gargantua and Pantagruel.*

Rabelais' account of the adventures of Gargantua and Pantagruel, originally the names of legendary medieval giants noted for their fabulous size and gross appetites, served as a vehicle for his lusty humor and his penchant for exuberant narrative as well as for the expression of his philosophy of naturalism. To some degree, Rabelais drew on the precedents of Christian humanism. Thus, like Erasmus, he satirized religious ceremonialism, ridiculed Scholasticism, scoffed at superstitions, and pilloried every form of bigotry. But much unlike Erasmus, who wrote in a highly cultivated classical Latin style comprehensible to only the most learned readers, Rabelais chose to address a far wider audience by writing in an extremely down-to-earth French, often loaded with the crudest vulgarities. Likewise, Rabelais wanted to avoid seeming in any way "preachy" and therefore eschewed all suggestions of moralism in favor of giving the impression that he wished merely to offer his readers some rollicking good fun. Yet, aside from the critical satire in *Gargantua and Pantagruel,* there runs through all five volumes a common theme of glorifying the human and the natural. For Rabelais, whose robust giants were really life-

Chambord. Built in the early sixteenth century by an Italian architect in the service of King Francis I of France, this magnificent Loire Valley château combines Gothic and Renaissance architectural traits.

The West Side of the Square Court of the Louvre by Pierre Lescot. The enlargement of the Louvre, begun by Lescot in 1546, took more than a century to complete. Drawing on the work of Bramante (see above, p. 432), he achieved a synthesis of the traditional château and the Renaissance palace.

loving human beings writ very large, every instinct of humanity was healthy, provided it was not directed toward tyranny over others. Thus in his ideal community, the utopian "abbey of Thélème," there was no repressiveness whatsoever, but only a congenial environment for the pursuit of life-affirming, natural human attainments, guided by the single rule of "do what thou wouldst."

Were we to imagine what Rabelais' fictional abbey of Thélème might have looked like, we would do best to picture it as resembling one of the famous sixteenth-century French Renaissance châteaux built along the River Loire, for the northern European Renaissance had its own distinctive architecture that often corresponded in certain essentials to its literature. Thus, just as Rabelais recounted stories of medieval giants in order to express an affirmation of Renaissance values, so French architects who constructed such splendid Loire châteaux as Amboise, Chenonceaux, and Chambord, combined elements of the late-medieval French flamboyant Gothic style with an up-to-date emphasis on classical horizontality to produce some of the most impressively distinctive architectural landmarks ever constructed in France. Yet much closer architectural imitation of Italian models occurred in France as well, for just as Ronsard and du Bellay modeled their poetic style very closely on Petrarch, so Pierre Lescot, the French architect who began work on the new royal palace of the Louvre in Paris in 1546, hewed closely to the classicism of Italian Renaissance masters in constructing a facade that emphasized classical pilasters and pediments.

It only remains to treat the accomplishments of northern Renaissance painting, another realm in which links between thought and art can be discerned. Certainly the most moving visual embodiments of

Northern Renaissance architecture

Left: *St. Jerome in his Study* by Dürer. St. Jerome, a hero for both Dürer and Erasmus, represents inspired Christian scholarship. Note how the scene exudes contentment, even down to the sleeping lion which seems rather like an overgrown tabby cat. Right: *The Four Apostles* by Dürer. This painting in two separate panels is a moving statement of the artist's intense religious faith.

Albrecht Dürer

See color plates facing page 449 for the *Self-Portrait* by Dürer

the ideals of Christian humanism were conceived by the foremost of northern Renaissance artists, the German Albrecht Dürer (1471–1528). From the purely technical and stylistic points of view, Dürer's greatest significance lies in the fact that, returning from his native Nuremberg after a trip to Venice in 1494, he became the first northerner to master Italian Renaissance techniques of proportion, perspective, and modeling. Dürer also shared with contemporary Italians a fascination with reproducing the manifold works of nature down to the minutest details and a penchant for displaying various postures of the human nude. But whereas Michelangelo portrayed his naked David or Adam entirely without covering, Dürer's nudes are seldom lacking their fig leaves, in deference to more restrained northern traditions. Moreover, Dürer consistently refrained from abandoning himself to the pure classicism and sumptuousness of much Italian Renaissance art because he was inspired primarily by the more traditionally Christian ideals of Erasmus. Thus Dürer's serenely radiant *St. Jerome* expresses the sense of accomplishment that Erasmus or any other contemporary Christian humanist may have had while working quietly in his study, his *Knight, Death, and Devil* offers a stirring visual depiction of Erasmus's ideal Christian knight, and his *Four Apostles* intones a solemn hymn to the dignity and penetrating insight of Dürer's favorite New Testament authors, Saints Paul, John, Peter, and Mark.

Dürer would have loved nothing more than to have immortalized Erasmus in a major painted portrait, but circumstances prevented him from doing this because the paths of the two men crossed only once, and after Dürer started sketching his hero on that occasion his work was interrupted by Erasmus's press of business. Instead, the accomplishment of capturing Erasmus's pensive spirit in oils was left to the second greatest of northern Renaissance artists, the German Hans Holbein the Younger (1497–1543). As good fortune would have it, during a stay in England Holbein also painted an extraordinarily acute portrait of Erasmus's friend and kindred spirit, Sir Thomas More, which enables us to see clearly why a contemporary called More "a man of . . . sad gravity; a man for all seasons." These two portraits in and of themselves point up a major difference between medieval and Renaissance culture because whereas the Middle Ages produced no convincing naturalistic likenesses of any leading intellectual figure, Renaissance culture's greater commitment to recapturing the essence of human individuality created the environment in which Holbein was able to make Erasmus and More come to life.

Sir Thomas More. Portrait by Hans Holbein the Younger.

6. RENAISSANCE DEVELOPMENTS IN MUSIC

Music in western Europe in the fifteenth and sixteenth centuries reached such a high point of development that it constitutes, together with painting and sculpture, one of the most brilliant aspects of Renaissance endeavor. While the visual arts were stimulated by the study of ancient models, music flowed naturally from an independent evolution which had been in progress in medieval Christendom. As earlier, leadership came from men trained in the service of the Church, but secular music was now valued as well, and its principles were combined with those of sacred music to bring a decided gain in color and emotional appeal. The distinction between sacred and profane became less sharp; most composers did not restrict their activities to either field. Music was no longer regarded merely as a diversion or an adjunct to worship but came into its own as a serious independent art.

The evolution of music as an independent art

See color plates facing page 449 for *Erasmus* by Holbein

Different sections of Europe vied with one another for musical leadership. As with the other arts, advance was related to the generous patronage afforded by the prosperous cities of Italy and the northern European princely courts. During the fourteenth century a pre- or early Renaissance musical movement called Ars Nova (new art) flourished in Italy and France. Its outstanding composers were Francesco Landini (c. 1325–1397) and Guillaume de Machaut (1300–1377). The madrigals, ballads, and other songs composed by the Ars Nova musicians testify to a rich secular art, but the greatest achievement of the

Leadership provided by Italy and France

Renaissance Trumpeters and Singers. Reliefs by Luca della Robbia.

period was a highly complicated yet delicate contrapuntal style adapted for ecclesiastical motets. Machaut, moreover, was the first known composer to provide a polyphonic version for the singing of the Mass.

The fifteenth century was ushered in by a synthesis of French, Flemish, and Italian elements that took place in the ducal court of Burgundy. This music was melodious and gentle, but in the second half of the century it hardened a little as northern Flemish elements gained in importance. As the sixteenth century opened, Franco-Flemish composers appeared in every important court and cathedral all over Europe, gradually establishing regional-national schools, usually in attractive combinations of Flemish with German, Spanish, and Italian musical cultures. The various genres thus created show a close affinity with Renaissance art and poetry. In the second half of the sixteenth century the leaders of the nationalized Franco-Flemish style were the Flemish Roland de Lassus (1532–1594), the most versatile composer of the age, and the Italian Giovanni Pierluigi da Palestrina (c. 1525–1594), who specialized in highly intricate polyphonic choral music written for Catholic church services under the patronage of the popes in Rome. Music also flourished in sixteenth-century England, where the Tudor monarchs Henry VIII and Elizabeth I were active in patronizing the arts. Not only did the Italian madrigal, imported toward the end of the sixteenth century, take on remarkable new life

Synthesis of national elements

in England, but songs and instrumental music of an original cast anticipated future developments on the Continent. In William Byrd (1543–1623) English music produced a master fully the equal of the great Flemish and Italian composers of the Renaissance period. The general level of musical proficiency seems to have been higher in Queen Elizabeth's day than in ours: the singing of part-songs was a popular pastime in homes and at informal social gatherings, and the ability to read a part at sight was expected of the educated elite.

In conclusion, it may be observed that while accomplishments in counterpoint were already very advanced in the Renaissance period, our modern harmonic system was still in its infancy, and thus there was much room for later experimentation. At the same time one should realize that the music of the Renaissance constitutes not merely a stage in evolution but a magnificent achievement in itself, with masters who rank among the great of all time. The composers Lassus, Palestrina, and Byrd are as truly representative of the artistic triumph of the Renaissance as are the painters Leonardo, Raphael, and Michelangelo. Their heritage, long neglected, has within recent years begun to be appreciated, largely by means of phonograph records, and is now gaining in popularity as interested groups of musicians devote themselves to its revival.

*The greatness of the
Renaissance musical
achievement*

7. THE SCIENTIFIC ACCOMPLISHMENTS OF THE RENAISSANCE PERIOD

Some extraordinarily important accomplishments were made in the history of science during the sixteenth and early seventeenth centuries, but these were not preeminently the achievements of Renaissance humanism. The educational program of the humanists placed a low value on science because it seemed irrelevant to their aim of making people more eloquent and moral. Science for humanists like Petrarch, Leonardo Bruni, or Erasmus was part and parcel of the "vain speculation" of the Scholastics which they attacked and held up to ridicule. Accordingly, none of the great scientists of the Renaissance age belonged to the humanist movement.

*The nonscientific
orientation of Renaissance
humanism*

Nonetheless, at least two intellectual trends of the period did prepare the way for great new scientific advances. One was the currency of Neoplatonism. The importance of this philosophical system to science was that it proposed certain ideas, such as the central position of the sun and the supposed divinity of given geometrical shapes, that would help lead to crucial scientific breakthroughs. It is ironic that Neoplatonism seems very "unscientific" from the modern perspective because it emphasizes mysticism and intuition instead of empiricism or strictly rational thought. Yet it helped scientific thinkers to reconsider older notions which had impeded the progress of medieval science; in

*Renaissance foundations of
modern science: (1)
Neoplatonism*

(2) a mechanistic view of the universe

A Cannon Foundry by Leonardo da Vinci

(3) the integration of theory and practice

other words, it helped them to put on a new "thinking cap." Among the most important of the scientists who were influenced by Neoplatonism were Copernicus and Kepler.

A second trend that contributed to the advance of science was very different: the growth in popularity of a *mechanistic* interpretation of the universe. Renaissance mechanism owed its greatest impetus to the publication in 1543 of the works of the great Greek mathematician and physicist Archimedes. Not only were his concrete observations and discoveries among the most advanced and reliable in the entire body of Greek science, but Archimedes taught the view that the universe operates on the basis of mechanical forces, like a great machine. Because his view was diametrically opposed to the occult outlook of the Neoplatonists, who saw the world inhabited by spirits and driven by supernatural forces, it took some time to gather strength. Nonetheless, mechanism did gain some very important late-Renaissance adherents, foremost among whom was the Italian scientist Galileo. Ultimately mechanism played an enormous role in the development of modern science because it insisted upon finding observable and measurable causes and effects in the world of nature.

One other Renaissance development which contributed to the rise of modern science was the breakdown of the medieval separation between the realms of theory and practice. In the Middle Ages Scholastically trained clerics theorized about the natural world but never for a moment thought of tinkering with machines or dissecting corpses because this empirical approach to science lay outside the Scholastic framework. On the other hand, numerous technicians who had little formal education and knew little of abstract theories had much practical expertise in various aspects of mechanical engineering. Theory and practice began to come together in the fifteenth century. One reason for this was that the highly respected Renaissance artists bridged both areas of endeavor: not only were they marvelous craftsmen, but they advanced mathematics and science when they investigated the laws of perspective and optics, worked out geometric methods for supporting the weight of enormous architectural domes, and studied the dimensions and details of the human body. In general, they helped make science more empirical and practically oriented than it had been earlier. Other reasons for the integration were the decline in prestige of the overly theoretical universities and a growing interest in alchemy and astrology among the leisured classes. Here again we can see some irony: alchemy and astrology are today properly dismissed as unscientific superstitions, but in the sixteenth and seventeenth centuries their vogue led some wealthy amateurs to start building laboratories and measuring the courses of the stars. Thereby scientific practice was rendered eminently respectable. When that happened modern science was on the way to some of its greatest triumphs.

The actual scientific accomplishments of the Renaissance period were international in scope. The achievement par excellence in as-

St. Lawrence Enthroned, Fra Filippo Lippi (1406–1469). A master of the Florentine Renaissance, Fra Filippo Lippi exhibited in this work his gift for portraying pensive melancholy. (MMA)

The Flight into Egypt, Giotto (1276–1337). Giotto is regarded as the founder of the modern tradition in painting. A fresco in the Arena Chapel, Padua. (MMA)

The Birth of Venus, Sandro Botticelli (1444–1510). Botticelli was a mystic as well as a lover of beauty and the painting is most often interpreted as a neo-Platonic allegory. (Scala)

The Virgin of the Rocks, Leonardo da Vinci (1452–1519). This painting reveals not only Leonardo's interest in human character, but also his absorption in the phenomenon of nature. (Louvre)

Mona Lisa, Leonardo da Vinci. Unlike most other Renaissance painters who sought to convey an understandable message, Leonardo created questions to which he gave no answer. Nowhere is this more evident than in the enigmatic countenance of Mona Lisa. (Louvre)

The Last Supper, Leonardo da Vinci. This great fresco depicts the varying reactions of Jesus' disciples when He announces that one of them will betray Him. (Santa Maria della Grazie, Milan)

Above: *The Madonna of the Chair,* Raphael (1483–1520). Raphael's art was distinguished by warmth, serenity, and tenderness. (Pitti Palace, Florence) Right: "Christ and Madonna." From *The Last Judgment,* Michelangelo (1475–1564). This painting above the altar in the Sistine Chapel, Rome, shows Christ as judge condemning sinners to perdition. Even the Madonna at His side seems to shrink from His wrath. (Sistine Chapel)

Pope Paul III with His Nephews, Titian (1488–1576). This painting emphasizes action far more than its forebear, Raphael's portrait of Pope Leo X with his nephews, shown in black and white on p. 473. (National Museum, Naples)

The Emperor Charles V, Titian. (Alte Pinakothek)

Self-Portrait, Albrecht Dürer (1471–1528). Dürer was the first major artist to paint self-portraits at different phases of his life. Here, aged twenty-eight, he makes himself seem almost Christlike. Note also the prominent initials "A.D." under the date of the painting at the upper left. (Alte Pinakothek)

Erasmus, Hans Holbein the Younger (1497–1543). This portrait is generally regarded as the most telling visual characterization of "the prince of the Christian umanists." (Louvre)

The Harvesters, Pieter Brueghel (1525–1569). Brueghel chose to depict both the hard work and recreation of the peasantry. (MMA)

tronomy—the formulation and proof of the heliocentric theory that the earth revolves around the sun—was primarily the work of the Pole Copernicus, the German Kepler, and the Italian Galileo. Until the sixteenth century the Ptolemaic theory that the earth stands still at the center of the universe went virtually unchallenged in western Europe. Nicholas Copernicus (1473–1543), a Polish clergyman who had absorbed Neoplatonism while studying in Italy, was the first to posit an alternative system. Copernicus made few new observations, but he thoroughly reinterpreted the significance of the old astronomical evidence. Inspired by the Neoplatonic assumptions that the sphere is the most perfect shape, that motion is more nearly divine than rest, and that the sun sits "enthroned" in the midst of the universe, "ruling his children the planets which circle around him," Copernicus worked out a new heliocentric theory. Specifically, in his *On the Revolutions of the Heavenly Spheres*—which he completed around 1530 but did not publish until 1543—he argued that the earth and the planets move around the sun in concentric circles. Copernicus's system itself was still highly imperfect: by no means did it account without difficulties for all the known facts of planetary motion. Moreover, it asked people to reject their commonsense assumptions that the sun moves because observation shows it moving across the sky and that the earth stands still because no movement can be felt. More serious, Copernicus contradicted passages in the Bible, such as the one wherein Joshua commands the sun to stand still. As a result of such problems, believers in Copernicus's heliocentric theory remained distinctly in the minority until the early seventeenth century.

It was Kepler and Galileo who ensured the triumph of Copernicus's revolution in astronomy. Johann Kepler (1571–1630), a mystical thinker who was in many ways more like a magician than a modern scientist, studied astronomy in order to probe the hidden secrets of God. His basic conviction was that God had created the universe according to mathematical laws. Relying on the new and impressively accurate astronomical observations of the Dane Tycho Brahe (1546–1601), Kepler was able to recognize that two assumptions about planetary motion that Copernicus had taken for granted were simply not in accord with the observable facts. Specifically, Kepler replaced Copernicus's belief in uniform planetary velocity with his own "First Law" that the speed of planets varies with their distance from the sun, and he replaced Copernicus's view that planetary orbits were circular with his "Second Law" that the earth and the other planets travel in *elliptical* paths around the sun. He also argued that magnetic attractions between the sun and the planets keep the planets in orbital motion. That approach was rejected by most seventeenth-century mechanistic scientists as being far too magical, but in fact it paved the way for the law of universal gravitation formulated by Isaac Newton at the end of the seventeenth century.

As Kepler perfected Copernicus's heliocentric system from the

Progress in astronomy: Copernicus's heliocentric theory

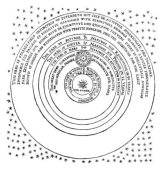

"*A Perfect Description of the Celestial Orbes.*" A diagram by Copernicus, showing the relationship of stars, the planets, and the sun.

Kepler's laws of planetary motion

Galileo's confirmation of the Copernican revolution

Galileo

Leonardo da Vinci and Galileo as physicists

point of view of mathematical theory, so Galileo Galilei (1564–1642) promoted acceptance for it by gathering further astronomical evidence. With a telescope which he manufactured himself and raised to a magnifying power of thirty times, he discovered the moons of Jupiter, the rings of Saturn, and spots on the sun. He was able also to determine that the Milky Way is a collection of celestial bodies independent of our solar system and to form some idea of the enormous distances of the fixed stars. Though many held out against them, these discoveries of Galileo gradually convinced the majority of scientists that the main conclusion of Copernicus was true. The final triumph of this idea is commonly called the Copernican Revolution. Few more significant events have occurred in the intellectual history of the world, for it overturned the medieval worldview and paved the way for modern conceptions of mechanism, skepticism, and the infinity of time and space. Some thinkers believe that it contributed also to the degradation of man, since it swept man out of his majestic position at the center of the universe and reduced him to a mere particle of dust in an endless cosmic machine.

In the front rank among the physicists of the Renaissance were Leonardo da Vinci and Galileo. If Leonardo da Vinci had failed completely as a painter, his contributions to science would still entitle him to considerable fame. Not the least of these were his achievements in physics. Though he actually made few complete discoveries, his conclusion that "every weight tends to fall toward the center by the shortest way" contained the kernel of the law of gravity. In addition, he worked out the principles of an astonishing variety of inventions, including a diving board, a steam engine, an armored tank, and a helicopter. Galileo is especially noted as a physicist for his law of falling bodies. Skeptical of the traditional theory that bodies fall with a speed directly proportional to their weight, he taught that bodies dropped from various heights would fall at a rate of speed which increases with the square of the time involved. Rejecting the Scholastic notions of absolute gravity and absolute levity, he taught that these are purely relative terms, that all bodies have weight, even those which, like the air, are invisible, and that in a vacuum all objects would fall with equal velocity. Galileo seems to have had a broader conception of a universal force of gravitation than Leonardo da Vinci, for he perceived that the power which holds the moon in the vicinity of the earth and causes the satellites of Jupiter to circulate around that planet is essentially the same as the force which enables the earth to draw bodies to its surface. He never formulated this principle as a law, however, nor did he realize all of its implications, as did Newton some fifty years later.

The record of Renaissance achievements in medicine and anatomy is also a most impressive one. Attention must be called above all to the work of the German Theophrastus von Hohenheim, known as Paracelsus (1493–1541), the Spaniard Michael Servetus (1511–1553), and the Belgian Andreas Vesalius (1514–1564). The physician Paracelsus resembled Copernicus and Kepler in believing that spiritual rather than material forces governed the workings of the universe. Hence he was a firm believer in alchemy and astrology. Nevertheless, Paracelsus relied on observation for his knowledge of diseases and their cures. Instead of following the teachings of ancient authorities, he traveled widely, studying cases of illness in different environments and experimenting with many drugs. Above all, his insistence on the close relationship of chemistry and medicine foreshadowed and sometimes directly influenced important modern achievements in pharmacology and healing. Michael Servetus, whose major interest was theology, but who practiced medicine for a living, discovered the lesser or pulmonary circulation of the blood, in an attempt to prove the veracity of the Virgin birth. He described how the blood leaves the right chambers of the heart, is carried to the lungs to be purified, then returns to the heart and is conveyed from that organ to all parts of the body. But Servetus had no idea of the return of the blood to the heart through the veins, a discovery that was made by the Englishman William Harvey in the early seventeenth century.

Purely by coincidence the one sixteenth-century scientific treatise that came closest to rivaling in significance Copernicus's work in astronomy, Vesalius's *On the Structure of the Human Body,* was published in 1543, the same year that saw the issuance of Copernicus's

Michael Servetus

Two Plates from Vesalius's On the Structure of the Human Body. On the left is a portrait of Vesalius himself displaying the sinews of the forearm. Note the striking similarity to the anatomical drawings of Leonardo, shown above, p. 426. On the right we see "the human skeleton shown from the side." The presence of the sarcophagus with the Latin warning "we live by the spirit, all else will die" shows that scientific illustrations still had to be justified by moralistic sententiousness in the early-modern period.

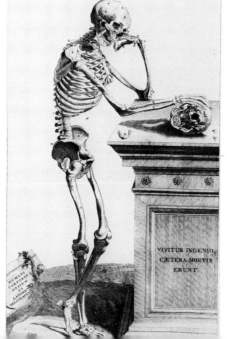

Revolutions of the Heavenly Spheres. Vesalius, a cosmopolitan who was born in Brussels and studied in Paris but later migrated to Italy where he taught anatomy and surgery at the University of Padua, approached his research from the correct point of view that much of ancient anatomical doctrine was in error. For him the ancient anatomy of Galen (so to speak, the Ptolemy of medicine) could only be corrected on the basis of direct observation. Hence he applied himself to frequent dissections of human corpses to see how various parts of the body actually appear when the skin covering is stripped away. Not content with merely describing in words what he saw, Vesalius then collaborated with an artist—Jan van Calcar, a fellow Belgian who had come to Italy to study under the Renaissance master Titian—in portraying his observations in detailed engravings. Art historians are uncertain as to whether van Calcar was directly inspired in executing his illustrations for Vesalius by knowledge of earlier anatomical drawings of Leonardo da Vinci, but even if not, he certainly relied on a cumulative tradition of expert anatomical depiction bequeathed to him by Italian Renaissance art. Gathered in Vesalius's *Structure of the Human Body* of 1543, van Calcar's plates offered a new map of the human anatomy just when Copernicus was laying out a new map of the heavens. Since Vesalius in the same work offered basic explanations of how parts of the body move and interact in addition to discussing and illustrating how they look, he is often counted as the father of modern physiology as well as the father of modern anatomy. With his landmark treatise we come to a fitting end to our survey of Renaissance accomplishments inasmuch as his *Structure of the Human Body* represented the fullest degree of fruitful international intellectual exchanges as well as the fullest merger of theory and practice, and art and science.

SELECTED READINGS

• *Items so designated are available in paperback editions.*

Baker, Herschel, *The Image of Man: A Study of the Idea of Human Dignity in Classical Antiquity, the Middle Ages, and the Renaissance,* Cambridge, Mass., 1947. An outstanding and engagingly written survey from the perspective of a modern liberal.
• Baxandall, Michael, *Painting and Experience in Fifteenth Century Italy,* Oxford, 1972.
Benesch, O., *The Art of the Renaissance in Northern Europe,* rev. ed., New York, 1965.
• Berenson, B., *The Italian Painters of the Renaissance,* New York, 1952.
• Boas, Marie, *The Scientific Renaissance: 1450–1630,* New York, 1962. An excellent, straightforward survey.
• Burckhardt, J., *The Civilization of the Renaissance in Italy,* many eds. The nineteenth-century work that formulated the modern view of the Renaissance.

Burke, Peter, *Culture and Society in Renaissance Italy, 1420–1540*, New York, 1972.
- Bush, D., *The Renaissance and English Humanism*, Toronto, 1939.
Butterfield, H., *The Origins of Modern Science*, London, 1949. Clear and wide ranging. Shows how science developed from major changes in intellectual orientations.
Chabod, F., *Machiavelli and the Renaissance*, London, 1958.
- Chambers, R. W., *Thomas More*, London, 1936. A spirited defense of the view that More was a life-long committed Catholic.
- Clark, Kenneth M., *Leonardo da Vinci*, 2nd ed., Cambridge, 1952.
De Tolnay, C., *Michelangelo: Sculptor, Painter, Architect*, Princeton, N.J., 1975.
Ferguson, W., ed., *The Renaissance: Six Essays*, rev. ed., New York, 1962.
Fox, Alistair, *Thomas More: History and Providence*, Oxford, 1982. More reliable in its judgments than Chambers.
- Gilmore, M., *The World of Humanism*, New York, 1952. A well-written survey.
Gould, Cecil, *An Introduction to Italian Renaissance Painting*, London, 1957.
Hale, J. R., *Machiavelli and Renaissance Italy*, New York, 1960.
- ———, *Renaissance Europe: The Individual and Society, 1480–1520*, London, 1971. A different kind of survey that does not treat the great events but examines the quality of life.
- Hay, D., ed., *The Renaissance Debate*, New York, 1965. A collection of readings on the question of how to define the Renaissance.
- Kearney, H., *Science and Change, 1500–1700*, New York, 1971. Supplements Butterfield in arguing that science progressed as the result of contributions made by three different "schools."
- Kristeller, P. O., *Eight Philosophers of the Italian Renaissance*, Stanford, Calif., 1964. Admirably clear.
- ———, *Renaissance Thought: The Classic, Scholastic, and Humanist Strains*, New York, 1961. Very helpful in defining main trends of Renaissance thought.
- Kuhn, Thomas S., *The Copernican Revolution: Planetary Astronomy in the Development of Western Thought*, Cambridge, Mass., 1957. Admirably clear.
Larner, John, *Culture and Society in Italy, 1290–1420*, New York, 1971.
- Levey, M., *Early Renaissance (Style and Civilization)*, Baltimore, 1967. Art history.
- Martines, L., *Power and Imagination: City-States in Renaissance Italy*, New York, 1979. An expert account of the interrelationships between political and material circumstances and cultural expressions.
Panofsky, E., *Albrecht Dürer*, 3rd ed., Princeton, N.J., 1948.
- ———, *Renaissance and Renascences in Western Art*, Stockholm, 1960. A difficult but rewarding attempt to distinguish the Italian Renaissance from its medieval predecessors.
Phillips, Margaret M., *Erasmus and the Northern Renaissance*, London, 1949.
Pope-Hennessy, J., *The Portrait in the Renaissance*, Princeton, N.J., 1966.
- Ralph, Philip L., *The Renaissance in Perspective*, New York, 1973. Both a useful summary and a stimulus to thought.
Reese, Gustave, *Music in the Renaissance*, rev. ed., New York, 1959. The leading work on the subject.

• Rice, E. F., Jr., *The Foundations of Early Modern Europe, 1460–1559*, New York, 1970.

Seigel, J., *Rhetoric and Philosophy in Renaissance Humanism*, Princeton, N.J., 1968. Treats a basic tension in the thought of early Renaissance thinkers.

Stechow, W., *Northern Renaissance Art: 1400–1600*, Englewood Cliffs, N.J., 1966.

Tracy, James, *Erasmus: The Growth of a Mind*, Geneva, 1972. The best intellectual biography.

Whitfield, J. H., *A Short History of Italian Literature*, Baltimore, 1960.

• Wittkower, R., *Architectural Principles in the Age of Humanism*, rev. ed., New York, 1965. An art-historical classic.

SOURCE MATERIALS

Alberti, Leon Battista, *The Family in Renaissance Florence*, tr. R. N. Watkins, Columbia, S.C., 1969.

• Cassirer, E., et al., eds., *The Renaissance Philosophy of Man*, Chicago, 1948. Leading works of Petrarch, Pico, etc.

• Castiglione, B., *The Book of the Courtier*, tr. C. S. Singleton, New York, 1959.

• Erasmus, D., *The Praise of Folly*, tr. J. Wilson, Ann Arbor, Mich., 1958.

• ———, *Ten Colloquies*, tr. C. R. Thompson, Indianapolis, 1957.

• Kohl, B. G., and R. G. Witt, eds., *The Earthly Republic: Italian Humanists on Government and Society*, Philadelphia, 1978. New translations with excellent introductions.

• Machiavelli, N., *The Prince*, tr. R. M. Adams, New York, 1976. In addition to Machiavelli's text, this edition provides related documents and an excellent selection of scholarly interpretations.

• Montaigne, M. de, *Essays*, tr. J. M. Cohen, Baltimore, 1958.

• More, Sir Thomas, *Utopia*, tr. R. M. Adams, New York, 1975. In the same series as Adams's translation of Machiavelli's *Prince;* provides background materials and selected scholarly interpretations as well as the text.

• Rabelais, F., *Gargantua and Pantagruel*, tr. J. M. Cohen, Baltimore, 1955. A robust modern translation.

Chapter 15

EUROPE EXPANDS AND DIVIDES: OVERSEAS DISCOVERIES AND PROTESTANT REFORMATION

Formerly we were at the end of the world, and now we are in the middle of it, with an unprecedented change in our fortunes.

—Hernán Pérez de Oliva, addressing the city fathers
of Cordova, Spain, 1524

Since then your serene majesty and your lordships seek a simple answer, I will give it in this manner, neither horned nor toothed: unless I am convinced by the testimony of Scripture or by clear reason . . . I am bound by the Scripture I have quoted, and my conscience is captive to the Word of God. I cannot and I will not retract anything, since it is neither safe nor right to violate one's conscience. I cannot do otherwise, here I stand, may God help me. Amen.

—Martin Luther, addressing the Diet of Worms, 1521

M uch as the civilization of the Renaissance made fundamental contributions toward the shaping of the modern world, the two most dramatic developments in the transition from the Middle Ages to the early-modern period of western European history were the overseas ventures of Spain and Portugal, and the Protestant Reformation. More or less overnight, these two developments changed the course of European history forever. Whereas European Christian civilization had been geographically self-contained throughout the thousand years of its prior history (excepting the relatively brief Crusade episode), in just a few decades, from about 1490 to about 1520, Europeans sailed out on the open seas to take commanding positions in Southeast Asia and lay claim to the whole Western Hemisphere. Ever since, the course of European history has been inseparable from interactions between events on the landmass of Europe and European engagements in the rest of the world.

*Overseas expansion of
Spain and Portugal*

But just when Europe was expanding it was also dividing. Up until the early sixteenth century, despite growing national differences, there remained a distinct European "Community of Christendom," presided over by the pope. Wherever one traveled one could hear the same Latin mass, see infants baptized and couples wed according to the same ecclesiastical formulae, and receive blessings from priests who were all ordained by virtue of the same papal authority. As quickly as Europeans took hold of the world, however, they lost their spiritual unity. The Protestant Reformation initiated by Martin Luther in 1517, as well as the Catholic response to it, were both to have numerous progressive effects, but the most obvious immediate results were that Europe rapidly became divided along several different religious lines and that Europeans quickly started warring with one another in the name of faith.

Although the overseas discoveries and Protestant Reformation were roughly contemporaneous, it is important to recognize that in their origins they had nothing directly to do with each other. The early explorers sailed prior to or in disregard of European religious dissensions, and the early Protestants gave little thought to the opening up of new trade routes or the discovery of continents. Yet there is warrant for treating the discoveries, the Protestant Reformation, and the Catholic Counter-Reformation all in the same chapter because their effects very quickly became interrelated and also because all these movements were full of incidents of great heroism. As Columbus sailed fearlessly into the unknown and Balboa viewed a new ocean, "silent, upon a peak in Darien," so Luther struggled fearlessly for a new understanding of "the justice of God" and the crippled soldier Ignatius Loyola found inspiration by inward "spiritual exercises," thereby opening up new vistas of their own.

1. THE OVERSEAS DISCOVERIES AND CONQUESTS OF PORTUGAL AND SPAIN

At first glance the speed with which Europeans in the years around 1500 began to traverse the high seas appears bewildering and almost incomprehensible. With good reason most contemporaries perceived Christian civilization to be on the defensive, not the offensive, in the second half of the fifteenth century. In 1453 Constantinople, a hitherto impregnable barrier to Islamic advance, fell to the Turks, commanded by Sultan Muhammad II "the Conqueror"; Serbia was lost in 1459 and Albania followed in 1470. Most frightening of all to western Europeans was a Turkish landing on the Italian peninsula itself in 1480, which saw the city of Otranto occupied and half the inhabitants slaughtered. Only the death of Sultan Muhammad in 1481 caused the Turks to abandon their Italian foothold, but many feared that the "Infidels" might soon return. In the midst of an unsuccessful attempt to organize united European resistance to the Turks, Pope Pius II (1458–1464) observed: "I see nothing good on the horizon."

Yet Pius II could hardly have been more wrong, for while Christians remained on the defensive against the Turks in eastern Europe until the later sixteenth century, Portuguese and Spanish sailing ships on the Atlantic horizon soon made Christians lords of the world. A few facts speak eloquently for themselves: in 1482 the Portuguese built a fortress at Elmina, in modern-day Ghana, which quickly dominated trade on the West African "Gold Coast"; in 1492 Columbus sighted the West Indies; in 1500 the Portuguese established their first trading base on the west coast of India; and in the two years from 1519 to 1521 the Spaniard Cortés seized hold of the Mexican empire of Montezuma. *Sudden overseas
expansion*

How did this all happen so quickly? Two different schools of scholarly interpretation offer substantially different responses. Proponents of what may be called the "Renaissance School" point out that the Portuguese and Spanish voyages of discovery occurred at the same time as the spread of Renaissance civilization (Columbus was a direct contemporary of Leonardo da Vinci) and argue that European overseas expansion can only be explained as a manifestation of allegedly new Renaissance principles of curiosity and self-reliance in practical affairs. But this interpretation assumes falsely that medieval people were not curious and self-reliant. Proponents of the Renaissance school also call attention to the fact that many of the mariners who sailed for Portugal and Spain were Italian born, but here they dodge the reality that some Italian voyagers, like Columbus himself, came from Genoa, a city which hardly participated in Italian Renaissance civilization. More important, the Renaissance interpretation seems weak because the leading Italian Renaissance states did not patronize the voyages of discovery at all. Undeniably some bits of classical geographical knowledge acquired in Italy by Renaissance humanists strengthened the resolve of some explorers to pursue certain ocean routes, but otherwise the alternative to the Renaissance explanation, namely the view that the movement of overseas expansion came from medieval preparations, seems far preferable. *Explanations for voyages:
"Renaissance School"*

Simply stated, the motives, the knowledge, and the wherewithal for the great discoveries were all essentially medieval. Certainly the single most dominant motive for the oceanic voyages was economic—the quest for Asiatic spices and other luxury goods. Pepper, cinnamon, nutmeg, ginger, and cloves could all be grown only in the tropical climates of Southeast Asia, and all were greatly prized throughout the High and late Middle Ages because of their preservative qualities. (Imagine a civilization without refrigeration and one can easily understand why wealthy Europeans hankered after tangy spices to keep their food from putrifying and to relieve the monotony of salt.) In the late Middle Ages, Asiatic spices, as well as luxury cloths and precious gems, reached European households by means of the enterprise of Islamic, *Medieval background to
voyages: economic motives*

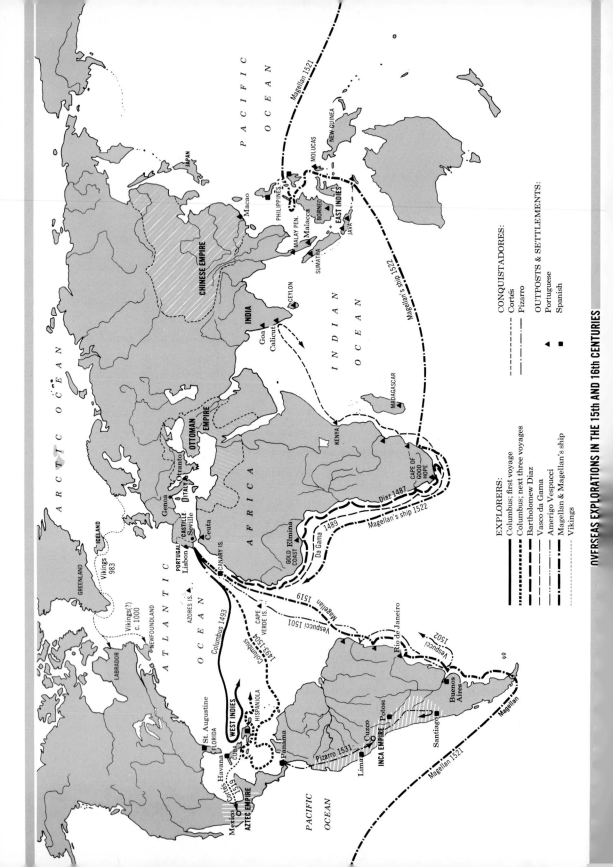

OVERSEAS EXPLORATIONS IN THE 15th AND 16th CENTURIES

EXPLORERS:
— Columbus; first voyage
— Columbus; next three voyages
— Bartholomew Diaz
— Vasco da Gama
— Amerigo Vespucci
— Magellan & Magellan's ship
— Vikings

CONQUISTADORES:
— Cortés
— Pizarro

OUTPOSTS & SETTLEMENTS:
▲ Portuguese
■ Spanish

ARCTIC OCEAN

PACIFIC OCEAN

ATLANTIC OCEAN

INDIAN OCEAN

CHINESE EMPIRE

OTTOMAN EMPIRE

AFRICA

INDIA

JAPAN

Macao

PHILIPPINES

MALAY PEN.
Malacca
BORNEO
EAST INDIES
SUMATRA
JAVA
MOLUCCAS
NEW GUINEA

CEYLON

Goa
Calicut

MADAGASCAR

KENYA

CAPE OF GOOD HOPE

GOLD COAST
Elmina

CANARY IS.

CAPE VERDE IS.

AZORES IS.

ICELAND

GREENLAND

LABRADOR

NEWFOUNDLAND

Vikings 983

Vikings(?) c. 1000

Genoa
ITALY
Otranto
PORTUGAL
Lisbon
CASTILLE
Seville
Ceuta

Magellan 1521

Magellan's ship 1522

Magellan's ship 1522

Diaz 1487

Da Gama 1489

Vespucci 1501

Vespucci 1502

Magellan 1519

Columbus 1493

Columbus 1493-1504

Rio de Janeiro

Buenos Aires

Santiago

Potosí

Cuzco
INCA EMPIRE

Lima
Pizarro 1531

Panama

Havana
CUBA
WEST INDIES
HISPANIOLA

St. Augustine
FLORIDA

Mexico
AZTEC EMPIRE
Cortés 1519

Magellan 1521

Magellan

Venetian, and Genoese middlemen, but the costs were exorbitant and a fortune was to be made by anyone who could go directly to the source by sea. (Land routes were out of the question because turbulent conditions in central Asia made them extremely unsafe; moreover, until the invention of railroads it normally was vastly more expensive to transport goods by land than by water.) Complementing the economic motives for overseas exploration were religious ones—hopes for converting unbaptized heathens and of finding imagined "lost Christians" in the East who might serve as allies against Islam. Needless to say, these hopes, like the lust for spices, flourished in the Middle Ages quite independently of the Italian Renaissance.

Then too the most important knowledge that lay behind the great discoveries and also the technological means to execute them were as medieval as the motivations. The popular notion that Europeans before Columbus believed the earth to be flat is simply a mistake: it would have been impossible after the twelfth century to have found an educated person or a mariner who did not accept the fact that the earth is a sphere. Nor did this knowledge remain solely in the realm of theory. As early as 1291 two Genoese, the Vivaldi brothers, sailed out on the Atlantic with the aim of reaching the East Indies by a "westward route." Although the Vivaldis never came back, by the middle of the fourteenth century Portuguese mariners were sailing regularly back and forth on the Atlantic as far west as the Azores Islands. These Portuguese sailings offer proof that by about 1350 European shipbuilding and navigational technology were fully up to the challenge of reaching new continents: since the Azores are one-third of the distance between Europe and America, from the strictly technological point of view any ship that could sail from Portugal to the Azores could have sailed all the way to the New World.

Medieval background to voyages: technology

Why, then, was America not discovered a century before it actually was? Historians are at their greatest disadvantage in trying to explain things that did not happen, but two hypotheses may be offered. One relates to the fact that the fourteenth and fifteenth centuries were times of acute economic depression and political turmoil throughout western Europe. Since the major states of the Atlantic—France, England, and Castile (the dominant kingdom on the Spanish peninsula)—were all weakened by economic contraction and caught up in seemingly interminable wars, it is no wonder that none of them commissioned expensive and risky sailing ventures to the west. The second, less speculative hypothesis pertains to the change in routes pursued by Portugal, the one Atlantic state already deeply involved in ambitious seaward expeditions. After establishing colonies in the second half of the fourteenth century on the Atlantic islands of the Azores and Madeira that yielded a lucrative trade in sugar and wine, the Portuguese in the early fifteenth century quite understandably turned their attention to exploring the coast of West Africa because Africa promised even greater wealth in gold and slaves. Thereafter one Portuguese African

Timing of voyages of discovery

Prince Henry the Navigator. By
a fifteenth-century Portuguese
painter.

discovery led to another until the Cape of Good Hope was rounded
in 1487 and the race for Asiatic spices that led to the most dramatic of
European overseas exploits had begun. Thus seen from the perspective of late-medieval Portuguese sailing and trading history, the great
discoveries look much less startlingly revolutionary than they do at
first glance.

The fifteenth-century Portuguese voyages that served as the major
connecting link to the dramatic achievements of the years around 1500
were commissioned by Portugal's Prince Henry "the Navigator" from
1418 until his death in 1460. Starting from an initial base of Ceuta in
North Africa, Portuguese ships advanced steadily southward along
the West African coastline, braving the ever-hotter sun and establishing forts and trading posts as they went. The extraordinary heroism
of the sailors on these ships can easily be appreciated from a mid–
fifteenth-century account, according to which four galleys "were
provisioned for several years and were away three years, but only one
galley returned and even on that galley most of the crew had died.
And those which survived could hardly be recognized as human. They
had lost flesh and hair, the nails had gone from hands and feet. Their
eyes were sunk deep in their heads and they were as black as Moors.
They spoke of heat so incredible that it was a marvel that ships and
crews were not burnt. They said also that they found no houses or
land and they could sail no farther. The farther they sailed, so the sea
became more furious and the heat grew more intense. They thought
that the other ships had sailed too far and it was impossible that they
should be able to return." But return they did, and despite the terrifying tales that such crews told, new expeditions continually were sent
out that ventured still farther.

After Henry the Navigator's death in 1460 some slackening in the
Portuguese enterprise ensued, but it regained vigor with the accession
of King John II (1481–1495). Inasmuch as the Portuguese had already
gained full control of the African Gold Coast and slave trade, they
naturally began to set their sights on reaching the wealth of Asia. The
literal as well as figurative turning point in this effort was the accidental rounding of the tip of southernmost Africa by the Portuguese captain Bartholomew Dias in 1487. Since Dias had only accomplished
this feat by being caught in a gale, he pessimistically called this pro-
montory the "Cape of Storms," but John II took a more optimistic
view of the matter and renamed it the Cape of Good Hope. Furthermore, John resolved to organize a major naval expedition designed to
travel beyond the cape all the way to India.

After several delays John's successor, Manuel I (1495–1521), finally
sent off a fleet in 1497 captained by Vasco da Gama which accomplished all that was planned. Da Gama's exploits were so heroic that
they later became the basis for the Portuguese national epic, *The Lusiad*.
After four months beyond sight of land the intrepid captain rounded
Africa, sailed up Africa's east coast to Kenya, and then crossed the

*Discovery of Cape of
Good Hope*

*Vasco da Gama's voyage
to India*

Left: *The Tower of Belem*. Right: *A Portuguese Galleon*. The Tower of Belem, a fifteenth-century fort, stands at the beach where Vasco da Gama departed in 1497 to sail beyond the Cape of Good Hope to India. The galleon shown at the right is the sort of ship da Gama might have sailed in.

Indian Ocean to western India, where he loaded his ships with spices. Two years after his departure da Gama returned, having lost half of his fleet and one-third of his men. But his pepper and cinnamon were so valuable that they made his losses seem worthwhile. Now master of the quickest route to riches in the world, King Manuel swiftly capitalized on da Gama's accomplishment. After 1500 Portuguese trading fleets sailed regularly to India; by 1510 Portuguese arms had established full control of the western Indian coastline, and in 1511 Portuguese ships seized Malacca, a center of the spice trade on the Malay peninsula. The Cape of Good Hope thus had lived up to John II's prophetic name and Europeans had arrived in the Far East to stay.

The decision of the Spanish rulers to underwrite Columbus's famous voyage was directly related to the progress of the Portuguese ventures. Specifically, given the strong likelihood that the Portuguese would dominate the sea lanes leading to Asia by the east in the wake of Dias's successful return in 1488, the only alternative for Portugal's Spanish rivals was to finance someone bold enough to try to reach Asia by sailing west. The popular image of Christopher Columbus (1451–1506) as a visionary who struggled to convince hardened ignoramuses that the world was round does not bear up under scrutiny. In fact Columbus was not "right" but "wrong" insofar as the sphericity of the earth was never in doubt and the stubborn Genoese seaman who had settled in Spain erred in vastly underestimating the distance westward from Europe to Asia. Had Columbus known the actual circum-

Reasons for Columbus's westward voyage

ference of the earth, even he would not have dared to set out because he would have realized that the distance to Asia, assuming no barriers lay between, was too great for ships of his day to traverse. America, then, was discovered as the result of a colossal error in reckoning, but when Columbus, with the financial backing of Queen Isabella of Castile, reached what we know today as the Bahamas and the island of Hispaniola in 1492 after only a month's sailing, he felt fully vindicated.

The "discovery" of
America

Strictly speaking, it cannot be said that Columbus "discovered America" for two reasons. In the first place, experts now agree that the earliest Europeans to reach the Western Hemisphere were the Vikings, who touched on present-day Newfoundland, Labrador, and perhaps New England in voyages made around the year 1000. Second, Columbus did not "discover America" because he never knew what he found, dying in the conviction that all the new land he encountered was merely the outer reaches of Asia. Yet neither of these arguments diminishes Columbus's achievement because the Viking landings had been forgotten or ignored throughout Europe for hundreds of years, and if Columbus did not know what he had found, others, following immediately in his path, came to the realization soon thereafter. Although Columbus brought back no Asiatic spices from his voyage of 1492, he did return with some small samples of gold and a few natives who gave promise of entire tribes that might be enslaved. (Columbus and all his contemporaries saw no conflict between converting heathen to Christianity and enslaving them.) This provided sufficient incentive for the Spanish monarchs, Ferdinand and Isabella, to finance three more expeditions by Columbus and many more by others. Soon the mainland was discovered as well as islands, and although Columbus refused until his death to accept the truth, the conclusion quickly became inescapable around 1500 that a new world had indeed been found. Since the recognition that Columbus had really stumbled upon a new world was most widely publicized by the Italian geographer Amerigo Vespucci (one of Vespucci's writings of 1504 was actually called *Mundus novus* or *A New World*), the Western Hemisphere soon became known as "America" after Vespucci's first name.

The search for a
"southwest passage" to
Asia

One might well think that the discovery of a new world around 1500 would have delighted the Spanish rulers who had invested in it, but in fact it came as a disappointment, for with a major landmass standing between Europe and Asia, Spain hardly could hope to beat Portugal in the race for spices. Any remaining doubt that two vast oceans separated Europe from East Asia instead of one was completely removed when Vasco Nuñez de Balboa first viewed the Pacific from the Isthmus of Panama in 1513. Not entirely admitting defeat, Ferdinand and Isabella's grandson King Charles accepted Ferdinand Magellan's offer in 1519 to see whether a feasible route to Asia could be found by sailing around South America. But Magellan's voyage merely demonstrated that the perils of a journey around southern Argentina

Ferdinand and Isabella Worshiping the Virgin. A contemporary Spanish painting: the royal pair are shown with two of their children in the company of saints from the Dominican order.

were simply too great: of five ships that left Spain, only one returned three years later, having been forced to circumnavigate the globe. Nor did Magellan himself live to tell this tale; instead, eighteen survivors out of an original crew of two hundred eighty reported that most of their comrades had died from scurvy or starvation and that their captain had been killed in a skirmish with East Indian natives. After this fiasco, all hope for an easy "southwest passage" came to an end.

But if it was disappointing that America loomed as a barricade to the East, it gradually became clear to the Spanish that the New World had much wealth of its own. From the start Columbus's gold samples, in themselves rather paltry, had nurtured hopes that somewhere in America gold might lie piled in ingots, and rumor fed rumor until a few Spanish adventurers really did strike it rich beyond their most avaricious imaginings. At first riches were seized by dint of astonishing feats of arms. In two years, from 1519 to 1521, the *conquistador* (Spanish for conqueror) Hernando Cortés, commanding six hundred men, subjugated the Aztec empire of Mexico numbering a million, and carried off all of the Aztecs' fabulous wealth. Then in 1533 another *conquistador,* Francisco Pizarro, this time with a mere hundred eighty men, plundered the fabled gold of the Incas in conquering Peru. Cortés and Pizarro had the advantage of some cannon and a few horses, but they achieved their victories primarily by sheer courage, treachery, and cruelty. Never before or since have so few men won such great realms against such enormous odds, but seldom have men acted in so ruthless and repugnant a manner.

The conquistadors *plunder the New World for gold*

Left: *The Aztec Ruler Montezuma Coming Forth to Meet Cortés*. Although Cortés here holds out his hand in friendship, he would soon destroy Montezuma and enslave the Aztec nation. From a German book of 1599. Right: *The Silver-mines of Potosí (Bolivia)*. A French engraving of 1602: some of the miners work naked because of the heat.

Economic rewards for Spain in the New World

Cortés, Pizarro, and their fellow *conquistadors* fought only for themselves, not for Spain, and knew only how to plunder, not produce, but by the middle of the sixteenth century the Spanish crown had taken governmental control of all Central and South America (except for Brazil, which was colonized by Portugal), and great quantities of bullion were being mined instead of stolen. Most important by far was the mining of silver. Gold, of course, was the more sought-after metal, but after quickly hauling off the stores of gold amassed for centuries by pre-Columbian native civilizations, the Spanish were able to mine only small quantities of gold on their own. On the other hand, however, they soon realized that in areas of Bolivia and Mexico they were sitting on some of the richest silver deposits in the world. By means of forced native labor and new refining techniques, Spanish overlords produced such vast quantities of silver bars by the second half of the sixteenth century that the relative lack of gold was hardly a disappointment. Since livestock farming and the production of sugar-cane in sixteenth-century Spanish America also became highly re-munerative, the Spanish crown could have had no regrets after all that Columbus had lighted on a new world instead of Asia.

Consequences of European expansion overseas

Subsequent chapters will pursue the continued development of European overseas expansion and colonization; here it may be said that the overall results of the initial achievements were extremely profound in their implications for at least three reasons. First of all, the emergence of Portugal and Spain as Europe's leading long-distance traders in the sixteenth century permanently moved the center of gravity of European economic power away from Italy and the Mediterranean toward the Atlantic. Deprived of their role as conduits of Oriental trade, Genoa became Spain's banker and Venice gradually a tourist attraction, while Atlantic ports bustled with vessels and shone with wealth. Admittedly the prosperity of Portugal and Spain themselves was fleeting, but the other Atlantic states of England, Holland, and France quickly inherited their mantle as the preeminent economic powers of the world. Second, throughout Europe the increase in the circulation of imported goods and the sudden influx of bullion stimulated entrepreneurial ambitions. Simply stated, the opening of the seas around 1500 provided marvelous opportunities for people with ability and daring to make new fortunes, inspiring a sense that success could only lead to success. Thus not only were many enterprising individuals enriched overnight, but the entire sixteenth century was one of great overall economic growth for western Europe.

Unfortunately, however, the enormous riches of America were gained only at an appalling cost in human life. Although exact figures are not available, of an estimated indigenous population of 250,000 on the island of Hispaniola in 1492, only about 500 remained in 1538. As for the far larger population of Mexico, it declined by about 90 percent in the first century of Spanish rule. Not all this loss of life was due to conscious ruthlessness; on the contrary, huge numbers of natives died from epidemic diseases such as small pox and measles introduced by the Europeans to which they had no biological resistance. But countless innocent people also died as the result of merciless exploitation—literally worked so hard by their conquerors that they expired from exhaustion and lack of care. Thus however much Europeans profited from their colonization of the New World, for the original inhabitants the appearance of the white man was an unmitigated disaster.

The human costs

A Spaniard Kicking an Indian. As this sixteenth-century drawing makes clear, the Spanish treatment of the indigenous American population was brutal.

2. THE LUTHERAN UPHEAVAL

Martin Luther. A portrait by
Lucas Cranach.

Causes of the Lutheran
Reformation

Background to Luther's
revolt: superstition

While the Portuguese and Spanish were plowing new paths on the
seas, a German monk named Martin Luther (1483–1546) was searching
for a new path to the understanding of human salvation, and though
his discoveries were made in the quiet of a monastic cell rather than in
exotic tropical climes, their effects were no less momentous. Indeed,
many Europeans felt the impact of Luther's activities much more
immediately and directly than they did the results of the overseas discoveries, because once the German monk started attacking the institutions of the contemporary Roman Church he set off a chain reaction
which rapidly resulted in the secession of much of northern Europe
from the Catholic faith, thereby quickly affecting the religious practices of millions.

In searching for the causes of the Lutheran revolt in Germany, three
main questions need to be dealt with: (1) why Martin Luther happened
to instigate a break with Rome; (2) why large numbers of Germans
rallied to his cause; and (3) why several ruling German princes decided
to put the Lutheran Reformation into effect. Reduced to the barest
essentials, the answers to these questions are that Luther himself broke
with Rome because of his doctrine of justification by faith, that the
German masses followed him primarily because they were swept away
by a surge of religious nationalism, and that the princes were moved
to institute Lutheranism above all because of their desire for absolute
governmental sovereignty. Within a decade preacher, populace, and
princes, so to speak, would all sing the same stirring Lutheran hymn,
"A Mighty Fortress Is Our God," in the same church, but it should
be emphasized that they arrived there by rather different paths.

Many people think that Luther rebelled against Rome because he
was disgusted with contemporary religious abuses—superstitions,
frauds, and the offer of salvation for money—but that is only part of
the story. Certainly abuses in Luther's day were grave and intensely
upsetting to religious idealists. In a world beset by disease and disaster, frail mortals clutched at supernatural straws to seek health on earth
and salvation in the hereafter. Some superstitious men and women,
for example, believed that viewing the consecrated host during Mass
in the morning would guard them from death throughout the day,
and others neglected to swallow the consecrated wafer so that they
could use it later either as a charm to ward off evil, an application to
cure the sick, or a powder to fertilize their crops. Similarly, belief in
the miraculous curative powers of saints was hard to distinguish from
belief in magic. Every saint had his or her specialty: "for botches and
biles, Cosmas and Damian; St. Clare for the eyes, St. Apolline for
teeth, St. Job for pox. And for sore breasts, St. Agatha." Because
alleged relics of Christ and the saints were thought to radiate marvelous healing effects, traffic in relics boomed. Even Luther's patron, the

Elector Frederick the Wise of Saxony, had a collection in his castle church at Wittenberg of 17,000 relics, including a supposed remnant of Moses's burning bush, pieces of the holy cradle, shreds from Christ's swaddling clothes, and thirty-three fragments of the holy cross. As Mark Twain once sardonically observed, there were indeed enough splinters of the holy cross throughout Europe "to shingle a barn."

Superstitions and gross credulity were offensive enough to religious idealists of Luther's stamp, but worse still were the granting of dispensations and the promises of spiritual benefits for money. If a man wished to marry his first cousin, for example, he could usually receive an official religious dispensation allowing the marriage for a fee, and annulments of marriage—divorce being prohibited—similarly came for a price. Most malodorous to many, however, was the sale of indulgences. In Catholic theology, an indulgence is a remission by papal authority of all or part of the temporal punishment due for sin— that is, of the punishment in this life and in purgatory—after the guilt of sin itself is absolved by sacramental confession. As we have seen, the practice of granting indulgences began at the end of the eleventh century as an incentive for encouraging men to become Crusaders. Once it became accepted in the course of the High Middle Ages that the pope could dispense grace from a "Treasury of Merits" (that is, a storehouse of surplus good works piled up by Christ and the saints), it soon was taken for granted that the pope could promise people time off in purgatory as well. But indulgences originally granted for extraordinary deeds gradually came to be sold for money; by the fourteenth century, popes started granting indulgences to raise money for any worthy cause whatsoever, such as the building of cathedrals or hospitals; and finally, in 1476 Pope Sixtus IV (the patron of the Sistine chapel) took the extreme step of declaring that the benefits of indulgences could be extended to the dead already in purgatory as well as to the living. Money, then, could not only save an individual from works of penance but could save his dearest relatives from eons of agonizing torments after death.

Background to Luther's revolt: sale of dispensations and indulgences

Certainly Luther was horrified by the traffic in relics and the sale of indulgences; indeed, the latter provided the immediate grounds for his revolt against Rome. But it was by no means the abuses of the late-medieval Church so much as medieval Catholic theology itself that he came to find thoroughly unacceptable. To this degree the term "Lutheran Reformation" is misleading, for Luther was no mere "reformer" who wanted to cleanse the current religious system of its impurities. Many Christian humanists of Luther's day were reformers in just that sense, but they shrank from breaking with Rome because they had no objections to the basic principles of medieval Catholicism. Luther, on the other hand, by no means would have been satisfied with the mere abolition of abuses because it was the entire Catholic "religion of works" that appalled him.

Luther's opposition to medieval Catholic theology

Simply stated, Luther preferred a rigorously Augustinian system of theology to a medieval Thomistic one. As we have seen, around the year 400 St. Augustine of Hippo had formulated an uncompromising doctrine of predestination which maintained that God alone determined human salvation and that His decisions concerning whom to save and whom to damn were made from eternity, without any regard to merits that given humans might show while sojourning on earth. This extreme view, however, left so little room for human freedom and responsibility that it was modified greatly in the course of the Middle Ages. Above all, during the twelfth and thirteenth centuries theologians such as Peter Lombard and St. Thomas Aquinas (hence the term "Thomistic") set forth an alternative belief system which rested on two assumptions: (1) since God's saving grace is not irresistible, humans can freely reject God's advances and encompass their own doom; and (2) since the sacramental ministrations of the Church communicate ongoing grace, they help human sinners improve their chances of salvation. Except in emergencies, none of the sacraments could be administered by persons other than priests. Having inherited this power from the Apostle Peter, the members of the clergy alone had the authority to cooperate with God in forgiving sins and in performing the miracle of the Eucharist, whereby the bread and wine were transubstantiated into the body and blood of the Saviour. All of this amounted, in Luther's opinion, to saying that humans could be saved by the performance of "good works," and it was this theology of works that he became prepared to resist even unto death.

Martin Luther may ultimately have been a source of inspiration for millions, but at first he was a terrible disappointment to his father. The elder Luther, who had risen from Thuringian German peasant stock and gained prosperity by leasing some mines, wanted his son Martin to rise still further. The father thus sent young Luther to the University of Erfurt to study law, but while there in 1505, possibly as the result of unconscious psychological rebellion against parental pressure, Martin shattered his father's ambitions by becoming a monk instead. Afterward, throughout his life Martin Luther was never to "put on airs." Even at the time of his greatest fame he lived simply and always expressed himself in the vigorous and sometimes earthy vernacular of the German peasantry.

Like many great figures in the history of religion, Luther arrived at what he conceived to be the truth by a dramatic conversion experience. Once a monk, young Martin zealously pursued all the traditional medieval means for achieving his own salvation. Not only did he fast and pray continuously, but he confessed so often that his exhausted confessor would sometimes jokingly say that his sins were actually trifling and that if he really wanted to have a rousing confession he should go out and do something dramatic like committing adultery. Yet, try as he might, Luther could find no spiritual peace because he feared that he could never perform enough good deeds to placate an angry God. But then, in 1513 he hit upon an insight that granted him relief and changed the course of his life.

Luther's guiding insight pertained to the problem of the justice of God. For years he had worried that God seemed unjust in issuing commandments that He knew men would not observe and then in punishing them with eternal damnation for not observing them. But after becoming a professor of biblical theology at the University of Wittenberg (many members of his monastic order were expected to teach), he was led by the Bible to a new understanding of the problem. Specifically, while meditating on the words in the Psalms "deliver me in thy justice," it suddenly struck him that God's justice had nothing to do with His disciplinary power but rather with His mercy in saving sinful mortals through faith. As Luther later wrote, "At last, by the mercy of God, I began to understand the justice of God as that by which God makes us just in his mercy and through faith . . . and at this I felt as though I had been born again, and had gone through open gates into paradise." Since the fateful moment of truth came to Luther in the tower room of his monastery, it is customarily called his "tower experience."

His "tower experience"

After that, everything seemed to fall into place. Lecturing on the Pauline Epistles in Wittenberg in the years immediately following 1513, Luther dwelled on the text of St. Paul to the Romans (1:17) "the just shall live by faith" to reach his central doctine of "justification by faith alone." By this he meant that God's justice does not demand endless good works and religious ceremonies, for no one can hope to be saved by his own works. Rather, humans are "justified"—that is, granted salvation—by God's saving grace alone, offered as an utterly unmerited gift to those predestined for salvation. Since this grace is manifested in humans in thoroughly passive faith, men and women are justified from the human perspective by faith alone. In Luther's view those who had faith would do good works anyway, but it was the faith that came first. Although the essence of this doctrine was not original but harked back to the predestinarianism of St. Augustine, it was new for Luther and the early sixteenth century, and if followed to its conclusions could only mean the dismantling of much of the contemporary Catholic religious structure.

Justification by faith

At first Luther remained merely an academic lecturer, teaching within the realm of theory, but in 1517 he was goaded into attacking some of the actual practices of the Church by a provocation that was too much for him to bear. The story of the indulgence campaign of 1517 in Germany is colorful but unsavory. The worldly Albert of Hohenzollern, archbishop of Mainz and youngest brother of the elector of Brandenburg, had sunk himself into enormous debt for several discreditable reasons. In 1513 he had to pay large sums for gaining dispensations from the papacy to hold the bishoprics of Magdeburg and Halberstadt concurrently, and for assuming these offices even

The scandalous indulgence campaign

though at twenty-three he was not old enough to be a bishop at all. Not satisfied, when the see of Mainz fell vacant in the next year, Albert gained election to that too, even though he knew full well that the costs of becoming archbishop of Mainz meant still larger payments to Rome. Obtaining the necessary funds by loans from the German banking firm of the Fuggers, he then struck a bargain with Pope Leo X (1513–1521). According to this, Leo proclaimed an indulgence in Albert's ecclesiastical territories on the understanding that half of the income raised would go to Rome for the building of St. Peter's Basilica, with the other half going to Albert so that he could repay the Fuggers. Luther did not know the sordid details of Albert's bargain, but he did know that a Dominican friar named Tetzel soon was hawking indulgences throughout much of northern Germany with Fugger banking agents in his train, and that Tetzel was deliberately giving people the impression that the purchase of an indulgence regardless of contrition in penance was an immediate ticket to heaven for oneself and one's dear departed in purgatory. For Luther this was more than enough because Tetzel's advertising campaign flagrantly violated his own conviction that people are saved by faith, not works. So on October 31, 1517, the earnest theologian nailed a statement of ninety-five theses objecting to Catholic indulgence doctrine onto the door of the castle church of Wittenberg, an act by which the Protestant Reformation is conventionally thought to have begun.

Luther's theses and break
with Rome

It is seldom realized that in posting his theses Luther by no means intended to bring his criticism of Tetzel to the public. Quite to the contrary, he wrote his objections in Latin, not German, and meant them only for academic dispute within the confines of Wittenberg University—the castle church door serving as something like the university's bulletin board. But some unknown person translated and published Luther's theses, an event which immediately gained the hitherto obscure monk wide notoriety. Since Tetzel and his allies outside the university did not mean to let the matter rest, Luther was immediately called upon to withdraw his theses or defend himself. At that point, far from backing down, he became ever bolder in his attacks on the government of the Church. In 1519 in public disputation before throngs in Leipzig, Luther defiantly maintained that the pope and all clerics were merely fallible men and that the highest authority for an individual's conscience was the truth of Scripture. Thereupon Pope Leo X responded by charging the monk with heresy, and after that there was no alternative for Luther but to break with the Catholic faith entirely.

Theology of the new
Lutheran faith

Luther's year of greatest creative activity came in 1520 when, in the midst of the crisis caused by his defiance, he composed three seminal pamphlets formulating the outlines of what was soon to become the new Lutheran religion. In these writings he put forth his three theological premises: justification by faith, the primacy of Scripture, and "the priesthood of all believers." We have already examined the meaning of the first. By the second he simply meant that the literal meaning of Scripture was always to be preferred to the accretions of tradition, and that all beliefs (such as purgatory) or practices (such as prayers to saints) not explicitly grounded in Scripture were to be rejected. As for "the priesthood of all believers," that meant that the true spiritual estate was the congregation of all the faithful rather than a special club of ordained priests.

From these premises a host of practical consequences followed. Since works themselves had no intrinsic value for salvation, Luther discarded such formalized practices as fasts, pilgrimages, and the veneration of relics. Far more fundamentally, he recognized only baptism and the Eucharist as sacraments (in 1520 he also included penance, but he later changed his mind on this), denying that even these had any supernatural effect in bringing down grace from heaven. For Luther, Christ was really present in the consecrated elements of the Lord's Supper, but there was no grace in the sacrament as such; rather, faith was essential to render the Eucharist effective as a means for aiding the believer along the road to eternal life. To make the meaning of the ceremony clear to all, Luther proposed the substitution of German for Latin in church services, and, to emphasize that those who presided in churches had no supernatural authority, he insisted on calling them merely ministers or pastors rather than priests. On the same grounds there was to be no ecclesiastical hierarchy since neither the pope nor anyone else was a custodian of the keys to heaven, and monasticism was to be abolished since it served no purpose whatsoever. Finally, firm in the belief that no sacramental distinction existed between clergy and laity, Luther argued that ministers could marry, and in 1525 took a wife himself.

Practical implications

Luther and his Wife, Katherine von Bora. Portraits done by Cranach for the couple's wedding in 1525.

Widely disseminated by means of the printing press, Luther's pamphlets of 1520 electrified much of Germany, gaining him broad and enthusiastic popular support. Because this response played a crucial role in determining the future success of the Lutheran movement—emboldening Luther to persevere in his defiance of Rome and soon encouraging some ruling princes to convert to Lutheranism themselves—it is appropriate before continuing to inquire into its causes. Of course, different combinations of motives influenced different people to rally behind Luther, but the uproar in Germany on Luther's behalf was above all a national religious revolt against Rome.

Ever since the high Middle Ages many people throughout Europe had resented the centralization of Church government because it meant the interference of a foreign papacy in local ecclesiastical affairs and the siphoning off of large amounts of ecclesiastical fees and commissions to the papal court. But certain concrete circumstances made Germany in the early sixteenth century particularly ripe for religious revolt. Perhaps greatest among these was the fact that the papacy of that time had clearly lost the slightest hint of apostolic calling but was demanding as much, if not more money from German coffers as before.

Susceptibility of Germany to religious rebellion

Left: *Luther with Dove and Halo*. Right: *Luther as German Hercules*. These two engravings, both executed before the end of 1522 while Luther was still garbed as a monk, exemplify the style of artistic propaganda that helped fuel the Lutheran movement in its earliest years. At the left, the artist Hans Baldung Grien has conceived Luther as a saint inspired by the Holy Spirit in the form of a dove. At the right, an engraving by Hans Holbein the Younger depicts Luther as the "German Hercules," smiting a Catholic theologian. Scholastic authorities such as Aristotle, St. Thomas (Aquinas), and Ockham already lie overwhelmed at Luther's feet.

Although great patrons of the arts, successive popes of Luther's day were worldly scoundrels or sybarites. As Luther was growing up, the Borgia pope, Alexander VI (1492–1503), bribed the cardinals to gain the papacy, used the money raised from the jubilee of 1500 to support the military campaigns of his son Cesare, and was so lascivious in office that he was suspected of seeking the sexual favors of his own daughter Lucrezia. Alexander's scandals could hardly have been outdone, but his successor, Julius II (1503–1515), was interested only in enlarging the papal states by military means (a contemporary remarked that he would have gained the greatest glory had he been a secular prince), and Leo X, the pope obliged to deal with Luther's defiance, was a self-indulgent esthete who, in the words of a modern Catholic historian, "would not have been deemed fit to be a doorkeeper in the house of the Lord had he lived in the days of the apostles." Under such circumstances it was bad enough for Germans to know that fees sent to Rome were being used to finance papal politics and the upkeep of luxurious courts, but worse still to pay money in the realization that Germany had no influence in Italian papal affairs, for Germans, unlike French or Spaniards, were seldom represented in the College of Cardinals and practically never gained employment in the papal bureaucracy.

In this overheated atmosphere, reformist criticisms voiced by both traditional clerical moralists and the new breed of Christian humanists exacerbated resentments. Ever since about 1400 prominent German critics of the papacy had been saying that the entire Church needed to be reformed "in head and members," and as the fifteenth century progressed, anonymous prophecies mounted to the effect, for example, that a future heroic emperor would reform the Church by removing the papacy from Rome to the Rhineland. Then in the early years of the sixteenth century, Christian humanists began to chime in with their own brand of satirical propaganda. Most eloquent of these humanists, of course, was Erasmus, who lampooned the religious abuses of his day with no mercy for Rome. Thus in the *Praise of Folly*, first published in 1511 and frequently reprinted, Erasmus stated that if popes were ever forced to lead Christlike lives, no one would be more disconsolate than themselves, and in his more daring pamphlet called *Julius Excluded*, published anonymously in Basel in 1517, the clever satirist imagined a dialogue held before the pearly gates in which Pope Julius II was locked out of heaven by Saint Peter because of his transgressions.

Pope Leo X. A portrait by the Italian Renaissance master, Raphael.

In addition to the objective reality of a corrupt Rome and the circulation of anti-Roman propaganda, a final factor that made Germany

Pope Alexander VI: "Appearance and Reality." Even before Luther initiated the German Reformation, anonymous critics of the dissolute Alexander VI surreptitiously spread propaganda showing him to be a devil. By lifting a flap Alexander is transformed into a monster who proclaims "I am the pope."

ready for revolt in Luther's time was the belated growth of universities. All revolts need to have some general headquarters; universities were the most natural centers for late-medieval religious revolts because groups of enthusiastic, educated young people assembled in universities who were accustomed to working together, who could formulate doctrinal positions with assurance, and who could turn out militant manifestoes at a moment's notice. There had hardly been any universities on German soil until a spate of new foundations between 1450 and 1517 provided many spawning grounds for cultural nationalism and religious resistance to Rome. Luther's own University of Wittenberg was founded as late as 1502, but soon enough it had become the cradle of the Lutheran Reformation, offering immediate support to its embattled hero.

Still, of course, there would have been no Lutheran Reformation without Luther himself, and the daring monk did the most to enflame Germany's dry kindling of resentment in his pamphlets of 1520, above all in one entitled *To the Christian Nobility of the German Nation*. Here, in highly intemperate colloquial German, Luther stated that "if the pope's court were reduced ninety-nine percent it would still be large enough to give decisions on matters of faith"; that "the cardinals have

Left: *The Seven-Headed Papal Beast*. Right: *The Seven-headed Martin Luther*. Around 1530 a Lutheran cartoon was circulated in Germany which turned the papacy into the "seven-headed beast" of the Book of Revelation. The papacy's "seven heads" consist of pope, cardinals, bishops, and priests; the sign on the cross reads "for money, a sack full of indulgences"; and a devil is seen emerging from an indulgence treasure chest below. In response, a German Catholic propagandist showed Luther as Revelation's "beast." In the Catholic conception Luther's seven heads show him by turn to be a hypocrite, a fanatic, and "Barabbas"—the thief who should have been crucified instead of Jesus.

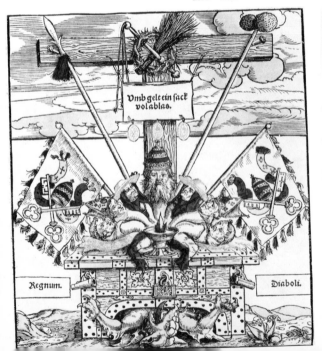

sucked Italy dry and now turn to Germany"; and that, given Rome's corruption, "the reign of Antichrist could not be worse." Needless to say, once this savage indictment was lodged, everyone wanted to read it. Whereas the average press run of a printed book before 1520 had been one thousand copies, the first run of *To the Christian Nobility* was four thousand, and these copies were sold out in a few days with many more thousands following.

Meanwhile, even as Luther's pamphlets were selling so rapidly, his personal drama riveted all onlookers. Late in 1520 the German rebel responded to Pope Leo X's bull ordering his recantation by casting not only the bull but all of Church law as well onto a roaring bonfire in front of a huge crowd. With the lines so drawn, events moved with great swiftness. Since Luther in the eyes of the Church was now a stubborn heretic, he was formally "released" to his lay overlord, the Elector Frederick the Wise, for proper punishment. Normally this would have meant certain death at the stake, but in this case Frederick was loath to silence the pope's antagonist. Instead, claiming that Luther had not yet received a fair hearing, he brought him early in 1521 to be examined by a "diet" (that is, a formal assembly) of the princes of the Holy Roman Empire convening in the city of Worms.

His appearance at the Diet of Worms

At Worms the initiative lay with the presiding officer, the newly elected Holy Roman Emperor, Charles V. Charles was not a German; rather, as a member of the Habsburg family by his paternal descent, he had been born and bred in his ancestral holding of the Netherlands. Since he additionally held Austria, and as grandson of Ferdinand and Isabella by his maternal descent, all of Spain, including extensive Spanish possessions in Italy and America, the emperor had primarily international rather than national interests and surely thought of Catholicism as a sort of glue necessary to hold together all his far-flung territories. Thus from the start Charles had no sympathy for Luther, and since Luther fearlessly refused to back down before the emperor, declaring instead "here I stand," it soon became clear that Luther would be condemned by the power of state as well as by Church. But just then Frederick the Wise once more intervened, this time by arranging a "kidnapping" whereby Luther was spirited off to the elector's castle of the Wartburg and kept out of harm's way for a year.

Luther vs. the Emperor Charles V

Thereafter Luther was never again to be in danger of his life. Although the Diet of Worms did issue an edict shortly after his disappearance proclaiming him an outlaw, the Edict of Worms was never properly enforced because, with Luther in hiding, Charles V soon left Germany to conduct a war with France. In 1522 Luther returned in triumph from the Wartburg to Wittenberg to find that all the changes in ecclesiastical government and ceremonial he had called for had spontaneously been put into practice by his university cohorts. Then, in rapid succession, several German princes formally converted to Lutheranism, bringing their territories with them. Thus by around

Lutheranism triumphant

The Wartburg. The castle in central Germany where Luther was hidden after the Diet of Worms.

1530 a considerable part of Germany had been brought over to the new faith.

At this point, then, the last of the three major questions regarding the early history of Lutheranism arises: Why did German princes, secure in their own powers, heed Luther's call by establishing Lutheran religious practices within their territories? The importance of this question should by no means be underestimated, because no matter how much intense admiration Luther may have gained from the German populace, his cause surely would have failed had it not been for the decisive intervention and support of constituted political authorities. There had been heretics aplenty in Europe before, but most of them had died at the stake, as Luther would have without the intervention of Frederick the Wise. And even had Luther lived, spontaneous popular expressions of support alone would not have succeeded in instituting Lutheranism because such could easily have been put down by the power of the state. In fact, although in the early years of Luther's revolt he was more or less equally popular throughout Germany, only in those territories where rulers formally established Lutheranism (mostly in the German north) did the new religion prevail, whereas in the others Luther's sympathizers were forced to flee, face death, or conform to Catholicism. In short, the word of the prince in religious matters was simply law.

This distinction between populace and princes, however, should not obscure the fact that the motivations of both for turning to Lutheranism were similar, with the emphasis on the princely side being the search for sovereignty. As little as common people liked the idea

Importance of German princely support

of money being pumped off to Rome, princes liked it less: German princes assembled at the Diet of Augsburg in 1500, for example, went so far as to demand the refund of some of the ecclesiastical dues sent to Rome on the grounds that Germany was being drained of its coin. Since such demands fell on deaf ears, many princes were quick to perceive that if Lutheranism were adopted, ecclesiastical dues would not be sent to support ill-loved foreigners and much of the savings would directly or indirectly wind up in their own treasuries.

Yet the matter of taxation was only part of the larger issue of the search for absolute governmental sovereignty. Throughout Europe the major political trend in the years around 1500 was toward making the state omnicompetent in all walks of life, religious as well as secular. Hence rulers sought to control the appointments of Church officials in their own realms and to limit or curtail the independent jurisdictions of Church courts. Because the papacy in this period had to fight off the attacks of internal clerical critics who wanted recognition of the "conciliarist" principle that general councils of prelates rather than popes should rule the Church (see Chapter 13), many popes found it advantageous to sign concordats with the most powerful rulers in the West—primarily the kings of France and Spain—whereby they granted the rulers much of the sovereignty they wanted in return for support against conciliarism. Thus in 1482 Sixtus IV conceded to the Spanish monarchs Ferdinand and Isabella the right to name candidates for all major Church offices; in 1487 Innocent VIII consented to the establishment of a Spanish Inquisition controlled by the crown which gave the rulers extraordinary powers in dictating religious policies; and in 1516, by the Concordat of Bologna, Leo X granted the choice of bishops and abbots in France to the French king, Francis I. In Germany, however, primarily because there was no political unity, princes were not strong enough to gain such concessions. Hence what they could not achieve by concordats some decided to wrest by force.

In this determination they were fully abetted by Luther. Certainly as early as 1520 the fiery reformer recognized that he could never hope to institute new religious practices without the strong arm of the princes behind him, so he implicitly encouraged them to disappropriate the wealth of the Catholic church as an incentive for creating a new order. At first the princes bided their time, but when they realized that Luther had enormous public support and that Charles V would not act swiftly to defend the Catholic faith, several moved to introduce Lutheranism into their territories. Motives of personal piety cannot be discounted from case to case, but the common aim of gaining sovereignty by naming pastors, cutting off fees to Rome, and curtailing the jurisdiction of Catholic church courts ultimately must have been the most decisive consideration. Given the added fact that under Lutheranism monasteries could be shut down and their wealth simply pocketed by the princes, the temptation to ordain the new faith regardless of any deeply felt religious convictions must have been simply overwhelming.

Once safely ensconced in Wittenberg as the protégé of princes, Luther began to express ever more vehemently his own profound conservatism in political and social matters. In a treatise of 1523, *On Temporal Authority,* he insisted that "godly" rulers must always be obeyed in all things and that even ungodly ones should never be actively resisted since tyranny "is not to be resisted but endured." Then, in 1525, when peasants throughout Germany rose up in economic revolt against their landlords—in some places encouraged by the religious radical Thomas Münzer (c. 1490–1525), who urged the use of fire and sword against "ungodly" powers—Luther responded with intense hostility. In his vituperative pamphlet of 1525, *Against the Thievish, Murderous Hordes of Peasants,* he went so far as to urge all who could to hunt the rebels down like mad dogs, to "strike, strangle, stab secretly or in public, and remember that nothing can be more poisonous than a man in rebellion." Once the princes had ruthlessly put down the Peasants' Revolt of 1525, the firm alliance of Lutheranism with the powers of the state helped ensure social peace. In fact, after the bloody punishment of the peasant rebels there was never again to be a mass lower-class uprising in Germany.

As for Luther himself, he concentrated in his last years on debating with younger, more radical, religious reformers, and on offering spiritual counsel to all who sought it. Never tiring in his amazingly prolific literary activity, he wrote an average of one treatise every two weeks for twenty-five years. To the end Luther was unswerving in his faith: on his deathbed in 1546 he responded to the question "Will you stand firm in Christ and the doctrine which you have preached?" with a resolute "Yes."

3. THE SPREAD OF PROTESTANTISM

Originating as a term applied to Lutherans who "protested" an action of a German Imperial Diet of 1529, the word "Protestant" has come to mean any non-Catholic, non–Eastern Orthodox Christian. In fact it was soon applied to non-Lutherans after 1529 because the particular form of Protestantism developed by Luther did not prove to be popular much beyond its native environment of Germany. To be sure, Lutheranism was instituted as the state religion of Denmark, Norway, and Sweden by official decrees of rulers made during the 1520s, and remains the religion of most Scandinavians today. But elsewhere early Protestantism spread in different forms. In England a break with Rome was introduced from above, just as in Germany and Scandinavia, but since Lutheranism appeared too radical for the reigning English monarch, a compromise variety of religious belief and practice, subsequently known as Anglicanism (in America, Episcopalianism), was worked out. On the other extreme, Protestantism spread more spontaneously in several cities of Switzerland and there soon took on forms that were more radical than Lutheranism.

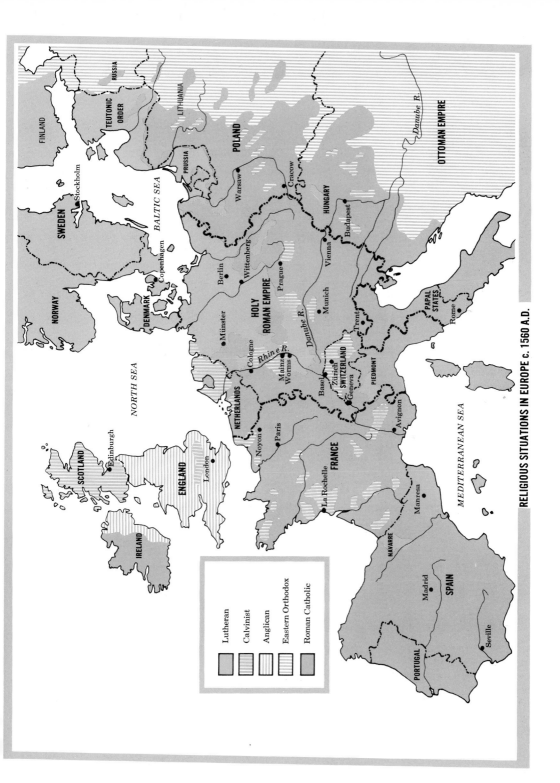

RELIGIOUS SITUATIONS IN EUROPE c. 1560 A.D.

Lutheran

Calvinist

Anglican

Eastern Orthodox

Roman Catholic

RUSSIA

FINLAND

TEUTONIC ORDER

LITHUANIA

POLAND

Danube R.

OTTOMAN EMPIRE

PRUSSIA

SWEDEN

Stockholm

BALTIC SEA

Warsaw

Cracow

HUNGARY

Budapest

NORWAY

DENMARK

Copenhagen

Berlin

Wittenberg

Prague

Vienna

Danube R.

Munich

Trent

PAPAL STATES

Rome

HOLY ROMAN EMPIRE

Münster

Cologne

Rhine R.

Mainz

Worms

Basel

Zürich

SWITZERLAND

Geneva

PIEDMONT

NORTH SEA

NETHERLANDS

Noyon

Paris

Avignon

FRANCE

SCOTLAND

Edinburgh

ENGLAND

London

IRELAND

La Rochelle

Manresa

MEDITERRANEAN SEA

NAVARRE

Madrid

SPAIN

Seville

PORTUGAL

*Henry VIII. Portrait by Hans
Holbein.*

Although the original blow against the Roman Church in England
was struck by the head of the government, King Henry VIII (1509–
1547), in breaking with Rome the English monarch had the support
of most of his subjects. For this there were at least three reasons. First,
in England, as in Germany, many people in the early sixteenth century
had come to resent Rome's corruption and the siphoning off of the
country's wealth to pay for the worldly pursuits of foreign popes.
Second, England had already been the scene for some time of protests
against religious abuses voiced by John Wyclif's heretical followers
known as Lollards. The Lollards had indeed been driven underground
in the course of the fifteenth century, but numbers of them survived
in pockets throughout England, where they promulgated their anticlerical ideas whenever they could and enthusiastically welcomed
Henry VIII's revolt from Rome when it occurred. Finally, soon after
the outbreak of the Reformation in Germany, Lutheran ideas were
brought into England by travelers and by the circulation of printed
tracts. As early as 1520 a Lutheran group was meeting at the University of Cambridge, and Lutheranism began to gain more and more
clandestine strength as the decade progressed.

*King Henry VIII's
divorce suit*

Despite all this, England would never have broken with Rome had
Henry VIII not issued the command because of his marital difficulties.
In 1527 the imperious Henry had been married for eighteen years to
Ferdinand and Isabella's daughter, Catherine of Aragon, yet all the
offspring of this union had died in infancy, save only the Princess
Mary. Since Henry needed a male heir to preserve the succession of
his Tudor dynasty, and since Catherine was now past childbearing
age, Henry had good reasons of state to rid himself of her, and in 1527
an immediate incentive arose when he became infatuated with the dark-
eyed lady-in-waiting, Anne Boleyn, who would not give in to his
advances out of wedlock. The king hence appealed to Rome to allow
the severance of his marriage to Catherine so that he could make Anne
his queen. Although the law of the Church did not sanction divorce,
it did provide that a marriage might be annulled if proof could be
given that conditions existing at the time of the wedding had made it
unlawful. Accordingly, the king's representatives, recalling that Queen
Catherine had previously been married to Henry's older brother, who
had died shortly after the ceremony was performed, rested their case
on a passage from the Bible which pronounced it "an unclean thing"
for a man to take his brother's wife and cursed such a marriage with
childlessness (Leviticus 20:31).

Henry's break with Rome

Henry's suit put the reigning pope, Clement VII (1523–1534), in a
quandary. If he rejected the king's appeal, England would probably
be lost to Catholicism, for Henry was indeed firmly convinced that
the Scriptural curse had blighted his chances of perpetuating his
dynasty. On the other hand, if the pope granted the annulment he
would provoke the wrath of the Emperor Charles V, Catherine of
Aragon's nephew, for Charles was then on a military campaign in

Italy and threatening the pope with a loss of his temporal power. There seemed nothing for Clement to do but to procrastinate. At first he made a pretense of having the question settled in England, empowering his officials to hold a court of inquiry to determine whether the marriage to Catherine had been legal. Then, after a long delay, he suddenly transferred the case to Rome. But meanwhile Henry had lost patience and resolved to take matters into his own hands. In 1531 the king obliged an assembly of English clergy to recognize him as "the supreme head" of the English Church. Next he induced Parliament to enact a series of laws abolishing all payments to Rome and proclaiming the English Church an independent, national unit, subject alone to royal authority. With the passage of the parliamentary Act of Supremacy (1534), declaring "the King's highness to be supreme head of the Church of England [having] the authority to redress all errors, heresies, and abuses," the last bonds uniting the English Church to Rome had been cut.

Yet these enactments did not yet make England a Protestant country. Quite to the contrary, although the break with Rome was followed by the dissolution of all England's monasteries, with their lands and wealth being sold to many of the king's loyal supporters, the system of Church government by bishops (episcopalianism) was retained, and the English Church remained Catholic in doctrine. The Six Articles, promulgated by Parliament in 1539 at Henry VIII's behest, left no room for doubt as to official orthodoxy: oral confession to priests, masses for the dead, and clerical celibacy were all confirmed; moreover, the Catholic doctrine of the Eucharist was not only confirmed but its denial made punishable by death.

The conservative nature of the Henrician Reformation

Nonetheless, the influence of Protestantism in the country at large at this time was growing, and during the reign of Henry's son, Edward VI (1547–1553), Protestantism gained the ascendancy. Since the new king (born from Henry's union with his third wife, Jane Seymour) was only nine years old when he inherited the crown, it was inevitable that the policies of the government should be dictated by powers behind the throne. The men most active in this regard were Thomas Cranmer, archbishop of Canterbury, and the dukes of Somerset and Northumberland, who successfully dominated the regency. Inasmuch as all three had strong Protestant leanings, the creeds and ceremonies of the Church of England were soon drastically altered. Priests were permitted to marry; English was substituted for Latin in the services; the veneration of images was abolished; and new articles of belief were drawn up repudiating all sacraments except baptism and communion and affirming the Lutheran doctrine of justification by faith alone. Thus when the youthful Edward died in 1553 it seemed as if England had definitely entered the Protestant camp.

The consolidation of English Protestantism

But Edward's pious Catholic successor, Mary (1553–1558), Henry VIII's daughter by Catherine of Aragon, thought otherwise. Because Mary associated the revolt against Rome with her mother's humilia-

The Burning of Archbishop Cranmer. In this Protestant conception an ugly Catholic, "Friar John," directs the proceedings, while the martyred Cranmer repeats Christ's words, "Lord, receive my spirit." John Foxe's *Book of Martyrs* (1563), in which this engraving first appeared, was an extraordinarily successful piece of English Protestant propaganda.

Popular resistance to Queen Mary's Catholicism

tions and her own removal from direct succession, upon coming to the throne she attempted to turn the clock back. Not only did she restore the celebration of the Mass and the rule of clerical celibacy, but she prevailed upon Parliament to vote the unconditional return of England to papal allegiance. Yet her policies ended in failure for several reasons. First of all, not only had Protestantism by then already sunk in deeply among the English masses, but many of the leading families which had profited from Henry VIII's dissolution of the monasteries had become particularly committed to Protestantism because a restoration of Catholic monasticism would have meant the loss of their newly acquired wealth. Then too, although Mary ordered the burning of Cranmer and a few hundred Protestant extremists, these executions were insufficient to wipe out religious resistance—indeed, Protestant propaganda about "Bloody Mary" and the "fires of Smithfield" soon actually hardened resistance to Mary's rule, making her seem like a vengeful persecutor. But perhaps the most serious cause of Mary's failure was her marriage to Philip, Charles V's son and heir to the Spanish throne. Although the marriage treaty stipulated that in the event of Mary's death Philip could not succeed her, patriotic Englishmen never trusted him. Hence when the queen allowed herself to be drawn by Philip into a war with France on Spain's behalf, in which England lost Calais, its last foothold on the European continent, the nation became highly disaffected. No one knows what might have happened next because death soon after ended Mary's troubled reign.

The question of whether England was to be Catholic or Protestant was thereupon settled definitively in favor of Protestantism by Elizabeth I (1558–1603). Daughter of Anne Boleyn and one of the most capable and popular monarchs ever to sit on the English throne, Elizabeth was predisposed in favor of Protestantism by the circumstances of her father's marriage as well as by her upbringing. But Elizabeth was no zealot, and wisely recognized that ordaining radical Protestantism in England posed the danger of provoking bitter sectarian strife because some English people were still Catholic and others resisted extremism. Accordingly, she presided over what is customarily known as "the Elizabethan compromise." By a new Act of Supremacy (1559), Elizabeth repealed all of Mary's Catholic legislation, prohibited the exercise of any authority by foreign religious powers, and made herself "supreme governor" of the English Church—a more Protestant title than Henry VIII's "supreme headship" insofar as most Protestants believed that Christ alone was the head of the Church. At the same time she accepted most of the Protestant ceremonial reforms instituted in the reign of her brother Edward. On the other hand, she retained Church government by bishops and left the definitions of some controversial articles of the faith, especially the meaning of the Eucharist, vague enough so that all but the most extreme Catholics and Protestants could accept them. Long after Elizabeth's death this settlement remained in effect. Indeed, as a result of the Elizabethan compromise, the Church of England today is broad enough to include such diverse elements as the "Anglo-Catholics," who differ from Roman Catholics only in rejecting papal supremacy, and the "low-church" Anglicans, who are as thoroughgoing in their Protestant practices as members of most other modern Protestant denominations.

The Elizabethan religious settlement

Philip of Spain and Mary Tudor. This double portrait was done on the occasion of the royal marriage.

Protestantism in
Switzerland

Zwinglianism

Anabaptism

If the English compromise came about through royal decision-making, in Switzerland more spontaneous movements to establish Protestantism resulted in the victory of greater radicalism. In the early sixteenth century Switzerland was neither ruled by kings nor dominated by all-powerful territorial princes; instead, prosperous cities there were either independent or on the verge of becoming so. Hence when the leading citizens of a Swiss municipality decided to adopt Protestant reforms no one could stop them, and Protestantism in Switzerland could usually take its own course. Although religious arrangements tended at first to vary in detail from city to city, the three main forms of Protestantism that emerged in Switzerland from about 1520 to 1550 were Zwinglianism, Anabaptism, and, most fateful for Europe's future, Calvinism.

Zwinglianism, founded by Ulrich Zwingli (1484–1531) in Zürich, was the most moderate form of the three. At first a somewhat indifferent Catholic priest, around 1516 Zwingli was led by close study of the Bible, as Luther was, to conclude that contemporary Catholic theology and religious observances conflicted with the Gospel. But he did not speak out until Luther set the precedent. Then, in 1522, Zwingli started attacking the authority of the Catholic church in Zürich, and soon all Zürich and much of northern Switzerland had accepted his leadership in instituting reforms that closely resembled those of the Lutherans in Germany. Yet Zwingli did differ from Luther concerning the theology of the Eucharist: whereas Luther believed in the real presence of Christ's body, for Zwingli Christ was present merely in spirit. Thus for him the sacrament conferred no grace at all and was to be retained merely as a memorial service. This disagreement may seem trifling to many of us today, but then it sufficed to prevent Lutherans and Zwinglians from uniting in a common Protestant front. Going his way, Zwingli fell in battle against Catholic forces in 1531, whereupon his successors in Zürich lost their leadership over Swiss Protestantism, and the Zwinglian movement was soon after absorbed by the far more radical Protestantism of John Calvin.

Before that happened, however, the phenomenon of Anabaptism briefly flared up in Switzerland and also Germany. The first Anabaptists were members of Zwingli's circle in Zürich, but they quickly broke with him around 1525 on the issues of infant baptism and their conception of an exclusive church of true believers. The name Anabaptism means "rebaptism," and stemmed from the Anabaptists' conviction that baptism should only be administered to adults because infants had no understanding of the meaning of the service. Yet this was only one manifestation of the Anabaptists' main belief that men and women were not born into any church. Although Luther and Zwingli alike taught the "priesthood of all believers," they still insisted that everyone, believer or not, should attend services and be part of one and the same officially instituted religious community. But the Anabaptists were sectarians or separatists, firm in the conviction that joining the true Church should be the product of an individual's inspired decision. For them, one had to follow the guidance of one's own "inner light" in opting for Church membership, and the rest of the world could go its own way. Since this was a hopelessly apolitical doctrine in an age when almost everyone assumed that Church and state were inextricably connected, Anabaptism was bound to be anathema to the established powers, both Protestant and Catholic. Yet in its first few years the movement did gain numerous adherents in Switzerland and Germany, above all because it appealed to sincere religious piety in calling for extreme simplicity of worship, pacifism, and strict biblical morality.

Unhappily for the fortunes of Anabaptism, a highly unrepresentative group of Anabaptist extremists managed to gain control of the city of Münster in northwestern Germany in 1534. When fellow extremists from surrounding areas came pouring in, Münster became a new Jerusalem where all the vagaries of the lunatic fringe of the movement were put into practice. The property of unbelievers was confiscated and polygamy was introduced. A former tailor named John of Leyden assumed the title of king, proclaiming himself the successor of David, with a mission to conquer the world and destroy the heathen. But after a little more than a year Münster was recaptured by Catholic forces and the leaders of Zion were put to death by excruciating tortures. Given that Anabaptism was already proscribed by many govern-

The turning point at Münster

The Anabaptists' Cages, Then and Now. After the three Anabaptist leaders who had reigned in Münster for a year were executed in 1535, their corpses were prominently displayed in cages hung from a tower of the marketplace church. As can be seen from the photo on the right, the bones are now gone but the iron cages remain to this very day as a grisly reminder of the horrors of sixteenth-century religious strife.

The Siege of Münster in 1534

ments, this episode thoroughly discredited the movement and all of its adherents were subjected to ruthless persecution throughout Germany, Switzerland, and wherever else they could be found. Among the few who survived were some who banded together in the Mennonite sect, named for its founder, the Dutchman Menno Simons (1492–1559). This sect, dedicated to the pacifism and simple "religion of the heart" of original Anabaptism, has continued to exist until the present. Various Anabaptist tenets were also revived later by religious groups such as the Quakers and different Baptist and Pentecostal sects.

A year after events in Münster sealed the fate of Anabaptism, a twenty-six-year-old French Protestant named John Calvin (1509–1564), who had fled to the Swiss city of Basel to escape religious persecution, published the first version of his *Institutes of the Christian Religion,* a work which was soon to prove the single most influential systematic formulation of Protestant theology ever written. Born in Noyon in northern France, Calvin originally had been trained for the law and around 1533 was studying the Greek and Latin classics while living off the income from a Church benefice. But then, as he later wrote, while he was "obstinately devoted to the superstitions of Popery," a stroke of light made him feel that God was extricating him from "an abyss of filth," and he thereupon opted for becoming a Protestant propagandist. Though some of these details resemble the early career of Luther, there was one essential difference: namely, whereas Luther was always a highly volatile personality, Calvin remained a cool French legalist through and through. Thus, whereas Luther never wrote systematic theology but only responded to given problems as they arose or as the mood struck him, Calvin resolved in his *Institutes* to set forth all the principles of Protestantism comprehensively, logically, and consistently. Accordingly, after several revisions and enlargements (the

John Calvin

John Calvin. A recently discovered anonymous portrait.

definitive edition appeared in 1559), Calvin's *Institutes of the Christian Religion* became the most theologically authoritative statement of basic Protestant beliefs and the nearest Protestant equivalent of St. Thomas Aquinas's *Summa Theologica*.

The hallmark of Calvin's rigorous theology in the *Institutes* is that he started with the omnipotence of God and worked downward. For Calvin the entire universe is utterly dependent on the will of the Almighty, who created all things for his greater glory. Because of the original fall from grace, all human beings are sinners by nature, bound hand and foot to an evil inheritance they cannot escape. Nevertheless, the Lord for reasons of His own has predestined some for eternal salvation and damned all the rest to the torments of hell. Nothing that human beings may do can alter their fate; their souls are stamped with God's blessing or curse before they are born. But this does not mean, in Calvin's opinion, that Christians should be indifferent to their conduct on earth. If they are among the elect, God will implant in them the desire to live right. Upright conduct is a sign, though not an infallible one, that whoever practices it has been chosen to sit at the throne of glory. Public profession of faith and participation in the sacrament of the Lord's Supper are also presumptive signs of election to be saved. But most of all, Calvin required an active life of piety and morality as a solemn obligation resting upon members of the Christian commonwealth. For him, good Christians should conceive of themselves as chosen instruments of God with a mission to help in the fulfillment of His purposes on earth, not striving for their souls' salvation but for the glory of God. In other words, Calvin clearly did not encourage his readers to sit with folded hands, serene in the knowledge that their fate was sealed.

Calvin's theology

Although Calvin always acknowledged a great theological debt to Luther, his religious teachings differed from those of the Wittenberg reformer in several essentials. First of all, Luther's attitude toward proper Christian conduct in the world was much more passive than Calvin's: for the former, the good Christian should merely endure the trials of this life in suffering, whereas for the latter the world was to be mastered in unceasing labor for God's sake. Second, Calvin's religion was more legalistic and more nearly an Old Testament faith than Luther's. This can be illustrated in the attitude of the two men toward Sabbath observance. Luther's conception of Sunday was similar to that which prevails among most Christians today. He insisted, of course, that his followers attend church, but he did not demand that during the remainder of the day they refrain from all pleasure or work. Calvin, on the other hand, revived the Jewish Sabbath with its strict taboos against anything faintly resembling worldliness. Finally, the two men differed explicitly on basic matters of Church government and ritual. Although Luther broke with the Catholic system of a gradated ecclesiastical hierarchy, Lutheran district superintendents were not unlike bishops, and Luther also retained a good many features of Roman worship such as altars and vestments (special clothing for the

Calvinism and Lutheranism compared

Services in a Calvinist Church. "Four bare walls and a sermon."

clergy). On the other hand, Calvin utterly rejected everything that smacked to him of "popery." Thus he argued for the elimination of all traces of the hierarchical system, instead having congregational election of ministers and assemblies of ministers and "elders" (laymen responsible for maintaining proper religious conduct among the faithful) governing the entire Church. Further, he insisted on the barest simplicity in church services, prohibiting all ritual, vestments, instrumental music, images, and stained-glass windows. When these teachings were put into practice, Calvinist services became little more than "four bare walls and a sermon."

Calvinist theocracy in Geneva

Not content with mere theory, Calvin was intent upon putting his teachings into practice. Sensing an opportunity to influence the course of events in the French-speaking Swiss city of Geneva, then in the throes of combined political and religious upheaval, he moved there late in 1536 and began preaching and organizing immediately. In 1538 his activities caused him to be expelled, but in 1541 he returned to Geneva, and this time soon had both the government and the religion of the city completely under his sway. Under Calvin's guidance Geneva's government became theocratic. Supreme authority in the city was vested in a "Consistory," made up of twelve lay elders and five ministers. (Although Calvin himself was seldom the presiding officer, he usually dominated the Consistory's decisions until his death in 1564.) In addition to passing on legislation submitted to it by a congregation of ministers, the Consistory had as its main function the supervision of morals. This activity was carried out not merely by the punishment of antisocial conduct but by a persistent snooping into the private life of every individual. Geneva was divided into districts, and a committee of the Consistory visited every household without warning to check on the habits of its members. Even the mildest forms of self-indulgence were strictly prohibited. Dancing, card-playing, attending the theater, working or playing on the Sabbath—all were outlawed as works of the devil. Innkeepers were forbidden to allow anyone to consume food or drink without first saying grace, or to permit any patron to stay up after nine o'clock. Needless to say, penalties were severe. Not only were murder and treason classified as capital crimes, but also adultery, "witchcraft," blasphemy, and heresy. During the first four years after Calvin gained control in Geneva, there were no fewer than 58 executions out of a total population of only 16,000.

As reprehensible as such interference in the private sphere may seem today, in the middle of the sixteenth century Calvin's Geneva appeared as a beacon-light of thoroughgoing Protestantism to thousands throughout Europe. Calvin's disciple John Knox, for example, who brought Calvinism to Scotland, declared that Geneva under Calvin was "the most perfect school of Christ that ever was on earth since the days of the Apostles." Accordingly, many foreigners flocked to the "perfect school" for refuge or instruction, and usually returned home to become ardent proselytizers of Calvinism. Moreover, since Calvin himself thought of Geneva as merely a way station for bringing Calvinism to France and the rest of the world, he encouraged the dispatching of missionaries and propaganda into hostile territories, with the result that from about the middle of the sixteenth century Geneva became the center of a concerted and militant attempt to spread the new faith far and wide. Soon Calvinists became a majority in Scotland, where they were known as Presbyterians; a majority in Holland, where they founded the Dutch Reformed Church; a substantial minority in France, where they were called Huguenots; and a substantial minority in England, where they were called Puritans. In addition, Calvinist preachers zealously tried to make converts in most other parts of Europe. But just as the Calvinists were fanning out through Europe, the forces of Catholicism were hardening in their determination to head off any further Protestant advances. The result, as we will see in the next chapter, was that many parts of a hitherto united Christendom became mired in bloody religious wars for decades after.

4. THE PROTESTANT HERITAGE

Inasmuch as Luther's revolt from Rome and the spread of Protestantism occurred after the height of the civilization of the Renaissance and before some particularly fundamental advances in modern European political, economic, and social development, it is tempting to think of historical events unfolding in an inevitably cumulative way: Renaissance, Reformation, "Triumphs of the Modern World." But history

Calvin as Seen by His Friends and His Enemies. Above, an idealized contemporary portrait of Calvin as a pensive scholar. Below, a Catholic caricature in which Calvin's face is a composite made from fish, a toad, and a chicken drumstick.

The place of Protestantism in Europe's historical development

is seldom as neat as that. Although scholars will continue to disagree on points of detail, most agree that the Protestant Reformation inherited little from the civilization of the Renaissance, that indeed in certain basic respects Protestant principles were completely at odds with major assumptions of Renaissance humanists. As for the relationship between "Protestantism and Progress," the most apt formulation appears to be a statement from a book of that title by the great German religious historian Ernst Troeltsch, according to which "Protestantism has furthered the rise of the modern world . . . [but nowhere] does it appear as its actual creator."

*Renaissance and
Reformation*

In considering the relationship between the Renaissance and the origins of the Protestant Reformation, it would admittedly be false to say that the one had absolutely nothing to do with the other. Certainly, criticisms of religious abuses by Christian humanists helped prepare Germany for the Lutheran revolt. Furthermore, close humanistic textual study of the Bible led to the publication of new, reliable biblical editions used by the Protestant reformers. In this regard a direct line ran from the Italian humanist Lorenzo Valla to Erasmus to Luther insofar as Valla's *Notes on the New Testament* inspired Erasmus to produce his own Greek edition and accompanying Latin translation of the New Testament in 1516, and that in turn enabled Luther in 1518 to reach some crucial conclusions concerning the literal biblical meaning of penance. For these and related reasons, Luther addressed Erasmus in 1519 as "our ornament and our hope."

*The Christian humanists'
opposition to Protestantism*

But in fact Eramus quickly showed that he had no sympathy whatsoever with Luther's first principles, and most other Christian humanists shunned Protestantism as soon as it became clear to them what Luther and other Protestant reformers actually were teaching. The reasons for this were that most humanists believed in free will while Protestants believed in predestination, that humanists tended to think of human nature as basically good while Protestants found it unspeakably corrupt, and that most humanists favored urbanity and tolerance while the followers of Luther and Calvin emphasized faith and conformity. Thus when Erasmus, for example, defended *The Freedom of the Will* in a treatise of 1524, Luther attacked it vehemently in his *Bondage of the Will* of the following year, insisting that original sin makes all humans "bound, wretched, captive, sick, and dead." And when Henry VIII introduced the Reformation into England, England's foremost Christian humanist, Sir Thomas More, resisted the break with Rome even unto martyrdom, mounting the scaffold with some stirring words about the primacy of the individual conscience.

*Protestantism and the rise
of the modern state*

If the Protestant Reformation, then, was by no means the natural outgrowth of the civilization of the Renaissance, it very definitely contributed to certain traits most characteristic of modern European historical development. Foremost among these was the rise of the untrammeled powers of the sovereign state. As we have seen, those German princes who converted to Protestantism were moved to do so primarily by the search for sovereignty, and the kings of Denmark, Sweden, and England followed suit for the same reasons. Not at all accidentally, the earliest act of the English Parliament announcing Henry VIII's break with Rome, the Act in Restraint of Appeals of 1533, put forth the earliest official statement that England is a completely independent country, "governed by one supreme head and king," possessed of "plenary, whole, and entire power. . . . to render and yield justice and final determination to all manner of folk." Since Protestant leaders—Calvin as well as Luther—preached absolute obedience to "godly" rulers, and since the state in Protestant countries assumed direct control of the Church, the spread of Protestantism definitely resulted in the growth of state power. But, as we have also seen, the power of the state was growing anyway, and it continued to grow in Catholic countries like France and Spain where kings were granted most of the same rights over the Church that were forcibly seized by Lutheran German princes or Henry VIII.

Catholic and Protestant Views of a Cardinal. A genuine papal medal (shown above) depicted a cardinal (right-side up) merged with a bishop (upside down). In response, a Protestant replica (shown below), probably struck in the Netherlands, depicted a cardinal merged with a grinning fool.

As for the growth of nationalism, a sense of national pride was already present in sixteenth-century Germany that Luther played upon in his appeals of 1520. But Luther himself then did the most to foster German cultural nationalism by translating the entire Bible into a vigorous German idiom. Up until then Germans from some regions spoke a language so different from that of Germans from other areas that they could not understand each other, but the form of German given currency by Luther's Bible soon became the linguistic standard for the entire nation. Religion did not help to unite the German nation politically because the non-German Charles V opposed Lutheranism and as a result Germany soon became politically divided into Protestant and Catholic camps. But elsewhere, as in Scotland and Holland, where Protestants fought successfully against Catholic overlords, Protestantism enhanced a sense of national identity. And perhaps the most familiar case of all is that of England, where a sense of nationhood had existed before the advent of Protestantism even more markedly than it had in Germany, Scotland, or Holland, but where the new faith, as we shall see, helped underpin the greatest accomplishments of the Elizabethan age.

Protestantism and modern economic development

The problem of Protestantism's relationship to modern commercial and industrial economic development is more controversial. Around 1900 the great German sociologist Max Weber, noticing that the economically advanced territories of England, Holland, and North America had all been Protestant, argued that Protestantism, particularly in its Calvinist forms, was especially conducive to acquisitive economic enterprise. According to Weber, this was because Calvinistic theology, as opposed to Catholicism, sanctified the ventures of profit-oriented traders and moneylenders, and gave an exalted place in its ethical system to the business virtues of thrift and diligence. But historians have found shortcomings in Weber's thesis. Although Calvin did indeed praise diligence and acknowledge that merchants could be "sanctified in their calling," he no more approved of exorbitant interest rates than Catholics did. Moreover Calvin argued vehemently that people should put their excess wealth at the service of the poor rather than piling up capital for the sake of gain or subsequent investments. Thus it appears that the "work ethic" necessary for economic success in commercial ventures did have some Calvinistic roots, but that Calvin's ideal merchant would by no means have been a great speculator or maker of fortunes. Bearing in mind that the European economy had already made great strides forward in the High Middle Ages and was advancing again in the early-modern period, not least because of the overseas ventures initiated by the Catholic powers of Portugal and Spain, Calvinism thus was at most just one of many contributory factors to the triumph of modern capitalism and the Industrial Revolution.

Finally, there arises the subject of Protestantism's effects on social relationships, specifically those between the sexes. As opposed to the question of Protestantism and economic development, this topic is still relatively unstudied. What is certain is that Protestant men as individuals could be just as ambivalent about women as Catholics, heathens, or Turks. John Knox, for example, inveighed against the Catholic regent of Scotland, Mary Stuart, in a treatise called *The First Blast of the Trumpet Against the Monstrous Regiment of Women,* yet maintained deeply respectful relationships with women of his own faith. But if one asks how Protestantism as a belief system rising above individual vagaries affected women's lot, the answer appears to be that it enabled women to become just a shade more equal to men, albeit still clearly within a subject status. Above all, since Protestantism, with its stress on the primacy of Scripture and the priesthood of all believers, called on women as well as men to undertake serious Bible study, it sponsored primary schooling for both sexes and thus enhanced female as well as male literacy. But Protestant male leaders never hesitated to insist that women were naturally inferior to men and thus should always defer to men in case of arguments. As Calvin himself said, "let the woman be satisfied with her state of subjection and not take it ill that she is made inferior to the more distinguished sex." Both Luther and Calvin appear to have been happily married, but that clearly meant being happily married on their own terms.

Protestantism's effects on
relations between the sexes

5. CATHOLIC REFORM

The historical novelty of Protestantism in the sixteenth century inevitably tends to cast the spotlight on such religious reformers as Luther and Calvin, but it must be emphasized that a powerful internal reform movement within the Catholic church exercised just as profound an effect on the course of European history as Protestantism did. Historians differ about whether to call this movement the "Catholic Ref-

Catholic reform before and
after Luther

ormation" or the "Counter-Reformation." Some prefer the former term because they wish to show that significant efforts to reform the Catholic church from within antedated the posting of Luther's theses and that therefore Catholic reform in the sixteenth century was no mere counterattack to check the growth of Protestantism. Others, however, insist quite properly that for the main part sixteenth-century Catholic reformers were indeed inspired primarily by the urgency of resisting what they regarded as heresy and schism. Fortunately the two interpretations are by no means irreconcilable, for they allude to two complementary phases: a Catholic Reformation that came before Luther and a Counter-Reformation that followed.

The Catholic Reformation beginning around 1490 was primarily a movement for moral and institutional reform inspired by the principles of Christian humanism and carried on with practically no help from the dissolute Renaissance papacy. In Spain around the turn of the fifteenth century, reform activities directed by Cardinal Francisco Ximénes de Cisneros (1436–1517) with the cooperation of the monarchy led to the imposition of strict rules of behavior for Franciscan friars and the elimination of abuses prevalent among the diocesan clergy. Although Ximénes aimed primarily at strengthening the Church in its rivalry with Jews and Muslims, his work had considerable effect in regenerating the spiritual life of the nation. In Italy there was no similarly centralized reform movement, but a number of earnest clerics in the early sixteenth century labored on their own to make the Italian Church more worthy of its calling. The task was a difficult one on account of the entrenchment of abuses and the example of profligacy set by the papal court, but despite these obstacles, the Italian reformers did manage to establish some new religious orders dedicated to high ideals of piety and social service. Finally, it cannot be forgotten that such leading Christian humanists as Erasmus and Thomas More were in their own way Catholic reformers, for in criticizing abuses and editing sacred texts, men like these certainly helped to enhance spirituality.

The Catholic Reformation

Once Protestantism began threatening to sweep over Europe, however, Catholic reform of the earlier variety clearly became inadequate to defend the Church, let alone turn the tide of revolt. Thus a second, more aggressive, phase of reform under a new style of vigorous papal leadership gained momentum during the middle and latter half of the sixteenth century. The leading Counter-Reformation popes—Paul III (1534–1549), Paul IV (1555–1559), St. Pius V (1566–1572), and Sixtus V (1585–1590)—were collectively the most zealous crusaders for reform who had presided over the papacy since the High Middle Ages. All led upright personal lives. Indeed, some were so grimly ascetic that contemporaries were unsure whether they were not too holy: as a Spanish councillor wrote in 1567, "We should like it even better if the present Holy Father were no longer with us, however great, inexpressible, unparalleled, and extraordinary his holiness may be." But in

The Counter-Reformation popes

A Session of the Council of Trent. The pope is not present, but the cardinals who represent him are enthroned, facing the semicircle of bishops. The orator with a raised right hand is a theologian advancing an opinion.

The Council of Trent: doctrinal matters

the circumstances of the Protestant onslaught, a pope's reputation for excessive asceticism was vastly preferable to a reputation for profligacy. More than that, becoming fully dedicated to activist revitalization of the Church, the Counter-Reformation popes reorganized their finances and filled ecclesiastical offices with bishops and abbots as renowned for austerity as themselves, and these appointees in turn set high standards for their own priests and monks.

These papal activities were supplemented by the actions of the Council of Trent, convoked by Paul III in 1545 and meeting at intervals thereafter until 1563. This general council was one of the most important in the history of the Church. Concerning basic matters of doctrine, the Council of Trent without exception reaffirmed all the tenets challenged by the Protestant Reformers. Good works were held to be as necessary for salvation as faith. The theory of the sacraments as indispensable means of grace was upheld. Likewise, transubstantiation, the apostolic succession of the priesthood, the belief in purgatory, the invocation of saints, and the rule of celibacy for the clergy were all confirmed as essential elements in the Catholic system. On the question as to the proper source of Christian belief, the Bible and the traditions of apostolic teaching were held to be of equal authority. Not only was papal supremacy over every bishop and priest expressly maintained, but the supremacy of the pope over the Church council itself was taken for granted in a way that left the monarchical government of the Church undisturbed. The Council of Trent also reaffirmed the doctrine of indulgences which had touched off the Lutheran revolt, although it did condemn the worst scandals connected with the selling of indulgences.

The legislation of Trent was not confined to matters of doctrine, but also included provisions for the elimination of abuses and for reinforcing the discipline of the Church over its members. Bishops and priests were forbidden to hold more than one benefice, so that absentees could not grow rich from a plurality of incomes. To eliminate the evil of an ignorant priesthood, it was provided that a theological seminary must be established in every diocese. Toward the end of its deliberations the council decided upon a censorship of books to prevent heretical ideas from corrupting those who still remained in the faith. A commission was appointed to draw up an index or list of writings which ought not to be read. The publication of this list in 1564 resulted in the formal establishment of the Index of Prohibited Books as a part of the machinery of the Church. Later, a permanent agency known as the Congregation of the Index was set up to revise the list from time to time. Altogether more than forty such revisions have been made. The majority of the books condemned have been theological treatises, and probably the effect in retarding the progress of learning has been slight. Nonetheless, the establishment of the Index must be viewed as a symptom of the intolerance which had come to infect both Catholics and Protestants.

The Council of Trent: practical reform and discipline

In addition to the independent activities of popes and the legislation of the Council of Trent, a third main force propelling the Counter-Reformation was the foundation of the Society of Jesus, commonly known as the Jesuit order, by St. Ignatius Loyola (1491–1556). In the midst of a youthful career as a worldly soldier, the Spanish nobleman Loyola was wounded in battle in 1521 (the same year in which Luther defied Charles V at Worms), and while recuperating, decided to change his ways and become a spiritual soldier of Christ. Shortly afterward he lived as a hermit in a cave near the Spanish town of Manresa for ten months, during which, instead of reading the Bible as a Luther or a Calvin might have done, he experienced ecstatic visions and worked out the principles of his subsequent meditational guide, *The Spiritual Exercises*. This manual, completed in 1535 and first published in 1541, offered practical advice on how to master one's will and serve God by a systematic program of meditations on sin and the life of Christ. Soon made a basic handbook for all Jesuits, and widely studied by numerous Catholic laypeople as well, Loyola's *Spiritual Exercises* had an influence second only to Calvin's *Institutes* of all the religious writings of the sixteenth century.

St. Ignatius Loyola

Nonetheless, St. Ignatius's foundation of the Jesuit order itself was certainly his greatest single accomplishment. Originating as a small group of six disciples who gathered around Loyola in Paris in 1534 to serve God in poverty, chastity, and missionary work, Ignatius's Society of Jesus was formally constituted as an order of the Church by Pope Paul III in 1540, and by the time of Loyola's death already numbered fifteen hundred members. The Society of Jesus was by far the most militant of the religious orders fostered by the Catholic reform move-

Ignatius Loyola. Engraving by Lucas Vorstiman, 1621.

ments of the sixteenth century. It was not merely a monastic society but a company of soldiers sworn to defend the faith. Their weapons were not to be bullets and spears but eloquence, persuasion, instruction in the right doctrines, and, if necessary, more worldly methods of exerting influence. The organization was patterned after that of a military company, with a general as commander-in-chief and iron discipline enforced on all members. Individuality was suppressed, and a soldierlike obedience to the general was exacted of the rank and file. The Jesuit general, sometimes known as "the black pope" (from the color of the order's habit), was elected for life and was not bound to take advice offered by any other member. But he did have one clear superior, namely the Roman pope himself, for in addition to the three monastic vows of poverty, chastity, and obedience, all senior Jesuits took a "fourth vow" of strict obedience to the Vicar of Christ and were held to be at the pope's disposal at all times.

Jesuit militancy;
educational
accomplishments

The activities of the Jesuits consisted primarily of proselytizing not just heathens but Christians, and establishing schools. Originally founded with the major aim of engaging in missionary work abroad, the early Jesuits by no means abandoned this goal, preaching to the heathen reached by the voyages of discovery in India, China, and Spanish America. For example, one of St. Ignatius's closest early associates, St. Francis Xavier (1506–1552), baptized thousands of natives and covered thousands of miles missionizing in the Indies. Yet, although Loyola had not at first conceived of his society as comprising shock-troops against Protestantism, that is what primarily became of it as the Counter-Reformation mounted in intensity. Working by means of preaching and diplomacy—sometimes at the risk of their lives—Jesuits in the second half of the sixteenth century fanned out through Europe in direct confrontation with Calvinists. In many places the Jesuits succeeded in keeping rulers and their subjects loyal to Catholicism, in others they met martyrdom, and in some others—notably Poland and parts of Germany and France—they actually succeeded in regaining territory temporarily lost to the Protestant faith. And wherever they were allowed to settle, the Jesuits set up schools and colleges, for they firmly believed that a vigorous Catholicism could rest only on widespread literacy and education. Indeed their schools were often so efficient that, after the fires of religious hatred began to subside, upper-class Protestants would sometimes send their children to receive a Jesuit education.

Results of the
Counter-Reformation

From the foregoing it should be self-evident that there is a "Counter-Reformation Heritage" every bit as much as there is a Protestant one. Needless to say, for committed Catholics, the greatest achievement of sixteenth-century Catholic reform was the defense and revitalization of the faith. Without any question, Catholicism would not have swept over the globe and reemerged in Europe as the vigorous spiritual force it remains today had it not been for the heroic efforts of the sixteenth-century reformers. But there were more practical results stemming

The Triumph of the Counter-Reformation. In this early–seventeenth-century fresco from the cathedral of Naples the Virgin intercedes for the faithful while personifications of Protestantism are trampled below.

from the Counter-Reformation as well. One was the spread of literacy in Catholic countries due to the educational activities of the Jesuits, and another was the growth of intense concern for acts of charity. Since Counter-Reformation Catholicism continued to emphasize good works as well as faith, charitable activities took on an extremely important role in the revived religion: hence spiritual leaders of the Counter-Reformation such as St. Francis de Sales (1567–1622) and St. Vincent de Paul (1576–1660) urged alms-giving in their sermons and writings, and a wave of founding orphanages and houses for the poor swept over Catholic Europe.

Two other areas in which the Counter-Reformation had less dramatic but still noteworthy effects were in the realm of women's history and intellectual developments. Whereas Protestantism encouraged female literacy for the purpose of making women just a little bit more like men in the ability to read the Bible, reinvigorated Catholicism pursued a different course. Most Catholic women were kept in a more subordinate position in the life of the faith than women under Protestantism, but Catholicism fostered a distinctive role for a female religious elite—countenancing the mysticism of a St. Teresa of Avila (1515–1582), or allowing the foundation of new orders of nuns such as the Ursulines and the Sisters of Charity. Under both Protestantism and Catholicism women remained subordinate, but in the latter model they were able to pursue their religious impulses more independently.

Effects of the Counter-Reformation on women

Finally, it unfortunately cannot be said that the Counter-Reformation perpetuated the tolerant Christianity of Erasmus, for Christian humanists lost favor with Counter-Reformation popes and all of Erasmus's writings were immediately placed on the Index. But sixteenth-

The Counter-Reformation and reason

century Protestantism was just as intolerant as sixteenth-century Catholicism, and far more hostile to the cause of rationalism. Indeed, because Counter-Reformation theologians returned for guidance to the scholasticism of Saint Thomas Aquinas, they were much more committed to acknowledging the dignity of human reason than their Protestant counterparts who emphasized pure Scriptural authority and blind faith. Thus although a hallmark of the subsequent seventeenth-century Scientific Revolution was the divorce between spirituality of any variety and strict scientific work, it does not seem entirely coincidental that René Descartes, one of the founders of the scientific revolution who coined the famous phrase "I think, therefore I am," was trained as a youth by the Jesuits.

SELECTED READINGS

• *Items so designated are available in paperback editions.*

OVERSEAS EXPANSION

Boxer, C. R., *The Portuguese Seaborne Empire, 1415–1825,* New York, 1969. The standard work on the subject.

Elliott, J. H., *The Old World and the New, 1492–1650,* Cambridge, 1970. A superb short analysis of the many ways in which the discovery of the New World affected life in the Old.

• Hale, J. R., *Renaissance Exploration,* New York, 1968. A scintillating brief introduction. Highly recommended as a point of departure.

• Morison, S. E., *Christopher Columbus, Mariner,* New York, 1955. A convenient abridgment of the master storyteller's definitive biography of Columbus, *Admiral of the Ocean Sea* (1942).

• Parry, J. H., *The Age of Reconnaissance,* London, 1963. Probably the best one-volume survey of the entire subject of early-modern European expansion; particularly strong on details of shipbuilding and navigation.

———, *The Spanish Seaborne Empire,* London, 1966. The counterpart to Boxer for the early Spanish colonial experience.

• Penrose, B., *Travel and Discovery in The Renaissance, 1420–1620,* Cambridge, Mass., 1960. Engrossing narratives of the major voyages.

PROTESTANT REFORMATION

• Bainton, R. H., *Here I Stand: A Life of Martin Luther,* Nashville, Tenn., 1950. The best introductory biography in English: absorbing and authoritative, though clearly partisan in Luther's favor.

———, *Women of the Reformation,* 3 vols., Minneapolis, 1970–1977. Full of interesting narrative, but little analysis.

• Brandi, K., *The Emperor Charles V,* New York, 1939. The standard narrative biography of the emperor who faced Luther and ruled much of Europe as well.

• Davis, Natalie Z., *Society and Culture in Early Modern France,* Stanford, Calif., 1975. A collection of pioneering essays in historical anthropology, including a brilliant piece on the role of women in sixteenth-century religious movements.

- Dickens, A. G., *The English Reformation,* New York, 1964. The best introduction.

    ———, *Reformation and Society in Sixteenth-Century Europe,* London, 1966. A highly stimulating introductory survey, with the added advantage of being profusely illustrated.

- Erikson, E. H., *Young Man Luther,* New York, 1958. A classic psychobiography that analyzes the young Luther's "identity crisis."

    Grimm, Harold J., *The Reformation Era: 1500–1650,* 2nd ed., New York, 1973. The best college-level text; consistently informative, balanced, and reliable.

- Harbison, E. H., *The Age of Reformation,* Ithaca, N.Y., 1955. A magnificent elementary introduction by a master of the field.

    ———, *The Christian Scholar in the Age of the Reformation,* New York, 1956. Discusses the relationship between Christian humanism and early Protestantism.

- Hillerbrand, H., *The World of the Reformation,* London, 1975. A stimulating overview.

- Hurstfield, Joel, ed., *The Reformation Crisis,* London, 1965. Lively essays on all major aspects of Reformation history.

- McNeill, John T., *The History and Character of Calvinism,* New York, 1945. A basic, reliable, older work.

    Monter, E. William, *Calvin's Geneva,* New York, 1967. Standard on the history of Calvin's Geneva.

    Mullett, M., *Radical Religious Movements in Early Modern Europe,* London, 1980. Thematic analysis of some of the major effects of Protestantism, with as much attention given to the seventeenth as to the sixteenth century. Contains a particularly valuable annotated bibliography.

    Oberman, H. A., *Masters of the Reformation,* Cambridge, 1981. A challenging study of the emergence of Protestantism as seen from the perspective of activities at the University of Tübingen. For more advanced readers.

    Samuelsson, K., *Religion and Economic Action,* New York, 1961. The standard critical evaluation of Max Weber's thesis that Calvinism fostered the modern "spirit of capitalism."

- Skinner, Q., *The Foundations of Modern Political Thought: 2. The Age of Reformation.* In a class by itself as the best analysis of Reformation and Counter-Reformation trends in political theory.

- Smith, Lacey B., *Henry VIII: The Mask of Royalty,* Boston, 1971. A breathtaking interpretation of the last years of Henry VIII and the age in which he lived.

- Spitz, Lewis W., ed. *The Reformation: Basic Interpretations,* 2nd ed., Lexington, Mass., 1972. A collection of readings on points of scholarly dispute.

    Tawney, R. H., *Religion and the Rise of Capitalism,* New York, 1926. The most sophisticated and elegantly written defense of the "Weber thesis."

    Troeltsch, E., *Protestantism and Progress,* New York, 1931. An enduring classic.

    Wendel, F., *Calvin,* London, 1963. A standard biography.

    Williams, George H., *The Radical Reformation,* 1962. Detailed account of Anabaptism and the "left wing" of the Protestant Reformation.

CATHOLIC REFORM

Broderick, James, *The Origin of the Jesuits,* London, 1940. An older work, but still unsurpassed.

Delumeau, J., *Catholicism between Luther and Voltaire: A New View of the Counter-Reformation,* Philadelphia, 1977. A sympathetic account stressing the positive aspects of Reformed Catholicism.

• Dickens, A. G., *The Counter Reformation,* London, 1968. A splendid counterpart to Dickens's *Reformation and Society;* like its companion, profusely illustrated.

Janelle, P., *The Catholic Reformation,* Milwaukee, 1949. A reliable brief introduction.

Jedin, H., *A History of the Council of Trent,* 2 vols., London, 1957–1961. Authoritative and exhaustive.

Knowles, D., *From Pachomius to Ignatius: A Study in the Constitutional History of the Religious Orders,* Oxford, 1966. In less than one hundred masterful pages Knowles places the organizational principles of the Jesuits in historical perspective.

SOURCE MATERIALS

Dillenberger, J., ed., *John Calvin: Selections from His Writings,* Garden City, N.Y., 1971.

———, *Martin Luther: Selections from His Writings,* Garden City, N.Y., 1961.

Hillerbrand, H. J., ed., *The Protestant Reformation,* New York, 1967.

St. Ignatius Loyola, *The Spiritual Exercises,* tr. R. W. Gleason, Garden City, N.Y., 1964.

Ziegler, D. J., *Great Debates of the Reformation,* New York, 1969.

Chapter 16

A CENTURY OF CRISIS FOR EARLY-MODERN EUROPE
(c. 1560—c. 1660)

I do not wish to say much about the customs of the age in which we live.
I can only state that this age is not one of the best, being a century of iron.

—R. Mentet de Salmonet, *History of the Troubles in Great Britain* (1649)

What in me is dark
Illumine, what is low raise and support.

—John Milton, *Paradise Lost*

On the night before St. Bartholomew's Day in August of 1572 the Catholic queen mother of France, Catherine de Medici, authorized the ambush of French Protestant leaders who happened to be in Paris to attend a wedding. Thereupon, during the hours after midnight, unsuspecting people found themselves awakened to be stabbed in bed or thrown out of windows. Soon all the targeted Protestants were eliminated, but the killing did not stop because roving bands of Parisian Catholics seized the opportunity of licensed carnage to slaughter at will any enemies they happened upon, Protestant or otherwise. By morning the River Seine was clogged with corpses and scores of bodies hung from gibbets in witness to an event known ever since as the Massacre of St. Bartholomew's Day.

A massacre in Paris

Had this lamentable incident been an isolated event it hardly would be worth mentioning, but in fact throughout the hundred years from roughly 1560 to roughly 1660 outbreaks of religious mayhem—with Protestants the ruthless killers in certain cases as Catholics were in others—recurred in many parts of Europe. Moreover, to make matters far worse, economic hardships and prolonged wars accompanied religious riots to result in a century of pronounced crisis for European civilization.

A century of crisis

The St. Bartholomew's Day Massacre. A contemporary painting depicts the merciless slaughter of Huguenots in Paris. At the top left (in front of the large gate next to the Seine) the Queen Mother Catherine looks over a pile of naked dead bodies; to the right a Huguenot leader is being pushed out of a window.

Lack of uniformity in causes and effects

In many respects Europe's early-modern period of crisis resembled the terrible times of the late Middle Ages, but the early-modern crisis was much less uniform in its nature and extent. From the economic point of view, there were two different major difficulties—first a dramatic price inflation lasting from about 1560 to 1600 that hurt the poor far worse than it did the rich, and then a period of overall economic stagnation which was marked, however, by significant exceptions from place to place. Similarly, although the main theme of political history during the entire era was intense warfare, the causes of war differed greatly according to place and time, with some areas occasionally even managing to bask in intervals of peace. Nonetheless, seen from the broadest perspective the period from 1560 to 1660 was western Europe's "iron century"—an age of enormous turbulence and severe trials.

1. ECONOMIC, RELIGIOUS, AND POLITICAL TESTS

Impending crisis

Europe's time of troubles crept up on contemporaries unawares. For almost a century before 1560 most of the West had enjoyed steady economic growth, and the discovery of the New World seemed to harbinger even greater prosperity to come. Political trends too seemed auspicious, since most western European governments were becoming ever more efficient and providing more internal peace for their subjects. Yet around 1560 thunderclouds were gathering in the skies that would soon burst into terrible storms.

Although the causes of these storms were interrelated, each may be examined separately, starting with the great price inflation. Nothing like the upward price trend which affected western Europe in the second half of the sixteenth century had ever happened before. The cost of a measure of wheat in Flanders, for example, tripled from 1550 to 1600, grain prices in Paris quadrupled, and the overall cost of living in England advanced well over 100 percent during the same period. Certainly the twentieth century has seen even more dizzying inflations than this, but since the skyrocketing of prices in the later sixteenth century was a novelty, most historians agree on calling it the "price revolution."

If experts agree on the terminology, however, very few of them agree on the exact combination of circumstances that caused the price revolution, for early-modern statistics are patchy and many areas of economic theory remain under dispute. Nonetheless, for present purposes two widely accepted dominant explanations for the great inflation may be offered with confidence. The first is demographic. Starting in the later fifteenth century, Europe's population began to mount again after the plague-induced fall-off: roughly estimated, there were about 50 million people in Europe around 1450 and 90 million around 1600. Since Europe's food supply remained more or less constant owing to the lack of any noteworthy breakthrough in agricultural technology, food prices inevitably were driven sharply higher by greater demand. In contrast, the prices of manufactured goods did not rise as steeply because there was a greater match between supply and demand. Yet prices of manufactured items did rise nonetheless, especially in cases where the supply of agricultural raw materials crucial to the manufacturing process remained relatively inelastic.

Population trends therefore explain much, but since Europe's population did not grow nearly as rapidly in the second half of the sixteenth century as prices, complementary explanations for the great inflation are still necessary, and foremost among these is the enormous influx of bullion from Spanish America. Around 1560 a new technique of extracting silver from silver ore made the working of newly discovered mines in Mexico and Bolivia highly practical, soon transforming the previous trickle of silver entering the European economy into a flood. Whereas in the five years between 1556 and 1560 roughly 10 million ducats worth of silver passed through the Spanish entry point of Seville, between 1576 and 1580 that figure had doubled, and between 1591 and 1595 it had more than quadrupled. Inasmuch as most of this silver was used by the Spanish crown to pay its foreign creditors and its armies abroad or by private individuals to pay for imports from other countries, Spanish bullion quickly circulated throughout Europe, where much of it was minted into coins. This dramatic increase in the volume of money in circulation further fueled the spiral of rising prices.

Soaring prices

Causes of inflation: (1) population increase

(2) influx of silver

Aggressive entrepreneurs and landlords profited most from the changed economic circumstances, while the masses of laboring people were hurt the worst. Obviously, merchants in possession of sought-after goods were able to raise prices at will, and landlords either could profit directly from the rising prices of agricultural produce or, if they did not farm their own lands, could always raise rents. But laborers in country and town were caught in a squeeze because wages rose far more slowly than prices, owing to the presence of a more than adequate labor supply. Moreover, because the cost of food staples rose at a sharper rate proportionately than the cost of most other items of consumption, poor people had to spend an ever-greater percentage of their paltry income on necessities. In normal years they barely managed to survive, but when disasters such as wars or poor harvests drove grain prices out of reach, some of the poor literally starved to death. The picture that thus emerges is one of the rich getting richer and the poor getting poorer—splendid feasts enjoyed amid the most appalling suffering.

In addition to these direct economic effects, the price inflation of the later sixteenth century had significant political effects as well because higher prices placed new pressures on the sovereign states of Europe. The reasons for this were simple. Since the inflation depressed the real value of money, fixed incomes from taxes and dues in effect yielded less and less. Thus merely to keep their incomes constant governments would have been forced to raise taxes. But to compound this problem, most states needed much more real income than previously because they were undertaking more wars, and warfare, as always, was becoming increasingly expensive. The only recourse, then, was to raise taxes precipitously, but such draconian measures incurred great resentments on the part of subject populations—especially the very poor who were already strapped more than enough by the effects of the inflation. Hence governments faced continuous threats of defiance and potential armed resistance.

Less need be said about the economic stagnation that followed the price revolution because it interfered little with most of the trends just discussed. When population growth began to ease and the flood of silver from America began to abate around 1600, prices soon leveled off. Yet because the most lucrative economic exploitation of the New World only began in the late seventeenth century and Europe experienced little new industrial development, the period from about 1600 to 1660 was at best one of very limited overall economic growth, even though a few areas—notably Holland—bucked the trend. Within this context the rich were usually able to hold their own, but the poor as a group made no advances since the relationship of prices to wages remained fixed to their disadvantage. Indeed, if anything, the lot of the poor in many places deteriorated because the mid–seventeenth century saw some particularly expensive and destructive wars, causing helpless civilians to be plundered either by rapacious tax collectors, looting soldiers, or sometimes by both.

It goes without saying that most people would have been far better off had there been fewer wars during Europe's iron century, but given prevalent attitudes, newly arisen religious rivalries made wars inevitable. Simply stated, until religious passions began to cool toward the end of the period, most Catholics and Protestants viewed each other as minions of Satan who could not be allowed to live. Worse, sovereign states attempted to enforce religious uniformity on the grounds that "crown and altar" offered each other mutual support and in the belief that governments would totter where diversity of faith prevailed. Rulers on both sides felt certain that religious minorities, if allowed to survive in their realms, would inevitably engage in sedition; nor were they far wrong since militant Calvinists and Jesuits were indeed dedicated to subverting constituted powers in areas where they had not yet triumphed. Thus states tried to extirpate all potential religious resistance, but in the process sometimes provoked civil wars in which both sides tended to assume there could be no victory until the other was exterminated. And of course civil wars might become international in scope when one or more foreign powers resolved to aid embattled religious allies elsewhere.

Religious wars

Compounding the foregoing problems were more strictly political ones: namely, while strapped by price trends and racked by religious wars, governments brought certain provincial and constitutional grievances down upon themselves. Regarding the provincial issue, most of the major states of early-modern Europe had been built up by conquests or dynastic marital accretions, with the result that many smaller territories had been subjected to absentee rule. At first some degree of provincial autonomy was usually preserved and hence the inhabitants of such territories did not object too much to their annexation. But in the iron century, when governments were making evergreater financial claims on all their subjects or trying to enforce religious uniformity, rulers customarily moved to destroy all semblances of provincial autonomy in order to implement their financial or religious policies. Naturally the province-dwellers were usually not inclined to accept total subjugation without a fight, so rebellions might break out on combined patriotic and economic or religious grounds. Nor was that all, since most governments seeking money and/or religious uniformity tried to rule their subjects with a firmer hand than before, and thus sometimes provoked armed resistance in the name of traditional constitutional liberties. Given this bewildering variety of motives for revolt, it is by no means surprising that the century between 1560 and 1660 was one of the most turbulent in all European history.

Governmental crises

2. A HALF CENTURY OF RELIGIOUS WARS

Despite the multiplicity of overlapping causes for instability, the greatest single cause of warfare in the first half of Europe's iron cen-

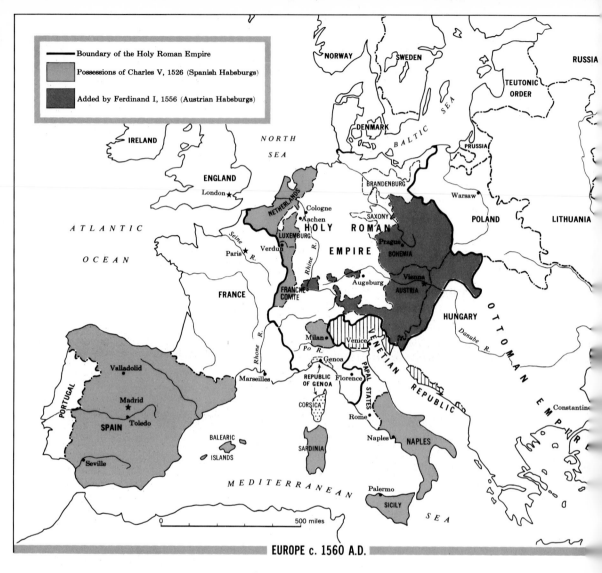

NORWAY

SWEDEN

RUSSIA

TEUTONIC ORDER

DENMARK

BALTIC SEA

PRUSSIA

IRELAND

NORTH SEA

ENGLAND

London ★

BRANDENBURG

Warsaw •

ATLANTIC

Cologne •

SAXONY

POLAND

LITHUANIA

•Aachen

HOLY ROMAN

OCEAN

Seine R.

LUXEMBURG

EMPIRE

Prague •

Paris ★

Verdun

Rhine R.

BOHEMIA

FRANCE

FRANCHE COMTÉ

Augsburg •

Vienna ★

AUSTRIA

HUNGARY

Rhone R.

Milan •

Po R.

Venice •

Danube R.

OTTOMAN EMPIRE

Genoa

PAPAL STATES

Marseilles •

REPUBLIC OF GENOA

Florence •

Valladolid •

CORSICA

Madrid ★

Rome •

Constantinople

Toledo •

SPAIN

BALEARIC ISLANDS

SARDINIA

Naples •

NAPLES

Seville •

MEDITERRANEAN

Palermo •

PORTUGAL

SICILY

SEA

0   500 miles

EUROPE c. 1560 A.D.

Religious wars in Germany until the Peace of Augsburg

tury was religious rivalry. Indeed, wars between Catholics and Protestants began as early as the 1540s when the Catholic Holy Roman Emperor Charles V tried to reestablish Catholic unity in Germany by launching a military campaign against several German princes who had instituted Lutheran worship in their principalities. At times thereafter it appeared as if Charles was going to succeed in reducing his German Protestant opponents to complete submission, but since he was also involved in fighting against France, he seldom was able to devote concerted attention to affairs in Germany. Accordingly, religious warfare sputtered on and off until a compromise settlement was reached in the Religious Peace of Augsburg (1555). This rested on the principle of *"cuius regio, eius religio"* ("as the ruler, so the religion"), which meant that in those principalities where Lutheran princes ruled,

Lutheranism would be the sole state religion, and the same for those with Catholic princes. Although the Peace of Augsburg was a historical milestone inasmuch as Catholic rulers for the first time acknowledged the legality of Protestantism, it boded ill for the future in assuming that no sovereign state larger than a free city (for which it made exceptions) could tolerate religious diversity. Moreover, in excluding Calvinism it ensured that Calvinists would become aggressive opponents of the *status quo*.

Background of the French wars of religion

Even though wars in the name of religion were fought in Europe before 1560, those that raged afterward were far more brutal, partly because the combatants had become more fanatical (intransigent Calvinists and Jesuits customarily took the lead on their respective sides), and partly because the later religious wars were aggravated by political and economic resentments. Since Geneva bordered on France, since Calvin himself was a Frenchman who longed to convert his mother country, and since Calvinists had no wish to displace German Lutherans, the next act in the tragedy of Europe's confessional warfare was played out on French soil. Calvinist missionaries had already made much headway in France in the years between Calvin's rise to power in Geneva in 1541 and the outbreak of religious warfare in 1562. Of the greatest aid to the Calvinist (Huguenot) cause was the conversion to Calvinism of many aristocratic French women because such women usually won over their husbands, who in turn maintained large private armies. The foremost example is that of Jeanne d'Albret, queen of the tiny Pyrenean kingdom of Navarre, who brought over to Calvinism her husband, the prominent French aristocrat Antoine de Bourbon, and her brother-in-law, the prince de Condé. Not only did Condé take command of the French Huguenot party when civil war broke out in 1562, but he later was succeeded in this capacity by Jeanne's son, Henry of Navarre, who came to rule all of France at the end of the century as King Henry IV. In addition to aristocrats, many people from all walks of life became Huguenots for a variety of motives, with Huguenot strength greatest in areas of the south which had long resented the dominance of northern rule from Paris. In short, by 1562 Calvinists comprised between 10 and 20 percent of France's population of roughly 16 million, and their numbers were swelling every day.

Jeanne D'Albret

Since both Catholics and Protestants assumed that France could have only a single *roi, foi,* and *loi* (king, faith, and law), civil war was inevitable, and no one was surprised when a struggle between the Huguenot Condé and the ultra-Catholic duke of Guise for control of the government during a royal minority led in 1562 to a show of arms. Soon all France was aflame. Churches were ransacked and local scores were settled by rampaging mobs who often were incited on both sides by members of their clergy. After a while it became clear that the Huguenots were not strong or numerous enough to gain victory, but they were also too strong to be defeated. Hence, despite intermittent

French warfare: The St. Bartholomew's Day Massacre

truces, warfare dragged on at great cost of life until 1572. Then, during an interval of peace, the cultivated queen mother Catherine de Medici, normally a woman who favored compromise, plotted with members of the Catholic Guise faction to kill all the Huguenot leaders while they were assembled in Paris for the wedding of Henry of Navarre. In the early morning of St. Bartholomew's Day (August 24) most of the Huguenot chiefs were murdered in bed and two to three thousand other Protestants were slaughtered in the streets or drowned in the Seine by Catholic mobs. When word of the Parisian massacre spread to the provinces, some ten thousand more Huguenots were killed in a frenzy of blood lust that swept through France.

*Henry IV establishes
French religious peace*

The St. Bartholomew's Day episode effectively broke the back of Huguenot resistance, but even then warfare did not cease because the neurotic King Henry III (1574–1589) tried to play off Huguenots against the dominant Catholic Guise family and because die-hard Huguenots sometimes were able to ally with Catholics revolting against overburdensome taxes or inequities in tax assessments. Only when the politically astute Henry of Navarre succeeded to the French throne as Henry III[1](1589–1610), initiating the Bourbon dynasty that would rule until 1792, did civil war finally come to an end. In 1593 Henry abjured his Protestantism in order to placate France's Catholic majority ("Paris is worth a mass") and then, in 1598, offered limited religious freedom to the Huguenots by the Edict of Nantes. According to the terms of this proclamation, Catholicism was recognized as the official religion, but Huguenot nobles were allowed to hold Protestant services privately in their castles, other Huguenots were allowed to worship at specified places (excluding Paris and all cities where bishops and archbishops resided), and the Huguenot party was permitted to fortify some towns, especially in the south, for military defense if the need arose. Thus, although the Edict of Nantes certainly did not counte-

[1]Here, as elsewhere, dates following a ruler's name refer to dates of reign.

The Assassination of Henry IV. This contemporary engraving shows Henry seated in an open carriage without any concern for his personal danger while his assassin climbs on the spoke of the carriage wheel to attack him. The entire composition conveys a vivid impression of early-modern Paris.

The Emperor Charles V. This portrait by the Venetian painter Titian depicts the emperor in a grandiloquent equestrian pose. (Another depiction of Charles V by Titian appears in the section of color plates following p. 448.)

nance absolute freedom of worship, it nevertheless represented a major stride in the direction of toleration. With religious peace established, France quickly began to recover from decades of devastation, but Henry IV himself was cut down by the dagger of a Catholic fanatic in 1610.

Contemporaneous with the religious warfare in France was equally bitter religious strife between Catholics and Protestants in the neighboring Netherlands, where national resentments gravely compounded religious hatreds. For almost a century the Netherlands (or Low Countries), comprising modern-day Holland in the north and Belgium in the south, had been ruled by the Habsburg family. Particularly the Belgian part of the Netherlands prospered greatly from trade and manufacture: southern Netherlanders had the greatest per capita wealth of all Europe and their metropolis of Antwerp was northern Europe's leading commercial and financial center. Moreover, the half-century-long rule of the Habsburg Charles V (1506–1556) had been extremely popular because Charles, who had been born in the Belgian city of Ghent, felt a sense of rapport with his subjects and allowed them a large degree of local self-government.

Habsburg rule in the Netherlands

But around 1560 the good fortune of the Netherlands began to ebb. When Charles V retired to a monastery in 1556 (dying two years later) he ceded all his vast territories outside of the Holy Roman Empire and Hungary—not only the Netherlands, but Spain, Spanish America, and close to half of Italy—to his son Philip II (1556–1598). Unlike Charles, Philip had been born in Spain, and thinking of himself as a Spaniard, made Spain his residence and the focus of his policy. Thus he viewed the Netherlands primarily as a potentially rich source of income necessary for pursuing Spanish affairs. (Around 1560 silver was only

Philip II and the impending crisis

Philip II of Spain. Titian's portrait shows Philip's resemblance to his father, Charles V, particularly in the protruding lower jaw of the Habsburgs.

beginning to flood through Seville.) But in order to tap the wealth of the Netherlands Philip had to rule it more directly than his father had, and such attempts were naturally resented by the local magnates who until then had dominated the government. To make matters worse, a religious storm also was brewing, for after a treaty of 1559 ended a long war between France and Spain, French Calvinists had begun to stream over the Netherlandish border, making converts wherever they went. Soon there were more Calvinists in Antwerp than in Geneva, a situation that Philip II could not tolerate because he was an ardent Catholic who subscribed wholeheartedly to the goals of the Counter-Reformation. Indeed, as he wrote to Rome on the eve of conflict: "rather than suffer the slightest harm to the true religion and service of God, I would lose all my states and even my life a hundred times over because I am not and will not be the ruler of heretics."

Evidence of the complexity of the Netherlandish situation is found in the facts that the leader of resistance to Philip, William the Silent, was at first not a Calvinist and that the territories which ultimately succeeded in breaking away from Spanish rule were at first the most Catholic ones in the Low Countries. William "the Silent," a prominent nobleman with large landholdings in the Netherlands, was in fact very talkative, receiving his nickname rather from his ability to hide his true religious and political feelings when the need arose. In 1566, when still a nominal Catholic, he and other local nobles not formally committed to Protestantism appealed to Philip to allow toleration for Calvinists. But while Philip momentarily temporized, radical Protestant mobs proved to be their own worst enemy—ransacking Catholic churches throughout the country, methodically desecrating hosts, smashing statuary, and shattering stained-glass windows. Though local troops soon had the situation under control, Philip II nonetheless

Protestants Ransacking a Catholic Church in the Netherlands. The "Protestant fury" of 1566 was responsible for the large-scale destruction of religious art and statuary in the Low Countries, provoking the stern repression of Philip II.

decided to dispatch an army of ten thousand commanded by the steely Spanish duke of Alva to wipe out Protestantism in the Low Countries forever. Alva's tribunal, the "Council of Blood," soon examined some twelve thousand persons on charges of heresy or sedition, of whom nine thousand were convicted and one thousand executed. William the Silent fled the country and all hope for a free Netherlands seemed lost.

But the tide turned quickly for two related reasons. First, instead of giving up, William the Silent converted to Protestantism, sought help from Protestants in France, Germany, and England, and organized bands of sea-rovers to harass Spanish shipping on the Netherlands coast. And second, Alva's tyranny helped William's cause, especially when the hated Spanish governor attempted to levy a repressive 10 percent sales tax. With internal disaffection growing, in 1572 William, for tactical military reasons, was able to seize the northern Netherlands even though the north until then had been predominantly Catholic. Thereafter geography played a major role in determining the outcome of the conflict. Spanish armies repeatedly attempted to win back the north, but they were stopped by a combination of impassable rivers and dikes which could be opened to flood out the invaders. Although William the Silent was assassinated by a Catholic in 1584, his son continued to lead the resistance until the Spanish crown finally agreed by a truce in 1609 to stop fighting and thus implicitly recognized the independence of the northern Dutch Republic. Meanwhile, the pressures of war and persecution had made the whole north Calvinistic, whereas the south—which remained Spanish—returned to uniform Catholicism.

The Duke of Alva. The gaunt Spanish general who attempted in vain to extirpate Calvinism in the Netherlands.

Predictably, religious strife which could take the form of civil war, as in France, or war for national liberation, as in the Netherlands, could also take the form of warfare between sovereign states, as in the case of the late-sixteenth-century struggle between England and Spain. After narrowly escaping domination by the Catholic Queen Mary and her Spanish husband Philip II, English Protestants rejoiced in the rule of Queen Elizabeth I (1558–1603) and naturally harbored great antipathy for Philip II and the Counter-Reformation. Furthermore, English economic interests were directly opposed to those of the Spanish. A seafaring and trading people, the English in the later sixteenth century were steadily making inroads into Spanish naval and commercial domination, and were also determined to resist any Spanish attempt to block England's lucrative trade with the Low Countries. But the greatest source of antagonism lay in naval contests in the Atlantic, where English privateers, with the tacit consent of Queen Elizabeth, could not resist raiding silver-laden Spanish treasure ships. Beginning around 1570, and taking as an excuse Spanish oppression of Protestants in the Netherlands, English admirals or pirates (the terms were really interchangeable) such as Sir Francis Drake and Sir John Hawkins began plundering Spanish vessels on the high seas. In a particularly dramatic sailing exploit lasting from 1577 to 1580, lust for booty and prevailing winds propelled Drake all the way around the world, to

Antagonism between England and Spain

Left: *The Defeat of the Spanish Armada*. Right: *Queen Elizabeth I.* The contemporary English oil painting of the great sea battle gives only a schematic idea of its turbulence. Note, however, the prominence of the papal insignia (tiara over crossed keys of St. Peter) on the ship in the middle foreground: Englishmen were convinced that had they not defeated the Spanish Armada in 1588 the pope would have planted his banner on their shores. At the right is a typically overblown portrait of Queen Elizabeth, known to her admiring subjects as "Gloriana," standing on a map of England.

return with stolen Spanish treasure worth twice as much as Queen Elizabeth's annual revenue.

All this would have been sufficient provocation for Philip II to have retaliated against England, but because he had his hands full in the Netherlands he resolved to invade the island only after the English openly allied with the Dutch rebels in 1585. And even then Philip did not act without extensive planning and a sense of assurance that nothing could go wrong. Finally, in 1588 he dispatched an enormous fleet, confidently called the "Invincible Armada," to punish insolent Britannia. After an initial standoff in the English Channel, however, English fireships outmaneuvered the Spanish fleet, setting some Spanish galleons ablaze and forcing the rest to break formation. "Protestant gales" did the rest and a battered flotilla soon limped home with almost half its ships lost.

The defeat of the Spanish Armada was one of the most decisive battles of Western history. Had Spain conquered England it is quite likely that the Spanish would have gone on to crush Holland and perhaps even to destroy Protestantism everywhere. But, as it was, the Protestant day was saved, and not long afterward Spanish power began to decline, with English and Dutch ships taking ever-greater command of the seas. Moreover, in England itself patriotic fervor became intense. Popular even before then, "Good Queen Bess" was virtually revered

The defeat of the Spanish Armada

The salvation of Protestantism

The Crucifixion, Tintoretto (1518–1594). This Venetian master of Mannerism combined typically Venetian richness of color with an innovative concern for movement and emotion. (Scala)

Saint Andrew and St. Francis, El Greco (c. 1541–1614). A striking exemplification of the artist's penchant for elongation as well as his profound psychological penetration. (The Prado)

View of Toledo, El Greco. One of the most awesomely mysterious paintings in the entire Western tradition. (MMA)

The Maids of Honor, Diego Velásquez (1599–1660). The artist himself is at work on an idealized double portrait of the king and queen of Spain (who may be seen in the rear mirror), but reality is more obvious in the foreground in the persons of the delicately impish princess, her two maids, and a misshapen dwarf. The twentieth-century Spanish artist Picasso gained great inspiration from this work. (The Prado)

Pope Innocent X, Velásquez. A trenchant portrait of a decisive man of affairs. (Doria-Pamphili Collection)

England and Scotland Crowning Charles I, Peter Paul Rubens (1577–1640). A typical piece of Baroque propaganda, in this case painted to glorify the English monarch of the Stuart family in the years before his ill-fated demise. (Minneapolis Institute of Art)

The Horrors of War, Rubens. The war god Mars here casts aside his mistress Venus and threatens humanity with death and destruction. In his old age Rubens took a far more critical view of war than he did for most of his earlier career. (Gall. Palatina)

Aristotle Contemplating the Bust of Homer, Rembrandt van Rijn (1606–1669). One of the greatest painters' view of one of the greatest of philosophers caught up by the aura of one of the greatest poets. (MMA)

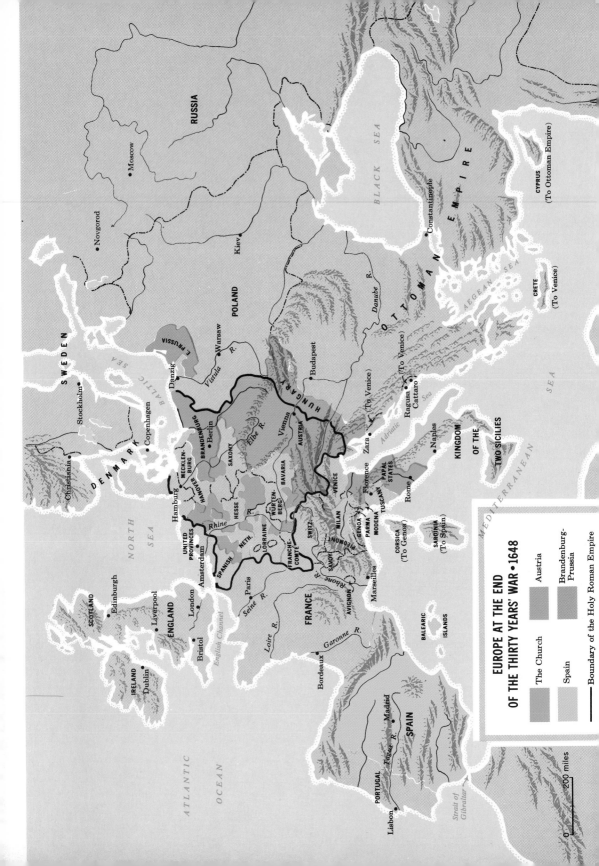

**EUROPE AT THE END
OF THE THIRTY YEARS' WAR • 1648**

The Church

Austria

Spain

Brandenburg-
Prussia

Boundary of the Holy Roman Empire

0   200 miles

SWEDEN

RUSSIA

Moscow

Novgorod

Kiev

Stockholm

Copenhagen

DENMARK

Christiania

POLAND

Warsaw

E. PRUSSIA

Danzig

Vistula R.

Elbe R.

Berlin

BRANDENBURG

MECKLEN-
BURG

SAXONY

Budapest

HUNGARY

Vienna

AUSTRIA

Danube R.

BLACK SEA

OTTOMAN EMPIRE

Constantinople

CYPRUS
(To Ottoman Empire)

CRETE
(To Venice)

AEGEAN SEA

SEA

Ragusa (To Venice)

Cattaro (To Venice)

Zara

Adriatic Sea

Naples

KINGDOM
OF THE
TWO SICILIES

MEDITERRANEAN

Rome

PAPAL
STATES

Florence

TUSCANY

Venice

VENICE

MODENA

PARMA

GENOA

MILAN

PIEDMONT

SAVOY

SWITZ.

Hamburg

HANOVER

HESSE

Rhine R.

WÜRTEN-
BERG

BAVARIA

NETH.

UNITED
PROVINCES

Amsterdam

SPANISH
NETH.

LORRAINE

FRANCHE-
COMTÉ

SCOTLAND

Edinburgh

IRELAND

Dublin

Liverpool

Bristol

London

ENGLAND

English Channel

NORTH
SEA

BALTIC SEA

Paris

Seine R.

Loire R.

FRANCE

Bordeaux

Garonne R.

Marseilles

Rhône R.

AVIGNON

CORSICA
(To Genoa)

SARDINIA
(To Spain)

BALEARIC
ISLANDS

SPAIN

Madrid

Tagus R.

PORTUGAL

Lisbon

*Strait of
Gibraltar*

ATLANTIC

OCEAN

by her subjects until her death in 1603, and England embarked on its golden "Elizabethan Age" of literary endeavor. War with Spain dragged on inconclusively until 1604, but the fighting never brought England any serious harm and was just lively enough to keep the English people deeply committed to the cause of their queen, their country, and the Protestant religion.

3. YEARS OF TREMBLING

With the promulgation of the Edict of Nantes in 1598, the peace between England and Spain of 1604, and the truce between Spain and Holland of 1609, religious warfare tapered off and came to an end in the early seventeenth century. But in 1618 a major new war broke out, this time in Germany. Since this struggle raged more or less unceasingly until 1648 it bears the name of the Thirty Years' War. Meanwhile, far from returning to enduring peace, Spain and France became engaged in the Thirty Years' War and war with each other, and internal resentments in Spain, France, and England flared up in the decade of the 1640s in concurrent outbreaks of uprisings and civil turmoil. As an English preacher said in 1643, "these are days of shaking, and this shaking is universal." He might have added that while in some instances religion remained one of the contested issues, secular disputes about powers of government were now becoming predominant.

A new phase of turmoil

The clearest example is that of the Thirty Years' War, which began in a welter of religious passions as a war between Catholics and Protestants but immediately raised basic German constitutional issues and ended as an international struggle in which the initial religious dimension was almost entirely forgotten. Between the Peace of Augsburg

The Thirty Years' War

Two Artistic Broadsides from the Thirty Years' War. On the left the German peasantry is ridden by the soldiery; on the right is an allegorical representation of "the monstrous beast of war."

in 1555 and the outbreak of war in 1618, Calvinists had replaced Lutherans in a few German territories but the overall balance between Protestants and Catholics within the Holy Roman Empire had remained undisturbed. In 1618, however, when a Protestant uprising against Habsburg Catholic rule in Bohemia (not a German territory, but nonetheless part of the Holy Roman Empire) threatened to upset the balance, German Catholic forces ruthlessly counterattacked, first in Bohemia and then in Germany proper. Led by Charles V's Habsburg descendant Ferdinand II, who was archduke of Austria, king of Hungary, and from 1619 to his death in 1637, Holy Roman Emperor, a German Catholic league seized the military initiative and within a decade seemed close to extirpating Protestantism throughout Germany. But Ferdinand, who was intent on pursuing political goals as well, imposed firm direct rule in Bohemia in order to build up the strength of his own Austro-Hungarian state, and attempted to revive the faded authority of the Holy Roman Empire in whatever ways he could.

*The involvement of
Sweden and France*

Thus when the Lutheran king of Sweden, Gustavus Adolphus, marched into Germany in 1630 to champion the nearly lost cause of Protestantism, he was welcomed by several German Catholic princes who preferred to see the former religious balance restored rather than stand the chance of surrendering their sovereignty to Ferdinand II. To make matters still more ironic, Gustavus's Protestant army was secretly subsidized by Catholic France, then governed by a cardinal of the Church, because Habsburg Spain had been fighting in Germany on the side of Habsburg Austria and France's Cardinal Richelieu was determined to resist any possibility of being surrounded by a strong Habsburg alliance on the north, east, and south. In the event, the military genius Gustavus Adolphus started routing the Habsburgs, but when the Swedish king fell in battle in 1632, Cardinal Richelieu had little choice but to send ever-greater support to the remaining Swedish troops in Germany, until in 1639 French armies entered the war directly on Sweden's side. From then until 1648 the struggle was really one of France and Sweden against Austria and Spain, with most of Germany a helpless battleground.

*The toll of warfare in
Germany*

The result was that Germany suffered more from warfare in the terrible years between 1618 and 1648 than it ever did before or after until the twentieth century. Several German cities were besieged and sacked nine or ten times over, and soldiers from all nations, who often had to sustain themselves by plunder, gave no quarter to defenseless civilians. With plague and disease adding to the toll of outright butchery, some parts of Germany lost more than half their populations, although it is true that others went relatively unscathed. Most horrifying was the loss of life in the last four years, when the carnage continued unabated even while peace negotiators had already arrived at broad areas of agreement and were dickering over subsidiary clauses.

Nor did the Peace of Westphalia, which finally ended the Thirty

A Swearing of Oaths at the Peace of Westphalia, 1648

Years' War in 1648, do much to vindicate anyone's death, even though it did establish some abiding landmarks in European history. Above all, from the international perspective the Peace of Westphalia marked the reemergence of France as the predominant power on the continental European scene, replacing Spain—a position France was to hold for two centuries more. In particular, France moved its eastern frontier directly into German territory by taking over large parts of Alsace. As for strictly internal German matters, the greatest losers were the Austrian Habsburgs, who were forced to surrender all the territory they had gained in Germany and to abandon their hopes of using the office of Holy Roman Emperor to dominate central Europe. Otherwise, something very close to the German *status quo* of 1618 was reestablished, with Protestant principalities in the north balancing Catholic ones in the south and Germany so hopelessly divided that it could play no united role in European history until the nineteenth century.

The Peace of Westphalia

See color map facing page 513

Still greater losers from the Thirty Years' War than the Austrian Habsburgs were their Spanish cousins, for Spain had invested vast sums in the struggle it could not afford and ceased being a great power forever after. The story of Spain's swift fall from grandeur is almost like a Greek tragedy in its relentless unfolding. Even after the defeat of the "Invincible Armada," around 1600 the Spanish empire—comprising all of the Iberian peninsula (including Portugal, which had been annexed by Philip II in 1580), half of Italy, half of the Netherlands, all of Central and South America, and even the Philippine Islands—was the mightiest power not just in Europe but in the world. Yet a bare half century later this empire on which the sun never set had come close to falling apart.

The decline of Spain

Spain's greatest underlying weakness was economic. At first this may seem like a very odd statement considering that in 1600, as in the three or four previous decades, huge amounts of American silver were being unloaded on the docks of Seville. Yet as contemporaries themselves recognized, "the new world that Spain had conquered was conquering Spain in turn." Lacking either rich agricultural or mineral resources, Spain desperately needed to develop industries and a balanced trading pattern as its rivals England and France were doing. But since the dominant Spanish nobility had prized ideals of chivalry over practical business ever since the medieval days when it was engaged in winning back Spanish territory from the Muslims, the Spanish governing class was only too glad to use American silver to buy manufactured goods from other parts of Europe in order to live in splendor and dedicate itself to military exploits. Thus bullion left the country as soon as it entered, virtually no industry was established, and when the influx of silver began to decline after 1600 the Spanish economy remained with nothing except increasing debts.

Nonetheless, the crown, dedicated to supporting the Counter-Reformation and maintaining Spain's international dominance, would not cease fighting abroad. Indeed, the entire Spanish budget remained on such a warlike footing that even in the relatively peaceful year of 1608 four million out of a total revenue of seven million ducats were paid for military expenditures. Thus when Spain became engaged in fighting France during the Thirty Years' War it fully overextended itself. The clearest visible sign of this was that in 1643 outnumbered French troops at Rocroi inflicted a stunning defeat on the famed Spanish infantry, the first time that a Spanish army had been overcome in battle since the reign of Ferdinand and Isabella. Yet worse still was the fact that by then two territories belonging to Spain's European empire were in open revolt.

In order to understand the causes of these revolts one must recognize that in the seventeenth century the real "nation of Spain" was Castile—all else was acquired territory. After the marriage of Isabella of Castile and Ferdinand of Aragon in 1469, geographically central Castile emerged as the dominant partner in the Spanish union, becoming even more dominant when Castile conquered the Muslim kingdom of Granada in southern Spain in 1492 and annexed Portugal in 1580. In the absence of any great financial hardships, semi-autonomous Catalonia (the most fiercely independent part of Aragon) endured Castilian hegemony. But in 1640, when the strains of warfare induced Castile to limit Catalonian liberties in order to raise more money and men for combat, Catalonia revolted. Immediately afterward the Portuguese learned of the Catalonian uprising and revolted as well, followed by southern Italians who revolted against Castilian viceroys in Naples and Sicily in 1647. At that point only the momentary inability of Spain's greatest external enemies, France and England, to take advantage of its plight saved the Spanish empire from utter collapse. Nothing if not determined, the Castilian government quickly put down the Italian revolts and by 1652 also brought Catalonia to heel. But

The Escorial. Philip II of Spain ordered the building between 1563 and 1584 of this somber retreat—part royal residence, part monastery—on an isolated spot, well removed from Madrid. Conceived on a grid-iron plan to honor the grid-iron martyrdom of St. Lawrence (on whose feast day Philip had won a decisive victory against the French), the Escorial symbolizes for many the Spanish crown's dedication to the ideals of the Counter-Reformation as well as its attempt to impose rationalized central government on the refractory outlying provinces of the Iberian Peninsula and Spanish Empire.

Portugal retained its independence forever, and by the Peace of the Pyrenees, signed with France in 1659, Spain in effect conceded that it would entirely abandon its ambitions of dominating Europe.

A comparison between the fortunes of Spain and France in the first half of the seventeenth century is highly instructive because some striking similarities existed between the two countries, but in the end differences turned out to be most decisive. Spain and France were of almost identical territorial extent and both countries had been created by the same process of accretion. Just as the Castilian crown had gained Aragon in the north, Granada in the south, and then Portugal, so the kingdom of France had grown by adding on such diverse territories as Languedoc, Dauphiné, Provence, Burgundy, and Brittany. Since the inhabitants of all these territories cherished traditions of local independence as much as the Catalans or Portuguese, and since the rulers of France, like those of Spain, were determined to govern their provinces ever more firmly—especially when the financial stringencies of the Thirty Years' War made ruthless tax collecting urgently necessary—a direct confrontation between the central government and the provinces in France became inevitable, just as in Spain. But France weathered the storm whereas Spain did not, a result largely attributable to France's greater wealth and the greater prestige of the French crown.

Spain and France compared

In good times most French people, including those from the outlying provinces, tended to revere their king. Certainly they had excellent reason to do so during the reign of Henry IV. Having established religious peace in 1598 by the Edict of Nantes, the affable Henry, who declared that there should be a chicken in every French family's pot each Sunday, set about to restore the prosperity of a country devastated by four decades of civil war. Fortunately France had enormous

The reign of Henry IV

Cardinal Richelieu. A contemporary portrait emphasizing the cardinal's awesome bearing.

Cardinal Richelieu

The Fronde

economic resiliency, owing primarily to its extremely rich and varied agricultural resources. Unlike Spain, which had to import food, France normally had been able to export it, and Henry's finance minister, the duke of Sully, quickly saw to it that France became a food exporter once more. Among other things, Sully distributed throughout the country free copies of a guide to recommended farming techniques and financed the rebuilding or new construction of roads, bridges, and canals to help expedite the flow of goods. In addition, Henry IV was not content to see France rest its economic development on agricultural wealth alone; instead he ordered the construction of royal factories to manufacture luxury goods such as crystal glass and tapestries, and he also supported the growth of silk, linen, and woolen cloth industries in many different parts of the country. Moreover, Henry's patronage allowed the explorer Champlain to claim parts of Canada as France's first foothold in the New World. Thus Henry IV's reign certainly must be counted as one of the most benevolent and progressive in all French history.

Far less benevolent was Henry's *de facto* successor as ruler of France, Cardinal Richelieu (1585–1642), yet Richelieu fully managed to maintain France's forward momentum. The cardinal, of course, was never the real king of France—the actual title was held from 1610 to 1643 by Henry IV's ineffectual son Louis XIII. But as first minister from 1624 to his death in 1642 Richelieu governed as he wished, and what he wished most of all was to enhance centralized royal power at home and expand French influence in the larger theater of Europe. Accordingly, when Huguenots rebelled against restrictions placed on them by the Edict of Nantes, Richelieu put them down with an iron fist and emended the Edict in 1629 by depriving them of all their military rights. Since his armed campaigns against the Huguenots had been very costly, the cardinal then moved to gain more income for the crown by abolishing the semi-autonomy of Burgundy, Dauphiné, and Provence so that he could introduce direct royal taxation in all three areas. Later, to make sure all taxes levied were efficiently collected, Richelieu instituted a new system of local government by royal officials known as *intendants* who were expressly commissioned to run roughshod over any provincial obstructionism. By these and related methods Richelieu made French government more centralized than ever and managed to double the crown's income during his rule. But since he also engaged in an ambitious foreign policy directed against the Habsburgs of Austria and Spain, resulting in France's costly involvement in the Thirty Years' War, internal pressures mounted in the years after Richelieu's death.

A reaction against French governmental centralization manifested itself in a series of revolts between 1648 and 1653 collectively known as "the slingshot tumults," or in French, the *Fronde*. By this time Louis XIII had been succeeded by his son Louis XIV, but because the latter was still a boy, France was governed by a regency consisting of Louis's mother Anne of Austria and her paramour Cardinal Mazarin. Considering that both were foreigners (Anne was a Habsburg and Mazarin originally an Italian adventurer named Giulio Mazarini), it is not surprising that many of their subjects, including some extremely powerful nobles, hated them. Moreover, nationwide resentments were greater still because the costs of war and several consecutive years of bad harvests had brought France temporarily into a grave economic plight. Thus when cliques of nobles expressed their disgust with Mazarin for primarily petty and self-interested reasons, they found much support throughout the country, and uncoordinated revolts against the regency flared on and off for several years.

France, however, was not Spain, and thus did not come close to falling apart. Above all, the French crown itself, which retained great reservoirs of prestige owing to a well-established national tradition and the undoubted achievements of Henry IV and Richelieu, was by no means under attack. On the contrary, neither the aristocratic leaders of the *Fronde* nor the commoners from all ranks who joined them in revolt claimed to be resisting the young king but only the alleged corruption and mismanagement of Mazarin. Some of the rebels, it is true, insisted that part of Mazarin's fault lay in his pursuance of Richelieu's centralizing, antiprovincial policy. But since most of the aristocrats who led the *Fronde* were merely "outs" who wanted to be "in," they often squabbled among themselves—sometimes even arranging agreements of convenience with the regency or striking alliances with France's enemy, Spain, for momentary gain—and proved completely unable to rally any unified support behind a common program. Thus when Louis XIV began to rule in his own name in 1651 and pretexts for revolting against "corrupt ministers" no longer existed, all opposition was soon silenced. As so often happens, the idealists and poor people paid the greatest price for revolt: in 1653 a defeated leader of popular resistance in Bordeaux was broken on a wheel and not long afterward a massive new round of taxation was proclaimed. Remembering the turbulence of the *Fronde* for the rest of his life, Louis XIV resolved never to let his aristocracy or his provinces get out of hand again and ruled as the most effective royal absolutist in all of French history.

French absolutism triumphant

Compared to the civil disturbances of the 1640s in Spain and France, those in England proved the most momentous in their results for the history of limited government. Whereas all that the revolts against Castile accomplished was the achievement of Portuguese independence and the crippling of an empire that was already in decline, and all that happened in France was a momentary interruption of the steady advance of royal power, in England a king was executed and barriers were erected against royal absolutism for all time.

The case of England

England around 1600 was caught up in a trend toward the growth of centralized royal authority characteristic of all western Europe. Not only had Henry VIII and Elizabeth I brought the English Church fully

*Henry VIII and
Elizabeth I increase royal
power*

James I. "The wisest fool in
Christendom."

*Causes of antagonism to
James I*

under royal control, but both monarchs employed so-called prerogative courts wherein they could proceed against subjects in disregard of traditional English legal safeguards for the rights of the accused. Furthermore, although Parliament met regularly during both reigns, members of Parliament were far less independent than they had been in the fifteenth century: any parliamentary representative who might have stood up to Henry VIII would have lost his head, and almost all parliamentarians were so charmed by Elizabeth that they were glad to do her bidding. Thus when the Stuart dynasty succeeded Elizabeth, the last of the Tudors, it was only natural that the Stuarts would try to increase royal power still more. And indeed they might have succeeded had it not been for their ineptness and an extraordinary combination of forces ranged against them.

Lines of contention were drawn immediately at the accession of Elizabeth's nearest relative, her cousin James VI of Scotland, who in 1603 retained his Scottish crown but also became king of England as James I (1603–1625). Homely but vain, addled but erudite, James fittingly was called by Henry IV of France "the wisest fool in Christendom," and presented the starkest contrast to his predecessor. Whereas Elizabeth knew how to gain her way with Parliament without making a fuss about it, the schoolmasterish foreigner insisted on lecturing parliamentarians that he was semi-divine and would brook no resistance: "As it is atheism and blasphemy to dispute what God can do, so it is presumption and high contempt in a subject to dispute what a king can do." Carrying these sentiments further, in a speech to Parliament of 1609 he proclaimed that "kings are not only God's lieutenants on earth . . . but even by God Himself they are called gods."

That such extreme pretentions to divine authority would arouse strong opposition was a result even James should have been able to foresee, for the English were still intensely committed to the theory of parliamentary controls on the crown. Yet not just theory was at stake since the specific policies of the new king antagonized large numbers of his subjects. For one, James insisted upon supplementing his income by modes of money-raising which had never been sanctioned by Parliament; and when the leaders of that body remonstrated, he angrily tore up their protests and dissolved their sessions. Worse, he interfered with the freedom of business by granting monopolies and lucrative privileges to favored companies. And, worst of all in the eyes of most patriotic Englishmen, James quickly put an end to the long war with Spain and refused thereafter to become involved in any foreign military entanglements. Today many of us might think that James's commitment to peace was his greatest virtue; certainly his pacifism was well advised financially since it spared the crown enormous debts. But in his own age James was hated particularly for his peace policy because it made him seem far too friendly with England's traditional enemy, Spain, and because "appeasement" meant leaving seemingly heroic Protestants in Holland and Germany in the lurch.

Although almost all English people (except for a small minority of clandestine Catholics) objected to James I's pacific foreign policy, those who hated it most were a group destined to play the greatest role in overthrowing the Stuarts, namely, the Puritans. Extremist Calvinistic Protestants, the Puritans believed that Elizabeth I's religious compromises had not broken fully enough with the forms and doctrines of Roman Catholicism. Called Puritans from their desire to "purify" the English Church of all traces of Catholic ritual and observance, they most vehemently opposed the English "episcopal system" of church government by bishops. But James I was as committed to retaining episcopalianism as the Puritans were intent on abolishing it because he viewed royally appointed bishops as one of the pillars of a strong monarchy: "No bishop, no king." Since the Puritans were the dominant party in the House of Commons and many Puritans were also prosperous businessmen who opposed James's monopolistic policies and money-raising expediencies, throughout his reign James remained at loggerheads with an extremely powerful group of his subjects for a combination of religious, constitutional, and economic reasons.

The Puritans

Nonetheless, James survived to die peacefully in bed in 1625, and had it not been for mistakes made by his son Charles I (1625–1649), England might have gone the way of absolutistic France. Charles held the same inflated notions of royal power and consequently was quickly at odds with the Puritan leaders of Parliament. Soon after his accession to the throne Charles became involved in a war with France and needed revenue desperately. When Parliament refused to make more than the customary grants, he resorted to forced loans from his subjects, punishing those who failed to comply by quartering soldiers in their homes or throwing them into prison without a trial. In reaction to this, Parliament forced the Petition of Right on the king in 1628. This document declared all taxes not voted by Parliament illegal, condemned the quartering of soldiers in private houses, and prohibited arbitrary imprisonment and the establishment of martial law in time of peace.

Charles I

Charles I. This portrait by Van Dyck vividly captures the ill-fated monarch's arrogance.

Angered rather than chastened by the Petition of Right, Charles I soon resolved to rule entirely without Parliament—and nearly succeeded. From 1629 to 1640 no Parliaments were called. During this "eleven-years' tyranny," Charles's government lived off a variety of makeshift dues and levies. For example, the crown sold monopolies at exorbitant rates, revived highly antiquated medieval financial claims, and admonished judges to collect the stiffest of fines. Though technically not illegal, all of these expedients were deeply resented. Most controversial was the collection of "ship money," a levy taken on the pretext of a medieval obligation of English seaboard towns to provide ships (or their worth in money) for the royal navy. Extending the payment of ship money from coastal towns to the whole country, Charles threatened to make it a regular tax in contravention of the Petition of Right, and was upheld in a legal challenge of 1637 brought against him on these grounds by the Puritan squire John Hampden.

By such means the king managed to make ends meet without the aid of taxes granted by Parliament. But he became ever more hated by most of his subjects, and above all the Puritans, not just because of his constitutional and financial policies but also because he seemed to be pursuing a course in religion that came much closer to Catholicism than to Calvinism. Whether the English Puritans would have risen up in revolt on their own is a moot question, but they were ultimately emboldened to do so by a chain of events beginning with a revolt in Scotland. The uprising in Scotland of 1640 against the policy of an English king was not unlike those in Catalonia and Portugal of the same year against the Spanish crown except that the Scottish rising was not just nationalistic but also explicitly religious in nature. Like his father, Charles believed in the adage "no bishop, no king" and hence foolhardily decided to introduce episcopalian church government into staunchly Presbyterian Scotland. The result was armed resistance by Charles's northern subjects and the first step toward civil war in England.

In order to obtain the funds necessary to punish the Scots, Charles had no other choice but to summon Parliament and soon found himself the target of pent-up resentments. Knowing full well that the king was helpless without money, the Puritan leaders of the House of Commons determined to take England's government into their own hands. Accordingly, they not only executed the king's first minister, the earl of Strafford, but they abolished ship money and the prerogative courts which ever since the reign of Henry VIII had served as instruments of arbitrary rule. Most significantly, they enacted a law forbidding the crown to dissolve Parliament and requiring the convening of sessions at least once every three years. After some indecision, early in 1642 Charles replied to these acts with a show of force. He marched with his guard into the House of Commons and attempted to arrest five of its leaders. All of them escaped, but an open conflict between crown and Parliament could no longer be avoided. Both parties collected troops and prepared for an appeal to the sword.

These events initiated the English Civil War, a conflict at once political and religious, which lasted from 1642 to 1649. Arrayed on the royal side were most of England's most prominent aristocrats and largest landowners, who were almost all "high-church" Anglicans. Opposed to them, the followers of Parliament included smaller landholders, tradesmen, and manufacturers, the majority of whom were Puritans. The members of the king's party were commonly known by the aristocratic name of Cavaliers. Their opponents, who cut their hair short in contempt for the fashionable custom of wearing curls, were derisively called Roundheads. At first the royalists, having obvious advantages of military experience, won most of the victories. In 1644, however, the parliamentary army was reorganized, and soon afterward the fortunes of battle shifted. The Cavalier forces were badly beaten, and in 1646 the king was compelled to surrender.

The struggle would now have ended had not a quarrel developed within the parliamentary party. The majority of its members, who had allied with the Presbyterian Scots, were ready to restore Charles to the throne as a limited monarch under an arrangement whereby a uniform Calvinistic Presbyterian faith would be imposed on both Scotland and England as the state religion. But a radical minority of Puritans, commonly known as Independents, distrusted Charles and insisted upon religious toleration for themselves and all other non-Presbyterian Protestants. Their leader was Oliver Cromwell (1599–1658), who had risen to command the Roundhead army. Taking advantage of the dissension within the ranks of his opponents, Charles renewed the war in 1648, but after a brief campaign was forced to surrender. Cromwell now resolved to end the life of "that man of blood," and, ejecting all the Presbyterians from Parliament by force of arms, obliged the remaining so-called Rump Parliament to vote an end to the monarchy. On 30 January 1649 Charles I was beheaded, a short time later the hereditary House of Lords was abolished, and England became a republic.

But founding a republic was far easier than maintaining one, and the new form of government, officially called a Commonwealth, did not last long. Technically the Rump Parliament continued as the legislative body, but Cromwell, with the army at his command, possessed the real power and soon became exasperated by the attempts of the legislators to perpetuate themselves in office and to profit from confiscating the wealth of their opponents. Accordingly, in 1653 he marched a detachment of troops into the Rump, and, saying "Come, I will put an end to your prating," ordered the members to disperse. Thereby the Commonwealth ceased to exist and was soon followed by the "Protectorate" or virtual dictatorship established under a constitution drafted by officers of the army. Called the Instrument of Government, this text was the nearest approximation of a written constitution England has ever had. Extensive powers were given to Cromwell as Lord Protector for life, and his office was made hereditary. At first a Parliament exercised limited authority in making laws and levying taxes, but in 1655 its members were abruptly dismissed by the Lord Protector. Thereafter the government became a thinly disguised autocracy, with Cromwell now wielding a sovereignty even more absolute then any the Stuart monarchs would have dared to claim.

Given the choice between a Puritan military dictatorship and the old royalist regime, when the occasion arose England unhesitatingly opted for the latter. Above all, years of Calvinistic austerities such as the prohibition of any public recreation on Sundays—then the workingperson's only holiday—had discredited the Puritans, making most people long for the milder Anglicanism of the original Elizabethan settlement. Thus not long after Cromwell's death in 1658, one of the deceased Protector's generals seized power and called for elections for a new Parliament which met in the spring of 1660 and proclaimed as

Oliver Cromwell

The Stuart Restoration

Cromwell Felling the Royal Oak of England. A Royalist print of 1656 which portrays Oliver Cromwell as a destructive villain.

king Charles I's exiled son, Charles II. With the reign of Charles II (1660–1685) Anglicanism was immediately restored, but by no means the same was true for untrammelled monarchical power. Rather, stating with characteristic good humor that he did not wish to "resume his travels," Charles agreed to respect Parliament and observe the Petition of Right. Of greatest constitutional significance was the fact that all the legislation passed by Parliament immediately before the outbreak of the Civil War, including the requirement to hold Parliaments at least once every three years, remained as law. Thus in striking contrast to absolutistic France, England became a limited monarchy. Putting its constitutional struggles behind it after one brief further test in the late seventeenth century, the realm of England would soon live up to the poet Milton's prediction of "a noble and puissant nation rousing herself like a strong man after sleep."

4. QUESTS FOR LIGHT OUT OF DARKNESS

Witchcraft and philosophy

Caught up in economic uncertainty, religious rivalries, and political turmoil, many Europeans between 1560 and 1660 understandably cast about for emotional or intellectual resolutions of their most pressing problems. Sometimes, as in the case of the great witchcraft delusion, this quest led merely to an intensification of hysteria. But in the case of more dispassionate reflections, the search for ways of resolving Europe's crises led to some of the most enduring statements of moral and political philosophy of all time.

Although no one simple explanation can be offered for the outbreak of western Europe's fearful witchcraft hysteria that reached its peak between 1580 and 1660, it is certain that persecutions of witches in those years were fiercest during times of greatest disaster and that people who burned witches genuinely thought they were fighting the powers of darkness. Looking for the origins of the great early-modern witchcraft delusion, historians recognize that peasant culture throughout the Middle Ages included belief in the possibilities of sorcery. In other words, most simple rural people assumed that certain unusual individuals could practice good, or "white," magic in the form of healing, divination for lost objects, and fortune-telling, or perhaps also evil, "black" magic that might, for example, call up tempests or ravage crops. Yet only in the later Middle Ages did learned authorities begin to insist on theological grounds that black magic could be practiced only as a result of pacts with the devil. Naturally, once this belief became accepted, judicial officers soon found it urgent to prosecute all "witches" who practiced black magic because warfare against the devil was paramount to Christian society and "the evil one" could not be allowed to hold any sway. Accordingly, as early as 1484 Pope Innocent VIII ordered papal inquisitors to root out alleged witchcraft with all the means at their disposal, and the pace of witch hunts gained momentum in the following decades. Nor were witch trials curtailed in areas that broke with Rome, for Protestant reformers believed in the insidious powers of Satan just as much as Catholics did. Indeed, Luther himself once threw an inkpot at a supposed apparition of the devil and Calvin saw Satan's evil workings wherever he looked. Thus both urged that alleged witches be tried more peremptorily and sen-

The origins of the witchcraft delusion

Supposed Witches Worshiping the Devil in the Form of a Billy-Goat. In the background other "witches" ride bareback on flying demons. This is one of the earliest visual conceptions of witchcraft, dating from around 1460.

tenced with less leniency than ordinary criminals, and persecutions of innocent people continued apace in Protestant as well as Catholic lands.

Yet the outbreak of a real mania for catching and killing "witches" did not begin until about 1580. Therefore it can only be supposed that the witchcraft hysteria was connected in some way with Europe's general crisis—all the more since it continued for about as long as the age of crisis itself and was most severe in just those localities where warfare or economic dislocation was most intense. In such places, whenever crops failed or cattle sickened people assumed that a "witch"—usually a defenseless old woman—was responsible, and rushed to put her to death. If not always old, the victims were most frequently women, no doubt in part because preachers had encouraged their flocks to believe that evil had first come into the world with Eve and in part because men in authority felt psychologically most ambivalent about members of the opposite sex. Pure sadism certainly cannot have been the original motive for such proceedings, but once trials began, horrendous sadism very often was unleashed. Thus old women, young girls, and sometimes even mere children might be brutally tortured by having needles driven under their nails, fires placed at their heels, or their legs crushed under weights until marrow spurted from their bones, in order to make them confess to having had filthy orgies with demons. The final death toll will never be known, but in the 1620s there was an average of one hundred burnings a year in the German cities of Würzburg and Bamberg, and around the same time it was said the town square of Wolfenbüttel "looked like a little forest, so crowded were the stakes."

Why persecution quickly ended in the years immediately after 1660 will remain a matter for scholarly speculation. Aside from the fact that better times returned to most of Europe around then, probably the best explanation is that shortly after 1660 educated magistrates began to adhere to a mechanistic view of the universe. In other words, once the leaders of society came to believe that storms and epidemics arose from natural rather than supernatural causes, they ceased to countenance witch hunts.

Burning of Witches at Dernberg in 1555. From a sixteenth-century German pamphlet denouncing witchcraft.

Fortunately, other attempts of Europeans between 1560 and 1660 to master the darkness around them were not in themselves so dark. Indeed, one of the most "enlightened" of all European moral philosophers was the Frenchman Michel de Montaigne (1533–1592), who wrote during the height of the French wars of religion. The son of a Catholic father and a Huguenot mother of Jewish ancestry, the well-to-do Montaigne retired from a legal career at the age of thirty-eight to devote himself to a life of leisured reflection. The *Essays* which resulted were a new literary form originally conceived as "experiments" in writing (French *essai* simply means "trial"). Because they are extraordinarily well written as well as being searchingly reflective, Montaigne's *Essays* ever since have ranked securely among the most enduring classics of French literature and thought.

Montaigne

Although the range of subjects of the *Essays* runs a wide gamut from "The Resemblance of Children to Their Fathers" to "The Art of Conversing," two main themes are dominant. One is a pervasive skepticism. Making his motto "Que sais-je?" (What do I know?), Montaigne decided that he knew very little for certain. According to him, "it is folly to measure truth and error by our own capacities" because our capacities are severely limited. Thus, as he maintained in one of his most famous essays, "On Cannibals," what may seem indisputably true and proper to one nation may seem absolutely false to another because "everyone gives the title of barbarism to everything that is not of his usage." From this Montaigne's second main principle followed—the need for tolerance. Since all people think they know the perfect religion and the perfect government, no religion or government is really perfect and consequently no belief worth fighting for to the death.

Montaigne's Essays:
skepticism and tolerance

If the foregoing description makes Montaigne sound surprisingly modern, it must be emphasized that he was by no means a rationalist. On the contrary, he believed that "reason does nothing but go astray in everything," and that intellectual curiosity "which prompts us to thrust our noses into everything" is a "scourge of the soul." Moreover, concerning practical affairs Montaigne was a fatalist who thought that in a world governed by unpredictable "fortune" the best human strategy is to face the good and the bad with steadfastness and dignity. Lest people begin to think too highly of their own abilities, he reminded them that "sit we upon the highest throne in the world, yet we do sit upon our own behinds." Nonetheless, despite his passive belief that "fortune, not wisdom, rules the life of mankind," the wide circulation of Montaigne's *Essays* did help combat fanaticism and religious intolerance in his own and subsequent ages.

Antirationalism and
fatalism

If Montaigne sought refuge from the trials of his age in skepticism, tolerance, and resigned dignity, his contemporary, the French lawyer Jean Bodin (1530–1596), looked for more light to come out of darkness from the powers of the state. Like Montaigne, Bodin was particularly troubled by the upheavals caused by the religious wars in

Jean Bodin

France—he had even witnessed the frightful St. Bartholomew's Day Massacre of 1572 in Paris. But instead of shrugging his shoulders about the bloodshed, he resolved to offer a political plan to make sure turbulence would cease. This he did in his monumental *Six Books on the Commonwealth* (1576), the earliest fully developed statement of governmental absolutism in Western political thought. According to Bodin, the state arises from the needs of collections of families, but once constituted should brook no opposition, for the maintenance of order is paramount. Whereas writers on law and politics before him had groped toward a theory of governmental sovereignty, Bodin was the first to offer a succinct definition; for him, sovereignty was "the most high, absolute, and perpetual power over all subjects," consisting principally in the power "to give laws to subjects without their consent." Although Bodin acknowledged the theoretical possibility of government by aristocracy or democracy, he assumed that the nation-states of his day would be ruled by monarchs and insisted that such monarchs could in no way be limited, either by legislative or judicial bodies, or even by laws made by their predecessors or themselves. Expressing the sharpest opposition to contemporary Huguenots who were saying (in contravention of the original teachings of Luther and Calvin) that subjects had a right to resist "ungodly princes," Bodin maintained that a subject must trust in his ruler's "mere and frank good will." Even if the ruler proved a tyrant, Bodin insisted that the subject had no warrant to resist, for any resistance would open the door "to a licentious anarchy which is worse than the harshest tyranny in the world." Since in his own day Bodin knew much "licentious anarchy" but had hardly any notion of how harsh the "harshest tyranny" could be, his position is somewhat understandable. Yet in the next century his *Commonwealth* would become the point of departure for justifications of an increasingly oppressive French royal absolutism.

Quite understandably, just as the French civil wars of the sixteenth century provoked a variety of responses, so did the English Civil War of the seventeenth. Drawing on a tradition of resistance to untrammelled state power expressed by French Huguenots and earlier English parliamentarians and Puritans, the great English Puritan poet John Milton enunciated a stirring defense of freedom of the press in his *Areopagitica* (1644). Similarly bold upholders of libertarianism were a party of Milton's Puritan contemporaries known as Levellers, the first exponents of democracy since Greek times. Organizing themselves as a pressure group within Cromwell's army in the later 1640s when Charles I's monarchy seemed clearly doomed, the Levellers—who derived their name from their advocacy of equal political rights for all classes—agitated in favor of a parliamentary republic based on nearly universal manhood suffrage. For them, servants and other wage-laborers had no right to vote because they formed part of their employer's "family" and allegedly were represented by the family head. More-

John Milton and the Levellers

over, the Levellers did not even deign to argue about women's rights. Otherwise, however, in the immortal words of one of their spokesmen, they argued that "the poorest He that is in England hath a life to live as the greatest He, and therefore . . . every man that is to live under a government ought first by his own consent to put himself under that government." But since Oliver Cromwell, who believed that the only grounds for suffrage was sufficient property, would have none of this, once Cromwell assumed virtually dictatorial powers the Leveller party disintegrated. More radical still were the communistic Diggers, so called from their attempts to cultivate common lands in 1649. Claiming to be "true Levellers," the Diggers argued that true freedom lies not in votes, but "where a man receives his nourishment," and hence argued for the redistribution of property. Cromwell, however, dispersed them quickly and thus the Diggers have merely historical interest as vanguards of movements to come.

Far to the other extreme of the libertarian Puritans was the political philosopher Thomas Hobbes (1588–1679), whose reactions to the English Civil War led him to become the most forceful advocate of unrestrained state power of all time. Like Bodin, who was moved by the events of St. Bartholomew's Day to formulate a doctrine of political absolutism, Hobbes was moved by the turmoil of the English Civil War to do the same in his classic of political theory entitled *Leviathan* (1651). Yet Hobbes differed from Bodin in several respects. For one, whereas Bodin assumed that the absolute sovereign power would be a royal monarch, the more radical Hobbes, writing without any respect for tradition in Cromwell's England two years after the beheading of a king, thought the sovereign could be any ruthless dictator whatsoever. Then too, whereas Bodin defined his state as "the lawful government of families" and hence did not believe that the state could abridge private property rights because families could not exist without property, Hobbes's state existed to rule over atomistic individuals and thus was licensed to trample over both liberty and property.

The Title Page of Hobbes's Leviathan

But the most fundamental difference between Bodin and Hobbes lay in the latter's uncompromisingly pessimistic view of human nature. Whereas Bodin was pessimistic about mankind only by implication, Hobbes posited that the "state of nature" which existed before civil government came into being was a condition of "war of all against all." For Hobbes, since man naturally behaves as "a wolf" toward man, and hence increasing fear of violent death in the state of nature made human life "solitary, poor, nasty, brutish, and short," people for their own good at some purely theoretical point in time surrendered their liberties to a sovereign ruler in exchange for his agreement to keep the peace. Having thus granted away their liberties, subjects have no right whatsoever to seek them back, and the sovereign can tyrannize as he likes—free to oppress his charges in any way other than to kill them, an act which would negate the very purpose of his

Hobbes's pessimism

rule. It is a measure of the relentless logic and clarity of Hobbes's abstract exposition that his *Leviathan* is widely regarded as one of the four or five greatest political treatises ever written, for practically nobody really likes what he says. Indeed, even in his own age Hobbes's views were vastly unpopular—libertarians detested them for obvious reasons, and royalists hated them as much because Hobbes was contemptuous of dynastic claims based on blood lineage and rationalized absolutistic rule not on the grounds of powers granted from God, as most royalists did, but on powers surrendered by society. Yet because many important thinkers felt compelled to argue against Hobbes, he had enormous influence, if only in provoking the responses of others.

Perhaps fittingly, the most moving and in certain ways most modern attempt to bring light out of pervasive darkness was that of the seventeenth-century French moral and religious philosopher Blaise Pascal (1623–1662). In certain superficial ways Pascal's most enduring legacy, his *Pensées* (*Thoughts*), resemble Montaigne's *Essays* because both are highly introspective collections of informal short pieces written with great literary power. But Pascal, who turned away in a conversion experience from scientific rationalism to become a firm adherent of Jansenism (the most puritanical wing of French Catholicism), was as ardent a religious believer as Montaigne was a cool skeptic. Thus while Pascal agreed with Montaigne that human life on earth was fraught with peril—he defined man as "a thinking reed"—he had no doubt that a just Providence ruled the world and he believed as firmly as did Luther or Calvin that faith alone could show the way to salvation. Yet, recognizing that skeptics or secular rationalists could never be brought to the true faith by dogmatic authority, he hoped to convert doubters by appealing simultaneously to their intellects and their emotions in a major defense of Christianity. Unfortunately, premature death prevented him from accomplishing this ambitious goal, but the *Pensées* survive as previews of his approach. In these he conceded his own sense of terror and anguish in the face of evil and eternity, but made the awe itself a sign of the existence of God. Individuals today will be moved by Pascal's *Pensées* in varying degrees according to their own convictions, but few people of any persuasion will dispute Pascal's famous paradox that "man knows he is wretched; he is therefore wretched because he is so; but he is very great because he knows it."

Blaise Pascal

5. LITERATURE AND THE ARTS

*Major statements
concerning the human
condition*

The combined wretchedness and greatness of humanity may be taken as the theme for the extraordinary profusion of towering works of literature and art produced during western Europe's period of crisis from 1560 to 1660. Of course not every single writing or painting of the era expressed the same message. During a hundred years of extraordinary literary and artistic creativity, works of all genres and sentiments were produced, ranging from the frothiest farces to the darkest tragedies, the serenest still lifes to the most grotesque scenes of religious martyrdom. Nonetheless, the greatest writers and painters of the period all were moved by a realization of the ambiguities and ironies of human existence not unlike that expressed in different ways by Montaigne and Pascal. They all were fully aware of the horrors of war and human suffering so rampant in their day, and all were directly or indirectly aware of the Protestant conviction that men are "vessels of iniquity"; but they also inherited a large degree of Renaissance affirmativeness, and most of them accordingly preferred to view life on earth as a great dare.

Cervantes

From the host of remarkable writers who flourished during what was probably the most extraordinary century in the entire history of western European poetry and drama, we may take the very greatest: Cervantes, the Elizabethan dramatists—Shakespeare to the fore—and John Milton. Although Miguel de Cervantes (1547–1616) was not strictly speaking either a poet or a dramatist, his masterpiece, the satirical romance *Don Quixote,* exudes great lyricism and drama. The plot recounts the adventures of a Spanish gentleman, Don Quixote of La Mancha, who has become slightly unbalanced by constant reading of chivalric epics. His mind filled with all kinds of fantastic adventures, he sets out at the age of fifty upon the slippery road of knight-errantry, imagining windmills to be glowering giants and flocks of sheep to be armies of infidels whom it is his duty to rout with his spear. In his distorted fancy he mistakes inns for castles and serving girls for courtly ladies on fire with love. Set off in contrast to the "knight-errant" is the figure of his faithful squire, Sancho Panza. The latter represents the ideal of the practical man, with his feet on the ground and content with the modest but substantial pleasures of eating, drinking, and sleeping. Yet Cervantes clearly does not wish to say that the realism of a Sancho Panza is categorically preferable to the "quixotic" idealism of his master. Rather, the two men represent different facets of human nature. Without any doubt, *Don Quixote* is a devastating satire on the anachronistic chivalric mentality that would soon help hasten Spain's decline. But for all that, the reader's sympathies remain with the protagonist, the man from La Mancha who dares to "dream the impossible dream."

Miguel de Cervantes

Directly contemporaneous with Cervantes were the English Elizabethan dramatists who collectively produced the most glorious age of theater known in the Western world. Writing after England's victory over the Spanish Armada, when national pride was at a peak, all exhibited great exuberance but none was by any means a facile optimist. In fact a strain of reflective seriousness pervades all their best works, and a few, like the tragedian John Webster (c. 1580–c. 1625), who "saw the skull beneath the skin," were if anything morbid pessimists. Literary critics tend to agree that of a bevy of great Elizabe-

Elizabethan drama

than playwrights the most outstanding were Christopher Marlowe (1564–1593), Ben Jonson (c. 1573–1637), and, of course, William Shakespeare (1564–1616). Of the three, the fiery Marlowe, whose life was cut short in a tavern brawl before he reached the age of thirty, was the most youthfully energetic. In plays such as *Tamburlaine* and *Doctor Faustus* Marlowe created larger-than-life heroes who seek and come close to conquering everything in their path and feeling every possible sensation. But they meet unhappy ends because, for all his vitality, Marlowe knew that there are limits on human striving, and that wretchedness as well as greatness lies in the human lot. Thus though Faustus asks a reincarnated Helen of Troy, conjured up by Satan, to make him "immortal with a kiss," he dies and is damned in the end because immortality is not awarded by the devil or found in earthly kisses. In contrast to the heroic tragedian Marlowe, Ben Jonson wrote corrosive comedies which expose human vices and foibles. In the particularly bleak *Volpone* Jonson shows people behaving like deceitful and lustful animals, but in the later *Alchemist* he balances an attack on quackery and gullibility with admiration for resourceful lower-class characters who cleverly take advantage of their supposed betters.

William Shakespeare

Incomparably the greatest of the Elizabethan dramatists, William Shakespeare, was born into the family of a tradesman in the provincial town of Stratford-on-Avon. His life is enshrouded in more mists of obscurity than the careers of most other great people. It is known that he left his native village, having gained little formal education, when he was about twenty, and that he drifted to London to find employment in the theater. How he eventually became an actor and still later a writer of plays is uncertain, but by the age of twenty-eight he had definitely acquired a reputation as an author sufficient to excite the jealousy of his rivals. Before he retired to his native Stratford about 1610 to spend the rest of his days in ease, he had written or collaborated in writing nearly forty plays, over and above 150 sonnets and two long narrative poems.

Shakespeare's three periods: (1) confidence

As everyone knows, Shakespeare's plays rank as a kind of secular Bible wherever the English language is spoken. The reasons lie not only in the author's unrivaled gift of expression, and in his scintillating wit, but most of all in his profound analysis of human character seized by passion and tried by fate. Shakespeare's dramas fall rather naturally into three groups. Those written during the playwright's earlier years are characterized by a sense of confidence. They include a number of history plays, which recount England's struggles and glories leading up to the triumph of the Tudor dynasty; the lyrical romantic tragedy *Romeo and Juliet;* and a wide variety of comedies including the magical *Midsummer Night's Dream* and Shakespeare's greatest creations in the comic vein—*Twelfth Night, As You Like It,* and *Much Ado about Nothing.* Despite the last-named title, few even of the plays of Shakespeare's early, lightest period are "much ado about nothing." Rather, most explore with wisdom as well as wit fundamental problems of psychological identity, honor and ambition, love and friendship. Occasionally they also contain touches of deep seriousness, as in *As You Like It,* when Shakespeare has a character pause to reflect that "all the world's a stage, and all the men and women merely players" who pass through seven "acts" or stages of life.

Such touches, however, never obscure the restrained optimism of Shakespeare's first period, whereas the plays from his second period are far darker in mood. Apparently around 1601 Shakespeare underwent a crisis during which he began to distrust human nature profoundly and indict the whole scheme of the universe. The result was a group of dramas characterized by bitterness, frequent pathos, and a troubled searching into the mysteries of things. The series begins with the tragedy of indecisive idealism represented by *Hamlet,* goes on to the cynicism of *Measure for Measure* and *All's Well That Ends Well,* and culminates in the cosmic tragedies of *Macbeth* and *King Lear,* wherein characters assert that "life's but a walking shadow . . . a tale told by an idiot, full of sound and fury signifying nothing," and that "as flies to wanton boys are we to the gods; they kill us for their sport." Despite all this gloom, however, the plays of Shakespeare's second period generally contain the dramatist's greatest flights of poetic grandeur.

(2) crisis

Although *Macbeth* and *Lear* suggest an author in the throes of deep depression, Shakespeare managed to resolve his personal crisis and end his dramatic career with a third period characterized by a profound spirit of reconciliation. Of the three plays (all idyllic romances) written during this final period, the last, *The Tempest,* is the greatest.

(3) reconciliation

Mr. WILLIAM
SHAKESPEARES
COMEDIES,
HISTORIES, &
TRAGEDIES.

Publiſhed according to the True Originall Copies.

William Shakespeare. Portrait made for the First Folio edition of his works, 1623.

John Milton. From the First Edition of his poems, 1645.

Here ancient animosities are buried and wrongs are righted by a combination of natural and supernatural means, and a wide-eyed, youthful heroine rejoices on first seeing men with the words "O brave new world, that has such people in it!" Here, then, Shakespeare seems to be saying that for all humanity's trials life is not so unrelentingly bitter after all, and the divine plan of the universe is somehow benevolent and just.

Though less versatile than Shakespeare, not far behind him in eloquent grandeur stands the Puritan poet John Milton (1608–1674). The leading publicist of Oliver Cromwell's regime, Milton wrote the official defense of the beheading of Charles I as well as a number of treatises justifying Puritan positions in contemporary affairs. But he was also a man full of contradictions who loved the Greek and Latin classics at least as much as the Bible. Hence he could write a perfect pastoral elegy, *Lycidas,* mourning the loss of a dear friend in purely classical terms. Later, when forced into retirement by the accession of Charles II, Milton, though now blind, embarked on writing a classical epic, *Paradise Lost,* out of material found in Genesis concerning the creation of the world and the fall of man. This magnificent poem, which links the classical tradition to Christianity more successfully than any literary work written before or since, is surely one of the greatest epics of all time. Setting out to "justify the ways of God to man," Milton in *Paradise Lost* first plays "devil's advocate" by creating the compelling character of Satan, who defies God with boldness and subtlety. But Satan is more than counterbalanced in the end by the real "epic hero" of *Paradise Lost,* Adam, who learns to accept the human lot of moral responsibility and suffering, and is last seen leaving Paradise with Eve, the world "all before them."

The ironies and tensions inherent in human existence also were portrayed with extraordinary eloquence and profundity by several immortal masters of the visual arts who flourished between 1560 and 1660. The dominant style in painting in Italy and Spain in the second half of the sixteenth century was Mannerism. Originally a term of opprobrium for alleged imitators—supposedly second-rate artists who painted in the "manner" of Michelangelo's late phase—the term *Mannerism* in current analysis has come to mean much more than that; indeed art historians now rank some Mannerist painters among the West's greatest masters. Unquestionably Mannerism did take as its point of departure Michelangelo's tendency toward anticlassicism and distortion of nature for emotional effects, but Mannerist painters went so much further in emphasizing restlessness, imbalance, and distortion that they left Michelangelo far behind. Admittedly many of them lacked skill and depth of vision, contenting themselves with portraying brawn instead of muscle, melodrama instead of drama. But some others fully succeeded in balancing great artistic virtuosity with the communication of radiant inner light.

*Italian and Spanish
Mannerism*

Of the latter, the two most outstanding are the Venetian Tintoretto (1518–1594) and the Spaniard El Greco (c. 1541–1614). Combining Manneristic distortion and restlessness with a traditionally Venetian taste for rich color, Tintoretto produced an enormous number of monumentally large canvases devoted to religious themes that still inspire awe with their broodingly shimmering light and gripping theatricality. More emotional still is the work of Tintoretto's disciple, El Greco. Born Domenikos Theotokopoulos on the Greek island of Crete, this extraordinary painter absorbed some of the stylized elongation characteristic of Greco-Byzantine icon painting before traveling to Italy to learn from great contemporary Mannerist painters such as Tintoretto and then finally settling in Spain, where he was nicknamed "El Greco"—Spanish for "the Greek." El Greco's paintings were too bizarre to be greatly appreciated in his own age, and even now they often appear so unbalanced as to seem the work of one almost deranged. Yet such a view slights El Greco's deeply mystical Catholic fervor as well as his technical achievements. Best known today is his transfigured landscape, the *View of Toledo,* with its somber but awesome light breaking where no sun shines, but equally inspiring are his swirling religious allegories such as *The Burial of the Count of Orgaz* (thought by the painter to be his masterpiece), and his myriad stunning portraits in which gaunt, dignified Spaniards radiate a rare blend of austerity and spiritual insight.

The dominant artistic school of southern Europe succeeding Mannerism was that of the Baroque, a school not just of painting but of sculpture and architecture lasting from about 1600 until the early eighteenth century. The term *Baroque* is derived from a Portuguese word for an irregular, rough pearl, and this reveals much about its meaning.

Fray Felix Hortensio Paravicino, by El Greco. More restrained in composition than most of the artist's other work, this portrait nonetheless communicates a sense of deep spiritual intensity.

See color plates following page 512 for the *Crucifixion* by Tintoretto and the *View of Toledo* by El Greco

The Laocoön, by El Greco. An extreme example of Manneristic stress on restlessness and distortion. Note that the Spanish painter here drew for inspiration on the famous Hellenistic sculpture group shown on p. 158.

The Church of S. Carlo alle Quattro Fontane, Rome. Built by Bernini's contemporary Francesco Borromini in 1665, the facade of S. Carlo well exemplifies the frontage "in depth" characteristic of Baroque architecture.

Picking up where Mannerism left off, the Baroque style emphasized the emotional, the antinaturalistic, and the swirling as much as Mannerism, but Baroque works of art characteristically were less shrouded by somber mystery and were far more affirmative than Manneristic paintings. One major explanation for this is that Baroque art in all genres was usually semi-propagandistic. Originating in Rome as an expression of the ideals of the Counter-Reformation papacy and the Jesuit order, Baroque architecture in particular aimed to gain adherence for a specific worldview. Similarly, Baroque painting often was done in the service of the Counter-Reformation Church, which at its high tide around 1620 seemed everywhere to be on the offensive, and when Baroque painters were not celebrating Counter-Reformation ideals, most of them worked in the service of monarchs who sought their own glorification.

Indubitably the most imaginative and influential figure of the original Roman Baroque was the architect and sculptor Gianlorenzo Bernini (1598–1680), a frequent employee of the papacy who created one of the most magnificent celebrations of papal grandeur in the sweeping colonnades leading up to St. Peter's basilica. Breaking with the serene Renaissance classicism of Palladio, Bernini's architecture retained the use of classical elements such as columns and domes, but combined them in ways meant to express both aggresssive restlessness and great power. In addition Bernini was one of the first to experiment with church facades built "in depth"—building frontages, that is, not conceived as continuous surfaces but which jutted out at odd angles

Left: *David,* by Bernini. Whereas the earlier conceptions of David by the Renaissance sculptors Donatello and Michelangelo were reposeful (see pp. 429 and 430), the Baroque sculptor Bernini chose to portray his young hero at the peak of physical exertion. Right: *St. Theresa in Ecstasy,* by Bernini. As David is seen at the peak of bodily exertion, St. Theresa is shown at the peak of spiritual transport.

The Surrender of Breda, by Velásquez. Celebrating a Spanish victory over the Dutch in an early phase of the Thirty Years' War, the Spanish lances point proudly skyward in contrast to the desolate Dutch smoke, but the Spanish commander displays magnanimity for the defeated enemy.

and seemingly invaded the open space in front of them. If the purpose of these innovations was to stir the viewer and draw him emotionally into the ambit of the work of art, the same may be said for Bernini's aims in sculpture. Harking back to the restless motion of Hellenistic statuary—particularly the Laocoön group—and building on tendencies already present in the later sculpture of Michelangelo, Bernini's statuary emphasizes drama and incites the viewer to respond to it rather than serenely observe.

Since most Italian Baroque painters lacked Bernini's artistic genius, to view the very greatest masterpieces of southern European Baroque painting one must look to Spain and the work of Diego Velásquez (1599–1660). Unlike Bernini, Velásquez, a court painter in Madrid just when Spain hung on the brink of ruin, was not an entirely typical exponent of the Baroque style. Certainly many of his canvases display a characteristically Baroque delight in motion, drama, and power, but Velásquez's best work is characterized by a more restrained thoughtfulness than usually found in the Baroque. Thus his famous *Surrender at Breda* shows muscular horses and splendid Spanish grandees on the one hand, but un-Baroque humane and deep sympathy for defeated, disarrayed troops on the other. Moreover, Velásquez's single greatest painting, *The Maids of Honor,* done around 1656 after Spain's collapse, radiates thoughtfulness rather than drama and is one of the most probing artistic examinations of illusion and reality ever executed.

Southern Europe's main northern rival for artistic laurels in the "iron century" was the Netherlands, where three extremely dissimilar painters all explored the theme of the greatness and wretchedness of

See color plates following page 512 for the *Maids of Honor* and *Pope Innocent X* by Velásquez

A Dwarf, by Velásquez. The great Spanish artist had an enduring fascination with the less favored of the earth.

*Painting in the
Netherlands: (1) Peter
Brueghel*

See color plates facing
page 449 for the
Harvesters by Brueghel

man to the fullest. The earliest, Peter Brueghel (rhymes with frugal)
(c. 1525–1569), worked in a vein related to earlier Netherlandish realism. But unlike his predecessors, who favored quiet urban scenes
Brueghel exulted in portraying the busy, elemental life of the peasantry. Most famous in this respect are his rollicking *Peasant Wedding*
and *Peasant Wedding Dance,* and his spacious *Harvesters,* in which guz-
zling and snoring fieldhands are taking a well-deserved break from
their heavy labors under the noon sun. Such vistas give the impression
of uninterrupted rhythms of life, but late in his career Brueghel became
appalled by the intolerance and bloodshed he witnessed during the
time of the Calvinist riots and the Spanish repression in the Netherlands and expressed his criticism in an understated yet searing manner
In *The Blind Leading the Blind,* for example, we see what happens when
ignorant fanatics start showing the way to each other. More powerfu
still is Brueghel's *Massacre of the Innocents,* which from a distance look
like a snug scene of a Flemish village buried in snow. In fact, however
heartless soldiers are methodically breaking into homes and slaughtering babies, the simple peasant folk are fully at their mercy, and the
artist—alluding to a Gospel forgotten by warring Catholics and Protestants alike—seems to be saying "as it happened in the time of Christ
so it happens now."

Vastly different from Brueghel was the Netherlandish Baroque
painter Peter Paul Rubens (1577–1640). Since the Baroque, unlike

The Massacre of the Innocents. This painting by Brueghel shows how effectively
art can be used as a means of social commentary. Many art historians believe
that Brueghel was tacitly depicting the suffering of the Netherlands at the
hands of the Spanish in his own day.

The Triumph of the Eucharist, by Rubens. A typical Baroque work, this painting proclaims the victory of the Cross and the Eucharistic Chalice, symbols of Counter-Reformation Catholicism.

Mannerism, was an international movement closely linked to the spread of the Counter-Reformation, it should offer no surprise that Baroque style was extremely well represented in just that part of the Netherlands which, after long warfare, had been retained by Spain. In fact, Rubens of Antwerp was a far more typical Baroque artist than Velásquez of Madrid, painting literally thousands of robust canvases that glorified resurgent Catholicism or exalted second-rate aristocrats by portraying them as epic heroes dressed in bearskins. Even when Rubens's intent was not overtly propagandistic he customarily revelled in the sumptuous extravagance of the Baroque manner, being perhaps most famous today for the pink and rounded flesh of his well-nourished nudes. But unlike a host of lesser Baroque artists, Rubens was not entirely lacking in subtlety and was a man of many moods. His gentle portrait of his son Nicholas catches unaffected childhood in a moment of repose, and though throughout most of his career Rubens had celebrated martial valor, his late *Horrors of War* movingly portrays what he himself called "the grief of unfortunate Europe, which, for so many years now, has suffered plunder, outrage, and misery."

In some ways a blend of Brueghel and Rubens, the greatest of all Netherlandish painters, Rembrandt van Rijn (1606–1669), defies all attempts at facile characterization. Living across the border from the Spanish Netherlands in staunchly Calvinistic Holland, Rembrandt belonged to a society which was too austere to tolerate the unbuckled realism of a Brueghel or the fleshy Baroque pomposity of a Rubens. Yet Rembrandt managed to put both realistic and Baroque traits to new uses. In his early career he gained fame and fortune as the painter of biblical scenes which lacked the Baroque's fleshiness but retained its grandeur in their swirling forms and stunning experiments with

(2) Peter Paul Rubens

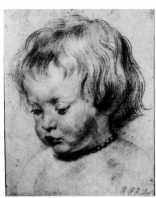

Rubens's Portrait of his Son Nicholas.

See color plates following page 512 for the *Horrors of War* and *England and Scotland Crowning Charles I* by Rubens

The Polish Rider, by Rembrandt. Unlike Titian's equestrian Charles V (above, p. 509), Rembrandt's rider is self-reflective and hence more humane.

(3) Rembrandt

See color plates following page 512 for *Aristotle Contemplating the Bust of Homer* by Rembrandt

light. In this early period too Rembrandt was active as a realistic portrait painter who knew how to flatter his self-satisfied subjects by emphasizing their Calvinistic steadfastness, to the great advantage of his purse. But gradually his prosperity faded, apparently in part because he grew tired of flattering and definitely because he made some bad investments. Since personal tragedies also mounted in the painter's middle and declining years his art inevitably became far more pensive and sombre, but it gained in dignity, subtle lyricism, and awesome mystery. Thus his later portraits, including those of himself, are imbued with introspective qualities and a suggestion that only the half is being told. Equally moving are explicitly philosophical paintings such as *Aristotle Contemplating the Bust of Homer,* in which the supposedly earthbound philosopher seems spellbound by the otherworldy luminous radiance of the epic poet, and the *The Polish Rider,* in which realistic and Baroque elements merge into a higher synthesis portraying a pensive young man setting out fearlessly into a perilous world. Like Shakespeare, Rembrandt knew that life's journey is full of perils, but his most mature paintings suggest that these can be mastered with poetry and courage.

SELECTED READINGS

• Items so designated are available in paperback editions.
• Ashton, Robert, *The English Civil War: Conservatism and Revolution, 1603–1649,* New York, 1978. A highly scholarly account: very informative, but not for beginners.

Aston, T., ed., *Crisis in Europe: 1560–1660,* London, 1965. A collection of highly valuable essays.

• Braudel, F., *The Mediterranean and the Mediterranean World in the Age of Philip II,* New York, 1972. One of the most brilliant history books of our age. Treats life in the Mediterranean regions in the second half of the sixteenth century with particular emphasis on how geography determines the course of human history.

• Chute, M., *Shakespeare of London,* New York, 1949. The best popular biography.

• Dean, Leonard F., ed., *Shakespeare: Modern Essays in Criticism,* New York, 1957. A variety of scholarly appraisals.

• Dunn, Richard S., *The Age of Religious Wars, 1559–1715,* 2nd ed., New York, 1979. The best college-level text on this period. Extremely well written.

• Elliot, J. H., *Imperial Spain, 1469–1716,* London, 1963. A masterpiece of sophisticated synthesis.

• ———, *Europe Divided: 1559–1598,* London, 1968. An extremely lucid narrative of complex events.

• Elton, G. R., *England under the Tudors,* 2nd ed., London, 1977. Engagingly written and authoritative.

• Ford, Boris, ed., *The Age of Shakespeare,* Baltimore, 1955. A good shorter handbook.

Frame, D., *Montaigne: A Biography,* New York, 1965. By far the best study in English.

Fraser, Lady Antonia, *Oliver Cromwell,* London, 1973. A popular biography.

Held, J. S., and D. Posner, *17th and 18th Century Art: Baroque Painting, Sculpture, Architecture,* New York, 1979. The most complete introductory review of the subject in English.

• Hibbard, Howard, *Bernini,* Baltimore, 1965. The basic study in English of this central figure of Baroque artistic activity.

• Hill, Christopher, *A Century of Revolution: 1603–1714,* 2nd ed., New York, 1982. A valuable survey of English developments that holds narrative to a minimum and stresses economic and social trends.

• Kahr, M. M., *Velázquez: The Art of Painting,* New York, 1976.

Kamen, Henry, *The Iron Century: Social Change in Europe, 1559–1660,* New York, 1971. One of the most detailed and persuasive statements of the view that there was a "general crisis" in many different aspects of European life.

Le Roy Ladurie, E., *Carnival in Romans,* New York, 1979. A closeup view of social turmoil in France in 1580.

• Mattingly, Garrett, *The Armada,* Boston, 1959. Fascinating narrative; thoroughly reliable but reads like a novel.

• Monter, E. W., ed., *European Witchcraft,* New York, 1969. Selected readings with fine introductions by one of the world's leading experts.

Parker, Geoffrey, *The Dutch Revolution,* Ithaca, N.Y., 1977. Now the standard survey in English on the revolt of the Netherlands.

• ———, *Europe in Crisis: 1598–1648,* Brighton, Sussex, 1980. A primarily political narrative of war and revolution in Europe exclusive of England.

• Pennington, D. H., *Seventeenth-Century Europe,* London, 1970. An extremely thorough and reliable survey that follows the conventional periodization of treating a century bounded by the round numbers 1600 and 1700.

Pierson, Peter, *Philip II of Spain,* London, 1975. An absorbing attempt to study Philip's personality and actions in terms of the dominant assumptions of his age.

• Rabb, T. K., *The Struggle for Stability in Early Modern Europe,* New York, 1975. A stimulating essay arguing for a shift from crisis to stability around 1660.

Roots, Ivan, ed., *Cromwell, A Profile,* New York, 1973. A collection of readings on problems in interpretation; complements Fraser.

• Rosenberg, Jakob, *Rembrandt, Life and Work,* London, 1964.

• Russell, Conrad, *The Crisis of Parliaments: English History, 1509–1660,* New York, 1971. The best survey covering this broad range of time.

• Shearman, John, *Mannerism,* Baltimore, 1967. Treats trends in late-sixteenth-century architecture and sculpture as well as Manneristic painting.

• Steinberg, S. H., *The Thirty Years' War and the Conflict for European Hegemony, 1600–1660,* New York, 1966. The best scholarly account.

• Stone, Lawrence, *The Causes of the English Revolution, 1529–1642,* New York, 1972. A judicious analysis by one of the foremost social historians of our age.

• Thomas, Keith, *Religion and the Decline of Magic,* London, 1971. A marvelously insightful study of popular belief in England.

• Trevor-Roper, H. R., *The Crisis of the Seventeenth Century: Religion, the Reformation and Social Change,* New York, 1968. A collection of path-breaking essays including one on the witch craze.

• Walzer, Michael, *The Revolution of the Saints: A Study in the Origins of Radical Politics,* Cambridge, Mass., 1965. An attempt by a political scientist to demonstrate that English Puritanism was the earliest form of modern political radicalism.

• Wedgwood, C. V., *William the Silent,* London, 1944. A laudatory and urbanely written biography.

———, *Richelieu and the French Monarchy,* New York, 1950. A somewhat slight but still useful introduction.

SOURCE MATERIALS

• Cervantes, Miguel de, *Don Quixote,* tr. Walter Starkie, New York, 1957.

Hobbes, Thomas, *Leviathan,* abridged by F. B. Randall, New York, 1964.

Montaigne, Michel de, *Essays,* tr. J. M. Cohen, Baltimore, 1958.

Pascal, Blaise, *Pensées,* French-English ed., H. F. Stewart, London, 1950.

Sprenger, Jakob, and H. Kramer, *The Malleus Maleficarum,* tr. M. Summers, 2nd ed., London, 1948. A frightful yet fascinating work, the *Malleus* ("The Hammer of Witches") was the most frequently used handbook of early-modern witchcraft prosecutors.

Chapter 17

THE ECONOMY AND SOCIETY
OF EARLY-MODERN EUROPE

We ought to esteem and cherish those trades which we have in remote or far countries, for besides the increase in shipping and mariners thereby, the wares also sent thither and received from thence are far more profitable unto the kingdom than by our trades near at hand.

—Thomas Mun, *England's Treasure by Foreign Trade,* 1630

In nearly every state in Europe citizens are divided into the three orders of nobles, clergy, and people. . . . Even Plato, although he intended all his citizens to enjoy an equality of rights and privileges, divided them into the three orders of guardians, soldiers and labourers. All this goes to show that there never was a commonwealth, real or imaginary, even if conceived in the most popular terms, where citizens were in truth equal in all rights and privileges. Some always have more, some less than the rest.

—Jean Bodin, *Six Books of the Commonwealth,* 1570

A ny study of early-modern European society must concern itself with change, with the factors that in the two hundred years after 1600 were powerful enough to produce the political upheaval of the French Revolution and the economic stimulus for the Industrial Revolution. Unquestionably, the most profound change during that period was economic. By the latter part of the eighteenth century, the freebooting overseas expansionism that had begun in the sixteenth century with the Spanish conquistadors had ended with Europe at the center of a vast system of worldwide trade. Commerce on this increasingly global scale had given birth to institutions fashioned for its support, and had altered patterns of living among those caught up in its overpowering dynamic. Banks and joint-stock companies financed international commercial ventures. New urban workshops responded to the intensified demand for manufactured goods.

Economic change

As international banking developed into a highly sophisticated profession, its practitioners became powerful men. As urban workshops imposed new conditions and habits, the urban artisan was forced to bend uncomfortably to unfamiliar demands.

European society as a whole found bending no more comfortable. Change was imposed upon national communities which, in many cases, were still defined according to the hierarchies of the Middle Ages: landlord and peasant, nobleman and serf. Each order was expected to acknowledge its inherent obligations and responsibilities, as each was assumed to be part of an organic and divinely sanctioned communal whole. Where, within this preordained structure, was the independent commercial entrepreneur or the dispossessed laborer supposed to fit? Tension of this sort between old forms and new realities was further exacerbated by the general crisis that we analyzed in the preceding chapter. Change produced by economic expansion and dislocation occurred against the background of civil and religious turmoil that tore much of Europe to pieces in the seventeenth century, and against an equally disruptive cycle of demographic swings caused by warfare and disease, by good weather one year, bad weather—and hence famine—the next. Those were the changes closest to the lives of most Europeans, the men and women still bound to the land, for whom, as the French historian Pierre Goubert has observed, "death was at the center of life, just as the graveyard was at the center of the village." The concerns of this chapter are thus both the economic and social circumstances that represented change, and the habits and traditions that were making change complex and difficult.

1. CAPITALISM, MERCANTILISM, AND THE COMMERCIAL REVOLUTION

The early-modern world of commerce and industry was governed by the assumptions of capitalism and mercantilism. Reduced to its simplest terms, capitalism may be defined as a system of production, distribution, and exchange, in which accumulated wealth is invested by private owners for the sake of gain. Its essential features are private enterprise, competition for markets, and business for profit. Generally it involves also the wage system as a method of payment of workers; that is, a mode of payment based not on the amount of wealth they create, but rather upon their ability to compete with one another for jobs. Capitalism represented a direct challenge to the semi-static economy of the medieval guilds, in which production and trade were supposed to be conducted for the benefit of society and with only a reasonable charge for the service rendered, instead of unlimited profits. Capitalism is a system designed to encourage commercial expansion beyond the local level, on a national and international scale. Guildmasters had neither the money (capital) to support nor the knowledge to organize and direct commercial enterprises beyond their own towns. Activity on that wider scale demanded the resources and expertise of wealthy and experienced entrepreneurs. These men, who usually started as merchants operating over a wide area and ended as bankers, could afford to invest in large quantities of manufactured goods, and if necessary, to hold them unsold until they could command a high price. The capitalist entrepreneur studied patterns of international trade. He knew where markets were and how to manipulate them to his advantage.

Capitalism is a system designed to reward the individual. In contrast, mercantilist doctrine emphasized direct governmental intervention in economic policy to increase the general prosperity of the state. Mercantilism was by no means a new idea. It was in fact a variation on the medieval notion that the populace of any particular town comprised a community with a common wealth, and that the economic well-being of such communities depended on the willingness of that populace to work at whatever task God or their rulers assigned them to benefit the community as a whole. Membership in a particular order within the community ensured to men and women the privileges of that order. In the case of the poor, this meant no more than protection from unfair prices and from starvation. In return for such protection, members of the community willingly placed themselves under the regimentation that guild restrictions and town ordinances imposed.

The medieval origins of mercantilism

The mercantilism of the seventeenth and eighteenth centuries translated this earlier concept of community as a privileged, but regimented, economic unit from the level of towns to the level of the entire state. This translation represented not so much a complete change as it did the extension and elaboration of theories and practices that had governed the policies of earlier rulers. The conquest and subsequent plundering of the New World by Spain was an instance of mercantilism at work on a grand scale. The Statute of Artificers, passed by the English Parliament in 1563, which established a customary "fair" wage scale applicable to all laborers, instituted economic privilege and regimentation at the national level.

Mercantilism and the state

Mercantile theory held that a state's power depended on its actual, calculable wealth, expressed in terms of the amount of gold and silver bullion in its possession at any given time. A state amassed bullion by ensuring itself as favorable a balance of trade as possible. Hence the degree to which a state could remain self-sufficient, importing as little as necessary while exporting as much as possible, was the clearest gauge not only of its economic prosperity but of its power. This doctrine had profound effects on state policy. First, it led to the establishment and development of overseas colonies. Colonies, mercantilists reasoned, would, as part of the national community, provide it with raw materials, including precious metals in some instances, which would otherwise have to be obtained outside the community. Second,

Definition of wealth

it inspired state governments to encourage industrial production and trade, both sources of revenue which would increase the state's income. And finally, it persuaded policy-makers to discourage domestic consumption, since goods purchased on the home market reduced the goods available for export. Government policy was thus to keep wages low, so that laborers would not have money to spend for more than it took to provide them with basic food and shelter.

Mercantilism in practice

Although most western European statesmen were prepared to endorse mercantilist goals in principle, the degree to which their policies reflected those goals varied according to national circumstance. Spain, despite its insistence on closed colonial markets and its determination to amass a fortune in bullion, never succeeded in attaining the economic self-sufficiency that mercantilist theory demanded. The Spaniards therefore found it necessary to exchange their bullion for Flemish, French, and English manufactured goods which they were unable to supply to either their home market or to their colonies. Madrid's mercantilism, however, had little appeal in Amsterdam. The Dutch rejected the governmental centralization implicit in the mercantilist notion of the sovereign state as an economic unit which they associated with the hated regime of Philip II of Spain. They further recognized that the United Provinces were too small to permit them to achieve economic self-sufficiency. Throughout the seventeenth and eighteenth centuries the Dutch remained dedicated in principle and practice to free trade, often investing, contrary to mercantilist doctrine, in the commercial enterprises of other countries and promoting national prosperity by encouraging the rest of Europe to rely upon Amsterdam as a hub of international finance and trade. The Dutch commitment to free trade did not extend to their colonial preserves which remained closed to their commercial rivals. It was the French and the English who combined, in differing degrees, governmental centralization and independent commercial enterprise most consistently and effectively and who became the most successful practitioners of mercantilism in early-modern Europe.

*Capitalism and
mercantilism: a
commercial revolution*

The goal of capitalism was a commercial system that would make individuals rich. The goal of mercantilism was a system that would make the state powerful. Though they differed as to ends, the two systems functioned compatably together for most of the early-modern period. Together, governments and entrepreneurs designed new institutions that facilitated the expansion of global commerce during the seventeenth and eighteenth centuries and effected what has come to be called a Commercial Revolution.

*Elements of the
Commercial Revolution:
(1) increased capital*

Enterprise on this new scale depended on the availability of capital for investment. And that capital was generated primarily by a gradual increase in agricultural prices throughout much of the period. Had that increase been sharp, it would probably have produced enough hunger and suffering to retard rather than stimulate economic growth.

Merchants' Houses in Seventeenth-Century Amsterdam. This engraving depicts not only the opulence of middle-class life in a thriving commercial capital, but also the spirit of civic unity, expressed by the crowds gathered for a public celebration. (Several of the principal thoroughfares of Amsterdam are canals.)

Had there been no increase, however, the resulting stagnation produced by marginal profits would have proved equally detrimental to expansion. Agricultural entrepreneurs had surplus capital to invest in trade; bankers put that surplus to use to expand their commercial enterprises. Together, capitalist investors and merchants profited.

Banks played a vital role in the history of this expansion. Strong religious and moral disapproval of lending money at interest meant that banking had enjoyed a dubious reputation in the Middle Ages. Because the Church did come to allow profit-making on commercial risks, however, banks in Italy and Germany were organized under family auspices, the most notable examples being the fourteenth- and fifteenth-century operations of the Medici in Florence and the Fuggers of Augsburg. The Fuggers lent money to kings and bishops, and served as broker to the pope for the sale of indulgences. The rise of these private financial houses was followed by the establishment of government banks, reflecting the mercantilist goal of serving the monetary needs of the state. The first such institution, the Bank of Sweden, was founded in 1657. The Bank of England was established in 1694, at a time when England's emergence as a world commercial power guaranteed that institution a leading role in international finance.

The growth of banking was necessarily accompanied by the adoption of various aids to financial transactions on a large scale, further

(2) the rise of banking

evidence of a commercial revolution. Credit facilities were extended in such a way that a merchant in Amsterdam could purchase goods from a merchant in Venice by means of a bill of exchange issued by an Amsterdam bank. The Venetian merchant would obtain his money by depositing the bill of exchange in his local bank. Later, the two banks would settle their accounts by comparing balances. Among the other facilities for the expansion of credit were the adoption of a system of payment by check in local transactions and the issuance of bank notes as a substitute for gold and silver. Both of these devices were invented by the Italians and were gradually adopted in northern Europe. The system of payment by check was particularly important in increasing the volume of trade, since the credit resources of the banks could now be expanded far beyond the actual amounts of cash in their vaults.

*(4) changes in business
organization; the growth
of regulated companies*

International commercial expansion called forth larger units of business organization. The prevailing unit of production and trade in the Middle Ages was the shop or store owned by an individual or a family. Partnerships were also quite common, in spite of the grave disadvantage of unlimited liability of each of its members for the debts of the entire firm. Obviously no one of these units was well adapted to business involving heavy risks and a huge investment of capital. The attempt to devise a more suitable business organization resulted in the formation of *regulated companies*. The regulated company was an association of merchants banded together for a common venture. Members did not pool their resources but agreed merely to cooperate for their mutual advantage and to abide by certain definite regulations. Usually the purpose of the combination was to maintain a monopoly of trade in some part of the world. Assessments were often paid by the members for the upkeep of docks and warehouses and especially for protection against "interlopers," as those traders were called who attempted to break into the monopoly. A leading example of this type of organization was an English company known as the Merchant Adventurers, established for the purpose of trade with the Netherlands and Germany.

The Commercial Revolution was facilitated in the seventeenth century when the regulated company was largely superseded by a new type of organization at once more compact and broader in scope. This was the *joint-stock company,* formed through the issuance of shares of capital to a considerable number of investors. Those who purchased the shares might or might not take part in the work of the company. Whether they did or not, they were joint owners of the business and therefore entitled to share in its profits in accordance with the amount they had invested. The joint-stock company had numerous advantages over the partnership and the regulated company. First, it was a permanent unit, not subject to reorganization every time one of its members died or withdrew. And second, it made possible a much larger accumulation of capital, through a wide distribution of shares

In short, it possessed nearly every advantage of the modern corporation except that it was not a person in the eyes of the law with the
rights and privileges guaranteed to individuals. While most of the early
joint-stock companies were founded for commercial ventures, some
were organized later in industry. A number of the outstanding trading
combinations were also *chartered companies*. They held charters from
the government granting a monopoly of the trade in a certain locality
and conferring extensive authority over the inhabitants, and were thus
an example of the way capitalist and mercantilist interests might
coincide. Through a charter of this kind, the British East India Company undertook the exploitation of vast territories on the Indian subcontinent, and remained virtual ruler there until the end of the
eighteenth century.

A final important feature of the Commercial Revolution was the
development of a more efficient money economy. Money had been
used widely since the revival of trade in the eleventh century. Nevertheless, there were few coins with a value that was recognized other
than locally. By 1300, the gold ducat of Venice and the gold florin of
Florence had come to be accepted in Italy and also in the international
markets of northern Europe. But no country could be said to have
had a uniform monetary system. Nearly everywhere there was great
confusion. Coins issued by kings circulated side by side with the money
of foreign states. Moreover, the types of currency were modified frequently, and the coins themselves were often debased. A common
method by which kings expanded their own personal revenues was to
increase the proportion of cheaper metals in the coins they minted.
But the growth of trade and industry in the Commercial Revolution
accentuated the need for more stable and uniform monetary systems.
The problem was solved by the adoption of a standard system of
money by every important state to be used for all transactions within
its borders. Much time elapsed, however, before the reform was complete. England began the construction of a uniform coinage during the
reign of Queen Elizabeth, but the task was not finished until late in
the seventeenth century. Indeed, the French did not succeed in reducing their money to its modern standard of simplicity and convenience
until the early nineteenth century.

(5) a money economy

The Commercial Revolution, although it contributed to the prosperity of both individuals and states, was accompanied by serious risks
and consequences occasionally disastrous to investors and to national
economies. One major result of overseas expansion was the severe
inflation caused by the increase in the supply of silver, which plagued
Europe at the end of the sixteenth century (see above, p. 503). Price
fluctuations, in turn, produced further economic instability. Businessmen were tempted to expand their enterprises too rapidly; bankers
extended credit so liberally that their principal borrowers, especially
nobles, often defaulted on loans. Spain and Italy were among the first
to suffer setbacks. In both, failure of wages to keep pace with rising

The dangers of expansion

prices brought severe and continuing hardships to the lower classes. Impoverishment was rife in the cities, and bandits flourished in the rural areas. In Spain, some ruined aristocrats were not too proud to join the throngs of vagrants who wandered from city to city. At the end of the fifteenth century the great Florentine bank of the Medici closed its doors. The middle of the century that followed saw numerous bankruptcies in Spain and the decline of the Fuggers in Germany. Meanwhile, England, Holland, and to some extent France waxed prosperous. This prosperity was especially characteristic of the "age of silver," which lasted from about 1540 to 1620. In the seventeenth century decline set in once more after inflation had spent its force, and as a consequence of religious and international wars and civil strife.

The South Sea Bubble

The alternation of booms and recessions was followed by outbreaks of feverish speculation. These reached their climax early in the eighteenth century. The most notorious were the South Sea Bubble and the Mississippi Bubble. The former was the result of inflation of the stock of the South Sea Company in England, whose offer to assume the national debt led to unwarranted confidence in the company's future. When buoyant hopes gave way to fears, investors made frantic attempts to dispose of their shares for whatever they would bring. A crash which came in 1720 was the inevitable result.

The Night-Share Crier and His Magic Lantern. A Dutch caricature of John Law's Mississippi Bubble, correctly suggesting that its promised financial rewards were illusory.

During the years when the South Sea Bubble was being inflated in England, the French were going through a similar wave of speculative madness. In 1715 a Scotsman by the name of John Law, who had been compelled to flee from British soil for killing his rival in a love intrigue, settled in Paris, after various successful gambling adventures in other cities. He persuaded the regent of France to adopt his scheme for paying off the national debt through the issuance of paper money and to grant him the privilege of organizing the Mississippi Company for the colonization and exploitation of Louisiana. As the government loans were redeemed, those who received the money were encouraged to buy stock in the company. Soon the shares began to soar, ultimately reaching a price forty times their original value. Nearly everyone who could scrape together a bit of surplus cash rushed forward to participate in the scramble for riches. Stories were told of butchers and tailors who were supposed to have become millionaires by buying a few shares and holding them for a rise in price. But as the realization grew that the company would never be able to pay more than a nominal dividend on the stock at its inflated value, the more cautious investors began selling their holdings. The alarm spread, and soon all were as anxious to sell as they had been to buy. In 1720 the Mississippi Bubble burst in a wild panic. Thousands of people who had sold good property to buy the shares at fantastic prices were ruined.

The Mississippi Bubble

The role of the state

Joint-stock companies in France were more directly dependent on the state than was the case elsewhere, a reflection of French dedication to mercantilist theory. In most cases French companies were floated under governmental auspices; courtiers—and the king himself—were heavy investors. Agents of the state played a direct role in their management, sometimes to the company's ultimate disadvantage. The French East India Company, for example, was compelled by state direction to govern its colonies in accordance with the laws of Paris, a fact which, one historian has remarked, "reminds one of the complaint that French progress in the Sahara was retarded by the refusal of the camel to accommodate its habits to administrative regulations made in Paris." [1] Even though companies elsewhere were less subject to governmental regulation than they were in France, government and commerce generally worked to promote each other's interests. In time of war, governments called upon commercial capitalists to assist in the financing of their campaigns. When England went to war against France in 1689, for example, the government had no long-range borrowing mechanism available to it; during the next quarter century the merchant community, through the Bank of England, assisted the government in raising over £170 million and in stabilizing the national debt at £40 million. In return, trading companies used the war to increase long-distance commercial traffic at the expense of their French enemy, and exerted powerful pressure on the government to secure treaties that would work to their commercial advantage.

2. COLONIZATION AND OVERSEAS TRADE

The institutions of the Commercial Revolution—banks, credit facilities, joint-stock companies, monetary systems—were designed specifically to assist both capitalist entrepreneurs and mercantilist policymakers in the development and exploitation of overseas colonies and trading posts, the most visible evidence of the economic expansionism of early-modern Europe. Following the exploits of the conquistadors, the Spanish established colonial governments in Peru and in Mexico, which they controlled from Madrid in proper mercantilist fashion by a Council of the Indies. In return for a protection fee, as distinct from the royalty of one-fifth of all bullion extracted from the colonies, the Spanish navy attempted to protect treasure ships from attacks by the French, English, and Dutch. The mercantilist governments of Philip II and his successors were determined to defend their monopoly in the New World. They issued trading licenses to none but Spanish merchants; exports and imports passed only through the port of Seville (later the more navigable port of Cadiz), where they were registered at the government-operated Casa de Contratación, or customs house.

Spanish colonization

These precautions did not deter other countries from attempting to win a share of the treasure for themselves. Probably the boldest challengers were the English, and their leading buccaneer the "sea dog" Sir Francis Drake, who three times raided the east and west coasts of

[1] G. N. Clark, *The Seventeenth Century* (New York, 1961), p. 39.

GREENLAND

HUDSON BAY
COMPANY

Québec
NEW
FRANCE
ACADIA
NEWFOUNDLAND

LOUISIANA

Boston
New Amsterdam
(New York after 1667)

VIRGINIA
Jamestown

Charlestown

FLORIDA

*Gulf
of Mexico*

NEW
SPAIN

Mexico

CUBA
HISPANIOLA

SPANISH MAIN
See enlargement below

Panama

NEW
GRANADA
SURINAM
FR. GUYANA

*ATLANTIC
OCEAN*

BRITAIN

Bristol
Amsterdam
NETHERLANDS
FRANCE

PORTUGAL
Lisbon
Madrid
SPAIN
Cadiz

AFRICA

St. Louis
GAMBIA
GOLD
COAST
GUINEA

SLAVES

KENYA

ANGOLA

MADAGA

MOZAMBIQUE

CAPE OF
GOOD HOPE

*PACIFIC
OCEAN*

Lima

BRAZIL

Rio de Janeiro

PERU

Buenos Aires

	Spanish
	Portuguese
	French
	British
	Dutch

Havana
CUBA
Bahamas (Br.)

Puerto
Rico
St. Domingue
(Fr.)
HISPANIOLA
Guadeloupe (Fr.)

Belize (Br.)
Jamaica (Br.)
Martinique (Fr.)

CARIBBEAN   SEA
Barbados

NEW SPAIN
Curaçao (Dutch)
Trinidad (Sp.)

NEW GRANADA

THE ATLANTIC WORLD IN 1713

Spanish America and who, in 1587, the year before the Armada set sail on its ill-fated voyage north, "singed the beard of the Spanish king" by attacking the Spanish fleet at its anchorage in Cadiz harbor. Yet despite dashing heroics of that sort, the English could do no more than dent the Spanish trade. Reluctantly foresaking the search for the quick profits Spain was extracting from its colonial gold and silver mines, English colonists began to establish agricultural settlements in North America and the Caribbean basin. The first permanent, though ultimately unsuccessful, colony was established at Jamestown, in Virginia, in 1607. Over the next forty years, 80,000 English emigrants founded over twenty autonomous settlements in the New World. At first, English governments did far less than the Spanish to control these enterprises by means of mercantilist-inspired policies. Agriculture did not seem to promise rewards large enough to warrant state regulation. In addition, since many of the colonies were settled by religious dissenters escaping the attempts of James I and Charles I to impose religious uniformity, those monarchs were not disposed to encourage their economic prosperity by direct subsidy, or by the introduction of tariffs to prevent foreign competitors from underselling the colonists in the English home market.

English colonization

By the mid–seventeenth century, however, English policy had changed. Agricultural colonies were producing crops in high demand throughout Europe. The profits of colonial planters encouraged the governments of both Oliver Cromwell and Charles II to intervene in the management of their overseas economy. Navigation Acts, passed in 1651 and 1660, and rigorously enforced thereafter, decreed that all exports from English colonies to the mother country be carried in English ships, and forbade the direct exporting of certain "ennumerated" products directly from the colonies to continental ports.

The growth of English colonial regulation

The most valuable of those products were sugar and tobacco. Sugar, virtually unknown in Europe earlier, had become a popular luxury by the end of the sixteenth century. Where once it had been considered no more than a medicine, one observer now noted that the wealthy were "devouring it out of gluttony." Sugarcane was raised in the West Indies after 1650 in rapidly increasing amounts. In the eighteenth century, the value of the sugar that England imported from its small island colonies there—Barbados, Jamaica, St. Kitts, and others— exceeded the value of its imports from the vast subcontinents of China and India. Although the tobacco plant was imported into Europe by the Spaniards about fifty years after the discovery of America, another half century passed before Europeans contracted the habit of smoking. At first the plant was believed to possess miraculous healing powers and was referred to as "divine tobacco" and "our holy herb nicotian." (The word "nicotine" derives from the name of the French ambassador to Portugal, Jean Nicot, who brought the tobacco plant to France.) The practice of smoking was popularized by English explorers, especially by Sir Walter Raleigh, who had learned to smoke

Sugar and tobacco

The Dutch East India Company Warehouse and Timber Wharf at Amsterdam. The substantial warehouse, the stockpiles of lumber, and the company ship under construction in the foreground illustrate the degree to which overseas commerce could stimulate economy of the mother country.

while living among the Indians of Virginia. It spread rapidly through all classes of European society. Governments at first joined the Church in condemning the use of tobacco because of its socially and spiritually harmful effects, but by the end of the seventeenth century, having realized the profits to be made from its production, they were encouraging its use.

The Dutch were even more successful than the English in establishing a flourishing commercial empire in the seventeenth century. Their *The Dutch in the Far* joint-stock East India Company, founded in 1602, rivaled its English *East* counterpart in Asia, gaining firm control of Sumatra, Borneo, and the Moluccas, or Spice Islands, and driving Portuguese traders from an area where they had heretofore enjoyed an undisturbed commercial dominion. The result was a Dutch monopoly in pepper, cinnamon, nutmeg, mace, and cloves. The Dutch also secured an exclusive right to trade with the Japanese, and maintained outposts in China and India as well. In the Western hemisphere, their achievements were less spectacular. Following a series of trade wars with England, they surrendered their North American colony of New Amsterdam (subsequently renamed New York) in 1667, retaining Surinam, off the northern coast of South America, as well as the islands of Curaçao and Tobago in the West Indies in compensation.

French colonial policy matured during the administration of Louis XIV's mercantilist finance minister, Jean Baptiste Colbert (1619–1683), *The French in America* who perceived of overseas expansion as an integral part of state economic policy. He organized joint-stock companies to compete with those of the English. He encouraged the development of lucrative sugar-producing colonies in the West Indies, the largest of which was St. Dominique (present-day Haiti). France also dominated the interior of the North American continent. Frenchmen traded furs and preached Christianity to the Indians in a vast territory that stretched from Acadia and the St. Lawrence River in the northeast to Louisiana in the west. Yet the financial returns from these lands was hardly commensurate with their size. Furs, fish, and tobacco were exported to home markets, but not in sufficient amounts to match the profits from the sugar colonies of the Caribbean or from the line of trading posts the French maintained in India.

The fortunes of these commercial empires rose and fell in the course of the seventeenth and eighteenth centuries. The Spanish, mired in a persistent economic lassitude and embroiled in a succession of expensive wars and domestic rebellions, were powerless to preserve the sanctity of their empire. Their merchant marine, once a match for cunning pirate-admirals like Drake, was by the middle of the seventeenth century unable to protect itself from attack by its more spirited commercial rivals. In a war with Spain in the 1650s, the English captured not only the island of Jamaica but treasure ships lying off the Spanish harbor of Cadiz. Further profit was obtained by bribing Spanish customs officials on a grand scale. During the second half of the century, two-thirds of the imported goods sold in Spanish colonies were smuggled in by Dutch, English, and French traders. By 1700, though Spain still possessed a colonial empire, it was one which lay at the mercy of its more dynamic rivals. Portugal, too, found it impossible to prevent foreign penetration of its colonial economies. The English worked diligently and successfully to win commercial advantages. They obtained concessions to export woolens duty-free into Portugal itself in return for similar preferential treatment for Portuguese wines. (The notorious affection of the English upper class for port wine dates from the signing of the Treaty of 1703.) English trade with the mother country led in time to English trade with the Portuguese colony of Brazil, indeed to the opening of commercial offices in Rio de Janeiro.

The decline of the Spanish and Portuguese empires

"The Solid Enjoyment of Bottle and Friend." An eighteenth-century English satire on the drinking habits of the upper classes.

The Dutch, whose merchant fleet of over 16,000 vessels was the largest in seventeenth-century Europe, continued to dominate world trade until eclipsed by the French and British after the late seventeenth century. Dutch ships—about half the European total—not only sailed the high seas, but dominated the European coastal carrying trade as well. The Dutch merchant marine force ensured the position of Amsterdam as the world's premier trading center, the volume of Dutch commerce allowing Amsterdam merchants to undersell their English and French rivals. During the eighteenth century a growing Anglo-French rivalry in India stole the commercial spotlight from the Dutch spice monopoly in the Far East. The French and English East India Companies employed mercenaries to establish and expand trading areas

The Dutch eclipsed; Anglo-French rivalry

such as Madras, Bombay, and Pondichéry. By exploiting indigenous industries, European capitalists continued to increase the flow of fine cotton textiles, tea, and spices which passed through these commercial depots on their way to Europe. The struggle for economic dominance in India was resolved in mid-century in England's favor following a series of military clashes. As a sign of France's defeat, in 1769 the French East India Company was dissolved.

*Increasing dominance of
western trade routes*

Despite the commercial importance of India, however, patterns of world trade came increasingly to be dominated by western routes that had developed in response to the lucrative West Indian sugar industry, and to the demand for slaves from Africa to work the plantations in the Caribbean. Here Britain, again, eventually assumed the lead. Typically, an English ship might begin its voyage with a consignment of Jamaican rum and sail to Africa, where the rum would be exchanged for a cargo of slaves. From the west coast of Africa the ship would then cross the South Atlantic to the sugar colonies of Jamaica or Barbados, where slaves would be traded for molasses, which would make the final leg of the journey to New England. A variant triangle might see cheap manufactured goods move from Bristol or Liverpool, in England, to Africa, where they would be traded for slaves. Those slaves would then be shipped to Virginia and exchanged for tobacco, which would be shipped to England and processed there for sale in continental markets. Other eighteenth-century trade routes were more direct: the Spanish, French, Portuguese, and Dutch all engaged in the slave trade between Africa and Central and South America; the Spanish attempted, vainly, to retain a mercantilist monopoly on direct trade between Cadiz and their South American colonies; others sailed from England, France, or North America to the Caribbean and back again. And of course trade continued to flourish between Europe and the Near and Far East. But the triangular western routes, dictated by the grim economic symbiosis of sugar and slaves, remained dominant.

The slave trade

The cultivation of sugar and tobacco depended on slave labor; and as demand for those products increased, so did the traffic in black slaves, without whose labor those products could not be raised or harvested. At the height of the Atlantic slave trade in the eighteenth century, somewhere between 75,000 and 90,000 blacks were shipped across the Atlantic yearly: six million in the eighteenth century, out of a total of over nine million for the entire history of the trade. About 35 percent went to English and French Caribbean plantations, 5 percent (roughly 450,000) to North America, and the rest to the Portuguese colony of Brazil and to Spanish colonies in South America. Although run in the sixteenth and early seventeenth centuries as a monopoly by various governments, in its heyday the slave trade was open to private entrepreneurs, who operated ports on the West African coast. Traders exchanged cheap Indian cloth, metal goods, rum, and firearms with African slave merchants in return for their human cargo. Already disoriented and degraded by their capture at the hands

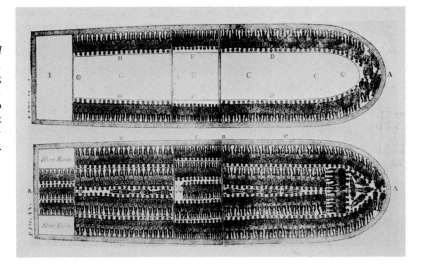

How Slaves Were Stowed Aboard Ship during the Middle Passage. Men were "housed" on the right; women on the left; children in the middle. The human cargo was jammed onto platforms six feet wide without sufficient headroom to permit an adult to sit up. This diagram is from evidence gathered by English abolitionists and depicts conditions on the Liverpool slave ship *Brookes.*

of rival tribes, black men, women, and children were packed by the hundreds into the holds of slave ships for the gruesome "middle passage" across the Atlantic (so called to distinguish it from the ship's voyage from Europe to Africa, and from the slave colony back to Europe again). Shackled to the decks, without sanitary facilities, the black "cargo" suffered horribly; the mortality rate, however, remained at about 10 or 11 percent, not much higher than the rate for a normal sea voyage of one hundred days or more. Since traders had to invest as much as £10 per slave in their enterprise, they ensured that their consignment would reach its destination in good enough shape to be sold for a profit.

Not until the very end of the eighteenth century did Europeans protest this ghastly traffic. Though the trade was risky, dependent as it was on a good wind and fair weather, profits often reached as much as 300 percent. Demand for slaves remained high throughout the eighteenth century. By the 1780s, there were over 500,000 slaves on the largest French plantation island, St. Dominique, and 200,000 or more on the English counterpart, Jamaica. Those numbers reflected the expanding world market for slave-grown crops. As long as demand for the crops cultivated by slaves continued to rise—as long as the economy relied to the extent it did upon slave labor—governments would remain unwilling to put an end to the system that, as one Englishman wrote in 1749, provided "an unexhaustible fund of wealth to this nation." Philosophers argued that though there was reason to rejoice that slavery had been banished from the continent of Europe (forgetting, apparently, the extent to which it continued to exist east of the Elbe in the form of serfdom), it remained a necessity in other parts of the world. Public pressure, first from Quakers and then from others motivated either by religious or humanitarian zeal, helped put an end to the trade in England in 1807, and to slavery itself in British

The ending of the trade

colonies in 1833. Slavery in French colonies was abolished in 1793, but only after slaves had risen in massive revolt on St. Dominique. Elsewhere, in Latin and North America, slavery lasted well into the nineteenth century—in the United States, until the Civil War of 1861–1865.

The slave trade is an integral part of the history of the dramatic rise of English and French commerce during the eighteenth century. France experienced a striking rise in trade. French colonial trade, valued at 25 million livres in 1716, rose to 263 million livres in 1789. In England, during roughly the same period, foreign trade increased in value from £10 million to £40 million, the latter amount more than twice that for France. These figures suggest the degree to which statecraft and private enterprise were bound to each other. If merchants depended on their government to provide a navy to protect and defend their overseas investments, governments depended equally on entrepreneurship, not only to generate money to build ships, but to sustain the trade upon which national power had come to rely so heavily.

3. AGRICULTURE AND INDUSTRY

The pace of industrial change in early-modern Europe was not as dynamic as that of the Commercial Revolution and the expansion of overseas colonization and trade. Changes did occur, but less uniformly and dramatically than those we have been tracing. This is not surprising, since the major economic enterprise remained agricultural production, which, throughout much of the period, was generally carried on according to traditional techniques that kept the volume of production low. Yet by the end of the eighteenth century, tradition was beginning to yield to innovation, with the result that production in some areas was increasing dramatically.

Most of the agricultural regions of seventeenth-century Europe were farmed in open fields. In the north, these fields were usually large sections of land, divided into long, narrow strips; in the south, the strips tended to reflect the more irregular shape of local landscapes. Although one or two rich aristocrats might own as much as three-fourths of the land in an open-field village, that land did not comprise one solid block. Instead it was made up of a great many plots, seldom contiguous, within the various open fields that surrounded the village. A large property owner's *desmesne* farm—which he worked with hired laborers for his own direct profit—and his tenant farms—those which he leased out to peasants—all consisted of these bits and pieces of land which lay alongside other bits and pieces that belonged to other landowners—very often small peasant proprietors. Each large open field thus resembled a patchwork quilt. Under these circumstances, in order for the fields to be cultivated with any degree of efficiency, all the "patches" had to be planted with the same crop, and sown, cultivated, and harvested together. Once the harvest was in, livestock was often turned into the fields to graze. One consequence of this practice was that crops were cut with a primitive sickle, which left more stubble for sheep and cattle, rather than with the far more efficient scythe. Inefficiency was indeed the hallmark of the open-field system, an inefficiency which those who owned large tracts of land grew more and more unwilling to tolerate. The Commercial Revolution encouraged landlords, particularly those in England and Holland, to compete for markets as capitalist agricultural entrepreneurs. In doing so, they looked for ways to improve the yield on their lands.

By the end of the eighteenth century a great many had resolved the problem of low production by adopting a full range of innovative farming techniques, the most drastic of which was the enclosure of open fields to allow for more systematic and therefore more productive farming. "Enclosure" was the term for land reorganization within a traditional village community. The earliest enclosures in England took place in the fifteenth and sixteenth centuries and entailed the conversion of lands into fenced-off sheep meadows. Because of the great profits to be accrued from wool, some landlords decided to convert common pastures that hitherto had supported peasant livestock into their own preserves for sheep-raising. Sometimes they also succeeded in converting grain fields into sheep pastures by evicting peasants whose leaseholds were none too secure. This caused grave hardships for the peasants concerned. As Thomas More wrote in his *Utopia* (1516), "sheep that used to be so meek and eat so little now are becoming so greedy and wild that they devour men themselves . . . for they leave no land free for the plough." The humanitarian More, however, was exaggerating somewhat. In fact, no more than about 3 percent of arable land had been enclosed before 1525 and part of that was not for sheep pasturage.

Enclosure

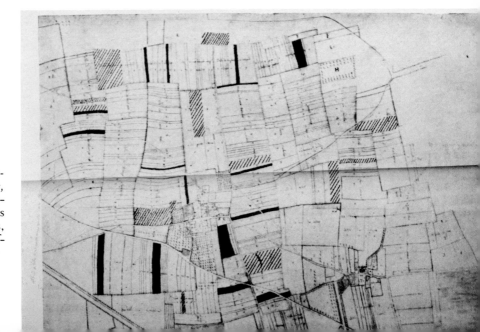

The Open-Field System in Northern France, 1738. Note the subdivision of large tracts into narrow strips, each owned by different proprietors.

The really dramatic enclosure movement in England took place between 1710 and 1810 and aimed not to free land for sheep but to increase the efficiency of crop-raising. In this period landlords became convinced of the necessity for "scientific farming." Above all, they realized that by introducing new crops and farming methods they could reduce the amount of fallow lands and bring in higher yields, and thus higher profits. Some of the important new crops with which they experimented were clover, alfalfa, and related varieties of leguminous plants. These reduced fertility much less than cereal grains and actually helped to improve the quality of the soil by gathering nitrogen and making the ground more porous. Another new crop that had a similar effect was the turnip. The greatest propagandist for the planting of this unattractive vegetable was Viscount Charles Townshend (1674–1738), a prominent aristocrat and politician, who toward the end of his life left the royal court to experiment with agriculture. In this he became a model for subsequent aristocratic interest in scientific farming. Townshend gained the nickname of "Turnip" Townshend because he was so dedicated to converting people to the use of the turnip in new crop-rotation systems.

Clover, alfalfa, and turnips not only helped in doing away with the fallow but they provided excellent winter food for animals, thereby aiding the production of more and better livestock. And more livestock also meant more manure. Accordingly, intensive manuring became another way in which scientific farmers could eliminate the need for letting land lie fallow. Other improvements in farming methods introduced in the period were more intensive hoeing and weeding, and the use of the seed drill for planting grain. The latter eliminated the old wasteful method of sowing grain broadcast by hand, most of it remaining on top to be eaten by birds.

Scientific farming dictated the necessity of enclosures because the "improving" landlord needed flexibility to experiment as he wished. He simply could not try to plant one narrow open strip with turnips while peasants were continuing to rotate all the contiguous areas on the basis of the age-old three-field system. Instead, it was necessary for him to have fenced-off compact plots to leave no doubt as to which territory was his own, to maximize efficiency in experimentation, and to keep away stray grazing animals. When the enclosure movement gathered momentum, landlords were not above using the principle of reorganizing and enclosing territories to gain new lands from freeholders that hitherto had in no way belonged to them. In all this they had the government on their side. Parliament stopped trying to prohibit enclosures in 1640 and actually started directing them in 1710, not surprising in view of the fact that Parliament was dominated by large landowners. Thereafter, throughout the eighteenth century, parliamentary "acts of enclosure" provided that all the lands of a given village be completely redistributed into compact, fenced parcels, with the leading landlords of an area gaining far and away the most land.

Here was a change that had major social consequences where it occurred. Village life under the open-field system was communal, since decisions as to which crops were to be grown where and when had to be arrived at jointly. Often land was held under customary right by the village as a whole; and this common land afforded the poor not only a place to tether a cow, to fish, or to gather firewood, but to breathe at least a bit of the air of social freedom. In most cases the acts of enclosure included the common land in the redistribution. Hence enclosure cost villagers their modest freedoms, as well as the traditional right to help determine how the community's subsistence economy was to be managed. Cottagers (very small landholders) and squatters, who had over generations established a customary right to the use of common lands, were reduced to the rank of landless laborers.

The social consequences of enclosure

On the Continent, except for Holland, there was nothing comparable to the English advance in scientific farming. Nor, with the notable exception of Spain, was there a pronounced enclosure movement as in England and the Low Countries. Wherever small peasant proprietorship was firmly entrenched, as in France and in some areas of Germany, enclosure was successfully opposed. Yet despite that fact, European food production became increasingly capitalistic in the seventeenth and eighteenth centuries. Landlords leased farms to tenants and reaped profits as rent. Often they allowed tenants to pay rent in the form of half their crops. This system of sharecropping was most prevalent in France, Italy, and Spain. Farther east, in Prussia, Poland, Hungary, and Russia, landowners continued to rely on unpaid serfs to till the land. Wherever the market economy replaced the economy of local self-sufficiency, it brought change in its wake.

The increasingly capitalistic basis of European agriculture

The eighteenth century saw the introduction of two crops from the New World, maize (Indian corn) and the potato, that eventually resulted in the provision of a more adequate diet for the poor. Since maize can only be grown in areas with substantial periods of sunny and dry weather, its cultivation spread through Italy and the southeastern part of the Continent. Whereas an average ear of grain would yield only about four seeds for every one planted, an ear of maize would yield about seventy or eighty. That made it a "miracle" crop, filling granaries where they had been almost empty before. The potato was an equally miraculous innovation for the European north. Its advantages were numerous: potatoes could be grown on the poorest, sandiest, or wettest of lands where nothing else could be raised; they could be fitted into the smallest of patches. Raising potatoes even in small patches was profitable because the yield of potatoes was extraordinarily abundant. Finally, the potato provided an inexpensive means of improving the human diet. It is rich in calories, and contains many vitamins and minerals. Northern European peasants initially resisted growing and eating potatoes. Some feared the plant because it is not mentioned in the Bible. Some claimed that it transmitted leprosy. Still

Introduction of maize and potatoes

others insisted that it was a cause of flatulence, a property acknowledged by the French *Encyclopédie* in 1765, although the writers added: "What is a little wind to the vigorous organs of the peasants and workers?" Yet in the course of the eighteenth century the poor grew accustomed to the potato, although sometimes after considerable pressure. Frederick the Great of Prussia at first practically forced potatoes down his peasants' throats until the crop achieved acceptence and became a staple throughout much of northern Germany. By about 1800 the average north German peasant family ate potatoes as a main course at least once a day. In the same period the potato was also introduced into Ireland and England. In the 1840s, it was all that stood between millions of Irish and starvation.

Agriculture was, of course, not the only commercial enterprise in early-modern rural Europe. Increasingly, manufactured goods—particularly textiles—were being produced in the countryside, as entrepreneurs battled to circumvent artisanal and guild restrictions that limited production in urban manufacturing centers. The so-called putting-out system, which had grown increasingly common since the sixteenth century, was used by entrepreneurs as a way of realizing the highest profit on their investments. Unhampered by guild regulations, which in medieval times had restricted the production and distribution of textiles to maintain price levels, merchants would buy up a stock of raw material, most often wool or flax, which they would then "put out," or supply, to rural workers for carding (combing the fibers) and spinning. Once spun, the yarn or thread was collected by the merchant and passed to rural weavers, who wove it into cloth. Collected once more, the material was processed by other workers at bleaching or dyeing shops, and collected for a final time by the entrepreneur who then either sold it to a wholesaler or directly to retail customers.

*Rural manufacturing: the
putting-out system*

Rural workers accepted the putting-out system as a means of staving off poverty, or possible starvation in years of particularly bad harvests. Domestic textile production involved the entire family. Even the youngest children could participate in the process of cleaning the raw wool. Older children carded. Wives and husbands spun or wove. Spinning, until the invention of the jenny at the end of the eighteenth century (see below, p. 719) was a far more time-consuming process than weaving, which was speeded considerably by the invention of the fly-shuttle by the Englishman John Kay in the early eighteenth century, a mechanical device that automatically returned the shuttle to its starting place after it had been "thrown" across the loom.

Family production

In addition to extra income, the putting-out system provided other advantages to rural homeworkers. They could regulate the pace of their labor to some degree, and could abandon it altogether when farm work was available during the planting and harvest seasons. Their ability to work at home was not an unmixed blessing, for conditions in cottages that were wretchedly built and poorly ventilated were often exceedingly cramped and unpleasant, especially when they were com-

Advantages of putting-out

Left: *"Rustic Courtship."* This detail from an etching (1785) by the English satirist Thomas Rowlandson suggests the advantages of doorstep domestic industry: natural lighting, improved ventilation, and a chance to converse with visitors. Work under these self-paced conditions, though usually long and hard, was carried on to a personal rhythm. Right: *Artisan and Family* by Gerard ter Borch. This seventeenth-century wheelwright, though a skilled artisan, is nevertheless depicted as living on the brink of poverty. Sickness, a bad harvest, unemployment—any of these might easily drive him and his family over the edge.

pelled to accommodate a bulky loom within their already crowded living quarters. But domestic labor, however unpleasant, was preferable in the minds of most to work away from home in a shop, where conditions might be even more oppressive under the watchful eye of an unsympathetic master. There were also advantages for the merchant-entrepreneur, who benefited not only from the absence of guild restrictions, but from the fact that none of his capital was tied up in expensive equipment. (Spinners usually owned their spinning wheels; weavers either owned or rented their looms.) Governments appreciated the advantages of the system too, viewing it as one way to alleviate the ever-present problem of rural poverty. The French abolished the traditional privileges of urban manufacturers in 1762, acknowledging by law what economic demand had long since established: the widespread practice of unrestricted rural domestic production. By that time, the putting-out system prevailed not only in northern France, but in the east and northeast of England, in Flanders, and in much of northern Germany—all areas where a mixed agricultural and manufacturing economy made economic sense to those engaged in it as entrepreneurs and producers.

Later generations, looking back nostalgically on the putting-out system, often compared it favorably to the factory system which displaced it. Life within the system's "family economy" was seldom other

Quality of life under the family system

than hard, however. While workers could set their own pace to some extent, they remained subject to the demands of small, often inexperienced entrepreneurs who, misjudging their markets, might overload spinners and weavers with work at one moment, then abandon them for lack of orders the next. Though it often kept families from starvation, putting-out did little to make their lives anything other than monotonous and harsh. The pressures of the system are crudely if eloquently expressed in an English ballad, in which the weaver husband responds to his wife's complaint that she has no time to sit at the "bobbin wheel," what with the washing and baking and milking she must do. No matter, the husband replies. She must "stir about and get things done./ For all things must aside be laid,/ when we want help about our trade."

Other rural manufacturing activities

Textiles were not the only manufactured goods produced in the countryside. In France, for example, metal-working was as much a rural as an urban occupation, with migrant laborers providing a workforce for small, self-contained shops. In various parts of Germany, the same sort of unregulated domestic manufacturing base prevailed: in the Black Forest for clock making, in Thuringia for toys. English production of coal increased from 200,000 tons a year in the 1550s to more than three million tons by the end of the seventeenth century; that of iron, another essentially rural enterprise, grew fivefold in the same period.

Rudimentary transportation systems

Rural industry flourished despite the fact that for most of the early-modern period transportation systems remained rudimentary. In all but a very few cases, roads were little more than ill-defined tracks, full of holes as much as four feet deep, and all but impassable in the rain, when carts and carriages might stay mired in deep ruts for days.

Roadside Inn by Thomas Rowlandson. Coaching inns brought the outside world into the lives of isolated villagers. Note the absence of any clearly defined roadway.

The Duke of Bridgewater Canal

One of the few paved roads was that from Paris to Orléans, the main
river port of France, but that was a notable exception. In general, no
one could travel more than twelve miles an hour—"post haste" at a
gallop on horseback—and speed such as that could be achieved only
at the expense of fresh horses at each stage of the ride. A journey of
60 miles over good roads could be accomplished in twenty-four hours,
provided that the weather was fair. To travel by coach from Paris to
Lyons, a distance of approximately 250 miles, took ten days. Merchants ran great risks when they shipped perishable goods. Breakables
were not expected to survive for more than fifteen miles. Transportation of goods by boat along coastal routes was far more reliable than
shipment overland. In 1675, English merchants calculated that it was
cheaper to ship coal 300 miles by water than to send it fifteen miles
overland, so impassable were the roads to heavy transport. In 1698, a
bronze statue of Louis XIV was sent on its way from the river port of
Auxerre, southeast of Paris, to the town of Dijon. The cart in which
it was dispatched was soon stuck in the mud, however, and the statue
remained marooned in a wayside shed for twenty-one years, until the
road was improved to the point that it could continue its belated journey.

Gradually in the eighteenth century transportation improved. The
French established a Road and Bridge Corps of civil engineers, with a
separate training school, in 1747. Work began in 1777 on a series of
canals which eventually linked the English Channel to the Mediterranean. By the end of the century, France was spending seven million
livres a year on road construction. In England, private investors,
spearheaded by that inveterate canal builder the duke of Bridgewater,
constructed a network of waterways and turnpikes linking provincial

*Transportation
improvements*

towns to each other and to London. With improved roads came stage-coaches, feared at first for their speed and recklessness much as automobiles were feared in the early twentieth century. People objected to being crowded into narrow carriages designed to reduce the load pulled by the team of horses. "If by chance a traveller with a big stomach or wide shoulders appears," an unhappy passenger lamented, "one has to groan or desert." Improvements such as stagecoaches and canals, much as they might increase the profits or change the pattern of life for the wealthy, meant little to the average European. Barges plied the waterways from the north to the south of France, but most men and women traveled no farther than to their neighboring market town, on footpaths or on rutted cart tracks eight feet wide, which had served their ancestors much as they served them.

*Urban manufacturing
centers*

That industry flourished to the extent it did, despite the hazards and inefficiencies of transport, is a measure of the strength of Europe's ever-increasing commercial impulse. Rural "putting-out" did not prevent the growth of important urban manufacturing centers. In northern France, many of the million or so men and women employed in the textile trade lived and worked in cities such as Amiens, Lille, and Rheims. The eighteenth-century rulers of Prussia made it their policy to develop Berlin as a manufacturing center, taking advantage of an influx of French Protestants to establish the silk-weaving industry there. Even in cities, however, work was likely to be carried out in small shops, where anywhere from five to twenty journeymen labored under the supervision of a master to manufacture the particular products of their craft. Despite the fact that manufacturing was centered in homes and workshops, by 1700 these industries were increasing significantly in scale as many workshops grouped together to form a single manufacturing district. Textile industries led this trend, but it was true as well of brewing, distilling, soap and candle making, tanning, and the manufacturing of various chemical substances for the bleaching and dying of cloth. These and other industries might often employ several thousand men and women congregated together into towns—or larger communities of several towns—all dedicated to the same occupation and production.

*Response to changing
machinery and techniques*

Techniques in some crafts remained much as they had for centuries. In others, however, inventions changed the pattern of work as well as the nature of the product. Mechanically powered saws were introduced into shipyards and elsewhere across Europe in the seventeenth century. The technique of calico printing, the application of colored designs directly to textiles, was imported from the Far East. New and more efficient printing presses appeared, first in Holland and then elsewhere. The Dutch invented a machine, called a "camel," by which the hulls of ships could be raised in the water so that they could be more easily repaired.

Innovations of this kind were not readily accepted by workers. Labor-saving machines such as mechanical saws threw men out of work. Artisans, especially those organized into guilds, were by nature conservative, anxious to protect not only their restrictive "rights," but the secrets of their trade. Often, too, the state would intervene to block the widespread use of machines if they threatened to increase unemployment. The Dutch and some German states for example, prohibited the use of what was described as a "devilish invention," a ribbon loom capable of weaving sixteen or more ribbons at the same time. Sometimes the spread of new techniques was curtailed by states in order to protect the livelihood of powerful commercial interest groups. On behalf of both domestic textile manufacturers and importers of Indian goods, calico printing was for a time outlawed in both France and England. The cities of Paris and Lyons, and several German states banned the use of indigo dyes because they were manufactured abroad. Changes in manufacturing processes, like changes in agriculture, though they promised greater profits to enterpreneurs, threatened the livelihood of workers and their families. Facing the disruptions that capitalism and the Commercial Revolution were producing, they tried to cling to a pattern of life they knew, which, if harsh, was at least predictable.

Adverse reaction to new machinery and processes

4. POPULATION PATTERNS

The patterns of life for most seventeenth-century Europeans centered on the struggle to stay alive. They lived and worked within a subsistence economy, considering themselves extremely fortunate if they could grow or earn what it took to survive. In most instances their enemy was not an invading army, but famine. At least once a decade, climatic conditions—usually a long period of summer rainfall—would produce a devastatingly bad harvest, which in turn would result in widespread malnutrition often leading to serious illness and death. A family might survive for a time by eating less; but eventually, with its meager stocks exhausted and the cost of grain high, the human costs would mount. The substitution of grass, nuts, and tree bark for grain on which the peasants depended almost entirely for nourishment was as inadequate for them as it appears pathetic to us.

The threat of famine

Widespread crop failures occurred at fairly regular intervals—the worst in France, for example, about every thirty years (1597, 1630, 1662, 1694). They helped to produce the series of population crises that are the outstanding feature of early-modern demographic history. Poor harvests and the high prices produced by a scarcity of grain meant not only undernourishment and possible starvation, but increasing unemployment: with fewer crops to be harvested, more money was spent on food and, consequently, less on manufactured goods. The despair such conditions could easily breed would in turn contribute to a postponement of marriage and of births, and thus to a

Population crises

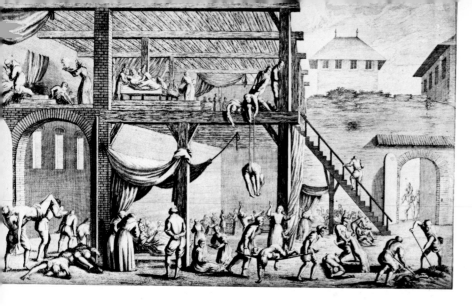

A Plague Hospital in Vienna. The efforts to contain outbreaks of plague by gathering the sick in establishments such as this and burying the dead on the site proved unsuccessful.

population decline. The patterns of marriages and births revealed in local parish registers indicate that throughout Europe the populations of individual communities rose and fell dramatically in rhythm with the fortunes of the harvest.

An undernourished population is a population particularly susceptible to disease. Bubonic plague had ravaged seventeenth-century Europe. Severe outbreaks occurred in Seville in 1649, in Amsterdam in 1664, and in London the following year. By 1700 it had all but disappeared; it last appeared in western Europe in a small area of southern France in 1720. But Moscow suffered an outbreak as late as 1771. Despite the gradual retreat of the plague, however, other diseases took a dreadful toll, in an age when available medical treatment was little more than crude guesswork, and in any event, beyond the reach of the poor. Epidemics of dysentery, smallpox, and typhus occurred with savage regularity. As late as 1779, over 100,000 people died of dysentery in the French province of Brittany. Most diseases attacked rich and poor impartially. Water supplies in towns and in the country were contaminated by heedless disposal of human waste and by all manner of garbage and urban filth. Bathing, feared at one time as a method of spreading disease, was by no means a weekly habit, whatever the social status of the household. Samuel Pepys, a prosperous servant of the crown in seventeenth-century London, recorded in his diary that his housemaid was in the habit of picking the lice from his scalp, that he took his first bath only after his wife had taken hers and experienced the pleasures of cleanliness, and that he had, on occasion, thought nothing of using the fireplace in his bedroom as a toilet, the maid having failed to provide him with a chamberpot. If such was Pepys's attitude toward hygiene and sanitation, imagine that of the poverty-stricken and ignorant peasant, and the threat to health implicit in such attitudes.

Health and sanitation

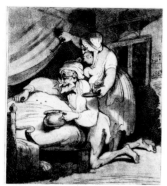

"Summer Amusement: Bugg Hunting." In this joking treatment of one of the facts of everyday life the bedbugs meet sudden death in a full chamber pot.

The precariousness of life encouraged most men and women in early-modern Europe to wed much later than in other traditional societies in Asia and Africa. This exceptional pattern found women marrying, on average, at twenty-five years of age, men at twenty-seven or twenty-eight, by which time they hoped to have accumulated sufficient resources to establish a household. Young couples lived on their own, and not, as in societies elsewhere, as part of "extended" families of three generations. In those extended families, a farm might pass from father to son before the death of the former. But in Europe this was not the custom. Since a son could not inherit until his father died, he was compelled to establish himself independently, and to postpone starting his own family until he had done so. Late marriage helped to control the birth rate. Once married, however, a couple generally produced their first child within a year. Although subsequent children appeared with annual or biannual regularity, long periods of breast-feeding, which tends to reduce the mother's fertility, and community disapproval of extramarital sexual relations went some way toward limiting childbirth.

Implications of the European marriage pattern

Until the middle of the eighteenth century, populations continued to chart their rise and fall according to the outbreak of warfare, famine, and disease. From about 1750 on, however, there was a steady and significant population increase, with almost all countries experiencing major growth. In Russia, where territorial expansion added further to the increases, the population rate may have tripled in the second half of the eighteenth century. Gains elsewhere, while not usually as spectacular, were nevertheless significant. The population of Prussia and Spain doubled; Hungary's more than tripled; and England's population, which was about 5.5 million in 1700, reached 9 million in 1800. France, already in 1700 the most heavily populated country in Europe (about 20 million), added a further 6 million before 1790. Although reasons for the population increase remain something of mystery, historians are inclined to agree that it was the cumulative result of a very gradual decline in the death rate, due in large measure to an equally gradual increase in the food supply. Better transportation facilitated the shipment of food over greater distances. Land clearances, particularly in England, and in Prussia and Russia, where territories were opened to colonization, provided an essential ingredient for increased production. New staples—the potato and maize—supplemented the diets of the very poor. And although evidence here is only fragmentary, it appears that whereas the climate of seventeenth-century Europe was abnormally bad, that of the succeeding hundred years was on the whole favorable.

Population growth

Population increase brought with it new problems and new attitudes. For example, the decline in the death rate among infants—along with an apparent increase in illegitimacy at the end of the eighteenth century—created a growing population of unwanted babies among the poor. Some desperate women resorted to infanticide, though since

New problems and attitudes

children murdered at birth died without benefit of baptism, the crime was stigmatized as especially heinous by the Church as well as by society in general. More often, babies were abandoned at the door of foundling hospitals. As an English benefactor of several such institutions, Jonas Hanway, remarked in 1766, "it is much less difficult to the human heart and the dictates of self-preservation to drop a child than to kill it." In Paris during the 1780s from seven to eight thousand children were being abandoned out of a total of thirty thousand new births. Paradoxically, some historians now argue that during this same period the decrease in infant and child mortality encouraged many parents to lavish care and affection on their offspring in a way that they had not when the repeated early deaths of their sons and daughters had taught them the futility of that emotional bond. The eighteenth century witnessed the rise of the children's book industry; in England between 1750 and 1814, over 2400 titles were published. Toy shops appeared in cities and towns; dolls and dollhouses began to be mass produced for the first time. All of this suggests the willingness of parents to invest in a new relationship that was the result of major demographic change.

5. LIFE WITHIN A SOCIETY OF ORDERS

*Orders, privilege, and
freedom*

Despite the economic and demographic alterations that were occurring in early-modern Europe, it remained a society divided into traditional orders. Jean Bodin, the French philosopher, wrote in 1570 that the division of the citizenry into "the three orders of nobles, clergy and people" was no more than natural. "There never was a commonwealth, real or imaginary, where citizens were in truth equal in all rights and privileges. Some always have more, some less than the rest." And some had none. Orders were demarcated by those rights and privileges. "Freedom" was understood as one such privilege, as a benefit, bestowed not upon all men and women, but upon special groups whose position "freed" them to do certain things others could not do, or freed them from the burden of doing certain things that were required of others. An English landowner was, because of the position his property conferred upon him, privileged, and therefore "free," to participate directly in the election of his government. A French nobleman was privileged, and therefore "free," to avoid the heavy burden of taxation levied upon the unprivileged orders. A German tailor who had served out his seven-year apprenticeship was free to set up his own shop for profit, something an unapprenticed man could not do, no matter what his degree of skill with needle and thread. The master tailor's position conferred this freedom, just as the position of aristocrat and property owner conferred theirs.

The members of the higher orders attempted at all times to live their lives in a particular style which accorded with their rank. The nobility

Middle-Class Fashion. In this seventeenth-century portrait of a Dutch burgo-
master and his family, the patriarch and his wife are wearing the costume of
an earlier generation, while the children are clothed in the current style. All
display the opulence characteristic of their prosperous class.

was taught from birth to consider itself a class apart. Merchants and
manufacturers were just as insistent upon maintaining the traditional
marks of privilege that separated them from artisans and peasants.
Sumptuary laws decreed what could be worn and by whom. An edict
promulgated in the German principality of Brunswick in 1738, for
example, forbade servant girls to use silk dress materials, to wear gold
or silver ornaments, or shoes of anything but plain black leather. A
similar law in the Polish city of Posen prohibited the wives of burghers from wearing capes or long hair. Style was not simply a matter of
current whim. It was a badge of status and was carefully adhered to
as such. An aristocratic lady powdered her hair and rouged her cheeks
as a sign that she was an aristocrat. Life within a society of orders
demanded a certain degree of theatricality, especially from those at the
top of the social hierarchy. Aristocrats "acted" their part in a calculat-
edly self-conscious way. Their manner of speech, their dress, the ceremonial sword they were privileged to wear, the title by which they
were addressed, were the props of a performance which constantly
emphasized the distinctions between those above and those below.
Noble families lived in castles, chateaux, or country houses whose size
and antiquity were a further proclamation of superiority. When they
built new mansions, as the *nouveau riche* capitalist English gentry did
in the eighteenth century, they made certain their elaborate houses and
spacious private parks declared their newfound power. The English
politician Robert Walpole had an entire village moved to improve the
view from his grand new residence.

The vast majority of men and women defined and understood social

*The theater of a society of
orders*

*Banquet Given in Paris by the Spanish Duke
of Alva in Honor of the Prince of Asturias.*
The scene illustrates the ostentatious
display this powerful nobleman believed
suitable to his rank and fortune.

hierarchy in terms of the rural communities in which they lived. At
the head of those communities, in all likelihood, stood a representative
of the noble elite. Aristocrats probably numbered about 3 percent of
the total population of Europe. The percentage was higher in Russia,
Poland, Hungary, and Spain; lower in Germany, France, and England.
Land was the hallmark of aristocratic position. And, generally speaking, the more land one possessed, the higher one stood within the
aristocracy. In Hungary, five noble families owned about 14 percent
of the entire country; the greatest of these, Prince Esterházy, controlled the lives of over half a million peasants. Most noblemen were
not nearly so rich and powerful. Some, indeed, could rely on little
more than inherited privilege to distinguish themselves from peasants.

The pattern of noble life varied considerably from country to country. In England and Prussia, the nobility tended to reside on its estates;
in south and west Germany, and in France, aristocrats were more likely
to leave the management of their estates to stewards and to live at the
royal court. Although the nobility claimed to disdain commerce, by
the end of the eighteenth century they were involving themselves in
increasing numbers in a variety of commercial enterprises. Some
exploited mineral deposits on their estates; others invested in overseas
trade. In France, two of the four largest coal mines were owned and
operated by noblemen, while the duke of Orléans was an important
investor in the newly established chemical dye industry. In eastern
Europe, because there were few middle-class merchants, aristocrats
frequently undertook to market their agricultural produce themselves.

The nobility

Nobility and commerce

In no country was the aristocracy a completely closed order. Men who proved of use to the crown as administrators or lawyers, men who amassed large fortunes as a consequence of judicious—and often legally questionable—financial transactions, moved into the ranks of the nobility with increasing frequency during the late seventeenth and eighteenth century. Joseph II of Austria was making financiers into noblemen by the dozen in the late eighteenth century. In France, it was possible to attain nobility through the purchase of expensive offices from the crown. There was also a growing legal nobility of the "robe," headed by members of the thirteen provincial *parlements* whose function it was to record, and thereby sanction, the laws of the kingdom.

In time, severe tensions arose, most particularly in France but elsewhere as well, between the older nobility and those much more active and frequently more intelligent men of a new noble order, whom aristocrats with a longer pedigree considered upstarts. Tradition had it that noble service meant military service, that the ideal of noble honor involved heroism on the battlefield, not cunning at the law courts or conniving in palace antechambers.

Whether recently enobled or members of one of those ancient families that existed throughout Europe and which the French called—simply and eloquently—*les grandes,* most aristocrats owned large landed estates. Landownership helped them not only to establish their position but to define it as well, by bringing them into direct relationship with the peasants and laborers who worked that land and over whose lives the aristocracy exercised dominion. The status of the peasantry varied greatly across the face of rural Europe. In the East—Russia, Poland, Hungary, and in parts of Germany beyond the Elbe—the desire for profit in agriculture and the collusion of the state with the aristocracy led to the growth of a "second serfdom," a serf system much stronger than that which had existed during the Middle Ages. In East Prussia, serfs often had to work from three to six days a week for their lord, and some had only late evening or night hours to cultivate their own lands.

Peasants throughout eastern Europe found their destinies controlled in almost all respects by their masters. Noble landlords dispensed justice in manorial courts and even ruled in cases to which they were themselves interested parties. These men were a combination of sheriff, chief magistrate, and police force in one, able to sentence their "subjects" to corporal punishment, imprisonment, exile, or in many cases death, without right of appeal. Peasants could not leave their land, marry, or learn a trade unless permitted to do so by their lord. In Russia, where half the land was owned by the state, peasants were bound to work in mines or workshops if their masters so ordered, and could be sold to private owners. Although Russian peasant serfs were said to possess a "legal personality" that distinguished them from slaves, the distinction was obscured in practice.

In western Europe, the position of the peasantry reflected the fact that serfdom had all but disappeared by the sixteenth century. Peas-

A French Peasant. Tattered and overworked, this peasant farmer is shown feeding his livestock as the tax collector at his door relieves him of all of his profits.

Poverty and the peasantry

Peasant bread and board

ants might theoretically own land, although the vast majority were either tenants or laborers. Hereditary tenure was in general more secure than in the East; peasants could dispose of their land and had legal claim to farm buildings and implements. Although far freer than their eastern European counterparts, the peasantry of western Europe still lived to a great degree under the domination of landowners. They were in many cases responsible for the payment of various dues and fees: an annual rent paid to landlords by those who might otherwise own their land outright; a special tax on recently cleared land; a fee, often as much as one-sixth of the assessed value of the land, collected by the manorial lord whenever peasant property changed hands; and charges for the use of the lord's mill, bakery, or wine press. In France, peasants were compelled to submit to the *corvée,* a requirement that they labor for several weeks a year maintaining local roads. Even access to the often questionable justice meted out in the manorial courts, which endured throughout the early-modern period in almost all of western Europe, was encumbered with fees and commissions. To many peasants, however, the most galling badge of their inferiority was their inability to hunt within the jurisdiction of their landlord's manor. The slaughter of game was a privilege reserved to the nobility, a circumstance generating sustained resentment on the part of a population that looked upon deer and pheasant not as a symbol of aristocratic status but as a necessary supplement to its meager diet. Noble landlords rarely missed an opportunity to extract all the money they could from their peasants while constantly reminding them of the degree to which their destiny was controlled by the lord of the manor.

That destiny was shaped as well by the level of economic prosperity a particular peasant might enjoy. A few were genuinely independent, literate, influential members of the communities where they lived, owning not only land but considerable livestock. Most, however, were far less fortunate. Those with claim to a small piece of land usually worked it into infertility in the course of one or two generations as they scrambled to make it produce as much as possible. Each time a peasant proprietor died, his property was divided among his male heirs, encouraging the sort of marginal economic existence that was the fate of most rural laborers.

Poor peasants often lived, contrary to the biblical injunction, by bread alone—two pounds a day if they were lucky, the dark dough a mixture of wheat and rye flour. Bread was supplemented by peas and beans, beer, wine, or, far less often, skimmed milk. Their houses usually contained no more than one or two rooms, and were constructed of wood, plastered with mud or clay. Roofs were most often thatched with straw, which was used as fertilizer when replaced, and provided fodder for animals at times of scarcity. Furnishings seldom consisted of more than a table, benches, pallets for sleeping, a few earthenware plates, and simple tools—an axe, a wooden spade, a knife.

Left: *"Russian Soup."* Interior of a sparsely furnished peasant's cottage. Note the cradle suspended from the ceiling. Right: *Market Scene* by Jean Michelin. Peasant women and children bringing produce to a nearby market town.

Wives of peasants tended livestock and vegetables, and managed the dairy, if there was one. Wives of agricultural laborers went out themselves as field workers, or worked at home at knitting, spinning, or weaving in order to augment the family income. A popular seventeenth-century poem has a laborer's wife lamenting her lot with a refrain that has echoed down the ages: ". . . my labor is hard,/ And all my pleasures are debarr'd;/ Both morning, evening, night and noon,/ I'm sure a woman's work is never done."

The peasant wife

Although somewhere between 80 and 90 percent of the population lived in small rural communities, towns and cities were coming to play an increasingly important role in the life of early-modern Europe. One must speak of the "rise" of towns and cities with some caution, however, since the pace of urbanization varied greatly across the Continent. Russia remained almost entirely rural: only 2.5 percent of its population lived in towns in 1630, and that percentage had increased by only 0.5 percent by 1774. In Holland, on the other hand, 59 percent of the population was urban centered in 1627 and 65 percent in 1795.

The growth of urban centers

As the fortunes of towns and cities rose and fell, so did their populations. Capital cities grew dramatically. By the middle of the eighteenth century, Madrid, Berlin, and St. Petersburg all had populations of over 100,000. London grew from 674,000 in 1700 to 860,000 a century later. Paris a city of approximately 180,000 in 1600, increased to over half a million by 1800. Berlin presents a particularly interesting example of urban expansion. From a population of 6500 in 1661, it swelled to 60,000 in 1721 and 140,000 in 1783. Its increase was due in

Urban populations

part to the fact that successive Prussian rulers undertook to improve its position as a trade center by the construction of canals which linked it with Breslau and Hamburg. Its population rose as well, however, because of the marked increase in Prussian army and bureaucratic personnel based in the capital city. Of the 140,000 citizens of Berlin in 1783, approximately 65,000 were state employees or members of their families.

*Commerce and urban
growth*

The population of other cities was related to the growth of trade. Amsterdam, the hub of early-modern international commerce, grew from 30,000 in 1530 to 115,000 in 1630 and 200,000 by 1800. Naples, the busy Mediterranean port, went from a population of 300,000 in 1600 to nearly half a million by the late eighteenth century. Populations could fluctuate considerably as a result of economic growth or decline. For example, that of Norwich, in England, increased when the manufacture of woolen goods shifted away from older industrial centers on the English Channel to the north. That of the important German market center of Frankfurt declined during and after the period of the Thirty Years' War, when difficulties of communication and the general instability caused by frequent military campaigns diverted much of its former business to Amsterdam.

*Urban living conditions:
emigration, housing*

Those towns and cities that grew did so because of the decline in the death rate, but also because commerce, industry, and government were attracting new urban recruits from the countryside. An eighteenth-century commentator noted that the laborers in Paris were "almost all foreigners"—that is, men and women born outside the city: carpenters from Savoy, water carriers from Auvergne, porters from Lyons, stonecutters from Normandy, wigmakers from Gascony, shoemakers from Lorraine. In the case of industries such as textile manufacturing, whose workshops required more space than was available inside the medieval walls of the city center, new workers settled in industrial suburbs. In capital cities, suburbs also served as fashionable neighborhoods for the ruling elite, places "where the want of London smoke is supplied by the smoke of Virginia tobacco," as one Englishman remarked wryly. Houses in areas inhabited by the wealthy were increasingly built of brick and stone, which replaced the wood, lath, and plaster of the Middle Ages. This change was a response to the constant danger of fire. The great fire of London in 1666, which destroyed three-quarters of the town—12,000 houses—was the largest of the conflagrations that swept cities with devastating regularity. Urban dwellings of the laboring poor remained firetraps. Workers' quarters were badly overcrowded; entire families lived in one-room accommodations in basements and attics that were infested with bugs and fleas.

Urban society was, like its rural counterpart, a society of orders. In capital cities, noble families occupied the highest social position, as they did in the countryside, living a parasitic life of conspicuous consumption at court. The majority of cities and towns were dominated by a nonnoble *bourgeoisie*. That French term originally designated a burgher or townsman who was a long-term, resident property owner or leaseholder and taxpayer. By the eighteenth century it had come to mean a townsman of some means who aspired to be recognized as a person of local importance, and evinced a willingness to work hard, whether at counting-house or government office, and a desire to live a comfortable, if by no means extravagant, existence. A bourgeois gentleman might derive his income from rents; he might, as well, be an industrialist, banker, or merchant, a professional, lawyer, or physician. If he served in the central bureaucracy, he would consider himself the social superior of those provincials whose affairs he administered. Yet he would himself be looked down upon by the aristocracy, who tended to think of the *bourgeoisie* as a class of vulgar social climbers. The French playwright Molière's comedy *The Bourgeois Gentleman* (1670) reflected this attitude, ridiculing the manners of the commercial class who were trying to ape their betters. "Bourgeois," another French writer observed, "is the insult given by noblemen to anybody they deem slow-witted or out of touch with the court." The *bourgeoisie* usually constituted about 20 to 25 percent of a town's population. As its economic elite, these men were almost always its governing elite as well. Municipal offices were considered a privilege of this order and were distributed accordingly.

Next within the urban hierarchy was a vast middle range of shopkeepers and artisans. Many of the latter continued to learn and then to practice their craft as members of guilds, which in turn contained their own particular ascending hierarchy of apprentice, journeyman, and master, thus preserving a society of orders. Throughout the early-modern period, however, commercial expansion threatened the rigid hierarchy of the guild structure. The expense and curtailed output resulting from restrictive guild practices met with serious opposition in big cities such as Paris and London, where expanding markets called for cheaper and more readily available goods. Journeymen tailors and shoemakers in increasing numbers set up shops without benefit of mastership and produced cheaper coats and shoes in defiance of guild regulations. In the silk workshops of Lyons, both masters and journeymen were compelled to labor without distinction of status for piece rates (wages paid per finished article, rather than per hour) set by merchandising middlemen far below an equitable level in the opinion of the silk workers. Artisans like these, compelled to work for low wages at the behest of profiteering middlemen, grew increasingly restive. In France and Germany, journeymen's associations had originated as social and mutual-aid organizations for young men engaged in "tramping" the country to gain experience in their trade. In some instances, however, these associations fostered the development of a trade consciousness that led to strikes and boycotts against masters and middlemen

Urban society: the bourgeoisie

Urban society: shopkeepers and artisans

over the issues of wages and working conditions. An imperial law passed in Germany in 1731 deprived the associations of their right to organize, and required journeymen to carry a certificate of identification as testimony of their respectability during their travels.

Urban society: the poor

At the bottom of urban society was a mass of semi-skilled and unskilled workers: carters and porters; stevedores and dockers; water carriers and sweepers; seamstresses, laundresses, cleaners, and domestic servants. These men and women, like their rural counterparts, lived on the margins of urban life, constantly battling the trade cycles, seasonal unemployment, and epidemics that threatened their ability to survive. A number lived in shanties on the edge of towns and cities. In Genoa, the homeless poor were sold as galley slaves each winter. In Venice, the poor lived on decrepit barges under the city's bridges. A French ordinance of 1669 ordered the destruction of all houses "built on poles by vagabonds and useless members of society." Derpived of the certainty of steady work, these people were prey not only to economic fluctuations and malevolent "acts of God," but to a social system that left them without any "privilege" or "freedom" whatsoever.

Attitudes toward poverty

Attitudes toward poverty varied from country to country. Most localities extended the concept of orders to include the poor: "the deserving"—usually orphans, the insane, the aged, the infirm; and "the undeserving"—able-bodied men and women who were out of work or who, even though employed, could not support themselves and their families. The authorities tended to assume in the latter case that poverty was the result of personal failings; few made a connection between general economic circumstances and the plight of the individual poor. For the deserving, private charitable organizations, such as those in France, founded by the order of St. Vincent de Paul and by

Beggars at the Doorway by Louis LeNain. A seventeenth-century depiction of poverty, sentimentalized so as to celebrate the virtues of deference.

Hanging Thieves. This seventeenth-century engraving is designed to teach a lesson. Troops stand by and priests shave the heads of the condemned criminals as they are executed by the dozen. "At last," the engraver's caption reads, "these infamous lost souls are hung like unhappy fruit."

the Sisters of Charity, provided assistance. For the undeserving, there was harsh treatment at the hands of the state whose concern to alleviate extreme deprivation arose more from a desire to avert public disorder than from motives of human charity. Food riots were common occurrences. In times of scarcity the French government frequently intervened to reduce the price of grain, hoping thereby to prevent an outbreak of rioting. Yet riots nevertheless occurred. When property damage resulted, the ringleaders were always severely punished, usually by hanging, but the remainder of the crowd was often left untouched by the law, a fact suggesting the degree to which governments were prepared to tolerate rioting itself as a means of dealing with the chronic problem of poverty. Poor vagrants were perceived as a serious threat to social tranquility. They were therefore frequently rounded up at harvest time to keep them from plundering the fields.

Vagrants and other chronically unemployed persons were placed in poorhouses where conditions were little better than those in prisons. Often the very young, the very old, the sick, and the insane were housed together with hardened criminals. Poor relief in England was administered parish by parish in accordance with a law passed in 1601. Relief was tied to a "law of settlement," which stipulated that paupers might receive aid only if still residing in the parish of their birth. An unemployed weaver who had migrated fifty miles in search of work could thus expect assistance only if he returned home again. In the late eighteenth century, several European countries established modest public works programs in an attempt to relieve poverty by reducing unemployment. France, for example, undertook road-building projects in the 1770s under the auspices of its progressive finance minister,

The treatment of paupers

Louis XIV Visiting the French Academy of Sciences. Royal patronage sustained such academies by guaranteeing members rewards suitable to their station.

Turgot. But generally speaking, indigence was perceived not as a social ill for which a remedy might be sought, but as an indelible stigma demarking the lowest of a community's social orders.

Early-modern Europe fashioned its institutions to reflect the patterns of social hierarchy. Nowhere was this more apparent than in the field of education. One barrier—a knowledge of Latin—separated aristocrats and a fair number of scholars and professionals from the commercial middle ranks; a second—the ability to read and write—separated the middle from the rest. Noblemen were generally educated by private tutors; though they might attend university for a time, they did so not in preparation for a profession but to receive further educational "finishing." Indeed during the late seventeenth and eighteenth centuries universities more or less surrendered intellectual leadership to various academies established with royal patronage by European monarchs to enhance their own reputations as well as to encourage the advancement of science and the arts: the Royal Society of London, founded by Charles II in 1660; the French Academy of Sciences, a project upon which Louis XIV lavished a good deal of ostentatious attention; and the Berlin Royal Academy of Science and Letters, patronized by Frederick the Great of Prussia in the eighteenth century. Few noblemen had the interest or the intelligence to participate in the activities of these august organizations, which were not, in any case, teaching institutions. Far better suited to their needs and inclinations was "the grand tour," often of many months' duration,

Education in a society of orders: the nobility

which led the aristocrat through the capitals of Europe, and during which he was expected to acquire a kind of international *politesse*.

Endowed, fee-charging schools for the training of a governmental elite existed in France (the *collège*) and Spain (the *collegio mayor*) and in Germany and Austria (the *gymnasium*). Here the emphasis was by no means on "practical" subjects such as modern language or mathematics, but on the mastery of Greek and Latin translation and composition, the intellectual badge of the educated elite. An exception was the Prussian University of Halle, designed to teach a professional elite; a contemporary described that institution as teaching only what was "rational, useful, and practical."

Male children from the middle orders destined to enter the family business or profession as a rule attended small private academies where the curriculum included the sort of "useful" instruction ignored in the *collèges* and *gymnasia*. Female children, from both the upper and middle orders, were almost invariably educated at home, receiving little more than rudimentary instruction in gentlewomanly subjects such as modern language, belles lettres, and music, if from the noble ranks, and a similar, if slightly more practical training, if from the bourgeoisie.

No European country undertook the task of providing primary education to all its citizens until the mid–eighteenth century, when Frederick the Great in Prussia and the Habsburg monarchs Maria Theresa and her son Joseph II in Austria instituted systems of compulsory attendance. Available evidence suggests that their results fell far short of expectation. An early–nineteenth-century survey from the relatively enlightened Prussian province of Cleves revealed dilapidated schools, poorly attended classes, and an incompetent corps of teachers. Educational conditions were undoubtedly worse in most other European communities.

Although educational opportunities for peasants and workers remained meager by modern standards, available evidence suggests that literacy rates increased considerably in the seventeenth and eighteenth centuries; in England, from one in four males in 1600 to one in two by 1800; in France, from 29 percent of the male population in 1686 to 47 percent in 1786. Literacy among women increased as well, though their rate of increase generally lagged behind that of men: only 27 percent of the female population in France was literate in 1786. Naturally, such rates varied according to particular localities and circumstances, and from country to country. Literacy was higher in urban areas which contained a large proportion of artisans. In rural eastern Europe, literacy remained extremely low (20–30 percent) well into the nineteenth century. Notwithstanding state-directed efforts in Prussia and Austria, the rise in literacy was largely the result of a growing determination on the part of religiously minded reformers to teach the poor to read and write as a means of encouraging obedience to divine and secular authority. A Sunday-school movement in eigh-

Training for government service

Education for the middle orders

Education for the poor

Increasing literacy

teenth-century England and similar activities among the Christian Brotherhood in France are clear evidence of this trend.

Though the majority of the common people were probably no more than barely literate, they possessed a flourishing culture of their own. Village life, particularly in Roman Catholic countries, centered about the church, to which men and women would go on Sundays not only to worship but to socialize. Much of the remainder of their day of rest would be devoted to participation in village games. Religion provided the opportunity for association and for a welcome break from the daily work routines. Pilgrimages, for example, to a nearby shrine would include a procession of exuberant villagers led by one of their number carrying an image of the village's patron saint and accompanied by drinking, dancing, and picnicking. In towns, Catholics joined organizations, called confraternities in France, Italy, Austria, and the Netherlands, which provided mutual aid and a set of common rituals and traditions centered upon a patron saint. Religious community was expressed as well in popular Protestant movements which arose in the eighteenth century: Pietism on the Continent and Methodism in England. Both emphasized the importance of personal salvation through faith and the potential worth of every human soul regardless of station. Both therefore appealed particularly to people whose position within the community had heretofore been presumed to be without any value. Though Methodism's founder, John Wesley (1703–1791), preached obedience to earthly authority, his willingness to rely on working men and women as preachers and organizers gave them a new sense of personal importance.

While much popular culture was directly linked to religious traditions and practices, much was now growing secular. Carnival, that vibrant prelenten celebration indigenous not only to Mediterranean

Cockfight by William Hogarth. This London scene suggests the degree to which men from different social orders came together for sport, drinking, and adventure. Here a clergyman and a young gentleman consort with the London riff-raff.

French Tavern. Often located outside the city limits so as to avoid the payment of municipal taxes, taverns such as this provided a gathering place for workers to drink, gossip, and relax after the day's labors. The tavern also served as a convenient place for public readings and for airing common grievances.

Europe but to Germany and Austria as well, represented an opportunity for common folk to cast aside the burdens and restraints imposed upon their order by secular authority. Performances and processions celebrated a "world turned upside down," a theme popular throughout much of Europe from the Later Middle Ages, appealing to commoners for a variety of ambiguous psychological reasons, but in large part, certainly, as a way of avenging symbolically the economic and social oppression under which they lived. For a few days, the oppressed played the role of the oppressor and rulers were made to look like fools and knaves. In parades, men dressed as kings walked barefoot while peasants rode on horseback or in carriages; the poor threw pretend money to the rich. Annual harvest festivals, once sponsored by the church, were also increasingly secular celebrations of release from backbreaking labor, punctuated by feasting, drinking, sporting, and lovemaking. Fairs and traveling circuses brought something of distant places and people into lives bound to one spot. The drudgery of everyday life was also relieved by horseraces, cock fights, and bear baiting. Taverns played an even more constant role in the daily life of the village, providing a place for men to gather over tobacco and drink to gossip and gamble.

Carnival and other amusements

Laboring men and women depended on an oral tradition of myth, legend, and superstition to steady their lives, and give them point and purpose. Stories in books sold at fairs by peddlers were passed on by those who could read. They told of heroes and saints, and of kings like Charlemagne whose paternal concern for his common subjects led him into battle against his selfish nobility. Belief in villains matched

The role of the oral tradition

Gin Lane by William Hogarth. Hogarth believed in portraying human nature as he found it. In this famous engraving, he is preaching a sermon against the gin trade, one of the besetting evils of eighteenth-century London.

belief in heroes. Witchcraft, as we have seen, was a reality for much of the period to superstitious men and women. So was Satan. So was any supernatural force, whether for good or evil, which could help them make sense of a world in which they, more than any, were victims of events beyond their control.

Stability and change

Though increasingly secularized, popular customs, celebrations, and beliefs remained a stabilizing force in early-modern Europe. They were the cultural expression of that social order to which the vast majority of Europeans belonged. Popular culture in the main tended to reinforce the traditions and assumptions of order and hierarchy. As such, it helped to bind men and women to what civilization had been, as capitalism and mercantilism impelled them in the direction of what it would become.

SELECTED READINGS

- *Items so designated are available in paperback editions.*
- Blum, Jerome, *Lord and Peasant in Russia,* Princeton, N.J., 1961. A good study of Russian society.
- Braudel, F., *Capitalism and Material Life, 1400–1800,* London, 1973. A fascinating review of evidence pertaining to the entire world by one of the greatest of living historians.

————, *The Structures of Everyday Life: The Limits of the Possible,* New York, 1981. A survey of the material conditions of life; profusely illustrated.

• Burke, Peter, *Popular Culture in Early Modern Europe,* London, 1978. Synthesizes the most recent work on the period between 1500 and 1800; fascinating.

Chambers, J. D., and G. E. Mingay, *The Agricultural Revolution, 1750–1880,* London, 1966. Now the standard work.

• Cipolla, C. M., *Before the Industrial Revolution: European Society and Economy, 1000–1700,* 2nd ed., New York, 1980. Wide-ranging and full of deft observations.

• Curtin, Philip D., *The Atlantic Slave Trade,* Madison, Wisc., 1969. Reinterprets the character of the trade.

• Davis, Natalie Z., *Society and Culture in Early Modern France,* Stanford, Calif., 1975. Eight scintillating essays by a pioneer in the use of anthropological methods for the study of early-modern European history.

Forster, Robert, *The Nobility of Toulouse in the Eighteenth Century,* Baltimore, Md., 1960. A careful analysis of the extent and nature of aristocratic power.

Glass, D. V., and D. E. C. Eversley, eds., *Population in History,* New York, 1965. Contains useful essays on demographic patterns.

Heckscher, E., *Mercantilism,* rev. ed., 2 vols., London, 1955. The most influential, but controversial, work on the subject.

Hufton, Olwen H., *The Poor of Eighteenth Century France,* Oxford, 1974. One of the first studies of a preindustrial "underclass."

Kamen, Henry, *The Iron Century: Social Change in Europe, 1560–1660,* New York, 1971. Especially suggestive and interesting in its exploration of the bleak side of life.

Kaplow, Jeffry, *The Names of Kings: The Parisian Laboring Poor in the Eighteenth Century,* New York, 1972. A valuable study of the urban poor.

• Laslett, Peter and Richard Wall, eds., *Household and Family in Past Times,* New York, 1972. A suggestive collection of essays.

LeRoy Ladurie, Emmanuel, *The Peasants of Languedoc,* Urbana, Ill., 1974. A classic on peasant life and demography.

Levine, David, *Family Formation in an Age of Nascent Capitalism,* New York, 1977. A thoughtful, recent treatment of patterns of social formation.

Mousnier, R., *Peasant Uprisings in Seventeenth-Century France, Russia and China,* New York, 1970. A comparative analysis.

• Ranum, Orest, *Paris in the Age of Absolutism,* New York, 1968. A useful view of urban life.

Rich, E. E., and C. H. Wilson, eds., *The Cambridge Economic History of Europe:* Volume 5, *The Economic Organization of Early Modern Europe,* New York, 1977. An indispensable guide to the study of the period's economy and society.

• Stone, Lawrence, *The Family, Sex and Marriage in England, 1500–1800,* New York, 1977. An important, controversial book which argues important changes in attitudes over the course of three centuries.

Wilson, Charles, *England's Apprenticeship, 1603–1763,* London, 1965. A reliable economic survey.

• Wrigley, E. A., *Population and History,* New York, 1969. A good introduction to family history.

SOURCE MATERIALS

Barnett, G. E., ed., *Two Tracts by Gregory King,* Baltimore, 1936. An introduction to the work of the modern world's first real statistician.

• Goubert, P., *The Ancien Régime: French Society, 1600–1750,* London, 1973. Particularly strong in its descriptions of rural life. Includes selections from illuminating documents.

Young, Arthur, *Travels in France during the Years 1787, 1788, 1789,* London, 1912. Vivid observations by an English traveler.

Chapter 18

THE AGE OF ABSOLUTISM
(1660-1789)

There are four essential characteristics or qualities of royal authority.
First, royal authority is sacred.
Second, it is paternal.
Third, it is absolute.
Fourth, it is subject to reason.

— Jacques Bossuet, *Politics Drawn from the Very Words of Holy Scripture*

The period from the accession to personal rule of Louis XIV of France until the French Revolution is known as the age of absolutism. The label is accurate if we define absolutism as the conscious extension of the legal and administrative power of state sovereigns over their subjects, and over the vested interests of the social and economic orders in which those subjects were ranked. The dates are suggestive in that for the period as a whole the activities of French monarchs most clearly expressed the doctrines of absolutist government. Yet both the dates and the label need to be treated with some caution. We have already noted that from about 1500 on, a general trend to make the state omnicompetent had manifested itself in England and on the Continent. Sixteenth-century kings saw in Protestantism a way of asserting the sovereignty of their states as a challenge to papal and aristocratic power. And political thinkers such as Bodin were championing absolutist theory in ther writings well before Louis XIV assumed personal rulership of France. By establishing the French monarchs as prototypical early-modern rulers, we risk ignoring variant modes of centralized government instituted by the rulers of Prussia, Russia, and Austria. And we exclude the crucially important exception of England, where after 1688 absolutist tendencies gave way to oligarchy, and political power was shared among monarchy, aristocracy, and plutocracy.

Absolutism defined

Finally, the term "absolutism" needs qualification. As practiced by western European eighteenth-century rulers, absolutism was not despotism. They did not understand it as a license for untrammeled and arbitrary rule, such as that practiced by Oriental potentates. Despite the best efforts of these European monarchs to consolidate their authority, they could not issue irresponsible decrees and achieve lasting compliance. Aristocrats, churchmen, merchants, and entrepreneurs remained strong enough within their respective orders to ensure that kings and queens would need to justify the actions they took. Moreover, rulers tended to respect not only the strength of their political adversaries but the processes of law; they quarreled openly and broke with tradition only under exceptional circumstances. No matter how "absolute" monarchs might wish to be, they were limited as well by rudimentary systems of transportation and communication from interfering with any degree of consistency and efficiency in the daily lives of their subjects. In this chapter we will measure the extent of royal power throughout Europe in the late seventeenth and eighteenth centuries, examine the varieties of absolutism as instituted and practiced by different monarchs, and take note of the way in which the centralization of power contributed to the rise of an international state system.

1. THE APPEAL AND JUSTIFICATION OF ABSOLUTISM

Absolutism appealed to many Europeans for the same reason that mercantalism did. In theory and practice, it expressed a desire for an end to the constant alarms and confusions of Europe's "iron century." The French religious wars, the Thirty Years' War in Germany, and the English Civil War all had produced great turbulence. The alternative, domestic order, absolutists argued, could come only with strong, centralized government. Just as mercantilists maintained that economic stability would result from regimentation, so absolutists contended that social and political harmony would be realized when subjects recognized their duty to obey their divinely sanctioned rulers.

Absolutist monarchs insisted, in turn, upon *their* duty to teach their subjects, even against their will, how to order their domestic affairs. As Margrave Karl Friedrich, eighteenth-century ruler of the German principality of Baden, expressed it: "We must make them, whether they like it or not, into free, opulent and law-abiding citizens." Looking back to the seventeenth-century wars that had torn Europe apart, rulers can be excused for believing that absolutism's promise of stability and prosperity—"freedom and opulence"—presented an attractive as well as an imperative alternative to disorder. Louis XIV of France remembered the experience of the *Fronde* as a threat to the welfare of the nation which he had been appointed by God to rule wisely and justly. When marauding Parisians entered his bedchamber one night in 1651 to discover if he had fled the city with Mazarin, Louis saw the intrusion as a horrid affront not only to his own person, but to the state. Squabbles among the nobility and criticisms of royal policy in the Paris Parlement during his minority left him convinced that he must exercise his powers and prerogatives rigorously if France was to survive and prosper as a great European state.

In order to achieve that objective, absolutist monarchs worked to control the disposition of the state's armed forces, the administration of its legal system, and the collection and distribution of its tax revenues. This ambitious goal required an efficient bureaucracy that owed its primary allegiance not to some particular social or economic order with interests antithetical to the monarchy, but to the institution of the monarchy itself. One hallmark of absolutist policy was its determination to construct a set of institutions strong enough to withstand, if not destroy, the privileged interests that had stood in the path of royal power in the past. The church and the nobility, the semi-autonomous regions, and the would-be independent representative bodies (the English Parliament and the French Estates-General) were all obstacles to the achievement of strong, centralized monarchical government. And the history of absolutism is, as much as anything, the history of the attempts of various rulers to bring these institutions to heel.

*Goals of absolute
monarchs: army,
administration, and
revenue*

In those major European countries where Roman Catholicism still remained the state religion—France, Spain, and Austria—successive monarchs throughout the eighteenth century made various attempts to "nationalize" the Church and its clergy. We have already noted the way in which in the fifteenth and sixteenth centuries, popes had conceded certain powers to the temporal rulers of France and Spain. Later absolutists, building on those earlier precedents, wrested further power from the Church in Rome. Even Charles III, the devout Spanish king who ruled from 1759 to 1788, pressed successfully for a papal concordat granting the state control over ecclesiastical appointments, and established his right to sanction the proclamation of papal bulls. Powerful as the Church was, it did not rival the aristocracy as an opponent of a centralized state. Monarchs combatted the noble orders in various ways. Louis XIV controlled the ancient French aristocracy by depriving it of political power while increasing its social prestige. Peter the Great, the talented and erratic tsar of early eighteenth-century Russia, coopted the nobility into government service. Later in the century, Catherine II struck a bargain whereby in return for the granting of vast estates and a variety of social and economic privileges such as exemption from taxation, the Russian aristocracy virtually surrendered the administrative and political power of the state into the empress's hands. In Prussia under Frederick the Great, the army was staffed by nobles: again, as in Peter's Russia, a case of cooption. Yet

*Absolutism and the control
of church and nobility*

in late–eighteenth-century Austria, the emperor Joseph II adopted a policy of confrontation rather than accommodation, denying the nobility exemption from taxation and deliberately blurring the distinctions between nobles and commoners.

These struggles between monarchs and nobles had implications for the additional struggle between local privileges and centralized power. Absolutists in France waged constant war against the autonomy of provincial institutions, often headed by aristocrats, much as Spanish rulers in the sixteenth century had battled independent-minded nobles in Aragon and Catalonia. Prussian rulers intruded into the governance of formerly "free" cities, assuming police and revenue powers over their inhabitants. These various campaigns, constantly waged and usually successful for a time, were evidence of the nature of absolutism and of its continuing success.

Absolutism had its theoretical apologists as well as its able practitioners. In addition to the political philosophies of men such as Bodin, defenders of royal power could rely on treatises such as Bishop Jacques Bossuet's *Politics Drawn from the Very Words of Scripture* (1708), written during the reign of Louis XIV, to sustain the case for extended monarchical control. Bossuet argued that absolute government was not the same as arbitrary government, since God, in whom "all strength and all perfection were united," was united as well with the person of the king. "God is holiness itself, goodness itself, and power itself. In these things lies the majesty of God. In the image of these things lies the majesty of the prince." It followed that the king was answerable to no one but God himself, and that the king was as far above other mortals as God was above the king. "The prince, as prince, is not regarded as a private person; he is a public personage, all the state is in him. . . .

Bishop Jacques Bossuet

The Château of Versailles. Dramatically expanded by Louis XIV in the 1660s from a hunting lodge to the principal royal residence and the seat of government, the château became a monument to the international power and prestige of the Grand Monarch.

Louis XIV, the Sun King. This portrait by Rigaud illustrates the degree to which absolute monarchy was defined in terms of studied performance.

As all perfection and all strength are united in God, all the power of individuals is united in the Person of the prince. What grandeur that a simple man should embody so much." What grandeur indeed! Bossuet's treatise was the most explicit and extreme statement of the theory of the divine right of kings, the doctrine that James I had tried to foist upon the English. Unlikely as it may sound to modern ears, the political philosophy of Bossuet was comforting to men and women who craved peace and stability after a century or more of international and domestic turmoil.

2. THE ABSOLUTISM OF LOUIS XIV

Examine a portrait of Louis XIV [1] (1643–1715) in court robes; it is all but impossible to discern the human being behind the facade of the absolute monarch. That facade was carefully and artfully constructed by Louis, who recognized, perhaps more clearly than any other early-modern ruler, the importance of theater as a means of establishing authority. Well into the eighteenth century, superstitious commoners continued to believe in the power of the king's magic "touch" to cure disease. Louis and his successors used this belief to enhance their position as divine-right rulers endowed with God-like powers and far removed from common humanity.

Absolutism as theater: Louis XIV

The advantages of strategic theater were expressed most clearly in Louis's palace at Versailles, the town outside of Paris to which he

[1]Here, as elsewhere, dates following a ruler's name refer to dates of reign.

One of the 1400 Fountains in the Gardens at Versailles. The grounds as well as the palace were part of the backdrop for the theater of absolutism.

Versailles

moved his court. The building itself was a stage, upon which Louis mesmerized the aristocracy into obedience by his performance of the daily rituals of absolutism. The main facade of the palace was a third of a mile in length. Inside, tapestries and paintings celebrated French military victories and royal triumphs. Outside, in gardens containing 1400 fountains, statues of Apollo, god of the sun, recalled Louis's claim to be the "Sun King" of the French. Noblemen vied to attend him when he arose from bed, ate his meals (usually stone-cold, having traveled the distance of several city blocks from royal kitchen to royal table), strolled in his gardens, or rode to the hunt. As Louis called himself the Sun King, so his court was the epicenter of his royal effulgence. Its glitter, in which France's leading aristocrats were required by their monarch to share, was deliberately manufactured so as to blind them to the possibility of disobedience to the royal will. Instead of plotting some sort of minor treason on his estate, a marquis enjoyed the pleasure of knowing that on the morrow he was to be privileged to engage the king in two or three minutes of vapid conversation as the royal party made its stately progress through the vast palace halls (whose smells were evidence of the absence of sanitation facilities and of the seamy side of absolutist grandeur).

Louis XIV on his duties

Louis understood this theater as part of his duty as sovereign, a duty which he took with utmost seriousness. Though far from brilliant, he was hard-working and conscientious. Whether or not he actually remarked "L'état, c'est moi" ("I am the State"), he believed himself personally responsible for the well-being of his subjects. "The deference and the respect that we receive from our subjects," he wrote in a memoir he prepared for his son on the art of ruling, "are not a free gift from them but payment for the justice and the protection that they expect from us. Just as they must honor us, we must protect and defend them."

Louis defined this responsibility in absolutist terms: as a need to concentrate royal power so as to produce general domestic tranquility. While taming the aristocracy, he conciliated the upper bourgeoisie by enlisting its members to assist him in the task of administration. He appointed them as intendants, responsible for the administration and taxation of the thirty-six *generalités* into which France was divided. Intendants never served in the regions where they were born, and were thus unconnected with the local elites over which they exercised authority. They held office at the king's pleasure, and were clearly "his" men. Other administrators, often from families newly ennobled as a result of administrative service, assisted in directing affairs of state from Versailles. These men were not actors in the theater of Louis the Sun King; they were the hard-working assistants of Louis the royal custodian of his country's welfare. Much of the time and energy of Louis's bureaucrats was expended on the collection of taxes, necessary above all in order to finance the large standing army on which France's ambitious foreign policy depended. In addition to the *taille,* or land tax, which increased throughout the seventeenth century and upon which a surtax was levied as well, the government introduced a capitation tax, payable by all, and pressed hard for the collection of indirect taxes such as that on salt (the *gabelle*) and on wine and tobacco. Since the nobility was exempt from the *taille,* its burden fell most heavily on the peasantry, whose periodic local revolts Louis easily crushed.

Regional opposition—and indeed regionalism generally—was curtailed during Louis's reign. Although intendants and lesser administrators came from afar, did not speak the local dialect, ignored local custom, and were therefore despised, they were generally obeyed. The semi-autonomous outer provinces of Brittany, Languedoc, and Franche Comté (a part of that territory known collectively as the *pays d'état*) came to heel as central administration crippled their provincial Estates. To put an end to the power of regional *parlements* (the courts responsible for registering laws), Louis decreed that members of those bodies which vetoed legislation would be summarily exiled. The Estates-General, the national French representative assembly last summoned in 1614 during the troubled regency following the death of Henry IV, did not meet again until 1789.

Louis was equally determined, for reasons of state and of personal conscience, to impose religious unity upon the French. That task proved to be difficult and time-consuming. The Huguenots were not the only source of theological heterodoxy. Jesuits, Quietists, and Jansenists—all three claiming to represent the "true" Roman faith—battled among themselves for adherents to their particular brand of Catholicism. Jesuits served Louis's interests best, since they advocated obedience to the secular power of the French state. Quietists preached

The administration of French absolutism: intendants and revenue

Curbing regional opposition

Louis XIV's religious policies

a retreat into personal mysticism. Jansenism—a movement named for its founder Cornelius Jansen, a seventeenth-century bishop of Ypres—was a French version of Calvinism which stressed the doctrine of original sin and rejected the belief in free will that was central to Jesuit teaching. Louis, adhering to the absolutist doctrine of *un roi, une loi, une foi* (one king, one law, one faith) which had served as a rallying cry for both Catholics and Protestants in France during the preceding century, took drastic steps to achieve religious conformity as part of his program of national unification. He persecuted Quietists and Jansenists, offering them the choice of recanting or of prison and exile. Against the Huguenots he waged an even sterner war. Protestant churches and schools were destroyed; Protestant families were forced to convert. In 1685, Louis revoked the Edict of Nantes, the legal foundation of the toleration Huguenots had enjoyed since 1598. French Protestants were thereafter denied civil rights, and their clergy was exiled. Thousands of religious refugees fled France for England, Holland, the Protestant states of Germany, and America, where their particular professional and artisanal skills made a significant contribution to economic prosperity. (The silk industry of Berlin and of Spitalfields, an urban quarter of London, was established by Huguenots.)

Jean Baptiste Colbert

Louis's drive for unification and centralization was assisted by his ability to rely upon increased revenues to fuel the domestic and military machinery of his absolutist monarchy. Those revenues were largely the result of policies and programs initiated by Jean Baptiste Colbert (1619–1683), the country's finance minister from 1664 until his death. Colbert was an energetic and committed mercantilist who believed that until France could put its fiscal house in order it could not achieve economic greatness. Colbert assumed office at a time when France, because of costly wars, was deeply in debt. Although he could not rid the country of that burden, he did for a time establish an interest rate of no higher than 5 percent, significantly lower than those the government had been accustomed to paying, and began negotiating directly with major creditors, rather than relying, as in the past, on fee-charging middlemen. Meanwhile, he tightened the process of tax collection, hounding corrupt officials who skimmed off a share of the taxes for themselves. He eliminated wherever possible the practice of tax farming, the system whereby collection agents were permitted to withhold a certain percentage of what they gathered for themselves. When Colbert assumed office, only about 25 percent of the taxes collected throughout the kingdom was reaching the treasury. By the time he died, that figure had risen to 80 percent.

The financial policies of Colbert

As a mercantilist, Colbert did all he could to increase the nation's income by means of protection and regimentation. Tariffs he imposed in 1667 and 1668 were designed to discourage the importation of foreign goods into France. He invested in the improvement of France's roads and waterways. And he used state money to promote the growth of national industry, and in particular the manufacture of goods such

Colbert as mercantilist

as silk, lace, tapestries, and glass, which had long been imported. Yet Colbert's efforts to achieve national economic stability and self-sufficiency could not withstand the insatiable demands of Louis XIV's increasingly expensive wars. Nor did his overseas trading companies ever achieve the stature of those of England and Holland. Unquestionably, however, France's economy was generally healthier as a result of his policies. And his championing of industrial enterprise did much to enhance the image of businessmen and entrepreneurs in the eyes of a nation which in the past had tended to disdain commerce and manufacturing.

3. ABSOLUTISM IN CENTRAL AND EASTERN EUROPE, 1660–1720

The degree of success enjoyed by Louis XIV as an absolutist monarch was in part the result of his own abilities, and of those of his advisors. Yet it was due as well to the fact that he could claim to stand as supreme embodiment of the will of all his people. Despite its internal division into territories and orders that continued to claim some right to independence, France was already unified before the accession of Louis XIV, possessed of a sense of itself as a nation. In this, it differed from the empires, kingdoms, and principalities to the east, where rulers faced an even more formidable task than did Louis as they attempted to weld their disparately constructed monarchies into a united, centralized whole. The Thirty Year's War had delivered a final blow to the pretensions of the Holy Roman Empire, which the French philosopher Voltaire dubbed neither holy, Roman, nor an empire. Power, in varying degrees, passed to the over three hundred princes, bishops, and magistrates who governed the assorted states of Germany throughout the remainder of the seventeenth and eighteenth centuries.

Absolutism and national unity

Despite the minute size of their domains, many of these petty monarchs attempted to establish themselves as absolutists in miniature, building lesser versions of Louis XIV's Versailles, maintaining standing armies, and paying for their expensive pretensions by tariffs and tolls that severely hampered the development of any sort of economic unity within the region as a whole. Although these rulers often prided themselves on their independence from imperial control, in many instances they were client states of France. A sizable portion of the money Louis devoted to the conduct of foreign affairs went to these German princelings. States like Saxony, Brandenburg-Prussia, and Bavaria, which were of a size to establish themselves as truly independent, were not averse to forming alliances against their own emperor.

Absolutism in the German states

Most notable among these middle-sized German states was Brandenburg-Prussia, whose emergence as a power of consequence during this period was the result of the single-minded determination of its rulers, principally Frederick William, elector of Brandenburg from

1640 to 1688, whose abilities have earned him the title of "Great Elector." The rise of Brandenburg-Prussia from initial insignificance, poverty, and devastation in the wake of the Thirty Years' War resulted from three basic achievements that can be credited to the Great Elector. First, he pursued an adroit foreign policy which enabled him to establish effective sovereignty over the widely dispersed and underdeveloped territories under his rule: Brandenburg, a large but not particularly productive territory in north-central Germany; Prussia, a duchy to the east that was dangerously exposed on three sides to Poland; and a sprinkling of tiny states—Cleves, Mark, and Ravensberg—to the west. By siding with Poland in a war against Sweden in the late 1650s, the Great Elector obtained the Polish king's surrender of nominal overlordship in East Prussia. And by some crafty diplomatic shuffling in the 1670s, he secured his western provinces from French interference by returning Pomerania, captured in a recent war, to France's Swedish allies.

Frederick William's second achievement was the establishment of a large standing army, the primary instrument of his diplomatic successes. By 1688, Brandenburg-Prussia had 30,000 troops permanently under arms. That he was able to sustain an army of this size in a state with comparatively limited resources was a measure of the degree to which the army more than repaid its costs. It ensured the elector and

Prussians Swearing Allegiance to the Great Elector at Königsberg, 1663. The occasion upon which the Prussian estates first acknowledged the overlordship of their ruler, this ceremony marked the beginning of the centralization of the Prussian state.

his successors absolute political control by fostering obedience among the populace, an obedience they were prepared to observe if their lands might be spared the devastation of another Thirty Years' War.

The third factor contributing to the emergence of the Great Elector's state as an international power was his imposition of an effective system of taxation and his creation of a government bureaucracy to administer it. Here he struck an important bargain with the powerful and privileged landlords (*Junkers*) without whose cooperation his programs would have had no chance of success. In return for an agreement which allowed them to reduce their peasant underlings to the status of serfs, the Junkers gave away their right to oppose a permanent tax system, provided, of course, that they were made immune from the payment of taxes themselves. (As in other European countries, taxes in Prussia fell most heavily on the peasantry.)

Henceforth, the political privileges of the landlord class diminished; secure in their right to manage their own estates as they wished, the Junkers were content to surrender management of the Hohenzollern possessions into the hands of a centralized bureaucracy. Its most important department was a military commissariat, whose functions included not only the dispensing of army pay and matériel, but the development of industries to manufacture military equipment. Frederick William's success was due primarily to his ability to gain the active cooperation of the Junker class, something he needed even more than Louis XIV needed the support of the French nobility. Without it, Frederick William could never have hammered together his absolutist state from the disparate territorial pieces that were his political raw material. To obtain it, he used the army not only to maintain order, but as a way of coopting Junker participation. The highest honor that could befall a Brandenburg squire was commission and promotion as a military servant of the state.

Like Brandenburg-Prussia, the Habsburg monarchy was confronted with the task of transforming three different regions into a cohesive state. In the case of Austria, this effort was complicated by the fact that these areas were ethnically and linguistically diverse: the southernmost Germanic lands that roughly comprised the present-day state of Austria; the northern Czech- (Slavic-) speaking provinces of Bohemia and Moravia; the German-speaking Silesia, inherited in 1527; and Hungary, where the Magyar population spoke a non-Slavic, Finno-Ugric language, also acquired in 1527 but largely lost to Turkish invasion just a few years afterward. For the next 150 years the Habsburgs and the Turks vied for control of Hungary. Until 1683 Turkish pashas ruled three-fourths of the Magyar kingdom, extending to within eighty miles of the Habsburg capital of Vienna. In 1683 the Turks besieged Vienna itself, but were repulsed by the Austrians, assisted by a mixed German and Polish army under the command of King John Sobieski of Poland. This victory was a prelude to the Habsburg reconquest of virtually all of Hungary by the end of the century.

The task of constructing an absolutist state from these extraordinarily varied territories was tackled with limited success by the seventeenth-century Habsburg emperors Ferdinand III (1637–1657) and Leopold I (1658–1705). Most of their efforts were devoted to the establishment of productive agricultural estates in Bohemia and Moravia, and to taming the independent nobility there and in Hungary. Landlords were encouraged to farm for export, and were supported in this effort by a government decree which compelled peasants to provide three days of unpaid *robot* service per week to their masters.[2] For this support, Bohemian and Moravian landed elites exchanged the political independence that had in the past expressed itself in the activities of their territorial legislative Estates.

Habsburg rulers tried to effect this same sort of bargain in Hungary as well. But there the tradition of independence was stronger and died harder. Hungarian (or Magyar) nobles in the west claimed the right to elect their king, a right they eventually surrendered to Leopold in 1687. But the central government's attempts to further reduce the country by administering it through the army, by granting large tracts of land to German aristocrats and settlers, and by persecuting non-Catholics were an almost total failure. The result was a powerful nobility which, while it insisted upon its right to exploit its serfs as it saw fit, nevertheless remained fiercely determined to retain its traditional constitutional and religious "liberties." The Habsburg emperors could boast that they too, like absolutists elsewhere, possessed a large standing army and an educated (in this case German-speaking) bureaucracy. But the exigencies imposed by geography and ethnicity kept them at some distance from the absolutist goal of a unified, centrally controlled and administered state.

Peter the Great. An eighteenth-century mosaic.

Undoubtedly the most dramatic episode in the history of early-modern absolutist rule was the dynamic reign of Tsar Peter I of Russia (1682–1725). Peter's accomplishments alone would clearly have earned him his history-book title, Peter the Great. But his gigantic height—he was nearly seven feet tall—as well as his mercurial personality—jesting one moment, raging the next—certainly helped. Peter is best remembered as the tsar whose policies brought Russia into the world of western Europe. Previously the country's rulers had set their faces firmly against the West, disdaining a civilization at odds with the Eastern Orthodox, semi-Oriental culture that was their heritage, while laboring to keep the various ethnic groups—Russians, Ukrainians, and a wide variety of nomadic tribes—within their ever-growing empire from destroying not only each other but the tsarist state itself. Since 1613 Russia had been ruled by members of the Romanov dynasty, who had attempted with some success to restore political stability following the chaotic "time of troubles" that had occurred after the death of the bloodthirsty, half-mad Tsar Ivan the Terrible in 1584. The early Romanovs' severest test had come between 1667 and 1671, when a

---

[2] The English usage of the term *robot* derives from the Czech designation of a serf.

Cossack leader (the Russian Cossacks were semi-autonomous bands of peasant cavalrymen) named Stenka Razin led much of southeastern Russia into rebellion. Stenka Razin's uprising found widespread support from hordes of serfs who had been oppressed by their masters as well as from non-Russian tribes in the lower Volga area who longed to cast off domination from Moscow. But ultimately Tsar Alexis (1645–1676) and the Russian nobility whose interests were most at stake were able to raise an army capable of defeating Razin's zealous but disorganized bands. Before the rebellion was finally crushed, over 100,000 rebels had been slaughtered.

This campaign was but a prelude to the deliberate and ruthless drive to absolutist power launched by Peter after he overthrew the regency of his half-sister Sophia and assumed personal control of the state in 1689. Within ten years he had scandalized aristocrats and churchmen alike by traveling to Holland and England to recruit highly skilled foreign workers and to study the craft of shipbuilding. Upon his return he distressed them still further by declaring his intention to Westernize Russia, and initiating this campaign by cutting off the "Eastern" beards and flowing sleeves of leading noblemen at court. Determined to "civilize" the nobility, he published a book of manners which forbade spitting on the floor and eating with one's fingers, and encouraged the cultivation of the art of polite conversation between the sexes.

Much as Peter wished to consider himself a Westerner, his particular brand of absolutism differed from that of other contemporary monarchs. As we have seen, the autocracy imposed by Ivan III in the fifteenth cetury had a decidedly Eastern caste. Peter was the willing heir to much of that tradition. He considered himself above the law

Russian absolutism: the situation before Peter the Great

Peter Cutting a Nobleman's Beard. In this Russian woodcut Peter the Great is portrayed as a diminutive pest.

Peter the Great's Execution of the Streltsy. This contemporary print shows scores of corpses gibbeted outside the walls of the Kremlin. Peter kept the rotting bodies on display for months to discourage his subjects from opposing his efforts to Westernize Russian society.

and thus his own absolute master to a degree that was alien to the absolutist theories and traditions of the Habsburgs and Bourbons. Autocrat of all the Russias, he ruled despotically, with a ferocious individual power that western European rulers did not possess. Armed with such arbitrary power in theory, and intent on realizing its full potential in practice, Peter set out to turn Russia to the West and to modernize his state. He would brook no opposition.

The suppression and reconstruction of the army

Confronted with a rebellion among the *streltsy,* the politically active, elite corps of the army who were most opposed to his innovations and who favored the restoration of his half-sister to the throne, Peter reacted with a savagery that astonished his contemporaries. Roughly 1200 suspected conspirators were summarily executed, many of them gibbeted outside the walls of the Kremlin, where their bodies remained for months as a graphic reminder of the fate awaiting those who would dare to challenge his absolute authority. Applying a lesson from the West, Peter proceeded to create a large standing army recruited from the ranks of the peasantry and scrupulously loyal to the tsar. One of every twenty males was conscripted for lifelong service. He financed his army, as did other absolutists, by increasing taxes, with their burden falling most heavily on the peasantry. To equip his new military force, he fostered the growth of the iron and munitions industries. Factories were built and manned by peasant laborers whose position was little better than that of slaves. Serfs were also commandeered for other public works projects, such as road and canal building, necessary for the modernization of the state.

Absolutism and the new bureaucracy

In an effort to further consolidate his absolute power, he replaced the Duma—the nation's rudimentary national assembly—with a rubber-stamp senate, and appointed a procurator, dependent directly on him, to manage the affairs of the tradition-bound Russian Orthodox church, which essentially became an extension of the state. At the same time, Peter was fashioning new, larger, and more efficient administrative machinery to cope with the demands of his modernization program. Although he preferred to draw "new" men, whose loyalty to the tsar would be unerring, into the bureaucracy, he was compelled to rely upon the services of the aristocrat—or *boyar*—class as well, rewarding them by increasing their control over their serfs. Nevertheless, membership in his new bureaucracy did not depend on birth. One of his principal advisers, Alexander Menshikov, began his career as a cook and finished as a prince. Bureaucratic status replaced noble rank as the key to power. The administrative machinery devised by Peter furnished Russia with its ruling class for the next two hundred years.

The influence of foreign and domestic policy

Peter the Great's Eurocentric worldview also manifested itself in his foreign policy, as witnessed by his bold drive to gain a Russian outlet on the Baltic Sea. To this end he engaged in a war with Sweden's meteoric soldier-king Charles XII (1697–1718), who devoted most of his reign to campaigns in the field against the Danes, the Poles, and

The St. Petersburg Palaces. The first of six versions of the Winter Palace here depicted (left) was erected in 1711. It quickly proved to be too modest for Peter's needs. Within a decade he had created a far more elaborate complex called Peterhof (right), complete with fountains fashioned after those of Versailles.

the Russians. By defeating Charles decisively at the Battle of Poltava in 1709, Peter was able to secure his window to the West. He promptly outdid his absolutist counterparts to the West, who moved their courts the outskirts of their capital cities, by moving the capital itself from Moscow to an entirely new city on the Gulf of Finland. An army of serfs was employed to erect the baroque city of St. Petersburg around a palace intended to imitate and rival Louis XIV's Versailles. It was not enough that Peter looked to the West; he wanted the Russian people to share the view.

Not surprisingly, Peter's drastic programs met with concerted resistance. Resentment smoldered under his imposing hand, even within the palace. His son Alexis, who had dared to declare himself opposed to his father's innovations, became a rallying point for the forces of resistance to the tsar and his policies, and died under torture inflicted at his father's command in 1718. Upon Peter's death in 1725, *boyar* determination to undo his reforms surfaced during the succession struggle. A series of ineffective tsars followed Peter, thus allowing the resentful nobles to rescind many of his reforms, until, in 1762, the crown passed to Catherine II, a ruler whose ambitions and determination were equal to those of her august predecessor.

Peter the Great of Russia, Leopold I of Austria, Frederick William of Brandenburg-Prussia, and above all Louis XIV of France: these were the "great" seventeenth-century absolutists. Elsewhere, the fortunes of absolutism fared far less well. The ineffectual, weak-minded

Peter's successors

The failure of absolutism to take root elsewhere

Spanish monarch Charles II found himself besieged by rebellions in Portugal and Sicily. In 1668, after years of fighting, he was forced to recognize Portuguese independence. In Sweden, Charles X and Charles XI managed to extend their territories at the expense of the Danes and to quell the independence of the aristocracy by confiscating their fiefdoms. During the reign of Charles XII, however, that legacy was dissipated by an adventurous but ultimately unproductive foreign policy. The opposition of the landed gentry—or *szlachta*—to any form of centralized government in Poland produced a political stalemate that amounted to little more than anarchy. Foreign powers took advantage of this situation to intervene in Polish affairs and, in the eighteenth century, to carve up the country and distribute it among themselves.

4. THE ENGLISH EXCEPTION

The policies of Charles II

But what of England, which had experienced a taste of absolutist centralization under the Tudors and early Stuarts, and indeed under Oliver Cromwell, but which possessed in its Parliament the longest tradition and most highly developed form of representative government in western Europe? England's political history in the late seventeenth century provides the most striking contrast to continental absolutism. Charles II, son of the beheaded Charles I, who returned from exile and ascended the throne in 1660, was initially welcomed by most English men and women. He pledged himself not to reign as a despot, but to respect Parliament and to observe Magna Carta and the Petition of Right, for he admitted that he was not anxious to "resume his travels." His delight in the unbuttoned moral atmosphere of his court and the culture it supported (risque plays, dancing, and marital infidelity) mirrored a public desire to forget the restraints of the puritan past. The wits of the time suggested that Charles, "that known enemy to virginity and chastity," played his role as the father of his country to the fullest. However, as Charles's admiration of things French grew to include the absolutism of Louis XIV, he came to be regarded as a threat to more than English womanhood by a great many powerful Englishmen who, however anxious they were to restore the monarchy, were not about to surrender their traditional rights to another Stuart autocrat. By the late 1670s, the country found itself divided politically into those who supported the king (called by their opponents "Tories," a popular nickname for Irish Catholic bandits) and those opposed to him (called by *their* opponents "Whigs," a similar nickname for Scottish Presbyterian rebels).

Charles II of England

Religion and the political reaction

As the new party labels suggest, religion remained an exceedingly divisive national issue. Charles was sympathetic to Roman Catholicism, even to the point of a deathbed conversion in 1685. He therefore opposed the stiff code of ecclesiastical regulations, known as the Clarendon Code, which had reestablished Anglicanism as the official state religion and which penalized Roman Catholics and Protestant dissenters. In 1672, Charles suspended the Clarendon Code, although the public outcry against this action compelled him to retreat. This controversy, and rising opposition to the probable succession of Charles's ardent Roman Catholic brother James, led to a series of Whig electoral victories between 1679 and 1681. But Charles found that increased revenues, plus a secret subsidy he was receiving from Louis XIV, enabled him to govern without resort to Parliament, to which he would otherwise have had to go for money. In addition to ignoring Parliament, Charles further infuriated and alarmed Whig politicians by arranging the execution of several of their most prominent leaders on charges of treason, and by remodeling local government in such a way as to make it more dependent on royal favor. Charles died in 1685 with his power enhanced; but he left behind him a political and religious legacy that was to be the undoing of his successor.

James II was the very opposite of his brother. A zealous Catholic convert, he alienated his Tory supporters, all of whom were of course Anglicans, by dismissing them in favor of Roman Catholics, and by once again suspending the penal laws against Catholics and dissenters. *James II as religious zealot* His stubbornness, as one historian has remarked, made it all but impossible for him to take "yes" for an answer. Whereas Charles had been content to defeat his political enemies, James was determined to humiliate them. Like Charles, James interfered in local government, but his appointments were so personally distasteful and so mediocre as to arouse active opposition. James made no attempt to disguise his Roman Catholicism. He publically declared his wish that all his subjects might be converted, and paraded papal legates through the streets of London. When, in June 1688, he ordered all Anglican clergymen to read his decree of toleration from their pulpits, seven bishops refused and were clapped into prison on charges of seditious libel. At their trial, however, they were declared not guilty, to the vast satisfaction of the English populace.

The trial of the bishops was one event that brought matters to a head. The other was the birth of a son to James and his second wife, the Roman Catholic daughter of the duke of Modena. This male infant, *The succession question* who was to be raised a Roman Catholic, replaced James's much older Protestant daughter Mary as heir to the British throne. Despite a rumor that the baby boy was an imposter smuggled into the royal bedchamber in a warming pan, political leaders of both parties were prepared not only to believe in the legitimacy of the child but to take active steps to prevent the possibility of his succession. A delegation of Whigs and Tories crossed the channel to Holland with an invitation to Mary's husband William of Orange, the *stadholder* or chief executive of the United Provinces and the great-grandson of William the Silent. William was asked to cross to England with an invading army to restore

English religious and political freedom. As leader of a continental coalition determined to put a spoke in Louis XIV's expansionist policies, he accepted, welcoming the chance such a move represented to bring England into active opposition to the French (see below, p. 609).

William's conquest was a bloodless coup. James fled the country, thereby allowing Parliament to declare the throne vacant and clearing the way for the accession of William and Mary as joint sovereigns of England. A Bill of Rights, passed by Parliament and accepted by the new king and queen, reaffirmed English civil liberties such as trial by jury, habeas corpus (guaranteeing the accused a speedy trial), and the right of petition and redress, and established that the monarchy was subject to the law of the land. An Act of Toleration, passed in 1689, granted dissenters the right to worship, though not the right to full political protection. In 1701, with the son of the exiled James II now reaching maturity in France, an Act of Succession ordained that the English throne was to pass first to Mary's childless sister Anne, who ruled from 1702 to 1714, and then to George, elector of the German principality of Hanover, who was the great-grandson of James I. The connection was a distant one, but the Hanoverian dynasty was Protestant, and George reputed to be a capable enough ruler. The act was further evidence of the degree to which Parliament could dictate its terms. Henceforth, all English sovereigns were to be communicants of the Church of England. If foreign born, they could not engage England in the defense of their native land, nor leave the country, without Parliamentary consent.

William III

A "glorious" revolution?

The events of 1688 and 1689 were soon referred to by the English as "the Glorious Revolution." Glorious for the English in that it occurred without bloodshed (although James is reputed to have been suffering from a nosebleed at the moment of crisis). Glorious, too, for defenders of Parliamentary prerogative. Although William and Mary and their royal successors continued to enjoy a large measure of executive power, after 1688 no king or queen attempted to govern without Parliament, which met annually from that time on. Parliament strengthened its control over the collection and expenditure of public money. Future sovereigns were henceforth unable to conduct the country's business without recourse to the House of Commons for the funds to do so. Glorious, finally, for advocates of the civil liberties now guaranteed within the Bill of Rights.

1688 as a defense of status quo

Yet 1688 was not all glory. It was a revolution that consolidated the position of large property holders, local magnates whose political and economic power base in their rural constituencies and on their estates had been threatened by the interventions of Charles II and James II. If it was a revolution, it was one designed to restore the *status quo* on behalf of a wealthy social and economic order that would soon make itself even wealthier as it drank its fill of government patronage and war profits. And it was a revolution that brought nothing but misery to the Roman Catholic minority in Scotland, which joined with England and Wales in the union of Great Britain in 1701, and the Catholic majority in Ireland where, following the Battle of the Boyne in 1690, repressive military forces imposed the exploitive will of a self-interested Protestant minority upon the Catholic majority.

Although the "Glorious Revolution" was an expression of immediate political circumstance, it was a reflection as well of anti-absolutist theories that had risen in the late seventeenth century to challenge the ideas of writers such as Bodin, Hobbes, and Bossuet. Chief among these opponents of absolutism was the Englishman John Locke (1632–1704), whose *Two Treatises of Civil Government* (1690) was used to justify the events of the previous two years. Locke maintained that originally all humans had lived in a theoretical state of nature in which absolute freedom and equality prevailed, and in which there was no government of any kind. The only law was the law of nature, which each individual enforced for himself in order to protect his natural rights to life, liberty, and property. It was not long, however, before men began to perceive that the inconveniences of the state of nature greatly outweighed its advantages. With individuals attempting to enforce their own rights, confusion and insecurity were the unavoidable results. Accordingly, the people agreed among themselves to establish a civil society, to set up a government, and to surrender certain powers to it. But they did not make that government absolute. The only power they conferred upon it was the executive power of the law of nature. Since the state was nothing but the joint power of all the members of society, its authority could "be no more than those persons had in a state of nature before they entered into society, and gave it up to the community." All powers not expressly surrendered were reserved to the people themselves. If the government exceeded or abused the authority explicitly granted in the political contract, it became tyrannical; the people then had the right to dissolve it or to rebel against it and overthrow it.

Locke condemned absolutism in every form. He denounced despotic monarchy, but he was no less severe in his strictures against the absolute sovereignty of parliaments. Though he defended the supremacy of the law-making branch, with the executive primarily an agent of the legislature, he nevertheless refused to concede to the representatives of the people an unlimited power. Arguing that state government was instituted among people for the preservation of property, he denied the authority of any political agency to invade the natural rights of a single individual. The law of nature, which embodied these rights, was an automatic limitation upon every branch of the government. Locke's theoretical defense of political liberties emerged in the late eighteenth century as an important element in the intellectual background of the French Revolution. In 1688, however, it served a far less radical purpose. The landed magnates responsible for the

John Locke

Defense of 1688: the political theories of John Locke

Locke and limited sovereignty

exchange of James II for William and Mary could read Locke as an apoligia for their conservative revolution. James II, rather than protecting their property and liberties, had encroached upon them; hence their right to overthrow the tyranny he had established and replace it with a government that would, by ensuring their rights, defend their interests.

5. WARFARE AND DIPLOMACY: THE EMERGENCE OF A STATE SYSTEM

Emergence of state interests

The rise of absolutist monarchies in the late seventeenth century resulted in the emergency of an international state system. To the extent that absolutists succeeded in attaining their goals of unification and centralization, their states took shape as individual, identifiable political and economic entities. Although the achievements of various monarchs in this regard were limited, they were significant enough to encourage diplomats to speak more commonly than in the past of the "interests" of a particular state, as if that state somehow had a corporate personality of its own, and of the way in which those interests might coincide or conflict with the interests of another state. Often the interests of a monarch might clash with those of the country over which he ruled. Bourbon kings and Habsburg emperors worried about the future of their family dynasties to the detriment of the future of France or Austria. Religion, the factor that had torn Europe apart in the preceding century, remained an international issue in 1700. But increasingly, both dynasty and religion were superseded by newer "interests"—commerce and international balance and stability. The emergence of something approaching the modern state was to result, by 1715, in a significant redefinition of the aims and calculations of diplomacy and warfare.

The growth of diplomacy

The organization of diplomatic bureaucracies was a major accomplishment of absolutist monarchies. Had most foreign ministers and ambassadors read the Dutchman Hugo Grotius's treatise on *The Law of War and Peace* (1625), they would have agreed with him about the necessity of establishing a body of rules that would help to bring reason and order to relations between governments. In practice, of course, reason and order gave way to bribery and improvisation. Yet the rationalization of diplomatic processes and the establishment of foreign ministries and embassies in European capitals, with their growing staffs of clerks and ministers, reflected a desire to bring order out of the international chaos that had gripped Europe during its "war century." International relations in the late seventeenth century was, among other things, a history of diplomatic coalitions, an indication of the degree to which negotiation was now a weapon in the armory of the absolutist state.

The Capture of Cambrai by Louis XIV in 1677. This print illustrates the tactics of siege warfare as practiced by early-modern armies. Louis is shown receiving an emissary from the city, whose walls have been breeched by siege guns.

Warfare, however, continued to play an integral and almost constant role in the international arena. The armies of the period grew dramatically. When Louis XIV acceded to power in 1661, the French army numbered 20,000 men; by 1688, it stood at 290,000; by 1694, 400,000. These armies were increasingly professional organizations, controlled directly by the state, and under the command of trained officers recruited from the nobility. In Prussia, common soldiers were mostly conscripts; in other European countries they were volunteers, either native or foreign, though often "volunteers" in no more than name, having been coerced or tricked into service. Increasingly, however, enlistment was perceived by common soldiers as an avenue to a career, one which included the possibility of promotion to corporal or sergeant, and in the case of France, the promise of a small pension at the end of one's service. However recruited, common soldiers became part of an increasingly elaborate and efficient fighting force. The maneuvers of infantry, cavalry, and artillery were coordinated as never before. Soldiers were drilled with a thoroughness necessitated by tactics which depended on the accurate firepower of cannon and flintlock muskets. They were taught to stand their ground in formations of long, rigid lines in the face of direct enemy assault. They mastered the use of the bayonet (short steel spikes attached to the end of muskets, first manufactured in Bayonne, France, in the seventeenth century); the most effective procedure: stabbing the man

The growth of professional armies

in his left side as he raised his right arm to fire. Above all, they were made to understand the dire consequences of disobedience, breaking rank, or desertion. Soldiers were expected to obey instantly and unquestioningly. Failure to do so resulted in brutal punishment, often flogging, sometimes execution. Commissioned and noncommissioned officers carried sticks and prods with which to "encourage" correct military behavior in their men. Drill, not only on the battlefield but on the parade ground, in brilliant, elaborate uniforms and intricate formations, was designed to reduce individuals to automaton-like parts of an army whose regiments were moved across battlefields as a chess player moves pawns across the board—and with about the same concern for loss of human life.

The foreign policies of Louis XIV

The patterns of international relations during the period from 1660 to 1715 show European monarchs making use of the new machinery of diplomacy and warfare to resolve the conflicting interests of dynasty, stability, and commerce. At the center of that pattern, as at the center of Europe, stood Louis XIV. From 1661 until 1688, in a quest for glory, empire, and even revenge, he waged war across his northern and eastern frontiers on the pretext that the lands in question belonged both to the Bourbons and to the French by tradition, by former treaty, or by dynastic inheritance. His aggressively expansionist policies, alarming to other European rulers, led William of Orange, in 1674, to form an anti-French coalition with Austria, Spain, and various smaller German states. Yet Louis continued to push his frontiers eastward, invading territories that had been Germanic for centuries, and capturing Strassburg in 1681 and Luxembourg in 1684. Louis's seizure of Strassburg (subsequently called Strasbourg by the French), completing the conquest of the German-speaking province of Alsace begun in 1634 by Richelieu, irreversibly incorporated the seeds of a Franco-German animosity centered on this region that would bear bitter fruit in the great wars of the nineteenth and twentieth centuries. A second coalition, the so-called League of Augsburg—Holland, Austria, Sweden, and further German allies—was only somewhat more successful than the first.

Europe on the verge of war

These allies were concerned above all to maintain some sort of European balance of power. They feared an expansionist France would prove insatiable, as it pressed its boundaries farther and farther into Germany and the Low Countries. Louis, mistakenly expecting that William would be forced to fight an English army under James to establish his right to his new throne and would therefore be too preoccupied to devote his full attention to developments on the Continent, kept up the pressure. In September 1688 he invaded the Palatinate and occupied the city of Cologne. The following year the French armies crossed the Rhine and continued their eastward drive, burning Heidelberg and committing numerous atrocities throughout the middle Rhine area. Aroused at last to effective action, the coalition, led by

William and now including in addition to its former members both England and Spain, engaged Louis in a war that was to last until 1697.

The major campaigns of this War of the League of Augsburg were fought in the Low Countries. William managed to drive an army under his predecessor, James II, from Ireland in 1690; from that point on, he took command of the allied forces on the Continent. By 1694 Louis was being pressed hard, not only by his allied foes, but by a succession of disastrous harvests that crippled France. Fighting remained stalemated until a treaty was signed at Ryswick in Holland which compelled Louis to return most of France's post-1679 gains, except for Alsace, and to recognize William as the rightful king of England.

Ryswick did nothing, however, to resolve the dynastic tangle known as the Spanish Succession. Since Charles II of Spain had no direct heirs, and since he appeared to be on his deathbed in 1699, European monarchs and diplomats were obsessed by the question of who would succeed to the vast domain of the Spanish Habsburgs: not only Spain itself, but also its overseas empire, as well as the Spanish Netherlands, Naples, Sicily, and other territories in Italy. Both Louis XIV and Leopold I of Austria were married to sisters of the decrepit, unstable Charles; and both, naturally, eyed the succession to the Spanish inheritance as an exceedingly tempting dynastic plum. Yet it is a measure of the degree to which even absolutists were willing to keep their ambitions within bounds that both Leopold and Louis agreed to William's suggestion that the lion's share of the Habsburg lands should go to six-year-old Joseph Ferdinand, the prince of Bavaria, who was Charles II's grandnephew. Unfortunately, in 1699 the child died. Though the chances of war increased, William and Louis were prepared to bargain further and arranged a second treaty that divided the Spanish empire between Louis's and Leopold's heirs. Yet at the same time, Louis's diplomatic agents in Madrid persuaded Charles to sign a will in which he stipulated that the entire Spanish Habsburg inheritance should pass to Louis's grandson Philip of Anjou. This option was welcomed by many influential Spaniards, willing to endure French hegemony in return for the protection France could provide to the Spanish empire. For a time, Louis contemplated an alternative agreement which would have given France direct control of much of Italy. When Charles finally died in November 1700, Louis decided to accept the will. As if this was not enough to drive his former enemies back to war, he sent troops into the Spanish Netherlands and traders to the Spanish colonial empire, while declaring the late James II's son—the child of the warming pan myth—the legitimate king of England.

Once it was clear to the allies that Louis intended to treat Spain as if it were his own kingdom, they again united against him in the cause of balance and stability. William died in 1702, just as the War of the Spanish Succession was beginning. His position as first general of the coalition passed to two brilliant strategists, the English John Chur-

War of the League of Augsburg

The problem of the Spanish Succession

War: the battle of Blenheim

chill, duke of Marlborough, and his Austrian counterpart, Prince Eugene of Savoy, an upper-class soldier of fortune who had been denied a commission by Louis. Under their command the allied forces engaged in battle after fierce battle in the Low Countries and Germany, including an extraordinary march deep into Bavaria, where the combined forces under Marlborough and Eugene smashed the French and their Bavarian allies decisively at Blenheim (1704). While the allies pressed France's armies on land, the English navy captured Gibraltar and the island of Minorca, thus establishing a strategic and commercial foothold in the Mediterranean, and helping to open a fourth major military theater in Spain itself.

Military stalemate

The War of the Spanish Succession was a "professional" war that tested the highly trained armies of the combatants to the fullest. At the battle of Malplaquet in northeastern France in 1709, 80,000 French soldiers faced 110,000 allied troops. Though Marlborough and Eugene could claim to have won that battle, in that they forced the French to retreat, they suffered 24,000 casualties, twice those of the French. Neither Malplaquet nor other such victories brought the allies any closer to their final goal, which now appeared to be not the containment, but the complete destruction of the French military force. Queen Anne of England (Mary's sister and William's successor), once Marlborough's staunchest defender, grew disillusioned with the war and fired her general.

Dynastic changes and the pursuit of peace

More than war-weariness impelled the combatants toward negotiation, however. The War of the Spanish Succession had begun as a conflict about the balance of power in Europe and the world. Yet dynastic changes had by 1711 compelled a reappraisal of allied goals. Leopold I had died in 1705. When his elder son and successor Joseph I died in 1711, the Austrian monarchy fell to Leopold's youngest son, the Archduke Charles, who had been the allies' candidate for the throne of Spain. With Charles now the Austrian and the Holy Roman Emperor as Charles VI (1711–1740), the prospect of his accession to the Spanish inheritance conjured up the ghost of Charles V and threatened to give him far too much power. International stability therefore demanded an end to hostilities and diplomatic negotiation toward a solution that would reestablish some sort of general balance.

The Treaty of Utrecht

The Treaty of Utrecht, which settled the conflict in 1713 to the extent that it redistributed territory and power in equitable portions, was a serious attempt to do just that. No one emerged a major winner or loser. Philip, Louis's grandson, remained on the throne of Spain, but Louis agreed that France and Spain would never be united under the same ruler. Austria gained territories in the Netherlands and Italy. The Dutch, victims of French aggression during the war, were guaranteed protection of their borders against future invasion. The English retained Gibraltar and Minorca, as well as territory in America: Newfoundland, Acadia, Hudson Bay, and in the Caribbean, St. Kitts. Perhaps most valuable of all, the English extracted the *asiento* from Spain

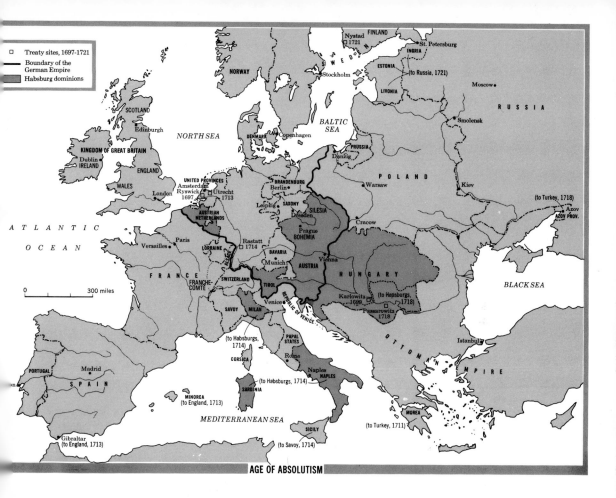

Treaty sites, 1697-1721
Boundary of the German Empire
Habsburg dominions

AGE OF ABSOLUTISM

which gave them the right to supply Spanish America with African slaves. The settlement reflected the degree to which new interests had superseded old. Balance of power and stability among states were the major goals of the negotiations, goals that reflected a departure from the world of seventeenth-century turmoil when religious fanaticism had been a major factor in international conflict. The eventual "winners" were undoubtedly the English, whose dynastic concerns were limited to a general acceptance of the Hanoverian settlement, and who could therefore concentrate their efforts on amassing overseas territories that would contribute to the growth of their economic prosperity and hence their international power.

6. ENLIGHTENED ABSOLUTISM AND LIMITED MONARCHY IN THE EIGHTEENTH CENTURY

Eighteenth-century absolutism was a series of variations on the dominant themes composed in the previous century by Louis XIV. That it has earned itself the historical distinction of "enlightened" absolut-

"Enlightened" absolutism

Louis XV

Absolutism under the successors of Louis XIV

ism suggests that those variations were of some consequence. Eighteenth-century rulers backed their sovereign claims not in the language of divine right, but in terms of their determination to act, as Frederick the Great of Prussia declared, as "first servant of the state." Enlightened rulers served their subjects by introducing reformist legislation and administration designed, at least in theory, to serve the well-being of the state community as a whole. They moved to curtail the privileges of old institutions. The Roman Catholic Church, for example, was compelled to suffer the expulsion of the Jesuits from most Catholic countries. Customary laws benefiting particular orders or interests were reformed. Serfdom was abolished or limited in some German states. Innovative policies in the areas of taxation, economic development, and education were instituted. As we shall see in Chapter 19, rational schemes of this sort reflected the spread of Enlightenment ideals as manifested in the writings of thinkers such as Beccaria, Diderot, and Voltaire. (The last was, in fact, a guest at Frederick's court for several years.) Assisting enlightened "first servants" in the implementation of these changes was a growing cadre of lesser servants: bureaucrats, often recruited from the nobility, but once recruited, expected to declare primary allegiance to their new master, the state. Despite innovation, "enlightened" absolutists continued to insist, as their predecessors had, that state sovereignty rested with the monarchy. Power remained their overriding concern, and to the extent that they combatted efforts by the estates of their realms to dilute that power, they declared their descent from their seventeenth-century forebears.

Louis XIV's successors, his great-grandson Louis XV (1715–1774) and that monarch's grandson Louis XVI (1774–1792), were unable to sustain the energetic drive toward centralization that had taken place under the Sun King. Indeed, during his last years, while fighting a desperate defensive war against his allied enemies, Louis XIV had seen his own accomplishments begin to crumble under the mounting pressure of military expenses. His heir was only five years old when he assumed the throne. As he grew up, Louis XV displayed little of his great-grandfather's single-minded determination to act the role of Sun King. The heroic, baroque grandeur of the main palace at Versailles yielded to the rococo grace of the Grand and Petit Trianons, pleasure pavillions built by Louis XV in the palace gardens. Both Louis XIV and Louis XV solaced themselves with the company of mistresses. The difference in their tastes, however, is a mark of the difference in their reigns. Madame de Maintenon, the Sun King's mistress, was a stern, devout Catholic, who interested herself directly in policies of state. Madame du Pompadour, Louis XV's favorite for many years, was a stylish, witty sensualist whose legacy was the elaborate hairstyle to which she bequeathed her name.

During the minority of Louis XV, the French *parlements,* those courts of record responsible for registering and thereby legalizing royal decrees, enjoyed a resurgence of power which they retained throughout the century. No longer tame adjuncts of absolutist governmental machinery as they had been under Louis XIV, these bodies now proclaimed themselves the protectors of French "liberties." In fact they were protectors of little more than the privileges of the elite, although a growing number welcomed the *parlements'* willingness to block new taxes. In the late 1760s, hoping to emulate the success of his illustrious predecessor, and encouraged by his chancellor René Maupeou, Louis XV issued an edict effectively ending the right of *parlements* to reject decrees. Protest on the part of the magistrates resulted in their imprisonment or banishment. The *parlements* themselves were replaced by new courts charged not only with the responsibility of rubber-stamping legislation but also with administering law more justly and less expensively. When Louis XVI ascended the throne in 1774, his ministers persuaded him to reestablish the *parlements* as a sign of his willingness to conciliate his trouble-making aristocracy. This he did, with the result that government—particularly the management of finances—developed into a stalemated battle.

Stalemate was what the Prussian successors to Frederick William, the Great Elector, were determined to avoid. Absolutism, to thrive, needed to remain a dynamic force: precisely what it was in eighteenth-century Prussia. Frederick I (1688–1713), the Great Elector Frederick William's immediate successor, enhanced the appearance and cultural life of Berlin. As the Roman numeral by his name attests, he also succeeded in bargaining his support to the Austrians during the War of the Spanish Succession in return for the coveted right to style himself king.[3]

Frederick William I(1713–1740), cared little for the embellishments his father had made to the capital city. His overriding concern was the building of a first-rate army. So single-minded was his attention to the military that he came to be called "the sergeant king." Military display became an obsession. His private regiment of "Potsdam Giants" was comprised exclusively of soldiers over six feet in height. The king traded musicians and prize stallions for such choice specimens and delighted in marching them about his palace grounds. Frederick William I's success as the builder of a military machine can be measured in terms of numbers: 30,000 men under arms when he came to the throne; 83,000 when he died twenty-seven years later, commander of the fourth-largest army in Europe, after France, Russia, and Austria. Since he could hardly count on volunteers, most of his soldiers were conscripts, drafted from the peasantry for a period of years and required to attend annual training exercises lasting three months. Conscription was supplemented by the kidnapping of forced recruits in neighboring

Frederick William I

---

[3] The Austrian monarch was the Holy Roman Emperor and therefore had the right to create kings.

German lands. To finance his army, Frederick William I increased taxes and streamlined their collection through the establishment of a General Directory of War, Finance, and Domains. He instituted a system of administration by boards, hoping thereby to eliminate individual inefficiency through collective responsibility and surveillance. In addition, he created an inspectorate to uncover and report to him the mistakes and inefficiencies of his officialdom. Even then, he continued to supervise personally the implementation of state policy while shunning the luxuries of court life; for him, the "theater" of absolutism was not the palace but the office, which placed him at the helm of the state and the army. Perceiving the resources of the state to be too precious to waste, he pared costs at every turn to the point where, it was said, he had to invite himself to a nobleman's table in order to enjoy a good meal.

The apprenticeship of Frederick the Great

A hard, unimaginative man, Frederick William I had little use for his son, whose passion was not the battlefield but the flute, and who admired French culture as much as his father disdained it. Not surprisingly, young Frederick rebelled; in 1730, when he was eighteen, he ran away from court with a friend. Apprehended, the companions were returned to the king, who welcomed the fledgling prodigal with something other than a fatted calf. Before Frederick's eyes, he had the friend executed. The grisly lesson took. Thenceforward Frederick, though he never surrendered his love of music and literature, bound himself to his royal duties, living in accordance with his own image of himself as "first servant of the state," and earning himself history's title of Frederick the Great.

Frederick the Great and Voltaire. Although Frederick offered asylum to the French *philosophe,* this "enlightened despot" did not permit his intellectual pursuits to interfere with matters of state.

Frederick William I's zealous austerity and his compulsion to build an efficient army and administrative state made Prussia a lean, strong state. Frederick the Great, building on the work of his father, raised his country to the status of a major power. As soon as he became king in 1740, Frederick mobilized the army his father had never taken into battle and occupied the poorly protected Austrian province of Silesia to which Prussia had no legitimate claim. Although he had earlier vowed to make morality rather than expediency the hallmark of his reign, he seemingly had little difficulty in sacrificing his youthful idealism in the face of an opportunity to make his Prussian state a leading member of the concert of nations. The remaining forty-five years of his monarchy were devoted to the consolidation of this first bold stroke.

Such a daring course required some adjustments within the Prussian state. The army had to be kept at full strength, and to this end, Frederick staffed its officer corps with young noblemen. In expanding the bureaucracy, whose financial administration kept his army in the field, he relied on the nobility as well, reversing the policy of his father, who had recruited his civil servants according to merit rather than birth. But Frederick was not one to tolerate mediocrity; he fashioned the most highly professional and efficient bureaucracy in all of Europe. The degree to which both army and bureaucracy were staffed by the nobility is a measure of his determination to secure the unflagging support of the most privileged order in his realm, in order to ensure a united front against Prussia's external foes.

Frederick's domestic policies reflected that same strategy. In matters where he ran no risk of offending the aristocracy, he followed his own rationalist bent, prohibiting the torture of accused criminals, putting an end to the bribing of judges, and establishing a system of elementary schools. He promoted religious toleration, declaring that he would happily build a mosque in Berlin if he could find enough Muslims to fill it. (Yet he was strongly anti-Semitic, levying special taxes on Jews and making efforts to close the professions and the civil service to them.) On his own royal estates he was a model "enlightened" monarch. He abolished capital punishment, curtailed the forced labor services of his peasantry, and granted them long leases on the land they worked. He fostered scientific forestry and the cultivation of new crops. He opened new lands in Silesia and brought in thousands of immigrants to cultivate them. When wars ruined their farms, he supplied the peasants with new livestock and tools. Yet he never attempted to extend these reforms to the estates of the Junker elite, since to have done so would have alienated that social and economic group upon which Frederick was most dependent.

Although the monarchs of eighteenth-century Austria eventually proved themselves even more willing than Frederick the Great to undertake significant social reform, the energies of Emperor Charles VI (1711–1740) were concentrated on guaranteeing the future dynastic

The seizure of Silesia

The Prussian army and the nobility

Frederick the Great as an enlightened absolutist

Charles VI and the "pragmatic sanction"

and territorial integrity of the Habsburg lineage and domain. Without a male heir, Charles worked to secure the right of his daughter Maria Theresa to succeed him as eventual empress. By his death in 1740 Charles had managed to persuade not only his subjects but all the major European powers to accept his daughter as his royal heir—a feat known as the "pragmatic sanction." Yet his painstaking efforts were only partially successful. As we have seen, Frederick the Great used the occasion of Charles's death to sieze Silesia. The French, unable to resist the temptation to grab what they could, entered the lists in this War of the Austrian Succession against the new empress, Maria Theresa (1740–1780).

With most of her other possessions already occupied by her enemies, Maria Theresa appealed successfully to the Hungarians for support. The empress was willing to play the role of the wronged woman when, as on this occasion, it suited her interests to do so. Hungary's vital troops combined with British financial assistance helped to enable her to battle Austria's enemies to a draw, although she never succeeded in regaining Silesia. The experience of those first few years of her reign persuaded Maria Theresa, who was both capable and tenacious, to reorganize her dominions along the tightly centralized lines characteristic of absolutist Prussia and France. Ten new administrative districts were established, each with its own "war commissar" appointed by and responsible to the central administration in Vienna—an Austrian equivalent of the French intendant. Property taxes were increased to finance an expanded army, which was modernized and professionalized so as to remain on a par with the military establishments of the other great powers. Centralization, finances, army: once more those three crucial elements in the formula of absolute rule came into play.

Maria Theresa of Austria

Austrian absolutism did not stop there, however. Together Maria Theresa and her son Joseph II, with whom she ruled jointly from 1765 to 1780, and who then succeeded her for another ten years, instituted a series of social reforms which has earned them their reputation as "enlightened" absolutists. Although both mother and son were devout Roman Catholics, they moved to assert control of the church, removing the clergy's exemption from taxation and decreeing the state's ability to block the publication of papal bulls in Austria. In 1773, following the papal suppression of the Jesuits, they used the order's assets to finance a program of state-wide primary education. Although the General Schools Ordinance of 1774 never achieved anything like a universally literate population, it did succeed in educating hundreds of thousands, and in financing not only schools for children but schools as well for those who taught the children. Joseph followed these reforms with an "Edict on Idle Institutions" in 1780, which resulted in the closing of hundreds of monastic houses, whose property went to support charitable institutions now under state control. These

"Enlightened" absolutism in Austria

Joseph II of Austria Visiting a Farm. The royal estates provided Joseph with the opportunity to experiment with agrarian reforms by raising the serfs to the status of free peasants.

reforms and others—rationalization of criminal procedures, a relaxation of censorship, and an attempt to eradicate superstition by curbing the practice of pilgrimages and celebration of saint's days—made Joseph more enemies than friends, among both the noble elite and the common people. Joseph's brother Leopold II, who succeeded him in 1790, attempted to maintain the reformist momentum. His death two years later and the accession of his reactionary brother Francis II (1792–1835), put an end to liberalizing experiments. "Enlightened" though Joseph II was, however, he nevertheless remained a staunch absolutist, as concerned with the maintenance of a strong army and an efficient bureaucracy as with the need to educate his peasantry.

Unlike Joseph II, Catherine the Great of Russia (1762–1796) felt herself compelled to curry the favor of her nobility by involving them directly in the structure of local administration, by exempting them from military service and taxation, and probably most important, by granting them absolute control over the serfs on their estates. Her policy grew out of her strong ties to powerful nobles and her involvement in the conspiracy which led to the assassination of her husband, Tsar Peter III, the last of a series of weak rulers who followed Peter the Great. Catherine was herself a German, and prided herself on her devotion to Western principles of government. Ambitious to establish a reputation as an intellectual and enlightened monarch, she corresponded with French philosophers, wrote plays, published a digest of William Blackstone's *Commentaries on the Laws of England,* and even began a history of Russia. Her contributions to social reform did not extend much beyond the founding of hospitals and orphanages, and

Catherine the Great

Catherine the Great of Russia

the expression of a pious hope that someday the serfs might be liberated. Although she did summon a commission in 1767 to codify Russian law, its achievements were modest: a minor extension of religious toleration; a slight restriction of the use of torture by the state.

Any plans Catherine may have had for improving the lot of the peasants, however, were abruptly cancelled after their frustration with St. Petersburg's centralization efforts erupted in a violent peasant-serf rebellion in 1773–1774. Free peasants in the Volga valley region found themselves compelled to provide labor services to nobles sent by the crown to control them, Cossacks were subjected to taxation and conscription for the first time, and factory workers and miners were pressed into service in the state's industrial enterprises. These and other disparate but dissatisfied groups, including serfs, united under the rebel banner of Emelyan Pugachev, an illiterate Cossack who claimed to be the late Tsar Peter III. The hapless Peter spoke as a reformer in life, and in death became a larger-than-life hero for those opposed to the determined absolutism of his successor. As Pugachev marched, he encouraged his followers to strike out not only against the empress but also against the nobility and the church. Over 1500 landlords and priests were murdered and the ruling classes terrified as the revolt spread. While Catherine's forces initially had little success against the rebel army, the threat of famine plagued Pugachev's advance and finally led to disrray among his troops. Betrayed in 1774, he was captured and taken in an iron cage to Moscow, where he was tortured and killed. Catherine responded to this uprising with further centralization and tightening of aristocratic authority over the peasantry.

Emelyan Pugachev Shackled and Encaged after His Capture

The significance of Catherine the Great

The brutal suppression and punishment of the rebels reflected the ease with which the German-born Catherine took to the despotic authoritarianism that characterized Russian absolutism. She was as outsized in her tastes and personality as was Peter the Great. Her sexual appetite was voracious; her current chief officers of state as often as not were also her current lovers. Catherine's chief significance lies in her ability to continue the work of Peter the Great in introducing Russia to Western ideas, to come to terms with the nobility in a way that brought stability to the state, and to make the country a formidable power in European affairs by extending its boundaries to include not only most of Poland but lands on the Black Sea.

The absolutist worldview

Eighteenth-century absolutist monarchs shared a desire to pursue policies that would mark their regimes as modern, befitting a world that was leaving obscurantism and fanaticism behind. They were modern, also, in their determination to press ahead with the task, begun by their seventeenth-century predecessors, of building powerful, centralized states by continuing to eliminate or harness the ancient privileges of still-powerful noble orders and provincial estates. The notion of a limited monarchy, in which power was divided between local and central authorities and shared by monarchs, nobles, and legislative assemblies, struck them as a dangerous anachronism. Yet as the century progressed, they found that conviction challenged by the emergence of England, under limited monarchy, as the world's leading commercial and naval power.

England (or Britain, as the country was called after its union with Scotland in 1707) prospered as a state in which power was divided between the king and Parliament. This division of political power was guaranteed by a constitution which, though unwritten, was grounded in common law and strengthened by precedent and by particular legal settlements such as those that had followed the restoration of the Stuarts in 1660 and the overthrow of James II in 1688. The Hanoverians George I (1714–1727) and his son George II (1727–1760) were by no means political cyphers. Though George I could not speak English, he could converse comfortably enough with his ministers in French. The first two Georges made a conscientious and generally successful effort to govern within their adopted kingdom. They appointed the chief ministers who remained responsible to them for the creation and direction of state policy. Yet because Parliament, after 1688, retained the right to legislate, tax, and spend, its powers were far greater than those of any European parlement, estate, or diet. During the reign of the first two Hanoverians, politics was on most occasions little more than a struggle between factions within the Whig party, composed of wealthy—and in many cases newly rich—landed magnates who were making fortunes in an expanding economy based on commercial and agricultural capitalism.

The Tories, because of their previous association with the Stuarts, remained political "outs" for most of the century. To the Whigs,

George I of England

The House of Commons. Despite its architectural division into two "sides," the House was composed of men of property whose similar economic interests encouraged them to agree on political fundamentals.

Left: *Sir Robert Walpole with Members of His Cabinet.* Right: *Walpole as a Roman Emperor.*

Local government

national politics was no longer a matter of clashing principles. Those principles had been settled—to their satisfaction—in 1688. Nor was politics a matter of legislating in the national interest. Britain was governed locally, not from the center, as in an absolutist state. Aristocrats and landed gentry administered the affairs of the particular counties and parishes in which their estates lay, as lords lieutenant, as justices of the peace, as overseers of the poor, unhampered, to a degree unknown on the Continent, by legislation imposed uniformly throughout the kingdom. The quality of local government varied greatly. Some squires were as "allworthy" as Henry Fielding's fictional character of that name in the novel *Tom Jones.* Others cared for little beyond the bottle and the chase. A French traveler noted in 1747 that the country gentleman was "naturally a very dull animal" whose favorite afterdinner toast was "to all honest fox hunters in Great Britain." These men administered those general laws that did exist—the Poor Law, game laws—which were drawn in such a way as to leave their administrators wide latitude, a latitude which they exercised in order to enhance the appearance of their own local omnipotence. Thus in Britain there was no attempt to pass a law establishing a state-wide system of primary education. Centralizing legislation of that sort, the hallmark of absolutist states, was anathema to the British aristocracy and gentry. They argued that education, if it was to be provided, should be provided at their expense, in village schoolrooms by schoolmasters in their employ. Those instructors would make it their business to teach their pupils not only rudimentary reading, writing, and figuring, but the deferential behavior that bespoke the obligation of the poor to their rich benefactors.

Politics, then, was neither first principles nor national legislation. It was "interest" and "influence," the weaving of a web of obligations into a political faction powerful enough to secure jobs and favors—a third secretaryship in the foreign office from a minister, an Act of Enclosure from Parliament. The greatest master of this game of politics was Robert Walpole (1676–1745) who was England's leading minister from the early 1720s until 1742. Walpole is sometimes called Britain's first prime minister, a less than entirely accurate distinction, since officially that position did not exist until the nineteenth century. Prime minister or not, he wielded great political power. He took advantage of the king's frequent absences in Hanover to assert control over the day-to-day governance of the country. He ruled as chief officer of his cabinet, a small group of like-minded politicians whose collective name derived from the small room in which they met. In time the cabinet evolved into the policy-making executive arm of the British political system; Britain is governed today by cabinet and Parliament, the cabinet comprised of leading politicians from the majority party in Parliament. Walpole was a member of a Norfolk gentry family who had risen to national prominence on the fortune he amassed while serving as paymaster-general to the armed forces during the War of the Spanish Succession. Adept at bribery and corruption, he used his ability to reward his supporters with appointments to ensure himself a loyal political following. By the end of his career, grossly fat and stuffed, seemingly, with the profits of his years in office, he was being depicted by cartoonists and balladeers as Britain's most accomplished robber. "Little villains must submit to Fate," lamented a typical lampoon, "while great ones do enjoy the world in state." Walpole was no more corrupt, however, than the political process over which he presided. The majority of seats in Parliament's lower House of Commons were filled by representatives from boroughs which often had no more than two or three dozen electors. Hence it was a relatively simple task to buy votes, either directly or with promises of future favors. Walpole cemented political factions together into an alliance that survived for about twenty years. During that time, he worked to ensure domestic tranquility by refusing to press ahead with any legislation that might arouse national controversy. He withdrew what was perhaps his most innovative piece of legislation—a scheme to increase excise taxes and reduce import duties as a means of curbing smugglers—in the face of widespread popular opposition.

Other Whig politicians succeeded Walpole in office in the 1740s and 1750s, but only one, William Pitt, later elevated to the House of Lords as the earl of Chatham, commanded public attention as Walpole had. George III (1760–1820), who came to the throne as a young man in 1760, resented the manner in which he believed his royal predecessors

Robert Walpole and the nature of British politics

George III: the battle over prerogative

had been treated by the Whig oligarchy. Whether or not, as legend has it, his mother fired his determination with the constant injunction "George, be king!" he began his reign convinced that he must assert his rightful prerogatives. He dismissed Pitt, and attempted to impose ministers of his own choosing on Parliament. King and Parliament battled this issue of prerogative throughout the 1760s. In 1770, Lord North, an aristocrat satisfactory to the king and with a large enough following in the House of Commons to ensure some measure of stability, assumed the position of first minister. His downfall occurred a decade later, as a result of his mismanagement of the overseas war which resulted in Britain's loss of its original thirteen North American colonies. A period of political shuffling was followed by the king's appointment, at the age of twenty-three, of another William Pitt, Chatham's son, and this Pitt directed Britain's fortunes for the next twenty-five years—a political reign even longer than Walpole's. Although the period between 1760 and 1780 witnessed a struggle between crown (as the king and his political following were called) and Parliament, it was a very minor skirmish compared with the titanic constitutional struggles of the seventeenth century. Britain saw the last of absolutism in 1688. What followed was the mutual adjustment of the two formerly contending parties to a settlement both considered essentially sound.

7. WAR AND DIPLOMACY IN THE EIGHTEENTH CENTURY

Diplomacy in mid-century: the "diplomatic revolution"

The history of European diplomacy and warfare after 1715 is one in which the twin goals of international stability and economic expansion remained paramount. The fact that those objectives often conflicted with each other set off further frequent wars, in which the ever-growing standing armies of absolutist Europe were matched against each other and in which the deciding factor often turned out to be not continental military strength, but British naval power. The major conflict at mid-century, known as the Seven Years' War in Europe and the French and Indian War in North America, reflects the overlapping interests of power balance and commercial gain. In Europe, the primary concern was balance. Whereas in the past France had seemed the major threat, now Prussia loomed—at least in Austrian eyes—as a far more dangerous interloper. Under these circumstances, in 1756 the Austrian foreign minister, Prince Wenzel von Kaunitz, effected the so-called diplomatic revolution, which put an end to the enmity between France and Austria, and resulted in a formidable threat to the Prussia of Frederick the Great. Frederick, meanwhile, was taking steps to protect his flanks. While anxious not to arouse his French ally, he nevertheless signed a neutrality treaty with the British, who were concerned to secure protection for their sovereign's Hanoverian domains. The French read Frederick's act as a hostile one, and thus fell all the more readily for Kaunitz's offer of an alliance. The French indeed perceived a pressing need for trustworthy European allies, since they were already engaged in an undeclared war with England in North America. By mid-1756 Kaunitz could count France, Russia, Sweden, and several German states as likely allies against Prussia. Rather than await retribution from his enemies, Frederick invaded strategic but neutral Saxony and then Austria itself, thus once again playing the role of aggressor.

Shifting power balances: the Seven Year's War

The configurations in this diplomatic gavotte are undoubtedly confusing. They are historically important, however, because they indicate the way in which the power balance was shifting, and the attempts of European states to respond to those shifts by means of new diplomatic alliances. Prussia and Britain were the volatile elements: Prussia on the Continent; Britain overseas. The war from 1756 to 1763 in Europe centered upon Frederick's attempts to prevent the dismemberment of his domain at the hands of the French-Austrian-Russian alliance. Time and again the Prussian army's superiority and Frederick's own military genius frustrated his enemies' attacks. Ultimately, Prussia's survival against these overwhelming odds—"the miracle of the House of Brandenburg"—was ensured by the death of the Tsarina Elizabeth (1741–1762), daughter of Peter the Great, and by the accession of Peter III (1762), whose admiration for Frederick was as great as was his predecessor's hostility. Peter withdrew from the war, returning the conquered provinces of East Prussia and Pomerania to his country's erstwhile enemy. The peace that followed, though it compelled Frederick to relinquish Saxony, recognized his right to retain Silesia, and hence put an end to Austria's hope of one day recapturing that rich prize.

The British navy as key to victory

Overseas, fighting occurred not only in North America but in the West Indies and in India, where Anglo-French commercial rivalry had resulted in sporadic, fierce fighting since the 1740s. Ultimate victory would go to that power possessing a navy strong enough to keep its supply routes open—that is, to Britain. Superior naval forces resulted in victories along the North American Great Lakes, climaxing in the Battle of Québec in 1759 and the eventual surrender of all of Canada to the British. By 1762 the French sugar islands, including Martinique, Grenada, and St. Vincent, were in British hands. Across the globe in India, the defeat of the French in the Battle of Plassey in 1757 and the capture of Pondichéry four years later made Britain the dominant European presence on the subcontinent. In the Treaty of Paris in 1763 which brought the Seven Years' War to an end, France officially surrendered Canada and India to the British, thus affording them an extraordinary field for commercial exploitation.

The success of the British in North America in the Seven Years' War was itself a major cause of the war which broke out between the mother country and her thirteen original colonies in 1775. To pay for

The Battle of Québec, 1759. Most often remembered for the fact that the British and French commanders, Generals Wolfe and Montcalm, were killed on the bluffs above the St. Lawrence River (the Plains of Abraham), this battle was most notable for the success of the British amphibious assault, a measure of Britain's naval superiority.

"Taxation without representation . . ."

the larger army the British now deemed necessary to protect their vastly expanded colonial possessions, they imposed unwelcome new taxes on the colonists. The North Americans protested that they were being taxed without representation. The home government responded that, like all British subjects, they were "virtually" if not actually represented by the present members of the House of Commons. Colonists thundered back that the present political system in Britain was so corrupt that no one but the Whig oligarchs could claim that their interests were being looked after.

The American Revolution

Meanwhile the British were exacting retribution for rebellious acts on the part of colonists. East India Company tea shipped to be sold in Boston at prices advantageous to the company was dumped in Boston harbor. The port of Boston was thereupon closed, and democratic government in the colony of Massachusetts curtailed. The British garrison clashed with colonial civilians. Colonial "minutemen" formed a counterforce. By the time war broke out in 1775, most Americans were prepared to sever ties with Britain and declare themselves an independent nation, which they did the following year. Fighting continued until 1781 when a British army surrendered to the colonists at Yorktown to the tune of a song entitled "A World Turned Upside Down." The French, followed by Spain and the Netherlands, were determined to do everything possible to inhibit the further growth of Britain's colonial empire, and allied themselves with the newly independent United States in 1778. A peace treaty signed in Paris in 1783 recognized the sovereignty of the new state. Though the British lost direct control of their former colonies, they reestablished their trans-atlantic commercial ties with America in the 1780s. Indeed, the brisk trade in raw cotton between the slave-owning southern states and Britain made possible the industrial revolution in textiles that began in the north of England at this time, and that carried Britain to world-wide preeminence as an economic power in the first half of the nine-teenth century. This ultimately profitable arrangement lay in the future. At the time, the victory of the American colonists seemed to contem-porary observers to right the world balance of commercial power, which had swung so far to the side of the British. In this instance, independence seemed designed to restore stability.

In eastern Europe, however, the very precariousness of Poland's independence posed a threat to stability and the balance of power. As an independent state, Poland functioned, at least in theory, as a buffer among the major central European powers—Russia, Austria, and Prussia. Poland was the one major central European territory whose landed elite had successfully opposed introduction of absolutist cen-tralization and a consequent curtailment of its "liberties." The result, however, had not been anything like real independence for either the Polish nobility or the country as a whole. Aristocrats were quite pre-pared to accept bribes from foreign powers in return for their vote in elections for the Polish king. And their continued exercise of their constitutionally guaranteed individual veto (the "liberum veto") in the Polish Diet meant that the country remained in a perpetual state of weakness that made it fair game for the land-hungry absolutist poten-tates who surrounded its borders.

Poland and the balance of power in eastern Europe

In 1764 Russia intervened to influence the election of King Stanis-laus Poniatowski, an able enough nobleman who had been one of Catherine the Great's lovers. Thereafter Russia continued to meddle in the affairs of Poland—and of Turkey as well—often protecting both countries' Greek Orthodox Christian minority. When war finally broke out with Turkey in 1769, resulting in large Russian gains in the Bal-kans, Austria made known its opposition to further Russian expan-sion, lest it upset the existing balance of power in eastern Europe. In the end Russia was persuaded to acquire territory in Poland instead, by joining Austria and Prussia in a general partition of that country's lands. Though Maria Theresa opposed the dismemberment of Poland, she reluctantly agreed to participate in the partition in order to main-tain the balance of power, an attitude which prompted a scornful Frederick the Great to remark that "She weeps, but she takes her share." According to the agreement of 1772, Poland lost about 30 percent of its kingdom and about half of its population.

The first partition of Poland

Following this first partition, the Russians continued to exercise virtual control of Poland. King Stanislaus, however, took advantage of a new Russo-Turkish war in 1788 to press for a more truly inde-pendent state with a far stronger executive than had existed previ-

The second and third partitions of Poland

European upheaval

ously. A constitution adopted in May 1791 established just that; but this rejuvenated Polish state was to be short-lived. In January 1792, the Russo-Turkish war ended and Catherine the Great pounced. Together the Russians and Prussians took two more enormous bites in 1793, destroying the new constitution in the process. A rebellion under the leadership of Thaddeus Kosciuszko, who had fought in America, was crushed in 1794 and 1795. A final swallow by Russia, Austria, and Prussia in 1795 left nothing of Poland at all. After this series of partitions of Poland, each of the major powers was a good deal fatter; but on the international scales by which such things were measured, they continued to weigh proportionately the same.

The final devouring of Poland occurred at a time when the Continent was once again engaged in a general war. Yet this most recent conflict was not just another military attempt to resolve customary disputes over commerce or problems of international stability. It was the result of violent revolution that had broken out in France in 1789, that had toppled the Bourbon dynasty there, and that threatened to do the same to other monarchs across Europe. The second and third partitions of Poland were a final bravura declaration of power by monarchs who already feared for their heads. Henceforth, neither foreign nor domestic policy would ever again be dictated as they had been in absolutist Europe, by the convictions and determinations of kings and queens alone. Poland disappeared as Europe fell to pieces, as customary practice gave way to new and desperate necessity.

The Royal Cake. A contemporary cartoon showing the monarchs of Europe at work carving up a hapless Poland.

SELECTED READINGS

• *Items so designated are available in paperback editions.*

Anderson, M. S., *Peter the Great,* London, 1978. A good, thorough biography.

• Avrich, Paul, *Russian Rebels, 1600–1800,* New York, 1972. A study of revolts against absolutist power.

Baxter, Stephen, *William III,* New York, 1965. The best study of the Dutchman who became England's king.

Bernard, Paul, *Joseph II,* New York, 1968.

• Carsten, F. L., *The Origins of Prussia,* Oxford, 1954. A survey which focuses on the reign of the Great Elector.

Churchill, W. S., *Marlborough,* New York, 1968. An abridged edition of Churchill's magnificently written biography of his ancestor.

• Dorn, Walter, *The Competition for Empire, 1740–63,* New York, 1940. A standard survey, still valuable.

Dukes, Paul, *Catherine the Great and the Russian Nobility,* Cambridge, 1967. A study of the limits of absolutism.

• Dunn, Richard S., *The Age of Religious Wars, 1559–1715,* 2nd ed., New York, 1979. A detailed and up-to-date survey, useful for the history of late seventeenth- and early eighteenth-century absolutism.

Florinsky, M. T., *Russia: A History and an Interpretation,* Vol. 1, New York, 1955. A useful text. Reviews divergent interpretations and emphasizes politics.

Ford, Franklin, *Robe and Sword: The Regrouping of the French Aristocracy after Louis XIV,* Cambridge, Mass., 1953. An important social study of the nobility of the robe and its striving for dominance before the revolution.

• Fraser, Antonia, *Royal Charles: Charles II and the Restoration,* New York, 1979. A readable, reliable life of the king and his times.

• Gagliardo, John, *Enlightened Despotism,* New York, 1967. A useful study of eighteenth-century absolutism.

Gershoy, Leo, *From Despotism to Revolution, 1763–1789,* New York, 1944. Valuable for the tensions leading up to the revolutionary period.

• Goubert, Pierre, *Louis XIV and Twenty Million Frenchmen,* New York, 1972. A valuable study, the starting point for an understanding of the Sun King's reign.

• Hatton, R. N., *Europe in the Age of Louis XIV,* New York, 1969. Thoughtful interpretation of the period; excellent illustrations.

• Herr, Richard, *The Eighteenth Century Revolution in Spain,* Princeton, N.J., 1958. The best introduction to Spain in this period.

Holborn, Hajo, *The Age of Absolutism,* New York, 1964. The best survey for Germany. Second volume of Holborn's *History of Modern Germany.*

• Krieger, Leonard, *Kings and Philosophers, 1689–1789,* New York, 1970. A thorough survey of the political and intellectual developments of this century.

• Lewis, W. H., *The Splendid Century: Life in the France of Louis XIV,* New York, 1953. A delightfully written survey.

• Palmer, R. R., *The Age of the Democratic Revolution: A Political History of Europe and America, 1760–1800,* Vol. 1, Princeton, N.J., 1964. Argues in favor of a general European aristocratic reaction prior to 1789.

Plumb, J. H., *Sir Robert Walpole,* 2 vols., Boston, 1956, 1961. A well-written, sympathetic biography of England's leading eighteenth-century politician.

• Ritter, Gerhard, *Frederick The Great: A Historical Profile,* Berkeley, Calif., 1968. A readable biography.

• Rosenberg, Hans, *Bureaucracy, Aristocracy, and Autocracy: The Prussian Experience, 1660–1815,* Cambridge, Mass., 1958.

Rudé, George, *Europe in the Eighteenth Century: Aristocracy and the Bourgeois Challenge,* New York, 1972. A survey which stresses social stratification and tension.

• Speck, W. A., *Stability and Strife: England, 1714–1760,* Cambridge, Mass., 1977. A good, recent survey.

Spielman, John P., *Leopold I of Austria,* New Brunswick, N.J., 1977. The only biography of the monarch in English.

• Wangermann, Ernst, *The Austrian Achievement, 1700–1800,* London, 1973. A suggestive introductory survey.

• Wolf, John B., *Louis XIV,* New York, 1968. The standard biography in English.

• ——, *The Emergence of the Great Powers, 1685–1715,* New York, 1951. A useful general survey of this critical period.

• Woloch, Isser, *Eighteenth Century Europe: Tradition and Progress, 1715–1789,* New York, 1982. A thoughtful, well-organized survey.

SOURCE MATERIALS

• Locke, John, *Two Treatises of Government.* (Many editions.) The argument against absolutism.

Saint-Simon, Louis, *Historical Memoirs.* (Many editions.) A brilliant source for evidence about life at the court of Louis XIV.

Chapter 19

THE SCIENTIFIC REVOLUTION AND ENLIGHTENMENT

This is the age wherein philosophy comes in with a spring-tide. . . . Methinks I see how all the old rubbish must be thrown away, and the rotten buildings be overthrown, and carried away with so powerful an inundation.

—Henry Power, *Experimental Philosophy* (1663)

Enlightenment is humanity's departure from its self-imposed immaturity. Immaturity is the inability to use one's intellect without the guidance of others. This immaturity is self-imposed when its cause is not a lack of intelligence but a failure of determination and courage to think without the guidance of someone else. Dare to know! This then is the slogan of the Enlightenment.

—Immanuel Kant, *What is Enlightenment?* (1784)

The years between roughly 1660 and 1789, which witnessed the prevalence of absolutism in western Europe, witnessed as well the most important mutation in all of European intellectual and cultural history to occur between the Middle Ages and the present. Just as the sweep of fresh winds can greatly change the weather, so in the last few decades of the seventeenth century the sweep of new ideas led to a bracing change in Europe's "climate of opinion." For purposes of analysis it is convenient to refer to two phases within the larger period: the triumph of the scientific revolution in the second half of the seventeenth century and the age of "Enlightenment" which followed for most of the eighteenth century. But without any doubt the same intellectual winds that swept into Europe during the later seventeenth century prevailed for well over a hundred years. Indeed, their influence is still felt today.

New ideas: 1660–1789

How did the new intellectual climate differ from the old? Concentrating on essentials, three points may be stressed. First, whereas medieval, Renaissance, and Reformation thinkers all assumed that past

*Changes in intellectual
environment*

knowledge was the most reliable source of wisdom, the greatest thinkers from the seventeenth century onward rejected any obeisance to ancient authority and resolved to rely on their own intellects to see where knowledge would lead them. Making their motto "dare to know," they stressed the autonomy of science and the free play of the mind in ways unheard of in the West since the golden age of Greece. Second, the new breed of thinkers believed strongly that knowledge was valueless if it could not be put to use. For a Plato, an Aristotle, or a St. Thomas Aquinas alike, the greatest wisdom was the most abstract wisdom since such wisdom helped to turn the human mind away from all earthly "corruptibility" and supposedly brought happiness by its sheer resemblance to timeless divinity. But after the change in Europe's climate of opinion in the late seventeenth century, all knowledge without practical value was belittled and thinkers from every realm of intellectual endeavor aimed directly or indirectly at achieving "the relief of man's estate." Finally, the new climate of opinion was characterized by the demystification of the universe. Up until the mid–seventeenth century, most people, learned and unlearned, assumed that the universe was driven and inhabited by occult forces that humans could barely understand and surely never control unless they were magicians. But around 1660 a mechanistic worldview swept away occultism, and pixies became consigned to the realm of children's storybooks. Thereafter nature was believed to work like the finest mechanical clock—consummately predictable and fully open to human understanding.

Causes of change

Why such a dramatic change in basic patterns of thought took place when it did will long remain a subject for speculation. Certainly the prior Scholastic stress on human rationality and the Renaissance reacquisition of classical Greek texts helped to bring European thought to a scientific threshold. Probably the most direct causes of the intellectual mutations, however, were the twin challenges to conventional assumptions introduced in the sixteenth century by the discovery of the New World and the realization that the earth revolves around the sun rather than vice versa, for neither the Bible nor ancient science allowed room for what one bewildered contemporary called "new islands, new lands, new seas, new peoples, and what is more, a new sky and new stars." At first many thinkers, daunted by all this novelty, experienced a sense of intellectual crisis. Some took refuge in skepticism, others in relativism, and others in a return to blind faith. Speaking for several generations, the poet John Donne lamented in 1611 that "new philosophy calls all in doubt, the element of fire is quite put out, the sun is lost, and the earth, and no man's wit can well direct him where to look for it. . . . 'tis all in pieces, all coherence gone." But just as Europe surmounted its early-modern political crisis around 1660, so did it surmount its intellectual one, above all because the last stages of a profound scientific revolution gave a new, completely convincing "coherence" to things. As Alexander Pope wrote in the early eighteenth century, almost as if in response to Donne: "Nature and Nature's Law's lay hid in night:/ God said, Let Newton Be! and all was light."

1. THE SCIENTIFIC REVOLUTION

Even though Europe did not begin to resolve its intellectual crisis until about 1660, the groundwork for that resolution was prepared earlier in the seventeenth century by four great individuals—Kepler, Galileo, Bacon, and Descartes. Kepler and Galileo—both practicing scientists—have been discussed earlier; suffice it here to say that they removed all doubts about the Copernican heliocentric theory of the solar system and helped lead the way to Sir Isaac Newton's theory of universal gravitation. As for Bacon and Descartes, their main achievements were not in the realm of original scientific discovery but rather in propagating new attitudes toward learning and the nature of the universe.

Sir Francis Bacon (1561–1626), lord chancellor of England, was also an extremely influential philosopher of science. In Bacon's view, expressed most fully in his *Novum Organum (New Instrument)* of 1620, science could not advance unless it departed entirely from the inherited errors of the past and established "progressive stages of certainty." For Bacon this meant proceeding strictly on the basis of empirical knowledge (knowledge gained solely by the senses) and by means of the "inductive method," meaning the arrival at truth by proceeding upward from particular observations to generalizations. Insisting that "the corruption of philosophy by superstition and an admixture of theology . . . does the greatest harm," and that thinking people thus should be "sober-minded, and give to faith that only which is faith's," Bacon advocated the advancement of learning as a cooperative venture proceeding by means of meticulously recorded empirical experiments. Unlike the arid speculations of the past, collective scientific research and observation would produce useful knowledge and result in bettering the human lot. Much of Bacon's ideology is vividly evoked in the cover illustration of his *Novum Organum,* wherein intrepid ships venture out beyond the Pillars of Hercules (Straits of Gibraltar) onto a fathomless sea in pursuit of unknown but great things to come.

Bacon's later contemporary, the French philosopher René Descartes (1596–1650), agreed with him on two points: that all past knowledge should be discarded, and that the worth of any idea depended on its usefulness. Yet Descartes otherwise proposed some very different approaches to science, for unlike the empiricist Bacon, Descartes was a rationalist and an apostle of mathematics. In his *Discourse on Method* (1637), Descartes explained how, during a period of solitude, he resolved to submit all inherited doctrines to a process of systematic

Title Page of Bacon's Novum Organum. Underneath the ship sailing out into the ocean is a quotation from the Book of Daniel: "Many shall venture forth and science shall be increased."

René Descartes

*A Diagram illustrating Cartesian
Principles.* Descartes maintained that the pineal gland, seen here at the back of the head, transmitted messages from the eyes to the muscles in purely mechanical fashion. But the pineal gland was also the link between the material body and the nonmaterial human mind. From the 1677 edition of Descartes' *De Homine.*

doubting because he knew that the "strangest or most incredible" things had previously been set down in learned books. Taking as his first rule "never to receive anything as a truth which [he] did not clearly know to be such," he found himself doubting everything until he came to the recognition that his mere process of thought proved his own existence ("I think, therefore I am"). Thereupon making rationality the point of departure for his entire philosophical enterprise, Descartes rebuilt the universe on largely speculative grounds that differed in almost every detail from the universe conceived by the Greeks, yet conformed fully to the highest principles of human rationality as expressed in the laws of mathematics. That most of his theories were not empirically verifiable did not trouble him at all, because he was confident that "natural processes almost always depend on parts so small that they utterly elude our senses."

Predictably, the details of Descartes' scientific system are now regarded as mere curiosities, but the French philosopher nonetheless was enormously influential in aiding the advance of science and in creating a new climate of opinion for several reasons. First of all, even though his systematic doubting did not succeed in establishing any solid new scientific truths, it did contribute to the discrediting of all the faulty science of the ancients. Then too, Descartes' stress on mathematics was salutary because mathematics has indeed proven to be an indispensable handmaiden to the pursuit of natural science. But undoubtedly Descartes' single most influential legacy was his philosophy of *dualism,* according to which God created only two kinds of reality—mind and matter. In Descartes' view, mind belonged to man alone and all else was matter. Thus he insisted that all created existence beyond man—organic and inorganic alike—operated solely in terms of physical laws, or the interplay of "extension and motion." In other words, for Descartes every single entity from the solar system to the realm of animals and plants was a self-operating machine propelled by a force arising from the original motion given to the universe by God. Indeed, Descartes thought that man himself was a machine—although, in this sole exception, a machine equipped with a mind. From this it followed that the entire universe could be studied objectively, without any aid from theology or appeals to the occult. Moreover, all apparent atributes of matter, such as light, color, sound, taste, or smell, which had no "extension" were to be classified as mere subjective impressions of the human mind unfit for proper scientific analysis. Based on such assumptions the pursuit of science could be dispassionate as never before.

Descartes' influence

Roughly speaking, for about a century after the work of Bacon and Descartes the English scientific community was Baconian and the French Cartesian (a name given to followers of Descartes). This is to say that the English concentrated primarily on performing empirical experiments in many different areas of physical science leading to concrete scientific advances, whereas the French tended to remain more

*The English and French
traditions*

oriented toward mathematics and philosophical theory. Among the numerous great seventeenth-century English laboratory scientists were the physician William Harvey (1578–1657), the chemist Robert Boyle (1627–1691), and the biologist Robert Hooke (1635–1703). Pursuing the earlier work of Vesalius and Servetus, but daring, unlike them, to practice vivisection, Harvey was the first to observe and describe the circulation of the blood through the arteries and back to the heart through the veins. Similarly committed to empirical experiment, Boyle used the air pump to establish "Boyle's law"—namely, that under constant temperature the volume of a gas decreases in proportion to the pressure placed on it. Boyle also was the first chemist to distinguish between a mixture and a compound (wherein the chemical combination occurs), and accomplished much to discredit alchemy. As for Hooke, although he conducted research in astronomy and physics as well as biology, he is best known for having used the microscope to discover the cellular structure of plants. Meanwhile, in France, Descartes himself pioneered in analytical geometry, Blaise Pascal worked on probability theory and invented a calculating machine before his conversion to religion, and Pierre Gassendi (1592–1655) sought to demonstrate the truth of the atomic theory. Also within the French realm of thought was the Dutch Jew Baruch Spinoza (1632–1677), a philosopher who tried to apply geometry to ethics and believed that he advanced beyond Descartes by interpreting the universe as being composed of a single substance—simultaneously God and nature—instead of two.

The dichotomy between English Baconianism and French Cartesianism, however, breaks down when one approaches the man commonly considered to have been the greatest scientist of all time, Sir Isaac Newton (1642–1727). A highly unattractive personality in his daily conduct—being secretive, petty, and vindictive—Newton was nonetheless a towering genius who drew on both the Baconian and Cartesian heritages. For example, following Bacon, and in the sharpest opposition to Descartes, Newton refused to dismiss the phenomenon of light as a mere subjective impression of "mind." Instead, by means of laboratory experiments he demonstrated that light behaves differently when filtered through different media, and hence offered an interpretation of light as a stream of particles that solidly established optics as an empirical branch of physics. Yet, on the other hand, Newton thoroughly approved of Descartes' stress on mathematics, and once in a burst of purely theoretical inspiration discovered the infinitesimal calculus.

Sir Isaac Newton

Of course Newton's supreme accomplishment lay in his formulation of the law of universal gravitation, which, as expressed in his monumental Latin *Principia Mathematica* (*Mathematical Principles of Natural Philosophy*) of 1687, integrated Copernican astronomy with Galileo's physics. In the *Principia* Newton broached the two major scientific questions of his day: (1) What keeps the heavy earth in motion?

Newton's law of gravitation

(before Copernicus the earth had been thought immobile) and (2) Why do terrestrial bodies tend to fall to the earth's center whereas planets stay in orbital motion? (before Copernicus the planets were thought to be embedded in crystalline spheres moved by angels or "divine intelligences"). In the early seventeenth century Kepler had already suggested the possibility of mutual attractions between all bodies in the solar system that kept the earth and other planets moving, but the Cartesians attacked this explanation as being too occult since attraction over space left out the crucial Cartesian ingredient of matter. Disregarding these Cartesian doubts because he saw no alternative, Newton returned to consider Kepler's theory of mutual attractions, and uniting Baconian observations with Cartesian mathematics, arrived at a single law of universal gravitation according to which "every particle of matter in the universe attracts every other particle with a force varying inversely as the square of the distance between them and directly proportional to the product of their masses." Since this law was verified by experience in both terrestrial and celestial realms, there could be no doubt that it explained all motion. Indeed, Newton's law was so reliable that it was employed immediately to predict the ebb and flow of tides. Later, in 1846, astronomers, noting irregularities in the motion of the planet Uranus, were able to deduce on Newtonian grounds the presence of the more distant planet Neptune before Neptune was actually located with the aid of high-power telescopes.

The impact of Newton's Principia

Historians of science consider Newton's law of gravity to be "the most stupendous single achievement of the human mind," finding that "no other work in the whole history of science equals the *Principia* either in originality and power of thought or in the majesty of its achievement." Certainly the publication of the *Principia* was the crowning event of the scientific revolution because it confirmed the most important astronomical and physical theories previously set forth by Copernicus, Kepler, and Galileo, and resolved beyond quarrel the major problems that Copernicus's heliocentric theory had created. Needless to say, scientific work did not thereafter come to a standstill. Quite to the contrary, since Newton's accomplishment proved inspirational to researchers in many other fields, scientific work advanced steadily after 1687. But a fundamental reconception of the nature of the physical universe had been made, and thinkers in all areas could proceed with their work confident that science rather than superstition was the new order of the day.

2. THE FOUNDATIONS OF THE ENLIGHTENMENT

Although the presuppositions for the Enlightenment were set by the triumph of the scientific revolution in the late seventeenth century, the Enlightenment itself was an eighteenth-century phenomenon, lasting for close to the entire century until certain basic Enlightenment postulates were challenged around 1790 by the effects of the French Revolution and the new movement of romanticism. Of course not every thinker who lived and worked in the eighteenth century was equally "enlightened." Some, such as the Italian philosopher of history G. B. Vico (1668–1744), were thoroughly opposed to everything the Enlightenment stood for, and others, most notably Jean Jacques Rousseau (1712–1778), accepted certain Enlightenment values but sharply rejected others. Moreover, patterns of Enlightenment ideology tended to vary from country to country and to change in each country over the course of the century. Yet, despite these qualifications, most thinkers of the eighteenth century definitely shared the sense of living in an exciting new intellectual environment in which "the party of humanity" would prevail over traditionalism and obscurantism by dint of an unflinching commitment to the primacy of the intellect.

*The Enlightenment: the
major pattern of
eighteenth-century thought*

Most Enlightenment thought stemmed from three basic premises: (1) the entire universe is fully intelligible and governed by natural rather than supernatural forces; (2) rigorous application of "scientific method" can answer fundamental questions in all areas of inquiry; and (3) the human race can be "educated" to achieve nearly infinite improvement. The first two of these premises were products of the scientific revolution and the third primarily an inheritance from the psychology of John Locke.

*Premises of the
Enlightenment*

Regarding the substitution of a natural for a supernatural world-view, explanations must start with the euphoria which greeted Isaac Newton's discovery of a single law whereby all motion in the heavens and earth became intelligible and predictable. If Newton could deal so authoritatively and elegantly with motion, it seemed to follow that all nature is governed neither by mysterious divine intervention nor by caprice, but by humanly perceivable universal laws. Hence most serious thinkers from about 1690 to 1790 became inveterate opponents of belief in miracles, and considered all varieties of revealed religion to be not just irrelevant to the pursuit of science, but positively antithetical to it. This is not to say that the Enlightenment abandoned belief in the existence of God: to the contrary, only the smallest number of Enlightenment thinkers were atheists, and very few even were avowed agnostics. Rather, most adhered to a religious outlook known as *Deism* which assumed that God existed but, having once created a perfect universe, no longer took an active interest in it. Expressed in the language of the Deists themselves, God was the "divine clockmaker" who, at the beginning of time, constructed a perfect timepiece and then left it to run on with predictable regularity. Most Deists continued to attend the churches of their ancestors (either Protestant or Catholic) from time to time, but they made little secret of their doubts about the efficacy of ritual and spoke out against all forms of religious intolerance.

*The rejection of
supernaturalism*

The Study of an Amateur Scientist. This late–seventeenth-century aristocratic dilettante collected all sorts of specimens from the natural world. The mounting of his crocodile must have offered some challenge.

Confidence in scientific method

As for the second Enlightenment premise, the accomplishments of the scientific revolution inspired a deep sense of assurance that "scientific method" was the only valid means for pursuing research in all areas of human inquiry. By scientific method Enlightenment thinkers usually meant the dispassionate, empirical observation of particular phenomena in order to arrive at general laws. Given the acknowledged triumph of Newtonian physics, it is not surprising that around 1700 western Europe was struck by a virtual mania for applying scientific method in studying all the workings of nature. Since most scientific work was still simple enough to be understood by amateurs without the benefit of years of specialized education, European aristocrats and prosperous people in all walks of life began to dabble in "research"—buying telescopes, chasing butterflies, or building home laboratories in the hope of participating in some new scientific breakthrough. Writing in 1710, the English essayist Joseph Addison satirized such pursuits by imagining a will written by one "Sir Nicholas Gimcrack," an earnest amateur who left his "recipe for preserving dead caterpillars" to his daughters, his "rat's testicles" to a "learned and worthy friend," and who disinherited his son for "having spoken disrespectfully of his little sister," whose mortal remains Sir Nicholas kept near his desk in "spirits of wine." Of course most of the aristocratic "Gimcracks" never progressed beyond pickling, but their enthusiasm for following the latest developments in scientific research led them to patronize the work of truly gifted scientists and contributed to creating an atmosphere wherein science was prized as humanity's greatest attainment.

Inevitably, in turn, such an atmosphere was conducive to an assumption which became dominant in the course of the eighteenth

century—that scientific method was the only proper means for studying human affairs as well as natural phenomena. Since the world of
physical nature seemed well on the way to being mastered, Enlightenment thinkers considered it mere common sense that the world of
human nature could soon be mastered as well by scientific means.
Thus students of religion started collecting myths from numerous different traditions, not to find any occult truth in them but to classify
their common traits and learn the steps by which humanity supposedly freed itself from superstition. Similarly, historians collected evidence to learn the laws governing the rise and fall of nations, and
students of politics compared governmental constitutions to arrive at
an ideal and universally applicable political system. In other words, as
the English poet Alexander Pope stated in his *Essay on Man* of 1733,
"the science of human nature [may be] like all other sciences reduced
to a few clear points," and Enlightenment thinkers became determined to learn exactly what those "few clear points" were.

It must be stressed, however, that if most thinkers of the Enlightenment supposed that the empirical study of human conduct could reduce
society's working to a few laws, most also believed that human conduct was not immutable but highly perfectible. In this they were
inspired primarily by the psychology of John Locke (1632–1704), who
was not only a very influential political philosopher, as we have seen,
but also the formulator of an extremely influential theory of knowledge. In his *Essay Concerning Human Understanding* (1690) Locke rejected
the hitherto dominant assumption that ideas are innate, maintaining
instead that all knowledge originates from sense perception. According to Locke, the human mind at birth is a "blank tablet" (Latin: *tabula
rasa*) upon which nothing is inscribed: not until the infant begins to
experience things, that is, to perceive the external world with its senses, is anything registered on its mind. From this point of departure,
Enlightenment thinkers concluded that environment determines
everything. For example, in their view, if some aristocrats were any
better than ordinary mortals it was not because they had inherited any
special knowledge or virtues, but only because they had been better
trained. It therefore followed that all people could be educated to
become the equals of the most perfect aristocrats, and that there were
no limits to the potentialities for universal human progress. Indeed, a
few Enlightenment thinkers became so optimistic as to propose that
all evil might be eradicated from the world, since whatever evil existed
was not the result of some divine plan but only the product of a faulty
environment that humans had created and humans could change.

3. THE WORLD OF THE PHILOSOPHES

France, the dominant country in eighteenth-century Europe, was the
center of the Enlightenment movement, and thus it is customary to
refer to the leading exponents of the Enlightenment, regardless of where

Voltaire by Houdon

they lived, by the French term *philosophe,* meaning philosopher. In fact the term philosophe is slightly misleading inasmuch as hardly any of the philosophes were really philosophers in the sense of being highly original abstract thinkers. Rather, most were practically oriented publicists who aimed to reform society by popularizing the new scientific interpretation of the universe and applying dispassionate "scientific method" to a host of contemporary problems. Since they sought most of all to gain converts and alter what they regarded as outmoded institutions, they shunned all forms of expression that might seem incomprehensible or abstruse, priding themselves instead on their clarity, and occasionally even expressing their ideas in the form of stories or plays rather than treatises.

By common consent the prince of the philosophes was the Frenchman born François Marie Arouet, who called himself Voltaire (1694–1778). Virtually the personification of the Enlightenment, much as Erasmus two centuries earlier had embodied Christian humanism, Voltaire commented on an enormous range of subjects in a wide variety of literary forms. Probably his greatest single accomplishment lay in championing the cause of English empiricism in previously Cartesian France. Having as a young man been exiled to England for the crime of insulting a pompous French nobleman, Voltaire returned after three years a thorough and extremely persuasive convert to the ideas of Bacon and Locke. Not only did this mean that he persuaded other French thinkers to accept Newton's empirically verifiable scientific system in place of Descartes' unverifiable one, but he also encouraged them to be less abstract and theoretical in all their intellectual inclinations and more oriented toward the solving of everyday problems. To be sure, throughout the eighteenth century France's intellectual world remained more rationalistic than England's, but Voltaire's lifelong campaign on behalf of empiricism nonetheless had a very salutary effect in making French thinkers more practically oriented than before.

Continually engaged in commenting on contemporary problems himself, Voltaire was an ardent spokesman for civil liberties. In this regard his battlecry was *Écrasez l'infâme*—"crush infamy"—meaning by infamy all forms of repression, fanaticism, and bigotry. In his own words, he believed that "the individual who persecutes another because he is not of the same opinion is nothing less than a monster." Accordingly, he wrote an opponent a line which forever after has been held forth as the first principle of civil liberty: "I do not agree with a word you say, but I will defend to the death your right to say it." Of all forms of intolerance Voltaire hated religious bigotry most of all because it seemed based on silly superstitions: "the less superstition, the less fanaticism; and the less fanaticism, the less misery." In addition to attacking religious repression, Voltaire also frequently criticized the exercise of arbitrary powers by secular states. In particular, he thought that the English parliamentary system was preferable to French absolutism and that all states acted criminally when their policies resulted in senseless wars. "It is forbidden to kill," he maintained sardonically, "therefore all murderers are punished unless they kill in large numbers and to the sound of trumpets."

Although Voltaire exerted the greatest effect on his age as a propagandist for the basically optimistic Enlightenment principle that by "crushing infamy" humanity could take enormous strides forward, the only one of his works still widely read today, the satirical story *Candide* (1759), is atypically subdued. Writing not long after the disastrous Lisbon earthquake of 1755, in which over 20,000 lives were lost for no apparent reason, Voltaire drew back in this work from some of his earlier faith that mankind by its own actions could limitlessly improve itself. Lulled into false security concerning what life has in store for him by the fatuous optimism of his tutor, Dr. Pangloss, the hero of the story, Candide, journeys through the world only to experience one outrageous misfortune after another. Storms and earthquakes are bad enough, but worse still are wars and rapacity caused by uncontrollable human passions. Only in the golden never-never land of "Eldorado" (clearly a spoof of the perfect world most philosophes saw on the horizon), where there are no priests, law courts, or prisons, but unlimited wealth and a "palace of sciences . . . filled with instruments of mathematics and physics," does Candide find temporary respite from disaster. Being a naturally restless mortal, however, he quickly becomes bored with Eldorado's placid perfection and leaves for the renewed buffetings of the real world. After many more lessons in "the school of hard knocks," he finally learns one basic truth by the end of the story: settling down on a modest farm with his once-beautiful but now hideously disfigured wife, he shrugs when Dr. Pangloss repeats for the hundredth time that "this is the best of all possible worlds," and replies: "that's as may be, but we must cultivate our garden." In other words, according to Voltaire, life is not perfect and probably never will be, but humans will succeed best if they ignore vapid theorizing and buckle down to unglamorous but productive hard work.

In addition to Voltaire, the most prominent French philosophes were Montesquieu, Diderot, and Condorcet. The baron de Montesquieu (1689–1755) was primarily a political thinker. In his major work, *The Spirit of Laws* (1748), Montesquieu sought to discover the ways in which differing environments and historical and religious traditions influence governmental institutions. Finding that unalterable differences in climates and geographic terrains affect human behavior, and hence governmental forms, Montesquieu throughout much of *The Spirit of Laws* seems to be saying that external conditions force humans to behave in different ways and that there is nothing they can do about this. But ultimately he was an idealist who preferred one particular political system, the English constitution, and hoped that all nations might overcome whatever environmental handicaps they faced to

Candide

Montesquieu

imitate it. For him, the greatest strength of the English system was that it consisted of separate and balanced powers—executive, legislative, and judicial: thus it guaranteed liberty inasmuch as no absolute sovereignty was given to any single governing individual or group. This idealization of "checks and balances" subsequently influenced many other Enlightenment political theorists and played a particularly dominant role in the shaping of the United States Constitution in 1787.

Diderot and the Encyclopedia

Unlike Voltaire, who was not a very systematic thinker, and Montesquieu, who wrote in a somewhat ambiguous and primarily reflective mode, the most programmatic of the philosophes was Denis Diderot (1713–1784). As a young firebrand Diderot was clapped into solitary confinement for his attacks on religion and thereafter worked under the ever-present threat of censorship and imprisonment. Yet throughout his life he never shrank from espousing a fully materialistic philosophy or criticizing what he considered to be backwardness or tyranny wherever he found it. Although, like Voltaire, Diderot wrote on a wide range of subjects in numerous different forms, including stories and plays, he exerted his greatest influence as the organizer of and main contributor to an extremely ambitious publishing venture, the *Encyclopedia*. Conceived as a summation and means for dissemination of all the most advanced contemporary philosophical, scientific, and technical knowledge, with articles written by all the leading philosophes of the day (including Voltaire and Montesquieu), the *Encyclopedia* first appeared between 1751 and 1772 in installments totaling seventeen large volumes and eleven more of illustrative plates. Whereas modern encyclopedias serve primarily as reference works, Diderot thought of his *Encyclopedia* as a set of volumes that people would read at length rather than merely using to look up facts. Therefore he hoped that it would "change the general way of thinking." Above all, by popularizing the most recent achievements in science and technology, Diderot intended to combat "superstition" on the broadest front, aid the further advance of science, and thereby help alleviate all forms of human misery. Dedicated to the proposition that all traditional beliefs had to be reexamined "without sparing anyone's sensibilities," he certainly would have excoriated all "irrational" religious dogmas openly if left to himself. But since strict censorship made explicitly antireligious articles impossible, Diderot thumbed his nose at religion in such oblique ways as offering the laconic cross-reference for the entry on the Eucharist: "see cannibalism." Not surprisingly, gibes like this aroused storms of controversy when the early volumes of the *Encyclopedia* appeared. Nonetheless, the project was not only completed in the face of prominent opposition, but as time went on the complete work became so popular that it was reprinted several times and helped spread the ideas of the philosophes not just in France but all over Europe.

Diderot. A contemporary portrait by Van Loo.

One of the youngest of the contributors to the *Encyclopedia,* the marquis de Condorcet (1743–1794), is customarily termed "the last of

Landscape with the Burial of Phocion, Nicolas Poussin (1594–1665). An outstanding example of the classical style in painting. As opposed to the Baroque stress on swirling movement, here there is practically no movement at all. Instead, nature is conceived in rigorously geometrical terms to convey a sense of permanence. Note too the presence of ancient classical buildings, making it seem as if the past is enduring. (Louvre)

A Dutch Interior, Pieter de Hooch (c. 1629–c. 1679). Seventeenth-century Dutch painters excelled at indoor genre compositions bathed in light. The restraint of the scene itself stands in contrast to the melodramatic Baroque painting in the background. (National Gallery, London)

Le Mezzetin, Antoine Watteau (1684–1721). Mezzetin was a popular character from Italian comedy. In portraying him in a relaxed pose Watteau succeeded in conveying a sense of dreamy elegance. (MMA)

The Blue Boy, Thomas Gainsborough (1727–1788). Gainsborough, eighteenth-century England's greatest portrait painter, combined Watteau's lushness with more traditional English gravity. (Huntington Library)

Madame de Pompadour, François Boucher (1703–1770). A characteristically frilly French Rococo portrait. Madame de Pompadour, King Louis XV's mistress, was a patroness of arts and letters, and for a time the virtual ruler of France. (The Wallace Collection, London)

The Stonemason's Yard, Canaletto (1697–1768). A quiet scene of everyday life, in strong contrast to the portrait below. (National Gallery, London)

Marriage à la Mode, William Hogarth (1697–1764). A satirical look at the arranged marriage: the financial needs of the nobleman and the social aspirations of his middle-class counterpart dominate the negotiations. (National Gallery, London)

Sarah Siddons as the Tragic Muse, Sir Joshua Reynolds (1723–1792). Mrs. Siddons, a famous actress of the seventeenth century, is here portrayed as the Queen of Tragedy, in accordance with Reynolds's habit of depicting wealthy patrons in impressive classical poses. (Huntington Library)

Madame Recamier, Jacques Louis David (1748–1825). David was the exponent of a new classicism during and after the French Revolution. The couch, the lamp, and the costume are copied from Rome and Pompeii. (Louvre)

A Laboratory, from Diderot's *Encyclopedia.* Each printed number refers to a detailed discussion in the text. Note the far greater stress on practical instruction here than in the illustration of the amateur scientist's study shown above, p. 636.

the philosophes" because his career, and the philosophes' activities in general, were cut short by the excesses of the French Revolution. In his early career Condorcet gained prominence as a brilliant mathematician, but he is best known as the most extreme Enlightenment exponent of the idea of progress. Already in the late seventeenth century, particularly as the result of the triumphs of science, several thinkers began arguing that the intellectual accomplishments of their own day were superior to any of the past and that greater intellectual progress in the future was inevitable. But since it was less clear to some that modern literature was superior to the Greek and Latin classics, around 1700 an argument raged concerning the relative claims of "ancients" and "moderns" wherein so able a critic as the English writer Jonathan Swift could regard what he called the "battle of the books" as a standoff. In the eighteenth century, however, the conviction grew that the present had advanced in all aspects of human endeavor beyond the accomplishments of any earlier time, and that the future was bound to see unlimited further progress on all fronts. Condorcet's *Outline of the Progress of the Human Mind* (1794) was the ultimate expression of this point of view. According to Condorcet, progress in the past had not been uninterrupted—the Middle Ages had been an especially retrogressive era—but, given the victories of the scientific revolution and Enlightenment, indefinite and uninterrupted progress in the future was assured. Venturing into prophecy, Condorcet confidently stated not only that "as preventive medicine improves . . . the average human life-span will be increased and a more healthy and stronger physical constitution guaranteed," but that "the moment will come . . . when

Condorcet and faith in progress

tyrants and slaves . . . will exist only in history or on the stage." Ironically, even while Condorcet was writing such optimistic passages he was hiding out from the agents of the French Revolution, who in fact soon counted him among the numerous victims of their "reign of terror."

Beyond France, philosophes in other countries also made significant contributions to the Enlightenment legacy. After France, the most "enlightened" country of Europe was Great Britain, where the most noteworthy philosophes were Gibbon, Hume, and Adam Smith. Edward Gibbon (1737–1794) was a man of letters and historian whose *Decline and Fall of the Roman Empire* (1776–1788) remains among the two or three most widely read history books of all time. Scintillatingly written, the *Decline and Fall* covers Roman and Byzantine history from Augustus to the fall of Constantinople in 1453. According to Gibbon, the Roman Empire was brought down by "the triumph of barbarism [i.e., the Germanic invasions] and religion [i.e., Christianity]," but the Europe of his day was no longer "threatened with a repetition of those calamities." For him the rise of Christianity was the greatest calamity because "the servile and pusillanimous reign of the monks" replaced Roman philosophy and science with a credulity which "debased and vitiated the faculties of the mind." Certainly Gibbon's antireligious bias vitiated the quality of his own work, and therefore he is read today not so much for his particular opinions as for his trenchant character portrayals and above all for his devastating wit.

The Scotsman David Hume (1711–1776), on the other hand, was a truly penetrating philosopher—certainly the only enduringly great original philosopher among all the philosophes. Dedicated like most Enlightenment thinkers to challenging preconceived opinions, Hume was an exponent of relativistic ethics, and pushed skepticism so far in his major work, *An Enquiry Concerning Human Understanding* (1742), that he undermined all assurance that anyone knew anything for certain. Yet despite this he joined in Voltaire's campaign to crush "infamy," or what Hume called "stupidity, Christianity, and ignorance," on the grounds that it is preferable to voyage amid a sea of uncertainties than to dwell in a forest of supernatural shadows.

The most practically oriented of the leading British philosophes was the Scottish economist Adam Smith, whose landmark treatise, *The Wealth of Nations* (1776), is recognized as the classic expression of "laissez-faire" economics. Strongly opposed to mercantilism—that is, any governmental intervention in economic affairs—Smith maintained that the prosperity of all could best be obtained by allowing individuals to pursue their own interests without competition from state-owned enterprises or legal restraints. The term *laissez-faire* comes from the French expression *laissez faire la nature* (let nature take its course), and Smith's advocacy of laissez-faire economic doctrine reveals how deeply indebted he was to the Enlightenment's idealization of

Edward Gibbon

Adam Smith

both nature and human nature. In other words, espousing "the obvious and simple system of natural liberty," Smith believed that just as the planets revolve harmoniously in their orbits and are prevented from bumping into each other by the invisible force of gravity, so humans can act harmoniously even while pursuing their selfish economic interests if only "the invisible hand" of competitive, free-market forces be allowed to balance equitably the distribution of wealth. Ironically, although Smith thought of himself as the champion of the poor against the economic injustices inherent in state-supported mercantile privileges, his laissez-faire doctrine later became the favored theory of private industrial entrepreneurs who exploited the poor as much if not more than mercantilistic governments ever did. Nevertheless, Smith's free-market economics, as will be seen in subsequent chapters, certainly represented the wave of the future.

Adam Smith

Elsewhere in Europe the circulation of Enlightenment ideas was by no means as widespread as in France and Britain, owing either to stiffer resistance from religious authorities, greater vigilance of state censors, or the lack of sufficient numbers of prosperous educated people to discuss and support progressive thought. Yet, aside from the Papal States, at least a few prominent philosophes flourished in virtually every country of western Europe. In Germany, for example, the literary critic and dramatist Gotthold Lessing (1729–1781) propounded the necessity for tolerance in much the same spirit as Voltaire. In his play *Nathan the Wise* (1779) Lessing argued that nobility of character has no relation to religious affiliations, and in his *On the Education of the Human Race* (1780) he maintained that the development of each of the world's great religions, Christianity included, was simply a step in the spiritual evolution of humanity, which would soon move beyond religion entirely toward pure rationality. The living model for Lessing's dramatic hero "Nathan the Wise" was his friend, the German Jewish sage Moses Mendelssohn (1729–1786), another philosophe who urged tolerance—in his case by writing a history of Judaism—but who also argued in favor of the immortality of the soul.

The Enlightenment in Germany

Nor was Italy without its prominent philosophes as well. Certainly the most influential of these was the Milanese jurist Cesare Beccaria (1738–1794), a legal reformer whose major publication was the treatise *On Crimes and Punishments* (1764). In this work Beccaria attacked the prevalent view that judicial punishments should represent society's vengeance on the malefactor, asserting instead that no person has the right to punish another unless some useful purpose is served. For Beccaria, the only legitimate purpose for punishing crimes was the deterrence of other crimes. This granted, he argued for the greatest possible leniency compatible with deterrence, because enlightened humanitarianism dictated that humans should not punish other humans any more than is absolutely necessary. Above all, Beccaria eloquently opposed the death penalty, then widely inflicted throughout Europe for the most trivial offenses, on the grounds that it was no deterrent and set

Cesare Beccaria

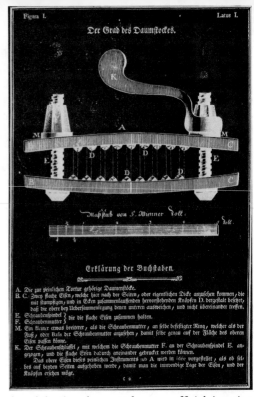

Instruments of Torture. The rack and the thumbscrew, from an official Austrian governmental handbook. Beccaria's influence helped phase out the use of such instruments by around 1800.

the bad example of public officials' presiding over murder rather than striving to deter it. *On Crimes and Punishments* was so favorably received that it was quickly translated into a dozen languages. Owing primarily to its influence, most European countries by around 1800 abolished torture, reserved the death penalty for capital crimes, and made imprisonment rather than any form of maiming the main form of judicial punishment.

In taking final stock of the Enlightenment movement, historians customarily raise two major questions. One is whether the philosophes were mere elitists who had no influence on the masses. Certainly, if one studies the sales figures of the philosophes' books or membership lists of eighteenth-century learned societies the answer is yes, for these reveal the philosophes' immediate audience to have been aristocrats, lawyers, government officials, prosperous merchants, and a scattering of members of the higher clergy. To some degree this class bias lay beyond the philosophes' control, for many of the poorer people throughout eighteenth-century Europe remained illiterate, and most of the masses in southern and southeastern Europe—literate and illiterate alike—lived under the sway of an extremely conservative Roman Catholic hierarchy that was determined to keep them ignorant of the philosophes' ideas by means of the strictest censorship. Yet it is also true that many of the philosophes, despite their avowed commitment

The audience of the philosophes

to clarity, wrote over the heads of most laboring people, and many did not even seek a lower-class audience because they feared that, if taken too far by the "uncouth" masses, their ideas might provoke open revolution. Typical philosophe elitism is well expressed in Gibbon's praise of imperial Roman religious policy whereby "the various modes of worship . . . were all considered by the people as equally true, by the philosopher as equally false, and by the magistrate as equally useful." Tradition also relates that whenever Voltaire discussed religion with his philosophe friends, he dismissed the servants so that they would not overhear any subversive remarks. Given this prevalent attitude, it is less surprising that Enlightenment ideas hardly percolated down to the masses than that they did have some effect on popular beliefs in France and England. For example, recent research on religious practices in southern France in the eighteenth century demonstrates that from 1760 to 1790 fewer and fewer people of all classes requested that masses be said for their souls after death. Apparently, then, some servants were overhearing the philosophes' drawing-room conversations after all.

The other major question often asked about the Enlightenment is whether the philosophes were not hopelessly impractical "dreamers rather than doers." Without ignoring the clear vein of utopianism in Enlightenment thought, the answer to this must surely be no. Admittedly, most philosophes were far more optimistic about the chances of human perfectibility than most people are today, after the total wars and gas ovens of the twentieth century. Yet even the most optimistic did not expect utopian miracles to occur overnight. Rather, almost all the philosophes were committed to agitating for piecemeal social reforms which they believed would culminate, step by inevitable step, in a new world of enlightenment and virtue. Often such agitation did lead to significant changes in the conduct of practical affairs, and in at least one case, that of the American Revolution, Enlightenment ideas were the main source of inspiration for con-

The philosophes' commitment to social reform

A Group of Philosophes *at Supper*. The commanding figure with his hand raised is Voltaire. It may be imagined that he will soon dismiss the servants so that he can begin to discuss religion.

structing a fully new political system. Moreover, sometimes even when Enlightenment propagandizing did not have any immediate practical impact, it did help to accomplish change in the future. For example, many philosophes condemned slavery on humanitarian or utilitarian grounds, thereby initiating a process of discussion that led cumulatively to the triumph of abolitionism throughout the West in the nineteenth century. In short, then, it is impossible to deny that the philosophes as a class were among the most practical-minded and influential intellectuals who ever lived.

4. THE ONWARD MARCH OF SCIENCE

Biology

Although several of the philosophes were natural scientists as well as publicists, it is preferable to treat the progress of eighteenth-century science separately because science, being highly international, is best broached by means of a topical rather than geographical method of review. The three scientific areas that witnessed the greatest progress from around the time of Newton to the end of the eighteenth century were descriptive biology, electricity, and chemistry. Regarding the first, four great pioneers in the use of newly invented high-power microscopes made enormous advances in observing small creatures and plant and cell structures during the last decades of the seventeenth century—the Italian Marcello Malpighi (1628–1694), the Englishman Robert Hooke, and two Dutchmen, Jan Swammerdam (1637–1680) and Antony van Leeuwenhoek (1632–1723). Perhaps most fundamental was the work of the last, a self-taught scientist who discovered bacteria and wrote the first description of human sperm. Building on such accomplishments as well as on numerous observations of his own, the Swedish botanist Karl von Linné (1707–1778)—commonly known by his Latinized name of Linnaeus—formulated the basic system of plant and animal classification that remains in use today. In the "Linnean Order" there are three realms—animal, vegetable, and mineral—and within the first two there are classes, "genera," and species. Furthermore, in Linnaeus's system every plant and animal is given two scientific Latin names—the first denoting the genus and the second the species. For example, robins are called *Planesticus migratorius:* the migrating species of the genus *Planesticus*.

Georges Buffon

Rivaling Linnaeus in eighteenth-century biology was the French naturalist Georges Buffon (1707–1788), whose massive *Natural History,* appearing in forty-four volumes from 1749 to 1778, was most advanced in its recognition of the close relationship between humans and other primates. Completely ignoring the biblical version of creation, yet never quite bringing himself to accept the full implications of a theory that located human origins in some form of evolution, Buffon admitted the possibility that the entire range of organic forms had descended from a single species and thus was a precursor of the evolutionism of Charles Darwin.

As opposed to developments in descriptive biology, where basic work hardly began before 1660, the "founding father" in the field of electricity was active well before the period under discussion. Around 1600 the Englishman William Gilbert discovered the magnetic properties of lodestones and introduced the word *electricity* into the language (*elektron* is the Greek word for amber, and Gilbert had observed that amber rubbed on fur will attract paper or straw). Yet because Gilbert worked before the triumph of mechanistic thought, he believed magnetism to be a purely occult force and therefore did not even dream of machines that could generate or harness electricity. Starting in the late seventeenth century, on the other hand, scientists from many different countries progressively began to master the science of electricity as we now know it. In 1672 the German Otto von Guericke published results of experiments wherein he generated electricity; in 1729 the Englishman Stephen Gray demonstrated that electricity could be conducted by means of threads and that certain other substances resisted conducting; and in 1745 a team of scientists at the Dutch University of Leyden invented a method for storing electricity in the "Leyden jar." In 1749 by using a kite-string to conduct lightning the American Benjamin Franklin charged a Leyden jar from a thunderstorm and thus was able to conclude that lightning and electricity are identical. This recognition allowed Franklin to invent the lightning rod, which saved houses from being destroyed in storms and is one of the best examples of the link between scientific theory and life-enhancing practice.

Electricity

Benjamin Franklin as the God of Electricity by Benjamin West

Probably the greatest theoretical breakthrough made in the second half of the eighteenth century lay in the field of chemistry, which had been languishing for about a century after the work of Robert Boyle. The reason for this delay lay mostly in the wide acceptance of errors concerning such matters as heat, flame, air, and the phenomenon of combustion. The most misleading error was the so-called phlogiston theory, based on the idea that "phlogiston" was the substance of fire— i.e., when an object burned, phlogiston was supposed to be given off. The remaining ash was said to be the "true" material. In the second half of the eighteenth century important discoveries were made which discredited this theory and cleared the way for a real understanding of basic chemical reactions. In 1766 the Englishman Henry Cavendish reported the discovery of a new kind of gas obtained by treating certain metals with sulfuric acid. He showed that this gas, now known as hydrogen, would not of itself support combustion and yet would be rapidly consumed by a fire with access to the air. In 1774 oxygen was discovered by another Englishman, the Unitarian minister Joseph Priestley. He found that a candle would burn with extraordinary vigor when placed in the new gas—a fact which indicated clearly that com-

Chemistry

Antoine Lavoisier

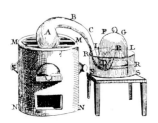

Lavoisier's Apparatus for the Decomposition of Air

*Comparative slowness of
medical progress*

*Inoculation and
vaccination*

bustion was not caused by any mysterious principle or substance in the flame itself. A few years after this discovery, Cavendish demonstrated that air and water, long supposed to be elements, are respectively a mixture and a compound, the first being composed principally of oxygen and nitrogen and the second of oxygen and hydrogen.

The final blow to the phlogiston theory was administered by the Frenchman Antoine Lavoisier (1743–1794), widely regarded as the greatest scientist of the eighteenth century, who lost his life in the French Revolution. Lavoisier proved that both combustion and respiration involve oxidation, the one being rapid and the other slow. He provided the names for oxygen and hydrogen, demonstrated that the diamond is a form of carbon, and argued that life itself is essentially a chemical process. But undoubtedly his greatest accomplishment was his discovery of the law of the conservation of mass. He found evidence that "although matter may alter its state in a series of chemical actions, it does not change in amount; the quantity of matter is the same at the end as at the beginning of every operation, and can be traced by its weight." This "law" has, of course, been modified by later discoveries regarding the structure of the atom and the conversion of some forms of matter into energy. It is hardly too much to say, however, that as a result of Lavoisier's genius chemistry became a true science.

Despite the notable scientific advances of the seventeenth and eighteenth centuries, the development of physiology and medicine progressed rather slowly during the same period for several reasons. One was the inadequate preparation of physicians, many of whom had begun their professional careers with little more training than apprenticeship under an older practitioner. Another was the common disrepute in which surgery was held as a mere trade, like that of a barber or blacksmith. Perhaps the most serious of all was the prejudice against dissection of human bodies for use in anatomical study. As late as 1750 medical schools which engaged in this practice were in danger of destruction by irate mobs. Despite these obstacles some progress was still possible. About 1670 Malpighi and Leeuwenhoek confirmed William Harvey's discovery of the circulation of the blood by observing the actual flow of blood through the network of capillaries connecting the arteries and veins. At approximately the same time an eminent physician of London, Thomas Sydenham, proposed a new theory of fever as a natural process by which diseased material is expelled from the system.

Medical progress during the eighteenth century was somewhat more rapid. Among the noteworthy achievements were the discovery of blood pressure, the founding of histology or microscopic anatomy, and the development of the autopsy as an aid to the study of disease. But the chief milestones of medical advancement in this period were the adoption of inoculation and the development of vaccination for smallpox. Knowledge of inoculation came originally from the Near

East, where it had long been employed by the Muslims. Information concerning its use was relayed to England in 1717 through the letters of Lady Mary Wortley Montagu, wife of the British ambassador to Turkey. The first systematic application of the practice in the Western world, however, was due to the efforts of the American Puritan leader Cotton Mather, who implored the physicians of Boston to inoculate their patients in the hope of curbing an epidemic of smallpox which had broken out in 1721. Thereafter inoculation had some success in saving lives, but the practice understandably was widely resisted because smallpox inoculation guaranteed the patient one bout with the disfiguring disease before inducing further immunity to it. Only in 1796 did the Englishman Edward Jenner, noticing that milkmaids always seemed to have clear complexions, conclude that in contracting the virus of cowpox from their daily occupation, milkmaids gained immunity to smallpox. Hence inoculation of humans with the deadly smallpox virus appeared unnecessary, and Jenner introduced *vaccination* (from *vacca*—Latin for cow), employing the mild cowpox virus instead. Once vaccination proved both harmless and marvelously effective, the vast possibilities opened up for the elimination of contagious diseases appeared to confirm the Enlightenment belief in the ability of science to make nature's laws work for the betterment of the human condition.

5. CLASSICISM AND INNOVATION IN ART AND LITERATURE

Although the spirit of the scientific revolution and Enlightenment was reflected in certain great artistic monuments, there were no simple, one-to-one correspondences between intellectual and artistic trends in the late seventeenth and eighteenth centuries. Artists and writers responded to a great variety of influences in addition to the new scientific view of the universe: national stylistic traditions, religious demands, differing political and sociological contexts, and, not least, the internal dynamics of artistic evolution within any given creative field. It is best, then, to look at certain major trends without forcing the explanations for them all to fit the same mold.

Manifold influences on artistic trends

As we have seen earlier, the dominant style in European art between about 1600 and the early eighteenth century was the Baroque. But a few countries resisted the dominance of Baroque influences—particularly France, Holland, and England. The French resistance was primarily nationalistic in inspiration. Since Baroque style was closely associated with the tastes of the Spanish and Austrian Habsburgs, against whom the French were continually fighting throughout most of the seventeenth and early eighteenth centuries, it seemed inappropriate for France to admit cultural inferiority by imitating the style of its political rivals. In opposition to the exuberant Baroque, then, French

French classicism

The Finding of Moses by Poussin. The artist has included a pyramid in the background (right) as a token of verisimilitude, but otherwise his scene appears to be set in ancient Rome. Note the stress on monumentality and perpendicular lines.

See color plates facing page 640 for *Landscape with the Burial of Phocion* by Poussin

East Entrance of the Louvre, Paris. Built by the French architect Charles Perrault between 1667 and 1670, this facade is an excellent example of the rigorously classical style patronized by Louis XIV.

artists and architects cultivated restrained classicism. Some of the best earlier examples of this are the canvases of seventeenth-century France's greatest painter, Nicolas Poussin (1594–1665), whose reposeful scenes from classical mythology, governed by the artist's programmatic commitment to "things well ordered," stand in the sharpest contrast to the swirling contortions of Poussin's Baroque contemporary, Rubens.

"Well-ordered" classicism continued to be the preferred style in France during the reign of Louis XIV (1651–1715) for three reasons. First of all, Louis in particular was determined to make sure that France cultivated its own characteristic national style for reasons of state. Second, Louis's own stylistic preferences tended toward the grand and sober. And third, the symmetrical qualities of classicism seemed to complement best the highly symmetrical natural order then being posited in France by Cartesian philosophers and scientists. Thus when Louis XIV decided to renovate his palace of the Louvre, the leading Baroque architect of the day, Bernini, submitted plans, but these were rejected in favor of those of a native Frenchman who emphasized severe classical monumentality. Later, when Louis erected his splendid new palace at Versailles, Baroque architectural features were introduced. Yet the Baroque of Versailles was a very restrained Baroque that emphasized massive symmetry rather than the jutting angles and startling curves favored by Bernini.

As classicism was the prevalent style in seventeenth-century French art, so too did it prevail in literature. This can be seen most clearly in the tragedies of Pierre Corneille (1606–1684) and Jean Racine (1639–1699). Both of these playwrights took as their subjects the heroes and heroines of classical mythology and history such as Medea, Pompey, Andromache, and Phaedra, and both strove as well to imitate the theoretical and structural principles of the classical Greek tragedians. Similarly, the great French writer of comedies, Jean Baptiste Molière (1622–1673), took the Roman comedies of Terence and Plautus for his models and was so committed to symmetrical formalism as to have his characters speak in rhyming couplets. Yet, unlike Corneille and Racine, Molière did set the action of his plays in the present because he believed that "the business of comedy is to represent in general all the defects of men and especially of the men of our time." Accordingly, his work was also highly satirical. In *Tartuffe,* for example, he pilloried religious hypocrisy, and in *The Bourgeois Gentleman* he mocked the vulgar pretentiousness of the social climber. Yet for all his satire, Molière had a measure of sympathy for the trials of human existence, rising to his greatest profundity in *The Misanthrope,* a play which pokes fun at a person who hates society but which also shows that the character has excellent reasons for his alienation. Thus mixing sympathy and occasional melancholy with wit and searing scorn, Molière was probably the most gifted European dramatic genius after Shakespeare.

In the other leading countries that resisted the Baroque, Holland and England, there can be little doubt that artistic preferences had religious as well as nationalistic causes. Since Holland and England were Protestant, they naturally preferred to limit Baroque influences emanating from Rome and the Catholic Spanish Netherlands. We have seen that the greatest seventeenth-century Dutch painter, Rembrandt, developed his own highly personal style which employed Baroque elements whenever he deemed them appropriate. Rembrandt's slightly

The Painter in his Studio by Vermeer. The model is posing as Clio, the muse of history, and thus stands for the timeless fame of painting. The fact that the source of light is concealed by the curtain may perhaps be be understood to mean that the artist works essentially by the interior illumination of his mind.

Left: *St. Peter's Basilica with Colonnade, Rome*. Right: *St. Paul's Cathedral, London*. The sweeping colonnade in front of St. Peter's was designed by the Baroque architectural master Bernini in 1656. Such showy effects were not to the taste of the English architect Christopher Wren, who in designing St. Paul's hewed more closely to the classicism implicit in the Renaissance style of the Vatican Basilica itself. Wren's "English answer to St. Peter's," however, makes classical columns even more prominent than they were in the Vatican. Note how Wren drew inspiration from Perrault's classical Louvre facade (above, p. 650) in designing St. Paul's second-level elevation.

later Dutch contemporary, Jan Vermeer (1632–1675), however, eliminated the Baroque entirely in painting the serenest realistic indoor genre scenes, as did most other seventeenth-century Dutch genre, landscape, and portrait painters. Similarly, the dominant stylistic commitment in England, after a brief flirtation with the Baroque during the reign of the Catholic-leaning Charles I, was to a classicizing restraint. Thus the most prominent of all English architects, Christopher Wren (1632–1723), did not hesitate to borrow Baroque elements when fitting, but emphasized classicism in his columns and domes, most notably in his masterwork, St. Paul's Cathedral (built from 1675 to 1710). More classical still was the "Palladian revival" which dominated English architecture in the first half of the eighteenth century. In this period numerous country houses commissioned by the landed gentry imitated the Renaissance master Palladio's serenely classical and highly symmetrical Villa Rotonda, just as that building had imitated the Roman Pantheon. Indeed, so many English town houses built in the fashionable resort spa of Bath around 1740 imitated Palladian models that Bath was soon called, after Palladio's main area of activity, "the English Vicenza."

Parallel to the artistic classicism of Wren and the English Palladians was the literary classicism which flourished in England from about

1660 to 1760. In fact, the writers of this period expressly called themselves "Augustans." This they did for two reasons: first, the restoration of royalty in 1660 after the English Civil War seemed to presage an age of peace and civility similar to the one installed by Augustus after civil war in ancient Rome; and second, the favored poetic models of the English Augustans were the Augustan Romans—Virgil, Horace, and Ovid. Still another reason why English literary taste became resolutely classical in the later seventeenth century was that the France of Louis XIV had enormous influence in setting fashions throughout Europe, and the English did not wish to be the slightest bit out of date in following the French lead. Finally, as in France, classicism appeared to be the one available style that came closest to being dispassionately "scientific." In other words, just when the English leisured classes were celebrating the triumphs of Newtonianism and endeavoring to make their own contribution to scientific advance by collecting natural specimens or gazing through telescopes, they patronized a form of writing which seemed to resemble Newtonian methods and laws in stressing simplicity, clarity, and symmetry.

Of the numerous members of the English Augustan school, the most outstanding were the prose writer Jonathan Swift (1667–1745) and the poet Alexander Pope (1688–1744). The former, a scathing satirist, was atypical of Augustan thinking in his pessimism concerning the potentialities of human nature: in Swift's masterpiece, *Gulliver's Travels*, humans at one point are dismissed as "the most pernicious race of little odious vermin that nature ever suffered to crawl upon the surface of the earth." Yet Swift's prose is fully Augustan in its economy and clarity; as opposed to earlier flowery stylists, Swift insisted on locating, as he said, "proper words in proper places." As for Pope, he was thoroughly Augustan in both style and thought—almost to a fault. A consistent exponent in highly regular rhyming verse of the naturalistic doctrines of the Enlightenment, Pope in such didactic poems as his *Essay on Man* and his *Essay on Criticism* held that humans must study and imitate nature if they were to bring any semblance of

Jonathan Swift and Alexander Pope

Chiswick House. Built near London around 1725, this country house initiated an English Palladian fad that had its echoes in Thomas Jefferson's Monticello, and later still in the Jefferson Memorial. Note how the design imitates Palladio's Villa Rotonda (above p. 432), just as that building itself was modeled on the Roman Pantheon (above, p. 189).

order into their affairs. Most necessary for mankind, in Pope's view, was unblinking self-knowledge, which the poet believed could be obtained entirely apart from theology or metaphysics. Summing up the secularistic spirit of his age, Pope responded to Milton's earlier poetic resolve to "justify the ways of God to man" in his most famous couplet: "Know then thyself, presume not God to scan;/ the proper study of Mankind is Man."

Rococo painting

As impressive as numerous artistic and literary productions of French and English classicism may have been, the classical movement self-evidently was not highly innovative. Two entirely separate developments of the eighteenth century, on the other hand, emphasized greater originality—namely, the emergence of the continental Rococo style in art, and the rise of the English novel. Regarding the former, the basic explanation for the emergence of Rococo art and architecture was the sense of relaxation experienced in France at the coming of peace and at the death of Louis XIV in 1715. Whereas the prolonged War of the Spanish Succession had begun to exhaust the country, and whereas Louis in his declining years had become ever more puritanical and ever more determined to enforce his own severe tastes and standards on everyone else, around 1715 the leisured classes of the nation breathed a deep sigh of relief. This reaction, not surprisingly, resulted in an artistic pendulum swing from classical severity to a cheerful abandonment which goes by the name of Rococo style. In painting, the earliest and most gifted Rococo artist was Antoine Watteau (1684–1721), who was influenced more by the Baroque artist Rubens than by any other single source, but who replaced Rubens's massiveness with airy French elegance and grace. Watteau was admitted into the French Academy of Fine Arts in 1717 for his masterpiece, *The Embarkation for Cythera*, even though none of the members would have dreamed of admitting him two years earlier. Moreover, since the Academy had no formal classification for the *Embarkation*—which merely showed graceful

See color plates following page 640 for *Le Mezzetin* by Watteau and *Madame de Pompadour* by Boucher

The Embarkation for Cythera by Watteau. This epoch-making painting broke with the severity of Poussin in favor of a greater stress on motion and lushness. No two art historians agree upon exactly what it means, but the evocation of dreamy pleasure is unmistakable.

A Reclining Nude by Boucher. The viewer is left to ponder the significance of the fallen flower.

people having a dreamily good time—it invented one for the purpose: "*fêtes galantes,*" best translated as stylish revels. At least Watteau's revellers were clothed, but the figures in the paintings of his Rococo successors François Boucher (1703–1770) and J. H. Fragonard (1732–1806) were usually half naked and displayed in postures that went well beyond sensuality in the direction of frank eroticism.

Most of the rest of Europe was too straightlaced to imitate the lasciviousness of French Rococo painting, but French Rococo architecture soon became the dominant style throughout the Continent and remained such for most of the eighteenth century. The reasons for this were, first, that the French architects who pioneered in Rococo building in the years shortly after 1715 took Baroque principles for their standards in replacing classical ones, thereby setting themselves in tune with the rest of their continental contemporaries, and second, that Rococo building design featured curvaceous elegance and thus appealed greatly to the vain European aristocrats who commissioned the major architectural projects of the day.

French Rococo architecture

Perhaps the easiest way to characterize the Rococo building style is to call it the "champagne of Baroque" or "Baroque with a French accent." Both Baroque and Rococo buildings emphasize dynamic movement, but whereas Baroque style exudes force and passion, the Rococo communicates a sense of delicacy and playfulness. Most amazing to initial viewers of Rococo interiors is how light and airy they are: as opposed to Baroque interiors, which are generally sombre, Rococo ones have walls and ceilings painted in white, gold, and pink. Among the leading European Rococo buildings are the Hôtel de Soubise in Paris, the pavilion known as the Zwinger in Dresden, the

Rococo and Baroque compared

Two German Rococo Interiors. The Vierzehnheiligen Church near Bamberg (left) and the Wieskirche near Munich (right) are the two foremost works of German Rococo interior decoration.

jewel-box Vierzehnheiligen church in Bavaria (near Bamberg), and the Cuvillies theater in Munich, which is still used for performances of eighteenth-century operas and plays. Although Rococo art and architecture unquestionably allowed great play for the imagination, from the long-term perspective of art history the Rococo style was an end rather than a beginning inasmuch as it represented the final phase of the Baroque.

Uniqueness of the novel In contrast, the only really new development in the artistic and literary history of the Enlightenment period that had a promising future was the emergence of the novel. In treating the rise of the novel in eighteenth-century England it must be stressed that the English novel was not invented out of nothing. To the contrary, works of prose fiction known as romances had been composed in classical antiquity and throughout western Europe from the twelfth century onward. Indeed, one European romance—Cervantes's *Don Quixote*—atypically had many of the characteristics of the modern novel. Moreover, in France, where the word *roman* means both romance and novel, prose fictions were written without interruption from the Middle Ages to the recognizably modern novels of the nineteenth-century writers Balzac and Flaubert. Nevertheless, there were such major differences between the best English prose fictions of the eighteenth century and all that came before (other than *Don Quixote*) as to make it possible to say that the modern novel was invented in eighteenth-century England.

The best way of characterizing the difference between the romance and the novel is that the former is patently a fabrication, whereas the latter (allowing a few inevitable exceptions) purports to be a reliable account of how humans behave. Assuming that a judge in a court of law were asked to accept the testimony of a romance as evidence for trying a case, he would have to throw it out and declare a mistrial because romances generally have little sense of verisimilitude, being written in an ornate style and recounting the adventures of clearly imaginary characters—usually from the mythical or semi-mythical past—who find themselves in preposterous situations. But a modern novel might stand up as excellent legal evidence, for in the novel, from the eighteenth-century English examples onward, experiences seem unique, plots and settings fully believable, and the manner of presentation dispassionately straightforward.

Two explanations may be offered for the emergence of the novel in eighteenth-century England. One is that the ideals of the Enlightenment unquestionably created the most conducive atmosphere for novel writing insofar as the "scientific," methodical study of human experience was widely regarded as the order of the day. Yet, because Enlightenment thinking predominated in France even more than in England, it remains to ask why England in particular was the modern novel's first home. The answer to this appears to relate to the distinctive nature of the English reading public. Specifically, England had a much larger nonaristocratic reading audience than France because of England's greater involvement in trade and industry; this class preferred novels to romances because novels were written in a gripping rather than "elevated" style and the action of the novel's more prosaic characters seemed more relevant to common, nonaristocratic experience. As will also presently be seen, it was by no means irrelevant to the novelistic form in England that the majority of novel readers were not men but women.

By common consent the three most influential novelists of eighteenth-century England were Daniel Defoe (1660–1737), Samuel Richardson (1689–1761), and Henry Fielding (1707–1754). All three portrayed recognizable, nonaristocratic characters doing their best to make their way in a perilous world, unaffected by any hint of divine intervention for good or ill. In the novels of Defoe and Richardson the narrator is usually a character who participates in the action and thus knows the "truth" of one side directly, but of course cannot be expected to understand every other character's point of view. On the other hand, in Fielding's *Tom Jones* an "omnipotent narrator" stands apart from the action, and accordingly has a fuller view of it, but seems by his obtrusive presence to be creating a rather more artificial fiction.

Tom Jones is the only eighteenth-century English novel universally considered to be an enduring classic of world literature, but at the very beginning of the next century the technical achievements of Defoe, Richardson, and Fielding were consolidated by Jane Austen (1775–1817), whose *Pride and Prejudice* and *Emma* represent for many readers the heights of novelistic perfection. That a woman should emerge around 1800 as a greater writer of novels than most men was almost inevitable, above all because early-modern European fiction writing was one of the very few areas of creative expression wherein society easily tolerated female contributions. Indeed, in seventeenth-century France the most widely read authors of romances—Madeleine de Scudéry (1607–1701) and the countess de La Fayette (1634–1692)—were women, and later in England Fanny Burney (1752–1840), Ann Radcliffe (1764–1823), and Maria Edgeworth (1767–1849) all wrote novels of great popularity and considerable distinction before Jane Austen went to work. Moreover, since the English novel-reading public was predominantly female, women readers understandably were particularly interested in characteristically female problems as seen from a feminine angle, a subject matter and perspective that Jane Austen bountifully provided. But of course Austen would not rank, as she does, among the handful of greatest novelists who ever lived had she been narrowly parochial in her views and lacking in extraordinary artistic skill. Rather, men as well as women can delight in her dry, ironic wit and admire her insight into human nature. Moreover, Jane Austen's technical accomplishments may well represent novelistic skills at their pinnacle. In particular, in compromising between Defoe's and Richardson's first-person narrator and Fielding's omnipotent third-person one by the use of a third-person narrator who remains unobtrusive and pursues events primarily from the point of view of a central character, Jane Austen created a delicate balance between subjectivity and objectivity that may well never have been surpassed.

6. BAROQUE AND CLASSICAL MUSIC

Innovation in Baroque and Classical music

The title of one of the most genial of eighteenth-century symphonic compositions, Haydn's *Surprise Symphony,* can be applied to the music of the entire age, for eighteenth-century music is continually full of surprises. Indeed, in contrast to developments in contemporary art and literature, where innovation was comparatively rare, the eighteenth century was the most fertile period of invention in all of western European musical history. Probably the major explanation for this is that early-modern composers, unlike artists and writers, did not have to concern themselves about how much they would borrow from the music of classical antiquity because the principles of ancient musical composition were virtually unknown. More free than painters and poets to strike out on their own, early-modern composers invented form after form in two successive major styles, the Baroque and the so-called classical, treating their listeners to surprise after surprise.

Baroque music, like Baroque art and architecture, emerged around 1600 in Italy as an artistic expression of the Counter-Reformation. Yet from the beginning Baroque composers were perforce more inventive than their artistic counterparts, having no equivalent of columns and domes with which to work. The first important figure in the history of Baroque music was the Italian Claudio Monteverdi (1567–1643), who reacted against the highly intricate Renaissance polyphonic style of his major predecessor, Palestrina. Pursuing the Baroque goal of dramatic expressiveness, Monteverdi found that deep human emotions were difficult to convey when members of a chorus were singing against each other as they did in the music of the late Renaissance, and that dramatic intensity becomes greatest when music is combined with theater. Having no classical models to draw upon, Monteverdi thus virtually single-handedly invented a new musical form, that of opera. In addition, to lend his opera singers greater emotional power than they would have had if they had sung alone, Monteverdi wrote instrumental accompaniments so forceful that they have earned him the title of "the father of instrumentation." Since Monteverdi's new form of opera fully suited the spirit of his times, within a generation operas were performed in all the leading cities of Italy. Staged within magnificent settings, and calling upon the talents of singers, musicians, dramatists, and stage designers, opera expressed as clearly as any art form the dedication of Baroque artistic style to grandeur, drama, and display.

With the notable exception of the Englishman Henry Purcell (1659–1695), there were no enduringly great Baroque composers in the second half of the seventeenth century. Nonetheless, many imaginative musicians began to create new forms during this period, most notably the instrumental forms of the sonata and the concerto. Moreover, whatever lull there may have been in the composition of masterpieces was more than compensated for in the last phase of the Baroque era by the appearance of Bach and Handel, two of the greatest composers of all time. Born in the same year very near each other in northern Germany, Johann Sebastian Bach (1685–1750) and George Frederick Handel (1685–1759) had very different musical personalities and very different careers. Bach was an intensely pious introvert who remained in the backwaters of provincial Germany all his life and wrote music of the utmost individuality, whereas Handel was a public-pleasing cosmopolitan whose music is more accessible than Bach's in its robust affirmativeness. Despite these differences, however, both Bach and Handel were distinctly late-Baroque stylists in their commitment to writing music of the deepest expressiveness.

Anyone who has any familiarity with classical music can identify in a moment a work of Bach even if he or she has never heard it before because Bach's music is so extraordinarily individualistic. This, however, does not mean that it is in any way predictable, for part of Bach's individuality lay in his very unpredictability. Combining an uncanny imagination and capacious intellect with heroic powers of discipline and an ability to produce music of the greatest genius on demand, Bach was an extremely prolific composer in the entire gamut of con-

Johann Sebastian Bach

Handel

"The Charming Brute." A contemporary caricature of Handel, engraved by Joseph Groupy, 1754.

temporary forms (excluding opera), from unaccompanied instrumental pieces to enormous works for vocal soloists, chorus, and orchestra. As a church musician in Leipzig for most of his mature career, Bach's professional duty was to provide new music regularly for Sunday and holiday services. Therefore much of his work consists of religious cantatas (over two hundred surviving), motets, and passions. One might think that the mere requirement to write such music on schedule might have made it routine and lifeless, but Bach, an ardent Protestant who was entirely unaffected by the secularism of the Enlightenment, seems to have written each one of his church pieces with such fervor that the salvation of the world appears to hang on every note. Not content with expressing himself in spiritual music alone, Bach also gloried in creating joyous concertos and suites for orchestra, and succeeded in composing the purest of "pure music"— extraordinarily subtle and complex fugues for keyboard in which the capacity of the human mind for apprehending abstraction appears to approach the celestial.

Much unlike the provincial, inner-directed Bach, Handel was a man of the world who sought primarily to establish rapport with large, secular audiences. After spending his early creative years in Italy, where he mastered Italian Baroque compositional techniques, Handel established himself in London. There he tried at first to make a living by composing Italian operas, but since the highly florid Baroque operatic style proved too foreign for more staid English tastes, Handel eventually realized that he would never survive unless he turned to some more saleable genre. This he found in the oratorio—a variety of music drama intended for performance in concert form. Marking a transition from the spiritual to the secular, Handel's oratorios were usually set to biblical stories but featured very worldly music, replete with ornate instrumentation and frequent flourishes of drums and trumpets. (Some music historians refer to Handel's "big bow-wow" manner.) These highly virile and heroic works succeeded in packing London's halls full of prosperous English people who interpreted the victories of the ancient Hebrews in such oratorios as *Israel in Egypt* and *Judas Maccabaeus* as implicit celebrations of England's own burgeoning national greatness. Of course Handel's music was not for one time but for all, as is demonstrated by the fact that his greatest oratorio, *The Messiah*, is sung widely throughout the English-speaking world every Christmas and its stirring "Hallelujah Chorus" certainly remains the most popular single choral piece in the entire classical repertory.

Although only a few decades separated the activity of Bach and Handel from that of their greatest eighteenth-century successors, the Austrians Franz Joseph Haydn (1732–1809) and Wolfgang Amadeus Mozart (1756–1781), the two pairs appear worlds apart because their compositional styles are utterly different. This is to say that whereas Bach and Handel were among the last and certainly the greatest composers of Baroque music, Haydn and Mozart were the leading representatives of the succeeding "classical" style. The latter term is slightly confusing because classicism in music had nothing to do with imitating music written in classical antiquity. Rather, the musical style that prevailed in Europe in the second half of the eighteenth century is called classical because it sought to imitate classical principles of order, clarity, and symmetry—in other words, to sound as a Greek temple looked. Moreover, composers of the classical school innovated in creating music that adhered rigorously to certain structural principles. For example, all classical symphonies have four movements, and all open with a first movement in "sonata form," characterized by the successive presentation of themes, development, and recapitulation. Undoubtedly the spread of the ideals of the Enlightenment influenced the development of the classical style, yet there were elements of elegant aristocratic Rococo influence at work as well, for the music of the classical era customarily has a lightness and gaiety about it that is most reminiscent of Rococo pastels.

Certainly the tastes of the same European aristocrats who commissioned Rococo buildings determined the personal fortunes of most composers in the second half of the eighteenth century because these men no longer had any interest in gaining a livelihood by writing church music as Bach had done, and as yet had no large concert-hall public (Handel's London audience being exceptional). The perils of struggling for a living by composing music in the later eighteenth century can be seen best in the sad career of the sublime genius Mozart. As a phenomenal child prodigy, the young Mozart—who began composing at four, started touring Europe as a keyboard virtuoso at six, and wrote his first oratorio at eleven—was the darling of the aristocracy. The Austrian empress Maria Theresa embraced him and the

The classical style in music

Mozart's career

Three Contemporary Impressions of Mozart. At the left is the child prodigy, aged seven, seated at a keyboard. The first name given as "Theoph." is not a mistake but is Greek for Mozart's real middle name, Amadeus, meaning "who loves God." The drawing of the mature Mozart in the middle is a highly idealized conception; no doubt the painting on the right comes closest to conveying what the composer really looked like.

Top: *Haydn in Livery.* Bottom:
The Composer in London. While
he worked in the pay of the
Esterházy family, Haydn was
little more than a high-level
servant. In London, on the
other hand, he was portrayed
as an inspired genius with a far-
away look in his eye and a sheet
of his own music in his hand.

Opera

pope made him "Knight of the Golden Spur." But as soon as Mozart
reached puberty he was no longer a curiosity and, owing partly to his
rather cantankerous personality, proved unable to gain steady
employment in the service of any single wealthy aristocrat. In lieu of
that, he strove to support himself as a freelance composer and keyboard performer in Vienna, but could make ends meet only with the
greatest difficulty. Although he spent every year of his mature life in
bountiful productivity, he had to live from hand to mouth until he
died at the age of thirty-five from the effects of an undiagnosed wast-
ing disease. Only a handful of people attended the funeral of one of
the greatest creative artists of all time, and he was buried in a pauper's
grave. Given these appalling circumstances, it is perfectly amazing
that Mozart's music is characteristically sunny and serene. Only rarely
did he write in a minor key, and even when he did so, he usually
paired a melancholy work with an exuberantly joyful one, as if to
demonstrate almost defiantly that the trials of his personal life had no
effect on his art.

Haydn's career provides an instructive contrast. Knowing much better how to take care of himself, "Papa Haydn" spent most of his life
in the comfortable employment of the Esterházys, an extremely
wealthy Austro-Hungarian aristocratic family that maintained its own
private orchestra. But this security entailed the indignity of wearing
the Esterházy livery, like any common butler. Only toward the end
of his life, in 1791, did Haydn, now famous, strike out on his own by
traveling to London, where for a year and a half he supported himself
handsomely by writing for a paying public, as Handel once did, rather
than for private patrons. The fact that London alone was able to provide opportunities for earning a commercial livelihood to two foreigners is clearly indicative of the city's unusual status in the eighteenth
century as one of the few localities where there was a mass market for
culture. In this regard, however, London definitely represented the
wave of the future because in the nineteenth century serious music
would definitively leave the aristocratic salon for the urban concert
hall all over Europe. It may also be noted that whereas in deeply aristocratic Austria Haydn was obliged to wear servants' livery, in London he was greeted as a creative genius—one of the earliest composers
to be regarded as such even though poets and painters had been celebrated as geniuses long before. Thus Haydn's *Miracle Symphony,* written for performance in a London concert hall, is so called because
during one performance a chandelier came crashing down and many
would have been killed had it not been for the fact that the entire
audience had moved up as close as possible to get a better view of the
"genius" Haydn who was conducting.

Haydn's stay in London foreshadowed the future in still another
way, for the music he wrote on that occasion was wholly secular, as
opposed to the semi-religious oratorios of Handel. Indeed, the music
of the entire classical era was predominantly secular, as most music

would remain until the present, and this secular writing advanced primarily on three fronts—opera, chamber music, and orchestral composition. In the field of opera, an important innovator of the classical period was Christoph Willibald von Gluck (1714–1787), who emphasized the necessity for dramatic action at a time when Monteverdi's many successors had made opera much too static. But by far the greatest operatic composer of the era was Mozart, whose *Marriage of Figaro, Don Giovanni,* and *The Magic Flute* remain among the most magnificent and best loved operas of all time. As for the realm of chamber music (music written for small instrumental ensembles), the classical era was the most fertile age of chamber music origins, for the genre of the string quartet was invented at the beginning of the period and was soon brought to the fullest fruition in the quartets of both Haydn and Mozart.

Yet probably the most impressive invention of the classical era was the symphony—so to speak the novel of music—for the symphony has since proven to be the most fertile and popular of all classical musical forms. Although not the very first writer of symphonies, Haydn is nonetheless usually termed the "father of the symphony" because in over one hundred works in the symphonic form—and preeminently in his last twelve symphonies, which he composed in London—Haydn formulated the most enduring techniques of symphonic composition and demonstrated to the fullest extent the symphony's creative potential. Yet Mozart's three last symphonies (out of that composer's total of forty-one) are generally regarded as greater even than those of Haydn, for the grace, variety, and utter technical perfection of these works is beyond comparison. Mere words cannot do justice to any of the marvelous musical creations of the eighteenth century, yet it may confidently be stated in conclusion that if just one or two of Mozart's musical compositions had survived instead of literally hundreds, they alone would be enough to place the century among the most inspired ages in the entire history of the human creative imagination.

The symphony

SELECTED READINGS

• Items so designated are available in paperback editions.

Baker, Keith, *Condorcet: From Natural Philosophy to Social Mathematics,* Chicago, 1975. Advances the view that Condorcet's greatest significance lies in his attempt to create a quantifiable social science rather than in his theory of historical progress.

Baumer, Franklin L., *Modern European Thought: Continuity and Change in Ideas, 1600–1950,* New York, 1977. An extraordinarily fine intellectual history, organized around major themes rather than the work of individuals.

• Becker, Carl, *The Heavenly City of the Eighteenth-Century Philosophers,* New Haven, Conn., 1932. Advances the thesis that the philosophes were just as impractical in their commitment to abstract secular rationalism as the medieval Scholastics were in their theological rationalism. Witty and stimulating but widely regarded as out of date in its views.

Briggs, Robin, *The Scientific Revolution of the Seventeenth Century*, New York, 1969. A very brief but extremely valuable survey, with a documentary appendix.

• Bronowski, J., and B. Mazlish, *The Western Intellectual Tradition*, New York, 1960. A superb, old-fashioned intellectual history which serves as an excellent complement to Baumer for the seventeenth and eighteenth centuries.

Bukofzer, M. F., *Music in the Baroque Era*, New York, 1947.

• Butterfield, H., *The Origins of Modern Science*, London, 1949. As important for its discussion of Newton's breakthrough regarding gravity and the impact of the scientific revolution on the Enlightenment as it is for the Renaissance period.

Darnton, Robert, *The Business of Enlightenment: A Publishing History of the Encyclopédie, 1775–1800*, Cambridge, Mass., 1979. A masterful and fascinating blend of intellectual, social, and business history.

• Gay, Peter, *The Enlightenment: An Interpretation;* Vol. 1, *The Rise of Modern Paganism;* Vol. 2, *The Science of Freedom*, New York, 1966–1969. A cross between an interpretation and a survey. Emphasizes the philosophes' sense of identification with the classical world and takes a generally positive view of their accomplishments. Contains extensive annotated bibliographies.

• Hall, Alfred R., *The Scientific Revolution, 1500–1800*, 2nd. ed., Boston, 1956. The best place to look for clear accounts of specific scientific accomplishments.

• Hampson, Norman, *The Enlightenment*, Baltimore, 1968. Probably the best shorter introduction.

• Hazard, Paul, *The European Mind: The Critical Years (1680–1715)*, New Haven, Conn., 1953. A basic and indispensable account of the changing climate of opinion which preceded the Enlightenment.

• Kimball, F., *The Creation of the Rococo*, Philadelphia, 1943.

• Levey, Michael, *Rococo to Revolution: Major Trends in 18th Century Painting*, New York, 1966.

Manuel, Frank E., *A Portrait of Isaac Newton*, Cambridge, Mass., 1968. A provocative psychobiography.

Shackleton, Robert, *Montesquieu: A Critical Biography*, London, 1961. The standard work on the man and his thought.

• Shryock, Richard H., *The Development of Modern Medicine: An Interpretation of the Social and Scientific Factors Involved*, London, 1948. Fascinating reading and still the basic work on the subject.

• Summerson, John, *Architecture in Britain, 1530–1830*, 6th ed., Baltimore, 1977. The best introduction to Wren and English Palladianism.

Wade, Ira O., *The Intellectual Development of Voltaire*, Princeton, N.J., 1969. A magnificent synthesis which stresses how Voltaire's "English experience" provided the cornerstone for all his subsequent thought.

• Waterhouse, Ellis K., *Painting in Britain, 1530–1770*, 4th ed., Baltimore, 1979. Very good on eighteenth-century developments.

• Watt, Ian, *The Rise of the Novel*, London, 1957. The basic work on the innovative qualities of the novel in eighteenth-century England.

Westfall, R. S., *Never at Rest: A Biography of Isaac Newton*, New York, 1980. Illuminates all aspects of Newton's scientific accomplishment.

SOURCE MATERIALS

• Beccaria, Cesare, *An Essay on Crimes and Punishments, with a Commentary by M. de Voltaire,* Stanford, Calif., 1953. A reprint of the original English translation of 1767.
• Gibbon, Edward, *The Portable Gibbon: The Decline and Fall of the Roman Empire,* ed. D. A. Saunders, New York, 1952. A convenient abridgment.
• Voltaire, *The Portable Voltaire,* ed. Ben Ray Redman, New York, 1949. An excellent anthology including the complete *Candide.*

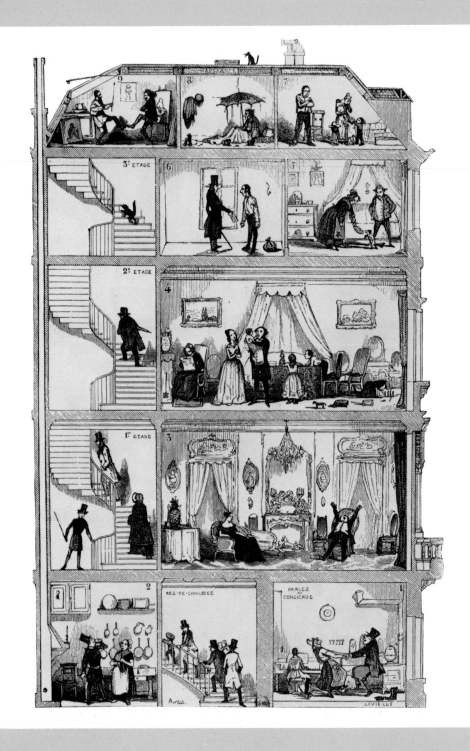

Part Five

THE FRENCH AND
INDUSTRIAL REVOLUTIONS
AND THEIR CONSEQUENCES

No two events more profoundly altered the shape of Western civilization than the French and Industrial Revolutions. "Modern" history begins with their occurrence. The major happenings of the nineteenth and early twentieth centuries—the spread of middle-class liberalism and economic success; the decline of the old, landed aristocracies; the growth of class consciousness among urban workers—all had their roots in these two revolutions.

The French and Industrial Revolutions took place at about the same time and affected many of the same people—though in different ways and to varying degrees. Together they resulted in the overthrow of absolutism, mercantilism, and the last vestiges of manorialism. Together they produced the theory and practice of economic individualism and political liberalism. And together they ensured the growth of class consciousness, and the culmination of those tensions between the middle and working classes that imparted new vitality to European history after 1800.

Each revolution, of course, produced results peculiarly its own. The French Revolution encouraged the growth of nationalism and its unattractive step-child, authoritarianism. The Industrial Revolution compelled the design of a new, urban social order. Yet despite their unique contributions, the two revolutions must be studied together and understood as the joint progenitors of Western history in the nineteenth and early twentieth centuries.

The French and Industrial Revolutions and Their Consequences

POLITICS	SCIENCE & INDUSTRY

1770

James Watt's steam engine, 1763
Spinning jenny patented, 1770

American War of Independence, 1775–1783

Beginning of factory system, 1780s

French Revolution begins, 1789

Lavoisier discovers the indestructibility of matter, 1789

France declared a republic, 1792
Declaration of Pillnitz, 1792
Reign of Terror, 1793–1794

Cotton gin invented, 1793
Edward Jenner develops smallpox vaccine, 1796

Treaty of Campo Formio, 1797

1800

Napoleon, first consul of France, 1799
Treaty of Lunéville, 1801
Napoleon declared first consul for life, 1802
Napoleon crowns himself emperor of the French, 1804
Continental System established, 1806

Reforms of Hardenberg and Stein, Prussia, 1808

Napoleon's invasion of Russia, 1812
Congress of Vienna, 1814–1815

Battle of Waterloo, 1815

"Peterloo Massacre," England, 1819
Congress of Verona, 1822
Monroe Doctrine, 1823

Louis Pasteur, 1822–1895

1825

"Decembrist" Revolt, Russia, 1825

First railway, England, 1825

Greek Independence, 1829
Revolution in France, 1830
"Young Italy," 1831
Reform Bill of 1832, England
Slavery abolished, British colonies, 1833
Poor Law reform, England, 1834
Chartist movement, England, 1838–1848

Corn Laws repealed, England, 1846
Revolutions in Europe, 1848
Karl Marx, *Communist Manifesto,* 1848
Second Republic, France, 1848
Frankfurt Assembly, Germany, 1848–1849
Reign of Louis Napoleon, 1851–1870

Great Exhibition, London, 1851
Invention of the sewing machine, 1850s

ECONOMICS & SOCIETY	ARTS & LETTERS	

Jean-Jacques Rousseau, *The Social Contract*, 1762

1770

Ludwig van Beethoven, 1770–1827

Adam Smith, *Wealth of Nations*, 1776

Immanuel Kant, *Critique of Pure Reason*, 1781

Jeremy Bentham, *The Principles of Morals and Legislation*, 1789
Utilitarianism, 1790–1870

Johann von Goethe, *Faust*, 1790–1808
Romantic movement, 1790–1850

Tom Paine, *The Rights of Man*, 1791–1792

Thomas Malthus, *An Essay on the Principle of Population*, 1798

William Wordsworth, *Lyrical Ballads*, 1798

1800

G. W. Hegel, *Phenomenology of the Spirit*, 1807
J. G. Fichte, *Addresses to the German Nation*, 1808

Louis Blanc, 1811–1882

Francisco Goya, *The Executions of the Third of May*, 1814

Founding of Prussian Zollverein, 1818

1825

Honoré de Balzac, *The Human Comedy*, 1829–1841
Eugène Delacroix, *Liberty Leading the People*, 1830

Realism in literature and art, 1840–1870

Friedrich Engels, *The Condition of the Working Class*, 1844

John Stuart Mill, *Principles of Political Economy*, 1848

Pre-Raphaelite Brotherhood formed, 1848

POLITICS	SCIENCE & INDUSTRY

1850

Crimean War, 1854–1856

Invention of the Bessemer process, 1856

Unification of Italy, 1858–1866

Charles Darwin, *Origin of Species,* 1859

Civil War, United States, 1861–1865
Otto von Bismarck's accession to power, 1862
First International, 1864

Parliamentary Reform Bill, England, 1867

Suez Canal opened, 1869
Union Pacific railroad, United States, 1869

Franco-Prussian War, 1870

CONOMICS & SOCIETY   ARTS & LETTERS

Giuseppe Verdi, *Il Trovatore*, 1853
Richard Wagner, *The Ring of the Nibelung*,
   1854–1874
Charles Dickens, *Hard Times*, 1854

Gustave Flaubert, *Madame Bovary*, 1857

mancipation of the serfs, Russia, 1861

arl Marx, *Capital*, 1867

Leo Tolstoy, *War and Peace*, 1866–1869

Pope Pius IX, *Syllabus of Errors*, 1869

Chapter 20

THE FRENCH REVOLUTION

Men are born, and always continue, free and equal in respect of their rights. Civil distinctions, therefore, can be founded only on public utility.

The nation is essentially the source of all sovereignty; nor can any individual, or any body of men, be entitled to any authority which is not expressly derived from it.

—*The Declaration of the Rights of Man and of the Citizen,* 1789

I n 1789, one European out of every five lived in France. And most Europeans, French or not, who thought beyond the boundaries of their own immediate concerns, perceived of France as the center of European civilization. It followed, therefore, that a revolution in France would immediately command the attention of Europe, and would from the first assume far more than mere national significance. Yet the French Revolution attracted and disturbed men and women for reasons other than the fact that it was French. Both its philosophical ideals and its political realities mirrored attitudes, concerns, and conflicts that had occupied the minds of Europeans for several decades. When the revolutionaries pronounced in favor of liberty, they spoke not only with the voice of the eighteenth-century *philosophes,* but with those of the English aristocracy in 1688 and the American revolutionaries of 1776. Absolutism was the bane of continental noblemen, jealous to preserve their ancient freedoms from monarchical inroads; it was also the bane of continental merchants, chafing under the constraints of mercantilist authority. Across Europe, monarch, nobility, and middle class confronted each other in uneasy hostilities that varied in intensity, but reflected common mistrust and uncertainty.

The era of revolution

I. THE COMING OF THE REVOLUTION

The character of Louis XVI

Louis XVI

Obstacles to administrative centralization

Resurgence of the Parlements

Faced with serious challenges to centralized power from resurgent noble elites as well as popularly based political movements in the eighteenth century, only the ablest absolutist ruler, possessing in equal measure the talents of administrative ability and personal determination and vision, could hope to rule successfully. The French king, Louis XVI, possessed neither of these talents. Louis came to the throne in 1774 at the age of twenty. He was a well-intentioned but dull-witted and ineffectual monarch, far more devoted to his hobbies—hunting and lock-making—than to the business of absolutist kingship. On July 14, 1789, when mobs stormed the Bastille, he wrote in his diary "Nothing." Fortunate at the outset in that he had as his principal financial minister the extremely able Anne Robert Jacques Turgot (1727–1781), Louis lost that advantage two years after his accession when he dismissed Turgot rather than press ahead with the economic reforms his minister advocated, when they encountered serious opposition from the nobility. From that time, national policy traced an unstable course, uncontrolled by the king and influenced by self-interested courtiers. As responsible as any for the king's indecisive misrule was the queen, Marie Antoinette, daughter of Austria's monarch Maria Theresa. Vain and strong-willed, fond of court entertainments and palace intrigue, she inspired the dedicated hatred of reformers, intellectuals, and the common people. Her reputation was completely dashed when it became apparent that she would even bestow her favors upon a cardinal of the church for the price of a diamond necklace. Both became the butt of jokes at court.

Conditions in France would have taxed the abilities of even the most talented king; for one with Louis XVI's personal shortcomings, the task was virtually insurmountable. Three factors, in particular, contributed to the breakdown that produced revolution. The first was the inability of the monarch to carry forward the centralized administrative processes which Louis XIV had instituted, and which even he had found it difficult to sustain. The various regions and orders continued to press for what they called their "liberties"—that is, their right to conduct their affairs without interference from the state. During the eighteenth century the efficacy of the intendant system declined in direct proportion to the crown's failure to keep the nobility isolated and impotent. By the 1780s intendants were themselves often noblemen, prepared to sacrifice state interests to those of their own privileged station.

As we have noted, the *Parlements*, France's powerful courts of record, had reasserted their independence during the early years of the reign of Louis XV. Throughout the century they had grown increasingly insistent upon what they began to call their "constitutional" rights—in reality, their traditional habit of opposing any legislation that did not serve the interests of their aristocratic members. When Louis XVI had pressed for new taxes to be levied on the nobility as well as the rest of the community after the expensive Seven Years War, the *Parlements* successfully blocked the proposal, insisting upon their right to exemption from major national taxes. In the mid-1770s this episode was reenacted when Turgot attempted to combat the government's indebtedness through a series of reforms that included the curtailing of court expenses, the abolition of the *corvée* (forced labor by the peasants on the royal roads) in favor of a small tax on landowners, and the abolition of certain guild restrictions in order to stimulate manufacturing. These innovations were steadfastly and successfully opposed by the Paris *Parlement,* whose members claimed that Turgot was trampling upon ancient prerogatives and privileges—as indeed he was.

This continued opposition to centralization on the part of the aristocracy was a symptom of the second major factor contributing to the outbreak of revolution: growing antagonism within and between the various social orders that composed French society. There was tension within the Roman Catholic church, the so-called first estate of the realm. Its rulers—bishops, archbishops, and cardinals—were in the main recruited from the aristocracy. They enjoyed large incomes, derived from property that had been willed to the Church over the centuries and that the Church continued to claim—successfully—was exempt from taxation by the state. In addition, the Church collected a tax—the tithe—on all land under cultivation, an average of between one-tenth and one-fifteenth of the annual harvest. Income from both property and tithe was inequitably distributed among the ranks of the clergy. The princes of the Church, along with the leading monastic orders, took the lion's share. Parish priests received very little. This imbalance in the distribution of revenues was resented not only by the priests, but by peasant tithepayers, who hated to see their taxes spent to support a distant and haughty ecclesiastical hierarchy, rather than their own, often very deserving, local clergy.

The Church: France's first estate

The ranks of the aristocracy, France's second estate, were also divided. Many determined reformers were themselves noblemen, but they were nobles of the robe, men who had, often by purchase, acquired administrative or judicial office (hence the "robe") which conferred a title of nobility, as well as the opportunity to amass a substantial fortune in land and other property. Included in this group were talented men such as the philosopher the baron de Montesquieu, the lawyer the comte de Mirabeau, and the statesman the marquis de Lafayette, who had represented France in America at the time of the revolutionary war. Among these nobles of the robe were men who would play prominent roles in the French Revolution.

Social antagonisms within the second estate: nobles of the robe

In contrast to this group stood the nobles of the sword—or *noblesse de race,* as the group enjoyed calling itself—whose title extended back to the Middle Ages. These aristocrats regarded the nobles of the robe as upstarts. In general, they lived at the royal court at Versailles, where

Nobles of the sword

they enjoyed making political mischief, leaving the management of their estates to bailiffs. In 1781, they pressed successfully for a law which restricted the sale of military commissions to men whose aristocratic lineage extended back at least four generations. If they could not prevent the general debasing of their order, they reasoned, they could at least ensure that the army remained their preserve. The tensions between the nobles of the robe and the sword kept the aristocracy fragmented and at odds with itself, and hence unable to form together into anything more than a negative and potentially destructive force.

The disdain of the *noblesse de race* for the nobility of the robe was mild compared with the contempt in which haughty aristocrats held the urban middle orders. This large group was by no means homogeneous. At the top stood government officials, talented professionals, and large-scale financiers and merchants. Lesser notables were to be found throughout the ranks of the third estate. For every major entrepreneur there were scores of small-scale masters, lodged in their workshops yet removed from the artisans and laborers below them by virtue of their ownership of those shops.

Movement from the upper ranks of the third estate into the nobility had been possible in the past for wealthy, ambitious members of the middle orders. The appointment or purchase of position—the route favored by nobles of the robe—or the marriage of a wealthy financier's daughter to the son of an impoverished aristocrat were the most common means of advancement. Yet to increasing numbers of the urban bourgeoisie it appeared by about 1780 that the nobility of the sword was more determined than ever to turn back their advances.

Their discontent would not have been so great had their birth and

Le Hameau. This rustic villa was constructed in the gardens of Versailles to allow the French court to amuse itself with the "return to nature" advocated by some of the *philosophes.*

A Gentleman of the Third Estate with His Family.
A contemporary engraving which illustrates the
respectability the third estate wished to see
translated into political power.

position within the third estate not excluded them from participation
in the political life of the nation. No matter how much money a merchant, manufacturer, banker, or lawyer might acquire, he was still
excluded from political privileges. He had almost no influence at the
court; he could not hold high political office; and except in the choice
of a few petty local officers, he could not even vote. As the middle
orders achieved affluence and greater self-esteem, their members were
bound to resent such discrimination. Above all, it was the demand of
the commercial, financial, and industrial leaders for political power
commensurate with their economic position that turned members of
the third estate into revolutionaries.

Lack of political power

Resentment of the aristocracy on the part of the urban bourgeosie
was dwarfed by the hatred rural peasants felt for their aristocratic
overlords. Those peasants who owned property, as well as those who
worked the land as tenant-farmers or laborers, remained obligated in
various ways to both the clergy and the nobility: a tithe and levy on
farm produce owed the church; fees, called *banalités,* for the use of a
landlord's facilities—a mill, a wine press; fees, as well, to the nobility
when land changed hands. In addition, peasants were forced to pay a
disproportionate share of both direct and indirect taxes—the most
onerous of which was the *gabelle* or salt tax—levied by the government. (For some time the production of salt had been a state monopoly; every individual was required to buy at least seven pounds a year
from the government works. The result was a commodity whose cost
was often as much as fifty or sixty times its actual value.) Further
grievances stemmed from the requirement that peasants work to

The peasantry

Pre-Revolutionary Propaganda, 1788–1789. These prints support the popular view that the third estate was carrying the burden of national taxation on its shoulders while the privileged orders enjoyed the fruits of the peasant's labors, tax-free.

maintain public roads (the *corvée*) and from the hunting privileges accorded the aristocracy, which for centuries had regarded the right to indulge in the diversions of the chase, to the exclusion of all others, as a distinctive badge of their order.

The effects of enclosure

The vestiges of manorial custom were not the only sources of peasant discontent. During the eighteenth century they also came under pressure as a result of the increasingly frequent enclosure of what had been common land. Fields allowed to lie fallow, together with those tilled only infrequently, were considered "common," land on which all persons might graze their livestock. These common lands, particularly extensive in the west of France, were an important resource for the peasants. In addition to the right to pasturage, they enjoyed that of gathering wood and of gleaning cultivated fields following a harvest. Now the king's economic advisors declared these collective rights to be obstacles in the path of agricultural improvement. Anxious to increase their income by increasing the efficiency of their estates, the landlords attempted to enclose these common lands, thereby depriving the peasants of the open pasturage they had come to depend on.

Financial crisis: rising taxes and rising prices

Social antagonism thus contributed in important ways to the tensions that eventually produced revolution. Those tensions were heightened by the third major, and eventually precipitating, cause of the revolution, a continuing and deepening financial crisis brought on by years of administrative improvidence and ineptitude. This crisis was compounded by a general price rise during much of the eighteenth century, which permitted the French economy to expand by providing capital for investment, but also worked hardship on the peasantry and urban artisans and laborers, who found their purchasing power considerably reduced. Their plight deteriorated further at the end of the 1780s when poor harvests encouraged landlords to extract even larger sums from their dependants in order to compensate for a sharp decline in profits, and when the high price of bread generated desperation among the urban poor. Families found themselves spending more than 50 percent of their income on bread in 1788; the following year the figure rose to as much as 80 percent. Poor harvests contributed to a marked reduction in demand for manufactured goods; families had little money to spend for anything other than food. Peasants could no longer rely on the system of domestic industry to help them make ends meet, since they were receiving so few orders for the textiles and other articles they were accustomed to making at home. Many left the countryside for the cities, hoping to find work there, only to discover that unemployment was far worse than in rural areas. Evidence indicates that between 1787 and 1789 the unemployment rate in many parts of urban France was as high as 50 percent. The financial despair produced by this unemployment fueled resentment and turned peasants and urban workers into potential revolutionaries.

The country's financial position was further weakened by an inefficient system of tax collection and disbursal. Not only was taxation tied to differing social status, it varied as well from region to region, some areas, for example, subject to a much higher *gabelle* than others. The myriad special circumstances and exemptions that prevailed made the task of collectors all the more difficult. Those collectors were in many cases so-called tax farmers, members of a syndicate which loaned the government money in return for the right to collect taxes and to keep for itself the difference between the amounts it took in and the amounts it loaned. The system of disbursal was at least as inefficient as was revenue collection. Instead of one central agency there were several hundred private accountants, a fact which made it impossible for the government to keep accurate track of its assets and liabilities. The financial system all but broke down completely under the increased expenses brought on by French participation in the American war. The cost of servicing the national debt of four million livres in the 1780s consumed 50 percent of the nation's budget. By 1788 the chaotic financial situation, together with severe social tensions and an inept monarch, had brought absolutist France to the edge of political disaster.

Administrative inefficiency: tax collection and disbursal

No event as all-encompassing as the French Revolution occurs in an intellectual vacuum. Although ideas may not have "caused" the revolution, they played a critical role in giving shape and substance to the discontent experienced by so many, particularly among the literate middle orders. The political theories of Locke, Voltaire, Montesquieu, and Condorcet appealed to both discontented nobility and bourgeoisie: Voltaire, because of his general execration of the privi-

The role of ideas: the Enlightenment

leged institutions of church and absolute monarchy; Condorcet because of his belief in progress; Locke and Montesquieu because of their defense of private property and limited sovereignty. Montesquieu's ideas were especially congenial to aristocrats, who read his doctrine of checks and balances as a defense of their ancient privileges—now elevated to the status of "liberties." The *Parlements* and provincial Estates, or governing assemblies, were the constituted bodies which would provide a check to royal power.

The physiocrats

The bourgeoisie also welcomed theoretical support from Enlightenment thinkers in its campaign for political recognition and against monarchical absolutism. That campaign was fueled as well by another group of libertarian thinkers, economic theoreticians called physiocrats in France, whose most influential member was Turgot, a contributor to the *Encyclopedia* as well as an experienced fiscal administrator, intendant, and royal minister. Their proposals were grounded in the ideas of the Enlightenment, particularly the notion of a universe governed by mechanistic laws. They argued that production and distribution of wealth were subject to laws as predictable and ultimately salutary as the laws of physics. Those laws would function beneficially, however, only if agriculture and trade were freed from mercantilist regulations. They urged the government to lift its controls on the price of grain, for example, which had been imposed to keep the cost of bread low, but which had not accomplished that goal. By allowing the laws of supply and demand to determine the market price, the government would encourage farmers to grow a crop that was more profitable to them, and an increase in supply would thus eventually reduce the cost to consumers.

The theories of one further thinker, Jean-Jacques Rousseau (1712–1778), played an important part in shaping the ideas and attitudes of French revolutionaries. The most significant of his writings on politics were *Discourse on the Origin of Inequality* (1753) and *Social Contract* (1762), the latter published in many editions before the revolution. Rousseau agreed with Locke that society had its origins in a state of nature. In contrast with Locke, however, he regarded the state of nature as a virtual paradise. Eventually, however, evils had arisen there, due primarily to quarrels over property rights which in turn produced social and economic inequality. To ensure general security, therefore, a civil society was established in which, according to Rousseau, individuals surrendered their rights to the community. This change was accomplished by means of a social contract, in which each person agreed to submit to the will of the majority. In the state that then emerged, citizens were leveled by their contract into democratic equality.

Jean-Jacques Rousseau

Rousseau vs. the Enlightenment

Rousseau developed an altogether different conception of sovereignty from that of other Enlightenment political theorists. Whereas Locke and his followers had argued that only a portion of sovereign power is surrendered to the state, the rest being retained by the people themselves, Rousseau contended that sovereignty is indivisible, and that all of it became vested in the community when civil society was formed. He insisted further that individuals in becoming a party to the social contract gave up their rights and agreed to submit absolutely to the general will. The sovereign power of the state was thus subject to no theoretical limitations.

Rousseau's appeal, though great, was not so much to those men whose thoughts and actions dominated the first stage of the revolution. Although they might have agreed with Rousseau's opposition to hereditary privilege, they were, as convinced individualists, unmoved by arguments in favor of surrender to a general will. Rousseau's influence upon the revolution was greatest during its second stage, when a more democratic and radical coterie emerged to lead events, first in the direction of democracy and then toward a new kind of "democratic absolutism" that accorded with Rousseau's notions of the sovereign state.

2. THE DESTRUCTION OF THE ANCIEN RÉGIME

The French Revolution occurred as a result of the various factors outlined above: tension between aristocrats and bourgeoisie; resentments on the part of urban artisans resulting from high prices and unemployment; and a generally depressed economy. It occurred when it did because of the inability of the king and his government to resolve the country's immediate financial crisis. When the king's principal ministers Charles de Calonne and Loménie de Brienne attempted in 1787 and 1788 to institute a series of financial reforms in order to stave off bankruptcy, they encountered not just opposition but entrenched aristocratic determination to extract further governmental concessions from the monarch. To meet the mounting deficit, the ministers proposed new taxes, notably a stamp duty and a direct tax on the annual produce of the soil. The king summoned an assembly of notables from among the aristocracy, in the hope of persuading the nobles to agree to his demands. Far from acquiescing, however, the nobles insisted that to institute a general tax such as the stamp duty the king would first have to call together the Estates General, representative of the three estates of the realm.

The summoning of this body, which had not met for over a century and a half, seemed to many the only solution to France's deepening problems. No doubt most of those aristocrats who argued for its calling did so from short-sighted and selfish motives. Yet the politically conscious population as a whole agreed with the idea in an unreasonable and desperate hope that this unusual event might, because of its very strangeness, work a miracle and save the country from ruin. During the period before the rise of monarchical absolutism, when the Estates General was convened more or less regularly, the representatives of each estate had met and voted as a body. Generally this

FRANCE IN 1789 · THE "GOVERNMENTS"

meant that the first and second estates combined against the third. By the late eighteenth century the third estate had attained such importance that it was not willing to tolerate such an arrangement. Consequently its leaders demanded that the three orders should sit together and vote as individuals. More important, it insisted that the representatives of the third estate should be double the number of the first and second. Leaving this issue unresolved, Louis XVI, in the summer of 1788, yielded to popular clamor and summoned the Estates General to meet in May of the following year.

In the ensuing months the question of "doubling the third" was fiercely debated. After having opposed the reform initially, in December 1788 the king agreed to it. His unwillingness to take a strong

The National Assembly

stand from the first, and his continuing vacillation on the matter of voting procedures, cost him support he might otherwise have obtained from the bourgeoisie. Shortly after the opening of the Estates General at Versailles in May 1789, the representatives of the third estate, angered by the king's attitude, took the revolutionary step of leaving the body and declaring themselves the National Assembly. "What is the third estate?" asked the radical clergyman Abbé Emmanuel Sieyès, one of the most articulate spokesmen for a new order, in his famous pamphlet of January 1789. The answer he gave then—"everything"—was the answer the third estate itself gave when it constituted itself the National Assembly of France. Sieyès, unlike most other revolutionaries at this point, derived his argument from Rousseau, and claimed that the third estate was the nation and that as the nation it was its own sovereign. Now the middle-class lawyers and businessmen of the third estate acted on that claim. Locked out of their meeting hall on June 20, the commoners and a handful of sympathetic nobles and clergymen moved to a nearby indoor tennis court.

Abbé Sieyès

Here, under the leadership of the volatile, maverick aristocrat Honoré Riqueti, comte de Mirabeau, and Sieyès, they bound themselves by a solemn oath not to separate until they had drafted a constitution for France. This Oath of the Tennis Court, on June 20, 1789, was the real beginning of the French Revolution. By claiming the authority to remake the government in the name of the people, the Estates General was not merely protesting against the rule of Louis XVI but asserting its right to act as the highest sovereign power in the nation. On June 27 the king virtually conceded this right by ordering the remaining delegates of the privileged classes to meet with the third estate as

The beginning of revolution

The Opening of the Estates General in Versailles, May 5, 1789

members of the National Assembly. The advocates of drastic change were inspired not only by the rhetoric of their leaders, but by the political debates which had occurred during the course of the preceding year. In preparation for the meeting of the Estates, the king had instructed local electoral assemblies to draw up *cahiers de doléances*—lists of grievances. Delegates took these instructions seriously. And the grievances they aired—financial chaos; aristocratic and clerical privileges; denial of political power to the bourgeoisie—became the basis for the radical reforms of the assembly in its initial weeks.

The first stage of the revolution

The course of the French Revolution was marked by three stages, the first of which extended from June 1789 to August 1792. During most of this period the destinies of France were in the hands of the National Assembly. In the main, this stage was moderate, its actions dominated by the leadership of liberal nobles and equally liberal men of the third estate. Yet three events in the summer and fall of 1789 furnished evidence that the revolution was to penetrate to the very heart of French society, ultimately touching both the urban populace and the rural peasants.

Municipal revolution and the fall of the Bastille

News of the events of late spring 1789 had spread quickly across France. From the very onset of debates on the nature of the political crisis, public attention was high. It was roused not merely by interest in matters of political reform, however, but also by the economic crisis that, as we have seen, brought the price of bread to astronomical heights. Belief was widespread that the aristocracy and king were together conspiring to punish an upstart third estate by encouraging scarcity and high prices. Rumors circulated in Paris during the latter days of June 1789 that the king was about to stage a reactionary coup d'état. The electors of Paris (those who had voted in the third estate)

The Tennis Court Oath by David. In the hall where royalty played a game known as *jeu de paume* (similar to tennis) leaders of the revolution swore to draft a constitution. In the center of this painting, with his arm extended, is Jean Bailly, president of the National Assembly. Seated at the table below him is Abbé Sieyès. Somewhat to the right of Sieyès, with both hands on his chest, is Robespierre. Mirabeau, with a hat in his left hand and wearing a black coat, stands somewhat farther to the right.

The Fall of the Bastille, July 14, 1789. A contemporary engraving celebrating the heroic actions of the citizenry of Paris.

feared not only a counterrevolution but the actions of the Paris poor, who had been parading through the streets and threatening violence. These electors were workshop masters, craftspeople, shopkeepers, petty tradespeople, the men and women who would soon come to be called sans-culottes—so called because the men did not wear upper-class breeches. They formed a provisional municipal government and organized a militia of volunteers to maintain order. Determined to obtain arms, they made their way on July 14 to the Bastille, an ancient fortress where guns and ammunition were stored. Built in the Middle Ages, the Bastille had served as a prison for many years, but was no longer much used. However, it symbolized hated royal authority. When crowds demanded arms from its governor, he at first procrastinated and then, fearing a frontal assault, opened fire, killing ninety-eight of the attackers. The crowd took revenge, capturing the fortress (which contained only seven prisoners—five common criminals and two lunatics) and decapitating the governor. At the same time the sans-culottes were establishing a revolutionary municipal government in Paris, similar groups assumed control in other cities across France. This series of events—dramatized by the fall of the Bastille—was the first to demonstrate the commitment of the common people to revolutionary change.

The second popular revolt occurred in the countryside, where the peasants were suffering the direct effects of economic privation. They too feared a monarchical and aristocratic counterrevolution. Eager for news from Versailles, their anticipation turned to fear when they began to understand that a middle-class revolution might not address itself to their problems. Frightened and uncertain, peasants in many areas of France panicked in July and August, setting fire to manor houses

The "Great Fear"

and the records they contained, destroying monasteries and the residences of bishops, and murdering some of the nobles who offered resistance.

The third instance of popular uprising, in October 1789, was also brought on by economic crisis. This time women, angered by the price of bread and fired by rumors of the king's continuing unwillingness to cooperate with the assembly, marched to Versailles on October 5 and demanded to be heard. Not satisfied with its reception by the assembly, the crowd broke through the gates to the palace, calling for the king to return to Paris. On the afternoon of the following day the king yielded. The National Guard, sympathetic to the agitators, led the crowd back to Paris, the procession headed by a soldier holding aloft a loaf of bread on his bayonet.

In each case, these three popular uprisings produced a decided effect on the course of political events as they were unfolding at Versailles. The storming of the Bastille helped persuade the king and nobles to treat the National Assembly as the legislative body of the nation. The "Great Fear" inspired an equally great consternation among the debaters in the assembly. On August 4, with one sweep, the remnants of manorialism were largely obliterated. Ecclesiastical tithes and the *corvée* were formally abolished. Serfdom was eliminated. The hunting privileges of the nobles were ended. Exemption from taxation and monopolies of all kinds were sacrificed as contrary to natural equality. While the nobles did not surrender all of their rights, the ultimate effect of these reforms of the "August Days" was to annihilate distinctions of rank and class and to make all French citizens of an equal status in the eyes of the law.

Following the destruction of privilege the assembly turned its attention to preparing a charter of liberties. The result was the Declaration of the Rights of Man and of the Citizen, issued in September 1789. Property was declared to be a natural right as well as liberty, security, and "resistance to oppression." Freedom of speech, religious toleration, and liberty of the press were declared inviolable. All citizens were guaranteed equality of treatment in the courts. No one was to

The Departure of the Women of Paris for Versailles, October 1789. Note that the contemporary caption refers to the "heroines of Paris." An early example of revolutionary propaganda.

Depart des Heroines de Paris pour Versailles le 5 Octobre 1789.

be imprisoned or otherwise punished except in accordance with due process of law. Sovereignty was affirmed to reside in the people, and officers of the government were made subject to deposition if they abused the powers conferred upon them.

The king's return to Paris during the October Days confirmed the reforms already underway and guaranteed further liberalization along lines decreed by the middle-class majority in the assembly. In November 1789, the National Assembly resolved to confiscate the lands of the Church and to use them as collateral for the issue of *assignats,* or paper money, which, it was hoped, would resolve the country's inflationary economic crisis. In July of the following year the Civil Constitution of the Clergy was enacted, providing that all bishops and priests should be elected by the people and should be subject to the authority of the state. Their salaries were to be paid out of the public treasury, and they were required to swear allegiance to the new legislation. The secularization of the Church also involved a partial separation from Rome. The aim of the assembly was to make the Catholic Church of France a truly national institution with no more than a nominal subjection to the papacy.

(3) secularization of the Church

An Assignat

Response to this clerical revolution was mixed. Because the Church had enjoyed a privileged position during the Old Regime, it had earned itself the hatred of many who resented its tolerance of clerical abuses and its exploitation of vast monastic land holdings. Bishops and other members of the higher clergy had often held several ecclesiastical appointments at the same time, had paid scant attention to their duties, and had led far from spiritual lives. Exempt from taxes itself, the Church had not hesitated to extract all it could from the peasantry. And its control of the country's educational system made it a target for those men and women who, influenced by Englightenment thinkers like Voltaire, had turned against the doctrines of Roman Catholicism. On the other hand, the practice of centuries had made the parish church and priest into institutions of great local importance. Peasants found it very difficult to shed habits of deference and respect overnight. It is not surprising, therefore, that the dramatic changes embodied in the Civil Constitution of the Clergy encountered considerable resistance in some parts of rural France, and thus eventually helped to strengthen the forces of counterrevolution.

Response to the clerical revolution

Not until 1791 did the National Assembly manage to complete its primary task of drafting a new constitution for the nation. The constitution as it finally emerged gave eloquent testimony to the dominant position now held by the middle class. The government was converted into a limited monarchy, with the supreme power virtually a monopoly of the well-to-do. Although all citizens possessed the same civil rights, the vote was allowed only to those who paid a certain amount in taxes. About half the adult males in France made up this latter category of "active" citizen. Yet even their political power was curtailed, for they were to vote for electors, whose property owner-

(4) constitution of 1791

ship qualified them for that position. Those electors, in turn, chose department officials and delegates to the National—or, as it was henceforth to be called, Legislative—Assembly. The king was deprived of the control he had formerly exercised over the army and local governments. His ministers were forbidden to sit in the assembly, and he was shorn of all powers over the legislative process except a suspensive veto, which in fact could be overridden by the issuance of proclamations.

(5) economic and governmental changes

The economic and governmental changes the National Assembly adopted were as much a reflection of Enlightenment liberalism as were its constitutional reforms. To raise money, it sold off Church lands, but in such large blocks that peasants seldom benefited by the sales as they had expected to. In opposition to the interests of the peasantry, the assembly proceeded with the enclosure of common lands in order to facilitate the development of capitalist agriculture. To encourage the growth of unfettered economic enterprise, guilds and trade unions were abolished. To rid the country of authoritarian centralization and of aristocratic domination, local governments were completely restructured. France was divided into eighty-three equal departments. All towns henceforth enjoyed the same form of municipal organization. All local officials were locally elected. This reorganization and decentralization expressed a liberal belief in the necessity of individual liberty and freedom from ancient privilege. As such these measures proclaimed, as did all the work of the assembly, that the "winners" of this first stage of the revolution were the men and women of the middle class.

3. A NEW STAGE: RADICAL REVOLUTION

The second stage: (1) disappointment of the common people

Their triumph did not go unchallenged, however. In the summer of 1792, the revolution entered a second stage, which saw the downfall of moderate middle-class leaders and their replacement by radical republicans claiming to rule on behalf of the common people. Three major reasons accounted for this abrupt and drastic alteration in the course of events. First, the politically literate lower classes grew disillusioned as they perceived that the revolution was not benefiting them. The uncontrolled free-enterprise economy of the government resulted in constantly fluctuating and generally rising prices. These increases particularly exasperated those elements of the Parisian population that had agitated for change in preceding years. Urban rioters demanded bread at prerevolutionary prices, while their spokesmen called for governmental control of the ever-growing inflation. Their leaders articulated as well the frustrations of a mass of men and women who felt cheated by the constitution. Despite their major role in the creation of a new regime, they found themselves deprived of any effective voice in its operation.

A second major reason for the change of course was a lack of effective national leadership during the first two years of the revolution. Louis XVI remained the weak, vacillating monarch he had been prior to 1789. Though outwardly prepared to collaborate with the leaders of the assembly, he remained essentially a victim of events. He was compelled to support measures personally distasteful to him, in particular the Civil Constitution of the Clergy. He was thus sympathetic to the plottings of the queen, who was in correspondence with her brother Leopold II of Austria. Urged on by Marie Antoinette, Louis agreed to attempt an escape from France in June 1791, in hopes of rallying foreign support for counterrevolution. The members of the royal family managed to slip past their palace guards in Paris, but were apprehended near the border at Varennes and brought back to the capital. Though the Constitution of 1791 declared France a monarchy, after Varennes that declaration was more fiction than fact. From that point on, Louis was little more than a prisoner of the assembly. The leadership of that body remained in Mirabeau's hands until his death in 1791. Yet he was a less than satisfactory leader. An outstanding orator, he was nevertheless mistrusted by many revolutionaries because of his dissolute, aristocratic youth. Nor, despite his continued support of a strong constitutional monarchy, did he enjoy the confidence of the king. Even with his shortcomings, Mirabeau was the most effective leader among the moderate constitutionalists, a group that generally failed to capitalize on its opportunities.

The third major reason for the dramatic turn of events was the fact that after 1792 France found itself at war with much of the rest of Europe. From the outset of the revolution, men and women across Europe had been compelled, by the very intensity of events in France, to take sides in the conflict. What we have called the first revolution won the support of a wide range of thoughtful intellectuals, politicians, businessmen, and artisans. Strikes and revolts broke out in Germany and Belgium. In England, philsophical radicals such as Joseph Priestley, the scientist, and Richard Price, a Unitarian minister, joined with businessmen such as James Watt and Matthew Boulton to welcome the overthrow of privilege and absolutism.

Others opposed the course of the revolution from the start. Exiled nobles, who had fled France for the haven of sympathetic royal courts in Germany and elsewhere, did all they could to stir up counterrevolutionary sentiment. The distressed clamoring of these emigrés, along with the plight of Louis XVI and his family, aroused the sympathy, if not, at first, the active support, of European defenders of absolutism and privilege. In England the cause was strengthened by the publication in 1790 of Edmund Burke's *Reflections on the Revolution in France*. A Whig politician who had sympathized with the American revolutionaries, Burke nevertheless attacked the revolution in France as a monstrous crime against the social order. He argued that by remodeling their government as they had, the French had turned their backs

Edmund Burke

Thomas Paine

Declaration of Pillnitz

on both human nature and history. Men and women were not constitutional abstractions, endowed with an objective set of natural rights, as the Declaration of the Rights of Man had insisted. Rights—and duties as well—were the consequence of the individual histories of the countries into which men and women were born. Those histories bound people to the past and entailed a commitment to the future, as well as the present. Hence they had no right to remake their country and its institutions without reference to the past or concern for the future, as Burke insisted the French had. Their failure to pay proper respect to tradition and custom had destroyed the precious fabric of French civilization woven by centuries of national history.

Burke's famous pamphlet, in which he painted a romantic and highly inaccurate picture of the French king and queen, helped arouse sympathy for the counterrevolutionary cause. It is questionable, however, whether that sympathy would have turned to active opposition, had not the French soon appeared as a threat to international stability and the individual ambitions of the great powers. It was that threat which led to war in 1792, and which kept the Continent in arms for a generation. This state of war had a most important impact on the formation of political and social attitudes during this period in Europe. Once a country declared war with France, its citizens could no longer espouse sympathy with the revolution without paying severe consequences. Those who continued to support the revolution, as did a good many among the artisan and small tradespeople class, were persecuted and punished for their beliefs. To be found in Britain, for example, possessing a copy of Tom Paine's revolutionary tract, *The Rights of Man* (1791–1792), a prorevolutionary response to Burke's *Reflections,* was enough to warrant imprisonment. As the moderate nature of the early revolution turned to violent extension, entrepreneurs and businessmen eagerly sought to live down their radical sentiments of a few years past. The wars against revolutionary France came to be perceived as a matter of national survival; to ensure internal security, it seemed that patriotism demanded not only a condemnation of the French but of French ideas as well.

The first European states to express public concern about events in revolutionary France were Austria and Prussia. They were not anxious to declare war; their interests at the time centered upon the division of Poland between themselves. Nevertheless, they jointly issued the Declaration of Pillnitz in August 1791, in which they avowed that the restoration of order and of the rights of the monarch of France was a matter of "common interest to all sovereigns of Europe." The leaders of the French government at this time were the moderate Girondists, many of whom came from the mercantile Gironde department. Afraid of losing political support in France, they pronounced the Declaration of Pillnitz a threat to national security, hoping that enthusiasm for a war would unite the French and result also in enthusiasm for their continued rule. They were aided in their scheme by the activities of monarchists, both within and outside France, whose plottings and pronouncements could be made to appear an additional threat, though to a greater extent than they actually were. On April 20, 1792, the assembly declared war against Austria and Prussia.

Almost all of the various political factions in France welcomed the war. The Girondists expected that their aggressive policy would solidify the loyalty of the people to their regime. Reactionaries hailed the intervention of Austria and Prussia as the first step in the undoing of all that had happened since 1789. Radicals hoped that initially the French would suffer reverses that would discredit the moderate Girondists and the monarchy, and thus hasten the advent of republican rule in France, and the triumph of people's armies and revolutionary ideals across Europe. As the radicals hoped, the forces of the French met serious reverses. By August 1792 the allied armies of Austria and Prussia had crossed the frontier and were threatening the capture of Paris. A fury of rage and despair seized the capital. The belief prevailed that the military disasters had been the result of treasonable dealings with the enemy on the part of the king and his conservative followers. On August 10 Parisian rioters, organized by their radical leadership, attacked the royal palace, slaughtering the king's guards and driving him to seek refuge in the meeting hall of the assembly. At the same time, radicals seized the municipal government in Paris, replacing it with a revolutionary Commune under their control. The Commune successfully demanded that the assembly suspend the king from his duties and hand him and his family over for imprisonment.

From this point, the country's leadership passed into the hands of an equalitarian-minded "middle" middle class. These new leaders called themselves Jacobins, after the political club to which they belonged, whose headquarters was in Paris, but whose membership extended throughout France. Like the Girondists, the Jacobins were mostly members of the bourgeoisie, professionals and businessmen, though an increasing number of artisans joined the club as it grew. They differed from the Girondists in their political philosophy, however. Girondists were loud in their defense of liberty, by which they often meant no more than freedom to pursue their own economic interests without state regulation. Because their political base was in the provinces, they tended to mistrust Parisians and were alarmed by the extremism of the Commune. Jacobins, in contrast, were the masterminds of the Commune. They were vigorous proponents of equality. They supported the elimination of civil and political distinctions, favored universal suffrage, and state programs for the maintenance of the poor. The Jacobins differed from the Girondists in that they were a tightly organized party. As such, again unlike the Girondists, they were able to move decisively and prepared to act ruthlessly in defense of their programs and their leadership.

One of the Jacobins' first actions was to call for an election by universal suffrage of delegates to a national convention, whose task would

Response to war

Jacobins. Contemporary drawings by Heuriot.

A Contemporary Engraving of the September Massacres in Paris, 1792

be to draft and enact a new and republican constitution. This convention became the effective governing body of the country for the next three years. It was elected in September 1792, at a time when disturbances across France reached a new height. The so-called September massacres occurred when patriotic Paris mobs, hearing a rumor that political prisoners were plotting to escape from their prisons, responded by hauling them before hastily convened tribunals and sentencing them to swift execution. Over one thousand supposed enemies of the revolution were killed in less than a week. Similar riots engulfed Lyons, Orléans, and other French cities.

The September massacres

When the newly elected convention met in September, its membership was far more radical than that of its predecessor, the Legislative Assembly, and its leadership was determined to demand an end to the monarchy and the death of Louis XVI. On September 21, the convention declared France a republic. In December it placed the king on trial and in January he was condemned to death by a narrow margin. The heir to the grand tradition of French absolutism met his end bravely as "Citizen Louis Capet," beheaded by the guillotine, the frightful mechanical headsman that had become the symbol of revolutionary fervor.

The death of Louis XVI

Meanwhile, the convention turned its attention to the enactment of further domestic reforms. Among its most significant accomplishments over the next three years were the abolition of slavery in French colonies; the prohibition of imprisonment for debt; the establishment of the metric system of weights and measures; and the repeal of primogeniture, so that property might not be inherited exclusively by the oldest son, but be divided in substantially equal portions among all immediate heirs. The convention also supplemented the decrees of the

Domestic reforms

assembly in abolishing the remnants of manorialism and in providing for greater freedom of economic opportunity for the commoner. The property of enemies of the revolution was confiscated for the benefit of the government and the lower classes. Great estates were broken up and offered for sale to poorer citizens on easy terms. The indemnities hitherto promised to the nobles for the loss of their privileges were abruptly canceled. To curb the rise in the cost of living, maximum prices for grain and other necessities were fixed by law, and merchants who profiteered at the expense of the poor were threatened with the guillotine. Still other measures of reform dealt with religion. An effort was made to abolish Christianity and to substitute the worship of Reason in its place. In accordance with this purpose a new calendar was adopted, dating the year from the birth of the republic (September 22, 1792) and dividing the months in such a way as to eliminate the Christian Sunday. Later, this cult of Reason was replaced by a Deistic religion dedicated to the worship of a Supreme Being and to a belief in the immortality of the soul. Finally, in 1794, the convention decreed simply that religion was a private matter, that church and state would therefore be separated, and that all beliefs not actually hostile to the government would be tolerated.

While effecting this political revolution in France, the convention's leadership at the same time accomplished an astonishingly successful reorganization of its armies. By February 1793, Britain, Holland, Spain, and Austria were in the field against the French. Britain's entrance into the war was dictated by both strategic and economic reasons. The English feared French penetration into the Low Countries directly across the Channel; they were also concerned that French expansion might pose a serious threat to Britain's own growing mercantile hegemony around the globe. The allied coalition ranged against France, though united only in its desire to contain this puzzling,

The revolutionary wars

The Execution of Louis XVI. A revolutionary displays the king's head moments after it had been severed by the guillotine in January 1793.

fearsome revolutionary phenomenon, was nevertheless a formidable force. To counter it, the French organized an army that was able to win engagement after engagement during these years. In August 1793, the revolutionary government imposed a levy on the entire male population capable of bearing arms. Fourteen hastily drafted armies were flung into battle under the leadership of young and inexperienced officers. What they lacked in training and discipline, they made up for in improvised organization, mobility, flexibility, courage, and morale. (In the navy, however, where skill was of paramount importance, the revolutionary French never succeeded in matching the performance of the British.) In 1793–1794, the French armies preserved their homeland. In 1794–1795, they occupied the Low Countries, the Rhineland, parts of Spain, Switzerland, and Savoy. In 1796, they invaded and occupied key parts of Italy and broke the coalition that had arrayed itself against them.

The dictatorship of the Committee of Public Safety

These achievements were not without their price, however. To ensure their accomplishment, the rulers of France resorted to a bloody authoritarianism that has come to be known as the Terror. Although the convention succeeded in 1793 in drafting a new democratic constitution, based upon manhood suffrage, it deferred its introduction because of wartime emergency. Instead, the convention prolonged its own life year by year, and increasingly delegated its responsibilities to a group of twelve leaders known as the Committee of Public Safety. By this time the moderate, upper-middle-class Girondists had lost all influence within the convention. Complete power had passed to the Jacobins, who, though from the middle class, continued to proclaim themselves disciples of Rousseau and champions of the urban workers.

The Death of Marat. This painting by the French artist David immortalized Marat. The bloody towel, the box, and the tub were venerated as relics of the revolution.

Foremost among the members of the Committee of Public Safety were Marat, Danton, and Robespierre. Jean Paul Marat (1743–1793) was educated as a physician, and by 1789 had already earned enough distinction in that profession to be awarded an honorary degree by St. Andrews University in Scotland. Almost from the beginning of the revolution he stood as a champion of the common people. He opposed nearly all of the dogmatic assumptions of his middle-class colleagues in the assembly, including the idea that France should pattern its government after that of Great Britain, which he recognized to be oligarchic in form. He was soon made a victim of persecution and was forced to take refuge in sewers and dungeons, but this did not put an end to his efforts to rouse the people to a defense of their rights. It did, however, leave him with a chronic skin affliction from which he could find relief only through frequent bathing. In 1793 he was stabbed through the heart during one of these soothing respites by Charlotte Corday, a young woman who was fanatically devoted to the Girondists. In contrast with Marat, Georges Jacques Danton (1759–1794) did not come into prominence until the revolution was three years old; but, like Marat, he directed his activities toward goading the masses into rebellion. Elected a member of the Committee of Public Safety in 1793, he had much to do with organizing the Terror. As time went on he appears to have wearied of ruthlessness and displayed a tendency to compromise that gave his opponents in the convention their opportunity. In April 1794 he was sent to the guillotine. Upon mounting the scaffold he is reported to have said: "Show my head to the people; they do not see the like every day."

The most famous and perhaps the greatest of all the extremist leaders was Maximilien Robespierre (1758–1794). Born of a family reputed to be of Irish descent, Robespierre was trained for the law and speedily achieved a modest success as an advocate. In 1782 he was appointed a criminal judge, but soon resigned because he could not bear to impose a sentence of death. Of a nervous and timid disposition, he was a less than able administrator, but he made up for this lack of talent by fanatical devotion to principle. He had adopted the belief that the philosophy of Rousseau held the one great hope of salvation for all mankind. To put this philosophy into practice he was ready to employ any means that would bring results, regardless of the cost to himself or to others. This passionate loyalty to a gospel that exalted the masses eventually won him a following. Indeed, he was so lionized by the public that he was allowed to wear the knee breeches, silk stockings, and powdered hair of the old society until the end of his life. In 1791 he was accepted as the oracle of the Jacobin Club. Later he became president of the National Convention and a member of the Committee of Public Safety. Though he had little or nothing to do with originating the Terror, he was nevertheless responsible for enlarging its scope. He came to justify ruthelessness as a necessary and therefore laudable means to revolutionary progress. In the last six weeks of his

Danton

Robespierre

government, no fewer than 1,285 heads rolled from the scaffold in Paris.

The years of the Terror were years of ruthless dictatorship in France. Pressed by foreign enemies from without, the committee faced sabotage from both the political Right and Left at home. In 1793, a royalist counterrevolution broke out in the western area of the Vendée. The peasantry there had remained generally loyal to church and king. Government attempts to conscript troops into the revolutionary armies fanned long-smoldering resentments into open rebellion. By the summer, the peasant forces there, led by noblemen in the name of a Royal Catholic Grand Army, posed a serious threat to the convention. Meanwhile, Girondist fugitives helped fuel rebellions in the great provincial cities of Lyon, Bordeaux, and Marseilles. This harvest of the decentralizing policies of the National Assembly was bitter fruit to the committee. At the same time they met with the scornful criticism of revolutionaries even more radical than themselves. This latter group, known as the *enragés,* was led by the journalist Jacques Hébert, and threatened to topple not only the government but the country itself by its extremist crusades. Determined to stabilize France, whatever the necessary cost, the committee dispatched commissioners into the countryside to suppress the enemies of the state. During the period of the Terror, from September 1793 to July 1794, the most reliable estimates place the number of executions as high as twenty thousand in France as a whole. The victims were by no means all aristocrats. Anyone who appeared to threaten the republic, no matter what his social or economic position, was at risk. Far more peasants and laborers than noblemen and women were killed. Among those executed was Marie Antoinette ("The Widow Capet"). When some time later the Abbé Sieyès was asked what he had done to distinguish himself during the Terror, he responded dryly, "I lived."

Three points need to be made with regard to the Committee of

Meeting of a Revolutionary Committee of Surveillance during the Terror

Public Safety. First, it dramatically reversed the trend toward decentralization which had characterized the reforms of the assembly. In addition to dispatching its own commissioners from Paris to quell provincial insurrection, the committee published a *Bulletin des loix,* to inform all citizens what laws were to be enforced and obeyed. And it replaced local officials, some of them still royalist in sympathy, with "deputies on mission," whose task was to conscript troops and generate patriotic fervor. When these deputies appeared too eager to act independently, they were in turn replaced by "national agents," with instructions to report directly to the committee. Second, by fostering, as it did, the interests of the lower middle class the committee significantly retarded the pace of industrial transformation in France. Through policies which assisted the peasant, the small craftsman, and the shopkeeper to acquire property, the government during this "second" revolution encouraged the entrenchment of a class at once devoted to the principle of republicanism while unalterably opposed to a large-scale capitalist transformation of the economy of France. Third, the ruthless Terror of the committee undoubtedly achieved its end by saving France from defeat at the hands of the coalition of European states. Whether the human price extracted in return for that salvation was worth the paying is a matter historians—and indeed all thoughtful humans beings—may well never finally resolve.

The achievements of the committee

The Committee of Public Safety, though able to save France, could not save itself. It failed to put a stop to inflation, thereby losing the support of those commoners whose dissatisfactions had helped bring the convention to power. The long string of military victories convinced growing numbers that the committee's demands for continuing self-sacrifice, as well as its insistence upon the necessity of the Terror, were no longer justified. By July 1794, the committee was virtually without allies. On July 27 (9 Thermidor, according to the new calendar) Robespierre was shouted down by his enemies while attempting to speak on the floor of the convention. Desperate, he tried to rally loyal Jacobins to his defense and against the convention. Discovered in the thick of this plot by convention troops, Robespierre tried unsuccessfully to shoot himself. The following day, along with twenty-one fellow conspirators he met his death as an enemy of the state on the guillotine. Now, the only remaining leaders in the convention were men of moderate sympathies, who, as time went on, inclined toward increasing conservatism. Gradually, the revolution came once more to reflect the interests of the upper middle class. Much of the extremist work of the radicals was undone. The law of maximum prices and the law against "suspects" were both repealed. Political prisoners were freed, the Jacobins driven into hiding, and the Committee of Public Safety shorn of its absolute powers. The new situation made possible the return of priests, royalists, and other emigrés from abroad to add the weight of their influence to the conservative trend.

*The Thermidorian
reaction: stage three*

The Fashionable Mama, 1796. An English cartoon lampooning the extreme style of dress adopted by the newly rich throughout Europe during the Directory period.

The plight of the Directory

In 1795 the National Convention adopted a new constitution, which lent the stamp of official approval to the victory of the prosperous classes. The constitution granted suffrage to all adult male citizens who could read and write. They were permitted to vote for electors, who in turn would choose the members of the legislative body. In order to be an elector, one had to be the proprietor of a farm or other establishment with an annual income equivalent to at least one hundred days of labor. The drafters of the constitution thus ensured that the authority of the government would actually be derived from citizens of considerable wealth. Since it was not practicable to restore the monarchy, lest the old aristocracy also come back into power, executive authority was vested in a board of five men known as the Directory, chosen by the legislative body. The new constitution included not only a bill of rights but also a declaration of the *duties* of the citizen. Conspicuous among the latter was the obligation to bear in mind that "it is upon the maintenance of property . . . that the whole social order rests."

The reign of the Directory has not enjoyed a good historical press. The collection of *nouveau riche* speculators and profiteers who rose to prominence as they labored to make a good thing for themselves out of the war were not a particularly attractive crew. They were lampooned as ostentatious and vulgar *"merveilleuses"*—outrageously overdressed men and underdressed women. But however anxious they were to live down the self-denying excesses of the past several years by self-indulgent excesses of their own, they were in no mood to see the major accomplishments of the revolution undone. They had no difficulty in disposing of threats from the Left, despite their failure to resolve that bugbear of all revolutionary governments, inflation and rising living costs. When in 1796 the radical "Gracchus" Babeuf[1] launched a campaign to abolish private property and parliamentary government, his followers were arrested, executed, and deported.

To dispatch threats from the Right was not so easy. Elections in March 1797—the first free elections held in France as a republic—returned a large number of constitutional monarchists to the councils of government. Leading politicians, among them some who had voted for the execution of Louis XVI, took alarm. With the support of the army, the Directory in September 1797 annulled most of the election results of the previous spring. Its bold coup did little, however, to end the nation's political irresolution. Two years later, after a series of further abortive uprisings and purges, and with the country still plagued by severe inflation, the Directors were desperate. This time they called their brilliant young general, Napoleon Bonaparte (1769–1821), to their assistance.

Bonaparte's first military victory in 1793, the recapture of Toulon from royalist and British forces, had earned him promotion from cap-

---

[1] Called "Gracchus" after the Roman tribune Gaius Gracchus, a hero of the people.

tain to brigadier general at the age of twenty-four. Though arrested as a terrorist following the fall of Robespierre, he was subsequently patronized by Viscount Paul Barras, a Directory politician. Bonaparte had gained further public fame and the gratitude of the Directory when on October 4, 1795 (13 Vendémiaire, new calendar), he had delivered the "whiff of grapeshot" that saved the convention from attack by opponents of the new constitution. Since that time he had registered a remarkable series of victories in Italy, which had resulted in Austria's withdrawal from the war. Most recently, he had attempted to defeat Britain by attacking its colonies in Egypt and the Near East. Despite initial successes on land, Bonaparte eventually found himself trapped by the British, following the defeat of the French fleet by Admiral Horatio Nelson at Abukir Bay in 1798. A year of further fighting had brought Bonaparte no nearer decisive victory in North Africa.

It was at this point that the call came from the Directory. Bonaparte slipped away from Egypt and appeared in Paris, already having agreed to participate in a coup d'état with the leading director, that former revolutionary champion of the third estate, the Abbé Sieyès. On November 9, 1799 (18 Brumaire), Bonaparte, along with Sieyès and one other director, was declared a "temporary consul." Bonaparte was the answer to the prayers of the Directory: a strong, popular leader who was not a king. Sieyès, who had once declared for revolution in the name of the third estate, now declared for counterrevolution in the name of virtual dictatorship: "Confidence from below, authority from above." With those words Sieyès pronounced the end of the revolutionary period.

The Eighteenth Brumaire. A detail from a painting by Bronchet depicting Napoleon as the man of the hour.

4. NAPOLEON AND EUROPE

Few men in Western history have compelled the attention of the world as Napoleon Bonaparte did during the fifteen years of his rule in France. And few men have succeeded as he has in continuing to live on as myth in the consciousness, not just of his own country, but of all Europe. Without doubt, part of the success of the Napoleonic myth can be credited to the fact that Napoleon never attempted to disguise his less-than-gentlemanly background. Although born in Corsica into a family that held a title of nobility from the Republic of Genoa, he cultivated the rude manners of an *arriviste,* losing his temper, cheating at cards, taking what he could get without regard to the conventions of polite society. As such, he appealed to the new citizens of a triumphantly middle-class Europe. In the minds of his admirers he would remain the "little corporal" who, without the privileges of the aristocrat, had made it to the top on his own.

Yet the myth was also grounded in the important fact of Bonaparte's undoubted abilities. Schooled in France and at the military academy in Paris, he possessed a mind congenial to the ideas of the

*The character of
Napoleon Bonaparte*

Enlightenment—creative, imaginative, and ready to perceive things anew. His primary interests were history, law, and mathematics. His particular strengths as a leader lay in his ability to conceive of financial, legal, or military plans and then to master their every detail; his capacity for inspiring others, even those initially opposed to him; and his belief in himself as the destined savior of the French. That last conviction eventually became the obsession that led to Napoleon's undoing. But supreme self-confidence was just what the French government had lacked since the first days of the revolution. Napoleon believed both in himself and in France. That latter belief was the tonic France now needed, and Napoleon proceeded to administer it in liberally revivifying doses.

His abilities

During the years from 1799 to 1804, Napoleon ruled under the title of first consul, but in reality as a dictator. Once again, France was given a new constitution. Though the document spoke of universal male suffrage, political power was retained, by the now familiar means of indirect election, in the hands of middle-class entrepreneurs and professionals. Recognizing, however, that his regime would derive additional substance if it could be made to appear the government of the people of France, Bonaparte instituted what has since become a common authoritarian device: the plebiscite. The voters were asked to approve the new constitution and did so by the loudly proclaimed vote of 3,011,107 in favor, 1,567 opposed.

Napoleonic reforms

Although the constitution provided for a legislative body, that body could neither initiate nor discuss legislation. The first consul made use of a Council of State to draft his laws; but in fact the government depended on the authority of one man. Bonaparte had no desire to undo the major egalitarian reforms of the revolution. He reconfirmed the abolition of estates, privileges, and local liberties, thereby reconfirming as well the notion of a meritocracy, of "careers open to talent," dear to the hearts of the middle class. Through centralization of the administrative departments, he achieved what no recent French regime had yet achieved, an orderly and generally fair system of taxation. His plan, by prohibiting the type of exemptions formerly granted the nobility and clergy, and by centralizing collection, enabled him to budget rationally for expenditures and consequent indebtedness. In this way he reduced the inflationary spiral that had entangled so many past governments. Napoleon's willingness to proceed against the decentralizing tendencies of the earlier years of the revolution marked him as a student of the absolutist policies of the Bourbons as well as an admirer of the egalitarian reforms of his more immediate predecessors. He replaced the elected officials and local self-government instituted in 1789 with centrally appointed "prefects" and "subprefects" whose administrative duties were defined in Paris, where local government policy was made as well.

Centralization and finance

Napoleon's most significant accomplishment was his completion of the educational and legal reforms begun during the revolutionary period. He ordered the establishment of *lycées* (high schools) in every major town and a school in Paris for the training of teachers. To supplement these changes, Napoleon brought the military and technical schools under state control and founded a national university to exercise supervision over the entire system. Like almost all his reforms, this one proved of particular benefit to the middle class; so did the new legal code promulgated in 1810. The Code Napoleon, as the new body of laws was called, reflected two principles which had threaded their way through all the constitutional changes since 1789: uniformity and individualism. The code made French law uniform, declaring past customs and privileges forever abolished. By underscoring in various ways a private individual's right to property, by authorizing new methods for the drafting of contracts, leases, and stock companies, and by once again prohibiting trade unions, the code worked to the benefit of individually minded entrepreneurs and businessmen.

To accomplish these reforms Napoleon called upon the most talented men available to him, regardless of their past political affiliations. He admitted back into the country emigrés of all political stripes. His two fellow consuls—joint executives, but in name only—were a regicide of the Terror and bureaucrat of the Old Regime. His minister of police had been an extreme radical republican; his minister of foreign affairs was the opportunist aristocrat Talleyrand. The work of political reconciliation was assisted by Napoleon's 1801 concordat with the pope, which reunited Church and state. Though the action disturbed former anti-Church Jacobins, Napoleon, ever the pragmatist, believed the reconciliation of Church and state necessary for reasons both of domestic harmony and of international solidarity. According to the terms of the concordat, the pope received the right to depose French bishops and to discipline the French clergy. At the same time, the Vatican agreed to lay to rest any claims against the expropriation of former Church lands. Hereafter, that property would remain unchallenged in the hands of its new middle-class rural and urban proprietors. In return, the clergy was guaranteed an income from the state. The concordat did nothing to revoke the principle of religious freedom established by the revolution. Although the Roman Catholic clergy received state money, so did Protestant clergy.

Napoleon's agreement won him the support of those conservatives who had feared for France's future as a godless state. To prove to the old Jacobins, in turn, that he remained a child of their revolution, he invaded the independent state of Baden in 1804 to arrest and then execute the duke of Enghien, a relative of the Bourbons, whom Napoleon falsely accused of a plot against his life. (Three years before he had deported over one hundred Jacobins on a similar charge, but with no permanent political repercussions.) The balancing act only served to increase Napoleon's general popularity. By 1802 the people of France were prepared to accept him as "consul for life." In 1804, they

(2) *education and law*

(3) *reconciliation*

Napoleon crowned emperor

Coronation of Napoleon and Josephine by David. Napoleon crowned himself and his wife and assumed the title of Napoleon I, emperor of the French.

rejoiced when, in the cathedral of Notre Dame, in Paris, he crowned himself Emperor Napoleon I.

Anti-French alliances

Across the boundaries of France, the nations of Europe had watched, some in admiration, others in horror, all in astonishment, at the phenomenon that was Napoleon. They had fought France since 1792 in hopes of maintaining European stability. Now they faced the greatest threat to that stability yet to arise. The detailed history of the wars fought to contain the French is complex, and of little direct relevance to the patterns of ideas, institutions, and societies we are tracing. Suffice it to say that from 1792 until 1795 France had been at war with a coalition of European powers—principally Austria, Prussia, and Britain. In 1795, Prussia retired from the fray, financially exhausted and at odds with Austria. In 1797, the Austrians, defeated by Bonaparte in northern Italy, withdrew as well, signing the Treaty of Campo Formio, which ceded to France territories in Belgium, recognized the Cisalpine Republic which Bonaparte had established in Italy, and agreed to France's occupation of the left bank of the Rhine.

Treaty of Lunéville

By the following year, Britain was left to fight the French alone. In 1798 it formed a second coalition against the French, this one with Russia and Austria. The results did not differ significantly from those of the first allied attempt to contain France. Russia and Austria had no success in driving the French from Italy; the French likewise failed to break Britain's advantage at sea. By 1801, the coalition was in tatters, Russia having withdrawn two years previously. The Treaty of Lunéville, signed by France and Austria, confirmed the provisions of Campo Formio; in addition the so-called Batavian, Helvetian, Cisalpine, and Ligurian republics—established by Napoleon from territories in the Low Countries, Switzerland, Italy, and Piedmont—were legitimized. The Austrians also acquiesced to a general redrawing of the map of Germany, which resulted eventually in an amalgamation of semi-independent states under French domination into the Confederation of the Rhine. The following year Britain, no longer able to fight alone, settled with the French as well, returning all the territories it had captured in overseas colonial engagements except Trinidad and Ceylon.

Under Napoleon's reign, the territories of central Europe underwent a revolution. This revolution was a thorough governmental reorganization, one which imposed the major egalitarian reforms of the French Revolution upon lands outside the borders of France, while building a French empire. Most affected were territories in Italy (the "Kingdom of Italy" as it was now called); Germany (the Confederation of the Rhine, including the newly formed Kingdom of Westphalia); Dalmatia (the Illyrian provinces); and Holland. (Belgium had been integrated directly into the empire.) Into all these territories Napoleon introduced a carefully organized, deliberate system of administration, based upon the notion of careers open to talent, equality before the law, and the abolition of ancient customs and privileges. The Napoleonic program of reform in the empire represented an application of the principles that had already transformed postrevolutionary France. Manorial courts were liquidated, and Church courts abolished. Provinces were joined into an enormous bureaucratic network that reached directly back to Paris. Laws were codified, the tax system modernized, and everywhere individuals were freed to work at whatever trade they chose. The one freedom denied throughout this new grand hegemony was that of self-government: i.e., all governmental direction emanated from Paris, and therefore from Napoleon. Despite that fact, middle-class business and professional men, who had chafed against restrictions imposed upon them by petty despotic traditions, welcomed this chance to exercise their talents to a fuller degree than they had ever before enjoyed.

Napoleon's reforms in Europe

Napoleon's motives in introducing these various radical changes were by no means altruistic. He understood that the defense of his enormous domain depended on efficient administration and the rational collection and expenditure of funds for his armies. His boldest attempt at consolidation, however, a policy forbidding the importation into the Continent of British goods, proved a failure. This "Continental System," established in 1806, was designed as a strategic measure in Napoleon's continuing economic war against Britain. Its purpose was to destroy Britain's commerce and credit—to starve it economically into surrender. The system failed for several reasons. Foremost was the fact that throughout the war Britain retained control of the seas. The British naval blockade of the Continent, implemented in 1807, served, therefore, as an effective counter to Napoleon's system. While the empire labored to transport goods and raw materials overland to avoid the British blockade, the British worked with success to develop a lively trade with South America. Internal tariffs were a second reason for the failure of the system. Napoleon was unable to per-

The Continental System

The Handwriting on the Wall. This English cartoon conjures up the biblical Feast of Belshazzar with a vice-ridden Paris, as the new Babylon, doomed to destruction. Headed by a crazed Napoleon and a grotesque Josephine, the banquet table offers a meal including the head of George III, the Tower of London, and the Bank of England.

suade individual territories to join a tariff-free customs union. As a result Europe remained divided into economic camps, fortified against each other by tariffs, and at odds with each other as they attempted to subsist on nothing more than what the Continent could produce and manufacture. The final reason for the system's collapse was the fact that the Continent had more to lose than Britain. Trade stagnated; ports and manufacturing centers grumbled as unemployment rose.

Reasons for Napoleon's fall

The Continental System was Napoleon's first serious mistake. As such it was one of the causes of his ultimate downfall. A second cause of Napoleon's decline was his constantly growing ambition and increasing sense of self-importance. Napoleon's goal was a united Europe modeled after the Roman Empire. The symbols of his empire—reflected in painting, architecture, and the design of furniture and clothing—were deliberately Roman in origin. But Napoleon's Rome was without question imperial, dynastic Rome. The triumphal columns and arches he had erected to commemorate his victories recalled the ostentatious monuments of the Roman emperors. He made his brothers and sisters the monarchs of his newly created kingdoms, which Napoleon controlled from Paris while their mother allegedly sat at court, anxiously wringing her hands and repeating to herself, "If only it lasts!" He divorced his first wife, the Empress Josephine, alleging her childlessness, and ensured himself a successor of royal blood by marrying into the monarchically respectable house of Habsburg. Even his admirers began to question if Napoleon's empire was not simply a larger, more efficient, and, therefore, ultimately more dangerous absolutism than the monarchies of the eighteenth century. War again broke out in 1805, with the Russians, Prussians, and Austrians joining the British in an attempt to contain France. But to no avail; Napoleon's military superiority led to defeats, in turn, of all three continental allies. Ultimately only the emperor's own unwillingness to recognize that his supply of men, matériel, and good fortune was not limitless brought military defeat upon him.

The Empress Josephine

THE EMPIRE OF NAPOLEON
AT ITS GREATEST EXTENT • 1812

French territory

French dependencies

Allied with Napoleon

Independent states

RUSSIA

Moscow

Borodino

NAPOLEON 1812

Tilsit

Friedland

DUCHY OF WARSAW

Warsaw

PRUSSIA

Berlin

Leipzig

Elbe R.

CONFEDERATION OF THE RHINE

AUSTRIAN EMPIRE

Austerlitz

Vienna

ILLYRIAN PROVINCES

BLACK SEA

OTTOMAN EMPIRE

AEGEAN SEA

ADRIATIC SEA

SWEDEN

NORWAY

DENMARK

Copenhagen

BALTIC SEA

NORTH SEA

HOLLAND

Amsterdam

Rhine R.

Ulm

HELVETIC REPUBLIC

KINGDOM OF ITALY

PO R.

PAPAL STATES

Rome

KINGDOM OF NAPLES

Naples

KDM. OF SICILY

MEDITERRANEAN SEA

CORSICA

KDM. OF SARDINIA

Marseilles

Brussels

Waterloo

Paris

FRENCH EMPIRE

Bordeaux

ENGLAND

London

IRELAND

English Channel

ATLANTIC OCEAN

SPAIN

Madrid

KDM. OF PORTUGAL

Lisbon

500 miles

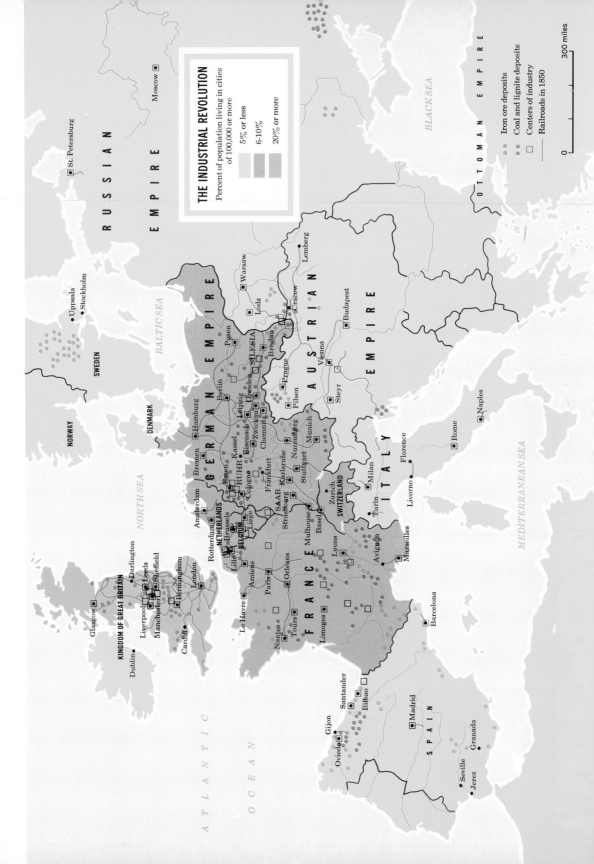

THE INDUSTRIAL REVOLUTION

Percent of population living in cities of 100,000 or more

5% or less
6-10%
20% or more

• Iron ore deposits
• Coal and lignite deposits
□ Centers of industry
— Railroads in 1850

0   300 miles

RUSSIAN EMPIRE

• St. Petersburg

• Moscow

SWEDEN

• Uppsala
• Stockholm

NORWAY

DENMARK

BALTIC SEA

NORTH SEA

KINGDOM OF GREAT BRITAIN

• Glasgow
• Darlington
• Leeds
• Sheffield
• Liverpool
• Manchester
• Birmingham
• Cardiff
• London
• Dublin

ATLANTIC OCEAN

GERMAN EMPIRE

• Hamburg
• Bremen
• Berlin
• Posen
• Warsaw
• Lodz
SILESIA
• Breslau
• Cracow
• Prague
• Pilsen
• Dresden
• Leipzig
• Zwickau
• Chemnitz
• Eisenach
• Kassel
RUHR
• Essen
• Cologne
• Frankfurt
• Nuremberg
• Munich
• Karlsruhe
• Stuttgart
SAAR
• Strasbourg
• Mulhouse
SWITZERLAND
• Zurich
• Basel

Amsterdam
Rotterdam
NETHERLANDS
BELGIUM
• Brussels
• Liège
• Lille
• Amiens
• Le Havre
• Paris
• Orleans
• Tours
• Nantes

FRANCE

• Limoges
• Lyons
• Avignon
• Marseilles

AUSTRIAN EMPIRE

• Lemberg
• Vienna
• Budapest
• Steyr

ITALY

• Milan
• Turin
• Florence
• Livorno
• Rome
• Naples

BLACK SEA

OTTOMAN EMPIRE

MEDITERRANEAN SEA

SPAIN

• Madrid
• Barcelona
• Santander
• Bilbao
• Gijon
• Oviedo
• Seville
• Jerez
• Granada

In 1808, Napoleon invaded Spain, as a first step toward the conquest of Portugal, which had remained a stalwart ally of the British. Napoleon was determined to bring the Iberian peninsula into the Continental System. Although he at first promised the senile Spanish king Charles IV that he would cede a part of Portugal to Spain, Napoleon proceeded to overthrow Charles and installed his brother Joseph Bonaparte on the throne. Napoleon then imposed a series of reforms upon the Spanish, similar to those he had instituted elsewhere in Europe. But he reckoned without two factors that led to the ultimate failure of his Spanish mission: the presence of British forces under Sir Arthur Wellesley (later the duke of Wellington), and the determined resistance of the Spanish people. They particularly detested Napoleon's interference in the affairs of the Church, actively opposing his ending of the Inquisition and his abolition of a number of monastic establishments. Together with the British, the Spanish maintained a concerted effort to drive Napoleon from their country, often employing guerrilla warfare to do so. Though at one point Napoleon himself took charge of his army, he could not achieve anything more than temporary victory. The campaign dragged on until 1813, when the French forces were finally driven back across the border. The Spanish campaign was the first indication that Napoleon could be beaten. As such, it helped to promote a spirit of anti-Napoleonic defiance that encouraged resistance elsewhere.

Invasion of Spain

A second stage in Napoleon's downfall began with the disruption of his alliance with Russia. As an agricultural country, Russia had suffered a severe economic crisis when it was no longer able, as a result of the Continental System, to exchange its surplus grain for British manufactures. The consequence was that Tsar Alexander began to wink at trade with Britain and to ignore or evade the protests from Paris. By 1811 Napoleon decided that he could endure this flouting of the Continental System no longer. Accordingly, he collected an army of 600,000 men and set out in the spring of 1812 to punish the tsar. The project ended in disaster. The Russians refused to make a stand, drawing the French farther and farther into the heart of their country. They permitted Napoleon to occupy their ancient capital of Moscow. But on the night of his entry, a fire of suspicious origin broke out in the city. When the flames subsided, little but the blackened walls of the Kremlin palaces remained to shelter the invading troops. Hoping that the tsar would eventually surrender, Napoleon lingered amid the ruins for more than a month, finally deciding on October 22 to begin the homeward march. The delay was a fatal blunder. Long before he had reached the border, the terrible Russian winter was upon his troops. Swollen streams, mountainous drifts of snow, and bottomless mud slowed the retreat almost to a halt. To add to the miseries of bitter cold, disease, and starvation, mounted Cossacks rode out of the blizzard to harry the exhausted army. Each morning the miserable remnant that pushed on left behind circles of corpses around the campfires

The Russsian debacle

The Retreat from Russia. In this painting by Charlet the horrors of the Russian winter can be seen.

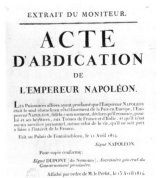

Napoleon's Abdication Proclamation, 1814

of the night before. On December 13 a few thousand broken solders crossed the frontier into Germany—a small fraction of what had once been proudly styled the *Grande Armée*. The lives of nearly 300,000 men had been sacrificed in Napoleon's Russian adventure.

Until the debacle of the Russian campaign, Napoleon's armies had enjoyed a striking series of victories. The Battle of Austerlitz, in December 1805, a mighty triumph for the French against the combined forces of Austria and Russia, had remained a symbol of the emperor's apparent invincibility. Subsequent victories in the following years—against the Prussians at Jena in 1806, the Russians at Friedland in 1807, and the Austrians at Wagram in 1809—increased the conviction on the part of Europe that it had no choice but to acquiesce in Napoleon's grand continental design. The great British naval victory at Trafalgar in 1805, which broke the maritime power of France, was perceived at the time by Napoleon's friends and foes alike as no more than a temporary check to his ambitions.

Now, however, following the retreat from Russia, the anti-Napoleonic forces took renewed hope. United by a belief that they might at last succeed in defeating the emperor, Prussia, Russia, Austria, and Britain renewed their attack. Most of the fighting during this so-called war of liberation took place in Germany. The climax of the campaign occurred in October 1813 when, at what was thereafter known as the Battle of the Nations, fought near Leipzig, the allies handed the French a resounding defeat. Meanwhile, allied armies won significant victories in the Low Countries and Italy. By the beginning of 1814, they had crossed the Rhine into France. Burdened with an inexperienced army of raw youths, Napoleon retreated to Paris, continuing, despite constant setbacks, to urge the French people to further resistance. On March 31, Tsar Alexander I of Russia and King Frederick William III of Prussia made their triumphant entry into Paris. Napoleon was forced to abdicate unconditionally, and was sent into exile on the island of Elba, off the Italian coast.

Less than a year later he once more set foot on French soil. The allies had in the interim restored the Bourbon dynasty to the throne, in the person of Louis XVIII, brother of Louis XVI.[2] Any sovereign would have suffered in the eyes of the French by comparison with Napoleon; Louis was particularly ill-suited to fill a space far too great for his mediocre talents. The French rallied enthusiastically to the former emperor. By the time he reached Paris, he had generated enough support to cause Louis to flee the country. The allies, meeting in Vienna to conclude peace treaties with the French, were stunned by the news of Napoleon's return. They dispatched a hastily organized army to counter the emperor's typically bold offensive push into the Low Countries. There, at the battle of Waterloo, fought on June 18, 1815, Napoleon suffered defeat for the final time. Shipped off to the bleak island of St. Helena in the South Atlantic, the once-mighty emperor, now the exile Bonaparte, lived out a dreary existence writing self-serving memoirs until his death in 1821.

Napoleon's return and final defeat

Napoleon's legacy was an impressive one. His administrative and legal reforms remained in place after his fall. The Napoleonic legal code persisted not only in France but in the Low Countries, Prussia, and various other German states. The institutions introduced during his reign—centralized bureaucracy, police and educational systems—became part of the machinery of government and society in many parts of nineteenth-century Europe.

Napoleon's legacy

To appreciate the larger impact of the revolutionary and Napo-

---

[2]Louis XVII, the young son of the executed king and queen, had died under mysterious circumstances in the hands of his revolutionary captors in 1795.

Napoleon Arrives in Paris after His Escape from Elba, March 20, 1815

leonic era on Western civilization, one must trace the ideas and institutions it fostered as they worked their way into the history of nineteenth- and twentieth-century Europe and America. Liberty—the right to act within the world with responsibility to no one but oneself—was a notion dear to those who made the French Revolution, and one which remained embodied in the reforms it produced. So was equality—the notion of rational laws applied even-handedly to all, regardless of birth or position. National pride, the era's third legacy, was bred in the hearts of the French people as they watched their citizen armies repel attacks against their newly won freedoms. It was instilled, as well, into those whose opposition to the French made them more conscious of their own national identity. The three concepts—liberty, equality, and nationality—were now no longer merely ideas; as laws and as a new way of addressing life, they rested at the center of European reality.

5. THE VIENNA SETTLEMENT

The European powers that met at the Congress of Vienna in 1814 to draw up a permanent peace settlement for Europe labored to produce an agreement that would as nearly as possible guarantee international tranquility. At the same time, however, they were by no means unwilling to advance the claims of their own countries to new territories, though such claims threatened conflict, or even war. Although the principal decisions of the congress were made by representatives of the major powers, it was attended by an array of dignitaries from almost all the principalities of Europe. No fewer than six monarchs attended: the tsar of Russia, the emperor of Austria, and the kings of Prussia, Denmark, Bavaria, and Württemberg. Great Britain was represented by Lord Castlereagh and the duke of Wellington. From France came the subtle intriguer Talleyrand, who had served as a bishop under

The Congress of Vienna. The figure to the left of center is Metternich. Seated at the right, with his arms on the table, is Talleyrand.

Louis XVI, as foreign minister at the court of Napoleon, and who now stood ready to espouse the cause of reaction.

The dominant roles at the Congress of Vienna were played by Tsar Alexander I (1801–1825) and by the Austrian diplomat Klemens von Metternich (1773–1859). The dynamic tsar is one of the most baffling figures in history. Reared at the court of Catherine the Great, he imbibed the doctrines of Rousseau from a French Jacobin tutor. In 1801 he succeeded his murdered father, Paul, as tsar and for the next two decades disturbed the dreams of his fellow sovereigns by becoming the most liberal monarch in Europe. After the defeat of Napoleon in the Russian campaign, Alexander's mind turned more and more to mystical channels. He conceived of a mission to convert the rulers of all countries to the Christian ideals of justice and peace. But the chief effect of his voluble expressions of devotion to "liberty" and "enlightenment" was to frighten conservatives into suspecting a plot to extend his power over all of Europe. He was accused of intriguing with Jacobins everywhere to substitute an all-powerful Russia for an all-powerful France.

Tsar Alexander I

The most commanding figure at the congress was Metternich, born at Coblenz in the Rhine valley, where his father was Austrian ambassador at the courts of three small German states. As a student at the University of Strassburg the young Metternich witnessed mob violence connected with the outbreak of the French Revolution, and to this he attributed his life-long hatred of political innovation. He had been active in fomenting discord between Napoleon and Tsar Alexander, after the two became allies in 1807, and had played some part in arranging the marriage of Napoleon to the Austrian archduchess, Marie Louise. Metternich once declared himself an admirer of the spider, "always busy arranging their houses with the greatest of neatness in the world." At the Congress of Vienna, he attempted at every turn to arrange international affairs with equal neatness, to suit his own diplomatic designs. His two great obsessions were hatred of political and social change and fear of Russia. Above all, he feared revolutions inspired by the tsar for the sake of establishing Russian supremacy in Europe. For this reason he favored moderate terms for France in its hour of defeat, and was ready at one time to sponsor the restoration of Napoleon as emperor of the French under the protection and overlordship of the Habsburg monarchy.

Klemens von Metternich

The basic idea that guided the work of the Congress of Vienna was the principle of *legitimacy*. This principle was invented by Talleyrand as a device for protecting France against drastic punishment by its conquerors, but it was ultimately adopted by Metternich as a convenient expression of the general policy of reaction. Legitimacy meant that the dynasties of Europe that had reigned in prerevolutionary days should be restored to their thrones, and that each country should regain essentially the same territories it had held in 1789. In accordance with this principle Louis XVIII was recognized as the "legitimate" sover-

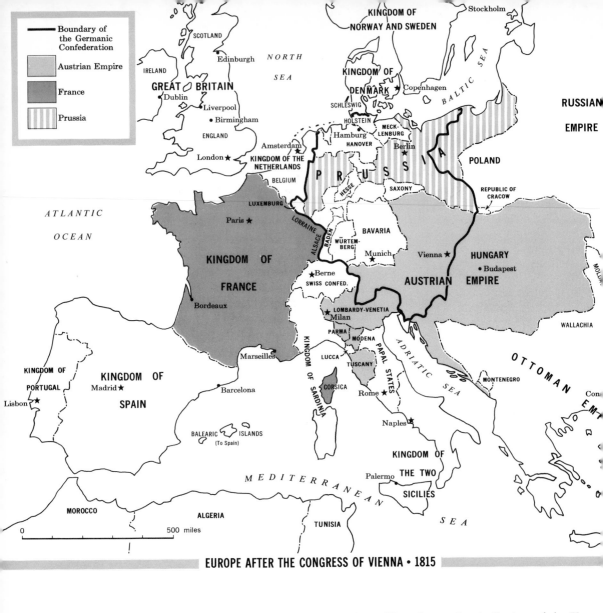

EUROPE AFTER THE CONGRESS OF VIENNA · 1815

eign of France; the restoration of Bourbon rulers in Spain and the Two
Sicilies was also confirmed. France was compelled to pay an indemnity of 700 million francs to the victorious allies, but its boundaries
were to remain essentially the same as in 1789.

To ensure that the French would not soon again overrun their
boundaries, however, a strong barrier was erected to contain them.

Barriers to French expansion

The Dutch Republic, conquered by the French in 1795, was restored
as the Kingdom of the Netherlands, with the house of Orange as its
hereditary monarchy. To its territory was added that of Belgium, formerly the Austrian Netherlands, with the hope that this now substantial power would serve to discourage any future notions of French ex-

pansion. For the same reason the German left bank of the Rhine was ceded to Prussia, and Austria was established as a major power in northern Italy.

The German settlement

The principle of legitimacy was not extended to the German principalities, however. There, despite pleas from rulers of the sovereign bits and pieces that had existed before 1789, the great powers agreed to retain the boundaries as redrawn by Napoleon. Fear of an aggressive Russia led the other European nations to support the maintenance—as an anti-Russian bulwark—of the Napoleonic kingdoms of Bavaria, Württemberg, and Saxony. At the same time, however, Tsar Alexander was demanding that Poland, partitioned into virtual extinction by Russia, Austria, and Prussia in the 1790s, be reconstituted a kingdom with himself as its constitutional monarch. Prussia was prepared to agree with this scheme, provided that it be allowed to swallow Saxony. National avarice for territorial expansion rapidly eclipsed legitimacy as a guiding principle in these negotiations. Metternich, horrified at the double threat thus presented to Austria by Prussia and Russia, allied himself with Talleyrand and Castlereagh, both of whom secretly agreed to go to war against Russia and Prussia, if necessary, in order to prevent them from consumating their Polish-Saxon deal. A compromise was eventually reached, allowing to Russia the major part of Poland and to Prussia a part of Saxony. Britain, no less anxious than the other victorious powers to gain compensation for its long years at war, received territories principally under French dominion in South Africa and South America and the island of Ceylon, thus adding further to its commercial empire.

Triumph of the state system

Legitimacy, as expressed in the treaties that concluded the Congress of Vienna, emerged as the latter-day expression of the principles of balance and stability that had shaped diplomacy during the eighteenth century. The age of absolutism had witnessed the emergence of an international state system dedicated to those principles. By enshrining

"Dividing the Cake." A contemporary cartoonist's impression of the work of the congress diplomats.

them in their settlement, the diplomats at Vienna ensured that such a state system would be part of the legacy passed to their nineteenth-century successors.

SELECTED READINGS

• *Items so designated are available in paperback editions.*

• Arendt, Hannah, *On Revolution,* New York, 1963. An analysis of the American and French Revolutions and their meaning for modern man.

• Bergeron, Louis, *France under Napoleon,* Princeton, N.J., 1981. Concentrates on the era of Napoleon rather than the man.

Bosher, J. F., *French Finances, 1770–1790: From Business to Bureaucracy,* Cambridge, 1970. An impressive study concerned with the financial apparatus of Old Regime and revolutionary France.

• Breunig, C., *The Age of Revolution and Reaction, 1789–1850,* 2nd ed., New York, 1978. A well-written survey.

• Brinton, Crane, *Anatomy of Revolution,* rev. ed., New York, 1961. Attempts to create a general model of revolutions by comparing the English, American, French, and Russian Revolutions.

• ———, *A Decade of Revolution, 1789–1799,* New York, 1934. An excellent European survey.

• Bruun, Geoffrey, *Europe and the French Imperium, 1799–1814,* New York, 1938. Describes the impact of Napoleon upon Europe.

• Cobb, R. C., *The Police and the People: French Popular Protest,* New York, 1970. A survey of peasants and sans-culottes.

Cobban, Alfred, *The Social Interpretation of the French Revolution,* Cambridge, 1964. A penetrating critique of the radical interpretation of the revolution, more important for its questions than its conclusions.

Egret, Jean, *The French Pre-Revolution, 1787–88,* Chicago, 1977. Describes the collapse of the Old Regime.

• Gershoy, Leo, *The French Revolution and Napoleon,* rev. ed., New York, 1964. A good survey with annotated bibliography.

Geyl, Pieter, *Napoleon: For and Against,* rev. ed., New Haven, Conn., 1964. The ways in which Napoleon was interpreted by French historians and political figures.

Goodwin, Albert, *The Friends of Liberty: The English Democratic Movement in the Age of the French Revolution,* Cambridge, Mass., 1979. Detailed, subtle analysis of English reform movements.

Greer, Donald, *The Incidence of the Terror during the French Revolution: A Statistical Interpretation,* Cambridge, Mass., 1935. An important study which reveals that the lower classes suffered most during the Terror, rather than the nobility or the clergy.

• Hampson, Norman, *A Social History of the French Revolution,* London, 1963. Deals with institutional development.

Herold, J. Christopher, *The Age of Napoleon,* New York, 1968. A well-written popular history.

• Kissinger, Henry, *A World Restored: Metternich, Castlereagh, and the Problem of Peace, 1812–1822,* Boston, 1957. By the former U.S. secretary of state, an admirer of Metternich.

- Lefebvre, Georges, *The Coming of the French Revolution,* Princeton, N.J., 1957. An excellent study of the causes and early events of the revolution.
———, *The French Revolution,* 2 vols., New York, 1963–64. An impressive synthesis by the greatest modern scholar of the revolution.
———, *The Great Fear of 1789,* New York, 1973. The best account of the rural disturbances.
  McManners, John, *The French Revolution and the Church,* New York, 1969. Describes the impact of revolutionary anticlericalism upon the French Church.
- Markham, Felix, *Napoleon,* New York, 1966. An excellent study.
- Nicolson, Harold, *The Congress of Vienna, a Study in Allied Unity,* New York, 1946. An excellent and very readable history, written by a British diplomat.
- Palmer, R. R., *The Age of the Democratic Revolution: A Political History of Europe and America, 1760–1800,* 2 vols., Princeton, N.J., 1964. Impressive for its scope; places the French Revolution in the larger context of a worldwide revolutionary movement.
———, *Twelve Who Ruled,* Princeton, N.J., 1958. Excellent biographical studies of the members of the Committee of Public Safety; demonstrates that Robespierre's role has been exaggerated.
- Rudé, George, *The Crowd in the French Revolution,* Oxford, 1959. An important monograph which analyzes the composition of the crowds which participated in the great uprisings of the revolution.
  Soboul, Albert, *The Sans-Culottes: The Popular Movement and Revolutionary Government, 1793–1794,* Garden City, N.Y., 1972. An outstanding example of "history from below"; analyzes the pressures upon the convention in the year of the Terror.
  Thompson, J. M., *Napoleon Bonaparte: His Rise and Fall,* Oxford, 1958. The standard work.
- ———, *Robespierre and the French Revolution,* London, 1953. An excellent short biography.
- Tilly, Charles, *The Vendée: A Sociological Analysis of the Counter-Revolution of 1793,* Cambridge, Mass., 1964. An important economic and social analysis of the factors that led to the reaction in the Vendée.
- Tocqueville, Alexis de, *The Old Regime and French Revolution.* Originally written in 1856, this remains a classic analysis of the causes of the French Revolution.
- Williams, Gwyn A., *Artisans and Sans-Culottes,* New York, 1969. Comparative history of English and French popular movements.

SOURCE MATERIALS

- Burke, Edmund, *Reflections on the Revolution in France,* London, 1790. (Many editions.) The great conservative statement against the revolution and its principles.
- Montesquieu, Baron de, *The Spirit of the Laws,* 1748. (Many editions). See especially Books I, II, III, XI.
- Paine, Thomas, *The Rights of Man,* 1791. (Many editions.) Paine's eloquent

response to Burke's *Reflections* resulted in his conviction for treason and banishment from England.

• Pernoud, G. and S. Flaisser, eds., *The French Revolution,* New York, 1960. Contains eyewitness reports.

• Rousseau, Jean-Jacques, *Discourse on the Origin of Inequality,* 1754. (Many editions.)

• ———, *The Social Contract,* 1762. (Many editions.) These two tracts provided a philosophical justification for both the American and French Revolutions.

Sieyès, Abbé, *What Is the Third Estate?,* 1789. (Many editions.) The most important political pamphlet in the decisive year 1789.

Stewart, John Hall, *A Documentary Survey of the French Revolution,* New York, 1951.

Thompson, J. M., *French Revolution Documents, 1789–1794,* Oxford, 1948.

Young, Arthur, *Travels in France during the Years 1787, 1788, 1789,* New York, 1972. France on the eve of revolution, as seen by a perceptive English observer.

Chapter 21

THE INDUSTRIAL REVOLUTION

Providence has assigned to man the glorious function of vastly improving the productions of nature by judicious culture, of working them up into objects of comfort and elegance with the least possible expenditure of human labor—an undeniable position which forms the basis of our Factory System.

     —Andrew Ure, *The Philosophy of Manufactures*

There have been many revolutions in industry during the history of Western civilization, and there will undoubtedly be many more. Periods of rapid technological change are often called revolutions, and justifiably so. But, historically, there is one Industrial Revolution. Occurring during the hundred years after 1780, it witnessed the first breakthrough from a rural, handicraft economy to one dominated by urban, machine-driven manufacturing.

  The uniqueness of the revolution

The fact that it was a European revolution was not accidental. Although Europe was, in the mid–eighteenth century, a continent still predominantly agricultural, although the majority of its people remained illiterate and destined to live out impoverished lives within sight of the place they were born—despite these conditions, which in our eyes might make Europe appear "underdeveloped," it was of course no such thing. European merchants and men of commerce were established as the world's foremost manufacturers and traders. Rulers relied upon this class of men to provide them with the wherewithal to maintain the economy of their states, both in terms of flourishing commercial activity and of victorious armies and navies. Those men, in turn, had for the most part extracted from their rulers the understanding that the property they possessed, whether invested in land, or commerce, or both, was theirs outright. That understanding, substantiated by the written contracts that were replacing unwritten, long-acknowledged custom, helped persuade merchants, bankers, traders, and entrepreneurs that they lived in a world that was stable, rational, and predictable. Believing the world was so, they

  A European revolution: the commercial class

moved out into it with self-confidence and in hopes of increasing their own, and their country's, prosperity. Only in Europe does one find these presuppositions and this class of men in the eighteenth century; only through the activities of such people could the Industrial Revolution have taken place.

These capitalists could not have prospered without an expanding market for their goods. The existence of this market explains further why it was in Europe that the Industrial Revolution took place. Ever since the beginning of the seventeenth century, overseas commercial exploration and development had been opening new territories to European trade. India, Africa, North and South America—all had been woven into the pattern of European economic expansion. The colonies and commercial dependencies took economic shape at Europe's behest. Even the new United States had not been able to declare its economic independence. Whatever commercial and industrial design Europe might devise, all would be compelled to accommodate themselves to Europe's demands.

A third factor helping to ensure that the revolution would occur in Europe was population growth which occurred throughout Western Europe in the eighteenth century. Increasing populations, along with overseas expansion, provided an ever-growing market for manufactured goods. It furnished, as well, an adequate pool—eventually a surplus—of laboring men, women, and children to work in the manufacture of those goods either at home or in factories.

See color map facing page 705

Yet these factors—a thriving commercial class, growing markets, and an expanding population—while helping to explain why the Industrial Revolution took place in eighteenth-century Europe, fail to tell us enough about its origins. For that understanding, we must change our focus from Europe as a whole to its most prosperous state, England.

1. THE INDUSTRIAL REVOLUTION IN ENGLAND

It was in England that the Industrial Revolution first took hold. England's economy had progressed further than that of any other country in the direction of abundance. In simplest terms: fewer people were engaged in the crude struggle to do no more than remain alive; more people were in a position to sell a surplus of the goods they produced to an increasingly expanding market; and more people had money enough to purchase the goods that market offered. English laborers, though poorly enough paid, enjoyed a higher standard of living than their continental counterparts. They ate white bread, not brown, and meat with some regularity. Because a smaller portion of their income was spent on food, they might occasionally have some to spare for articles which were bought rather than homemade.

Further evidence of this increasing abundance was the number of bills for the enclosure of agricultural land passed by an English Parliament sympathetic to capitalism during the last half of the eighteenth century. The enclosure of fields, pasture, and waste lands into large fenced tracts of land under the private ownership and individual management of capitalist landlords, although it deprived local agricultural laborers of the right to share in the use of common lands as they had in past times, meant an increased food supply to feed an increasing and increasingly urban population. Yet another sign of England's abundance was its growing supply of surplus capital, derived from investment in land or commerce, and available for further employment to finance new economic enterprises. London, already a leading center for the world's trade, served as a headquarters for the transfer of raw material, capital, and manufactured products. For example, Portugal alone channeled as much as £50,000 in Brazilian gold per week into London. Thus English capitalists had enough money on hand to underwrite and sustain an industrial revolution.

*Abundance: food and
capital*

But the revolution required more than money. It required habits of mind that would encourage investments in enterprises that were risky, but that represented an enormous potential for gain. In England, far more than on the Continent, the pursuit of wealth was perceived to be a worthy end in life. The aristocracy of Europe had, from the period of the Renaissance, cultivated the notion of "gentlemanly" conduct, in part to hold the line against social encroachments from below. The English aristocrats, whose privileges were meager when compared with those of continental nobles, had never ceased to respect men who made money; nor had they disdained to make whatever they could for themselves. They invested and speculated. Their scramble to enclose their lands reflected this sympathy with aggressive capitalism. Below the aristocracy, there was even less of a barrier separating the world of urban commerce from that of the rural gentry. Most of the men who pioneered as entrepreneurs in the early years of the Industrial Revolution sprang from the minor gentry or yeoman farmer class. To a degree unknown on the Continent, men from this sort of background felt themselves free to rise as high as their abilities might carry them on the social and economic ladder.

(2) climate of opinion

Eighteenth-century England was not by any means free of social snobbery: lords looked down upon bankers, as bankers looked down upon artisans. But a lord's disdain might well be tempered by the fact of his own grandfather's origins in the countinghouse. And the banker would gladly lend money to the artisan if convinced that the artisan's invention might make them both a fortune. The English, as a nation, were not afraid of business. They respected the sensible, the practical, and the financially successful. Robinson Crusoe, that desert island entrepreneur, was one of their models. In the novel (1719) by Daniel Defoe, the hero had used his wits to master nature and become lord

*Respect for financial
success*

of a thriving economy. His triumph was not diminished because it was a worldly triumph; far from it. "It is our vanity which urges us on," the economist Adam Smith, defender of laissez-faire capitalism, declared. And thank God, Smith implied, for our blessed vanity! An individual's desire to show himself a worldly success worked to produce prosperity for the country as a whole.

(3) increasing markets

England's eighteenth-century prosperity was based upon an expanding market for whatever goods it manufactured. Its small size and the fact that it was an island encouraged the development of a nationwide domestic market. The absence of a system of internal tolls and tariffs, such as existed on the Continent, meant that goods could be moved freely to the place where they could fetch the best price. This freedom of movement was assisted by a constantly improving transportation system. Parliament in the years just before the Industrial Revolution passed acts to finance turnpike building at the rate of forty per year; the same period saw the construction of canals and the further opening up of harbors and navigable streams. Unlike the government of France, whose cumbrous mercantilist adventures as often as not thwarted economic growth, the English Parliament believed that the most effective way in which it could help businessmen was to assist them in helping themselves.

Overseas expansion

Parliament's members had every reason to promote England's economic fortunes. Some were businessmen themselves; others had invested heavily in commerce. Hence their eagerness to encourage by statute the construction of canals, the establishment of banks, and the enclosure of common lands. And hence their insistence, throughout the eighteenth century, that England's foreign policy respond to its commercial needs. At the end of every major eighteenth-century war, England wrested overseas territories from its enemies. At the same time, England was penetrating hitherto unexploited territories, such as India and South America, in search of further potential markets and resources. In 1759, over one-third of all British exports went to the colonies; by 1784, if we include the newly established United States, that figure had increased to one-half. The English possessed a merchant marine capable of transporting goods across the world, and a navy practiced in the art of protecting its commercial fleets. By 1780 England's markets, together with its fleet and its established position at the center of world trade, combined to produce a potential for expansion so great as to compel the Industrial Revolution.

The cotton industry

English entrepreneurs and technicians responded to the compulsion by revolutionizing the production of cotton textile goods. Although far less cotton goods were made in eighteenth-century England than wool, the extent of their manufacture by 1760 was such as to make cotton more than an infant industry. Tariffs prohibiting the importation of East Indian cottons, imposed by Parliament to stimulate the sale of woolen goods, had instead served to spur the manufacture of domestic cotton goods. Thus the revolution, when it did occur, took

The Spinning Jenny. Invented by James Hargreaves in 1767

place in an already well-established industry. Yet without the invention of some sort of machinery which would improve the quality and at the same time dramatically increase the quantity of spun cotton thread, the necessary breakthrough would not have come. The invention of the fly-shuttle, which greatly speeded up the process of weaving, only made the bottleneck in the prior process of spinning the more apparent. The problem was solved by the invention of a series of comparatively simple mechanical devices, the most important of which was the spinning jenny, invented by James Hargreaves, a carpenter and hand-loom weaver, in 1767 (patented 1770). The spinning jenny, named after the inventor's wife, was a compound spinning wheel, capable of producing sixteen threads at once. The threads it spun were not strong enough, however, to be used for the longitudinal fibers, or warp, of cotton cloth. It was not until the invention of the water frame by Richard Arkwright, a barber, in 1769, that quantity production of both warp and woof (latitudinal fibers) became possible. This invention, along with that of the spinning mule, conceived of by Samuel Crompton in 1779, and combining the features of both the jenny and the frame, solved the problems that had heretofore curtailed the output of cotton textiles. They increased the mechanical advantage over the spinning wheel enormously. From six to twenty-four times the amount of yarn could be spun on a jenny as on the wheel, by the end of the century two to three hundred times as much on the mule. Just as important, the quality of the thread improved not only in terms of strength but also of fineness.

Once these machines came into general use, the revolution proceeded apace. Cotton suited the mule and the jenny because it was a

Eli Whitney

Growth of factories

The extent of the cotton trade

tougher thread than wool—fiber which could withstand the rough treatment it received at the mechanical hands of the crude early machines. In addition, the supply of cotton was expandable in a way that the supply of wool was not. The cotton gin, invented by the American Eli Whitney in 1793, separated seeds from fiber mechanically, thereby making cotton available at a lower price. The invention kept America's slave plantations profitable, and meant that supply would be available to meet increased demand.

The first machinery was cheap enough to allow spinners to continue to work at home. But as it increased in size, it was more and more frequently housed not in the cottages of individual spinners, but in workshops or mills located near water which could be used to power the machines. Eventually, with the further development of steam-driven equipment, the mills could be built wherever it might suit the entrepreneur—frequently in towns and cities in the north of England.

The transition from home to factory industry was of course not accomplished overnight. Cotton yarn continued to be spun at home at the same time that it was being produced in mills. Eventually, however, the low cost of building and operating a large plant, plus the efficiency realized by bringing workers together under one roof, meant that larger mills more and more frequently replaced smaller workshops. By 1851, three-fifths of those employed in cotton manufacture worked in medium- to large-size mills. Weaving remained a home industry until the invention of a cheap, practical power loom convinced entrepreneurs that they could save money by moving the process from home to mill. Hand-loom weavers were probably the most obvious victims of the Industrial Revolution in England. Their unwillingness to surrender their livelihood to machinery meant that they continued to work for less and less—by 1830, no more than a pitiful six shillings a week. In 1815 they numbered about 250,000; by 1850, there remained only 40,000; by 1860, only 3,000.

English cotton textiles flooded the world market from the 1780s. Here was a light material, suitable for the climates of Africa, India, and the more temperate zones of North America. Here was a material cheap enough to make it possible for millions who had never before enjoyed the comfort of washable body clothes to do so. And here was material fine enough to tempt the rich to experiment with muslins and calicos in a way they had not done before. Figures speak eloquently of the revolutionary change wrought by the expanding industry. In 1760, England exported less than £250,000 worth of cotton goods; by 1800 it was exporting over £5 million worth. In 1760, England imported 2.5 million pounds of raw cotton; in 1787, 22 million pounds; in 1837, 366 million pounds. By 1800, cotton accounted for about 5 percent of the national income of the country; by 1812, from 7 to 8 percent. By 1815, the export of cotton textiles amounted to 40 percent of the value of all domestic goods exported from Great Britain. Although the price of manufactured cotton goods fell dramatically, the market expanded so rapidly that profits continued to increase.

Unlike the changes in the textile industry, those occurring in the manufacture of iron were not great enough to warrant their being labeled revolutionary. Yet they were most significant. Britain's abundant supply of coal, combined with its advanced transportation network, allowed the English, from the middle of the eighteenth century, to substitute coal for wood in the heating of molten metal. A series of discoveries made fuel savings possible, along with a higher quality of iron, and the manufacture of a greater variety of iron products. Demand rose sharply during the war years at the end of the century. It remained high as a result of calls for plant machinery, agricultural implements, and hardware; it rose dramatically with the coming of railways in the 1830s and 1840s. Britain was exporting 571,000 tons of iron in 1814; in 1852, it exported 1,036,000 tons out of a world total of almost 2,000,000—more iron than was made by all the rest of the world combined.

The need for more coal required the mining of deeper and deeper veins. In 1712, Thomas Newcomen had devised a crude but effective steam engine for pumping water from mines. Though of value to the coal industry, it was of less use in other industries, since it was wasteful of both fuel and power. In 1763, James Watt, a maker of scientific instruments at the University of Glasgow, was asked to repair a model of the Newcomen engine. While engaged in this task he conceived the idea that the machine would be greatly improved if a separate chamber were added to condense the steam, so as to eliminate the necessity of cooling the cylinder. He patented his first engine incorporating this device in 1769. Watt's genius as an inventor was not matched by his business ability. He admitted that he would "rather face a loaded cannon than settle a disputed account or make a bargain." As a consequence, he fell into debt in attempting to place his machines on the market. He was rescued by Matthew Boulton, a wealthy hardware manufacturer of Birmingham. The two men formed a partnership,

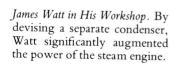

James Watt in His Workshop. By devising a separate condenser, Watt significantly augmented the power of the steam engine.

The Staffordshire Collieries. In the building to the right is a whimsey, or coal-powered steam engine, used to lift loads of coal from the mines.

with Boulton providing the capital. By 1800 the firm had sold 289 engines for use in factories and mines. The steam engine replaced water as the principle motive force in industry slowly. In 1850 more than a third of the power used in woolen manufacture and an eighth of that used in cotton was still produced by water. Nevertheless, there is no question that without the steam engine there could have been no industrial expansion on the scale that we have described.

Other advances

Other industries experienced profound changes during the hundred years of the Industrial Revolution. Many of those changes came in response to the growth of textile manufacture. The chemical industry, for example, developed new methods of dyeing and bleaching, as well as improved methods of production in the fields of soap and glass-making. Production of goods increased across the board, as profits from the boom in manufacturing increased the demand for new and more sophisticated articles. Pottery, metalware—these and other trades expanded to meet demands, in the process adopting methods that in most instances reduced cost and speeded manufacture.

The limits of the Industrial Revolution

To understand fully the nature of the Industrial Revolution in England one must not lose sight of two important factors: the first is that dramatic as the revolution was, it happened over a period of two or three generations, at varying paces in different industries. Some men and women continued to work at home, much as their grandfathers and grandmothers had. Old tools and old methods were not immediately replaced by new ones, any more than populations fled the countryside overnight for the city. Second, the revolution was accomplished from a very limited technological and theoretical base. Except in the chemical industry, change was not the result of scientific research. It was the product of empirical experimentation—in some cases, of little more than creative tinkering. To say this is not to disparage the work of men such as Arkwright, Hargreaves, Watt, and their like. It is to suggest, however, the reason why England, without a national system of education on any level, was nonetheless able to accomplish the revolution it did. Nor are these remarks intended to belittle the magnitude of the change. What occurred in England was a revolution because of the way in which it reshaped the lives, not just of the English, but of people across the globe. By responding as it did to the demands of its apparently insatiable markets, England made a revolution every bit as profound and long-lasting as that which occurred simultaneously in France.

2. THE INDUSTRIAL REVOLUTION ON THE CONTINENT

The Industrial Revolution came in time to the Continent, but not to any important degree before about 1830. Manufacturing in eighteenth-century France and Germany clustered in regions whose proximity to raw materials, access to markets, and traditional attachment to particular skills had resulted in their development as industrial centers. Flanders and Normandy in France, and Saxony in Germany were centers for the manufacture of woolen cloth; Switzerland, southern Germany, and Normandy, of cottons; Wallonia (the area around Liège in Belgium), the Marne valley, and Silesia in Germany, of iron. Yet for a variety of reasons, these areas failed to experience the late-eighteenth-century breakthrough that occurred in Britain. Nor were they capable at first of imitating Britain's success, once they began to perceive the great economic advantages that its pronounced lead was bringing it. There were a number of reasons for the delay of continental industrialization. Whereas England's transportation system was highly developed, those of France and Germany were not. France was far larger than England, its rivers were not as easily navigable, its seaports farther apart. Central Europe was so divided into tiny principalities, each with its own set of tolls and tariffs, as to make the transportation of raw materials or manufactured goods over any considerable distance most impractical. Nor was France itself free of the sorts of regulations that thwarted easy shipments. In addition, the Continent was not as blessed with an abundance of raw materials as England. France, the Low Countries, and Germany had to import wool. Europe lacked an abundant supply of the fuel that was the new source of industrial energy. Few major coal deposits were known to exist, while an abundant supply of timber discouraged exploration that might have resulted in their discovery.

Reasons for delay:
(1) lack of transport and raw materials

(2) *lack of entrepreneurial*
spirit

Distances and distinctions between social and economic ranks were far greater on the Continent than in England. Money was not the social solvent in France and Germany that it was across the Channel. Before the French Revolution, continental aristocrats were unwilling to invest in commercial enterprises they believed would damage their social standing. In some countries, laws prevented aristocrats from engaging in business. After the revolution middle-class Frenchmen, though free in theory to rise as high on the social and economic ladder as they might aspire, appear largely to have remained content to make only enough money to sustain a modest-size business. Those revolutionary constitutional changes which had favored the lower middle class by encouraging its acquisition of property, prevented the growth of industry by dispersing capital into the hands of innumerable small-scale enterprises. The entrepreneurial spirit that compelled Englishmen to drive competitors to the wall was not as highly developed in France and Germany in the years after 1815. Exhausted by the competitiveness of war, and fearful of the disruptions that war brought in its train, continental businessmen remained far more willing than the English to keep on manufacturing and selling on the same scale they always had.[1]

(3) *effect of wars*

The Continent did not simply stand idle as England assumed its industrial lead. The pace of mechanization was increasing in the 1780s. But the French Revolution and the wars which followed disrupted growth which might have otherwise taken place. Battles fought on French, German, and Italian soil destroyed factories and machinery. Although ironmaking increased to meet the demands of the wars, techniques remained what they had been. Commerce was badly hurt both by British destruction of French merchant shipping and by Napoleon's Continental System. Probably the revolutionary change most beneficial to industrial advance in Europe was the removal of previous restraints on the movement of capital and labor; for example, the abolition of trade guilds, and the reduction in the number of tariff barriers across the Continent. On balance, however, the revolutionary and Napoleonic wars clearly thwarted industrial development on the Continent, while at the same time intensifying it in England.

Increases after 1815: (1)
population rise

A number of factors combined to produce a climate more generally conducive to industrialization on the Continent after 1815. Population continued to increase, not only throughout Europe, but in those areas now more and more dependent upon the importation of manufactured goods—Latin America, for example. These increases, which doubled the populations of most European countries between 1800 and 1850, meant that the Continent would be supplied with a growing number of producers and consumers. More people did not necessarily mean further industrialization. In Ireland, for example, where other

---

[1] On this point, see David S. Landes, *The Unbound Prometheus*, pp. 132–33.

necessary factors were absent, more people meant less food. But in those countries with an already well-established commercial and industrial base—France and Germany, for example—increased population did encourage the adoption of the technologies and methods of production that had transformed Britain.

Transportation improved in western Europe both during and following the Napoleonic wars. The Austrian Empire added over 30,000 miles of roads between 1830 and 1847; Belgium almost doubled its road network in the same period; France built, in addition to roads, 2,000 miles of canals. In the United States, where industrialization was occurring at an increasingly rapid rate after 1830, road mileage jumped from 21,000 miles in 1800 to 170,000 in 1856. When these improvements were combined with the introduction of rail transport in the 1840s, the resulting increase in markets available to all Western countries encouraged them to introduce methods of manufacturing that would help meet new demands.

In this endeavor, governments played a more direct role on the Continent than in Britain. Napoleon's rationalization of French and imperial institutions had introduced Europe to the practice of state intervention. His legal code, which guaranteed freedom of contract and facilitated the establishment of joint-stock enterprises, encouraged other rulers to provide a similar framework for commercial expansion. In Prussia, lack of private capital necessitated state operation of a large proportion of that country's mines. In no European country but Britain would railways be built without the financial assistance of the state. In the private sector, as well, more attention was given on the Continent than in England to the need for artificial stimulation to produce industrial change. It was in Belgium that the first joint-stock investment bank—the Société Générale—was founded, an institution designed to facilitate the accumulation of ready capital for investment in industry and commerce. Europeans were also willing for the state

(2) improved transportation

(3) centralization

A Swedish Mining Town, 1790

Silk Weavers of Lyon, 1850. The first significant working-class uprisings in nineteenth-century France occurred here in 1831 and 1834. Note the domestic character of the working conditions.

to establish educational systems whose aim, among others, was to produce a well-trained elite capable of assisting in the development of industrial technology. What Britain had produced almost by chance, the Europeans began to reproduce by design.

Until the Continent produced its own technicians it was compelled to rely on British expertise. And another reason why the pace of continental, and also American, industrialization, even after 1815, remained far slower than in Britain was Britain's natural reluctance to see its methods of production pirated by others. British industrialists believed it their patriotic duty to prevent the exportation of their techniques, although they were more than willing to raid the Continent for technological experts: Matthew Boulton imported skilled workers from Vienna and Sweden. Continental entrepreneurs likewise argued that it was patriotism, not profit, that inspired them to compete with the British. "Our reasons for building our factory were exactly those which made you oppose it," a German firm wrote to Boulton; "that is patriotic zeal." Until 1825, British artisans were forbidden to emigrate; until 1842, much innovative machinery could not be exported. Laws did not, however, prevent the movement of creative technician-entrepreneurs and their particular skills; many Englishmen, during the first part of the nineteenth century, made fortunes as they taught others in Europe and America to do what they had taught themselves. One such man was William Cockerill, who began his career in England as a carpenter. He and his sons built cotton-spinning equipment on the Continent during the revolutionary wars. In 1817, they purchased the palace of the former bishops of Liège, converting it to a factory producing machinery and steam engines. Yet despite the presence of entrepreneurs like the Cockerills, or of continental counterparts such

(4) the lack of technicians

as the Westphalian Fritz Harkort, who built and sold steam engines across Europe in the 1820s and 1830s, the general lack of large numbers of European technicians, experts, and entrepreneurs undoubtedly hampered rapid industrial expansion in France, Germany, and elsewhere.

The growth of the textile industry in Europe was patterned by the circumstances of the Napoleonic wars. The supply of cotton to the Continent had been interrupted, thanks to the British blockade, but the military's greater demand for woolen cloth meant that expansion occurred more rapidly in the latter than in the former industry. By 1820, the spinning of wool by machine was the common practice on the Continent; weaving, however, was still accomplished largely by hand. Centers for the production of wool were located at Rheims and in Alsace, in France; in what is now Belgium; and, in Germany, in Saxony and Silesia. Mechanization was retarded because manual labor was cheap, and by the important fact that since Britain's market was so large, continental profits too often depended upon the manufacture of some particular specialty not made in England, and therefore without broad commercial appeal. Cotton manufacture was curtailed by the same circumstances. In France, as a result, mechanization occurred first in the silk industry and those sections of the cotton industry which produced finer specialty materials—lace, for example. A tradition of prestige associated with the production of luxury goods, dating back to the reign of Louis XIV, encouraged entrepreneurs to invest in this branch of the textile industry. They were willing to forgo mass markets in the hope that their products

Textiles

A German Textile Factory, 1848. This is an unusually large manufacturing facility for this period on the Continent.

would not meet with British competition. France nevertheless remained the largest continental producer of cotton goods, followed, again, by Belgium, the German territories of the Rhine valley, Saxony, Silesia, and Bavaria.

In the area of heavy industry on the Continent, the picture was much the same as in textiles: i.e., gradual advances in the adoption of technological innovation against a background of more general resistance to change. Here, however, because change came later than in Britain, it coincided with an increased demand for various goods that had come into being as a result of industrialization and urbanization: iron pipe, much in use by mid-century in cities for gas, water, and drainage; metal machinery, now replacing earlier wooden prototypes. Consequently, the iron industry took the lead over textiles on the Continent, accompanied by an increase, where possible, in the production of coal. Coal was scarce, however; in the Rhineland, wood was still used to manufacture iron. The result was an unwillingness on the part of entrepreneurs to make as extensive use of the steam engine as they might have otherwise; it used too much fuel. In France, as late as 1844, hydraulic (i.e., water-driven) engines were employed far more often for the manufacture of iron than were steam engines. One further problem hampered the development of continental heavy industry during the first half of the nineteenth century. British competition forced continental machine construction firms to scramble for whatever orders they could get. This need to respond to a variety of requests meant that it was difficult for firms to specialize in a single product. The result was a lack of standardization, and continued production to order, when rationalization and specialization would have resulted in an increased volume of production.

3. THE COMING OF RAILWAYS

By about 1840, then, European countries, and to some degree the United States, were moving gradually along the course of industrialization traced by Britain, producing far more than they had, yet nothing like as much as their spectacular pace setter. Within the next ten years, the coming of the railways was to alter that situation. Though Britain by no means lost its lead, the stimulus provided generally to Western economies by the introduction of railway systems throughout much of the world carried Europe and America far enough and fast enough to allow them to become genuine competitors with the British.

Railways came into being in answer to two needs. The first was the obvious desire on the part of entrepreneurs to transport their goods as quickly and cheaply as possible across long distances. Despite already-mentioned improvements in transportation during the years before 1830, the movement of heavy materials, particularly coal, remained a problem. It is significant that the first modern railway was built in England in 1825 from the Durham coal field of Stockton to Darlington, near the coast. "Tramways"—parallel tracks along which coal carts were pulled by horses—had long been in use at pitheads to haul coal short distances. The Stockton to Darlington railway was a logical extension of this device, designed to answer the transportation needs produced by constantly expanding industrialization. The man primarily responsible for the design of the first steam railway was George Stephenson, a self-made engineer who had not learned to read until he was seventeen. He talked a group of northern England investors into the merits of steam traction and was given full liberty to carry out his plans. The locomotives on the Stockton-Darlington line traveled at fifteen miles per hour, the fastest rate at which human beings had yet moved overland.

Railways were also built in response to other than purely industrial needs: specifically, the need for capitalists to invest their money. Englishmen such as those who had made sizable fortunes in textiles, once they had paid out workers' wages and plowed back substantial capital in their factories, retained a surplus profit for which they wanted a decent yet reliable return. Railways provided them with the solution to their problem. Though by no means as reliable as had been hoped, railway investment proved capable of more than satisfying the capitalists' demands. No sooner did the first combined passenger and goods service open in 1830, on the Liverpool to Manchester line, than plans were formulated and money pledged to extend rail systems throughout Europe, the Americas, and beyond. In 1830, there were no more than a few dozen miles of railway in the world. By 1840, there were

Railways as goods carriers

Railways as an investment opportunity

The New Railway Age. Left: Stephenson's *Rocket.* A reconstruction of the railway engine built by George Stephenson in 1829. Right: "The Railway Juggernaut of 1845." A cartoon from the English humor magazine *Punch* satirizing speculation—often financially disastrous—in railway stocks.

Thomas Brassey

Size and scope of the railway construction industry

The "navvies"

over 4,500 miles; by 1850, over 23,000. The English contractor, Thomas Brassey, the most famous, but by no means the only one of his kind, built railways in Italy, Canada, Argentina, India, and Australia.

The railway boom accelerated industrialization generally. Not only did it increase enormously the demand for coal and for a variety of heavy manufactured goods—rails, locomotives, carriages, signals, switches; by enabling goods to move faster from factory to salesroom, railways decreased the time it took to sell those goods. Quicker sales meant, in turn, a quicker return on capital investment, money which could then be reinvested in the manufacture of more goods. Finally, by opening up the world market as it had never been before, the railway boom stimulated the production of such a quantity of material goods as to ensure the rapid completion of the West's industrialization.

The building of a railway line was an undertaking on a scale infinitely greater than the building of a factory. Railway construction required capital investment beyond the capacity of any single individual. In Britain, a factory might be worth anything from £20,000 to £200,000. The average cost of twenty-seven of the more important railway lines constructed between 1830 and 1853 was £2 million. The average labor force of a factory ranged from 50 to 300. The average labor force of a railway, after construction, was 2,500. Because a railway crossed the property of a large number of individual landowners, each of whom would naturally demand as much remuneration as he thought he could get, the planning of an efficient and economical route was a tricky and time-consuming business. The entrepreneur and contractor had to concern themselves not only with the purchase of right-of-way. They also contended with problems raised by the destruction of sizable portions of already existing urban areas, to make room for stations and switching yards. And they had to select a route that would be as free as possible of the hills and valleys that would necessitate the construction of expensive tunnels, cuts, and embankments. Railway-builders ran tremendous risks. Portions of most lines were subcontracted at fixed bids to contractors of limited experience. A spate of bad weather might delay construction to the point where builders would be lucky to bring in the finished job within 25 percent of their original bid. Of the thirty major contractors on the London to Birmingham line, ten failed completely.

If the business of a contractor was marked by uncertainty, that of the construction worker was characterized by back-breaking labor. The English "navvies," who built railways not only throughout Britain but around the world, were a remarkable breed. Their name derived from "navigator," a term applied to the construction workers on England's eighteenth-century canals. The work that they accomplished was prodigious. Because there is little friction between a

Construction of the London to Birmingham Railway, London, 1838. This drawing of the building of retaining walls in a new railway cut evokes the chaos created by railway construction within urban areas.

train's wheels and its tracks, it can transport heavy loads easily. But lack of friction ceases to be an advantage when a train has to climb or descend a grade, thereby running the risk of slippage. Hence the need for comparatively level roadbeds; and hence the need for laborers to construct those tunnels, cuts, and embankments that would keep the roadbeds level. Navvies worked in gangs, whose migrations throughout the countryside traced the course of railway development. They were a rough lot, living in temporary encampments, often with women who were not their wives. The Irish navvies were a particularly tough breed. A sign posted by local residents in Scotland in 1845 warned that if all the Irish navvies were not "off the ground and out of the country" in a week, they would be driven out "by the strength of our armes and a good pick shaft."

The magnitude of the navvies' accomplishment was extraordinary. In England and in much of the rest of the world, mid–nineteenth-century railways were constructed almost entirely without the aid of machinery. An assistant engineer on the London to Birmingham line, in calculating the magnitude of that particular construction, determined that the labor involved was the equivalent of lifting 25 billion cubic feet of earth and stone one foot high. This he compared with the feat of building the Great Pyramid, a task he estimated had involved the hoisting of some 16 billion tons. But whereas the building of the pyramid had required over 200,000 men and had taken twenty years, the construction of the London to Birmingham railway was accomplished by 20,000 men in less than five years. Translated into individual terms, a navvy was expected to move an average of twenty tons of earth per day. Railways were laid upon an almost infinite base of human muscle and sweat.

The magnitude of the navvies' achievement

Railway Navvies. Without the aid of machinery, the burden of building Britain's railways fell on the backs of men such as these.

4. INDUSTRIALIZATION AFTER 1850

Britain still the leader

In the years between 1850 and 1870, Britain remained very much the industrial giant of the West. But France, Germany, Belgium, and the United States assumed the position of challengers. In the iron industry, Britain's rate of growth during these years was not as great as that of either France or Germany (5.2 percent for Britain, as against 6.7 percent for France and 10.2 percent for Germany). But in 1870 Britain was still producing half the world's pig iron; 3.5 times as much as the United States, more than 4 times as much as Germany, and more than 5 times as much as France. Although the number of cotton spindles increased from 5.5 to 11.5 million in the United States between 1852 and 1861, and by significant but not as spectacular percentages in European countries, Britain in 1861 had 31 million spindles at work in comparison with France's 5.5 million, Germany's 2 million, Switzerland's 1.3 million, and Austria's 1.8 million.

Continuing European advance

Most of the gains experienced in Europe came as a result of continuing changes in those areas we have come to recognize as important for sustained industrial growth. The improved transportation systems that resulted from the spread of railways helped encourage an increase in the free movement of goods. International monetary unions were established, and restrictions removed on international waterways such as the Danube. The Prussian *Zollverein,* or tariff union, an organization designed to facilitate internal free trade, was established in 1818 and was extended over the next twenty years to include most of the German principalities outside Austria. Free trade went hand in hand with further removal of barriers to the freedom to enter trades and to practice business unhampered by restrictive regulation. Control of guilds and corporations over artisan production was abolished in Austria in 1859 and in most of Germany by the mid-1860s. Laws against usury, most of which had ceased to be enforced, were officially abandoned in Britain, Holland, Belgium, and in many parts of Germany. Governmental regulation of the operation of mines was surrendered by the Prussian state in the 1850s, freeing entrepreneurs to develop resources as they saw fit. The formation of investment banks proceeded apace, encouraged by an important increase in the money supply, and therefore an easing of credit, following the opening of the California gold fields in 1849.

A further reason for increased European production was the growing trade in raw materials. Wool and hides imported from Australia helped diminish the consequences of the cotton shortage suffered after the outbreak of the United States Civil War and the Union blockade of the American South. Other importations—guano from the Pacific, vegetable oils from Africa, pyrites (sulfides) from Spain—stimulated the scale of food production and both altered and increased the manufacture of soap, candles, and finished textiles. Finally, discoveries of new sources of coal, particularly in the Pas-de-Calais region of France and in the Ruhr valley in Germany, had dramatic repercussions. Production of coal in France rose from 4.4 million to 13.3 million tons between 1850 and 1869; during the same years, German production increased from 4.2 million to 23.7 million tons.

By 1870 Europe had by no means turned its back on agriculture. Fifty percent of France's labor force remained on farms. Agricultural laborers were the single largest occupational category in Britain during the 1860s. Great stretches of the Continent—Spain, southern Italy, eastern Europe—were almost untouched by the Industrial Revolution. And in the industrialized countries, much work was still accomplished in tiny workshops or at home. Yet if Europe was by no means wholly industrial, it was far and away the most industrially advanced portion of the globe—and not by accident. In order to maintain its position of producer to the world, Europe, and Britain particularly, made certain that no other areas stood a chance to compete. Europe used its economic and, when necessary, its military strength to ensure that the world remained divided between the producers of manufactured goods—Europe itself—and suppliers of the necessary raw materials—everyone else. Often this arrangement suited those in other parts of the world who made their money by providing the raw materials that fueled the European economy. Cotton-growers in the southern United States, sugar-growers in the Caribbean, wheat-growers in the Ukraine—all remained content with arrangements as dictated by the industrialized West. Those countries which expressed their discontent—Egypt, for example, which in the 1830s attempted to establish its own cotton textile industry—were soon put in their place by a show of force. Western Europeans, believing in their right to industrial leadership in the world, saw nothing wrong with employing soldiers, if they had to, to make others understand their destiny.

Increased trade in raw materials

Europe's economy within the world

SELECTED READINGS

- *Items so designated are available in paperback editions.*
- Ashton, T. S., *The Industrial Revolution, 1760–1830*, London, 1948. A standard short introduction.

  Checkland, S. G., *The Rise of Industrial Society in England, 1815–1885*, New York, 1965. Emphasizes the economic organization of England.
- Deane, Phyllis, *The First Industrial Revolution*, Cambridge, 1965.

  Henderson, W. O., *The Industrialization of Europe, 1780–1914*, New York, 1969.

  ———, *The State and the Industrial Revolution in Prussia, 1740–1870*, Liverpool, 1958. A biographical approach. Good on technical education.
- Hobsbawm, Eric, *Industry and Empire: 1750 to the Present Day*, New York, 1968. A general survey of industrialization in Britain, written from a Marxist perspective.
- Landes, David S., *The Unbound Prometheus*, London, 1969. An excellent treatment of the technological innovations and economic results of the Industrial Revolution.

  McManners, John, *European History: Men, Machines and Freedom*, New York, 1967.

  Mantoux, Paul, *The Industrial Revolution in the Eighteenth Century*, rev. ed., New York, 1961. The beginnings of the modern factory system in England.
- Taylor, George Rogers, *The Transportation Revolution, 1815–1860*, New York, 1968.

  Usher, A. P., *A History of Mechanical Invention*, Cambridge, Mass., 1954.

SOURCE MATERIALS

  Dodd, George, *Days at the Factories; or the Manufacturing Industry of Great Britain Described, and Illustrated by Numerous Engravings of Machines and Processes*, Totawa, N.J., 1975. A reprint of the 1850 edition.

  Mitchell, Brian R., and Phyllis Deane, *Abstract of British Historical Statistics*, Cambridge, 1962. The single best source for statistics on population, trade, manufacturing, etc.
- Smith, Adam, *An Inquiry into the Nature and Causes of the Wealth of Nations*, Chicago, 1977. Written in 1776, this revolutionary work called for the end of mercantilism.

  Ward, J. T., *The Factory System, 1830–1855*, New York, 1970. Excerpts from contemporary documents describing, defending, and criticizing the factory system and industrialization.

Chapter 22

CONSEQUENCES OF INDUSTRIALIZATION: URBANIZATION AND CLASS CONSCIOUSNESS (1800–1850)

What Art was to the ancient world, Science is to the modern: The distinctive faculty. In the minds of men the useful has succeeded the beautiful. Yet rightly understood, Manchester is as great a human exploit as Athens.

—Benjamin Disraeli, *Coningsby*

The Industrial Revolution was more than an important event in the economic and technological history of the West. It helped to reshape the patterns of life for men and women, first in Britain, then in Europe and America, and eventually throughout much of the world. By increasing the scale of production, the Industrial Revolution brought about the factory system, which in turn compelled the migration of millions from the countryside and small towns into cities. Once in those cities, men and women had to learn a new way of life, and learn it quickly: how to discipline themselves to the factory whistle and survive in a slum, if they were first-generation urban workers; how to manage a workforce and achieve respectable prominence for themselves in the community, if they were businessmen and their wives. One particular lesson that industrialization and urbanization taught was that of class consciousness. Men and women, to a far greater degree than heretofore, began to perceive themselves as part of a class with interests of its own, and in opposition to the interests of men and women in other classes.

We shall examine this range of social and cultural changes as they occurred during the first fifty years or so of the nineteenth century, after looking briefly first at the condition of the bulk of the popula-

Consequences of the Industrial Revolution

tion, which, despite industrialization, remained on the land. Since the Industrial Revolution came first to Britain, our focus will be on that country. Yet the pattern set by the British was one that was repeated to a great extent in other European countries, as industrialization came to them in time.

1. PEOPLE ON THE LAND

The dramatic story of the growth of industrialization and urbanization must not be allowed to obscure the fact that, in 1850, the population of Europe was still overwhelmingly a peasant population. While in England, by 1830, a sizable minority lived in towns and cities, elsewhere society remained predominantly or overwhelmingly rural. In France and Italy, 60 percent lived in the country; in Prussia, over 70 percent; in Spain, over 90 percent; in Russia, over 95 percent. Demographic pressures which helped produce chaos in the cities, likewise caused severe hardship in the countryside. The populations of the predominantly agricultural nations lept forward with those that were industrializing. The population of Europe as a whole, estimated roughly at 187 million by 1800, had risen to 274 million by 1850. In Britain, with its comparatively high standard of living, the numbers increased from 16 million to 27 million. Yet the rural Irish, despite their periodic famines, increased too, from 5.5 to 8 million, and the Russians from 39 to 60 million, in the same period. The causes of this continuing population explosion remain as obscure as do those of the preceding century. As the death rate declined, a result, presumably, of advances in medical knowledge, improved agricultural technology, and the introduction of the potato, more people could expect to eat regularly, if not very well. The birth rate in most countries increased, but whether because of the higher incidence of earlier marriages, or illegitimacy, or of a desire on the part of parents to produce more potential family wage earners, historians have been unable to discover with any certainty.

Wretched rural conditions

Whatever the reasons for the population increase, conditions remained such as to make the life of the poorer rural inhabitants of Europe seldom more than bleak. Overpopulation brought underemployment, and hence poverty, in its train. Millions of tiny holdings produced a bare subsistence living, if that. Farmers still sowed and harvested by hand. Conditions in rural areas deteriorated sharply whenever there was a bad harvest, as there was with continuing regularity. The average daily diet for an entire family in a "good" year might amount to no more than two or three pounds of bread—a total of about 3,000 calories. Hunger—often near-starvation—as well as epidemic disease were still common occurrences. The result was a standard of living—if one can dignify the condition with that name—that for many rural inhabitants of many areas in Europe actually declined in the first half of the nineteenth century, although not enough to reverse general population growth. Governments in some countries attempted to solve the related problems of population pressure and impoverishment by passing laws raising the age of marriage. In some of the states of southern and western Germany, as well as in Austria, men were forbidden to marry before the age of thirty, and were also required to prove their ability to support a family.

Even had such laws acted as an effective curb on population growth—which, in the main, they did not—they would nevertheless have failed to prevent the rural stresses that resulted from the continuing spread of agricultural capitalism. The pace of this change varied across Europe; it was furthest advanced in England and Prussia. Wherever landed proprietors determined to meet increased demand for food by farming large areas as a capital investment, they imposed a series of transformations that were bound to affect the lives of agricultural laborers. First, land must be made a negotiable commodity. It must not, therefore, be tied to ancient customs which clouded its title—as was the case, for example, with common land, to which the poor within a community might have some right of access or cultivation. Second, land must be in the hands of those with capital enough to improve it, in order to make of it a profitable investment. It must be enclosed—"regulated" was the term in Prussia—so that, as we have seen, it could be properly fertilized and drained, or, if it was grazing land, so that breeds might be scientifically improved without fear of mongrelization. Finally, a mobile force of agricultural laborers must be available to work at the capitalists' behest. They must not be "tied" to a particular piece of land, either through systems of customary rights or bondage. They must be free to go where they were told to go, to work whatever land would bring most profit to its owners.

These requirements, as they were imposed, produced dislocation and hardship. In Scotland, workers were cleared from land which they

Agricultural capitalism

Interior of an English Farm Laborer's Cottage, 1846. Note the wooden crate used as an infant's cradle.

had farmed as tenants, in order to provide pasturage for the more profitable sheep. In Germany, those serfs emancipated by a reform-minded government in 1807 were compelled to forfeit somewhere between a third to a half of their land in return for their freedom; those who were able to retain small holdings were in most cases pressured to sell out to larger landholders. Not all landlords were ruthless. "Model" improvers among the wealthiest of the English landowners adjusted to capitalist competition without entirely forswearing traditional responsibilities. They built houses for tenants and laborers, and provided them with schools and churches. In eastern Europe there were among the Prussian landlords (Junkers) pietists who acknowledged obligations to their tenants as well as to the market.

The speed with which agricultural change occurred in various parts of Europe depended upon the nature of particular governments. Those more sympathetic to new capitalist impulses facilitated the transfer and reorganization of land by means of enabling legislation. They encouraged the elimination of small farms and an increase in larger, more efficient units of production. In England, over half the total area of the country, excluding waste land, was composed of estates of a thousand acres or more. In Spain, the fortunes of agricultural capitalism fluctuated with the political tenor of successive regimes: with the coming of a liberal party to power in 1820 came a law encouraging the free transfer of land; with the restoration of absolutism in 1823 came a repeal of the law. Russia was one of the countries least affected by agricultural change in the first half of the nineteenth century. There land was worked in vast blocks; some of the largest landowners possessed over half a million acres. Until the emancipation of the serfs in the 1860s, landowners claimed the labor of dependent peasant populations for as much as several days per week. At the same time, manorial serfdom, which bound hundreds of thousands of men, women, and children to particular estates for generations, prohibited the use of land as a negotiable commodity and therefore prevented the development of agricultural enterpreneurship. In France, despite the fact that manorialism had been abolished by the revolution, there was no rapid movement toward large-scale capitalist farming. An army of peasant proprietors, direct beneficiaries of the Jacobins' democratic constitution, continued to work the small farms they owned. The fact that France suffered far less agricultural distress, even in the 1840s, than did other European countries, and the fact that there was less migration in France from the country to the city and overseas than there was in Germany and England, are marks of the general success of this rural lower middle class in sustaining itself on the land. Its members were content to farm in the old way, opposed agricultural innovation, and, indeed, innovation generally. Despite their veneration of the revolution, they were among the most conservative elements in European society.

Rural populations, despite their isolation from urban centers, found themselves directly affected by the events of the Industrial Revolution. Factories brought about a decline in cottage industry and a consequent loss of vital income, especially during winter months. Improved communication networks not only afforded rural populations a keener sense of events and opportunities elsewhere, but also made it possible for governments to intrude upon the lives of these men and women to a degree previously impossible. Central bureaucracies now found it easier to collect taxes from the peasantry, and to conscript its sons into their armies.

Country people responded with sporadic violence against these and other harsh intrusions upon their lives. In southern England in the late 1820s, small farmers joined forces to burn barns and hayricks in protest to the introduction of threshing machines, a symbol of the new agricultural capitalism. They masked and otherwise disguised themselves, riding out at night under the banner of their mythical leader, "Captain Swing." Their raids were preceded by anonymous threats such as the one received by a large-scale farmer in the county of Kent: "Pull down your threshing machine or else [expect] fire without delay. We are five thousand men [a highly inflated figure] and will not be stopped." Other major rural disturbances occurred in Ireland, Silesia, and Galicia in the 1830s and 1840s, and indeed, to a lesser degree, right across Europe. In no country, however, was the agrarian population a united political force. Those who owned land, those who leased it as tenants, and those who worked it as laborers had interests as different from each other as from those of the urban populations.

2. URBANIZATION AND THE STANDARD OF LIVING

If the countryside continued to hold the bulk of Europe's population in the years between 1800 and 1850, the growth of cities nevertheless remains one of the most important facts in the social history of that period. Cities grew in size and number once the steam engine made it practical to bring together large concentrations of men, women, and children to work in factories. Previously, workshops had been located throughout the countryside, close to the water power that provided the primary means of operating machinery. Steam engines freed entrepreneurs from their dependence on water power and allowed them to consolidate production in large cities. In cities, transportation was more accessible than in the countryside. Hence it was less costly to import raw materials and ship out finished goods. Workers were more readily available in cities, as well, attracted as they were in large numbers in the hope—often false—of finding steady work at higher wages than those paid agricultural laborers. Industrialization was not the only reason for the growth of cities in the early nineteenth century, however. General population growth combined with industrialization forced cities to expand at an alarming rate.

In the ten years between 1831 and 1841 London's population grew by 130,000, Manchester's by 70,000. Paris increased by 120,000 between 1841 and 1846. Vienna grew by 125,000 from 1827 to 1847, into a city of 400,000. Berlin had as large a population by 1848, having increased by 180,000 since 1815. The primary result in these and other fast-growing centers was dreadful overcrowding. Construction lagged far behind population growth. In Vienna, though population rose 42 percent during the twenty years before 1847, the increase in housing was only 11.5 percent. In many of the larger cities, old and new, working men and women lived in lodging houses, apart from families left behind in the country. The poorest workers in almost all European cities dwelt in wretched basement rooms, often without any light or drainage. Governments did their best to encourage emigration to ease the overcrowding, the majority of emigrants relocating in the Americas. Emigration from England rose from 57,000 in 1830, to 90,000 in 1840, to 280,000 in 1850. Ireland, in the early years of the nineteenth century, witnessed the departure of over 1.5 million before the great potato famine of 1846, which increased the flow to a flood. In that year, approximately three out of every four acres of potatoes were blighted. Over 1 million died between 1846 to 1851, either from starvation, or as a result of their weakened physical condition which left them prey to disease.

With cities as overcrowded as they were, it is no wonder that they were a menace to the health of those who lived within them. The middle classes moved as far as possible from disease and factory

Urban population increases

Women and Boys Fetching Water from a Standpipe in Fryingpan Alley, London. Not until the beginning of the twentieth century did major European cities begin to provide poorer residents with an adequate water supply.

moke, leaving the poorest members of the community isolated and a prey to the sickness which ravaged working-class sections. Cholera, typhus, and tuberculosis were natural predators in areas without adequate sewerage facilities and fresh water, and over which smoke from factories, railroads, and domestic chimneys hung heavily. A local committee appointed to investigate conditions in the British manufacturing town of Huddersfield—not by any means the worst of that country's urban centers—reported that there were large areas without paving, sewers, or drains, "where garbage and filth of every description are left on the surface to ferment and rot; where pools of stagnant water are almost constant; where dwellings adjoining are thus necessarily caused to be of an inferior and even filthy description; thus where disease is engendered, and the health of the whole town perilled." Measures were gradually adopted by successive governments in an attempt to cure the worst of these ills, if only to prevent the spread of catastrophic epidemics. Legislation was designed to rid cities of their worst slums by tearing them down, and to improve sanitary conditions by supplying both water and drainage. Yet by 1850, these projects had only just begun. Paris, perhaps better supplied with water than any European city, had enough for no more than two baths per capita per year; in London, human waste remained uncollected in 250,000 domestic cesspools; in Manchester, no more than a third of the dwellings were equipped with toilets of any sort.

Conditions such as these are important evidence in the debate which has occupied historians for the past several decades. The question is: Did the standard of living rise or fall in Europe during the first half century of the Industrial Revolution? One school, the "optimists," argues that workers shared in the more general increase in living standards which occurred throughout Europe from 1800 onward. A variation on this optimistic theme maintains that whatever the hardships workers were compelled to suffer during the period of intense industrialization after 1800, they represent the necessary and worthwhile price society had to pay before it could "take off" into a period of "sustained economic growth." Sacrifices, in terms of standard of living, were required to permit accumulation of a capital base sufficient to guarantee economic expansion and an eventual level of general prosperity higher than any civilization had hitherto achieved. Other historians insist that such an analysis encourages one to ignore the evidence of physical squalor and psychological disruption that men, women, and children suffered as they provided the statistical "base" for future economic historians' abstract calculations.

The debate is hampered by an absence of reliable evidence about wage levels, hours of work, and cost of living. Some skilled workers within the new factories, along with some artisans in older trades as yet unaffected by industrialization, appear to have benefited from a slight rise in wages and a decline in living costs. But regional vari-

Wentworth Street by Gustav Doré. The artist was much concerned with the overcrowding squalor which resulted from early industrialization in London.

ables, along with a constantly fluctuating demand for labor in all countries, suggest that the more lowly paid, unskilled worker, whether in England or on the Continent, led a thoroughly precarious existence. Textile workers in England, if guaranteed something like full employment, could theoretically earn enough to support a family. Such was not the case in Switzerland, however, where similar work paid only half what was necessary, or in Saxony, where a large portion of the population was apparently dependent upon either poor relief or charity. One of the most depressing features of working-class life in these years was its instability. Economic depressions were common occurrences; when they happened, workers were laid off for weeks at a time, with no system of unemployment insurance to sustain them. Half the working population of England's industrial cities were out of work in the early 1840s. In Paris, 85,000 went on relief in 1840. One particularly hard-pressed district of Silesia reported 30,000 out of 40,000 citizens in need of relief in 1844. Nor should one overlook the plight of those whose skills had been replaced by machinery—the hand-loom weavers being the most notable examples. In the English manufacturing town of Bolton, a hand-loom weaver could earn no more than about three shillings per week in 1842, at a time when experts estimated it took at least twenty shillings a week to keep a family of five above the poverty line. On that kind of pay, workers were fortunate if they did not starve to death. Forced to spend something like 65 percent of their income on food, the per capita meat consumption of the average worker declined to about forty pounds per year in the early nineteenth century.

Such figures make the optimists' generalizations hard to countenance. Figures of whatever sort fail to take into account the stress that urban factory life extracted from the workers. Even workers making thirty shillings a week might well wonder if they were "better off," forced as they were to come to terms with the factory disciplines and living conditions imposed upon them. Though most of those who moved into factory towns—and of the more than 3 million men, women, and children living in England's sixty largest towns and cities in 1850, less than half had been born there—migrated but a short distance from their place of birth, the psychological distance they traveled was tremendous. These qualitative factors, admittedly difficult to assess, must be weighed along with more easily quantifiable evidence before reaching any conclusion as to the increased standard of living in early–nineteenth-century cities. Whether or not life in cities was pleasant or ghastly, however, it was, for rapidly increasing numbers, a fact of life. Once we examine that life we will better understand the full impact of industrialization and urbanization upon those who first experienced it.

The quality of life

3. THE LIFE OF THE URBAN MIDDLE CLASS

The urban middle class which emerged during this period was by no means one homogeneous unit, in terms of occupation or income. In a general category that includes merchant princes and humble shopkeepers, subdivisions are important. The middle class included families of industrialists, such as the Peels (cotton) in England and, at a

Soup Kitchen Run by Quakers, Manchester, England, 1862. Enterprises of this sort, which doled out charity "indiscriminately"—that is, without investigating the recipient's character — were condemned by many members of the middle class as encouraging the "worst" elements — idlers and loafers — among the poor.

Isambard Kingdom Brunel. Behind him are lengths of anchor chain from the steamship *The Great Western*.

Social mobility

later period, the Krupps (iron) in Germany. It included financiers like the internationally famed Rothschilds, and, on a descending scale of wealth and power, bankers and capitalists throughout the major money markets of Europe: London, Brussels, Paris, Berlin. It included entrepreneurs like Thomas Brassey, the British railway magnate, and John Wilkinson, the English ironmaster, who had himself buried in an iron coffin, and technicians, like the engineer Isambard Kingdom Brunel, designer of the steamship *The Great Western*. It included bureaucrats, in growing demand when governments began to regulate the pace and direction of industrialization, and to ameliorate its harshest social and economic results. It included those in the already established professions—in law particularly, as lawyers put their expertise to the service of industrialists. It included the armies of managers and clerks necessary to the continuing momentum of industrial and financial expansion, and the equally large army of merchants and shopkeepers necessary to supply the wants of an increasingly affluent urban middle-class population. Finally, it included the families of all those who lived their lives in the various subcategories we have listed.

Movement within these ranks was often possible, in the course of one or two generations. Movement from the working class into the middle class, however, was far less common. Most middle-class successes originated within the middle class—the children of farmers, skilled artisans, or professionals. Upward mobility was almost impossible without education; education was an expensive, if not unattainable luxury for the children of a laborer. Careers open to talents, that goal achieved by the French Revolution, frequently meant middle-class jobs for middle-class young men who could pass exams. The examination system was an important path for ascendancy within governmental bureaucracies. If passage from working class to middle class was not common, neither was the equally difficult social journey from middle class to aristocratic, landed society. This was particularly the case on the Continent, where the division between noble and commoner had traditionally been most pronounced. In Britain, mobility of this sort was easier. Children from wealthy upper-middle-class families, if they were sent, as occasionally they were, to elite schools and universities, and if they left the commercial or industrial world for a career in politics, might effect the change. William Gladstone, son of a Liverpool merchant, attended the exclusive educational preserves of Eton, a private boarding school, and Oxford University, married a connection of the aristocratic Grenville family, and became prime minister of England. Yet Gladstone was an exception to the rule in Britain, and Britain was an exception to the Continent. Movement, when it occurred, did so in less spectacular degrees.

Nevertheless, the European middle class helped sustain itself with the belief that it was possible to get ahead by means of intelligence, pluck, and serious devotion to work. The Englishman Samuel Smiles,

Young Gentlemen, 1834. It was to models such as these that the young men of the middle class aspired.

in his extraordinarily successful how-to-succeed book *Self Help,* preached a gospel dear to the middle class. "The spirit of self-help is the root of all genuine growth in the individual," Smiles wrote. "Exhibited in the lives of many, it constitutes the true source of national vigor and strength." Although Smiles's gospel declared that anyone willing to exert himself could rise to a position of responsibility and personal profit, however, and although some men actually did so, the notion remained no more than myth for the great majority.

Self-help

Seriousness of purpose was reflected in the middle-class devotion to the ideal of family and home. A practical importance attached to the institution of the family in those areas in England, France, and Germany where sons, sons-in-law, nephews, and cousins were expected to assume responsibility in family firms when it came their turn. Yet the worship of family more often ignored those practical considerations and assumed the proportions of sacred belief. Away from the business and confusion of the world, sheltered behind solid masonry and amid the solid comfort of their ornate furnishings, middle-class fathers retired each evening to enjoy the fruits of their daily labors. Inside the home, life was enclosed in a hierarchical and ritualistic system under which the husband and father was master. His wife was called his help-mate, and very occasionally within the middle class— especially in France—a wife might serve as shopkeeper or business associate with her husband. Far more frequently, however, a middle-class wife was treated by her spouse as a kind of superior servant. Her task was to keep the household functioning smoothly and harmoniously. She maintained the accounts and directed the activities of the servants—usually two or three women. Called in Victorian England

Family and home

Left: *A Salon in Vienna, 1830s*. A representation of middle-class home life on the Continent. Right: *A Victorian Family at Tea, 1860s*

the "Angel in the House," the middle-class woman was responsible for the moral education of her children. Yet she probably spent no more than two or three hours a day at most with her offspring. Until sent to school, they were placed in the custody of a nursemaid or governess. Much of a middle-class woman's day was spent in the company of other women from similar households. An elaborate set of social customs involving "calls" and "at homes" was established in European middle-class society. Women were not expected to improve their minds. They were not expected to be the intellectual companions of their husbands. Rather, they were encouraged to be dabblers, education for them usually consisting of little more beyond reading and writing, a smattering of arithmetic, geography, history, and a foreign language, embellished with lessons in drawing, painting in watercolor, singing, or piano-playing.

Queen Victoria as prototype

Queen Victoria, who ascended the British throne in 1837, labored to make her solemn—occasionally almost stolid—public image reflect the feminine middle-class virtues of moral probity and dutiful domesticity. Her court was eminently proper and preeminently bourgeois, a marked contrast to that of her uncle George IV, whose fleshly and unbuttoned ways had set the style for high life a generation before. Though possessing an imperious temper, Victoria trained herself to curb it in deference to her ministers and her public-spirited, ultra-respectable husband, Prince Albert of Saxe-Coburg. She was a successful queen because she embodied the traits dearest to the middle class, whose triumph she seemed to epitomize and whose habits of mind we have come to call Victorian.

Middle-class wives were indoctrinated to believe that they were superior to their husbands in one area only. A wife was "the better half" of a middle-class marriage because she was deemed pure—the untainted Vestal of the hearth, unsullied by cares of the world outside her home, and certainly untouched by those sexual desires which marked her husband, her natural moral inferior. A wife's charge was to encourage her husband's "higher nature." She must never respond to his sexual advances with equal passion; passion was, for her, a presumed impossibility. (Victoria, who gave birth to nine children, referred to sexual intercourse as "the shadow side" of marriage.) She must persuade her husband to seek, through love of home and family, a substitute for the baser instincts with which nature had unhappily endowed the male. Should she fail, she must accept the fact of her "failure" as she was bound to accept the rest of her life: uncomplainingly. That she often did fail was evidenced by the brisk trade in prostitution that flourished in nineteenth-century cities. In all European cities, prostitutes solicited openly. At mid-century the number of prostitutes in Vienna was estimated to be 15,000; in Paris, where prostitution was a licensed trade, 50,000; in London, 80,000. London newspaper reports of the 1850s catalogued the vast underworld of prostitutes and their followers: those who operated out of "lodging houses" run by unsavory entrepreneurs whose names—Swindling Sal, Lushing Loo—suggest their general character; the retinue of procurers, pimps, panderers, and "fancy men" who made the lives of common prostitutes little better than slavery; the relatively few "prima donnas" who enjoyed the protection of rich, upper-middle-class lovers, who entertained lavishly and whose wealth allowed them to move on the fringes of more respectable high society. The heroines of Alex-

Prince Albert and Queen Victoria. In this photograph by Roger Fenton the royal couple is depicted not as monarch and consort but as a conventional upper-middle-class married couple.

andre Dumas's novel *La Dame aux Camilles,* and of Giuseppe Verdi's opera *La Traviata*—"the lost one"—were prototypes of women of this sort.

If a middle-class wife should herself succumb to "unwomanly desires" and be discovered to have done so, she could expect nothing less than complete social banishment. The law tolerated a husband's infidelity and at all times respected a husband's rights both to his wife's person and to her property. It made quick work of an "unfaithful" wife, granting to her husband whatever he might desire in terms of divorce, property, and custody, to make him amends for the personal wrongs and embarrassments he had suffered at the hands of his "unnatural" spouse.

Middle-class family rituals helped to sustain this hierarchy. Daily meals, with the father at the head of the table, were cooked and brought to each place by servants, who were a constant reminder of the family's social position. Family vacations were a particularly nineteenth-century middle-class invention. Thanks to the advent of the railways, excursions of one or two weeks to the mountains or to the seashore were available to families of even moderate means. Entrepreneurs built large, ornate hotels, adorned with imposing names—Palace, Beau Rivage, Excelsior—and attracted middle-class customers by offering them on a grander scale exactly the same sort of comfortable and sheltered existence they enjoyed at home.

The houses and furnishings of the middle class were an expression of the material security the middle class valued. Solidly built, heavily decorated, they proclaimed the financial worth and social respectability of those who dwelt within. In provincial cities they were often

The Middle Class at Leisure. The "morning lounge" at Biarritz, a French resort on the Atlantic coast.

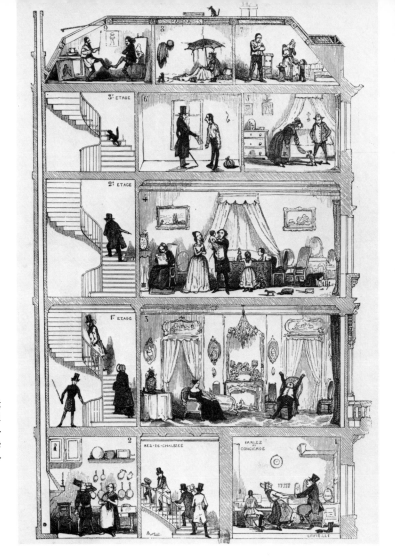

Apartment Living in Paris. This print shows that on the Continent rich and poor often lived in the same buildings, the rich on the lower floors, the poor at the top. This sort of residential mixing was unknown in Britain.

free-standing "villas." In London, Paris, Berlin, or Vienna, they might be rows of five- or six-story townhouses, or large apartments. Whatever particular shape they took, they were built to last a long time. The rooms were certain to be crowded with furniture, art objects, carpets, and wall hangings. Chairs, tables, cabinets, and sofas might be of any or all periods; no matter, so long as they were adorned with their proper complement of fringe, gilt, or other ornamentation. The size of the rooms, the elegance of the furniture, the number of servants, all depended, of course, on the extent of one's income. A bank clerk did not live as elegantly as a bank director. Yet in all likelihood both lived in obedience to the same set of standards and aspirations. And that obedience helped bind them, despite the differences in their material way of life, to the same class.

The European middle class had no desire to confront the unpleasant urban by-products of its own success. Members of the middle class

Houses

The Paris Opera. An exterior view of the Opera. Designed by Charles Garnier, it was constructed between 1861 and 1875. This grandiose display of wealth and luxury epitomized the taste of the new industrial middle class.

Cities and the middle class

saw to it that they lived apart from the unpleasant sights and smells of industrialization. Their residential areas, usually built to the west of the cities, out of the path of the prevailing breeze, and therefore of industrial pollution, were havens from the congestion for which they were primarily responsible. When the members of the middle class rode into the urban centers they took care to do so over avenues lined with respectable shops, or across railway embankments that lifted them above monotonous working-class streets en route to their destination. Yet the middle class, though it turned its face from what it did not want to see, did not turn from the city. Middle-class men and women celebrated the city as their particular creation and the source of their profits. They even praised its smoke—as a sign of prosperity—so long as they did not have to breathe it night and day. For the most part, it was they who managed their city's affairs. And it was they who provided new industrial cities with their proud architectural landmarks: city halls, stock exchanges, opera houses. These were the new cathedrals of the industrial age, proclamations of a triumphant middle class.

4. THE LIFE OF THE URBAN WORKING CLASS

Ranks within the working class

Like the middle class, the working class was divided into various subgroups and categories, determined in this case by skill, wages, and workplace. The working class included skilled workers in crafts that were centuries old—glassblowing and cabinetmaking, for example. It included as well mechanics equally skilled in new industrial technology. It included the men who built textile machinery and the women and children who tended it. It included the men, women, and children who together worked in mines and quarries. And it included the countless millions who labored at unskilled jobs—dock workers, coal porters, cleaning women, and the like. The nature of workers' experiences naturally varied, depending upon where they worked, where they lived, and, above all, how much they earned. A skilled textile worker lived a life far different from that of ditch digger, the former able to afford the food, shelter, and clothing necessary for a decent existence, the latter so busy trying to keep himself and his family alive that he would have little time to think about anything but the source of their next meal.

Some movement from the ranks of the unskilled to the skilled was possible, if children were provided, or provided themselves, with at least a rudimentary education. Yet education was considered by many parents a luxury, especially since children could be put to work at an early age to supplement a family's meager earnings. There was movement from skilled to unskilled also, as technological change—the introduction of the power loom, for example—drove highly paid workers into the ranks of the unskilled and destitute. Further variations within the working class were the result of the fact that though more men, women, and children were every year working in factories, the majority still labored either in workshops or at home. These variations mean that we cannot speak of a common European working-class experience during the years from 1800 to 1850. The life we shall be describing was most typical of English workers, during the first half century of their exposure to industrialization. Only in the years 1850–1900 did continental workers undergo to anything like the same extent, this harsh process of urban acclimatization.

Life in industrial cities was, for almost all workers, uncomfortable at best and unbearably squalid at worst. Workers and their families lived in housing that failed to answer the needs of its inhabitants. In older cities single-family dwellings were broken up into apartments of

Social mobility

Housing

Left: *An Urban Courtyard in London.* Right: *A Working-Class Tenement in Glasgow, Scotland.* Courtyards such as these were frequently the only available dumping grounds for household sewage and garbage.

often no more than one room per family. In new manufacturing centers, rows of tiny houses, located close by smoking factories, were built back-to-back, thereby eliminating any cross-ventilation or space for gardens. Whether housing was old or new, it was generally poorly built. Old buildings were allowed by landlords to fall into disrepair; new houses, constructed of cheap material, decayed quickly. Water often came from an outdoor tap, shared by several houses and adjacent to an outdoor toilet. Crowding was commonplace. Families of as many as eight lived in two or, at the most, three rooms. A newspaper account from the 1840s noted that in Leeds, a textile center in northern Britain, an "ordinary" worker's house contained no more than 150 square feet, and that in most cases those houses were "crammed almost to suffocation with human beings both day and night." When, after 1850, governments began to rid cities of some of their worst slums, many working-class men and women discovered that urban "improvement" meant relocation into dreary "model" tenements whose amenities were matched by their barracklike anonymity; or removal from one dilapidated structure to another in the wake of a clearance scheme—the nineteenth century called it "ventilation"—that replaced ancient, overcrowded housing with a more sanitary—and, for the landlord, more profitable—railway switching yard.

The life of women

The life of working-class wives and mothers was hard. Lack of cheap contraceptive devices and a belief that these devices were immoral helped to keep women pregnant through most of their childbearing years, thus endangering their general health and adding to the burden of their lives. Wives were usually handed a portion of the weekly wage packet by their husbands, and were expected to house, feed, and clothe the family on the very little they were given. Their daily life was a constant round of cooking, cleaning, shopping, and washing—in a tiny space and without enough money. Housewives could not rely, as in the country, on their own gardens to help supply them with food. Instead, they went to markets and catered to their needs with cheap goods, often stale or nearly rotten, or dangerously adulterated. Formaldehyde was added to milk to prevent spoilage. Pounded rice was mixed into sugar. Fine brown earth was introduced into cocoa. A woman's problems were compounded, of course, when she had to work, and therefore had far less time to accomplish the household tasks she was still expected to perform.

Women workers

Women were employed in growing numbers—along with children—in factories during the nineteenth century. Yet many more labored at home or in small workshops—"sweatshops," as they came to be called—for wretchedly low wages based not on the hours they worked but on the amount of work they did: so much per shirt stitched or matchbox glued. By far the greatest number of unmarried working-class young women worked as domestic servants, often a lonely occupation and one which occasionally trapped female servants into undesired sexual relationships with their male employers or their sons.

Female sexuality within the working classes of western Europe was acknowledged in a way that it was not within the middle class. Demographic evidence reveals a sharp rise in illegitimacy between 1750 and 1850. In Frankfurt, Germany, for example, where the illegitimacy rate had been a mere 2 percent in the early 1700s, it reached 25 percent in 1850. In Bordeaux, France, in 1840, one-third of the recorded births were illegitimate. Reasons for this increase are difficult to establish. Illegitimacy in Germany may have been the result of laws forbidding the poor to marry. Certainly, increased mobility meant weaker family ties, less parental supervision, and greater opportunity for an unrestricted life. This is not to say that the majority of working-class women were sexually promiscuous. Premarital intercourse was an accepted practice in preindustrial villages, but, because of the social controls that dominated village life, it was almost always a precursor to marriage. In the far more anonymous setting of a factory town, such control often did not exist. In addition, the economic uncertainties of the early industrial age meant that a young workingman's promise of marriage based on his expectation of a job might frequently be difficult to fulfill. The same economic uncertainty led some young working-class women to a career—usually temporary—as prostitutes. Middle-class men, prepared to postpone marriage until they could afford a house and furnishings reflecting the social position to which they aspired, turned to the sexual underworld to satisfy their desires. Class consciousness encouraged them to regard working-class women—prostitutes or not—as easy prey, possessed of coarser natures and therefore a lesser breed of womankind than the middle-class "ladies" they intended eventually to marry.

Sexuality

The anonymity of city life encouraged prostitution. New cities could be lonely places, particularly for working-class men and women struggling to cope with an alien environment. If possible, they would live near relatives who had already made the transition and who could

Loneliness

A Laundress and Her Children. Note the cramped and cluttered living quarters.

assist the newcomers in adjusting to their very different existence. In many cities working-class families lived in districts inhabited primarily by others working at the same trade—weavers in one place, miners in another—and in this way achieved some sense of commonality.

Adjustment to the demands of the factory was every bit as difficult for workers as was acceptance of urban living patterns. The factory system, emphasizing as it did standard rather than individual work patterns, denied skilled laborers the pride in craft that had previously been theirs. Many workers found themselves stripped of the reassuring protection of guilds and formal apprenticeships which had bound their predecessors to a particular trade or place, and which were outlawed or sharply curtailed by legislation in France, Germany, and Britain in the first half of the nineteenth century. Factory hours were long, before 1850 usually twelve to fourteen hours a day. Conditions were dirty and dangerous. Textile mills remained unventilated, so that bits of material lodged in workers' lungs. Machines were unfenced and were a particular danger to child workers, often hired, because of their supposed agility, to clean under and around the moving parts. Manufacturing processes were unhealthy. The use of poison lead in the making of glazed pottery, for example, was a constant hazard to men and women workers in that industry. Surveys by British physicians in the 1840s catalogued the toll that long factory hours and harsh working conditions were taking, particularly on young workers. Spinal curvature and other bone malformations resulted from standing hour after hour in unnatural positions at machines. Varicose veins and fallen arches were also common. One concerned doctor stated his belief that "from what I saw myself, a large mass of deformity has been produced by the factory system." And what was true of factories was true as well of mines, in which over fifty thousand children and young people were employed in Britain in 1841. Children were used to haul coal to underground tramways or shafts. The youngest were set to work—often for as long as twelve hours at a stretch—operating doors which regulated the ventilation in the mines. When they fell asleep, which, because of long hours, they frequently did, they jeopardized the safety of the entire workforce. Women—sometimes pregnant women—were employed to haul coal and perform other strenuous underground tasks. Lung diseases—popularly known as "black spittle"—and eye infections, not to mention the constant danger of explosions caused by trapped gas, were constant threats to life and limb in the mines.

As upsetting as the physical working conditions was the psychological readjustment demanded of the first-generation workers in the factories. Preindustrial laborers had to work long hours and for very little monetary reward. Yet, at least to some degree, they were free to set their own hours and structure their own activities, to move from their home workshops to their small garden plots and back again as they wished. In a factory, all "hands" learned the discipline of the whistle. To function efficiently, a factory demanded that all employees begin and end work at the same time. Most workers could not tell time; fewer possessed clocks. None was accustomed to the relentless pace of the machine. In order to increase production, the factory system encouraged the breaking down of the manufacturing process into specialized steps, each with its own assigned time, an innovation that upset workers accustomed to completing a task at their own pace. The employment of women and children was a further disturbing innovation. In preindustrial communities, women and children had worked, as well as men, but more often than not, all together and at home. In factory towns women and children were frequently hired instead of men: they could be paid less and were declared to be easier to manage. When this happened, the pattern of family life was severely disrupted, and a further break with tradition had to be endured. It is no wonder that workers began to see machinery itself as the tyrant that had changed their lives and bound them to a kind of industrial slavery. A radical working-class song written in Britain in the 1840s expressed the feeling: "There is a king and a ruthless king;/ Not a king of the poet's dream;/ But a tyrant fell, white slaves know well,/ And that ruthless king is steam."

Faced with a drastic reordering of their lives, working-class men and women reacted in various ways. Some sought "the shortest way out of Manchester" by taking to drink (there were 1,200 public houses in that city in 1850). Many more men and women struggled to make

Escape

"*Capital and Labour.*" In its earliest years, *Punch,* though primarily a humorous weekly, manifested a strong social conscience. In this 1843 cartoon, the capitalists are seen revelling in the rewards of their investments while the workers— men, women, and children— who toiled in the mines under cruel and dangerous conditions are found crippled and starving.

some sort of community out of the street where they lived or the factory where they worked. It was a long and discouraging process. Yet by mid-century their experiences were beginning to make them conscious of themselves as different from and in opposition to the middle class that was imposing a new way of life on them.

5. THE MIDDLE-CLASS WORLDVIEW

The middle class was not unaware of the many social problems it was generating as it created an industrial society. Despite its general confidence that the world was progressing—and at its own behest—the middle class was beset by uncertainties. Its belief in its own undoubted abilities was shadowed by concern as to whether its particular talents might ultimately prove irrelevant to the preservation of prosperity. Self-assurance could dissolve in the face of bankruptcy and prosperity vanish in the abyss of economic catastrophe. Those who had risen by their own exertions might fall victim to someone else's ambitions. Nor was it always a simple matter for the middle class to reconcile its own affluence with the poverty of the thousands of workers exploited under its aegis. The middle class was responsible for having wrenched European society out of old patterns of living and thrust it into new ones. To those willing to acknowledge that responsibility, the realization was enough to temper confidence with apprehension. No one was certain what the factory system and urbanization might eventu-

The Interior of the Crystal Palace. This building of iron and glass was constructed to house exhibits sent to the Exhibition of the Works of Industry of All Nations, held in London in 1851. The exhibition celebrated the triumph of middle-class industrialization.

ally produce. Evidence drawn from the reports of various official commissions and from the intentionally lurid writings of sensational journalists suggested that city life was already spawning an underclass of men and women who preferred a life of promiscuity and criminality to one of honest toil. French novelists began to use the sewers as a metaphor to describe the general condition of urban existence for what was assumed to be a vast number of Parisians. Poverty and crime were linked together in the public—middle-class—mind, until poverty itself began to be defined as criminal. All this was part of a middle-class compulsion to rationalize its own prosperity, and to legitimize its ascendancy over the urban working poor.

To assist themselves in constructing this congenial worldview, the members of the new industrial middle class made use of the theories of a number of political economists. It is important to recognize that a factory-owner or a banker was not likely to have read the works of these theorists. He might, however, have encountered popular journalistic condensations of their ideas, or have participated in discussions at which the conclusions, if not the reasoned arguments, of the economists were aired. Because those conclusions supported his own interests, he grew familiar with them, until, in time, he could talk of the ideas of these men as if they were his own.

Political economics and the worldview

We have noted already the manner in which the ideas of the economist Adam Smith sustained middle-class respect for individual enterprise. Smith's argument was reinforced by a second generation of economists—particularly the Englishmen Thomas Malthus (1766–1834) and David Ricardo (1772–1823)—whose writings embodied principles appealing to businessmen who desired a free hand to remake the economies of their countries. The chief elements in the theories of these economists were:

Classical economics

(1) Economic individualism. Individuals are entitled to use for their own best interests the property they have inherited or acquired by any legitimate method. People must be allowed to do what they like so long as they do not trespass upon the equal right of others to do the same.

(2) Laissez-faire. The functions of the state should be reduced to the lowest minimum consistent with public safety. The government should shrink itself into the role of a modest policeman, preserving order and protecting property, but never interfering with the operation of economic processes.

(3) Obedience to natural law. There are immutable laws operating in the realm of economics as in every sphere of the universe. Examples are the law of supply and demand, the law of diminishing returns, and so on. These laws must be recognized and respected; failure to do so is disastrous.

(4) Freedom of contract. Individuals should be free to negotiate the best kind of contract they can obtain from any other individual. In

Thomas Malthus

particular, the liberty of workers and employers to bargain with each other as to wages and hours should not be hampered by laws or by the collective power of labor unions.

(5) Free competition and free trade. Competition serves to keep prices down, to eliminate inefficient producers, and to ensure the maximum production in accordance with public demand. Therefore, no monopolies should be tolerated, nor any price-fixing laws for the benefit of incompetent enterprises. Further, in order to force each country to engage in the production of those things it is best fitted to produce, all protective tariffs should be abolished. Free international trade will also help to keep prices down.

Businessmen naturally warmed to theories so congenial to their own desires and intentions. But Malthus and Ricardo made further contributions to the middle-class worldview, based upon their perceptions of conflicting interests within society. Malthus, in his controversial *Essay on Population,* first published in 1798, argued that nature had set stubborn limits to the progress of mankind. Because of the voracity of the sexual appetite there was a natural tendency for population to increase more rapidly than the supply of food. To be sure, there were powerful checks, such as war, famine, disease, and vice; but these, when they operated effectively, further augmented the burden of human misery. It followed that poverty and pain were inescapable. Even if laws were passed distributing all wealth equally, the condition of the poor would be only temporarily improved; in a very short time they would begin to raise larger families, with the result that the eventual state of their class would be as bad as the earlier. In the second edition of his work, Malthus advocated postponement of marriage as a means of relief, but he continued to stress the danger that population would outrun any possible increase in the means of subsistence.

Malthus on population

Malthus's arguments allowed the middle class to acquiesce in the destruction of an older society which had made some attempt to care for its poor. In England, for example, officials in rural parishes had instituted a system of doles and subsidized wages to help sustain laborers and their families when unemployed. The attempt failed to prevent distress and was met with increasing resistance by taxpayers. Now Malthus told taxpayers that schemes designed to help the poor damaged both rich and poor alike. Poor relief took money, and therefore food, from the mouths of the more productive members of society and put it into the mouths of the least productive. Malthus helped shift the responsibility for poverty from society to the individual, a shift appealing to the middle class, which wished to be freed from the burden of supporting the urban unemployed.

The application of Malthusian doctrine

Ricardo on wages and rent

Malthusian assumptions played a large role in the development of the theories of the English economist Ricardo. According to Ricardo, wages seek a level which is just sufficient to enable workers "to subsist and perpetuate their race, without either increase or diminution." This

Ricardo held to be an inescapable iron law. If wages should rise temporarily above the subsistence standard, men and women would be encouraged to marry earlier and produce more children, the population would increase, and the ensuing competition for jobs would quickly force the rate of pay down to its former level. Ricardo devised a law of rent as well as a law of wages. He maintained that rent is determined by the cost of production on the poorest land that must be brought under cultivation, and that, consequently, as a country's population increases and more land is cultivated, and higher rents charged for more productive land, an ever-increasing proportion of the national income is absorbed by landlords.

Here again, a theorist provided arguments useful to the middle class in its attempt to define and defend itself within a new social order. The law of wages gave employers a useful weapon to protect themselves from their workers' petitions for higher pay. The law of rent justified middle-class opposition to the continuing power of landed interests: a class which derived its income not from hard work but simply from its role as rent-collector was profiting unfairly at the expense of the rest of society and deserved to have its profit-making curtailed.

As soon as the middle class began to argue in this fashion, however, it betrayed its devotion to the doctrine of laissez-faire. Businessmen and entrepreneurs vehemently opposed to government intervention which might deny them the chance to make as much money as they could, were nevertheless prepared to see the government step in and prevent profiteering landlords from making what *they* could from their property. How could this apparent inconsistency be justified? The answer lay in the theories of the Englishman Jeremy Bentham (1748–1832), without doubt among the most influential of middle-class apologists. Bentham, whose major work, *The Principles of Morals and Legislation,* was published in 1789, argued against the eighteenth-century notion that a satisfactory theory of social order could be grounded in a belief in the natural harmony of human interests. Men and women were basically selfish beings. To suppose that a stable and beneficent society could emerge unassisted from a company of self-interested egos was, Bentham believed, to suppose the impossible. Society, if it was to function properly, needed an organizing principle that would both acknowledge humanity's basic selfishness and at the same time compel people to sacrifice at least a portion of their own interests for the good of the majority. That principle, called utilitarianism, stated that every institution, every law, must be measured according to its social usefulness. And a socially useful law was one which produced the greatest happiness of the greatest number. If a law passed this test, it could remain on the books; if it failed, it should be abandoned forthwith, no matter how venerable. A selfish man would accept this social yardstick, realizing that in the long run he would do himself serious harm by clinging to laws that might benefit him, but produce such general unhappiness as to result in disruptions

Jeremy Bentham

detrimental to his own interests as well as to those of others.

In what ways did this philosophy particularly appeal to the industrial middle classes? First, it acknowledged the importance of the individual. The interests of the community were nothing more than the sum of the interests of those selfish egos who lived within it. Each individual best understood his or her own interests, and was therefore best left free, whenever possible, to pursue those interests as he or she saw fit. Only when they conflicted with the interests—the happiness—of the greatest number were they to be curtailed. Entrepreneurs could understand this doctrine as a license to proceed with the business of industrialization, since, they argued, industrialization was so clearly producing happiness for the majority of the world's population. At the same time, Bentham's doctrines could be used to justify those changes necessary to bring an industrial world into being. Was the greatest happiness produced, English factory-owners might ask, by an antiquated electoral system which denied representation to growing industrial cities? Obviously not. Let Parliament reform itself so that the weight of the manufacturing interests could be felt in the drafting of legislation.

Utilitarianism's appeal to the middle class

Utilitarianism was thus a doctrine that could be used to cut two ways—in favor of laissez-faire; in favor of governmental intervention. And the middle class proceeded to cut both ways at once. Benthamite utilitarianism provided the theoretical basis for many of the middle-class interventionist reforms, such as a revised poor law in Britain and an expanded educational system in France, achieved between 1815 and 1848.[1] At the same time utilitarianism, combined with the theories of Malthus and Ricardo, fortified the position of those businessmen who believed that unfettered individualism had produced the triumphs of the Industrial Revolution. To restrain that individualism was to jeopardize the further progress of industrialization and hence the greatest happiness of the greatest number.

Individualism and intervention

In arguing as it did, the middle class relied upon the conviction that industrialization and the factory system were together showering benefits on all—not just themselves. As we shall see, there were those who disagreed, who pressed, for example, for regulation of factory wages and hours. But the capitalists claimed intervention would inhibit the distribution of those benefits, and hence the proliferation of general happiness. In their support they could cite the English economist Nassau Senior, who claimed that the net profit of any industrial enterprise was derived solely from its last hour of daily operation. Reduce working hours, said Senior, and you eliminate profits, thereby compelling factories to close and workers to starve. The middle class believed Senior because it was clearly in its interest to do so. The middle class also believed him because the enterprise upon which

Belief in improvement

---

[1] These and other similar reforms will be discussed in the following chapter.

it was embarked was so new and so uncharted that it was hard to prove him wrong. Their uncertainty led them to believe those theories which provided them with the most reassurance and encouraged them to think that what they were doing was of benefit to their fellow men.

Political economists and philosophers in France as well as in England helped provide the new middle class with a congenial worldview. Count Claude de Saint-Simon (1760–1825), while a proponent of utopian schemes for social reorganization, nevertheless preached the gospel of "industrialism" and "industrialists" (two words which he coined). Disciples of Saint-Simon were among the leading proponents in France of industrial entrepreneurship and a standardized and centralized financial system.

Auguste Comte

Far more generally influential was the Positivist philosophy of Auguste Comte (1798–1857). Comte's philosophy, like utilitarianism, insisted that all truth is derived from experience or observation of the physical world. Comte rejected metaphysics as utterly futile; no one can discover the hidden essences of things—why events happen as they do, or what is the ultimate meaning and goal of existence. All one can really know is how things happen, the laws which control their occurrence, and the relations existing between them. Positivism derived its name from the assertion that the only knowledge of any current value was "positive," or scientific, knowledge. Comte argued that humankind's ability to analyze society scientifically and to predict its future had reached a point which would soon enable Europe to achieve a "positive" society, organized not in terms of belief but in terms of facts. Such an achievement would not be a simple matter, however; "positive" attitudes and institutions could not replace those of the "metaphysical" stage through which Europe had just passed without a struggle. By dividing the history of the world into progressive stages (a "religious" stage had preceded the "metaphysical"), and by declaring that the achievement of the highest stage was not possible without the turmoil of industrialization, Comte assured the middle class of its leading role in the better world that was to be.

The Positivism of Comte

6. EARLY CRITICS OF THE MIDDLE-CLASS WORLDVIEW

The middle-class worldview did not go unchallenged. Many writers deplored the social disintegration and moral hypocrisy they saw as the legacy of the Industrial Revolution. The Scot Thomas Carlyle (1795–1881), though a defender of the French Revolution and a believer in the need for a new aristocracy of industrialists ("captains of industry"), had nothing but contempt for the theories of the utilitarians. In Carlyle's view, they did no more than excuse the greed and acquisitiveness of the new middle class. Equally scathing in his attacks on the middle class was the English novelist Charles Dickens

The Greek Slave by Hiram Powers. The art of the bourgeoisie: titilation combined with a moral lesson.

(1812–1870). In such novels as *Oliver Twist, Hard Times,* and *Dombey and Son,* he wrote with sympathy of the tyrannization of industrial workers by the new rich. In France, the Abbé Felicité Lamennais (1782–1854), though preaching respect for private property, nevertheless attacked self-interest. He argued, in his *Book of the People,* that the "little people" of the world enjoyed far too small a share in the direction of their lives. Honoré de Balzac (1799–1850) wrote *The Human Comedy* to expose the stupidity, greed, and baseness of the middle class. Gustave Flaubert (1821–1880), in his foremost novel *Madame Bovary,* depicted the banal, and literally fatal, nature of bourgeois existence for women.

One of the most trenchant critics of early industrialization was the English philosopher and economist John Stuart Mill (1806–1873). Mill's father had been a close disciple of Bentham, and his son began his adult life a convinced utilitarian. A severe psychological crisis in early manhood compelled him to modify his acceptance of classical economic theory. First, he rejected the universality of economic laws. Though he admitted that there are unchangeable laws governing the field of production, he insisted that the distribution of wealth can be regulated by society for the benefit of the majority of its members. Second, he advocated more radical departures from laissez-faire than any recommended by his forerunners. He favored legislation, under certain conditions, for shortening the working day, and he believed that the state might properly take preliminary steps toward the redistribution of wealth by taxing inheritances and by appropriating the unearned increment of land. In the fourth book of his *Principles of Political Economy* he urged the abolition of the wage system and looked forward to a society of producers' cooperatives in which the workers would own the factories and elect the managers to run them. On the other hand, Mill was no socialist. He distrusted the state, and his real reason for advocating producers' cooperatives was not to exalt the power of the workers but to give them the fruits of their labor. In 1859 he wrote what many consider the classic defense of individual freedom, *On Liberty,* in which he attacked what he called "the tyranny of the majority." Yet his ringing defense of individualism was as much a treatise against middle-class conformism as it was against the threat of state control. "If all mankind were of one opinion," Mill wrote, "and only one person were of the contrary opinion, mankind would be no more justified in silencing that one person than he, if he had the power, would be justified in silencing mankind." Those sentiments were not the sort to appeal particularly to a society determined to define itself in accordance with rigid behavioral patterns and codes of conduct.

Middle-class art and its critics

Artists, too, attacked the values of industrial society in their painting and sculpture. The art preferred by the European middle class in the nineteenth century was that which in some way either told a story or, better still, preached a message. Beauty was surface decoration, which could be admired for its intrinsic richness and for what it therefore declared about its owner's wealth. Or beauty was a moralism, easily understood and, if possible, reassuring. When the Great Exhibition of the Works of Industry in All Nations was held at the Crystal Palace in London in 1851 to celebrate the triumph of industrialism, one of the most popular exhibits was *The Greek Slave,* a statue by the American sculptor Hiram Powers. Depicting a young Christian woman stripped bare and standing, according to the catalogue, before the gaze of an Eastern potentate, the work allowed its Victorian male admirers a chance to relish its salaciousness, while at the same time profiting from its depiction of the woman's righteous disdain for her captor.

Some of the artists most critical of the middle class, while repudiating the artificial and decorative, nevertheless reflected the middle-class obsession with art as morality. The self-designated Pre-Raphaelite Brotherhood of English painters was a group of men and women, led by the painter-poet Dante Gabriel Rossetti (1828–1882), determined to express its disdain for contemporary values. They called themselves Pre-Raphaelites as a way of announcing their admiration for the techniques of early Renaissance artists, untainted, supposedly, by corrupted artistic taste. Yet the works of the leading members of the Brotherhood exuded a degree of sentimentality that compromised their rebel nature and rendered them conventionally pietistic and ultimately innocuous as social protest. The same can be said, to a lesser degree, of the work of the Frenchman Jean-François Millet (1814–1875). His *Man with the Hoe* is a stark, bitter statement about peasant life; his *The Angelus* softens the statement to sentiment. In both England and France, however, some of the most talented painters seriously questioned many of the values the middle class revered. Gustave

John Stuart Mill

The Angelus by Jean-François Millet. The artist's peasants accept their humble lot in this sentimental portrayal.

The Third Class Carriage by Honoré Daumier. Daumier's realism did not mask his sympathy with the condition of the common people of France.

Courbet (1819–1877) and Honoré Daumier (1808–1879) both expressed sympathy toward the plight of the French working class, contrasting scenes of rural and urban misfortune with unflattering caricatures of the bourgeoisie. Daumier, in particular, was a powerful satirist of social and political evils, ridiculing the corruption of petty officials and the hypocritical piety of the rich. There was a harsh bite to most of the work of Daumier and Courbet that proscribed sentimentalizing.

These writers and artists, while critical of the Industrial Revolution and middle-class values, proposed nothing very tangible in the way of radical reform. If they opposed the triumph of a materialistic middle class, they opposed, as well, the idea of complete democracy. Carlyle, in particular, criticized the present by comparing it with a rosy past that had never been. In this he was like one of the doughtiest critics of the new middle-class society, the Englishman William Cobbett (1763–1835). Cobbett, in his newspaper the *Political Register,* argued against industrialization itself as well as its effects. His propaganda mirrored the dilemma most critics had to face: Granted industrialization has brought great social and economic hardship in its train, does this mean that we should try to return to the life of preindustrial society, also often harsh, and always confining, though probably more secure?

For some time, a small band of thinkers had been answering that question with a resounding "no." They argued that there could be no

Past or present?

See color plates facing page 800 for *The Gleaners* by Millet and the *Funeral at Ornans* by Courbet return to old times and old ways, but that society could be at the same time both industrial and humane. These radical thinkers were often explicitly utopian. Two of the most persuasive were the Englishman Robert Owen (1771–1858) and the Frenchman Charles Fourier (1772–1837). Owen, himself the proprietor of a large cotton factory at New Lanark in Scotland, argued against the middle-class belief that the profit motive should be allowed to shape social and economic organization. Having reorganized his own mills to provide free schooling and a system of social security for his workers, he proceeded to advocate a general reorganization of society on the basis of cooperation, with communities rewarding workers solely as a result of their actual labor. Fourier urged an even more far-reaching reconstitution, including the abolition of the wage system and the complete equality of the sexes. The numerous followers of Owen and Fourier sought escape from the confusions of the contemporary world in idealist communities founded according to the principles of their leaders. All these attempts failed after a time, victims of faulty leadership and, in the case of Fourierist communities in France, of charges of moral turpitude resulting from Fourier's revolutionary sexual doctrines.

Louis Blanc

Less utopian radical theories were proposed during the 1840s, years which witnessed recurring economic depressions and their horrifying consequences. The French politician and journalist Louis Blanc (1811–1882), stood, like many contemporary critics, against the competitiveness of the new industrial society and particularly opposed the exploitation of the working class. His solution was to campaign for universal male suffrage, which would give working-class men control of the state. Following their triumph, these workers would make the state the "banker of the poor" and institute "Associations of Production"—actually a system of workshops governed by workers—which would guarantee jobs and security for all. Once these associations became established, private enterprise would wither through competition, and with it the state, for which there would no longer be any need. As we shall see, these workshops were briefly instituted in Paris during the Revolution of 1848. Another Frenchman, Pierre Proudhon (1809–1865), condemned the profits accruing to employers at the expense of their employees. He, too, proposed new institutions, which he argued could be made to produce goods at a price fairer to the worker, a price based solely on the amount of labor devoted to the manufacture of any particular product.

Blanc and Proudhon

Few critics of industrialization availed themselves of the opportunity to examine its effect for an extended period at first hand. One who did, and who as a result wrote a stinging condemnation of industrial capitalism, was the young German Friedrich Engels (1820–1895), the son of a partner in a Manchester cotton factory. Engels spent almost two years in Manchester in the mid-1840s, not only serving his father's business interests, but observing the consequences of such businesses on the lives of the men and women who labored to produce their

Friedrich Engels

Friedrich Engels

profits. In *The Condition of the Working Class in England in 1844,* Engels described in vivid detail the overcrowded Manchester slums and the wretched lives led by those condemned to an existence there. He argued that factory work was turning laborers into no more than machines, separated from themselves as human beings because they were separated from the work over which they had no control. Yet he insisted that the experience of working-class life, depressing as it was for those forced to endure it, was producing in men and women a class consciousness—a distinctive sense of their interests as opposed to those of their masters in the middle class—that would bring about a revolution and the eventual triumph of their class.

Engel's argument, when coupled as it soon was with that of his fellow German, Karl Marx (see below, p. 812), produced a theory that not only examined the way in which society had come to its present, divided state, but that proposed a means whereby it might be altered to benefit those who were now its victims. The theories of Engels, and of those other writers whom we have been considering—both the defenders and the opponents of the middle-class industrial world—are historically important for two reasons. First, the ideas helped men and women better understand the new social order which had sprung up following the French and Industrial Revolutions, and the part they might play, as members of a class, in that new order. Second, the ideas themselves helped inspire the concrete political, social, and economic changes and events which are the subject of the next two chapters.

SELECTED READINGS

• *Items so designated are available in paperback editions.*
  Briggs, Asa, *Victorian Cities,* New York, 1963. A survey of British cities, stressing middle-class attitudes toward the new urban environment.
• Burn, W. L., *The Age of Equipoise,* London, 1964. A charming account of the mid-Victorian years.
  Chevalier, Louis, *Laboring Classes and Dangerous Classes,* New York, 1973. An intriguing though controversial study of the quality of life in Paris between 1815 and 1848 which concludes that social mobility was downward and that fear of crime dominated middle-class social consciousness.
• Halévy, Elie, *The Growth of Philosophical Radicalism,* rev. ed., London, 1949. The best introduction to the thought of Malthus, Ricardo, Bentham, and their philosophical heirs.
  ———, *England in 1815,* London, 1949. The classic work by the greatest historian of nineteenth-century England.
• Hammond, J. L., and Barbara Hammond, *The Town Labourer, 1760–1832,* London, 1917. An impassioned account of the economic changes which affected the quality of life of the English worker.
• Heilbroner, Rober L., *The Worldly Philosophers,* New York, 1967. An introduction to the thought of economic liberals.

- Hobsbawn, Eric, *The Age of Capital, 1848–1875,* London, 1975. A perceptive world survey which traces the global triumph of capitalism and its impact on the working class, written from a Marxist perspective.
  ———, *Labouring Men: Studies in the History of Labour,* London, 1964. A series of essays on workers and the working class in England.
- Houghton, Walter, *The Victorian Frame of Mind, 1830–1870,* New Haven, Conn., 1957. An outstanding synthesis of Victorian middle-class mentality.
- Langer, William L., *Political and Social Upheaval, 1832–1852,* New York, 1969. Comprehensive survey of European history, with excellent analytical chapters and thorough bibliographies.
  Manuel, Frank E., *The Prophets of Paris,* Cambridge, Mass., 1962. An entertaining introduction to the philosophers of progress, from Turgot to Comte.
- Rostow, W. W., *The Stages of Economic Growth,* rev. ed., Cambridge, 1971. A synthesis by the exponent of the "take-off" theory of economic development.
- Rudé, George, *The Crowd in History,* New York, 1964. A study of popular disturbances in France and England.
- Taylor, A. J. *The Standard of Living in Britain in the Industrial Revolution,* New York, 1975. A good introduction to the debate on the effects of industrialization.
  Tilly, Charles, and Edward Shorter, *Strikes in France, 1830–1848,* New York, 1974. A valuable study of early continental class consciousness.
- Tilly, Louise, and Joan W. Scott, *Women, Work and Family,* New York, 1978. Deals with women in nineteenth-century France and England.
- Thompson, E. P., *The Making of the English Working Class,* London, 1963. Argues that the coincidence of the French and Industrial Revolutions fostered the growth of working-class consciousness. A brilliant and important work.
  Walker, Mack, *German Home Towns: Community, State and General Estate, 1648–1871,* Ithaca, N.Y., 1971. Attempts to explain the absence of a strong middle class in Germany.
- Zeldin, Theodore, *France, 1848–1951,* 2 vols., Oxford, 1973–1977. A highly individualistic synthesis of French history, remarkable for its scope and insight.

SOURCE MATERIALS

- Engels, Friedrich, *The Condition of the Working Class in England,* New York, 1958. A much criticized but reliable firsthand account by the later collaborator of Marx, written in 1844. Presents a devastating portrait of living and working conditions, especially in Manchester.
- Malthus, Thomas R., *An Essay on Population,* London, 1798 and 1803. Malthus's famous essay relating population growth and food production.
- Mayhew, Henry, *London Labor and the London Poor,* New York, 1968. A reprint of the 1851 edition; provides a fascinating view of the population and trades of London. A good factual companion to Dickens.

• Mill, John Stuart, *Autobiography,* London, 1873. The intellectual coming-of-age of one of England's major nineteenth-century figures.

• ———, *On Liberty,* London, 1859. The classic defense of individual freedom.

Owen, Robert, *A New View of Society,* London, 1813. A proposed utopian society based on cooperative villages by the founder of British socialism.

Chapter 23

THE RISE OF LIBERALISM
(1815–1870)

The general thought, the hope of France, has been order and liberty reuniting under constitutional monarchy.

— François Guizot, "Speech on the State of the Nation," 1831

The history of nineteenth-century Europe was to a great extent shaped by the interplay of the forces of liberalism and nationalism. The middle classes of France and England, where liberalism was strongest, espoused a set of doctrines reflecting their concerns and interests. Liberalism to them meant (1) an efficient government prepared to acknowledge the value of commercial and industrial development; (2) a government in which their interests would be protected by their direct representation in the legislature—in all probability, a constitutional monarchy, and most certainly not a democracy; (3) a foreign policy of peace and free trade; and (4) a belief in individualism and the doctrines of the classical economists.

The components of liberalism

Many middle-class men and women in other European countries shared these beliefs and assumptions, and worked diligently and with some success to carry through specific liberal reforms. But for them, an equally important and often more immediate objective was the achievement of some form of national unity. The middle classes in Germany, Italy, Poland, and the Austrian Empire, however dedicated they were to liberalism, believed that their chances of achieving liberal goals would be greatly enhanced if they could unify the patchwork of principalities that surrounded them into a vigorous, "modern" nation-state. In this chapter, we shall examine the phenomenon of liberalism, primarily as it affected the fortunes of England and France. In the following chapter, we shall describe the way in which liberalism combined with nationalism to reshape the history of central Europe.

The compulsion of nationalism

1. CONSERVATIVE REACTION, 1815–1830

*The conservative
restoration*

The growth of liberalism occurred, in part, as a reaction to the conservative policies adopted by frightened governments anxious to restore domestic and international order following the Napoleonic wars. For a period of about fifteen years after 1815 the rulers of most European countries did their best to stem the advance of middle-class liberalism. In most instances, however, their repressive policies only made liberals more determined than ever to succeed. The primary concern of governments was to ensure that Europe would never again fall prey to the sort of revolutionary upheavals which it had experienced during the preceding quarter-century.

The system of alliances

Following Napoleon's final defeat at Waterloo in 1815, the major powers reconfirmed the Vienna settlement in the hope that their efforts might result in a permanently stable "Concert of Europe." To further ensure an end to revolutionary disturbances, they formed the Quadruple Alliance—Britain, Austria, Prussia, and Russia; when France was admitted as a fifth member in 1818 it became the Quintuple Alliance. Its members pledged to cooperate in the suppression of any disturbances which might arise from attempts to overthrow legitimate governments or to alter international boundaries. At the same time, Tsar Alexander, his mystic nature now in the ascendant, persuaded the allies to join him in the declaration of another alliance—a "Holy Alliance"—dedicated to the precepts of justice, Christian charity, and peace. The only result of this second league was to confuse Europe's leaders as to Alexander's intentions. Was he a liberal—a Jacobin even, as Metternich feared—or a reliable conservative? The confusion was cleared away, as in one country after another, liberal uprisings were stifled by stern reactionary policies of the allied governments, Alexander's among them.

*Suppression of liberal
uprisings*

Attacks against reactionary governments in Naples and in Spain brought the allies scurrying to a conference at Troppau in Austria in 1820. Secret brotherhoods of young liberals, many of them army officers, had spearheaded these revolts. These organizations, which originated in Italy, called themselves *Carbonari*. They were an active counterreactionary force, whose influence spread throughout Europe in the early 1820s. In both Naples and Spain, they succeeded in forcing the kings to take oaths to establish constitutions modeled on the liberal French constitution of 1789–1791. At Troppau, Austria, Prussia, and Russia reacted to these threats to international order and absolutism by pledging to come to each other's aid to suppress revolution. France and Britain declined to endorse the pledge, not so much because they opposed repression, but because they did not wish to curtail their freedom of action by binding themselves to detailed international treaties. Metternich nevertheless proceeded, with Russian and Prussian concurrence, in a repression of the *Carbonari* rebels through imprisonment or exile.

Two years later, in 1822, another congress was convened at Verona, this one to deal with the continuing liberal threat to stability in Spain, with the series of revolutions occurring in Spanish colonies in South America, and with an insurrection in the Near East. To resolve the Spanish problem, the French dispatched an army of 200,000 men to the Iberian peninsula in 1823. Without much difficulty, this force put an end to the Spanish liberals, who opposed King Ferdinand VII's attempt to undermine representative government. The French assisted Ferdinand in restoring his authority to rule as he pleased. Contrary to their experience in Spain, the defenders of the status quo were unable to succeed in stemming the move to independence and liberalism in the colonies of Central and South America. In 1823 President James Monroe of the United States issued the "Monroe Doctrine," which declared that attempts by European powers to intervene in the affairs of the New World would be looked upon as an unfriendly act by his government. Without British maritime support, the doctrine would have remained a dead letter. Britain was ready to recognize the independence of the South American republics, however, since as new countries they were prepared to trade with Britain instead of Spain. The British therefore used their navy to keep Spain from intervening to protect its vanishing empire.

*Defying the congress
system*

In the Near East, a Greek soldier, Alexander Ypsilanti, was attempting to encourage the formation of a Greek "empire," to be constructed on vaguely liberal principles. In doing so, he had engaged his band of armed followers in battles against the Turks who ruled over Greece. Though Ypsilanti was soon defeated, his movement lived on. Five years later its aims had been narrowed to the more accessible goal of an independent Greece. Supported for reasons of Mediterranean naval strategy by a joint Anglo-French-Russian naval intervention, and by a Russian invasion of the Balkans, the rebels this time succeeded. Their success signaled the extent of changes that had occurred since the Congress of Verona. No longer could Metternich and other reactionaries build alliances on the assumption that, for the powers of Europe, preservation of the status quo was, before everything else, the major goal. Britain, in particular, could not be relied upon. There, by the late 1820s, the liberal movement was gaining momentum fast.

Rebellion in Greece

2. LIBERAL GAINS IN WESTERN EUROPE, 1815–1830

Liberal gains in Britain came after an era of reaction that paralleled that which occurred on the Continent. The conservative Tory party had enjoyed almost unbroken political supremacy since the younger William Pitt had become first minister in 1783. Though Pitt had begun his career as something of a reformer, the French Revolution had turned him, along with his fellow Tories, into a staunch defender of the status quo. The Tories' political opponents, the Whigs, had throughout the long years of the revolutionary and Napoleonic conflicts remained to

British politics

The Peterloo Massacre, 1819. A contemporary rendering of the shootings which condemned the "wanton and furious attack by that brutal armed force The Manchester & Cheshire Yeomanry Cavalry."

"Peterloo" and the Six Acts

The liberalizing Tories

some degree conciliatory to the French. But Whigs were as unsympathetic as Tories to democratic notions and as defensive of their rights to the full fruits of their property.

Hence when rioting broke out in England after 1815 as a result of depression and consequent unemployment, there was general support among the well-to-do for the repressive measures adopted by the British government. Spies were hired to ferret out evidence against popular agitators. In the industrial north, where conditions were particularly severe, radical members of the middle and working classes capitalized on the general unrest to press their demands for increased representation in Parliament. At Manchester a crowd of 80,000, demonstrating for political reform in St. Peter's Fields, was fired upon by soldiers. Eleven persons were killed and over 400 injured, including 113 women. The massacre was thereafter called "Peterloo" by British radicals: i.e., a domestic Waterloo. It was the first of several repressive measures taken by the government to stifle reform. Another was the legislation known as the Six Acts, which was passed by Parliament in 1819, and outlawed "seditious and blasphemous" literature; levied a stamp tax on newspapers; allowed the searching of houses for arms; and restricted the rights of public meeting.

Yet within a surprisingly short time British political leaders reversed their opposition to everything new. Instead, they displayed an ability to compromise which kept their country free from revolution. George Canning, the foreign minister, and Robert Peel, the home secretary, son of a rich cotton manufacturer, were both sensitive to the interests of Britain's liberal-minded capitalist entrepreneurs. Under their direction, the government retreated from its commitment to the intransigent Quintuple Alliance; it was Canning who took the lead in recognizing the new South American republics. At home, these same politicians began to make order of the inefficient tangle of British laws; for example, they abolished capital punishment for about a hundred different offenses. And Canning liberalized, though he did not abolish, the Corn Laws. These laws levied a tariff on the importation of cheap foreign grain. As such, they benefited English landlords, but hurt manufacturers, who had to pay higher factory wages to enable their workers to purchase more expensive bread. These "liberalizers" among the still essentially conservative Tories went so far as to abolish the laws which had kept both dissenting Protestants (members of Protestant sects—Baptist, Congregationalist, Methodist—other than Anglican) and Roman Catholics from full participation in public political life.

What the conservatives would not do was reform the system of representation in the House of Commons, heavily weighted on the side of the landed interests. Here the Tories, the majority party in Parliament, drew the line and showed themselves still basically committed to the status quo. Yet members of the liberal middle class argued that such a reform was absolutely necessary before they could themselves play a constant and active role in shaping British policy to comply with their own interests. "Interest" was, indeed, the key word in the debate over parliamentary reform. For centuries Parliament had represented the interests of landowners, the major propertied class in England. About two-thirds of the members of the House of Commons were either directly nominated by or indirectly owed their election to the patronage of the richest landowners in the country. Many of the parliamentary electoral districts, or boroughs, which returned members to the House of Commons, were controlled by landowners who used the pressure of their local economic power—or, in many cases, outright bribery—to return candidates sympathetic to their interests. These were the "rotten" or "pocket" boroughs, so-called because they were said to be in the pockets of those men who controlled them. Those who favored the system as it was argued that it mattered little that electoral politics were corrupt, that electoral districts represented unequal numbers, or that very, very few (about one in a hundred) were enfranchised. What did matter, they claimed, was that the interests of the nation at large, which they perceived to coincide with the interests of landed property, were well looked after by a Parliament elected in this fashion.

Parliamentary reform

Of course the new industrial middle class did not agree with the arguments of the landowners. They insisted, for example, that the Corn Laws did not coincide with the nation's best interest. (If they were followers of the theories of Jeremy Bentham, they might argue that the Corn Laws did not produce "the greatest happiness of the greatest number.") Rather, the Corn Laws worked only for the benefit of landlords, by keeping the price of grain high; and they worked to the disinterest of everyone else. Therefore, said members of the mid-

*The middle class and
reform*

dle class, Parliament must be reformed to represent not only landlords but the interests of industrial England. It is important to note that the liberal middle class was *not* arguing in favor of reform on the basis of a belief in democracy. Some leaders within the emerging working class did make this argument—and, as we shall see, continued to make it after a reform bill was passed in 1832. Most of those who spoke in favor of reform, however, declared that the middle class was capable of representing the interests of the working class, as well as of itself, in Parliament. Reformers took this position either because they believed it; or because they were afraid of working-class representatives; or because they realized that to favor direct representation for the working class would frighten the more timid reformers and hence defeat their whole campaign.

A working-class alliance

Spurred by the example of liberal reformers on the Continent (see below, p. 776) and by the oratory and organizational abilities of middle-class and artisan radicals at home, the movement for reform intensified after 1830. It was strong enough to topple the Tories and to embolden the Whigs, under the leadership of Lord Grey, to make a party issue of reform by introducing a bill to modify the ancient electoral structure of the country. The government was clearly frightened. Revolution, if it were ever to come in England, would come as a result of the alliance now threatening between middle-class industrialists and the artisan/tradesman leadership of the new working class. In Birmingham, a middle-class banker, Thomas Attwood, organized a "Political Union of the Lower and Middle Classes of the People." By July 1830, there were similar organizations in Glasgow, Manchester, Liverpool, Sheffield, Newcastle, and Coventry, some willing to engage in bloody clashes with army units and police. Middle-class shopkeepers declared their determination to withhold taxes and, if necessary, to form a national guard. Plagued as well by an outbreak of cholera, the country appeared to be on the verge of serious general disorder, if not outright revolution. The king, William IV, wrote worriedly to Lord Grey that "miners, manufacturers, colliers, and labourers" appeared ready for some sort of open rebellion.[1] Sensing the grave danger of a possible union of the working and middle classes, the governing class once more accommodated to change, as it had in the 1820s.

The Reform Bill of 1832

The Reform Bill of 1832, however, was not a retreat from the notion of representation by interest. No attempt was made to create equal electoral districts. The franchise, though increased, extended the vote to no more than 3 percent of the total population. It was defined in terms of the amount of property owned and the length of time one had owned it. In the counties, for example, a man could vote if he paid at least ten pounds annual rental for land held on a long-term sixty-year lease. In other words, the vote was granted to the middle

[1] Asa Briggs, *The Age of Improvement*, New York, 1959, p. 248.

class, but to very few of the working class. Probably more significant than its extension of the franchise was the bill's scheme for a redistribution of seats. One hundred forty-three seats were reallocated, most of them from the rural south to the industrial north, thereby increasing representation in and around cities such as Manchester, Leeds, and Birmingham; and thereby increasing, in turn, the political power of the industrial middle classes. Though the bill was the product of change and itself brought change in its wake, it was understood as a conservative measure. It by no means destroyed the political strength of landed aristocratic interests, though it reduced that strength somewhat. And it preserved the notion of representation by interest. The liberal, industrial middle classes had been admitted into junior partnership with the landed oligarchy that had for centuries ruled Britain and was to rule it for at least one more generation.

Efforts to introduce liberal political reforms were not limited to Britain during this period. In the United States, the rule of eastern landed and commercial interests was superseded by the antiprivilege Democratic party, led by General Andrew Jackson, a war hero who had led American troops against the British when those two countries had gone to war over Britain's restrictive trade policies in 1812. Across the world, in Russia, a group of army officers revolted, following the death of Tsar Alexander in 1825, in hopes of persuading his liberally minded brother, Constantine, to assume the throne and guarantee a constitution. In this case, however, the attempt at reform failed. Constantine was unwilling to usurp power from the rightful heir, a third brother, Nicholas. The officers, called Decembrists (because of the month of their rebellion), were harshly punished; Nicholas I (1825–1855) continued to rule in the severely autocratic ways Alexander had adopted toward the end of his life, creating the Third Section, a political police force, to prevent further domestic disorder. Yet even under Nicholas, perhaps Europe's most unremitting reactionary, Russia evidenced signs of modernization. Bureaucracy, less dependent than in the past on the aristocracy, grew more centralized and more efficient. Laws were systematically codified in 1832. Stimulated by European demand for Russian grain, estates were reorganized for its more effective production, and railways built to transport it to Western markets.

For a time, autocracy threatened the liberal revolutionary and Napoleonic heritage in France. The upper middle class in France had remained generally content with the domestic settlement agreed upon by the major powers in 1814 and confirmed at the Congress of Vienna the following year. Louis XVIII, a clever yet self-indulgent man, had "granted" a "constitutional charter" upon his succession to the French throne. While refusing to deny himself absolute power in theory, in practice Louis XVIII had willingly enough agreed to support those principles most desired by French middle-class liberals: legal equality; careers open to talent; and a two-chamber parliamentary government, with the vote confined to property-holders. Yet by basing the fran-

Liberalism and modernization in other parts of the West

France

chise on age and property qualifications, which made it impossible for the vast majority of those born after 1789 to participate directly in the government of their country, Louis's charter divided France in a way that would contribute to eventual instability.

In 1824, Louis died and was succeeded by his brother Charles X (1824–1830). Charles was an honest, determined reactionary, who once declared that only he and LaFayette had not changed since 1789, the former still a liberal, Charles still a zealous monarchist. By his policies Charles immediately declared himself a foe of liberalism, modernization, and the general legacies of the revolutionary and Napoleonic eras. At his direction the French assembly voted indemnities to those aristocratic emigrés whose land had been confiscated by the state. The Church was allowed to reassert its traditionally exclusive right to teach in French classrooms. The upper middle class, strengthened by its role within the country's growing industrial economy, reacted by heading a rebellion against Charles's reactionary policies. In March 1830, members of the Chamber of Deputies, led by bankers, passed a vote of no confidence in the government. Charles dissolved the chamber, as he was constitutionally empowered to do, and called new elections for deputies. When those elections went against his candidates, Charles further retaliated by a series of ordinances, issued on his own authority, which (1) again dissolved the newly elected chamber before it had even met; (2) imposed strict censorship on the press; (3) further restricted suffrage so as to exclude the upper middle class almost completely; and (4) called for new elections.

What Charles got in return for these measures was revolution. Led by republicans—workers, artisans, students, writers, and the like—Parisians took to the streets. For three days of intense fighting behind hastily constructed barricades, they defied the army and the police, neither of which was anxious to fire into the crowds. Sensing the futility of further resistance, Charles abdicated. Those who had manned the barricades pressed for a genuine republic. But those with the power—bankers, merchants, and industrialists—wanted none of that. Instead they brought the duke of Orleans to the throne as King Louis Philippe (1830–1848) of *the French*—not of France—after extracting a promise from him to abide by the constitution of 1814 which had so suited their particular liberal needs. The franchise was extended, from about 100,000 to 200,000 males. But the right to vote was still based upon property ownership. The major beneficiaries of the change were members of the middle class, those whose interests the Revolution of 1830 primarily served.

Other countries in Europe caught the revolutionary fever in the summer of 1830. As we have already noted, middle- and working-class radicals in England were inspired by the French to press their own case for liberal reform. In Belgium, an insurrection which combined elements of liberal and national sentiment put an end to the

The July Revolution of 1830 in Paris. Workers construct street barricades to ward off government troops.

union of that country with the Dutch, instituted by the Congress of Vienna. The European powers strengthened Belgium's political structure, and hence its independence, by agreeing to the accession of Leopold of Saxe-Coburg, uncle of the future Queen Victoria of England, as king. Once again, a middle class had succeeded in establishing a constitutional monarchy to its liking, congenial to its liberal and entrepreneurial goals. No such fate awaited the liberal nationalists in Poland, who moved at this time to depose their ruler, the Russian Tsar Nicholas, whose hegemony extended to Poland as a result of the Vienna settlement of 1815. Western Europe did not intervene; Russian troops crushed the Polish liberal rebels, and Poland was merged into the tsarist empire.

Liberal forces in Spain enjoyed a greater success. There, middle-class liberalism was linked to the attempts of Queen Maria Christina, widow of King Ferdinand VII, to secure the throne for her daughter, *Spain* Isabella. Though no liberal herself, the queen was prepared to court the favor of urban middle-class elites to win her struggle against her late husband's brother, the reactionary Don Carlos. During the so-called Carlist Wars, which lasted from 1834 to 1840, liberals extracted from Isabella II (1833–1868) a constitution which ensured them a strong voice in the legislature, while restricting the franchise in such a way as to keep the more radical lower middle and artisan classes at bay. By mid-century, however, fear of these radicals led the middle class to acquiesce in a government that was nothing more or less than an authoritarian dictatorship, but that did not threaten directly their own economic interests.

3. LIBERALISM IN BRITAIN AND FRANCE, 1830–1848

The Revolution of 1830 in France and the Parliamentary Reform Bill of 1832 in England represented a setback for aristocratic power in both countries. Aristocrats and their supporters did not cease overnight to play an active role in politics, however. Lord Palmerston, for example, was one of England's most influential prime ministers at mid-century and one of Europe's most authoritative arbiters. But no longer would it be possible for the legislatures of France and England to ignore the particular interests of the middle class. Henceforth representatives would include members from that class in sufficient numbers to press successfully for programs which accorded with liberal beliefs.

One of the major accomplishments of the first British Parliament elected after 1832 was passage of a new law governing the treatment of paupers. In accordance with the law passed in 1598 under Elizabeth I, each parish in England had been declared responsible for the maintenance of its own poor, either through accommodation in poorhouses, or through a system of doles, coupled with local public employment programs. This system, although it by no means eliminated the debilitating effects of poverty, did provide a kind of guarantee against actual starvation. But by 1830 it had broken down. Population growth and economic depressions had produced a far larger number of underemployed men and women in Britain than had ever before existed, placing tremendous strain upon those funds, levied as taxes, which each parish used to provide relief. Industrialization also demanded that families move in search of employment from one part of the country to another; yet the old poor law provided assistance only to those who applied in the parish of their birth. The old law did not accord with liberal notions of efficiency; the new Parliament set about to amend it. The result, drafted by Jeremy Bentham's former private secretary,

An English Workhouse for the Able-Bodied Poor. This workhouse in the county of Devon was built in the late 1830s.

Edwin Chadwick, and passed almost without dissent, clearly reflected the liberal, middle-class notion of how to achieve "the greatest happiness of the greatest number." Doles were to cease forthwith. Those who could not support themselves were to be confined in workhouses. Here conditions were to be made so severe as to all but compel inmates to depart and accept either whatever work they might find outside, no matter how poorly paid, or whatever charity their friends and relatives might be able to provide them. Parishes were to be grouped together into more efficient unions; the law was to be administered by a central board of commissioners in London. Inspiring this new legislation were the liberal belief that poverty was a person's own fault and the liberal assumption that capitalism, though unregulated, was capable of providing enough jobs for all who genuinely wanted them. Economic depressions in the early 1840s proved that latter assumption false, and wrecked the tidy schemes of the poor-law administrators. Doles were once more instituted, taxes once more increased. Yet the law's failure did not shake the liberal conviction that poverty was, in the end, an individual and not an institutional problem.

Even more symbolic of the political power of Britain's middle class than the new poor law was the repeal of the Corn Laws in 1846. The laws, even after their modification in the 1820s, continued to keep the price of bread artificially high, forcing employers, in turn, to pay wages high enough to allow workers to keep food on their tables. More than that, the Corn Laws symbolized to the middle classes the unwarranted privileges of an ancient and, to their minds, generally useless order: the landed aristocracy. The campaign to accomplish repeal was superbly orchestrated and relentless. The Anti–Corn Law League, an organization of middle-class industrialists and their supporters, held large meetings throughout the north of England, lobbied members of Parliament, and, in the end, managed to persuade Sir Robert Peel, now prime minister, of the inevitability of their goal. They were aided, as well, by the potato famine in Ireland, whose existence argued in favor of ending restrictions against the importation of cheap foodstuffs. That Peel was willing to split the Tory—or as it was now coming to be called, Conservative—party to introduce repeal suggests the power of the middle class and its belief in the gospel of free trade.

Repeal of the Corn Laws

Robert Peel

Legislation during this period reflected other middle-class concerns, and in some cases, directly conflicted with the liberal doctrine of nonintervention. Many members of the urban middle class professed devotion to the tenets of Christianity, particularly that doctrine which argued that all human beings have within themselves a soul which they must work to preserve from sin for their eternal salvation. This belief in the ability of an individual to achieve salvation, which contradicted the older Calvinist doctrine of a predestined "elect," accorded well with more general middle-class notions about the importance of individualism and the responsibility of the individual for his or her own well-being. It produced legislation such as the abolition of the slave trade in British colonies (1833), and the series of Factory Acts which set limits on the working hours for child labor and which, in 1847, culminated in the curtailment of the workday in some trades to ten hours. Evangelicals such as William Wilberforce, who was throughout his life an eloquent spokesman for enslaved blacks, and Lord Shaftesbury, who campaigned to end the employment of women and children in mines, maintained that individual souls could not find God when imprisoned in the overworked bodies of plantation slaves or factory operatives. They were joined by others who argued, simply, that to keep people tied to their work for as long as twelve or fourteen hours a day was both inhuman and unnecessary.

The religious issue affected educational reform as well. England had no comprehensive system of state education before 1870. What state support there was came, after the 1830s, in the form of government grants to schools managed by the Church of England. Any move to increase this support, however, met with the strong opposition of middle-class dissenters, who saw it as no more than an attempt by the religious Establishment to extend its influence over the young. Middle-class liberals thus found arguments for reform confusing. The laws of classical economics clashed with other prejudices and beliefs, pulling men and women in various directions at once. Their uncertainty mirrored the extent to which no one could discern a right course in this world of new difficulties and fresh options.

The years of Louis Philippe's reign in France were not so marked as those in England with significant reforms. In the first place, France was not confronted with anything like the same degree of rapid industrialization that was compelling legislative activity on a number of fronts in England. France had nothing to compare with the problems generated by the growth of urban manufacturing centers in the north of England. Though the Chamber of Deputies contained representatives from the upper middle class, they tended to be bankers and merchants, not industrialists. Some were willing to espouse the notion of free trade, though not with the general enthusiasm of their British counterparts, whose unrivaled position as the world's leading manufacturers gave them a vested interest in that cause. Under the succession of governments dominated by France's leading politician of the period, François Guizot (1787–1874), the French expanded their educational system, thereby further underwriting their belief in the liberal doctrine of a meritocracy, or careers open to talent. A French law of 1833 provided for the establishment of elementary schools in every village. Children of indigent parents were to receive a free education; all others would pay a modest fee. In addition, larger towns were to provide training schools for trade and industry, and departments,

Louis Philippe

schools for teacher training. As a result, the number of pupils in France increased from about 2 million in 1831, to about 3.25 million in 1846. Little else of lasting importance was accomplished during the regime of Louis Philippe. Guizot became more and more an apologist for the status quo. Everyone was free, he argued, to rise to the upper middle class and thus to a position of political and economic power. His advice to those who criticized his complacency was: "enrich yourselves." Politicians followed his advice, finding in schemes for the modernization of Paris and the expansion of the railway system ample opportunities for graft. Louis Philippe did little to counteract the lifelessness and corruption that characterized his regime. Although he had played a minor part in the first stage of the revolution of 1789, he was no revolutionary. He did not have the dash and glamor of a Napoleon. He was a paunchy, fussy, and undistinguished person, easily caricatured by his enemies. He appeared to most to be nothing more or less than a typically successful plutocrat. He amassed a fortune which, in characteristic bourgeois fashion, he claimed he had accumulated in order to provide for his five sons and three daughters. He enjoyed the company of bankers and businessmen, though he attempted to develop a reputation as the friend of the people. Rumor had it that when he stopped to shake hands with shopkeepers he wore a special pair of dirty gloves, which he would replace with white kid when hobnobbing with the rich. Louis Philippe was unable to rise above his stodgy public image. The German poet Heinrich Heine reported that the young people of France "yearned for great deeds and scorned the stingy small-mindedness and huckstering selfishness" that the king seemed to embody.

Meanwhile radical members of the French and British lower middle and working classes who had assisted—if not propelled—the forces of liberalism to victory in 1830 and 1832 grew increasingly dissatisfied with the results of their efforts. In Britain they soon realized that the Reform Bill had done little to increase their chances for political participation. For a time they devoted their energies to the cause of trade unionism, believing that industrial, rather than political, action might bring them relief from the economic hardships they were suffering.

Trade union organization had been a goal of militant workers since the beginning of the century. Among the first workers' campaigns in the nineteenth century were those often-riotous revolts organized both in England and, later, on the Continent against the introduction of machinery. In some instances, factories were attacked by workers and machines smashed, in the belief that machines, by replacing skilled workers, were producing widespread unemployment. In England, the rioters were called Luddites, after "Ned Ludd," who was the mythical leader of the movement. In other instances, the hostility of trade unionists was not directed so much toward machinery as toward those workers who refused to join in unions against their masters. Yet no-

The slower pace of reform in France

Growing dissatisfaction of radicals

Trade unionism

where in Europe were trade unions able to organize themselves into effective bargaining agents before 1850. They came closest in England. There, artisans and skilled workers had banded together in the mid-1820s to form both Friendly Societies, really mutual aid and insurance organizations, and cooperatives, communal stores which cut prices by eliminating the middleman between producer and consumer. By 1831, there were about 500 cooperative societies in England, with a membership of something like 20,000. These organizations encouraged the parallel growth of trade unions, which, in the early 1830s, reached the peak of their early power and effectiveness. The National Association for the Protection of Labour comprised about 150 separate local unions in the textile and mining industries of the north; the Operative Builder's Union, about 30,000 workers throughout the country. In 1834, a new and potentially far more radical organization, the Grand National Consolidated Trades Union of Great Britain and Ireland, was organized by a group of London artisans. Its leadership declared that only by bringing the country to a standstill with a general strike could workers compel the governing class to grant them a decent life. At that point, the government decided to put an end to unions. In 1834, six organizers for the Grand National were convicted of administering secret oaths (unions were not themselves illegal) and sentenced to transportation (forced emigration to penal colonies in Australia). Subsequently employers demanded that their workers sign a document pledging their refusal to join a union, thereby stifling opportunities for further organization.

Chartism

After the defeat of the Grand National, the efforts of radical democratic reformers in England turned back from trade union to political activity, centering on attempts to force further political reform upon the uninterested government through the device of the "People's Charter." This document, circulated across the country by committees of Chartists, as they were known, and signed by millions, contained six demands: universal manhood suffrage; institution of the secret ballot; abolition of property qualifications for membership in the House of Commons; annual parliamentary elections; payment of salaries to members of the House of Commons; and equal electoral districts.

Varieties of Chartism

The fortunes of the Chartist movement waxed and waned. In some areas its strength depended upon economic conditions: Chartism spread with unemployment and depression. There were arguments among its leaders as to both ends and means: Did Chartism imply a reorganization of industry or, instead, a return to preindustrial society? Were its goals to be accomplished by petition only, or by more violent means if necessary? The Chartist William Lovett, a cabinetmaker, for example, was as fervent a believer in self-improvement as any member of the middle class. He advocated a union of educated workers to acquire their fair share of the nation's increasing industrial

*The Chartist Procession
to the Houses of Parlia-
ment, April 1848*

bounty. The Chartist Feargus O'Connor, on the other hand, appealed
to the more impoverished and desperate class of workers. He urged a
rejection of industrialization, and the resettlement of the poor on agricultural allotments. These polarities and disagreements regarding the
aims of the movement suggest the extent of the confusion within the
working class, whose consciousness as a separate political force was
only just beginning to develop. Events answered most of the Chartists' questions for them. In 1848, revolutionary outbreaks across the
Continent inspired Chartist leaders to plan a major demonstration and
show of force in London. A procession of 500,000 workers was called,
to bear to Parliament a petition containing 6,000,000 signatures
demanding the six points. Confronted, once again, with the spectre
of open class conflict, special constables and contingents of the regular
army were marshaled under the now-aged duke of Wellington to resist
this threat to order. In the end, fewer than 50,000 made the march to
Parliament, however. Rain, poor management, and unwillingness on
the part of many to do battle with the well-armed constabulary put an
end to the Chartists' campaign. Increased prosperity among skilled
workers disarmed the movement after mid-century.

In France, radical agitation produced very different results. There,
as well, those who had manned the barricades in 1830 soon grew disgusted with the liberalism for which they had risked their lives. In
their minds they carried memories or myths of the years of the first
French Republic—its domestic accomplishments, its foreign victories,
if not its Reign of Terror. They were opposed to constitutional monarchy, and unenthusiastic about parliamentary government, especially
by a *nouveau riche* upper middle class. They were prepared, if necessary, to use force in order to achieve their ends. Centered in an
increasingly industrialized Paris, they were for the most part either

*French republicans and
socialists*

Rue Transnomain. A drawing by Daumier to commemorate the victims of government repression in 1834.

writers, students, or working-class leaders. They met in secret, studied the works of the radical theorist, Gracchus Babeuf (see above, p. 698), whose socialist *Conspiracy of Equals,* written during the French Revolution, became their Bible, and succeeded in making constant trouble for the liberal, middle-class governments of Louis Philippe. Their leading spokesman was the socialist Auguste Blanqui (1805–1881). He decried the victimization of the workers by the middle class, and helped organize secret societies which were to become the instruments of eventual insurrection. Radicals waged some of their most successful campaigns in the press. Honoré Daumier's savage caricatures of Louis Philippe landed him in prison more than once. But campaigners took to the streets as well. In retaliation, the government in 1834 declared radical political organizations illegal. Rioting broke out in Lyon and Paris in protest, where for two days government troops massacred hundreds of insurgents, and arrested some 2,000 republican leaders. In 1835, following an attempt to assassinate Louis Philippe, the government passed a censorship law, which forbade the publication of articles attempting to inspire contempt for the king and which prohibited the printing of any drawing or emblem without prior governmental approval.

These repressive measures served only to increase dissatisfaction with the regime. Guizot was advised by more progressive members of the legislature to extend the franchise to professionals whose lack of wealth now denied them the vote, but whose general adherence to the doctrines of liberalism was unquestioned. Guizot unwisely refused, thereby driving these moderates into the camp of the more radical republicans. By 1847, various elements within the opposition were disaffected enough to instigate a general campaign of agitation throughout France. At political banquets, republicans such as the poet Alphonse de Lamartine (1790–1869) and socialist republicans such as Louis Blanc (see above, p. 765) preached drastic reform, though not

A Caricature of Louis Philippe by Daumier. The inscription reads "Louis Philippe, the Last King of the French." It reflects a popular sentiment of the time.

outright revolution. Contrary to the expressed wishes of the king, a giant protest meeting was announced for February 22, 1848. The day before, the government forbade the meeting. Rioting and barricading during the following two days ended in the abdication of Louis Philippe and increased demands for a republic.

4. THE REVOLUTION OF 1848 IN FRANCE

The February revolution in France was a catalyst which, as we shall see, helped to produce uprisings in the succeeding months throughout much of Europe. Meanwhile, in Paris, a provisional government was established consisting of ten men, seven of whom, including Lamartine, were middle-of-the-road republicans; three of whom, including Blanc, were socialists. The tensions between middle-class republicans and radical socialists, which had been masked by a common disgust with the government of Louis Philippe, now emerged to shape the political events of the ensuing months in several specific ways. Blanc insisted upon the establishment of national workshops, institutions he had championed as a writer, which were to be organized by trades as producers' cooperatives, where men and women workers would be trained if necessary, put to work, and paid two francs a day when employed and a smaller stipend when unemployed. Instead, the government established what it called workshops, but what amounted to nothing more than a program of public works in and around Paris, where economic conditions had resulted in widespread unemployment. Initially, plans had called for the employment of no more than ten or twelve thousand in projects throughout the city. But with unemployment running as high as 65 percent in construction trades and 51 percent in textiles and clothing, workers began to flood into the government's so-called workshops, as many as 66,000 by April, and 120,000 by June.

Republican-socialist split: Blanc's workshops

Paris meanwhile attracted numbers of radical writers, organizers, and agitators. The provisional government had removed all restric-

A National Workshop. When few could read, newspapers were heard rather than scanned. Under government auspices, these workshops achieved a good deal less than Louis Blanc had envisioned.

The Revolution of 1848 in France. A contemporary broadside celebrating the triumph of the people.

Continuing agitation

tions upon the formation of political clubs and the dissemination of political literature. As a result, 170 new journals and more than 200 clubs formed within weeks; the club headed by the socialist Auguste Blanqui boasted a membership of some 3,000. Delegations claiming to represent the oppressed of all European countries—Chartists, Hungarians, Poles—moved freely about the city, attracting attention, if not devoted followings, and contributing to tension which was convincing more and more members of the middle class that stern measures were needed to forestall further insurrectionary outbreaks. This sentiment was fortified as a result of elections held at the end of April. The provisional government had been pressured by Parisian radicals into decreeing universal manhood suffrage. Yet the election returned only a small proportion of radical socialists. The largest blocs consisted of "true," or moderate, republicans and monarchists—this latter group divided, however, between supporters of the Bourbon dynasty and the Orleanist Louis Philippe. The generally conservative tenor of the newly elected assembly strengthened the hand of those who pressed for the repession of the socialists. It also, naturally, convinced the socialists that once again, as in the 1790s, a potentially radical revolution had been betrayed by the timid, self-serving middle class.

The "June Days"

By late spring, a majority of the assembly believed that the workshop system represented both an unbearable financial drain and a serious threat to social order. At the end of May, the workshops were closed to new enrollment as a first step toward barring membership to all who had resided for less than six months in Paris and sending all members between the ages of eighteen and twenty-five to the army. Thousands of workers lost their state-financed jobs, and with them their best chance for survival. Desperate, they and their supporters once more threw up barricades across Paris. For four days, June 23–26, they defended themselves in an ultimately hopeless military battle against armed forces recruited, in part, from willing provincials eager enough to assist in the repression of the urban working class. Whether or not the Parisian insurrectionists were fighting as members of a beleaguered class, or simply as men and women on the brink of starvation, is a matter that historians continue to debate. That they were taken seriously as a revolutionary threat can be seen by the ferocity with which they were hunted out once the street fighting had ceased. About 3,000 were killed and 12,000 more arrested, the majority of whom were deported to Algerian labor camps.

In the aftermath of the "June Days," the French government moved quickly to bring order to the country. The assembly, faced with the task of drafting a republican constitution, contained a large number of men to whom the idea of a republic was anathema. Assembly members therefore arranged for the immediate election of a president. Their hope was that a strong leader might assist in bringing dissidents to heel. Four candidates stood: Lamartine, the moderate republican; General Eugène Cavaignac, who had commanded the troops in June; Alexander Ledru-Rollin, a socialist; and Louis Napoleon Bonaparte, nephew of the emperor, who polled more than twice as many votes as the other three candidates combined.

The imposition of order

The astonishing upstart Louis Napoleon had spent most of his life in exile. Returning to France after the Revolution of 1830, he was imprisoned a few years later for attempting to provoke a local uprising. But in 1846 he escaped to England, where he was supplied with funds by both British and French reactionaries. By the summer of 1848 the situation in France was such that he knew it was safe to return. In fact, he was welcomed by members of all classes. Conservatives were looking for a savior to protect their property against the onslaughts of the radicals. Workers were beguiled by his glittering schemes for prosperity in his book, *The Extinction of Pauperism,* and by the fact that he had corresponded with Louis Blanc and with Pierre Proudhon, the anarchist. In between these two classes was a multitude of patriots and hero-worshipers to whom the name Napoleon was a symbol of glory and greatness. It was chiefly to this multitude that the nephew of the Corsican owed his astounding triumph. As one old peasant expressed it: "How could I help voting for this gentleman—I whose nose was frozen at Moscow?"

The rise of Louis Napoleon

With dreams of emulating his uncle, Louis Napoleon was not long content to remain president of France. Almost from the first he used the power he already had to achieve the further power he desired. He enlisted the support of the Catholics by permitting them to regain control over the schools and by sending an expedition to Rome to restore to the pope the temporal power denied him during the revolutionary struggles of 1848. He courted the workers and the middle class by introducing old-age insurance and laws for the encouragement of business. In 1851, alleging the need for extraordinary mea-

A second emperor

Napoleon III's Decree Dissolving the National Assembly

sures to protect the rights of the masses, he proclaimed a temporary dictatorship and invited the people to grant him the power to draw up a new constitution. In the plebiscite held on December 21, 1851, he was authorized by an overwhelming majority (7,500,000 to 640,000) to proceed as he liked. The new constitution, which he put into effect in January 1852, made the president an actual dictator. After one year Louis Napoleon Bonaparte ordered another plebiscite and, with the approval of over 95 percent of the voters, assumed the title of Napoleon III, emperor of the French.[2]

The implications of the French Revolution of 1848

What is the significance of the French Revolution of 1848 and its political aftermath in the history of middle-class liberalism, which is our subject? Two points need particular emphasis. First, we must recognize the pivotal role of the liberal middle class. Under Louis Philippe, it increasingly perceived itself and its particular interests as neglected. Denied a direct political voice because of a severely limited franchise, it swung to the left, allying itself with radicals who, by themselves, would probably have stood no chance of permanent success. Yet no sooner had Louis Philippe abdicated than the liberal middle class began to wonder if "success" was not about to bring disaster upon its heels. And so it swung again, this time to the right, where it found itself confronting the mysterious and yet not entirely unattractive prospect of Louis Napoleon. He, in turn, was clever enough to understand this first lesson of 1848, that in France no government could survive that did not cater to the interests of the middle class. By assisting it to achieve its liberal economic goals, the emperor helped it forget just how heavily he was trampling on its political liberties.

[2] Napoleon I's son, Napoleon II, had died in Vienna in 1832.

Yet 1848 proved that there was now in France another element—class consciousness may, at this point, not yet be the correct term—that governments ignored at their peril. If mid–nineteenth-century Europe saw the middle class closer than ever to the center of power, it saw the workers moving rapidly in from the edge. Their barricades could, if necessary, be destroyed, and their demands ignored, but only at an increasingly grave risk to the fabric of the state. Middle-class liberalism, if it was to thrive, would not only have to pay lip service to working-class demands, but in some measure accommodate to them as well.

Napoleon III

5. LIBERALISM IN FRANCE AND BRITAIN AFTER 1850

Napoleon III recognized the vital role that public opinion had now assumed in the management of affairs of state. He labored hard and successfully to sell his empire to the people of France. He argued that legislative assemblies only served to divide a nation along class lines. With power residing in him, he would unite the country as it had not been for generations. The French, who craved order following their recent political misadventures, bought the program he was selling willingly enough. Napoleon III modeled his constitution upon that of his uncle. An assembly, elected by universal manhood suffrage, in fact possessed almost no power. It could do no more than approve legislation drafted at the emperor's direction by a Council of State. Elections were manipulated by the government to ensure the return of politically docile representatives. Control of finance, the army, and foreign affairs rested exclusively with the emperor. France was a democracy only in the sense that its people were periodically afforded a chance, through elections, to express their approval of Napoleon's regime.

Napoleon III's
constitution

In return for the gift of almost absolute power, Napoleon III gave the French what they appeared to want. For the middle class, he provided a chance to make a great deal of money. The device of the *Crédit Mobilier,* an investment banking institution, facilitated the expansion of industry by selling its shares to the public and using its income to underwrite various entrepreneurial schemes. In 1863 a limited liability law encouraged further investment by guaranteeing that stockholders could lose no more than the par value of their stock no matter how indebted the company in which they had invested. Railways, owned by the state, spread across the country, and spurred further industrial expansion. So prosperous did the French economy appear that Napoleon was prepared to follow Britain's lead in pressing for tariff-free trade between the two countries. A treaty was signed in 1860; though funds were set aside to compensate French industries for any loss they might suffer, they were never completely expended, suggesting that French manufacturers were now well enough established to meet the threat of British competition. The apparent satisfaction of the middle class with

Napoleon III and the
middle class

Paris under the Second Empire. The Avenue de l'Imperatrice was designed for the enjoyment of the middle class.

Empress Eugénie

Napoleon's regime provides a measure with which to assess the state of liberalism in France after 1850. The fact that the country no longer enjoyed a free press, that universities were politically controlled, and that political opposition was repressed seemed to matter very little to most. Liberalism, if it existed at all, existed as the freedom to have one's own economic way.

Napoleon III, though he catered to the middle class, did not fail to court the favor of the workers as well. He encouraged the establishment of hospitals and instituted a program of free medical assistance. More important, he permitted, if he did nothing to encourage, the existence of trade unions and in 1864 introduced legislation to legalize strikes. Ultimately, he appealed to the workers much as he appealed to the middle class, as a glamorous, if not heroic symbol of his country's reemergence as a leading world power. The activities of his court, and of his stylish empress, Eugénie, were well publicized. The reconstruction of Paris into a city of broad boulevards and grand open spaces was calculated to provide appropriate scenery for the theater of empire—as well as to lessen the chances for successful proletarian barricade-building across narrow streets.

Grandeur, however, appeared to Napoleon III to demand an aggressive foreign policy. Although early in his regime he declared himself in favor of that central liberal tenet—international peace—he was soon at war: first against Russia in the Crimea; then in Italy; then in Mexico, where he attempted to assist in the establishment of another empire; and finally and disastrously with Prussia. The details of these adventures are part of the subject of the following chapter. It is enough at this point to remark that Napoleon III's foreign policy reflects clearly how far he—and the rest of France with him—had subordinated the liberal heritage of the first French Revolution to that of another of its legacies: national glory.

What, meanwhile, of the liberal tradition in Britain? There the course of liberalism was altered by changes occurring within the working class. Industrialization had, by this time, begun to foster and sustain a growing stratum of labor "aristocrats," men whose particular skills, and the increasing demand for them, allowed them to demand wages high enough to ensure them a fairly comfortable standard of living. These workers—concentrated for the most part within the building, engineering, and textile industries—turned from the tradition of militant radicalism that had characterized the so-called hungry forties. Having succeeded within the liberal economic system imposed upon Britain by the middle class, they were now prepared to accept many liberal, middle-class principles as their own. They believed in self-help, achieved by means of cooperative societies or through trade unions, whose major function was the accumulation of funds to be used as insurance against old age and unemployment. They believed in education as a tool for advancement, and patronized the Mechanics Institutes and other similar institutions either founded by them or on their behalf.

Liberalism in Britain: the "labor aristocracy"

Yet the labor aristocracy, as it came to appreciate its ability to achieve a decent life for itself within the capitalist system, grew all the more dissatisfied with a political system which excluded it from any direct participation in the governmental process. Although some pressed for extension of the franchise as democrats, as many argued for it on the same grounds the middle class had used in 1832. They were responsible workers, whose loyalty to the state could not be questioned. As such, they were a bona fide "interest," as worthy of the vote and of direct representation as the middle class. They were joined in their campaign by many middle-class reformers who continued to chafe at the privileged position of national institutions which they associated with the landed society and the old order. Many middle-class men and women, for example, were dissenters from the Church of England; yet they were forced to pay taxes to support a church which was staffed, in the main, by sons of the gentry. Their sons were denied the facilities of the nation's ancient universities, Oxford and Cambridge, unless those sons subscribed to the articles of faith of the Anglican church.

Middle-class dissatisfaction

Together with working-class leaders, these middle-class dissidents organized a Reform League to campaign across the country for a new reform bill and a House of Commons responsive to their interests. Though by no means revolutionary, the reformers made it clear by their actions that they were determined to press their case to the utmost. Politicians in Britain in the 1860s were confronted by a situation not unlike that which had faced Guizot in France in 1848: middle class, lower middle class, and skilled workers discontented and demanding reform. Unlike Guizot, however, the leaders of both British politi-

Reform Bill of 1867

cal parties, Conservative (formerly Tory) and Liberal (formerly Whig), were prepared to concede what they recognized it would be dangerous to withhold. Once convinced of this need, the Conservative leader of the House of Commons and future prime minister, Benjamin Disraeli, seized upon reform as an issue with which to belabor the Liberals. In 1867 he steered a bill through Parliament more far-reaching than anything proposed by his political opponents. It doubled the franchise by extending the vote to any males who paid poor rates or rent of ten pounds or more a year in urban areas (this would mean, in general, the skilled workers), and to tenants paying rent of twelve pounds or more in the counties. Seats were again redistributed as in 1832, with large northern cities gaining representation at the expense of the rural south. The "responsible" working class had been deemed worthy to participate in the affairs of state. For the next twenty years it showed its appreciation by accepting its apprentice position without demur, and by following the lead prescribed by the middle class.

The triumph of British liberalism

The decade or so following the passage of the Reform Bill of 1867 marked the high point of British liberalism. The labor aristocracy was accommodated with an Education Act, virtually guaranteeing a primary education to all, with legalization of trade unions, and with a series of measures designed to improve living conditions in the great cities; yet it was the middle class that set the governmental tone. Under Disraeli and his Liberal counterpart William Gladstone, and with the cooperation of the newly enfranchised skilled workers, Britain celebrated the triumph of the liberal principles of free trade, representative—but not democratic—government, and general prosperity.

SELECTED READINGS

• *Items so designated are available in paperback editions.*

Anderson, R. D., *Education in France, 1848–1870,* New York, 1975. Covers every level of formal education and its practical and theoretical relationship to state and society.

• Artz, Frederick B., *Reaction and Revolution, 1814–1832,* New York, 1934. A European survey, dated but still useful.

Blake, Robert, *Disraeli,* London, 1966. A masterful biography.

Briggs, Asa, *The Age of Improvement,* New York, 1959. A survey of England from 1780 to 1870, particularly strong on Victorian attitudes.

Duveau, Georges, *1848: The Making of a Revolution,* New York, 1967. Focuses on the working class during the revolution in Paris: their unity at the outset, their division in the "June Days."

Finer, Samuel E., *The Life and Times of Edwin Chadwick,* London, 1952. An excellent biography of the great English Benthamite reformer.

Halévy, Elie, *A History of the English People*, Vols. II–IV, London, 1949–1952. The best survey of nineteenth-century England, comprehensive and analytical.

Harrison, Royden, *Before the Socialists: Studies in Labour and Politics, 1861–1881*, London, 1965. Examines the social and political background of franchise extension in Britain.

• Hobsbawm, E., and G. Rudé, *Captain Swing: A Social History of the Great English Agricultural Uprising of 1830*, New York, 1975.

Johnson, Douglas, *Guizot: Aspects of French History, 1787–1874*, London, 1963. Analytical essays about the leading politician of the July monarchy.

• Kissinger, Henry, *A World Restored: Metternich, Castlereagh, and the Problem of Peace, 1812–1822*, Boston, 1957. By an admirer of Metternich.

• Langer, William L., *Political and Social Upheaval, 1832–1852*, New York, 1969. (Several chapters have been published separately under the title *The Revolutions of 1848*.) A thorough general survey.

• McCord, Norman, *The Anti–Corn Law League*, London, 1955.

Magnus, Philip, *Gladstone: A Biography*, London, 1955. A readable and reliable biography.

Merriman, John M., ed., *1830 in France*, New York, 1975. Recent scholarship emphasizing the nature of revolution and examining events outside of Paris.

• Pinkney, David, *Napoleon III and the Rebuilding of Paris*, Princeton, N.J., 1972. An interesting account of the creation of modern Paris during the Second Empire.

——, *The French Revolution of 1830*, Princeton, N.J., 1972. A reinterpretation, now the best history of the revolution.

Roberts, David, *Victorian Origins of the British Welfare State*, New Haven, Conn., 1960. Examines various nineteenth-century reforms in England.

• Robertson, Priscilla, *The Revolution of 1848: A Social History*, Princeton, N.J., 1960. Surveys the revolutions across Europe.

de Sauvigny, G. de Bertier, *The Bourbon Restoration*, New York, 1967. An outstanding work; the best history of a neglected period.

• Stearns, Peter N., *1848: The Revolutionary Tide in Europe*, New York, 1974. Stresses the social background of the revolutions.

Thompson, J. M., *Louis Napoleon and the Second Empire*, Oxford, 1954. A good biography. Presents Louis Napoleon as a modern Hamlet.

Woodward, E. L., *The Age of Reform*, Oxford, 1962. An excellent survey from the Oxford History of England series.

• Wright, Gordon, *France in Modern Times: 1760 to the Present*, 3rd ed., New York, 1981. The best textbook on modern France.

• Zeldin, Theodore, *The Political System of Napoleon III*, New York, 1958. Examines the processes by which Napoleon maintained power as the first modern dictator.

——, *France, 1848–1951*, 2 vols., Oxford, 1973–77.

SOURCE MATERIALS

• Flaubert, Gustave, *L'Education Sentimentale*, London, 1961. Contains an unsympathetic but memorable portrait of the Revolution of 1848 and of the bourgeois style of life that contributed to its outbreak.

• Greville, Charles Fulke, *Memoirs,* ed. by Roger Fulford, New York, 1963. Originally published in seven volumes in 1875, these comprise the diaries of the secretary to the Privy Council for the years 1821–1861. An excellent source for the court and politics of the period.

• Price, Roger, ed., *1848 in France,* Ithaca, N.Y., 1975. An excellent collection of eyewitness accounts, annotated.

Stewart, John Hall, *The Restoration Era in France, 1814–1830,* Princeton, N.J., 1968. A brief narrative and a good collection of documents.

Chapter 24

NATIONALISM AND NATION-BUILDING (1815–1870)

The present problem, the first task . . . is simply to preserve the existence and continuance of what is German.

—Johann Fichte, *Addresses to the German Nation*

The great questions of the day will not be decided by speeches or by majority decisions—that was the mistake of 1848 and 1849—but by blood and iron.

—Otto von Bismarck, speech, 1862

I f the history of nineteenth-century Britain and France can be studied against a general background of middle-class liberalism, that of much of the rest of Europe during the same period must be understood in terms of a more complex combination of the forces of liberalism, nationalism, and nation-building. We shall define nationalism as a sentiment rooted in broad historical, geographical, linguistic, or cultural circumstances. It is characterized by a consciousness of belonging, in a group, to a tradition derived from those circumstances, which differs from the traditions of other groups. Nation-building is the political implementation of nationalism, the translation of sentiment into power.

Nationalism and nation-building defined

Men and women in Britain and France during the nineteenth century entertained national as well as liberal sentiments. When Britain's prime minister, Lord Palmerston, declared in 1850 that any British citizen, in any part of the world, had but to proclaim, like a citizen of the Roman Empire, "civis Romanus sum" ("I am a citizen of Rome") to summon up whatever force might be necessary to protect him from foreign depradations, he was echoing his countrymen's pride in the powers of their nationhood. When the French rejoiced in 1840 at the return of the Emperor Napoleon's remains from St. Helena to an elaborate shrine in Paris, they were reliving triumphs that had become

Nationalism in Britain and France

part of their nation's heritage. Palmerston's boast and Napoleon's bones were both artifacts of national traditions and sentiments bound up in the life of the English and the French.

*Nationalism
elsewhere*

Nineteenth-century nationalism in other areas of Europe was to be a more assertive phenomenon than it was in Britain and France, which had for centuries existed as particular geographical, cultural, and political entities. Elsewhere, common traditions and assumptions were less clearly articulated, because the political unity that might have helped define them did not exist. East Prussians or Venetians had no difficulty in perceiving of themselves as such; history had provided them with those identities. But history had not provided them, except in the most general way, with identities as Germans or Italians. They had to make a deliberate effort to think of themselves in those terms before the terms could have any political reality.

Nationalism and liberalism

Neither nationalism nor nation-building stood in necessary opposition to liberalism. Indeed, to the extent that nationalism celebrated the achievements of a particular common people over those of a cosmopolitan aristocratic elite, it reflected liberalism's abhorrence of traditional privilege. Yet to liberalism's readiness to accept the new, nationalism responded with an appreciation, if not veneration, of the past. And to the liberals' insistence upon the value and importance of individualism, nation-builders replied that their vital task might require the sacrifice of some measure of each citizen's freedom. The success of nation-building rested upon the foundation of a general balance of international power, achieved by the European states during the half century after 1815. The emergence of new nations—a unified Italy and Germany—would require readjustments to that balance. But accommodation remained possible, with only minor skirmishes marring the stability of the settlement achieved at the Congress of Vienna.

1. ROMANTICISM AND NATIONALISM

*Romanticism
defined*

As we noted in the preceding chapter, nationalism was in part a child of the French Revolution. It was closely related, as well, to the intellectual movement that has been called "romanticism." Romanticism was so broad and so varied that it all but defies definition, if not analysis. Perhaps as much as anything, romanticism represented a reaction against the rationalism of the eighteenth-century Enlightenment. Where the eighteenth century relied on reason, the romantics put their faith in emotion. The eighteenth century understood the mind as a blank tablet, which received knowledge from impressions imprinted upon it through the senses by the external world. Romantics also believed in the importance of sense experience. But they insisted that innate sensibility—that which constituted a person's own particular personality—was inherited, and therefore present in the mind from birth. Knowledge, then, for the romantic, was the product of both innate feelings *and* external perceptions. Romanticism thus stressed individualism, and the individual creativity that resulted from the interaction of unique personality with external experience. At the same time, by stressing the inheritance of attitudes, it also celebrated the past. And that celebration was its link with nationalism.

Romanticism and nationalism were connected by their common belief that the past should be made to function as a means of understanding the present and planning for the future. It was in Germany that this notion received its fullest airing and most enthusiastic reception. One of the earliest and most influential German romantics was Johann von Herder (1744–1803). A Protestant pastor and theologian, his interest in past cultures led him, in the 1780s, to set out his reflections in a lengthy and detailed treatise, *Ideas for a Philosophy of Human History*. Herder traced what he perceived to be the progressive development of European society from the time of the Greeks through the Renaissance. He believed that civilization was not the product of an artificial, international elite—a criticism of Enlightenment thinking—but of the genuine culture of the common people, the *Volk*. No civilization could be considered sound which did not continue to express its own unique historical character, its *Volksgeist*. Herder did not argue that one *Volksgeist* was either better or worse than any other. He insisted only that each nation must be true to its own particular heritage. He broke dramatically with the Enlightenment idea that human beings could be expected to respond to human situations in more or less the same fashion, and with the assumption that the value of history was simply to teach by example.

Johann von Herder

Herder's intellectual heirs, men like the conservative German romantics Friedrich Schlegel (1772–1829) and Friedrich von Savigny (1779–1861) condemned the implantation of democratic and liberal ideas—"foreign" to Germany—in German cultural soil. History, they argued, taught that institutions must evolve organically—a favorite word of the political romantics, and that proper laws were the product of historical growth, not simply deductions from universal first principles. This idea was not peculiar to German romantics. The English romantic poet and philosopher Samuel Taylor Coleridge (1772–1834) argued against the utilitarian state and in favor of giving that ancient institution, the national church, a larger role in the shaping of society. The French conservative Chateaubriand (1768–1848) made much the same case in his treatise, *The Genius of Christianity,* published in 1802. The past, and in particular the religious experiences of the past, are woven into the present, he declared. They cannot be unwoven without destroying the fabric of a nation's society.

The role of history and religion

The theory of the organic evolution of society and the state received its fullest exposition in the writings of the German metaphysician Georg Wilhelm Hegel (1770–1831). Professor of philosophy at the

Georg Wilhelm Hegel

Fichte

University of Berlin, he attracted many adherents. Hegel wrote of history as development: Social and political institutions grew to maturity, achieved their purposes, and then gave way to others. Yet the new never entirely replaced the old, for the pattern of change was "dialectic." When new institutions challenged established ones, there was a clash of "thesis" and "antithesis" producing a "synthesis," a reordering of society that retained elements from the past while adapting to the present. Hegel expected, for example, that the present disunity among the German states (thesis), which generated the idea of unity (antithesis), would inevitably result in the creation of a nation-state (synthesis). Hegel had no use for the theory of a state of nature, so popular with philosophers like Rousseau and Hobbes. Men and women have always lived within some society or other, Hegel argued. The institution of the state was itself a natural historic organism; only within that institution, protected by its laws and customs from personal depradations, could men and women enjoy freedom, which Hegel defined not as the absence of restraint but as the absence of social disorder.

These theories of history and of historical development articulated by the romantics relate directly to the idea of nationalism formulated during the same period. The French Revolution provided an example of what a nation could achieve. Nationhood had encouraged the French to raise themselves to the level of citizenship; it had also allowed them to sustain attacks from the rest of Europe. Applying the historical lessons of the French Revolution and the theories of romantics, Germans, in particular, were roused to a sense of their own historical destiny. The works of the philosopher J. G. Fichte (1762–1814) are an example of this reawakening. As a young professor at the University of Jena, Fichte had at first advanced a belief in the importance of an individual's inner spirit, the creator of its own moral universe. Devoid of national feeling, he welcomed the French Revolution as an emancipator of the human spirit. Yet when France conquered much of Germany, Fichte's attitude changed dramatically. He adopted Herder's notion of a *Volksgeist;* what mattered was no longer the individual spirit, but the spirit of a whole people, expressed in its customs, traditions, and history. In 1808, Fichte delivered a series of *Addresses to the German Nation,* in which he declared the existence of a German spirit, not just one among many such spirits, but superior to the rest. The world had not yet heard from that spirit; he predicted it soon would. Although the French military commander in Berlin, where Fichte spoke, believed the addresses too academic to warrant censorship, they expressed a sentiment that aided the Prussians in their conscious attempt to rally themselves, and, as a political *Volk,* to drive out the French.

Nationalism, derived from romantic notions of historical development and destiny, manifested itself in a variety of ways. The brothers Grimm, editors of *Grimm's Fairy Tales* (1812), traveled across Germany to study native dialects, and collected folktales that were published as part of a national heritage. The poet Friedrich Schiller's (1759–1805) drama of *William Tell,* the Swiss hero (1804), became a rallying cry for German national consciousness. In Britain, Sir Walter Scott (1771–1832) retold in many of his novels the popular history of Scotland, while the poet William Wordsworth (1770–1850) consciously strove to express the simplicity and virtue of the English people in collections such as his *Lyrical Ballads* (1798). Throughout Europe, countries assiduously catalogued the relics of their historical past as in the society for publishing the *Monumenta Germaniae Historica* (Monuments of German History), founded in 1819; the French École des Chartes (1821); and the English Public Records Office (1838). In France, the neoclassical style, typified by the paintings of David, and used by Napoleon to exalt his image, gave way to the turbulent romanticism of painters like Eugène Delacroix, whose *Liberty Leading the People* (1830) was a proclamation not only of liberty, but of the courage of the French nation. Music, too, reflected national themes, though not until a generation or so after 1815. Many of Giuseppe Verdi's (1813–1901) operas, *Don Carlo,* for example, contained musical declarations of faith in the possibility of an Italian *risorgimento:* a resurrection of the Italian spirit. The operas of Richard Wagner (1813–1883)—in particular, those based on the German epic, *Song of the Nibelung*—managed to raise veneration for the myths of Nordic gods and goddesses to the level of pious exaltation. Architects, though they found it difficult to escape entirely from the neoclassicism of the eighteenth century, often tried to resurrect a "national" style in their designs. Sir Charles Barry, assigned the task of redesigning the British Houses of Parliament following their destruction by fire in 1836, managed to mask a straightforward and symmetrical classical plan behind a Gothic screen, intended to acknowledge the coun-

Giuseppe Verdi

See color plates
following page 800 for
*Liberty Leading the
People* and *The Massacre
of Chios* by Delacroix

Houses of Parliament, London. Redesigned by Sir Charles Barry with a Gothic facade after the earlier structure was destroyed by fire.

A William Blake Etching for a Children's Book Written by Mary Wollstonecraft

George Sand

try's debt to its own past. All this creative activity was the spontaneous result of artists' and writers' enthusiastic response to the romantic movement. Yet politicians soon perceived how historical romanticism might serve their nationalist ends. They understood how an individual work of art, whether a painting, a song, a drama, or a building, could translate into a national symbol. And they did not hesitate to assist in that translation when they deemed it useful.

Though romanticism and nationalism shared a common devotion to the past, romantics were not necessarily nationalists. Indeed, romanticism was explicitly international in its celebration of nature, and above all, of individual creativity. The romantics declared that nature was best perceived not by reason, but by the senses. And they respected those elements of nature which appeared the product of chance, not rational order. Whether as a single flower or a mountain range, nature was welcomed as it impressed itself directly on the senses. Men and women were declared free to interpret nature—and life as well—in terms of their individual reactions to it, not simply as it might reflect a set of general rational precepts. The English poet Percy Shelley (1792–1822), the German poet Heinrich Heine (1797–1856), the French novelist Victor Hugo (1802–1885), the Spanish painter Franciso Goya (1746–1828)—all characteristic figures of the romantic movement—expressed in their works romanticism's concern for the experiences of human individuals, a concern that transcended national boundaries. Human experience, romantics believed, was not linked to any one national tradition or *Volksgeist,* but rather to transcendant nature. The paintings of the Englishmen William Blake (1757–1827) and J. M. W. Turner (1775–1851), although they often reflect "Englishness," transcend nationalism by recording a communion with the fundamental elements of nature.

Romantics were internationalists because they enjoyed freedom from the confinement of any boundary—metaphysical or political—which tended to restrict a person's ability to realize his or her potential. In this way romanticism encouraged women to make themselves heard. The Englishwoman Mary Wollstonecraft (1759–1797), author of *A Vindication of the Rights of Woman;* Madame de Staël (1766–1817), an emigré from France to Germany during the revolutionary period, whose essay *De l'Allemagne* (On Germany) was steeped in romanticism; George Sand (1804–1876), whose novels, and whose life, proclaimed allegiance to the standards of radical individualism—these women exemplify romanticism's readiness to break with the past, and its assumptions and stereotypes, if they stood in the path of individual expression.

Romantics, as worshipers of individuality, worshiped "genius." The genius was possessed of a spirit which could not be analyzed and must be allowed to make its own rules. (It was the particular genius of an entire people, of course, that Herder extolled as the *Volksgeist.*) And the human spirit must never allow itself to be fettered by national

The Gleaners, Jean François Millet (1814–1875). A Realist, Millet remained fascinated with color and setting to a degree that often made his paintings something other than a record of social change. (Louvre)

Funeral at Ornans, Gustave Courbet (1819–1877). Though a less strident Realist than his contemporary Daumier, Courbet was concerned to express human nature as he found it—neither more handsome nor more ugly. This painting, in which he used men and women from his village as models, reflects his commitment to personal, as opposed to social, Realism. (Louvre)

Execution of the Rioters, Francisco Goya (1746–1828). Unlike most artists of his time, Goya dealt unflinchingly with suffering, violence, fear, and death. Depicted here is the execution of Spanish rebels by Napoleon's soldiers in 1808. This harshness caused the rebellion to spread over the whole peninsula. (Prado)

The Raft of the Medusa, Théodore Géricault (1791–1824). Agony and suffering is vividly portrayed in Géricault's realistic figures. (Louvre)

Liberty Leading the People, Eugène Delacroix (1798–1863). Delacroix was a romantic painter of dramatic and emotional scenes. In this painting he celebrates the triumph of the revolutionary principle of liberty in a tempestuous allegory. (Louvre)

The Massacre of Chios, Eugène Delacroix. Here Delacroix again puts his brush to work for the cause of liberty, eulogizing the more than 20,000 Greeks slain by the Turks during the Greek war of independence in 1822. (Louvre)

The Last of England, Ford Madox Brown (1821–1893). A haunting scene of a couple emigrating from England by one of the most noted pre-Raphaelites. (The City Museum and Art Gallery, Birmingham, England)

Valley of Aosta—Snowstorm, Avalanche, and Thunderstorm, Joseph M. W. Turner (1775–1851). Turner's complete absorption in light, color, and atmosphere helped to prepare the way for the French Impressionists. (MMA)

A Woman Reading, Camille Corot (1796–1875). Corot was a Naturalist whose interest in the effects of light prefigured to a degree the work of the Impressionists. Sentimentality and a preference for scenes of innocence and simplicity distinguished him from the Realists. (MMA)

The Port of La Rochelle, Corot. (Louvre)

Apotheosis of Homer, Jean Auguste Ingres (1780–1867). Though he painted during the Romantic period, Ingres did not desert the neoclassical themes and style that dominated art during the Revolutionary and Napoleonic eras. (Louvre)

Beatrice and Dante, William Blake (1757–1827). Blake was a mystical Romantic whose work possesses a compelling uniqueness that defies exact categorization. This painting is from his series for *The Divine Comedy.* (The Tate Gallery, London)

Left: *A Page from the Score of Beethoven's Piano Sonata Opus 109 in E Major.* Right:
Ludwig van Beethoven

prescriptions, any more than by social conventions, in such a way as
to prevent enjoyment of its most precious possession, its freedom.

Freedom and the problem of self-recognition were major themes in
the work of two of the giants of the romantic movement, the composer Ludwig van Beethoven (1770–1827) and the writer Johann
Wolfgang von Goethe (1749–1832). The most remarkable quality
about Beethoven's compositions is their uniqueness and individuality.
In the Fifth Symphony Beethoven reaches the summit of symphonic
logic, the Sixth is a glorification of nature, the Seventh a Dionysian
revelry, the Eighth a genial conjuring up of the spirit of the eighteenth-century symphony. The deafness which afflicted Beethoven in
his later years seems to have encouraged him in his determination to
speak out through his music as one extraordinarily powerful, and at
times distressed, human being. Five piano sonatas, five string quartets, the Ninth Symphony, and the great Mass, *Missa Solemnis,* constitute his final legacy. They fill the listener with awe not so much
because of their unusual form or their vast proportions, but because
they express boundless individual will and power.

Goethe's dedication to the idea of individual freedom was, in part,
the product of his having been born and raised in the free imperial city
of Frankfurt. Frankfurt was an international center, a trading place
open to intellectual winds from all quarters. Goethe was, in terms of
his environment, free from the particularist, nationalist influences
which directed the work of other German romantics. Goethe's own
"genius" drove him first to the study of law, then medicine, then the

Beethoven

Goethe

An Illustration from Goethe's Sorrows of Werther

Immanuel Kant

fine arts and natural sciences. In 1775 he took up residence at the court of the young duke of Weimar. Weimar was a tiny German principality with a population of no more than half a million, another cosmopolitan community and in this respect not unlike Frankfurt. Influenced by Herder, Goethe had already published various romantically inclined works, including the immensely popular *Sorrows of Werther,* a novel expressive of Goethe's early restlessness and emotionalism. The almost excessive sensitivity characteristic of Goethe's earlier writings gave way, in his middle years, to the search for a new spirit, equally free and yet more ordered. This mode derived from his experiences in Italy and from his study of the ancient Romans and Greeks. In 1790 Goethe published the first part of his masterpiece, *Faust,* a drama in verse, which he completed a year before his death in 1832. The play, in its retelling of the German legend of the man who sold his soul to the devil in return for universal knowledge, reflects the romantic unwillingness to restrain the spirit; it also expresses Goethe's own recognition of the magnitude of humanity's daring in its desire for unlimited knowledge and its own fulfillment.

The theme of self-realization as humanity's ultimate goal, so characteristic of so much of romantic thinking, contrasted with the notions of those other romantics we have discussed, who, like Herder, insisted upon the subordination of one human spirit to the spirit of a whole people. Immanuel Kant (1724–1804), Goethe's only rival as a thinker during this period, expressed himself as opposed to the idea that unbounded individual freedom was the highest good. Kant, a retiring scholar who lived out his life in the city of Königsberg, where he was born, argued that there were limits to human knowledge, that beyond the world of appearances there lay an unknowable realm of what he called "things in themselves." This thesis, first expounded in his *Critique of Pure Reason* (1781), was further developed in his *Critique of Practical Reason* (1790), in which he attempted to establish proper criteria for personal behavior. If pure reason could neither prove nor disprove the existence of God, Kant argued, practical reason tells us that in the idea of God there exists a notion of moral perfection toward which all people must strive. They must live consistent with what Kant called the "categorical imperative": to act as if one's actions were to become a universal law of nature. Kant argued that only by living according to this categorical imperative could men and women enjoy true freedom. Freedom he defined in terms of self-imposed duty, rather than the absence of restraint or—as in Goethe's case—the compulsion to achieve self-fulfillment.

Whether or not Kant can be classed as a romantic is a question that historians have continued to debate. His devotion to reason has often led scholars to consider him a late Enlightenment figure. In one respect, however, Kant certainly thought with the romantics. His insistence that "things in themselves" were ultimately unknowable, reflected the romantics' willingness to surrender to the mysterious. "There is nothing beautiful, pleasing, or grand in life, but that which is more or less mysterious," Chateaubriand wrote, in his defense of Christianity. While Kant was not an explicit defender of Christianity, his philosophy helped perpetuate religious belief, and was thus one in its effect with romanticism. Certainly Kant was not a romantic nationalist, although nationalists used his arguments to support their claim that men and women had a duty to an authority higher than themselves. Kant himself, however, in his treatise *On Perpetual Peace,* published at the height of the revolutionary wars in 1795, argued vehemently against national aggrandizement and in favor of a kind of European federal union.

Kant as a romantic

Romanticism and nationalism bear much the same relationship to each other in the history of nineteenth-century Europe as they do in the thought of the men and women we have just surveyed. At some points, as in England, they appear to run separate courses. At others they join together, as they did in Germany, whose own history lies at the center of the history of both romanticism and nationalism.

The relationship between romanticism and nationalism

2. NATIONALISM AND NATION-BUILDING: 1800–1848

The humiliating French occupation of Prussia, combined with the growing sense of national destiny exemplified in Fichte's *Addresses,* resulted in a drive on the part of Prussian intellectuals and political reformers to bring their country once more to its former position among European powers. Prussia's crushing defeat by the French in 1806 had been the logical outcome of the inertia that had gripped the country during the half century or so since the aggressive achievements of Frederick the Great. Unlike the rest of the German states, however, allied directly with France in the Confederation of the Rhine, the separate kingdom of Prussia consciously avoided French "contamination," participating unwillingly in the Continental System, and otherwise holding itself aloof.

Nationalism and reform in Prussia, 1806–1815

Its major task was to rebuild its armies, since only by that means could Prussia reassert itself against Napoleon. To that end, two generals, Gerhard von Scharnhorst and August Gneisenau, instituted changes based on an essential lesson in nation-building they had learned from the French Revolution: that men were far more effective fighters if they believed themselves to have some direct stake in the wars they fought. A reconstituted national army, eventually based upon a system of universal military service, involved the country as a whole in its own defense and grew to become a far more consciously "Prussian" force than it had been heretofore. Officers were recruited and promoted on the basis of merit, not birth, although the large majority continued to come from the Junker (aristocratic) class. This breach with tradition encouraged the Prussian middle class to take a

Military reforms

Baron Heinrich vom Stein

*Stein's governmental
reforms*

Economic nationalism

more active and enthusiastic interest in its country's affairs. Old or inefficient officers, despite their social standing, were removed from positions of command; training at the royal cadet school in Berlin was modernized.

These reforms, which illustrate the way in which a liberal desire for modernization might combine with nationalism, paralleled similar changes instituted during the same period under the direction of Prussia's principal minister, Baron Heinrich vom Stein (1757–1831), and his successor, Prince Karl von Hardenberg (1750–1822). Stein was not himself a Prussian; he was initially less interested in achieving a Prussian nation-state than in uniting by some means or other all the various principalities of Germany. Only after the disasters wrought upon the Germans by Napoleon did Stein turn to Prussia as a last resort. He had read Kant and Fichte, and was convinced by them that a state must somehow make its citizens aware of their obligations to the national interest. A sense of duty to the state could hardly be kindled, however, without first convincing men and women that loyalty meant reward as well as obligation. Stein therefore labored to dismantle the caste system which had until that time characterized Prussia, in order to permit individuals to rise within society. Stein's Municipal Ordinance of 1808 was a conscious attempt to increase the middle-class Germans' sense of themselves as citizens—again, a goal shared by both liberals and nationalists. Cities and towns were henceforth required to elect their councilmen, while local justice and security continued to be administered by the central government in Berlin; all other matters, including finance, were left to individual communities. Education played a vital role in nation-building. Schools were ideal agencies for the dissemination of the doctrines of national duty. Recognizing this fact, the Prussian reformers expanded facilities for both primary and secondary education. The University of Berlin, founded in 1810, numbered among its faculty such ardent nationalists as Fichte and Savigny, and was the institutional embodiment of the new spirit that contributed to Prussia's eventual victory over the French.

The history of Prussia between 1815 and 1850 can most easily be understood in terms of its continuing struggle to establish itself as the leading independent national power among the thirty-nine states that comprised Germany after 1806, and as a successful rival to Austrian domination. The most important Prussian victory in this respect was the establishment of the *Zollverein,* or customs union. By the 1840s, the union included almost all of Germany except German Austria, and offered manufacturers a market of almost 34 million people. Meanwhile Prussia had produced in the work of the economist Friedrich List (1789–1846) a nationalist response to the internationalism of the liberal free-trade economists. List wrote that while free trade might suit the British, it did not suit Prussia. Economics, he argued, far from being an abstract science equally applicable everywhere, was a discipline which must be grounded in the particular national experience of individual countries. Germany's, and therefore Prussia's, experience demanded not free trade but high tariffs. Only when sheltered behind a protectionist system could Prussia build the factories and manufacture the goods that would guarantee its economic health.

The events which had altered the political shape of Britain and France in the early 1830s—revolution in the latter and liberal reforms in both—did not have lasting counterparts in Germany. A revolutionary movement of sorts, spawned in the universities and youthful secret societies, did result in temporary changes in a few German principalities. But Metternich, still in control of Austrian policy and determined to thwart Prussia's attempts to assert its nationality, used the occasion of those outbreaks to encourage a general antiliberal reaction throughout the German states by playing on the fears of the propertied classes. The diet of the German Confederation, the loose organization of sovereign powers that had replaced the finally defunct "Holy Roman Empire" after 1815, coordinated the repressions.

The failure of liberalism in Germany

Prussia avoided revolution as a result of the reforms instituted a generation before by Stein and Hardenberg. In 1840 Frederick William IV succeeded to the Prussian throne. Apparently devoted to liberal principles, he relaxed censorship laws and encouraged participation in the central government by provincial diets. It soon became apparent, however, that the king was no liberal, but some sort of romantic-nationalist, and an authoritarian as well. He crushed the revolt of thousands of Silesian weavers in 1844, when they protested the importation of English yarn and cotton goods and their consequent unemployment and poverty. He further declared himself opposed to constitutionalism, that central doctrine in the liberal canon of beliefs. When middle-class Prussian liberals pressed, in 1847, for control over legislative and budgetary matters in the recently convened assembly of diets (the *Landtag*), the king saw to it that their request was denied. Frederick William then turned his attention to a scheme whereby Prussia might play a far larger role in the confederation. But before his plan could receive a hearing, it was overtaken by the revolutionary movement of 1848, which, as we shall se, engulfed central Europe as it had western Europe, though with different results.

The politics of Frederick William IV

National sentiment, the spirit which served to unite the Prussians, was at the same time operating to divide the heterogeneous elements within the Austrian Empire. Its people, who lived within three major geographical areas—Austria, Bohemia, and Hungary—were composed of a considerable number of different ethnic and language groups: Germans, Czechs, Magyars, Poles, Slovaks, Serbs, and Italians, to name the most prominent. In some parts of the empire, these people lived in isolation; elsewhere they dwelt in direct proximity, if not much harmony, with others. The Austrian Empire attempted to unite these groups by means of a reigning house, the Habsburgs, and a supposedly benevolent bureaucracy. These devices failed increasingly to satisfy the various groups, in whom a spirit of cultural, if not politi-

Nationalism in the Austrian Empire

cal, nationalism grew persistently stronger in the years after 1815. In the Polish territories of the empire, where the gentry had for generations been conscious of themselves as Poles, the imperial government succeeded in stifling the sentiment by playing off the serfs against their masters, encouraging a class war as a means of preventing an ethnic one. Elsewhere within the empire they were less adroit. In Hungary, nationalism expressed itself in both cultural and political forms. In 1827, a Hungarian national theater was established at Budapest. The year before, Magyar was substituted for Latin as the official language of government. A political movement, whose most formidable leader was the radical nationalist Louis Kossuth (1802–1894), was at the same time seeking independence and a parliamentary government for Hungary.

Pan-Slavism

The most widespread of the eastern European cultural nationalist movements was Pan-Slavism, at this period just beginning. Slavs included Russians, Poles, Czechs, Slovaks, Slovenes, Croats, Serbs, and Bulgars. Before 1848 Pan-Slavism was an almost exclusively cultural movement, united by a generalized anti-Western sentiment, yet divided by a tendency to quarrel as to the primacy of this or that particular language or tradition. These divisions did not substantially lessen the effect of Pan-Slavism as a further problem of the Austrian Empire. The literature of the movement—for example, the historian Francis Palacky's (1798–1876) *History of the Bohemian People* and the poetry of the revolutionary Pole Adam Mickiewiez (1798–1855), fed the desires of those who wished to rid themselves of what they considered a foreign yoke. In Russia, slavophilism had been held in check by the Western-looking Alexander I. After his death, however, the notion that the Russian people possessed its particular *Volksgeist* increased in general popularity.

Nationalism in Italy

Two other national movements were growing beyond infancy during the years before 1848: one in Italy, the other in Ireland. Italy, at the beginning of the nineteenth century, was a peninsula divided into a multitude of states, most of them poor and ineffectually governed. The most efficient governments after 1815 were those imposed by Austria on the northern territories of Lombardy and Venetia (see map, p. 820) and by the introverted, visionary, yet intensely reform-minded king of Sardinia, Charles Albert (1831–1849). At the opposite pole were the Kingdom of the Two Sicilies and the Papal States, governed by equally obscurantist rulers, Francis I (1825–1830), a Bourbon, and thereafter by his son, Ferdinand II (1830–1859), and Pope Gregory XVI (1831–1846). Popular uprisings in Modena, Parma, and Bologna occurred in 1830, but with no lasting consequences, either for the initiation of local liberal reforms or for the cause of unification of the various disparate states into some sort of national whole. Among the pan-Italian organizations formed in the confused period at the end of the Napoleonic wars, none was louder in its nationalist proclamations than the Italian *Carbonari*. One member of that group, Joseph Mazzini

(1805–1872), founded a society of his own in 1831, Young Italy, which was dedicated to the cause of uniting the peninsula. In 1834, from Switzerland, Mazzini launched a totally unsuccessful verbal assault against the Kingdom of Sardinia, in the hope that the rest of Italy would join with him. Mazzini subsequently contented himself with propagandizing for the cause of Italian nationalism and republicanism, attracting a devoted following, particularly among British liberals. Liberals in Italy, however, mistrusted him. Although they too wished to see Italy one nation, they were dismayed, as "good" liberals, and members of the middle class, by Mazzini's insistence upon a republic, hoping instead to merge existing principalities together into some sort of constitutional monarchy.

If Italian nationalism was primarily a middle-class liberal phenomenon at this time, the same was not true of the Irish movement to repeal the union with England. Headed by Daniel O'Connell (1775–1847), it derived its strength from the support of Irish peasants. O'Connell's remarkably successful appeal was based on the hatred all Irish felt for the English, because of the centuries of oppression Irish Catholics had suffered under English Protestant rule. Both before and after the official union of 1801, the English had imposed on the Irish a foreign rule that had brought with it little but poverty and persecution. O'Connell's campaign for the repeal of the union was grounded in the hope that he would be able to negotiate some sort of moderate agreement with the English ruling class. The desires of his followers exceeded him in being far more radical in nature. Neither the separatist hopes of O'Connell, called by the Irish the "Liberator," nor the more genuinely nationalist hopes of his followers, however, were to achieve realization. Unlike the nationalist movements of central Europe, nationalism in Ireland faced a powerful and determined adversary—England—which would for a century deny it victory.

Joseph Mazzini

Nationalism in Ireland

3. NATIONALISM, LIBERALISM, AND REVOLUTION, 1848

The history of the revolutions of 1848 in central Europe can most easily be understood in terms of two major themes: the first, the struggle of various nationalities, particularly within the Austrian Empire, to assert their own autonomy; the second, the contention between the forces of liberalism and nationalism in Germany.

News of the February revolution in France traveled quickly eastward. By the end of March the Austrian Empire was split apart. Hungary, with Kossuth in the lead, severed all but the most tenuous of links with the House of Habsburg and prepared to draft its own constitution. In Vienna, workers and students imitated their counterparts in Paris, erecting barricades and invading the imperial palace. A measure of the political chaos was the fact that Metternich, veteran of a score of threats to the precarious stability he had crafted, found the

*The "March Days" in
Austria*

The March Days in Vienna, 1848

pressure this time too great, and fled in disguise to Britain. The feeble Habsburg emperor, Ferdinand, once he had been deserted by Metternich, yielded to nationalist demands from Bohemia and granted that kingdom its own constitution as well. To the south, Italians launched attacks against the Austrian-held territories in Milan, Naples, Venetia, and Lombardy, where the forces of the Sardinian ruler, King Charles Albert, routed the Austrians.

Yet the forces of national sentiment which had brought Austria to its knees then succeeded in allowing the empire to recoup its fortunes. The paradox of nationalism, as it manifested itself in central Europe, was that as soon as a cultural majority had declared itself an independent or semi-independent state, other cultural minorities within that new state complained bitterly about their newly institutionalized inferiority. This is precisely what happened in Bohemia. There the anti-German Czech majority refused to send delegates to an all-German assembly, meeting at Frankfurt to draft a German constitution. Instead, they summoned a confederation of Slavs to Prague. The delegates, most of them from within the boundaries of the old Austrian Empire, immediately recognized that the idea of a united Germany represented a far greater threat to their political and cultural autonomy than the fact of the empire ever had. The German minority in Bohemia, however, was naturally anxious to participate in discussions which might result in closer union with their ethnic counterparts. They resented the Bohemian government's refusal to do so. The resulting animosities made it all the easier for the Austrians to take advantage of a May 1848 insurrection in Prague, subdue the city, send the Slav congress packing, and reassert control in Bohemia. Although the Austrian gov-

ernment was at this time a liberal one, the product of the March revolution in Vienna, it was no less determined than its predecessor had
been to prevent the total dismemberment of the empire for economic
as well as political reasons. Hence it was quick to restore Lombardy
and Venetia to its realm when quarrels among the heretofore united
Italian allies had sufficiently weakened their common stand against the
Austrians.

Nationalism and counternationalism in Hungary set the stage for
the final act of the restoration of Austrian hegemony. Kossuth's radi-
cal party was, above all, a Magyar nationalist party. Once in power, in *Civil war in Hungary*
early 1849 it moved the capital from Pressburg, near the Austrian bor-
der, to Budapest, and again proclaimed Magyar as the country's official language. These actions offended national minorities within
Hungary, particularly the Croats, who prior to the revolution had enjoyed certain liberties under Austrian rule. The Croatians raised an in-
surgent army and launched a civil war. The Austrains, once more
encouraging division along nationalist lines, named the Croatian rebel
Josef von Jellachich their military commander against the Magyars.
By this time the Viennese liberals began to recognize—too late—that
their turn might come next. They were right. Despite a second uprising in Vienna in October, the revolution was spent. Forces loyal to the
emperor descended upon Vienna from Bohemia. On October 31, the
liberal government capitulated.

Once the imperial government had reasserted itself, it labored to
suppress nationalist impulses as thoroughly as possible. Austria's min-
isters recognized that, though tactically advantageous at times, nation- *Imperial nation-building*
alist movements operated generally to the detriment of the empire's
political and economic unity. The emperor's chief minister, Prince
Felix von Schwarzenberg, and the minister of the interior, Alexander
Bach, both nation-builders, together centralized the state within one
united political system. Hungary and Bohemia no longer enjoyed separate rights. Peasants of all ethnic groups, liberated from serfdom as
part of the general reform movement, were permitted to retain their
freedom, on the grounds of their loyalty to the empire. The law was
reformed, again to achieve uniformity, and railways and roads were
constructed to link the empire. Economic nationalism was encouraged
through tariffs designed to exclude foreign manufactures, while a free
trade area within the empire encouraged domestic industries. Having
done all it could to eradicate separatist movements, the Austrian government thus moved to secure its advantage by engaging in a vigorous
campaign of nation-building.

In Prussia, revolution ran a similar course. In March, King Frederick William found himself compelled to yield to demands for a popu-
larly elected legislative assembly. When it met, the body proved par- *The failure of revolution
in Prussia*
ticularly sympathetic to the plight of the Polish minority within
Prussia, and antagonistic toward the Russians, whom radical legislators saw as the major threat to the spread of enlightened political ideas

Procession of the German National Assembly to Its Opening Session at St. Paul's Church, Frankfurt, May 1848

in central Europe. When the assembly's sympathy with Polish nationalism extended to the granting of self-government to Prussian Poland, however, it generated the same feelings among the German minority there that we have seen arousing minorities within the Austrian Empire. In so doing, it precipitated the same eventual results. Germans in Posen, the major city of Prussian Poland, revolted against the newly established Polish government; not surprisingly, Prussian army units on duty sided with the Germans and helped them crush the new government. Power, it now became clear, lay with the army, professionalized since the days of Gneisenau and Scharnhorst, yet still dominated by the Junkers. Against the armed authority of the military, the radical legislators of Berlin were no match; revolution ended in Prussia as quickly as it had begun.

The Frankfurt Assembly   Meanwhile, at Frankfurt, Germans engaged in the debate that provides the history of central Europe in these revolutionary years with its second theme: liberalism vs. nationalism. Delegates had been chosen from across Germany and Austria to attend the Frankfurt Assembly. They were largely from the professional classes—professors, lawyers, administrators—and generally devoted to the cause of middle-class liberalism. Many had assumed that their task would resemble that of the assembly which had met in 1789 to draft a constitution for the French: i.e., they would draft a constitution for a liberal, unified Germany. That former convocation, however, had been grounded in the simple but all-important fact that a French nation-state already existed. The French assembly had been elected to give the nation a new shape and new direction. But a centralized sovereign power was there to reshape; there was an authority that could be either commandeered or, if necessary, usurped. The Frankfurt Assembly, in contrast, was grounded upon nothing but its own words. It was a collection of thoughtful, well-intentioned middle-class liberals, committed to a belief that a liberal-national German state could somehow be constituted out of abstract principles. These men, from the start of their deliberations, ruled out the use of violence to achieve their ends. At the same time, they failed to ally themselves with the urban workers. If by 1848 the workers were not yet a self-conscious and articulate class, they were nevertheless a force no reformer or revolutionary could reckon without. Yet the Frankfurt debaters by and large ignored them, and thus denied themselves the one source of power they might otherwise have called to their aid.

Almost from the start, the assembly found itself tangled in the problems of nationality. Who, they asked, were the Germans? A majority of the delegates argued that they were all those who, by language, culture, or geography, felt themselves bound to the enterprise now underway at Frankfurt. The German nation that was to be constituted must include as many of those "Germans" as possible. This point of view came to be known as the "Great German" position. Great Germans found themselves stymied, however, by the unwillingness of other nationalities to be included in their fold. The Czechs in Bohemia, as we have seen, wanted no part of Great Germany. In the end the Great Germans settled that the nation for which they were drafting a constitution should include, among other territories, all Austrian lands except Hungary. This decision meant that the crown of their new country might most logically be offered to the Habsburg emperor. At this point the voice of the "Little Germans" began to be heard. Prussian nationalism took precedence over German nationalism; a minority argued that Austria should be excluded altogether and the crown instead offered to King Frederick William of Prussia.

Great Germans vs. Little Germans

The liberalism of the assembly was put to the test by events in Austria and Poland in the fall of 1848. When the imperial forces crushed the Czech and Hungarian rebellions, when the Prussian Junkers put an end to Polish self-government, liberals found themselves forced to cheer. They were compelled to support the suppression of minority nationalities; otherwise there would be no new Germany. But their cheers were for the forces not only of German nationalism but of antiliberal authoritarianism. The assembly's most embarrassing moment occurred when it found itself compelled to take shelter behind the Prussian army. Riots broke out in Frankfurt protesting the assembly's willingness to withdraw from a confrontation with the

Liberalism vs. nationalism

The end of the assembly

Danes over the future of Germans in Schleswig, a Danish province. That particular area, which many considered to be part of Germany, had been annexed by the Danes in March 1848. The Frankfurters had been unable to do more than ask the Prussians to win Schleswig back for them; and the Prussians had refused. Hence the riots; hence a second request, this time heeded, for Prussian assistance.

Reduced to the status of dependents, the Frankfurt delegates nevertheless, in the spring of 1849, produced a constitution. By this time Austria, fearing its Prussian rival, had decided to have no more to do with Frankfurt. The Little Germans thus won by default and offered their constitutional monarchy to Frederick William of Prussia. Though tempted, he turned them down, arguing that their constitution was too liberal, embodying as it did the revolutionary notion that a crown could be offered to a monarch. Frederick wanted the crown, but on his own terms. The delegates went home, disillusioned by their experience, many of them convinced that their dual goal of liberalism and nationalism was an impossible one. Some, who refused to surrender that goal, emigrated to the United States, where they believed the goal had already been achieved. Many of those who stayed behind convinced themselves that half the goal was better than none, and sacrificed their liberalism to nationalism.

One German exile who took hope for the future from the events of the revolutions of 1848 was the young Karl Marx (1818–1883), whose radical ideas and activities had compelled his emigration to England. Like his friend and collaborator Friedrich Engels (see above, p. 765), Marx was the son of wealthy middle-class parents. After study at the university of Berlin, in 1842 he took a job as editor of the *Rhineland Gazette,* hoping to use that position to argue for the transformation of a society he was growing to despise. His radical policies soon put him at odds with his publishers, however. He moved first to Paris and then to Brussels, where he helped found the Communist League, a body whose declared aim was the overthrow of the middle class. While in Paris, Marx had renewed a former friendship with Engels. Together, during the late 1840s, they produced a theory of revolutionary change which was published by Marx at the request of the League in 1848, at the height of the struggles on the Continent, as *The Communist Manifesto.*

Karl Marx

*The Communist
Manifesto*

In the *Manifesto* Marx outlined a theory of history which owed a good deal to the German philosopher Hegel (see above, p. 798). Hegel, it will be recalled, had argued that ideas, the motive force of history, were in constant conflict with each other, and that this antithetical relationship between ideas in turn would produce an eventual synthesis, representing an advance in the history of the human race. Marx adapted this particular progressive notion of history to his own uses. Whereas Hegel perceived conflict and resolution (a dialectic) in terms of ideas, Marx saw them in terms of economic forces. Society, he argued, was at any time no more than the reflection of a hierarchy of classes dictated by those who own the means of production and control the distribution of its material goods. As history had progressed, so had the means changed. Feudalism and manorialism were vanquished by capitalism. And capitalism, Marx declared, would be vanquished in turn by communism. That process, however, would first involve the concentration of capitalist economic power into the hands of fewer and fewer members of the middle class (the bourgeoisie), and the consequent opposition of an ever-increasing and ever-debased working class (the proletariat). Once the proletariat overthrew the bourgeoisie by revolution, as it was bound to do eventually, society as a whole would be emancipated. An interim period in which a "dictatorship of the proletariat" rid the world of the last vestiges of bourgeois society would be followed by an end of the dialectical process and the emergence of a truly classless civilization.

Marx insisted that the *Manifesto* was not just another theory. His declaration that the proletariat together could consciously participate in the revolutionary process he described—could actually advance history through its own efforts—and that the revolutions of 1848 were part of that process, helps explain the document's eventual appeal. The writings of Marx and Engels did not bring about an immediate proletarian revolution. Though the *Manifesto,* in its famous declaration, called upon the workers of the world to unite, Marx and Engels realized that this goal would not be achieved quickly. Marx and Engels, however, more than any other political thinkers of the 1830s and 1840s, provided workers with a potential sense of their worth as human beings and of their vital role in the historical process. Engels made workers understand what factory work and urban living was doing to them. Marx gave workers the sense that those sufferings Engels described had an ultimate purpose, that they represented the workers' own particular contribution to the eventual and inevitable triumph of their class.

The Manifesto's *appeal*

4. NATION-BUILDING, 1850–1870

The twenty years between 1850 and 1870 were years of intense nation-building in the Western world. Of the master-builders, none was more accomplished than the man who brought Germany under Prussian rule, Otto von Bismarck (1815–1898). He was born into the Junker class. During the revolutionary period of 1848 and 1849, Bismarck had served in the Prussian parliament as a defender of the monarchy. Bismarck was really neither a liberal nor a nationalist; he was a Prussian. When he instituted domestic reforms, he did so not because he favored the "rights" of this or that particular group, but because he thought that his policies would result in a more united, and hence more powerful, Prussia. When he maneuvered to bring other German states under Prussian domination, he did so not in conformity with a

Bismarck

grand Germanic design but because he believed that some sort of union was almost inevitable and, if so, that it must come about at Prussia's behest. He prided himself on being a realist; and he became a first-rate practitioner of what has come to be called *Realpolitik*—the politics, not of idealism, but of what its practioners claim to be hard-headed reality. Bismarck readily acknowledged his admiration of power. He at one point had considered a career in the military—not at all surprising considering his Junker origins. He once wrote the emperor William I that he regretted that he was compelled to serve his country from behind a desk rather than at the front. But whatever his post, he intended to command. "I want to play the tune the way it sounds good to me or not at all," he declared. "Pride, the desire to command. . . . I confess I am not free from these passions." Nor did he consider those passions unworthy of the man who was to undertake the task of shaping the fortunes of the German state.

Bismarck and the liberals

When Bismarck came to power as minister-president of Prussia in 1862, he was confronted by a liberal parliamentary majority which, since 1859, had opposed a campaign to increase military expenditures despite pressure from the king. This majority had been produced by an electoral system that was part of the constitution granted by Frederick William to Prussia in 1850, following the collapse of the assembly. The parliament was divided into two houses, the lower one elected by universal male suffrage. Votes were apportioned according to one's ability to pay taxes, however; those few who together paid one-third of the country's taxes elected one-third of the legislators. A large landowner or industrialist exercised about a hundred times the voting power of a poor man. Contrary to the king's expectations, however, under this constitution a liberal majority was succeeding in thwarting the plans of the sovereign and his advisors. It was to break this deadlock that King William I, who succeeded his brother Frederick William in 1861, summoned Bismarck. In Bismarck the liberals more than met their match. When they refused to levy taxes, he collected them anyway, claiming that the constitution, whatever its purposes, had not been designed to subvert the state. When liberals argued that Prussia was setting a poor example for the rest of Germany, Bismarck replied that Prussia was admired not for its liberalism but its power.

The Crimean War

Whether or not the Germans—or the rest of Europe—admired Prussia's power, they soon found themselves confronted by it. Bismarck proceeded to build a nation that in the short space of eight years came into being as the German Empire. Bismarck was assisted in his task by his readiness to take advantage of international situations as they presented themselves, without concerning himself particularly with the ideological or moral implications of his actions. He was aided as well by developments over which he had no initial control but which he was able to turn to his advantage. The first of these, the Crimean War, had occurred in 1854–1856, prior to his taking office.

British Encampment near Sebastopol, 1854–1855. Photograph taken by Roger Fenton. The Crimean War was the first to be reported to the world by photograph as well as by news dispatch.

Russia and Turkey, perennial European squabblers, had precipitated the hostilities. Russia invaded the territories of Moldavia and Wallachia (later Rumania) in an attempt to take advantage of the continuing political rot that made the Ottoman Empire an easy prey. In 1854 France and then Britain came to the aid of the Turks by invading Russia's Crimean peninsula. These allies were soon joined by Austria and Sardinia. The quarrel had by this time enlarged to include the question of who was to protect the Christians in Jerusalem from the Turks; it was fueled from the start as well by Britain's continuing determination to prohibit a strong Russian presence in the Near East. The allies' eventual victory was the result primarily of a British blockade of Russia. The peace settlement was a severe setback for Russia, whose influence in the Balkans was drastically curbed. Moldavia and Wallachia were united as Rumania, which, along with Serbia, was granted power as a self-governing principality. Austria, though it had sided with the victor, lost more than it gained from the war. Austrian military resources were severely taxed during the invasion and occupation of Moldavia and Wallachia. It was the subsequent weakness of both Russia and Austria, the result of the Crimean War, that Bismarck used to his advantage in the 1860s.

In consolidating the German states into a union controlled by Prussia, Bismarck first moved to eliminate Austria from its commanding position in the Germanic Confederation. As a means to this end he inflamed the long-smoldering dispute with Denmark over the possession of Schleswig and Holstein. Inhabited largely by Germans, these two provinces had an anomalous status. Since 1815 Holstein had been included in the Germanic Confederation, but both were subject to the personal overlordship of the king of Denmark. When, in 1864, the Danish king attempted to annex them, Bismarck invited Austria to participate in a war against Denmark. A brief struggle followed, at the end of which the Danish ruler was compelled to renounce all his claims to Schleswig and Holstein in favor of Austria and Prussia. Then

Steps to German unification: (1) weakening of Austria

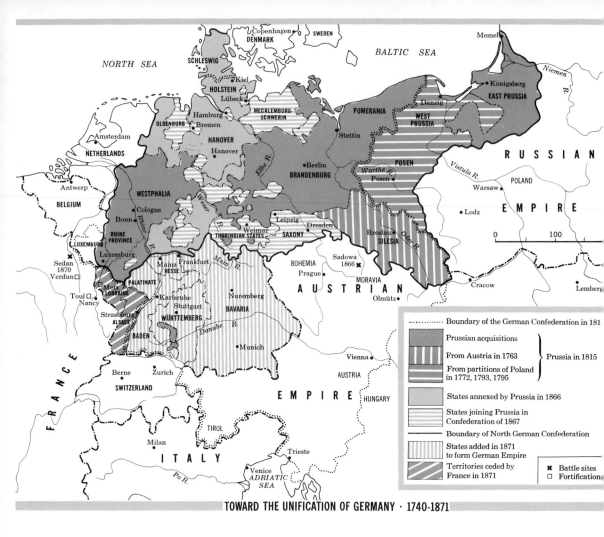

TOWARD THE UNIFICATION OF GERMANY · 1740-1871

the sequel occurred for which Bismarck ardently hoped: a quarrel between the victors over division of the spoils. The conflict which followed in 1866, known as the Seven Weeks' War, ended in an easy triumph for Prussia. Austria was forced to give up all claims to Schleswig and Holstein, to surrender Venetia, and to acquiesce in the dissolution of the Germanic Confederation. Immediately following the war Bismarck proceeded to isolate Austria by uniting all of the German states north of the Main River into the North German Confederation.

(2) courting the masses
To achieve the confederation Bismarck willingly turned himself into a democrat. He saw that if he was to attain his end, which was a strong union with Prussia at its head, he would need to cultivate a constituency hitherto untapped by any German politicians: the masses. He appreciated the manner by which Napoleon III had reinforced his regime through plebiscites. And Bismarck understood that the majority of Germans were not particularly enthusiastic supporters

of capitalist liberals, of the bureaucracies of their own small states, or of the Austrian Hapsburgs. The constitution he devised for his confederation provided for two chambers: the upper chamber represented the individual states within the union, though not equally; the lower chamber was elected by universal manhood suffrage. The liberal middle class, to say nothing of the Junkerdom, was astonished and dismayed, as well they might be. Bismarck's intention was to use popular support to strengthen the hand of the central government against the interests of both landlords and capitalists. To this end, he struck a bargain with German socialists, who agreed to exchange support for the confederation for universal suffrage.

Bismarck's final step in the completion of German unity was the Franco-Prussian War of 1870–1871. He hoped that a conflict with France would kindle the spirit of German nationalism in Bavaria, Würtemberg, and other southern states still outside the confederation. Taking advantage of a diplomatic tempest concerning the right of the Hohenzollerns (Prussia's ruling family) to occupy the Spanish throne, Bismarck worked hard to force a Franco–German misunderstanding. King William agreed to meet with the French ambassador at the resort spa of Ems in Prussia to discuss the Spanish succession. When William telegraphed Bismarck that the demands of the French for perpetual exclusion of the Hohenzollern family from the Spanish throne had been refused, Bismarck released portions of the message to the press so as to make it appear that King William had insulted the ambassador—which he had not done. When the garbled report of what happened at Ems was received in France, the nation reacted with a call for war. The call was echoed in Prussia, where Bismarck published evidence which he claimed proved French designs upon the Rhineland. Once war had been declared the south German states rallied to Prussia's side in the belief that it was the victim of aggression. The war was quickly fought. The French were no match for Prussia's professionally trained and superbly equipped forces. Nor did other European powers come to France's assistance. Austria, the most likely candidate, remained weakened by its recent war with Prussia. The Magyars, who at this time had assumed positions of influence within the Austrian government, were quite prepared to welcome a strengthened Prussia; Prussia's growing strength in Germany would further increase Austria's weakness there. And the weaker Austria was as a German power, the stronger would be the claims of the Magyars to predominance. Once more one nationalist consciousness was grinding against another. The war began in July; it ended in September with the defeat of the French and the capture of Napoleon III himself at Sedan in France.

(3) the Franco-Prussian War

Following the collapse of the French imperial government, insurrectionary forces in Paris continued to hold out against the Germans until the winter of 1871. Bismarck meanwhile proceeded to consummate the German union toward which he had worked so assiduously.

The German Empire

Meeting to Arrange Peace Terms at the End of the Franco-Prussian War. On the left is Otto von Bismarck, chancellor of the new German Empire. In the center is Jules Favre and to his right Louis-Adolphe Thiers, both representing the provisional government set up after the overthrow of Napoleon III.

On January 18, 1871, in the great Hall of Mirrors at Versailles the German Empire was proclaimed. All those states, except Austria, which had not already been absorbed into Prussia declared their allegiance to William I, henceforth emperor or kaiser. Four months later, at Frankfurt, a treaty between the French and Germans ceded the border region of Alsace to the new empire, condemned the French to an indemnity of five billion francs, and thereby broadcast to the world the remarkable success of Bismarck's nation-building.

Events in Italy ran a course almost parallel to that which had led to the unification of Germany. Italy before 1848, it should be remembered, was a patchwork of petty states. The most important of those possessing independence were the Kingdom of Sardinia in the north, the Papal States in the central region, and the Kingdom of the Two Sicilies in the south. The former republics of Lombardy and Venetia were held by Austria, while Habsburg dependents ruled in Tuscany, Parma, and Modena. As the revolutionary fervor of 1848 swept across the peninsula, one ruler after another granted democratic reforms. Charles Albert of Sardinia outdistanced all the others by providing for civil liberties and a parliamentary form of government. But it soon became evident that the Italians were as interested in nationalism as in liberalism. For some years romantic patriots had been dreaming of the *Risorgimento,* which would restore the nation to the position of glorious leadership it had held in Roman times and during the Renaissance. To achieve this, it was universally agreed that Italy must be welded into a single state. But opinions differed as to the form the new government should take. Young idealists followed the leadership of Mazzini. Religious-minded patriots believed that the most practicable solution would be to federate the state of Italy under the presidency of the pope. The majority of the more moderate nationalists advocated a constitutional monarchy built upon the foundations of the Kingdom

Italian unification

of Sardinia. The aims of this third group gradually crystallized under the leadership of a shrewd Sardinian nobleman, Count Camillo di Cavour (1810–1861). In 1850 he was appointed minister of commerce and agriculture of his native state and in 1852 prime minister.

The campaign for unification of the Italian peninsula began with efforts to expel the Austrians. In 1848 revolts were organized in the territories under Habsburg domination, and an army of liberation marched from Sardinia to aid the rebels; but the movement ended in failure. It was then that Cavour, as the new leader of the campaign, turned to less heroic but more practical methods. In 1855, to attract the favorable attention of Great Britain and France, he had entered the Crimean War on their side, despite the fact that he had no quarrel with Russia. In 1858 he held a secret meeting with Napoleon III and prepared the stage for an Italian War of Liberation. Napoleon agreed to cooperate in driving the Austrians from Italy for the price of the cession of Savoy and Nice by Sardinia to France. A war with Austria was duly provoked in 1859, and for a time all went well for the Franco-Italian allies. But after the conquest of Lombardy, Napoleon III suddenly withdrew, fearful of ultimate defeat and afraid of antagonizing the Catholics in his own country by aiding the avowedly anticlerical government of Cavour. Thus deserted by its ally, Sardinia was unable to expel the Austrians from Venetia. Nevertheless, extensive gains were made; Sardinia annexed Lombardy, and acquired by various means the duchies of Tuscany, Parma, and Modena, and the northern portion of the Papal States. Sardinia was now more than twice its original size and by far the most powerful state in Italy.

Camillo di Cavour

The second step in consolidating the unity of Italy was the conquest of the Kingdom of the Two Sicilies. This kingdom was ruled by a Bourbon, Francis II, who was thoroughly hated by his Italian subjects. In May 1860 a romantic adventurer, Giuseppe Garibaldi, set out with a regiment of one thousand "red shirts" to rescue his fellow Italians from oppression. Within three months he had conquered the island of Sicily and had then marched to the deliverance of Naples, where the people were already in revolt. By November the whole kingdom of Francis II had fallen to Garibaldi. He at first intended to convert the territory into an independent republic but was finally persuaded to surrender it to the Kingdom of Sardinia. With most of the peninsula now united under a single rule, Victor Emmanuel II, king of Sardinia, assumed the title of king of Italy (March 17, 1861). Venetia was still in the hands of the Austrians, but in 1866, following their defeat in the Seven Weeks' War, they were forced by the Prussians to cede it to Italy. All that remained to complete the unification of Italy was the annexation of Rome. The Eternal City had resisted conquest thus far, largely because of the military protection accorded the pope by Napoleon III. But in 1870 the outbreak of the Franco-Prussian War compelled Napoleon to withdraw his troops. In September 1870 Ital-

Giuseppe Garibaldi

SWITZERLAND

AUSTRIA

SAVOY
(To France in 1860)

KINGDOM OF
SARDINIA

PIEDMONT

LOMBARDY

• Milan

Po R.

Turin

FRANCE

PARMA

Genoa •

MODENA

LUCCA

Florence •

Arno R.

TUSCANY

UMBRIA

VENETIA

Venice

Bologna

ROMAGNA

Tiber R.

Rome ★

PAPAL STATES

CORSICA
(To France)

KINGDOM
OF
SARDINIA

T Y R R H E N I A N

S E A

★ Naples

KINGDOM OF THE TWO SICILIES

A D R I A T I C

S E A

0   200 miles

M E D I T E R R A N E A N

Palermo •

SICILY

• Messina

S E A

THE UNIFICATION OF ITALY

ian soldiers occupied Rome, and in July of the following year it was
made the capital of the by now united kingdom.

The occupation of Rome brought the kingdom of Italy into conflict
with the papacy. During the first years of his reign, which began in
1846, Pope Pius IX instituted a series of "modern" improvements:
gaslight, railways, vaccination. Yet Pius, who, like his reactionary
predecessor, Gregory XVI, continued to rule over the Papal States in
the manner of a secular prince, was no friend to either liberalism or
nationalism. And no wonder: the movement that had brought Italian
troops to Rome had from its inception expressed hostility to the Church

Italy and the Papal States

as an impediment to unification. Following the occupation of Rome in 1870, an attempt was made to solve the problem of relations between the state and the papacy. In 1871 the Italian parliament enacted the Law of Papal Guaranties, purporting to define the status of the pope as a reigning sovereign. This law the reigning pontiff, Pius IX, promptly denounced on the ground that issues affecting the pope could be settled only by an international treaty to which he himself was a party. Whereupon he shut himself up in the Vatican and refused to have anything to do with a government which had so shamefully treated Christ's vicar on earth. His successors continued this practice of voluntary imprisonment until 1929, when a series of agreements between the Italian government and Pius XI effected settlement of the dispute.

Nation-building was the preoccupation of another major country in the first half of the nineteenth century: the United States. The history of the expansion and consolidation of this newly born country into a nation of remarkable economic potential in little over half a century can best be understood in terms of several major factors. The first is the growth of political democracy.

Nation-building in the U.S.: (1) the growth of democracy

The United States did not begin its history as a democracy. No more than a few of the country's leaders professed genuine democratic ideals. The authors of the Constitution were not interested in the rule of the masses. The primary aim of the founders of the United States was to establish a *republic* that would promote stability and protect the rights of private property against the leveling tendencies of majorities. For this reason they adopted checks and balances between the branches of government, devised the Electoral College for choosing the president, created a powerful judiciary, and entrusted the selection of senators to the legislatures of the several states.

Thomas Jefferson by Gilbert Stuart

Following the establishment of a new and more firmly united government under the Constitution of 1789, democratic ideals began to win acceptance in the United States. Until 1801 the Federalists, the party of large landowners and successful merchant capitalists, held power. In the latter year the Democratic-Republicans gained control as a result of the election of Thomas Jefferson (1743–1826) to the presidency. Although this event is often referred to as the Jeffersonian Revolution, on the supposition that Jefferson was the champion of the masses and of the political power of the underprivileged, there is danger in carrying this interpretation too far. He strenuously opposed the unlimited sovereignty of the majority. His conception of an ideal political system was an aristocracy of "virtue and talent," in which respect for personal liberty would be the guiding principle.

Yet the Jeffersonian movement had a number of ultimately democratic objectives. Its leaders were vigorous opponents of special privilege, whether of birth or of wealth. They worked for the abolition of established churches. They led the campaign for the addition of a Bill of Rights to the Constitution and were almost exclusively responsible

Jeffersonian principles

Jacksonian democracy

for its success. Although professing devotion to the principle of the separation of powers, they actually believed in the supremacy of the representatives of the people and viewed with abhorrence the attempts of the executive and judicial branches to increase their power.

By 1820, these notions were being expressed in more direct and forceful terms. Urban populations grew increasingly conscious of their political importance and demanded attention to their interests. The predominance of the agricultural Old South (the South of the original thirteen colonies) had declined. As a result of the Louisiana Purchase (a vast tract bought from the French in 1803) and of increased settlement in the area known as the Northwest Territory (western New York State and Ohio), a new frontier had come into existence. Life there was characterized by a rugged freedom that left little room for class distinctions. In the struggle to survive, hard work and sharp wits counted for more than birth and education. As a consequence a new democratic spirit, which eventually found its leader in Andrew Jackson (1767–1845), took shape around the principle of equality. The Jacksonian Democrats transformed the doctrines of liberalism into a more radical creed. They pronounced all (excluding slaves, American Indians, and women) politically equal, not merely in rights but in privileges. They were devoted adherents to the causes of suffrage for all white males; the election, rather than appointment, of all governmental office-holders; and the frequent rotation of men in positions of political power—a doctrine that served to put more Democratic politicians into federal office. These democratic beliefs helped encourage a spirit of unity within the United States during a period of rapid territorial expansion.

As the United States continued to acquire more territories in the

"Meal Time." Between the decks on an immigrant ship to the United States in the mid–nineteenth century.

West (the most notable addition resulting from the conquest of lands in the southwest from Mexico in 1846), it not only faced the task of binding those areas and their settlers into the nation. There was, as well, the problem of assimilating the thousands of immigrants who came to America from Europe in the first half of the century. Many were Scottish and English; for them the difficulties of adjusting to a new life in a new country were generally not difficult, since they spoke a common language with their fellow-citizens. For others the problems were far greater. For the Irish, who immigrated in great numbers, particularly during the 1840s, there was the fact of their alien religion, Roman Catholicism. For Germans and others from the Continent, there was the language barrier. The United States's policy toward its immigrants was directed against the creation of any foreign nationalist enclaves apart from the main body of its citizenry. Although foreign-language newspapers were tolerated, and immigrants were free to attend churches and social gatherings as they chose, English remained the language of the public schools, the police, the law courts, and the government. To hold a job, a person was almost always forced to learn at least some English. In this way, the United States encouraged immigrants to shed their "foreign" ways and to commit themselves to their adopted nation.

(2) immigration

If there were enclaves in the United States, they existed in the South, where the institution of slavery and the economic dependence of the planters upon England produced two distinct minorities, neither of which was to be assimilated without resort to war. During the nineteenth century, slavery had been abolished throughout much of the Western world, for both economic and humanitarian reasons. Southern planters continued to insist that without the slave system they would go bankrupt. To humanitarians they responded with arguments based upon theories of racial inferiority and upon their self-professed reputation as benevolent masters. The position of these southern spokesmen grew increasingly distasteful and unconvincing to the North. As the country opened to the west, North and South engaged in a protracted tug-of-war as to which new states were to be "free" and which "slave." Northerners were motivated by more than concern for the well-being of blacks. The North was industrializing fast. Capitalists there were demanding protective tariffs to assist them in their enterprises. Southerners favored free trade, since they wished to import British goods in return for the cotton they sold to the manufacturers of Lancashire.

(3) slavery and the South

The American Civil War, when it came in 1861, was a war not about the issue of slavery so much as it was about preserving the union of American states and territories. President Abraham Lincoln undertook the war to defend the unity of the United States. European governments, while never recognizing the Confederacy officially, nevertheless remained sympathetic to its cause. They hoped that the fragmentation of the United States would result in the opening up of markets for their manufactured goods, much as the dissolution of the

The Civil War

Spanish Empire had proved a boon to European commercial interests. The victory of the North in 1865, however, ensured the continued growth of the United States as a nation. The Fourteenth Amendment to the Constitution stated specifically that all were citizens of the United States, and not of an individual state or territory. In declaring that no citizen was to be deprived of life, liberty, or property without due process of law, it established that "due process" was to be defined by the national, and not the state or territorial governments.

The years following the American Civil War witnessed the binding together of the nation economically under the direction of northern private enterprise. The symbol of the North's triumph as nation-builder came with the driving of the final spike of the transcontinental Union Pacific railroad in 1869. Nation-building in Europe and the United States helped ensure the continuing expansion of capitalism. Liberalism had provided a general climate of opinion and a set of attitudes toward government that encouraged industrialization. Nation-building, in its turn, produced the necessary economic units: large enough to generate the wherewithal to sustain economic growth; confident enough to enter into competition with the British Goliath.

SELECTED READINGS

• *Items so designated are available in paperback editions.*

Artz, Frederick B., *France under the Bourbon Restoration, 1814–1830,* New York, 1963. A basic survey with a good treatment of romanticism.

Beales, Derek, *The Risorgimento and the Unification of Italy,* New York, 1971. Objective, concise survey of Italian unification.

• Berlin, Isaiah, *Karl Marx: His Life and Environment,* New York, 1948. The best short account.

• Binkley, Robert C., *Realism and Nationalism, 1852–1871,* New York, 1935. An excelelnt synthesis despite some dated passages.

• Craig, Gordon, *The Politics of the Prussian Army,* Oxford, 1964. Much more than the title implies. An excellent analysis of Prussian social structure and the role of the army in social reform and unification.

Epstein, Klaus, *The Genesis of German Conservatism,* Princeton, N.J., 1966. Provides excellent early-nineteenth-century background.

• Eyck, Erich, *Bismarck and the German Empire,* London, 1958. The best one-volume study of Bismarck.

Eyck, Frank, *The Frankfurt Parliament, 1848–49,* New York, 1968. A detailed study of its composition and procedure.

Ford, Guy Stanton, *Stein and the Era of Reform in Prussia, 1807–1815,* New York, 1922. An old but still valuable work on a leading Prussian reformer.

• Hamerow, Theodore, *Restoration, Revolution, Reaction,* Princeton, N.J., 1966. An excellent social and economic history of Germany between 1815 and 1871.

• ———, *The Social Foundations of German Unification, 1858–1871,* 2 vols., Princeton, N.J., 1972. Concentrates on economic factors which determined the solution to the unification question. An impressive synthesis.

Hayes, C. J. H., *The Historical Evolution of Modern Nationalism,* rev. ed., New York, 1968. A valuable survey.

• Hobsbawm, Eric J., *The Age of Revolution, 1789–1848,* New York, 1962. An unrigidly Marxist interpretation, good for the entire period it covers.

Holborn, Hajo, *History of Modern Germany,* Vols. II and III, New York, 1964. The best survey of German history in English.

• Kohn, Hans, *The Idea of Nationalism,* New York, 1944. A perceptive analysis.

• Krieger, Leonard, *The German Idea of Freedom,* Boston, 1957. A difficult but rewarding study of German political thought.

Macartney, C. A., *The Hapsburg Empire, 1790–1918,* London, 1968. A worthwhile survey.

Mack Smith, Denis, *Garibaldi: A Great Life in Brief,* New York, 1956.

———, *The Making of Italy, 1796–1870,* New York, 1968. A narrative with documents.

• Mehring, Franz, *Karl Marx: The Story of His Life,* New York, 1976. A good, recent life.

Namier, Lewis B., *1848: TheRevolution of the Intellectuals,* London, 1964. A controversial analysis, highly critical of the Frankfurt Assembly.

Noyes, P. H., *Organization and Revolution: Working-Class Associations in the German Revolutions of 1848–49,* Princeton, N.J., 1966. An important monograph analyzing the degree of working-class consciousness at the time of the revolution.

• Pflanze, Otto, *Bismarck and the Development of Germany, 1815–1871,* Princeton, N.J., 1963. An impressive analysis of Bismarck's aims and policies.

• Rosenberg, Hans, *Bureaucracy, Aristocracy, and Autocracy: The Prussian Experience, 1660–1815,* Cambridge, Mass., 1958. A difficult but valuable book explaining the forces that molded the modern Prussian state.

Salvemini, Gaetano, *Mazzini,* London, 1956. Biography with excerpts from Mazzini's writings.

• Taylor, A. J. P., *The Hapsburg Monarchy. 1809–1918,* rev. ed., London, 1965. An idiosyncratic account by an eminent historian.

SOURCE MATERIALS

Bismarck, Otto von, *Bismarck, the Man and the Statesman, Written and Dictated by Himself,* London, 1899. Bismarck's memoirs, written after his fall from power.

• Clausewitz, Karl von, *On War,* London, 1968. Published posthumously, this work, in reality a philosophy of war, was perceived by the Prussian military bureaucracy as a mandate for total war—for the subjugation of all interests of the state to war.

Fichte, Johann Gottlieb, *Addresses to the German Nation,* New York, 1968. Presented in 1808 while French armies occupied Prussia, these lectures helped stir a German nationalist spirit.

• Marx, Karl, and Friedrich Engels, *The Marx-Engels Reader,* 2nd ed., by R. C. Tucker, New York, 1978. Reprints the basic texts.

Schurz, Carl, *The Reminiscences of Carl Schurz,* 3 vols., New York, 1907–1908. Especially valuable is Vol. I. A young German liberal in 1848 and a delegate to the Frankfurt Assembly, Schurz spent the rest of his life as an exile in the United States.

Part Six

THE WEST AT THE WORLD'S CENTER

The years between 1870 and 1945 found the West at the center of global affairs. The industrial supremacy of western Europe and the United States gave them a combined power greater than that possessed by any nation or empire in previous times. Yet world domination was by no means accompanied by any sense of general world order. The economic might of the Western nations, while it resulted in their ability to dominate the less developed quarters of the globe, resulted, as well, in their concern lest one of their number overpower the others. The old system of the balance of power, designed to preserve peace by ensuring that no one country achieved overwhelming predominance at the expense of its neighbors, was strained to the breaking point by economic rivalries that stretched around the world. Meanwhile, tensions mounted within each nation, as landed and middle classes, threatened by the possibility of social turmoil, tried to balance the mounting clamor for political concessions against their desire to retain power in their own hands. Twice during the period, in 1914 and 1939, international and domestic pressures exploded into global wars. Those wars and their results, generated by the rivalries and miscalculations of the Western nations, so sapped the strength of those nations as to depose them thereafter as the sole arbiters of the world's destinies.

POLITICS	SCIENCE & INDUSTRY

1870

First commercially practical electrical generator, 1870

Gilcrist-Thomas steel process, 1870s

Paris Commune, 1871
Kulturkampf, Germany, 1872
League of Three Emperors, 1873
Constitution for Third French Republic, 1875 — Germ theory of disease, 1875
End of First International, 1876 — Invention of telephone, 1876
Congress of Berlin, 1878

Triple Alliance, 1882
Berlin conference on imperialism, 1885
Second International formed, 1889
Pan-Slavism, 1890–1914

Dreyfus affair, 1894–1899

Discovery of the X-ray, 1895
Spanish-American War, 1898 — Marie Curie, discovery of radium, 1898

Boer War, 1899–1902 — Invention of wireless telegraph, 1899

1900

N. Lenin, *What Is to Be Done?,* 1902

First airplane flight, 1903
Russo-Japanese War, 1904–1905 — Ivan Pavlov, Nobel Prize for physiology, 1904
Revolution in Russia, 1905 — Albert Einstein, development of relativity theory 1905–1910

Triple Entente, 1907
Bosnian Crisis, 1908 — Model T Ford, 1908
Revolt of the Young Turks, 1908

Balkan Wars, 1912–1913

First World War, 1914–1918
Russian Revolution, 1917

Treaty of Versailles, 1919
Socialist revolution, Germany, 1919
League of Nations, 1920–1946

1920

NEP, Russia, 1921

Mussolini's March on Rome, 1922

Hitler's beer-hall putsch, 1923
New constitution, Soviet Union, 1924
Locarno agreements, 1925

Discovery of viruses, sulfa drugs, and penicillin 1930s
Hitler, chancellor of Germany, 1933 — World economic conference, 1933
New Deal, United States, 1933–1940

ECONOMICS & SOCIETY	ARTS & LETTERS	
	Impressionism in art, 1870–1900	*1870*
Growth of finance capitalism, 1880s Social welfare legislation, Germany, 1882–1884		
	Émile Zola, *Germinal*, 1885	
Sherman Anti-Trust Act, United States, 1890 Meline tariff, 1892	Henrik Ibsen, *Hedda Gabler*, 1890 Paul Cézanne, *The Card Players*, 1890–1892	
	George Bernard Shaw, *Plays Pleasant* and *Unpleasant*, 1898	
Women's suffrage movement, England, 1900–1914	Sigmund Freud, *The Interpretation of Dreams*, 1900	*1900*
Social welfare legislation, France, 1904; 1910	Cubism in art 1905–1930	
Social welfare legislation, England, 1906–1912		
	Marcel Proust, *Remembrance of Things Past*, 1913–1918	
	Oswald Spengler, *The Decline of the West*, 1918 Bauhaus established, 1919	
German inflation, 1920s	Writers of the "Lost Generation," 1920–1930 Surrealism and Dadaism, 1920s Ludwig Wittgenstein, *Tractatus Logico-philosophicus*, 1921 T. S. Eliot, *The Waste Land*, 1922 James Joyce, *Ulysses*, 1922	*1920*
Great Depression, 1929–1940	Neo-realism in art, 1930s	

POLITICS	SCIENCE & INDUSTRY
Italy conquers Ethiopia, 1935–1936	National rearmament programs, 1935
Rome-Berlin Axis, 1936	
Spanish Civil War, 1936–1939	
Germany annexes Austria, 1938	
Munich conference, 1938	
Nazi-Soviet pact, 1939	Discovery of atomic fission, 1939
Second World War, 1939–1945	
United States enters war, 1941	
Allied invasion of Normandy, 1944	
Bombing of Hiroshima and Nagasaki, 1945	First atomic bomb test, 1945
United Nations founded, 1945	

1940

. M. Keynes, *General Theory of Employment, Interest,*
and Money, 1936

1940

Jean-Paul Sartre, *Being and Nothingness,* 1943

Chapter 25

THE PROGRESS OF INTERNATIONAL INDUSTRIALIZATION AND COMPETITION (1870-1914)

We have conquered for ourselves a place in the sun. It will now be my task to see to it that this place in the sun shall remain our undisputed possession. . . .

—Kaiser William II, speech, **1901**

I f most historians now speak of a second industrial revolution oc-curring during the years after 1870, they are quick to qualify the term. Whatever the changes in technique and in scope—and they were significant—they do not compare to those which characterized the first revolution—*the* Industrial Revolution. There is, however, good reason to distinguish a second period of industrial development and advance from the first. Successful nation-building meant that the years 1870–1914 would be characterized by sharply increased interna-tional political and economic rivalries, culminating in a scramble after imperial territories in Africa and Asia. Britain, if it did not actually surrender its industrial primacy during this period, failed to counter with any real success the energetic and determined challenges from Germany and the United States to its constantly decreasing lead. New technology, particularly in the fields of metals, chemicals, and elec-tricity, resulted in new products. Larger populations and improving standards of living produced greater demand, which, in turn, increased the volume of production. And the need for increased production called forth significant reorganization to provide a freer supply of capital and to ensure a more efficient labor force. It is these changes that distin-guish the second stage of industrialization from the first, and therefore warrant its separate treatment. Yet they must be perceived as stem-ming not only from those economic conditions which were the result of the first stage, but also from the more general political, social, and cultural climate whose history we have been tracing.

A second industrial revolution

In analyzing the progress of industrialization, we shall deal with changes in three major areas: in technology; in scope and scale of production; and in the reorganization of the capitalist system. Finally we shall examine the phenomenon of late–nineteenth-century imperialism, and consider the extent to which that phenomenon can be attributed to increasing economic and industrial rivalries.

1. NEW TECHNOLOGIES

Technology in steel

A most important technological change in this period resulted in the mass production of steel. The advantages of steel over iron—a result of steel's lower carbon content—are its hardness, its malleability, and its strength. Steel can keep its cutting edge, where iron cannot; it can be worked more easily than iron, which is brittle and which, if it is to be used industrially, must almost always be cast (that is, poured into molds). And steel, because of its strength in proportion to its weight and volume, makes a particularly adaptable construction material. These advantages had been recognized by craftsmen for centuries. Until steel could be produced both cheaply and in mass, however, the advantages remained more theoretical than real. Two inventions, during the earlier years of the Industrial Revolution, had reduced the price and increased the output of steel to some degree. The crucible technique, discovered in the eighteenth century in England, called for the heating of relatively small amounts of iron ore to a point at which foreign matter could be removed by skimming, the carbon content reduced, and a proper proportion of carbon distributed evenly throughout the finished product. Although individual crucibles were not large, holding on the average no more than forty-five to sixty pounds, they could be poured together to produce steel ingots of several tons. A century later, in the early 1840s, two Germans adapted the puddling process, used in the production of iron, to the manufacture of steel. While it did not produce steel as hard as that made in crucibles, it reduced its price considerably.

Bessemer, Siemens-Martin, and Gilchrist-Thomas systems

Not until the invention of the Bessemer and Siemens-Martin processes, however, could steel begin to compete with iron. In the 1850s, an Englishman, Henry Bessemer, discovered that by blowing air into and through the molten metal he could achieve a more exact degree of decarbonization in much shorter time, and with far larger quantities of ore, than was possible with either the crucible or puddling methods. Bessemer soon found, however, that his "converters" were incapable of burning off sufficient quantities of phosphorous; and phosphorous in anything but the smallest quantities made the metal unworkable. A partial solution was achieved with the introduction of nonphosphoric hematite ores. Yet this was of little long-term use in most European countries, where supplies of hematite ore were not

The Manufacture of Steel by the Bessemer Process. An 1875 engraving.

abundant. This same problem plagued the German inventors Frederick and William Siemens, whose furnace made use of waste gases to increase heat. Not until Pierre Martin, a Frenchman, discovered that the introduction of scrap iron into the mix would induce proper decarbonization, could the Siemens furnace be used to make steel commercially. And not until the late 1870s was the problem of phosphoreting solved for both the Bessemer and the Siemens-Martin processes. The solution was a simple one, discovered by two Englishmen, a clerk and a chemist: Sidney Gilchrist Thomas and his cousin Sidney Gilchrist. They introduced limestone into the molten iron to combine with the phosphorus, which was then siphoned from the mix. And they lined the converter in such a way that the slag was prevented from eating away the walls and releasing phosphorus back into the molten metal.

Together, these three processes revolutionized the production of steel. Although the use of iron did not end overnight, steel soon moved into the lead. In the British shipbuilding industry, for example, steel had overtaken iron by 1890. In part because Siemens-Martin was particularly suited to the manufacture of steel plates used in shipbuilding, that process dominated the manufacture of steel in Britain, where shipbuilding was a major industry. Bessemer steel, which could be manufactured more cheaply and in larger plants, was more commonly produced on the Continent and in America. The result was a particular increase in the production of German steel: by 1901, German converters were capable of pouring annually an average of 34,000 tons, compared to Britain's 21,750. By 1914 Germany was producing twice as much steel as Britain, and the United States twice as much as Germany.

Increased steel production

A second and equally important technological development resulted in the availability of electric power for industrial, commercial, and domestic use. Electricity's particular advantages result from the facts that it can be easily transmitted as energy over long distances, and that it can be converted into other forms of energy—heat and light, for example. Although electricity had, of course, been discovered prior to the first Industrial Revolution, its advantages could not have been put to general use without a series of inventions which occurred during the nineteenth century. Of these, some of the most important were the invention of the chemical battery by the Italian Alessandro Volta in 1800; of electromagnetic induction by the Englishman Michael Faraday in 1831; of the electromagnetic generator in 1866; of the first commercially practical generator of direct current in 1870; and of alternators and transformers capable of producing high-voltage alternating current in the 1880s. These inventions meant that by the end of the century it was possible to send electric current from large power stations over comparatively long distances. Electric power could be manufactured by water—hence cheaply—and delivered from its source to the place where it was needed.

Once it had been delivered to its destination, the power was converted and put to use in myriad ways. Households quickly became one of the major users of electrical power. The invention by Thomas Edison of the incandescent filament lamp—or light bulb—was crucial in this regard. As individual houses were electrified to receive the power that was to be transformed into light, consumer demand for electricity resulted in further expansion of the electrical industry. Demand for electrical power was increasing in the industrial sector as well. Electric motors soon began to power subways, tramways, and, eventually, long-distance railways. Electricity made possible the development of new techniques in the chemical and metallurgical industries. Most important, electricity helped to transform the work patterns of the factory. Heavy steam engines had made equipment and machinery stationery; electric motors meant that comparatively lightweight power tools could be moved—often by hand—to the site of a particular piece of work. The result was far greater flexibility in terms of factory organization. Smaller workshop industries benefited as well; they could accommodate themselves to electrically powered motors and tools in a way they could not to steam.

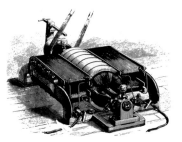

An Early Dynamo Used for Lighting

Steel and electricity were only two of the most important areas where technological changes were taking place. The chemical industry was significantly advanced by developments in the manufacture of alkali and organic compounds. Demand for alkali had increased with the demand for soaps and textiles, and with the changes in the manufacturing process of paper, which required large amounts of bleach. An older, more expensive and wasteful technique used extensively by the British was superseded after 1880 by a new process perfected by the Belgian Ernest Solvay. The result was, again, a rapid overtaking of the British by the Germans in the production not only of alkalis but of sulfuric acid, a by-product recoverable in the Solvay process, and used in the manufacture of fertilizers, petroleum refining, iron, steel, and textiles. In the field of organic compounds, the impetus for further discovery came as a result of demand for synthetic dyes. Although the British and French were the first successful pioneers in this area, the Germans once more moved ahead to a commanding lead by 1900. At the turn of the century German firms controlled about 90 percent of the world market.

The need for more and more power to meet increasing industrial demands resulted not only in developments in the field of electricity, already noted, but in the improved design and expanded capacity of steam engines. The most noteworthy invention in this area was the steam turbine, which permitted engines to run at speeds heretofore unobtainable. Internal combustion engines made their appearance during this period as well. Their major advantage lay in their efficiency; i.e., they could be powered automatically, and did not need to be stoked by hand like steam engines. Once liquid fuels—petroleum and distilled gasoline—became available, as they did increasingly with the discovery of oil fields in Russia, Borneo, and Texas about 1900, the internal combustion engine took hold as a serious competitor to steam. By 1914 most navies had converted from coal to oil, as had domestic steamship companies. The automobile and the airplane, both still in their infancies, made little impact upon the industrial world, however, before 1914.

Improved engines

2. CHANGES IN SCOPE AND SCALE

These technological changes must be understood as occurring against a background of—indeed in part as a result of—a constantly growing population and a generally increased standard of living for the majority of men and women in the Western world. Between 1870 and 1914,

Population increases

The First Successful Airplane Flight

The Interior of a Berlin Department Store, 1882

Europe's population increased from 295 million to 450 million. This was the case despite a declining birth rate in the more industrially advanced countries of western Europe, where more and more middle- and working-class men and women were postponing marriage and limiting the number of their children, confident that those children they did have stood a fairly decent chance of survival. Population growth was primarily the result of a sharp decline in infant mortality, caused by improved sanitation and diet, and by the virtual elimination of diseases such as cholera and typhus. Increases were greatest in the areas of central and eastern Europe, where the birth rate did not drop as dramatically as in the west. Britain's population grew from 34.9 to 45.2 million between 1881 and 1911; France's from 37.4 to 39.1. But Germany's advanced during the same period from 45.2 to 64.9 million, and Russia's from 94 to an estimated 129 million.

Higher living standards

Declining death rates were an indicator of generally increasing prosperity. There were, of course, still a great many very poor people, both in cities and in the country: casual laborers, the unemployed, those in declining industries and trades. Those skilled workers and their families whose real incomes did rise as a result of deflation and higher wage rates did not experience anything like the rate of increase enjoyed by most of the middle class. Nor could they expect to avoid altogether the stretches of unemployment that made life so chaotic for so many of their unskilled co-workers. Yet despite these qualifications, it is fair to say that more people enjoyed a higher standard of living than ever before. And a higher standard of living produced the demand for an increase in consumer goods.

Increased consumption of manufactured goods was by no means uniform; it was higher in urban and industrialized areas than in the country. But even in the country, traditional thrift was challenged as farmers and their wives journeyed by train into the cities, saw what they had not imagined they could have, and then decided they must spend their savings to have it. To accommodate the new and largely middle-class consumers, department stores and chain stores designed their products and their advertising to make shopping as easy and inviting as possible. Behind large plate-glass windows goods were displayed attractively and temptingly; periodic sales encouraged householders to purchase "bargains"; catalogues and charge accounts made it easy for customers to spend money without leaving home. The result was an enormous increase in the volume of manufactured goods produced for this rapidly expanding consumer market. Bicycles, clocks, appliances, furnishings—these and a great many other things were were being made in large quantities, and with new materials (cheap steel) and new techniques (electrical power). Many of these products were designed according to the correct assumption that women were more and more responsible for household purchases. Therefore, goods were fashioned to appeal directly to women, or to the children for whom women were responsible. The foot-powered sewing machine was a particular case in point—the first domestic appliance. Isaac Singer, the American responsible for the development of the treadle and straight needle in the 1850s, was as much an entrepreneur as an inventor. He was a pioneer in the field of advertising and promotion, encouraging purchase on the installment plan and providing courses for would-be domestic seamstresses.

New consumers

Advertisement for a German Sewing Machine. The company proclaims the machine's versatility: unsurpassed for use in the home as well as in the workshop or factory.

*The web of industrial
change*

*Industrial expansion and
consolidation*

*Effects of increase in scale
on workers: (1) relearning*

Sewing machines changed far more than the sewing habits of house-wives, however. They were cheap, lightweight tools, easily installed and easily operated. Workshop masters could set up several, employ a handful of young women at very low wages, and make a profit turning out cheap ready-made clothing in response to increasing markets. Here is just one of the ways in which the scale of manufacturing altered during the latter part of the nineteenth century, both demand and technology conspiring to produce the change. In metal-working, hard-edged steel allowed for the rapid cutting of patterns, which reduced price, which, in turn, encouraged the manufacture of a variety of inexpensive metal goods—kitchenware, for example. The sewing machine led to the development of other new tools that helped cut costs in the clothing industry: button-holers, lace-makers, leather-stitchers. Whereas it took one cobbler ten hours to make a pair of shoes in 1850 by hand, by the end of the century it took a team of cobblers but a few hours to produce ten pairs using machinery. In textiles, improved engines doubled the pace of mules and looms. In heavy industry, steam hammers performed the work of many men more precisely and with greater speed than before. New equipment of this sort was expensive. As a result, in heavy industry, it was the larger companies that prospered, and in the course of their prosperity, they grew even larger.

In all the countries of Europe, and in the United States, the pattern is one of expansion and consolidation. This was especially the case in Germany, where in the iron and steel industry nearly 75 percent of those employed worked in factories of a thousand or more, and where over 90 percent of the electrical equipment manufactured was made in factories with over fifty employees. Machinery was thus altering the scale of manufacturing in two directions at once. In the clothing industry, entrepreneurs could use inexpensive machines to make small workshops turn a profit. In steel foundries, the cost of new equipment forced small competitors to the wall, with the result that the foundries grew very much bigger.

The increase in the scale of manufacturing had important and often disturbing consequences for workers. The most obvious was the need for men and women to relearn their trades. They were compelled to adapt their older skills to the new machines. Very often this adaptation resulted in a loss of either pay or prestige, or both. Most machine work was not skilled work. A trainee could "pick up" a trade in a week or so. Workers who had prided themselves on a particular skill and had been paid according to their ability to perform it, had to face the fact that industrial change was not only forcing them to relearn, but was compelling them to tell themselves that their new "skills"—if they could be called that—did not amount to very much. For example, when the machine itself could cut metal with infinitesimal accuracy, there was far less need than there had been previously for the skills of a human "fitter." Even if workers were not forced to relearn in these ways in order to accommodate to increased scale, they often had at least to accommodate to factory reorganization and rationalization. In workplaces where the hand-carrying of materials had been a major factor in their final cost, mechanization to reduce that cost would produce a bewildering series of changes. Electric cranes, used together with huge magnets in the iron and steel industries, increased the speed with which goods could be moved, and demanded that workers defer to whatever changes their introduction might entail.

A second—and even more important—effect of the change in scale was the constant demand for further efficiency. The greater the scale of the operation, the more important it became to eliminate waste. One minute lost in the production of every ten pairs of shoes might not make much difference if only fifty pairs were produced in a day. But if hundreds were being made, it became crucial, in the eyes of management, to see that those minutes were no longer lost. In factories where capital had been spent on new machinery, the owners, conscious of the cost of their investment, increased output in order to realize a profit on that investment. In factories where older machinery was still in use, owners believed that the only way they could remain competitive with modernized operations was by extracting all they could from their less productive equipment. In both cases, workers were pressed to produce more and more. One result of this drive for efficiency was a restructuring of wage scales. Prior to this period, although there had been serious wage disputes, both management and labor appeared content to bargain from the traditional notion of "a fair day's wage for a fair day's work." Definitions of what was fair naturally varied. But the level of individual performance was generally set by custom. What workers produced in the course of a day continued to determine what they were expected to produce. From about 1870 onward, however, expectations and procedures began to

(2) efficiency

Technological Change and Production Speed-up. An early assembly line of the Ford Motor Company, United States, 1913. Car bodies slid down the ramp and were attached to the chassis as they passed through the line below. One thousand cars were produced each day.

change. Periodic economic depressions in the last quarter of the nineteenth century saw profits fall before wages. This pattern caused employers to insist on greater individual productivity from their employees. It was no longer enough to work at a job with customary speed. Workers were now asked to produce as much as the owners thought they were potentially capable of producing.

Scientific management

But who was to determine that potential? That question plagued industrial relations during these years. Employers, who were adopting precision tools in order to increase production, grew more and more convinced that worker output could be gauged with a like precision as well. The foremost theoretician of worker efficiency and what was called scientific management of labor was the American Frederick W. Taylor (1865–1915). Taylor devised a three-step system whereby a worker's output could be "scientifically" measured, a system which, he argued, would provide a precise method for the determination of wage scales. First, he observed, timed, and analyzed workers' movements on the job, in order to determine how long a particular task should take. Second, he figured the labor costs of these movements. Third, he produced "norms," or general standards, which all workers were expected to maintain. These norms were invariably higher than those which had prevailed under traditional conditions.

Piece rates

In order to encourage workers to accept these increased standards, Taylor urged all factory-owners to adopt piece rates (i.e., payment to workers according to the specific amount produced) rather than hourly or daily wages. Payment by piece rate was already a growing practice in many European and American factories. In theory, at least, workers were not opposed to this method of payment; they reasoned that their only hope for a share in increasing output lay in their chance to be paid directly for what they made. But when they were told that their pay would not increase unless they measured up to predetermined—and, to their mind, unrealistic—norms, they rebelled. They argued that rates were set according to the performance of the speediest workers. Even though workers might earn more money if they agreed to the new rates, they resented the intrusion of management upon the pace of their working lives. Despite this opposition, scientific management spread throughout the industrialized West. In England, the United States, and on the Continent, particularly in the engineering trades, factory after factory subscribed to the new gospel. Where it could not entirely succeed in introducing "efficiency" on the shop floor, management proceeded to rationalize its own procedures. Accounting departments were expanded, and encouraged to attend closely to the problem of cost control in all areas of production and distribution. These reforms were no more than a reflection of the general move in the direction of greater efficiency. They were brought on by the vastly increased scale of production, the need to reduce waste wherever possible, and the desire to derive maximum profits from the elimination of unnecessary motions and unproductive habits.

3. THE NEW CAPITALISM

Responding to the increased scope of production and to the consequent pressures for further efficiency, the institutions of capitalism began to reorganize toward the end of the nineteenth century. Hitherto, most firms had been small or at most middle-sized; now, as firms grew and their need for capital increased, they began to incorporate. Limited liability laws, enacted by most countries in the course of the century, worked to encourage this incorporation. "Limited liability" meant that an individual owning stock in a particular corporation could be held liable only for the amount of his or her shares, should that corporation bankrupt itself. Once insured in this way, many thousands of middle-class men and women considered corporate investment a safe and financially promising way of making money for themselves. A stockholding, "rentier" class emerged, brought into existence by the willingness of governments to encourage capitalism through friendly legislation, and by the desire of capitalist businessmen to expand their industrial undertakings to meet increased demands. More and more companies incorporated. In doing so, their management tended to be removed from the direct control of family founders or of company-based boards of directors. The influence of bankers and financiers, often situated in cities far removed from the factories they invested in, grew accordingly. These men were not investing their own money but the money of their clients; their power to stimulate or to discourage the growth of particular industries and enterprises encouraged a kind of impersonal "finance" capital.

The growth of incorporation

The New York Stock Exchange, 1893

Vertical organization

Horizontal organization: cartels

J. P. Morgan

Opposition to cartels

Corporate organization on a large scale facilitated the spread of industrial unification. Some industries—steel, for example—combined vertically. Steel companies, to ensure uninterrupted production, acquired their own coal and iron mines. By doing so, they could guarantee themselves a supply of raw materials at attractive prices. Often the same steel companies would obtain control of companies whose products were made of steel: for example, shipyards or railway factories. Now they would not only possess a ready stock of raw materials but an equally ready market for their manufactured products—steel plates, steel rails, whatever they might be. Such vertical integration was only possible as a result of the money available for investment through the institutions of finance capital.

A second form of corporate organization was a horizontal formation: the cartel. These were combinations of individual companies producing the same kind of goods, joined for the purpose of controlling, if not eliminating, competition. Since their products were identical, an identical price could be charged. Companies involved in the production of coal and steel were especially suited to the organization of cartels because of the costs of initial capitalization. It is very expensive to build, equip, and man a steel foundry; thus there were relatively few of them. And because there were few, they were the more easily organized into a combine. Cartels were particularly strong in Germany; less so in France, where there was not as much heavy industry, where the tradition of the small family firm was particularly entrenched, and where there was long-standing opposition to competition in the form of price-cutting and general intra-industrial warfare. In Britain, though some cartels were formed, continuing subscription to the policy of free trade meant that companies would find it difficult to maintain fixed prices. How could they do so if they could not exclude, by means of a tariff, foreign competitors who wanted to undersell them? Germany had abandoned the policy of free trade in 1879; the United States, where cartels were known as trusts, did the same after the Civil War, though not all at once. Britain, however, clung to free trade until well into the twentieth century.

Defenders of the cartel argued that the elimination of competition brought more stable prices and more continuous employment. They pointed out as well that cartels almost always reduced the cost of production. Opponents questioned, however, whether those reduced costs were reflected in lower prices, or, as they charged, in higher stockholder profits. Critics of cartels were vocal in the United States, where the so-called captains of industry, most prominently the financier J. P. Morgan (1837–1913), were attacked as a new breed of feudal barons. The Sherman Anti-Trust Act was passed by Congress in 1890 to curb the practice of industrial combination. It had little effect in retarding the process, however, until the trust-busting presidency of Theodore Roosevelt (1901–1908).

Elsewhere in the West at the end of the nineteenth century, governments and big business tended to develop close working relationships contrary to the laissez-faire theories of early industrial entrepreneurs. A significant manifestation of this new partnership was the appearance of businessmen and financiers as officers of state. Joseph Chamberlain, a Birmingham manufacturer, served as Britain's colonial secretary; the German banker Bernhard Dernberg was German secretary of state for colonies; the Frenchman Charles Jonnart, president of the Suez Canal Company and the Saint-Étienne steel works, was later governor-general of Algeria; Guilio Prinetti, a north Italian industrialist, was his country's foreign minister from 1901 to 1903. The interrelationship between government and industry, like the growth of cartels and combines, was seen as a natural development in the capitalist system which, its defenders argued, was showering its benefits on all classes of society.

4. INTERNATIONAL COMPETITION: BRITAIN VS. GERMANY

Throughout the period we have been examining, Britain and Germany were locked in industrial competition. By 1914, both the United States and Germany were outproducing Britain in a number of areas. Yet the German challenge was, for the British, the more significant. Industrial competition with Germany helped reshape international political alliances at the end of the century. Britain, moving to align itself with its ancient enemy France against the Germans, found itself engaged in a contest of naval superiority with the latter, determined that in that field the British would not lose their age-old advantage to the upstart challenger.

To what degree did the Germans succeed in overtaking the British? By 1914, Britain's industrial-commercial day was by no means over. The volume of German trade at the turn of the century was no more than 60 percent as great. Britain, more mature industrially than Germany, was shifting resources to the service sector of the economy, into areas such as the wider distribution of goods. If Britain's output of manufactured goods did no more than double between 1870 and 1913, as compared to Germany's sixfold increase, it was in part for this reason. Nor should one suppose that all areas of German industry were functioning as efficient, modernized, and technologically advanced units. For every up-to-date chemical plant, for every thriving steel mill, there were many smaller workshops where manufacturing took place on little more than a domestic scale. Having said this, however, the fact remains that the Germans *were* a powerful threat to the British. Even before 1870, Germany had ceased to provide a ready market for British manufactures; the Germans were supplying their

Reasons for Britain's lag: (1) the problem of priority

own needs. After 1870, Germany began to export to the rest of the world. Moving into markets that the British had considered exclusively their own, German salesmen promoted German goods in Australia, South America, China, and in Britain itself. In fields such as the manufacture of organic chemicals and electrical equipment, Germany outsold Britain across the globe.

How can Germany's success and, perhaps more important, Britain's inability to counter it be explained? To attempt an answer to the latter question first: Britain was handicapped because it had been the first nation to industrialize. Because of the capital they had invested in older factories and equipment, the British were reluctant to enter new fields or to exploit new methods. For example, because the British had constructed plants to manufacture alkali by an earlier, less efficient process, they found themselves trapped into continuing to produce in that way after the Solvay process had been discovered. Rather than make the expensive switch, British manufacturers attempted to make their alkali more competitive by cutting costs and improving worker efficiency. But when further refinements were introduced in the 1890s, British output not only failed to keep pace with German and also American increases, but actually decreased. The same difficulties arose with steel. Here again Britain was hampered by the problem of priority. Because the British were the first to industrialize, their manufacturing centers took shape in accordance with the scale of early- and mid–nineteenth-century production. Now there was need for large tracts of land, close to transportation, to accommodate steel mills. Because of the cramped layout of Britain's industrial cities, it could not build mills as large as those in Germany or the United States. The result was that by 1900 the largest British steel mills were no bigger than the average-sized mills in Germany. Even new plants built for other manufacturing purposes in Britain were only a third as

Interior of a Krupp Steel Mill, Essen, Germany

large as those constructed by its major rival. Because German plants were big, and because, therefore, they represented a large investment of capital, those who managed them did all they could to ensure their efficient operation. They rationalized design and standardized parts to an extent the British, with their smaller plants, continued to believe unnecessary. Smaller firms tended to receive smaller and more specialized orders which did not encourage standardization. Although standardization was accomplished by 1914 in Britain in some industries—notably iron and steel—in many others it remained more the exception than the rule.

Britain's industrial lead, which froze its urban areas into obsolete patterns and thus prevented growth, froze British attitudes as well. Because they had come so far so fast, the British had grown complacent. Nowhere is this fact more clearly reflected than in the British attitude toward education. If the achievements of the first Industrial Revolution—for example, the steam engine, the spinning jenny—were the result of what might be called creative tinkering, those of the second revolution were the product of a close and fruitful union of pure science with technology. Achievement now depended on a generally literate workforce, a trained body of mechanics, a scientifically grounded body of technicians, and a corps of highly trained, creative scientists. Germany was producing these cadres; Britain was not. Only in 1870 was a system of public elementary education instituted in Britain, and not until ten years later was it made compulsory. In Germany, compulsory education dated from the eighteenth century. The British governing class believed the primary purpose of education was social control: teaching a boy or girl not only how to read and write, but to accept his or her particular place within the social structure. Though German elementary education was authoritarian in many respects as well, the fact that it had begun earlier and was directly joined to systems of secondary education encouraged the development of abilities; it was in this respect far less wasteful than that of the British. As Britain lagged in the area of elementary education, it lagged in the development of scientific and technological laboratories and training centers. In Germany, the state established an elaborate network of such technical institutions; in Britain there were almost none before the First World War.

(2) attitudes

Complacency was the major reason for this lack. The British tended to believe, wrongly, that practical experience and on-the-job training would produce the skills necessary to keep abreast of change. In addition, the British upper middle class convinced itself that the goal of education was not the production of creative technologists but of "gentlemen." Fathers who had made their fortunes as entrepreneurs during the first Industrial Revolution sent their sons to private boarding schools and to the ancient universities of Oxford and Cambridge to receive a "gentleman's" education—training in Greek and Latin, pri-

Complacency

marily. Those sons, whose creative talents might otherwise have been channeled into science and technology, chose careers in politics, or in the imperial or domestic bureaucracies instead. The result was a severe narrowing of the pool of creative technologists and dynamic entrepreneurs. There were fewer men than in either Germany or the United States interested in organizing the increasingly large amounts of capital necessary to engage in industrial expansion. It was easier to invest money overseas than to undertake the revitalization of various enterprises at home. A suspicion of what was new, encouraged by the British tendency to rely upon practical experience of the past, prevented Britain from rising in more than a fitful way to the German challenge.

5. INTERNATIONAL COMPETITION: IMPERIALISM

A global economy

The rivalry between Britain and Germany was only the most intense aspect of international competitiveness during the last decades of the nineteenth century. As nations proceeded with the business of industrialization, their search for markets brought them into direct opposition with one another. One result was that the dogma of free trade was abandoned by all save Britain. As we have seen, the Germans rejected the policy of low tariffs in 1879. Austria and Russia had already done so. Spain instituted new scales of import duties in 1877 and again in 1891. In France, two decades of gradual abandonment were climaxed by the passage of the Méline Tariff in 1892. Although individual nations attempted to isolate themselves from each other in this way, developments in international economics mandated the continuing growth and development of an interlocking, worldwide system of manufacturing, trade, and finance. The general adoption by western Europe and the United States of the gold standard meant that the currencies of the so-called civilized world could be readily exchanged with each other against the measure of a common standard—the international price of gold. Hence countries needing to import from the United States, for example, did not have to sell goods directly to that country. They could sell to South America, exchange the money they received for gold, and then buy from America.

"Invisible" exports

Almost all European countries, dependent on vast supplies of raw materials to sustain their rate of industrial production, imported more than they exported. To avoid the mounting deficits that would otherwise have resulted from this practice, they relied upon "invisible" exports: i.e., shipping, insurance, and interest on money lent or invested. The extent of Britain's exports in these areas was far greater than that of any other country. London was the money market of the world, to which would-be borrowers looked for assistance before turning elsewhere. By 1914, Britain had $20 billion invested overseas, compared with the $8.7 of the French and the $6 billion of the Germans. The insurance firm of Lloyds of London served clients around the world. The British merchant fleet transported the manufactured goods and raw materials of every trading nation. It was the volume of its "invisible" exports that permitted Britain to remain faithful to the doctrine of free trade while other European nations were forced to institute tariffs.

Effects on Africa and Asia

The competition between the principal economic powers of this worldwide marketplace affected not only their relationships with each other but also with those less developed areas upon which they were increasingly dependent for both raw materials and markets. Some of those areas, such as India and China, were the seats of ancient empires. Others, such as central Africa, sheltered less complex tribal socieities. No matter what the nature of the indigenous civilization, the intrusion upon it of modern science and technology, systematic wage labor, financial and legal institutions caused enormous disruption. Though drawn into the world economy, these areas did not draw from it the benefits that the West did. Native industries such as Indian textile spinning and weaving stood no chance in competition with the factory-made products of Manchester. African herdsmen and hunters endured the disruption of their living habits by the activities of European ranchers and miners. Men who had made their living as boatmen and carters lost their livelihood to the railways constructed by Western nations. New jobs there might be; but they were jobs worked according to a Western style, dictated by Western economic demands, and threatened by Western economic disorders. In great measure the workers of this emerging world were assuming the role of a global unskilled working class under the hegemony of Western capitalism.

*Earlier
imperialism*

With this global background in mind, we can better understand the history of late–nineteenth-century imperialism—the subjugation by the European powers of vast tracts of land and indigenous populations, primarily on the continents of Africa and Asia. Imperialism was by no means a new phenomenon. During the nineteenth century, the French had penetrated Algeria and the British, India. In other parts of the world, where Western powers did not govern directly, they often exercised an indirect influence so powerful as to preclude "native" defiance. When the West "opened" China beginning in 1834, it left the Chinese in nominal charge of their state. But it ensured that affairs would be conducted to its advantage and within its "sphere of influence." Britain added to its "informal" empire in this way in South America, Africa, and south and east Asia.

*Imperialism
as economics:
Hobson*

As international rivalries increased, European powers moved with greater frequency and determination to control both the government and economy of underdeveloped nations and territories. The scope, intensity, and long-range consequences of this so-called new imperialism of the late nineteenth century have generated a debate about its causes as heated as that which surrounds the first Industrial Revolution. One influential group of social critics and historians has argued that the causes were predominantly, if not exclusively, economic. As early as 1902, the English social reformer and theorist, J. A. Hobson, charged that what he called "the scramble for Africa" had occurred as a result of the economic interests of a small group of extremely rich and influential financiers throughout western Europe. Hobson declared that the colonization of Africa had produced little economic gain for the taxpayers whose countries had dispatched armies of conquest and occupation at the behest of international capitalists. Profits went only to the rich, who ventured beyond the bounds of economically stagnant western Europe in search of a higher return on their investments than could be realized at home. Hobson concluded that late–nineteenth-century imperialism was "a depraved choice of national life," appealing primarily to "the lusts of self-seeking acquisitiveness and forceful domination."

Hobson's analysis inspired a more influential critique of imperialism by the Russian communist and future revolutionary leader, Nicolai Lenin. Lenin agreed with Hobson that imperialism was an economic phenomenon. But, unlike Hobson, he saw it as an integral and inevitable phase of the capitalist system, as the title of his 1916 treatise, *Imperialism: The Last Stage of Capitalism,* explicitly declared. Capitalist competition, Lenin argued, and the consequent monopolies that it had produced, had lowered domestic profits, and thus compelled the owners of surplus capital to invest it overseas. The alternative, enlarging home markets by raising wages, would serve only to further decrease profits. Imperialism was thus the creature of the internal contradictions of industrial capitalism.

Lenin

While most historians would agree that economic pressures were one important cause of imperialism, they have remained uncomfortable with analyses that ignore other factors they consider equally important. They remain prepared to acknowledge the role of economics when it seems to make sense to do so: in the case of Great Britain, for example, where about half its total of £4 billion in foreign investments was at work within its empire. In all western European countries, demand for raw materials made colonies a necessary investment and helped persuade governments that imperialism was a worthwhile policy. Yet the economic explanation begins to break down when one considers facts like the following: that colonial markets were generally too poor to answer the needs of European manufacturers; that Africa, the continent over which there was the greatest "scramble," was also the poorest and least profitable to investors; that only a very small portion of German capital was invested in German colonies before 1914; that only one-fifth of French capital was so invested; that, indeed, the French had more capital invested in Russia, hoping to stabilize that ally against the Germans, than in all their colonial possessions.

*Limits to the
economic
argument*

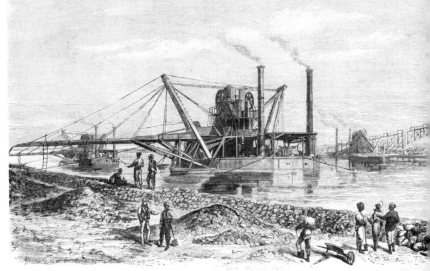

*Dredges and Elevators at Work
on the Construction of the Suez
Canal, 1869*

THE ISTHMUS OF SUEZ MARITIME CANAL: DREDGES AND ELEVATORS AT WORK.

Those in charge of the imperial building process decided policy in response to a combination of political and economic considerations, and as a corollary to the process of nation-building. National security and the preservation of a general balance of power were issues never far from the forefront of politicians' thinking and planning. Britain's domination of Egypt in the 1880s was the result, in large measure, of its fear of what might occur in the Near East should large portions of the decaying Ottoman Empire fall into Russian hands. Britain had purchased 44 percent of the shares in the Suez Canal Company in 1875, and considered the waterway a strategic lifeline to the east. The canal had been built by the French under the direction of the engineer Ferdinand de Lesseps. Begun in 1859 and completed in 1869, it was expected to assist France in its bid for commercial expansion to the East. Britain obtained its shares from the spendthrift khedive (viceroy) of Egypt at a time when he was threatened with bankruptcy. When, in 1882, nationalist rebels protested continuing British intervention in the internal affairs of Egypt, the British claimed they had no choice but to bombard the port of Alexandria and place the Egyptian ruler under their protection. A continuing British presence in Egypt, and the willingness of the British government to support Egyptian claims to the Upper Nile, worried the French, who were growing to fear Britain's political domination of the entire African continent. Moving to correct what they perceived as a severe political imbalance, the French challenged the British and at Fashoda, in the Sudan, came close to war in 1898. The British called the French bluff, however, and war was averted.

Imperialism and international politics

The power struggle over Suez, Egypt, and the Sudan provides an excellent example of the manner in which international politics was directly related to imperial advance. It suggests, as well, that what passed for "imperial policy" was less a matter of long-range planning

Imperial policy-making

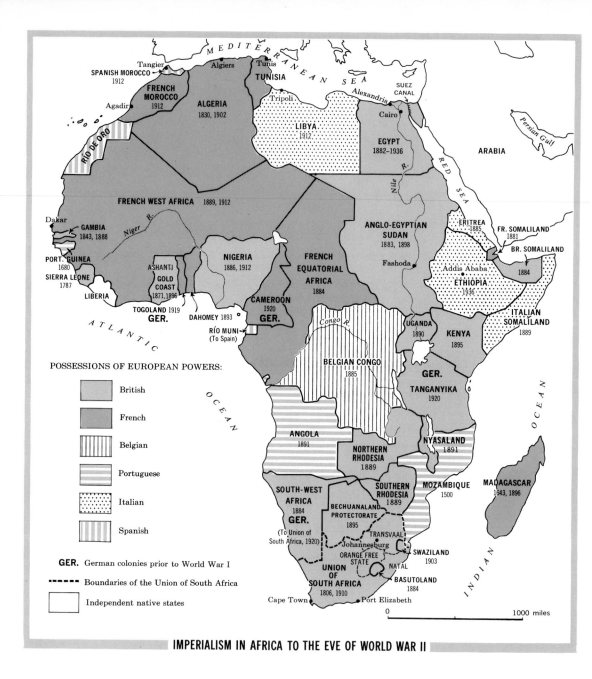

MEDITERRANEAN SEA

Tangier
SPANISH MOROCCO
1912
Algiers
Tunis
TUNISIA
Alexandria
SUEZ CANAL
FRENCH MOROCCO
1912
Agadir
Tripoli
Cairo
ALGERIA
1830, 1902
LIBYA
1912
EGYPT
1882-1936
ARABIA
Persian Gulf
RÍO DE ORO
Nile R.
RED SEA
FRENCH WEST AFRICA 1889, 1912
Dakar
GAMBIA
1843, 1888
Niger R.
ANGLO-EGYPTIAN SUDAN
1883, 1898
ERITREA
1885
FR. SOMALILAND
1881
BR. SOMALILAND
PORT. GUINEA
1680
SIERRA LEONE
1787
LIBERIA
ASHANTI
GOLD COAST
1871, 1896
NIGERIA
1886, 1912
FRENCH EQUATORIAL AFRICA
1884
Fashoda
Addis Ababa
ETHIOPIA
1936
1884
ITALIAN SOMALILAND
1889
TOGOLAND 1919
GER.
DAHOMEY 1893
CAMEROON
1920
GER.
RÍO MUNI
(To Spain)
Congo R.
UGANDA
1890
KENYA
1895
ATLANTIC
BELGIAN CONGO
1885
GER.
TANGANYIKA
1920

POSSESSIONS OF EUROPEAN POWERS:

OCEAN
ANGOLA
1891
NYASALAND
1891
OCEAN
British
French
Belgian
NORTHERN RHODESIA
1889
MOZAMBIQUE
1500
MADAGASCAR
1643, 1896
Portuguese
SOUTH-WEST AFRICA
1884
GER.
(To Union of South Africa, 1920)
SOUTHERN RHODESIA
1889
Italian
Spanish
BECHUANALAND PROTECTORATE
1895
TRANSVAAL
Johannesburg
ORANGE FREE STATE
SWAZILAND
1903
NATAL
INDIAN

GER. German colonies prior to World War I
------- Boundaries of the Union of South Africa
UNION OF SOUTH AFRICA
1806, 1910
BASUTOLAND
1884
Independent native states
Cape Town
Port Elizabeth
0   1000 miles

IMPERIALISM IN AFRICA TO THE EVE OF WORLD WAR II

than of a series of pragmatic and often spontaneous responses to particular colonial political and economic situations. Often those in charge of policy-making found themselves led beyond their original ambitions, not only by the demands of international rivalries, but by the actions of individual explorers and entrepreneurs who established claims to hitherto unknown territories which home governments then felt compelled to recognize and defend.

Imperialism must also be understood as something more than official policy, whether carefully conceived or accidental. A French diplomat once described the dynamic English imperial adventurer Cecil Rhodes as "a force cast in an idea"; the same might be said of imperialism itself. Imperialism as an idea excited the minds of explorers like the English missionary David Livingstone, who believed that his country's conquest of Africa would put an end to the East African slave trade, and "introduce the Negro family into the body of corporate nations." Rudyard Kipling, the English poet and novelist, wrote of "the white man's burden," of his mission to civilize the "half devil, half child" races that inhabited what most Europeans considered the "barbaric" and "heathen" quarters of the globe. To combat slave-trading, famine, filth, and illiteracy seemed to many a legitimate reason for invading the jungles of Africa and Asia.

Imperialism as an idea was also of use to European governments at home. A populace could be encouraged to forget domestic hardships as it celebrated its country's triumphs overseas. Patriotism—a not always attractive corollary to nation-building—was stimulated by arguments such as that expressed by the German historian Heinrich von Treitschke in 1887: that "the colonizing impulse has become a vital question for a great nation"—the implication clearly being that a nation was not great unless it possessed colonies. Associations with a semi-official standing—the Deutsche Kolonialgesellschaft, the Comité de l'Afrique Française, the Royal Colonial Institute—propagandized on behalf of empire, as did newspapers, which recognized in sensational stories of overseas conquest a means of attracting a newly literate clientele.

Imperial competition centered in Africa. In 1875, 11 percent of the continent was in European hands; by 1902, 90 percent. Germans pressed inward from the east; Frenchmen from the west. The Portuguese schemed to connect the ancient colonies of Angola, on the west, with Mozambique, on the east. Most active among the European powers during this initial period of late–nineteenth-century colonization was a privately financed group of Belgians under the leadership of that country's king, Leopold II. In association with H. M. Stanley, an American newspaperman and explorer, Leopold and a group of financiers founded the International Congo Association in 1878, which negotiated treaties with chieftains that opened the Congo River basin to commercial exploitation. A conference, called in Berlin in 1885 and attended by most European nations and the United States, attempted to establish certain ground rules for the game of imperial acquisition. The Congo was declared a Free State, under the trusteeship of Leopold (the first example of this later familiar device of protecting "backward" peoples). A European nation with holdings on the African coast was declared to have first rights to territory in the interior behind those coastal regions. Those rights, however, could be sustained only by what was termed "real" occupation—that is, the presence of either administrators or troops. The scramble was on! Occupation was accompanied by the exploitation of native labor. Agreements reached with local chieftains, whom the Europeans courted, authorized the employment of men and women as laborers under conditions little better than slavery. Often compelled to live in compounds apart from their families, Africans were victimized by a system which rooted out prevailing custom without attempting to establish anything like a new civilization in its place. In the Congo, the Arab slave trade was suppressed, replaced by a system of forced labor. Tribal lands were confiscated and rebellions brutally crushed.

The scramble for territory

The division of the geographical spoils accelerated after 1885. The Portuguese increased their hold in Angola and Mozambique. The Italians invaded Somaliland and Eritrea. They attempted to extend their controls to Ethiopia, but were repulsed by an army of 80,000 Ethiopians, the first instance of a major victory by native Africans over whites. Germany came relatively late to the game. Bismarck was reluctant to engage in an enterprise which, he believed, would do little to profit the empire either politically or economically. Eventually concluding, however, that they could not afford to let other powers divide the continent among them, the Germans established colonies in German East Africa, in the Cameroons and Togo on the west coast, and in the desertlike and economically valueless territory of South

"The Rhodes Colossus." The ambitions of Cecil Rhodes, the driving force behind British imperialism in South Africa, are satirized in this cartoon, which appeared in *Punch.*

Boer Commandos under Louis Botha. Botha became the first prime minister of the Union of South Africa following the Boer War.

West Africa. The French controlled large areas in West Africa and, in the Red Sea, the port of Obok. It was to further their plan for an east-west link that the French risked challenging the British at Fashoda. That scheme, however, fell afoul of Britain's need to dominate Egypt, and of its plans for a north-south connection through the African continent.

Cecil Rhodes, the English entrepreneur and imperial visionary, promoted the notion of a Capetown to Cairo railway both before and after his assumption of the prime-ministership of the Cape Colony in 1890. His plans were thwarted in the south, however, by the presence of two independent neighboring republics, the Transvaal and the Orange Free State, both inhabited by descendents of the original Dutch settlers in South Africa. These Boers—the Dutch word for "farmers"—had fled from the British in the Cape Colony and established themselves in their agricultural states in defiant opposition to the freebooting and exploitationist spirit of the British economic adventurers who had driven them from their original settlements. When diamonds and gold were discovered in the Transvaal in 1886, the tension between the British and the Boers grew. As British prospectors and entrepreneurs moved in, the Boers refused to pass laws permitting the exploitation of their resources by foreign firms. They also taxed the interlopers heavily. Rhodes retaliated by attempting to force a war with the republics. His first try, the dispatching of a force of irregular volunteers under the command of Dr. L. S. Jameson in 1895, failed to provoke a conflict, but precipitated general censure on the British for harassing a peaceful neighbor. Rhodes was forced to resign as prime minister of the Cape Colony in 1896. War broke out in 1899. Its course, however, did not run according to British plans. The Boers proved tough fighters. It took three years to secure an armistice; it took further long months and resort to brutal policies such as detention camps and farm-burning to bring the resilient republicans to heel.

Britain in India

Britain managed to increase its hold on its prize imperial possession—India—throughout the nineteenth century. The "informal" rule of the commercially motivated East India Company had proved ineffective in 1857, when native Indian troops and a large number of other disaffected elements within the subcontinent rebelled in what the British chose to call "The Indian Mutiny," but which was in fact a far more serious and deep-seated challenge to foreign control. Henceforth the British government administered the subcontinent. But at the same time, they decided to rule through the Indian upper classes, and not, as in the past, in opposition to them. Although instruction in British-sponsored schools continued in English, Indian customs were tolerated as they had not been before, and princes and their bureaucracies were incorporated as protectorates into the general scheme of government. A class of westernized, and yet devotedly Indian, civil servants and businessmen thus emerged by the end of the nineteenth century, trained by the British yet burdened by no sense of obligation to their tutors. This group provided the leadership for the nationalist movement that was to challenge British rule in India during the mid-twentieth century. Britain's aim in India was to promote order and stability. Civil servants administered justice even-handedly; they promoted improved sanitation, which, ironically, helped to increase the country's population beyond the point where it could sustain itself. The vast majority of Indians remained desperately poor, victims in many cases of the importation of cheap manufactured goods which threatened indigenous industries and testified to Britain's willingness to subordinate its colonies' economic well-being to its own.

British colonial rule

The pattern of British imperialism differed throughout the world. In areas dominated by white settlers, home rule was introduced in hopes of preventing the sort of disaffection that had produced the American Revolution. Australia was granted self-government in the 1850s, New Zealand in 1876. In 1867, a united Dominion of Canada, with its own federal governments and legislatures, was established.

Imperialism elsewhere

Elsewhere in the world, Western nations hastened to plant their colors upon those territories that promised rewards, either economic or strategic. Britain, France, Germany, and the Netherlands all staked claims in the East Indies, the Dutch achieving an overall hegemony there by 1900. China allowed itself to be victimized by a series of commercial treaties; among the predators was China's neighbor Japan, the only non-Western nation able to modernize in the nineteenth century. The United States played a double game. It acted as champion of the

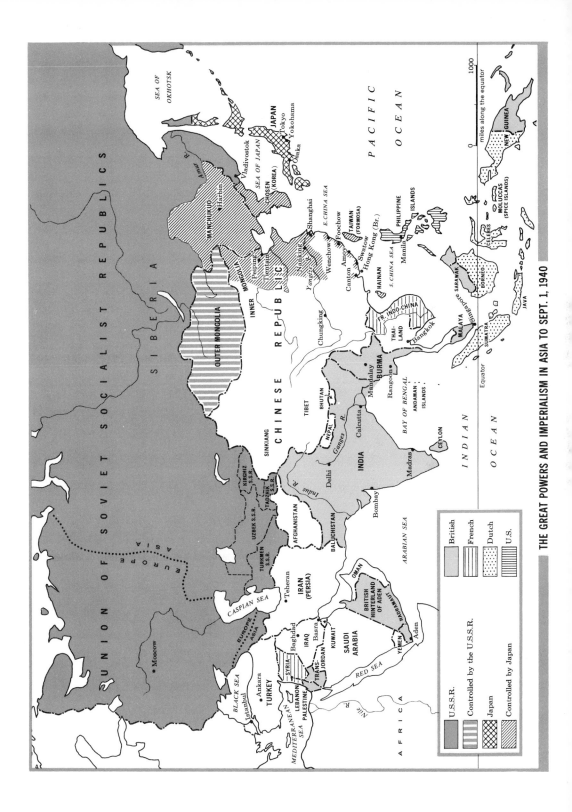

THE GREAT POWERS AND IMPERIALISM IN ASIA TO SEPT. 1, 1940

Imperialism. Left: Germans traveling in East Africa, 1907. Right: A British officer in India, c. 1900.

underdeveloped countries in the Western Hemisphere when they were threatened from Europe. Yet the Americans were willing, whenever it suited them, to prey on their neighbors, either "informally" or formally. When, at the end of the century, Spain's feeble hold on its Caribbean and Pacific colonies encouraged talk of rebellion, the United States stepped in to protect its investments and guarantee its maritime security. It declared and won a war against Spain in 1898 on trumped-up grounds. In the same year, the United States annexed Puerto Rico and the Philippines, and established a "protectorate" over Cuba. When Colombia's colony, Panama, threatened to rebel in 1903, the Americans quickly backed the rebels, recognized Panama as a republic, and then proceeded to grant it protection while Americans built the Panama Canal on land leased from the new government. Intervention in Santo Domingo and in Hawaii proved that the United States was no less an imperial power than the nations of western Europe. Together, by the end of the century, those countries had succeeded in binding the world together as it had never been before. The military and economic power with which they had accomplished that achievement meant that, for the time being at any rate, they would be the world's masters.

SELECTED READINGS

• *Items so designated are available in paperback editions.*
• Ashworth, W., *A Short History of the International Economy since 1850,* rev. ed., London, 1975. A good introduction.

Barkin, Kenneth D., *The Controversy over German Industrialization, 1890–1902*, Chicago, 1970. The political and social struggles between agricultural and industrial interests.

Cameron, Rondo E., *France and the Economic Development of Europe, 1800–1914*, Princeton, N.J., 1961. Emphasizes the export of French capital and skill in the economic growth of Europe.

• Headrick, Daniel R., *The Tools of Empire: Technology and European Imperialism in the Nineteenth Century*, Oxford, 1981. A study of the relationship between technological innovation and imperialism.

• Hobsbawm, Eric, *Industry and Empire: The Making of Modern English Society, 1750 to the Present Day*, New York, 1968. Emphasizes the economic background of imperialism.

• Fieldhouse, D. K., *The Colonial Empires*, London, 1966. A general survey from the eighteenth to the twentieth centuries.

———, *Economics and Empire, 1830–1914*, London, 1973. Argues against the primacy of economic factors in the spread of imperialism.

• Gollwitzer, Heinz, *Europe in the Age of Imperialism, 1880–1914*, London, 1969. A brief survey with excellent illustrations.

Kieran, V. G., *Marxism and Imperialism*, New York, 1975. Argues the Marxist position effectively.

• Kindleberger, C. P., *Economic Growth in France and Britain, 1851–1950*, Cambridge, Mass., 1963. A technical account.

• Landes, David S., *The Unbound Prometheus*, London, 1969. Particularly good on the Anglo-German rivalry.

Langer, William L., *The Diplomacy of Imperialism, 1890–1902*, New York, 1960. A thorough, standard work, useful for its analysis of the intellectual as well as political origins of imperialism.

Louis, William Roger, ed., *Imperialism: The Robinson and Gallagher Controversy*, New York, 1976. The best introduction to recent debate over the nature and causes of imperialism.

Milward, Alan S., and S. B. Saul, *The Development of the Economies of Continental Europe, 1850–1914*, Cambridge, Mass., 1977. An excellent, comprehensive text, particularly good on the smaller European nations.

Moorehead, Alan, *The White Nile*, London, 1971. Captures much of the excitement of imperial exploration.

Price, Roger, *The Economic Modernization of France*, New York, 1975. Rejects conventional periodizations; stresses the advent of railroads which transformed the market structure of France.

Robinson, Ronald, and J. Gallagher, *Africa and the Victorians: The Official Mind of Imperialism*, London, 1961. Contains their famous thesis that imperialism was not deliberately pursued as a policy of state, but rather was a response to events in colonial areas. The modern debate over imperialism begins with this work.

• Shannon, Richard, *The Crisis of Imperialism, 1865–1915*, St. Albans, England, 1976. An excellent survey of the transformation of British society in the wake of modern industrialization.

Stolper, Gustav, et al., *The German Economy, 1870 to the Present*, New York, 1967. A good introduction.

SOURCE MATERIALS

Court, W. H. B., *British Economic History, 1870–1914; Commentary and Documents,* Cambridge, 1965. An excellent collection of documents.

Hobson, J. A., *Imperialism: A Study,* London, 1902.

Lenin, Vladimir, *Imperialism: The Highest Stage of Capitalism,* 1916. (Many English editions.) Lenin's most significant contribution to Marxist ideology. He saw the essence of imperialism as the export of capital rather than goods which led to worldwide competition, of which World War I was an inevitable result.

Reitz, Deneys, *Commando: A Boer Journal of the Boer War,* London, 1929. A superb memoir of the Boer War.

Chapter 26

THE MIDDLE CLASS
CHALLENGED

The time of surprise attacks, of revolutions carried through by small conscious minorities at the head of unconscious masses, is past. Where it is a
question of a complete transformation of the social organization, the
masses themselves must also be in it, must themselves already have
grasped what is at stake, what they are going in for, with body and soul.
—Friedrich Engels, *The Class Struggles in France, 1848–50*

C apitalism's continuing expansion encouraged middle-class men
and women at the end of the nineteenth century to believe
themselves the necessary key to the progress of the human
race. At the same time, however, that belief was being challenged
from several directions. In each case, the challenges called into question assumptions close to the core of middle-class consciousness. Socialist doctrine, which was for the first time receiving a widespread
hearing, pronounced capitalism a threat, rather than a boon, to society. New scientific theories—particularly the theory of evolution—
declared that the key to progress was not the well-laid schemes of humanity, but chance. Psychologists discovered the irrationality of
human beings and philosophers their ultimate helplessness. Paintings,
poetry, and music proclaimed an artists' revolution on behalf of the
idea of art for its own sake, not for the edification of a middle-class
public. Together, these various intellectual and cultural currents threatened the notion that society would most successfully advance under
middle-class auspices, setting its course in accordance with middle-
class moral and economic precepts, and placing its faith in a belief in
the importance and inevitability of continued material progress.

*The dimensions of the
challenge*

I. THE CHALLENGE OF SOCIALISM

Marx in England

The history of socialism in the latter half of nineteenth century is, to a great degree, the biography of its most famous propagandist and theoretician, Karl Marx (1818–1883). Marx was both a social thinker and a political leader. At certain times theory dictated his actions; at others, political events led him to alter doctrine. But always he was at the center of the socialist movement, his moral passion, as much as his scholarly research, shaping the course of its events. The fact of his continuing influence is particularly remarkable for two reasons. First, although a German, he lived from 1849 until his death in London, an exile from the mainstream of continental socialism, in a country whose toleration of socialists was a mark of its comparative immunity from their doctrines. Second, Marx was not a leader who readily took others into his confidence. His antisocial nature was due, in part, to the poverty in which he was forced to live. He and his family were kept alive by gifts of money from his faithful friend and collaborator, Friedrich Engels, and by occasional stints as a political journalist—for a time Marx was a correspondent for the *New York Tribune*.

Capital

During the 1850s and 1860s Marx labored to produce his definitive analysis of capitalist economics, *Capital,* the first volume of which was published in 1867. The argument of *Capital* owed a great deal to that dialectical idealism and economic materialism which, as we have seen, shaped Marx's earlier thinking and writing. In *Capital* he synthesized ideas he and Engels had enunciated in their previous tracts. He described in detail the processes of production, exchange, and distribution as they operated within the capitalist system. He argued that under capitalism, workers were denied their rightful share of profits. The value of any manufactured item, Marx claimed, was determined by the amount of labor necessary to produce it. Yet workers were hired at wages whose value was far less than the value of the goods they produced. The difference between the value of workers' wages and the value of their work as sold was pocketed by members of the capitalist class, who, according to Marx, made off with far more than a justifiable portion of the sale price. This so-called labor theory of value, borrowed from a somewhat similar doctrine held by Ricardo and other classical economists, was the basis for Marx's claim that the working class was compelled to suffer under the capitalist system. Because workers were forced to sell their labor they became nothing more than commodities in the economic market.

So long as capitalists refused to pay wages more nearly equal to the labor value of their employees' work, those employees would remain exploited. Marx preached that the only class which, under capitalism, produced more wealth than it enjoyed was the working class, the proletariat. The bourgeoisie, which owned the means of production and was therefore able to appropriate that which was rightfully the work-

Karl Marx

ers', had a vested interest in maintaining the status quo; hence its willingness to make use of political, social, religious, and legal institutions to keep the proletariat in its place.

Marx predicted that capitalism would eventually do itself in. He argued that as time passed, market competition would compel the formation of ever-larger industrial and financial combinations. As the smaller enterpreneurial class—the petty bourgeoisie—was squeezed out by more powerful combines, its members would join with the proletariat, until society resembled a vast pyramid, with a much-enlarged proletariat at its base and an opposing force of a few powerful capitalists at its tip. At this point, Marx declared, the proletariat would rise in revolution against what was left of the bourgeoisie.

Marx as prophet

After capitalism had received its death blow at the hands of the workers, it would be followed by a socialist stage, characterized by the dictatorship of the proletariat; payment in accordance with work performed; and ownership and operation by the state of all means of production, distribution, and exchange. In time socialism would be succeeded by communism, the goal of historical evolution. Communism would bring with it a classless society. No one would live by owning, but solely by working. The state would now disappear, relegated to the museum of antiquities, "along with the bronze ax and the spinning wheel." Nothing would replace it except voluntary associations to operate the means of production and provide for social necessities. The essence of communism was payment in accordance with needs. The wage system would be abolished, and citizens would be expected to work in accordance with their faculties, entitled to receive from the total fund of wealth produced an amount in proportion to their needs.

The advent of communism

In the ten years after its publication, *Capital* was translated into English (Marx had written it in German), French, Russian, and Italian. The book's widespread appeal was the result of its compelling deterministic certainty and of its vigorous crusading temper. Though much that *Capital* predicted has failed to occur, middle- and working-class socialists reading it soon after its publication and measuring its pronouncements against the capitalistic world they knew had little difficulty in accepting Marx's reasoning. It seemed to them that he had constructed an objective science of society out of their own experiences. The book became the theoretical rallying point for a growing band of socialists who stood opposed to the world the middle class had made. For a time it breathed life into an organization of continental and British workers that had been founded in London in 1864: the International Workingmen's Association, usually referred to as the International. This body had been formed with the declared purpose of forging an international working-class alliance to overthrow capitalism and abolish private property. Marx delivered its inaugural address, in which he preached that workers must win political power for themselves if they were ever to escape their industrial bondage.

The First International

Various difficulties had prevented the formation of a radically oriented workers' organization prior to this time. There was, first of all, fear of official reprisal. Second, the irregular pace of industrialization across Europe meant that workers in one country could have little understanding of the particular plight of their fellow workers elsewhere. Finally, the period after 1850 had witnessed an increase in general prosperity which encouraged the more highly skilled—and more politically conscious—workers to forsake revolutionary goals and to pursue the more immediate end of accommodation with middle-class politicians. The German socialists' dealings with Bismarck (see below, p. 892), were a case in point. Meanwhile, however, the determination of a small band of dedicated radical socialists temporarily surmounted these problems to permit the formation of the first international workers' association.

Lassalle and Bakunin

Marx immediately assumed the direction of the International. He labored to exclude moderates from its councils and denounced the German socialists, and their leader Ferdinand Lassalle (1825–1864), for striking bargains with Bismarck. The duty of socialists, Marx argued, was not partnership with the state, but rather its overthrow. At the same time Marx battled the doctrines of the Russian anarchist Michael Bakunin (1814–1876), who opposed the socialist notion that social evil was the product of capitalism. Bakunin argued that the state was the ultimate villain, and preached its immediate destruction through isolated acts of terrorism. He also opposed centralization within the International, urging instead a kind of federal autonomy for each national workers' group. To Marx, these individualist notions represented nothing more than reversion to a kind of primitive rebellion, heroic but ultimately fruitless. He succeeded in having Bakunin banished from the International in 1872. The International prospered for a time during the 1860s. Individual trade unions in various countries were persuaded to join in its united campaign which preached revolution and, through the application of pressure both at the ballot box and in the factory, seemed to promise at least higher wages and shorter hours. Under Marx's direction the International was a highly organized and tightly controlled body, far more effective in this respect than any previous socialist organization.

The troubled International

Yet by 1876 it had faded from existence. Despite Marx's abilities as an authoritarian chief of staff, the International throughout its existence had to battle those same circumstances which delayed its foundation. In addition, Marx's insistence upon control from the center thwarted a growing desire on the part of individual socialist organizations to pursue programs of immediate benefit to themselves. These factors weakened the International. What probably brought about its demise was its association with events occurring in Paris after the defeat of France by Germany in 1870 in the Franco-Prussian War.

Following the collapse of Napoleon III, a new republic, generally conservative in tone, had been established by the French. In March

Above: *The Birth of Venus,* Alexandre Cabanel (1823–89). Below: *Luncheon on the Grass,* Edouard Manet (1823–83). Cabanel's painting is a typical product of the fashionable French Salon, and was at one time owned by Napoleon III. It won the Salon prize in 1863 and was copied several times by the artist (as were other Salon paintings), emphasizing the fact that it was considered as much a piece of "decoration" as a piece of art. This sort of "bestseller" was exceedingly popular with upper-middle-class collectors, who felt no need to apologize for its semi-pornographic nature because of its classical subject matter. Manet's painting, done in the same year, created an enormous furor. Its style broke with the soft, painterly techniques of the Salon school; instead it was painted with broad, flat strokes that presaged the coming of Impressionism. Its subject matter caused a sensation as well. Whereas voluptuous classical nudes were respectable art, a painting of a young woman seated without her clothing at a picnic with fully clothed gentlemen friends conveyed a sense of serious social impropriety to bourgeois viewers. (Louvre)

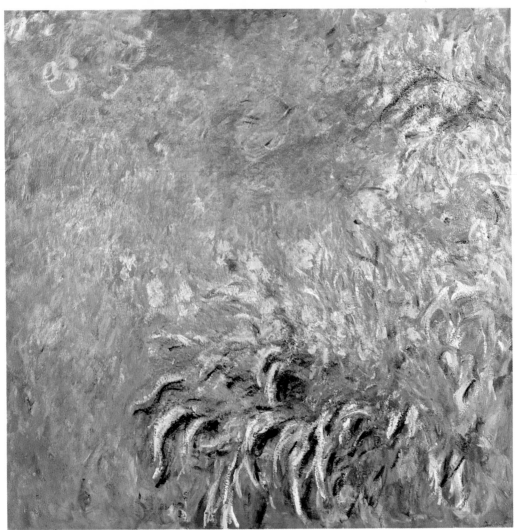

Iris beside a Pond, Claude Monet (1840–1926). Monet called some of his paintings Impressions, and the name soon came to designate a school. (Art Institute of Chicago)

Pink and Green, Edgar Degas (1834–1917). Degas was an Impressionist to the extent of his interest in fleeting motion. But as an admirer of the classicist Ingres, he emphasized line and careful composition. (MMA)

A Young Woman in the Sun, Auguste Renoir (1841–1919).
Though Renoir used Impressionist techniques, the results
sometimes bore little resemblance to the work of other
Impressionists. He believed that "a picture ought to be a
lovable thing, joyous and pretty." (Jeu de Paume)

Luncheon of the Boating Party, Renoir. (Phillips Memorial Gallery)

Still Life, Paul Cézanne (1839–1906). It has been said that when the Impressionists painted a haystack, there was light, but there was no haystack. When Cézanne painted an apple, there was the play of light; there was also the apple. (MMA)

Montagne Sainte-Victoire with Aqueduct, Cézanne. This landscape has been a source of inspiration for many of the tendencies of so called modern art. The composition is as structurally balanced and proportioned as a Greek temple. (MMA)

The Card Players, Cézanne. Here are exemplified Cézanne's skill in composition, his discriminating sense of color, and the sculptured qualities of solidity and depth he gave to his figures. (Stephen C. Clark)

Portrait of the Artist, Vincent van Gogh (1853–1890). This self-portrait shows a deep seriousness and intense concentration. (V. W. van Gogh)

Ia Orana Maria, Paul Gauguin (1848–1903). Gauguin revolted not only against the complexity and artificiality of European life, but against civilization itself. He finally fled to Tahiti to paint the lush, colorful life of an uncorrupted society. (MMA)

Sunflowers in a Vase, van Gogh. The feverish technique seems to have endowed the flowers with rhythmic motion. (V. W. van Gogh)

The Starry Night, van Gogh. This painting gives vivid expression to van Gogh's bold conceptions. (Museum of Modern Art)

The Piano Lesson, Henri Matisse (1869–1954). Matisse conveyed a freshness of approach and a vitality of line and color. (Museum of Modern Art)

Portrait of Gertrude Stein, Pablo Picasso (1881–1973). Picasso seems to have given this portrait of the great experimenter in poetry some elements of the distortion of form characteristic of the work of both. (Museum of Modern Art)

Three Musicians, Pablo Picasso. This painting, regarded by many as the masterpiece of Cubism, sums up the final stage of the movement. (Museum of Modern Art)

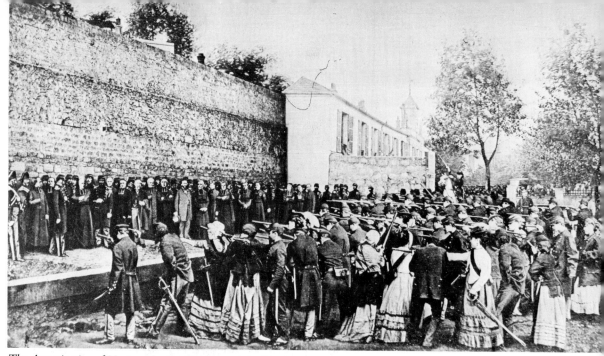

The Assassination of Hostages by the Communards in Paris, 1871. Note the presence of women among the firing squads. Hundreds of "citoyennes" participated in street fighting in the working-class quarters of Paris.

1871, the government attempted to disarm the Paris National Guard, a volunteer citizen army with radical political sympathies. The guard refused to surrender, declared its autonomy, deposed officials of the new government, and proclaimed a revolutionary committee—the Commune—as the true government of France. Though this movement is commonly described as a rebellion of dangerous radicals intent upon the destruction of law and order, most of its members resembled the Jacobins of the first French Revolution and belonged largely to the lower middle class. They did not advocate the abolition of private property but rather its wider distribution. Their respect for the deposits in the Bank of France was as scrupulous as any bourgeois financier might have wished. Their most radical political action was a symbolic one: the toppling of a statue of Napoleon I in the Place Vendôme. The movement was precipitated by bitterness over the defeat of Napoleon III and exhaustion by the long siege of Paris that followed. There were fears as well that the central government would be dominated by the rural population to the disadvantage of the urban masses in the capital. After several weeks of frustrating disputation, the conflict turned into a bloody civil war. The Communards killed about sixty hostages, including the archbishop of Paris. The government numbered its victims by the thousands. The courts-martial which were set up executed twenty-six. Thousands of others were sentenced to imprisonment or banishment in New Caledonia, in the South Pacific.

The Paris Commune

The Aftermath of the Paris Commune. A view of the Champs-Élysées showing damage resulting from the 1871 uprising. The Arc de Triomphe is seen in the distance.

The Commune and the International

While middle-class Europe reacted in horror at what it mistakenly perceived as a second Reign of Terror, Marx, in the name of the International, extolled the courage of the Communards, who, he wrote, had fought the first pitched battle in the class war he had predicted. In a pamphlet entitled *The Civil War in France* (1871), Marx claimed that the Commune was an example of the transitional form of government through which the working class would have to pass on its way to emancipation. Yet many of the less radical members of the International were frightened and disturbed not only by the events of the Commune itself, but by the possibility of reprisals against members of an organization that openly praised men and women who were considered by the middle class to be little more than murderers. In 1872 Marx acknowledged defeat by moving the seat of the International's council to the United States, a country far removed from the organization's affairs and from the criticisms that had begun to be heaped upon Marx for his misdirection. In 1876, the First International expired.

The spread of socialism

Although the International collapsed, socialism continued to gain ground as both a theory and a program. The German Social Democratic party was founded in 1875; a Belgian Socialist party in 1879; and in France, despite the disasters of the Commune, a Socialist party was established in 1905. In England, although socialism was much debated and discussed, no party proclaiming itself socialist emerged. When the Labour party came into being in 1901, however, various socialist societies were represented on its executive council, along with less radical, nonsocialist trade union groups. On the periphery of Europe—in Spain, Italy, and Russia—socialism made less headway. There the absence of widespread industrialization and the educational backwardness of large elements within the population retarded the development of a working-class consciousness, and of socialism as its political expression.

During the years before the First World War, socialists continuously and often bitterly debated the course they should follow as they attempted to achieve their goal of radical change. One group, led by Marx himself until his death, urged socialists to avoid collaboration with other parties to achieve such immediate ends as higher wages, shorter working hours, and unemployment insurance. These reforms, the "purists" declared, were the means by which the bourgeoisie could buy off the proletariat and hence indefinitely postpone revolution. On the other hand, "revisionist" socialists urged their followers to take advantage of the fact that many of them now could vote for socialist candidates in elections. They argued that those candidates, if elected, could help them obtain a better life in the immediate future. Socialist theory might proclaim a worldwide struggle of the proletariat against the bourgeoisie; but was this any reason to turn one's back on a chance to make real headway through the ballot box in achieving reforms that would put a better life within reach of workers and their families?

Revisionism spread despite efforts of the "purists" to put a stop to it. In Germany the pattern had been established by Lassalle, whose opportunism had led him to bargain with Bismarck. Following his death, his place as theorist was taken by Eduard Bernstein (1850–1932), a Social Democrat and member of the German parliament, the Reichstag. Bernstein was among the first to question the predictions Marx had made in *Capital*. In his appropriately titled book, *Evolutionary Socialism*, published in 1899, Bernstein pointed out that for most European workers the standard of living had risen since 1850, and that the lower middle class showed no evidence that it wished to identify its interests with those of the proletariat. At the same time, increasingly wider franchises meant that workers had an excellent chance of achieving reform by means of the ballot box. The program of the future was not revolution, but democratic social reform. Bernstein's most outspoken opponent in Germany was his fellow socialist Karl Kautsky, an orthodox Marxist who warned that collaboration would end in the total corruption and demoralization of the proletariat. In France, the same battle was waged by the "purist" Jules Guesde, who preached that the Socialist party's primary goal should be the development of proletarian class consciousness, and Jean Jaurès, socialist leader in the Chamber of Deputies, who advocated a revisionist course. In both Germany and France, revisionists outnumbered purists by a wide margin. This was, to an even greater degree, the case in Britain. There, Fabian socialists—so named from their policy of delay, in imitation of the tactics of Fabius, a Roman general—preached what they called "the inevitability of gradualism." They believed their country would evolve toward socialism by means of parliamentary democracy. Prominent among the Fabians were the social investigators Sid-

Jean Jaurès

ney and Beatrice Webb, the novelist H. G. Wells, and the playwright George Bernard Shaw.

The continued success of revisionism led its opponents to sharpen their attack and to advocate increasingly violent means to achieve their ends. Their campaigns, though they never managed to convince a majority of the working class, nevertheless attracted an increasing number of adherents. Some who had originally supported the revisionists grew disappointed when reforms did not come as quickly as expected. At the same time, in much of Europe, the cost of living began to rise for many workers. The comparative prosperity that some members of the working class had experienced vanished in the face of price rises that were not matched by wage increases. The result was a frustration which encouraged the adoption of a more militant stance. Germans rallied to the side of the radical socialists Rosa Luxemburg and Karl Liebknecht, while in France a new revolutionary socialist party disowned the reformist leader Alexandre Millerand, after he agreed to serve as cabinet member in a nonsocialist government. The Second International, which had been founded in 1889, demanded at a conference in 1906 that affiliated parties declare their goal to be the destruction of the bourgeois order and the state which served its interests.

This militant mood encouraged acceptance of the doctrines of anarchists and syndicalists. Anarchists preached the overthrow of capitalism by violence. They differed from socialists, however, in their hatred of the machinery of the state or any government based upon coercion. Socialists argued that until the communist millennium promised by Marx, the state would remain a necessary means to the achievement of that eventual end. Anarchists worked to see the immediate abolition of a state bureaucracy which, no matter who controlled it, they believed would result in tyranny. Bakunin, whom Marx had succeeded in expelling from the First International, was anarchism's most popular propagandist. Syndicalism, like anarchism, demanded the abolition of both capitalism and the state. It resembled socialism in its demand that workers share in the ownership of the means of production. Instead of making the state the owner and operator of the means of production, however, the syndicalist would delegate these functions to syndicates of producers. The steel mills would be owned and operated by the workers in the steel industry, the coal mines by the workers in the coal industry, and so on. These associations would take the place of the state, each one governing its own members in their activities as producers.

Syndicalism received its most sympathetic hearing in France, where a General Confederation of Labour, after 1902, resolved to seek solutions to economic problems outside the legally constituted framework of French politics. The most effective spokesman for syndicalism was the Frenchman Georges Sorel (1847–1922). Sorel, in his *Reflections on*

Violence, published in 1908, argued that workers should be made to believe in the possibility of a general strike by the proletariat which would result in the end of bourgeois civilization. The general strike might be nothing more than myth, Sorel acknowledged. Yet, as myth, it remained a powerful weapon in the hands of those whose goal was the destruction of society and who must not shy from the employment of violent means to achieve that end.

Socialism before the First World War, then, was not a unified force. It was divided by quarrels between purists and revisionists, and challenged by the even more radical proposals of anarchists and syndicalists. Socialists, intent on their goal of international solidarity among working classes, ignored the appeal that nationalism and imperialism might make to workers in France, Germany, and Britain. Yet despite its divisions and weaknesses, socialism appeared to the middle classes of Europe as a real threat to their continued prosperity. Capitalism had provided the machinery by which the bourgeoisie had achieved power. Socialism attacked capitalism and hence those who were its direct beneficiaries. Although most socialists disapproved of violence, violent acts were attributed by middle-class men and women to an amorphous, anticapitalist body easily labeled "socialist." Riots by trade unionists in Chicago's Haymarket Square in 1886 and in London's Trafalgar Square in 1887; the assassinations of President Sadi Carnot of France in 1894, of King Humbert of Italy in 1900, and of President William McKinley of the United States in 1901; strikes which grew in number and violence throughout Europe and America after 1900—all these events were perceived by members of the middle class as part of a larger movement whose professed goal was to tear from them their economic, political, and social security.

Georges Sorel

Socialism as a threat to the middle class

The Haymarket Riots, Chicago, 1886. A contemporary illustration depicting the results of attempts to unionize workers at the McCormick Harvester works.

Science and progress

Louis Pasteur

Marie Curie

2. THE CHALLENGE OF SCIENCE AND PHILOSOPHY

While socialism challenged middle-class self-confidence from one quarter, science and philosophy threatened from another. The fact that science might undermine, rather than sustain, certainty was all the more difficult to comprehend, given the manner in which science and technology had together assisted in the birth and continued development of industrialization. This is not to say that science abandoned its role as an instrument for the solving of human problems and as a vital aid to continuing progress. There were striking improvements in the field of medicine, for example. The Frenchman Louis Pasteur (1822–1895) proved that all forms of life, no matter how small, are reproduced only by living beings. Hitherto, according to the theory of spontaneous generation, it had commonly been supposed that bacteria and other microscopic organisms originated from water or from other decaying vegetable and animal matter. By locating the source of bacteria, Pasteur's discovery opened the way for major improvements in the areas of public sanitation and health: among others, the process of ridding food of objectionable bacteria by sterilization—pasteurization—that was named for him. Pasteur, along with the German Robert Koch (1843–1910), also proved conclusively that germs were not, as was commonly supposed, the result but rather the cause of disease. The discovery of the X ray by the German Wilhelm von Röntgen in 1895 and of radium by the Polish scientist Marie Curie in 1898 not only altered perceptions as to the nature of energy, but suggested ways in which energy could be put to use for medical purposes. These discoveries—along with similarly important ones in the areas of cell theory, anesthetics, and antiseptics—worked to convince the educated public that science was a friend of humanity. They reinforced as well a belief in the predictability of the universe and in its essential timelessness, the sense that the passage of time brought with it no fundamental change.

Against this psychologically reassuring fortress of a harmonious universe, biological scientists hurled the bomb of evolutionary theory. We have seen that this theory was at least as old as Anaximander in the sixth century B.C., and that it was accepted by many of the great minds of antiquity. We have learned also that it was revived in the eighteenth century by the scientists Buffon and Linnaeus. But neither of these men offered much proof or explained how the process of evolution might work. The first to develop a systematic hypothesis of evolution was the French biologist, Jean Lamarck (1744–1829). The essential principle in Lamarck's hypothesis, published in 1809, was the inheritance of acquired characteristics. He maintained that an animal, subjected to a change in environment, acquired new habits, which in turn were reflected in structural changes. These acquired characteristics of body structure, he believed, were transmissible to the offspring, with the result that after a series of generations a new species of animal was eventually produced. Lamarck's successors found little evidence to confirm this hypothesis, but it dominated biological thought for nearly fifty years.

A much more convincing hypothesis of organic evolution was that of the English naturalist Charles Darwin (1809–1882), published in 1859. The son of a small-town physician, Darwin began the study of medicine at the University of Edinburgh, but soon withdrew and entered Cambridge to prepare for the ministry. Here he instead devoted most of his time to natural history. In 1831 Darwin obtained an appointment as naturalist without pay with a government-sponsored expedition aboard H.M.S. *Beagle,* which had been chartered for scientific exploration on a trip around the world. The voyage lasted nearly five years and gave Darwin an unparalleled opportunity to become acquainted at first hand with the manifold variations of animal life. He noted the differences between animals inhabiting islands and related species on nearby continents, and observed the resemblances between living animals and the fossilized remains of extinct species in the same locality. It was a magnificent preparation for his life's work. Upon returning from the voyage he read Malthus's essay on population, and was struck by the author's contention that throughout the world of nature many more individuals are born than can survive, and that consequently the weaker ones must perish in the struggle for food. Finally, after twenty more years of research and analysis, he published his *Origin of Species* (1859).

Darwin's hypothesis was that of natural selection. He argued that it is nature, or the environment, which selects those variants among offspring that are to survive and reproduce. Darwin pointed out, first of all, that the parents of every species beget more offspring than can possibly survive. He maintained that, consequently, a struggle takes place among these offspring for food, shelter, warmth, and other conditions necessary for life. In this struggle for existence certain individuals have the advantage because of the factor of *variation,* which means that no two of the offspring are exactly alike. Some are born stronger than others; some have longer horns or sharper claws or perhaps a body coloration which enables them better to blend with their surroundings and thus to evade their enemies. It is these favored members of the species that win out in the struggle for existence and survive as the "fittest" of their generation; the others are eliminated generally before they have lived long enough to reproduce. Darwin regarded variation and natural selection as the primary factors in the origin of new species. In other words, he taught that individual plants and animals with favorable characteristics would transmit their inherited qualities to their descendants through countless generations, and that successive eliminations of the least fit would eventually produce a new species. Darwin applied his concept of evolution not only to plant and animal species but also to humans. In his second great work,

Charles Darwin

Illustrations from Darwin's First Edition of The Descent of Man. *The drawings were used to point up the similarities between a human embryo (top) and that of a dog (bottom).*

The Descent of Man (1871), he attempted to show that the human race originally sprang from some apelike ancestor, long since extinct, but probably a common forebear of the existing anthropoid apes and humans.

Refinements of the Darwinian hypothesis

The Darwinian hypothesis was elaborated and improved by several later biologists. The German August Weismann (1834–1914) flatly rejected the idea that acquired characteristics could be inherited. He conducted experiments to show that body cells and reproductive cells are entirely distinct, and that there is no way in which changes in the former can affect the latter. He concluded, therefore, that the only qualities transmissible to the offspring are those which have always been present in the reproductive cells of the parents. In 1901 the Dutch botanist Hugo De Vries (1848–1935) published his celebrated mutation hypothesis, based upon Darwin's original hypothesis and, in large part, upon laws of heredity discovered by the Austrian monk Gregor Mendel (1822–1884). De Vries asserted that evolution results not from minor variations, as Darwin had assumed, but from radical differences or mutations, which appear in more or less definite ratio among the offspring. When any of these mutations are favorable to survival in a given environment, the individuals possessing them naturally emerge triumphant in the struggle for existence. Not only do their descendants inherit these qualities, but from time to time new mutants appear, some of which are even better adapted for survival than their parents. Thus in a limited number of generations a new species may be brought into existence. The mutation theory of De Vries corrected one of the chief weaknesses in the Darwinian hypothesis. The variations which Darwin assumed to be the source of evolutionary changes are so small that an incredibly long time would be necessary to produce a new species. De Vries made it possible to conceive of evolution as proceeding by sudden leaps.

Evolution and chance

Clearly, the implications of this new theory were deeply disturbing for those who had until now believed in an orderly universe, or had taken as literal the words of the Bible. For the latter the task of reconciling Darwin's account of creation with the first chapter of Genesis, though troublesome, was often not insuperable. Outside fundamentalist sects, the Bible was, at this time, perceived by growing numbers as containing a combination of myths, legends, history, and profoundly important moral truths. The work of the German theologian David Friedrich Strauss (1808–1874) and of the French historian Ernest Renan (1832–1892) had cast doubt on the historical accuracy of the Bible, and dealt with its inconsistencies. These writers had defended the intentions of the Bible's various authors, while firmly insisting upon their human fallibilities. Their searching yet nevertheless sensitive critiques helped people understand that they need not abandon their Christian faith simply because Darwin insisted that the world and all that lived within it had been created over millions of years and not in six days. Far more difficult to deal with was the notion, explicit in Darwin, that nature was not a changeless harmony, but instead a constant and apparently undirected struggle. Chance, and not order, ruled the universe. Nothing was fixed, nothing perfect; all was in a state of flux. Good and bad were defined only in terms of an ability to survive. The "best" of a species were those that triumphed over their weaker rivals. All of a sudden, the universe had become a harsh and uncompromising place, deprived of pre-Darwinian certainties; belief in a benevolent God was now much harder to sustain.

Darwin's most vigorous defender, the philosopher Thomas Henry Huxley (1825–1895), was one of those who could no longer reconcile science with a belief in God. While he did not reject the possibility of a supernatural power, Huxley averred that "there is no evidence of the existence of such a being as the God of the theologians." He pronounced Christianity to be "a compound of some of the best and some of the worst elements of Paganism and Judaism, moulded in practice by the innate character of certain people of the Western World." Huxley coined the word *agnosticism* to express his contempt for the attitude of dogmatic certainty symbolized by the beliefs of the ancient Gnostics.[1] As propounded by Huxley, agnosticism was the doctrine that neither the existence nor the nature of God nor the ultimate character of the universe is knowable. Huxley earned himself the nickname of "Darwin's bulldog" because of his stout attacks upon orthodox Christians who refused to accept the implications of Darwinian theory. In a famous debate between Huxley and Samuel Wilberforce, the bishop of Oxford, in 1860, the bishop made the mistake of trying to turn Darwin into a joke, inquiring of the audience if anyone were willing to trace his descent from an ape, whether it was through his grandmother or grandfather. Huxley rejoined that the only ancestor of which he would feel ashamed was a man like the bishop, who so misused his talents to make light of such a serious issue. The sustained applause with which his remarks were greeted suggest the degree to which religious orthodoxy could now be safely challenged in public discussion.

The most uncompromising of the evolutionist philosophers was Ernst Heinrich Haeckel (1834–1919). Originally a physician, later a professor of biology, Haeckel was the first outstanding scientist on the Continent to subscribe wholeheartedly to Darwinism, summarizing his conclusions in a book entitled *The Riddle of the Universe*. Haeckel's philosophy contained three main doctrines: atheism, materialism, and mechanism. He would have nothing to do with Huxley's agnosticism; on the contrary, he dogmatically affirmed that nothing spiritual exists. The universe, he maintained, was composed of matter alone, in a pro-

Thomas Henry Huxley

Haeckel

[1] See above, p. 68.

cess of constant change from one form into another. Life, Haeckel stated, originated from the spontaneous combination of the essential elements of protoplasm. From these earliest forms of protoplasm all the complex species of the present gradually evolved through the process of natural selection. Haeckel regarded the mind of humans as just as much a product of evolution as the body. The human mind differs only in degree from the minds of the lower animals. Memory, imagination, perception, and thinking are mere functions of matter; psychology should be considered a branch of physiology. Such was the philosophy of materialism and determinism which appeared to Haeckel and his followers to be a logical deduction from the new biology.

The Social Darwinists

The middle classes of western Europe and the United States, disoriented by the antireligious implications of evolutionary theory, received some comfort from the writings of those who adapted Darwinian thought to the analysis of society—the so-called Social Darwinists. These thinkers argued that the apparent "success" of Western civilization was the result of its special fitness. The white race, they boasted, had proved itself superior to the black; non-Jews superior to Jews; rich superior to poor; the British Empire superior to the subject territories it controlled. If nature was a matter of competition, so was society, with the victory going to that race or nation which could demonstrate its fitness to survive by subduing others.

Though he never expressed his ideas that crudely, the English philosopher Herbert Spencer (1820–1903) extolled the virtues of competition in a way that made it easier for others to do so. Spencer grounded his philosophy upon evolutionary theory. He insisted upon the idea of evolution as a universal law. He was deeply impressed by Darwin's *Origin of Species* and enriched the hypothesis of natural selection with a phrase that has clung to it ever since—"the survival of the fittest." He contended that not only species and individuals are subject to evolutionary change, but also planets, solar systems, customs, institutions, and religious and ethical ideas. Everything in the universe completes a cycle of origin, development, decay, and extinction. When the end of the cycle has been reached, the process begins once more and is repeated eternally. As a political philosopher, Spencer was a vigorous champion of individualism. He condemned collectivism as a relic of primitive society, as a feature of the earliest stage of social evolution. Any so-called assistance individuals might receive from the state, Spencer argued, would result not only in their own degeneration, but in that of society as well.

Herbert Spencer

Anthropology

If Social Darwinists could reassure some by implying the biological right of Western civilization to survive as the "fittest" within the contemporary world, anthropologists—pioneers in what was essentially a new scientific discipline—argued, on the contrary, that no culture could be perceived as "better" than any other. All societies were adaptations to a particular environment. Each society produced its own customs, which could not be declared "good" or "bad," but only successful or unsuccessful, according to the degree to which they helped that society survive. This notion of cultural "relativism" was a theme in the influential work of the English anthropologist Sir James Frazer (1854–1941). In his masterpiece, *The Golden Bough,* he demonstrated the relationship of Christianity to primitive practices and magical rites. Christianity was nothing more or less than one society's response to the craving for an explanation of the apparently inexplicable.

Friedrich Nietzsche

Christianity was challenged far more directly in the writings of the German philosopher Friedrich Nietzsche (1844–1900). Nietzsche was not a scientist, nor was he interested in the nature of matter or in the problem of religious truth. He was essentially a romantic poet glorifying the struggle for existence to compensate for his own life of weakness and misery. Born in 1844, the son of a Lutheran minister, he was educated in the classics at Leipzig and Bonn and at the age of twenty-five was appointed professor of philology at the University of Basel. Ten years later repeated and severe attacks of nerves forced his retirement. He spent the next decade of his life in agony, wandering from one resort to another in a fruitless quest for relief. If we can believe his own statement, each year was made up of two hundred days of pain. In 1888 he lapsed into hopeless insanity, which continued until his death in 1900.

Nietzsche's philosophy is contained in such works as *Thus Spake Zarathustra, A Genealogy of Morals,* and *The Will to Power.* His cardinal idea was the notion that natural selection should be permitted to operate unhindered in the case of human beings as it does with plants and animals. Yet he did not accept the deterministic worldview upon which the theories of Darwin—and of Marx as well—ultimately rested. He asserted the possibility of a triumph of human will over external circumstance, a triumph which he believed could eventually produce a race of supermen—not merely a race of physical giants but men distinguished above all for their moral courage, for their strength of character. Those who would perish in the struggle were the moral weaklings, who had neither the strength nor the courage to battle nobly for a place in the sun. Before any such process of natural selection could operate, however, religious obstacles would have to be removed. Nietzsche therefore demanded that the moral supremacy of Christianity and Judaism be overthrown. Both of these religions, he alleged, glorified the virtues of the downtrodden. They exalted into virtues qualities which ought to be considered vices—humility, nonresistance, mortification of the flesh, and pity for the weak and incompetent. The enthronement of these qualities prevented the elimination of the unfit and preserved them to pour their degenerate blood into the veins of the race.

Scientists and philosophers, as they continued to explore the various and sometimes contradictory implications of evolutionary theory,

Nietzsche's philosophy

Pavlov

helped to undermine the comforting notion of humankind's essential superiority to the rest of the animal kingdom. The work of the Russian psychologist Ivan Pavlov (1849–1936) resulted in the discovery of the conditioned reflex. Although Pavlov experimented with animals, he insisted that his conclusions applied equally to human beings. The conditioned reflex is a form of behavior in which natural reactions are produced by an artificial stimulus. Pavlov showed that if dogs were fed immediately following the ringing of a bell, they would eventually respond to the sound of the bell alone and secrete saliva exactly as if confronted by the sight and smell of the food. This discovery suggested the conclusion that the conditioned reflex is an important element in human behavior and encouraged psychologists to center their attention upon physiological experiment as a key to understanding the mind.

Behaviorism

Pavlovians inaugurated a type of physiological psychology known as behaviorism. Behaviorism is an attempt to study the human being as a purely physiological organism—to reduce all human behavior to a series of physical responses. Such concepts as *mind* and *consciousness* are dismissed as vague and meaningless terms. For the behaviorist nothing is important except the reactions of muscles, nerves, glands, and visceral organs. There is no such thing as an independent psychic behavior; all that humans do is physical. Thinking is essentially a form of talking to oneself. Every complex emotion and idea is simply a group of physiological responses produced by some stimulus in the environment. Such was the mechanistic interpretation of human actions offered by followers of Pavlov.

Freud and psychoanalysis

The other important school of psychology to make its appearance after the turn of the century was psychoanalysis, founded by Sigmund Freud (1856–1939), an Austrian physician. Psychoanalysis interprets human behavior mainly in terms of the unconscious mind. Freud admitted the existence of the conscious mind (the ego), but he avowed that the unconscious (the id) is much more important in determining the actions of the individual. He considered humans as egoistic creatures propelled by basic urges of power, self-preservation, and sex. These urges are much too strong to be overcome; but inasmuch as society (the superego) has branded their unrestrained fulfillment as sinful, they are commonly driven into the unconscious, where they linger indefinitely as suppressed desires. Yet they are seldom completely submerged; they rise to the surface in dreams, or they manifest themselves in lapses of memory, in fears and obsessions, and in various forms of abnormal behavior. Freud believed that most cases of mental and nervous disorder result from violent conflicts between natural instincts and the restraints imposed by an unfortunate environment. Freud hoped that by elucidating his theory of the unconscious he could impose predictable patterns upon the irrationality that seemed to characterize so much human activity. His search for order, however, resembled that of the behaviorists by continuing to stress

Sigmund Freud

the extent to which men and women, like animals, were prey to drives, impulses, and reflexes over which they could exercise at best only minimal control.

Under the impact of these various scientific and philosophical challenges, the institutions responsible for the maintenance of traditional faith found themselves hard pressed. Protestantism had based its revolt against Roman Catholic orthodoxy upon the belief that men and women should seek to understand God with the aid of not much more than the Bible and a willing conscience. In consequence, Protestants had little in the way of authoritarian doctrine to support them when their faith was challenged. Some—the fundamentalists—chose to ignore the implications of scientific and philosophical inquiry altogether, and continued to believe in the literal truth of the Bible. Some were willing to agree with the school of American philosophers known as Pragmatists (Charles Pierce, William James), that if belief in a personal God produced mental peace or spiritual satisfaction, that belief must therefore be true. Truth, for the Pragmatists, was whatever provided useful, practical results. Other Protestants sought solace from religious doubt in religious activity, founding missions, and laboring among the poor. Many adherents to this "Social Gospel" were also "Modernists," determined to accept the ethical teachings of Christianity while discarding belief in miracles and the doctrines of original sin and the Incarnation.

Pope Pius IX

The Roman Catholic church was compelled by its tradition of dogmatic assertion to assist its followers in their response to the modern world. In 1864 Pope Pius IX issued a *Syllabus of Errors* condemning what he regarded as the principal religious and philosophical "errors" of the time. Among them were materialism, free thought, and "indifferentism," or the idea that one religion is as good as another. The *Syllabus* was condemned by critics as a "crusade against civilization." While heated discussions continued over the *Syllabus of Errors,* Pope Pius convoked a church council in 1869, the first to be summoned since the Catholic Reformation. The most notable pronouncement of the Vatican Council was the dogma of papal infallibility. In the language of this dogma the pope, when he speaks *ex cathedra*—that is, in his capacity "as pastor and doctor of all Christians"—is infallible in regard to all matters of faith and morals. Though generally accepted by pious Catholics, the dogma of papal infallibility evoked a storm of protest in many circles. Governments of several Catholic countries denounced it, including France, Spain, and Italy. The death of Pius IX in 1878 and the accession of Pope Leo XIII brought a more accommodating climate to the church. The new pope was ready to concede that there was "good" as well as "evil" in modern civilization. He added a scientific staff to the Vatican and opened archives and observatories. However, he made no concessions to "liberalism" or "anticlericalism" in the political sphere. He would go no farther than to urge capitalists and employers to be more generous in recognizing the

Roman Catholicism

Pope Leo XIII

rights of organized labor.

The effect of various scientific and philosophical challenges upon the men and women who lived at the end of the nineteenth century cannot be measured in any exact way. Millions undoubtedly went about the business of life untroubled by the implications of evolutionary theory, content to believe as they had believed. Certainly, for most members of the middle class, the challenge of socialism was understood as "real" in a way that the challenge of science and philosophy probably was not. Socialism was a threat to livelihood. Darwinism, relativism, materialism, and behaviorism, though "in the air" and troublesome to those who breathed that air, did not impinge upon consciousness to the same degree. Men and women can postpone thoughts about their origins and ultimate destiny in a way that they cannot postpone thoughts about their daily bread. And yet the impact of the changes we have been discussing was eventually profound. Darwin's theory was not so complicated as to prevent its popularization. If educated men and women had neither the time nor inclination to read the *Origin of Species,* they read magazines and newspapers which spelled out for them its implications. Those implications induced an uncertainty that tempered the optimism of capitalist expansion.

Men and women who had never read the German philosopher Arthur Schopenhauer (1788–1860) might well have agreed with his assessment of this world as one condemned to witness the devouring of the weak by the strong. Yet their commitment to the ways of the world prevented their acceptance of Schopenhauer's particular remedy: an escape into a life of personal asceticism and self-denial. Like the English poet and essayist Matthew Arnold, sensitive men and women might feel themselves trapped in a world resembling no more than "a darkling plain," where there was "neither joy, nor love, nor light, nor certitude, nor peace, nor help for pain."

3. THE CHALLENGE OF LITERATURE AND THE ARTS

After 1850 a handful of artists and a greater number of writers continued to challenge the middle-class worldview, as had their predecessors, by drawing attention to the shortcomings of industrial society. As the century drew to a close, however, one of the major problems these critics now faced was the question of audience: not merely what to say, but whom to say it to. Before the middle of the eighteenth century, that audience had been primarily aristocratic. Between 1750 and 1870 it was both aristocratic and upper middle class. Now, thanks to the fact of an increasingly literate general population, the potential audience appeared to have increased enormously. In 1850 approximately half the population of Europe had been illiterate. In subsequent decades, country after country introduced state-financed elementary and secondary education—in part as an attempt to provide citizens with an opportunity for social mobility, in part as a means of social control and as a preventive to the establishment of schools run by workers for workers, and in part as a measure to keep pace with changing technological knowledge. Britain instituted elementary education in 1870, Switzerland in 1874, Italy in 1877. France expanded its existing system between 1878 and 1881. Germany instituted after 1871 a state system modeled on Prussia's. By 1900, approximately 85 percent of the population in Britain, France, Belgium, the Netherlands, Scandinavia, and Germany could read. Elsewhere, however, the percentages were far lower, ranging between 30 and 60 percent.

In those countries where literacy rates were highest, capitalist publishers such as Alfred Harmsworth in England and William Randolph Hearst in the United States hastened to serve the new reading public. Middle-class readers had for some time been well supplied by newspapers catering to their interests and point of view. *The Times* of London had a readership of well over 50,000 by 1850; the *Presse* and *Siècle* in France, a circulation of 70,000. By 1900, however, other newspapers were appealing to a different mass market—the newly literate—and doing so by means of sensational journalism and spicy, easy-to-read serials.

These new developments encouraged writers and artists to distance themselves more and more from what seemed to them a vulgar, materialistic culture. They agreed with writers of the mid-century who had insisted that the purpose of art and literature was not to pander or sentimentalize. They went further, however, by declaring that art had no business preaching morality to a public that, in any event, had proved itself unwilling to heed the sermon. This generation of artists and writers argued that one did not look at a painting or read a poem to be instructed in the difference between good and evil, but to understand what was eternally true and beautiful—to appreciate art for its own sake. They were not so much interested in reaching a wider audience, whose standards of taste they generally deplored, as they were in addressing each other. This self-conscious desire not only to live apart but to think apart from society was reflected in their work. In 1850, educated men and women could read a Dickens novel or examine a Daumier print and understand it, even if they did not admire it or agree with its message. In 1900, men and women found it much harder to understand, let alone admire, a painting by Paul Cézanne or a poem by Paul Valéry. Artists and public were ceasing to speak the same language, a fact which contributed, as did the ideas of Darwin and Nietzsche, Pavlov and Freud, to the further confusion and fragmentation of Western culture.

These new perceptions of the artist's relationship to society did not surface to any measurable degree before the very end of the century. Until that time, the arts were dominated by what has come to be called *realism*. Realists were predominantly critics of contemporary so-

A new journalism

The distancing of art and literature from the public

Realism

ciety. Swayed by a fervor for social reform, they depicted the inequities of the human condition against the sordid background of industrial society. Like the romantics, the realists affirmed the possibility of human freedom, although realists emphasized more than romantics the obstacles that prevented its achievement. Realists differed most markedly from romantics in their disdain of sentiment and emotional extravagance. Adopting from natural science the idea of life as a struggle for survival, they tried to portray human existence in accordance with hard facts, often insisting that their characters were the irresponsible victims of heredity, environment, or their own animal passions.

Literary realism in France

Realism as a literary movement made its initial appearance in France. Its leading exponents included the novelists Honoré de Balzac and Gustave Flaubert,[2] whose work, as we have already noted, contained a stinging assessment of the dullness and greed of modern life. Émile Zola (1840–1902), another Frenchman, is often called a naturalist rather than a realist, to convey the idea that he was interested in an exact, scientific presentation of the facts of nature without the intrusion of personal philosophy. Naturalism was expected to dismiss moral values in a way that realism was not. Zola did have a definite moral viewpoint, however. His early years of wretched poverty imbued him with a deep sympathy for the common people and with a passion for social justice. Though he portrayed human nature as weak and prone to vice and crime, he was not without hope that a decided improvement might come from the creation of a better society. Many of his novels dealt with such social problems as alcoholism, poverty, and disease.

Realism in England

Realism in the writings of the Englishman Charles Dickens was overlaid with layers of sentimentality. Dickens was a master at depicting the evils of industrial society, but the invariable happy endings of his novels testify to his determined—and unrealistic—unwillingness to allow wrong to triumph over right. No such ambivalence marked the works of the later English novelist Thomas Hardy (1840–1928), however. In such well-known novels as *The Return of the Native, Jude the Obscure,* and *Tess of the D'Urbervilles,* he expressed his conception that humans are the playthings of an inexorable fate. The universe, though beautiful, was depicted as in no sense friendly, and the struggle of individuals with nature was a pitiable battle against almost impossible odds. If God existed, he watched with indifference while the helpless denizens of the human ant-heap crawled toward suffering and death. Yet Hardy pitied his fellow creatures, regarding them not as depraved animals but as the victims of cosmic forces beyond their control.

Realism in Germany and Scandinavia

Pity for humanity was a central theme in the work of the German Gerhard Hauptmann (1862–1946). Calling himself a naturalist, Hauptmann nevertheless reflected the realists' concern for suffering. His plays show the influence of Darwin in their emphasis upon deter-

[2] See above, p. 762.

minism and environment. *The Weavers,* which depicts the suffering of Silesian weavers in the 1840s, is probably his most outstanding work. Doubtless the most eminent playwright among realists and naturalists was the Norwegian Henrik Ibsen (1828–1906). The stark message of Ibsen's early dramas was not favorably received, and while still a young man he decided to abandon his native country. Residing first in Italy and then in Germany, he did not return permanently to Norway until 1891. His writings were characterized most of all by bitter rebellion against the tyranny and ignorance of society. In such plays as *The Wild Duck, A Doll's House, Hedda Gabler,* and *An Enemy of the People,* he satirized the conventions and institutions of respectable life, and showed, with great insight, how these oppressed women in particular. Along with his scorn for hypocrisy and social tyranny went a profound distrust of majority rule. Ibsen despised democracy as the enthronement of unprincipled leaders who would do anything for the sake of votes to perpetuate themselves in power. As one of his characters in *An Enemy of the People* says: "A minority may be right—a majority is always wrong."

Henrik Ibsen

The literature of the Russians, which flourished during the period of realism, includes within it themes that are both romantic and idealist as well. Russia's three most outstanding novelists of this period were Ivan Turgenev (1818–1883), Feodor Dostoevsky (1821–1881), and Leo Tolstoy (1828–1910). Turgenev, who spent much of his life in France, was the first of the Russian novelists to become known to western Europe. His chief work, *Fathers and Sons,* describes in brooding terms the struggle between the older and younger generations. The hero is a nihilist (a term first used by Turgenev), who is convinced that the whole social order has nothing in it worth preserving. Dostoevsky was almost as tragic a figure as any he projected in his novels. Condemned at the age of twenty-eight on a charge of revolutionary activity, he was exiled to Siberia, where he endured four horrible years. His later life was harrowed by poverty, family troubles, and epileptic fits. As a novelist, he chose to explore the anguish of people driven to shameful deeds by their raw, animal emotions and by the intolerable meanness of their lives. He was a master of psychological analysis, probing into the motives of distorted minds with an intensity that was almost morbid. At the same time he filled his novels with a broad sympathy and with a mystic conviction that humanity can be purified only through suffering. His best known works are *Crime and Punishment* and *The Brothers Karamazov.*

Russian literature: Turgenev and Dostoevsky

As an earnest champion of the simple life of the peasant, Tolstoy was somewhat less deterministic than the author of *Crime and Punishment.* Yet in *War and Peace,* a majestic epic of Russian conditions during the period of the Napoleonic invasion, he expounds the theme that individuals are at the mercy of fate when powerful elemental forces are unleashed. His other most celebrated novel, *Anna Karenina,* is a study of the tragedy which lurks in the pursuit of individual desire.

Tolstoy

Leo Tolstoy in His Study Dictating to His Secretary

Victor Hugo by Auguste Rodin. The artist's realism enhances his ability to impart human character to his work.

The hero, Levin, is really Tolstoy himself, who eventually finds refuge from doubt and from the vanities of worldly existence in a mystic love of humanity. As Tolstoy grew older he became more and more an evangelist preaching a social gospel. In such novels as *The Kreutzer Sonata* and *Resurrection* he condemned most of the institutions of civilized society and called upon men and women to renounce selfishness and greed, to earn their living by manual toil, and to cultivate the virtues of poverty, meekness, and nonresistance. His last years were devoted to attacks upon such evils as war and capital punishment and to the defense of victims of political persecution.

The works of all these realists and naturalists, whatever their individual differences, shared two things in common: they contained vigorous moral criticism of present-day middle-class society, and they were written in direct and forceful language that the middle class could understand, if it chose to read or listen. The same can be said of realist painters such as Courbet and Daumier, discussed previously, and of the sculptor Auguste Rodin (1840–1917), whose style and message were neither difficult to comprehend nor easy to ignore. Realist artists were still anxious to address the public, if only to attack its members for their shallowness and insensitivity. The advent of the *impressionist* movement in painting in the 1870s marks the first significant break in this tradition. It is at this point that artists began to turn away from the public and toward each other. The movement started in France, among a group of young artists whose work had been refused a place in the annual exhibitions of the traditionally minded French Royal Academy. They had been labeled "impressionists" in derision by critics who took them to task for painting not an object itself, but only their impression of that object. The name in fact suited the personal, private nature of their work. They were painting to please themselves, to realize their own potential as artists.

In a sense, impressionists were realists, for they were determined to paint only what they saw, and they were vitally interested in the scientific interpretation of nature. But impressionist technique was different from that of the older realist painters. Scenes from the world around them were not depicted as if the results of careful study. On the contrary, the works of impressionists sought to reveal immediate sense impressions, leaving it to the mind of the observer to fill in additional details. This often resulted in a type of work appearing at first glance to be nonnaturalistic. Figures were commonly distorted; a few significant details were made to represent an entire object; and dabs of primary color were placed side by side without a trace of blending. Convinced that light is the principal factor in determining the appearance of objects, the impressionists left the studio for the woods and fields in an attempt to capture the fleeting alterations of a natural scene with each transistory shift of sunlight and shadow. From science they had learned that light is composed of a fusion of primary colors visible in the spectrum. Accordingly, they decided to use these colors almost exclusively. They chose, for example, to achieve the effect of the green in nature by placing daubs of pure blue and yellow side by side, allowing the eye to mix them.

Impressionism

Impressionism differed from realism in one other important respect. In these new paintings artists remained detached from their subject. They did not paint to evoke pity, or to teach a lesson. They painted to proclaim the value and importance of painting *as painting*. In doing so, the artist was not deliberately setting out to exclude the viewers. It was clear, however, that the viewer must not expect to understand a painting except on the artist's terms. Probably the greatest of the impressionists were the Frenchmen Claude Monet (1840–1926) and Auguste Renoir (1841–1919). Monet was perhaps the leading exponent of the new mode of interpreting landscapes. His paintings have little structure or design in the conventional sense; they suggest, rather than depict, the outlines of cliffs, trees, mountains, and fields. Intensely interested in the problem of light, Monet would go out at sunrise with an armful of canvases in order to paint the same subject in a dozen momentary appearances. It has been said of one of his masterpieces that "light is the only important person in the picture." Renoir's subjects include not only landscapes but portraits and scenes from contemporary life. He is famous for his pink and ivory nudes, which, as expressions of frank sexuality, represented an additional threat to middle-class sensibilities.

Monet and Renoir

See color plates following page 864 for *Iris Beside a Pond* by Monet and *A Young Woman in the Sun* and *Luncheon of the Boating Party* by Renoir

The freedom explicit in the work of the impressionists encouraged other painters to pursue fresh techniques and to define different goals. The *expressionists* turned upon the impressionists, objecting to their preoccupation with the momentary aspects of nature and their indifference to meaning. Expressionists were not arguing a return to meaning in the sense of "message." They were instead insisting that a painting must represent the artist's particular intellect. Here again, they

Expressionism: Cézanne

Self-Portrait by Paul Gauguin

See color plates following page 864 for *The Starry Night* by van Gogh

were making art a private matter, removing it yet another step from the public. The artist who laid the foundations of expressionism was Paul Cézanne (1839–1906), now recognized as one of the greatest painters who ever lived. A native of southern France, Cézanne labored to express a sense of order in nature that he believed the impressionists had ignored. To achieve this end, he painted objects as a series of planes, each plane expressed in terms of a color change. While Cézanne was in this way equating form with color, he also began to reduce natural forms to their geometrical equivalents, hoping thereby to express the basic shapes of existence itself. He distorted form into geometrical regularity until abstraction became reality. In all this Cézanne was declaring the painter's right to recreate nature in such a way as to express an intensely personal vision.

Art as personal expression was the hallmark of two other painters in the so-called post-impressionist period, the Frenchman Paul Gauguin (1848–1903) and the Dutchman Vincent Van Gogh (1853–1890). Both, by their life as well as their art, declared war on traditional nineteenth-century values. Dismayed by the artificiality and complexity of civilization, Gauguin fled to the South Sea Islands and spent the last decade of his life painting the hot and luscious colors of an unspoiled, primitive society. Van Gogh, whose passionate sympathy for the sufferings of his fellow humans led him to attempt the life of a minister to poor mining families and undoubtedly contributed to his eventual insanity and ultimate suicide, poured out the full intensity of his feelings in paintings such as *The Starry Night,* which seem to swirl off the canvas.

In the years between 1900 and the First World War, art underwent still further revolutionary development. Henri Matisse (1869–1954) greatly extended Cézanne's use of distortion, thereby declaring once again the painter's right to create according to an individual definition

Joy of Life by Henri Matisse

Girl Before a Mirror by Pablo Picasso

of aesthetic merit. This declaration was given its most ringing prewar endorsement by Pablo Picasso (1881–1973). Picasso, a Catalan Spaniard who came to Paris in 1903, developed a style, *cubism,* that takes its name from an attempt to carry Cézanne's fascination with geometrical form to its logical conclusion. Influenced both by the work of Cézanne and by African sculpture, cubism results not only in distortion but in some cases in actual dismemberment. The artist may separate the various parts of a figure and rearrange them in other than their natural pattern. The purpose is partly to symbolize the chaos of modern life but also to express defiance of traditional notions of form—to repudiate once and for all the conception of art as representational prettiness.

See color plates following page 864 for representative works by Cézanne, Gauguin, Matisse, and Picasso

The artistic declaration of independence from middle-class society was enunciated most dramatically by painters, but was heard also in the realms of literature and music. In France, the work of a group calling itself the symbolists, and centered upon the poetry of Paul Verlaine, Arthur Rimbaud, Stéphane Mallarmé, and Paul Valéry attempted to intensify the personal while transcending reality in a way reminiscent of the impressionists, expressionists, and cubists. In music, as well, there was a break from the romantic tradition that dominated the nineteenth century and was expressed in the works of composers such as Robert Schumann (1810–1856), Felix Mendelssohn (1809–1847), and Franz Liszt (1811–1886). Already the late romantic operas of Richard Wagner had taken vast liberties with harmony and departed from stereotypical melodic patterns, producing music that

New directions in literature and music

was not subject to the tyranny of form but sensitive to personal expression. Now in the works of composers such as the Austrian Richard Strauss (1864–1949) and the Frenchman Claude Debussy (1862–1918) music moved even further in the direction of the intensely personal. Strauss's opera *Der Rosenkavalier* (1911), although based externally on the conventions of late–eighteenth-century plot, is nevertheless a musical expression of the inner realities of its characters, written to express those realities more directly than heretofore. Both Strauss and Debussy were, like the impressionists, determined to convey atmosphere; Debussy's piano compositions, and his symphonic sketch, *La Mer,* are musical manifestations of the impressionists' regard for association rather than formal structure.

Self-imposed isolation

Whether in painting, in literature, or in music, artists sought to escape to a position from which they could learn and then express what was closest to their own consciousness. Their direct, calculated dismissal of conventional form and content declared their fundamental disdain for—more important, their complete lack of interest in—the problems of the world at large. Their self-imposed isolation served only to increase the general sense of a fragmented world that, despite its material prosperity, was at war with itself.

SELECTED READINGS

• *Items so designated are available in paperback editions.*

SOCIALISM

• Avineri, S., *The Social and Political Thought of Karl Marx,* London, 1968.
• Cole, G. D. H., *A History of Socialist Thought,* Vols. I–III, London, 1953–1956. A comprehensive treatment of the period 1789–1914.
• Derfler, Leslie, *Socialism since Marx: A Century of the European Left,* New York, 1973. Survey and analysis of continental socialist movements.
Gay, Peter, *The Dilemma of Democratic Socialism: Eduard Bernstein's Challenge to Marx,* New York, 1952. A good study of German revisionism.
Goldberg, Harvey, *A Life of Jean Jaurès,* Madison, Wisc., 1962. A fine biography of the eminent French socialist.
• Joll, James, *The Anarchists,* London, 1965. Survey of various radical European groups.
Lichtheim, G., *A Short History of Socialism,* New York, 1970. Provides a useful overview.
• McBriar, A. M., *Fabian Socialism and English Politics, 1884–1918,* Cambridge, 1966. An extensive study of this important circle: their composition, their ideology, their methods.
Noland, Aaron, *The Founding of the French Socialist Party, 1893–1905,* Cambridge, Mass., 1956. Primarily a narrative account of the translation of ideology into political reality.
Schorske, Carl E., *German Social Democracy, 1905–1917,* Cambridge, Mass., 1955. A magnificent study of the problems of the Social Democrats in a time of imperialism and war.

• Butterfield, Herbert B., *The Origins of Modern Science,* rev. ed., New York, 1957. A standard survey.

Eiseley, Loren C., *Darwin's Century: Evolution and the Men Who Discovered It,* New York, 1961. The history of evolution after Darwin.

Gillespie, C. C., *The Edge of Objectivity,* Princeton, N.J., 1960. A history of scientific ideas.

• Hughes, H. Stuart, *Consciousness and Society,* New York, 1958. Examines the reaction to Positivism and the growing interest in the irrational by considering the work of Freud, Max Weber, and others.

• Jones, Ernest, *The Life and Work of Freud,* 3 vols., New York, 1953–1957. The official biography, by a close collaborator and eminent psychoanalyst.

Rieff, P., *Freud: The Mind of the Moralist,* New York, 1959. A useful, one-volume discussion.

THE ARTS AND PHILOSOPHY

Barzun, Jacques, *Darwin, Marx, and Wagner,* Boston, 1941. Argues that these men were not so much originators of new ideas as founders of systems which are mechanistic and pseudoscientific, and therefore threatening to the human cultural heritage.

Kaufmann, Walter A., *Nietzsche: Philosopher, Psychologist, Anti-Christ,* Princeton, N.J., 1974. A superb intellectual biography.

Lang, Paul, *Music in Western Civilization,* New York, 1941. Useful survey and reference.

• Masur, Gerhard, *Prophets of Yesterday,* New York, 1961. A broad survey of nineteenth-century European thinkers.

Mosse, G. L., *The Culture of Western Europe: The Nineteenth and Twentieth Centuries,* Chicago, 1961. Thoughtful analysis and overview.

Shattuck, Roger, *The Banquet Years: The Arts in France, 1885–1918,* New York, 1958. The emergence of modernism in French art, literature, and music.

SOURCE MATERIALS

• Arnold, Matthew, *Culture and Anarchy,* New York, 1971. Originally published in 1867. A perceptive criticism of English society and a call for an authoritarian principle in an increasingly democratic society.

• Darwin, Charles, *The Descent of Man,* Cambridge, Mass., 1964. See especially Chapter XXI.

• ———, *Origin of Species,* Cambridge, Mass., 1964. See especially Chapters IV, XV.

Edwards, Stewart, ed., *The Communards of Paris, 1871,* New York, 1976. Annotated eyewitness reports, documents, and accounts of the Paris Commune.

• Gosse, Edmund, *Father and Son,* New York, 1963. A moving autobiography by a distinguished Victorian literary critic, this work reveals the conflict between the religious fundamentalism of the father and the skepticism of the son in the wake of Darwinian theory.

Kohn, Hans, *The Mind of Modern Russia,* New Brunswick, N.J., 1955. An edited collection of historical, literary, and philosophical works of nineteenth- and twentieth-century Russian authors, designed to reveal the conflict between traditional and Western thought in Russia.

• Marx, Karl, *Capital,* intro. by G. D. H. Cole, New York, 1974. A good edition of the classic.

Webb, Beatrice, *My Apprenticeship,* London, 1926. Beatrice Webb was one of the leading Fabian Socialists, and in this first volume of her autobiography she explains how she, as a member of one of England's wealthier families, was converted to a socialist creed.

Zola, Émile, *L'Assommoir,* London, 1970. Written in 1877 and set in the Paris of the 1860s, this bitterly realistic novel portrays the brutalization of the French working class by the forces of industrial change, poverty, and alcohol.

Chapter 27

THE SEARCH FOR STABILITY
(1870–1914)

Ah! What a seething there has been, . . . customs worthy of the inquisition and despotism, the pleasure of a few gold-braided individuals setting their heels on the nation, and stifling its cry for truth and justice, under the mendacious and sacrilegious pretext of the interest of the State!

—Émile Zola, "J'accuse"

Between 1870 and 1914, the major powers of Europe worked to maintain both domestic and international stability. Accomplishment of this goal was facilitated by continuing industrialization. Despite periodic trade depressions, general prosperity increased for almost all classes of society at least until 1900. And prosperity, in its turn, helped to produce stability, allowing for the establishment in many countries of social welfare systems designed to benefit workers and their families, and thus to gain their political allegiance.

Continuing prosperity

At the same time, various factors operated to make the achievement of a generally stable Western world difficult, and ultimately impossible. First, the process of nation-building, which had resulted in the dramatic creation of a modern Germany and Italy, left potential conflict in its wake. Second, although the majority of citizens in most western European countries participated at least indirectly in the governance of their country and enjoyed certain guaranteed rights, heated debate continued as to the political usefulness of such arrangements. In France, monarchists threatened the republic; in Germany, democrats battled imperial and bureaucratic oligarchy; in Russia, liberals rose against tsarist autocracy. And across Europe, socialists contended against the political strength of the middle classes.

The roots of instability

Internal tension was resulting as well from shifts in class structure and class consciousness. One of the most dramatic occupational changes to occur in late-nineteenth-century Europe was the rapid growth of a lower- to middle-level, "white-collar" class of bureaucrats, employed in commerce and industry and in expanding government departments. The post office, the railways, the police, and the bureaus charged with the task of administering various social welfare and insurance programs, all demanded growing numbers of recruits. In Germany, for example, by 1914 there were over two million white-collar employees in private firms and two million lower- or middle-range civil servants. Members of this new class were particularly anxious to give sharp definition to the line separating them from skilled "labor aristocrats," who might earn as much money as they did, but whose blue collars were, in the eyes of the white-collar brigades, a badge of their inferior status. However, those same skilled "aristocrats," as we have seen, often found their skills made obsolete by technological change, with the result that they showed themselves more willing than in the past to make common cause with their unskilled fellow workers against the middle class.

One further important source of European instability during this period lay in the international rivalries that we have seen growing between nations as they reached out to build empires. Nations grouped into alliances, hoping that a balance between power blocs might continue to provide the international stability that Europe had enjoyed since 1815, and that had prevented general war. Instead, the alliances produced only further tensions, and ultimately general world conflict.

1. GERMANY: THE SEARCH FOR IMPERIAL UNITY

During the years immediately following the foundation of the German Empire, Bismarck was particularly anxious to achieve imperial unity under Prussian domination. In this he was aided by the economic and military predominance of the Prussian state, and by the organizational framework upon which the empire had been constructed. All powers not granted to the central government were reserved to the individual states. Each had control over its own form of government, public education, highways, police, and other local agencies. Even the enforcement of the laws was left primarily in the hands of the state governments, since the empire had no machinery for applying its laws against individuals. Despite their apparent autonomy, however, the states were in fact subordinate to the empire, and to the emperor himself, the Prussian William I. The German imperial units were once described as comprised of "a lion, a half-dozen foxes, and a score of mice." The Prussian "lion" exercised authority through the person of the emperor and his chancellor. The empire was not governed by a cabinet system, in which ministers of state were responsible to a popularly elected legislature. Instead, the chancellor and other ministers were responsible solely to the emperor. And William was no mere figurehead; he was vested with extensive authority over the army and navy, over foreign relations, and over the general enactment and execution of imperial laws. He had the authority to declare war if the coasts or territory of the empire were attacked. And as king of Prussia, he controlled that country's block of one-third of the votes in the generally conservative upper house, or Bundesrat, of the imperial parliament. The chairman of the Bundesrat, charged with the control and supervision of the federal administration, was also the Prussian prime minister, appointed by the king of Prussia.

The parliament was no mere rubber stamp, however. Money for the imperial treasury had to be voted by the lower house, the Reichstag, which was elected by universal manhood suffrage and whose membership was primarily middle class. Yet the Reichstag's powers were essentially negative. Although the parliament could veto proposals of the kaiser (emperor) and his ministers, it could not initiate legislation on its own. Hence, although Bismarck often found himself temporarily stymied by the activities of an unsympathetic legislature, he could expect, in the end, to have his way. That way was directed toward the goal of a unified Germany under Prussian domination: essentially conservative; antisocialist, though not necessarily opposed to social welfare schemes; protectionist, and thus sympathetic to the interests of German industrialists; and, in foreign affairs, anti-French, standing firm against any threat from that longtime antagonist.

William I of Germany

The Kulturkampf

Bismarck's first campaign on behalf of imperial unity was launched against the Roman Catholic church. Called the *Kulturkampf,* or "struggle for civilization," the attack was initiated, with some help from intellectual liberals, in 1872. Bismarck's motives were almost exclusively nationalistic. He perceived in some Catholic activities a threat to the power and stability of the empire he had just created. He resented, first of all, the support Catholic priests continued to give to the states'-rights movement in southern Germany and to the grievances of Alsatians and Poles. He was alarmed also by recent assertions of the authority of the pope to intervene in secular matters and by the promulgation in 1870 of the dogma of papal infallibility. For these reasons he resolved to deal such a blow to Catholic influence in Germany that it would never again be a major factor in national or local politics. His weapons were a series of laws and decrees issued between 1872 and 1875, designed to curb the independent power of the church. Bismarck's campaign backfired, however. The Catholic Center party appealed to the electorate so effectively on behalf of the persecuted clergy, while adopting an economic policy attractive to the upper middle class, that it won fully one-quarter of the seats in the Reichstag in 1874. Recognizing that he needed Catholic support for other elements of his program, Bismarck took the occasion of the election of the more conciliatory Pope Leo XIII to make his peace with the Vatican and to negotiate an alliance of convenience with the Catholic Center party. By 1886 almost all of his anticlerical legislation either

Bismarck and the Socialists

had been permitted to lapse or had been repealed.

Having forged a new political combination in 1878, Bismarck shifted the focus of his attacks to German socialism, now perceived by him as a far more immediate threat to the empire than Catholicism. The Social Democratic party, under the reformist leadership of the politician Wilhelm Liebknecht (1829–1900), successor to Ferdinand Lassalle, was building a substantial following. Bismarck, his memory of the Paris Commune (see above, pp. 865–866) still fresh, feared socialism as anarchy, and therefore as a direct challenge to the stability and unity he was attempting to achieve within the empire. Forgetting for the moment the manner in which he had courted the socialists when he needed their support in the 1860s, Bismarck now appeared determined to extinguish them. His attack was motivated not only by his personal perception of the socialist threat; he was by now anxious to continue to court the favor of industrialists whom he had won to his side by his policy of protective tariffs. In 1878, two separate attempts were made by unbalanced zealots on the life of the emperor. Although neither would-be assassin had anything but the most tenuous connection with the socialists, Bismarck used their actions as an excuse to secure legislation abolishing workers' rights to meet and to publish. The legislature also agreed to a law which gave the government the right to expel socialists from major cities, as was later done in Berlin, Breslau, and Leipzig. These laws in effect dissolved the Social Democratic party until after 1890, although individual socialist candidates were elected to the Reichstag.

Bismarck was too clever a politician to suppose that he could abolish socialism solely by means of repression. He was prepared to steal
Social welfare legislation at least a portion of the socialists' thunder by adopting parts of their legislative program as his own. In a speech in the Reichstag he frankly avowed his purpose of insuring the worker against sickness and old age so that "these gentlemen [the Social Democrats] will sound their bird call in vain." In addition, he had military purposes in mind. He hoped to make the German worker an effective potential soldier by safeguarding his health in some measure from the debilitating effects of factory labor. Bismarck's program of social legislation was initiated in 1883–1884 with the adoption of laws insuring workers against sickness and accidents. These acts were followed by others providing for rigid factory inspection, limiting the employment of women and children, fixing maximum hours of labor, establishing public employment agencies, and insuring workers against incapacity on account of old age. By 1890, Germany had adopted nearly all the elements, with the exception of unemployment insurance, in the pattern of social legislation that later became familiar in the majority of Western nations.

In that same year the Iron Chancellor was dismissed by the young emperor, William II (1888–1918), following the less-than-year-long reign of his father Frederick III. Bismarck's loss of power was to a degree the result of a personality clash between the two men. Wil-

Left: *William II of Germany and Bismarck*. Right: *Dropping the Pilot*. This cartoon appeared in the British magazine *Punch* on March 29, 1890, after the inexperienced but ambitious young emperor dismissed Bismarck as chancellor and personally assumed the helm of the ship of state. Note that Bismarck appears stripped of the insignia of office.

liam's father had remarked that his son had "a tendency to overestimate himself"; his tutor noted that he "imagined he knew everything—without having learned anything." William's arrogance was encouraged by the cult of imperial family worship which had by this time become part of the patriotic creed that was imposed by the state upon its citizens. Yet the quarrel between the young kaiser and his chancellor was a matter of substance as well as personality, involving policies directed at curbing the activities and popularity of the socialists. Bismarck's dismissal came in part over William's insistence that the antisocialist legislation of the past decade had achieved very little, and his mistaken belief that socialists would respond positively to his determination to rule in his own right and to create a more unified, stable, and powerful reich. William was arguing a line that appealed to the landowners, military leaders, and industrialists, whom he continued to court throughout his reign. He wooed the landowners by embarking on a policy of agricultural protection. And he wooed the military and the industrialists with a vast program of naval rearmament. Meanwhile, despite his decision to end the ban against the Social Democrats, he did all he could to undermine their growing political strength.

State schools were instructed to teach the dangers of socialism by stressing the virtues of patriotism and piety. Admission to the civil service was almost impossible unless one was an officer in the military reserve; and admission to that very influential body was not open to

William's politics

Combatting the socialists

socialists—or to Jews. Stealing a leaf from Bismarck's text, William authorized the extension of earlier programs of social insurance, hoping to dampen enthusiasm for the Social Democrats by granting some of the reforms for which they continued to campaign. But William steadfastly refused to extend any sort of meaningful political participation beyond the powerful industrial, military, and agricultural classes. The country was administered efficiently, but not democratically. With the exception of his first chancellor, Count Leo von Caprivi, a military officer, all were civil servants, a fact that underscored his determination to keep the administration of the country as far removed as possible from democratic control.

*Social Democrats and the
political stalemate*

Growing opposition to these policies brought the Social Democrats increasingly impressive electoral victories. In 1912 they polled a third of the votes cast, and elected 110 members—the largest single bloc—to the Reichstag. Yet they were thwarted, not only by William's determination to ignore his parliament, but by their inability to resolve the conflict within their own ranks between purist and revisionist theory (see above, pp. 867–868). The party continued to profess itself devoted to the principles of socialist purity. Yet its increasingly large following tended to push it in the direction of piecemeal reformist legislation. And even with their large bloc of Reichstag votes, the Social Democrats could not command a majority there unless they formed a coalition with center parties far less reformist—let alone revolutionary—than they were. By 1914, German politics were approaching stalemate. The country was spared a domestic constitutional crisis only by the infinitely more profound international crisis of the First World War.

2. FRANCE: THE EMBATTLED THIRD REPUBLIC

Politically divided France

Although France, in 1870, was not a newly constructed nation like the German Empire, it was a nation sorely in need of reunification and dedication to a common set of political purposes. Its history for the past century had left it torn between various factions. The conflicts it suffered after 1870 tended to be more ideological than social, a reflection not only of France's tumultuous political past, but of its comparatively slow rate of industrialization. Monarchists were divided between supporters of the Bourbon and Orleanist dynasties, their allegiance sustained by loyalties either to the descendents of Louis XVIII or of Louis Philippe. Bonapartists looked for political salvation to Napoleon III's son and heir Louis Napoleon. Republicans recalled the short-lived triumphs of their revolutionary ancestors. Socialists called down plagues on all political houses but their own. The result of this deep division was that not until 1875 did France have a constitution under which it could function.

Following the collapse of Napoleon III's empire a provisional government was organized to rule the country until a new constitution could be drafted. Elections held in 1871 for a national constituent assembly resulted in the choice of some 500 monarchists and only about 200 republicans. Conservative political sentiment was further reinforced by the events of the Paris Commune, which occurred during the period immediately following the elections. But the apparent winners, the monarchists, could not agree among themselves as to whether their king should be a Bourbon or an Orleanist. This stalemate led to the eventual passage in 1875—by one vote—of a series of constitutive laws which made France a republic. These laws established a parliament with a lower house elected by universal manhood suffrage (the Chamber of Deputies) and an upper house elected indirectly (the Senate); a cabinet of ministers presided over by a premier; and a president. Although at first the relative powers of president and premier were not clearly established, within two years the nation had declared itself in favor of a premier at the head of a government answerable to the Chamber of Deputies. An early president, Marshal Marie-Edmé MacMahon, attempted in 1877 to dismiss a premier with whom he disagreed but who was supported by a majority in the chamber. When new elections were held, MacMahon's policy was repudiated. Henceforth, premiers of the Third Republic were answerable to the chamber and not to the president, who became a figurehead. Yet the resolution of this constitutional question failed to produce political stability, since the premier had no authority to dissolve the legislature. This meant that members of the chamber could vote a premier and his fellow ministers out of office at will, with no risk of being forced to stand for reelection. If defeated on a vote, the premier and his colleagues had no alternative but to resign. The result was no fewer than fifty ministries in the years between 1870 and 1914. The Third Republic, for all its constitutional shortcomings, nevertheless managed to last until 1940—far longer than any system of French government since 1789. Its longevity was due, as much as anything, to the stability of other French institutions—the family, the law courts, and the police, for example. And its stability was attested to by the willingness of French men and women to invest their savings in state loans, rather than in industrial enterprises that appeared far less secure to them.

The formation of the Third Republic

In the years after 1875, the republicans, who had been feared at first as dangerous radicals, proved themselves to be generally moderate. It was the discontented monarchists and authoritarian sympathizers within the army, the Roman Catholic church, and among the families of the aristocracy who took to plotting the overthrow of duly constituted governmental authority. Much of the time of successive republican governments was taken up defending the country from these reactionary radicals. In the late 1880s, a general, Georges Boulanger,

Radical reactionaries

gathered about him a following not only of Bonapartists, monarchists, and aristocrats, but of workingmen who were disgruntled with their lot and who believed, with Boulanger, that a war of revenge against Germany would put an end to all their troubles. Thanks to the general's own indecisiveness, the threatened coup d'état came to nothing. But Boulanger was a symptom of deep discontents; he appealed, like Napoleon III, to disparate groups of disenchanted citizens, promising quick, dramatic solutions to tedious problems.

The Dreyfus affair

One further symptom of the divisions which plagued the republic during the later years of the nineteenth century was the campaign of anti-Semitism which the reactionaries adopted to advance their aims. The fact that certain Jewish bankers were involved in scandalous dealings with politicians lent color to the monarchist insistence that the government was shot through with corruption and that Jews were largely to blame. An anti-Semitic journalist, Edmond Drumont, insisted that "Jews in the army" were subverting the national interest. In 1889 he and others founded the Anti-Semitic League. This ugly and heated campaign furnished the background of the famous Dreyfus Affair. In 1894 a Jewish captain of artillery, Alfred Dreyfus, was accused by a clique of monarchist officers of selling military secrets to Germany. Tried by court-martial, he was convicted and sentenced for life to Devil's Island, a ghastly prison camp in the Caribbean. At first the verdict was accepted as the merited punishment of a traitor; but in 1897 Major Picquart, a new head of the Intelligence Division, announced his conclusion that the documents upon which Dreyfus had been convicted were forgeries. A movement was launched for a new trial, which the War Department promptly refused. Soon the whole nation was divided into friends and opponents of Dreyfus. On his side were the radical republicans, socialists, people of liberal and humanitarian sympathies, and such prominent literary figures as Émile Zola and Anatole France. The anti-Dreyfusards included monarchists,

Alfred Dreyfus Leaving His Court-Martial

clerics, anti-Semites, militarists, and a considerable number of conservative workingmen. A Roman Catholic newspaper insisted that the question was not whether Dreyfus was guilty or innocent, but whether Jews and unbelievers were not the secret masters of France. Dreyfus was finally set free by executive order in 1899, and six years later was cleared of all guilt by the Supreme Court and restored to the army. He was immediately promoted to the rank of major and decorated with the emblem of the Legion of Honor.

The history of the Dreyfus affair gave the republicans the solid ground they had lacked in order to end the plottings of the radical reactionaries once and for all. The leaders of the republic chose to attack their enemies by effectively destroying the political power of the Roman Catholic church in France. The anticlericalism expressed in this campaign was probably in part the product of a materialistic age, and of a long-standing mistrust by French republicans of the institution of the church. Its main source, however, was the nationalism which we have already seen fueling Bismarck's *Kulturkampf*.

Anticlericalism

The great majority of the leaders of the Third Republic were hostile to the church; and naturally so, for the Catholic hierarchy was aiding the monarchists at every turn. Clerics had conspired with monarchists, militarists, and anti-Semites in attempting to discredit the republic during the Dreyfus affair. But in the end they had overreached themselves. In 1901 the government passed a series of acts prohibiting the existence of religious orders not authorized by the state, forbidding members of religious orders to teach in either public or private schools, and finally, in 1905, dissolving the union of church and state, thereby prohibiting payment of the clergy from public funds. For the first time since 1801 the adherents of all creeds were placed on an equal basis.

Legislation to curb the church

The republic was, during these years, pressed from the Left as well as the Right. Socialism was a political force in France, as it was in Germany. Yet the response of republicans in France to socialist pressure differed markedly from that of Bismarck. There was no antisocialist legislation. Indeed, a law was passed in 1881 abolishing "crimes of opinion," thereby extending the freedom of the press considerably. In the same year, another law authorized public meetings without prior official approval. But if there was no attempt at repression, there was little positive social reform. The largest single party in the republic, the Radicals or Radical Socialists, was really a party representing small shopkeepers and lesser propertied interests. The Radicals were willing to found and maintain a democratic compulsory educational system, but they were reluctant to respond to demands for social legislation such as had been instituted in Germany. Those laws which were passed—establishing a ten-hour workday in 1904 and old-age pensions in 1910—were passed grudgingly and only after socialist pressure. The result was a growing belief among socialists and other workers that parliamentary democracy was worthless, that progress,

Pressure from the Left

if it was to be made, would be made only as a result of direct industrial action: the strike.

This attitude was reinforced by the same debate—revisionism vs. purism—that we have seen dividing the Social Democrats in Germany. Purists had called it "opportunism" when the socialist Alexander Mitterand had joined the nonsocialist cabinet of Prime Minister René Waldeck-Rousseau in 1899. Mitterand had insisted that his cooperation would help heal the wounds inflicted on French politics by the Dreyfus affair. His opponents charged that such collaboration was a sell-out. Their successors pointed to the lack of anything more than occasional and very mild social legislation in succeeding parliaments to prove their point. In response to this growing sentiment came a wave of strikes, which swept the country for several years before 1914, including one by postal workers in 1909 and by teachers and railwaymen in 1910. The government suppressed these actions by ruthless intervention. Tension increased after 1910 during debates over the extension of military conscription from two to three years, opposed by the socialists, and over the institution of an income tax, favored by the socialists as a way of financing social programs threatened as a result of increased military spending. By 1914, the republic, though hardly on the brink of revolution, remained divided and uncertain. If the threat from the radical Right had been quelled, the challenge from the Left was only just being faced.

3. GREAT BRITAIN: FROM MODERATION TO MILITANCE

During the half-century before 1914, the British prided themselves on what they believed to be a reasonable, orderly, and workable system of government. Following the passage of the Second Reform Bill in 1867, which extended suffrage to over a third of the nation's adult males, the two major political parties, Liberal and Conservative, vied with each other in adopting legislation designed to provide an increasingly larger proportion of the population the chance to lead fuller and healthier lives. Laws which recognized the legality of trade unions, allowed male religious dissenters to participate fully in the life of the ancient universities of Oxford and Cambridge, provided elementary education for the first time to all children, and facilitated the clearance and rebuilding of large urban areas, were among those placed on the books during the administrations of the two leading politicians of the period, the Conservative Benjamin Disraeli (1804–1881) and the Liberal William Gladstone (1809–1898). In 1884, suffrage was once more widened, to include over three-fourths of the adult males, and to allow rural workingmen the chance to vote for the first time. Coupled with a previous act which instituted the secret ballot, this electoral reform bill brought Britain nearer to representative democracy.

Benjamin Disraeli

Gladstone and Disraeli were remarkably different men. The former was a devout member of the Church of England, so dedicated to the cause of personal moral reform that he was willing to risk his political career by accosting prostitutes in the hope of persuading them to change their way of life. He devised his political programs—his long and ultimately unsuccessful campaign for Irish Home Rule, for example—on the basis of his moral convictions. Disraeli, on the other hand, was a pragmatist, willing to acknowledge the degree to which politics is an opportunistic game. When he became prime minister he celebrated the fact by declaring delightedly that he had at last climbed to "the top of the greasy pole." He thought Gladstone's morality a pose, and declared that he wouldn't mind the fact that his opponent had an extra ace up his sleeve, if only he didn't insist that God had put it there. Disraeli was probably correct, however, when he observed that Britain, "subject as it is to fogs and a middle class," preferred its statesmen to be properly grave. He was the exception, a converted Jew and former novelist, whose remarkably compelling political style had enabled him to overcome his unorthodox background.

Despite the personal differences between Gladstone and Disraeli, the political parties over which they presided were managed by a small ruling class of similar men drawn either from landed society or from the upper reaches of the middle class. As members of successive governmental cabinets they recognized their responsibility to Parliament and, in particular, to its lower House of Commons. It was their task, as cabinet ministers, to impose a legislative program upon the Commons. And if the House refused to agree to that program, they recognized, as well, their obligation either to resign forthwith—to make way for a cabinet of opposing party members—or to "go to the country," that is, to dissolve Parliament and order a new election to test the opinion of the voters. This system of "ministerial responsibility" meant that the cabinet retained full responsibility for the management of public affairs, subject, however, to the will of the people as represented by the House of Commons. It produced a generally stable government: although ministries had to answer to Parliament, Parliament would think twice before voting a ministry out of office when it knew that the ministry might well appeal to the voters for support in a general election. (The lack of this particular feature was what had condemned the French Third Republic to its succession of short-lived governments.) Political stability was ensured by more than the device of ministerial responsibility, however. Since both the Conservative and Liberal political leadership was drawn in large part from similar social and economic strata, there was little chance for violent change during these years. One party might espouse a particular cause—the Conservatives imperialism, the Liberals more self-government for Ireland, for example. But both parties generally agreed upon a course steered by men whose similar background and temperament promised programs that were neither radical nor reactionary. This moderation

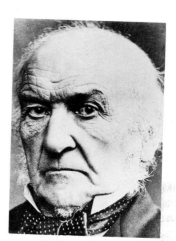

William Gladstone

"Ministerial responsibility"

*Liberal reforms,
1906–1914*

suited the electorate, which was content to defer to politicians whose leadership was secured by the undoubted fact of Britain's general prosperity.

By 1914, however, that leadership was being seriously challenged. Prosperity, though widespread enough, did not extend to the unskilled: dock workers, transport workers, and the like. These groups formed trade unions to press their claims. Their determination encouraged other unions to assume a more militant and demanding stance. In the 1890s this activity produced a reaction in the form of anti–trade union employers' associations and a series of legal decisions limiting the right of unions to strike. Workers, in turn, reacted by associating with middle-class socialist societies to form an independent Labour party, which was born in 1901 and five years later managed to send twenty-nine members to the House of Commons. Sensitive to this pressure from the Left, the Liberals, during their ministry which began in 1906, passed a series of reforms they hoped would ensure a minimum standard of living for those who had heretofore known little security. Sickness, accident, old-age, and unemployment insurance schemes were adopted. A minimum wage was decreed in certain industries. Labor exchanges, designed to help unemployed men and women find new jobs, were established. Restrictions on strikes and on the right of trade unions to raise money for political purposes were relaxed.

Lloyd George's budget

Much of this legislation was the work of David Lloyd George (1863–1945), chancellor of the exchequer (finance minister) in the Liberal cabinet of Prime Minister Herbert Asquith. Together with another young Liberal, Winston Churchill (1874–1965), Lloyd George, a radical middle-class lawyer from Wales, much feared by many within the political establishment, had hammered together legislation that was

Lloyd George and Winston Churchill on Their Way to the House of Commons on Budget Day, 1910

London Dock Strike, 1911. Police move to clear demonstrators from shops where they have taken refuge after having been fired upon.

both a reflection of his own political philosophy and a practical response to the growing political power of the working class. To pay for these programs—and for a larger navy to counter the German buildup— Lloyd George proposed a budget in 1909 that included progressive income and inheritance taxes, designed to make wealthier taxpayers pay at higher rates. His proposals so enraged the aristocratic members of the House of Lords that they declared themselves prepared to throw out the budget, an action contrary to constitutional precedent. Asquith countered with a threat to create enough new peers (titled noblemen) sympathetic to the budget to ensure its passage.[1] The House of Lords eventually surrendered; the result of the crisis was an act of Parliament which provided that the House of Lords could not veto legislation passed by the House of Commons.

The rancor aroused by this constitutional conflict was intense. Self-proclaimed defenders of the House of Lords screamed threats in a chamber unused to anything but gentlemanly debate. Angry threats were by no means confined to the Houses of Parliament during these years, however. Throughout Britain, men and women threw moderation to the winds as they disputed issues in an atmosphere little short of anarchic. The reasons for this continued agitation were various. A decline in real wages after 1900 kept the working class in a militant mood, despite Liberal reforms, and produced an unusually severe

Increased militance

[1] In Britain the monarch had the authority to elevate an unlimited number of men to the peerage. But since the crown acts only on the advice of the prime minister, it is this official who had the actual power to create new members of the House of Lords. If necessary, he could use this power to pack the upper house with his own followers.

Violent Suffragette Protest. Emily Davison was killed when she threw herself in front of the king's racehorse at the Epsom Derby, June 4, 1913. Her purpose was to call attention to the suffragette cause.

series of strikes in 1911 and 1912. A liberal plan to grant Home Rule (self-government) to Ireland produced not only panic in the Protestant minority counties of the north (Ulster) but arming and drilling of private militias with an intensity that seemed to forecast civil war.

Perhaps the most alarming—because the most unexpected—of the militant revolts that seized Britain in the years before 1914 was the campaign for women's suffrage. The middle-class women who engaged in this struggle enjoyed more freedom of opportunity than their mothers had known. Laws had been passed easing the process of divorce and permitting married women control of their own property. Some universities had started to grant degrees to women. Contraceptive devices—and feminist propaganda defending their use—had begun to result in changed attitudes toward sexuality within the middle class. Perhaps because of these gains, many women felt their lack of the vote all the more acutely. Although the movement began among middle-class women, it soon included some female members of the working class and the aristocracy. Agitation reached a peak after 1900, when militant suffragettes—under the leadership of Emmeline Pankhurst, her daughters Christabel and Sylvia, and others—resorted to violence in order to impress upon the nation the seriousness of their commitment. Women chained themselves to the visitors' gallery in the House of Commons; slashed paintings in museums; invaded that male sanctum, the golf course, and inscribed VOTES FOR WOMEN in acid on the greens; disrupted political meetings; burned politicians' houses; and smashed department store windows. The government countered violence with repression. When women, arrested for their disruptive activities, went on hunger strikes in prisons, wardens proceeded to

Suffragettes

feed them forcibly, tying them down, holding their mouths open with wooden and metal clamps, and running tubes down their throats. When hunger strikes threatened to produce deaths and thus martyrs for the cause, the government passed the constitutionally dubious Cat and Mouse Act, which sanctioned the freeing of prisoners to halt their starvation and then, once they had regained their health, authorized their rearrest. The movement was not to see the achievement of its goal until after the First World War, when reform came largely because of women's contributions to the war effort.

Whether Britain's militant mood might have led to some sort of general conflict had not the war begun in 1914, is a question historians continue to debate. Suffice it to say that national sentiment in the last few years before the outbreak of general hostilities was a far different one from that of the 1870s. Britain, so confident of itself and of its moderation, was proving no less a prey to instability than other European nations.

Instability

4. RUSSIA: THE ROAD TO REVOLUTION

In only one European country, Russia, did conditions pass from instability to insurrection during these prewar years. The early-twentieth-century Russian revolutionary movement had numerous forerunners. Waves of discontent broke out several times during the nineteenth century. Threatened uprisings between 1850 and 1860 persuaded Tsar Alexander II, who came to the throne in 1855, to grant local self-government, to reform the judicial system, and, most important of all, to liberate the serfs.

Reform and reaction in nineteenth-century Russia

The law of 1861 granted legal rights to some 22 million serfs, and authorized their title to at least a portion of the land they had worked. Yet the pattern of rural life in Russia did not change drastically. Large-scale landowners managed to retain the most profitable acreage for themselves. Newly liberated serfs faced the need to pay the state for the land they held (the state, in turn, recompensing the former owners). This expense, plus the fact that peasants were often left with less than enough land to sustain themselves and their families, and without adequate pasturage, water, and forest rights, meant that they were compelled to return to work as agricultural laborers for their previous masters.

Liberation of the serfs

The structure of local government instituted in 1861 placed responsibility in the hands of the *mir,* or village commune. Its officials regulated the assignment of land and collected taxes. They were also able to restrict the movement of residents in and out of their community, a regulation designed to ensure that peasants could not escape their obligation to pay for the land they now occupied as free men. At a higher level, district councils were authorized to administer their own

Local government

courts and tax collection. In 1864, indirectly elected provincial councils—*zemstvos*—were empowered to manage local welfare and educational programs.

Though only moderately reformist, these *zemstvos* provided forums for the debate of political issues and, along with the extension of educational opportunities, encouraged middle-class Russians to suppose themselves on the way to some sort of liberalized state. The government, however, grown fearful of the path it was treading, called a halt to reform and substituted repression in its place. By 1875, censorship had been extended not only to the *zemstvos,* which were forbidden to discuss general political issues, but to the press and to schools as well. The result of suppression was, not surprisingly, further discontent and active subversion. Middle-class Russians argued privately the virtues of utopian socialism, liberal parliamentarianism, and pan-Slavism. A growing number, calling themselves nihilists, espoused the doctrines of the anarchist Bakunin (see above, p. 864). Terrorists, believing that assassination of the tsar was the only solution to oppression, achieved their goal in 1881, when a bomb killed Alexander II.

Far from putting an end to authoritarian rule, however, the terrorist bombing triggered a floodtide of reaction against the entire policy of reform. The new tsar, Alexander III (1881–1894), governed under the theory that Russia had nothing in common with western Europe, that its people had been nurtured on despotism and mystical piety for centuries and would be utterly lost without them. Western ideals such as rationalism and individualism would undermine the deferential faith of the Russian masses and would plunge the nation into anarchy and crime. In like manner, Western institutions—trial by jury, parliamentary government, and free education—could never bear fruit if planted in Russian soil. With these doctrines as his guiding principles, Alexander III enforced a regime of stern repression. He curtailed in every way possible the powers of the local assemblies, increased the authority of the secret police, and subjected villages to government by wealthy nobles selected by the state. These policies were continued, though in somewhat less rigorous form, by his son, Nicholas II (1894–1917), a much less effective ruler. Both tsars were ardent proponents of Russification, a more ruthless counterpart of similar nationalistic movements in various countries. Its purpose was to extend the language, religion, and culture of Great Russia, or Russia proper, over all of the subjects of the tsar and thereby to simplify the problem of governing them. It was aimed primarily at the Poles, Finns, and Jews, since these were the nationalities considered most dangerous to the stability of the state. Russification meant repression. The Finns were deprived of their constitution; the Poles were compelled to study their own literature in Russian translations; and high officials in the tsar's government connived at *pogroms,* i.e., wholesale massacres, against the Jews.

Despite these attempts to turn Russia's back to the West, however, the nation was being drawn more closely than it had ever been before

A Railroad Yard in Eastern Russia, 1896

into the European orbit. Russia was industrializing, and making use of European capital to do so. Economic policies during the 1890s, when Count Sergei Witte was the tsar's leading minister, resulted in the adoption of the gold standard, which made Russian currency easily convertible. Railways and telegraph lines were constructed; exports and imports multiplied by factors of seven and five respectively from 1880 to 1913. In addition, Russian writers and musicians contributed in a major way to the enriching of Western culture. We have already noted the singular contributions of Tolstoy, Turgenev, and Dostoevsky. The musical works of Peter Tchaikovsky (1840–1893) and Nikolai Rimsky-Korsakov (1844–1908), while expressing a peculiarly Russian temperament and tradition, were recognized as important additions to the general body of first-rate contemporary composition.

Westernization

With Westernization came the growth of a new wage-earning class. Most of Russia's workers were recruited from the countryside. We have seen that regulations made migration outside the *mir* difficult if not impossible. To live permanently in cities meant surrendering all claim to one's land. The result was that peasant factory workers lived away from their villages only temporarily, returning to attend to farming's seasonal demands. Consequently, these workers could not easily master a trade, and were forced to take unskilled jobs at extremely low wages. They lived in large barracks; they were marched to and from factories where conditions were as unsafe and unhealthy as they had been in British factories in the early years of industrialization. An average working day in a textile mill was from twelve to fourteen hours. This sudden and extremely harsh transition from country to city living instilled deep discontent and a militant class consciousness in Russian workers.

A new working class

Worker's Quarters in St. Petersburg, c. 1900. These buildings, in which workers from the country were housed temporarily while they labored in factories, were breeding grounds for class consciousness.

Growth of political parties

The increase in class consciousness brought with it the emergence of new political parties. Middle-class businessmen and professionals combined with enterprising landowners in 1903 to form a Constitutional Democratic party, whose program included the creation of a nationally elected parliament or Duma to determine and carry out policies which would further the twin goals of liberalization and Westernization. Meanwhile, two essentially working-class parties, the Social Revolutionaries and the Social Democrats, began to agitate for far more radical solutions to the problems of Russian autocracy. The Social Revolutionaries concerned themselves with the onerous plight of the peasants, burdened with land purchase and high taxes. The Social Revolutionaries wanted to equalize the landholdings of peasants within their *mirs,* and to increase the power of the *mirs* in their continuing competition with large landowners. The Social Democrats were Marxists, who saw themselves as westerners and as part of the international working-class movement. In 1903 the leadership of the Social Democratic party split in an important disagreement over revolutionary strategy. One group, which achieved a temporary majority (and thus called itself the Bolsheviks—"Majority Group") favored a strongly centralized party of active revolutionaries, and opposed the notion of a postrevolutionary transitional bourgeois state, insisting instead that revolution be succeeded immediately by a socialist regime. The Mensheviks ("Minority Group"), whose position resembled that of other European revisionist socialists, soon managed to regain control of the party. The Bolshevik splinter party remained in existence, however, under the leadership of the young, dedicated revolutionary Vladimir Ulanov (1870–1924), who wrote under the pseudonym of Nikolai Lenin.

Lenin was a member of the middle class, his father having served as an inspector of schools and minor political functionary. He had been expelled from the University of Kazan for engaging in radical activity, following the execution of his elder brother for his involvement in a plot to assassinate Alexander III. Lenin spent three years as a political prisoner in Siberia; from 1900 until 1917 he lived as an exile in western Europe. His zeal and abilities as both a theoretician and a political activist are evidenced by the fact that he retained leadership of the Social Democrats even while residing abroad. Lenin continued to preach the gospel of Marxism and of a relentless class struggle. His treatise *What Is to Be Done?* was a stinging response to revisionists who were urging collaboration with less radical parties. Revolution was what was to be done, Lenin argued, revolution "made" as soon as possible by an elitist group of agitators working through the agency of a disciplined party. Lenin and his followers, by merging the tradition of Russian revolutionism with Western Marxism, and by endowing the result with a sense of immediate possibility, fused the Russian situation in such a way as to make eventual explosion almost inevitable.

The Young Lenin, 1897

The revolution that came in 1905, however, took even the Bolsheviks by surprise. Its unexpected occurrence was the result of a war between Russia and Japan, which broke out in 1904, and in which the Russians were soundly beaten. Both countries had conflicting interests in Manchuria and Korea; this fact was the immediate cause of the conflict. On land and sea the Japanese proved themselves the military superiors of the Russians. As dispatches continued to report the defeats of the tsar's army and navy, the Russian people were presented with dramatic evidence of the inefficiency of autocracy.

The Russo-Japanese War

Members of the middle class who had hitherto refrained from association with the revolutionists, now joined in the clamor for change. Radical workers organized strikes and held demonstrations in every important city. Led by a priest, Father Gapon, a group of 200,000 workers and their families went to demonstrate their grievances at the tsar's winter palace in St. Petersburg on January 22, 1905—known ever after as Bloody Sunday. The demonstrators were met by guard troops and many of them were shot dead. By the autumn of 1905 nearly the entire urban population had enlisted in a strike of protest. Merchants closed their stores, factory-owners shut down their plants, lawyers refused to plead cases in court, even valets and cooks deserted their wealthy employers. It was soon evident to Tsar Nicholas that the government would have to yield. On October 30, he issued a manifesto, pledging guarantees of individual liberties, promising a moderately liberal franchise for the election of a Duma, and affirming that henceforth no law would be valid unless it had the Duma's

The Revolution of 1905

Bloody Sunday. Demonstrating workers who sought to bring their grievances to the attention of the tsar were met and gunned down by government troops, January 1905.

approval. This was the high-water mark of the revolutionary movement. During the next two years Nicholas issued a series of sweeping decrees which negated most of the promises made in the October Manifesto. He deprived the Duma of many of its powers, and decreed that it be elected indirectly on a class basis by a number of electoral colleges. Thereafter the legislative body contained a majority of obedient followers of the tsar.

The reasons for setback

There were several reasons for the setback to this movement for major political reform. In the first place, the army remained loyal to its commander-in-chief. Consequently, after the termination of the war with Japan in 1905, the tsar had a large body of troops that could be counted upon if necessary to decimate the ranks of the revolutionists. An even more important reason was the split in the ranks of the revolutionists themselves. After the issuance of the October Manifesto, large numbers of the bourgeoisie became frightened at threats of the radicals and declared their conviction that the revolution had gone far enough. Withdrawing their support altogether, they became known henceforth as Octobrists. The more radical merchants and professional men, organized into the Constitutional Democratic party, maintained that opposition should continue until the tsar had been forced to establish a government modeled after that of Great Britain. This fatal division rendered the middle class politically impotent. Finally, disaffection appeared within the ranks of the workers. Further attempts to employ the general strike as a weapon against the government ended in disaster.

But the Russian revolutionary movement of 1905 was not a total failure. The vengeance taken by the tsar convinced many people that their government was not a benevolent autocracy, as they had been led to believe, but a stubborn and brutal tyranny. The uprising revealed the ability of working-class leaders to control the destiny of Russia. The general strike had proved a valuable revolutionary tool, as had workers' councils, elected from the factory floor and briefly operating as the only effective government in some areas. In addition, the revolt of 1905 persuaded some of the more sagacious advisors of the tsar that last-ditch conservatism was none too safe. The result was the enactment of a number of conciliatory reforms. Among the most significant were the agrarian programs sponsored by the government's leading minister, Peter Stolypin, between 1906 and 1911. These included transfer of five million acres of royal land to the peasants for a price; the granting of permission to peasants to withdraw from the *mir* and set up as independent farmers; and cancellation of the remaining installments owed by the peasants for their land. Decrees were issued permitting the formation of labor unions, providing for a reduction of the working day (to not more than ten hours in most cases), and establishing sickness and accident insurance. Yet the hopes of some liberals that Russia was on the way to becoming a progressive nation on the Western model proved illusory. The tsar remained stubbornly autocratic. Few peasants had enough money to buy the lands offered for purchase. In view of the rising cost of living, the factory workers considered their modest gains insufficient. A new revolutionary outbreak merely awaited a convenient spark.

Gains from the revolutionary movement

5. THE SEARCH FOR STABILITY ELSEWHERE IN THE WEST

Other European countries generally found it just as difficult to attain internal stability in the early twentieth century as did those whose history we have surveyed. Italy was burdened with the problems of a rapidly increasing population, the need to industrialize quickly, and a stark disparity between a relatively prosperous industrial north and an impoverished agricultural south. As the population increased, so did the stream of rural migration into cities, where there were few jobs available. In its drive to create jobs and to industrialize, the government intervened directly in the economy by placing large orders for military equipment and by undertaking an ambitious program of railway construction. By the First World War the share of industrial production in the national economy had risen to 25 percent.

Problems in Italy

These strides were largely the result of policies instituted by Giovanni Giolitti (1842–1928), who was prime minister for almost the entire period between 1900 and 1914. Yet his efforts to spur industrialization widened the division between north and south. Relying on opportunistic maneuvering which he called *trasformismo,* and which argued the

Trasformismo

pointlessness of party politics, Giolitti rewarded the support of southern politicians for his program of industrial expansion by allowing the south to remain under the domination of the great landowners, the church, and—in Sicily—the Mafia, none of which were interested in furthering the economic well-being or political consciousness of the average citizen. Thus whereas illiteracy was reduced in northern Italy to about 11 percent, in the south it remained at 90 percent. By failing to address the desperate economic conditions in the south, *trasformismo* denied the country an opportunity to develop a much needed internal market for its goods.

Socialist split

Hoping to gain support for his program from the socialists, Giolitti engineered passage of laws legalizing trade unions, improving factory conditions, and extending the suffrage to virtually all males over thirty. But attempts to satisfy the Left did not sit well with more conservative elements in Italian society, who remembered bread riots in Milan in 1896, the assassination of King Humbert by radicals in 1900, and widespread strikes in 1902 and 1904. Meanwhile, socialists in Italy were as divided on the matter of strategy as they were elsewhere in Europe. Reformists competed with radicals, organized into chambers of labor—local trade union councils with a revolutionary outlook—which assisted in the takeover of the Socialist party by a militant left wing in 1912.

Nationalism in Austria-Hungary

Nationalist aspirations continued to be a major problem in eastern Europe. In 1867 an attempt had been made to resolve national differences in Austria by dividing the empire in two—an Austrian empire west of the river Leith, and a kingdom of Hungary to its east. Each of the two components in this so-called Dual Monarchy was to be the equal of the other, though the two were joined by the same Habsburg monarch, by several common ministries, and by a kind of superparliament. This solution failed to put an end to nationalist divisions, however. Czechs and Slavs in both of the new territories nursed resentment against what they perceived as domination by alien German or Magyar culture. Despite the division of reponsibilities between Austria and Hungary, the government remained centralized under the rule of the Emperor-King Francis Joseph. Social agitation was countered, as in Germany, by repression coupled with welfare measures. Universal male suffrage was introduced into Austria in 1907; in Hungary it was opposed by the Magyar majority which saw it as a device whereby the Slavic minority might increase its power.

The Ottoman Empire

In southeastern Europe nationalist agitation continued to rend the ever-disintegrating Ottoman Empire. Before 1829 the entire Balkan peninsula—bounded by the Aegean, Black, and Adriatic Seas—was controlled by the Turks. But during the next eighty-five years a gradual dismemberment of the Turkish Empire occurred. In some instances the slicing away of territories had been perpetrated by rival European powers, especially by Russia and Austria; but generally it

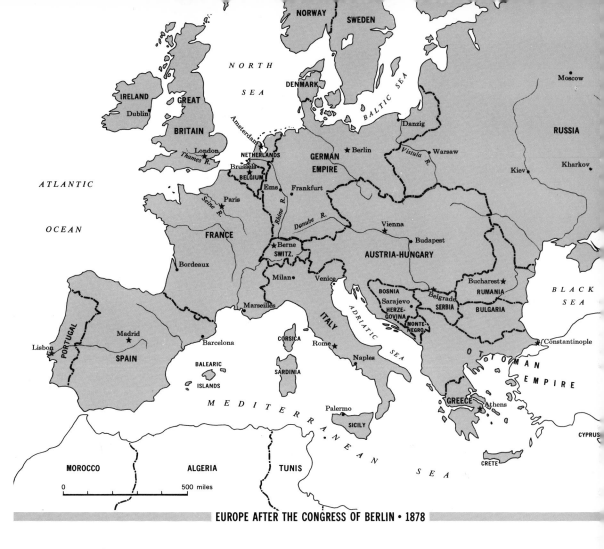

EUROPE AFTER THE CONGRESS OF BERLIN · 1878

was the result of nationalist revolts by the sultan's Christian subjects. In 1829, at the conclusion of a war between Russia and Turkey, the Ottoman Empire was compelled to acknowledge the independence of Greece and to grant autonomy to Serbia and to the provinces which later became Rumania. As the years passed, resentment against Ottoman rule spread through other Balkan territories. In 1875–1876 there were uprisings in Bosnia, Herzegovina, and Bulgaria, which the sultan suppressed with effective ferocity. Reports of atrocities against Christians gave Russia an excuse for renewal of its age-long struggle for domination of the Balkans. In this second Russo-Turkish War (1877–1878) the armies of the tsar won a smashing victory. The Treaty of San Stefano, which terminated the conflict, provided that the sultan surrender nearly all of his territory in Europe, except for a remnant around Constantinople. But at this juncture the great powers intervened. Austria and Great Britain, especially, were opposed to granting Russia jurisdiction over so large a portion of the Near East. In 1878 a congress of the great powers, meeting in Berlin, transferred Bessarabia to Russia, Thessaly to Greece, and Bosnia and Herzegovina to the control of Austria. Seven years later the Bulgars, who had been granted some degree of autonomy by the Congress of Berlin, seized the province of Eastern Rumelia from Turkey. In 1908 they established the independent Kingdom of Bulgaria.

The Young Turk revolution

In the very year when this last dismemberment occurred, Turkey itself was engulfed by a tidal wave of nationalism. For some time the more enlightened Turks had grown increasingly disgusted with the weakness and incompetence of the sultan's government. Those who had been educated in European universities were convinced that their country should be rejuvenated by the introduction of Western ideas of science, patriotism, and democracy. Organizing themselves into a society known as the Young Turks, they forced the sultan in 1908 to establish constitutional government. The following year, in the face of a reactionary movement, they deposed the reigning sultan, Abdul Hamid II, and placed on the throne his brother, Mohammed V, as a titular sovereign. The real powers of government were now entrusted to a grand vizier and ministers responsible to an elected parliament. This revolution did not mean increased liberty for the non-Turkish inhabitants of the empire. Instead, the Young Turks launched a vigorous movement to Ottomanize all of the Christian subjects of the sultan. At the same time the disturbances preceding and accompanying the revolution opened the way for still further dismemberment. In 1908 Austria annexed the provinces of Bosnia and Herzegovina, which the Treaty of Berlin had allowed it merely to administer, and in 1911–1912 Italy entered into war with Turkey for the conquest of Tripoli.

Of all the major nations of the West, the United States probably underwent the least domestic turmoil during the several decades before 1914. The Civil War had exhausted the country; until the end of the century the ever-expanding frontier provided an alternative for those discontented with their present lot. Yet the United States also felt, to some degree, the pressures that made stability so hard to sustain in Europe. Though the Civil War had ended, the complex moral problem of racism remained to block all attempts to truly heal the nation. Severe economic crises, particularly an economic depression in the 1890s, accompanied by the collapse of agricultural prices and the closing of factories, caused great suffering and aroused anger at capitalist adventurers who seemed to be profiting at the expense of the country as a whole. Many grew convinced that a restricted money supply had produced the depression. Demand for the issuance of paper money and the increased coinage of silver were at the heart of the programs of the Greenback and the Populist parties, which attracted large followings, and which campaigned as well for an income tax and govern-

Eugene Debs

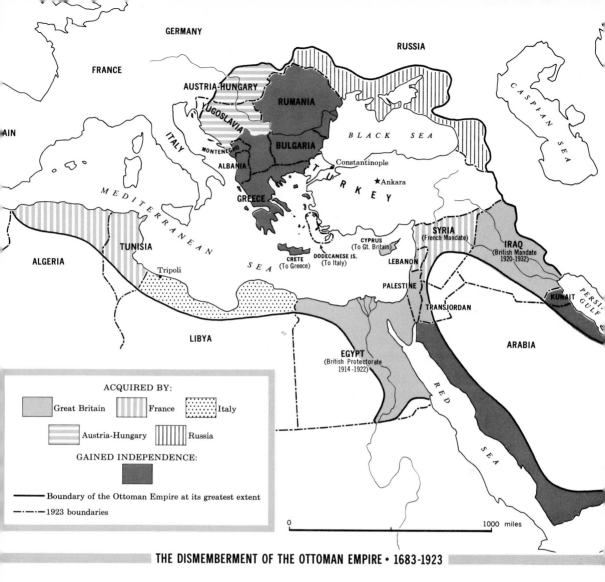

GERMANY · FRANCE · RUSSIA · AUSTRIA-HUNGARY · YUGOSLAVIA · RUMANIA · MONTENEGRO · BULGARIA · ALBANIA · ITALY · GREECE · SPAIN · ALGERIA · TUNISIA · Tripoli · LIBYA · EGYPT (British Protectorate 1914-1922) · Constantinople · Ankara · T U R K E Y · B L A C K   S E A · CASPIAN SEA · M E D I T E R R A N E A N   S E A · CRETE (To Greece) · DODECANESE IS. (To Italy) · CYPRUS (To Gt. Britain) · SYRIA (French Mandate) · LEBANON · PALESTINE · TRANSJORDAN · IRAQ (British Mandate 1920-1932) · KUWAIT · PERSIAN GULF · ARABIA · RED SEA

ACQUIRED BY:

Great Britain   France   Italy

Austria-Hungary   Russia

GAINED INDEPENDENCE:

——— Boundary of the Ottoman Empire at its greatest extent

—·—·— 1923 boundaries

0   1000 miles

THE DISMEMBERMENT OF THE OTTOMAN EMPIRE · 1683-1923

ment ownership of railways, and telephone and telegraph lines. Socialism of a reformist brand was espoused by Eugene V. Debs (1855–1926), leader of a mildly Marxist Socialist party. It failed to appeal to the generally un–class-conscious American worker, who continued to have faith in the dream of economic mobility. More radical was the membership of the Industrial Workers of the World, a general union whose goal was to organize the unskilled and immigrant worker. Perceived as a device of foreign agitators, the IWW was repressed both by the government and by industrial management. Characteristic of the generally moderate tone of American reformism, the Progressive movement captured both the imagination and votes of a vocal minority of middle-class Americans whose hostility over the accumulation of private economic power and the political corrup-

Unrest in the United States

tion of urban "bosses" was balanced by their belief in the democratic process and in the possibility of continuing progress. The movement, many of whose ideas were embodied in the programs of Presidents Theodore Roosevelt and Woodrow Wilson, was curtailed by the new realities that emerged with the advent of the First World War.

6. INTERNATIONAL RIVALRIES: THE ROAD TO THE FIRST WORLD WAR

The end of a century of peace

Despite the domestic instabilities and uncertainties that characterized the Western world in the years before 1914, a great many men and women retained a faith in the notion of peaceful progress. There had been an absence of multinational armed conflict—with the exception of the Crimean War—for a century. European countries—even autocratic Russia—had been moving gradually toward what most agreed was the worthy goal of democracy. Indeed, instability could be understood as the result of either an overzealous or an overdelayed movement in that direction. Above all, industrialization seemed to be providing a better standard of living for all—or at least all within the Western world. There is little wonder, therefore, that men and women reacted with disbelief as they saw their world crumbling during the days of frantic diplomatic maneuvering just prior to the outbreak of war in August 1914.

The balance of power

The key to an understanding of the coming of the World War lies in an understanding of international diplomacy during the years after 1870. Europe had prided itself on the establishment of a balance of power, which had kept any one nation from assuming a position so powerful as to threaten the general peace. During his years as chancellor, Bismarck played a diplomatic variation upon this general theme, in order to ensure that France would not engage in a war of revenge against the German victors of 1870. There was little prospect that the French would attempt war singlehanded. Therefore, Bismarck determined to isolate France by attaching all of its potential allies to Germany. In 1873 he managed to form an alliance with both Austria and Russia, the so-called League of the Three Emperors, a precarious combination that soon foundered. Bismarck then cemented a new and much stronger alliance with Austria. In 1882 this partnership was expanded into a Triple Alliance with Italy. The Italians joined out of fear of the French. They resented the French occupation of Tunisia (1881), a territory which they regarded as properly theirs. Moreover, Italian politicians, still at odds with the Roman Catholic church, feared that supporters of the papacy in France might gain the upper hand and send a French army to defend the pope. In the meantime, the Three Emperors' League had been revived. Though it lasted officially for only six years (1881–1887), Germany managed to hold the friendship of Russia until 1890, by means of a Reinsurance Treaty (1887) providing for the neutrality of either power if the other went to war.

Thus after more than a decade of diplomatic maneuvering, Bismarck had achieved his ambition. By 1882 France was cut off from nearly every possibility of obtaining aid from powerful friends. Austria and Italy were united with Germany in the Triple Alliance, and Russia after a three-year lapse was back once more in the Bismarckian camp. The only conceivable quarter from which help might come to the French was Great Britain; but, with respect to continental affairs, the British were maintaining a policy of "splendid isolation." Therefore, so far as the danger of a war of revenge was concerned, Germany had little to fear. Bismarck's complicated structure of alliances appeared to answer the purpose for which he claimed it had been built—to keep the peace. But the alliance system was a weapon that could cut two ways. In Bismarck's hands, it kept the peace. In hands less diplomatically capable, it might become less an asset than a liability, as was the case after 1890.

*Bismarck's diplomatic
success*

During the years between 1890 and 1907, European nations, competing across the globe for trade and territory, became more suspicious of each other. This general international insecurity produced a diplomatic revolution that obliterated Bismarck's handiwork, resulting in a new alignment which threatened the Germans. The Germans

A diplomatic revolution

Grand Palace, Paris Exposition, 1900. European nations continued to promote exhibitions of this sort, patterned after the Crystal Palace exhibition of 1851. Designed to celebrate the growth of Western industrialism, they also served to promote international rivalry.

retained the support of Austria, but they lost the friendship of both Russia and Italy, while Britain abandoned its isolation to enter into agreements with Russia and France. This shift in the balance of power had fateful results. It helped convinced the Germans that they were surrounded by a ring of enemies, and that consequently they must do everything in their power to retain the loyalty of Austria-Hungary.

The Triple Entente

The first of the major results of this diplomatic revolution was the formation of the Triple Entente between Russia, France and Great Britain. William II of Germany, mistrustful of Russian ambitions in the Balkans, refused to renew the Reinsurance Treaty following Bismarck's dismissal in 1890. A growing coolness between the two countries led to Russia's political flirtation with France. Secret military conventions signed by the two countries in 1894 provided that each would come to the aid of the other in case of an attack by Germany, or by Austria or Italy supported by Germany. This Dual Alliance of Russia and France was followed by an Entente Cordiale between France and Great Britain. During the last two decades of the nineteenth century, the British and the French had been involved in frequent altercations over colonies and trade, as in the Sudan. By 1904, however, France, fearing Germany, had buried its differences with Britain and in that year signed the Entente. This was not a formal alliance but a friendly agreement, covering a variety of subjects. The final step in the formation of the Triple Entente was the conclusion of a mutual understanding between Great Britain and Russia in 1907. Again there was no formal alliance, but the ability of the two powers to reconcile their ambitions in Asia suggested a willingness to ally in case of war.

Strains within the two camps

Thus by 1907 the great powers of Europe were arrayed in two opposing combinations, the Triple Alliance of Germany, Italy, and Austria-Hungary, and the Triple Entente of Britain, France, and Russia. Nevertheless, these new groupings were not without internal strains. Italy and Austria, though allied, were bitterly at odds over the disposition of territory in the Adriatic region—Trieste in particular, which the Austrians held and which the Italians claimed as *Italia Irredenta* (unredeemed Italy). The Italians had designs on portions of Africa as well. In the 1890s, under the premiership of Francesco Crispi, a hero of the Risorgimento, they had attempted to establish a protectorate over the Ethiopians, only to suffer a devastating loss at Aduwa in 1896—the first defeat of a European army by African forces. Now the Italians coveted Tripoli in North Africa, which they believed they might more easily obtain, over the objections of Turkey, if they supported the Moroccan claims of their French adversaries. Strains within the Entente were equally apparent. Britain viewed Russia's growing determination to control the Dardenelles as a threat to its supply routes to the East.

The generally fragile state of international relations was certainly one of the important causes of the First World War. Yet it was by no

The Baghdad Railroad. German and Turkish officials celebrate the launching of the enterprise.

means the only one. Recent scholars—most notably the German historian Fritz Fischer—ignited a controversy by insisting that the paramount reason was Germany's internally generated drive to power, its compulsion to aggrandize itself at the expense of the rest of Europe— not simply to achieve what the emperor had called its "place in the sun," but to see to it that the sun shone no more than fitfully on anyone else. Scholars of this persuasion, reacting to a more conventional view that has all nations sharing the blame, point to Germany's rapid commercial expansion, the growth, in particular, of its coal and steel industries, and its dockyards and overseas shipping as indications of its intentions. German capitalists financed the construction of a Berlin to Baghdad railway, as part of a concerted *drang nach osten* (drive to the east). At the same time, the Germans launched a massive campaign to increase the size of their navy, a prospect particularly pleasing to the industrial bourgeoisie, who would profit directly from the new construction, and whose sons, excluded from the aristocratically based army, manned the naval officer corps. The naval buildup was accompanied by a brash and effective propaganda campaign—perhaps the first of its kind—directed by the secretary of the navy, Admiral Alfred von Tirpitz, and concerted through "navy leagues," organizations devoted to trumpeting Germany's intention of matching the strength of the British navy.

German "war guilt"

Others have taken issue with the notion that Germany faced the prospect of a preemptive war with equanimity, and that this posture in the end made war unavoidable, on the grounds that, in part, it ignores the fact that many German industrialists did not want war, since they had heavy investments in the economies of both Russia and France. They further argue that it is a mistake to view the problem of the war's outbreak through the single lens of Germany. They maintain that Britain's rapprochement with Russia and France, for example, reflected the demands of its own imperial policies and not simply

Others' responsibility

a response to overweening German ambition.

Certainly, the spirit of militarism prevailed beyond the borders of Germany. Serbia and Rumania, two very real threats to Austro-Hungarian security, possessed armies of over 400,000 men each. In 1913, Russia embarked on a military training program that was to bolster its army by 500,000, to over two million men. Germans were not alone in praising the therapeutic value of war. The French historian Ernest Renan had justified it as a condition of progress, "the sting which prevents a country from going to sleep." We have seen that in all the major countries of Europe clashes between the political forces of Left and Right threatened internal stability. The notion that revolution and counterrevolution were on the prowl heightened a mood that seemed to proclaim the inevitability of conflict. "Almost one might think the world wished to suffer," Winston Churchill wrote after the war was over. "Certainly men were everywhere eager to dare."

Militarism

Nationalism, too, fed the conflict. From the beginning of the twentieth century, Serbia moved to extend its jurisdiction over all those alleged to be similar to its own citizens in race and in culture. Some of these peoples inhabited what were then the two Turkish provinces of Bosnia and Herzegovina. Others included Croatians and Slovenes in the southern provinces of Austria-Hungary. After 1908, when Austria suddenly annexed Bosnia and Herzegovina, Serbian activity was directed exclusively against the Habsburg Empire. It took the form of agitation to provoke discontent among the Slav subjects of Austria, in the hope of drawing them away and uniting the territories they inhabited with Serbia. It resulted in a series of dangerous plots against the peace and integrity of the Dual Monarchy.

Nationalism

In many of their activities the Serbian nationalists were aided and abetted by the Pan-Slavists in Russia. The Pan-Slav movement was founded upon the theory that all of the Slavs of eastern Europe constituted one cultural nation. Therefore, it was argued that Russia, as the most powerful Slavic state, should act as the protector of the smaller Slavic nations of the Balkans. Pan-Slavism was not merely the wishful sentiment of a few ardent nationalists; it was a part of the official policy of the Russian government, and went far toward explaining Russia's aggressive stand in every quarrel that arose between Serbia and Austria.

Pan-Slavism

All these factors—diplomatic instability, international militarism, domestic unrest, and nationalism—combined to produce a series of crises between 1905 and 1913. They were not so much causes as they were symptoms of international animosity. Yet each left a heritage of suspicion and bitterness that made war all the more probable. In some cases hostilities were averted only because one of the parties was too weak at the time to offer resistance. The result was a sense of humiliation, a smoldering resentment that was almost bound to burst into flame in the future. Two of the crises were generated by disputes over Morocco. Both Germany and France wanted to control Morocco; in

Moroccan crises

The Iron Fist of the Kaiser Strikes Agadir. This British cartoon depicts the Germans' use of gunboat diplomacy in Morocco in 1911 to secure colonial concessions from the French as an overtly hostile and sinister act. In precipitating this Second Moroccan Crisis the Germans hoped to drive a wedge between Britain and France but succeeded only in driving the Entente powers closer together.

1905 and 1911 the two powers stood on the brink of war. Each time the dispute was smoothed over, but not without the usual legacy of suspicion.

In addition to the clash over Morocco, two flare-ups occurred in the Near East, the first in Bosnia in 1908. At the Congress of Berlin in 1878 the two Turkish provinces of Bosnia and Herzegovina had been placed under the administrative control of Austria, though actual sovereignty was still to be vested in the Ottoman Empire. Serbia also coveted the territories; they would double the size of its kingdom and place it within striking distance of the Adriatic. Suddenly, in October 1908, as we have seen, Austria annexed the two provinces, in flat violation of the Treaty of Berlin. The Serbs were furious and appealed to Russia. The tsar's government threatened war, until Germany addressed a sharp note to St. Petersburg announcing its firm intention to back Austria. Since Russia had not yet fully recovered from its war with Japan and was plagued by internal troubles, Russian intervention was postponed.

Still more bad blood between the nations of eastern Europe was created by the Balkan Wars. In 1912 Serbia, Bulgaria, Montenegro, and Greece, with encouragement from Russia, joined in a Balkan alliance for the conquest of the Turkish province of Macedonia. The war started in October 1912; in less than two months the resistance of the Turks was shattered. Then came the problem of dividing the spoils. In secret treaties negotiated before hostilities began, Serbia had been

Serbian crisis

Balkan Wars

promised Albania, in addition to a generous slice of Macedonia. But now Austria, fearful as always of any increase in Serbian power, intervened at the peace conference and obtained the establishment of Albania as an independent state. For the Serbs this was the last straw. It seemed to them that at every turn their path to western expansion was certain to be blocked by the Habsburg government. From this time on, anti-Austrian agitation in Serbia and in the neighboring province of Bosnia became ever more venomous.

A world at war

It was the assassination of the Austrian Archduke Francis Ferdinand by a Serbian sympathizer on June 28, 1914, that ignited the conflict. The four-year war that ensued altered the Western world immeasurably. Yet many changes which came either during or after the First World War were the result, not of the war itself, but of pressures and forces we have seen at work during the prewar years, when European power, at its height, was challenged by forces which that power had unleased and which it proved unable to contain.

SELECTED READINGS

• *Items so designated are available in paperback editions.*

Blum, J., *Lord and Peasant in Russia from the Ninth to the Nineteenth Century*, Princeton, N.J., 1961. Contains a thorough discussion of emancipation.

• Berghahn, Victor, *Germany and the Approach of War in 1914*, New York, 1973. Examines the domestic background of German foreign policy, especially the naval program.

Brogan, D. W., *France under the Republic, 1870–1930*, New York, 1940. An excellent survey, comprehensive and analytical.

• Dangerfield, George, *The Strange Death of Liberal England*, New York, 1961. Examines England's three major crises of the prewar period: women's suffrage, labor unrest, and Irish home rule.

• Fischer, Fritz, *Germany's Aims in the First World War*, New York, 1967. An extremely controversial study which seeks to lay major blame for the coming of the First World War on Germany.

• Haimson, L., *The Russian Marxists and the Origins of Bolshevism*, Cambridge, Mass., 1955. Analyzes the revolutionaries as part of the Russian radical tradition.

Hale, Oron J., *The Great Illusion, 1900–1914*, New York, 1971. A general synthetic treatment of the period that is particularly concerned with mood and spirit.

Jenks, William A., *Austria under the Iron Ring, 1879–1893*, Charlottesville, Va., 1965. An examination of Austria's attempts at political and social reform, set in the context of a struggle for autonomy from German domination.

Johnson, Douglas, *France and the Dreyfus Affair*, London, 1966. A good survey, with breadth.

• Jones, Gareth Stedman, *Outcast London*, Oxford, 1971. A remarkable book which examines the breakdown in the relationship between classes in London during the latter half of the nineteenth century.

Mack Smith, Denis, *Italy: A Modern History,* rev. ed., Ann Arbor, Mich., 1969. An excellent survey.

- McManners, John, *Church and State in France, 1870–1914,* New York, 1972. Particularly good on the question of education and the final separation of church and state.
- May, Arthur J., *The Hapsburg Monarchy, 1867–1914,* Cambridge, Mass., 1951. A detailed narrative of the period.
- Mosse, W. E., *Alexander II and the Modernization of Russia,* New York, 1958. Brief but useful biography.
- Pulzer, Peter, *The Rise of Political Anti-Semitism in Germany and Austria,* New York, 1964. An excellent study of the roots of anti-Semitism and the part it played in shaping politics.

Ralston, David B., *The Army of the Republic: The Place of the Military in the Political Evolution of France, 1871–1914,* Cambridge, Mass., 1967. Useful for background to the Dreyfus affair.

Rémond, René, *The Right Wing in France from 1815 to De Gaulle,* Philadelphia, 1969. Traces the survival of royalism and Bonapartism in French thought and politics.

Stavrianos, L. S., *The Balkans, 1815–1914,* New York, 1963. Surveys domestic and international affairs within the entire, troubled region.

Seton-Watson, Hugh, *The Russian Empire, 1801–1917,* Oxford, 1967. Standard survey.

- Taylor, A. J. P., *The Struggle for Mastery in Europe, 1848–1918,* Oxford, 1971. An excellent diplomatic history.

Thayer, John A., *Italy and the Great War: Politics and Culture, 1870–1915,* Madison, Wisc., 1964. Written to explain Italian policy and its origins in the prewar period.

Vicinus, Martha, *A Widening Sphere: Changing Roles of Victorian Women,* Bloomington, Ind., 1977. Essays which trace the slow emancipation of Victorian womanhood.

Weber, Eugen, *Peasants into Frenchmen: The Modernization of France, 1870–1914,* Stanford, Calif., 1977. Argues that the great achievement of the Third Republic was the consolidation of France, accomplished by bringing rural areas into the mainstream of modern life.

- Williams, Roger L., *The French Revolution of 1870–1871,* New York, 1969. A good narrative account.

SOURCE MATERIALS

Booth, Charles, ed., *Life and Labour of the People in London,* 9 vols., London, 1892–1897. A remarkable document for its time. A street-by-street survey of London's labor and poverty. One of the most comprehensive social surveys ever.

Childers, Erskine, *The Riddle of the Sands,* New York, 1978. A bestseller in England in 1903, this novel concerns a future war between England and Germany. Its reception gives evidence of the rise of anti-German sentiment prior to the First World War.

- Hamerow, Theodore S., ed., *The Age of Bismarck: Documents and Interpretations,* New York, 1973.
- Lenin, Nikolai, *What Is To Be Done?* London, 1918. Written in 1902, this is

Lenin's most famous pamphlet. In it he called for the proletarian revolution to be led by elite cadres of bourgeois intellectuals, like himself.

• Mackenzie, Midge, ed., *Shoulder to Shoulder,* New York, 1975. A richly illustrated documentary history of the British movement for women's suffrage.

• Pankhurst, Emmeline, *My Own Story,* New York, 1914. The memoirs of one of the leaders of England's militant suffragettes.

• Turgenev, Ivan, *Fathers and Sons,* New York, 1966. Turgenev's greatest novel is set in Russia in the 1860s and portrays the ideological conflict between generations at the time of the emancipation of the serfs and the rise of nihilism.

• Zola, Émile, *Germinal,* New York, 1964. Zola's realistic novel describes class conflict in France's coal-mining region.

Chapter 28

THE FIRST WORLD WAR

Nevertheless, except you share
With them in hell the sorrowful dark of hell,
Whose world is but the trembling of a flare,
And heaven but as the highway for a shell,

You shall not hear their mirth:
You shall not think them well content
By any jest of mine. These men are worth
Your tears. You are not worth their merriment.

—Wilfred Owen, "Apologia Pro Poemate Meo"

The war that broke out in 1914 was not really the "first world war." The wars against Napoleon at the beginning of the nineteenth century had extended beyond the European continent. Yet the war that took place between 1914 and 1918 had an impact that far exceeded any ever fought before. It quickly became a "people's war," to which civilians as well as soldiers and sailors were directly and totally committed. It bore fruit in revolution, and sowed the seeds of new and even more deadly conflicts in the future. It set the pattern for an age of violence that has continued through most of the twentieth century.

The world at war

1. PRELUDE TO WAR

The assassination of the Austrian archduke was the immediate cause of the First World War. Francis Ferdinand was soon to become emperor of Austria-Hungary. The reigning monarch, Francis Joseph, had reached his eighty-fourth year, and his death was expected momentarily. The murder of the heir to the throne was therefore considered in a very real sense as an attack upon the state. The actual murderer of Francis

The assassination of Francis Ferdinand

The Assassination at Sarajevo. Left: The Archduke Francis Ferdinand greets Bosnian notables a few hours before his death. Right: The police seize Princip after he had killed the heir to the Habsburg monarchy.

Ferdinand was a Bosnian student, Gavrilo Princip, the tool of Serbian nationalists. The murder, though committed in Sarajevo, the capital of Bosnia, was the result of a plot hatched in Belgrade, the Serbian capital. The conspirators were members of a secret society officially known as Union or Death, but commonly called the Black Hand. Their opposition to Francis Ferdinand stemmed from his support for a plan which would have resulted in the reorganization of the Habsburg Empire. This plan, designated as *trialism,* entailed changing the Dual Monarchy into a triple monarchy. In addition to German Austria and Magyar Hungary, already virtually autonomous, there was to be a third semi-independent region to accommodate the Slavs. Serbian national extremists opposed this scheme, fearing that if it were put into effect, their Slovene and Croatian kinsmen would be content to remain under Habsburg rule. They therefore determined to assassinate Francis Ferdinand before he could become emperor and press ahead with his reform.

Austrian ultimatum to Serbia   The Austrians were immediately convinced that the Serbian government was behind this violent act. Austria waited for more than three weeks before acting on its suspicions and seizing the opportunity to extract a high price from Serbia for its transgressions. The delay was due in part to Austria's inability to decide how to proceed and in part to its unwillingness to mobilize its forces until after the harvest. On July 23 the Austrian government dispatched a severe ultimatum to the Serbians consisting of eleven demands: among them Serbia was to suppress anti-Austrian newspapers; to crush secret patriotic societies; to eliminate from the government and from the army all persons guilty of anti-Austrian propaganda; and to accept the collaboration of Austrian officials in stamping out the subversive movement against the Habsburg Empire. Two days later the Serbian government transmitted its reply. Of the total of eleven demands, only one was emphatically refused, and five were accepted without reservations. The Austrians, however, pronounced the Serbian reply unsatisfactory, severed diplomatic relations, and mobilized parts of their army. The Serbs themselves had been under no illusions about pleasing Austria, since, three hours before transmitting their reply, they had issued an order to mobilize their troops.

The Austrian intransigence vis-à-vis the Serbian response was actually the culmination of a belligerence which had been growing among European nations prior to the events which followed the assassination. *Russia and France* As early as July 18 Sergei Sazonov, the Russian foreign minister, warned Austria that Russia would not tolerate any effort to humiliate Serbia. On July 24 Sazonov informed the German ambassador: "I do not hate Austria; I despise her. Austria is seeking a pretext to gobble up Serbia; but in that case Russia will make war on Austria." In the adoption of this attitude, Russia had the support of France. On the twentieth of July, Raymond Poincaré, president of France, paid a visit to St. Petersburg to strengthen the Russian resolve to "be firm" and to avoid any compromise which might result in a loss of prestige for the Triple Entente. He warned the Austrian ambassador that "Serbia has very warm friends in the Russian people. And Russia has an ally, France."

The attitude of Germany in these critical days was ambiguous. Although the kaiser was shocked and infuriated by the assassination, his government did not make any threats until after the actions of Russia *The attitude of Germany*

Nicholas II and Raymond Poincaré, the President of the French Republic, in St. Petersburg on July 23, 1914

See color map
following page 961

Mobilizations begin

*The German ultimatums
to Russia and France*

gave cause for alarm. Yet both William II and the chancellor, Theobald von Bethmann-Hollweg, adopted the premise that stern punishment must be meted out to Serbia without delay. They hoped in this way to confront the other powers with an accomplished fact. The kaiser declared on June 30: "Now or never! Matters must be cleared up with the Serbs, *and that soon."* On July 6 Bethmann-Hollweg gave a commitment to the Austrian foreign minister which was interpreted by the latter as a blank check. The Austrian government was informed that the emperor would "stand true by Austria's side in accordance with his treaty obligations and old friendship." The Germans apparently hoped that by taking quick punitive action against Serbia, the Austrians would be able to counter a very real Serbian threat before Russia and its allies could recover from the shock of the assassination and mobilize either diplomatically or militarily.

Austria declared war against Serbia on July 28, 1914. For a fleeting, anxious moment there was a possibility that the conflict might be contained. But it was quickly transformed into a war of larger scope by the action of Russia. On July 24 the Russian government decided to respond to any Austrian military initiative against Serbia with a partial mobilization. However, by July 30 Sazonov and a prowar military clique persuaded Tsar Nicholas II to issue an order mobilizing all troops, not only against Austria but against Germany as well, on the grounds that such a vast country as Russia would require considerable time to get its military machine into operation.

There was now no drawing back from the abyss. The Germans were alarmed by Russian preparations for war. The latest action by the tsar's government made the situation far more critical, since in German military circles, and also in French and Russian, general mobilization meant war. Upon learning that the tsar's decree had gone into effect, William II's government sent an ultimatum to St. Petersburg demanding that mobilization cease within twelve hours. On the afternoon of August 1, the German ambassador requested an interview with the Russian foreign minister. He appealed to Sazonov for a favorable answer to the German ultimatum. Sazonov replied that mobilization could not be halted, but that Russia was willing to continue negotiations. The ambassador repeated his question a second and a third time, emphasizing the terrible consequences of a negative answer. Sazonov finally replied: "I have no other answer to give you." The ambassador then handed the foreign minister a declaration of war and, bursting into tears, left the room. In the meantime, the kaiser's ministers had also dispatched an ultimatum to France demanding that its leaders make known their intentions. Premier René Viviani replied on August 1 that France would act "in accordance with her interests," and immediately ordered a general mobilization of the army. On August 3 Germany declared war upon France.

These grim timetables had doomed the efforts of Britain's foreign secretary, Sir Edward Grey, to convene a conference to settle the Aus-

August 1, 1914. A German officer reads the declaration of war in the streets of Berlin.

tro-Serbian dispute. Perhaps if Britain had declared its readiness to go to war on the side of France and Russia earlier, that declaration would have compelled Germany and Austria to draw back. Yet Grey was not certain enough of his country's willingness to fight to make such a commitment. Although military conversations between the British and French had bound the former to an expeditionary force on French soil in case of war, the British public did not know this. Opinion was divided: Conservatives generally favored war; the Liberals, still in power, disagreed among themselves; Labour was opposed.

The British position

Fortunately for Grey and the prime minister, Herbert Asquith, both of whom wanted a British declaration of war, Germany's invasion of neutral Belgium brought together parliamentary and public support for intervention. In 1839, along with the other great powers, Britain had signed a treaty guaranteeing the neutrality of Belgium. Moreover, it had been British policy for a century or more to try to prevent domination of the Low Countries, lying directly across the Channel, by any powerful continental nation. The Germans planned to attack France through Belgium. Accordingly, they demanded of the Belgian government permission to send troops across its territory, promising to respect the independence of the nation and to pay for any damage to property. When Belgium refused, the kaiser's legions began pouring across the frontier. The British foreign secretary immediately went before Parliament and urged that his country rally to the defense of international law and to the protection of small nations. The next day, August 4, the cabinet sent an ultimatum to Berlin demanding that

Britain enters the war

Germany respect Belgian neutrality, and that the Germans give a satisfactory reply by midnight. The kaiser's ministers offered no answer save military necessity, arguing that it was a matter of life and death for Germany that its soldiers reach France by the quickest route. As the clock struck twelve, Great Britain and Germany were at war.

The conflagration spreads

Other nations were quickly drawn into the struggle. On August 7 the Montenegrins joined with their kinsmen, the Serbs, in fighting Austria. Two weeks later the Japanese declared war upon Germany, partly because of their alliance with Great Britain, but mainly for the purpose of conquering German possessions in the Far East. On August 1 Turkey negotiated an alliance with Germany, and in October began the bombardment of Russian ports on the Black Sea. Italy, though still technically a member of the Triple Alliance, proclaimed neutrality. The Italians insisted that the Germans were not fighting a defensive war, and that consequently they were not bound to go to their aid. Italy remained neutral until May 1915, when it entered the war on the side of the Triple Entente.

Diplomacy and the question of guilt

The diplomatic maneuvers during the five weeks that followed the assassination at Sarajevo have probably best been characterized as "a tragedy of miscalculation." Because the war brought such disaster in its train, debate about immediate responsibility for its outbreak has been continual and often acrimonious. The eventual victors—Britain, France, the United States, and their allies—insisted at the war's end that Germany assume that responsibility, and wrote German war "guilt" into the postwar settlement. Historians during the 1920s and 1930s challenged that harsh assessment, arguing instead that all the major European nations—and the alliance systems they had constructed—had driven the world into conflict in those fatal weeks during the summer of 1914. More recently, Fritz Fischer has insisted that William II and Bethmann-Hollweg did everything they could to encourage the Austrians to go to war against Serbia, knowing that such a war would almost certainly engage the Russians on the side of the Serbians and the French on the side of the Russians. Undoubtedly there were those in positions of power in Germany arguing that war was inevitable, that to wait until Russia had fully recovered from its war with Japan, and until France's armies had been strengthened by its three-year conscription law, was to invite defeat. Better to do battle now, from a position of strength. To what extent William II and Bethmann-Hollweg shared these views is uncertain. It is clear, however, that they did perceive Russia as a serious threat to Germany and that they saw Austria as Germany's only reliable bulwark against that threat.

2. THE ORDEAL OF BATTLE

Because the war soon demanded the wholehearted support of entire civilian populations, national leaders felt compelled to depict it as a noble conflict rather than a widespread quarrel between imperialist powers or the unexpected outcome of nationalist jealousies. The socialist Second International had declared that workers should respond to a call to arms with a general strike. Although none of the European socialist parties heeded that call, governments continued to fear subversion of the war effort from "below," and attempted to head off any such movement by ceaseless appeals to patriotism. Propaganda became as important a weapon as the machine gun. The task of the Allies was at first made easier by Germany's treatment of the neutral Belgians: their execution of civilian hostages, destruction of the ancient library at Louvain, and massacre of over six hundred civilians at Dinant.

Prime Minister Asquith on August 6, 1914, declared that Britain had entered the conflict to vindicate "the principle that smaller nationalities are not to be crushed by the arbitrary will of a strong and overmastering Power." Across the Channel, President Poincaré was assuring his fellow citizens that France had no other purpose than to stand "before the universe for Liberty, Justice and Reason." Later, as a consequence of the writings of individuals such as H. G. Wells and Gilbert Murray, and the pronouncements of the American president, Woodrow Wilson, the crusade of the Entente powers became a war to redeem mankind from the curse of militarism. In the opposing camp, the subordinates of the kaiser were doing all in their power to justify Germany's military efforts. The struggle against the Entente powers was represented to the German people as a crusade on behalf of a superior *Kultur* and as a battle to protect the fatherland against the wicked encirclement policy of the Entente nations. German socialist politicians were persuaded to vote for the war on the grounds that a German war with Russia would help liberate the Russian people from the tsarist yoke.

The First World War fooled military experts who believed it would end quickly. Open warfare soon disappeared from the Western Front—the battle line that stretched across France from Switzerland to the North Sea, where the fighting was concentrated for four years. Germany's initially successful advance into France followed war plans drawn up by General Alfred von Schlieffen and adopted in 1905. Schlieffen's strategy called for Austria to hold against the Russians while Germany dealt a quick blow to the French, knocking them out of the war. Germany was then to turn, with Austria, to the major task of defeating the Russians. Contrary to expectation, however, the advance to the west, which brought German troops to within thirty miles of Paris, was halted. A series of flanking maneuvers by both sides ended in the extension of the battle lines in a vast network of trenches. Attacks to dislodge the enemy from their positions on the line failed to achieve more than very limited gains. Protected by barbed wire and machine guns—both making their first major appearance in a European war—defenders had the advantage. The one weapon with

British Propaganda Poster. During the war governments, confronted with the bitter fruit of prewar militarism and nationalist rivalry, resorted to using any image that seemed likely to stir the passions of their populations against their foes.

Trench Warfare. After the first few battles, the war on the Western Front settled into static or position warfare. During the four-year period, veritable cities of mud, stone, and timber sprang up behind the trenches.

War of attrition

the potential to break the stalemate, the tank, was not introduced into battle until 1916, and then with such reluctance by tradition-bound commanders that its half-hearted employment made almost no difference. Airplanes were used almost exclusively for reconnaissance, though occasional "dog-fights" did occur between German and Allied pilots. The Germans sent Zeppelins to raid London, but they did little significant damage. Commanding officers continued to believe that the war would have to be won on the ground. Only by battering their enemies first with artillery and then with thousands of men armed with rifles, grenades, and bayonets, did they believe they could achieve the always-elusive "breakthrough." On more than one occasion those in charge of the war attempted to end the stalemate by opening military fronts in other areas of the world. In 1915, Britain and France attempted a landing at Gallipoli, in Asia Minor, in the hope of driving Turkey from the war. The campaign was a disaster for the Entente powers, however, failing, as did others, to refocus the fighting or to free it from the immobility of the trenches.

Life in the trenches

Life for the common soldier on the Western Front alternated between the daily boredom and extreme unpleasantness of weeks spent in muddy and vermin-ridden trench communities, and the occasional and horrifying experience of battle, a nightmare not only of artillery, machine guns, and barbed wire, but of exploding bullets, liquid fire, and poison gas. Morale among most troops remained remarkably steady, given the dreadful conditions in the trenches and the endless series of battles fought without significant gain to either side. Mutinies did occur among French troops in 1917, when soldiers moved forward in attack bleating like sheep, their pathetic way of protesting their commanders' continued willingness to lead them like lambs to the slaughter.

By 1916 the war, which appeared to have settled into an interminable stalemate, had extracted a fearful cost. Over 600,000 were killed and wounded when the Germans unsuccessfully besieged the French stronghold of Verdun, near France's eastern border, in the spring of that year. The Germans acknowledged that their aim was not so much to take the fortified city, which they knew the French would defend with desperation, but to "bleed France white of all able-bodied men"; yet the Germans lost as many men as the French. In August 1916 the British launched an enormous attack along the Somme River to ease the pressure on Verdun. Lasting from July to October, the battle cost the Germans 500,000, the British 400,000, and the French 200,000 in return for an Allied advance of seven miles across the front. On the first day of fighting alone, over 57,000 British troops were killed or wounded. Meanwhile, conditions within Germany worsened, as an Allied blockade slowly reduced the country's raw materials and food supply.

In time such losses fueled an unsuccessful move on the part of a minority on both sides to press for a negotiated peace. But in the minds of those who were making decisions, both military and civilian, the immediate effect of the carnage was to reinforce determination to press ahead for total victory. This intransigence led, in turn, to changes in leadership. In Britain, the ineffectual prime minister Asquith was replaced by Lloyd George, a buccaneer politician who, if he had little new to propose, nevertheless projected a properly fervent public image. In France, the following year, Georges Clemenceau assumed the premiership, again with a mandate to counter a growing defeatist attitude within the military high command. And in Germany, control continued to pass into the hands of Generals Paul von Hindenburg and Erich Ludendorff, the men responsible as well for the overall military strategy of the Central Powers.

The enormous human cost

Changes in leadership

German and British Planes Engage in a Dogfight

The expansion of the conflict

As the conflict dragged on, other countries were drawn into the war. Italy was bribed by the Allies with a promise of Austrian territories and a generous slice of the eastern shore of the Adriatic. Bulgaria joined the Central Powers in September 1915, and Rumania sided with the Allies a year later. It was the intervention of the United States on the Allied side, however, in April 1917, that tipped the balance. The United States entered the war vowing, in the words of its president, Woodrow Wilson, to "make the world safe for democracy," to banish autocracy and militarism, and to establish a league or society of nations in place of the old diplomatic maneuvering. Undoubtedly the primary reason for the American decision to enter the war, though, was the government's concern to maintain the international balance of power. For years it had been a cardinal doctrine in American diplomatic and military circles that the security of the United States depended upon a balance of forces in Europe. So long as Great Britain was strong enough to prevent any one nation from achieving supremacy in Europe, the United States was safe. American officials had grown so accustomed to thinking of the British navy as the shield of American security that they found it difficult to contemplate any different situation. Germany, however, presented not merely a challenge to British naval supremacy; it threatened to starve the British nation into surrender and to establish a hegemony over all of Europe.

Submarine warfare

The direct cause of United States participation in the First World War was the U-boat, or submarine, warfare of the Germans. Once it became clear that the war would be one of attrition, the Germans recognized that unless they could break the Entente's stranglehold on their shipping, they would be defeated. In February 1915, the kaiser's government announced that neutral vessels headed for British ports would be torpedoed without warning. President Wilson replied by declaring that the United States would hold Germany to a "strict accountability" if any harm should come to American lives or property. The warning caused Germany to discontinue the campaign, but

Wartime Leaders. Left: Haig, Joffre, and Lloyd George discuss strategy. Right: Reviewing a map are Hindenburg, William II, and Ludendorff, members of the German high command.

The Lusitania *Leaving New York Harbor.* In February 1915 the *Lusitania* was torpedoed and sunk by a German U-boat. Among the 1,200 people drowned were 119 Americans. The disaster was one step in the chain of events which led to the entry of the United States into the war on the side of Britain and France.

only temporarily. The Germans were convinced that the U-boat was one of their most valuable weapons, and they considered themselves justified in using it against the British blockade. They also believed, correctly, that the British were receiving war matériel clandestinely shipped aboard passenger ships from the United States, and continued to sink them, thus appearing to violate United States neutrality. When the kaiser's ministers announced that, on February 1, 1917, they would launch a campaign of unrestricted submarine warfare, Wilson cut off diplomatic relations with the Berlin government. On April 2 he went before Congress and requested and received a declaration of war.

The immediate result of U.S. entry was an increase in the amount of war matériel and food—later, in the number of troops—shipped unmolested in armed convoys across the Atlantic. New ship construction overcame earlier losses; submarine warfare, Germany's most effective weapon against the Allies, had been neutralized.

The success of the Atlantic convoys

3. REVOLUTION IN THE MIDST OF WAR

In the midst of world war came revolution. Russia, already severely weakened by internal conflicts before 1914, found itself unable to sustain the additional burden of continuous warfare. In a nation ruled as autocratically as was Russia, a successful war effort depended greatly on the determination and talents of its ruler, the tsar. Nicholas II was, by nature, irresolute and weak. His limited capabilities were further undermined by the irrationality of his wife, Alexandra, a religious fanatic, and of her spiritual mentor, the monk Rasputin. The latter had gained the tsarina's sympathy by his ability to alleviate the sufferings of her hemophiliac son, and used his influence over her to shape policy to his own self-aggrandizing ends. Russia's armies proved incapable of sustained success in the field. Although they managed to advance against the Austrians into Galicia in the south, they had suffered two stunning defeats in 1914, at Tannenberg and the Masurian lakes in the

Rasputin

Tsar Nicholas II and His Family on the Eve of the Revolution

north, losing almost 250,000 men in the process. In some instances soldiers were sent to the front without rifles; their clothing supplies were inadequate. Medical facilities were scarce. The railway system broke down, producing a shortage of food not only in the army but in cities as well. By the end of 1916, Russia's power to resist had all but collapsed.

The March 1917 revolution

The revolution in Russia followed a pattern of successive radicalization not unlike that of the French Revolution. It began in March 1917 with the forced abdication of the tsar. For this the immediate cause was disgust with the conduct of the war. The Russians had attempted a major offensive in the summer of 1916, to coincide with the campaign along the Somme in the west. The offensive, though initially successful, turned into a humiliating retreat, however, thanks to transportation breakdowns and a lack of ammunition. In addition to military disasters, inflation and consequent high prices, and shortages of food and fuel had produced a rebellious urban population. Demands for a popularly elected, broad-based government were met by the tsar's determination to retain power in his own hands until bread riots in Petrograd precipitated the abdication. (The city had abandoned its supposedly Germanic name of St. Petersburg at the beginning of the war.) Troops summoned to quell the fighting broke ranks and joined the protesters, further evidence of the collapse of both civilian and military order. With the overthrow of the tsar, the authority of the government passed into the hands of a provisional ministry organized by leaders in the Duma in conjunction with representatives of workers in Petrograd, calling themselves a *soviet* or government council. With the exception of Alexander Kerensky (1881–1970), who was a member of the rurally based Social Revolutionary party, nearly all of the ministers were middle-of-the-road bourgeois liberals. Their hope was to transform the Russian autocracy into a constitutional monarchy modeled after that of Great Britain. In accordance with this aim, they issued a proclamation of civil liberties, released thousands of prisoners, and made plans for the election of a constituent assembly.

The increasingly powerful soviets of workers and soldiers pressed for social reform, the redistribution of land, and a negotiated settlement with the Central Powers. Yet ministers of the provisional government insisted that demands for domestic change must be subordinated to the war effort, which they defined in terms of previously declared imperialistic aims. They argued that basic governmental and economic reform should await the convening of the constituent assembly. Because the provisional ministers could not govern without the cooperation of the soviets, Kerensky, vice-president of the Petrograd soviet by the summer of 1917, became prime minister. He orga-

The Kerensky government

Scenes from the Russian Revolution. Right: Mass demonstration sponsored by the First All-Russian Congress of Soviets in which Bolshevik banners far outnumber the rest, spring 1917. Bottom left: Street fighting in Petrograd, summer 1917. Bottom right: Russian soldiers join the Bolsheviks in front of the Winter Palace, fall 1917.

nized a government which managed to retain power for several months. Meanwhile, opposition to the growing radicalization of the ministry—reflected in Kerensky's elevation—encouraged conservatives and liberals to make common cause, and to mount a military action led by General Lavr Kornilov, the commander-in-chief of the army, against the government. The attempted coup was crushed. Yet Kerensky's own position had been undermined, his enemies on the Left arguing that Kornilov's ability to mount a counterrevolutionary effort was a sign of Kerensky's ineffectual leadership and willingness to compromise revolutionary aims.

Lenin and the Bolsheviks

On April 3, 1917, Nikolai Lenin, who had been living in exile in Switzerland, was smuggled into Russia by the Germans, who recognized his potential as a revolutionary, and hence his value to them as a troublemaker. They correctly reasoned that his opposition to Russia's participation in the war would further weaken their enemy to the east. Throughout the spring and summer of 1917, while Kerensky was struggling to hold his government together, Lenin led the Bolsheviks on a bolder course which shunned all collaboration with the bourgeoisie and condemned their war policies. He soon became the leader of a vast popular uprising of workers, soldiers, and peasants; the Bolsheviks at this time clearly spoke to the people's needs as no other party did. Lenin, determined to sieze power from Kerensky, after Kornilov's failure waited on the advice of his fellow Bolsheviks until the convening of the All-Russian Congress of Soviets on November 7. The preceding day, a coup d'état, centered in Petrograd and directed by Lenin's ally Leon Trotsky (1879–1940), succeeded in overturning the provisional government.

Revolutionary changes

Lenin immediately proceeded to issue decrees that would give substance to the Bolsheviks' slogan of "Peace, Bread, and Land." The "People's Commissars" (ministers) ordered the partition of land and its distribution to peasants, without compensation to former owners;

Kerensky (second from right) *and His Aides in the Winter Palace.* This is the last known photograph of Kerensky in Petrograd.

Strife in Ireland, 1916. British troops raiding the office of a Dublin printer who supported the rebellion.

nationalized banks, confiscating private accounts in the process; handed factory control over to workers; and began to negotiate a treaty with the Germans. The resulting agreement, signed at Brest-Litovsk in March 1918, surrendered Poland, Finland, and the Ukraine to the Germans. The treaty aroused the fury of Lenin's political enemies, both moderates and reactionaries, who were still a force to be reckoned with and who were prepared to plunge Russia into civil war rather than accept the revolution.

Yet another outbreak of revolution in this period was the so-called Easter Rebellion in Ireland. At the beginning of the World War, Irish nationalists, who resented the rule of their country by the British, were ripe for revolt. They had been promised self-rule on the eve of the war, but the British later reneged on the ground that a national emergency must take preeminence over everything else. This greatly angered the Roman Catholic majority of southern Ireland. They scheduled Easter Monday, 1916, as a day for revolt. British forces quelled the uprising, but not until a hundred people had been killed. Sporadic outbreaks kept the island in turmoil for years thereafter, but were finally brought to a temporary end by an agreement constituting southern Ireland as a free republic. The northern counties, or the province of Ulster, were to continue subject to the British crown.

The Easter Rebellion in Ireland

4. ARMISTICE AND PEACE

While the fighting raged on for four years, various attempts were made to bring about peace negotiations. In the spring of 1917, Dutch and Scandinavian socialists summoned an international socialist conference to meet at Stockholm to draft plans to end the fighting which would be acceptable to all the belligerents. The Petrograd soviet embraced the idea and on May 15 issued an appeal to socialists of all nations to send delegates to the conference and to induce their govern-

Peace proposals

ments to agree to a peace "without annexations and indemnities, on the basis of the self-determination of peoples." The socialist parties in all the principal countries on both sides of the war accepted this formula and were eager to send delegates to the conference, but when the British and French governments refused to permit any of their subjects to attend, the project was abandoned. That the rulers of the Entente states were not afraid of these proposals merely because they emanated from socialists is indicated by the fact that a similar formula suggested by the pope was just as emphatically rejected. Nowhere was there a disposition to take peace proposals seriously. Woodrow Wilson, as spokesman for the Allies, declared that negotiation of peace under any conditions was impossible so long as Germany was ruled by the kaiser. The Central Powers professed to regard with favor the general import of the papal suggestions, but they refused to commit themselves on indemnities and restorations, especially the restoration of Belgium.

The Fourteen Points

The best known of all the peace proposals was President Wilson's program of Fourteen Points, which he incorporated in an address to Congress on January 8, 1918. Summarized as briefly as possible, this program included: (1) "open covenants openly arrived at," i.e., the abolition of secret diplomacy; (2) freedom of the seas; (3) removal of economic barriers between nations; (4) reduction of national armaments "to the lowest point consistent with safety"; (5) impartial adjustment of colonial claims, with consideration for the interests of the peoples involved; (6) evacuation of Russia by foreign armies; (7) restoration of the independence of Belgium; (8) restoration of Alsace and Lorraine to France; (9) a readjustment of Italian frontiers "along clearly recognizable lines of nationality"; (10) autonomous development for the peoples of Austria-Hungary; (11) restoration of Rumania, Serbia, and Montenegro, with access to the sea for Serbia; (12) autonomous development for the peoples of Turkey, with the straits from the Black Sea to the Mediterranean "permanently opened"; (13) an independent Poland, "inhabited by indisputably Polish populations," and with access to the sea; (14) establishment of a League of Nations. On several other occasions Wilson reiterated in public addresses that his program would be the basis of the peace for which he would work. Thousands of copies of the Fourteen Points were scattered by Allied planes over the German trenches and behind the lines, in an effort to convince both soldiers and civilians that the Entente nations were striving for a just and durable peace.

Domestic conflict in Germany

With Russia now no longer a combattant, Germany appeared to have gained an advantage that would almost guarantee ultimate victory. Yet by the late spring of 1918 the Germans were suffering acutely, not only because of the continued effectiveness of the Allied blockade, but because of a growing domestic conflict over war aims. German socialists attacked expansionist goals—control of the steel- and coal-producing areas of Belgium and of the agricultural regions in eastern

German Supplies Moving toward the Somme during the Last German Offensive in 1918

Europe—which conservatives continued to urge and which the government endorsed. Socialists were alarmed as well by the reactionary administration imposed upon the territories taken from Russia at Brest-Litovsk. By the fall of 1918, Germany was a country on the verge of civil war.

Meanwhile, fighting continued as it had for four years on the Western Front. A great offensive launched by the British, French, and United States forces in July dealt one shattering blow after another to the German battalions and forced them back almost to the Belgian frontier. By the end of September the cause of the Central Powers appeared hopeless. Bulgaria withdrew from the war on September 30. Early in October the new chancellor of Germany, the liberal Prince Max of Baden, appealed to President Wilson for a negotiated peace on the basis of the Fourteen Points. But the fighting went on, Wilson now demanding that Germany agree to depose the kaiser. Germany's remaining allies tottered on the verge of collapse. Turkey surrendered at the end of October. The Habsburg Empire was cracked open by rebellions on the part of the empire's subject nationalities. A German-Austrian offensive in Italy in October 1917 had gained them a major victory at Caporetto, where Italian military police were ordered to shoot their own soldiers, if necessary, to stem the retreat. Yet a year later, the Italians responded to a similar attack with a counteroffensive that cost Austria the city of Trieste and 300,000 prisoners. On November 3 Emperor Charles, who had succeeded Francis Joseph in 1916, signed an armistice which took Austria out of the war.

The collapse of the Central Powers

Germany was now left with the impossible task of carrying on the struggle alone. The morale of its troops was rapidly breaking. The blockade was causing such a shortage of food that there was real danger of starvation. Revolutionary tremors that had been felt for sometime swelled into an earthquake. On November 8 a republic was proclaimed in Bavaria. The next day nearly all of Germany was in the throes of revolution. A decree was published in Berlin announcing the

The signing of the armistice

kaiser's abdication, and early the next morning he was moved across the frontier into Holland. In the meantime, the government of the nation had passed into the hands of a provisional council headed by Friedrich Ebert, leader of the socialists in the Reichstag. Ebert and his colleagues immediately took steps to conclude negotiations for an armistice. The terms as now laid down by the Entente powers provided for acceptance of the Fourteen Points with three amendments. First, the item on freedom of the seas was to be stricken (in accordance with the request of the British). Second, restoration of invaded areas was to be interpreted in such a way as to include reparations, that is, payment to the victors to compensate them for their losses. Third, the demand for autonomy for the subject peoples of Austria-Hungary was to be changed to a demand for independence. In addition, troops of the Entente nations were to occupy cities in the Rhine valley; the blockade was to be continued in force; and Germany was to hand over 5,000 locomotives, 150,000 railway cars, and 5,000 trucks, all in good condition. The Germans could do nothing but accept these terms. At five o'clock in the morning of November 11, two delegates of the defeated nation met with the commander of the Entente armies, Marshal Foch, in the dark Compiègne forest and signed the papers officially ending the war. Six hours later the order "cease fire" was given to the troops. That night thousands of people danced through the streets of London, Paris, and Rome in the same delirium of excitement with which they had greeted the declarations of war four years before.

A harsh peace

The peace concluded at the various conferences in 1919 and 1920 more closely resembled a sentence from a court than a negotiated settlement. Propaganda had encouraged victorious soldiers and civilians to suppose that their sacrifices to the war effort would be compensated for by payments extracted from the "wicked" Germans. The British prime minister, David Lloyd George, campaigned during the election of 1918 on the slogan "Hang the Kaiser!", while one of his partisans demanded "Squeeze the German lemon until the pips squeak!" In all the Allied countries nationalism and democracy combined to make compromise impossible and to reassert the claim that the war was a crusade of good against evil. The peace settlement drafted by the victors inevitably reflected these feelings.

The Paris Conference

The conference convoked in Paris[1] to draft a peace with Germany was technically in session from January until June of 1919, but only six plenary meetings were held. All of the important business of the conference was transacted by small committees. At first a Council of Ten was made up of the president and secretary of state of the United States, and the premiers and foreign ministers of Great Britain, France, Italy, and Japan. By the middle of March this body had been found too unwieldy and was reduced to the Council of Four, consisting of

[1] The conference did most of its work in Paris. The treaty of peace with Germany, however, takes its name from Versailles, the suburb of Paris in which it was signed.

The Council of Four. Meeting to draft a peace treaty in Paris were Orlando of Italy, Lloyd George of Britain, Clemenceau of France, and Wilson of the United States.

the American president and the English, Italian, and French premiers. A month later the Council of Four became the Council of Three when Premier Vittorio Orlando withdrew from the conference in a huff because Wilson refused to give Italy all it demanded.

The final character of the Treaty of Versailles was determined almost entirely by the so-called Big Three—Wilson, Lloyd George, and Clemenceau. These men were as different in personality as any three rulers who have ever come together for a common purpose. Wilson was an inflexible idealist, accustomed to dictating to subordinates and convinced that the hosts of righteousness were on his side. When confronted with unpleasant realities, such as secret treaties among the Entente governments for division of the spoils, he had a habit of dismissing them as unimportant and eventually forgetting that he had ever heard of them. Though he knew little of the devious maneuvers of European diplomacy, his unbending temperament made it difficult for him to take advice or to adjust his views to those of his colleagues. Lloyd George, the canny Welshman, possessed cleverness and Celtic humor that enabled him to succeed, on occasions, where Wilson failed; but he was above all a politician—shifty, and not particularly sympathetic to particular European problems such as nationalism.

The Big Three: Wilson and Lloyd George

The third member of the great triumvirate was the aged and cynical French premier, Georges Clemenceau. Born in 1841, Clemenceau had been a journalist in the United States just after the Civil War. Later he had won his nickname of "the Tiger" as a relentless foe of clericals and monarchists. He had fought for the republic during the stormy days of the Boulangist episode, the Dreyfus affair, and the struggle for separation of church and state. Twice in his lifetime he had seen France invaded and its existence gravely imperiled. Now the tables were turned, and the French, he believed, should take full advantage of their

Clemenceau

Emasculating the Fourteen Points

opportunity. Only by keeping a strict control over a prostrate Germany could the security of France be preserved.

From the beginning a number of embarrassing problems confronted the chief architects of the Versailles treaty. The most important was what to do about the Fourteen Points. There could be no doubt that they had been the basis of the German surrender on November 11. It was beyond question also that Wilson had represented them as the Entente program for a permanent peace. Consequently there was every reason for the peoples of the world to expect that the Fourteen Points would be the model for the Versailles settlement—subject only to the three amendments made before the armistice was signed. In actuality, however, no one among the highest dignitaries at the conference, with the exception of Wilson himself, gave more than lip service to the Fourteen Points. In the end, the American president was able to salvage, in unmodified form, only four parts of his famous program: point seven, requiring the restoration of Belgium; point eight, demanding the return of Alsace and Lorraine to France; point ten, providing for independence for the peoples of Austria-Hungary; and the final provision calling for a League of Nations. The others were ignored or modified to such an extent as to change their original meanings.

Germany sentenced

By the end of April 1919 the terms of the Versailles treaty were ready for submission to the enemy, and Germany was ordered to send delegates to receive them. On April 29, a delegation headed by Count von Brockdorff-Rantzau, foreign minister of the provisional republic,

Crowds Greet President Wilson in Paris after the War. Despite public demonstrations of this sort, Wilson's attempt to shape the peace was a failure.

arrived in Versailles. When Brockdorff-Rantzau protested that the terms were too harsh, he was informed by Clemenceau that Germany would have three weeks to decide whether or not to sign. Eventually the time had to be extended, for the heads of the German government resigned their positions rather than accept the treaty. Their attitude was summed up by Chancellor Philip Scheidemann in the pointed statement: "What hand would not wither that sought to lay itself and us in those chains?" The Big Three now made a few minor adjustments, mainly at the insistence of Lloyd George, and Germany was notified that seven o'clock on the evening of June 23 must bring either acceptance or invasion. Shortly after five a new government of the provisional republic announced that it would yield to "overwhelming force" and accede to the victors' terms. On June 28, the fifth anniversary of the murder of the Austrian archduke, representatives of the German and Allied governments assembled in the Hall of Mirrors at Versailles and affixed their signatures to the treaty.

The provisions of the Treaty of Versailles can be outlined briefly. Germany was required to surrender Alsace and Lorraine to France, northern Schleswig to Denmark, and most of Posen and West Prussia to Poland. The coal mines of the Saar Basin were to be ceded to France, to be exploited by the French for fifteen years. At the end of this time the German government would be permitted to buy them back. The Saar territory itself was to be administered by the League of Nations until 1935, when a plebiscite would be held to determine whether it should remain under the league, be returned to Germany, or be awarded to France. Germany's province of East Prussia was cut off from the rest of its territory, and the port of Danzig, almost wholly German, was subjected to the political control of the League of Nations and the the economic domination of Poland. Germany was disarmed, surrendering all its submarines and navy of surface vessels, with the exception of six small battleships, six light cruisers, six destroyers, and twelve torpedo boats. The Germans were forbidden to possess an air force, and their army was limited to 100,000 officers and men, to be recruited by voluntary enlistment. To make sure that Germany would not launch any new attack upon France or Belgium, it was forbidden to keep soldiers or maintain fortifications in the Rhine valley. Last, Germany and its allies were held responsible for all the loss and damage suffered by the Entente governments and their citizens, "as a consequence of the war imposed upon them by the aggression of Germany and her allies." This was the so-called war-guilt provision of the treaty (Article 231), and also the basis for German reparations. The exact amount that Germany should pay was left to a Reparations Commission. In 1921 the total was set at $33 billion.

The main provisions of the Treaty of Versailles

For the most part, the Treaty of Versailles applied only to Germany. Separate pacts were drawn up to settle accounts with Germany's allies—Austria-Hungary, Bulgaria, and Turkey. The final form of these treaties was determined primarily by a Council of Five,

The goal of self-determination

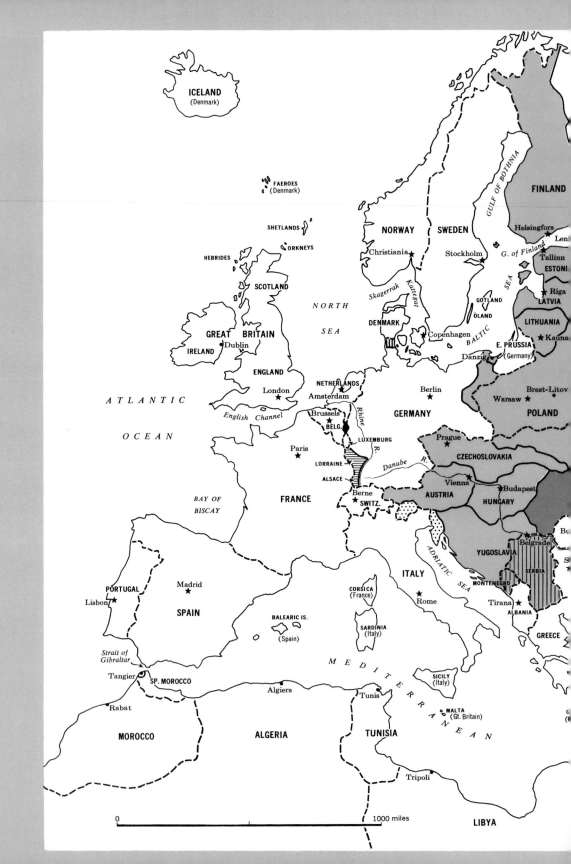

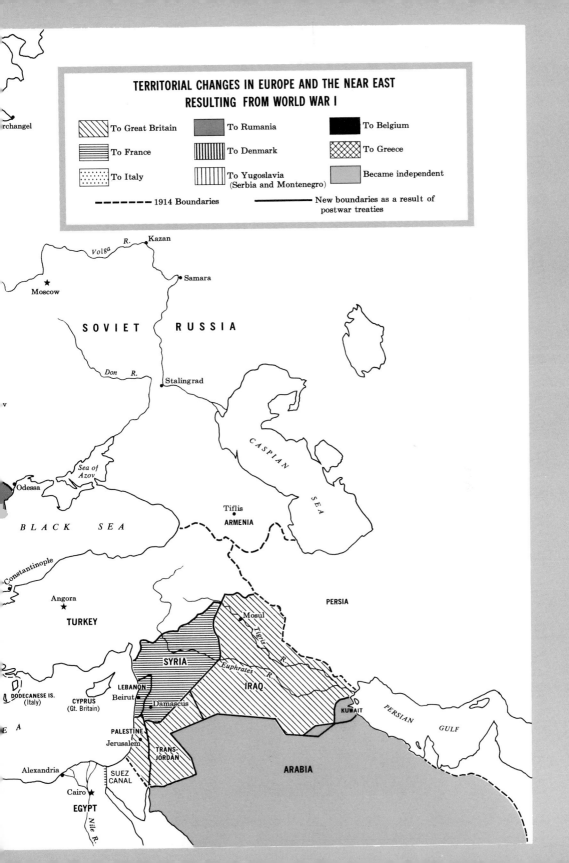

TERRITORIAL CHANGES IN EUROPE AND THE NEAR EAST
RESULTING FROM WORLD WAR I

To Great Britain

To France

To Italy

To Rumania

To Denmark

To Yugoslavia
(Serbia and Montenegro)

To Belgium

To Greece

Became independent

- - - - - 1914 Boundaries

——— New boundaries as a result of
postwar treaties

rchangel

Kazan

Volga R.

Samara

★ Moscow

S O V I E T   R U S S I A

Don R.

Stalingrad

*Sea of
Azov*

Odessa

C A S P I A N   S E A

B L A C K   S E A

Tiflis
ARMENIA

Constantinople

Angora
★

PERSIA

TURKEY

Mosul

Tigris R.

SYRIA

Euphrates R.

DODECANESE IS.
(Italy)

LEBANON

IRAQ

CYPRUS
(Gt. Britain)

Beirut

Damascus

KUWAIT

PERSIAN   GULF

E A

PALESTINE

Jerusalem

TRANS-
JORDAN

ARABIA

Alexandria

SUEZ
CANAL

Cairo ★

EGYPT

Nile R.

composed of Clemenceau as chairman and one delegate each from the United States, Great Britain, France, and Italy. The treaties reflected a desire on the part of their drafters to recognize the principle of national self-determination. The experience of the prewar years convinced diplomats that they must draw national boundaries to conform as closely as possible to the ethnic, linguistic, and historical traditions of the people they were to contain. Yet practical, political difficulties made such divisions impossible.

*The treaty with Austria:
the compromising of
national self-determination*

The settlement with Austria, completed in September 1919, was known as the Treaty of St. Germain. Austria was required to recognize the independence of Hungary, Czechoslovakia, Yugoslavia, and Poland, and to cede to them large portions of its territory. In addition, Austria had to surrender Trieste, the south Tyrol, and the Istrian peninsula to Italy. Altogether the Austrian portion of the Dual Monarchy was deprived of three-fourths of its area and three-fourths of its people. Contrary to the principles of self-determination, in several of the territories surrendered the inhabitants were largely German-speaking—for example, in the Tyrol, and the region of the Sudeten mountains awarded to Czechoslovakia. The Austrian nation itself was reduced to a small, land-locked state, with nearly one-third of its population concentrated in the city of Vienna.

*The treaties with
Bulgaria and Hungary*

The second of the treaties with lesser belligerents was that with Bulgaria, which was signed in November 1919 and called the Treaty of Neuilly. Bulgaria was forced to give up nearly all of the territory it had gained since the First Balkan War. Land was ceded to Rumania, to the new kingdom of Yugoslavia, and to Greece. Here again, self-determination was compromised. All of these regions were inhabited by large Bulgarian minorities. Since Hungary was now an independent state, it was necessary that a separate treaty be imposed upon it. This was the Treaty of the Trianon Palace, signed in June 1920. It required that Slovakia be ceded to Czechoslovakia, Transylvania to Rumania, and Croatia-Slovenia to Yugoslavia. Nowhere was the principle of self-determination of peoples more flagrantly violated. Numerous sections of Transylvania had populations that were more than half Hungarian. Included in the region of Slovakia were not only Slovaks but almost a million Magyars and about 500,000 Ruthenians. As a consequence, a fanatical irredentist movement flourished in Hungary after the war, directed toward the recovery of these lost provinces. The Treaty of the Trianon Palace slashed the area of Hungary from 125,000 square miles to 35,000, and its population from 22 million to 8 million.

*The Treaties of Sèvres
and Lausanne with
Turkey*

The settlement with Turkey was a product of unusual circumstances. The secret treaties had contemplated the transfer of Constantinople and Armenia to Russia and the division of most of the remainder of Turkey between Britain and France. But Russia's withdrawal from the war after the Bolshevik Revolution, together with insistence by Italy and Greece upon fulfillment of promises made to them, necessitated considerable revision of the original scheme. Finally, in August 1920, a treaty was signed at Sèvres, near Paris, and submitted to the government of the sultan. It provided that Armenia be organized as a Christian republic; that most of Turkey in Europe be given to Greece; that Palestine and Mesopotamia become British "mandates," i.e., to remain under League of Nations control but to be administered by Britain; that Syria become a mandate of France; and that southern Anatolia be set apart as a sphere of influence for Italy. About all that would be left of the Ottoman Empire would be the city of Constantinople and the northern and central portions of Asia Minor. The decrepit government of the sultan, overawed by Allied military forces, agreed to accept this treaty. But a revolutionary government of Turkish nationalists, which had been organized at Ankara under the leadership of Mustapha Kemal (later called Atatürk), determined to prevent acceptance of the settlement of Sèvres. The forces of Kemal obliterated the republic of Armenia, frightened the Italians into withdrawing from Anatolia, and conquered most of the territory in Europe which had been given to Greece. At last, in November 1922, they occupied Constantinople, deposed the sultan, and proclaimed Turkey a republic. The Allies now consented to a revision of the peace. A new treaty was concluded at Lausanne in Switzerland in 1923, which permitted the Turks to retain practically all of the territory they had conquered. Though much reduced in size compared with the old Ottoman Empire, the Turkish republic still had an area of about 300,000 square miles and a population of 13 million.

Kemal Atatürk

Incorporated in each of the five treaties which liquidated the war with the Central Powers was the Covenant of the League of Nations. The establishment of a league in which the states of the world, both great and small, would cooperate for the preservation of peace had long been the cherished dream of President Wilson. Indeed, that had been one of his chief reasons for taking the United States into the war. He believed that the defeat of Germany would mean the deathblow of militarism, and that the road would thenceforth be clear for setting up the control of international relations by a community of nations instead of by the cumbersome and ineffective balance of power. But to get the league accepted he found himself compelled to make numerous compromises. He permitted his original idea of providing for a reduction of armaments "to the lowest point consistent with domestic safety" to be changed into the altogether different phrasing of "consistent with national safety." To induce the Japanese to accept the league he allowed them to keep former German concessions in China. To please the French, he sanctioned the exclusion of both Germany and Russia from his proposed federation, despite his long insistence that it should be a league of *all* nations. These handicaps were serious enough. But the league received an even more deadly blow when it was repudiated by the very nation whose president had proposed it.

Established under such unfavorable auspices, the league never

The League of Nations

League of Nations Buildings, Geneva, Switzerland

achieved the aims of its founder. In only a few cases did it succeed in allaying the threat of war, and in each of these the parties to the dispute were small nations. But in every dispute involving one or more major powers, the league failed. It did nothing about the seizure of Vilna by Poland in 1920, because Lithuania, the victimized nation, was friendless, while Poland had the powerful backing of France. When, in 1923, war threatened between Italy and Greece, the Italians refused to submit to the intervention of the league, and the dispute was settled by direct mediation of Great Britain and France. Thereafter, in every great crisis the league was either defied or ignored. Its authority was flouted by Japan in seizing Manchuria in 1931 and by Italy in conquering Ethiopia in 1936. By September 1938, when the Czechoslovakian crisis arose, the prestige of the league had sunk so low that scarcely anyone thought of appealing to it. Yet the league justified its existence in other, less spectacular, ways. It reduced the international opium traffic and aided poor and backward countries in controlling the spread of disease. Its agencies collected invaluable statistics on labor and business conditions throughout the world. It conducted plebiscites in disputed areas, supervised the administration of internationalized cities, helped find homes for racial and political refugees, and made a notable beginning in codifying international law. Such achievements may well be regarded as providing a substantial groundwork for a later effort at international organization, the United Nations, formed after the Second World War.

Successes and failures of the league

The league, with all its failings, was seen as the one promising result of the war that many soon recognized as a hideously wasteful carnage. The price would have been enormous even if all the results which were supposed to flow from an Entente victory had really been achieved. Altogether 8.5 million men died and more than twice that number

A war of waste

were wounded. The total casualties—killed, wounded, and missing—numbered over 37 million. Germany lost 6 million and France almost as many, a larger proportion, indeed, of its total population. But despite these appalling losses, almost nothing was gained. The war which was to "end all wars" sowed the seeds of a new and more terrible conflict in the future. The autocracy of the kaiser was destroyed, but the ground was prepared for new despotisms. The First World War did nothing to abate either militarism or nationalism. Twenty years after the fighting had ended, there were nearly twice as many men under arms as in 1913; and national and ethnic rivalries and hatreds were as deeply ingrained as ever.

If the war failed to make the world less of an armed camp, it nevertheless altered it drastically in other ways. In the first place, it strengthened a belief in the efficacy of central planning and coordination. To sustain the war effort, the governments of all the major belligerents were forced to manage their economies by regulating industrial output, exercising a close control over imports and exports, and making the most effective use of manpower—both civilian and military. Second, the war upset the world trade balance. With few manufactured goods coming from Europe, Japanese, Indian, and South American capitalists were free to develop industries in their own countries. When the war was over, Europe found it had lost many of its previously guaranteed markets, and that it had become a debtor to the United States which, throughout the war, had lent large sums to the Allies. Third, while war was altering the patterns of world trade, it was also producing worldwide inflation. To finance their fighting,

Changes brought by the war

Women at Work. The all-out war effort combined with a manpower shortage at home brought women into factories across Europe in unparalleled numbers. On the left, men and women work side-by-side in a British shell factory. At the right, women toil in a German gun factory.

governments resorted to policies of deficit financing (spending above their income) and increased paper money which, with the shortage of goods, inflated their price. Inflation hit hardest at the middle class, those men and women who had lived on their income from invested money, and now saw that money worth far less than it once had been. Fourth, the war, while it brought hardships to most, brought freedom to many. Women were emancipated by their governments' need for them in factories and on farms. The contribution of women to the war effort undoubtedly explains the granting of female suffrage in both Great Britain and the United States in 1918 and 1920. Finally, despite this legacy of liberation, the war's most permanent contribution to the spirit of the postwar years was disillusion—particularly within the middle classes. A generation of men had been sacrificed—"lost"—to no apparent end. Many of those left alive were sickened by the useless slaughter, to which they knew they had contributed and for which they believed they must share at least part of the guilt. They were disgusted by the greedy abandonment of principles by the politicians at Versailles. Hatred and mistrust of the "old men" who had dragged the world into an unnecessary conflict, who had then mismanaged its direction with such ghastly results, and who had betrayed the cause of international peace for national gain soured the minds of many younger men and women in the postwar period. The British poet Edmund Blunden expressed this profound disillusionment when he took as the title for a poem, written to celebrate New Year's Day 1921, the biblical verse: "The dog is turned to his own vomit again, and the sow that was washed to her wallowing in the mire."

SELECTED READINGS

• *Items so designated are available in paperback editions.*

THE WORLD WAR AND THE PEACE SETTLEMENT

Albertini, Luigi, *The Origins of the War of 1914,* 3 vols., New York, 1952–1957. An exhaustive, valuable study.
• Falls, Cyril, *The Great War,* New York, 1961. A military history.
Feldman, Gerald D., *Army, Industry, and Labor in Germany, 1914–1918,* Princeton, N.J., 1966. The effect of war on the domestic economy.
Ferro, Marc, *The Great War, 1914–1918,* London, 1973. Social and economic developments receive particular treatment.
Fischer, Fritz, *War of Illusions,* New York, 1975. Deals with Germany within the context of internal social and economic trends. See also his *Germany's Aims in the First World War,* mentioned in the preceding chapter.
• Fussell, Paul, *The Great War and Modern Memory,* New York, 1975. A brilliant examination of British intellectuals' attitudes toward the war.

Hardach, Gerd, *The First World War, 1914–1918,* Berkeley, Calif., 1977. An excellent economic history of the war.

Horne, Alastair, *The Price of Glory: Verdun, 1916,* New York, 1963.

• Lafore, Laurence D., *The Long Fuse: An Interpretation of the Origins of World War I,* Philadelphia, 1971. Argues that the war was the result of obsolete institutions and ideas.

Laqueur, Walter, and G. L. Mosse, eds., *1914: The Coming of the First World War,* New York, 1969. An excellent series of essays by modern scholars.

Mayer, Arno, *Politics and Diplomacy of Peacemaking: Containment and Counterrevolution at Versailles, 1918–1919,* New York, 1967. Emphasizes the role of the Russian Revolution in the peacemaking process.

Moorehead, Alan, *Gallipoli,* London, 1956. A study of the British campaign.

Nicolson, Harold, *Peacemaking, 1919,* Boston, 1933. Written by a participant, provides a good account of the atmosphere of Versailles.

• Steiner, Zara S., *Britain and the Origins of the First World War,* New York, 1977. Argues that external rather than internal strains brought Britain into the war.

• Taylor, A. J. P., *English History, 1914–1945,* New York, 1965. An excellent treatment of the war and its impact on British society.

• Turner, L. C. F., *Origins of the First World War,* New York, 1970. Stresses Russia's role in the prewar diplomatic situation.

• Tuchman, Barbara, *The Guns of August,* New York, 1962. A popular account of the outbreak of war.

• Wheeler-Bennett, J. W., *The Forgotten Peace: Brest-Litovsk, March 1918,* London, 1939. An excellent study of personalities involved in the Russo-German peace treaty.

Williams, John, *The Home Fronts: Britain, France and Germany, 1914–1918,* London, 1972. A survey of life away from the battlefield and the impact of the war on domestic life.

Wohl, Robert, *The Generation of 1914,* Cambridge, Mass., 1979. Uses generational analysis to explain attitudes toward the war.

Zeeman, Z. A. B., *The Break-up of the Hapsburg Empire, 1914–1918,* New York, 1961.

THE RUSSIAN REVOLUTION

• Deutscher, Isaac, *The Prophet Armed,* New York, 1954. The first volume of a magnificent biography of Trotsky; covers the years 1879–1921.

Fischer, Louis, *The Life of Lenin,* New York, 1964. A lengthy, somewhat popularized biography by a journalist who was present during the revolution.

Keep, John L. H., *The Russian Revolution,* New York, 1977.

• Pares, Bernard, *A History of Russia,* rev. ed., New York, 1953. A useful, straightforward survey.

• Rabinowitch, Alexander, *The Bolsheviks Come to Power,* New York, 1976. A well-researched and carefully documented account.

• Wolfe, Bertram D., *Three Who Made a Revolution,* rev. ed., New York, 1964. A study of Lenin, Trotsky, and Stalin.

SOURCE MATERIALS

Carnegie Foundation, Endowment for International Peace, *The Treaties of Peace, 1919–1923,* 2 vols., New York, 1924.

Gooch, G. P., and H. Temperley, eds., *British Documents on the Origins of the War, 1898–1914,* London, 1927.

Keynes, John Maynard, *The Economic Consequences of the Peace,* London, 1919. A contemporary attack upon the peace settlement, particularly the reparations agreements, by the brilliant economist who served on the British delegation to the peace conference.

Owen, Wilfred, *Collected Poems,* London, 1963. Moving evidence of the horror of life at the front by Britain's most talented war poet.

• Reed, John, *Ten Days That Shook the World,* New York, 1919. (Many editions.) A contemporary account by a sympathetic American journalist of the Bolshevik revolution.

• Remarque, Erich Maria, *All Quiet on the Western Front,* 1929. (Many editions.) A famous novel describing the war on the Western Front.

Chapter 29

THE WEST BETWEEN THE WARS

Democracy of the West today is the forerunner of Marxism, which would
be inconceivable without it. It is democracy alone which furnishes this
universal plague with the soil in which it spreads. In parliamentarianism,
its outward form of expression, democracy created a monstrosity of filth
and fire. . . .

—Adolf Hitler, *Mein Kampf*

Among the claims made by the Allied Powers during the First
World War was that an Allied victory would make the world
"safe for democracy." The boast was grounded in a belief in
the inevitability of progress, fostered by a century of growing material
prosperity and by a habit of mind that found it all but impossible to
equate the events of history with something other than the "advance"
of civilization. The history of Europe in the 1920s and 1930s, however, would make it increasingly difficult for men and women to
believe in progress as they had, or to assume that war might prove of
ultimate benefit to mankind. These were decades of disillusionment
and desperation, a circumstance brought about not only by the war
itself but by the events which followed in the wake of war. Rather
than encourage the growth of democracy, those events were often the
direct cause of its decline and fall. A number of Western nations
remained democracies—Great Britain, France, and the United States
being the most notable cases—yet they nevertheless experienced the
same pressures and strains which in other countries resulted in the
demise of democracy altogether.

Decline of democracy

Although the reasons for the decline of democracy in the West varied according to particular national circumstances, its failure can be
attributed to several major causes. First, class conflict increased in many
countries during the interwar years. The real issue in most parts of
continental Europe was whether control of the government and economic system would continue in the possession of aristocracies,
industrialists, and financiers, or some combination of these elements.

Reasons for the decline

None of them were willing to surrender more than a fraction of their considerable power to the less privileged majorities which, at great sacrifice, had made major contributions to the war effort. The common people expected and had been promised that those contributions would be rewarded by greater attention to their political rights and economic needs. When they were ignored, they were naturally embittered, and hence prey to the blandishments of political extremists. Second, economic conditions worked against the establishment of stable democracies. The creation of new nations encouraged debilitating economic rivalries. War had disoriented the world's economy, leaving in its wake first inflation and then depression. Finally, nationalist sentiment encouraged discontent among minorities in the newly established states of central Europe. Countries weakened by conflicts between national minorities were an unlikely proving ground for democracy, a political system which functions best in an atmosphere of unified national purpose.

Rise of totalitarianism

The political history of the interwar years must be understood not only in terms of the decline of democracy, however, but also against the background of the rise of the totalitarian state. Totalitarianism, whatever it promised, preached the destruction of the political systems that had failed to grapple successfully with the problems of class conflict, economic chaos, and nationalism. Although there were significant differences between the communism of the Soviet Union under Joseph Stalin, the fascism of Italy under Benito Mussolini, and the National Socialism—or, as it was called, Nazism—of Germany under Adolf Hitler, all three systems can be defined as totalitarian.

Totalitarianism defined

These systems demanded the total subordination of individuals and classes to the greater good of the state as defined and directed by an all-powerful single political party. To this end, violent force, intimidation, and propaganda were employed to divert men and women from the pursuit of their individual interests, to deny them their freedom as citizens, and to compel them to labor on behalf of goals defined as useful to the nation. Churches, trade unions, even parliamentary government were either subverted or suppressed completely. The state, through the party, imposed its will on the total life of society.

Its ideology and appeal

Totalitarian governments framed their programs in ideology. In the case of Soviet Russia, the ideology was a nationalistic version of Marxist socialism. In the case of Italy and Germany, it was a peculiar concoction of nineteenth-century nationalism and socialism. These ideologies proclaimed the necessity of revolutionary change and encouraged belief in the ability of the party and its leader to effect that change. They thus appealed to those who saw themselves dispossessed by the system as it was, or as it had become, and who believed that nothing but desperate measures would suffice to bring society to rights. During the interwar years the ranks of those people in Europe were legion.

I. THE RISE OF TOTALITARIANISM IN COMMUNIST RUSSIA

Soon after the 1917 revolution in Russia, the country's desperate plight—a result of wartime devastation and governmental corruption and mismanagement—compelled the Bolshevik leaders to undertake a drastic program of authoritarian centralization. During this transformation, Lenin showed himself as capable a revolutionary administrator and politician as he had been a strategist. He commanded the respect and loyalty of his fellow Bolshevik ministers. His dedication to his own theory of revolution and his readiness to apply that theory with a ruthless disregard for human lives, if necessary, was combined with a willingness to heed the opinions of his close adherents. He welcomed free discussion during the decision-making process. Once a decision had been reached, however, discussion gave way to unquestioning implementation. Lenin won the confidence of the Russian people by speaking frankly to them of the dangers and difficulties inherent in a revolution as bold and all-consuming as theirs was. He was what he appeared to be: a selfless man, unwilling to claim special privileges for himself, wholly dedicated to the revolution which he had done so much to bring about. He cared nothing for luxury or personal glory, living an almost monklike existence in two rooms in the Kremlin, and dressing little better than an ordinary worker.

Lenin

Lenin's ablest and most prominent lieutenant was Leon Trotsky (1879–1940). Originally named Lev Bronstein, Trotsky was born of middle-class Jewish parents in the Ukraine. Before the revolution he had refused to identify himself with any particular faction, preferring to remain an independent Marxist. For his part in the revolutionary movement of 1905 he was exiled to Siberia; he escaped, and for some years led a roving existence in various European capitals. He was expelled from Paris in 1916 for pacifist activity and took refuge in the

Trotsky

Lenin Speaking to Crowds in Moscow. To the right of the platform, in uniform, is Trotsky.

The civil war

United States. Upon learning of the overthrow of the tsar, he attempted to return to Russia. Captured by British agents at Halifax, Nova Scotia, he was eventually released through the intervention of Kerensky. He arrived in Russia in April 1917 and immediately began plotting the overthrow of the provisional government and later of Kerensky himself. He became minister of foreign affairs in the government headed by Lenin, and later, commissar for war.

Scarcely had the Bolsheviks concluded the war with the Central Powers than they were confronted with a desperate civil war at home. Landlords and capitalists did not take kindly to the loss of their property. The result was a prolonged and bloody combat between the Reds, or Bolsheviks, and the Whites, including not only reactionary tsarists but also disaffected liberals, Social Revolutionaries, Mensheviks, and peasants. The Whites were assisted for a time by expeditionary forces of British, French, American, and Japanese troops—hoping to defeat the Bolsheviks in order to bring Russia back into the war against Germany—and later by the armies of the newly created republic of Poland. Under the direction of Trotsky, who appealed to the Russian people both in the name of revolution and the fatherland, the Red army was mobilized to a degree that allowed it to withstand both the foreign invaders and the Russian insurgents. By 1922, the Bolsheviks had managed to stabilize their boundaries, although to do so they were forced to cede former Russian territory to the Finns, to the Baltic states of Latvia and Estonia, to Poland, and to Rumania. Internally, the Bolsheviks responded to the White counter-revolution by instituting a "Terror" far more extensive than the repression that had earned that name during the French Revolution. A secret police force shot thousands as suspects or merely as hostages. The tsar and tsarina and their children were executed by local Bolsheviks in July 1918 as White forces advanced on the town of Ekaterinburg, where the family was held prisoner. That same year "enemies of the state" were hunted down in large numbers following the attempted assassination of Lenin.

See color map
following page 960

The Red Army, 1919. This scene near the southern front was the celebration of the victory over the counterrevolutionary forces.

The Terror abated when the regime had satisfied itself that it had destroyed its internal opposition.

The civil war was accompanied by an appalling economic breakdown. In 1920 total industrial production was only 13 percent of what it had been in 1913. To make up for the shortage of goods, the government abolished the payment of wages and distributed supplies among the workers in the cities in proportion to their need. All private trade was prohibited, and everything produced by the peasants above what they required to subsist was requisitioned by the state. This system was an expedient to crush the bourgeoisie and to obtain as much food as possible for the army in the field. It was soon abandoned after the war had ended. In 1921 it was superseded by the New Economic Policy (NEP), which Lenin described as "one step backward in order to take two steps forward." The NEP authorized private manufacturing and private trade on a small scale, reintroduced the payment of wages, and permitted peasants to sell their grain in the open market. In 1924 a constitution was adopted, replacing imperial Russia with the Union of Soviet Socialist Republics. The union represented an attempt to unite the various nationalities and territories that had constituted the old empire. Each separate republic was, in theory, granted certain autonomous rights. In fact, government remained centralized in the hands of a few leaders. Further, central authority was maintained by means of the one legal political party—the Communist party—whose Central Committee was the directing force behind both politics and government, and whose organizational apparatus reached out into all areas of the vast country.

Economic and constitutional changes

The philosophy of Bolshevism, now known as communism, was developed primarily by Lenin during these years. It was proclaimed not as a new body of thought, but as a strict interpretation of Marx's writings. Nevertheless, from the beginning it departed at several important points from Marx's teachings. These changes were the necessary result of the fact that Marx had expected revolution to occur first in highly industrialized countries, whereas it had in fact broken out and succeeded in one of the least industrialized nations in Europe. Marx had assumed that a capitalist stage must prepare the way for socialism; Lenin denied that this was necessary, insisting rather that Russia could leap directly from a feudal to a socialist economy. In the second place, Lenin emphasized the revolutionary character of socialism much more than did its original founder. Marx did believe that in most cases revolution would be necessary, but he was inclined to deplore the fact rather than to welcome it. Finally, communism differed from Marxism in its conception of proletarian rule. When Marx spoke of the "dictatorship of the proletariat," he meant by this a dictatorship of the whole working class over the remnants of the bourgeoisie. Within the ranks of this class, democratic forms would prevail. Lenin, however, proclaimed the necessity of the dictatorship of an elite, a select minority, wielding supremacy not only over the bour-

The tenets of communism

Left: *Lenin's Casket Is Carried through the Streets of Moscow*. It was not known with certainty until 1956 that, prior to his death, Lenin had discredited Stalin. Right: *Lenin and Stalin*. Under Stalin this picture was used to show his close relationship with Lenin. In fact, the photograph has been doctored.

geoisie but over the bulk of the proletarians themselves. In Russia this elite was the Communist party.

The death of Lenin in January 1924 precipitated a struggle between two of his lieutenants to inherit his mantle of power. Outside of Russia it was generally assumed that Trotsky would succeed the fallen leader. But the fiery commander of the Red army had a formidable rival in the tough and mysterious Joseph Stalin (1879–1953). The son of a peasant shoemaker in the province of Georgia, Stalin received part of his education in a theological seminary. Expelled at the age of seventeen for "lack of religious vocation," he thereafter dedicated his career to revolutionary activity.

The struggles between Trotsky and Stalin

In 1917 Stalin assumed the secretary-generalship of the Communist party which, in the years that followed, became the heart of the government. Theoretically, Soviet Russia was ruled by a Central Executive Committee, which in turn represented local, provincial, and regional Councils of Workers and Peasants. Because the Central Executive did not remain in continuous session, however, power increasingly fell into the hands of that body responsible for day-to-day operations and decisions: the Council of the People's Commissars—that is, the various departmental ministers. These commissars were nominated by, and were themselves members of, the Communist party. In his position as the party's secretary-general, Stalin was able to control nominations to the Council of Commissars, and thus to fill the government with party members loyal to him. When the commissars picked Lenin's successor, they perceived Trotsky as brilliant but erratic; Stalin as predictable and safe.

Stalin and the party

The battle beween Stalin and Trotsky was not simply a struggle for personal power; fundamental issues of political policy were also involved. Trotsky maintained that socialism in Russia could never be entirely successful until capitalism was overthrown in surrounding countries. Therefore, he insisted upon a continuous crusade for world revolution. Stalin was willing to abandon the program of world revolution, for the time being, in order to concentrate on building socialism in Russia itself. His strategy for the immediate future was essentially nationalist. The outcome of the duel was a complete triumph for Stalin. In 1927 Trotsky was expelled from the Communist party, and two years later he was driven from the country. In 1940 he was murdered in Mexico City by Stalinist agents. Lenin did not hold either Stalin or Trotsky in lofty esteem. In a "testament" to the Council written shortly before his death, he criticized Trotsky for "far-reaching self-confidence" and for being too preoccupied with administrative detail. But he dealt far less gently with Stalin, condemning him as "too rough" and "capricious" and urging that the commissars remove him from his position at the head of the party.

Once Stalin consolidated his position, he reinforced the role of the party as a state within a state, with its own bureaucrats—the *apparatchiki*—assuming ever-increasing influence in the administration of the country and in the determination of its fortunes. He insisted that Russia's first priority was economic well-being. His major reform was the introduction of the so-called Five-Year Plan, based on the conviction that the Soviet Union had to take drastic steps to industrialize and thereby achieve economic parity among the nations of the world. The plan instituted an elaborate system of national priorities. It decreed how much of each major industrial and agricultural commodity the nation should produce, the wages workers should receive, and the prices that should be charged for goods sold at home and abroad. The first plan, instituted in 1928, was succeeded by others during the 1930s. In some areas goals were met, in a few they were exceeded, in some they fell short. One of the major results of the Five-Year Plans was the creation of an extensive state bureaucracy, charged with the task of organization and supervision at all levels.

Included in the first plan was a program for agricultural collectivization. The scheme was designed to bring rural farms together into larger units of several thousand acres, under the communal proprietorship of peasants. Only with this sort of reorganization, Russia's rulers declared, could the new and expensive processes of mechanization be introduced, and the country's agricultural yield thereby increased. Not surprisingly, the argument failed to win the support of the more prosperous farmers—the kulaks—who had been allowed to retain ownership of their land. Their opposition led to another Terror, made all the more deadly by a famine which occurred in southeastern Russia in 1932. The kulaks were liquidated, either killed or transported to

"The Five-Year Plan in Four Years." Stalin faces down reactionary capitalist enemies in this Soviet propaganda poster of the 1930s.

distant labor camps: the rural bourgeoisie was eliminated, to be replaced by a rural proletariat. Collectivization was an accomplished fact by 1939. It represented to a vast number of Russians a revolution far more immediate than that of 1917. Twenty million people were moved off the land, which, once it had been reorganized into larger units, and production mechanized, required fewer laborers. They were sent to cities, where most went to work in factories. Although· agricultural output did not increase during the early years of collectivization, the scheme was nevertheless of benefit to the government. By controlling production, the central bureaucracy was able to regulate the distribution of agricultural products, allocating them for export, where necessary, to pay for the importation of much-needed industrial machinery.

The Third International

As part of Stalin's campaign to put the interests of Russia ahead of those of international communism, the Bolshevik regime adopted a new and more conservative foreign policy during the 1930s. Its international goals contradicted the militant socialist internationalism of the 1920s. Lenin had supported revolutionary leftist movements in Europe, sending money and lending moral support to the radical German Marxists Karl Liebknecht and Rosa Luxemburg in 1919, and to the short-lived Soviet regime of the Bolshevik Béla Kun in Hungary in the same year. Shortly thereafter, the Third International—later called the Comintern—was formed. It declared its allegiance to international communism; its policy was to oppose cooperation or collaboration with the capitalist governments of the West and to work for their overthrow.

With Stalin's suppression of the internationalism advocated by Lenin and Trotsky, however, came a change in tactics and the revival of an interest in playing the game of power politics. The Russian army

Panel (3), Wassily Kandinsky (1866–1944). The Expressionist painters carried their explorations of the psychological properties of color and line to the point where subject matter was deemed unnecessary and even undesirable. (Museum of Modern Art)

Nude Descending a Staircase, Marcel Duchamp (1887–1968). An example of the impact of film on painting. The effect is that of a series of closely spaced photographs coalescing to create motion. (Philadelphia Museum of Art)

The Table, Georges Braque (1881–1963). An example of later Cubism showing the predominance of curvilinear form and line instead of geometric structure. (Museum of Modern Art)

I and the Village, Marc Chagall (1889–). The subject refers to the artist's childhood and youth in Vitebsk, Russia. The profile on the right is probably that of the artist himself. (Museum of Modern Art)

The Persistence of Memory, Salvador Dali (1904–). The Spaniard Dali is the outstanding representative of the Surrealist school. Many objects in his paintings are Freudian images. (Museum of Modern Art)

Barricade, José Clemente Orozco (1883–1949). The
Mexican muralist Orozco was one of the most celebrated of contemporary painters with a social message. His themes were revolutionary fervor, satire of
aristocracy and the Church, and deification of the
common man. (Museum of Modern Art)

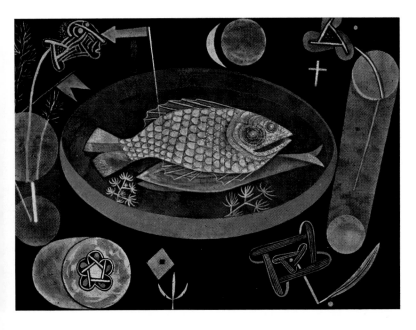

Around the Fish, Paul Klee
(1879–1940). Klee is recognized as the most subtle
humorist of twentieth-century
art. The central motif of a fish
on a platter suggests a banquet,
but many of the surrounding
objects sppear to be products of
fantasy. (Museum of Modern
Art

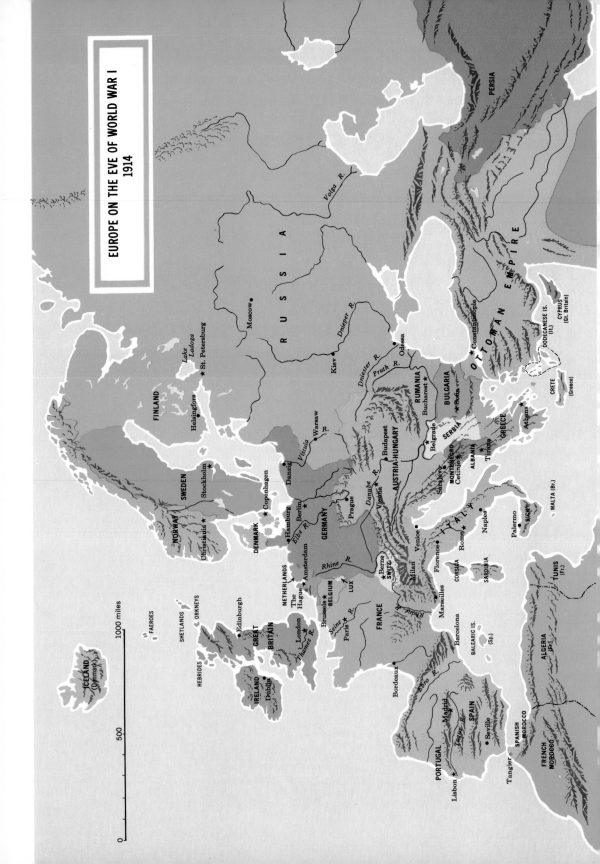

EUROPE ON THE EVE OF WORLD WAR I
1914

0   500   1000 miles

ICELAND
(Denmark)

FAEROES

SHETLANDS

ORKNEYS

HEBRIDES

IRELAND
Dublin

GREAT
BRITAIN
Edinburgh
London
Thames R.

NETHERLANDS
The Hague
Brussels
BELGIUM
LUX.

FRANCE
Seine R.
Paris

Bordeaux

Rhône R.
Marseilles

SPAIN
Madrid
Tagus R.
Seville
Barcelona
BALEARIC IS.
(Sp.)
Ebro R.

PORTUGAL
Lisbon

Tangier

SPANISH
MOROCCO

FRENCH
MOROCCO

ALGERIA
(Fr.)

TUNIS
(Fr.)

NORWAY
Christiania

SWEDEN
Stockholm

DENMARK
Copenhagen

Hamburg
Elbe R.
Berlin

GERMANY
Prague
Rhine R.
Amsterdam

Danzig
Vistula

SWITZ.
Berne
Milan
Venice

ITALY
Florence
CORSICA
Rome
Naples
SARDINIA
Palermo
SICILY

MALTA (Br.)

FINLAND
Helsingfors

Lake
Ladoga
St. Petersburg

R U S S I A
Moscow

Volga R.

Dnieper R.
Kiev

Warsaw
R.

AUSTRIA-HUNGARY
Vienna
Budapest
Danube R.

Dniester R.
Pruth R.
Odessa

RUMANIA
Bucharest

Belgrade
SERBIA
BULGARIA
Sofia

MONTENEGRO
Cetinje
Sarajevo
ALBANIA
Tirana

GREECE
Athens

Constantinople

O T T O M A N   E M P I R E

DODECANESE IS.
(It.)

CYPRUS
(Gt. Britain)

CRETE
(Greece)

PERSIA

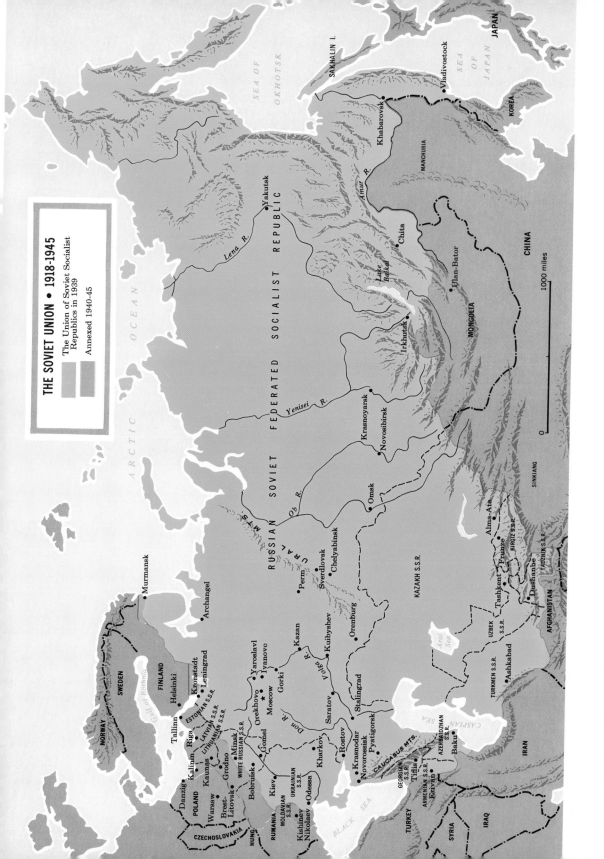

THE SOVIET UNION • 1918-1945

The Union of Soviet Socialist
Republics in 1939

Annexed 1940-45

0   1000 miles

JAPAN

SEA OF OKHOTSK

SAKHALIN I.

SEA OF JAPAN

Vladivostock

KOREA

Khabarovsk

MANCHURIA

Amur R.

Chita

Ulan-Bator

MONGOLIA

CHINA

SINKIANG

Yakutsk

Lena R.

Lake Baikal

Irkutsk

Krasnoyarsk

Novosibirsk

Omsk

KAZAKH S.S.R.

Alma-Ata

Frunze

KIRGIZ S.S.R.

TADZHIK S.S.R.

Dushanbe

Tashkent

UZBEK S.S.R.

AFGHANISTAN

TURKMEN S.S.R.

Ashkabad

Aral Sea

CASPIAN SEA

IRAN

SOVIET FEDERATED SOCIALIST REPUBLIC

RUSSIAN

URAL MTS.

Yenisei R.

Ob R.

Perm

Sverdlovsk

Chelyabinsk

Orenburg

Kuibyshev

Kazan

Volga R.

Saratov

Stalingrad

Pyatigorsk

CAUCASUS MTS.

Baku

AZERBAIDZHAN S.S.R.

GEORGIAN S.S.R.

Tiflis

ARMENIAN S.S.R.

Erivan

TURKEY

ARCTIC OCEAN

Murmansk

Archangel

Kama R.

Gorki

Ivanovo

Yaroslavl

Orekhovo

Moscow

WHITE RUSSIAN S.S.R.

Minsk

Gomel

Bobruisk

Kiev

UKRAINIAN S.S.R.

Odessa

Nikolaev

Kishinev

MOLDAVIAN S.S.R.

Kharkov

Rostov

Krasnodar

Novorossisk

Don R.

BLACK SEA

SYRIA

IRAQ

NORWAY

SWEDEN

Gulf of Bothnia

FINLAND

Helsinki

Kronstadt

Leningrad

Tallinn

ESTONIAN S.S.R.

Riga

LATVIAN S.S.R.

LITHUANIAN S.S.R.

Kaunas

Grodno

Kalinin

Brest-Litovsk

Danzig

POLAND

Warsaw

CZECHOSLOVAKIA

HUNG.

RUMANIA

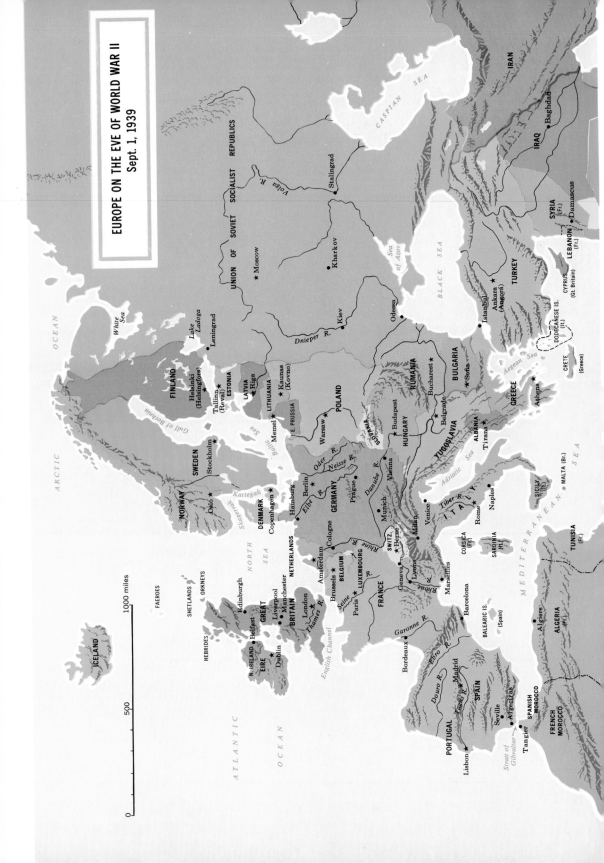

EUROPE ON THE EVE OF WORLD WAR II
Sept. 1, 1939

ARCTIC OCEAN

ICELAND

FAEROES

SHETLANDS

ORKNEYS

HEBRIDES

N. IRELAND
Belfast

EIRE
Dublin

GREAT
BRITAIN
Edinburgh
Liverpool • Manchester
London
Thames R.

English Channel

ATLANTIC OCEAN

NORTH SEA

PORTUGAL
Lisbon

Douro R.
Tagus R.
SPAIN
Madrid
Seville • Algeciras
Strait of Gibraltar
Tangier
SPANISH MOROCCO
FRENCH MOROCCO

Ebro R.

BALEARIC IS.
(Spain)

Barcelona

Garonne R.
Bordeaux

FRANCE
Paris
Seine R.
Lyons
Geneva
Marseilles
Rhône R.

NETHERLANDS
Amsterdam
BELGIUM
Brussels
LUXEMBOURG
Cologne
Rhine R.

SWITZ.
Berne

Milan
CORSICA (Fr.)
SARDINIA (It.)

ALGERIA (Fr.)
Algiers

TUNISIA (Fr.)

MEDITERRANEAN SEA

MALTA (Br.)

ITALY
Tiber R.
Rome
Naples
Venice
Genoa
Adriatic Sea
SICILY (It.)

GERMANY
Hamburg
Berlin
Elbe R.
Oder R.
Neisse R.
Prague
Munich
Danube R.
Vienna

DENMARK
Copenhagen

Kattegat
Skagerrak

NORWAY
Oslo

SWEDEN
Stockholm

Gulf of Bothnia

Baltic Sea

E. PRUSSIA
Memel
LITHUANIA
Kaunas (Kovno)
LATVIA
Riga
ESTONIA
Tallinn (Reval)

FINLAND
Helsinki (Helsingfors)

White Sea

Lake Ladoga
Leningrad

UNION OF SOVIET SOCIALIST REPUBLICS
Moscow ★
Volga R.
Stalingrad
Kharkov
Dnieper R.
Kiev

POLAND
Warsaw
SLOVAKIA

HUNGARY
Budapest

RUMANIA
Bucharest

YUGOSLAVIA
Belgrade

ALBANIA
Tirana

GREECE
Athens

Aegean Sea

BULGARIA
Sofia

Odessa

Sea of Azov

BLACK SEA

CASPIAN SEA

TURKEY
Ankara (Angora) ★
Istanbul

CRETE (Greece)

DODECANESE IS. (It.)

CYPRUS (Gt. Britain)

SYRIA (Fr.)
Damascus
LEBANON (Fr.)

IRAN

IRAQ
Baghdad

0   500   1000 miles

was more than doubled in size and was reorganized in accordance with the western European model. Patriotism, which strict Marxists despised as a form of capitalist propaganda, was exalted into a Soviet virtue, again a symptom of totalitarianism. When Germany once again appeared to threaten Russian security, as it did in the 1930s, the Soviet leadership looked abroad for allies. Along with their efforts to build up a great army and to make their own country self-sufficient, they adopted a policy of cooperation with the western European powers. In 1934 they entered the League of Nations, and in 1934 they ratified a military alliance with France.

In June 1936, the Soviets adopted a new constitution, some of whose provisions suggested the possibility of a more liberal regime. Power continued to reside in a governing body (the Presidium) and an administrative agency (the Council of Ministers), both of which were chosen by a two-chamber parliament, the Supreme Soviet, which was elected, in turn, by universal suffrage. This pyramidal structure was not unlike that which it superseded and which, because of the dominant position of the Communist party, had resulted in the concentration of power in the person of Stalin. Now, however, the constitution provided citizens with a bill of rights guaranteeing freedom of speech, of assembly, and of religion. In addition, they were promised the right to employment, the right to leisure, and the right to maintenance at the expense of the state in case of old age or disability.

These guarantees meant very little, however, so long as all aspects of life in the Soviet Union continued to be dominated by the Communist party, whose membership of about 1 million in 1930 was but a small fraction of the total population of 150 million. That the new "bill of rights" was a sham was quickly proved by a series of purges which began shortly after the constitution was adopted. In August 1936, the first of several "show trials" occurred, at which persons alleged to be "Trotskyites" and spies were publically condemned and either imprisoned, executed, or exiled to Siberia. Although the accused for the most part confessed to their "crimes," those confessions were obtained by physical and psychological torture.

Stalin's victims were people at all levels who had opposed his personal rule, men such as Nikolai Bukharin, editor of the newspaper *Izvestia,* who had spoken out against the elimination of the kulaks; Karl Radek, a leading political theorist; and a number of "old" Bolsheviks, who had been unwilling to acquiesce in Stalin's refusal to debate policy, who had opposed his increasingly nationalistic foreign policy, or who had hoped that revolution did not mean the complete suppression of personal liberty. The purges were the result of Stalin's own psychological instability and pathological distrust. They were as well, however, the logical result of totalitarianism's inability to tolerate any dissent whatsoever. Whatever their cause, the purges took a toll of almost nine million imprisoned, banished, or killed. By ridding the country of his opposition Stalin forestalled further revolution—

not an unlikely possibility, given discontent with his policies—and solidified his position as virtual dictator of Russia.

The results of the Soviet revolution were profound. No other regime in the history of western Europe had ever attempted to reorder completely the politics, economy, and society of a vast nation as the Russians had in the short space of twenty years. By 1939 private manufacturing and trade had been almost entirely abolished. Factories, mines, railroads, and public utilities were exclusively owned by the state. Stores were either government enterprises or cooperatives in which consumers owned shares. Agriculture had been almost completely socialized. At the same time, the nation had been industrialized. By 1932 over 70 percent of Russia's national product was industrial in origin. In the area of social reform, illiteracy was reduced from at least 50 percent to about 20 percent, and higher education was made available to increasingly large numbers. Government assistance for working mothers and free hospitalization did a great deal to raise the national standard of health.

But, as we have seen, those achievements were purchased at a very high price. In addition to the liquidation of millions of kulaks and political dissidents and the internment of millions of others in slave-labor camps, the Russian people were subjected to an unrelenting campaign of indoctrination that encompassed every aspect of their lives. The Soviet leadership set out to shatter those prevailing belief systems which threatened to impede the achievement of its goals. Subtle forms of persecution were implemented to discourage religious orthodoxy while the nation's youth were inculcated with the new Soviet ideals of steadfast loyalty to the Soviet state and unquestioning obedience to the Communist party. Over time, experiments in the arts and literature, which had been promoted during the early years of the revolution under Lenin, gave way to the culture of totalitarian bureaucracy. Education became a tool of the revolution, much as violence and intimidation had. Control of the minds of the populace was regarded as a prerequisite to building a new society in which individual interests would be sacrificed to those of the state. After two decades of revolutionary change, the Stalinist regime had fastened upon the Russian people a tyranny as heavy as any imposed by the tsars.

2. THE EMERGENCE OF TOTALITARIAN FASCISM IN ITALY

That Italy turned to totalitarianism may at first seem surprising, in view of the fact that the Italians emerged as victors after the First World War. Yet Italy's difficulties were rooted in long-standing problems that the war had done little to resolve. Italy continued to be divided into two sharply contrasting halves: a relatively prosperous industrialized north, and a wretchedly poor agrarian south. In addition to the problems the country faced as a result of that unhealthy economic split, it was also the victim of an unrequited imperialist impulse which had existed since the 1890s. Its unsuccessful attempts to establish itself as a power in North Africa had left the country with a sense of frustration and humiliation. Before the war, the ruling class was held in public contempt by a younger generation anxious to cleanse the nation of rulers widely perceived to be at once cynical and corrupt, vaccilating and defeatist.

But the establishment of a dictatorship in Italy would never have been possible without the demoralizing and humiliating effects of the First World War. The chief business of the Italian armies had been to keep the Austrians occupied on the Southern Front while the British, French, and Americans hammered Germany into submission along the battle lines in the west. To accomplish this assignment, Italy had mobilized more than 5,500,000 men; of these nearly 700,000 were killed. The direct financial cost of Italian participation in the struggle was over $15 billion. These sacrifices were no greater than those made by the British and the French, but Italy was a poor country. Moreover, in the division of the spoils after the fighting, the Italians got less than they expected. While Italy did receive most of the Austrian territories promised in the secret treaties, the Italians maintained that these were inadequate rewards for their sacrifices and for their valuable contribution to an Entente victory. At first the nationalists vented their spleen for the "humiliation of Versailles" upon President Wilson, but after a short time they returned to castigating their own rulers. They alleged Premier Orlando had been so cravenly weak and inept that he and those who governed with him had allowed their country to be cheated of its just desserts.

The demoralizing and humiliating effects of the war

The war contributed to the revolutionary mood in a multitude of other ways. It resulted in inflation of the currency, with consequent high prices, speculation, and profiteering. Normally wages would have risen also, but the postwar labor market was glutted by the return to civilian life of millions of soldiers. Furthermore, business was demoralized, owing to extensive and frequent strikes and to the closing of foreign markets. In the minds of the upper and middle classes the most ominous consequence of the war was the growth of socialism. As hardship and chaos increased, the Italian socialists embraced a philosophy akin to Bolshevism. They voted as a party to join the Third International. In the elections of November 1919, they won about a third of the seats in the Chamber of Deputies. During the following winter socialist workers took over about a hundred factories and attempted to run them for the benefit of the workers. Radicalism also spread through the rural areas, where so-called Red Leagues were organized to break up large estates and to force landlords to reduce their rents. Two large political parties with mass appeal, the Socialists and the Catholic People's party, drained strength from other parties of the Center and moderate Left. Neither preached revolution; yet

Inflation, radicalism, and economic chaos

both urged far-reaching social and economic reforms. Industrialists and landowners were badly frightened and were therefore ready to accept totalitarianism as a less dangerous form of radicalism that might save at least part of their property from confiscation.

How much the Fascist movement depended for its success upon the leadership of Benito Mussolini is difficult to say. Mussolini was born in 1883, the son of a socialist blacksmith. His mother was a schoolteacher, and in deference to her wishes he eventually became a teacher. But he was restless and dissatisfied, soon leaving Italy for further study in Switzerland. Here he gave part of his time to his books and the rest to writing articles for socialist newspapers. He was eventually expelled from the country for fomenting strikes. Returning to Italy, he became a journalist, and eventually editor of *Avanti,* the leading socialist daily. His ideas in the years before the war were a contradictory mixture of radicalisms. He professed to be a Marxist socialist, but he mingled his socialism with doctrines of corporatism, adapted from the French syndicalists.

Mussolini in fact believed in no particular set of doctrines. No man with a definite philosophy could have reversed himself so often. When war broke out in August 1914, Mussolini insisted that Italy should remain neutral. He had scarcely adopted this position when he began urging participation on the Entente side. Deprived of his position as editor of *Avanti,* he founded a new paper, *Il Popolo d'Italia,* and dedicated its columns to arousing enthusiasm for war. He regarded the decision of the government the following spring to go in on the side of the Entente allies as a personal victory.

The word *fascism* derives from the Latin *fasces,* the ax surrounded by a bundle of sticks representing the authority of the Roman state; the Italian *fascio* means group or band. *Fasci* were organized as early as October 1914, as units of agitation to drive Italy into the war. Their members were young idealists, fanatical nationalists, and frustrated white-collar workers. The original platform of the Fascist movement was drafted by Mussolini in 1919. It was a surprisingly radical document, which demanded universal suffrage, abolition of the conservative Senate, the establishment by law of an eight-hour day, a heavy capital levy, a heavy tax on inheritances, confiscation of 85 percent of war profits, acceptance of the League of Nations, and "opposition to all imperialisms." This platform was accepted more or less officially by the movement until May 1920, when it was supplanted by another of a more conservative character. Indeed, the new program omitted all reference to economic reform. On neither of these platforms did the Fascists achieve much political success.

The Fascists made up for their initial lack of numbers by disciplined aggressiveness and strong determination. As the old regime crumbled, they prepared to take over the government. In September 1922, Mussolini began to talk openly of revolution. On October 28 an army of about 50,000 Fascist militia, in blackshirted uniforms, marched into

Left: *"On to Rome."* Mussolini (wearing a suit) and uniformed Fascists march into Rome in October 1922. Right: *Mussolini Addressing a Crowd of His Followers from the Balcony of the Palazzo Venezia in Rome*

Rome and occupied the capital. The premier resigned, and the following day the king, Victor Emmanuel III, invited Mussolini to form a cabinet. Thus, without firing a shot the blackshirts had gained control of the Italian government. The explanation is to be found not in the strength of fascism, but in the chaos created by the war and in the weakness and irresolution of the old ruling classes. By the end of the next three years Mussolini's revolution was virtually complete.

Italian fascism embodied a variety of doctrines that were an expression of its totalitarian nature:

(1) Statism. The state was declared to incorporate every interest and every loyalty of its members. There was to be "nothing above the state, nothing outside the state, nothing against the state." *Major doctrines of fascism*

(2) Nationalism. Nationhood was the highest form of society. It had a life and a soul of its own apart from the lives and souls of the individuals who composed it. Yet there could be no real harmony of interests between two or more distinct nations. Hence internationalism was a perversion of human progress.

(3) Militarism. Strife was the origin of all things. Nations which did not expand would eventually wither and die. War exalted and ennobled man and regenerated sluggish and decadent peoples.

Declaring his allegiance to these principles, Mussolini began to rebuild Italy in accordance with them. He abolished the cabinet system and all but extinguished the powers of the Parliament. In characteristic totalitarian fashion, he made the Fascist party an integral part of the Italian constitution. The king was compelled to select a prime minister from a list compiled by the party's Great Council. Voters, as well, were left with no real choice; they were forced to select their candidates from lists prepared by the party. Within a few years, there *Mussolini's fascist state* were no other political parties left in Italy. Mussolini assumed the dual position of prime minister and party leader (*duce*). A potent and effective mechanism of political discipline was the party's militia, which Mussolini used to eliminate his enemies by violent means. Police supervision, censorship of the press and of academic life—the hallmarks of totalitarian regimes—were soon fastened upon the Italian people by the party.

His bid for worker support

Mussolini reorganized the economy while preaching the end of class conflict as fascist doctrine. He secured worker support by instituting massive public works and building projects, along with state-sponsored programs of library-building, vacations, and social security. He won further popular acclaim when, in 1929, he settled Italy's sixty-year-old conflict with the Roman Catholic church by a treaty granting independence to the papal residence in the Vatican City and establishing Roman Catholicism as the official religion of the nation's schools.

Corporatism

At the same time that Mussolini was attempting to pacify the Italian working class, he was pulling the teeth of the country's labor movement. The Italian economy was placed under the management of twenty-two corporations, each responsible for a major industrial enterprise. In each corporation were representatives of trade unions, whose members were organized by the Fascist party, the employers, and the government. Together, the members of these corporations were given the task of determining working conditions, wages, and prices. In fact, however, the decisions of these bodies were closely managed by the government and favored the position of management.

Its failure

Although the Italian economy did improve somewhat—along with the economies of other European countries—in the late 1920s, fascism did little to lessen Italy's plight during the years of worldwide depression which occurred in the 1930s. Although he managed to make his country appear more efficient—his admirers often bragged that he had at last "made the trains run on time"—Mussolini failed to solve its major problems, particularly those of the peasantry, whose standard of living remained desperately low. Mussolini's fascism was little more than illusion. It is a measure of the Italians' disgust with their past leaders that they were so ready to be taken in by him.

3. THE RISE OF NAZI GERMANY

Germany: the Spartacists

Germany succumbed to totalitarianism later than Italy. For a brief period following the First World War, events seemed to be moving the country to the Left. Most of the leading politicians in the immediate postarmistice government were socialists, members of the Social Democratic party. Their reformist policies, which had seemed radical enough to many prior to the war, now appeared too mild to a group of extreme Marxists who had been encouraged by the revolution in

Russia. Calling themselves Spartacists,[1] and led by the able Rosa Luxemburg and Karl Liebknecht, they attempted an uprising in 1919 designed to bring the proletarian revolution to Germany. Despite assistance from the Russian Bolsheviks, the rebellion was crushed; Liebknecht and Luxemburg were killed by soldiers while being taken to prison. In engineering the Spartacists' defeat, the German government had recourse to private vigilante groups headed by disillusioned former army officers, men whose true sympathies lay no more with democratic socialism than with Russian communism, and whose discontent would soon focus on the government they had helped to salvage.

With the Spartacist revolt only just behind them, the leaders of a coalition of socialists, Catholic centrists, and liberal democrats in 1919 drafted a constitution for the new German republic reflecting a generally progressive political and social philosophy. It provided for universal suffrage, for women as well as men; the cabinet system of government; and for a bill of rights, guaranteeing not only civil liberties but the right of the citizen to employment, to an education, and to protection against the hazards of an industrial society. But the republic established under this constitution was beset with troubles from the start. Reactionaries and other extremists plotted against it. Moreover, the German people had had little experience with democratic government. The Weimar Republic (named for the city where its constitution was drafted) did not spring from the desires of a majority of the nation. It was born of change forced upon Germany in its hour of defeat. Its instability made it a likely victim of the forces it was desperately attempting to tame.

The Weimar Republic

[1] After the Roman, Spartacus, who led a slave revolt.

Karl Liebknecht (center) and Rosa Luxemburg

Various factors led to the eventual triumph of German totalitarianism. First was the sense of humiliation arising from defeat in the war. Between 1871 and 1914 Germany had risen to lofty heights of political and cultural prestige. German universities, science, philosophy, and music were known and admired all over the world. The country had likewise attained a remarkable prosperity, by 1914 surpassing Britain and the United States in several fields of industrial production. Then came the defeat of 1918, with Germany left to the mercy of its powerful enemies. It was too much for the German people to understand. They found it difficult to believe that their invincible armies had really been worsted in battle. Quickly the legend grew that the nation had been "stabbed in the back" by socialists and Jews in the government. Though there was no truth in this charge, it helped to salve the wounded pride of German patriots. Those in search of a scapegoat also blamed the laxity and irresponsibility that appeared to distinguish the republican regime. It was alleged that Berlin had displaced Paris as the most frivolous and decadent city of Europe. What the country seemed to need was authoritative leadership to spearhead a campaign to regain the world's respect.

The sense of humiliation was increased by two of the provisions imposed on the Germans in the Versailles treaty. First, Germany was compelled to reduce its army to 100,000 men, a requirement that produced bitter discontent among the politically powerful corps of officers that remained at the head of its ranks. Second, the enormous burden of reparations payments continued to arouse the anger of the Germans. Opponents of the reparations settlement urged an obstructionist policy of nonpayment, arguing that the sum of $33 billion demanded would doom the German economy for the foreseeable future. German politicians of all persuasions agreed that the sum was impossibly large. Yet Weimar's foreign minister in the early 1920s, Walter Rathenau, opposed the obstructionists, and attempted to reach a compromise with the former Allied powers. Rathenau's assassination in 1922, by a secret organization of obstructionist army officers, produced a reaction which led to the German government's refusal to make further payments. The result was French occupation of the Ruhr valley in early 1923, in a fruitless attempt to compel German miners there to produce for France. The ensuing stalemate, which lasted for several months, was ended by the German chancellor, Gustav Stresemann, who recognized the futility of obstructionist tactics. His success in persuading the Germans to accept his point of view was aided by an international agreement to renegotiate reparations under the guidance of a committee of experts headed by the American Charles G. Dawes. Crisis was temporarily averted, but the psychological wounds caused by the reparations controversy did not heal.

Another major reason for totalitarianism's appeal in Germany was the inflation the country suffered in the 1920s. When Germans began

Depression in Germany. Following the defeat in the First World War, inflation was rampant and food in short supply. Here a fallen horse is torn to shreds by hungry citizens.

to experience severe unemployment, the government increased the supply of paper money—eventually to a flood—in order to finance programs of unemployment insurance and to try to provide its citizenry with the economic wherewithal to survive. The result was a period of wild inflation, particularly demoralizing to the middle class. Salaries could not keep up with the vast increase in the cost of living. Those who existed on fixed incomes—pensioners, stockholders—saw their security vanish. As they lost their faith in the ability of the government to come to their aid, these men and women began, as well, to lose whatever faith they may have had in the republic. The middle class, traumatized by inflation, continued its search for a government that promised attention to its needs and sympathy with its problems. That search intensified with the advent of the Great Depression of 1929. As we shall see, the depression was a major disaster for most of the world. In few countries, however, were its effects more keenly felt than in Germany. Farmers were angered by the collapse of agricultural prices and by their burden of debts and taxes. University students saw little prospect of gaining a place in already-overcrowded professions. Six million workers were unemployed. Once again the middle class saw its savings vanish.

(2) economics

For a brief period in the late 1920s, however, it had appeared that the German economy, and the Weimar Republic with it, might recover. Low German wages meant that the country was able to make its reparations payments, scaled down in accordance with the Dawes Committee recommendations, and to earn money abroad with cheaply priced exports. Building programs, sponsored by socialist municipal governments in large cities such as Frankfurt, Düsseldorf, and Berlin—schools, hospitals, and low-cost worker housing—suggested that the country was both politically and economically healthier than it actually was. In fact the Dawes Plan, by stressing the need for immediate increases in production, ensured that the economy would remain

Weimar's later years

in the hands of the country's leading industrialists. These were very conservative men, whose sympathies lay with the restoration of a more authoritarian form of government than Weimar represented. They were allied with equally conservative landowners, bound together by their mutual desire for a protective economic policy that would stimulate the sale of domestically produced goods and foodstuffs. This alliance was augmented by the army and civil service, staffed with men opposed to the traditions of parliamentary democracy and international cooperation embodied in the republic.

Parties polarized

By the end of the decade, party politics had polarized much as they had in Italy. The Center parties attracted diminishing support while candidates for the Communist party on the Left and the monarchist German People's party on the Right were enjoying increased success. In 1932 discontent with the republic manifested itself in the national elections, which resulted in the continued presidency of the war hero Marshall von Hindenburg. What was significant, however, was not Hindenburg's return to power, but the fact that the Communists polled about five million votes, and that the candidate of the radical Right, Adolph Hitler, received over eleven million, more than one-third of those cast. The Weimar Republic was doomed. And Hitler was its logical nemesis.

The founding of the Nazi party; the early career of Hitler

Hitler's rise to power dated from 1919, when he met with six other men to found the National Socialist Workers' party.[2] Hitler was born in 1889, the son of a petty customs official in the Austrian civil service. Hitler's early life was unhappy and maladjusted. Rebellious and undisciplined from childhood, he seems always to have been burdened with a sense of frustration. He was a failure in school, decided that he would become an artist, and went to Vienna in 1909, hoping to enter the Academy. But he failed the required examinations: for the next four years he was compelled to eke out a dismal existence as a casual laborer and a painter of watercolors. Meanwhile he developed violent political prejudices. He became an ardent admirer of certain vociferously anti-Semitic politicians in Vienna; and since he associated Judaism with Marxism, he learned to hate that philosophy as well. When war broke out, Hitler was living in Munich. Though an Austrian citizen, he immediately enlisted in the German army. Following the war, he joined with other disaffected Germans to denounce the Weimar Republic. In 1923, Hitler led an attempt in Munich by the Nazis' private army, the Brownshirts, to stage a "putsch," or sudden overthrow of the government. The Brownshirts were quickly dispersed, and Hitler sentenced to a term in prison, where he composed a declaration of his beliefs, *Mein Kampf* (My Struggle). In this rambling treatise he expressed his hatred of Jews and communists, his sense of Germany's betrayal by its enemies, and his belief that only with strong leadership

[2] The name of the party was soon abbreviated in popular usage to Nazi.

One Step Away from Power. President Hindenburg followed by Hitler, Göring on the extreme right, and other Nazi party members.

could the country regain its rightful place within the European concert of nations.

Hitler's message appealed to an ever-growing number of his disillusioned and economically threatened countrymen and women. In the election of 1928 the Nazis won 12 seats in the Reichstag. In 1930 they won 107 seats, their popular vote increasing from 800,000 to 6,500,000. During the summer of 1932 the parliamentary system broke down. No chancellor could retain a majority in the Reichstag, for the Nazis declined to support any cabinet not headed by Hitler, and the communists refused to collaborate with the socialists. In January 1933, a group of reactionaries—industrialists, bankers, and Junkers—prevailed upon President Hindenburg to designate Hitler as chancellor, in the mistaken belief that they could control him. It was arranged that there should be only three Nazis in the cabinet, and that Franz von Papen, a Catholic aristocrat, should hold the position of vice-chancellor. The sponsors of this plan failed to appreciate the tremendous popularity of the Nazi movement, however. Hitler was not slow in making the most of his new opportunity. He persuaded Hindenburg to dissolve the Reichstag and to order a new election on March 5. When the new Reichstag assembled, it voted to confer upon Hitler practically unlimited powers. Soon afterward the flag of the Weimar Republic was lowered and replaced by the swastika banner of the National Socialists. The new Germany was proclaimed to be the Third Reich, the successor of the Hohenstaufen Empire of the Middle Ages and of the Hohenzollern Empire of the kaisers.

During the next few months, other sweeping changes converted Germany from Bismarck's federalized state into a highly centralized totalitarian regime. As both chancellor and leader of the Nazi party,

The Nazi revolution

Nazi rule

Hitler was in a unique position to put the powers of the state to the purposes of the party. To this end, all other political parties were declared illegal. Nazi party luminaries were appointed heads of various government departments, and party *gauleiters,* or regional directors, assumed administrative responsibility throughout the country. Hitler made use of paramilitary Nazi "storm troopers" (the S.A.) to maintain discipline within the party and to impose order on the populace through calculated intimidation and violence. Not even the S.A. itself was immune to the imperatives of totalitarian terror: when the aspirations of the S.A. leadership to supplant the established army hierarchy threatened to undermine Hitler's support within the military at a critical moment, he unleashed a bloody purge in which more than a thousand high-ranking S.A. officials were summarily executed. Hitler and his associates would brook no interference with their plans to achieve absolute power.

Nazism and the workers

Like Mussolini, Hitler moved to abolish class conflict by robbing working-class institutions of their power. He outlawed trade unions and strikes, froze wages, and organized workers and employers into a National Labor Front. At the same time, Hitler increased welfare benefits for workers and battled unemployment with large state-financed construction projects: highways, public housing, and reforestation. Later in the decade, rearmament and a substantial increase in the size of the military establishment all but ended the German unemployment problem. These programs met with the approval of the middle and upper classes, who were as anxious as the working class to see an end to depression. Industrialists welcomed the military buildup that brought orders to their factories. In addition, they and the still-influential Junkers saw Hitler as a bulwark against Communist subversion.

The Nazi Party Congress in Nuremburg, 1934. The Nazis were masters of the use of humanity *en masse* as propaganda. Hitler stands at attention in the center.

Despite the fact that Germany was one of the most highly industrialized countries in the world, National Socialism had a peculiar peasant flavor. The key to Nazi theory was contained in the phrase *Blut und Boden* (blood and soil). The word *soil* reflected not only a deep reverence for the homeland but an abiding affection for the peasants, who were considered to embody the finest qualities of the German race. No class of the population was more generously treated by the Nazi government. This high regard for country folk came partly, no doubt, from the circumstance that they had the highest birth rate of the nation's citizens and therefore were most valuable for military reasons. It was explainable also by the reaction of the Nazi leaders against everything that the city stood for—not only intellectualism and radicalism but high finance and the complicated problems of industrial society.

The dreary patterns of totalitarian repression were imposed on the lives of the German people, and for the most part they accepted them willingly. Censorship, restriction of movement, political persecution, and political murder became the norm, as they had elsewhere. Nazism differed from other forms of totalitarianism, however, in its single-minded persecution of the Jews. The Nazis argued that the so-called Aryan race, which was supposed to include the Nordics as its most perfect specimens, was the only one ever to have made any notable contributions to human progress. They contended further that the accomplishments and mental qualities of a people were determined by blood. Thus the achievements of the Jew forever remained Jewish, no matter how long he or she might live in a Western country. It followed that no Jewish science or Jewish literature or Jewish music could ever truly represent the German nation. This racial doctrine was mere rationalization. The Nazis persecuted the Jews because Hitler was himself rabidly anti-Semitic and because they needed a scapegoat to blame for their nation's troubles. A series of laws passed in 1935 deprived Jews and people of Jewish blood of their German citizenship, and prohibited marriage between Jews and other Germans. Jews were compelled to wear an identifying Star of David when they appeared in public. Eventually, millions of Jews were rounded up, tortured, and murdered in concentration camps. Other representatives of "imperfect" racial and social groups—homosexuals, gypsies, and anti-Nazi intellectuals—met a similar fate. The extremism of Hitler's anti-Semitic campaigns underscores the fact that National Socialism was more fanatical than Italian fascism. It was a new religion, not only in its dogmatism and its ritual, but in its fierce intolerance and its zeal for expansion.

German Jews Wearing Identifying Yellow Stars. Part of the Nazis' anti-Semitic campaign of the 1930s.

The significance of German and Italian totalitarianism remains a subject of controversy among students of modern history. Some argue that it reflected the enthronement of force by capitalists in an effort to save their dying system from destruction. And it is true that the success of both movements in gaining control of the government depended on support from great landowners and captains of industry. Others explain German and Italian totalitarianism as a reaction of debtors against creditors, of farmers against bankers and manufacturers, and of small businessmen against high finance and monopolistic practices. Still others interpret it as a reaction to Communist threat, a reversion to primitivism, a result of the despair of the masses, a protest against the weaknesses of democracy, or a supreme manifestation of nationalism. Undoubtedly it was all of these things combined. One further argument holds that fascism and Nazism were extreme expressions of tendencies prevalent in all industrialized countries. If official policies in most Western countries in the 1930s took on more and more of an authoritarian semblance—a tightly controlled economy, limitation of production to maintain prices, and expansion of armaments to promote prosperity—it was because nearly all nations in that period were beset with similar problems and, in varying degrees, frightened of their implications.

4. THE DEMOCRACIES BETWEEN THE WARS

Class conflict in France

The histories of the three Western democracies—Great Britain, France, and the United States—run roughly parallel during the years after the First World War. In all three countries there was an attempt by governments to trust to policies and assumptions that had prevailed before the war. The French, not surprisingly, continued to fear Germany and to take whatever steps they could to keep their traditional enemy as weak as possible. Under the leadership of the moderate conservative, Raymond Poincaré, who held office from 1922 to 1924, and again from 1926 to 1929, the French pursued a policy of deflation, which attempted to keep the price of manufactured goods low, by restraining wages. This policy pleased businessmen, but was hard on the working class. Edouard Herriot, a Radical Socialist who served as premier from 1924 to 1926 was, despite his party's name, a spokesman for the small businessman, farmer, and lower middle class. Herriot declared himself in favor of social reform, but refused to raise taxes in order to pay for it. Class conflict lay close to the surface of French national affairs throughout the 1920s. While industries prospered, employers rejected trade unionists' demands to bargain collectively. A period of major strikes immediately after the war was followed by a sharp decline in union activity. Workers remained dissatisfied, even after the government passsed a modified social insurance program in 1930, insuring against sickness, old age, and death.

Britain's economic difficulties

Class conflict flared in Britain as well. Anxious to regain its now irretrievably lost position as the major industrial and financial power in the world, Britain, like France, pursued a policy of deflation, designed to lower the price of manufactured goods and thus make them more attractive on the world market. The result was a reduction in wages

Labor Troubles in Britain. Mounted police escorting delivery wagons through a mob of angry strikers during the general strike of 1926.

which undermined the standard of living of many British workers. Their resentment helped to elect a Labour party government in 1924 and 1929. But its minority position in Parliament left it little chance to accomplish much of consequence, even had its leader, Prime Minister J. Ramsay MacDonald, been a more adventurous socialist than he was. In 1926 British trade unions grew increasingly militant because of the particularly distressing wage levels in the coal mining industry, and because the Conservative government, returned to power under Stanley Baldwin in 1925, refused to be deflected from its deflationary stance. The unions staged a nationwide general strike which, though it failed as an industrial strategy, turned the middle class more than ever against the workers.

The United States was undoubtedly the most impregnable fortress of conservative power among the democracies. The presidents elected during the 1920s—Warren G. Harding, Calvin Coolidge, and Herbert Hoover—upheld a social philosophy formulated by the barons of big business in the nineteenth century, and the Supreme Court used its power of judicial review to nullify progressive legislation enacted by state governments and occasionally by Congress.

Conservatism in the U.S.

The course of Western history was dramatically altered by the advent of worldwide depression in 1929. We have already seen the way in which depression contributed to the rise of Nazism. But all countries were forced to come to terms with the economic and social devastation it produced. The Great Depression had its roots in a general agricultural slump in the 1920s, the result of increased postwar production which drove down the price of grain and other commodities to the point of bankrupting farmers, though not far enough to benefit the urban poor. To chronic agricultural distress was added the financial crisis that began with the collapse of prices on the New York Stock Exchange in 1929. With a drop in the value of stocks, banks found themselves short of capital and forced to close. International investors called in their debts. Industries, unable to sell their products, stopped manufacturing and started laying off workers. Unemploy-

The Great Depression

The Stock Market Crash, October 24, 1929. Crowds milling outside the New York Stock Exchange on the day of the big crash.

ment further contracted markets—fewer people had money with which to buy goods or services—and that contraction led to more unemployment.

The results of the depression took varied forms throughout the West. In 1931 Great Britain abandoned the gold standard; the government of the United States followed suit in 1933. By no longer pegging their currencies to the price of gold, these countries hoped to make money cheaper, and thus more available for programs of public and private economic recovery. This action was the forerunner of a broad program of currency management, which became an important element in a general policy of economic nationalism. As early as 1932 Great Britain abandoned its time-honored policy of free trade. Protective tariffs were raised in some instances as high as 100 percent.

Domestically, Britain moved cautiously to alleviate the effects of the depression. A national government, which came to power in 1931 with a ministry composed of members from the Conservative, Liberal, and Labour parties, was reluctant to spend beyond its income, as it would have to in order to underwrite effective programs of public assistance. Of the European democracies, France adopted the most advanced set of policies to combat the inequalities and distress that followed in the wake of the depression. In 1936, responding to a threat from ultraconservatives to overthrow the republic, a Popular Front government, under the leadership of the socialist Léon Blum (1872–1950), was formed by the Radical, Radical Socialist, and Communist parties, and lasted for two years. The Popular Front nationalized the munitions industry and reorganized the Bank of France so as to deprive the 200 largest stockholders of their monopolistic control over credit. In addition, it decreed a forty-hour week for all urban workers and initiated a program of public works. For the benefit of the farmers it established a wheat office to fix the price and regulate

Léon Blum

the distribution of grain. Although the threat from the political Right
was for a time quelled by the Popular Front, conservatives were generally uncooperative and unimpressed by its attempts to ameliorate
the conditions of the French working class. The anti-Semitism that
had appeared at the time of the Dreyfus affair resurfaced; Blum was
both a socialist and a Jew. Businessmen saw him as the forerunner of
a French Lenin, and were heard to opine, "better Hitler than Blum."
They got their wish before the decade was out.

The most dramatic changes in policy occurred not in Europe, but
in the United States. The explanation was twofold. The United States
had clung longer to the economic philosophy of the nineteenth century. Prior to the depression the business classes had adhered firmly
to the dogma of freedom of contract and insisted upon their right to
form monopolies and to use the government as their agent in frustrating the demands of both workers and consumers. The depression in
the United States was also more severe than in the European democracies. Industrial production shrank by about two-thirds. The structure of agricultural prices and of common stocks collapsed. Thousands
of banks were forced to close their doors. Unemployment rose to one-
third of the total labor force. An attempt to alleviate distress was contained in a program of reform and reconstruction known as the New
Deal. The chief architect and motivator of this program was Franklin
D. Roosevelt (1882–1945), who succeeded Herbert Hoover in the
presidency on March 4, 1933.

The New Deal

The aim of the New Deal was to preserve the capitalist system, by
managing the economy and undertaking programs of relief and public
works to increase mass purchasing power. Although the New Deal
did assist in the recovery both of individual citizens and of the country, through programs of currency management and social security, it
left the crucial problem of unemployment unsolved. In 1939, after six
years of the New Deal, the United States still had more than nine
million jobless workers—a figure which exceeded the combined
unemployment of the rest of the world. Ironically, only the outbreak
of a new world war could provide the full recovery that the New Deal
had failed to assure, by directing millions from the labor market into
the army and by creating jobs in the countless factories that turned to
the manufacture of war matériel.

Its achievements

5. INTELLECTUAL AND CULTURAL TRENDS IN THE INTERWAR YEARS

The First World War, which proved so disillusioning to so many, and
the generally dispiriting political events which followed in its train,
made it difficult to hold fast to any notion of a purposeful universe.
Philosophers, to a greater degree than their predecessors, declared that

Antimetaphysics

Bertrand Russell

Religion as a cultural force

there was little point in attempting to discover answers to questions about the nature of ultimate reality. These antimetaphysicians broke dramatically with the philosophers of the past century, who had grounded their speculations in a belief in progress and in a search for all-encompassing explanations of human behavior. Probably the most influential of these new thinkers was the Viennese Ludwig Wittgenstein (1889–1951), founder, with the Englishman Bertrand Russell (1872–1970), of the school of Logical Positivism. Developed further by the so-called Vienna Circle, whose leader was Rudolf Carnap, Logical Positivism emerged as an uncompromisingly scientific philosophy. It is not concerned with values or ideals except to the extent that they may be demonstrable by mathematics or physics. In general, the Logical Positivists reject as "meaningless" everything that cannot be reduced to a "one-to-one correspondence" with something in the physical universe. They reduce philosophy to a mere instrument for the discovery of truth in harmony with the facts of the physical environment. They divest it almost entirely of its traditional content and use it as a medium for answering questions and solving problems. They are concerned especially to attack political theory, regarding that subject as particularly burdened with unproved assumptions and questionable dogmas.

Sociologists reinforced philosophers in denying the value of metaphysics. One of the most important was the German Max Weber (1864–1920), who, in his book *The Protestant Ethic and the Spirit of Capitalism* (1905), argued that religion must be understood as a cultural force, in this case assisting directly in the spread of capitalism. By making work a cardinal virtue and idleness a supreme vice, Protestantism had encouraged the work ethic, which, in turn, had fueled the energies of early capitalist entrepreneurs. When he turned to a study of the contemporary world, Weber concluded that societies would inevitably fall more and more under the sway of ever-expanding and potentially totalitarian bureaucracies. Recognizing the extent to which such a development might threaten human freedom, Weber posited the notion of "charismatic" leadership as a means of escaping the deadening tyranny of state control. A term derived from the Greek word for gift, "charisma" was, according to Weber, an almost magic quality which could induce hero worship and which, if properly directed by its possessor, might produce an authority to challenge bureaucracy. Weber himself recognized the dangers as well as the attractions of charismatic authority, dangers which the careers of Stalin, Hitler, and Mussolini soon made all too apparent. Another thinker who treated religion as a powerful social and psychological force, rather than as a branch of metaphysics, was the Swiss psychologist Carl Jung (1875–1961). Originally a student and disciple of Freud, Jung broke with his intellectual mentor by proclaiming the existence of a force behind individual id, ego, and superego: the "collective unconscious."

Jung's literary background and his personal penchant for mysticism helped persuade him of the enduring psychological and therapeutic value of myth and religion, something Freud refused to acknowledge.

The writings of some philosophers during the interwar years not only reflected a sense of crisis and despair but, because of the influence of those works, contributed to it as well. Foremost among these were the Italian Vilfredo Pareto (1848–1923) and the German Oswald Spengler (1880–1936), who agreed in their contempt for the masses, in their belief that democracy was impossible, in their anti-intellectual viewpoint, and in their admiration for strong and aggressive leaders. Spengler was, in many respects, more extreme than Pareto. In his *Decline of the West,* completed in 1918, and even more in his later writings, he gave vent to attitudes that reflect the extent to which totalitarianism might appeal to an "anti-intellectual" intellectual. In his *Hour of Decision,* published in 1933, he fulminated against democracy, pacifism, internationalism, the lower classes, and nonwhite peoples. He sang the praises of those "who feel themselves born and called to be masters," of "healthy instincts, race, the will to possession and power." Spengler despised the analytical reasoning of urban intellectuals and called upon men to admire the "deep wisdom of old peasant families." Human beings, he maintained, are "beasts of prey," and those who deny this conclusion are simply "beasts of prey with broken teeth."

Literary movements during the interwar period showed tendencies similar to those in philosophy. Like the philosophers, the major novelists, poets, and dramatists were disillusioned by the brute facts of world war and by the failure of victory to fulfill its promises. Many were profoundly affected also by revolutionary developments in science and especially by the probings of the new science of psychoanalysis into the hidden secrets of the mind. Much of the literature of the interwar period reflected themes of frustration, cynicism, and disenchantment. The general mood of the era was expressed individually by different writers; for example, by the early novels of the American Ernest Hemingway (1899–1961), by the poetry of the Anglo-American T. S. Eliot (1888–1965), and by the plays of the German Bertolt Brecht (1898–1956). In *The Sun Also Rises,* Hemingway gave the public a powerful description of the essential tragedy of the so-called lost generation and set a pattern which other writers, like the American F. Scott Fitzgerald, were soon to follow. In his poem *The Waste Land* (1922), T. S. Eliot presented a philosophy that was close to despair. Once you are born, he seemed to be saying, life is a living death, to be endured as boredom and frustration. The German Brecht, in plays written to be performed before the proletarian patrons of cabarets, proclaimed the corruption of the bourgeois state and the pointlessness of war.

T. S. Eliot

The works of many writers in the interwar period reflected to an increasing extent the isolation of self-conscious intellectuals and the

Virginia Woolf

Influence of the depression

Jean-Paul Sartre

constricting of their audience that characterized the years before the First World War. While Brecht carried his revolutionary messages into the streets of Berlin, others wrote primarily for each other or for the small elite group who could understand what they were saying. Eliot crammed his poetry with esoteric allusions. The Irishman James Joyce (1882–1941), whose ability to enter his characters' minds and to reproduce their "stream-of-consciousness" on paper made him a writer of the very first order, nevertheless wrote with a complexity that only few could appreciate. The same was true, though to a lesser extent, of the novels of the Frenchman Marcel Proust (1871–1922) and the Englishwoman Virginia Woolf (1882–1941). In her novels and essays, Woolf was, as well, an eloquent and biting critic of the ruling class of Britain, focusing in part on the enforced oppression of women even in that class.

The depression of the 1930s forced a reexamination of the methods and purposes of literature. In the midst of economic stagnation and threats of totalitarianism and war, literature was politicized. Authors came to believe that their work must indict meanness, cruelty, and barbarism, and point the way to a more just society, that it should also be a literature addressed not to fellow intellectuals, but to common men and women. The American John Steinbeck (1902–1968), in *The Grapes of Wrath,* depicted the sorry plight of impoverished farmers fleeing from the "dust bowl" to California only to find that all the land had been monopolized by companies that exploited their workers. Pervading the novels of the Frenchman André Malraux (1901–1976) was the strong suggestion that the human struggle against tyranny and injustice is that which gives meaning and value to life. Young British writers such as W. H. Auden, Stephen Spender, and Christopher Isherwood declared, as Communist sympathizers, that artists had an obligation to politicize their art for the benefit of the revolution. They rejected the pessimism of their immediate literary forebears for the optimism of political commitment to a common cause.

In this they differed radically from their French contemporary, Jean-Paul Sartre (1905–1980), whose pessimistic philosophy of Existentialism was receiving its first hearing at this time. Sartre was a teacher of philosophy in a Paris *lycée* and subsequently a leader of the French Resistance movement against the Germans during the Second World War. His philosophy takes its name from its doctrine that the *existence* of human beings as free individuals is the fundamental fact of life. But this freedom is of no help to humanity; instead it is a source of anguish and terror. Realizing, however vaguely, that they are free agents, morally responsible for all their acts, individuals feel themselves strangers in an alien world. They can have no confidence in a benevolent God or in a universe guided by purpose, for, according to Sartre, all such ideas have been reduced to fictions by modern science. The only way of escape from despair is the path of "involvement," or active participation in human affairs. It should be noted that in addition to the atheistic Existentialism of Sartre, there was also a prior Christian version, which had its origin in the teachings of Søren Kierkegaard (1813–1855), a Danish theologian of the mid–nineteenth century. Like its atheistic counterpart, Christian Existentialism also teaches that the chief cause of human agony and terror is freedom, but it finds the source of its freedom in original sin.

Another writer who refused to allow himself the luxury of political optimism was the Englishman George Orwell (1903–1950). Although sympathetic to the cause of international socialism, Orwell continued to insist that all political movements were to some degree corrupted. He urged writers to recognize a duty to write only on the basis of what they had themselves experienced. Above all, writers should never simply parrot party propaganda. Orwell's last two novels, *Animal Farm* and *1984,* written during and immediately after the Second World War, are powerful expressions of his mistrust of political regimes—whether of the Left or the Right—that profess democracy but in fact destroy human freedom.

George Orwell

Optimism during the 1930s was generally the property of those writers who were prepared to advocate a violent change in the social order, most notably men and women sympathetic to the doctrines of communism and the achievements of Soviet Russia. An exception to this rule was the British economist John Maynard Keynes (1883–1946), who argued that capitalism could be made to work if governments would play a part in its management, and whose theories helped shape the economic policies of the New Deal. Keynes had served as an economic adviser to the British government during the 1919 treaty-making at Paris. He was disgusted with the harsh terms imposed upon the Germans, recognizing that they would serve only to keep alive the hatreds and uncertainties that breed war. Keynes believed that capitalism with its inner faults corrected could provide a just and efficient economy. Capitalism, though, would require a thorough rethinking. First, Keynes abandoned the sacred cow of balanced budgets. He did not advocate continuous deficit financing. He would have the government deliberately operate in the red whenever private investment was too scanty to provide for the economic needs of the country. When depression gave way to recovery, private financing could take the place of deficit spending for most purposes. He favored the accumulation and investment of large amounts of venture capital, which he declared to be the only socially productive form of capital. Finally, Keynes recommended monetary control as a means of promoting prosperity and full employment. He would establish what is commonly called a "managed currency," regulating its value by a process of contraction or expansion in accordance with the needs of the economy. Prosperity would thus be assured in terms of the condition of the home market, and no nation would be tempted to "beggar its neighbor" in the foolish pursuit of a favorable balance of trade.

John Maynard Keynes

John Maynard Keynes

Trends in art tended to parallel those in literature. For much of the

Big Julie by Fernand Léger. Note the artist's fascination with industrial shapes and images.

Trends in art

period, visual artists continued to explore aesthetic frontiers far removed from the conventional taste of average men and women. Picasso followed his particular genius as it led him further into cubist variations and inventions. So did others, such as the Frenchman Fernand Léger (1881–1955), who combined devotion to cubist principles and a fascination with the artifacts of industrial civilization. A group more advanced, perhaps, than the cubists, the expressionists argued that since color and line express inherent psychological qualities which can be represented without reference to subject matter, a painting need not have a "subject" at all. The Russian Wassily Kandinsky (1866–1944) carried the logic of this position to its conclusion by calling his untitled paintings "improvisations," and insisting that they meant nothing. A second group of expressionists rejected intellectuality for what they called "objectivity," by which they meant a candid appraisal of the state of the human mind. Their analysis took the form of an attack upon the greed and decadence of postwar Europe. Chief among this group was the German George Grosz (1893–1959), whose cruel, satiric line has been likened to a "razor lancing a carbuncle." Another school expressed its disgust with the world by declaring that there was in fact no such thing as aesthetic principle, since aesthetic principle was based on reason and the world had conclusively proved by fighting itself to death that reason did not exist. Calling themselves dada-ists (after a name picked at random, allegedly, from the dictionary) these artists, led by the Frenchman Marcel Duchamp (1887–1968), the German Max Ernst (1891–1976), and the Alsatian Jean Hans Arp (1887–1966), concocted "fabrications" from cut-outs and juxtapositions of wood, glass, and metal, and gave them bizarre

See color plates following page 1056 for representative works by Kandinsky, Duchamp, Dali, and Orozco names: *The Bride stripped bare by her Bachelors, even* (Duchamp), for example. These works were declared by critics, however, to belie their professed meaninglessness, to be, in fact, expressions of the subconscious. Such certainly were the paintings of the surrealists, artists such as the Italian Giorgio de Chirico (1888–1978) and the Spaniard Salvador Dali (1904–), whose explorations of the interior of the mind produced irrational, fantastic, and generally melancholy images.

For a time in the 1930s artists, like writers, responded to the sense of international crisis by painting to express their pain and outrage directly to a mass audience. Among the chief representatives of the new movement were the Mexicans Diego Rivera and Jose Clemente Orozco, and the Americans Thomas Hart Benton, Reginald Marsh, and Edward Hopper. The fundamental aim of these artists was to depict the social conditions of the modern world and to present in graphic detail the hopes and struggles of peasants and workers. While they scarcely adhered to the conventions of the past, there was nothing unintelligible about their work; it was intended to be art that any-

Art and the depression

Left: *The Funeral Procession* by George Grosz. Painted in the late stages of the First World War, this portrayal of a funeral procession gone mad shows death triumphant as humanity is swept into a hell of its own making. The work expressed an anger and a loathing felt by an entire generation. Right: *Mural of Kansas City, Missouri* by Thomas Hart Benton. The mural protests the corruption of American politics and the depression misery and degradation of farm workers and industrial laborers. The man in the armchair is the political boss of Kansas City in the 1930s, Tom Pendergast.

Igor Stravinsky

Development of functional architecture

one could understand. Much of it bore the sting or thrust of social satire. Orozco, in particular, delighted in pillorying the hypocrisy of the church and the greed and cruelty of plutocrats and plunderers.

Music, along with the rest of the arts, continued its movement away from nineteenth-century form and intentions. Impressionists, such as Debussy, were succeeded by expressionists, whose work is concerned more with form than with sensuous effects and tends toward abstraction. Expressionism, more radical and more influential than impressionism, comprises two main schools: atonality, founded by the Viennese Arnold Schoenberg (1874–1951), and polytonality, best typified by the Russian Igor Stravinsky (1882–1971). Atonality abolishes key. In this type of music, dissonances are the rule rather than the exception, and the melodic line commonly alternates between chromatic manipulation and strange unsingable leaps. In short, the ordinary principles of composition are reversed. The atonalists attempt, with some success, to let musical sound become a vehicle for expressing the inner meaning and elemental structure of things.

Polytonality, of which Stravinsky is the most famous exponent, is essentially a radical kind of counterpoint, deriving its inspiration partly from baroque practices of counterpoint that were placed in the service of new ideas. However, it does not simply interweave independent melodies which together form concord, but undertakes to combine separate keys and unrelated harmonic systems, with results that are highly discordant. While the atonalists have retained elements of romanticism, the polytonalists have tried to resurrect the architectural qualities of pure form, movement, and rhythm, stripping away all sentimentality and sensuous connotations.

Architects during this period were also intent upon denying sentimentality. Between 1880 and 1890 designers in Europe and America announced that the prevailing styles of building construction were out of harmony with the facts of modern civilization, and declared as well their intention of restoring that harmony. The chief pioneers of this "functionalism" were Otto Wagner (1841–1918) in Germany and Louis Sullivan (1856–1924) and Frank Lloyd Wright (1869–1959) in the

Taliesin East by Frank Lloyd Wright. A famous example of the functional style, with the pattern of the house conforming to the natural surroundings.

Contrasting Architectural Styles in Germany between the Wars. Left: The Bauhaus by Walter Gropius. This school in Dessau, Germany, is a starkly functional prototype of the interwar "international style." Right: The Chancellery in Berlin by Albert Speer. Note the massive qualities of the Nazi state style.

United States. The basic principle of functionalism is the idea that the appearance of a building should proclaim its actual use and purpose. There must be no addition of friezes, columns, tracery, or battlements merely because some people consider such ornaments beautiful. True beauty consists in an honest adaptation of materials to the purpose they are intended to serve. Functionalism also embodies the notion that architecture should express either directly or symbolically the distinguishing features of contemporary culture. Ornamentation must therefore be restricted to such elements as will reflect an age of science and machines. A leading European practitioner of functionalism was the German, Walter Gropius (1883–1969), who in 1919 established a school—the *Bauhaus*—in Dessau to serve as a center for the theory and practice of modern architecture. Gropius and his followers declared that their style of design, which in time came to be called "international," was the only one which permitted an honest application of new material—chromium, glass, steel, and concrete.

Gropius was one of the multitude of German intellectuals—both Jewish and non-Jewish—to leave their country after Hitler's rise to power. Totalitarianism had its own cultural aesthetic. Functionalism, which celebrated the qualities of material, line, and proportion, had no place in a totalitarian regime, where the arts were obliged to adver-

The arts under Hitler

tise the virtues of the state, its tradition, and the aspirations of its people. Instead of Gropius, Hitler had Albert Speer, an architect of unimpressive talents, who produced for him grandiose designs whose vacuous pretentiousness was an unconscious parody of Nazi ideology. Atonality in music was banished along with functionalism in architecture, to be replaced by a state-sponsored revival of the mystical and heroic nationalism of Wagner.

Propaganda

Art was an important part of the new and cultural arm of totalitarianism: propaganda, the practice of indoctrinating populations to believe only what governments wished them to believe. It mattered not at all that belief was based on falsehood, as in the "superiority of the Aryan race," for example. If it served the interest of the state, it was disseminated as truth. Never before had so many of the world's people been able to read. Nineteenth- and twentieth-century governments had encouraged literacy, fearing an ignorant working class as a revolutionary threat. Now totalitarian regimes used education unashamedly as a means of propagating a party line. "All effective propaganda has to limit itself to a very few points and to use them like slogans," Hitler wrote in *Mein Kampf*. "It has to confine itself to little and to repeat this eternally." Books critical of the state were banned, their places on school and library shelves taken by others specifically written to glorify the present leadership. Youth programs instructed children in the virtues of discipline and loyalty to the state. Mass gymnastic displays suggested the ease with which well-trained bodies could be made to respond to the military needs of the nation. Propagandizing was made more effective by the advent of mass-circulation publishing, the radio, and the motion picture. Newspapers which printed only what the state wanted printed reached a wider audience than ever before. Party political broadcasts, beamed into homes or blared through loudspeakers in town squares, by their constant repetitiveness made people begin to accept—if not believe—what they knew to be untrue. Films could transform German youths into Aryan gods and goddesses, as they could Russian collective farms into a worker's paradise. Sergei Eisenstein (1898–1948), the Russian director, rewrote Russian history on film to serve the ends of the Soviet state. Hitler commissioned the filmmaker Leni Riefenstahl to record a political rally staged by herself and Speer. The film, entitled *Triumph of the Will,* was a visual hymn to the Nordic race and the Nazi regime. (And the comedian Charlie Chaplin riposted in his celebrated lampoon, *The Great Dictator,* an enormously successful parody of totalitarian pomposities.)

The media in the democracies

In Western democracies, although the media were not manipulated by the state as they were elsewhere, their effectiveness as propagandizers was nevertheless recognized and exploited. Advertising became an industry when manufacturers realized the mass markets that newspapers, magazines, and radio represented. Much that was printed and

A Scene from John Ford's film of Steinbeck's The Grapes of Wrath

aired was trivialized by writers and editors who feared that serious or difficult material would antagonize the readers or listeners upon whom they depended for their livelihood. This is not to say that the new media were uniformly banal, or that artists and performers were unable to use them to make thoughtful protests. The film version of Steinbeck's *Grapes of Wrath,* directed by John Ford, though an exception to the normal run of escapist Hollywood comedies and adventures, was perhaps as stinging an indictment of capitalism as the novel, and it reached far more people. During these years popular culture, whatever else it was, remained a powerful and alarming new fact of life: powerful in terms of its vast audience; alarming because of its particular applicability as a means of controlling the minds of men and women.

SELECTED READINGS

• *Items so designated are available in paperback editions.*

GENERAL

Carsten, F. L., *Revolution in Central Europe, 1918–1919,* London, 1972. A useful treatment of the postwar revolts.
• Collaer, P., *A History of Modern Music,* Cleveland, Ohio, 1961. Useful introduction.

Galbraith, John Kenneth, *The Great Crash, 1929*, Boston, 1955. An entertaining and informative account by the celebrated economist.

• Hamilton, George Heard, *Painting and Sculpture in Europe, 1880–1940*, Baltimore, 1967. An excellent survey.

Hartnack, Justus, *Wittgenstein and Modern Philosophy*, Garden City, N.Y., 1965. Clear introduction to a difficult subject.

• Kahler, Erich, *The Tower and the Abyss*, New York, 1957. A survey of the arts in the context of contemporary culture.

Kindleberger, C. P., *The World in Depression, 1929–1939*, Berkeley, Calif., 1973. A first-rate study of the worldwide aspects of the slump.

Laqueur, W., and G. L. Mosse, eds., *The Left-Wing Intellectuals between the Wars, 1919–1939*, New York, 1966. Recent essays by modern historians.

Mosse, George L., *The Naturalization of the Masses: Political Symbolism and Mass Movements in Germany from the Napoleonic Wars through the Third Reich*, New York, 1975. Attempts to trace the roots of Nazism in naturalist movements.

Payne, Stanley G., *Fascism: Comparison and Definition.* Madison, Wisc., 1980. A review of various European fascist movements, written with balance and careful thought.

• Rothschild, Joseph, *East Central Europe between the Two World Wars*, Seattle, 1975. An authoritative survey; does not include Austria.

Shapiro, Theda, *Painters and Politics: The European Avant-Garde and Society, 1900–1925*, New York, 1976. An analysis of the political and social attitudes of a revolutionary generation in the arts.

• Sontag, Raymond J., *A Broken World, 1919–1939*, New York, 1971. A fine, detailed survey of interwar Europe.

THE SOVIET UNION

Carr, E. H., *The Russian Revolution: From Lenin to Stalin*, New York, 1979. A distillation from his ten-volume *History of Soviet Russia.* A fine starting point for the general reader.

• Daniels, Robert U., *The Conscience of the Revolution*, Cambridge, Mass., 1960. Discusses the opposition to Bolshevism in the 1920s.

Deutscher, Isaac, *The Prophet Armed*, London, 1954; *The Prophet Unarmed*, London, 1959; *The Prophet Outcast*, London, 1963. A superb, three-volume biography of Leon Trotsky.

Tucker, Robert C., *Stalin as Revolutionary, 1879–1929: A Study in History and Personality*, New York, 1973. An excellent account of Stalin's rise to power, and of the change from revolution to dictatorship in Russia.

GERMANY AND ITALY

• Bracher, Karl Dietrich, *The German Dictatorship: The Origins, Structure, and Effects of National Socialism*, New York, 1970. A penetrating and exhaustive study of the Nazi state by a political scientist.

• Bullock, Alan, *Hitler: A Study in Tyranny*, rev. ed., New York, 1971. The standard biography.

• Eyck, Erich, *History of the Weimar Republic*, 2 vols., Cambridge, Mass., 1962. A sympathetic account by a prominent German liberal.

Hale, Oron J., *The Captive Press in the Third Reich*, Princeton, N.J., 1964. Examines the manner in which totalitarianism invades journalism.

Mack Smith, Denis, *Mussolini's Roman Empire,* New York, 1976. An able treatment of Italian fascism by the foremost English scholar of Italy.

Gay, Peter, *Weimar Culture: The Outsider as Insider,* New York, 1970. Examines the failure of commitment to the Weimar Republic by German intellectuals.

• Nolte, Ernst, *The Three Faces of Facism,* New York, 1966. A difficult but rewarding study of Germany, Italy, and France, from a philosophical perspective.

• Schoenbaum, David, *Hitler's Social Revolution: Class and Status in Nazi Germany, 1933–39,* Garden City, N.Y., 1966. Hitler's impact upon the various social and economic classes in Germany.

• Stern, Fritz, *The Politics of Cultural Despair: A Study in the Rise of Germanic Ideology,* Berkeley, Calif., 1961. Assesses the way in which cultural beliefs influence politics.

• Zeman, Z. A. B., *Nazi Propaganda,* New York, 1973. Examines an important bulwark of the authoritarian state.

THE DEMOCRACIES

Bullock, Alan, *The Life and Times of Ernest Bevin: Trade Union Leader, 1881–1940,* London, 1960. An excellent study of the British trade unionist and the political and social history of Britain between the wars.

• Burns, James M., *Roosevelt: The Lion and the Fox,* New York, 1956. A readable analysis.

Colton, Joel, *Léon Blum: Humanist in Politics,* New York, 1966. A first-rate biography that illuminates the history of the Popular Front.

• Graves, Robert, and Alan Hodge, *The Long Week-End: A Social History of Great Britain, 1918–1939,* London, 1940. A striking portrait of England in the interwar years.

Harrod, R. F., *The Life of John Maynard Keynes,* New York, 1951. A solid biography by an admirer of Keynes.

Hughes, H. Stuart, *The Obstructed Path: French Social Thought in the Years of Desperation, 1930–1960,* New York, 1968. Detailed analysis of major French thinkers.

• Leuchtenburg, W. E., *Franklin Roosevelt and the New Deal, 1932–1940,* New York, 1964. A good introduction.

Mowat, Charles L., *Britain between the Wars, 1918–1940,* Chicago, 1955. A detailed political and social history, especially valuable for its extensive biographical footnotes.

• Taylor, A. J. P., *English History, 1914–1945,* New York, 1965. The best survey of the period; witty, provocative, insightful.

• Weber, Eugen, *Action Française: Royalism and Reaction in Twentieth Century France,* Stanford, Calif., 1962. The best study of this protofascist movement.

SOURCE MATERIALS

Cole, G. D. H., and M. I. Cole, *The Condition of Britain,* London, 1937. A contemporary analysis by English socialists.

• Ehrenburg, Ilya, *Memoirs, 1921–1941,* New York, 1964. The intellectual at work within the Stalinist regime.

• Greene, Nathanael, comp., *European Socialism Since World War I,* Chicago, 1971. A collection of contemporary accounts.

Gruber, H., *International Communism in the Era of Lenin: A Documentary History,* Greenwich, Conn., 1967. A very useful collection of primary materials.

• Hitler, Adolf, *Mein Kampf,* New York, 1962. Hitler's autobiography, written in 1925. Contains his version of history and his vision for the future. Especially important for his insight into the nature of the masses and the use of propaganda.

Noakes, Jeremy, and Geoffrey Pridham, *Documents on Nazism, 1919–1945,* New York, 1975. An excellent sourcebook; comprehensive and annotated.

• Speer, Albert, *Inside the Third Reich,* New York, 1970. The self-serving but informative memoirs of one of the leaders of Nazi Germany.

Tucker, Robert C., ed., *The Great Purge Trial,* New York, 1965. An annotated edition of the transcript of one of the Soviet "show-trials" that so puzzled Western observers.

Chapter 30

THE SECOND WORLD WAR

The President [Roosevelt] and the Prime Minister [Churchill], after a complete survey of the world situation, are more than ever determined that peace can come to the world only by a total elimination of German and Japanese war power. This involves the simple formula of placing the objective of this war in terms of an unconditional surrender by Germany, Italy, and Japan.

—Franklin D. Roosevelt, Casablanca, January 24, 1943

In September 1939, Europe was drawn again into a general war. The peace of 1919–1920 proved to be no more than an armistice; once more millions of people were locked in a conflict whose devastation surpassed any that had occurred heretofore. As had happened in 1914–1918, the new struggle soon became worldwide. Although the Second World War was not merely a continuation of, or a sequel to, the First, the similarity in causes and characteristics was more than superficial. Both were precipitated by threats to the balance of power, and both were conflicts between peoples, entire nations, rather than between governments. On the other hand, there were notable differences between the two conflicts. The methods of warfare in the Second World War had little in common with those of the earlier conflict. Trench warfare was superseded by bombing and by sudden aerial (Blitzkrieg) attacks, with highly mobile armies, on both civilian populations and military installations. Because so many were now vulnerable to the ravages of warfare, the distinction between those on the battlefield and those at home was more completely obliterated in the second war than it had been in the first. Finally, this war was not greeted with the almost universal, naïve enthusiasm that had marked the outbreak of the other. Men and women still remembered the horrors of the First World War. They entered the Second with determination, but also with a keener appreciation of the frightful devastation that war could bring than their predecessors had possessed.

A comparison of the two world wars

Defects of the peace treaties

The causes of the Second World War related to the failure of the peace terms of 1919–1920. Those terms, while understandable in view of the passions and hatreds engendered by the First World War, created almost as many problems as they solved. By yielding to the demands of the victors for annexation of territory and the creation of satellite states, the peacemakers sowed new seeds of bitterness and conflict. By proclaiming the principle of self-determination while acquiescing in the distribution of national minorities behind alien frontiers, the treaties raised expectations while at the same time frustrating them. Perhaps most important, by imposing harsh terms on Germany, the treatymakers gave the Germans what seemed to many to be legitimate grievances, by depriving them of their rightful share of international power and saddling them with the entire burden of war "guilt."

Power politics

Power politics were a second cause of war. Although Woodrow Wilson and other sponsors of the League of Nations had acclaimed the league as a means of eliminating power struggles, it did nothing of the sort. It merely substituted a new and more precarious balance for the old. The signatures on the peace treaties had scarcely dried when the victors began the construction of new alliances to maintain their supremacy. A neutralized zone consisting of the Baltic states, Poland, and Rumania was created as a buffer against Soviet Russia. A "Little Entente" composed of Czechoslovakia, Yugoslavia, and Rumania was established to prevent a revival of Austrian power. These combinations, together with a Franco-Belgian alliance and a Franco–Polish alliance, would also serve to isolate Germany. Even the league itself was fundamentally an alliance of the victors against the vanquished. That there would be fears and anxieties over a disturbance of the new power arrangement was natural. The first sign of such a disturbance appeared in 1922 when Germany and Russia negotiated the Treaty of Rapallo. Though disguised as a mere trade agreement, it opened the way for political and, according to some accounts, even military collaboration between the two states.

Attempts to preserve international amity

Diplomats made various attempts to preserve or restore international amity during the 1920s and 1930s. Some saw in disarmament the most promising means of achieving their purpose. Accordingly, a succession of conferences was called in the hope of at least limiting a race to rearm. In 1925 representatives of the chief European powers met at Locarno and acted on the suggestion of the German and French foreign ministers, Gustav Stresemann and Aristide Briand, that Germany and France pledge themselves to respect the Rhine frontiers as established in the Versailles treaty. They agreed also that they would never go to war against each other except in "legitimate defense." More widely celebrated than the Locarno Agreements was the Pact of Paris, or Kellogg-Briand Pact of 1928. Its purpose was to outlaw war

Members of the Council of the League of Nations. In the front row, from the right, are Chamberlain of Britain, Vandervelde of Belgium, Stresemann of Germany, and Briand of France.

as an international crime. Eventually, nearly all the nations of the world signed this agreement renouncing war as "an instrument of national policy" and providing that the settlement of international disputes "of whatever nature or of whatever origin" should never be sought "except by peaceful means." Neither the Locarno Agreements nor the Pact of Paris was much more than a pious gesture. The signatory nations adopted them with so many reservations and exceptions in favor of "vital interests" that they could never be effective instruments for preserving peace. Had the League of Nations been better organized, it might have relieved some of the tensions and prevented clashes between nations still unwilling to relinquish their absolute sovereignty. Yet it was not a league of all nations, since both Germany and Russia were excluded for much of the interwar period.

Economic conditions were a third important cause of the outbreak of war. The huge reparations imposed upon the Germans, and the French occupation of much of Germany's industrial heartland, helped, as we have seen, to retard Germany's economic recovery and bring on the debilitating inflation of the 1920s. The depression of the 1930s contributed to the coming of the war in several ways. It intensified economic nationalism. Baffled by problems of unemployment and business stagnation, governments resorted to high tariffs in an attempt to preserve the home market for their own producers. The depression was also responsible for a marked increase in armaments production, which was seen as a means of reducing unemployment. Despite the misgivings of some within the governments of Britain and France, Germany was allowed to rearm. Armaments expansion, on a large scale, was first undertaken by Germany about 1935, with the result that unemployment was substantially reduced and business boomed. Other nations followed the German example, not simply as a way of boosting their economies, but in response to Nazi military power. The depression helped as well to produce a new wave of militant expansionism directed toward the conquest of neighboring territories

Economic conditions

The Krupp Shipworks in Germany. Seen here are German submarines in the final stages of assembly.

as a means of solving economic problems. Japan took the lead in 1931 with the invasion of Manchuria. The decline of Japanese exports of raw silk and cotton cloth meant that the nation as a consequence was unable to pay for needed imports of coal, iron, and other minerals. Japanese militarists were thus furnished with a convenient pretext for seizing Manchuria, where supplies of these commodities could then be purchased for Japanese currency. Mussolini, in part to distract the Italians from the domestic problems brought on by economic depression, invaded and annexed Ethiopia in 1936. Finally, the depression was primarily responsible for the triumph of Nazism, whose expansionist policies contributed directly to the outbreak of war.

Nationalism   Nationalism was a further cause of the general discontent that helped increase the chances for world war. In eastern Europe, national and ethnic minorities remained alienated from the sovereign states into which the treaty-makers had placed them. This was particularly the case of the Sudetenland Germans, who had been included in the newly created state of Czechoslovakia. That country could in fact boast no national majority, including as it did Czechs, Slovaks, Poles, Ruthenians, and Hungarians, as well as Germans. Although it possessed an enlightened policy of minority self-government, the patchwork state of Czechoslovakia remained unstable. And its instability was to prove a key factor as the tensions mounted in the late 1930s.

Appeasement   A final cause of war was the policy of "appeasement" which was pursued by the Western democracies in the face of German, Italian, and Japanese aggression. The appeasers' strategy was grounded in three commonly held assumptions. The first was that the outbreak of another war was unthinkable. With the memory of the slaughter of 1914–1918 fresh in their minds, many in the West embraced pacifism, or at any rate adopted an attitude that kept them from realistically addressing the implications of Nazi and fascist policies and programs. Second, many in Britain and the United States argued that Germany had been mistreated in the Versailles treaty, that the Germans had legitimate grievances which should be acknowledged and resolved. Finally, the appeasers were, for the most part, staunch anti-Communists. They believed that by assisting Germany to regain its former military and economic power, they were constructing a bulwark to halt the westward advance of Soviet communism. When Japan invaded Manchuria, the West refused to impose sanctions against the Japanese through the League of Nations, arguing that Japan, too, could serve as a counterweight to Russia.

Hitler took advantage of this generally tolerant attitude to advance the expansionist ambitions of Germany. As the country rearmed, Hitler played upon his people's sense of shame and betrayal, proclaiming their right to regain their former power within the world. In 1933, he removed Germany from the League of Nations—and thus from any obligation to adhere to its declarations. In 1935 Hitler tore up the disarmament provisions of the Treaty of Versailles, announcing the revival of conscription and the return to universal military training. In 1936 he repudiated the Locarno Agreements and invaded the Rhineland. Britain and France did nothing to stop him, as they had done nothing to prevent Mussolini's invasion and conquest of Ethiopia the previous year. Hitler's move tipped the balance of power in Germany's favor. While the Rhineland remained demilitarized and German industry in the Ruhr valley unprotected, France had held the upper hand. Now it no longer did so.

Hitler's aggressive moves

In 1936 civil war broke out in Spain; a series of weak republican governments had proved unable to prevent the country's political disintegration. Although they had signed a pact of nonintervention with the other Western powers, Hitler and Mussolini both sent troops and equipment to assist the forces of the rebel fascist commander, Francisco Franco. Russia countered with aid to the Communist troops serving under the banner of the Spanish republic. Again, Britain and France failed to act decisively. The Spanish Civil War lasted three years,

The Spanish Civil War

Guernica by Pablo Picasso. This painting, a protest against the bombing of an undefended city during the Spanish Civil War, has come to be recognized as one of the century's most profound antiwar statements.

The Munich Conference, 1938. Left: Prime Minister Chamberlain of Britain and Hitler during the Munich conference. Right: Chamberlain addressing a crowd on his return from the Munich conference.

with the forces of the fascists finally victorious over those of the republicans. The conflict engaged the commitment of many young European and American leftists and intellectuals, who saw it as a test of the West's determination to resist totalitarianism. The fighting was brutal; aerial bombardment of civilians and troops was employed for the first time on a large scale. Because of this, the Spanish war has often been seen as a "dress rehearsal" for the much larger struggle that was shortly to follow. The war also served to confirm Hitler's belief that if Britain, France, and Russia did decide to attempt to contain fascism, they would have a difficult time concerting their policies—another reason, indeed, why Britain and France did remain content to do nothing.

Munich and after

In March of 1938, Hitler annexed Austria, declaring it his intention to bring all Germans into his Reich. Once more, there was no official reaction from the West. Hitler's next target was the Sudetenland in Czechoslovakia. With Austria now a part of Germany, Czechoslovakia was almost entirely surrounded by its hostile expansionist neighbor. Hitler declared that the Sudetenland was a natural part of the Reich and that he intended to occupy it. The British prime minister, Neville Chamberlain, determined to negotiate, but on Hitler's terms. On September 28, Hitler agreed to meet with Chamberlain, Premier Édouard Daladier of France, and Mussolini in a four-power conference in Munich. The result was another capitulation by France and Britain. Ignoring the vital interests of a nation whose territory the Versailles treaty had guaranteed, the four negotiators bargained away a major slice of Czechoslovakia, while that country's representatives were left to await their fate outside the conference room. Chamberlain returned to England proclaiming "peace in our time." Hitler soon

See color map facing page 961

proved that fatuous boast untrue. In March 1939 he invaded what was
left of Czechoslovakia and established a puppet regime in its capital,
Prague. This action convinced British public opinion of the foolhar-
diness of appeasement. Chamberlain, compelled to shift his policies
dramatically, guaranteed the sovereignty of the two states now directly
in Hitler's path: Poland and Rumania. France followed suit.

Meanwhile, the appeasement policies of Britain and France had
fueled Stalin's fears that the timid Western democracies might strike a
bargain with Germany at Soviet expense by diverting Nazi expansion
eastward. This, combined with the suspicion that they might make
unreliable allies, convinced Stalin that he must look elsewhere for
security. Tempted by the traditional Russian desire for territory in
Poland, and promised a share of both Poland and the Baltic states by
Hitler, Stalin signed a pact with the Nazis in August 1939. In going
to Munich, Britain and France had put their interests first; Russia would
now look after its own.

Nazi-Soviet pact

2. THE OUTBREAK OF HOSTILITIES

Following the extinction of Czechoslovakia, and despite Chamberlain's guarantee, Hitler demanded the abolition of the Polish Corridor,
a narrow strip of territory connecting Poland with the Baltic Sea. The
corridor contained a large German population, which Hitler declared
must be reunited with the Fatherland. Judging Britain and France by
past performance he believed their pledges to Poland worthless. With
the Soviets now in his camp, he expected that Poland would quickly
capitulate, and that the Western allies would back down once more as
they had done at Munich. When Poland stood firm, Hitler attacked.
On September 1, 1939, German tanks crossed the Polish border. Britain and France sent a joint warning to Germany to cease its aggression.
There was no reply; on September 3, Britain and France declared war
against Germany.

Beginning of the war

The conflict with Poland proved to be a brief encounter. In less than

*The Beginning of the Second World
War.* A long line of German tanks
crossing into Poland.

three weeks the Polish armies had been routed, Warsaw had been captured, and the chiefs of the Polish government had fled to Rumania. For some months after that the war resolved itself into a kind of siege, a "phony war" or "sitzkrieg," as it was sometimes called. Such fighting as did occur was largely confined to submarine warfare, aerial raids on naval bases, and occasional battles between naval vessels. In the spring of 1940 the sitzkrieg was suddenly transformed into a Blitzkrieg, or "lightning war." The Germans struck blows at Norway, Denmark, Belgium, the Netherlands, and France, conquering them in short order, and driving the British and French forces back against the English Channel at Dunkirk in Belgium. Despite heavy German air attacks, the British were able to evacuate over 300,000 troops, many of them in commercial and pleasure boats which had been pressed into emergency service. Northern France, including Paris, was occupied by the Germans. In the south, a puppet government loyal to the Germans was established at Vichy under the leadership of the aged First World War hero, Marshal Henri-Philippe Pétain.

Before launching an invasion across the Channel, the Nazis decided to attempt the reduction of Britain's military strength and civilian will by air raids. From August 1940 to June 1941, in the so-called Battle of Britain, thousands of planes smashed at British ports, industrial centers, and air defenses throughout the country. Despite the fact that whole sections of cities were laid in ruins and more than 40,000 civilians killed, the British held firm. Winston Churchill had by this time succeeded Neville Chamberlain as prime minister of Britain. A maverick Conservative, who had served in Britain's First World War government as a Liberal, Churchill was not trusted by his party's

Left: *London during the Blitz.* This picture conveys a vivid impression of the agony which the British capital suffered during the Battle of Britain, which lasted from August 1940 to June 1941. Behind the tumbling ruins brought down by firebombs is St. Paul's Cathedral. Right: *French Refugees Driven from Their Homes during the Early Years of the Nazi Occupation*

Pearl Harbor, December 7, 1941. This photo shows American battleships sunk at their moorings, following the Japanese raid on what President Franklin D. Roosevelt declared was "the day that will live in infamy."

leadership, particularly since he had been one of the few who had spoken out in favor of British rearmament during the years of appeasement. Now that his warnings had proved true, he was given direction of the war as head of a national government composed of ministers from the Conservative, Liberal, and Labour parties. Churchill, an exceedingly compelling orator, used the radio to persuade his countrymen and women—and the rest of the free world—that Britain must not, and would not, surrender to the Nazis. His friendship with President Roosevelt, and the latter's conviction that the United States must come to Britain's aid, resulted in the shipment of military equipment and ships to the British under the Lend-Lease Act passed by the U.S. Congress in 1941.

Meanwhile, Germany moved eastward into the Balkans, subduing the Rumanians, Hungarians, Bulgarians, and Yugoslavs. The Italians, less successful in their campaigns in Greece and North Africa, required German assistance to accomplish their missions. Scornful of Mussolini's military inadequacies, Churchill called him Hitler's "jackal." Frustrated in his attempt to subjugate Britain, Hitler broke with his erstwhile ally Russia, and turned eastward, on June 22, 1941, with a massive invasion. Before the end of the year his armies had smashed their way to the gates of Moscow but never actually succeeded in capturing it. The defense of Moscow by the Russian armies marked one of the war's important early turning points.

The German invasion of Russia

The war was converted into a global conflict when Japan struck at Pearl Harbor on December 7 of the same year. The Japanese had been involved in a costly war with China since 1937. To wage it successfully they needed the oil, rubber, and extensive food resources of the Netherlands Indies, the Malay Peninsula, and Southeast Asia. They had allied with Germany in 1940. (Germany, Italy, and Japan were together known as the Axis powers, a name derived from the Rome-Berlin diplomatic axis formed in the 1930s.) Now, before attacking

Pearl Harbor

A German V-2 Rocket. Used in the later years of the war, it was the forerunner of the early space launch vehicles.

south, they considered it necessary to secure their position to the rear by crushing American naval and air power on the base of Pearl Harbor. The next day the United States Congress recognized a state of war with Japan, and on December 11 Germany and its allies declared war upon the United States.

In the course of the next two and a half years, events turned slowly but inexorably against the forces of Germany, Italy, and Japan. Churchill and Roosevelt, meeting shortly after the United States' entry into the war, agreed that victory in the West would be their first priority. As an initial step toward that goal, the British succeeded in turning the North African advance of Germany's brilliant tank commander, General Erwin Rommel, who had driven the British back across the Sahara to the Egyptian border. That victory was the prelude to a joint Anglo-American invasion of North Africa in November 1942. The success of this first major combined Allied offensive led in turn to further Mediterranean campaigns in the next year, first in Sicily and then in Italy. Mussolini's government was overthrown, and his successors sued for peace. The Germans, however, sent troops into Italy and resurrected Mussolini as the ruler of a puppet state in the north, where he reigned a virtual prisoner of the Nazis until his death at the hands of his countrymen at the time of the general defeat of the Axis powers in Europe. Despite Allied attempts to break the German grip on the peninsula, the Nazi forces continued to hold central and northern Italy until the spring of 1945.

The battle of Stalingrad

In eastern Europe, meanwhile, the Germans had continued to press the war against the Russians, turning in 1942 to the south and the rich agricultural and industrial areas of the Ukraine, the Donets Basin, and the Caucasus oilfields. The German advance was stopped at Stalingrad, in a military struggle of great strategic and symbolic importance for both sides. The battle saw 300,000 Germans for a time in control of the city, then enclosed by the counterattacking Russians in a pincers movement, and eventually, by the time of their surrender, reduced to fewer than half their original number. The loss of the battle of Stalingrad compelled the Germans to undertake a general retreat. By the spring of 1943, they were no further east than they had been the previous year.

The D-Day invasion

Stalin continued to pressure his allies to open a second front in the west to relieve the concerted Nazi drive against Russia. The North African and Italian campaigns were a response to that plea. But not until June 1944 did Allied troops invade France. On June 6 (D-Day) a massive invasion force landed on the Normandy coast. Air superiority, plus a tremendous buildup of matériel and manpower, produced a series of successful advances and the liberation of Paris on August 25. Despite a final German assault in December 1944, the Allied armies penetrated deep into Germany itself by the early spring of 1945.

At the same time, Soviet troops were approaching from the east. On April 21, 1945, they hammered their way into the suburbs of Berlin. During the next ten days a savage battle raged amid the ruins and heaps of rubble. On May 2 the heart of the city was captured, and the Soviet red banner flew from the Brandenburg Gate. A few hours earlier Adolf Hitler killed himself in the bomb-proof shelter of the Chancellery. On May 8 representatives of the German High Command signed a document of unconditional surrender.

End of the war in Europe

The war in the Pacific came to an end four months later. Important victories won by the United States Navy against the Japanese at the battles of the Coral Sea and Midway in the spring of 1942 forestalled Japanese attempts to capture Australia and the Hawaiian Islands, and thus deprive the United States of advance bases for a counteroffensive against Japan. Final Allied victory followed further naval battles, island assaults, and land battles in Southeast Asia. In June 1945, the island of Okinawa was taken, after eighty-two days of desperate fighting. The American forces now had a foothold less than 500 miles from the Japanese homeland. The government in Tokyo was anticipating an invasion and calling upon its citizens for supreme endeavors to meet the crisis.

The Pacific war

On July 26 the heads of the United States, British, and Chinese governments issued a joint proclamation calling upon Japan to surrender or be destroyed. In the absence of a reply the United States resolved to make use of a new and revolutionary weapon to end the war quickly. This weapon was the atomic bomb, recently developed in secrecy by Allied scientists. Many high military and naval officers contended that use of the bomb was not necessary, on the assumption that Japan was already beaten. Harry Truman, who had succeeded Roosevelt following the latter's death in April 1945, decided otherwise. On August 6, a single atomic bomb was dropped on Hiroshima, completely obliterating about 60 percent of the city. Three days later a second bomb was

The atomic bomb

Left: *D-Day.* Cargo ships are seen pouring supplies ashore during the invasion of France. Balloon barrages float overhead to protect the ships from low-flying enemy planes. Right: *Signing the German Surrender, May 7, 1945*

View of Hiroshima after the First Atom Bomb Was Dropped, August 6, 1945. This photo, taken one month later, shows the utter devastation of the city. Only a few steel and concrete buildings remained intact.

dropped, this time on Nagasaki. President Truman warned that the United States would continue to use the atom bomb as long as might be necessary to bring Japan to its knees. On August 14, Tokyo transmitted to Washington an unconditional acceptance of Allied demands.

Total war

To an even greater extent than was the case in the First World War, total populations were mobilized as part of the war effort. Governments imposed the rationing of food and clothing and the regulation of manpower. Production quotas demanded that factories produce around the clock. In Russia, all men between the ages of sixteen and fifty-five and all women between the ages of sixteen and forty-five were pressed into service, either in the armed forces or on the home front. The Germans destroyed much of Russia's industrial plant and existing war matériel in the early months of the war—over 90 percent of Russia's tanks, for example. To produce what was necessary, factories were rebuilt in the security of the Ural mountain region, and whole populations moved there to work in them.

The Resistance

In countries conquered and occupied by the Germans and Italians, the Axis powers installed administrations willing to follow their commands without question. (Vidkun Quisling, the Norwegian Nazi leader, made his name synonymous with the word "traitor.") Life for civilians was harsh at best. Rations in occupied France, for example, were less than half the amount considered to be a healthy minimum. There and elsewhere, Resistance movements emerged, composed of men and women of various political persuasions united in their determination to assist the Allies in driving the Axis powers from their native lands. By transmitting intelligence reports, aiding prisoners to escape, distributing newspapers to counter official propaganda, and undertaking acts of direct sabotage to military and industrial targets, these groups helped the Allied cause immeasurably. The success of the Normandy invasion was in part the result of information concerning German military emplacements sent to Britain by the French Resistance.

The war brought devastation in the form of street fighting and air bombardment to most of the major urban centers of Europe. The Allies proved to be fully as ruthless and even more efficient than the Axis powers in this regard. After some debate, British and American strategists abandoned pinpoint bombing in favor of the nighttime aerial bombardment of entire cities. The result was the deliberate fire-bombing of civilian populations, climaxing in Europe in early 1945 with the brutal obliteration of Dresden, a German city without significant industry and filled with refugees. These attacks were equaled by the German bombing of French, Belgian, Dutch, Russian, and British cities and civilian populations. Such raids were, of course, dwarfed by the United States' atomic bomb attacks on the Japanese cities of Hiroshima and Nagasaki.

The war's devastation of cities

Ghastly as was the destruction meted out by the armed forces to each other and to civilians, none of it matched in premeditated, obscene horror the systematic persecution by the Nazis of whole Jewish populations, not only in Germany itself, but in occupied countries as well. When allied armies opened the concentration camps in Germany and elsewhere in what had been German-occupied Europe, they found the starved, diseased, and brutalized remnants of a total of six million prisoners, those who had been able to survive the ghastly experience of Nazi persecutions. Most of the men, women, and children who had been imprisoned, tortured, and killed, were Jews, although Poles, Russians, Gypsies, homosexuals, and other "traitors" to the Reich had been incarcerated, used for forced labor, and executed also.

The concentration camps

German Civilians Compelled to View the Bodies of Concentration Camp Victims at the Landesburg Camp in 1945 as an American army Officer Lectures Them on the Horrors of the Nazis' "Final Solution"

Postwar plans

Allied conflicts

The Teheran conference

The Yalta conference

3. THE PEACE SETTLEMENT

During the war the Allied leaders had come together on several occasions to discuss war aims and postwar goals. The public rhetoric of government propaganda spoke of the need for a world without conflict and of the right of all people to political self-determination, objectives expressed in the "Atlantic Charter" issued by Roosevelt and Churchill in August 1941, and in a declaration signed by twenty-six nations, including Britain, the United States, the Soviet Union, and China, the following year. Yet those worthy goals, like most of Wilson's Fourteen Points, fell eventual victim to the realities of international politics.

Stalin, Churchill, and Roosevelt convened in two conferences that were of major importance in determining the shape and political complexion of postwar Europe. In both cases, tensions between the three major participants were to some degree glossed over in their desire to present a united front to the world. Yet those tensions were real. The focus of disagreement was central Europe, and particularly the future of Germany and Poland. Stalin insisted that Russia retain the Polish territory annexed in 1939 at the time of the Nazi-Soviet pact, an expression of his understandable desire to build a bulwark against any future German aggression, and a reflection of his unwillingness to see postwar Western influence extended too far in Russia's direction. His memories of Anglo-American participation in the attempt by White Russians to overthrow the newly created Communist regime in 1919 were matched by American perceptions of the Soviet Union as an expansionist and politically alien and dangerous regime. All three leaders were also confronted by conflicting plots and aspirations on the part of governments-in-exile from Nazi-occupied countries, and of extra-governmental Resistance groups—often led by Communists—whose struggles to retain or to assume leadership in their homelands were exceeded only by their determination to oust the Germans.

When the three leaders met in Teheran in December 1943, they managed to put forward a declaration of unified purpose only by postponing the really knotty problems that confronted them. The invasion of France was agreed to for the following year; Stalin undertook to enter the war against Japan following the defeat of Germany. But on the question of Poland, only the most tentative agreement was reached regarding boundary lines, and the nature of the postwar Polish government was left for further negotiation.

By the time Stalin, Churchill, and Roosevelt met again, in February 1945 at Yalta, the military situation favored Russia's position. Soviet troops had occupied Poland the previous spring; they now held part of Czechoslovakia as well, and were poised to invade Germany. Once more the matter of Poland's future arose, as well as that of the com-

The Yalta Conference. Churchill, Molotov, Secretary of State Stettinius, at the left, and Stalin, in the center, with glasses raised in a toast. Roosevelt is also to Stalin's left.

position of postwar regimes. A general declaration outlined plans for Russian expansion westward into Poland, and the compensation of Poland with territory taken from the Germans. As to Poland's government, though communiqués spoke of the need for free elections there and elsewhere among the occupied countries, the fact remained that the Soviets had already established a Communist government in Warsaw, and were unlikely to tolerate its replacement by an anti-Communist faction still in London, whatever the results of an election. Yalta produced accord on several important issues: the establishment of a United Nations Organization to keep the peace; the terms for Russian entry into the Japanese war; the positioning of zones of Allied occupation in Germany and Austria; and agreement in principle to a policy of German reparation payments—though in goods and equipment rather than in gold, as had been the case after the First World War.

Little more than two months after Germany's surrender, the Allies met again, this time at Potsdam, a suburb of Berlin and the former residence of Prussian kings. Roosevelt had died the previous spring; his place at the conference was taken by his successor, President Harry Truman. Churchill represented Britain until replaced, as the result of elections at home, by the new prime minister and Labour party leader, Clement Attlee. Stalin remained to negotiate for the Soviets. As at past conferences, less was settled than was allowed to remain unresolved. Peace treaties were to be prepared with the "recognized democratic governments" of previously occupied lands. Yet the question as to whether those governments set up by the Soviets in Poland and—by this time—elsewhere in eastern Europe were truly democratic was not settled. Polish boundaries were redrawn to conform to the general agreement reached at Yalta. An inter-Allied war tribunal was established to try major Nazi leaders for "war crimes." In November 1945, the trials began in Nuremberg, Germany. The following September,

The Potsdam conference

The Potsdam Conference. Churchill, a cigar in his mouth, is seated in the back to the left; Stalin is at the right; Truman is seated with his back to the camera.

eighteen of the twenty-two defendants were found guilty and received sentences ranging from ten-years' imprisonment to death.

The Potsdam conference was shadowed by the East-West conflict that had darkened all the wartime meetings and was to do the same to *East-West tensions* international politics in the immediate postwar years. The division of Germany into four occupied zones—American, British, French, and Soviet—and the agreement to structure reparations payments on the basis of those zones rather than on a united Germany, forecast the unwillingness of either the Soviet Union or the Western powers to trust each other, or to tolerate the extension of the other's influence in that country which, though devastated, still remained vital to the security and peace of Europe as a whole.

The treaty with Japan, though it too produced disagreement between Russia and the West, did not reflect conflicts as immediate as those *The treaty with Japan* that characterized the European negotiations. The treaty deprived the Japanese of all the territory they had acquired since 1854—their entire overseas empire. They surrendered the southern half of Sakhalin Island and the Kuril Islands to Soviet Russia, and the Bonins and Ryukyus to control by the United States. They also renounced all rights to Formosa, which was left in an undefined status. They yielded as well to the United States the right to continue maintaining military installations in Japan until the latter was able to defend itself. The treaty went into effect in April 1952 despite opposition from the Russians, who feared a United States military presence in the Far East.

As in the case of the Versailles treaty one of the most significant elements in the settlements was their provision for an international organization. The old League of Nations had failed to avert the outbreak of war in 1939, and in April 1946 it was formally dissolved. Yet Allied statesmen continued to recognize the need for some international organization. In February 1945, they agreed at Yalta that a conference to respond to that need should be convoked the following April. Despite the sudden death of Roosevelt two weeks earlier, the conference met as scheduled. A charter was adopted on June 26, providing for a world organization to be known as the United Nations and to be founded upon the principle of "the sovereign equality of all peace-loving states." Its important agencies were to be (1) a General Assembly composed of representatives of all the member states; (2) a Security Council composed of reresentatives of the United States, Great Britain, the Soviet Union, the Republic of China, and France, with permanent seats, and of six other states chosen by the General Assembly to fill the nonpermanent seats; (3) a Secretariat consisting of a secretary-general and a staff of subordinates; (4) an Economic and Social Council composed of eighteen members chosen by the General Assembly; (5) a Trusteeship Council, and (6) an International Court of Justice.

Establishment of the United Nations

Although the United Nations has failed to live up to the hopes of its founders, it continues to function as the world's longest lived international assembly of nations. By far the most important functions of the new organization were assigned by the charter to the Security Council. This agency has the "primary responsibility for the maintenance of international peace and security." It has authority to investigate any dispute between nations, to recommend methods for settlement, and, if necessary to preserve the peace, to employ diplomatic or economic measures against an aggressor. If, in its judgment, these have proved, or are likely to prove, inadequate, it may "take such action by air, naval, or land forces" as may be required to maintain or restore international order. The member states are required by the charter to make available to the Security Council, on its call, armed forces for the maintenance of peace.

The Security Council

The Security Council was so organized as to give almost a monopoly of authority to its permanent members, since no action of any kind could be taken without the unanimous consent of Great Britain, France, the United States, the Republic of China, the Soviet Union, and two other members besides. This absolute veto given to each of the principal states, instead of bolstering the peace of the world, crippled the council and rendered it helpless in the face of emergencies.

The veto power of the Big Five

The remaining agencies of the U.N. were given a wide variety of functions. The Secretariat, composed of a secretary-general and a numerous staff, is chiefly an administrative authority. Its duties, though, are by no means routine, for the secretary-general may bring to the attention of the Security Council any matter which, in his opinion,

Other agencies of the U.N.

threatens international peace. The functions of the Economic and Social Council are the most varied of all. Composed of eighteen members elected by the General Assembly, it has authority to initiate studies and make recommendations with respect to international social, economic, health, educational, cultural, and related matters, and may perform services within such fields at the request of U.N. members.

During its first three decades the work of various U.N. agencies helped the organization achieve a modestly impressive record of accomplishment. But against its successes must be recorded major failures as well. The U.N. was unable to establish control of nuclear weapons. And it was powerless in the face of any determined effort by a major power to have its own way, as in the case of the Soviet suppression of a revolt in Hungary in 1956; or the massive intervention by the United States in Vietnam in the 1960s and early 1970s. If the United Nations acted upon occasion to defuse potentially explosive world situations, it failed to achieve the lofty peace-making and peace-keeping goals set for it by its founders.

SELECTED READINGS

• *Items so designated are available in paperback editions.*

Carr, E. H., *The Twenty-Years Crisis,* London, 1942. Stimulating, though somewhat dogmatic.

• Carr, Raymond, *The Spanish Tragedy: The Civil War in Perspective,* London, 1977. A thoughtful introduction to the Spanish Civil War and the evolution of Franco's Spain.

• Dawidowicz, Lucy S., *The War Against the Jews, 1933–1945,* New York, 1975. A full account of the Holocaust.

• Divine, Robert A., *Roosevelt and World War II,* Baltimore, 1969. A diplomatic history.

• Feis, Herbert, *Churchill–Roosevelt–Stalin: The War They Waged and the Peace They Sought,* Princeton, N.J., 1957. A standard survey.

Géraud, André, *The Gravediggers of France,* Garden City, N.Y., 1944. A critical and impassioned account of the fall of France.

Gilbert, Martin, and R. Gott, *The Appeasers,* Boston, 1963. Excellent study of British pro-German sentiment in the 1930s.

Holborn, Hajo, *The Political Collapse of Europe,* New York, 1951. Examines Europe's position in light of the rise of Russia and the United States as superpowers.

• Jackson, Gabriel, *The Spanish Republic and the Civil War, 1931–1939,* Princeton, N.J., 1965. A solid, useful account.

Milward, Alan S., *War, Economy, and Society, 1939–1945,* Berkeley, Calif., 1977. Analyzes the impact of the war on the world economy and the ways in which economic resources of the belligerents determined strategies.

• Paxton, Robert D., *Vichy France: Old Guard and New Order,* New York, 1972. A bitter account.

- Taylor, A. J. P., *The Origins of the Second World War,* New York, 1962. A controversial but provocative attempt to prove that Hitler did not want a world war.

  Wheeler, Bennett, J. W., *Munich: Prologue to Tragedy,* London, 1966. A sensitive treatment of prewar diplomatic negotiations, outdated to some extent, but still evocative.

- Wright, Gordon, *The Ordeal of Total War, 1939–1945,* New York, 1968. Particularly good on the domestic response to war and the mobilization of the resources of the modern state.

SOURCE MATERIALS

- Bloch, Marc, *Strange Defeat: A Statement of Evidence Written in 1940,* London, 1949. An analysis of the fall of France, written by one of France's greatest historians, who later died fighting for the Resistance.

- Churchill, Winston S., *The Second World War,* 6 vols., London, 1948–1954. The war as Churchill saw it and as he wanted history to see it. Especially useful is the first volume on the 1930s, *The Gathering Storm.*

- De Gaulle, Charles, *The Complete War Memoirs,* New York, 1964. De Gaulle's apologia.

- Hershey, John, *Hiroshima,* New York, 1946. A moving account of the aftermath of the U.S. atomic bombing written very soon after the event.

  Noakes, Jeremy, and Geoffrey Pridham, *Documents on Nazism, 1919–1945,* New York, 1975. A helpful collection.

Part Seven

THE EMERGENCE OF
WORLD CIVILIZATION

Western civilization, as we have described and analyzed it, no longer exists today. Instead, we speak in terms of a world civilization, one that owes much of its history and many of its most perplexing problems to the West, but one which is no longer shaped by those few nations that for so many centuries dominated the globe.

The great powers of the nineteenth century—Britain, France, and Germany—are powers now only insofar as they have agreed to pool their interests in an all-European Common Market. The mid–twentieth century superpowers, the United States and the Soviet Union, after two decades of confrontation, have begun to understand the limitations of their power and to adjust their expectations accordingly. Power, and with it the attention of the world, is shifting from the West to the emerging nations of Africa, the Middle East, Asia, and Latin America. Their vast natural resources are affording many of them the chance to play the old Western game of power politics, and in a world arena wider than ever before. The equally vast dimensions of their internal problems—economic, racial, nutritional, and political—suggest that their solution will have to be worldwide as well. We are all, as the American designer Buckminster Fuller has said, partners for better or worse on "spaceship earth."

The Emergence of World Civilization

POLITICS	SCIENCE & INDUSTRY

1945

Truman Doctrine, 1947
Independence of India, 1947
Communist regimes established in eastern Europe,
    1947–1948
Marshall Plan, 1948
Division of Germany, 1949
Victory of Chinese communists, 1949
NATO, 1949
Korean war, 1950–1953

                                    Hydrogen bomb, 1952

Death of Stalin, 1953   Discovery of polio vaccine, 1953

                                      Discovery of DNA, 1953

Hungarian revolt, 1956
Suez crisis, 1956

                                      Sputnik launched, 1957

1960

Conflict in the Congo, 1960
Nigerian Civil War, 1960s
Berlin wall, 1961

Cuban missile crisis, 1962
Assassination of John F. Kennedy, 1963
War in Vietnam, 1964–1975
Assassination of Malcolm X, 1965
Civil war in Nigeria, 1966–1970
Arab-Israeli war, 1967
Assassination of Martin Luther King, Jr., 1968

                                      Manned U.S. spacecraft lands on moon, 1969

1970   Advent of automation, 1970s

Civil war in India, 1971

First SALT agreements signed, 1972
Arab-Israeli war, 1973

Egyptian-Israeli peace treaty, 1979
Iranian revolution, 1979

1980

Zimbabwe established, 1980
Assassination of Anwar Sadat, 1981
U.S. rejection of SALT II agreement, 1981

Solidarity movement in Poland, 1982–
War in Lebanon, 1982–

ECONOMICS & SOCIETY	ARTS & LETTERS	
	Richard Wright, *Native Son,* 1940	
	Abstract expressionism in art, mid-1940s	**1945**
	Albert Camus, *The Plague,* 1947	
	Simone de Beauvoir, *The Second Sex,* 1949–1950	
	Samuel Beckett, *Waiting for Godot,* 1952	
	Boris Pasternak, *Doctor Zhivago,* 1957	
European Common Market established, 1958		
Black civil rights movement, United States, 1960–1968	"Pop" art, 1960s	**1960**
Youth "revolution," 1960s	Francois Truffant, *Jules and Jim,* 1961	
Women's liberation movement, 1960s–1970s	James Baldwin, *The Fire Next Time,* 1963	
Worldwide inflation and unemployment, late 1970s and early 1980s	Arthur Penn, *Bonnie and Clyde* (1967)	
		1970
	Aleksandr Solzhenitsyn, *The Gulag Archipelago,* 1973	
		1980

Chapter 31

NEW POWER RELATIONSHIPS

Africa, all I ask from you is the courage to know: to look about you and
see what is happening in this old and tired world; to realize the extent and
depth of its rebirth and the promise which glows on your hills.

—W. E. B. Du Bois, *Autobiography*

The Second World War left the political world of Europe, Asia,
and the United States in a state of disorder. As victory
approached, wartime allies began to mistrust each other and
to protect themselves against those whom they now perceived as pro-
spective rivals. In addition, the war spawned nationalist revolts
throughout the world. Many of these struggles were attempts by colonies to gain independence. Although these wars were often no more
than local, they threatened to lead to major conflict and, because of
the increasing proliferation of nuclear weapons, to general holocaust.
Yet this last threat, if it did not reduce tensions, may in fact have
operated to prevent nations from pursuing their interests to the point
of no return.

Tensions in the postwar world

1. SOVIET-AMERICAN WORLD RIVALRY

As a result of the Second World War, world power relationships were
drastically altered. Germany, Italy, and Japan had been defeated so
overwhelmingly that they seemed for a time destined to play a subordinate role in world affairs. Officially, the list of great powers included five states—the Soviet Union, the United States, Great Britain,
France, and the Republic of China. These were the Big Five that, as
the war ended, seemed fated to rule the world. China was soon overwhelmed by a Communist revolution, however, while for a time
Britain and France became increasingly dependent on the United States.
As a consequence, the world of nations, during the ten years after
1945, took on a bipolar character, with the United States and the Soviet

Changing power relationships

Union contesting for supremacy and striving to draw the remaining states into their orbits. This rivalry was based on long-standing apprehensions of both countries. Prior to its temporary wartime alliance with the Soviets, the United States had never hesitated to express its antagonism to Stalinist communism. And that antagonism was matched by a growing fear on the part of Russia's leaders of U.S.-inspired military and economic encirclement.

From the standpoint of economic power, the United States far outdistanced the other nations of the world. Since 1939 Americans had doubled their national income and quadrupled their savings. Though they constituted only 7 percent of the world's population, they enjoyed over 30 percent of the world's estimated income. For the first time in its history the United States was in a position to be the economic and military arbiter of at least half the earth. Japan was virtually its colony; the United States controlled both the Atlantic and Pacific Oceans, policed the Mediterranean, and shaped the development of international policy in western Europe. And until 1949, America had a monopoly of death-dealing atomic weapons.

Soviet Russia emerged from the Second World War as the second-strongest power on earth. Though its navy was small, its land army and possibly its air force by 1948 were the largest in the world. Soviet population was climbing rapidly toward 200 million and this in spite of the loss of 7 million soldiers and about 8 million civilians during the war. In mineral wealth and petroleum resources Russia's position compared favorably with that of the richest countries. On the other hand, its industrial machine had been badly crippled by the war. No fewer than 1700 Russian cities and towns had been totally destroyed along with 40,000 miles of railway and 31,000 factories. Stalin declared in 1946 that it would probably require at least six years to repair the damage and rebuild the devastated areas.

In part because of the need to recoup their enormous industrial losses, the Soviets were particularly determined to maintain political, economic, and military control of those countries in eastern Europe which they had liberated from Nazi control. Building on the agreements reached at Yalta, the Russians remained as an occupying force throughout the area, working meanwhile to establish "people's republics" sympathetic to the Soviet regime. By 1948, governments which owed allegiance to Moscow were established in Poland, Hungary, Rumania, Bulgaria, and Czechoslovakia. Albania and Yugoslavia, liberated by their own anti-Nazi forces, were not directly linked to Russia as satellites, although the governments of those two countries were also Communist. The nations of eastern Europe did not all succumb without a struggle. Greece, which the Russians wished to include within their sphere of influence, was torn by civil war until 1949, when with Western aid its monarchy was restored. The most direct challenge to the Yalta guarantee of free, democratic elections occurred in Czechoslovakia, where in 1948 the Soviets crushed the coalition government of liberal leaders Eduard Beneš and Jan Masaryk.

The United States countered these moves with massive programs of economic and military aid to western Europe. In 1947, President Truman proclaimed the so-called Truman Doctrine, which provided assistance programs to prevent further Communist infiltration into the governments of Greece and Turkey. The following year, the Marshall Plan, named for Secretary of State George Marshall who first proposed it, provided funds for the reconstruction of western European industry. The plan was notable in two respects: first, it represented an attempt by the United States to restore the strength of its most serious economic competitors, and of its former enemy Germany, under the notion that an economically independent Europe would be less likely to fall prey to Soviet domination. Second, it relied upon a willingness on the part of the western European nations to coordinate their economic efforts, substituting, at least to some degree, cooperation for competition.

The Marshall Plan

At the same time, the United States moved to shore up the military defenses of the West. In April 1949, a group of representatives of North Atlantic states together with Canada and the United States signed an agreement providing for the establishment of the North Atlantic Treaty Organization (NATO). Subsequently Greece, Turkey, and West Germany were added as members. The treaty declared that an armed attack against any one of the signatory parties would be regarded as an attack against all, and that they would combine their armed strength to whatever extent necessary to repel the aggressor. The joint military command, or NATO army, established in 1950, was increased from thirty to fifty divisions in 1953, with a rearmed West Germany contributing twelve of the divisions.

NATO

The Russians reacted with understandable alarm to the determination of the United States to strengthen western Europe economically and militarily. They organized an international political arm, the Cominform, responsible for the coordination of worldwide Communist policy and programs, that is, for the development and imposition of a party line. In addition the Soviets rejected an original offer of Marshall Plan aid, and instead organized an eastern European counterpart for economic recovery, the Council for Mutual Economic Assistance. They responded to NATO with the establishment of military alliances, confirmed by the Warsaw Pact of 1955. This agreement set up a joint armed forces command among its signatories, and more important, authorized the continued stationing of Russian troops in Albania, Czechoslovakia, Hungary, Poland, Rumania, and the eastern portion of Germany, which had remained under Soviet domination since the end of the war.

Russian response

Germany was, in fact, the focal point of East-West tensions during these years. After the war, the Russians had continued to insist on $10 billion worth of reparations from Germany in the form of industrial

Focus on Germany

Crises in Berlin. Left: The Berlin Airlift, 1948. For fifteen months the United States, Britain, and France airlifted over two million tons of supplies into West Berlin, around which the Russians had imposed a land blockade. Right: The Berlin Wall, 1961. Thirteen years after the blockade, the East German government constructed a wall between East and West Berlin to stop the flow of escapees to the West. This manifestation of the "iron curtain" remains in place today.

production. Although the Soviets' desperate economic condition and their fear of a revived Germany played a role in this posture, Britain and the United States read this demand as a reflection of a Soviet desire to keep Germany weak and therefore susceptible to political instability—specifically, to the spread of communism.

The Berlin Blockade

By 1946 the joint administration of Germany by the four former Allied powers had collapsed. The Soviet Union remained in control of its satellite, which eventually became the nominally independent German Democratic Republic (East Germany), while the Western powers continued to support the industrial recovery of that area under their control—in its turn to emerge as the Federal Republic of Germany (West Germany). A crisis of grave proportions arose in 1948 when, in retaliation for the reunification of the western zones of control under one authority, the Russians closed down road and rail access from the west to Berlin. Berlin, though within the territory of East Germany, was administered by all four powers. The Western powers countered with an airlift of food and other necessary supplies which prevented the collapse of the city into Soviet hands. After almost a year the Russians lifted the blockade. For many years to come, however, Berlin was to remain one of the hottest spots in the ongoing "Cold War," as it came to be called, between the Soviet Union and the West. The city symbolized opposition to a divided Germany, as well as the determination of the Western powers to ensure that nation's economic recovery.

The tensions that produced the Cold War were the result of a set of misconceptions on both sides. Americans, who had been persuaded by wartime government propaganda to admire the Russians as stalwart anti-fascists, were naïvely disillusioned when they discovered that their erstwhile allies were in fact not democrats. Concerned about the economic weakness throughout postwar western Europe, U.S. leaders allowed themselves to believe that the Russians were hatching a vast plan to take advantage of that weakness by establishing Communist regimes throughout the west, as they had in the east. *The Cold War: U.S. attitudes*

In fact, scholars have recently argued convincingly that there was no grand Soviet strategy of this sort. The Russians were not willing to undertake any such campaign, primarily because they were economically and militarily incapable of doing so. However, since the Soviets had long feared encirclement by hostile capitalist powers, they saw the Truman and Marshall programs as a direct form of neoimperialism, an American plot to subject western Europe to the economic hegemony of the United States. Stalin found it useful to orchestrate his propaganda to this theme. As a result of wartime destruction, he needed to convince the Russian people that they must undergo a further series of rugged Five-Year Plans stressing the production of heavy industrial materials rather than consumer goods. He could demand sacrifices more convincingly if he could point to an international anti-Russian conspiracy. *Russian attitudes*

Stalin himself remained deeply suspicious, not only of the West, but of threats to his own rule from within the Communist bloc. In 1948, when the Yugoslavs under the wartime hero, Marshall Josip Tito, broke with the Soviets to pursue a communism of their own design, Stalin banished Yugoslavia from the Cominform and purged leaders in other eastern European countries whom he suspected of political deviationism. At home he tightened his control through the agency of a powerful and deadly secret police force. *Stalinism*

The Soviet-American rivalry did not deter the postwar recovery of western Europe. In Britain, France, Germany, and Italy, governments made their first priority the reestablishment of their economies. They were aided in this effort not only by economic support from the United States, but by various internal factors, the most significant of which was population growth. Population in western Europe increased in the 1950s by about 12 percent. That rise in turn stimulated national economies by increasing the demand for consumer goods. During the 1950s western European production grew by about 80 percent. Mass production and sales served not only to make western Europe an economic bulwark against the Soviet Union, but they eventually came to express as well a kind of economic "declaration of independence" from the United States. That declaration was most clearly pronounced in 1957 with establishment of a Common Market, or tariff union. By the mid-1970s, most of the major western European nations, including Britain, France, and West Germany, were members. Although the *European recovery* market was by no means the equivalent of a United States of Europe, its formation and continuing operation declared the existence of a new and important power bloc which, while more generally sympathetic to U.S. than to Soviet aims, nevertheless was determined to speak with a voice of its own.

The Korean war

The most serious clash between Communist and non-Communist forces in the first postwar decade occurred not in Europe but in Korea, where armed conflict broke out in 1950. Treaties with Japan at the end of the Second World War had provided that Korea, under Japanese rule since 1910, would become an independent and united country. The United States and the Soviet Union left occupying forces there until 1949, however, the Americans south of the thirty-eighth parallel, the Russians to the north of it. During this period of occupation, the Soviets refused to cooperate with the United Nations–sponsored plan to hold free elections for the entire country. Instead, they established in the north a people's republic similar to those they had erected in eastern Europe. In June 1950, troops from North Korea crossed the thirty-eighth parallel and invaded the south. Taking advantage of a temporary Russian boycott of the United Nations, the United States was able to avoid a Soviet veto of its plan to counter this invasion by sending a contingent of troops to oppose it. The troops, though nominally under United Nations command, were largely American, directed and supplied by the United States. Initial military gains by this force were countered in November by the invasion into Korea of troops from the newly established People's Republic of China (see below, p. 1026), sent to aid the North Koreans. A stalemate ensued, President Truman and his advisors being as unwilling to widen the conflict into China—fearing a third world war—as they were to abandon their South Korean allies. After two years of military and diplomatic deadlock, a peace settlement was concluded, recognizing the existence of both North and South Korea and abandoning any scheme for their reunion.

Effects of the Korean war

The Korean war adversely affected relationships between the United States and the nations of the Far East. While Japan welcomed American intervention as a sign of its determination to halt the spread of communism, other countries looked on America's role with suspicion. The United States claimed to be acting in accordance with United Nations principles. Powers such as India, Burma, and Indonesia, however, saw the war as a neocolonialist intrusion by America on behalf of its client state, South Korea. China's determination to understand the war in this light contributed greatly to the deep hostility that characterized Sino-American relations during the next twenty years.

The "thaw"

Tensions between the United States and Russia eased considerably during the late 1950s and 1960s. America, it is true, continued to adhere to a policy of Soviet "containment," seeking as allies those most willing to oppose by military force, if necessary, the spread of international communism. And Russia was never afraid to risk Western military reaction when suppressing revolts within the countries of its satellite allies. Yet the period has not incorrectly been labeled one of "thaw." A change in direction was signaled by the death of Stalin in 1953 and the accession to power after a brief interregnum of Nikita Khrushchev (1894–1971) in 1955. Khrushchev possessed a kind of earthy directness which, despite his hostility to the West, nevertheless helped for a time to ease tensions. Abandoning the seclusion of the Kremlin where Stalin had immured himself, he traveled throughout the world. On visits to the United States in 1958 and 1960 he traded quips with Iowa farmers and was entertained at Disneyland. Attending a meeting of the United Nations in New York, he underscored his disagreement with the speaker by banging his desk with his shoe.

Nikita Khrushchev

As testimony to his desire to reduce international conflict, Khrushchev soon agreed to the first of a series of summit meetings with the leaders of Britain, France, and the United States. This new Soviet determination to lower international tensions grew out of Khrushchev's need to consolidate his regime at home and to prevent the threatened crumbling of the Communist bloc in eastern Europe. The harsh demands of the Stalin regime had generated discontent among the Russian people. Dissenters, their voices no longer silenced by the Stalinist police, began to demand a shift from the production of heavy machinery and armaments to the manufacture of consumer goods. Meanwhile, throughout the other Communist states growing resentment of Soviet demands for rapid industrialization and collectivization generated arguments for an easing of the restrictions that Stalinism had imposed. In response to these pressures the Soviet leaders altered their economic goals and began preaching that there was "more than one road to socialism."

Khrushchev's policies

The Soviet Union's new posture toward its client states in eastern Europe received its severest test in 1956 when Poland and Hungary demanded greater autonomy in the management of their domestic affairs. In Poland, the government at first responded to major strikes with military repression and then with a promise of liberalization. The anti-Stalinist Polish leader Wladyslav Gomulka was able to win Soviet permission for his country to pursue its own "ways of socialist development" by pledging Poland's continued loyalty to the terms of the Warsaw Pact. Events in Hungary produced a different result. There, protests against Stalinist policies developed into a much broader anti-Communist struggle. If the Russians were prepared to entertain a liberalization of domestic policy, they would not tolerate a repudiation of the Warsaw Pact. On November 4, 1956, Russian troops occupied Budapest; leaders of the Hungarian liberation were taken prisoner and executed.

Revolts in Poland and Hungary, 1956

Despite these events, Khrushchev did not abandon his policy of "peaceful coexistence" with the West. Though he did not renounce his ultimate belief in the triumph of communism, he argued that victory could be achieved by other than military means. Yet Soviet lead-

The limits of coexistence: the Berlin Wall

ers remained unyielding in their determination to reduce any possible German military threat to eastern Europe. They continued to nurture the fear that Germany might launch a new war, abetted by its capitalist allies. For this reason, they staunchly opposed the reunification of the country. In 1961 the East German government built a high wall separating the two sectors of Berlin in order to cut off the escape of thousands of East Germans to West Berlin and thence to western Germany. The wall remained as a symbol of Soviet determination to prevent the formation of a united Germany.

Czech and Polish revolts

Khrushchev eventually fell prey to political rivals and was deposed in 1964, with the reins of Soviet power passing to Aleksei Kosygin as premier and Leonid Brezhnev as secretary of the Communist party. The Soviets continued to hold the governments of eastern Europe in check. In 1968 the Soviets sent troops into Czechoslovakia after the leadership there had attempted to meet criticisms by decentralizing the administration, democratizing the Communist party, and permitting a brief flowering of intellectual life. In 1980, calling their movement "Solidarity," Polish workers organized strikes which brought the government of the country to a standstill. The strikers were objecting to working conditions imposed by the government to combat a severe economic crisis which had produced high prices. Again the Russians assisted a puppet military regime in reimposing authoritarian rule. Though the Soviet Union did not intervene directly, the implied threat that it might do so, reinforced by the presence of increasing numbers of Russian troops near the Polish border, reemphasized Soviet unwillingness to permit its eastern European neighbors autonomy over their internal affairs.

Arms limitation

During the 1970s, the Soviets showed, by their intervention in the affairs of newly emerging nations of the so-called Third World—Africa, Asia, and Latin America—that they remained vitally interested in extending their sphere of influence wherever they could. At the same time they continued to adhere to a policy which allowed for a further easing of tensions, a policy pursued with some enthusiasm, as well,

The Occupation of Czechoslovakia. In 1968 the liberalized regime of Alexander Dubček was suppressed by the Soviets. The violent response by the citizens was put down by military force.

Defiance in Poland. Thousands of striking workers take part in religious services in the Lenin Shipyards in Gdansk on August 24, 1980. This was the scene of the first in a series of strikes that paralyzed an already troubled economic and political system and challenged Soviet domination of Polish governmental policy.

by American diplomats. Henry Kissinger, secretary of state under Presidents Richard Nixon and Gerald Ford in the 1970s, proclaimed détente with the Russians as his goal, and devoted much time to negotiations aimed at defusing potentially explosive areas of conflict between the two nations. Both countries were concerned to curb the spread of nuclear weapons and to limit, if possible, the apparently endless expansion of their own arsenals. The Strategic Arms Limitation Treaty (SALT) talks, in which the Russians and Americans engaged during the 1970s and early 1980s, were an indication of mutual willingness to recognize and tackle a problem of awesome dimensions. Yet the talks produced little in the way of concrete agreement. President Ronald Reagan, who took office in 1981, denounced a second stage of the SALT negotiations during his campaign, and has continued to press for dramatic increases in his military budgets for sophisticated armaments. Brezhnev's death in 1982 and the succession of Yuri Andropov, former head of the Soviet secret police, has thus far not produced a change in the essentially intransigent position of the Russians. The continued stalemate has resulted in vigorous disarmament campaigns in both western Europe and the United States. Yet both East and West continue to arm themselves with arsenals capable of destroying each other many times over.

See color map facing page 1057

Yuri Andropov

2. IMPERIAL DECLINE IN ASIA AND THE MIDDLE EAST

Probably more significant in the long run than U.S.-Soviet rivalry in the postwar period has been the decline of the Western imperial pow-

The Third World

Relations with the West

ers and the concurrent emergence of what has come to be called the Third World—newly independent states in Africa and Asia, along with older nations there as well as in Latin America. Many of these countries have established themselves in territories which were formerly part of European empires. Others—China and the various nations of the Middle East and Latin America, for example—while nominally independent of the West before 1945, nevertheless existed under European hegemony and were forced to acquiesce to European demands. Such is the case no longer. Although many of these so-called emerging nations are poor, and although the people of the Third World are by no means a united bloc, they represent a new and increasingly independent factor in the world power equation.

Many of these countries are rich in natural resources. Nations in the Middle East, Venezuela in South America, and Nigeria in Africa, possess oil in quantities sufficient to make their every move of vital importance to the West. Other African nations, Zaire and Angola, for example, are immensely rich in many mineral resources. Population is both a liability and an asset in the Third World. The people of China, by their sheer numbers, constitute an implicit threat to the balance of power at all times. The people of India, again by their sheer numbers, and lack of food, represent a perpetual threat to the stability of their own country and hence to all Asia. Every area in the Third World is a potential "trouble spot." This is so not only because the problems of racism, poverty, hunger, and over-population make them particularly vulnerable to violent civil conflicts. It is so, as well, because the superpowers—the United States, Russia, the European nations, and China itself—are prepared to engage each other through the medium of Third World adversaries, thus increasing the possibility of conflict by their willingness to encourage it. To protect themselves from direct confrontation with each other, these developed nations interfere in the civil wars of others, on opposite sides and with an intensity that frequently belies their declared interest in avoiding general world war.

A final general observation concerning the Third World: Although the governments of most countries have pursued the twin goals of industrialization and urbanization, this policy has not gone unchallenged. In the spring of 1979, for example, the extremely repressive regime of one of the Third World's most devoted "Westernizers," the shah of oil-rich Iran, was overthrown by the revolutionary forces of an equally repressive religious fanatic, the Ayatollah Khomeini, whose explicit policy was to turn his country's back not only on the West but on "progress" as the West had defined that term for the past two hundred years.

The most radical Third World change resulting from the events of the Second World War was the Chinese revolution. A civil war had raged in China since 1927, when the forces of the nationalists, under Chiang Kai-shek (1887–1975), had engaged in battle first in the south,

The Ayatollah Khomeini

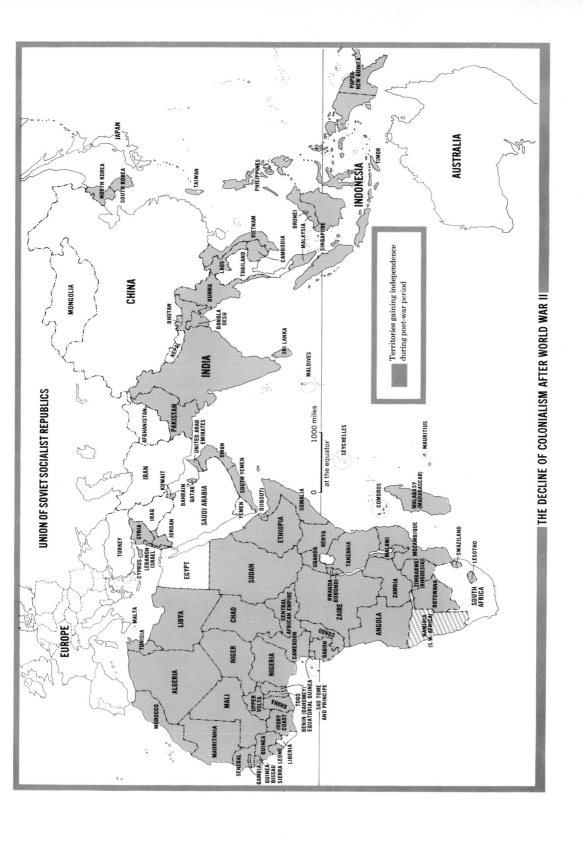

THE DECLINE OF COLONIALISM AFTER WORLD WAR II

Territories gaining independence
during post-war period

0   1000 miles
at the equator

UNION OF SOVIET SOCIALIST REPUBLICS

EUROPE

MONGOLIA

CHINA

JAPAN

NORTH KOREA

SOUTH KOREA

TAIWAN

TURKEY

SYRIA

CYPRUS

LEBANON

ISRAEL

JORDAN

IRAQ

IRAN

AFGHANISTAN

PAKISTAN

NEPAL

BHUTAN

INDIA

BANGLA DESH

BURMA

LAOS

THAILAND

VIETNAM

CAMBODIA

MALTA

TUNISIA

MOROCCO

ALGERIA

LIBYA

EGYPT

KUWAIT

BAHRAIN

QATAR

UNITED ARAB EMIRATES

SAUDI ARABIA

OMAN

YEMEN

SOUTH YEMEN

DJIBOUTI

SUDAN

ETHIOPIA

SOMALIA

SRI LANKA

MALDIVES

SEYCHELLES

MAURITANIA

SENEGAL

GAMBIA

GUINEA-BISSAU

GUINEA

SIERRA LEONE

LIBERIA

MALI

UPPER VOLTA

IVORY COAST

GHANA

TOGO

BENIN (DAHOMEY)

NIGER

NIGERIA

EQUATORIAL GUINEA

SAO TOME AND PRINCIPE

CHAD

CAMEROON

CENTRAL AFRICAN EMPIRE

CONGO

GABON

ZAIRE

UGANDA

KENYA

RWANDA

BURUNDI

TANZANIA

ANGOLA

ZAMBIA

MALAWI

ZIMBABWE (RHODESIA)

MOZAMBIQUE

NAMIBIA (S. W. AFRICA)

BOTSWANA

SWAZILAND

LESOTHO

SOUTH AFRICA

COMOROS

MALAGASY (MADAGASCAR)

MAURITIUS

PHILIPPINES

BRUNEI

MALAYSIA

SINGAPORE

INDONESIA

TIMOR

PAPUA-NEW GUINEA

AUSTRALIA

then the north with Communist insurgents under the leadership of Mao Tse-tung (1893–1976), a former teacher and union organizer. A truce in 1937 had allowed both sides to wage common battle against the Japanese. At the end of the war, however, the Communists, still led by Mao Tse-tung, refused to surrender the northern provinces under their control, and civil war broke out again. The United States intervened, first as mediator, then with massive military assistance, as an ally of Chiang—all to no avail. The nationalists, corrupt and unrepresentative of the people, surrendered in 1949 to the Communists and decamped to the island of Taiwan. Intensely hostile to the capitalist West, the Chinese Communists soon found themselves engaged, as well, in a series of skirmishes, verbal and otherwise, with their erstwhile Marxist co-revolutionaries, the Russians. The Sino-Soviet rivalry, and the willingness of the United States in the 1970s to reach an accommodation with the Chinese in order to capitalize on that rivalry, suggest that however much power has shifted since the Second World War, power politics remains a game nations believe themselves compelled to play—if necessary, in opposition to their professed ideological commitments.

Mao Tse-tung. A photograph taken in 1933 when he was the leader of the radical left opposition to the Kuomintang under Chiang Kai-shek.

The Second World War, which had assisted the course of Chinese revolution by dissolving older power structures, served the same purpose within the colonial empires of the West. The first major British colony to establish self-government after the World War was India. Rebel movements had harassed the representatives of Britain in that country throughout the nineteenth century. The flames of revolt burned more fiercely during the First World War and after; another World War added more tinder. By 1945 anti-British resentment had reached such a pitch that the country was ripe for revolution. Resolutions by nationalist bodies such as the Indian National Congress called upon Britain to "quit India." The congress had taken the position that India would fight only as a free nation without limitations imposed by the mother country. Protests and disturbances mounted more

Indian independence

Gandhi and Nehru at a Meeting of Indian Leaders in 1946

strongly than ever. It is noteworthy, however, that the foremost Indian nationalist leader, Mohandas K. Gandhi (1869–1948) did not approve of armed attacks on rulers and their institutions. His methods were noncooperation and civil disobedience. By 1947 he and his comrade and disciple, Jawaharlal Nehru (1889–1964), had gained such support that the British found it expedient to grant autonomy to India and its neighboring area, Pakistan. In 1950 both countries organized themselves as independent republics. Disorders continued to plague the two countries, however, finally resulting in a bloody war in 1971. An important outcome of this conflict was the establishment of the independent republic of Bangladesh, formerly East Pakistan.

In recent years India has struggled to maintain itself as a democracy in the face of mounting economic and social problems. In the mid-1970s, Prime Minister Indira Gandhi (the daughter of Nehru) assumed authoritarian powers after declaring the country in a state of emergency. Her defeat, in free elections which she sanctioned following more than a year of virtual dictatorship, and her subsequent political comeback, leaves unresolved the question of whether a country as dominated by the internal problems of poverty, illiteracy, overpopulation, and near-starvation as India can afford what many Third World leaders claim is the luxury of a slow-moving and comparatively inefficient democracy.

Indira Gandhi Campaigning on the Eve of Her Return to Power in Early 1980

India was only the most important of the colonies surrendered by Britain after the war. Over a period of years Britain liberated Ceylon, Malaysia, Mauritius, Fiji, and Singapore, among others, together with the Caribbean colonies of Guyana, Trinidad and Tobago, Jamaica, and Antigua, and, as we shall see, significant territories in sub-Saharan Africa as well. More significant was Britain's forced departure from Egypt. In 1951 Egyptian nationalists compelled the British to withdraw their troops from Egyptian territory. A year later a group of nationalist army officers seized control of the government. They deposed the playboy king, Farouk, alleged to be subservient to the British, and proclaimed the state a republic. Shortly thereafter an Egyptian colonel, Gamal Abdel Nasser (1918–1970), assumed the presidency of the country. The British misread Nasser's nationalist ambitions. Anthony Eden, prime minister at the time, called Nasser the Mideastern equivalent of Adolph Hitler, and accused him, without foundation, of widespread imperial designs. When Nasser nationalized the Suez Canal Company in 1956 in order to finance the construction of a high dam on the Nile at Aswan, the British and French, dependent on the canal as their major trade route to the East, interpreted the Egyptian action as a direct threat to their economic security. Together with Israel, the three countries launched an abortive, ill-fated invasion of the canal zone as a way not only of recovering control of the company but, as Eden put it, of "punishing" Nasser. World opinion turned against the invaders, who were forced to with-

Further liquidation: Egypt and others

Anti-Imperialist Revolt in Algeria, 1960. At Dar-es-Saada, Muslims take furniture from the homes of Europeans and burn it in the streets.

draw. Britain's resounding defeat symbolized the extent to which its status as an imperial power had eroded.

The French in Algeria

The French were no more successful in surrendering their colonial possessions without conflict. For France, the most difficult withdrawal occurred in its North African colony of Algeria, inhabited by about 1,000,000 immigrants, mainly French, in a total population of 10,300,000. These immigrants monopolized not only government positions but also the best economic opportunities in industry, trade, and finance. The Arab and Berber inhabitants were chiefly peasants and laborers. In 1954 Arab and Berber nationalists rose in revolt when their demand for equal status with the French was denied by the government. The war continued for seven years. It was complicated by the fact that many of the European settlers feared the French government almost as much as they did the Algerian nationalists. They were determined to keep Algeria "French" and correctly foresaw that a settlement by President Charles de Gaulle (1890–1970) would make the former colony independent and subject the immigrant governing class to the rule of the Arabs and Berbers. The upshot was a revolt by four French generals, who seized government buildings, arrested French officials, and threatened to invade France. De Gaulle proclaimed a state of emergency and ordered a total blockade of Algeria. In the face of such determined opposition the revolt collapsed. On a promise of self-government the nationalists laid down their arms in 1962, and Algeria soon after achieved independence. Additional portions of the French empire in North Africa were surrendered as well. In 1955 the French withdrew from their protectorate over Morocco, which was established as an independent kingdom. And a short time afterward they renounced their protectorate over Tunisia as well.

British and French withdrawal from North Africa came at a time of mounting tensions in the Middle East, an area fated to become one of the most troubled in the postwar world. These conflicts focused on the creation and continued existence of the state of Israel. At the end of the First World War, the country now known as Israel, then called Palestine, was a province of Turkey. Its population was about 70 percent Arab and 30 percent Jewish and Christian. Following Turkey's defeat, Palestine was mandated to the League of Nations as a protectorate of Britain. Meanwhile, Zionist organizations in Europe and America worked to convert Palestine into a national home for the Jewish people. Heeding their cause, the British issued the so-called Balfour Declaration, promising to assist in the achievement of that goal.

Palestine under British mandate

For a time Palestine flourished under the British mandate. By 1929, however, tension between Arabs and Jews had become severe. The prosperous, well-educated Jews were arousing the fear and envy of the Arabs, who saw them buying up lands and forcing Arab farmers to leave the country for the cities at a time when the international economic depression made it increasingly difficult for the unskilled to find jobs. The paramount cause of Arab concern, however, was the increasing flow of Jews into Palestine. Arabs foresaw a relentless immigrant wave of Europeans and Americans, backed by foreign capital and flaunting a culture alien to the ways of the Muslim majority. This anxiety manifested itself in a series of armed attacks and terrorist raids by Arabs against the Jews in the late 1920s and early 1930s. As news spread of the Nazi persecution of the Jews, pressure increased

Growing Arab-Jewish tensions

Immigration to Palestine. Left: British soldiers guard the shore as a ship loaded with unauthorized refugees attempts to land in 1947. Right: A view of the unbearably crowded conditions aboard ships bringing refugees to Palestine.

on the British to allow more and more Jewish immigrants into Palestine. During the period from 1930 to 1933 more than 130,000 Jews were admitted; uncounted thousands more entered the country illegally. The Arabs rose in open rebellion. Guerrilla attacks in rural areas and looting, burning, and sabotage in towns and cities kept the population in turmoil. By 1939, though the British had 20,000 troops in Palestine, they were unable to maintain order.

Termination of the mandate and establishment of the state of Israel

Little progress toward a lasting settlement had been achieved when, in April 1947, the British government referred the Palestine problem to the United Nations and announced that a year later it would terminate its mandate and withdraw all its troops from the country. On May 15, 1948, the British mandate came to an end; on the same day a Jewish provisional government proclaimed the establishment of an independent state of Israel.

The Arab-Israeli wars

Meanwhile, from the day of proclaimed independence until the spring of 1949, Israel and its Arab neighbor countries were at war. United Nations efforts brought about temporary truces, but nothing lasting was achieved until Israel, Egypt, Jordan, and Syria signed general armistice agreements in early February 1949. The status of the ceasefire was regarded as a victory for Israel and a defeat for the Arab powers. Neither, however, accepted it as final. Violent incidents continued to occur, including retaliatory massacres.

Continued conflicts

Despite wars with the Arabs, Israel embarked on a concerted program of industrialization to strengthen the economy. Large sums of money flowed into the country, mainly from the United States, Britain, and West Germany, as restitution for the outrages of Nazi persecution. Yet Israel's conflict with its Arab neighbors continued unabated, fueled by Israel's inability to resolve the question of the rights of Palestinian Arabs who still claim the state of Israel as their home. These tensions were exacerbated by Israeli participation in a poorly conceived action against Egypt in 1956. In 1967 President Nasser of Egypt, in alliance with Jordan and Syria, closed the port of Aqaba, Israel's only

Israeli Tanks Move into Jerusalem. A scene during the Arab-Israeli War of June 1967.

On the Path to Peace in the Middle East. From left to right, Egyptian President Anwar Sadat, U.S. President Jimmy Carter, and Israeli Prime Minister Menachem Begin shake hands at the announcement of the Camp David accord which laid the groundwork for a peace treaty between Egypt and Israel.

direct outlet to the Red Sea. The Israelis responded with a lightning war against Egypt and its allies, whose forces were routed in six days. An eventual ceasefire did nothing to ease regional animosities. New outbreaks flared sporadically for more than two years. The Arabs were tormented by loss of confidence and fearful of their own future as a result of their defeat. The Israelis were obsessed with security and determined to preserve it regardless of cost.

Another war of longer duration in 1973 once again failed to resolve the impasse. In that conflict, the Arabs threatened to withhold their immense oil reserves from the West, in hopes that the West would in turn put pressure on the Israelis to negotiate. This tactic succeeded only to the extent of convincing Europe and America of their dependence on Arab oil, and of their need to escape from that dependence. Since that time, prospects for peace have waxed and waned. In 1978, President Anwar Sadat, Nasser's successor, traveled to Jerusalem in a dramatic bid to break the deadlock. And in the fall of that year U.S. President Jimmy Carter, having persuaded Sadat and Israeli Prime Minister Menachem Begin to meet with him at Camp David outside Washington, engineered their agreement to a treaty draft, which was signed in final form by Israel and Egypt in Washington in 1979. Yet factors such as Israel's reluctance to surrender Arab territory in the Sinai peninsula, and the continuing terrorist campaigns of non-Jewish Palestinians deprived of a homeland by the Israelis, guaranteed that peace would not come easily or soon to the Middle East. Proof of that unhappy truth came yet again in 1982, when Israel launched a savage attack against Palestinian forces based in Lebanon. During the conflict the Israelis bombed civilian populations in Tyre, Sidon, and Beirut,

Uncertain prospects for peace in the Middle East

The oil crisis

the Palestine Liberation Organization (PLO) used the civilian populations as human shields for its military activities in those cities, and Lebanon Christian terrorists allied with the Israelis slaughtered hundreds of unarmed civilians in two Palestine refugee camps.

Influencing the attitudes of United States and European governments toward Israel and its Arab enemies was the fact of Western dependence on the Arabs for oil. The Organization of Petroleum Exporting Countries (OPEC), formed in 1960 to regulate the production and pricing of crude oil, assumed an increasingly militant posture in the 1970s under the leadership of its Middle Eastern Arab members. For a time a majority appeared willing to follow the lead of militant Middle Eastern nationalists such as Muammar Qaddafi, Libyan chief of state, in attempting to extract a high price—both economic and political—from the West. Western powers tempered their support of Israel and designed their policies toward the PLO at least in part on the basis of their continuing need for oil. In the mid-1980s overproduction and a decrease in the demand for oil brought about by economic depression in western Europe and the United States made it far more difficult for the OPEC countries to keep the price of oil uniformly high. Yet the resulting price reductions were not an unalloyed boon to Western economies. Many oil-producing nations in the Third World had borrowed large sums of money from Western financial institutions in the 1970s using their "black gold" as collateral. When reduced oil prices resulted in financial crisis for some of those nations—as in Mexico in 1982, for example—Western lenders were threatened with default. The problems of oil production and pricing illustrate convincingly the degree to which the world is now locked together, for better or worse, in one giant economy.

3. THE RISE OF BLACK AFRICA

During the quarter century following the Second World War the colonial territories of sub-Saharan Africa one after another struggled first to throw off the colonial rule of the European powers and then to cope with the myriad problems of establishing viable independent states. In the forefront of the African colonial revolt was Ghana, formerly called the Gold Coast, a colony of Britain. The drive for Ghanian independence was led by Kwame Nkrumah (1909–1972). The son of an illiterate goldsmith, he was a gifted student, educated in the United States and England. Nkrumah returned to his homeland in 1948 and launched a campaign of intense political pressure and agitation which resulted in a grant of self-government in 1954, independence in 1957, and the establishment of a republic in 1960. He was one of the first and most persuasive spokesmen for African self-rule, insisting that it was absurd that Central Africans, with their proud heritage and ancient culture, should be ruled by Europeans. Nkrumah called himself a Marxist and

Kwame Nkrumah (center, seated) and Members of His Government in Ghana

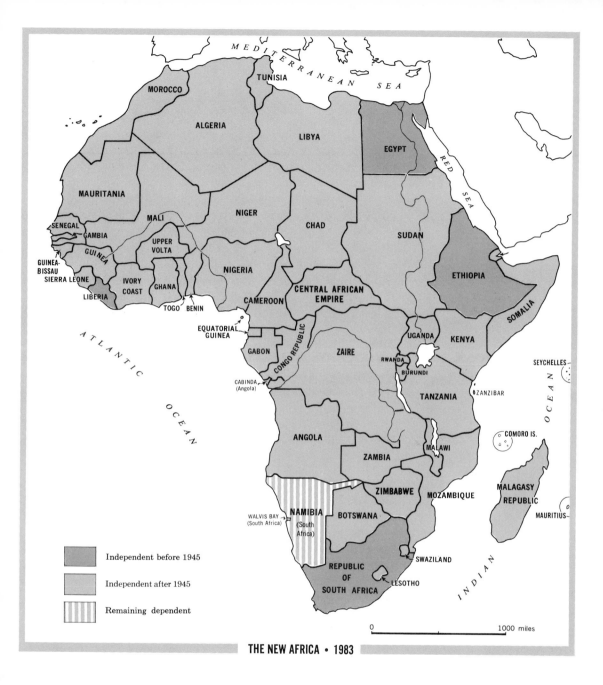

THE NEW AFRICA · 1983

Independent before 1945

Independent after 1945

Remaining dependent

0   1000 miles

looked to the Soviets for support of his policies. For a time Nkrumah ruled benevolently even after he established a one-party political system. He pressed for the raising of literacy standards and the building of hospitals and schools. Accused of extravagance and corruption, he was driven from power in 1966 by an army coup financed by the U.S. Central Intelligence Agency. Nkrumah died a refugee in Guinea in 1972.

Ghana and Nkrumah

Conflict in the Congo

One of the most violent independence struggles in Africa occurred in the Congo. Conditions there had been unstable since the end of the Second World War. In 1960, fearing an outbreak among disaffected colonial subjects, Belgium granted the Congolese independence. This was the signal for the beginning of a series of rebellions and assassinations that raged for more than five years. The disorders centered in the southeastern province of Katanga, the source of rich copper resources controlled by Belgian capitalists. At one time the copper mines of Katanga had produced revenues sufficient to defray 50 percent of the costs of the Belgian colonial government. In July 1960, Katanga seceded and attempted to gain control of the entire country. In the course of the revolt several former premiers and other high-ranking officers were murdered, including the leftist Congolese leader Patrice Lumumba, whose assassination was arranged with the aid of the American C.I.A. The U.N. Security Council sent a contingent to guard against revival of civil war. Strong-man rule was revived by President Sese Seko Mobutu, who changed the name of the country to Zaire in 1971 and managed to restore a degree of stability.

Nigerian civil war

Other African territories—Nigeria, Kenya, and Rhodesia, for example—seemed to promise a less painful transition to independence. All three were former British colonies. Apologists for British colonial rule claimed that by training indigenous elites and gradually transferring to them responsibility for local administration, British colonies would make that transition more smoothly than would French and Belgian colonies, where self-government came with little preparation. Yet in each of these cases the path to independence and stability proved no less difficult than it was for their neighbors. Nigeria is richly endowed with natural resources: oil, natural gas, coal, and the world's greatest abundance of columbium (used in the manufacture of steel). These natural riches meant that the economic stakes were high and that conflicting forces would battle all the harder for control of the country. Charges of inefficiency and corruption, true or not, led to the overthrow of the government in 1966. After further assassinations, a group of military officers seized control. Within a year the eastern region of the country seceded and proclaimed itself the Republic of Biafra. During the late 1960s civil war raged in Nigeria between the central government and the Biafrans. Thousands were killed in battle; far more died of starvation. A total of over one million lost their lives before the rebel forces surrendered in 1970.

Kenya: the Mau Mau

Unlike Nigeria, Kenya is a poor country. The northern three-fifths of its territory is barren and almost waterless. In Kenya the conflict that preceded independence was both racial and tribal: the Mau Mau was a secret terrorist organization whose members were drawn from the Kikuyu tribe. Their targets were the whites in Kenya, a large Indian merchant middle class, and the blacks who refused to join the Mau Mau. The British managed to subdue the rebellion by 1958; five years later Kenya was a free nation.

The leader who did most to promote the growth and progress of an independent Kenya was the Kikuyu tribesman Jomo Kenyatta, socialist president of his country from 1963 until his death in 1978. Kenyatta devoted a long career to the defense of his homeland against white exploitation. While imprisoned for his Mau Mau activities in the 1950s, Kenyatta developed his philosophy of African socialism, which was reformist in nature, resembling that of European social democrats far more closely than it did communism. He urged his followers to forget the wrongs of the past and to concentrate on building a better future, a future that would not be dependent on either East or West. The African way, Kenyatta declared, had little to do with either capitalism or communism.

Though race was clearly a factor in the Kenyan turmoil, it was not as dominant an issue there as it was in both Rhodesia and South Africa. White Rhodesians for many years refused to acknowledge the inevitability of black rule. Rather than see power transferred to the blacks in Rhodesia, its prime minister, Ian Smith, in 1965 declared his country's unilateral independence from the British Commonwealth, that loose confederation of sovereign states which still maintains economic ties with Britain. Smith held firm in his determination to resist black rule until 1977, when combined pressure from the United States and Britain finally budged him. The compromise plan he favored, which promised gradual increase in black political power, and resulted in the election of Rhodesia's first black president in 1979, failed to satisfy the more militant rebel forces who claimed that the elections had been rigged, and that whites would continue to exercise real power in Rhodesia. Following further negotiations and elections monitored by the British, black nationalists led by Robert Mugabe established a government in 1980. Rhodesia, named for the most famous of the European imperialists, Cecil Rhodes, became the independent state of Zimbabwe, named for the capital of the great Katangan kingdom of the thirteenth century.

Meanwhile, South Africa continued to oppose appeals and pressures both from within and without to relax its racial policy of "apartheid," which has for years decreed a separate and desperately inferior existence for its black and mixed-race population. In 1976, blacks rioting to protest racial inequality in the Johannesburg ghetto of Soweto were suppressed by the police, leaving a death toll of over 200. The following year Steve Biko, a powerful black leader and advocate of nonviolent protest, died under extremely suspicious circumstances in jail following his intensive campaign against apartheid practices. Because many countries and many internationally powerful corporations have large investments in South Africa, the weapon of economic boycott, though threatened, has not been employed to try to force the government to change its racial policy. Political power may change hands, but the power of money remains a prime mover in the affairs of the world.

Jomo Kenyatta Addressing an All-Africa Congress in London

White Rhodesian opposition

Prime Minister Robert Mugabe of Zimbabwe

Apartheid in South Africa. A policeman and an interpreter check the passports of black men coming to work in the mines of Johannesburg.

4. THE LIMITS OF POWER

A nuclear balance of power

Although the world's leading nations retained or acquired enormous power in the postwar years, they often found themselves unable to exercise that power as they once had, or as they might want. Possession of nuclear weapons did not necessarily mean that a nation could impose its will upon another. Fear that their use might unleash a war that would destroy civilization forced nations to keep their powder dry.

The issue had been raised first during the Korean war, when the United States government deliberately refrained from extending the war into China for fear that such a move might lead irrevocably to a nuclear world war. This policy puzzled and angered many Americans, however, accustomed to the concepts of all-out war and unconditional surrender. Especially galling to them was the fact that President Harry Truman saw fit to fire General Douglas MacArthur, hero of the Pacific theater in the Second World War and now commander of the United Nations forces, because MacArthur refused to fight a limited war. In 1962 the United States and the Soviet Union were again forced to ask themselves how much they were willing to risk in order to protect their own strategic interests. During the early 1960s, United States President John F. Kennedy (1917–1963) and his advisors grew increasingly concerned about the activities of Premier Fidel Castro of Cuba. Castro was a Communist revolutionary who had led a successful revolt against a repressive Cuban dictatorship. He had subsequently arranged to have the Russians supply him with "offensive" missiles and other war matériel. In October 1962 Kennedy ordered a naval blockade of the island to prevent a delivery of promised equipment. The Soviet government, alarmed by the threat of war, agreed to withdraw and

Fidel Castro

to remove the bombers and missiles already on Cuban soil. The incident posed an extremely difficult question for the two superpowers: How could one nation convince another of its determination to brook no further interference with its plans, if its adversary could be fairly certain that because of the fear of nuclear war the threat was no more than a bluff?

In this instance, the Russians chose not to call America's bluff, thereby appearing to much of the world as the more statesmanlike of the two nations. The United States, however, read the results of the Cuban missile crisis as a triumph for confrontation, a policy it soon began to employ with disastrous consequences in Vietnam. After the defeat of Japan in 1945, France had sought to recover its lost empire in the Far East. These efforts ended in failure, however. The French were immediately confronted by a rebellion of Vietnamese nationalists under the leadership of Ho Chi Minh (1890–1969). The rebels resorted to guerrilla warfare and inflicted such costly defeats upon the French that the latter decided to abandon the struggle. An agreement was signed at Geneva in 1954 providing for the division of Vietnam into two zones, pending elections to determine the future government of the entire country. Ho Chi Minh became president of North Vietnam and established his capital at Hanoi. His followers, the Viet Cong, were numerous in both halves of the country. Had elections been held as provided by the Geneva Agreement, Ho Chi Minh would probably have been elected president of all of Vietnam. But the government of South Vietnam, backed by the United States, refused to permit elections to be held.

From this point on, involvement by the United States in the Vietnamese civil war escalated steadily. President Kennedy was convinced that a Chinese Communist juggernaut would soon roll over all of Southeast Asia: Vietnam, Laos, Cambodia, Malaysia, and Singapore; then Thailand, Burma, and India. How far Kennedy would have gone in his crusade to confront communism had he escaped assassination in 1963 is impossible to say. Kennedy's successor, Lyndon B. Johnson (1908–1973), hoped that a relatively small force of perhaps 100,000 men would be sufficient to defeat the Viet Cong and drive them back into their own country. Little consideration was given to the fact that these forces were solidly entrenched in both states of Vietnam, and that they had been waging a bitter national struggle for upward of eighteen years. They had succeeded in driving out the French in 1954 and were not likely to surrender to a new invader, as they conceived the Americans to be. The Viet Cong and the North Vietnam regulars, though less well equipped, nevertheless fought the South Vietnamese and their American allies to a standstill on several occasions. During the Tet offensive of 1968 they came close to capturing Saigon, the South Vietnamese capital.

Exasperated by failure to win an easy victory in South Vietnam, the American civilian and military chiefs undertook a campaign of heavy

Ho Chi Minh

Kennedy's intrusion into Vietnam

War in Vietnam. Confronted with a new kind of warfare, the American military sought to adapt its methods to the Vietnamese situation.

aerial bombardment. A series of incidents in 1964 were contrived so as to provide them with justification. Reports, of doubtful veracity, indicated that North Vietnamese ships had attacked American naval vessels in the Tonkin Gulf. President Johnson pronounced these incidents acts of war and immediately obtained from Congress authorization to use whatever measures might prove necessary to repel Communist aggression. Soon afterward the first American raids began. Although evidence accumulated which cast doubt on the efficacy of these raids, they continued. At least as much tonnage in nonnuclear bombs was dropped on tiny Vietnam as was unloaded by the Allied forces on all of Germany in the Second World War. As the struggle entered its fifth year, with no end in sight, disillusionment spread throughout the United States. Criticism of President Johnson was so harsh in 1968 that he was forced to abandon his plans to run for a second term.

President Johnson escalates the war

Johnson's successor, Richard M. Nixon, elected on the strength of promises to end the war, instead continued its escalation. In May 1970, the United States invaded Cambodia and a few months later the kingdom of Laos. In April 1972, the North Vietnamese, with aid from Russia and China, launched a powerful counteroffensive with the objective of conquering South Vietnam and driving all foreign armies out of the country. A number of South Vietnamese strongholds were captured. Nixon countered with increased bombing of North Vietnam's factories and railroads and by mining its harbors, savage raids which continued while negotiations were underway in December 1972.

The Nixon policies

A ceasefire, early in 1973, did no more than postpone the inevitable. Two years later, South Vietnam fell to the Viet Cong and the North Vietnamese. The massive intervention had proved a ghastly failure. The lesson of Vietnam—that in a nuclear age there are limits to national power—was one that the United States, Russia, and other countries

The limits to power

of the world were beginning to learn in the 1970s. The Soviet Union had suffered its share of setbacks too: in border clashes with China, and in its attempts to penetrate the governments of the Third World. In 1979 the Russians invaded Afghanistan to support the overthrow of a government they perceived as unsympathetic to their interests. Four years later, a force of 100,000 Russian troops had been unable to quell guerrilla opposition to this action. An ability to accommodate goals to limitations was a talent difficult for the superpowers to master. Yet it remained their best hope for a continuing, if uneasy, peace.

SELECTED READINGS

• *Items so designated are available in paperback editions.*

• Barnett, A. Doak, *A New U.S. Policy Toward China,* Washington, D.C., 1971. Discusses the diplomatic revolution of the early 1970s.

• Beer, Samuel, *British Politics in the Collectivist Age,* New York, 1965. A comprehensive treatment of welfare-state Britain.

Berger, Earl, *The Convenant and the Sword: Arab-Israeli Relations, 1948–1956,* London, 1965. An impartial account.

• Dehio, Ludwig, *Germany and World Politics in the Twentieth Century,* London, 1959. A series of essays assessing Germany's twentieth-century drive for European hegemony.

Ehrmann, Henry W., *Politics in France,* Boston, 1968. French politics since 1958.

• Erikson, Erik, *Gandhi's Truth: On the Origins of Militant Nonviolence,* New York, 1969. An analysis of Gandhi by a modern psychologist.

• Fairbank, J. K., *The United States and China,* rev. ed., Cambridge, Mass., 1971. A reliable survey by the leading U.S. historian of modern China.

Fall, Bernard B., *The Two Vietnams: A Political and Military Analysis,* rev. ed., New York, 1967. A journalist's compelling account.

Fejtö, François, *A History of the People's Democracies: Eastern Europe since Stalin,* London, 1971. Analyzes the various eastern European states as they succumbed to Soviet domination.

Fitzgerald, C.P., *Mao Tse-tung and China,* New York, 1976. A reliable study.

• Herring, George C., *America's Longest War: The United States and Vietnam, 1950–1975,* New York, 1979. Probably the best history of the war; balanced and thorough.

Hoffman, Stanley, et al., *In Search of France,* Cambridge, Mass., 1965. Essays providing perceptive analyses of postwar French politics and society.

Kolko, Gabriel, *The Politics of War: The World and United States Foreign Policy, 1943–45,* New York, 1969. Argues that the blame for the Cold War rests with the Western allies.

• Laqueur, Walter, *Europe since Hitler,* rev. ed., New York, 1982. A very useful survey.

• Rotberg, Robert I., *The Rise of Nationalism in Central Africa,* Cambridge, Mass., 1965. A skillful survey.

• Ulam, Adam B., *The Rivals: America and Russia since World War II,* New York, 1972. A survey of the Cold War in all its ramifications.

• Williams, W. A., *The Tragedy of American Diplomacy,* rev. ed., New York, 1962. The major "revisionist" study of the Cold War.
• Yergin, Daniel, *Shattered Peace: The Origins of the Cold War and the National Security State,* Boston, 1977. Another "revisionist" study, arguing that American diplomats failed to read Russia's challenge correctly.

SOURCE MATERIALS

Adenauer, Konrad, *Memoirs, 1945–53,* Chicago, 1966. Adenauer served as chancellor of the Federal Republic of Germany from 1949 to 1963 and sought both American support and the reunification of dismembered Germany.

Barnes, Thomas G., and Gerald D. Feldman, comps., *Breakdown and Rebirth: 1914 to the Present,* Boston, 1972. An excellent documentary collection of contemporary history, primarily European.

Brandt, Conrad, Benjamin Schwartz, and John Fairbank, eds., *A Documentary History of Chinese Communism,* Cambridge, Mass., 1952.

• Caputo, Philip, *A Rumor of War,* New York, 1977. The best memoir of the American experience in the Vietnam war.

De Gaulle, Charles, *Memoirs of Hope: Renewal and Endeavor,* New York, 1971.

• Fanon, Frantz, *The Wretched of the Earth,* New York, 1968. A brilliant, bitter denunciation by a black of Third World oppression.

Kennan, George F., *Memoirs, 1925–1950,* New York, 1967. Kennan, a career diplomat, was America's leading expert on Russia and instrumental in the formation of the containment policy.

Servan-Schreiber, J. J., *The American Challenge,* New York, 1968. A Frenchman's assessment of the impact of American economy and technology on Europe.

Chapter 32

PROBLEMS OF WORLD CIVILIZATION

This conjunction of an immense military establishment and a large arms industry is new in American experience. The total influence—economic, political, even spiritual—is felt in every city, every statehouse, every office of the federal government. . . . We must guard against the acquisition of unwarranted influence, whether sought or unsought, by the military-industrial complex. The potential for the disastrous rise of misplaced power exists and will persist.

—Dwight D. Eisenhower, "Farewell Address"

The writing of a final chapter in a textbook of this sort is, for the authors, a difficult task. Not only are they called upon to attempt an instant analysis of their own society and time; they are expected as well to discern in present events patterns that will continue to be of some consequence five to ten years hence. In other words, they are called upon to pick historical winners, to decide not what *has* mattered, which is difficult enough, but what *will* matter. Historians, whose job it is to acknowledge the way in which human idiosyncrasies make prediction a tricky business, are particularly loath to single out this movement or that trend and to pronounce it "significant" in terms of the future. We shall therefore merely content ourselves with a discussion of some of the most serious problems confronting society in the 1970s and 1980s, calling attention at the outset to the fact that these problems are rooted in many of the historical developments—industrialization, urbanization, and international competition, for example—that we have traced in the preceding chapters.

The present as history

1. THE GROWTH OF CENTRALIZED GOVERNMENT AND ITS CONSEQUENCES

The responsibilities central governments assumed, and the power they arrogated to themselves to discharge those responsibilities, increased

Centralization and social welfare

significantly around the world after the Second World War. In almost all countries, successive administrations either initiated or expanded social welfare programs, ensuring that entire populations would receive protection from the depredations of unemployment, sickness, and old age. Building upon the examples set by Germany and Britain before the First World War, Western nations instituted increasingly comprehensive national programs for health and social security. Socialist and Third World countries likewise moved, in some cases with remarkable speed, to alleviate the problems and disabilities of people who for generations had been denied the chance of a healthy and secure existence.

Reasons for the increase

This movement to expand social welfare systems resulted in an increased tendency on the part of governments to manage and control their citizenry. Programs of social insurance were designed to benefit and hence to regulate the lives of all classes of men and women, not just the destitute. New agencies, staffed by armies of newly recruited bureaucrats, imposed rules while they dispensed assistance to a clientele that grew to include the entire citizenry. As government planning became more sophisticated this increasingly large and powerful class of technocrats argued that decisions could only be based on expert knowledge that lay beyond the reach of elected representatives. The European Economic Community, whose headquarters was a bureaucratic hive staffed by thousands of supranational civil servants, seemed to critics in the 1980s a particularly potent breeder of a protechnocratic, antidemocratic attitude toward representative government.

Central governments and the economy

Concern to improve, or at any rate to stabilize, a nation's international position within a world in which power relationships were constantly shifting, contributed further to the growth of centralized government. New nations wanted to attain some new measure of international power. Older nations wanted to retain whatever measure had been theirs. In either case, governments recognized the need for a stable economy. Few countries, old or new, managed to attain that goal in the 1970s and 1980s to the extent they deemed necessary. Inflation was the first of the problems that thwarted their designs. Rates of inflation soared in the late 1970s and early 1980s to more than 20 percent in Britain and Italy. Other European countries experienced less severe but nevertheless alarming increases in prices. A second related problem confronting central governments in the 1980s was unemployment. In Britain and the United States unemployment was, to some degree at least, the result of government-imposed monetary policies designed to curb inflation by making money harder to borrow and thus curtailing its circulation. Inflation rates did drop. But restrictive monetary policies also slowed consumer spending and business investment, and thereby eliminated jobs. In Britain, by 1982, 12 percent of the workforce was without employment, the highest figure since the depression of the 1930s. In the United States the number topped 10 percent; in France and Italy, 8 percent; in Germany, 6 percent. Unemployment was exacerbated by industrial competition from non-Western countries: Japan, to be sure, but also Third World nations in the Far East, Africa, and Latin America, where Western capital had built factories and where cheap labor made it possible to manufacture goods at lower cost than in the highly industrialized West. Shoe factories in France closed because they could not compete with shoe factories in South Korea. Throughout these struggles with inflation and unemployment governments tightened their hold on the economy, working to do so with the forces of both management and labor. The result of these activities was a further growth of the power and control of government.

What have been the consequences of such growth? Some observers have argued that the general worldwide increase in the authority of central governments is a symptom of a decline in the importance of political and economic ideology. Whether a nation declares itself to be a capitalist democracy (as does the United States), a socialist commonwealth (as does the Soviet Union) or something in between (as do many of the nations of western Europe), all appear to some degree to have blunted ideological differences as they have attempted to rationalize—or nationalize—their industries, manage their economies, provide for the well-being of their citizens, and arm themselves against the possibilities of future war. Fewer socialists now advocate collective ownership of the means of production; they have become instead exponents of the welfare state. Defenders of capitalism still exist in theory, but few would recognize it if they saw it in full swing. Capitalist economies are no longer free-enterprise systems but "mixed" economies, involving government controls, managed currencies, and forced distribution of profits.

Political reaction to centralization

To suggest that there has been some ideological blurring in the movement toward more generally accepted goals does not mean, however, that men and women do not continue to call themselves capitalists or socialists, or that those terms have lost their meaning. Nor should it imply that there is not continuing and heated debate about both ends and means. During the mid-1970s a reaction of some magnitude occurred in several Western countries against the notion that governments should manage the lives of their citizens to the extent they were. Social reform, critics said, has cost too much, and has not really achieved what it was supposed to. There is still poverty and misery. Admit that they will always exist, these people argued, and moderate your goals accordingly; in the process, put an end to big government. This viewpoint was occasionally translated into political victory. The socialist government of Sweden, in power for decades, was succeeded by a conservative one. Margaret Thatcher, arch-conservative leader of Britain's Tory party, became the first woman prime minister of that country in 1979, as well as the first woman head of state of a Western nation, on a platform which blamed her country's economic decline in the 1970s on the fact that the government

Margaret Thatcher

Alexsandr Solzhenitsyn

President Nixon Resigns. Here Nixon bids his last farewell to the White House in the wake of his resignation.

had overextended itself. In the United States, Ronald Reagan was elected president in 1980 after promising to undo much of the social legislation passed in the 1960s and early 1970s. As president, he continued to blame the country's economic problems—inflation, flagging production, unemployment—on the willingness of past administrations to spend borrowed money on programs in the areas of housing, education, and family assistance. (Reagan remained willing, however, to spend vast sums on armaments.)

This debate has been carried on not only in the political arena but in the writings of thoughtful and angry critics of modern society. Two of the most powerful voices raised against the growth of worldwide governmental expansion and authoritarianism were those of Alexsandr Solzhenitsyn and Herbert Marcuse. Solzhenitsyn, an exiled Russian novelist, attacked the brutal methods employed by the Soviet Union in its rapid climb to world power. His *Gulag Archipelago,* published in 1973, is a fictionalized account of the fate of those whose willingness to stand in the way of Soviet "progress" sentenced them to life in Siberian labor camps. Marcuse, an American, charged that authoritarianism was just as much a fact of life under capitalism as under communism. He argued that industrial capitalism had produced a "one-dimensional" society, in which the interests of individual citizens had been ruthlessly subordinated to those of the powerful corporate interests which were the true governors of the world.

Marcuse urged the adoption of revolutionary measures to accomplish the overthrow of authoritarian capitalist imperialism. Those unwilling to follow him to that extreme nevertheless concurred in his denunciation of the manner in which big government and big business together appeared to be draining power from individual citizens. Indeed, as devoted a capitalist as Dwight D. Eisenhower, general in the U.S. Army during the Second World War and president of the United States in the 1950s, warned in his farewell presidential address of the growing might of what he called "the military-industrial complex." In those countries calling themselves democracies, democracy seemed to many to have less and less meaning, as people appeared to enjoy little control over their government and hence over their lives. Concerns of this sort received apparent confirmation in the late 1960s and early 1970s, when the United States was at war in Vietnam. Evidence subsequently published showed that the democratically elected Congress was misled by President Lyndon Johnson and his advisors into believing that hostile North Vietnamese attacks on American ships had compelled U.S. intervention, whereas the attacks had instead been "manufactured" to allow the government to pursue its own aggressive policies. Concern about the arrogance of governmental power reached its peak in the United States during the Watergate investigations leading to the resignation of President Richard Nixon in 1974, when it was learned that Nixon had authorized domestic spying in the name of national security but without proper regard for the constitutional rights of American citizens. Following that dramatic episode came revelations about the role played in secret by the U.S. Central Intelligence Agency in subverting leftist Third World governments, along with the intervention of giant multinational corporations and the C.I.A. together in assisting to overthrow a democratically elected socialist government in Chile. Knowledge of these events brought home the extent to which centralized authority in supposedly democratic governments had removed itself from popular control and accountability.

2. COMMITMENT: THE GROWTH OF BLACK CONSCIOUSNESS

Partly in response to revelations of this sort, partly as a result of long-standing grievances and dissatisfactions, groups that had hitherto lived as subordinates in society, kept powerless and in large part silenced, raised their voices in the 1960s and 1970s, demanding not only to be heard but to have their demands met. At the very time when democracies were being charged with ignoring the wishes of their constituents, blacks, youth, and women, in particular, began to assert their right to equality.

*Society's subordinates
speak out*

The growth of insurgency among American blacks has paralleled the rise of black nations in Africa and the Caribbean. Through most of the years from the Civil War to 1900, black people were condemned, in the North as well as the South, to a subordinate role within a predominantly white culture. The emancipation of slaves and the Thirteenth and Fourteenth Amendments to the Constitution brought little change in a quality of existence which was centuries-old and which was underwritten by the racist attitudes and practices of most whites. These attitudes and practices were realized in substandard education, lack of jobs, poor housing, inequality under the law, lynching of both black men and women, and other oppressive conditions of life with which black people were faced. Any changes in this reality might have been indefinitely postponed had it not been for the spread of black political consciousness and the rise of a number of black leaders, both male and female, during the course of the twentieth century. Black political consciousness and black leaders were not unknown before the turn of the century: Harriet Tubman, Sojourner Truth, Frederick Douglass, Nat Turner, and others, were eloquent and powerful spokespeople and activists. But with the twentieth century came a massive emigration of blacks from the South to the North. Although the North shared most of the attitudes of the South, there were more opportunities for blacks in the industrial cities than in the primarily agrarian South. Many thousands of black people emigrated to the

*U.S. blacks after the
Civil War*

W. E. B. Du Bois

Martin Luther King, Jr.

North during the years of the First World War, when the lack of white labor created a need for their services; over 400,000 blacks were drafted into the military even though, in most parts of the United States, they were essentially disenfranchised citizens. During the postwar depression, however, black workers were the first to suffer and to lose their jobs. Yet despite setbacks, emigration was producing a changed political consciousness for black people.

In 1910 the National Association for the Advancement of Colored People was founded and contributed to this political progress and the growing awareness among black people that they were an oppressed group and that this should be changed. The work of the NAACP was supplemented in 1911 with the founding of the National League on Urban Conditions Among Negroes (later known as the National Urban League). The work of black leaders of this time—for example, Ida Wells-Barnett (1862–1931), A. Philip Randolph (1889–1979), W. E. B. Du Bois (1868–1963), Mary Mcleod Bethune (1875–1955)—who were visible and vocal opponents of lynching, promoters of educational opportunities for blacks, and of the organization of blacks into labor unions, kept the movement for equality alive.

The Second World War saw another influx of blacks into northern cities and intensified their drive for dignity and independence. The Congress of Racial Equality (CORE) was founded by James Farmer in 1942. His announced aim was to translate "love of God and man" into specific crusades against discrimination and injustice. By 1960 CORE had combined its efforts with those of other political and civil rights organizations seeking the same goals. Together they helped to promote "freedom rides" on behalf of civil rights and boycotts directed at private businesses and public sources that discriminated against blacks in the South. The leader of these protests, and the undoubted leader of the black movement in the United States in the 1960s, was Martin Luther King, Jr. (1929–1968), a Baptist minister. Like Farmer, King embraced the Gandhian philosophy of nonviolence. His personal participation in countless demonstrations, his willingness to go to jail for a cause that he believed to be just, and his ability as an orator to arouse both blacks and whites with his message led to his position as the most highly regarded—and widely feared—defender of black rights. His career was ended by assassination in 1968.

The goal of King and of organizations like CORE was a fully integrated nation. That of other charismatic black leaders was complete independence from white society. Marcus Garvey (1887–1940), a native of Jamaica who lived in the black New York City ghetto of Harlem, emphasized the African origins of black Americans. He claimed that his people were the descendants of the "greatest and proudest race who ever peopled the earth." In his campaign for black separatism he generated a movement of black emigration from America to Africa. Another black separatist was Malcolm X (1925–1965), who assumed the "X" after having discarded his "white" surname. For most of his adult life a spokesman for the Black Muslim movement, Malcolm X urged blacks to renew their commitment to their own heritage—the Muslim religion, for example—and to establish black businesses as a way of maintaining economic and psychological distance from white domination. Like King, he was assassinated, in 1965 while addressing a rally in Harlem.

Civil rights laws enacted under the Johnson administration in the 1960s brought American blacks some measure of equality with regard to voting rights—and, to a much lesser degree, school desegregation. In other areas, such as housing and job opportunities, blacks continue to suffer disadvantage and discrimination, as a result of white racism, which lies beneath arguments that blacks should be satisfied with the gains they have made, and the general recalcitrance of administrations following Lyndon Johnson's domestically innovative one. These problems are not confined to the United States. In Great Britain, for example, where there has been a large immigration of blacks from former colonies, extreme discrimination in jobs and housing menaces the chances for early or satisfactory integration. Because most black workers are "last hired, first fired," they were particular victims of Britain's rising unemployment. In the summer of 1981 black frustrations resulted in serious rioting in London and other British cities. Disturbances broke out again in the United States in 1982 in Miami, where an influx of Latin American refugees, most of them Cuban, had created further tensions. Response to these outbreaks followed the pattern established in the 1960s: immediate concern and investigation, but little else, particularly in terms of solving the problems of economic inequality. Black leadership in the United States is not as centrally organized as in recent decades. Because the momentum for reform has slowed, black leaders are less able than in the 1960s to chart their movement's direction. Meanwhile black people derive continued strength not only from the conviction that the battle for equality is both justified and still to be won, but from the example of African and Caribbean nations emerging into independent statehood.

Blacks in the 1970s and 1980s

3. COMMITMENT: YOUTH AND WOMEN

The years from 1964 through 1972 were marked by widespread protests and upheaval among the younger generation. Its members were committed, as were blacks, to the assertion of their right to be heard. In the United States this rebellion was fueled by the war in Vietnam. Young men, drafted to fight in a war they despised, rebelled against the idea that it was their "duty" to serve. Together, young men and women proclaimed instead their duty to question anew the presuppositions that had led the U.S. into its unhappy military predicament. Science antagonized them because of its association with war-making. Knowledge that was not "relevant" to the world's problems was

The youth rebellion

Vietnam Protest, 1971. Veterans of the U.S. Armed Forces march on the Capitol to protest continued U.S. involvement in the war in Vietnam.

questioned with regard to its worth. Young leaders urged their peers to leave their college books and address the problems of the "real" world: overpopulation, industrial pollution, mistreatment of blacks and other minorities. It was this rebellion that exposed the inhumanity of the American adventure in Southeast Asia. Long before adult liberals spoke out against the bombing raids and body-counts of that war, students in colleges and universities stormed the institutions of the Establishment in angry protest. Although they did not stop the war, they helped to bring about President Johnson's retirement in 1968. Their *compères* in France, who rioted in May 1968, contributed to the defeat of President Charles de Gaulle.

Terrorism in the 1970s and 1980s

Political radicalism no longer shapes the mind of the West's youth as it did in the late 1960s, a fact explained in large part by the end of hostilities in Vietnam. Radicalism's much-distorted reflection, however, appears in the activities of terrorist gangs which appeared in the late 1970s and early 1980s. Irish Catholic (Irish Republican Army, or IRA) and Protestant extremists have continued to wage guerrilla war not only against each other but against the British who have for over a decade attempted vainly to impose peace upon Northern Ireland. Palestine Liberation Organization terrorists killed Israeli athletes at the 1972 Olympic Games in Munich. Basque nationalists, seeking to free themselves from Spanish rule, took to terrorist killings of Spanish soldiers and civilians. In Germany, leftist terrorists kidnapped businessmen and politicians. Red Brigades in Italy gained brief worldwide notoriety by kidnapping and murdering the highly respected politician and former prime minister Aldo Moro in 1978. The Italian government's determination to face down terrorist threats was tested successfully in 1982 when an American NATO commander was rescued from his captors who were themselves brought to trial. Though terrorism remained a serious threat to stability in the 1980s, its practice had no profound effect on the course of world events. Hoping their extremist tactics would somehow speed revolution, terrorists have in fact done no more than conduct a series of isolated exercises in irrationality, immediately horrifying but ultimately sterile.

Not all young rebels in the 1960s and 1970s committed themselves to a life of radical political activism. Some turned for spiritual or psychological comfort to fundamentalist religious movements. Some declared their disgust with the world by "dropping out," living in communities of their own design apart from society. Others devoted themselves to a counterculture reflected in the intensely personal music and lyrics of young popular musicians, in the custom of drug-taking, and in the freedom to live with each other without marriage. Social rebellion of this sort infected various countries to various degrees. It was primarily a movement of urban middle-class youths. Though in some cases their rejection of older values was the result of deeply held and enduring convictions, in many others their declaration of independence was short-lived, amounting to little more than the customary behavior of uncertain and impatient adolescents. In contrast to their predecessors of the 1960s and 1970s, the middle-class youth of the 1980s was being criticized for its "selfish" attention to career goals and materialism.

Youthful counterculture

Women, like blacks and young people, began to assert themselves during the 1960s and 1970s. As was the case with the youth rebellion, the women's movement began in the United States and was first directed from within the middle class. Some women in western European countries joined in the struggle for equal rights; by the mid-seventies the movement had spread worldwide, including the Third World nations, and was no longer limited to the middle class. Many of the early activists within the movement had been part of the youth

The women's movement

Students of the University of Paris during the Uprisings of 1968

rebellion during its most intense phase in the sixties. Their activism, in part, stemmed from a realization that even in a radical political atmosphere, women were relegated to second place. Women's position within society had changed radically since the nineteenth century. The assumption that the middle-class woman's place was in the home had been challenged by the ever-increasing demand for women workers and by the need experienced by more and more women to hold a job—either for financial reasons or because housework was for a growing number an unfulfilling occupation. The increased availability and social acceptance of birth-control devices meant that women were having fewer children, and that they could begin to exercise more control over the pattern of their lives.

Yet society seemed loath to acknowledge the implication of these changes: that women are equal to men. Women were paid less than men for similar work. Women with qualifications no different from men were turned down because of their gender when they applied for jobs. Women with excellent employment records were forced to rely on their husbands to establish credit. Political action helped alleviate some of these inequities in the late 1960s and the 1970s. The U.S. government instituted programs of "affirmative action" which mandated the hiring of qualified women as well as members of racial minority groups. The campaign for equality did not meet with universal approval, however. A particularly volatile subject was a woman's right to an abortion. Feminists argued that women must enjoy the freedom to plan for their future unencumbered by the responsibilities of motherhood if they choose, and that their bodies are theirs to govern. Their opponents, which included members of the so-called right-to-life

Margaret Sanger, a Leader in the Movement to Awaken the World to the Necessity of Birth Control

The Women's Movement in France. French women demand equal pay for equal work.

movement, countered with the argument that abortion encouraged sexual irresponsibility; some declared that abortion is the equivalent of murder. By the mid-1980s the campaigners for women's equality, despite the failure in the United States of passage of a constitutional Equal Rights Amendment, had a good many successes to their credit. Unlike the youth rebellion, which had run its course by that time, the women's movement, like that of black people, was based not on the disaffections of only one generation, but on a history of discrimination experienced by great numbers and recognized as unjust by a sizable proportion of majority opinion.

4. LITERATURE AND ART AS REFLECTIONS OF CONTEMPORARY PROBLEMS

Not surprisingly, the work of many of the West's leading writers reflect the difficulties and commitments we have been surveying. During the immediate postwar years novelists concerned themselves with the horrors of war and of the totalitarian systems which had spawned the conflict of the 1940s. The Americans James Jones and Norman Mailer, in *From Here to Eternity* and *The Naked and the Dead,* portrayed the coarseness and cruelty of military life with ruthless realism. The German Günter Grass's first and probably most important novel, *The Tin Drum,* depicted the vicious and politically diseased life of Nazi Germany in the 1930s. In France, Jean-Paul Sartre, as a result of his own and his country's wartime experiences, recommitted himself in his novels, plays, and other writings to a life of active political involvement as a Marxist. Whereas he had previously defined hell in terms of individual hostilities, he now defined it in terms of class inequality. Unlike Sartre, his compatriot Albert Camus (1913–1960) was unable to construct a secular faith from his own perceptions of the world and its apparent absurdities. Though idealist enough to participate in the French resistance movement against the German occupation in the Second World War, and though proclaiming the virtues of rebellion, Camus remained tortured in novels such as *The Fall, The Plague,* and *The Rebel* by the problem of humanity's responsibility for its own miserable dilemma and by the limitations placed upon the ability of men and women to help each other.

Postwar authors

The theme of individual alienation and helplessness, a reflection of the problems arising from the growth of state power, was one to which writers addressed themselves with increasing frequency in the 1960s and 1970s. The Russian Boris Pasternak, in his novel *Dr. Zhivago,* indicted the Soviet campaign to shape all its citizens to the same mold. Although both Pasternak and his compatriot Solzhenitsyn were awarded the Nobel Prize for literature, the former in 1958 and the latter in 1970, their works were condemned by the Soviet government and Solzhenitsyn was sent into exile. Western novelists dealt with the

Alienation and helplessness

threat to individuality as well, building upon a prewar tradition most forcefully expressed in the writings of the Austrian Franz Kafka (1883–1924). Kafka's novels present a vision of humans in a hostile universe, hopelessly striving to come to terms with a remote and unknown power. His best-known work, *The Castle,* is at once a satire on bureaucracy and a philosophical representation of the isolation of the individual in the universe. The American novelist Saul Bellow (1915–   ) was concerned with many of these same themes, though Bellow spoke with a far gentler, if less compelling, voice than Kafka. He chose the modern city as the milieu for his fiction. His heroes in novels such as *The Adventures of Augie March, Henderson the Rain King,* and *Mr. Sammler's Planet* were all men trapped in a world turned upside down, condemned to seek personal understanding—indeed to maintain their sanity—in an environment at worst savage, at best absurd.

Women authors wrote not only of the general loneliness of the human condition, but of the particular plight of women trapped in a world not of their own making. The Frenchwoman Simone de Beauvoir (1908–   ) in *The Second Sex,* a germinal study of the female condition, denounced the male middle class for turning not only workers but also its own women into objects for its own ends. American writers like Adrienne Rich, Tillie Olsen, and the philosopher Mary Daly helped define the politics and culture of the women's movement.

Simone de Beauvoir

The specific issues that drove men and women to committed action in the mid-1960s compelled writers to take sides as well. Günter Grass, in *Local Anaesthetic,* published in 1970, wrote of student unrest and political involvement. The movement for black equality encouraged a tradition in America that had burgeoned in the wake of the depression and the Second World War. One initiator of this tradition was Richard Wright (1908–1960), who grew up amid the rural poverty and violent racism of Mississippi. As a youth Wright drifted to Chicago and became a resident of and spokesman for the black ghetto. In his novel, *Native Son,* and his autobiography, *Black Boy,* he portrayed with scathing realism the oppression of working-class blacks. Despite the pretensions of the New Deal, he found that the burdens of that group had not been appreciably lightened. One of the most effective articulaters of black aspiration and disenchantment in the 1960s was James Baldwin, the son of a Harlem clergyman. Living under the dual stigmas of his blackness and his homosexuality, Baldwin remained a self-exile in Paris for ten years following the Second World War. He returned to the United States to warn, in his most powerful book, *The Fire Next Time,* that unless whites awoke soon to the extent and pervasiveness of their racism, American society would be consumed by its own animosities.

James Baldwin

Some authors, although they agreed with indictments of contemporary civilization, believed the human condition too hopeless to warrant direct attack. These writers expressed their despair by escaping into the absurd and fantastic. In the plays of Samuel Beckett (1906–   ), an Irishman who wrote in French, and of the Englishman Harold Pinter (1930–   ), nothing happens. Characters speak in the banalities that have become the hallmark of modern times. Words which are meaningless when spoken by human beings nevertheless take on a logic of their own; yet they explain nothing. Other authors, less willing, perhaps, to attempt to make a statement out of nothingness, have invaded the realms of hallucination, science fiction, and fantasy. The novels of the Americans William Burroughs and Kurt Vonnegut convey their readers from interior fantasizing to outer space. Significantly one of the most popular books among the youth of the sixties and seventies was *The Lord of the Rings,* a pseudosaga set in the fantasy world of "Middle Earth," written before the Second World War by the Englishman J. R. R. Tolkien.

The absurd and fantastic

Filmmakers, in the decades after the Second World War, made films which mirrored the problems and concerns of society, with a depth and artistic integrity seldom attempted or achieved previously. The Swede Ingmar Bergman, the Frenchmen Jean-Luc Godard and François Truffaut, the Italians Frederico Fellini and Michelangelo Antonioni, to name but a few of the most gifted directors, dealt in their films with the same themes that marked the literature of the period: loneliness, war, oppression, and corruption. One important factor facilitating the achievement of artistic quality was the general willingness on the part of censors—state or industry sponsored—to reflect public taste by permitting filmmakers great license in the handling of themes such as racism, violence, and sexuality. While there is no question that this relaxation led to exploitation, it cleared the way for extraordinarily powerful film statements, such as the American Arthur Penn's *Bonnie and Clyde* (1967) and the Italian Bernardo Bertolucci's *Last Tango in Paris* (1972), shocking declarations about humanity made possible by explicit depictions of violence and sex. Film, while gaining a general maturity it had heretofore lacked, did not desert its role as entertainment. The international popularity of the British rock-and-roll group, the Beatles, was translated, for example, into equally successful films, charming, slapstick escapism which nevertheless proclaimed the emancipation of youth from the confining formalities and conventions of their elders.

Film

Unlike writers or filmmakers, the majority of postwar artists did not use their work as a vehicle to express either ideological commitment or a concern for the human situation. Following trends established by the impressionists and cubists, they spoke neither about the world or to the world, but instead to each other and to the extremely small coterie of initiates who understood their artistic language. Foremost among the postwar schools of art was abstract expressionism, whose chief exponents were the painters Jackson Pollack

Fine arts

Mahoning by Franz Kline. A work representative of the abstract expressionists' desire to explore the varieties of light, texture, and surface.

See color plates following page 1056 for representative works by Johns, Stella, Rothko, and Hanson

(1912–1956), William deKooning (1904–   ), and Franz Kline (1910–1962). Their interests lay in further experimentation with the relationships between color, texture, and surface, to the total exclusion of "meaning" or "message" in the traditional sense. Jasper Johns's painting of the American flag insisted that the viewer see it not as *a* painting—that is, something to be interpreted—but instead as painting, the treatment of canvas with paint. Robert Rauschenberg, in revolt against the abstract expressionists, exhibited blank white panels, insisting that by so doing he was pressing art to the ultimate question of a choice of medium. Painters fought the notion that their work in some way expressed disgust with an empty civilization. "My paintings are based on the fact that only what can be seen is there," declared the American Frank Stella, who painted stripes on irregularly shaped canvases. "Pop" art, a phenomenon of the late sixties which took as its subject everyday objects such as soup cans and comic-strip heroes, was likewise, according to its practitioners, not a protest against the banality of industrialism but another experiment in abstractions.

Rothko

Even the remote and yet extraordinarily compelling abstractions of Mark Rothko (1903–1970), glowing or somber rectangles of color imposed upon other rectangles, were said by the artist himself to represent "nothing but content—no associations, only sensation." Only with the coming, in the 1970s, of the so-called hyper-realists, artists such as the American Duane Hanson, who recreates his invariably depressing human subjects in plastic down to the last eyelash, can we perhaps say that some artists are making a statement not only about technique but about what they perceive as the vacuity of life.

5. THE CRISIS OF ECOLOGY AND POPULATION

Pessimism about the human condition derived not only from concern for the problems of the present that we have been considering. It stemmed as well from a fear about the future, the future of the earth's human beings, of the earth itself, and of what is termed its ecology. The word *ecology* is often used to refer to human beings and their environment, but it is much broader than that. Ecologists think of humans as related to a vast chain of life which extends through mammals, amphibians, invertebrates, and the simplest microorganisms, either plants or animals. In popular usage ecology may be synonymous with pollution problems. Again this is an oversimplification. The causes and prevention of pollution make up important elements in the study of ecology, but they are not its whole subject. Equally important is the use of our environment in ways that will safeguard the heritage of fertile soil, pure air, fresh water, and forests for those who come after us.

The meaning of ecology

Ecological violations consist not merely of poisoning the atmosphere and contaminating oceans, rivers, and lakes by dumping wastes into them, but of any assault upon them that makes them less valuable for human survival. The excessive construction of dams, for example, causes the silting of rivers and the accumulating of nitrates at a faster rate than the surrounding soil can absorb. The use of insecticides, especially those containing DDT, may result in upsetting the balance of nature. An example in the recent history of Malaysia illustrates such an occurrence. The Malaysian government resorted to extensive spraying of remote areas with DDT in the hope of stamping out malaria-carrying mosquitoes. The DDT killed the mosquitoes but also poisoned the flourishing cockroaches. The cockroaches in turn were eaten by the village cats. The cats died of the DDT poison. The net result was a multiplication of rats formerly kept from a population explosion by their natural enemies, the cats. So badly disturbed was the balance of nature that a fresh supply of cats had to be airlifted from other regions. Other assaults upon the balance of nature have been even more serious. The Aswan High Dam of Egypt, undoubtedly valuable for increasing the water supply of that country, has at the same time cut down the flow of algal nutrients to the Mediterranean, with damaging effects on the fishing industry of various countries. From the ecological standpoint the rapid development of industry in modern times is an almost unmitigated disaster. For thousands of years the human race introduced into the environment no more waste substances than could easily be absorbed by the environment. But modern technology has introduced a variety of wastes never abundant before. Among them are carbon monoxide, sulfur dioxide, and nitrogen oxides. And this is to say nothing of the discharge into nature of pesticides, the great host of synthetic products that are not biologically

Other assaults upon nature

Industrial Pollution. This photo shows steel mills in Westfalenhuette, West Germany. While polluting gases and particular matter are released into the air, industrial wastes, both thermal and chemical, are released into nearby waters.

degradable, and the fallout of nuclear weapons testing. As the nature and gravity of these problems have become apparent, governments have been pressured to take preventive and remedial action. In late 1982 the United States government was actually compelled to purchase the entire town of Times Beach, Missouri, where a highly dangerous pesticide had been sprayed (with permanently damaging effects to the health of its citizens), before it could proceed with a detoxification program.

Ecology and the population explosion

The ecological problem is caused not simply by the dumping of harmful and nondegradable products. It is also the result of wastage of land as our most valuable natural resource. In many parts of the world rivers run brown because they are filled with earth washed from the fields bordering them. In some of the largest American cities two-thirds to three-quarters of the land area is paved with streets and parking lots. A close link exists between the problems of ecology and the population explosion. Indeed, if population had not increased alarmingly in recent years, the problems of ecology might well have passed unnoticed. For example, New York City on the eve of the Civil War had a total population of 700,000. The area was not essentially smaller than what it is now. Yet the inhabitants of the five boroughs constituting the city have multiplied ten times over. This increase has been accompanied by physical transformations that have facilitated crowded living by masses of people. Oil lamps were replaced by gaslight and then by electricity, horse-drawn wagons and carriages by trolley cars, automobiles, subways, and buses. While some of these inventions eliminated a few forms of pollution, the general effect was to multiply

Four Darks in Red, Mark Rothko (1903–1970). Oil on canvas. Rothko became obsessed with the need to reduce both color and form, achieving thereby a kind of gloomy mysticism. (The Whitney Museum of American Art)

Summer Rental No. 2, Robert Rauschenberg (born 1925). Oil on canvas. Rauschenberg experiments with problems of dimensionality and painterly technique as he strives to achieve a total harmony out of disparate elements. (Collection Whitney Museum of American Art). Gift of the Friends of the Whitney Museum of American Art.

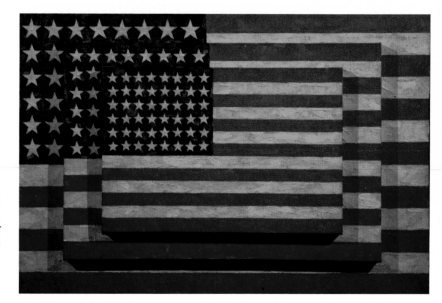

Three Flags, Jasper Johns (born 1930). Encaustic on canvas. Painted with absolute objectivity Johns' objects, in this case three American flags, cease to be mere reproductions and take on distinctive identities of their own. (The Whitney Museum of American Art)

Woman with Dog, Duane Hanson (born 1925). Polvinyl, polychromed in oil, life size. Hanson recreates the human artifacts of Middle-American culture as symbols of a hollow society. (Collection Whitney Museum of American Art). Gift of Frances and Sydney Lewis.

Green Coca Cola Bottles, Andy Warhol (born 1931). Oil on canvas. Warhol, who stands as the high priest of the "pop art" movement in the public imagination, turns mass production into art. Here he takes a commercial product and presents it in row after row, much as it might appear on a grocery store shelf. (Collection Whitney Museum of American Art). Gift of the Friends of the Whitney Museum of American Art.

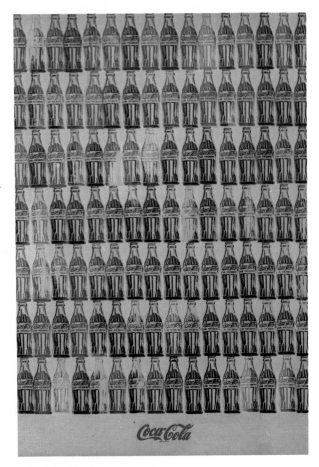

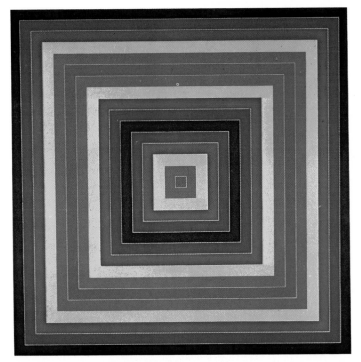

Gran Cairo, Frank Stella (born 1936). Synthetic polymer paint on canvas. The artist employs absolute symmetry and a rectilinear pattern with compelling effect. (Collection Whitney Museum of American Art). Gift of the Friends of the Whitney Museum of American Art.

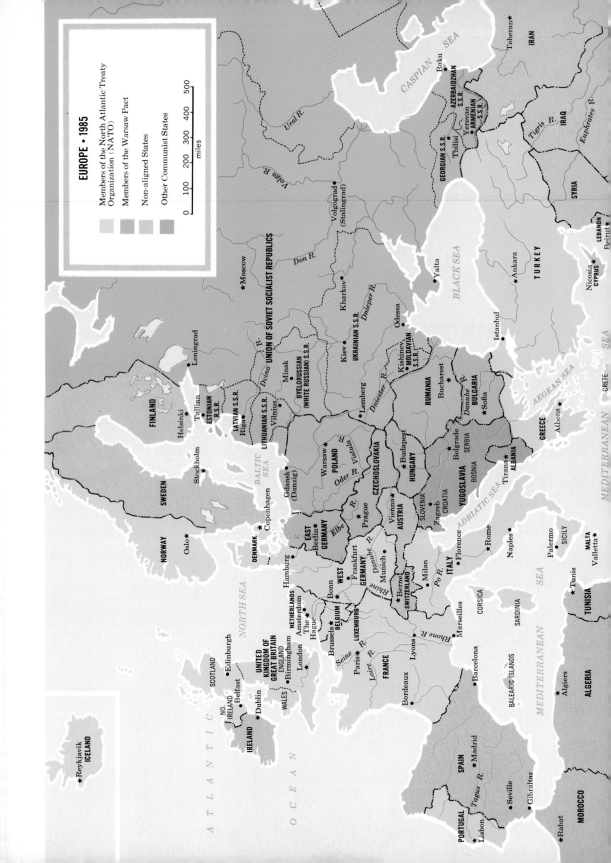

sources of contamination and abuse of the natural environment. The example of New York City can be duplicated in many other overcrowded areas, not only in America but especially in Asia. Calcutta now has a population of 7.5 million, compared with 3 million in 1961. Tokyo has grown from 9 million to over 12 million in little more than twenty years.

As the population increases, human beings create more and more problems and the damage done by each person escalates rapidly. Conditions in Los Angeles illustrate the danger. Increases in the number of smog-producers nullify every victory the smog-control experts succeed in gaining. The worst offenders in vitiating ecological progress are the big industrial powers. They combine exhaustion of natural resources with contamination of the environment by industrial poisons, and consume hundreds of times more natural products than do most of the inhabitants of the Third World. The oil shortages of the 1970s, produced by the uncertain political state of the Middle East, forced the West—and particularly the United States—to become aware of its wasteful ways. Whether those shortages will also compel the West to expend its resources less extravagantly remains to be seen.

Effects of population explosion

Most nations of the contemporary world are in danger of being overwhelmed by a population explosion. Its major cause has been what the experts call the demographic revolution. By this is meant an overturning of the ancient balance between births and deaths, which formerly kept the population on a stationary or slowly rising level. This balance is a biological condition common to nearly all species. For thousands of years humankind was no exception. The total population of the earth at the beginning of the Christian era was about 250 million. More than sixteen centuries passed before another quarter-billion had been added to the total. Not until 1860 did the population

The demographic revolution

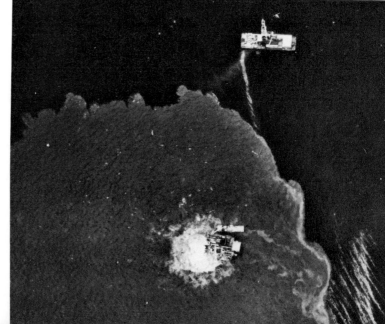

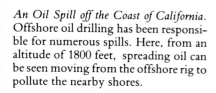

An Oil Spill off the Coast of California. Offshore oil drilling has been responsible for numerous spills. Here, from an altitude of 1800 feet, spreading oil can be seen moving from the offshore rig to pollute the nearby shores.

of the globe approximate 1 billion. From then on the increase was vastly more rapid. The sixth half-billion, added about 1960, required scarcely more than ten years.

Causes of the demographic revolution

What have been the causes of this radical imbalance known as the demographic revolution? Fundamentally, what has happened has been the achievement of a twentieth-century death rate alongside a medieval birth rate. Infant mortality rates have markedly declined. Deaths of mothers in childbirth have also diminished. The great plagues, such as cholera, typhus, and tuberculosis, take a much smaller toll than they did in earlier centuries. Wars and famines still number their victims by the millions, yet such factors are insufficient to counteract an uncurbed rate of reproduction. Though the practice of contraception had been approved by the governments of such nations as India, China, and Japan, only in the last decade have the effects of that policy been noticeable. In some countries poverty, religion, and ignorance have made the widespread use of contraceptives difficult. Leaders in Third World countries charge that attempts by Western powers to encourage them to limit population growth, either by contraceptive devices or by sterilization, is a not-so-subtle form of genocide.

The uneven growth of world population

The demographic revolution has not affected all countries uniformly. Its incidence has been most conspicuous in the underdeveloped nations of Central and South America, Africa, and Asia. Whereas the population of the world as a whole will double, at present rates of increase, in thirty-five years, that of Central and South America will multiply twofold in only twenty-six years. An outstanding example is that of Brazil. In 1900 its population was estimated to be 17 million. By 1975 this total has grown to 98 million, and by 1981 to 125 million, a more than sevenfold increase in less than one hundred years. The population of Asia (excluding the USSR) grew from 813 million in 1900 to approximately 2.8 billion in 1981— approximately 60 percent of the world's population. A situation in which the poorest nations are also the most overpopulated does not augur well for the future of world stability.

6. ACHIEVEMENTS AND LIMITATIONS OF SCIENCE AND TECHNOLOGY

Science and technology: cause and cure of the world's problems

The magnitude of the world's problems has encouraged doubt and pessimism among some of its most creative thinkers. Yet the majority of those charged with the responsibility of finding solutions to the problems—primarily politicians and civil servants—remain cautiously optimistic. For solutions they have continued to turn, paradoxically, to those agencies responsible, in many cases, for the creation of the problems: science and technology. Scientists and technicians invented and perfected the internal combustion engine and the chemical DDT.

Now other scientists and technicians are seeking ways to combat their deleterious effects. Scientific research has been responsible for the medical advances which have helped to produce worldwide population increase. No one would argue, of course, that the research should not have taken place, or that the continuing battle against disease is not one of humanity's most worthwhile engagements. Most would agree, however, that science must move as quickly as possible to come up with a safe and simple method of controlling birth, as it continues to fight to prolong life.

The achievements of science in the field of health during the past half-century have been truly remarkable. Two discoveries of great importance have enabled scientists to understand more clearly the ways in which the human body receives and transmits disease. The discovery of viruses was the result of experimentation conducted chiefly by the American biochemist Wendell Stanley in the 1930s. Viruses are microscopic organisms which show signs of life—including the ability to reproduce—only when existing inside living cells. They are the cause of many human diseases, including measles, poliomyelitis (infantile paralysis), and rabies. Not until the nature of viruses was understood could scientists begin to develop means of treating and preventing the virus-produced illnesses in human beings. A second most important discovery that has increased our understanding of human life occurred in 1953, when the Englishman F. H. C. Crick and the

The discovery of viruses; DNA

The Decoding of DNA. Left: F. H. C. Crick and James D. Watson discuss their efforts to analyze the molecular structure of DNA. Right: A model of the molecular structure of DNA. The dual spiral chains are called a double helix.

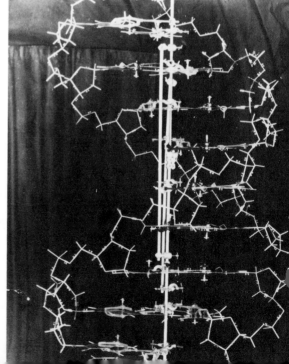

American James D. Watson further unlocked the mysteries of genetic inheritance that had been explored by Gregor Mendel at the end of the nineteenth century. Crick and Watson successfully analyzed deoxyribonucleic acid, or DNA, the chemical molecular structure that occurs in the nuclei of gene cells. They discovered that DNA is composed of smaller molecules of four different kinds, linked together in spiral chains. The arrangement of these molecules in each cell forms a distinct chemical message which determines the character of the genes and therefore of the human organism of which they are a part. The knowledge gained through analysis of DNA has enabled scientists and doctors to understand the causes of hereditary disease and also, by altering a patient's body chemistry, to prevent it. Despite the great benefits that have resulted from this recent discovery, scientists and others have warned that an understanding of the workings of DNA could lead to dangerous tampering with the genetic processes, as, for example, in attempts to produce artificially a breed of more "perfect" human beings.

Medical advances: sulfa drugs, antibiotics, tranquilizers

Experimentation based upon a fuller understanding of the causes of disease has led to the discovery of new medicines to treat it. In 1935 the German Gerhard Domagk discovered the first of the sulfa drugs, which he called sulfanilamide. Soon others were added to the list. Each was found to be marvelously effective in curing or checking such diseases as rheumatic fever, gonorrhea, scarlet fever, and meningitis. About 1930, the Englishman Sir Alexander Fleming discovered the first of the antibiotics, which came to be known as penicillin. Antibiotics are chemical agents produced by living organisms and possessing the power to check or kill bacteria. Many have their origin in molds, fungi, algae, and in simple organisms living in the soil. Penicillin was eventually found to be a drug that could produce spectacular results in the treatment of pneumonia, syphilis, peritonitis, tetanus, and numerous other maladies hitherto frequently fatal. Scientists used knowledge obtained through the analysis of DNA to strengthen the cultures used to develop penicillin. In the 1940s the second most famous of the antibiotics—streptomycin—was discovered by the American Dr. Selman W. Waksman. Streptomycin seems to hold its greatest promise in the treatment of tuberculosis, though it has been used for numerous other infections that do not yield to penicillin. Tranquilizers are another of the so-called miracle drugs. Introduced in 1955, they came to be used frequently in the treatment of mental disorders such as manic-depression and have achieved success in making violent patients more tractable. Although these drugs do not themselves effect cures, they help make patients more accessible to other forms of therapy and enable them in many instances to lead relatively normal lives outside institutions in which they would otherwise be incarcerated. That tranquilizers have been misused by men and women indiscriminately as a dangerously simple method of achieving a desired state of mind is no more than further confirmation of the fact that science continues to create new problems as it solves old ones.

As important as the discovery of new drugs to treat disease has been the development of new means of preventing it. Sir Edward Jenner discovered the first successful vaccine, used to prevent smallpox, in 1796. But not until the 1950s were vaccines found that could protect from diseases such as mumps, measles, and cholera. One of the most exciting breakthroughs occurred with the development of an innoculation against poliomyelitis by the American Dr. Jonas Salk, in 1953. Still to be discovered are effective agents for the successful treatment of two of the world's most deadly killers, heart disease and cancer. The technique of transplanting a heart from a recently dead human being to a live but ailing heart patient, first perfected by the South African, Dr. Christiaan Barnard, has proved of limited usefulness. More effective have been operations substituting plastic valves for defective arteries leading to the heart, and the insertion of electrical devices—"pacemakers"—to steady or stimulate heartbeat. An attempt in 1983 to implant an artificial heart failed to keep the patient alive for more than several months. Though the first attempt, it will certainly not be the last. Testing has produced a definite link between cancer and cigarette smoking, as well as industrial and urban pollution—another example of the way in which technology generates difficulties as it resolves others. Doctors continue to experiment with cancer treatment by X-ray and chemical therapy. But despite the dedication of researchers and the expenditure of large sums to assist their work, a cure eludes them.

Few would today oppose continued campaigns by scientists intent upon eradicating disease. Governments have found it increasingly difficult, however, to justify the spending of vast sums of public money on programs designed to facilitate the exploration of outer space. From their inception, these "experiments" have resembled international competitions between the United States and the Soviet Union as much as they have scientific and technological investigations. On October 4, 1957, the government of the Soviet Union rocketed the first artificial satellite into space at a speed of about 18,000 miles an hour. Though it weighed nearly 200 pounds, it was propelled upward higher than 500 miles. This Russian achievement gave the English language a new word—Sputnik, the Russian for satellite or fellow traveler. A month later the Soviet scientists surpassed their first success by sending a new and much larger Sputnik to an altitude of approximately 1000 miles. These Sputniks were the forerunners of others of greater significance. In April 1961, the Russians succeeded in sending the first man into orbit around the earth. Meanwhile, scientists and military specialists in the United States had been competing to match the Soviets' achievements. After a number of successes with animals and "uninhabited" capsules, and the suborbital journey of a manned

Dr. Jonas Salk in His Laboratory

Space exploration

The First Lunar Landing. Astronaut Edwin E. Aldrin, Jr., is photographed walking near the lunar module of Apollo 11. Astronaut Neil Armstrong, who took the picture, and part of the lunar module are reflected in Aldrin's face plate.

capsule, they succeeded, on February 20, 1962, in launching the first American manned spaceship into orbit around the earth. The successful astronaut was Lieutenant-Colonel John H. Glenn, Jr., who circled the globe three times at a top speed of over 17,000 miles per hour. In 1966 a United States Navy officer left the cabin of his spacecraft and walked in space for forty-four minutes, hundreds of miles above the earth. His feat was surpassed in July 1969, when Neil Armstrong, a civilian astronaut, left his lunar landing module and became the first man on the moon's surface. All over the world these successful voyages and those that followed were hailed as events of capital importance. They did promise an extension of our knowledge of outer space and could doubtless prepare the way for exploration of the moon and eventually of distant planets. But by the mid-1970s, both the United States and the Soviet Union had drastically cut back their space programs in response to demands on their economies from other quarters. A space "shuttle" and laboratory, plus continuing experiments of a minor nature, kept the programs alive. But their value was being questioned, in view of the billions required to keep them operational.

Undoubtedly it was in the area of nuclear science that the largest and most disturbing questions arose as to the capabilities, limitations, and implications of science and technology. Most of the eventual twentieth-century developments in this area were based upon the pioneering work of the physicist Albert Einstein (1879–1955). In 1905

Nuclear science: Einstein's discoveries

Einstein began to challenge not merely the older conceptions of matter but practically the entire structure of traditional physics. The doctrine for which he is most noted is his principle of relativity. During the greater part of the nineteenth century, physicists had assumed that space and motion were absolute. Space was supposed to be filled with an intangible substance known as *ether,* which provided the medium for the undulations of light. But experiments performed by English and American physicists near the end of the century exploded the ether hypothesis. Einstein then set to work to reconstruct the scheme of the universe in accordance with a different pattern. He maintained that space and motion, instead of being absolute, are relative to each other. Objects have not merely three dimensions but four. To the familiar length, breadth, and thickness, Einstein added a new dimension of *time* and represented all four as fused in a synthesis which he called the *space-time continuum.* In this way he sought to explain the idea that mass is dependent upon motion. Bodies traveling at high velocity have proportions of extension and mass different from those they would have at rest. Einstein also posited the conception of a finite universe— that is, finite in space. The region of matter does not extend into infinity; the universe has limits. While these are by no means definite boundaries, there is at least a region beyond which nothing exists. Space curves back upon itself so as to make of the universe a gigantic sphere within which are contained galaxies, solar systems, stars, and planets.

The Einstein theories had a major influence in precipitating other revolutionary developments in physics. By 1960 it had been discovered that the conception of the subatomic world as a miniature solar system was much too simple. The atom was found to contain not only positively charged protons and negatively charged electrons, but *positrons,* or positively charged electrons; *neutrons,* which carry no electric charges; and *mesons,* which may be either negative or positive. Mesons, it was discovered, exist not only within the atom (for about two millionths of a second) but are major components of the cosmic rays that are constantly bombarding the earth from somewhere in outer space.

Several of the developments in physics outlined above helped to make possible one of the most spectacular achievements in the history of science, the splitting of the atom to release the energy contained within it. Ever since it became known that the atom is composed primarily of electrical energy, physicists had dreamed of unlocking this source of tremendous power and making it available for man. As early as 1905 Einstein became convinced of the equivalence of mass and energy and worked out a formula for the conversion of one into the other, which he expressed as $E = mc^2$. E represents the energy in ergs, m the mass in grams, and c the velocity of light in centimeters per second. In other words, the amount of energy locked within the

Albert Einstein

Releasing the energy within the atom

atom is equal to the mass multiplied by the square of the velocity of light. But no practical application of this formula was possible until after the discovery of the neutron by the Englishman Sir James Chadwick in 1932. Since the neutron carries no charge of electricity, it is an ideal weapon for bombarding the atom. It is neither repulsed by the positively charged protons nor absorbed by the negatively charged electrons. Moreover, in the process of bombardment it produces more neutrons, which hit other atoms and cause them in turn to split and create neutrons. In this way the original reaction is repeated in an almost unending series.

The development of the atomic bomb

In 1939 two German physicists, Otto Hahn and Fritz Strassman, succeeded in splitting atoms of uranium by bombarding them with neutrons. The initial reaction produced a chain of reactions, in much the same way that a fire burning at the edge of a piece of paper raises the temperature of adjoining portions of the paper high enough to cause them to ignite. Scientists in Germany, Great Britain, and the United States were spurred on by governments anxious to make use of these discoveries for military purposes during the Second World War. The first use made of the knowledge of atomic fission was in the preparation of an atomic bomb. The devastating weapon was the achievement of scientists working for the War Department of the United States. Some were physicists who had been exiled by Nazi or Fascist oppression. (Einstein himself, a native of Germany and a Jew, had left that country in the 1930s for the United States.)

The hydrogen bomb

Even more disturbing than the results of the bombs dropped on Japan at the end of World War II were the first tests of a hydrogen bomb by the United States Atomic Energy Commission in Novem-

An H-Bomb Mushrooms. The cloud spreads into a huge mushroom following a 1952 explosion of a hydrogen bomb in the Marshall Islands of the Pacific. The photo was taken 50 miles from the detonation site at about 12,000 feet. The cloud rose to 40,000 feet two minutes after the explosion. Ten minutes later the cloud stem had pushed about 25 miles. The mushroom portion went up to 10 miles and spread 100 miles.

Calder Hall. Built in 1956 in England, this was the world's first large-scale atomic power station. The two towers on the left are for cooling. Since this time such power plants have proliferated around the world. However, the near-catastrophic accident at the Three Mile Island Power Station close to Harrisburg, Pennsylvania, in March 1979 has spurred opponents to press even harder for a reexamination of the use of nuclear power.

ber 1952. The tests were conducted at Eniwetok Atoll in the South Pacific; an entire island disappeared after burning brightly for several hours. The hydrogen bomb, or H-bomb, is based upon fusion of hydrogen atoms, a process which requires the enormous heat generated by the splitting of uranium atoms to start the reaction. The fusion results in the creation of a new element, helium, which actually weighs less than the sum of the hydrogen atoms. The "free" energy left over provides the tremendous explosive power of the H-bomb. The force of hydrogen bombs is measured in *megatons,* each of which represents 1,000,000 tons of TNT. Thus a 5-megaton H-bomb would equal 250 times the power of the A-bombs dropped on Hiroshima and Nagasaki.

Clearly the scientists had, at the behest of their government, unleashed a weapon of devastating proportions upon the world. By the 1970s, not only the United States, but the Soviet Union, China, Britain, France, India, Israel, and other nations either possessed atomic weapons or were in the process of developing the technology to do so. Science was once and for all proved to be something other than "pure," that is, without practical and political implications. The application of its discoveries had become a burdensome fact of life for humanity the world over.

The proliferation of nuclear weapons

Governments experimented with schemes to harness nuclear energy for peaceful purposes. Some progress has been made in the development of atomic power as an alternative source of domestic and industrial fuel. But the dangers of radiation as a by-product suggest that this scheme may prove of limited value. During the late 1970s, when the West's supplies of oil were threatened, heated debate continued between advocates of further construction of atomic power plants and

The uses of atomic energy; electronics

The Age of Television. Left: The first working television pickup camera, 1929. Right: The Telstar communications satellite. Weighing only 170 pounds, and measuring 34 inches in diameter, it is powered by 3600 solar cells. It circles the earth at a speed of 1600 miles per hour, at a height of from 500 to 3000 nautical miles.

those who argued in favor of other energy forms—among them solar—as safer and cheaper alternatives. Meanwhile, technologists working for private industry made use of discoveries in atomic physics to pioneer the field of electronics. Electronics derives from that branch of physics which deals with the behavior and effects of electrons, or negatively charged constituents within the atom. Electronic devices have multiplied in staggering profusion since the Second War. Among them are devices to measure the trajectory of missiles, to give warnings of approaching missiles or aircraft, to make possible "blind" landings of airplanes, to store and release electrical signals, to amplify and regulate the transmission of light and sound images, and to provide the power for photoelectric cells that open doors and operate various automatic machines. The spacecraft industry, which has made possible the exploration of outer space, is closely dependent upon electronics.

Automation

The use of electronic devices for radio reception led to initial progress in automation. Automation should not be confused with mechanization, though it may be considered the logical extension of that process. More correctly, automation means a close integration of four elements: (1) a processing system; (2) a mechanical handling system; (3) sensing equipment; and (4) a control system. Though all of these elements are necessary, the last two are the most significant. Sensing equipment performs a function similar to that of the human senses. It observes and measures what is heppening and sends the information thus gained to the control unit. It employs such devices as photoelectric cells, infrared cells, high-frequency devices, and devices making use of X rays, isotopes, and resonance. It operates without fatigue and much faster and more accurately than do the human senses. Moreover, its observations can be made in places unsafe for, or inaccessible to, human beings. A control system receives information from a sensing element, compares this information with that required by the "program," and then makes the necessary adjustments. This series of operations is continuous, so that a desired state is constantly maintained without any human intervention, except for that initially involved in "programming." This revolution has been greatly extended by the invention of lasers. A laser is a device for amplifying the focus and intensity of light. High-energy atoms are stimulated by light to amplify a beam of light. Lasers have demonstrated their value recently in medicine. They have been used effectively in arresting hemorrhaging in the retina in eye afflictions. Through automation, expensive and complicated machines are constantly taking the place of much human labor. Data-processing machines and electronic computers are employed to control switching operations in railroad yards, to operate assembly lines, to operate machines that control other machines, and even to maintain blood pressure during critical operations in hospitals.

Electronic inventions have proved no more an unmixed blessing than have the other discoveries and developments of scientists and technicians. One obvious problem generated by devices that can do the work of humans is that they put humans out of work. Technological unemployment has become an important problem for the modern world. Though new industries absorbed many workers, others were bound to be displaced by automation. While the demand for skilled labor remained high, the so-called entry jobs performed by the unskilled were fast disappearing. They were being eliminated not by computers so much as by fork-lift trucks and motorized conveyors and sweepers. Mechanization of agriculture also eliminated thousands of jobs for unskilled and uneducated workers.

Technological Unemployement

Science and technology provide no panaceas for the problems of the world. If those problems are to be solved, men and women, not machines, will have to do the work. They will be better equipped to do so if they possess some sense of their own past. The lesson of history is not that it repeats itself. The lesson is, rather, that the present can be clearly perceived, and the future intelligently planned for, only when those responsible for the world's destiny understand the workings of human nature. And for knowledge of that extraordinarily complicated and fascinating mechanism, there is no better source than history.

Science, technology, and an understanding of human nature

SELECTED READINGS

• *Items so designated are available in paperback editions.*

Allsop, Kenneth, *The Angry Decade: A Survey of the Cultural Revolt of the 1950s,* London, 1964. Deals effectively with the phenomenon of postwar disillusionment.

Barr, A. H., Jr., *What Is Modern Painting?* New York, 1966. Especially useful for beginning students of art history.

• Bell, Daniel, *The End of Ideology: On the Exhaustion of Political Ideas in the Fifties,* Glencoe, Ill., 1960. Major spokesman for the point of view expressed in the title.

Bowges, Hervé, comp., *The Student Revolts: The Activists Speak,* London, 1968. Interviews with participants in the student riots of May 1968 which shook France and almost toppled the government.

Collins, Doreen, *The European Economic Community, 1958–72,* London, 1975. A thorough analysis of the Common Market, emphasizing the social policies that have emerged in Europe since 1958.

Cornish, Edward, *The Study of the Future: An Introduction to the Art and Science of Understanding and Shaping Tomorrow's World,* Washington, D.C., 1977. An introduction to the world of the "futurists."

• Erlich, Paul, *The Population Bomb,* New York, 1968. Discusses the threat of overpopulation.

• Galbraith, John Kenneth, *The New Industrial State,* Boston, 1967. A penetrating analysis of the changes in capitalism wrought by advanced technology.

• Gamow, George, *Thirty Years That Shook Physics,* New York, 1966. A lucid account by a physicist.

• Harrington, Michael, *The Other America: Poverty in the United States,* New York, 1962. An influential polemic of the early 1960s.

Heilbroner, Robert L., *An Inquiry into the Human Prospect,* New York, 1974, 1980. Pessimistic assessment of the future of humanity.

Infeld, Leopold, *Albert Einstein: His Work and Its Influence on Our World,* New York, 1950. A general introduction.

• Jackson, George, *Soledad Brother: The Prison Letters of George Jackson,* New York, 1970. The testimony of a black radical.

• Marcuse, Herbert, *Counterrevolution and Revolt,* Boston, 1972.

• Popper, Karl, *The Open Society and Its Enemies,* rev. ed., London, 1962. A vigorous comparison of the totalitarian and democratic philosophies by a libertarian.

• Rich, Adrienne, *On Lies, Secrets, and Silence,* New York, 1979. Essays by a leading feminist thinker.

Rosenberg, Harold, *The Anxious Object: Art Today and Its Significance,* New York, 1964. Written by a leading apologist for contemporary art trends.

Servan-Schreiber, J. J., *The World Challenge,* New York, 1981. Analyzes problems of distribution of world resources.

Snow, C. P., *The Two Cultures and a Second Look: An Expanded Version of the Two Cultures and the Scientific Revolution,* Cambridge, 1965. Argues that in the modern world the great divergence between science and the humanities has been a disastrous process.

• Solzhenitsyn, Alexsandr, *The Gulag Archipelago, 1918–1956,* New York, 1974–1975. An account of prison camps during the Stalinist era by the exiled Russian novelist.

• Sullerot, E., *Women, Society, and Change,* New York, 1971. A good introduction to the recent history of changing roles for women.

• Toffler, Alan, *Future Shock,* New York, 1971. An extended essay on the consequences of rapid change in modern industrial society.

RULES OF PRINCIPAL EUROPEAN STATES SINCE 700 A.D.

The Carolingian Dynasty

Pepin, Mayor of the Palace, 714
Charles Martel, Mayor of the Palace, 715–741
Pepin I, Mayor of the Palace, 741; King, 751–768
Charlemagne, King, 768–814; Emperor, 800–814
Louis the Pious, Emperor, 814–840

MIDDLE KINGDOMS

Lothair, Emperor, 840–855
Louis (Italy), Emperor, 855–875
Charles (Provence), King, 855–863
Lothair II (Lorraine), King, 855–869

WEST FRANCIA

Charles the Bald, King, 840–877; Emperor, 875
Louis II, King, 877–879
Louis III, King, 879–882
Carloman, King, 879–884

EAST FRANCIA

Ludwig, King, 840–876
Carloman, King, 876–880
Ludwig, King, 876–882
Charles the Fat, Emperor, 876–887

Holy Roman Emperors

SAXON DYNASTY

Otto I, 962–973
Otto II, 973–983
Otto III, 983–1002
Henry II, 1002–1024

FRANCONIAN DYNASTY

Conrad II, 1024–1039
Henry III, 1039–1056
Henry IV, 1056–1106
Henry V, 1106–1125
Lothair II (of Saxony), King, 1125–1133; Emperor, 1133–1137

HOHENSTAUFEN DYNASTY

Conrad III, 1138–1152
Frederick I (Barbarossa), 1152–1190
Henry VI, 1190–1197
Philip of Swabia, 1198–1208 ⎱ Rivals
Otto IV (Welf), 1198–1215 ⎰
Frederick II, 1220–1250
Conrad IV, 1250–1254

INTERREGNUM, 1254–1273

EMPERORS FROM VARIOUS DYNASTIES
Rudolf I (Habsburg), 1273–1291

Adolf (Nassau), 1292–1298
Albert I (Hapsburg), 1298–1308
Henry VII (Luxemburg), 1308–1313
Ludwig IV (Wittelsbach), 1314–1347
Charles IV (Luxemburg), 1347–1378
Wenceslas (Luxemburg), 1378–1400
Rupert (Wittelsbach), 1400–1410
Sigismund (Luxemburg), 1410–1437

HABSBURG DYNASTY

Albert II, 1438–1439
Frederick III, 1440–1493
Maximilian I, 1493–1519
Charles V, 1519–1556
Ferdinand I, 1556–1564
Maximilan II, 1564–1576
Rudolf II, 1576–1612
Matthias, 1612–1619
Ferdinand II, 1619–1637
Ferdinand III, 1637–1657
Leopold I, 1658–1705
Joseph I, 1705–1711
Charles VI, 1711–1740
Charles VII (not a Habsburg), 1742–1745
Francis I, 1745–1765
Joseph II, 1765–1790
Leopold II, 1790–1792
Francis II, 1792–1806

Rulers of France from Hugh Capet

CAPETIAN KINGS

Hugh Capet, 987–996
Robert II, 996–1031
Henry I, 1031–1060
Philip I, 1060–1108
Louis VI, 1108–1137
Louis VII, 1137–1180
Philip II (Augustus), 1180–1223
Louis VIII, 1223–1226
Louis IX, 1226–1270
Philip III, 1270–1285
Philip IV, 1285–1314
Louis X, 1314–1316
Philip V, 1316–1322
Charles IV, 1322–1328

HOUSE OF VALOIS

Philip VI, 1328–1350
John, 1350–1364
Charles V, 1364–1380
Charles VI, 1380–1422
Charles VII, 1422–1461
Louis XI, 1461–1483
Charles VIII, 1483–1498
Louis XII, 1498–1515
Francis I, 1515–1547

Henry II, 1547–1559
Francis II, 1559–1560
Charles IX, 1560–1574
Henry III, 1574–1589

BOURBON DYNASTY

Henry IV, 1589–1610
Louis XIII, 1610–1643
Louis XIV, 1643–1715
Louis XV, 1715–1774
Louis XVI, 1774–1792

AFTER 1792

First Republic, 1792–1799
Napoleon Bonaparte, First Consul, 1799–1804
Napoleon I, Emperor, 1804–1814
Louis XVIII (Bourbon dynasty), 1814–1824
Charles X (Bourbon dynasty), 1824–1830
Louis Philippe, 1830–1848
Second Republic, 1848–1852
Napoleon III, Emperor, 1852–1870
Third Republic, 1870–1940
Pétain regime, 1940–1944
Provisional government, 1944–1946
Fourth Republic, 1946–1958
Fifth Republic, 1958–

Rulers of England

ANGLO-SAXON KINGS

Egbert, 802–839
Ethelwulf, 839–858
Ethelbald, 858–860
Ethelbert, 860–866
Ethelred, 866–871
Alfred the Great, 871–900
Edward the Elder, 900–924
Ethelstan, 924–940
Edmund I, 940–946
Edred, 946–955
Edwy, 955–959
Edgar, 959–975

Edward the Martyr, 975–978
Ethelred the Unready, 978–1016
Canute, 1016–1035 (Danish Nationality)
Harold I, 1035–1040
Hardicanute, 1040–1042
Edward the Confessor, 1042–1066
Harold II, 1066

HOUSE OF NORMANDY

William I (the Conqueror), 1066–1087
William II, 1087–1100
Henry I, 1100–1135
Stephen, 1135–1154

HOUSE OF PLANTAGENET

Henry II, 1154–1189
Richard I, 1189–1199
John, 1199–1216
Henry III, 1216–1272
Edward I, 1272–1307
Edward II, 1307–1327
Edward III, 1327–1377
Richard II, 1377–1399

HOUSE OF LANCASTER

Henry IV, 1399–1413
Henry V, 1413–1422
Henry VI, 1422–1461

HOUSE OF YORK

Edward IV, 1461–1483
Edward V, 1483
Richard III, 1483–1485

HOUSE OF TUDOR

Henry VII, 1485–1509
Henry VIII, 1509–1547
Edward VI, 1547–1553
Mary, 1553–1558
Elizabeth I, 1558–1603

HOUSE OF STUART

James I, 1603–1625
Charles I, 1625–1649

COMMONWEALTH AND PROTECTORATE, 1649–1659

HOUSE OF STUART RESTORED

Charles II, 1660–1685
James II, 1685–1688
William III and Mary II, 1689–1694
William III alone, 1694–1702
Anne, 1702–1714

HOUSE OF HANOVER

George I, 1714–1727
George II, 1727–1760
George III, 1760–1820
George IV, 1820–1830
William IV, 1830–1837
Victoria, 1837–1901

HOUSE OF SAXE-COBURG-GOTHA

Edward VII, 1901–1910
George V, 1910–1917

HOUSE OF WINDSOR

George V, 1917–1936
Edward VIII, 1936
George VI, 1936–1952
Elizabeth II, 1952–

Prominent Popes

Silvester I, 314–335
Leo I, 440–461
Gelasius I, 492–496
Gregory I, 590–604
Nicholas I, 858–867
Silvester II, 999–1003
Leo IX, 1049–1054
Nicholas II, 1058–1061
Gregory VII, 1073–1085
Urban II, 1088–1099
Paschal II, 1099–1118
Alexander III, 1159–1181

Innocent III, 1198–1216
Gregory IX, 1227–1241
Boniface VIII, 1294–1303
John XXII, 1316–1334
Nicholas V, 1447–1455
Pius II, 1458–1464
Alexander VI, 1492–1503
Julius II, 1503–1513
Leo X, 1513–1521
Adrian VI, 1522–1523
Clement VII, 1523–1534
Paul III, 1534–1549

Paul IV, 1555–1559
Gregory XIII, 1572–1585
Gregory XVI, 1831–1846
Pius IX, 1846–1878
Leo XIII, 1878–1903
Pius X, 1903–1914
Benedict XV, 1914–1922

Pius XI, 1922–1939
Pius XII, 1939–1958
John XXIII, 1958–1963
Paul VI, 1963–1978
John Paul I, 1978
John Paul II, 1978-

Rulers of Austria and Austria-Hungary

*Maximilian I (Archduke), 1493–1519
*Charles I (Charles V in the Holy Roman Empire),
  1519–1556
*Ferdinand I, 1556–1564
*Maximilian II, 1564–1576
*Rudolph II, 1576–1612
*Matthias, 1612–1619
*Ferdinand II, 1619–1637
*Ferdinand III, 1637–1657
*Leopold I, 1658–1705
*Joseph I, 1705–1711
*Charles VI, 1711–1740
Maria Theresa, 1740–1780

*Joseph II, 1780–1790
*Leopold II, 1790–1792
*Francis II, 1792–1835 (Emperor of Austria as
  Francis I after 1804)
Ferdinand I, 1835–1848
Francis Joseph, 1848–1916 (after 1867 Emperor
  of Austria and King of Hungary)
Charles I, 1916–1918 (Emperor of Austria and King
  of Hungary)
Republic of Austria, 1918–1938 (dictatorship
  after 1934)
Republic restored, under Allied occupation, 1945–1956
Free Republic, 1956–

*Also bore title of Holy Roman Emperor.

Rulers of Prussia and Germany

*Frederick I, 1701–1713
*Frederick William I, 1713–1740
*Frederick II (the Great), 1740–1786
*Frederick William II, 1786–1797
*Frederick William III, 1797–1840
*Frederick William IV, 1840–1861
*William I, 1861–1888 (German Emperor after 1871)

Frederick III, 1888
William II, 1888–1918
Weimar Republic, 1918–1933
Third Reich (Nazi Dictatorship), 1933–1945
Allied occupation, 1945–1952
Division into Federal Republic of Germany in west
  and German Democratic Republic in east, 1949–

*Kings of Prussia.

Rulers of Russia

Ivan III, 1462–1505
Vasily III, 1505–1533
Ivan IV, 1533–1584
Theodore I, 1584–1598
Boris Godunov, 1598–1605

Theodore II, 1605
Vasily IV, 1606–1610
Michael, 1613–1645
Alexius, 1645–1676
Theodore III, 1676–1682

Ivan V and Peter I, 1682–1689
Peter I (the Great), 1689–1725
Catherine I, 1725–1727
Peter II, 1727–1730
Anna, 1730–1740
Ivan VI, 1740–1741
Elizabeth, 1741–1762
Peter III, 1762

Catherine II (the Great), 1762–1796
Paul, 1796–1801
Alexander I, 1801–1825
Nicholas I, 1825–1855
Alexander II, 1855–1881
Alexander III, 1881–1894
Nicholas II, 1894–1917
Soviet Republic, 1917–

Rulers of Italy

Victor Emmanuel II, 1861–1878
Humbert I, 1878–1900
Victor Emmanuel III, 1900–1946
Fascist Dictatorship, 1922–1943
   (maintained in northern Italy until 1945)

Humbert II, May 9–June 13, 1946
Republic, 1946–

Rulers of Spain

Ferdinand { and Isabella, 1479–1504
{ and Philip I, 1504–1506
{ and Charles I, 1506–1516
Charles I (Holy Roman Emperor Charles V),
   1516–1556
Philip II, 1556–1598
Philip III, 1598–1621
Philip IV, 1621–1665
Charles II, 1665–1700
Philip V, 1700–1746
Ferdinand VI, 1746–1759
Charles III, 1759–1788
Charles IV, 1788–1808

Ferdinand VII, 1808
Joseph Bonaparte, 1808–1813
Ferdinand VII (restored), 1814–1833
Isabella II, 1833–1868
Republic, 1868–1870
Amadeo, 1870–1873
Republic, 1873–1874
Alfonso XII, 1874–1885
Alfonso XIII, 1886–1931
Republic, 1931–1939
Fascist Dictatorship, 1939–1975
Juan Carlos I, 1975–

Index

Guide to Pronunciation

The sounds represented by the diacritical marks used in this Index are illustrated by the following common words:

āle	ēve	īce	ōld	ūse	bo͞ot
ăt	ĕnd	ĭll	ŏf	ŭs	fo͝ot
fåtality	évent		ȯbey	ůnite	
câre			fôrm	ûrn	
ärm					
ȧsk					

Vowels that have no diacritical marks are to be pronounced "neutral," for example: Aegean = ė-je′an, Basel = bäz′el, Basil = bă′zil, common = kŏm′on, Alcaeus = ăl-sē′us. The combinations ou and oi are pronounced as in "out" and "oil."

ii